D0722210

58 16

ISSN 0276-8178

Volume 14

Twentieth-Century Literary Criticism

Excerpts from Criticism of the Works of Novelists, Poets, Playwrights, Short Story Writers, and Other Creative Writers Who Died between 1900 and 1960, from the First Published Critical Appraisals to Current Evaluations

Dennis Poupard
James E. Person, Jr.
Editors

Thomas Ligotti
Associate Editor

Gale Research Inc. • DETROIT • LONDON

STAFF

The paper used in this publication meets the minimum requirements
of American National Standard for Information Sciences—Permanence
Paper for Printed Library Materials, ANSI Z39.48-1984. ♾™

Library of Congress Catalog Card Number 76-46132
ISBN 0-8103-0228-4
ISSN 0276-8178

Printed in the United States of America

Published simultaneously in the United Kingdom
by Gale Research International Limited
(An affiliated company of Gale Research Inc.)

Contents

Preface

It is impossible to overvalue the importance of literature in the intellectual, emotional, and spiritual evolution of humanity. Literature is that which both lifts us out of everyday life and helps us to better understand it. Through the fictive lives of such characters as Anna Karenin, Jay Gatsby, or Leopold Bloom, our perceptions of the human condition are enlarged, and we are enriched.

Literary criticism can also give us insight into the human condition, as well as into the specific moral and intellectual atmosphere of an era, for the criteria by which a work of art is judged reflects contemporary philosophical and social attitudes. Literary criticism takes many forms: the traditional essay, the book or play review, even the parodic poem. Criticism can also be of several types: normative, descriptive, interpretive, textual, appreciative, generic. Collectively, the range of critical response helps us to understand a work of art, an author, an era.

Scope of the Series

Twentieth-Century Literary Criticism (TCLC) is designed to serve as an introduction for the student of twentieth-century literature to the authors of the period 1900 to 1960 and to the most significant commentators on these authors. The great poets, novelists, short story writers, playwrights, and philosophers of this period are by far the most popular writers for study in high school and college literature courses. Since a vast amount of relevant critical material confronts the student, *TCLC* presents significant passages from the most important published criticism to aid students in their location and selection of criticism on authors who died between 1900 and 1960.

The need for *TCLC* was suggested by the usefulness of the Gale series *Contemporary Literary Criticism (CLC),* which excerpts criticism on current writing. Because of the difference in time span under consideration *(CLC* considers authors who were still living after 1959), there is no duplication of material between *CLC* and *TCLC*. For further information about *CLC* and Gale's other criticism series, users should consult the Guide to Gale Literary Criticism Series preceding the title page in this volume.

Each volume of *TCLC* is carefully compiled to include authors who represent a variety of genres and nationalities and who are currently regarded as the most important writers of this era. In addition to major authors, *TCLC* also presents criticism on lesser-known writers whose significant contributions to literary history are important to the study of twentieth-century literature.

Each author entry in *TCLC* is intended to provide an overview of major criticism on an author. Therefore, the editors include approximately twenty authors in each 600-page volume (compared with approximately sixty-five authors in a *CLC* volume of similar size) so that more attention may be given to an author. Each author entry represents a historical survey of the critical response to that author's work: some early criticism is presented to indicate initial reactions, later criticism is selected to represent any rise or decline in the author's reputation, and current retrospective analyses provide students with a modern view. The length of an author entry is intended to reflect the amount of critical attention the author has received from critics writing in English, and from foreign criticism in translation. Critical articles and books that have not been translated into English are excluded. Every attempt has been made to identify and include excerpts from the seminal essays on each author's work. Additionally, as space permits, especially insightful essays of a more limited scope are included.

An author may appear more than once in the series because of the great quantity of critical material available, or because of a resurgence of criticism generated by events such as an author's centennial or anniversary celebration, the republication of an author's works, or publication of a newly translated work or volume of letters. Several author entries in each volume of *TCLC* feature criticism on single works by major authors who have appeared previously in the series. Only those individual works that have been the subjects of vast amounts of criticism and are widely studied in literature classes are selected for this in-depth treatment. F. Scott Fitzgerald's *The Great Gatsby* and Thomas Mann's *Death in Venice* are examples of such entries in *TCLC,* Volume 14.

Organization of the Book

An author entry consists of the following elements: author heading, biographical and critical introduction, principal works, excerpts of criticism (each followed by a bibliographical citation), and an additional bibliography for further reading.

- The *author heading* consists of the author's full name, followed by birth and death dates. The unbracketed portion of the name denotes the form under which the author most commonly wrote. If an author wrote consistently under a pseudonym, the pseudonym will be listed in the author heading and the real name given in parentheses on the first line of the biographical and critical introduction. Also located at the beginning of the introduction to the author entry are any name variations under which an author wrote, including transliterated forms for authors whose languages use nonroman alphabets. Uncertainty as to a birth or death date is indicated by a question mark.

- The *biographical and critical introduction* contains background information designed to introduce the reader to an author and to the critical debate surrounding his or her work. Parenthetical material following many of the introductions provides references to biographical and critical reference series published by Gale. These include *Contemporary Authors, Dictionary of Literary Biography, Something about the Author,* and past volumes of *TCLC.*

- The *list of principal works* is chronological by date of first book publication and identifies the genre of each work. In the case of foreign authors where there are both foreign language publications and English translations, the title and date of the first English-language edition are given in brackets. Unless otherwise indicated, dramas are dated by first performance, not first publication.

- *Criticism* is arranged chronologically in each author entry to provide a useful perspective on changes in critical evaluation over the years. All titles by the author featured in the critical entry are printed in boldface type to enable the user to ascertain without difficulty the works being discussed. Also for purposes of easier identification, the critic's name and the publication date of the essay are given at the beginning of each piece of criticism. Unsigned criticism is preceded by the title of the journal in which it appeared. When an anonymous essay is later attributed to a critic, the critic's name appears in brackets at the beginning of the excerpt and in the bibliographical citation.

- Important critical essays are prefaced by *explanatory notes* as an additional aid to students using *TCLC.* The explanatory notes provide several types of useful information, including: the reputation of a critic; the importance of a work of criticism; the specific type of criticism (biographical, psychoanalytic, structuralist, etc.); a synopsis of the criticism; and the growth of critical controversy or changes in critical trends regarding an author's work. In many cases, these notes cross-reference the work of critics who agree or disagree with each other. Dates in parentheses within the explanatory notes refer to a book publication date when they follow a book title and to an essay date when they follow a critic's name.

- A complete *bibliographical citation* designed to facilitate location of the original essay or book by the interested reader follows each piece of criticism. An asterisk (*) at the end of a citation indicates that the essay is on more than one author.

- Most *TCLC* entries include *illustrations* of the author. Many entries also contain illustrations of materials pertinent to an author's career, including holographs of manuscript pages, title pages, dust jackets, letters, or representations of important people and events in an author's life.

- The *additional bibliography* appearing at the end of each author entry suggests further reading on the author. In some cases it includes essays for which the editors could not obtain reprint rights. An asterisk (*) at the end of a citation indicates that the essay is on more than one author.

An appendix lists the sources from which material in each volume has been reprinted. It does not, however, list every book or periodical consulted in the preparation of the volume.

Cumulative Indexes

Each volume of *TCLC* includes a cumulative index to authors listing all the authors who have appeared in *Contemporary Literary Criticism, Twentieth-Century Literary Criticism, Nineteenth-Century Literature Criticism,* and *Literature Criticism from 1400 to 1800,* along with cross-references to the Gale series *Children's Literature Review, Authors in the News, Contemporary Authors, Contemporary Authors Autobiography Series, Dictionary of Literary Biography, Something about the Author,* and *Yesterday's Authors of Books for Children.* Users will welcome this cumulated author index as a useful tool for locating an author within the various series. The index, which lists birth and death dates when available, will be particularly valuable for those authors who are identified with a certain period but whose death date causes them to be placed in another, or for those authors whose careers span two periods. For example, F. Scott Fitzgerald is found in *TCLC,* yet a writer often associated with him, Ernest Hemingway, is found in *CLC.*

Each volume of *TCLC* also includes a cumulative nationality index. Author names are arranged alphabetically under their respective nationalities and followed by the volume numbers in which they appear.

A cumulative index to critics is another useful feature in *TCLC.* Under each critic's name are listed the authors on whom the critic has written and the volume and page where the criticism may be found.

Acknowledgments

No work of this scope can be accomplished without the cooperation of many people. The editors especially wish to thank the copyright holders of the excerpted criticism included in this volume, the permissions managers of many book and magazine publishing companies for assisting us in securing reprint rights, and Jeri Yaryan for assistance with copyright research. We are also grateful to the staffs of the Detroit Public Library, the Library of Congress, University of Detroit Library, University of Michigan Library, and Wayne State University Library for making their resources available to us.

Suggestions Are Welcome

In response to various suggestions, several features have been added to *TCLC* since the series began. Recently introduced features include explanatory notes to excerpted criticism that provide important information regarding critics and their work, a cumulative author index listing authors in all Gale literary criticism series, entries devoted to criticism on a single work by a major author, and more extensive illustrations.

Readers who wish to suggest authors to appear in future volumes, or who have other suggestions, are cordially invited to write the editors.

Authors to Be Featured in *TCLC,* Volumes 15 and 16

Ryūnosoke Akutagawa (Japanese short story writer)—Author of the classic novella "Rashomon," Akutagawa is celebrated for his Poe-like tales of the horrific and the bizarre, which critics often view as a literary reflection of his brief and traumatic life.

Charles A. Beard (American historian)—An important historian who examined the influence of economics on all aspects of American history, including the drafting of the U.S. Constitution.

Mikhail Bulgakov (Russian novelist, short story writer, and dramatist)—Bulgakov's works are grotesque and satiric mockeries of Soviet society in particular and communist utopias in general. First translated into English in the late 1960s, Bulgakov's fiction and dramas have since received increasing critical attention in the West.

Colette (French novelist)—Colette's fiction is noted for its depictions of passionate and independent female protagonists. *TCLC* will devote an entire entry to criticism of recently translated collections of Colette's short stories and letters.

Stephen Crane (American novelist)—Author of *The Red Badge of Courage,* Crane was one of America's foremost Realist writers and is credited with establishing American literary Naturalism.

Ford Madox Ford (English novelist)—A major novelist of manners, Ford has been the subject of a critical revival in recent years.

Anne Frank (Dutch diarist)—Composed while in hiding from the Nazis in Amsterdam, *The Diary of Anne Frank* is one of the most enduring and widely read documents of the Holocaust, as well as a testament to the suffering and creative talent of its young author.

Rémy de Gourmont (French critic, novelist, and dramatist)—Gourmont was one of the most prominent French men of letters of the modern era. Displaying an encyclopedic range of learning, his critical writings were extremely influential among early twentieth-century English and American critics.

Thomas Hardy (English novelist)—Hardy's novel *Tess of the D'Urbervilles* was controversial in the late nineteenth century for its sympathetic depiction of an independent female protagonist. *TCLC* will devote an entire entry to the critical reception of this classic work of English fiction.

William Dean Howells (American novelist and critic)—Howells was the chief progenitor of American Realism and the most influential American literary critic of the late nineteenth century. Several of his early novels have been recently reissued, and discussion of his work is growing.

Henrik Ibsen (Norwegian dramatist)—Ibsen's *The Wild Duck* is one of the major works of the twentieth-century stage. *TCLC* will devote an entire entry to critical discussions of this important drama.

William James (American philosopher)—The foremost philosopher America has produced, James examined the metaphysical dilemmas of modern life. *TCLC* will present a summary and explanation of his thought as well as critical reactions to his work.

James Joyce (Irish novelist)—Joyce's *A Portrait of the Artist as a Young Man* examines the nature of youthful idealism and the role of the artist in modern society. In an entry devoted solely to that work, *TCLC* will present the major critical essays on the novel.

Vladislav Khodasevich (Russian poet)—Called the greatest Russian poet of the twentieth century by Vladimir Nabokov, Khodasevich has been the subject of recent critical interest in the United States.

D. H. Lawrence (English novelist)—Once known primarily as the controversial author of such banned works as *Lady Chatterly's Lover,* Lawrence is one of modern literature's major delineators of the romantic quest for personal freedom, as well as one of the first twentieth-century authors to employ theories of modern psychology in his writing. *TCLC* will devote an entire entry to *Sons and Lovers,* which is among Lawrence's most popular novels.

David Lindsay (English novelist)—An important writer in the genre of fantasy, Lindsay addressed metaphysical and spiritual questions in novels that strongly influenced the works of C.S. Lewis and J.R.R. Tolkien.

Liu E (Chinese novelist)—His *Travels of Lao Ts'an* is one of the most important Chinese novels of the twentieth century.

Jack London (American novelist)—Although often considered an adventure writer, London examined issues of social equality and personal morality in his fiction. Recent years have witnessed greatly renewed interest in his works.

George Meredith (English novelist and poet)—A prolific author and an associate of England's most famous Victorian literary figures, Meredith ranks among the outstanding writers of his era.

J. Middleton Murry (English critic)—A noted magazine editor and influential literary critic, Murry has contributed important studies on the works of his wife Katherine Mansfield, and his intimate friend, D. H. Lawrence.

George Orwell (English novelist and essayist)—During the past two years, his novel *Nineteen Eighty-Four* has been more widely discussed than at any other time since its initial publication. *TCLC* will present the critical history of the work and an extensive survey of recent criticism on *Nineteen Eighty-Four* in 1984.

Rainer Maria Rilke (German poet and novelist)—Rilke's *The Notebooks of Malte Laurids Brigge,* a loosely autobiographical novel that explores the angst-ridden life of a hypersensitive man in Paris, is considered the author's most accomplished prose work. To mark a new translation of this novel, *TCLC* will devote an entire entry to critical discussion of this important work.

Dorothy L. Sayers (English novelist)—Sayers was an accomplished Dante scholar, a respected writer on Christian themes, and the creator of Lord Peter Wimsey, the sophisticated detective-hero of such acclaimed novels as *Murder Must Advertise, The Nine Tailors,* and *Gaudy Night.*

Robert W. Service (Canadian poet)—Known as "the Canadian Kipling," Service is remembered for jauntily rhythmic verse that celebrates life and adventure in the Yukon.

Montague Summers (English critic and historian)—A scholar of Restoration and Gothic literature and a historian of occult subjects such as vampirism and witchcraft, Summers was renowned as one of the most remarkable figures of his time, both for his erudition and his eccentricity.

Leo Tolstoy (Russian novelist)—His *Anna Karenin* is considered one of the greatest novels in world literature. *TCLC* will devote an entire entry to the critical history of this work.

Paul Valéry (French poet)—Valéry is widely recognized as one of France's outstanding poets and literary theoreticians. His work bridges the movements of nineteenth-century Symbolism and twentieth-century Modernism.

Robert Walser (Swiss novelist and short story writer)—Considered among the most important Swiss authors writing in German, Walser was praised by such major figures of German literature as Franz Kafka and Robert Musil. His fiction is distinguished by a grotesque imagination and black humor suggestive of the Expressionist and Surrealist movements.

Beatrice and Sydney James Webb (English social writers)—Prominent members of the progressive Fabian society, the Webbs wrote sociological works significant to the advent of socialist reform in England and influenced the work of several major authors, including H. G. Wells and Bernard Shaw.

Additional Authors to Appear in Future Volumes

Abbey, Henry 1842-1911
Abercrombie, Lascelles 1881-1938
Adamic, Louis 1898-1951
Ade, George 1866-1944
Agustini, Delmira 1886-1914
Akers, Elizabeth Chase 1832-1911
Akiko, Yosano 1878-1942
Aldanov, Mark 1886-1957
Aldrich, Thomas Bailey 1836-1907
Aliyu, Dan Sidi 1902-1920
Allen, Hervey 1889-1949
Archer, William 1856-1924
Arlen, Michael 1895-1956
Austin, Alfred 1835-1913
Austin, Mary 1868-1934
Bahr, Hermann 1863-1934
Bailey, Philip James 1816-1902
Barbour, Ralph Henry 1870-1944
Benét, William Rose 1886-1950
Benjamin, Walter 1892-1940
Bennett, James Gordon, Jr. 1841-1918
Benson, E(dward) F(rederic) 1867-1940
Benson, Stella 1892-1933
Berdyaev, Nikolai Aleksandrovich 1874-1948
Beresford, J(ohn) D(avys) 1873-1947
Bergson, Henri 1859-1941
Binyon, Laurence 1869-1943
Bishop, John Peale 1892-1944
Blackmore, R(ichard) D(oddridge) 1825-1900
Blake, Lillie Devereux 1835-1913
Blum, Leon 1872-1950
Bodenheim, Maxwell 1892-1954
Bosschere, Jean de 1878-1953
Bourne, Randolph 1886-1918
Bowen, Marjorie 1886-1952
Brennan, Christopher John 1870-1932
Broch, Hermann 1886-1951
Byrne, Donn 1889-1928
Caine, Hall 1853-1931
Campana, Dina 1885-1932
Cannan, Gilbert 1884-1955
Chand, Prem 1880-1936
Churchill, Winston 1871-1947
Coppée, Francois 1842-1908
Corelli, Marie 1855-1924
Croce, Benedetto 1866-1952
Crofts, Freeman Wills 1879-1957
Crothers, Rachel 1878-1958
Cruze, James (Jens Cruz Bosen) 1884-1942
Curros, Enriquez Manuel 1851-1908
Dagerman, Stig 1923-1954
Dall, Caroline Wells (Healy) 1822-1912
Daudet, Leon 1867-1942
Davidson, John 1857-1909
Day, Clarence 1874-1935
Delafield, E.M. (Edme Elizabeth Monica de la Pasture) 1890-1943
Deneson, Jacob 1836-1919
DeVoto, Bernard 1897-1955
Douglas, (George) Norman 1868-1952
Douglas, Lloyd C(assel) 1877-1951
Dovzhenko, Alexander 1894-1956
Drinkwater, John 1882-1937
Drummond, W.H. 1854-1907
Durkheim, Émile 1858-1917
Duun, Olav 1876-1939
Eaton, Walter Prichard 1878-1957
Eggleston, Edward 1837-1902
Erskine, John 1879-1951
Fadeyev, Alexander 1901-1956
Ferland, Albert 1872-1943
Feydeau, Georges 1862-1921
Field, Rachel 1894-1924
Flecker, James Elroy 1884-1915
Fletcher, John Gould 1886-1950
Fogazzaro, Antonio 1842-1911
Francos, Karl Emil 1848-1904
Frank, Bruno 1886-1945
Frazer, (Sir) George 1854-1941
Freud, Sigmund 1853-1939
Fröding, Gustaf 1860-1911
Fuller, Henry Blake 1857-1929
Futabatei, Shimei 1864-1909
Futrelle, Jacques 1875-1912
Gladkov, Fydor Vasilyevich 1883-1958
Glaspell, Susan 1876-1948
Glyn, Elinor 1864-1943
Gogarty, Oliver St. John 1878-1957
Golding, Louis 1895-1958
Gosse, Edmund 1849-1928
Gould, Gerald 1885-1936
Gray, John 1866-1934
Grimke, Charlotte L. 1837-1914
Guest, Edgar 1881-1959
Gumilyov, Nikolay 1886-1921
Gyulai, Pal 1826-1909
Hale, Edward Everett 1822-1909
Hall, James 1887-1951
Harris, Frank 1856-1931
Hawthorne, Julian 1846-1934
Hernandez, Miguel 1910-1942
Hewlett, Maurice 1861-1923
Heyward, DuBose 1885-1940
Hilton, James 1900-1954
Hope, Anthony 1863-1933
Howe, Julia Ward 1819-1910
Hudson, W(illiam) H(enry) 1841-1922
Huidobro, Vincente 1893-1948
Hulme, T(homas) E(rnest) 1883-1917
Hurban Vanjansky, Svetozar 1847-1916
Hviezdoslav (Pavol Orszagh) 1849-1921
Ilyas, Abu Shabaka 1903-1947
Imbs, Bravig 1904-1946
Ishikawa Takuboku 1885-1912
Ivanov, Vyacheslav Ivanovich 1866-1949
Jacobs, W(illiam) W(ymark) 1863-1943
James, Will 1892-1942
Jammes, Francis 1868-1938
Jerome, Jerome K(lapka) 1859-1927
Johnston, Mary 1870-1936
Jorgensen, Johannes 1866-1956
Kaye-Smith, Sheila 1887-1956
King, Grace 1851-1932
Kirby, William 1817-1906
Kline, Otis Albert 1891-1946
Kohut, Adolph 1848-1916
Korolenko, Vladimir 1853-1921
Kuzmin, Mikhail Alexseyevich 1875-1936
Lamm, Martin 1880-1950
Lang, Andrew 1844-1912
Lawson, Henry 1867-1922
Ledwidge, Francis 1887-1917
Leipoldt, C. Louis 1880-1947
Lemonnier, Camille 1844-1913
Leverson, Ada 1862-1933
Lewisohn, Ludwig 1883-1955
Liliencron, Detlev von 1844-1909
Lima, Jorge De 1895-1953
Lindsay, (Nicholas) Vachel 1879-1931
Locke, Alain 1886-1954
Long, Frank Belknap 1903-1959
Louÿs, Pierre 1870-1925
Lucas, E(dward) V(errall) 1868-1938
Lugones, Leopoldo 1874-1938
Lyall, Edna 1857-1903
Maghar, Josef Suatopluk 1864-1945
Manning, Frederic 1887-1935
Maragall, Joan 1860-1911
Marais, Eugene 1871-1936
Martin du Gard, Roger 1881-1958
Masaoka Shiki 1867-1902
Masaryk, Tomas 1850-1939
McClellan, George Marion 1860-1934
McCoy, Horace 1897-1955
Mirbeau, Octave 1850-1917
Mistral, Frederic 1830-1914
Molnar, Ferenc 1878-1952
Monro, Harold 1879-1932
Moore, Thomas Sturge 1870-1944
Morley, Christopher 1890-1957
Morley, S. Griswold 1883-1948
Mqhayi, S.E.K. 1875-1945
Murray, (George) Gilbert 1866-1957

Murry, J. Middleton 1889-1957
Nansen, Peter 1861-1918
Nathan, George Jean 1882-1958
Nobre, Antonio 1867-1900
Nordhoff, Charles 1887-1947
Norris, Frank 1870-1902
Obstfelder, Sigborn 1866-1900
O'Dowd, Bernard 1866-1959
Ophuls, Max 1902-1957
Orczy, Baroness 1865-1947
Owen, Seaman 1861-1936
Page, Thomas Nelson 1853-1922
Papini, Giovanni 1881-1956
Parrington, Vernon L. 1871-1929
Peck, George W. 1840-1916
Pereda, Jose Maria de 1833-1906
Peret, Benjamin 1899-1959
Phillips, Ulrich B. 1877-1934
Pickthall, Marjorie 1883-1922
Pinero, Arthur Wing 1855-1934
Pontoppidan, Henrik 1857-1943
Porter, Gene(va) Stratton 1886-1924
Prévost, Marcel 1862-1941
Quiller-Couch, Arthur 1863-1944
Radnoti, Miklos 1909-1944
Randall, James G. 1881-1953
Rappoport, Solomon 1863-1944
Read, Opie 1852-1939
Reisen (Reizen), Abraham 1875-1953
Remington, Frederic 1861-1909
Renard, Jules 1864-1910
Riley, James Whitcomb 1849-1916
Rinehart, Mary Roberts 1876-1958
Ring, Max 1817-1901
Rohmer, Sax 1883-1959
Rolland, Romain 1866-1944
Rólvaag, O(le) E(dvart) 1876-1931
Roumain, Jacques 1907-1944
Roussel, Raymond 1877-1933
Rozanov, Vasily Vasilyevich 1856-1919
Ruskin, John 1819-1900
Saar, Ferdinand von 1833-1906
Sabatini, Rafael 1875-1950
Saintsbury, George 1845-1933
Sakutarō, Hagiwara 1886-1942
Sanborn, Franklin Benjamin 1831-1917
Santayana, George 1863-1952
Sardou, Victorien 1831-1908
Schickele, Rene 1885-1940
Seabrook, William 1886-1945
Seton, Ernest Thompson 1860-1946
Shestov, Lev 1866-1938
Shiels, George 1886-1949
Skram, Bertha Amalie 1847-1905
Sodergran, Edith Irene 1892-1923
Solovyov, Vladimir 1853-1900
Sorel, Georges 1847-1922
Spector, Mordechai 1859-1922
Spengler, Oswald 1880-1936
Squire, J(ohn) C(ollings) 1884-1958
Stavenhagen, Fritz 1876-1906
Stockton, Frank R. 1834-1902
Subrahmanya Bharati, C. 1882-1921
Sudermann, Hermann 1857-1938
Sully-Prudhomme, René 1839-1907
Talev, Dimituv 1898-1966
Thoma, Ludwig 1867-1927
Tolstoy, Alexei 1882-1945
Trotsky, Leon 1870-1940
Tuchmann, Jules 1830-1901
Turner, W(alter) J(ames) R(edfern) 1889-1946
Vachell, Horace Annesley 1861-1955
Van Dine, S.S. (William H. Wright) 1888-1939
Van Doren, Carl 1885-1950
Van Dyke, Henry 1852-1933
Vazov, Ivan Minchov 1850-1921
Veblen, Thorstein 1857-1929
Villaespesa, Francisco, 1877-1936
Wallace, Edgar 1874-1932
Wallace, Lewis 1827-1905
Walsh, Ernest 1895-1926
Webb, Mary 1881-1927
Webster, Jean 1876-1916
White, Walter Francis 1893-1955
Whitlock, Brand 1869-1927
Wilson, Harry Leon 1867-1939
Wister, Owen 1860-1938
Wolf, Emma 1865-1932
Wood, Clement 1888-1950
Wren, P(ercival) C(hristopher) 1885-1941
Yonge, Charlotte Mary 1823-1901
Zangwill, Israel 1864-1926
Zecca, Ferdinand 1864-1947
Zeromski, Stefan 1864-1925
Zoshchenko, Mikhail 1895-1958
Zweig, Stefan 1881-1942

Readers are cordially invited to suggest additional authors to the editors.

Innokenty Annensky

1856-1909

(Also transliterated as Innokentij; also Ánnensky and Annenskij; also wrote under pseudonym of Nik. T.O.) Russian poet, dramatist, critic, and translator.

Annensky is considered an important figure of the Silver Age of Russian letters, a literary epoch that spanned the 1890s and early 1900s and marked a revolt against the optimistic spirit and subordination of art to social duty characteristic of earlier Russian literature. A major poet whose importance was only fully recognized after his death, Annensky was also a sensitive and original critic capable of great psychological insight. In evaluating Annensky's career, critics generally consider not only the intrinsic merit of his works, but also his profound influence on his fellow writers. His verses exercised a catalytic effect on the generation of poets who succeeded him, and critics agree that his aesthetic ideas were instrumental in leading to the inception of the Acmeist, or anti-Symbolist movement in Russian letters. Although Annensky's writings have received a great deal of thoughtful critical attention in Russia, there is no book-length collection of his work available in English translation.

Annensky was born in Omsk, Siberia, but his father, an important government official, moved the family to St. Petersburg while Annensky was still a child. Raised in St. Petersburg, Annensky studied classical languages and literature at the university, with the intention of earning an advanced degree and becoming a professor. He abandoned this plan, however, when he was offered an opportunity to teach classical languages at the gymnasium at Tsarkoye Selo. Annensky eventually became the director of schools for the district of Tsarkoye Selo, a position that he held until shortly before his death. In 1903 Nikolai Gumilev, the future founder of the Acmeist movement, enrolled at the Tsarkoye Selo gymnasium. Evidence from many sources indicates that Annensky and Gumilev became well acquainted at this time, and that Gumilev often read his poems to Annensky. Annensky's acquaintance with Anna Akhmatova and Osip Mandelstam, the other important Acmeist poets, also dates from this period. Akhmatova met Gumilev—who later became her husband—during her student days at Tsarkoye Selo, and he introduced her to Annensky. Mandelstam lived in nearby Pablovsk and shared Annensky's interest in Pushkin, a bond through which he came to know Annensky well. Annensky's popularity with the younger generation was to prove important to his reputation in later years.

While in St. Petersburg in 1908, Gumilev introduced Annensky to Sergei Makovsky, who was then planning a classically oriented literary journal to be called *Apollon*. Prior to this meeting, Annensky had published his critical essays only in scholarly journals, while his first volume of poetry, *Tikhi pesnie,* had been met for the most part with critical indifference. Makovsky asked Annensky to contribute to *Apollon* and to advise him in its production. Many of Annensky's important critical essays and several of his poems first appeared in this journal which, shortly after Annensky's death, became the official forum of the Acmeist movement, led by Gumilev, Akhmatova, and Mandelstam. Annensky's involvement with *Apollon* led to his acceptance in St. Petersburg literary circles that had formerly been closed to him, and this brought long-denied critical recognition for his poetry. But Annensky had little opportunity to enjoy his new celebrity; he died of a heart attack in 1909, shortly before the publication of his *Kiparisovy larets,* a volume of poetry that is still regarded as a masterpiece.

By permission of Ardis Publishers

Critics often compare Annensky's poetry, with its stylistic borrowings from the French Symbolists and jaded outlook reminiscent of the Decadents, to that of Stéphane Mallarmé and Paul Verlaine. But despite the poet's use of subjects and techniques associated with these authors and movements, there are certain characteristics of Annensky's work that set it apart from French influences. For example, Annensky strove for a clarity of expression in his poetry that was foreign to Symbolist writing, and his use of concrete imagery and colloquial expressions stood in sharp contrast to the mystical and indefinite quality of Symbolist verse. His determination that the external, sensual world was the most suitable subject for poetry also separated his work from the Russian Symbolists. It was this artistic principle that especially influenced the thinking of youthful poets such as Mandelstam, Akhmatova and Gumilev. Whereas the Russian Symbolists viewed poetry primarily as a vehicle for achieving mystical transcendence, Annensky and the Acmeists after him celebrated the beauties and the limitations of the physical world. Annensky's essentially classical approach to literature, his emphasis on aesthetic form, and his interest in

Western European literature in general also influenced the Acmeists. It is for these reasons that Annensky is viewed by most critics as a transitional figure between the Symbolist and the Acmeist eras, and is typically given credit for helping shape the Acmeist aesthetic, despite the fact that the Acmeist doctrine was not officially formulated as such by Gumilev and Mandelstam until several years after Annensky's death.

Among Annensky's other works are his translations of Euripides' plays. Although critics generally acknowledge them to be of high quality, these translations have nonetheless provoked controversy over the years, because Annensky's intent in undertaking them was to modernize and popularize the Greek poet, and not simply to make his works accessible to Russian readers in verbatim translations. Thus, although Annensky's translations retain the classical form of the Greek originals, they also contain many colloquial expressions and neologisms of the type found in Annensky's own poetry.

In addition to his translations of Euripides' plays, Annensky also wrote several original dramas, including *Laodamia, Melanippa-filosof,* and *Famira kifared,* that utilize settings, dramatic forms, and plots borrowed from the classical theater and Greek mythology. Annensky used these classical devices to construct dramas that present contemporary social issues and ethical questions. Simon Karlinsky has noted, for example, that Annensky's best-known play, *Famira-kifared,* which is set in ancient Greece, shares the essentially Freudian theme of the devouring mother-figure with Anton Chekhov's more conspicuously "modern" drama *The Sea Gull.*

Annensky was also a respected and influential literary critic. His critical works, *Kniga otrazheniy* and *Vtoraya kniga otrazheniy,* have been widely praised for their psychological and artistic insights, and the poetic quality of their prose. Annensky's criticism, like his poetry, reveals the impressionistic influence of the French Symbolists and the emphasis on form, intellectual process, and the autonomy of the creative work that characterize both French Parnassianism and classical art.

Despite the brevity of Annensky's career and his failure to achieve recognition during his lifetime, his independent thinking and theorizing in the realm of aesthetics helped renew the interest of a generation of Russian writers in the classical perfection of form that later came to characterize the modernist approach to art of all types. Similarly, his wide range of literary interests helped draw Russian authors into the mainstream of European literature.

(See also *Contemporary Authors,* Vol. 110.)

PRINCIPAL WORKS

Melanippa-filosof [first publication] (drama) 1901
Tsar' Iksion [first publication] (drama) 1902
Tikhie pesni [as Nik. T.O.] (poetry) 1904
Laodamia [first publication] (drama) 1906
Kniga otrazheniy (criticism) 1907
Teatr Evripida [translator] (dramas) 1907
Vtoraya kniga otrazheniy (criticism) 1909
Kiparisovy larets (poetry) 1910
Famira kifared (drama) 1916
Posmertnye stikhi (poetry) 1923
Stikhotvoreniya i tragedii (poetry, letters, and dramas) 1959

Translated selections of Annensky's poetry have appeared in the following publications: *A Book of Russian Verse, Modern Russian Poetry, The Penguin Book of Russian Verse* and *A Second Book of Russian Verse.*

ALEKSANDR BLOK (essay date 1906)

[Blok was the foremost poet of the Silver Age in Russian letters, a literary epoch that spanned the 1890s and early 1900s and which marked a revolt against the optimism and subordination of art to social duty that was characteristic of earlier Russian art. During the first decade of the twentieth century, Blok was the acknowledged leader of the Russian Symbolist movement, and he is remembered today as the creator of the controversial poem The Twelve *(1918), the greatest poetic celebration of the October Revolution. In the following excerpt from a review that originally appeared in 1906, Blok offers a generally favorable reading of Annensky's* Tikhie pesnie, *which was published under the pseudonym "Nik. T.O." ("Nobody").]*

The greater part of the poems [***Tikhie pesni***] of Mr. Nik-to bears the stamp of a fragile fineness and a true poetic sensitivity, despite the naive lack of taste in several lines and the decadent excesses which this poet allows himself. It is even easy to pass up this book completely because of its ugly exterior, the crookedness of its lines, which stand out under a cursory glance, its pale epigraph and its doubtful pseudonym. But somehow, having become interested in it you read it—and it becomes all right—and you cannot believe that what you have read could have been written by Mr. Nik-to.

Aleksandr Blok, in an extract from a review of "Tikhie pesni," in Studies in the Life and Work of Innokentij Annenskij *by Vsevolod Setchkarev, Mouton & Co., 1963, p. 31.*

INNOKENTY ANNENSKY (essay date 1909)

[In the following excerpt from an essay on the works of Mikhail Lermontov originally published in 1909, Annensky digresses from his main topic to discuss Russian poetry and Russian poets, in the process revealing much about his own ideas on art and his anti-Romantic approach to poetry.]

The Russian poet was the first to finish celebrating his marriage with life, or, more precisely, he accepted its yoke on the day when Gogol *not without affectation* pronounced the terrible word *poshlost'* [*vulgarity*]. It was from that time that life became for us a soiled peasant woman, and although consciousness of this is occasionally very humiliating, we take consolation in the fact that each of us now has at least a warm corner where he may hide, and the cockroaches in this peculiarly Russian corner scarcely interfere with our speculation. This warm corner is not devoid of sentimental distractions, but the peasant woman who tends it wearies us with two in particular; we must play her game—either penitence or self-pity. But one must give us our due, for, although we sometimes play this game with slightly soiled cards, we play it fervently. (p. 58)

Gentlemen, I am not a Romantic. I cannot, indeed, and I would not want to escape from the hopeless decrepitude of my vulgar world. I have observed ever so closely such tempting abysses, I have visited—and with you, with you, gentlemen, don't deny it, please—such dubious little corners that stars and waves, no matter how they glitter and twinkle, can no longer always charm me.

But strength is always pleasing, and although it is foolish to quarrel with the past and even more foolish so to invoke it (and from where, I would like to know, could it come?), still it is sometimes difficult not to lose oneself in admiration of the past. (pp. 60-1)

Do I love people or not? What business is it of yours? I understand that you want to know if I love freedom and the dignity of man. Yes, I love them, because I love snow-covered mountains which recede into the heavens and a sail which summons a storm. I love independence. That is why I love the quiet of a lunar night, and why I so love and so value the quiet tonight that when one star speaks with another I pause in my stride on a cobbled road and let them speak in a language of silence which I cannot attain. I love strength, but because force is senseless, it is unnatural to desire and love it. What right, in fact, do you have to soil a river with blood that pure snow melts to feed? This is why I love strength which only sleeps and does not overpower or kill. . . . And what else? Death sometimes seems to me a magical midday dream, which sees far, in a calm and clear fashion. But death can and must be beautiful in another way, too, because it is the soul-child of my will and it can be, if I wish it, also a golden luminary in the harmony of the world's order. It must have an indifference about it, the indifference of Lermontov. (p. 62)

Innokenty Annensky, "Innokenty Annensky on Mikhail Lermontov," in The Complection of Russian Literature: A Cento, *edited and translated by Andrew Field, Atheneum, 1971, pp. 57-62.**

VYACHESLAV IVANOV (essay date 1910)

[*Ivanov was a prominent Russian Symbolist poet. Influenced by the mystic philosophy of the poet Vladimir Solovyov, he, like fellow Russian Symbolists Aleksandr Blok and Andrey Bely, perceived the visible world as laden with symbols of transcendent realities and promoted a new consciousness in which the metaphysical element should prevail. In the following excerpt from an essay that originally appeared in 1910, Ivanov defines and discusses Annensky's "post-Symbolist" vision.*]

Innokenty Annensky is a lyric poet and a Symbolist of the sort that we may term *associative*. This type of poet-Symbolist takes as a point of departure something physically or psychologically concrete, and, without defining it immediately, often without naming it at all, he makes a series of associations with it. The laying bare of such associative connections helps to realize vividly and fully the spiritual meaning of the phenomenon that the poet experiences. Sometimes he may succeed in naming it for the first time, in replacing its heretofore common and vacuous name with a name full of significance.

Such a poet loves, as Mallarmé did, to surprise us with unexpected and occasionally mysterious combinations of images and ideas, forcing us to realize their inter-relationships and correlations. He also frequently employs the impressionistic device of "laying bare." An object is "laid bare" by poetic contemplation when its name finally registers clearly in the reader's consciousness, seems new and, as it were, is perceived for the first time, when its perspective deepens.

This limited technique of "correspondence" in Mallarmé and Annensky reminds us of the hermetically sealed riddle of the same phenomenon. For those who choose the path of depictive Symbolism, a phenomenon is a symbol insofar as it is a doorway and an exit to a secret; but for poets such as Annensky, the Symbol is a prison window through which a prisoner stares, and after he has grown weary of the fixed and limited landscape before him he turns his attention again to the dark and limited immediacy of his cell. The sole result of choosing such prison martyrdom for oneself or someone else's self is the opportunity to run in lyrical transport the gamut of negative emotions—despair, despondency, bitter scepsis, self-pity, and pity for one's neighbor who is also in solitary confinement. In Annensky's poetry pity is the note sounded most consistently. It is pity which, as the constant firmament of all lyricism and sensitivity, makes this quasi-Frenchman, quasi-Hellene of the decline into a deeply Russian poet, as though he has made contact again with our original Christian roots. Like the Sceptics of old he doubts everything—except the reality of the suffering he experiences.

Annensky, the Russian translator of Euripides, seemed to understand the ancient "new man" of Euripides, in whom he detected the same discord and division that he felt in himself. His personality had freed its consciousness and self-consciousness from the bonds of the old communalism and religious collectivism, but it ended locked within itself and deprived of true intercourse with others, not knowing any way of breaking through the cage door which had thudded shut. (pp. 179-80)

Tragedy in any real sense of the word could have no place in this psychology. Nonetheless, Annensky may be said to have been faithful to the Euripidean formula of tragedy and to have followed this track to the natural end Euripides indicated. (p. 180)

Vyacheslav Ivanov, "Vyacheslav Ivanov on Innokenty Annensky," in The Complection of Russian Literature: A Cento, *edited and translated by Andrew Field, Atheneum, 1971, pp. 179-80.*

NIKOLAI GUMILEV (essay date 1914)

[*Gumilev was one of the founders and major figures of the Acmeist movement in early twentieth-century Russian poetry. The Acmeists reacted against the earlier school of the Russian Symbolists, whose work they criticized as abstract, diffuse, and alienated by mysticism from the beauties and the value of the physical world. Gumilev and other Acmeists, including his wife Anna Akhmatova and the poet Osip Mandelstam, briefly established a poetics that demanded concise and concrete renderings of physical reality, emphasizing a Neoclassic formalism that contrasted with what the Acmeists considered the loose transcendental verbiage of the Symbolists. As a young man, Gumilev was Annensky's pupil at Tsarkoye Selo. In the following excerpt, originally published in 1914, Gumilev discusses Annensky's drama* Famira kifared.]

Innokenty Annensky's bacchic drama, ***Famira Kifared*** . . . is, after ***The Cypress Chest,*** the deceased poet's most significant book. It is a continuation and completion of his earlier attempts to revive antiquity, like ***Ixion, Melannippe the Philosopher, Laodamia*** and the treatise **"The Ancient World in Contemporary French Poetry,"** important for the depth and novelty of the ideas expressed in it. Innokenty Annensky, all impulse, all trembling, was equally far from both the Renaissance idea that the world is not ahead of, but behind us, that is, with the ancient Greeks, and from the contemporary desire to pillage that strange and beautiful world, using ready-made thoughts and sonorous proper names. He has a deep feeling for myth, as a situation existing from the beginning of time, or rather, as a relation between two intransient unities, that is only very superficially connected with the epoch that discovered it. Only good taste and a striving toward the beautiful difficulty (he speaks of this, by the way, in the above-mentioned treatise) prevented him from creating symbolic-allegorical dramas within a mythical framework. Not for anything did he want to abandon the present, with its vivid, graphic language and psychological nuances, for the sake of dismal abstraction; but in treating myth a touch of the unusual was indispensable, and he achieved it, capriciously combining the ancient with the contemporary. His characters are taken from the ancient world; they do nothing that would be uncharacteristic for their epoch, but their conversations, with the exception of the general poetic intensification (the drama was written in 1906), are strikingly contemporary. Of course, we do not know how the ancient Greeks spoke, the language of their poets is not conversational language, but still, it is impossible to believe that echoes of Balmont and Verlaine could be heard in their words. Innokenty Annensky does this quite consciously, almost as though with defiance, as is shown by such anachronisms as Apollo's famous violin. In ***Famira Kifared,*** there are two musical motives, separate, but indispensable to each other: the story of Famira and the background against which it is played out, the choruses now crazed maenades, now jovial satyrs. This is the framework of the story: "Famira or Famirid, the son of the Thracian king Philammon and the nymph Argiope, was renowned for playing the cithara; his arrogance reached the point that he challenged the Muses to a contest, but was defeated, and as punishment, deprived of sight and the gift of music." Annensky complicates this scheme with the nymph's unexpected love for her son, and portrays him as a dreamer, for whom love is alien, but who still perishes in the net of the woman in love with him. Fate appears in the image of the splendidly indifferent muse, Euterpe, of whom one of the characters says:

> Haughty—when she passes among us,
> She gathers up her dress with her hand. Fingers—
> And rings are beautiful on her pink
> And slender fingers—only, I suppose, her hands
> Are cold—and she is always looking at them
> With a smile—she is so content . . .

Famira burns out his eyes with coals and goes off to beg alms; the guilty mother, transformed into a bird, accompanies him in his wanderings and draws lots from the useless cithara. They set off, as if they had hangovers, and behind, the exultant and languorous call of the maenades still sounds, even more audible in memory. . . . (pp. 137-39)

Nikolai Gumilev, "Bryusov, Severyanin, Khlebnikov, Komarovsky, Golike and Vilborg, Annensky, Sologub," in his Nikolai Gumilev on Russian Poetry, *edited and translated by David Lapeza, Ardis, 1977, pp. 129-39.**

D. S. MIRSKY (essay date 1926)

[Mirsky was a Russian prince who fled his country after the Bolshevik Revolution and settled in London. While in England, he wrote two important and comprehensive histories of Russian literature, Contemporary Russian Literature *(1926) and* A History of Russian Literature *(1927). In 1932, having reconciled himself to the Soviet regime, Mirsky returned to the USSR. He continued to write literary criticism, but his work eventually ran afoul of Soviet censors and he was exiled to Siberia. He disappeared in 1937. In the following excerpt from* Contemporary Russian Literature, *Mirsky briefly describes Annensky's work as "uncommonly original and interesting" and discusses the influence on Annensky's poetry of the works of such French poets as Paul Verlaine, Stéphane Mallarmé, and Charles Baudelaire.]*

In 1904 [Ánnensky] published a book of lyrics (half of which was occupied by translations from French poets and from Horace) entitled ***Quiet Songs*** **[*Tikhie pesni*]** and under the whimsical pseudonym of *Nik. T. O.* (read: *Niktó*—nobody). He means it to be an allusion to the Polyphemus episode in the *Odyssey*. This farfetched and elaborate allusion is typical of Ánnensky. ***Quiet Songs*** passed unnoticed, even by the symbolists. Poetry over his name continued to appear from time to time in the magazines, and he brought out two books of critical essays, which are remarkable both for the subtlety and penetration of his criticism and for the perverse pretensions of his style. In 1909 a few people began to realize that Ánnensky was an uncommonly original and interesting poet. He was "taken up" by the Petersburg symbolists and introduced to their poetical circles, where he at once became a central figure. He was on his way to becoming a principal influence in literature when he suddenly died of heart failure. He had prepared for the press a second book of verse—***The Cypress Chest*** **[*Kiparisovy larets*]**—which was published in 1910 and recognized in the inner circle of Russian poets as a classic.

Ánnensky's poetry is in many ways different from that of all his contemporaries. It is not metaphysical, but purely emotional—or rather, perhaps, nervous. He had no Russian masters. In so far as he had any masters at all, they were Baudelaire, Verlaine, and Mallarmé. But on the whole his lyrical gift is remarkably original. It is a rare case of a very late development. Nor did he at once attain to perfection. ***Quiet Songs*** is distinctly immature (although written at forty-eight). But in ***The Cypress Chest*** the majority of the poems are flawlessly perfect jewels. Ánnensky is a symbolist, in so far as his poetry is based on a system of "correspondences." But they are purely emotional correspondences. His poems are developed in two interconnected planes—the human soul and the outer world; each of them is an elaborate parallel between a state of mind and the external world. Ánnensky is akin to Chékhov, for his material is also the pinpricks and infinitesimals of life. His poetry is essentially human, and its appeal would be universal, for it deals with the common stuff of humanity. His poems are constructed with disconcerting and baffling subtleness and precision. They are compressed and laconic—much of the structure has been pulled away, and only the essential points remain for the reader to reverse the process and grasp the unity of the poem. Few readers, however, feel themselves capable of the creative effort required. But the work is worth the while. Those who have mastered him usually prefer him to all other poets. For he is unique and always fresh. The extent of his poetry is small, his two books do not contain more than a hundred lyrics all told, and most of them are not over twenty lines long. This makes it comparatively easy to study. It must be added that Ánnensky's diction is studiously common and trivial. It is the unbeautiful language of every day—but his poetical alchemy transforms the ugly dross of vulgarity into the purest poetical gold.

Ánnensky's tragedies written in imitation of Euripides are not on the level of his lyrics. The most interesting is the posthumous ***Thamiras Cytharede*** **[*Famira kifared*]**. The subject is the Apollonian myth of the proud harpist who challenged the god to a contest in music and expiated his arrogance by the loss of his eyes. There is much poignant poetry in the tragedy, but it is eminently unclassical. Still less classical are his most curious translations from Horace. Altogether, considering his lifelong connection with the ancients, Ánnensky is quite disconcertingly free from any kinship with antiquity. (pp. 447-48)

D. S. Mirsky, "The Symbolists," in his A History of Russian Literature Comprising "A History of Russian Literature" and "Contemporary Russian Literature," *edited by Francis J. Whitfield, Alfred A. Knopf, 1949, pp. 430-84.**

MARC SLONIM (essay date 1953)

[*In the following excerpt, Slonim briefly outlines Annensky's principal poetic subjects of suffering, death, and beauty. Slonim also describes Annensky's poetic style, concluding that his style places him midway between the Symbolists and the anti-Symbolists (Acmeists). For further discussions of Annensky's themes, see the excerpts by Avrahm Yarmolinsky (1969) and Janet Grace Tucker (1973).*]

An intermediate position between the Decadents and Symbolists was occupied by Innokenty Annensky . . . , an exquisite poet and the beloved teacher of the younger generation. His influence grew steadily; by 1917 he was recognized as one of the masters of Russian poetry. (p. 101)

The three themes of poetry, Annensky maintained, are suffering, death, and beauty—and to these he devoted his murmurous rhythms. He felt intensely 'the pangs of being,' the decay of things, and that subtle melancholy which a flutter of beauty—a woman, a flower, a quotation from Aeschylus—evokes in those who are disturbed by the coarseness and inanity of the world. With a refinement bordering on snobbishness he returned again and again to the same themes: the 'venom of poetry,' the 'intoxication of creative work,' the 'opium of dreaming'—to the tedium and futility of life, which can be dispelled only through art and love. This aesthetic attitude was, however, strangely blended with a sense of genuine compassion for 'all things that suffer.' Annensky felt compassion not only for men and animals but also for objects, and his poems on vernal landscapes (he hated spring) or on flowers cease to be mere descriptions: in the light of pity and preciousness things start to move and distill a sweet poison of resignation.

The delicate insinuating musicality and the emotional symbolism of his lines are conveyed in changing, though perfectly constructed, meters. Nothing is loose in his poems; poignancy and concentration are blended. This poet's formal achievements were so varied that their echo resounds not only in the works of such Symbolists as Blok, but also in such anti-Symbolists as Gumilev, Pasternak, and Mandelstamm. Annensky's works never reached a large public but they had an indisputable place in the revival of modern Russian verse. (pp. 101-02)

Marc Slonim, "The Modernist Movement," in his Modern Russian Literature: From Chekhov to the Present, *Oxford University Press, New York, 1953, pp. 79-102.**

RENATO POGGIOLI (essay date 1960)

[*Poggioli was an Italian-born American critic and translator. Much of his critical writing is concerned with Russian literature, including* The Poets of Russia, 1890-1930, *which is one of the most important examinations of this literary era. In the following excerpt from that work, Poggioli states that Annensky's place among modern Russian poets may be second only to Aleksandr Blok's. He compares the "feverish and electric quality" of Annensky's inspirations to those of Charles Baudelaire, stating that their temper and vision are alike "in quality if not in degree."*]

[Annenskij] bared his own rare gift to himself and to others all too late and too briefly, just before his own death; and that revelation coincided with what at the time seemed to be the "crisis," or even the "agony," of Russian Symbolism. He conveyed the decadent mood with such genuineness of feeling as to change it into a personal experience; and if he used for the purpose the visionary imagery and suggestive music of the Symbolists, it was only because he found those media the expressive vehicles most congenial to his psyche. This is but one of the reasons why many readers of keen taste, as well as many critics of deep insight, consider him a lyricist of the first rank; and some of them do not hesitate to place him, within the gallery of the Russian poetry of his time, in a place second only to Blok's. (pp. 170-71)

He was about forty-five when he published his first book of poems, under the strange pseudonym *Nik. T. O.*, a partial anagram of his Christian name, forming the Russian word meaning "no one." The choice of that pseudonym, obviously patterned after the Ουτιδ [Nobody] by which Homer's Ulysses cunningly names himself to Polyphemus, reflects the author's awareness of his own obscurity. That first book, ***Still Songs*** . . . , half of which was taken up by very personal translations, mainly from modern French verse, passed almost unnoticed, but the poems which appeared later in many periodicals were enthusiastically received. Annenškij died shortly before 1910, when his masterpiece, ***The Cypress Chest,*** was published. The rest of his literary heritage is made up of verse fragments and minor pieces, collected, under the title ***Posthumous Poems,*** as late as 1923; and of two volumes of sensitive and well-written critiques: ***A Book of Reflections*** and ***A Second Book of Reflections,*** published respectively in 1906 and 1909, the last the very year of the poet's death.

The whole lyrical output of Annenskij amounts to about a hundred pieces, rarely consisting of more than three or four stanzas each. At first impression it seems that his poetry tends to move in an atmosphere similar to that of Verlaine. This is particularly true of his earlier poems, where, like that French poet at his best, Annenskij tries to catch vague impressions and to convey indefinite feelings, to fix transitory experiences or to shape impalpable things. The most frequent background of such poems is a garden, painted in the chiaroscuro of twilight rather than in the *plein air* [*fuller atmosphere*] of mid-day. That garden may well symbolize Annenskij's spiritual and physical world, which is indeed a *hortus conclusus* [*enclosed garden*], preserving the faded flowers of being, while his heart might in turn be compared to a smaller, private shrine, or to use the image of one of his titles, to a quaint coffer or "cypress chest" embalming the relics of feeling.

Yet, if we look deeper, we shall see that if Annenskij is a Verlaine, he is a Verlaine in a saturnine mood. His voice sounds so intimate and discreet, his tone so unassuming and subdued, that it seems his poetry should be called, as Verlaine named his own, a *chanson grise* [*gray song*]. As for the tender musicality of his tunes it is so fluid and vague that his lyrics should be likewise defined with the Verlainian title of *romances sans paroles* [*romances without words*]. Annenskij himself must have been aware of this, since he entitled the first of his collections ***Still Songs.*** Yet at second glance that "stillness" reveals the feverish and electric quality of this poet's inspirations, and we discover that the "songs without words" are in reality wordless plaints, that the *chanson grise* is in reality a mournful and wailing chant. Thus, while looking at first like a Russian Verlaine, Annenskij turns out to be the only poet of his nation and time whose temper and vision could be compared, in quality if not in degree, to those of Baudelaire.

Annenskij's landscapes, being *états d'âme* [*states of the soul*] in the most literal sense of the term, cannot be simply inter-

ИННОКЕНТІЙ АННЕНСКІЙ

КИПАРИСОВЫЙ ЛАРЕЦЪ

ВТОРАЯ
КНИГА СТИХОВЪ
(ПОСМЕРТНАЯ)

ОБЛОЖКА А. АРНШТАМА

КНИГОИЗДАТЕЛЬСТВО
„ГРИФЪ“
МОСКВА — 1910

Title page of the first edition of Annensky's Kiparisovy larets. *By permission of Ardis Publishers.*

preted as the emblems of a timid and petty decadence, mirroring itself in the twilights or glimmers of late autumn. As Baudelaire said of himself, Annenskij is a painter working not with light but with darkness. His palette neglects all bright and wholesome colors for vanishing shades or fading hues. Yet it is through such shadows and nuances that he succeeds in depicting the purgatory of life and the hell of the world. Thus in substance all his landscapes are but imaginative projections of the innermost experiences of his psyche; one could say that few modern poets ever turned the pathetic fallacy to a better advantage, by sharing with nature at large the shame of the self and the pain of life. Annenskij resembles Baudelaire also in his tendency to see sin and evil even in the most lovely flowers of the earth. All his poetry is in essence but the pathetic revery or morbid fancy of the sense of being, full of a poignant melancholy intoxicating the soul. Annenskij himself saw the spring of his inspiration in "the subtle poison of remembrance," by which he meant a reminiscence mixing loathing and disgust with longing and regret. And it was the poet's awareness of the wicked charm of his craft that led him to avow that he loved his verses "as only a mother can adore her sick children."

In brief, like Baudelaire, Annenskij transformed the mystic dreams of Symbolism into the nightmares of the self. The poet of insomnia and ennui, he conveyed his obsessive and yet lucid vision with direct simplicity of utterance, in almost colloquial speech. Mirskij saw a splendid paradox in the fact that this classical scholar, unlike his colleague Vjacheslav Ivanov, always refused to be tempted by that grand style and lofty diction which are the nemesis of modern classicism. Of all the dimensions of form, the ones for which Annenskij showed greatest concern were meter and rhythm. He was no innovator in that field; all he sought was to recapture in his verse that trancelike music which may be found in the best of the Romantics. His own is but "chamber music," yet the quality of his poetry may be likened, more fairly than to that of his contemporaries, to the most quintessential lyrics of Tjutchev and even Pushkin: in the case of the latter, especially to such a brief piece as **"Lines Written on a Sleepless Night,"** with its uncanny sense of all the perceptions and hallucinations which may haunt a brain morbidly awake, from "the Parque's stammering gossip" to "the mouselike rustlings" of daily life. (pp. 171-73)

Renato Poggioli, "Symbolists and Others," in his The Poets of Russia: 1890-1930, *Cambridge, Mass.: Harvard University Press, 1960, pp. 153-78.**

VSEVOLOD SETCHKAREV (essay date 1963)

[*Setchkarev is the author of the only book-length study in English of Annensky's work. In the following excerpt from that study, Setchkarev discusses the influence of the French Parnassians on Annensky's poetry, as well as the aesthetic principles, themes, and techniques that helped shape his verse and dramas. In particular, Setchkarev discusses the important influence of the Symbolists on Annensky's best-known drama,* Famira kifared, *which the critic claims represents Annensky's attempt to "embody the Symbolist idea of a synthetic work of art, in which Poetry, Music and Painting are united."*]

The development of modern Russian poetry shows with increasing clarity that the poet whose work has been most influential was Innokentij Annenskij.

The impact of Blok, Esenin, and Majakovskij was, to be sure, of a much larger scope and received wider publicity, yet the outstanding poets of the last decades did not follow them, preferring rather to accept Annenskij's achievements.

By Russian poetry I mean the 'individualistic' poetry outside of Russia, not the rather dubious 'collectivistic' productions of the Soviet poets. With very few exceptions, for example, Anna Axmatova or Osip Mandel'štam, who certainly are not Soviet poets, the verses of the poets inside Russia cannot—for obvious reasons—be measured and evaluated in the usual way as products of the aesthetic feeling in men. But the unsupervised poetry of the most gifted among the emigrants, such as Georgij Ivanov, Boris Poplavskij, Anatolij Štejger, Igor' Činnov—to mention only a few—is largely indebted to the work of Annenskij.

The influence of the Acmeists is of course very distinct too; but can they be separated from Annenskij's poetry? Gumilëv, Axmatova, Mandel'štam—the greatest of this school—gratefully recognized their indebtedness to him. (p. 5)

As a poet, Annenskij belongs to the "elder Symbolists". This statement can be found in any history of Russian literature. But as so often is the case, this literary label does not fit completely and some of his most important characteristics do not correspond to it at all.

There is unquestionably a very strong connection between Annenskij and French symbolism. Baudelaire, Verlaine, Mallarmé and many minor symbolist poets influenced him so strongly that he tried to write exactly as they did. Yet he wrote without giving up his own personality and his own specific range of metaphysical and literary interests and beliefs. The result was a poetry that is thoroughly original in spite of its clear literary genealogy—a kind of paradox which succeeded because the personality of the poet was great enough to make the contrasts unite on a higher level.

This specific original undercurrent brought Annenskij very close to another literary movement in Russia—Acmeism. The school in between elder Symbolism and Acmeism—the so-called "younger Symbolism"—was absolutely foreign to him.

French symbolism in Russia developed in two ways: the first was mysticism; the second was a return to the principles of the Parnasse, but enriched with the experiences of Symbolism.

It was the first that was the Russian road par excellence. The second stayed in the European tradition, avoiding above all the pitfalls of mystic nationalism and at the same time moving steadily away from religion. Its "religion" became more and more aesthetics, a kind of "aesthetics of life", a search for beauty in real objects and the attempt to recreate it in art.

The youngest poets of the first decade of this century, disagreeing with the mystic development of symbolism, saw in Annenskij an uncompromising champion of pure art. This does not mean a fight for the *l'art pour l'art* principle, but life transposed into art and intuitively explained and clarified to the highest possible degree by the transposition.

Annenskij's poetry does not contain hints at a "beyond" which would imply a religious revelation and therefore be truer than the "here". This "here" is an emanation of Beauty, but spoiled and degenerated; art makes the connecting link between Beauty and real life—it is able to prove their original connection.

To a certain degree this theory might also be termed mysticism, but it is not a mysticism that requires faith and it does not want to have anything to do with religion. It is an "aesthetic mysticism" which only presupposes a feeling for the creative power of an artist in order to be accepted as a *kind* of solution for the enigma of life.

This last cautious formulation indicates the drop of scepticism which is constantly present in "aesthetic mysticism" and which is always prepared to dissolve it into an avowal of complete ignorance. The aesthetic attitude is aware of its own fragility, and its ardent belief in Beauty seems sometimes to be a deliberate turning away from the terrible recognition that the whole of life is an unexplainable bit of ugly nonsense. The attempt to make life beautiful by transposition is made, and now and again it succeeds very well. But the "unbeautiful" intrudes with a violence which makes one fear that the metaphysical power might be on its side, that evil and ugliness might be victorious at the end.

This feeling of anxiety for the beautiful, the feeling of the constant danger to beauty from "real" life, is the basic motif of Annenskij's poetry. He is not afraid of death itself; he fears the unbeautiful manifestations of death in life—and this is why he fears life and fears for life.

The fear for the beautiful in life results in a second main theme: compassion for life, which might be beautiful in all its stages—starting from a stone and rising up to God. One of the points at which Annenskij and Acmeism converge is this loving interest in the objects of reality, whatever they may be. In Annenskij the accent on pity is much stronger, while the Acmeists try to keep a cooler attitude. Both have a keen interest in things and try to find and to point out what makes them beautiful.

Sometimes it is very difficult to see this beauty, and then life with its powerful metaphysical ingredient of evil becomes a nightmare—a nightmare containing clear-cut objects, which are the more menacing in the suddenly unreal atmosphere into which they are put.

Annenskij is not a poet with "a hope". There are no reassuring aspects in his view on life. The hope for Beauty, poignant as it may be, is too vague, too endangered. It can only give a temporary consolation, a temporary respite—then it dies away. And it is so difficult to get a glance at it. Art demands torture; its creation is a constant sacrifice. But it is a sacrifice which is worthwhile because it leads through ugliness and evil to the fragile kernel of Beauty.

Annenskij is deliberately "unpoetic" in his imagery and in his epithets. His themes, such as rainy days and nights, shadows, fear, growing cold, sorcery, loneliness, railway coaches, melting snow, dirt on roads, decay, sleeplessness, banality, are unbeautiful as such, but they are *made* beautiful because they are put into poetic words. There are combinations of sounds which can transform real ugliness into poetic beauty. Annenskij was very sensitive to those combinations. . . . And in his poetry we have a constant preoccupation with the word in its full shape—meaning and sound combined.

Osip Mandel'štam, the best theoretician of Acmeism, apart from Gumilëv, praises Annenskij as a representative of "heroic Hellenism", of "militant philology". Being imbued with ancient Greek poetry, with the "snake's poison of wise Hellenic speech", Annenskij did not try to "hellenize" the Russian language. He tried to give it an "inner Hellenism" which is suitable to its spirit. He wanted to give Russian a "domestic Hellenism" (*domašnij èllinizm*). What Mandel'štam means are those small details, those unpoetic everyday-life features which receive a poetic touch because Annenskij knows how to make the word designating them glow in a specific light. (pp. 54-6)

It is rarely possible to *describe* exactly what the special quality of poetic speech is, but its existence can be strongly felt in Annenskij's plain, apparently unpretentious verse.

The main influences on Annenskij, apart from the immense impact of French symbolism, were Puškin, Boratynskij and Tjutčev. They are so obvious that it is hardly necessary to point them out. Puškin's clear diction and his all-comprising conciseness, Boratynskij's passionate metaphysical attitude and his clear thought imbued with emotion, as well as Tjutčev's philosophical and oratorical pathos can be traced in a great number of Annenskij's poems. (pp. 56-7)

[The] three volumes of his verse have exactly the same quality.

It has been said repeatedly—without proof—that there is an enormous progress from ***Quiet Songs*** to ***The Cypress Chest.*** This is not true; ***Tixie Pesni*** contains many of the best poems Annenskij wrote. Moreover, who can prove that many poems in ***Kiparisovyj larec*** were not written before those in the earlier publication (not to mention those in ***Posthumous Verse***)?

It is doubtful that the interval between the first two volumes (1904 and 1909) is big enough to have allowed for a really significant progress. (p. 57)

The most important achievement of Annenskij as a classical philologist is his translation of Euripides. He translated the nineteen surviving tragedies and wrote introductions to nearly all of them. (p. 150)

Annenskij himself formulates his attitude to his task as translator of Euripides clearly in the introduction to ***Phoenissae:*** "Shying away from a literal rendering, so different from a real exactness, I tried however in my translation not to omit a single shade of meaning which I understood and noticed, but most of all, of course, I sought to preserve at least a weak reflection of the poetical individuality of Euripides, as I imagined it myself, at least a shadow of that individual blend, unique in its kind, of tenacious sophistry and scorching pathos."

Concerning the accuracy of Annenskij's translations there were no doubts in any of his critics. He used not one edition of Euripides, but was familiar with all variants and selected the one of which he could fully approve. From this point of view his translation might be valued as a critical commentary to Euripides' unclear spots. (pp. 151-52)

Annenskij's attitude toward antique tragedy is clearly expressed in his foreword to the first volume of the Euripides edition of 1907. . . . In this brilliant essay [***Antique Tragedy***], full of unusual formulations and spirited aperçus, Annenskij—starting from the description of a modern performance of Aeschylus' *Prometheus* in the open air theater at Bézier—surveys the development of Greek tragedy. He notes that one of the main differences between modern and Greek tragedy is that the Greeks paid more attention to the details of their plays; the mythological content was known to everyone and a complete development of the particular plot was unnecessary. The strength lay in the small strokes. (pp. 153-54)

The peak of Greek tragedy for Annenskij is Euripides: "The tragedies of Euripides appear to me sometimes as links of a unique gigantic drama of mankind: these links, forged together by the mastery of genius, have fallen asunder and a timid pupil has fixed beginnings and ends to them in order to give them the appearance of independent tragedies." . . . (p. 154)

Famira Kifared . . . is the last tragedy written by Annenskij and the only one to be staged. . . . (p. 194)

It is a complicated psychological play, comprising decadence in antique forms, and its end does not satisfy as do the clear, logical conclusions of the three previous tragedies. Annenskij abandoned a division of the play into acts, which as a matter of fact, was also unnecessary in ***Melanippa*** and ***Laodamija.*** He divides the continuous action into twenty scenes, of which almost all bear a name and mark the progress of the day.

The skeleton of the legend, which forms the plot (Sophocles used it to write a tragedy, which was lost), is in Annenskij's own words the following: "The son of the Thracian king Philammon and the nymph Argiope, Thamyras (or Thamyrides), became famous by his playing of the cythara and his pride grew so much that he challenged the Muses. He was defeated, and as a punishment was deprived of his eyes and his musical gift." . . . (pp. 194-95)

This basis is the theme for free variations—partly in old Greek literature, partly by Annenskij himself. . . .

The unity of time, space, and action is as strictly observed as in the other tragedies—as a matter of fact, there is hardly a break in the action. (p. 195)

The musical quality of Annenskij's conception of the tragedy is nowhere clearer than it is in [***Famira Kifared***]. At times it seems to be an opera with a complicated and well worked out sequence of choruses, arias and recitatives. (p. 196)

In ***Famira Kifared*** Annenskij apparently tries to embody the symbolist idea of a synthetic work of art, in which Poetry, Music, and Painting are united. The titles of the scenes suggest colors—they do not only mark the unity of time. Colors are constantly mentioned in the dialogue. The frequent musical interludes, the dances of the Chorus, the arias, the frequent changes from dramatic speech in blank verse to rhymes and widely different meters—everything works towards the unification of the branches of art. In a letter Annenskij says that he put into ***Famira*** the "Grenzfragen" from the region of musical psychology and aesthetics, which interested him in an exciting way. . . . This interest corresponded to the problems of his time, and certainly he knew the dramatic output of Maurice Maeterlinck. But Maeterlinck and most of the other symbolists in Europe chose mainly "romantic" or "symbolistic" subjects. Annenskij tries to transpose classical antiquity into symbolist settings and on the whole he succeeds very well. This transposition goes by steps. It is still cautious in ***Melanippa,*** stronger in ***Car' Iksion,*** very outspoken in ***Laodamija,*** and at it highest in ***Famira.*** Here Annenskij even gives up the classical constant presence of the Chorus: it comes and goes and is not always the same Chorus (Maenads, non-initiated Bacchantes, Satyrs, etc. alternate). So the role of the Choragus nearly disappears.

In speech, Annenskij goes so far as to use prose and does not hesitate to introduce "picturesque" things which do not occur in his antique patterns, (at least not in this context): Argiope's transformation into a bird for example is not "classical", but it would certainly fit into Maeterlinck!

The main problem of ***Famira*** is the artist's creative power and its opposition to life. The motif of Thamyras' erotic feelings towards the Muse is antique. In most antique sources the punishment is double: loss of the musical gift and the piercing of his eyes. The first is punishment for his pride; the second, for his eroticism. Strangely enough D. S. Mirsky writes in his well-known *A History of Russian Literature* [see excerpt above, 1926] about the challenge of Apollo and about the loss of the sight only (which certainly would not prevent Thamyras from singing!). The same is repeated by Renato Poggioli, though Apollo is mentioned neither in the myths nor in Annenskij.

Annenskij changes the old myth completely in causing Thamyras to blind himself. Much more refined is the explanation of why he wants to challenge the Muse: it is not pride, but the desire to know the ideal. When he hears it, he has to realize how human, how insolent his wishes were. He does not even try to sing, and if the Muse had not taken the musical gift from him, he would have certainly blinded himself in order not to be distracted by reality. After the loss of his musical gift, his blinding himself is a more cruel punishment committed in despair from the dejection of the moment. Annenskij has prepared it very well psychologically. Thamyras is cold as stone on the surface, but he has a heart able to suffer and to love. He feels that he has to be cold to preserve his gift as an artist; but being a man he vacillates—and perishes. The conflict between art and life is not solved.

Thamyras wants to love. But poets are doomed. They have to be cold and still they have the constant longing for love. Only the Gods (here the Muse) can have the holy art, because they are not able to love. Thamyras wanted to unite art to the love of the Muse. She punishes him for his unholy desire, as well as for his too high daring—and he punishes himself because longing for love entered his mind through his eyes. He is a poet who could not live up to his gift. He tried to break out and failed. Art with men is loveless (*bezljuboe*). Only the Gods can bear the curse of art. Thamyras cannot endure *bezljubost'*, but the Muse can. So in the final issue it is the tragedy of a poet, who is too weak to sustain his cursed gift.

The character of Argiope is more simple. She substitutes her love for her lover with the love for her son, and destroys him by her egoism. (pp. 203-05)

In his attitude towards the Gods, Annenskij accepts the attitude of Euripides: they are worse than men, who at least love and pity and try to understand.

The impression left by ***Famira*** is ambiguous. Excellent lyrical passages and great dramatic spots suffer at times from irony as their counterpoint, and the mythological "painting" apparatus is perhaps a little too big. But, with [Annenskij's] three other tragedies, it certainly belongs to the best plays in Russian literature. (pp. 205-06)

Annenskij saw in Euripides the "antique new man", who, standing on the border of two epochs felt in himself the same schism, the same dualness, as the poet felt in his own soul.

Like Euripides he had freed himself from the conventions, superstitions and beliefs of his time and found himself alone—an outstanding personality—but caged in his own mind without any communication with his fellow men.

This attitude (the attitude of most of the Euripidean heroes) cannot bring forth tragedy in the strict sense of the word. There is no freedom of decision for sacrifice in it. When in contact with their fellows these heroes are driven, by necessity, to the last sufferings, to the last possibilities of human endurance.

This feeling of necessity, lacking the feeling that a free sacrifice would be worthwhile, introduces a new touch into antique tragedy. Here is no heroic greatness, only decadence; no suffering on a grand scale, but the division of heroic greatness into a sequence of small, sometimes contradictory, half-conscious moods and sensations.

Euripides was the first Greek tragedian for whom the masks worn by the actors became an obstacle. The mask forces the dialogue to be only typical or rhetorical; it concentrates psychology in some decisive culmination points of the drama.

This is the point which Annenskij develops. He preserves the outward features of antique tragedy, but his personages do not wear masks. The nuances of suffering in the doomed human soul, the changing traits of the human face, the uncertainty of appearing and disappearing moods—all these become the real contents of tragedy. The Chorus, which was the incarnation of objective norm in classical tragedy, changes into the expression of lyrical subjectivism in Euripides and is consistently led along this way by Annenskij until it reaches the last possibilities of lyrical atmosphere.

The common thought in Annenskij's tragedies is the impossibility of love on earth. The distance between the celestial and the earthly is vast. But true love, love which is worthwhile, is love for the eternal, the absolute and therefore infinitely, distant. The "pathos of distance" between the human and the godlike is the tragic pathos of Annenskij's work.

True love may choose between the *eternally existing* in the beyond or its reflection on earth. In the first instance the lover is accused of pride and blasphemy, and is destroyed, as were Ixion and Thamyras. In the second he leads a life of suffering upon earth, without satisfaction, as in the case of Melanippe and, to a certain degree, Laodamia. It is perhaps interesting to note that Annenskij chose men for the first and women for the second possibility. The guilt of Annenskij's heroes is that they love "too far"—but true love does not exist on an earthly level, in the poet's opinion.

So suffering is the distinguishing feature of true love, which is always, in this way or that, directed toward the unattainable. Yet this suffering in love is what differentiates men from the gods; it makes them more than gods. The gods lack the quality of love: they live in blissfulness (*oni-blaženny*). (pp. 206-07)

Annenskij knows only one thing: man, on earth, has forgotten everything he may have known in heaven. He is unaware of his god-likeness. No remembrance of it appears in his consciousness. Only at times is the virtue of goodness apparent in the exercise of virtue; it manifests itself in the feeling and in the existence of a love for something which is not upon earth, and in a "lack of love" for the earthly. Annenskij does not attempt to say whether or not these longings might at the last transform man and enable him to return to his celestial fatherland. He travels this road only as far as the terrestrial level and stops where revelation or faith become necessary. This skepticism (which Annenskij calls *nedoumen'e* in *Moja toska*) is mitigated by his love for Beauty. He constantly seeks it and constantly refuses to accept it in its earthly guise. He does not believe in a quiet, self-sufficient Apollonian beauty; on earth he finds it but a bad and false translation of the divine, fit only to satisfy the Pharisean tendencies of the human mind. The distorted mask of suffering, the shameless grin of a satyr, are nearer to him than the perfectly proportioned, but dead and untransmuted, form of heavenly Aphrodite. (pp. 207-08)

Annenskij's attitude toward literary criticism was very peculiar. In the foreword to his ***Book of Reflections***, he explains in his usual, precise manner what he means by "reflection". Ordinarily a critic stands outside the work, analyzing and evaluating it. Not only is he located somewhere outside the work, but he is somewhere above it. "I have written here only about things which *governed* me, about things which I *followed, gave myself to,* about things which I wished to retain within myself having made them a part of myself." . . . Thus the word *reflection* is by no means a metaphor. It is a spiritual reflection, of a special kind to be sure, but nevertheless a real reflection. A poetical reflection cannot be presented as though it were a geometrical blueprint, nor can it be passive or disinterested: "Poets do not write for mirrors nor for stagnant waters." . . . But thus the more complicated and active the "fixing" of our impression becomes!

The selection of the works is already determined by this attitude: "I chose only those things which I felt were higher than myself but at the same time consonant." . . . The second criterion which Annenskij applied in selecting his subjects was determined primarily by the degree of interest which he had for the creator of a given work. He even states that he was guided more by his interest in "the owners of the marionettes" than by the "marionettes" themselves. We are therefore in the fortunate position of seeing clearly what appeared striking to him. In the first book the "owners" are Gogol', Dostoevskij, Turgenev, Pisemskij, Tolstoj, Gor'kij, Čexov, and Bal'mont; in the second, Lermontov, Turgenev, Leonid Andreev, Heine,

Shakespeare, Ibsen and Dostoevskij. At the end of his short introduction to the first book Annenskij states that he has used two different methods of approach: the analytic and the synthetic. He leaves it to the reader to discover the difference between the two. In the foreword to the ***Second Book of Reflections,*** briefer even than the foreword to the first, the subjective attitude is developed: "I am writing here only about things which everyone knows, and only of those who are close to all of us. I am only reflecting the same things that you are."

Annenskij energetically stresses the fact that his book is not an anthology, not a mere unity containing a plurality, but also a unity in itself. All of his reflections were stimulated and chained together by his one old anxiety: "And they are all penetrated by the one anxiety with which, like you, I am looking for a justification of life—the problem of creation." Thus the main theme of Annenskij's poetry: beauty, death and the torture of life, appear here on a theoretical level.

It will be more convenient to discuss Annenskij's individual essays in connection with his aesthetic theory which is clearly developed in the first essay of his ***Second Book of Reflections,*** **"The Reverse Side of Poetry"** ***(Iznanka poèzii).***

The first part of the essay is titled "The Dreamer and the Chosen One". It begins with a treatment of one of Dostoevskij's main themes: the weaker one's contact with real life, the smaller the role one plays in it, the more magnificent and more powerful one feels oneself to be in the realm of fantasy. Here the weak man is strong for he can do whatever he desires with the life which he has created for himself. Here the Ego becomes a radiant, resplendent sun vivifying a world entirely of its own making. Annenskij of course quotes from *White Nights* in exemplifying his meaning and he sees quite vividly, as did Dostoevskij, the dangers and the different gradations of fantasy life where a naive and ecstatic egoism takes possession of such a dreamer and transforms him into a furry caterpillar for which the whole world consists of nothing but the green "cud" of its dreams. But at times the dreamer ("one in a myriad") happens to be not the *balagannyj car' mečty* but its madman and its martyr. (pp. 209-10)

The poet does not love life with the ridiculous self-centered love of the "furry caterpillar" but with the mad desire to be dissolved in it completely.

In the second part of his essay "Symbols of Beauty in Russian Writers" Annenskij states that poets have only three themes: suffering, death, and beauty. Even laughter in poetry contains a grain of suffering, and it is precisely this small particle of suffering which induces the poet to accept laughter.

The poet has to suffer in order to be able to create, and in the opinion of Annenskij he likes to simulate suffering. And this suffering is neither a lie nor a deliberate fraud; although the poet may induce his own suffering, he nevertheless suffers as though his suffering were absolutely genuine.

Poetry, therefore, in its essence is a complete negation of real suffering and compassion despite the fact that the simulated torture is very genuine. In this paradox of the genuine and yet simulated vs. the simulated and yet genuine, Annenskij sees the true source of artistic creation. Genuine torture does not speak and genuine compassion has no words; genuine compassion does not dream of Prometheus on the rock: it need only silently unwind the bandages while the chisel of the surgeon pierces the rotten bones of the pale child. Certainly poetry is not reality, but it must be able to imagine reality so vividly that the imagination exceeds reality in stringency, clarifies and even perhaps explains it. (p. 211)

The poet is so much in love with life that he is unable to conceive of death as "le néant"; it becomes for him a form of life. Annenskij quotes Rémy de Gourmont in saying that the intellect simply cannot acquire the habit of connecting the idea of death with that of annihilation, which one would suppose to be particularly near to it, that is, the idea of nothingness. "Le néant" acquires a symbolic value which, in its relation to others, transforms this nothing into something. Because it is a symbol it achieves power and beauty and its own mysterious meaning.

Beauty, which is the third subject, does not remain a pure idea either. In poetry it becomes a feeling, a desire of the poet. It continues to live as something infinitely more concrete and complicated and, above all, more narrow than it is by definition or in pure reasoning. Annenskij quotes Stendhal as having said somewhere that beauty is "la promesse de bonheur" and it is of course a tradition among poets to see beauty in woman, or beauty as a woman. It is at this that Annenskij arrives at his great synthesis where the negative, morbid force of torture is balanced in poetry by the force of beauty which contains the promise of happiness. At times the ideas of torture and beauty approach one another and their combinations give rise to certain peculiar symbols, but even then we do not cease to feel their original contradiction with one another. In poetry as in life beauty and torture are not neutralized. They only offer more or less interesting combinations (*spletenija*).

This very consistent and persuasive theory of art explains much in Annenskij's own poetry. (p. 212)

Annenskij persuasively defines the contrast between the concept of the poet and his individuality in romanticism and symbolism. In romanticism it was the ego which opposed itself to the whole world which did not understand the poet; in symbolism it is the ego which ardently seeks to imbibe this world and to become this world in causing it to become the ego. "New poetry is searching for exact symbols for *feelings,* i.e., the real substratum of life, and for *moods,* i.e., that form of spiritual life which most relates men, and which enters into mass psychology with the same rights that it enters into individual psychology." . . . (p. 214)

Vsevolod Setchkarev, in his Studies in the Life and Work of Innokentij Annenskij, *Mouton & Co., 1963, 270 p.*

AVRAHM YARMOLINSKY (essay date 1969)

[*In the following excerpt, Yarmolinsky examines the "strain of morbidity" in Annensky's poetry as it is manifested in his depictions of ailing and dying. For further discussion of Annensky's preoccupation with death, see the excerpts by Marc Slonim (1953) and Janet Grace Tucker (1973).*]

If there is a strong strain of morbidity in the small body of verse left by Innokenty Annensky, it is qualified by grim humor, by courageous confrontation of invalidism and the thought of death waiting on the doorstep. Evening and autumn are his favored death symbols, but winter and even spring serve the same purpose, the poet hearing "the call of death in the Easter hymn." Though free of self-pity, his lyrics dwell on waning, ailing, dying: his habitual cast of mind is one of anguish and hopelessness. Sometimes he is drawn to what he fears. He plays variations on such themes as loneliness, insomnia, dreams (chiefly nightmares). As might be expected of a Modernist who translated some of the French Symbolists, Annensky readily turns to music and moonlight and flowers (withering ones). Beauty redeems existence for him but, alas, life holds little of it, and that little is fragile. Poetry, like music, can adumbrate it faintly. Yet words are so inadequate that the making of verse is a torment, mitigated by the exhilaration of attempting a well-nigh impossible task. Although he occasionally touches upon the ideal world and his poems sometimes have an esoteric quality, there is nothing mystical about them. He wanted poetry to be concrete, dealing with three-dimensional objects and avoiding riddles, but he did not always practice what he preached. (p. 198)

Avrahm Yarmolinsky, "Russian Poetry—A Survey," in his The Russian Literary Imagination, *Funk & Wagnalls, 1969, pp. 187-259.**

JANET GRACE TUCKER (essay date 1973)

[*In the following excerpt, Tucker discusses Annensky's role as a transitional literary figure whose works, although reflecting some of the aesthetic values of the Russian Symbolists, also anticipate the more realistic verse of the Acmeists. Tucker examines Annensky's themes, style, and techniques, comparing them to those of both the Symbolists and the Acmeists. For further discussion of Annensky's themes, see the excerpts by Marc Slonim (1953) and Avrahm Yarmolinsky (1969).*]

The complexity of Annenskij's relationship to Russian Symbolism is one facet of the link between him and the Acmeists. . . . In a sense, Annenskij seems almost to symbolize the state of Russian poetry of his time, for he displays a certain degree of flux in his verse technique and in his aesthetic values as well. (p. 209)

Although Annenskij has been classified as a Symbolist by some critics, he should rather be regarded as a transitional figure between Symbolism and later poetic developments. . . . [The] fact that he was not involved in the polemics of the Symbolist movement might parallel Annenskij's emphasis upon poetry as an artistic phenomenon rather than as a literary school. Annenskij's feeling that poetry has intrinsic importance extends to his avoidance of mysticism, whereby poetry is the vehicle rather than the goal of artistic creativity. His abstention from mysticism and from literary polemics represents a desire to maintain the self-importance of art, thus preventing its prostitution for other ends. This would later be extremely important for the Acmeists, particularly for Mandel'štam.

Annenskij differs from the other Symbolists in his aesthetic beliefs and in poetic technique. The differences between him and the poets of the second generation of Symbolism, such as Belyj and Blok, are marked, but he displays certain similarities to the other older Symbolists. Thematically, for example, he is close to the other early Symbolists. The theme of death plays a significant role in his poetry, and he also composed a number of poems in which dream, disorientation, and nightmare figure prominently. Unlike the other early Symbolists, however, Annenskij does not dwell upon death and morbidity to the exclusion of other poetic themes; he differs, therefore, from such poets as Fedor Sologub and Valerij Brjusov. Although Annenskij wrote several poems in which an escape from temporality (symbolized by such themes as death and the dream, as well as by the intrusion of the conception of "infinity" in certain nature poems) is significant, his most important single theme, aside from his metapoetry, is time. It is the theme of time that provides a means of linking together all of Annenskij's poetic themes. . . . Annenskij's constant awareness of time and of poetry places him in sharp contrast to the other Symbolists, both older and younger.

Annenskij differs from the first generation of Symbolists, then, in several basic ways. In the first place, even though the themes of death and dream are important in his poetry, they do not dominate all of his other poetic themes. Instead, death is subordinated to time; time relates all of his themes to one another. His poetic orientation, therefore, is more definite and immediate than that of his contemporaries. Furthermore, Annenskij separates the theme of poetry from all of his other poetic themes; only poetry (art) is not dominated by time. He focuses, therefore, upon the significance of poetry as a means of expression and as a cultural phenomenon which represents man's only possibility for escaping time. Also, in his verses about art, Annenskij concentrates upon poetry and not upon the figure and personality of the poet. For him, the poet becomes an announcer, a medium of artistic expression. . . . Thus, he is dissimilar from, for example, Brjusov, for whom the poet himself was of primary significance with the work of art only a secondary import resulting from the poet's inspiration or experiences. For Annenskij, therefore, the emphasis was upon time and art rather than upon death and escape (through dream).

Annenskij seems closer to the older Symbolists stylistically than thematically. In many of his poems, he employs the verb infrequently. Like the other older Symbolists, he uses suggestion in his verse. Many of his poems are puzzles which must be solved by the reader. Annenskij, on the other hand, differs significantly from the older Symbolists in poetic style and technique as well as in terms of poetic themes. His poems are marked by a frequent use of devices that produce *concrete* images. Unlike some of the other early Symbolists (such as Valerij Brjusov) who concentrated upon the use of the adjective, Annenskij is a poet of the noun who displays an interest in concrete objects and in the more familiar aspects of nature.

The ambiguities that can be found in Annenskij's literary criticism are perhaps a facet of the slight indefiniteness that marks his relationship to the other Symbolists of the first generation. In his belief that the poet is, first of all, a craftsman and in his emphasis upon the importance of language, i.e., the word, he exhibits convictions that would place him within the aesthetic traditions of Classical poetry and the poetic theories which the Acmeists would later espouse. Like Annenskij, Brjusov also felt that the poet was a craftsman rather than a seer. Brjusov, however, considered the poet and his reactions to be of primary importance, while Annenskij held that art came first, the poet functioning merely as a transmitter of beauty into communicable terms. Annenskij's stressing of the suffering which accompanies the creative act and his feeling that the poet is somehow separate from the crowd demonstrate the fact that he held some aesthetic beliefs which were similar, to at least a certain extent, to the conceptions of the poet held by the other Symbolists. In addition, Annenskij's remarks concerning a possible link between ethics and aesthetics (beauty and a higher good) would set him apart from the Acmeists, although his feelings about this are not necessarily similar to those of the other early Symbolists, pointing instead to some sort of connection with earlier Russian poetry.

Annenskij differed markedly from the second generation of Russian Symbolists. Unlike the later poets, his orientation was mainly aesthetic rather than philosophical. He regarded the expression of beauty through poetry as a self-sufficient goal.

Annenskij felt that the creation of a work of art was outside of time because the beauty of art can endure (even though it does not always do so), and he considered the poet to be a craftsman whose purpose in life is to transmit into art the beauty that he is able to perceive. Annenskij rejected the mysticism of the younger Symbolists. His emphasis upon time established an immediacy and definiteness in his verse that was in stark contrast to the lack of clarity of, for example, Andrej Belyj's poems and the mysticism of Blok. Annenskij's denial of the possibilities of a mystical escape for the artist is very definitely indicated in such poems as **"Toska sinevy,"** in which he posits the boundaries symbolized by the clouds as the outward limits of man's knowledge. (Annenskij's views on this matter are somewhat ambiguous, however, for in the poem **"Nojabr"** he paints a picture of unlimited space and time that might perhaps be equated with a mystical escape. Even in this poem, though, the removal of spatial and temporal boundaries does not affect the rational basis which the poet has established.)

The spatial and temporal immediacy of Annenskij's themes is reflected stylistically in his tendencies to concretize poetic images rather than to make them less definite or more abstract. Stylistically, as well as thematically, he is in marked contrast to the later Symbolists. For them, poetry was a means of attaining a sort of mystical escape from their surroundings. Hence, their poems were characterized by an emphasis upon mood and atmosphere rather than upon the concreteness of the physical world. To a certain extent, of course, any differences between Annenskij and the second generation of Symbolists may be ascribed to the fact that Annenskij, as one of the older Symbolists, would be more like such poets as Brjusov, Sologub, and Bal'mont. However, Annenskij differed from these earlier poets (as well as from the later Symbolists) in his emphasis upon the intrinsic value of art. In addition, the physical immediacy of his poetic world is in contrast to the aesthetic beliefs of the earlier Symbolists and the later Symbolists as well.

Annenskij's aesthetic values, as they are expressed in his literary criticism, stand in marked contrast to the tenets of the younger Symbolists. In the very range of his artistic interest, which included the dramas of ancient Greece, the poetry of the French Symbolists and Parnassians, the poetry of the Russian Symbolists and of the newest Russian poets, Annenskij exhibited a catholic taste that was the antithesis of the later Symbolists' concentration upon German philosophy and Russian mystical philosophy. In his orientation specifically toward French art and culture, he differed from the younger Symbolists, whose interests lay in German philosophy and in the mystical philosophy of Vladimir Solov'ev.

Annenskij differs from the younger Symbolists in his emphasis upon art as a self-sufficient goal for the poet. He did not regard art as a means to a higher end (that end being the mystical transcendence of reality). Annenskij's statements concerning the possibility of a connection between ethics and aesthetics (beauty and a higher good), along with his belief in the intrinsic value of art, points to a certain degree of ambiguity in his aesthetic theory. He did not, however, deny the fact that the creation of beauty might be a sufficiently well motivated goal for the poet. His orientation toward the work of art rather than the creator of that work (the poet) sets him off from the other Symbolists, both older and younger. For Annenskij, the poet was primarily a craftsman, an artisan, who transmitted the beauty he perceived into art. For the other Symbolists, even for Brjusov, the poet was a member of the elect, and it was the poet, not the work of art, which occupied first place. (Aleksandr Blok is somewhat closer to Annenskij in this matter than are some of the other Symbolists; for him, the poet was important principally in his ability to transform the sounds which he could hear into poetry.)

One very significant difference between Annenskij and the other Symbolists lay in their utilization of the means of perception. For the other Symbolists, sound was extremely important. Blok, for example, was a poet of sound, and Bal'mont, following the French Symbolists, was interested in musicalness in verse. Annenskij, on the other hand, is primarily a poet of visual images who was, therefore, more concerned with concrete objects which could be seen by the poet (and by the reader as well). His preference for visual images in his verse may correspond stylistically to his emphasis upon the concrete, the objective, which is in marked contrast to the poetry of the older Symbolists and certainly to that of the younger ones. (pp. 209-19)

There are some basic affinities between the themes of Annenskij's poetry and the ideas put forth in the Acmeist doctrine. Annenskij's major themes, those of time and of poetry, are connected with the aesthetic theories and the philosophy of the Acmeist doctrine; Annenskij's utilization of nature as a theme also ties in with the basic tenets espoused by the Acmeists. Annenskij's emphasis upon time thematically demonstrates his focus upon the immediate world and points up the fact that, in the main, he eschewed any tendencies toward mysticism. . . . [Time] is not Annenskij's only poetic theme, but it is the one that provides a link between and, hence, encompasses, all of the other themes except for poetry. The fact that Annenskij accepts, at least poetically, the strictures imposed upon man by the inevitability of time underlines his similarities to the Acmeist doctrine. Both Gumilev and Gorodeckij emphasized the poet's duty to be a part of the physical world, with its implication of temporality. Both critics scolded the later Symbolists for their attempts to escape from the world through mysticism, for which their medium was poetry. In "Utro akmeizma," Mandel'štam stressed the artist's acceptance of the three dimensions of existence as a prerequisite to the act of artistic creation. He criticized the later Symbolists for their disregard of earthly existence, their quest for psychological escape. Annenskij, it would seem, comes closer to the Acmeist ideal that the poet remain within the points of reference which are immediate and tangible than does any other Symbolist poet, including Brjusov. Brjusov's emphasis upon eroticism, death, and the special position of the poet constitutes a denial of reality which, although less pronounced and obvious than the mysticism of the younger Symbolists, is nevertheless present. The fact that Annenskij and the Acmeists are quite close in this matter does not . . . "prove" that Annenskij "influenced" the Acmeists. Rather, he and the Acmeists were similar so far as their conceptions of the place of man within the world is concerned. On the other hand, the personal connection between Annenskij and the Acmeists and the fact that there was a certain degree of similarity between their ideas points to the existence of a definite relationship between the aesthetic beliefs and philosophy of the older poet and of the younger ones as well.

Like Annenskij's use of time as a poetic theme, his employment of the theme of death may also indicate his acceptance of the world surrounding him and, therefore, might be regarded as a point of contact between him and the Acmeists. Annenskij's poems about death are immediate rather than escapist or morbid. He posits death as an inevitable and banal end to life; it is the end result of the flow of time. In Annenskij's poetry, death and time are connected. In his poems about death, Annenskij hints at a denial of the possibility of a mystical escape from the unpleasant or demeaning aspects of existence. Like his emphasis upon time, therefore, Annenskij's interest in death demonstrates his accentuation of the immediate and temporal and underlines his similarities to the Acmeists' tenets.

In addition to emphasizing time and dealing with death in his poetry, Annenskij also devotes a number of verses to nature. Some of the poems about nature are closer to another theme (death, life, or time). Since Annenskij often employs nature as a means of setting off another theme, his interest in it is evident. Like his concern with time (and death), Annenskij's use of nature theme or images points to an avoidance of mysticism in poetry. The theme of nature, as well as that of death, is tied in with Annenskij's treatment of time. Annenskij's thematic emphasis upon time, nature, and death (connected by time) bespeaks an acceptance of the boundaries of the physical world. His temporal and spatial orientation, so different from the attitudes of the younger Symbolists, indicates the presence of a metaphysical link between him and the Acmeists. The Acmeists' advocacy of the three-dimensional world as the basis for art indicates that there is a connection between them and Annenskij as regards the acceptance of reality and the rejection of mysticism. Again, the question of the "influence" of Annenskij upon the Acmeists is one which must remain unanswered, since this cannot be proved.

One of the most significant points of contact between Annenskij and the Acmeists, as far as Annenskij's poetic themes are concerned, is in his treatment of art and the artist (which may be seen as representing poetry and the poet in this instance). Although a certain amount of ambiguity exists in Annenskij's treatment of this subject, on the whole he is consistent in his conception of poetry and the role of the poet. Annenskij considers the poet to be an artisan of clear verse. This is demonstrated in a number of his poems, including **"V volšebnuju prizmu," "Drugomu,"** and **"Poètu."** In the first, Annenskij employs the prism to symbolize the poet, who transforms the clear light of inspiration into the colors of the work of art. It is interesting that Annenskij equates visual perception with art. He uses the image of light or fire to stand for art or artistic inspiration in several poems. Generally, the Acmeists also have a visual conception of art. In **"Drugomu,"** Annenskij contrasts himself to the Symbolist poet, referring to him as a "god" while he himself is only a "moralist." In **"Poètu,"** Annenskij pictures the muse of the Symbolist poet as the veiled goddess Isis, while at the same time identifying himself with the clear art and the emphasis upon the physical world which characterized the art of classical Greece. Annenskij, said Setchkarev, insisted on the "objective, concrete conciseness of his own poetry" as opposed to the "sweet airiness" of Symbolist poetry. It is not possible to determine whether Annenskij referred to all of the Symbolists in his metapoetry, or whether he only meant to compare himself to the later Symbolists. Most probably, he was alluding to the later Symbolists, whose dependence upon mysticism in their poetry had resulted in a lack of clarity and concreteness.

Annenskij's conception of the poet as a craftsman of clear verse is linked with his rejection of the later Symbolists' position that the poet was primarily a seer and that art was, first of all, a religion. The Symbolists, asserted A. Fedorov, adopted poses, while the hero of Annenskij's poems was the simple poetic "I." Annenskij's ideas regarding the poet are not completely clear. He maintained (in his verse) that the poet was an artisan who consciously created clear and objective art by means of poetic inspiration. On the other hand, Annenskij felt that the poet was subject to torment during the creative act. (See **"Smyčok i struny"** and **"Staraja šarmanka."**) The poet would seem to be, to at least a certain extent, segregated from others. Even though the poet differs from others, he is not necessarily superior to them in the way that the other Symbolist poets imagined themselves to be. (pp. 240-46)

Although Annenskij does separate the artist from the "masses" in **"Posle koncerta," "Bronzovyj poèt,"** and **"Smyčok i struny,"** he basically subordinates the artist to the work of art. This can be seen in the poem **"V volšebnuju prizmu,"** where the poet, identified with the prism, is only a medium who "absorbs" inspiration and produces art. For Annenskij, the poet was primarily a craftsman who was important for the art that he produced; this can be seen from such poems as **"Poètu"** and **"Drugomu."** (p. 249)

Annenskij's feelings about art are, not surprisingly, closely related to his view of the artist. The poet is an artisan of understandable verse. Hence, clarity is a hallmark of a work of art. The importance of clarity accentuates form, making it the central property of art. The Acmeists, too, stressed clarity of expression and the significance of form. Sharply delineated form, symmetry, and clarity form a basic whole that is in stark contrast to the amorphousness and inexactness of the art of the later Symbolists. (p. 250)

Annenskij is close to the Acmeists stylistically in several fundamental ways. His emphasis upon clarity of expression, his use of colloquialisms in verse, his employment of devices that produce a concrete image demonstrate his stylistic similarity to the Acmeists. All of these devices are characteristic of poetry that is realist rather than abstract or mystical in orientation; concreteness and reality are essential features of the Acmeist poetic doctrine. (p. 251)

The clarity recommended by Annenskij (in his criticism and verse) and by the Acmeists in their literary doctrine is linked to their emphasis upon the word (the unit of expression) and to their advocacy of conversational elements in poetry. The stressing of the word points to logical expression in poetry. For Annenskij, the writing of poetry was primarily an intellectual exercise based upon the logical use of words. In his essay "Utro akmeizma," Mandel'štam spoke of the importance of logic in poetry, asserting that logic is a component of the highest achievements of art. In positing a logical basis for poetry, the Acmeists rejected the mysticism of the later Symbolists; this was an important part of their doctrine. Annenskij did not single out mysticism to repudiate it but either ignored it stylistically or else "spoke" against it briefly in his poetic themes (and in his critical essays).

The Acmeists advocated a return to basic conversational language in poetry. In doing this, they were interested in rejecting the mysticism of the later Symbolists, stressing the worldly nature of poetry, emphasizing the word as the unit of poetic expression, and underlining the basic logical structure of the poem and its formal comprehensibility. Annenskij made wide use of conversational stylistic elements in his poetry. In his "letters," Gumilev spoke of Annenskij's employment of conversational speech. Annenskij's conversational elements consisted in large part of prosaisms, words which normally would appear in prose writing or conversation rather than in poetry. D. S. Mirsky felt that Annenskij's "diction is studiously common and trivial. It is the unbeautiful language of everyday . . ." [see excerpt above, 1926]. Annenskij did not make use of prosaisms and colloquialisms to the exclusion of all other means of expression. In his nature poems, there are stylistic reminders of his nineteenth-century predecessors Tjutčev and Fet. Even here, however, conversational elements intrude, and the combination of the structure of the traditional nature lyric with some discordant stylistic components shatters the impression which a nature lyric would normally be expected to give. Like Annenskij's thematic emphasis upon time, his employment of conversational stylistic elements and prosaisms points to a rejection of mysticism and incomprehensibility and an acceptance of reality. This is also true for the Acmeists. (pp. 253-56)

Although Annenskij made use, to some extent, of suggestion in his verse and cannot be divorced completely from Symbolism, he nevertheless was far more concerned with reality than were the other Symbolists; this can be seen from Annenskij's emphasis upon time, as well as from the differences in their respective styles. (Annenskij, however, is more readily comparable to a similarly transitional figure such as Puškin than he is to a purely realistic writer.) Like Puškin, Annenskij combined certain classical and Romantic elements in his verse to form a new poetic medium; he rejected neither "Classicism" nor "Romanticism," his verse displaying elements of both. (p. 258)

Janet Grace Tucker, in her Innokentij Annenskij and the Acmeist Doctrine, *Indiana University, 1973, 284 p.*

SIMON KARLINSKY (essay date 1974)

[*Karlinsky is an American educator and essayist who is well known for his many perceptive critical articles on the works of such twentieth-century Russian writers as Marina Tsvetaeva and Anton Chekhov. In the following excerpt, Karlinsky discusses the thematic and conceptual similarities between Annensky's mythical drama* Famira Kifared *and Chekhov's modern masterpiece* The Sea Gull *(1896).*]

From the outwardly angelic, inwardly murderous Mrs. Phelps in Sidney Howard's 1926 Broadway hit *The Silver Cord* to the grotesque Madame Rosepettle in Arthur L. Kopit's more recent *Oh Dad, Poor Dad, etc., etc., etc.,* the figure of the power-hungry matriarch who gratifies her bloated ego at the expense of her male offspring has been one of the most recurrent themes of American twentieth-century drama. In most plays that have featured this type of character (including the two just mentioned) the mother is shown as ostensibly encouraging her son to develop his artistic gifts and then using his need for self-expression to enslave him, to control his life or to deprive him of his career. It would be easy to relate the popularity of this theme in America to the spread of Freudian theories, with the advent of which Sidney Howard's play, the probable originator of this theme on the American stage, chronologically coincided. However, this same theme was also central to two important Russian dramas of the turn of the century, Anton Čechov's *The Seagull* . . . and Innokentij Annenskij's ***Thamyras the Cythara Player***. . . . Neither of these writers experienced any impact of Freudian theories, nor were they even likely to have known of their existence. In this case, as in so many others, the creative momentum of the Russian Silver Age had once more anticipated an important aspect of the twentieth-century sensibility that was to be developed in the West several decades later.

The thematic and conceptual similarities of *The Seagull* and ***Thamyras*** are not immediately apparent. The two plays belong to two entirely different literary traditions and are written in two widely divergent dramatic modes. . . . *The Seagull* is . . . a *pièce à thèse*. In it Čechov postulates two possible approaches to creative fulfillment. The traditionalist actress Irina Arkadina and the non-innovative writer Boris Trigorin achieve success by exploiting what is safe, established and accepted in their respective arts. They are contrasted in the play with two innovators, Konstantin Treplev and Nina Zarečnaja, whose path to art takes them through personal tragedy, but whose willingness to take risks enables them ultimately to achieve originality and genuine creativity. Treplev's defeat is brought about by his failure to attain his ideal in art, by his mother's perfidy and withdrawal of support, and by the loss of the young woman he loves who proves to be a more enduring and selfless artist than he is. This, in a nutshell, is also the situation of Thamyras in Annenskij's Bacchic drama, for Thamyras is also an ambitious young artist undone by his own high ideals and by the excessive demands he places on his art.

Annenskij's nymph Argiope neglected her son during the twenty years she was pursued by the wrath of Zeus. Irina Arkadina neglected hers because of the exigencies of her stage career. Each one seeks out her son's place of residence when it is expedient to do so. Argiope tries to use her son's artistic ambition to gain ascendancy over him and to control his life. Arkadina jeopardizes her son's future as an artist by mocking his search for originality, by treating his later success with indifference and by switching her allegiance to Trigorin, her son's rival both in art and in love. Both Annenskij's mythical Greek nymph and Čechov's provincial turn-of-the-century Russian actress coldly manipulate the younger women who could have given their sons happiness (Nina in Čechov and the muse Euterpe in Annenskij), and both cruelly sacrifice their sons' artistic future out of nakedly selfish motives.

Annenskij knew and liked Čechov's plays, as his essay "Theater of Mood" makes amply clear. But it would be wrong to see ***Thamyras the Cythara Player*** as an imitation or even a parallel of *The Seagull*. What we have, rather, is a convergent treatment of two themes basic to much of twentieth-century literature: the high price an artist pays for failure in his art and the selfish maternal love that particularly gifted sons can arouse. Čechov treated these interrelated themes in a play which under its modest, quasi-realistic garb dealt a blow to the conventions of the nineteenth-century well-made play from which that genre never recovered. Annenskij's poetic drama, written only ten years later, is a richly imaginative attempt to write a post-Wagnerian *Gesamtkunstwerk,* incorporating elements of painting, music and dance within its literary framework.

The drama that unfolds in the Franco-Russian, herb-scented, psychedelically illuminated *fin de siècle* Greece of Annenskij's play (it is also, obviously, the Greece of Leon Bakst's designs for the Djagilev productions of Ravel's "Daphnis and Chloe" and Debussy's "Afternoon of a Faun") coincides with the drama that Čechov had situated on a modest lakeshore estate in provincial Russia in many major and a few minor points (among the latter are Dr. Dorn's comparison of Arkadina's sabotage of her son's play to the anger of Jupiter, evoking the ominously smiling countenance of Zeus that peers from the sunlit clouds in ***Thamyras,*** and, for that matter, Arkadina's suspiciously Grecian surname).

"The main problem of ***Thamyras*** is the artist's creative power and its opposition to life," Vsevolod Setchkarev justly observed. Many other Russian twentieth-century writers stated this problem in some of their most important works: Majakovskij in "About This," Cvetaeva in "The Pied Piper," Pasternak in "Doctor Zhivago" and Nabokov in almost everything he has written. It is interesting and possibly significant that both Čechov and Annenskij connected it with the destructive potential of maternal love. (pp. 229-31)

Simon Karlinsky, "Frustrated Artists and Devouring Mothers in Čechov and Annenskij," in Mnemozina: Studia litteraria Russica in honorem Vsevolod Setchkarev, *edited by Joachim T. Baer and Norman W. Ingham, Wilhelm Fink Verlag, 1974, pp. 229-31.**

VICTOR ERLICH (essay date 1975)

[In the following excerpt, Erlich briefly discusses Annensky's essay on Nikolai Gogol's novel Dead Souls, *maintaining that Annensky was essentially an impressionistic critic.]*

[The] subhuman, freakish, "soulless" quality of Gogolian humanity is evoked in Innokentij Annenskij's **"The Aesthetics of Gogol's *Dead Souls* and Its Legacy"** (1910). Another note sounded in this suggestive and intensely personal essay is stubborn insistence on the aesthetic enchantment of the Gogolian universe. The poet in Annenskij is properly and richly alive to the creative exuberance of Gogol's art, to the paradoxical quality of aesthetic joy, so clearly at odds with the essential hopelessness of the writer's moral vision.

Annenskij's impressionistic manner has its pitfalls. His habit of drifting in and out of the viscous prose of *Dead Souls* without actually quoting can be disconcerting to a layman. Nor is Annenskij above being willfully wrongheaded on occasion: his view of Chekhov as a melancholy and feeble writer is utterly misguided. Yet he has an imaginative grip on an essential and rarely acknowledged aspect of Gogol and manages to convey it arrestingly, if at times idiosyncratically. (pp. 8-9)

Victor Erlich, "Introduction: Modern Russian Criticism from Andrej Belyj to Andrej Sinjavskij, Trends, Issues, Personalities," in Twentieth-Century Russian Literary Criticism, *edited by Victor Erlich, Yale University Press, 1975, pp. 3-32.**

DAVID BORKER (essay date 1977)

[In the following excerpt, Borker illustrates the manner in which Stéphane Mallarmé's poem "Le vierge, le vivace et le bel aujourd'hui," *in all probability, provided the subtext for Annensky's poem* "Ledjanaja tjur'ma" ("Ice Prison"). *For further discussion of Mallarme's influence on Annensky, see the excerpt by Richard Byrns and M. Kotzamanidou (1977).]*

In the introduction to a series of articles he wrote on contemporary Russian poetry in 1909 shortly before his unexpected death, Annenskij indicates the unity between the great French Symbolist tradition and early Russian Symbolism—as essentially one literary culture for the Russians. In this early period, Annenskij singles out Mallarmé and Maeterlinck as the two Western European poets representative of the movement. The only foreign poems cited are by Mallarmé. One of these is "Don du poème." Another passage is from the early poem "L'azur," offered as a statement symptomatic of a general Symbolist attitude toward art. The appearance of such a citation suggests, perhaps, Annenskij's general familiarity with Mallarmé's poems, as well as an awareness of the poet's pronounced metapoetic themes. (pp. 50-1)

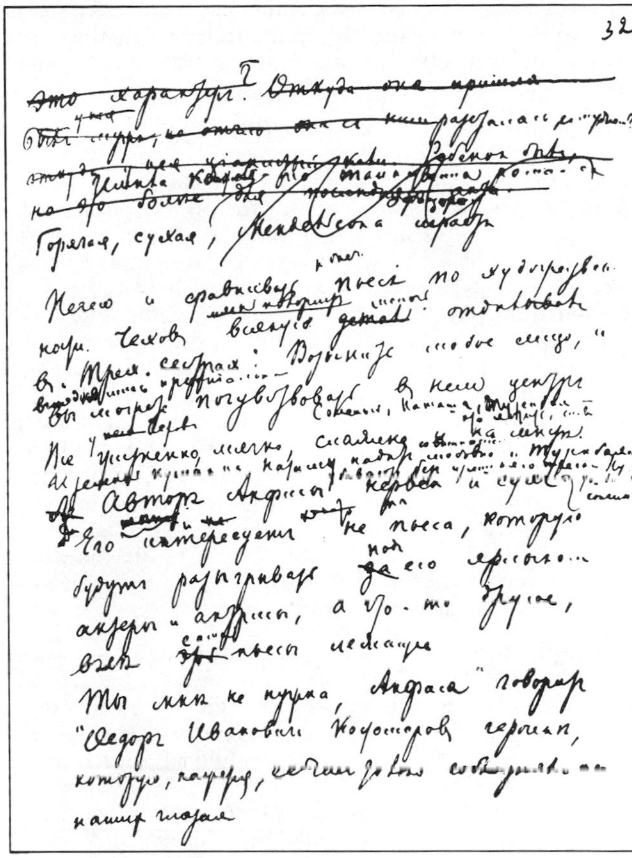

Holograph copy of a portion of Annensky's essay "The Theater of Leonid Andreyev." By permission of Ardis Publishers.

Vjačeslav Ivanov, in an article written about Annenskij shortly after his death, described Annenskij's poetic method as being a form of "associative symbolism," like that of Mallarmé, in which the poet takes as a starting point something physically or psychologically concrete, and without directly defining it, produces a range of associations connected with it, which once understood properly, allows one to realize the multifaceted spiritual meaning of the poet's experience [see excerpt above, 1910]. Such an underlying concrete situation or setting can be uncovered (or deciphered) in **"Ledjanaja tjur'ma."** The setting is a hole in the ice over water . . . momentarily illuminated by the sun. The poet-speaker apparently gazes into the opening while standing over it. The rippling patch of water . . . perhaps reflects the face of the poet, who is perturbed to see himself, like the water, encircled by the enclosing ice. . . . It is already clear in the first stanza of the poem that the status of the poet's addressee is a central problem of the poem and the basis of the poem's multi-leveled significance. The addressee . . . unifies a variety of values, ranging from, on the level of concrete setting, the open water itself, which once reflected the spring skies, to the spiritual longing of the poet-speaker whose face is reflected in the water. The object of this longing is expressed in terms of the concrete setting as the liberation of the water from the ice prison by the spring thaw. Stanzas one and two can be seen as depicting the water's figurative torment and frustration over the momentary illumination of the winter sun which will not accomplish this. Continuing on this level, stanza three begins by contrasting the spring flowers that were once reflected in the water with the snow flowers or crystals of winter.

The personification of the ice hole setting suggests the speaker's growing feeling of identification with the open water. This can be seen in the anguish and longing for liberation he shares with the addressee. As a double for the poet's spiritual self, as well as his creative inspiration, the addressee's longing for liberation from the ice prison can be seen on various levels as escape from paralysis and death in the encroaching ice, spiritual liberation from physical bonds in general, or the unfettered, infinite expansion of the poet's creative consciousness. In the final stanza the poet foresees the actual coming of spring as a destructive deluge which symbolically threatens to obliterate the very definition of the self. Thus the dream-addressee is rejected as a false longing ("ty ne mečta"), while the poet's spiritual and creative self are seen as incapable of transcendence, and thus perishable. . . . The final contrast in stanza four of the roaring unleashed waves with the silent addressee, already seen as much as a creature of the ice as of the water, asserts the muteness of the poet's own longing for expression in the face of the fury of the natural cycle.

Although the dominant theme of this rather pessimistic poem is perhaps a rejection of the hopeless struggle of the spiritual self against the material forces of death, the poem can also be taken as dealing in part with the problem of poetic self expression. This is evidenced by the traditional resonances of "mečta" in Russian and French Symbolist poetry, as well as Annenskij's use of the significant auditory contrast which closes the poem. Even the poet's contradictory negation of "mečta" in the final stanza introduces a metapoetic observation about the poem's preceding metaphoric associations, in the sense that it comments on the poem's structure.

The symbolic self-portrayal of the poet as a creature trapped in the winter ice and struggling to free itself is reminiscent of Mallarmé's celebrated sonnet "Le vierge, le vivace et le bel aujourd'hui." . . . As in Annenskij's poem, the victim is trapped in the surface of the ice. The ice itself is described as painfully and oppressively bright . . . , like the hopeless gleaming of the ice prison which is a source of anguish for the speaker and addressee in the Russian poem. Though obviously highly divergent protagonists, Mallarmé's swan and Annenskij's "mečta vesny" are both depicted as creatures from a happier past in which they were free from the ice's confinement. . . . Both are conscious of their past. The encircled water remembers its former unboundedness, the warm sun, and the flowers of spring, while Mallarmé's swan would seem to recall past flights and the fact that he should have flown away to the south . . . at the first signs of cold weather. The swan, like Annenskij's addressee, struggles helplessly and vainly, although perhaps more energetically, to free itself from its entrapment. . . . Escape, however, proves impossible for both. The swan will no more break the hold of the ice "avec un coup d'aile ivre" than the winter sun will miraculously melt the water's ice prison. The plight of the earthbound swan, like that of the addressee, is to freeze and die. . . . (pp. 51-3)

A thoughtful comparison of Annenskij's poem with the Mallarmé text shows significant thematic differences which are revealing in distinguishing the two poets' divergent views of the poet. One of the most striking differences can be found in the contrasting attitudes of the two imprisoned protagonists. Mallarmé's swan is depicted as a noble, independent figure, magnificently proud and scornful in the face of its fate. Annenskij's dream, on the other hand, is, in spite of its struggling, portrayed as a more passive, feminine creature plaintively pining and anguishing over its fate. Annenskij's addressee has no past or present control over its condition. All hope of liberation is seen in the sun and the forces of spring. Its sole emotion is its desperate hope for spring and salvation. Mallarmé's swan on the other hand is by no means a passive victim of winter. On the poem's most literal level captivity is viewed as the result of choosing not to migrate south in the winter as swans normally do. Even where it gives up active struggle, it maintains an attitude of proud dignity, showing scorn and contempt for the space that binds it. As it grows still upon the ice, its freezing is figuratively portrayed as the "cold dream" of contempt it "dons" in exile.

To be sure, the swan and the "dream of spring" are intrinsically two very different poetic images. The selection and development of each as the central image reflects profound differences in symbolic content. Mallarmé's poem treats the theme of the poet's inability to create, represented by the allegory of a swan locked in the ice. The elegant swan symbolizes the poet, while the act of flight is equated with writing, and soaring of poetic inspiration. The sterile winter, in whose ice the swan is trapped, symbolizes the poet's own impotence to create and his resultant "ennui." Within this allegory its struggle against the painful white space is a struggle against the emptiness of the blank page and a challenge to fill the creative void. Although the struggle seems to end in defeat, it offers in its magnificence a new value in place of the poetic flight. The proud spiritual struggle within the poet, his proud negation of the space that would negate him, is offered as a spiritual value in itself, the preeminence of the inner value of poetic consciousness over the outer value of the finished work. In his "dream of scorn" in the final tercet, the poet affirms himself as a self-contained value, the radiance of which figuratively illuminates the ice around it. Thus, in the final line of the poem the protagonist, "le Cygne," now capitalized to mark its transcendence, occupies the weighty final rhyme position.

Annenskij constructs an entirely different set of associations around the image of the ice hole. The personified patch of water encircled in a wall of ice suggests an amorphous creature, shaped by the icy space that contains it and dependent for its pattern and color on the objects reflected, or perhaps refracted, upon it. Unlike Mallarmé's swan, which assigns its own pure brightness to the surrounding setting, Annenskij's "dream of spring" is itself defined by the values around it. For Annenskij the soul of the poet, like the ice hole, is a sort of empty container of reflected images which is itself contained within the physical body symbolized by the ice prison. The amorphous image of the poet's self or consciousness as a bare container is a recurring image pattern in Annenskij's poetry.

The Annenskij text, when viewed in juxtaposition to the Mallarmé subtext, can be seen to take on additional thematic values. Its significance as a statement about art, as a metaphorical portrayal of the poet's inability to achieve transcendent expression, a theme within the poem which coexists with and complements the existential theme of the futility of survival, is intensified by such a comparison. Both Annenskij and Mallarmé portray through the metaphor of entrapment the poet's inability to achieve artistic expression, yet from diverse perspectives. The absence in Annenskij's poem of the central protagonist of the Mallarmé poem, the swan, underscores profound differences in each writer's poetic concept of self. All that remains of the setting is a hole in the ice. The emptiness of Annenskij's setting, devoid of the direct portrayal of animate life, is indicative of Annenskij's general system of imagery in which the poet expresses greatest affinity between self and the inanimate world of objects. (pp. 53-5)

David Borker, "Annenskij and Mallarmé: A Case of Subtext," in The Slavic and East European Review, *Vol. 21, No. 1, Spring, 1977, pp. 46-55.**

RICHARD BYRNS AND M. KOTZAMANIDOU (essay date 1977)

[In the following excerpt, Byrns and Kotzamanidou compare Annensky's aesthetic theories and poetic techniques to those of Stéphane Mallarmé, who is commonly recognized as one of Annensky's most important influences. For further discussion of Mallarmé's influence on Annensky, see the excerpt by David Borker (1977).]

There is certainly no doubt that Annensky knew the work of Mallarmé; indeed, he had translated into Russian two of Mallarmé's poems, "Don du poème," and "Tombeau d'Edgar Poe." However, individualism was for Annensky a necessary quality which poetry demanded from the initiated. This impressionistic attitude characterizes his translations of Euripides, as well as his critical articles, and may well be summed up by his comments in the introduction to a book of these articles, significantly titled the ***Book of Reflections:*** "I have written here only about that which ruled me, which I followed, which I devoted myself to, that I wanted to preserve within myself, having made it part of myself." Annensky's translations of Mallarmé demonstrate in their turn the personal element in the process. They are reworkings from the inside, re-creations based on the Russian poet's interpretation. . . . But Annensky's aesthetic kinship with the French poet can be seen more clearly in the Russian's own works, through a study of surfaces of and textures within the poems.

Mallarmé's relation to the changing aesthetic awareness in the transitional period from nineteenth to twentieth century art is well known. Art critics have mentioned Mallarmé's affinities with the impressionism of Cézanne and his influence on the cubists, and the surrealists claimed him as their own. Markov sees Mallarmé as tied more to Russian futurism than Russian symbolism.

Annensky, too, partakes of various aesthetic currents. He was classified among the "elder Symbolists," preceding the generation of Blok, Biely, and Ivanov, although his poetry collections appeared much after they had started writing. Yet, he was distinguished by Mandelstamm and Akhmatova for the concreteness of his imagery, and Ginzburg acknowledges that "The poets of 1910 need Annensky with his psychologism and materiality, so far as the reaction against the outdated symbolism came about under the sign of aspiration toward the concrete." Karlinsky notes that Annensky in his mature poetry has elements which relate less to symbolism than to acmeism and cubo-futurism, and mentions the poet in connection with *art nouveau* and *Jugendstil.*

But what actually were these changing concepts of art that essentially became differentiated into these "avant-gard" movements? Perhaps one might try to stress—certainly in relation to Mallarmé and Annensky—a new point of view. New art involved new means of perception and expression. . . . Cézanne's definition of art as a "harmony parallel to nature" . . . has important implications for the poetic art of Mallarmé and Annensky. That is, the artist no longer attempts to reproduce the world of experience; rather, he transforms natural appearance to create a "reality" which implicitly expresses some relationship between the observer and the objects observed. *New Art* involved an attempt at synthesis, the artist drawing from objects the necessary elements—forms and colors—inspired by emotion to create a work. (pp. 223-25)

Both Mallarmé and Annensky believe in the power of the word to create an image, evoke a mood, elicit a response from the reader. In a famous comment to Degas, Mallarmé indicates that poetry is not written with ideas but with words, and a conversation with René Ghil leads him to say that "Il convient de nous servir des mots de tout le monde, dans le sens que tout le monde croit comprendre" ["It is proper for us to use common words in the sense that common people believe they understand (these words)"]. When transposed into poetry, however, common words may well attain a cryptic power all their own, as Mallarmé recognizes, for he goes on to say that the bourgeoisie no longer understand these words because they have been rewritten by a poet. Annensky echoes Mallarmé's point of view, and dramatically recognizes the impact of such words, when he claims that many do not understand "that the most frightening and powerful word—the most enigmatic—is perhaps just the everyday word."

The poetic word thus possesses new value, and the verse becomes magic, Mallarmé's "trait incantatoire" ["incantatory quality"], which develops and gains meaning until the illusion invoked has power to equal anything seen in the external world. These "diamond words of the poet," as Annensky puts it, the expression of the poet's world view, are invested with a strange creative force. In a letter to Voloshin, which might well be applied to his own concept of art, the Russian poet writes: "You have not only luminous spots but every dark brown path of unawakened still crepuscular grasses entangled during the night . . . knows, that they are the *Word* and that they—the luminous spots—can be nothing but the *Word* and from here they derive their beauty, their jewel-like brilliance, their unrest, their dejection."

Words are also evocative; they never describe directly. Rather, they attempt to suggest, through the image formed, something else, perhaps some higher state of awareness which the poet feels and would communicate to others. . . . Annensky at one point inveigles against the clear cut images of painting—for him, what is important is not the purely imitative aspect of imagery but something that lies beyond; images for Annensky should be suggestive and have symbolic force: "In general poetry must speak in words, that is, in symbols of psychic actions." The images of new poetry are important as the expression of an inner life, the poetic experience, but in a universal way: "New poetry is searching for exact symbols for feeling, i.e. the real substance of life, and for moods, i.e. that form of spiritual life which most attracts people to each other."

Hence, the relationship of the reader to the poem is also important as he, too, must become involved in the poetic act. Both Mallarmé and Annensky feel that the word, through its "musicality," deeply affects the reader. Mallarmé believes that the musical expressiveness of poetic language can evoke chords within the soul . . . Annensky, too, believes that the reader must participate creatively in the poem, and in this manner become a poet whose existence is varied. To attain this end, the reader-poet needs the "musical potentiality of the word . . . to stimulate a creative mood in the reader which should help him . . . fill in between the lines of the piece and to give

self returning from the desert, as the animate agent yet to be revealed. The combination *zvezdnaja pustynja,* interpretable as either the "star-covered desert" or the starry expanse of the sky itself, might accordingly suggest the celestial kinship of this agent with the starry realm he has taken leave of.

The noun subject and main verb of the sentence revealed in line 3 contradict our expectations from the preceding lines of an animate agent involved in spiritual departure. *Verbnaja nedelja* is a segment of time, and, as such, is only capable of temporal departure. The verb *uplyvat'* 'to float away' thus also takes on its temporal meaning. . . . The result of the metaphorical collision of these two lines is that both lines are rendered more polysemous. The Palm Week which is passing away becomes personified as a person who is floating away on a journey, while at the same time the departure from the wilderness in line 2 is seen figuratively as the temporal transition from Lent as Palm Week (or Palm Sunday, which begins on its eve) draws to a close.

This tension between spatial and temporal meanings of *uplyvat'* shifts again toward the spatial pole in line 4, where the Palm Week becomes concretized as an actual figure resting on a block of ice. The image of the ice block, presumably floating downstream along a river, incorporates itself as part of the earlier concrete setting at dusk in the wilderness, which is now clearly identifiable as a northern landscape. The modified *poslednij* 'last' identifies the ice block as a last chunk of ice departing downstream during the spring thaw. Such an image complements folk associations about Palm Week according to which the flowing away of the last ice block in the river is taken as signalling the arrival of the Palm Week and the coming of spring. The use of the adjective *pogiblyj* 'lost, perished,' although colloquial in style, introduces an unexpected note of pessimism not customarily associated with these themes. The adjective further personifies the passing of the Palm Week by metaphorically equating the ice block's journey and final melting with the process of dying. By this metaphorical association of melting with dying, the final line of the stanza introduces an additional non-spatial meaning of *uplyvat'*—namely, the process of metaphysical departure, or ceasing to be.

Taken as a fateful journey which will ultimately end in death, the ice block's journey may be viewed as symbolizing Christ's own journey as narrated in the Bible. Following his arrival in Jerusalem, celebrated at the end of the Palm Week, he will be arrested, judged, and crucified. Annenskij's pessimistic reference to the ice block may thus be seen as an anticipation of the more somber mood of the Biblical events which will be commemorated during Passion Week (*Strastnaja nedelja*)—a mood which is in contrast to the celebration normally associated with Palm Week. At the same time, line 4 can be interpreted as characterizing the actual temporal passing of Lent, which itself can be seen as symbolized by the departing block of ice. Palm Week is itself the last week (and Palm Sunday the last day) of Lent, and its passing away may be viewed metaphorically as perishing. Thus, through the tension of spatial, temporal, and metaphysical notions of the process of *uplyvala,* the poet achieves a polysemous synthesis of meanings which dramatizes the unity of the Holy Week with the events it commemorates. (pp. 494-95)

The metaphorical and sound organization of the stanza's internal structure . . . is complemented by an instance of extratextual literary allusion occurring in line 4. The image of the ice block floating downstream with its metaphorical associations of dying is reminiscent of a Tjutčev poem in which the metaphor is expanded to the dimensions of an entire poem. . . . In Annenskij's poem as in Tjutčev's, the floating away of the ice block during the spring is equated with a journey toward death. The lexical and thematic overlap of the two texts suggests that Tjutčev's poem may function as a subtext for line 4 of **"Verbnaja nedelja."** The allusion to the earlier text underscores the existential issue of self-annihilation raised in the Tjutčev poem and also sets Annenskij's image of the final solitary ice block in thematic contrast with Tjutčev's imagery of impersonal mass death. The result is a subtle new poetic tension in which the reader senses both the personal, intimate nature of a solitary departure to one's fate, perhaps modelled on Christ's own journey, and the general, impersonal nature of death as humanity's common fate. (p. 496)

The second stanza of **"Verbnaja nedelja"** continues the theme of the complex journey or movement portrayed in the previous stanza. Here, however, the setting has shifted from the outdoors to the interior of a church, perhaps during the Palm Saturday service. Within the stanza the dominant meaning of *uplyvala* is that of the temporal passing of the Holy Week, or more specifically the final day of that week. The events of the service are represented in terms of concrete aspects of church ritual (ringing bells, incense, icons) as well as allusions to a major theme of the liturgy read at this time—the Lazarus tale. Of these references, lines 5 and 6 present imagery of diffusion suggestive of temporal and metaphysical passing from presence to absence and non-being. Lines 7 and 8, on the other hand, portray the theme of humanity, represented by the faces of the icons and by the *Lazari,* who are seen as, in a sense, abandoned by the departing week. Clearly, this latter notion of abandonment reactivates for the reader the notion of spatial displacement in terms of Christ's imminent departure from earth which will be commemorated during the following Holy Week. . . . The unusual plural reference to Lazarus juxtaposes a new general notion of lost humanity to the single Biblical character whom Christ singles out for salvation. The reference need not be taken as obviously ironic or antireligious, as the critic Fedorov suggests. The association is, however, in distinct discordance with the mood of the Palm Week celebration and the function of the Lazarus text within the liturgy of Palm Sunday eve. It reflects more, perhaps, the poet's anticipation of the feelings of apprehension and desolation experienced by believers as they relive the events commemorated in the Holy Week to follow—Passion Week.

The final stanza opens with a new visual and temporal setting, again in the outdoors, which is similar to the one portrayed in the first stanza of the poem. The time frame would seem to have shifted to later in the evening, as is indicated by the rising of the moon, not mentioned in the first stanza. The reference to the moon's waning phase at the end of line 9 recapitulates the theme of dissipation and dying present in the preceding stanzas. However, by its cyclical nature, the imagery of the moon's phases introduces the implicit countertheme of cyclical renewal, dormantly present in the dead April of the first stanza. The reference . . . in line 10, returns us to the theme of the forgotten dead, or Lazari, here identified in universal terms as all who have died. Specifically, the use of the adjective *nevozvratima* underscores the motif of the journey—"irrevocable" journey towards death—which resonates throughout the poem. The preposition *za,* anticipating some gesture or expression in honor of the dead, stands in contradistinction to *ot* in line 8 of the previous stanza, characterizing the abandoning of the dead.

The final two lines of the poem seem to portray in a curiously indirect, disembodied manner an emotional response to separation by death. In line 11 the tears running down the willow branch . . . would seem to suggest an animate agent who is crying for the dead and whose tears have fallen onto the willow branch which he is holding. In terms of such an expectation, the *rumjanye ščeki xeruvina,* "rosy cheeks of a cherub," in line 12 would seem to be an appropriate source for the tears, were it not for the strange placement of the preposition *na* which precedes it. Rather than suggesting that the tears have fallen from the cheeks of a cherub (child) onto the willow branch, the poet reverses the expected order of things and depicts the tears flowing from the willow onto the cherub's cheeks. The use of the verb *plyli* 'floated' (rather than the more expected *tekli* 'flowed') is perhaps in the idiomatic sense of overflowing or melting into liquid. A possible interpretation of these lines is that they depict a rosy-cheeked child (much like Annenskij's grandson Valja) carrying a willow branch home from the church service. During the Palm Saturday service children traditionally carried willow branches which were blessed with holy water by the priest. Thus the tears falling from the willow branch could refer to drops of holy water dripping from the branch onto the child's cheeks. (pp. 497-98)

The flowing of the tears onto the cheeks of a cherub can be interpreted as symbolizing the ideal of an innocent child crying compassionately for the dead and is clearly reminiscent of the crying altar boy at the end of Blok's 1905 poem "Devuška pela v cerkovnom xore," a poem exhibiting many similarities to **"Verbnaja nedelja"** in theme and style. Furthermore, the motif of the child is itself symbolic of the process of renewal traditionally associated with the Palm Week. The falling of the tears onto the cherub can thus be taken as symbolizing as well the bestowal of a lifegiving baptismal blessing onto a newborn child. Such an association is all the more plausible in view of the willow's symbolism of renewal and regeneration as well as the traditional association of holy water with Christ's tears. In this manner the themes of dying and renewal are both unified in the poem in the image of Christ's tears, expressing compassion for the dead and dying and spiritual invigoration for those to come. (p. 500)

"Verbnaja nedelja" can be seen as Annenskij's expression of the flow of his subjective impressions on the eve of Palm Sunday, when he and his grandson Valja most probably attended the holiday service. These impressions are strongly colored by aspects of the actual setting within and outside of the church as well as by literary and religious associations from the poet's past experience. Specifically, the alternation between the outdoor and indoor settings from stanza to stanza would seem to indicate the chronological sequence of arriving at the church (stanza I), standing through the service (stanza II), and departing from the church (stanza III). The impressions of this experience are organized into a cyclic art pattern expressing the poet's feelings of both fatalism and compassion in response to the inevitability of passing and human loss. Beyond his pessimism, however, we sense in this pattern a larger vision of life as the constant alternation of phases of decline and renewal from which we can derive at least some faint hope of the possibility of resurrection. Thus, behind the seemingly irrational and noncontextual surface of the poem's linear development, which led Setchkarev to call it surrealistic in style, we find a highly organized and meaningful verbal construct of great semantic density. (p. 503)

David Borker, "Intrinsic and Extrinsic Aspects of Structure in Annenskij's 'Verbnaja Nedelja'," in The Slavic and East European Review, *Vol. 23, No. 4, Winter, 1979, pp. 491-504.*

ADDITIONAL BIBLIOGRAPHY

Agushi, Irina. "The Poetry of Georgy Ivanov." *Harvard Slavic Studies* V (1970): 116, 125-27.*

Briefly compares Annensky's use of imagery to that of Georgy Ivanov. Agushi also notes similarities in the two poets' choice of themes.

Mihály Babits

1883-1941

Hungarian poet, novelist, short story writer, critic, dramatist, translator, editor, and historian.

Babits was one of the most versatile and erudite contributors to modern Hungarian literature. His highly intellectual poetry earned him the sobriquet of *poeta doctus,* or "learned poet," and reveals his studied expertise of modernist trends in European literature. Largely influenced by the French Parnassians and Symbolists, Babits's works display a mastery of technical form, while thematically they express a deep concern with the perennial struggles of human existence, primarily those of love, war, and religion. In addition to his poetry, Babits was distinguished for his brilliant translations, many from the works of important authors who had never been translated into the Hungarian language. Among these are translations from Dante, Shakespeare, Johann Wolfgang von Goethe, Charles Baudelaire, and Edgar Allan Poe.

Courtesy of Europa Verlag A.G., Zuerich

Born in Szekszárd, Babits was raised in an intellectually stimulating, somewhat conservative middle-class environment. He attended a Cistercian secondary school, which reinforced his early Catholic upbringing, and matriculated in the humanities at the University of Budapest. During his university days, Babits also began a career as a writer, publishing his early verse in *Nyugat.* This journal was the principal organ of a small coterie of writers and artists whose modernist thinking broke with the romantic traditions of their national literature, which had largely consisted of works glorifying Hungary's past. Within this group, Babits shared his contemporaries' enthusiasm not only for the aestheticism of the French Symbolists, but also for the poetic innovations of several English and American poets, for theories of Naturalism in fiction and Impressionism in art, and for the philosophical ideas of Friedrich Nietzsche and Henri Bergson. Influences of the Symbolist movement are most evident in Babits's early poetry, including his first two collections of verse, *Levelek Irisz koszorújából* and *Herceg, hátha megjön a tel is,* which are also strongly influenced by Babits's classical learning. Babits combined his writing career with a teaching career until 1919 when the Communist regime, incensed by his pacifist poetry, pressured him to resign his professorial position at the University of Budapest. Thereafter, he devoted his life solely to literary pursuits.

Babits wrote successfully in a variety of genres and, with *A Gólyakalifa (The Nightmare), Timár Virgil fia,* and *Halálfiai,* earned a prominent reputation as a novelist with acute insight into the psychology of the middle class of the nineteenth century. In 1929 Babits accepted the editorship of *Nyugat,* becoming one of the most influential and respected literary figures in Hungary. In addition, he was chosen to administer the Baumgarten Prize, a distinguished literary award presented annually to the writer "who had remained faithful to his principles." Occasionally, both of these large responsibilities fostered hostile feelings toward Babits by some of his contemporaries who did not agree with his decisions, which favored aesthetic over political concerns. For the most part, however, he retained a respectful following of students and critics throughout his life.

Although he was stricken with throat cancer several years before his death in 1941, Babits continued to contribute to Hungarian literature, drawing from a reserve of spiritual strength despite his painful illness. During this time, he wrote his last volume of poetry, *Jónás Könyre,* which is considered by many critics to be his best. Unlike his earlier collections of poetry, *Jónás Könyre,* along with *Az istenek halnak, az ember él,* and *Versenyt as esztendökkel,* displays a new sense of mysticism. As Joseph Reményi has stated of these works: "There is an element of *consolatio mystica* in them, an admission that 'only God sees with the eyes of everyone'; but also a fascinating and fantastic conclusion about the 'holy pain' that throws opposites into oneness." In 1940 Babits completed one of his finest literary endeavors and one of which he was especially proud—the translation of Dante's *Divine Comedy.* The work was well-received and shortly before his death earned him the Italian San Remo Prize as the best translation of Dante's work in existence.

Critics agree that Babits was one of the most important benefactors of modern Hungarian literature. While his works are sometimes criticized for their "emotional sterility," they are more often praised for their evocative language and classic style. Miklós Szabolcsi echoed the critical consensus when he commented: "Babits was one of the most versatile and most complex figures in Hungarian letters, an outstanding representative of twentieth-century bourgeois humanism, and one of the most distinguished links between Hungarian and European literature."

PRINCIPAL WORKS

Levelek Irisz koszorújából (poetry) 1909
Herceg, hátha megjön a tél is (poetry) 1911
Dante isteni színjátéka. 3 vols. [translator] (poetry) 1913-1923
A gólyakalifa (novel) 1915
[*King's Stork*, 1948; also published as *The Nightmare*, 1966]
Recitativ (poetry) 1916
Shakespeare: A vihar [translator] (poetry) 1916
Karácsonyi Madonna (novel) 1920
Laodameia (drama) 1921
Gondolat és írás (essays) 1922
Timár Virgil fia (novel) 1922
Kártyavár (novel) 1923
Sziget és tenger (poetry) 1925
Halálfiai (novel) 1927
Versek (poetry) 1927
Az istenek halnak, az ember él (poetry) 1929
Élet és irodalom (essays) 1929
A torony árnyéka (short stories and fables) 1931
Oedipus király és egyéb műfordítások [translator] (drama) 1931
Elza pilóta vagy a tökéletes társadalom (novel) 1933
Versenyt as esztendőkkel (poetry) 1933
Az európai irodalom története, 1760-1925 (criticism) 1934
Hat holdas rózsakert (short stories) 1937
Összes művei. 10 vols. (poetry, novels, short stories, and essays) 1937-38
Jónás Könyre (poetry) 1938
Keresztülkasul as életemen (autobiography) 1939

Translated selections of Babits's poetry have appeared in the following publications: *A Little Treasury of Hungarian Verse, The Magyar Muse*, and *Modern Magyar Lyrics*.

WATSON KIRKCONNELL (essay date 1933)

[*In the following excerpt, Kirkconnell offers a general evaluation of Babits's poetry and his translations of poetry.*]

Michael Babits . . . is, if anything, even more of a technical virtuoso [in his poetry than his contemporary, Andre Ady], although inferior to him as a lyrist. Much of Babits's astonishing mastery of metre has been gained in the apprenticeship of verse translation from many languages. The general level of his original work is unusually high. (p. 26)

[Babits's] masterful verse translation of Dante's Inferno and Purgatorio is one of the best in any language. He has also translated from Shakespeare, Wilde, Goethe, Baudelaire, and Verlaine; and has published two anthologies of translations. . . . (p. 180)

Watson Kirkconnell, "Introduction" and "Michael Babits," in The Magyar Muse: An Anthology of Hungarian Poetry, 1400-1932, *edited and translated by Watson Kirkconnell, Kanadai Magyar Ujság Press, 1933, pp. 15-26, 180.**

JOSEPH REMÉNYI (essay date 1944)

[*Reményi was a Hungarian-born American editor, literary critic, and educator who worked to foster a greater understanding of Hungarian culture in the English-speaking world. His critical work* Hungarian Writers and Literature: Modern Novelists, Critics, and Poets *was a major effort in that direction. In the following excerpt from that work, Reményi provides one of the most comprehensive surveys in English of Babits's works. This essay originally appeared in the* Slavonic and East European Review, *Vol. XXII (1944).*]

Mihály Babits, modern Hungary's most erudite poet, represents (though he never participated actively in politics) the enlightened principles of Count István Széchenyi, the nineteenth-century statesman. Count Széchenyi was considered by Lajos Kossuth "the greatest Hungarian," despite their political differences. Babits, Széchenyi-like, believed that politically, socially, economically, and culturally Hungary should be an equal of Western Europe, without ignoring the obligations of her Central and Southeastern European geographical position.

However, Babits was not only a twentieth-century literary expression of Széchenyi's spirit; his aesthetic and philosophical temper, accompanied by catholic taste and interest, induced him to explore the universe in his own fashion. His roots were Hungarian, his outlook universal. In one of his poems he points out "how small this earth is"; but he also speaks about "the little house" where he was born. In the madness of modern life he was attached to spiritual and moral order. He knew that to reach it there were no short cuts, but he also knew that, in an age of shifting values, slippery slogans, and poorly administered national and international institutions, self-respect and faith in human dignity were necessary in order to rise above the exploiting tendencies of mere opportunism. He adhered to this conviction.

Babits was the most important poetic contemporary of Endre Ady, whose greatness he acknowledged. Like that apocalyptic poet of modern Hungary, Babits was conscious of the iniquities of Hungarian life, yet he differed from him in many ways. His creative freedom was closer to ideas of intellectual perspective than those of Ady; he went further on the road of philosophical restlessness than his poetic confrere. On the other hand, he possessed less intuitive spontaneity; he lacked Ady's powerful and matchless hallucinations. For a considerable time "radicals" and "conservatives" likewise frowned on him. Their attitude could be explained by Babits' unwillingness to be a football for political roughnecks, or drowsy reactionaries, or ideologists whose honesty he did not question, but with whose judgment he often disagreed. (p. 306)

As one of the chief contributors of *Nyugat* (West), an important literary periodical, and later as its editor, he shared with Endre Ady, Ignotus, Margit Kaffka, Zsigmond Móricz, Ernő Osvát, Aladár Schöpflin, Árpád Tóth and other more or less untraditional creators and critics the precarious reputation of a "radical."

Nevertheless, Babits was not politically minded; he was a pacifist in a humanitarian sense, which is frequently misinterpreted by politicians. By this time his voice was heard and to a certain extent feared by the representatives of literary vested interests. . . . After World War I, when differences developed between him and some of his friends, he confined his work mostly to the editing of *Nyugat*, to the chairmanship of the Baumgarten committee of literary prizes, to pure creative and interpretative writing, and to the elaboration of the idea (akin to that of Julien Benda, the French writer) that poets and writers should be first of all artists, and that they should not be willing tools of political interests or truculent protagonists of political views. In an essay entitled ***A halhatatlanság halála (The Death of Immortality),*** though recognizing the "magnificent past" of Ignotus, *Nyugat's* former editor, he carried his creed into a verbal battle, namely, that he should always be governed by literary postulates, whereas, according to Babits, Ignotus subjected his convictions to the practice of politics in literature. It was unfortunate that these two capable leaders of modern Hungarian literature should have come to the parting of the ways; the truth is that both demonstrated faith in the maximum values of the creative spirit, but they did it with opposing temperaments.

From the end of World War I till the time of his death in 1941, the prestige of Babits as a creator and as a critic increased. Younger writers and poets with diverse social and political interests but true artistic and intellectual aims judged him as one of the foremost spokesmen of twentieth-century Hungarian literature. He had imitators in the realm of poetry and disciples in the sphere of essay writing. While there was a countercurrent—either accentuating the realistic romanticism of Dezső Szabó, the novelist, and of his "neoprimitive" followers, or the champions of the avant-garde who were interested in "revolutionary" social and aesthetic creeds—on the basis of authentic critical consideration it was Babits who stayed in the spotlight of Hungarian literary life.

To gossiping critics he remained impenetrable. They called him a *poeta doctus,* using the words disparagingly. He was modern and classical, logical and irrational, complex and simple, vague and positive, bored and vital, sensuous and spiritual, austere and joyful; indeed, catholic in his taste to such a degree that he visioned life in its totality. He was a major poet in an age of disillusioning confusion; ironic in an environment that eulogized uncritical and self-centered enthusiasms. He never paid mere lip service to values since values were the sublime and supreme realities of his world, hence the burning issue of his own existence. He disliked organized optimism. He believed in literary workmanship when many writers believed solely in "best sellers" or in propaganda. His *bête noire* was pseudo-literary journalism that vulgarized public taste. Crude or homespun individualism in the disguise of "honest folkways" aroused his critical resentment.

The incorruptible creative sensitivity of Babits was in profound contrast with the poetic beliefs and psychological manners of his predecessors who were writing at the turn of the century. It was mostly due to this fact that critics who admitted his ability were liable to be confused by his "never-to-be-satisfied" warring spirit. He was not unintelligible, but he had no panacea for every national problem and did not espouse "causes" with evangelistic fervor. Babits, as a poet, novelist, short-story writer, poetic dramatist, essayist, critic, literary historian, translator of ancient and recent poetry, occupies a unique place in Hungarian literature. In a disorganized world he stood for the kind of artistic probity which was in direct opposition to the slick and breezy competence of "timely" writers and poets. With some exceptions, his older contemporaries were much less interested in the inexorable forces of fate than in the expediencies of the moment. Bombastic diction or transitory wit, principles smoothly adjusted to the riddle of selfishly applied "historical necessities," or cynical repudiations of legitimate ethnic images, ideas that were merely sentimental in relation to ideals, and ideals that resembled the imaginative scenery of assumed national importance narrowed the horizon of Hungarian creators to a spiritual existence that Babits rejected.

Consequently, this poet of imponderables remained solitary for many years. His unexpected metaphors, his baffling technique, his learnedness were not exciting to critics or readers who looked for thrills or for the obvious. No doubt there are tedious parts in his writing. In his yearning for clarity Babits was prone to use too many definitive terms. As a whole, however, those attributes predominate that show an unfailing directive, concentrating on the essence of ideas, things, and experiences. Here and there the harshness and bookishness of his images, his sensuous and abstruse concern with the incongruent, remind one of certain seventeenth-century English metaphysical poets. But Babits' raptures have a noticeably Catholic language, deriving from his Catholic upbringing and resulting, despite a mild baroque fancifulness, in less mystical shudders or whimsical effects. His Hungarianism produced mental and spiritual landscapes for which he found gracious and unorthodox utterances in which few Hungarian poets ever equaled him. His sense of form was such that it embodied the freedom not only of an intellectual vocabulary but also of colloquialism and all the variations that derive from the Protean instincts and judgments of his personality.

The lyric, dramatic, narrative, and critical substance of Babits' art springs from a tragic sense that has a Sophoclean perspective. While his opponents admit his importance as an aesthetician and literary historian, they are less magnanimous in recognizing his poetry and fictional prose. They seem to forget that feeling and thinking are not diffused in the art of Babits, but move on the same level. Babits rejected what John Crowe Ransom calls "the belletristic theory of poetry," unrelated to the essence of creativeness. He was the author of nine volumes of poetry; seven of these were collected in one volume, entitled ***Versek (Poems),*** containing his poems written between 1902 and 1927. Spiritually and aesthetically Babits is the best example in modern Hungarian poetry of the organic relationship between talent shaped by tradition and talent creating tradition. His indignations and opinions, the light and darkness of his words, should be regarded as instinctive and deliberate representations of a spirit that without the conscience of universality would have considered itself a heretic of literature. (pp. 307-10)

In his first volume, entitled ***Levelek Irisz koszorújából (Leaves from Iris' Wreath),*** he introduced a concept of beauty hitherto unknown in Hungarian poetry. In the formative process of his poetic work he subjected himself to rigorous self-criticism. He was immersed in antique culture; this fact and a poetic commentary on strange or strangely expressed experiences distinguished his work from the work of those poets whose bulky outputs, fixed views, maudlin beliefs were close to conventional taste. One of his first sonnets, **"Hegeso sírja" (The Tomb of Hegeso),** reveals his connection with the antique past. (p. 310)

In his early poetry Babits' taste was Parnassian; it seems that José María de Heredia's *Les Trophées* influenced him. Later he was disposed to eye the world with the sensitive discrimination of the Symbolists. Detachment and subjectivity in a background of indeterministic attitudes (though constantly tempted by unspeculative determinism) placed him above the empiricism of the moment; he did not permit time to make him dependent on transitoriness. His private vocabulary and his public vocabulary were valid because of the congenital poetic assurance they suggested. Too bad that so little of his work has been translated into English; it would be interesting to show how he avoided the blind alley of merely stimulating versification. There were few poetic forms that he did not master; and his knowledge of world literature was so vast that in the receptive stage of youth he was able to blend contrasts of influences without betraying his own voice.

In his first volume the underlying psychological motive of his images was an attempt to integrate pride and courage into a manner of expression that would repudiate the omnipotent power of "incurable stupidity." He called himself "the priest of the Muses." Throughout this volume the craftsman struggles with sensibilities; the somber spirit with hedonistic freedom. **"In Horatium,"** one of his finest poems, **"Óda a bűnhöz" (An Ode to Sin), "Himnusz Iriszhez" (A Hymn to Iris), "Sunt Lacrimae Rerum,"** are poems in which he handles his complex emotions with effectiveness, and with the appropriate voice of a young poet excited "by difference that is color, and by life that is different." He sings about the "brown gipsy clouds of eternity," about "fire, this immortal flag." One is likely to note in these poems a sense of historical dimensions made significant through creativeness; one also notes self-consciousness and a fear of wasting energies upon unimportant or worthless matters. **"Messze . . . Messze" (Far, Far Away)** is impressive in its intellectual romanticism, but disciplined by a classical sense of order. The poet visualizes Spain, Italy, Greece, Switzerland, Germany, France, England, Sweden; the scenes are the projections of a fertile imagination; the organic form of the poem reaches its climax in these two lines:

How many towns there are, how many folk,
How many far, fair regions to invoke!

The volume suggests excessive restlessness. **"Tüzek" (Flames), "A csendéletekből" (Still Life), "A vásár" (The Market), "Mozgófénykép" (Film), "A világosság udvara" (The Courtyard of Light), "Fekete ország" (Black Land), "A lírikus epilógja" (The Epilogue of the Lyricist),** reveal the crystallized subjectivity of a poet who lives in his "own prison." His poems illustrate an almost grim defiance of a resolute, yet vexed, tense, and intense poet who seems to say that he will attain his end by always following his daimon.

In ***Herceg, hátha megjön a tél is (But, Prince, if Winter Should Come)*** one feels a strong regard for self-imposed poetic patterns. In this second volume there are allusions to a weary spirit, struggling with the settings of a drab existence, careful at the same time not to have his intensity impaired by the attacks of indifference of the moment. The poet is confused; in the poem, dedicated to János Arany, the great Hungarian lyric and epic poet, he admits bewilderment. This second volume contains a number of short poems; the images are rich, emanating from a sensitiveness that is eager to comprehend, to live, to conquer the darkness of nothingness. The poems **"Ballada Irisz fátyoláról" (Ballad of the Veil of Iris), "A sorshoz" (To Fate), "Mindenek szerelme" (Love of All), "Oda a szépségről" (An Ode to Beauty), "Klasszikus álmok" (Classical Dreams),** and **"A Danaidák" (The Danaïdes)** show the matured expressiveness of the poet. The spirit of these poems, though subscribing to the realities of the objective world, is a continual reflection of that "prison" existence with which Babits invested his poetic realm. Several poems have English or French titles, indicating the poet's affectionate and lively interest in the "exoticism of the Occident," made pictorial or musical through the consciousness of English or French words. (pp. 311-12)

The first two volumes present the course of a poetic mentality which proceeds with certainty only when pragmatism is ignored. The third volume, ***Recitativ (Recitative),*** reveals the wounded spirit of the poet in a new light. As professor of literature in provincial secondary schools outside the cosmopolitan orbit of Budapest, or as a visitor to his native town, his cultivated soul registered obstacles which provoked his compassionate and his ironic nature. Deep melancholy carried the poet to grounds which were, after all, his native land, yet threatened his heightened sensitiveness with silence because of indifference or hopelessness. "Hurting, freezing songs," "vinegar songs" were the expression of his pale or forlorn heart; then again poems of loneliness fighting tiresome or problematically amusing trifles. References to his sweetheart and to his relatives, images of piety and nightmares, were the varied directions of his interests; sometimes, but only on rare occasions, a buoyant voice merged into the inherent sadness of these poems; "warmth and soaring feeling," of which he speaks in the preface of one of his books, claimed his impatience with himself. He is now more closely allied with the outside world; he either invites realistic reality, or is invaded by it. **"Augusztus" (August), "A költő életének pusztájáról" (From the Desert of the Poet's Life), "Anyám nagybátyja régi pap" (An Old Priest Is My Mother's Uncle), "Vakok a hídon" (The Blind on the Bridge), "Régi magyar arckép" (An Old Hungarian Portrait), "Cigánydal" (Gypsy Song), "Levél Tomiból" (Letter from Tomi),** are poems abundant in direct expressions, melodius through assonances, alliterations, onomatopoetic qualities.

His fourth volume, ***Isten kezében (In the Hands of God),*** containing his poems written between 1914 and 1916, will be remembered for their pacifistic eloquence. Some of the pacifistic poems were, indeed, a test of Babits' "nonpolitical" poetic theory. At any rate, they incensed certain power interests (the war would not favor the "triviality" of peace); those who quibbled with the poet's patriotism were unable to understand his humaneness, and much less his fearlessness. . . . His fifth volume, ***A nyugtalanság völgye (The Valley of Restlessness),*** joins hands with the preceding volume in the panegyric of peace. By now Babits had become the master of his medium. The emotional and imaginative, the ideal and brutal interactions of his expressions, related to immediateness and convictions that transcend immediateness, make this one of his most important volumes. **"Egy filozófus halálára" (At the Death of a Philosopher)** is not only a Miltonian tribute to a friend who was killed on a Galician battlefield, it is also an attack against the Teutons "responsible for senseless wars" and a sorrowful utterance of regret because "forms and rules shatter their own mirrors." Written with the "sad supremacy of words," **"A jóság dala" (The Song of Goodness), "Zsoltár férfihangra" (Psalm for Man's Voice), "A könnytelenek könnyei" (The Tears of the Tearless), "Csillagokig" (To the Stars),** all are magnificent expressions of a poet who was not deterred in his devotion to truth as he knew it. . . . The poet's tragic sense, affected by the fatal position of his native land and by man's disloyalty to his own humaneness, speaks with dauntless honesty and irrevocable faithfulness to those principles without which the human mind and the human heart would be nothing but a foolish or diabolical battleground of unnecessary plots and counterplots.

With each successive volume, his poems revealed sagacity as well as unwillingness to succumb to flag-waving policies, accompanied by ingratiating or "noble" slogans. The core of his human and poetic issues was always a symbol of human dignity. In an inchoate civilization and culture, in a more mystifying than enigmatic age of destructiveness, he approached reality first with the authority of a poet, then with the frankness of human warmth, conscious of disappointments and of greatness. When his enemies or those who were unable to understand him stated that he was a ''cold'' poet, they only expressed an opinion that proved nothing. Babits was not merely aesthetically and philosophically versatile but well versed in history, psychology, and natural sciences. His work does not suggest spontaneity, it suggests intensity. There was intensity in Sophocles; true, less than in Euripides, yet it was there. How could he have written about doom without intensity? Babits' feet remained on earth but the rhythmic variety of his work touched eternity. His classicism has heart and intelligence, and, indeed, it is difficult to understand why his ''feelings'' (sometimes ebullient) were not recognized by many readers and critics. The only answer seems to be that he did not play to the gallery or that his intellectuality made ''hard reading'' for those used to platitudinous tidbits.

There is a characteristic confession in his sixth volume, entitled ***Sziget és tenger (Island and Sea).*** In the poem **"Örökkék ég a felhők mögött" (Eternal Blue Skies Back of the Clouds)** he declares his belief in the worthwhileness of living, in struggle, in brotherhood and truth, in the wisdom of the superfluous, in pictures that portray a new world, in the soul that loves the universe, in matter to be conquered, and in his Hungarian heredity which he could not and would not discard, because such action would impoverish the world, and he believed in the enrichment of the world. (pp. 312-14)

His last three volumes of poems, ***Az istenek halnak, az ember él (The Gods Die, Man Lives On), Versenyt az esztendőkkel (Race with the Years),*** and ***Jónás könyve (The Book of Jonah),*** are timeless realizations of a human and poetic will that learned to treasure life for what it is and what it seems to be. There is an element of *consolatio mystica* in them, an admission that ''only God sees with the eyes of everyone''; but also a fascinating and fantastic conclusion about the ''holy pain'' that throws opposites into oneness. There is self-pity and mercy in the poet's soul. This feeling, however, does not mean an intellectual deadlock, and it does not imply separation from irony. Paradoxical religious images and outward and inward forces appear with equal necessity in the poet's work, trying to understand the momentary and the ultimate. (p. 318)

As any poet worthy of the name, in his prose work too Babits viewed the world *sub species aeternitatis*. The discord between his sense of values and the stereotyped or indifferent culture of his surroundings, of course, has bearing upon his fiction. To come to grips with the simple albeit significant fact that one must face readers, accustomed to jingoistic trash or to tepid perhaps counterfeit honesty, required not only a truth-detecting disposition but in order to overcome the clumsiness of this situation, it required a tenacity of purpose and a predisposition to face misunderstanding without fear. Babits knew how to translate experiences into fiction; and no trickiness of his opponents, no melodramatic homily, no plotting, mordant or pedantic animosity could make him servile to views in which he had no confidence. (pp. 319-20)

He published eight volumes of novels, short stories, fables, harmonizing traditional habits of writing with modern psychology. His knowledge of modern psychology affected the outlook and technique of his work. For the background of his tales he has chosen either contemporary scenes or the subterranean sphere of the psyche. The progression of his stories is assisted by effective probabilities. It should be pointed out that he was fond of the detective stories of Edgar Allan Poe and recognized in their contrived structure the kind of brilliancy which appealed to him when he enjoyed reconstructing exciting meaningfulness from vague premises. Influenced by William James (this is rather an assumption), he was interested in the spiritual mask of alternating entities. He was susceptible to Freudian influences, but never to such an extent that his stories would have been plain case histories, illustrating the validity of the psychoanalytical method. (p. 320)

Karácsonyi Madonna (Christmas Madonna) reveals the writer's interest in the fantastic. ***Gólyakalifa (The Stork Caliph)*** shows Babits' curiosity for the subconscious. ***A torony arnyéka (The Shadow of the Tower)*** contains fables and tales; the inimitable qualities of a literary artist, the delicate shades of the tangible and the intangible, make this collection valid. ***Hat holdas rózsakert (Six-Acre Rose Garden)*** is a representative collection of short stories. ***Kártyavár (Castle of Cards)*** is a satirical novel of social criticism, portraying the political, social, and economic bleakness and unscrupulousness of a modern Hungarian industrial and commercial community. It is a city of poor taste and bluff, keeping up with the loud tone of sordid and, from an ethical point of view, parasitic ''modernity.'' The writer's character delineation is refreshing; his ''busy people'' are cheap and pretentious opportunists or coarse entrepreneurs. This is a Hungarian ''Main Street'' story, not typical of the agrarian communities but instructive as a travesty of ''sophisticated'' and brutal individual and collective egotism, unfit from a desirable social point of view and inclined to overemphasize and embrace purely materialistic objectives. ***Elza pilóta vagy a tökéletes társadalom (Pilot Elza or the Perfect Society)*** comes very close to the sort of sardonic despair that one observes in some of Aldous Huxley's symbols. The central theme of the novel is related to a ''civilization'' that accepted ''eternal warfare'' as unavoidable. There is a story within a story; didactic in its implication but not shoutingly so, suggesting an ideal microcosm that is on the level of realizable human capacities. Technically and psychologically the novel is a meritorious achievement of Babits the introspective man and Babits the ironic recorder of human unhappiness. In ***Halálfiai (The Sons of Death)*** the writer exceeded the usual length and ignored the bizarre features of his other stories. There seems much paraphrased autobiography in this novel; it was evidently motivated by a profound conscience revealing anxieties about the Fool's Paradise of the Hungarian middle class and its disintegration. There are splendidly drawn figures; for example, the character of an old lady, ''Cenci néni,'' who seems to be the wisest person in an environment of tired and tiring people. The reader participates in a world whose customs became anachronistic and the characters pathetic or silly. For these qualities of characterization the novel deserves praise. (pp. 320-21)

Timár Virgil fia (The Son of Virgil Timár) is Babits' best novel. In fact, it is a long short story, persuasive, absorbing, coherent. Introduction, presentation, and denouement create an atmosphere of expectation and fulfillment. One's emotional response is immediate. The analysis of the three major characters is complete, therefore convincing. The love of Virgil Timár, who is a teacher and a member of a religious order, for a half-orphan student, Pista Vagner, his feeling that he is his ''spiritual father,'' and the return of the ''real father,'' Vilmos Vitany, an able but skeptical and materialistic journalist, the real father's ability to impress the boy with his fatherhood, though he had neglected him theretofore, the boy's decision to follow his father, thus betraying his faithfulness to his spiritual father, the conflict of attitudes and instincts, of evident and ineffable factors, the entire plot is knit together with an artistic sureness, with a creative sense of understanding, with an intuitive and positive concentration on the comedy and tragedy of the possessive and unpossessive traits of human nature. No glittering embellishment, no conspicuous imagery, no verbal dressing-up, no lifelessness spoil the unity of the story or the delight that its psychology of contrasts offers.

Referring to Babits' prose, his three volumes of literary essays, ***Irodalmi problémák (Literary Problems), Gondolat és írás (Thought and Letter), Élet és irodalem (Life and Literature),*** his literary history ***Az europai irodalom története (The History of European Literature),*** and his autobiography ***Keresztülkasul az életemen (Crisscross Through My Life),*** must be mentioned. The aesthetic and moral critic and historian, the philosophically and psychologically trained appraiser of values, the spirit that respected the cultural legacy of the past and endeavored to find values in the often uncongenial flux of modern life upholds in these studies those principles which were destroyed or were in danger of destruction by organically insensitive and amoral forces. Regardless of whether Sophocles or St. Augustine of the ancients, Bergson of the moderns, or Hungarian writers and poets of the past or of more recent times were the subjects of his critical evaluation, Babits, attracted to their loftiness, made them attractive to those who in the age of "progress," of decaying or decayed taste, were not sufficiently conversant or were unconcerned with them. (pp. 321-22)

As a translator, [Babits'] taste was eclectic but never superficial. He asserted that poetic translations were independent creations; there is no impassive translation while conveying the rhythm of other poets. In view of all this, it is natural that he never violated his responsibility as a translator and that his translations are as much a part of his creative spirit as is his original work.

The translations of Sophocles' *Oedipus Tyrannus,* Dante's *Divina Commedia,* to which Babits wrote a scholarly preface, Shakespeare's *Tempest,* Goethe's *Iphigenia,* his *Amor Sanctus,* a collection of fifty Latin hymns, *Erato,* a book of antique and modern erotic poems, and his poetic anthology of foreign poets entitled ***Pávatollak (Peacock Feathers)*** prove his admiration for the task he set before himself. . . . His translations (transplantations) are not inferior to the original. In most instances the impression one gains is of a *total* poetic experience in the Hungarian language. Wordsworth, Tennyson, Meredith, Wilde, Swinburne, Rossetti of the English poets, Baudelaire, Richepin, Verlaine of the French, Carducci of the Italian, Vogelweide, Lenau, Heine, Liliencron of the German inspired Babits to translations. This list is not particularly revealing of Babits' taste; it is not a unit of the poet's sole sympathies as to the kind of foreign poets he was fond of. By translating them Babits stressed aesthetic perceptions which, prior to him, had not been generally accepted by Hungarian poetic translators. Most of these translations, with all their admirable characteristics, were, in a pioneering sense, matters of aesthetic importance. Dante or Shakespeare, of course, and other great writers and poets of foreign countries had their good Hungarian translators in the past; but it was Babits, and among his contemporaries Dezső Kosztolányi and Árpád Tóth, who included in their list of translations poets theretofore unknown to the Hungarian public.

Babits as a playwright was less exceptional. ***Laodameia*** is a closet drama. The theme is not fully developed. In ***Vihar (Storm)*** he used the theme of a fable, written by János Garay, a nineteenth-century Hungarian writer of ballads and patriotic lyric verses. It is an unfinished play. ***A literator (The Literator)*** is Babits' tribute in dramatic form to Ferenc Kazinczy, the enlightened nineteenth-century Hungarian writer and critic whose life and work were a source of encouragement to his friends and to later generations. The play, in its intent, is a comedy, but not a thoroughly successful one. Babits, absorbed in ideas, ideals, and images, was not destined to be a playwright according to box-office terms. But even in these book-dramas we meet the virtuoso of the Hungarian language and the spirit of a poetic nonconformist.

In the literary and political babel of twentieth-century Hungary Babits knew that he was fighting a more or less losing battle. His complete works were published in ten volumes, the various literary societies were proud to claim him as a member, some of his work was translated into German, French, English, Italian, and other languages; nevertheless, his real achievement was that of *succès d'estime*. In his quest for values he never yielded to greedy external success, which is a parody of appreciation. He was always a literary artist with an independent spirit.

As a witness and as an expression of the tragic lot of the cultured man in his native land and all over the world, he offered evidence of understanding and intellectual bravery that should make his importance clear to his own people as well as to the people of other countries. His tragic sense, . . . akin to a Sophoclean acceptance of the ceaseless warring of the human spirit (although much less conservative in its political and social aspect), was immune to the marginal intelligence of those who were satisfied with the clever or meaningless technique of adjustment. He possessed the faculty of an inspiring and impartial intelligence, relying on ideas and ideals, never desisting from the duty of critical consciousness. He said that "the poem gives birth to the poet," thus admitting, in a Kantian sense, the relationship of meaning to awareness. (pp. 322-24)

One could quarrel with some of Babits' canons regarding his pamphleteering contemporaries, rightist and leftist, and their political casuistry. One could say that his concept of enduring worth in literature was sometimes subject to justified criticism. One could discern in his loneliness, in its lyrical and ironic manifestation, a self-designated policy, sincere but occasionally too arbitrary in its relation to those who did not see eye to eye with him. The flesh-and-blood richness of some other great writers and poets was not one of his characteristic attributes. Nonetheless, his grasp of ideal values and his superb talent entitle him to universal recognition. This recognition should save Babits from the linguistic solitariness of a Hungarian poet. (pp. 324-25)

Joseph Reményi, "Twentieth Century Hungarian Writers and Literature: Mihály Babits, 'Poeta Doctus' (1883-1941)," in his Hungarian Writers and Literature: Modern Novelists, Critics, and Poets, *edited by August J. Molnar, Rutgers University Press, 1964, pp. 306-25.*

G. F. CUSHING (essay date 1956)

[*In the following excerpt, Cushing comments on Babits's attributes as a Hungarian author.*]

The development of individual characteristics [in Hungarian literature] became very much more marked during the early years of the present century. The literary periodical 'West' (*Nyugat*) became a rallying-point for a new generation of writers whose desire was to be linked with West European thought, but it did not stifle individual ability. . . .

Of the *Nyugat* circle, Babits strove to achieve a synthesis between Hungarian traditions and the wider European and classical ideals. He was a humanist of wide scholarship—his **'His-**

tory of European Literature' pays remarkable tribute to this—and a poet with an unrivalled mastery of sound and rhythm, which could occasionally carry him away. His work was just as subjective as that of [his contemporary Andre] Ady, but contained an element of polished dignity and nobility which befitted the translator of Dante and lent him a certain reserve. His spiritual pilgrimage was a long and complicated journey, from the formal verse of his early years through the first world war and the various fashions of the post-war period to the prophetic majesty of his **'Book of Jonah'.** (p. xxix)

G. F. Cushing, in an introduction to his Hungarian Prose and Verse, *The Athlone Press, 1956, pp. xi-xxxv.**

MIKLÓS SZABOLCSI (essay date 1964)

[*In the following excerpt, Szabolcsi presents an overview of Babits's career, focusing on his literary development.*]

Babits started his career as a believer in art for art's sake, a virtuoso in playing with various styles, a master of verse forms displaying high artistry in his use of the language. An admirer of the end-of-the-century poets, especially Swinburne, he was of the type of the *poeta doctus,* with whom the polished forms serve only to conceal his fevered inward disquietude, his tormented solitude, the dilemma between thought and action. He is a thinking type of poet, one with a philosophical turn of mind, an outstanding representative of idealist philosophy, a past master in bold and unusual verse constructions, and in the use of words. He did not follow Ady's revolutionary fervour and desire for action. In politics, too, he was rather on the conservative side—the populace scared and repulsed him. Nevertheless, the horrors of the world war moved him to determined protest—the cry of pain that bursts forth from his poem ***Before Easter,*** makes this verse a masterpiece of Hungarian anti-war poetry.

After the revolution, his poetry, too, took a new course. Gone were the stiff, set forms, the playful masquerades—weariness, lethargy, and loss of direction are mirrored by his near-expressionist poems written in these years. The bookish idyll of the earlier years had been lost, but it was now compensated for by closer ties with national life, by the protest of a staunch liberal intellectual at the sight of the new inhumanity. By the end of the 20's, Babits had established a new equilibrium: from his essays, novels and poems alike emerged the position of a man who, standing on the ground of nineteenth-century liberal humanism, now took up the defence of all that was positive in culture and literature, against challenges from both the Right and the Left. His stand was that of a new classicism, representing the aspiration towards a "Silver Age"—a rather precarious and unrealistic programme to put forward in an age so bedevilled by troubles. As the editor of the *Nyugat* and curator of the most important Hungarian literary prize, the Baumgarten foundation, he pursued from the early 30's a consistent literary policy, a liberal-conservative view of literature free of politics, an attitude characteristic of him, but one for which he was attacked from both Right and Left.

Babits changed his attitude and views in the last few years of his life. The spread of fascism and the approach and eventual advent of the Second World War drove him on to change his course. He sensed the approaching danger, and surveyed the pitfalls on the road he had travelled thus far; his dramatic search for a new way, his agony, his loyalty to higher ideas and his awareness of the need for taking a more militant stand are mirrored in poems like his ***The Book of Jonah*** . . . , a self-avowal transposed into a Biblical setting. His fatal disease—cancer of the throat—caused him torment and physical suffering that inspired him to some extraordinarily forceful poems of classic purity in which he cast off all formal trappings.

Lyrics form but part of Babits's immense work. In his great novel, ***Sons of Death*** . . . , he paints a canvas of the Hungarian intelligentsia of the late nineteenth century. This is a psychological, analytical novel, encumbered with some philological ponderousness, which views with scorn both conservatives and radicals. He made an attempt at a—slightly mystic—portrayal of the industrialising capital of Hungary of the 1910's (***House of Cards*** . . .); wrote one novel about a split personality, based on Freudian teachings (***King Stork*** . . .); and gave vent to his fears, to the loss of direction induced by those disjointed times, in a great utopian war-novel (***Flyer Elsa or Perfect Society*** . . .). His novelettes and short stories, too, extend over a wide gamut, and his essays fill volumes. A man of great erudition, and equipped with a superior knowledge of Hungarian and European culture, he had a conservative humanist view of the world. His work as essayist and philologist culminated in ***A History of European Literature*** . . . , a survey based on wide learning and full of personal experiences.

Art translation was an almost natural form of expression with this erudite poet, who had such strong ties with world literature. From the time when he became a novice to poetry till the last years of his life, he produced translations; we are indebted to him for the adequate interpretation of a number of masterpieces. Perhaps his greatest achievement in this direction is the Hungarian version—perfectly true to form and supported by penetrating studies—of the full *Divine Comedy.* Close rivals to this are Babits's very learned and appealing interpretations of several Greek tragedies, of Shakespeare's *Tempest,* Baudelaire's poems, and his rendering of medieval Latin poets, of Goethe and George Meredith.

Babits was one of the most versatile and most complex figures in Hungarian letters, an outstanding representative of twentieth-century bourgeois humanism, and one of the most distinguished links between Hungarian and European literature. (pp. 210-12)

Miklós Szabolcsi, "The Twentieth Century: The Rise of Modern Hungarian Literature (1905-1914)," translated by István Farkas, in History of Hungarian Literature *by Tibor Klaniczay, József Szauder and Miklós Szabolcsi, edited by Miklós Szabolcsi, Collet's, 1964, pp. 187-228.**

ADDITIONAL BIBLIOGRAPHY

Konnyu, Leslie. "Michael Babits." In his *Modern Maygar Literature: A Literary Survey and Anthology of the XXth Century Hungarian Authors,* pp. 10-12. Richmond Heights, Mo.: American Hungarian Review, 1964.

Brief biography.

Kunz, Egon F. Introduction to *Hungarian Poetry,* edited by Egon F. Kunz, pp. 7-16. Sydney: Pannonia, 1955.*

Short critical assessment of Babits. Kunz comments that Babits's works are similar to those of T. S. Eliot in "spirit and activity."

Arturo Barea

1897-1957

Spanish autobiographer, novelist, critic, essayist, and short story writer.

Although the violent spectacle of the Spanish Civil War was depicted firsthand by many writers during the 1930s, Barea's autobiography *La forja de un rebelde (The Forging of a Rebel)* is the only account of this conflict written by a native of Madrid and a participant in the war on the side of the defeated Republicans. With the acute insight of an insider and an uncompromising honesty that has been universally praised by critics, Barea described the political chaos, military adventurism, and inequitable social conditions that led to the outbreak of civil war in 1936. The essential facts about the war as presented by Barea correspond closely with such fictionalized accounts as Ernest Hemingway's *For Whom the Bell Tolls*. However, *The Forge, The Track,* and *The Clash*—the three volumes that form *The Forging of a Rebel*—also describe, in rich detail, life in the Spanish middle classes at the turn of the century, as well as features of Spanish culture that were destroyed or altered irrevocably by the war. The book has been particularly praised for its portrait of prewar Madrid, with many critics asserting that the city itself takes on a role as important as Barea's own.

Barea was born in Badajoz in 1897. His father died shortly after his birth, and his mother became a laundress and did housework in order to support the family. A well-to-do and childless uncle and aunt took Barea to live with them, thus enabling him to attend school and to escape the effects of the poverty in which his mother and sisters lived. Barea later believed that this early experience with social injustice and the class system was instrumental in shaping his socialist beliefs: in *The Forge* he describes his family's life in the slums of Madrid, his life in his relative's comfortable home, and his first disillusioning experience with Spanish capitalism as a badly treated and poorly paid apprentice in a Madrid bank. When he was twenty-three, Barea was drafted into the army. His experiences as a conscript during the ill-conceived Moroccan campaign of 1921, when thousands of Spanish troops were slaughtered by Moroccan revolutionaries while defending one of Spain's last colonies, are related in *The Track,* which also describes his impressions of General Francisco Franco and the other generals who later fought to overthrow the Republican government of Spain. After Barea was released from the army he returned to Madrid, where he worked as a patent agent and later—in the service of the Republican authorities—as the chief of the Foreign Censorship Office during the seige of Madrid. Barea later recounted in *The Clash*—the concluding volume of his autobiography—the horrifying events of the seige and his final flight from Madrid with his Austrian wife, Ilsa. In 1939 Barea settled in England with his wife and began a career as a writer and as a broadcaster for the British Broadcasting Corporation. He died in 1957, having never returned to Spain.

Barea's varied career and his experiences with many different levels of Spanish society gave him a knowledge of his country that critics believe contributed greatly to the value of his autobiography as a social document. The stature of Barea's work has also been enhanced by the passionate sincerity of its author; he consistently strove to present objectively even those events in which he was involved as a staunch partisan. This quality is especially evident in the chapters from *The Track* that describe the despotic Franco as the idol of the Spanish and Moorish troops in Morocco, and in the sections of *The Clash* containing Barea's account of the internal dissension among the Republicans and of their ineptness in suppressing the Falangist rebellion in its early stages. However, in spite of its merits as an autobiography, *The Forging of a Rebel,* published as a unit in 1946, has posed unique problems for critics because of its novelistic format. Throughout the narrative, Barea employed the present tense; changed the names of some of the real-life characters; and paid close—some critics have termed it ''poetic''—attention to colors, sounds, textures, and details. Because Barea chose to use a style generally reserved for works of fiction, his autobiography is often judged by two distinct sets of critical standards, and of the three volumes that form *The Forging of a Rebel,* only the second, *The Track,* is generally deemed successful by both artistic and autobiographical criteria. This is because the novelistic elements of *The Forge* and *The Clash* often prove inadequate to the confusion of the unsettling events portrayed therein, but in *The Track,* as Anthony West has pointed out, Barea succeeded in making ''a personal experience carry the whole story of the Spanish Moroccan tragedy, he understood what had happened to himself in Morocco, and what had happened to Spain there, and out of the two sorts of knowledge . . . made a balanced whole.''

Barea's only novel, *La raiz rota (The Broken Root),* also deals with the consequences of the revolution in Spain. However, unlike his trilogy, *The Broken Root* is marred by the intrusion of the author's political prejudices and by an improbable plot. Critics have also expressed disappointment at the novel's lack of Spanish atmosphere—an important element in Barea's earlier works—though some have suggested that Barea probably deliberately omitted this element in an effort to broaden his theme of the tragedy of youth in an age of revolution and war. Although most critics have expressed sympathetic support for his political views, Barea's novel was only a limited popular and critical success.

Barea also wrote two well-known works of criticism on Spanish authors: *Unamuno* and *Lorca, el poeta y su pueblo (Lorca: The Poet and His People).* In *Unamuno,* Barea briefly introduced and explicated the diverse and seemingly contradictory writings of the great Basque philosopher Miguel de Unamuno. In examining this work, critics agree that Barea possessed a firm understanding of Unamuno's thought, and that his book has much value for students who might otherwise have difficulty following Unamuno's often complex reasoning. However, some critics have complained that Barea's examination of Unamuno fails to convey the force of the philosopher's unique personality. Barea was apparently more sympathetic with his subject in *Lorca,* a work that has been widely praised for its qualities as both a biographical portrait of the murdered Republican poet Federico García Lorca and as a work of criticism. Prior to the publication of Barea's study, few critics had realized the extent to which Andalusian folk elements had figured in García Lorca's poetry. Many had mistakenly interpreted the folk expressions as merely uncommon terms that the poet employed for their value as obscure symbols. Barea's understanding of Spanish country people enabled him to comprehend this aspect of García Lorca's work, and his findings in this area led many critics to conclude that García Lorca was not a Symbolist in the sense that they had previously thought.

Barea's works were banned in many Spanish-speaking countries until 1951, when an edition of *The Forging of a Rebel* was published in Argentina. Although Barea wrote in Spanish, his works first appeared in English translations that were published in England and North America. Critics agree that these translations, undertaken by Barea's wife, are of excellent quality, and they commend the translator for preserving the Spanish atmosphere that Barea created in the originals. Critics also concur that Barea has made both his country and its literature much more accessible to the world. *The Forging of a Rebel,* in particular, is still valuable today for its firsthand account of a decaying society on the brink of a conflict that many historians regard as the true beginning of World War II.

(See also *Contemporary Authors,* Vol. 111.)

PRINCIPAL WORKS

Valor y miedo (short stories) 1938
**La forja de un rebelde* (autobiography) 1951
[Published in three volumes: *The Forge,* 1941; *The Track,* 1943; *The Clash,* 1946; also published as *The Forging of a Rebel,* 1946]
The Struggle for the Spanish Soul (nonfiction) 1951
**La raiz rota* (novel) 1955
[*The Broken Root,* 1951]
**Lorca, el poeta y su pueblo* (criticism) 1957
[*Lorca: The Poet and His People,* 1944]
**Unamuno* (criticism) 1959
[*Unamuno,* 1952]
El centro de la pista (short stories) 1960

*These works, although written in Spanish, were first published in English translation, and, for political reasons, were not published in Spanish for several years.

GEORGE ORWELL (essay date 1941)

[*An English novelist and essayist, Orwell is significant for his unwavering commitment, both as a man and an artist, to personal freedom and social justice. His unpretentious self-examination and his ability to perceive the social effects of political theories inspired Irving Howe to call him "the greatest moral force in English letters during the last several decades." Throughout his career Orwell attacked exploitation of the weak by the powerful, whether in a modern democracy or a totalitarian state. He was particularly attuned to the confining effects of class and social standing in modern life. Foremost among Orwell's work is his novel* Nineteen Eighty-Four, *one of the most influential books of the century. An attack on totalitarianism, it warns that absolute power in the hands of any government can deprive a people of all basic freedoms. Orwell's prose style, especially that of his essays, has become a model for its precision, clarity, and vividness. Many of his essays, which combine observation and reminiscence with literary and social criticism, are considered modern masterpieces. Orwell fought on the Republican side in the Spanish Civil War and wrote a classic account of the failure of the Republicans and the collapse of democratic ideals in* Homage to Catalonia *(1938). In the following excerpt, Orwell reviews* The Forge, *the first part of Barea's autobiographical trilogy, and discusses the explosive nature of societies plagued by the type of social injustices Barea describes as everyday facts of life in prewar Madrid.*]

If some Russian writer were at this moment to produce a book of reminiscences of his childhood in 1900, it would be difficult to review it without mentioning the fact that Soviet Russia is now our ally against Germany, and in the same way it is impossible to read ***The Forge*** without thinking at almost every page of the Spanish Civil War. In fact there is no direct connection, for the book deals only with Senor Barea's early youth and ends in 1914. But the civil war made a deep and painful impression on the English intelligentsia, deeper, I should say, than has yet been made by the war now raging. The man in the street, misled by frivolous newspapers, ignored the whole business, the rich mechanically sided with the enemies of the working class, but to all thinking and decent people the war was a terrible tragedy that has made the word 'Spain' inseparable from the thought of burnt bodies and starving children. One seems to hear the thunder of future battles somewhere behind Senor Barea's pages, and it is as a sort of prologue to the civil war, a picture of the society that made it possible, that his book is most likely to be valued. (p. 214)

All his good memories are of country places, especially of the forge belonging to his uncle in Mentrida, a magnificent independent peasant of the type now extinct in the industrialized countries. On the other hand his memories of Madrid are low and squalid, a tale of poverty and overwork far more extreme than anything to be found in England. (pp. 214-15)

[In the Spain that Senor Barea writes of,] injustice was unmistakable, politics was a struggle between black and white, every extremist doctrine from Carlism to Anarchism could be held with lunatic clarity. 'Class war' was not merely a phrase, as it has come to be in the Western democracies. But which state of affairs is better is a different question.

This is not primarily a political book, however. It is a fragment of autobiography, and we may hope that others will follow it, for Senor Barea has had a varied and adventurous life. (p. 216)

George Orwell, in a review of "The Forge," in Horizon, *London, Vol. IV, No. 21, September, 1941, pp. 214-17.*

ANTONIA WHITE (essay date 1941)

[*An English critic, editor, and translator, White is best known as a Catholic novelist whose works, notably* Frost in May *(1933) and the Clara Batchelor trilogy (1950-54), reflect her troubled life and spiritual struggles. In the following excerpt, she offers high praise for* The Forge, *but suggests that Barea has, in several sections of the book, inaccurately portrayed the Catholic clergy and Church teachings. For further discussion of Barea's portrayal of Spanish Catholicism, see the excerpt by John Devlin (1966).*]

The first time I read [***The Forge***] I had simply given myself up to the sheer sensuous pleasure of watching the flow of pictures. I don't know any writer except Colette who has that same power of evoking, not only shapes and colours, but smells and textures.

Lawrence's descriptions, vivid as they are, are cloying compared to the fine sharp edge of Barea's. Lawrence forces you to see plants and animals through a quivering heat haze of his own projected emotions. But Barea gives you the illusion of looking at whatever object he presents to you . . . a woman's hand, a blacksmith at his anvil, a junk shop in Madrid, the bubbles on a tube of shaving soap—through clear glass and not through someone else's distorting lens. It is the ability to produce that illusion which makes Barea an artist and not merely a brilliant reporter.

Do you know Edward Weston's photographs? He never, as far as I know, fakes or arranges his subjects, but his pictures have a peculiar quality that you don't find even in the most intelligent 'creative' photographers. (p. 217)

To me Barea's writing has the same quality as Weston's photography. It is so purely visual that I imagine it could be translated into any language and produce the same effect. Therefore things that might have been irritating, such as his use of the eternal present, and a rather loose and choppy style (which may be due to translation difficulties) didn't worry me.

It seemed a profoundly uneasy book—uneasy as a man who can't sleep and shifts restlessly from his right side to his left—the classic predicament of the day in fact. Barea, more keenly than most of us, has a particular right to feel the predicament. . . . He knows from the inside the lives of beggars, bank-clerks, shop assistants, bourgeois and peasants. He has been rich and poor, employer and employed, submissive and rebellious, believer and sceptic.

Since ***The Forge*** only takes the author up to his twentieth year, one doesn't expect him to have found any solutions. It is enough that he should state his predicament and leave it at that. There is only one point where I feel at all competent to judge whether or not he has stated it exactly; that is in his indictment of Catholicism. Not that I don't believe there may be usurers, neurotics, lechers and exploiters among the Spanish clergy. His scandals are as likely to be true as the far more sensational scandals St. Catherine of Siena castigated in the Italian clergy of her time. Barea draws at least one admirable priest in the Father Rector of his school as well as many indifferent, and downright bad ones. But I had a shock when Father Joachim, whom he had described as a kind of St. Francis, suddenly produced a 'wife' and a son. I can accept the woman and the son (Father Joachim was an excellent man who made it quite clear that he had not a vocation) but not the fact that, still wearing the soutane, saying mass, and administering the sacraments (and incidentally encouraging Barea to attend them) he should introduce his child's mother as 'my wife'. The episode may have been true, yet given everything he has said of Father Joachim, it didn't *ring* true.

But these details of behaviour are irrelevant compared to some of the curious statements he makes about Catholic doctrine. Are Spanish children really taught, not that there are three persons in God, but that there are 'three Gods, but only one true God' . . .? And does even the most ignorant Catholic believe that, however much individual priests may flatter the rich and despise the poor, 'when you are rich you have everything including heaven' . . .? In this connection he goes on to make some extraordinary statements about indulgences which are almost incredible in anyone who has ever been a Catholic.

If Barea really believes such things, his priests were obviously more competent to teach him advanced mathematics than elementary dogma. But if he only wants to make you think he believes them in order to pile on the agony, you are left only with the entrancing picture book and no means of knowing how many of the pictures transcribe real experiences. It may be crude of me to worry about their 'truth' . . . he is, after all, composing an autobiographical work of art, which may be a blend of the real and the fantastic like Rilke's *Malte Laurids Brigge,* and not a sociological manual. Incidentally both Rilke's book and ***The Forge*** produced very much the same effect on me: complete intoxication on the first reading; considerable uneasiness on the second. But it is Barea's own fault if he writes with such an air of conviction that one feels cheated if one has to stop, even for a moment, to question such apparently disingenuous sincerity. (pp. 217-19)

Antonia White, in a review of "The Forge," in Horizon, *London, Vol. IV, No. 21, September, 1941, pp. 217-19.*

HORIZON **(essay date 1941)**

[*In the following excerpt, the critic calls Barea's* The Struggle for the Spanish Soul *an informative "hybrid" between a book and a pamphlet. The critic maintains that the work is useful as an illustration of the German Nazis' insidious meddling in the affairs of other peoples and governments.*]

Arturo Barea's book [***The Struggle for the Spanish Soul***] is an excellent survey of the historic roots, the economic and mass-psychologic realities of Spanish fascism; the only point to criticize is the pompous title. In fact it is a little masterpiece of that new branch in writing: the hybrid between book and pamphlet, which seems to gain an ever-increasing importance in mass-education. I have read quite a number of voluminous books on Spain, and was surprised how many new facts I learned from Barea's 30,000 word booklet; among other things the first plausible character-analysis of that strange little monster-caudillo.

Yet the main topical value of the book is its demonstration of the uncannily efficient way in which Nazism is able to fit in foreign national aspirations into its New Order scheme:

> . . . Germany fully realizes the possibilities of a Hispanic Fascism which would group together the South American raw material exporting countries under the hegemony of a falangist Spain, as a most valuable complement to the European industrial countries under German domination. . . . German organizations in the South American countries collaborate with Falange organizations, but leave the Spaniards to do the more conspicuous work. Hitler's own dreams of world power may well coincide with the most extravagant hopes of Spanish imperialists.

This is only one example of the magic attraction which Hitler's New Order is able to exert on the ambitious ruling castes in a number of European countries. On the other hand, there are about one million Spaniards in prisons and concentration camps and about ten times as much opposed to the Christian Gentleman's regime. Yet Barea makes it politely but unmistakably clear that 'it would be impossible to link up this great potential force with England's struggle if these Spaniards had the feeling that the English remembered them only as a last resort, when things are going badly. To mobilize the latent strength of the common people in Spain who are unconquered and unconquerable by despotism and fascism, England will have to make it plain that she really stands for the freedom and self-determination of *all* peoples.' (pp. 219-20)

X., in a review of "The Struggle for the Spanish Soul," in Horizon, *London, Vol. IV, No. 21, September, 1941, pp. 219-20.*

ANTHONY WEST (essay date 1946)

[*The son of Rebecca West and H. G. Wells, West is an English author who has written several novels concerned with the moral, social, psychological, and political disruptions of the twentieth century. As a critic he has written a study of D. H. Lawrence and many reviews published in various magazines. In the following excerpt, West discusses* The Clash*—the final volume of Barea's trilogy—which he finds a bewildering book that gets lost in the "confusing maze of intrigue and violent events that made up the Spanish Civil War." Of the trilogy as a whole, West writes that only the second volume,* The Track, *is entirely successful as a work of art, because in it Barea "made a personal experience carry the whole story of the Spanish Moroccan tragedy."*]

With ***The Clash*** Mr. Arturo Barea rounds off his trilogy describing the road by which he came to England as a refugee. The pattern followed is that invented by Restif De La Bretonne when he wrote *Monsieur Nicolas* or *The Human Heart Unveiled,* a work which begins with an address from writer to reader:

> Lover of truth, fear not to read me! You will not be beguiled by tinsel trappings, nor deceived on matters of fact. I have written novels enough which, though founded on reality, did not exclude imagination: I thirst for the simple truth; I give it you; for truth alone can serve the purpose of this book.

Restif's book still lives because it is a complete revelation of a private mind, an exposure of what a man usually keeps secret from the world. But the story is not the simple truth: it is rather a complicated web in which fantasy is inextricably interwoven with truth. We know for certain that many things that are most vivid in *Monsieur Nicolas* are in the domain of psychological reality—events imagined by Restif which had greater force in framing his attitudes than things which actually happened. All this is by way of edging up to the point of saying that Mr. Barea in following the same path as Restif has placed his critics in an acutely difficult position—at least a highly embarrassing one. A critic faced by a novel must bring his critical standards to bear on it without ulterior considerations. He cannot remember that the writer is a charming fellow with nice friends, or a member of a political group with laudable intentions, or that he has had a hard time; he can only remember the standards by which he judges Proust, Balzac, Flaubert, Dostoievsky, Henry James or Turgenev. By those standards ***The Forge,*** the first part of Mr. Barea's trilogy was a confusion, redeemed only by its deep feeling for the life of Madrid which was known and understood; the second part—***The Track***—was a success as a work of art. In it Mr. Barea made a personal experience carry the whole story of the Spanish Moroccan tragedy, he understood what had happened to himself in Morocco, and what had happened to Spain there, and out of the two sorts of knowledge had made a balanced whole. The third part—***The Clash,*** which is now before us—is a confusion again. In it there is Mr. Barea's personal story, there is the story of the defence of Madrid, there is the story of the division and corruption among the Republicans, and there is as a pendant the story of what was happening to France in 1939. Here the critic's embarrassment rises up to choke him; there is a great deal to be said about the thing as a work of art, or rather about why it is not a work of art—but as one shapes the words there is Mr. Barea repeating Restif's address to the reader. If the thing were the novel, which it is in form, it would be possible to say that the study of a ruthless egotist overwhelmed by war was excellent. The picture of his disregard for any personal feelings his wife Aurelia might have could not be improved as a study in egotism, nor could the picture of his relations with the typist Maria. . . . (pp. 363-64)

The creation of these private hells of personal relationship is masterly, so is the handling of the mechanism of release—an appointment as Republican Press Censor after the outbreak of civil war. . . .

But at this point precision departs, and we are lost, as indeed Mr. Barea was, in a maze of back stairs intrigue among the various component factions of the Republic. So disturbing and complex was the maze that Mr. Barea's nerves failed to stand the strain. The story of his breakdown is moving, but it is reminiscence and not art, and the pain and distress of it colour the account of the progress of the war. Aurelia and Maria simply drop from sight, the situation is not worked out. All that one can say of what follows is that Mr. Barea makes the reader share the bewilderment and unhappiness of an individual lost in great events. (p. 364)

Anthony West, "Behind the Scenes," in The New Statesman & Nation, *Vol. XXXI, No. 795, May 18, 1946, pp. 363-64.*

IRVING HOWE (essay date 1947)

[*A longtime editor of the leftist magazine* Dissent *and a regular contributor to* The New Republic, *Howe is one of America's most highly respected literary critics and social historians. He has been a socialist since the 1930s, and his criticism is frequently informed by a liberal social viewpoint. Howe is widely praised for what F. R. Dulles has termed his "knowledgeable understanding, critical acumen and forthright candor." Howe has written: "My work has fallen into two fields: social history and literary criticism. I have tried to strike a balance between the social and the literary; to fructify one with the other; yet not to confuse one with the other. Though I believe in the social approach to literature, it seems to me peculiarly open to misuse; it requires particular delicacy and care." In the following excerpt, from a review of* The Forging of a Rebel, *Howe commends many aspects of Barea's work, particularly his portrait of the city of Madrid. However, he also maintains that Barea's lack of concern with political ideas undermines the content of his work.*]

[Although Arturo Barea] has written an autobiography, in which form one expects the writer's personality to be central, the I of [***The Forging of a Rebel***] is its least important figure. Things happen to him; his senses register; but he neither manipulates his past nor attempts to give it retrospective order. He merely allows his laden memory to flow freely. The center of the book then becomes a city, Madrid; and since the twentieth-century history of Madrid reflects the transformations of Spanish civilization—the never completed transition to modernity so painful in backward countries—what would otherwise be a mere atomized and indiscriminate sequence of recollection acquires more general validity.

Even when writing about his private concerns, as in the movingly scrupulous description of his neurotic paralysis before the issues thrust upon him by the 1936 civil war, Barea succeeds in making them seem a symbolic fraction of the tragedy which struck Spain and Europe. The result is a book fringeing on the first rate, a work of social autobiography which, if not history itself, contains the ores from which history is fused, and which bears a palpable, sensuous quality seldom present in formal historical writings.

Through Barea's unforced recollections of his childhood in Madrid there appear the gradual social reformations of modern Spain: a sluggish middle class in disintegration, a cohering proletariat scenting the western winds of Marxism and in part responding with an indigenous anarchism, the product of its position as a militant class in a primitive country. The inns; the gutters; the washwomen at the rivers; the static peasants, bearing in themselves the richness of an old civilization; the impatient counterpoint of Madrileños hemmed in by a dying past and a stillborn future—all of this, the actual material and substance of life unthinned by theory and unsorted by perspective, filters through his recollections.

The course of Barea's life coincided with the central events of modern Spain. As a youth, he served in the colonial army in Morocco and his account of the disastrous expeditions against the Moors (as impressively dry and bare as the desert in which these expeditions took place) is an addition to the literature of anti-imperialism. The Spanish army lives in his book as a remarkably corrupt institution; a pure chain of pilfering from general to batman. One senses in this long section on Morocco, the best in the book, all the decay and putrefaction which was to reach its tragic head in 1936. (pp. 310-11)

Reading this massive work, one is reminded of an Elder Breughel with its movement of differentiated but not thoroughly individualized figures in which no attempt is made to accentuate but in which the action is so inviting and warm that the spectator finds himself merged with its context. Much the same sympathetic inclusion is effected by Barea's book, which lacks only that sense of purposeful control that gives a Breughel its unity. And that is where Barea pays for his greatest weakness: his lack of concern with ideas. Absence of self-consciousness permits a rich recollection, but the selectivity essential to form demands a highly trained intelligence as well.

If Spain is vivid in the book, Barea is dim. Between his personal history and the movement of the book there is a disturbing lack of harmony. At each crucial juncture of his life, the book blacks out. At one moment a child, the next a man; at one moment apolitical, the next a socialist. The personal biography is like a series of jerky slides from which the decisive ones have been omitted. But the book is redeemed by its vision of Spain's tragedy, by now a symbol of our age. (p. 311)

Irving Howe, "Personal History," in Partisan Review, *Vol. XIV, No. 3, Spring, 1947, pp. 310-12.*

CARL SANDBURG (essay date 1949)

[Sandburg was one of the central figures in the "Chicago Renaissance," an early twentieth-century flowering of the arts, which vanquished the myth that the Eastern cities were the only centers of legitimate creativity in America and established the Midwest as the home of major writers, sculptors, and painters, as well as an important source of artistic subject matter. A lifelong believer in the worth of the common, unsung individual, Sandburg expressed his populist beliefs in poetry and songs, and in his Pulitzer Prize-winning biography of Abraham Lincoln. In the following excerpt, Sandburg praises Lorca, *stating that Barea sketches the life of Federico García Lorca "with rare skill and the sympathy of a complete friend."]*

Who was Lorca? Why does his name linger in Spain and elsewhere? What kind of a poet was he? What would you think of a Spaniard who reminded you of Vachel Lindsay, Patrick Henry, Alfred Kreymborg, Edwin Arlington Robinson and Salvador Dali? . . .

With rare skill and the sympathy of a complete friend Arturo Barea sketches the life of Lorca [in **"Lorca: The Poet and His People"**], giving free renditions of many poems, summaries of plays, paragraphs from lectures. "He had no politics," we are told, and yet, "The emotional forces he released became part of the shapeless revolutionary movements of Spain, whether he intended or not." How this can happen as between a poet and a people he loves makes a dark fascinating piece of historical narrative—and Barea can tell it. By profuse quotation from Lorca's writings we are given much of his story in his own words. . . .

A somber and thoughtful book steeped in the soul of ancient and modern Spain, its shadows reaching far back and beyond reading a long stretch into the future. In degree it unriddles the Spanish for us and brings us in slight measure closer to the Spain that now broods over yesterday and wonders about tomorrow.

Carl Sandburg, "A Great Spanish Poet," in New York Herald Tribune Weekly Book Review, *October 16, 1949, p. 1.*

RAMON SENDER (essay date 1950)

[Although forced to spend over half his life in exile from his native Spain, Sender is nevertheless regarded as one of that nation's most distinguished novelists. Like Barea, he was forced to flee Spain during the Civil War after supporting the Republican cause. In the following excerpt, Sender praises Barea's Lorca *as a most insightful and compelling work of criticism.]*

Barea's book [***Lorca: The Poet and His People***] clarifies the more accessible zones in the problem of the social personality of the poet and it shows us the roots of his popularity. The chapters "The Poet and Sex," "The Poet and Death" and "The Poet and His Art" have a luminosity that surpasses the literary analysis. With the purpose of showing Lorca integrated in the Spanish character Barea makes a suggestive differentiation of the elements making up that character, independently of the poet.

I am sure that these pages will be to the liking of American readers, whether they know Lorca or not. The book offers bilingual examples of all the stages of the poet's production that quicken nostalgia in us Spaniards, and in Americans will doubtless awaken zones of sensibility undiscovered or unknown to themselves. (p. 17)

Ramon Sender, "Lorca, Poet of the People," in The New York Times Book Review, *January 1, 1950, pp. 3, 17.*

FREDERIC MORTON (essay date 1951)

[In the following excerpt Morton, an American novelist, biographer, and short story writer, reviews Barea's novel The Broken Root, *praising Barea for presenting the tragedy of Spain without resorting to emotionalism or propaganda.]*

Five years ago Artura Barea published **"The Forging of a Rebel,"** an autobiography which not only told the story of an extraordinary life but also recreated much of the experience of the Spanish people in the first forty years of this century. Now

Mr. Barea gives us [in **"The Broken Root"**] a novel about Spain as it has lived—or tried to live—since Franco's victory. What he has written is not free of political preconceptions or narrative flaws. But it makes for a story illumined at all times by an overpowering sincerity and a soul-deep knowledge of the tragedy of contemporary Spain.

Mr. Barea's hero, Don Antolin, was a Loyalist soldier who escaped to London after the defeat of the Republican army. In England he found peace, employment, even a woman he could love. But he had left his family as well as his heart on the hot bright pavements of Madrid. A British citizen after ten years, he decided to go back for a visit, if not to stay. **"The Broken Root"** enacts the drama of a wanderer who returns to a home no longer his.

The Spain of 1949 which Don Antolin enters is a country not reconcilable to his memory. It looks rather like an immense slum so rotten with bureaucrats, procurers, black marketeers, so gnawed-at and fevered with hunger that its inhabitants are driven to the most desperate compensations. Don Antolin's own family stares at him with greed-distorted faces. . . .

Yet in the last analysis Don Antolin emerges as the most tragic figure in the novel. It is not merely that the hovering terror and the squalor everywhere defeat each of his attempts to ameliorate the position of his loved ones, but the very money he has painfully saved up over the years as a waiter in Soho, and which he wants to use toward his family's welfare, turns into an instrument of calamity. For the rumor that he has one thousand pounds to invest brings all the hyenas of the city on his trail and changes his wife and children into wolves. . . .

The most frighteningly effective feature of the book is its measured tone. Sometimes I searched almost hopefully for the heat or hollowness of propaganda. But there is not a trace of it in these chapters. Thus one must accept, no matter how reluctantly, much of Mr. Barea's picture of his country as the terrible truth. He has a rare capacity for writing moderately about immoderate things, and with the sorrowful, calm certitude of one who knows the grief whereof he speaks.

The implications of **"The Broken Root"** reach out beyond the geographical boundaries of its setting. For in his protagonist Mr. Barea has mirrored the dilemma of the liberal everywhere. He shows that in a world where effective political action grows more and more the monopoly of totalitarianism, the liberal is frightened into impotence. Don Antolin's lack of decisiveness contributes to the final catastrophe. The social idealism which once sustained him is no longer his, just as the golden colors and the warm music of Spain have vanished. He must return to England without country and without creed, a double exile.

That a book of such comprehensive scope should have some faults is not surprising. Its *dramatis personae,* for instance, are too patly arranged as a complete cross-section of Spanish society. The top-heavy and synthetically hopeful symbolism of the funeral scene at the end seems unconvincing.

Nothing in **"The Broken Root,"** however, can overshadow its masterful portrayal of a beautiful and stricken country whose song and sun are now more than ever only a tourist-catching slogan. Mr. Barea's comments have the ring of cool and appalling authenticity. He has performed a sad but vital service for all who have a stake in freedom.

Frederic Morton, "A Masterful Picture of a Beautiful and Stricken Country," in New York Herald Tribune Book Review, *March 18, 1951, p. 5.*

THE TIMES LITERARY SUPPLEMENT **(essay date 1952)**

[In the following excerpt from a review of the Spanish edition of The Forging of a Rebel, *the critic contends that Barea's book occupies a unique place between autobiography and the novel, and supports this theory by citing the work's unaffected realism and objectivity, as well as its "creation of a fresh dimension of realism," and its "invention of an appropriate language."]*

The recent publication in Spanish of ***The Forging of a Rebel,*** an autobiographical trilogy by Arturo Barea, allows us to examine, in its true literary perspective, a work known through versions in nine other European languages before it was published in its original tongue. Arturo Barea's work now takes its place in the tradition of the realistic Spanish novel; in a succession that begins with the nineteenth-century novels of Benito Pérez Galdós, continues through the vast and monotonous world of Pío Baroja, the baroque world of Valle-Inclán, and the journalistic and symbolic one of Ramón J. Sender, to end among the stories inspired by the Spanish civil war—in Max Aub's *Closed Land* and *Land of Blood,* in *The Lamb's Head* of Francisco Ayala. Among these Mr. Barea's trilogy is outstanding for the ardent strength of the testimony, the brutal directness of the narrative and the sustained objectivity of its standpoint, as well as for its stylistic quality.

There are few autobiographies in Spanish literature. The Spaniard seems to be more jealous of his inner life, more fiercely proud of his weaknesses, than his European neighbours, so that only exceptionally does there appear in his vast and rich literature a work of confession or personal testimony. This rarity makes more notable ***The Forging of a Rebel,*** which takes a middle course between autobiography and fiction. Centred in one man's experience, the work does not set out to tell everything. The narrative concentrates on those episodes, and those only, which illuminate "the forging of a rebel."

The story is not continuous. Between the first and the second parts (**"The Forge"** and **"The Track"**) there is a lapse of some six years, 1914-1920. Between the second and the third (**"The Clash"**) the interval is about 10 years, 1925-1935. Occasionally a glimpse backwards, a "racconto," bridges the gaps, gathering together the uneventful years, the unrecorded experiences. Undoubtedly the author's selectiveness is not for the purpose of schematizing his own life. When Mr. Barea skips something it is because, in his judgment, it contributes nothing. He selects and concentrates. The events of his own life appear to be organized round three centres of interest: his childhood on the Manzanares, his youth in Morocco, his experience of the civil war in Madrid. The remaining elements are subordinated to these.

Each of these basic experiences has a double value. On the one side is the collective experience. On the other is the personal experience through which the rebel is being fashioned; and through the story of this rebel is seen a generation scattered by the civil war, a world destroyed and irrecoverable. For a whole human group first Morocco and, later, the civil war were determining experiences.

The characteristic quality of the book is its objectivity. Mr. Barea does not want to appear better than he is; nor does he take delight, as others have done, in similar circumstances, in multiplying the charges against himself. He takes himself for granted and, after this acceptance (which does not imply unqualified approval), he relates his experiences. Hence the directness of his story from which nothing essential is omitted. But in his sincerity and objectivity Mr. Barea reaches still farther. He does not fail to record his egoism towards women, the harsh treatment it could not escape; with detachment, he discusses the affairs called sentimental; that is to say, all that others more moderate (or more cowardly) leave in obscurity. He writes:

> I understood Maria's attitude and hopes, but I had no intention of realizing them. A divorce followed by a joint household or marriage would have meant no more than an exchange of one woman for another, with the prospect of more children and the boredom of married life without love. Maria was in her own right while she worked with me as my secretary and listened to my personal worries and problems; she was in her own right as my comforter. She would lose all this in a marriage. I would lose the secretary and the comforting listener. . . . My attitude and line of action were coldly and pointedly selfish. I knew that. It gave me a chill feeling in the pit of my stomach. I did not like myself, and I did not like her.

This is not a retouched portrait.

When Mr. Barea comes to describe the Spanish civil war he adheres rigorously to the dual principle of telling only what he has seen and of telling it without constituting himself a judge. From the pages of **"The Clash"** surge up the resisting people of Madrid, surrounded by the mutinous army improvizing defences from nothing; the people who rush through the night demanding "Arms, arms," as in a long chant; the people who in anger destroy themselves for the possession of a city ward; the people who yield to brutal instincts, to the dictates of fear, and begin to hunt out fascists, bringing down many of the innocent. No writer before has given with such simplicity, with less aim at propaganda, an account of the impossible and pathetic resistance of the people of Madrid, a resistance of two years, four months and three weeks. This same objectivity obliges Mr. Barea to denounce the administrative chaos, the rivalries of the different political groups, the suicidal struggle for power, which darkened the final hours of the Spanish Republic. His testimony is not only to the heroism of the Spanish people but also to its blindness, to its monstrous madness.

> For better and for worse—and I believe for better—we can no longer perceive reality through the medium of a novel, unless it makes us see the interplay of forces, the inner life of people, the third dimension as it were.

These words of his in an article on **"Realism in the Modern Spanish Novel"** . . . define his position as a realistic writer. At first sight it might be thought that his work is simply documentary. But although this autobiography is so skilfully constructed, it is not merely an artistic elaboration. Reality itself appears to be treated with a sensitiveness that selects and reacts. This is nowhere better exemplified than in the first volume, **"The Forge."** In describing his infancy and adolescence Mr. Barea uses the present indicative. He has rebuilt the world of his childhood just as it appeared to his childish eyes. Nothing is farther from photographic (or phonographic) realism. Thanks to this the book conveys impressions, in all their freshness, of a world which is discovered in the seeing, the world of childhood.

Occasionally, as if to accentuate the distinct narrative planes, there are interpolated, in **"The Forge,"** certain reflections on maturity, some pages of the present (and not of that timeless present) which enrich the narrative with a double significance, carrying the reader away from the evoked world into this world of to-day, away from conscious reminiscence, from digging into the depth of self. . . .

Nobody would deny that Mr. Barea achieves realism in the first volume, but the treatment is less obvious in the other two. The world is already created, the man himself circulates before a reality which he knows, or believes he knows. He holds readymade answers to all the problems. But this, too, is a superficial appearance, a mask of reality. For the vision offered by Mr. Barea in his chronicle is dual; on the one side there is the daily reality in its confusion, its inexpressibility, its loathsomeness, its overwhelming mediocrity; on the other—and sensing it only as an underlying emptiness, a hunger, a dull pain which does not rise to the surface, which is not localized—Mr. Barea himself, searching for a deep meaning in the world, who is not resigned merely to living, who questions and struggles in an inner agony.

This man is alone from the beginning, even before he knows what he is; he cannot conform to his surroundings, he does not accept what destiny has given him: poverty, the petty job of the adolescent, the loveless marriage, the destruction of his Spain. Already in childhood his equivocal position—the son of a widowed washerwoman, brought up by rich relations; a poor child in a religious establishment for the rich—makes him feel himself different. . . .

This difference has haunted him all his life, in all the surroundings in which he has found himself. Because of his intelligence, his sensibility, his strength of character, he lives apart from the other recruits in Morocco; separated from his fellow-passengers in the bus that carries him to Novés, the village in which he lives anonymously with those who possess more and those who possess nothing; isolated from his fellow townsmen at the start of the siege of Madrid ("But that evening I felt leaden. The fight was on, it was my own fight, and I was repelled and chilled to the core"); far away also from his exiled compatriots in France, even to the extent of understanding that in his own profession he has no ties:

> The conceptions of art of the professional writers [he writes towards the end of the work] did not help me; they hardly interested me. Twice a French writer had taken me along to a literary gathering, but the self-conscious statements of people gyrating round one "master" here and another "master" there had only filled me with astonished boredom and an embarrassing disgust. Now it depressed me to think that I belonged nowhere.

Mr. Barea was to continue to feel himself alone until the moment when he discovered—now mature and apparently liquidated by the disaster to his native land—not only the woman who gave meaning to his personal life but also his true and profound vocation. This latter discovery is gradual. . . .

> I tried to see where I might fit in, because it was torturing to know that nothing of what I had to give was exploited in the war. But the only thing I found to do for myself was to write the book of Madrid which I had planned. I was just a vessel that must empty itself of its contents.

In the end, Mr. Barea accepts his true destiny and affirms: ". . . for writing was to me part of action, part of our war against death and for life, and not just self-expression." A crude, superficial realism is, then, transcended by this profound vision of man and his destiny. It leads to a world infinitely more complex and rich; where, to quote the author's own words, are to be found "the hidden source of things."

There is a third form of creation in the work, the creation of a language. Mr. Barea's almost self-taught style explains his unorthodoxy in contemporary Spanish literature. He confronts the literary groups, the intellectual coteries, from an iconoclastic and non-conformist standpoint, opposes himself even to the very notion of the intellectual. He creates his own work, from the very midst of the people. Significant, in this respect, is his experience with Don Ramón del Valle Inclán, the irascible dictator of café literary circles, or his attitude to the French writers (as conveyed in a passage already quoted).

Clearly, in asserting that Mr. Barea creates his work from the heart of the people, it is not possible to forget the ambiguity implied in the world *pueblo,* the plurality of worlds that it implies. The "people" from whose heart Mr. Barea writes are the people of the Avapies sector of Madrid, of the Brunete of his holidays, of the Morocco of the Colonial War, of the Patents Office in Madrid, of the Central Telephone Building in which he worked and struggled as a censor. There he was to acquire that spoken language which so impressed his listeners in the civil war, "this style rough and devoid of linguistic flourishes," as he describes it. Contrasted with the literary style of a Valle Inclán (now resurrected and amplified by Max Aub), or with a vocabulary like that of Ayala in which are heard echoes of the writers of the Golden Age, the style of Mr. Barea displays the directness and effectiveness, the faultiness and force of popular speech. This does not mean that his work has no literary antecedents. It is not difficult to detect there traces of Baroja (although not of the diffuseness into which that writer has recently fallen). Neither is there absent another voice—the unexpected voice of Ramón Gómez de la Serna. Although Mr. Barea never degenerates into the merely baroque he appears to share with Ramón Gómez a hunger for the material, a sensibility wounded by things—"the things which I had smelt, seen, touched, felt."

Through these associations Arturo Barea's work finds its place in the tradition of the Spanish novel, to which it is already related by the naturalness of its testimony, by the profound realism of its vision. This tradition is enriched, in his hands, by objective testimony to a world destroyed, by the creation of a fresh dimension of realism, by the invention of an appropriate language.

"The Mask of Realism," in The Times Literary Supplement, *No. 2622, May 2, 1952, p. 296.*

DUDLEY FITTS (essay date 1952)

[An American poet, critic, educator, and translator, Fitts is one of the twentieth century's foremost translators from the ancient Greek. He has been especially praised for his modern colloquial translations of Aristophanes's plays, particularly The Birds. *In the following excerpt, Fitts offers lukewarm praise for* Unamuno, *indicating several shortcomings in Barea's study. He compares* Unamuno *with L. S. Salzberger's study of the German poet Johan Christian Friedrich Hoelderlin, both books being published in 1952 as volumes in the series* Studies in Modern European Literature and Thought.]

[Neither L. S. Salzberger's *Hoelderlin* nor Arturo Barea's ***Unamuno***] runs to much more than 60 pages; yet in the *Hoelderlin,* at least, we feel as though we had been given a reasoned Life, Aesthetic, and Critique. The ***Unamuno*** is less satisfactory in its criticism; but even so, it is a remarkably full book. Sleight of hand? A happy *tour de force*? Not indicated by investigation: simply thorough understanding, enlightened scholarship, and good writing. . . .

Señor Barea's study is largely concerned with the philosophical development of Unamuno. The writing itself is scanted. I do not mean that the book is top-heavy or lopsided: on the contrary, the expository passages, the re-creation of the various ambients in which Unamuno moved, are brilliantly handled. Yet considering the fact that he is concerned here with a figure who was primarily a man of letters, after all, it seems a pity that the author has limited himself so straitly in his literary criticism. *Del sentimiento tragico* (1913) is one of the decisive books of our century, and Señor Barea is right in devoting so much time to it; but that astonishing sequence of poems *El Cristo de Velasquez,* which tells us so much not only about Unamuno, but about the Spanish set of mind in general, whether positively or negatively—this work is not even mentioned in the Bibliography! The omission seems almost unbelievable.

Dudley Fitts, "Studies of Hoelderlin and Unamuno," in The New Republic, *Vol. 127, No. 23, December 8, 1952, p. 25.**

ANGEL FLORES (essay date 1953)

[A Puerto Rican-born American educator, critic, and translator, Flores is the author of numerous studies of the works of Spanish and Latin American writers. In the following excerpt, he praises Barea's Unamuno *as a valuable critical work.]*

There was nothing of the exquisite or the literary *recherché* in Unamuno. His poetry is the direct, often crude loud thinking of a passionate man, and, perhaps because of this, terrifyingly sincere and pervasive. He is, in short, a philosopher meditating poetically rather than a poet philosophizing. . . .

This light of poetico-philosophical fusion, perhaps the best for seeking the core of Miguel de Unamuno, has been overlooked by Arturo Barea in his otherwise perceptive volume, **"Unamuno."** . . . Barea, a fine Spanish novelist and critic now living in exile in London, has collaborated with his wife, Ilsa, who is responsible for the smooth and clear-cut English style of the essay. In remarkably few pages Barea succeeds in recreating the stage setting, geographically and historically, of Unamuno's life. His opening chapter, "Unamuno and the National Problem," on the definition and meaning of the so-called "Generation of 1898," is especially fine for its conciseness and the clear and direct vision of the sociological moment. After this it becomes easier to follow step by step the development of Unamuno's thought, particularly his constant shifts, his contrasting emphases and never-ending paradoxes. Barea retells the plot of every novel and short story, thus providing an excellent brief introduction to the man and his writings; though the book will perhaps be less useful to the initiated, particularly those who know Spanish and have followed the numerous exegeses and studies which have appeared in Spain and Latin America about this turbulent thinker and tragic protagonist of our times.

Angel Flores, "Soul Struggles of a Spanish Philosopher," in New York Herald Tribune Book Review, *February 15, 1953, p. 7.**

JOHN DEVLIN (essay date 1966)

[*In the following excerpt, Devlin discusses Barea's anticlericalism as it is manifested in* The Forging of a Rebel. *For further discussion of Barea's portrayal of Spanish Catholicism, see the excerpt by Antonia White (1941).*]

Arturo Barea's greatest work was ***The Forging of a Rebel***. . . . It is an autobiographical trilogy that tells the story of the author's tumultuous, varied life which reached a climax in 1936. In so doing the book also provides a vivid history of tortured Spain from the beginning of the reign of Alfonso XIII to the climactic period of the Civil War, which Barea terms "a war of two Cains." (p. 161)

Barea was born in humble circumstances in Badajoz. In relating the trials of his childhood he takes his readers to the very heart of Spanish life among the poorer classes where the pattern of protest was beginning to engage the forces of tradition. The conflicts in the three basic areas [of educational programs and intellectual movements; the status of the monarchy and the Directorate, and the Republic and the New Constitution] shaped his life. In his boyhood he attended the Escuela Pía in Madrid. It was the time when educational problems and policy were beginning to cause volcanic rumblings beneath the surface of society. He personally experienced the conflict between the religious and secular drives in this area. In adolescence he was apprenticed in a bank and participated in the struggle between labor, associated with the parties rising on the left, and capital, long aligned with the predominantly rightist monarchical structure. Later, in early manhood, he witnessed monarchical policy in the military arena, during his service in Morocco. In his maturity he lived the culmination of this cycle of history during the Republic and the Civil War. Like a person standing upon an elevation that reveals the contours and winding paths in a landscape, he writes in retrospect and presents his readers with a unified picture of the origin and development of the important tensions, whose misunderstandings and clash of interests caused the conflict. Barea's anticlericalism is three-pronged; that is, it extends chiefly to those areas which I have designated as the three keys, although he does not always speak specifically under these topics. (pp. 161-62)

Barea's life story is written in a style which is blunt and bare—born of its time. It reads like a saga and is peopled with innumerable real figures representative of every possible type and status. Beginning with his youth in ***The Forge*** the author introduces his urchin companions bathing naked in the river. There pass in review child laborers, beggars, laundresses, *beatas* [sanctimonious people], laborers, farmers, poor relatives, wealthy relatives, relatives with true charity, relatives exuding avarice; the wealthy fail to pay his mother; the peasants struggle for the land; and Barea writes "I needed God . . . but I could not pray." Upon the author's entrance into the bank, another view of society is opened up. It is a world peopled by unpaid apprentices, underprivileged clerks, overpaid directors, prostitutes, working girls, timorous socialists, political reactionaries. The forces of tension are beginning to be heard in shouts of "Maura—yes!" "Maura—no!" In ***The Track,*** during his army years, the procession of types reveals flea-bitten Moors, soldiers who deliberately contract venereal disease to escape combat; more down-trodden of the earth, more generous souls; Lieutenant Colonel Millán Astray who delivers panegyrics on Spanish courage; an officer who confiscates books by Anatole France, Blasco Ibáñez, and Victor Hugo; other officers who dally in the houses of prostitution. The power of the *juntas* grows amid an atmosphere that points toward dictatorial leadership. In ***The Clash*** we get a variegated view of the political maelstrom of the Republican years, which Gerald Brenan also evoked in his study, *The Spanish Labyrinth*. Anarchists, socialists, democrats, monarchists, syndicalists, communists, falangists, and their various subdivisions vie with each other to make their own particular ideology prevail. These pages are peopled by those who chose the Republic freely; those who chose it through fear; those who chose the Falange through conviction; those who chose it through ignorance; those who chose it through cowardice; those who chose it for the sake of having a cause. We meet Republican generals and Republican officials; officials with whom Barea could work and officials who sought to destroy him as the Republican movement crumbled under the Civil War. Staunch clerical supporters of Gil Robles are apparent. Sincere priests loyal to the Republic are not unknown even during the Civil War.

In presenting this picture the author in no sense accuses the Church of being the cause of the pattern of historical woe. He criticizes severely, however, when he feels that in given situations churchmen were aligned with or committed to the entrenched interests of the right; he castigates the political efforts to maintain these alignments and the prejudices which contributed to the failure of the clergy to appreciate the aspirations of the people, which, given more understanding, direction, and encouragement, need not have become antireligious. The book is, thus, anticlerical in the most generic understanding of the term. Barea, in other words, presents an intense personal reaction set in an historical matrix of the type which Conrad Bonacina has penetratingly analyzed. Although Barea's feeling is strong and bitter, it is not basically antireligious. He summed up his position shortly before the elections of 1936, in a conversation with Don Lucas, the parish priest at Novés:

> You're pushing me into the personal sphere. It is possible that you yourself are one of those exceptional priests I've mentioned, and some of whom I have known and still know. But if you want to hear what I would do in your place if I were a priest, it's quite simple; I would drop the post of Chairman of Catholic Action—that's what you are, I think—so as to obey your Master's law, "Render unto Caesar that which is Caesar's," and that other word which says that his reign is not of this world. And then I would use the pulpit for teaching the Word of Christ, not for political propaganda, and I would try to convince all people to live together in peace, so that the poor need no longer perish, lined up along the stone wall of the road waiting for a piece of bread as for a miracle, while the rich let the soil lie waste and each night gamble away enough money to wipe out all the hunger in Novés. . . .

These ideas need to be counter-balanced by the author's contact with Don Leocadio Lobo, a workers' priest who had remained loyal to both the Church and the Republic:

> The deepest hurt to him [Father Lobo] was not the fury vented against churches and priests by maddened, hatefilled, brutalized people, but his knowledge of the guilt of his own caste, the clergy, in the existence of that brutality, and in the abject ignorance and misery at the root of it. It must have been infinitely hard on him to know that the princes of his Church were

> doing their level best to keep his people subjected, and they were blessing the arms of the generals and overlords and the guns that shelled Madrid.

Barea's anticlerical reactions did not suddenly crystalize with these political considerations during the Republic. They began during his early contact with religion years before when his aunt, a *beata* [*sanctimonious person*] and a good woman in many ways, forced him into almost monastic ritual of religious exercises. Initial distaste was heightened by his experience in school, particularly in the confessional, where he had the misfortune to encounter a priest who had a totally perverted notion of good and evil, especially in matters of sex. Personal dislike rises in pitch when he witnesses the position of the clergy with regard to the social order. Thus, his own humanly understandable emotional reactions color his anticlericalism and lead him to emphasize the darker side. He does not portray only reactionary priests, yet, the "good priests" are exceptions. The priests whom he does not like or with whom he has strong, well-reasoned ideological differences are either monstrously fat or otherwise ugly to look at. . . . In other instances, Barea reacts almost puritanically to priests who use wine; none are drunkards but many are topers—a situation certainly not scandalous in a Latin land. In another sketch, the tortures of the flesh which a certain priest is probably undergoing redound to his discredit. On the other hand, the priests whom the author admires are almost invariably the victims of "beatific" mothers who forced their sons into the Church. This is implied even of Father Lobo. Thus, these clerics represent the impossible situation of apostolic dedication flowing from insincere motivation.

Another important insight into the anticlerical movement in Spain is offered by the circumstances of the author's life which placed him in proximity to popular sources of the phenomenon. Barea's grandmother, for example, is a hard-bitten old woman, not unlike Tomasa in Blasco Ibáñez' *La Catedral*. She frequently denounces religion and priests, and proclaims herself an atheist. The study of the inner reaction of such people in their *milieu* offers a psychological insight into the various violent outbreaks of anti-religious demonstrations and church burnings which in Spain have unfortunately been associated with the economic-political impetus of the uneducated working classes.

Further insights into Barea's anticlericalism can be gleaned from some of his subjective, youthful reactions. Circumstances had of course moved him externally to the left. But the author probes deeper and powerfully relates incidents and emotional reactions which suggest how certain tenets of communist ideology can germinate in the social conditions which he knew. For example, he analyses the subjective content of one of his own youthful outbursts. Angered during a family conversation and ever mindful of the poverty of his class, young Arturo had blurted out: "Parents have no rights. We children are here, because they brought us here for their own pleasure. And so they must put up with what had been their pleasure. I never asked my mother to bring me into the world, and so I can't allow her any right over me such as you claim over your son." Barea adds: "My mother said slowly, 'Yes. Having children is a pleasure for which you pay dearly.'" But a deeper subjective penetration was able to probe the weakness of his thorough-going, all-inclusive stand:

> At that I saw tumbling visions of my uncle's house, of heaps of dirty linen, of her lye bitten hand and her meek silent forbearance, a smile forever on her lips. Kisses in the kitchen and behind the curtain of the Café Español. The struggle for centimos. Her falling into a chair utterly worn out. Her fingers in my rumpled hair, my head on her lap. It all surged up in me and it put me in the wrong, but not the outcries and protests of the others who disputed and shouted.

Throughout his turbulent days during the Republic and the Civil War, Barea did not identify himself with any ideological group defined more specifically than by the rather general concepts of "leftist", "U.G.T.", "republican", and "strongly socialist." At one time he admitted to being almost a communist. During the last months in Madrid, as the communists gained greater ascendency in the government, he found himself surrounded with an increasing number of communist colleagues. He does not mention actually becoming a member of the communist party and stresses his role as a "loyalist" in the sense of remaining loyal to the Republic. He sympathized with the communists who he believed were honestly working for social justice. In fact, precisely at the moment that the hard-core communists reached their maximum power Barea faced another crisis. He felt his own power waning and realized that his life and Ilsa's were in danger. They both realized that their efforts in the social struggle were now fruitless and fled to France. Thus, Barea, whether or not he formally professed communism, certainly witnessed its genesis, passed through its intellectual *milieu* and transcended beyond its doctrinaire alignments. Strongly indicative of this transit are his reflections on the personality of "Poldi" (Leopold Kulcsar), Ilsa's first husband. . . . It was [his] . . . fanatical power that drove Ilsa from Kulcsar to Barea, with whom she shared a belief in "the human individual" as "the final value" in the social struggle.

The Forging of a Rebel is a shocking book. Its clear crisp prose, rapid action, concise character portrayals, and accurate historical recall make it easy to read. It is a book that is "hard to put down." On the other hand, the bare realistic narration of terrible but real history combined with the bitter rebellious and revolutionary reaction to that same reality could well cause a person to put the book down quickly—unfinished. Within that paradox lies its value. Beneath the vinegar, there is a warmth and a value structure that is bedrock in the ideology of Catholicism or any western religion, for that matter. The frequently tragic turns in Barea's life symbolize the tragedy of many other Spanish liberals who became embittered lapsed Catholics. (pp. 162-68)

John Devlin, "Anticlericalism in 'Belles Lettres' in the Era 1931-1936," in his Spanish Anticlericalism: A Study in Modern Alienation, *Las Americas Publishing Company, 1966, pp. 161-92.**

HUGH THOMAS (essay date 1975)

[*Thomas is an English novelist and historian who has been actively involved in politics as a disarmament adviser for the United Nations. He is the author of* The World's Game *(1957), a novel based on the Suez crisis of 1956, and* The Spanish Civil War *(1961), a history of that conflict. In the following excerpt, Thomas discusses* The Forging of a Rebel, *concluding that its chief merits are the pictures it provides of the Spanish middle class and the war in Morocco, as well as its portrayal of the role of the church and the position of women in Spanish society.*]

The three books [***The Forge, The Track*** and ***The Clash*** by Arturo Barea] are separate studies linked by two things: the developing personality of the author and the city of Madrid, as it used to be before it was ruined by the war. ***The Forge*** describes Barea's childhood in that city before 1914. ***The Track*** is chiefly an interpretation of the author's experiences in the Army during the Moroccan wars against Abd-el Krim in the Rif. ***The Clash*** is a more diffuse work and takes Barea into the Socialist Party at a time of rapidly increasing politicization. He follows this with a reconstruction of his time as a censor in the Foreign Office during the Civil War itself and ends with his exile in 1938 at a time when the *mystique* with which the Republicans began the Civil War was giving way to *politique,* in no uncertain way. (p. 535)

Of the three sections of the book, the last is probably the best known because of the Civil War which dominates it. That is understandable, for there are in this some very vivid passages which are a pleasure to reread. There is a good picture of the Foreign Ministry in the emptying capital before the battle. There is a vivid exchange between the author and a man who is brought to confess that the reason he is so busy killing alleged Fascists is that he himself had been friendly with the by-then dissolved right-wing Christian Democratic Party, the CEDA. An election meeting just before the Civil War is brilliantly described. There is too in this section of the book an unforgettable picture of the city of Madrid improvising its defense in the face of innumerable difficulties, not least the suspicion that certain prominent people were traitors.

Nevertheless I have recently found ***The Clash,*** as it happens, the least satisfactory of the three sections. First, this is because it is less well organized than the other two. It sprawls from 1935 to 1938, from the world of micro-politics to that of international military missions and thoughts on world wars. The international figures whom Barea introduces briefly—General Goriev, Sefton Delmer, Gustav Regler, Herbert Matthews—are one-dimensional figures in comparison with the aunts and uncles who make such a vivid impression in the first part of the book.

The last part of this book is also rather unsatisfactory. It is far from clear exactly why Barea left Spain, and anyone who knows anything of the Spanish Civil War cannot help thinking that there may be more to the story here than Barea allows. For example, he tells us that Leopold Kocsar, his wife Ilsa's Austrian first husband, was working for the SIM, the military intelligence service which persecuted the POUM and the anarchists so relentlessly. But we are made to feel a little sorry for "Poldi," who "looked very ill and was suffering pain; he confessed to a serious stomach complaint rendered worse by his way of living, the late nights, the irregular food, the black coffee. . . ." But these late nights were caused by his endless interrogations and even tortures of alleged Trotskyists. "My historic mission," "Poldi" said to Katia Landau, "is to find the proofs that, among twenty Trotskyists, eighteen are the agents of Hitler and Franco."

The Forge and ***The Track*** are free from the problems that these recollections arouse, and I think that the writing is better as well. In the first, there are brilliant, self-confident pictures of Barea's family, all, as it were, peering over the edge of the giant cauldron of Spanish working-class feelings to see what sort of mixture will result. Don Luis, the blacksmith of Brunete, with his breakfasts of rabbit and brandy, is a particularly compelling figure. These 200 or so pages seem to me to be among the two or three best pieces of writing ever done which are inspired by working-class life. Or can one call that world of craftsmen about to sink, or about to rise, as fate determines, really "working class"? I think not: indeed, the whole sweep of this section of Barea's work reminds one of the diversity of the class whom some would quite neglect in their efforts to reach a simple and stark interpretation of politics. Priests and engine drivers, lion tamers and cashiers, matadors and beggars—all live forever caught by one short sentence or anecdote, thanks to Barea's acute and selective memory. A particularly important function of these pages is that they show, through the analysis of relations between men and women, just how authoritarian modern Spain was—perhaps still is.

The war in Morocco is especially well illustrated. It reminds the reader just how important that war was in modern Spanish history. For it was there that the generals of the Civil War generation were in effect brutalized by an atrocious colonial war carried out to "write a brilliant page in history" by entering sacred Xauen. The pen picture of General Millán Astray is extremely vivid, though perhaps a little contrived. Then the scene in the brothel in Tetuán in which the author sleeps with the General's girl is also very good. So too is Barea's accidental meeting with the dictator Primo de Rivera in the Villa Rosa night club. But no doubt the passages here which will leave a more profound impression are those which show how Barea, from observation of the disease, corruption, dirt and incompetence of the Spanish Army at war, gradually became a Socialist and subsequently a writer. The events outside Melilla in 1921 must have been compelling so far as Barea's later political views were concerned: "I cannot tell the story of Melilla. . . . I was there, but I do not know where: somewhere in the midst of shots, shells, and machine-gun rattle, sweating, shouting, running, sleeping on stone and on sand, but above all ceaselessly vomiting, smelling of corpses, finding at every step another dead body, more horrible than any I had known at any moment before. . . ."

This scene was to be repeated often in Barea's experience and the outrage which he never ceased to feel is very well conveyed. But though Barea is particularly good, and honest, about scenes of violence, he can also conjure up "salt plains by the shimmering Mediterranean; the palm trees of Elche in the noon haze; eyeless, blindingly white Moorish houses on the slope of bare yellow dunes, petrified in the shape of waves; gnarled oak and pines on rocky ridges unbearably lonely under the infinite dome of the sky. . . ." And then there was Father Vesga, the priest whom the children tried to avoid going to for confession, since he frightened them so much with his tales of sin. . . . (pp. 535-36)

Barea's book gives a fine picture of an old society in decay. It is no less compelling because, from the standpoint of the much more conventional, clean, characterless Madrid of today, one cannot help a certain nostalgia for the fascinating slum life of Barea's childhood: poor, often wretched, but what vigor, what eccentricity! (p. 536)

Hugh Thomas, "Spain before the Falange," in The Nation, *Vol. 220, No. 17, May 3, 1975, pp. 535-36.*

ADDITIONAL BIBLIOGRAPHY

Brenan, Gerald. "An Honest Man." *The New York Review of Books* XXII, No. 3 (6 March 1975): 3-4.

A sympathetic biographical essay by a friend of Arturo and Ilsa Barea.

Brickell, Herschel. "Of Moral Wreckage." *The Saturday Review of Literature* XXXIV, No. 12 (24 March 1951): 17, 38.
Review of *The Broken Root*. Brickell concludes that the protagonist is weakly characterized and that the novel lacks the Spanish atmosphere so accurately evoked in *The Forging of a Rebel*.

Devlin, John. "Arturo Barea and José María Fironella—Two Interpreters of the Spanish Labyrinth." *Hispania* XLI, No. 2 (May 1958): 143-48.*
Discusses Barea's autobiography. Devlin emphasizes Barea's apt depiction of the political chaos of the Spanish republic, and his attitude toward the Catholic clergy.

Mattingly, Garrett. "Autobiography of a Spanish Exile." *The Saturday Review of Literature* XXIX, No. 52 (28 December 1946): 11.
Compares *The Forging of a Rebel* to Leo Tolstoy's *War and Peace* and Victor Hugo's *Ninety-Three*, finding that, like them, "it reveals the essential shape and meaning of a public series of events with . . . density of impact and richness."

Parkinson, Tom. "After Lorca." *Prairie Schooner* XXXIII, No. 4 (Winter 1959-1960): 289-93.
Review of *Lorca*, concluding that "every poet and student of poetry should know [Barea's] book."

Weber, Brom. "Individual, Spanish Universal." *The Sewanee Review* LVIII, No. 4 (October-December 1950): 728-31.
Discusses *Lorca*, emphasizing the insightfulness of Barea's study of the symbolism and imagery in Federico García Lorca's poems.

Weeden, Margaret. "Arturo Barea: An Appreciation." *Meanjin* XVIII, No. 1 (1959): 96-9.
On Barea's life and literary achievement.

Wolfe, Bertram D. "In One Man's Life We Have the Soul of Spain." *New York Herald Tribune Weekly Book Review* (22 December 1946): 3.
Reviews *The Forging of a Rebel*. Wolfe praises Barea's honesty and notes the breadth of his experience.

Kate (O'Flaherty) Chopin

1851-1904

American novelist, short story writer, poet, and essayist.

A popular local colorist during her lifetime, Chopin is best known today for her psychological novel *The Awakening,* which realistically depicts a woman's search for spiritual and sexual freedom in the repressive society of nineteenth-century America. When *The Awakening* appeared in 1899, critical and public indignation over the novel's frank treatment of guiltless adultery caused Chopin to abandon her literary career, and the novel itself was all but forgotten for several decades. Since the 1950s, however, serious critical attention has focused on the pioneering psychological realism, symbolic imagery, and artistic integrity of the work. Interest in *The Awakening* has also led to reappraisals of Chopin's short stories.

Born in St. Louis, Chopin was the daughter of a prominent businessman and his wife. Her father died when Chopin was four years old, and her childhood was most profoundly influenced by her mother, grandmother, and great-grandmother, women descended from French Creole pioneers. Chopin also spent much time with her family's Creole and mulatto slaves, whose dialects she mastered. A bookish child, she often retreated to an attic hideaway to read the works of Walter Scott, Edmund Spenser, and other writers who were not represented among the encyclopedias and religious books in the family library. Despite her early interest in literature, Chopin was an undistinguished student at the convent school she attended. She graduated at age seventeen and spent two years as a belle of fashionable St. Louis society. In 1870 she married a wealthy Creole cotton factor, Oscar Chopin, and moved with him to New Orleans. For the next decade, Chopin pursued the demanding social and domestic schedule of a wealthy wife, the recollection of which would later serve as material for the novel *The Awakening*. But by 1880, financial difficulties made it necessary for Chopin's steadily growing family to move to Cloutierville in Natchitoches Parish, which is located in Louisiana's Red River bayou region. There, Chopin's husband managed the family plantations until his death in 1883. Afterward, Chopin insisted upon assuming her husband's managerial responsibilities, which brought her into contact with almost every aspect of the family business and every segment of the community. She was particularly intrigued by the French Acadian, Creole, and mulatto sharecroppers who worked the plantations. The impressions she gathered of these people and Natchitoches Parish life was to later influence her fiction.

In the mid-1880s Chopin sold most of her property and left Louisiana to live with her mother in St. Louis. Family friends, who had found her letters entertaining, encouraged Chopin to write professionally, and she soon began writing short stories. These early works evidence the influence of her favorite authors: the French writers Guy de Maupassant, Alphonse Daudet, and Molière. At this time Chopin also read the works of Charles Darwin, Thomas Huxley, and Herbert Spencer in order to keep abreast of trends in scientific thinking, and began questioning the benefits of certain mores and ethical constraints imposed upon human nature. After an apprenticeship marked by routine rejections, Chopin began to publish her stories in the most popular American periodicals. Between 1894 and

Missouri Historical Society, C-001-000859

1897 she published the collections *Bayou Folk* and *A Night in Acadie,* the success of which solidified her growing reputation as a skillful local colorist. Financially independent and encouraged by success, Chopin now turned her creative interest to longer works. Although she had published the novel *At Fault* in 1890, the work displayed many of the shortcomings of an apprentice novel, and failed to interest readers or critics. A later novel and some short stories were rejected for publication on moral grounds, for editors perceived in them an unseemly interest in female self-assertion and sexual liberation. Undaunted, Chopin completed the ambitious novel *The Awakening,* which was published in 1899. It was received with hostility by critics, despite general acknowledgment of Chopin's mature writing skills. Chopin's career was ruined by the critical and public reaction; she had difficulties finding publishers for later works and was ousted from local literary groups. Demoralized, she wrote little during the rest of her life, which a cerebral hemorrhage ended abruptly when Chopin was fifty-three.

The short stories collected in *Bayou Folk* and *A Night in Acadie* established Chopin as an important writer of local-color fiction. Set primarily near Natchitoches Parish, these tales of Creole and Cajun life are noted for meticulous descriptions of setting, precise rendering of characters' dialect, and an objective point of view. Most contemporary reviews of Chopin's short stories emphasized her skillful delineation of character. Early twentieth-century critics, however, were more interested in Chopin's psychologically complex characterizations, and considered locale unimportant to an understanding of the stories's wider significance. Modern critics have concentrated on both aspects of the stories, noting the equal importance of setting, theme, and characterization, elements that Chopin linked through the use of symbolic imagery to achieve an interdependent balance. Many of the stories in *Bayou Folk* and *A Night in Acadie* build to an ironic plot reversal reminiscent of the technique Maupassant employed. Some critics argue that frequent dependence upon this technique weakens the artistry of such a story as "Désirée's Baby," but other critics regard it as an inevitable outgrowth of the types of plots and themes Chopin used during the early period of her career, which was devoted to popular-magazine fiction. Later, essentially plotless stories like "The Storm," are more realistically structured and do not lend themselves to the commercially expedient resolutions of earlier stories. Although they sometimes have a slick quality, the stories in *Bayou Folk* and *A Night in Acadie* attempt honest examinations of sexuality, repression, freedom, and responsibility—themes Chopin was to explore more fully in *The Awakening*.

The Awakening is considered Chopin's best work as well as a remarkable novel to have been written during the morally uncompromising America of the 1890s. Psychologically realistic, *The Awakening* is the story of Edna Pontellier, a conventional wife and mother who experiences a spiritual epiphany and an awakened sense of independence that change her life. The theme of sexual freedom and the consequences one must face to attain it is supported by sensual imagery that acquires symbolic meanings as the story progresses. This symbolism emphasizes the conflict within Pontellier, who realizes that she can neither exercise her new-found sense of independence nor return to life as it was before her spiritual awakening: the candor of the Creole community on Grand Isle, for example, is contrasted with the conventional mores of New Orleans; birds in gilded cages and strong, free-flying birds are juxtaposed; and the protagonist selects for her confidants both the domesticated, devoted Adele Ratignolle and the passionate Madame Reisz, a lonely, unattractive pianist. The central symbol of the novel, the sea, also provides the frame for the main action. As a symbol, the sea embodies multiple pairs of polarities, the most prominent being that it is the site of both Edna Pontellier's awakening and suicide.

After the initial furor over morality and sexuality in *The Awakening* had passed, the novel was largely ignored until the 1930s, when Daniel S. Rankin published a study of Chopin's works that included a sober assessment of *The Awakening*'s high literary quality and artistic aims. During the succeeding decades, critical debate surrounding *The Awakening* has focused on Chopin's view of women's roles in society, the significance of Pontellier's awakening, her subsequent suicide, and the possibility of parallels between the lives of Chopin and her protagonist. George Arms, for example, has contended that Chopin was a happily married woman and devoted mother whose emotional life bore no resemblance to Pontellier's, while Chopin's principal biographer, Per Seyersted, has noted her compellingly secretive, individualistic nature and her evident enjoyment of living alone as an independent writer. Priscilla Allen has posited that male critics allow their preconceptions about "good" and "bad" women to influence their interpretations of Chopin's novel, arguing that they too often assume that Edna's first priority should have been to her family and not to herself. Like Allen, Seyersted brings a feminist interpretation to *The Awakening*, and points out that the increasing depiction of passionate, independent women in Chopin's other fiction supports the theory that she was in fact concerned about the incompatibility of motherhood and a career for women living during the late nineteenth century. These questions about Chopin's depictions of women's roles in society have led to a debate about the significance of Pontellier's suicide. The ambivalence of the character as she wrestles with the new choices that confront her has left the suicide open to many interpretations. Carol P. Christ, like Seyersted, interprets the death as a moral victory and a social defeat—the act of a brave woman who cannot sacrifice her life to her family, but will not cause her children disgrace by pursuing a scandalous course. In a contrasting assessment of Pontellier's choice to die, James H. Justus likens the protagonist's gradual withdrawal from society and responsibility to a regression into childhood selfishness because she refuses to compromise and cannot control her urge for self-assertion. Often compared to the protagonist of Gustave Flaubert's *Madame Bovary*, Pontellier differs primarily in her desire for selfhood, even at the risk of loneliness, while Madame Bovary seeks romantic fulfillment.

Once considered a minor author of local-color fiction, Chopin is today recognized for her examination of sexuality, individual freedom, and the consequences of actions—themes and concerns important to many later twentieth-century writers. While the psychological examinations of female protagonists have made *The Awakening* and several of Chopin's stories seminal works in the historical development of feminist literature, her works also provide a broad examination of societies that stifle self-expression, illustrating, as Peggy Skaggs has observed, that "having a secure place . . . is not enough in life; that one's sexual nature is a powerful part of the self, whether feminine or masculine."

(See also *TCLC*, Vol. 5; *Contemporary Authors*, Vol. 104; and *Dictionary of Literary Biography*, Vol. 12: *American Realists and Naturalists*.)

PRINCIPAL WORKS

At Fault (novel) 1890
Bayou Folk (short stories) 1894
A Night in Acadie (short stories) 1897
The Awakening (novel) 1899
The Complete Works of Kate Chopin. 2 vols. (novels, short stories, poetry, and essays) 1969
The Awakening, and Other Stories (novel and short stories) 1970
The Awakening, and Selected Stories (novel and short stories) 1976

THE NATION (essay date 1894)

[*In the following excerpt, the reviewer notes the artistry of Chopin's style in the stories collected in* Bayou Folk.]

Of writing many stories of Louisiana life there is no end. It is not surprising, for the material embraces all that is most picturesque, whether the scenes of action be New Orleans or the inland parishes, whether Creoles or negroes be the actors. Kate Chopin has written of the **'Bayou Folk'** dwelling in Natchitoches Parish, who are of every race and admixture of race that can be evolved from stems American, French, Spanish, Indian, Negro. Her stories are among the most clever and charming that have seen the light. Her pen is an artist's in choice of subject, in touch, and in forbearance. There is never a word nor an idea too much, and in the score of sketches in which the same names often recur, there is no repetition, nevertheless, of herself or of others. Hers is good work, and as interesting as the good often is not.

A review of "Bayou Folk," in The Nation, *Vol. LVIII, No. 1513, June 28, 1894, p. 488.*

***THE NATION* (essay date 1898)**

[*In the following excerpt from an early review of* A Night in Acadie, *Chopin's stories are favorably compared to those of New England local colorist Mary Wilkins Freeman.*]

Kate Chopin tells a story like a poet, and reproduces the spirit of a landscape like a painter. Her stories [collected in ***A Night in Acadie***] are to the bayous of Louisiana what Mary Wilkins's are to New England, with a difference, to be sure, as the Cape jessamine is different from the cinnamon rose, but like in seizing the heart of her people and showing the traits that come from their surroundings; like, too, in giving without a wasted word the history of main crises in their lives. That Cape jessamine is sometimes a thought too heavy is perhaps inevitable in the heated South. But enough there is of artistic in the best sense to hold the reader from cover to cover, transported for the time to a region of fierce passions, mediaeval chivalry, combined with rags and bad grammar, a soft, sliding Creole accent, and the tragedies and comedies that loom with special meaning in a sparsely settled country.

A review of "A Night in Acadie," in The Nation, *Vol. LXVI, No. 1719, June 9, 1898, p. 447.*

***PUBLIC OPINION* (essay date 1899)**

[*The following excerpt is from an early, unfavorable review of* The Awakening. *For a contrasting opinion, see the excerpt from* The New York Times Book Review *(1899).*]

"The Awakening," by Kate Chopin, is a feeble reflection of Bourget, theme and manner of treatment both suggesting the French novelist. We very much doubt the possibility of a woman of "solid old Presbyterian Kentucky stock" being at all like Mrs. Edna Pontellier who has a long list of lesser loves, and one absorbing passion, but gives herself only to the man for whom she did not feel the least affection. If the author had secured our sympathy for this unpleasant person it would not have been a small victory, but we are well satisfied when Mrs. Pontellier deliberately swims out to her death in the waters of the gulf.

A review of "The Awakening," in Public Opinion, *Vol. XXVI, No. 25, June 22, 1899, p. 794.*

***THE NEW YORK TIMES BOOK REVIEW* (essay date 1899)**

[*The following excerpt is from a favorable review of* The Awakening. *For an opposing view, see the excerpt from* Public Opinion *(1899).*]

Would it have been better had Mrs. Kate Chopin's heroine [in ***The Awakening***] slept on forever and never had an awakening? Does that sudden condition of change from sleep to consciousness bring with it happiness? Not always, and particularly poignant is the woman's awakening, as Mrs. Chopin tells it. The author has a clever way of managing a difficult subject, and wisely tempers the emotional elements found in the situation. Such is the cleverness in the handling of the story that you feel pity for the most unfortunate of her sex.

A review of "The Awakening," in The New York Times Book Review, *June 24, 1899, p. 408.*

FRED LEWIS PATTEE (essay date 1915)

[*An American literary historian and critic, Pattee viewed literature as popular rather than elitist expression. In the following excerpt from his* A History of American Literature since 1870, *he discusses the narrative artistry of Chopin's short stories, which he considers among the best by an American. He also briefly compares Chopin's work with that of Grace King, a New Orleans-born writer of local-color stories who was a contemporary of Chopin.*]

[Kate Chopin's] work is equal to the best that has been produced in France or even in America. She wrote but little, two volumes of stories, notably ***Bayou Folk,*** containing all that is now accessible of her shorter work. Many of her sketches and stories have never been republished from the magazines.

The strength of Mrs. Chopin's work came partly from the strangeness of her material—she told of the Grand Pré Acadians in the canebrakes of central Louisiana—and from her intimate knowledge of her field, but it came more from what may be described as a native aptitude for narration amounting almost to genius. (p. 364)

No writer of the period was more spontaneously and inevitably a story teller. There is an ease and a naturalness about her work that comes from more than mere art. She seldom gave to a story more than a single sitting, and she rarely revised her work, yet in compression of style, in forbearance, in the massing of materials, and in artistry she ranks with even the masters of the period. A story like **"Désirée's Baby,"** with its inevitableness and its culminating sentence that stops for an instant the reader's heart, is well-nigh perfect. She was emotional, she was minutely realistic, and, unlike Grace King, used dialect sometimes in profusion; she was dramatic and even at times melodramatic, yet never was she commonplace or ineffective. She had command at times of a pervasive humor and a pathos that gripped the reader before he was aware, for behind all was the woman herself. She wrote as Dickens wrote, with abandonment, with her whole self. There is art in her work, but there is more than art. One may read again and again such bits of human life as **"Madame Celestin's Divorce":** it is the art that is independent of time and place, the art indeed that is universal. (pp. 364-65)

Fred Lewis Pattee, "The Triumph of the Short Story," in his A History of American Literature Since 1870, *1915. Reprint by Cooper Square Publishers, Inc., 1968, pp. 355-84.**

SHIELDS McILWAINE (essay date 1939)

[*McIlwaine is an American writer who has written several studies of Southern culture and literature. In the following excerpt from* Southern Poor White, *he credits Chopin and George Washington Cable with introducing the picturesque customs and idiosyncrasies of Louisiana Cajun culture into American fiction. However, the critic considers Chopin's stories to be more realistic than Cable's because her characters, unlike the regional stereotypes found in much of Cable's work, cope with more realistic emotions.*]

[What primarily interested] writers like Cable and Mrs. Chopin in the Cajuns was their picturesque community life and their Latin natures. Yet both authors in dealing with them were more than local colorists. (p. 148)

Like the later James Lane Allen, Mrs. Chopin joined the movement away from local color and propaganda toward a purer art.

And, for the interpretation of the Cajun, this was fortunate; inasmuch as ten stories in her volumes, ***Bayou Folk*** . . . and ***A Night in Acadie*** . . . , concern poor-whites and constitute an even wider view of them than that in Cable's novel [*Bonaventure*]. Besides, her fictional emphasis was different. She concentrated upon the emotions called forth, both by the French natures and by the daily grooves and conditions of the Cajuns. The description of the locale of her Cajun stories around and west of Natchitoches—a pine and cotton country to the north of Cable's Bayou Teche—was to her unimportant in comparison with the making of an artistic record of Cajun sentiments. And, be it said to her credit, that, more often than any other writer in the Southern Revival, she kept sentiment from melting into sentimentality. As a result, her Cajuns, though displayed on their quaint and sweeter sides, are not merely picturesque types in a pastoral such as *Bonaventure,* but humble human beings, feeling and thinking according to long-set patterns. Consequently, at the end of nearly every story, Mrs. Chopin crystallized the feeling which she had already built up beforehand. Emotional reality—that was her primary concern.

And this she might have achieved in tragedy had public taste been different. But Kate Chopin, a widow with a family to support, knew that the market demanded sentiment, comedy, and at least a few dashes of local color. As a result, she used tragic elements merely to give a glow to sentiment. In **"A Visit to Avoyelle,"** Doudouce went to see his old love, Mentine, now the misshapen, shrill-voiced mother of six, living desperately on a worn-out farm. Yet when the old lover started home, he realized that Mentine was watching not him, but her sorry husband going back to the plough-tail. Lalie, the heroine of **"Love on the Bon Dieu,"** "slender with a frailness that indicated a lack of wholesome and plentiful nourishment," had "a pathetic uneasy look—in her gray eyes." When she crossed the churchyard after mass, the Cajuns who were better off whispered: "She's real canaille, her," because Lalie lived near the swamp with a half-crazy grandmother in a cabin which even the darkies had refused to rent. Nevertheless, Azenor, a young carpenter, found that love could level ranks and therefore married her. Such typical narratives show that Mrs. Chopin evaded the tragic implications of her material.

Nevertheless, within the province of comedy and sentiment, she penned three short stories of poor-white life that were unsurpassed until the advent of Erskine Caldwell. And even today, they stand apart as faultless art records of poor-whites who happened to be French. In the two and a half pages of **"Boulôt and Boulotte,"** Kate Chopin left a comic miniature of Cajun childhood. (pp. 149-50)

"In Sabine" is Mrs. Chopin's story of 'Tite Reine, a gay, illiterate girl of Natchitoches parish, who had eloped with the roving, drunken Texan, Bud Aiken. After this, 'Tite's life had been one backwoods clearing after another in three parishes; now Bud swore that "Sabine's a damn sight worse than any of 'em. . . . I'm fixin to sell out an' try Vernon." And so, when an old acquaintance, Gregoire Sentien, chanced upon the Aiken cabin, 'Tite poured out her woes to him. Bud had treated her like a dog, forced her to pick cotton while he lay around drunk, and put her on his bucking mustang to laugh at her being thrown. Worse than that: "I tell you," 'Tite Reine whispered to Gregoire. "He beats me; my back and arms—you ought to see—it's all blue." . . . No wonder, 'Tite Reine, lost in the pinelands, crawled in the dark to Gregoire's pallet on the porch and convinced him that he should take her away. One morning, Bud discovered that he had no wife, no mustang, and no guest.

Azélie and 'Tite Reine, along with Lalie in **"Love on the Bon-Dieu,"** stand out as the only memorable poor-white girls created during the Southern Revival. Also, in so far as their lives are mixtures of sentiment and fairly sordid conditions, they assume added significance as literary ancestors of the tenant women depicted by Paul Green and other sensibilitists in the next century.

To the literature of Cajun life, Cable contributed pastoral background, folkways, and propaganda; Kate Chopin, the emotional values of these facts presented by Cable. (pp. 151-53)

Shields McIlwaine, "The South Claims the Poor-White for War and Literature," in his The Southern Poor-White: From Lubberland to Tobacco Road, *University of Oklahoma Press, 1939, pp. 75-162.**

VAN WYCK BROOKS (essay date 1952)

[*An American critic and biographer, Brooks is noted chiefly for his biographical and critical studies of such writers as Mark Twain, Henry James, and Ralph Waldo Emerson, and for his influential commentary on the history of American literature. His career can be neatly divided into two distinct periods: the first, from 1908 to 1925, dealt primarily with the negative impact of European Puritanism on the development of artistic genius in America. Brooks argued that the puritan conscience in the United States, carried over from Europe, produced an unhealthy dichotomy in American writers and resulted in a literature split between stark realism and what he called "vaporous idealism." During this early period, Brooks believed that in reality America had no culture of its own, and that American literature relied almost exclusively on its European heritage. After 1925, and his study on Emerson, Brooks radically altered his view of American literary history. He began to see much in America's past as unique and artistically valuable, and he called for a return in literary endeavors to the positive values of Emerson, as opposed to the modern pessimism of such writers as T. S. Eliot and James Joyce. Despite the radical difference in these two critical approaches, one element remained constant throughout Brooks's career, namely his concern with the reciprocal relationship between the writer and society. In the following excerpt, Brooks praises* The Awakening.]

[During the 1890s,] the South was notable for the cultural lag that sociologists talked about and the good old ways in literature continued to prevail in the writings of John Fox, Jr., for instance, Mary Johnston's historical novels and F. Hopkinson Smith's *Colonel Carter*. What Henry James called in *The American Scene* the Southern "pretence of a social order founded on delusions and exclusions" had plenty of defenders, while local-colour writers still liked to dwell on the piney-woods folk who referred to a wedding-dinner as an "infair." . . . But there was one novel of the nineties in the South that should have been remembered, one small perfect book that mattered more than the whole life-work of many a prolific writer, a novel of Kate Chopin, who wrote Creole stories, like one or two others in New Orleans who carried on the vein of George W. Cable. ***The Awakening*** was more mature than even the best of Cable's work, so effortless it seemed, so composed in its naturalness and grace was this tragic tale of Grand Isle, the fasionable New Orleans summer resort where the richer merchants deposited their wives and children. There, with the carelessness and lightness of a boy, the young Creole idler Robert awakened, with sorrowful results, from the dull dream of her existence the charming young woman whose husband adored her while he made the sad mistake of leaving her alone with her reveries and vague desires.

But this beautiful novel was rare indeed. (pp. 340-41)

Van Wyck Brooks, "South of the James," in his The Confident Years: 1885-1915, *E. P. Dutton & Co., Inc., 1952, pp. 337-52.**

STANLEY KAUFFMANN (essay date 1966)

[*Kauffmann is one of America's most well-known contemporary film and theater critics. A contributor of reviews to several magazines, he is currently the film critic of* The New Republic. *Although the theater and cinema are of primary concern to Kauffmann as a critic, he is knowledgable in many other areas of world literature. In the following excerpt, Kauffmann notes Larzer Ziff's apt comparison of* The Awakening *to Gustave Flaubert's* Madame Bovary *(see* TCLC, *Vol. 5). Kauffmann argues that while there are similarities, Chopin's novel is more realistic and honest because it depicts sexual fulfillment in the absence of marriage or romance, and because the protagonist is motivated by desires rather than manipulated by plot contrivances.*]

Wilson compares ***The Awakening*** to D. H. Lawrence [see *TCLC*, Vol. 5], but Ziff's comparison to *Madame Bovary* seems more apt [see *TCLC*, Vol. 5]. Like Emma Bovary, Edna Pontellier is an attractive young woman married to a well-meaning dullard, she is a mother, she is involved with two men, she commits suicide. Mrs. Chopin is not Flaubert's equal; her book does not have Flaubert's complexity of character or subtlety of orchestration; it lacks the breadth of context to make its intense anguish seem like an ironic winking moment in cosmic nonchalance; and there is no one scene in ***The Awakening*** that is conceived with the genius of such an episode as the one between Emma and Rodolphe at the agricultural fair. But there are two respects in which Mrs. Chopin's novel is *harder* than Flaubert's, more ruthless, more insistent on truth of inner and social life as sole motivation. Edna Pontellier has her first affair out of sexual hunger, without romantic furbelow. She is in love, but the young man she loves has left New Orleans (where most of the novel takes place). Increasingly aware that her life is increasingly empty, she has a sheerly sexual affair with an accomplished amorist. And, second, Mrs. Chopin uses no equivalent of the complicated financial maneuvers with which Flaubert finally corners his heroine. Edna kills herself solely because of the foredoomed emptiness of life stretching ahead of her. It is purely a psychological motive, untouched by plot contrivance.

The patent theme is in its title (a remarkably simple one for its day): the awakening of a conventional young woman to what is missing in her marriage, and her refusal to be content. Below that theme is the still-pertinent theme of the disparity between woman's sexual being and the rules of marriage. And below *that* is the perennial theme of nature versus civilization. The atmosphere of the book is that of frilled and formal New Orleans society (for, unlike Emma, Edna is not a provincial); but the book begins and ends with the sea.

It opens on Grand Isle in the Gulf of Mexico where the Pontelliers are summering, and it closes there. The very same sentence, about "the voice of the sea," occurs twice in the book. The first time, early in the story. . . . The sentence about the sea occurs once more, near the very end, just after the following:

> Despondency had come upon her there in the wakeful night, and had never lifted. There was no one thing in the world that she desired. There was no human being whom she wanted near her except Robert [the young man she loves]; and she even realized that the day would come when he, too, and the thought of him would melt out of her existence, leaving her alone. The children appeared before her like antagonists who had overcome her; who had overpowered and sought to drag her into the soul's slavery for the rest of her days. But she knew a way to elude them. She was not thinking of these things when she walked down to the beach.

I submit that this is an extraordinary paragraph for an American novel published in 1899. It is neither Nora Helmer nor Susan B. Anthony. It is an anachronistic, lonely, existentialist voice out of the mid-20th century.

Such anachronisms, inexplicable and marvelous, appear in all the arts from time to time: Vermeer, anticipating by two centuries the light of the French Impressionists; Büchner, anticipating by a century the German Expressionist drama. Kate Chopin was at least a generation ahead of her time. Her style is not free of Victorian upholstery: "spun-gold hair"; two lips "that were so red one could only think of cherries"; a cook serves "a delicious repast"; and so on. But these mannerisms of the day only make the other elements in the book all the more remarkable: the impatience with moral mythology; the insistence on emotional truth; the confrontation of the resultant consequences without plot contrivance or escape; the humane but unsparing eye for character; the dynamics of the story's cruel progress, step by inexorable step.

In the post-Freudian age, a certain patronizing view creeps into our reading of novels like this one, as if we thought that the author did very well considering that he didn't know as much about these matters as we do. An accompanying aspect is that we tend to give credit, even to Flaubert, on extra-literary grounds—pats on the head for being a pioneer. Still, after those aspects are either discounted or reckoned on, ***The Awakening*** remains a novel of high quality, fine in itself and astonishing for its day.

To discover a novel of such stature in the American past is both a happiness and an occasion for some shame. Not many readers would claim to know all of American literature, but some of us like to think that at least we know the best of it. ***The Awakening*** has been too much and too long neglected. (p. 38)

Stanley Kauffmann, "The Really Lost Generation," in The New Republic, *Vol. 155, No. 23, December 3, 1966, pp. 22, 37-8.**

PER SEYERSTED (essay date 1969)

[*A professor of American literature at the University of Oslo, Seyersted is the author of* Kate Chopin: A Critical Biography, *and editor of* The Complete Works of Kate Chopin, *published simultaneously in 1969. These works introduced Chopin's previously unpublished or uncollected writings and sparked new interest in the novel* The Awakening *as well. In the following excerpt, Seyersted surveys Chopin's career and discusses* The Awakening *as a feminist novel, noting the suppression of several of her other novels and short stories for their depictions of passionate, independent women. In an opinion similar to that expressed in the excerpt by Carol P. Christ (1980), Seyersted interprets Edna Pontellier's suicide as both a social defeat and a victory of self-knowledge. For other discussions of the significance of Pontellier's suicide, see the excerpts by James E. Rocks (1972), James H. Justus (1978), and Carol P. Christ (1980).*]

Many of the views which informed Kate Chopin's fiction from the start are suggested in her essays of the middle 1890's. She insisted here that no author can be true to life who refuses to pluck from the Darwinian tree of knowledge and to see human existence in its true meaning. Reflecting the tenet that man is a higher animal, she once told a friend that she would rather be a dog than a nun because the existence of the one was "a little picture of life" and that of the other only a "phantasmagoria." To her, nature was amoral, playing with man, and morality was man-made and relative. That she drifted away from Catholicism did not mean that she became an atheist, however, but only that she sought God in nature rather than through the Church. She could not share Spencer's belief in progress, and she did not believe in idealism or reform. In her view, man is basically the same today as he has ever been, that is, ruled by imperative, immutably selfish drives. At the same time she did not deterministically deprive man of the ability to choose between right and wrong and to exert his will and influence his fate; nor did she ever view man as bestial. She was, she said, a lover of "brightness and gaiety and life and sunshine," and though she was not blind to evil, she was unable to see and paint life in the dark colors so often used by the naturalists.

Even while calling Zola "the great French realist," she complained that he took life "too clumsily and seriously." She objected to the "rampant sentimentality" of his *Lourdes,* and also to the gloom and lack of humor in Hardy's *Jude the Obscure*. She objected to Zola's "mass of prosaic data" and his design to instruct, and she saw Hardy's characters as "so plainly constructed with the intention of illustrating the purposes of the author, that they do not for a moment convey any impression of reality." To her, true art was incompatible with a thesis and with a zeal for reform. (pp. 23-4)

As for herself, Kate Chopin concentrated on the immutable impulses of love and sex, and Whitman and Maupassant were two of the authors who spoke most deeply to her, probably because they acknowledged the existence of Eros and because they are helped to extend the literary limits to the treatment of sex. Though she leaned to the French school, she believed that American writers, with their "wider and more variegated field of observation," might equal, and perhaps even surpass, the French authors, "were it not that the limitations imposed upon their art by their environment hamper a full and spontaneous expression." Mrs. Chopin wanted to express herself freely, but she did not so much aspire to the somewhat external realism of a Zola as to the more inward, psychological realism of a Maupassant. Her ideal was the invisible and impersonal author who wrote with an objectivity coupled with humor and sympathy. (p. 24)

In September, 1890, she brought out the novel ***At Fault*** in St. Louis at her own expense. Its heroine, who is opposed to divorce, makes the man she loves and who loves her remarry the woman he divorced because she drank. The wife soon falls back into drinking, and the heroine questions what earlier had been absolute moral truths to her and her right to force her views on others.

In reviewing the novel, St. Louis critics paid tribute to the author's style, but objected to her view that man was unimprovable. In a lone eastern review, the *Nation* also praised her artistry while criticizing the book on moral grounds.

Stimulated by her modest success, Kate Chopin soon finished a second novel. All we know about it is that a number of publishers refused it and that she later destroyed it. She had more luck with her stories, which soon appeared locally, then in national children's magazines, and finally—from 1893—in such well-known eastern periodicals as *Vogue,* the *Century,* and the *Atlantic*. She reached the high-point of her public success when Houghton Mifflin Company in March, 1894, published ***Bayou Folk,*** which included half of the fifty tales and sketches she had then written. She was welcomed in more than a hundred press notices as a distinguished local colorist. The *Atlantic,* meanwhile, suspected that a wider role might be cut out for her when it observed that her occasional "passionate note" was "characteristic of power awaiting opportunity."

The sudden national fame inspired Kate Chopin to write **"The Story of an Hour,"** a most remarkable account of a woman who exclaims: "Free! free! free!" when she hears of her husband's sudden death. A month later Kate Chopin declared in a diary entry that she would now be willing to "forget the past ten years of [her] growth—real growth" and with a new, "perfect acquiescence" join Oscar were it possible for him to come back to earth. The story and the diary entry suggest that Mrs. Chopin may have felt repressed in her marriage, perhaps because of an unfulfilled literary ambition, and that the success with ***Bayou Folk*** gave her a release from her frustration. What is certain is that her subsequent writings reflect an increasing self-confidence and daring.

"The Story of an Hour" was refused by Richard Watson Gilder of the *Century,* no doubt because he felt it lacked "ethical value," as he expressed it in connection with another tale she submitted. The reason why editors now turned down a number of her stories was very likely that her women became more passionate and emancipated. The heroine of **"Two Portraits,"** for example, insists on giving herself "when and where she chooses." When ***A Night in Acadie,*** Mrs. Chopin's second collection, was published in Chicago in November, 1897, it received less notice than its predecessor. The critics again praised her art, but they objected to "coarsenesses" in the book and to its sensuous ambiance. While these reviews appeared, the author was completing ***The Awakening,*** her masterpiece.

By 1897, Kate Chopin had written three novels and nearly a hundred stories and sketches. A large number of her works are set in Natchitoches, which she made her special literary province, and inevitably they have many traits in common with the local color literature of her time. Discreetly, yet forcefully, she evokes her particular locality with the enchanting Cane River atmosphere, the quaint idioms, and the charming idiosyncrasies of the Natchitoches people. But though she concentrated on what was then a distant, exotic community, she never emphasized the strange or remote; and though, like George W. Cable and Grace King, she commanded a wealth of local material, she did not join them in focusing on old Creole days. She was concerned with the living present rather than the past,

Oscar Chopin at the time of his marriage. Missouri Historical Society, C-76-001-000863.

with universal rather than regional aspects of life, and the fact that she gave only a few early stories to certain Southern issues which necessarily affected her suggests that she wanted to free her mind of them and move on to more timeless or immutable matters.

When Kate Chopin dealt with such problems as slavery, miscegenation, and integration, she concentrated on the psychology of the individual rather than the social issue as such. If she exposes the institution of slavery in **"La Belle Zoraïde,"** she does so only indirectly as she depicts the pride of a woman who forbids her mulatto slave girl to marry a Negro. Likewise, the subject is pride rather than race when Mrs. Chopin treats mixed marriage in her best-known story, **"Désirée's Baby,"** and when she treats segregation in **"A Little Free-Mulatto."**

Regarding the author's own attitudes, we may perhaps say there are indications that she condemns slavery in **"La Belle Zoraïde"**; belittles desegregation in the tale **"In and Out of Old Natchitoches"**; reflects the sentimentality of her time about devoted former slaves in **"Nég Créol"**; and suggests in **"Ma'ame Pélagie"** that the legend of the glorious Southern past should be discarded. But even in these stories, she is so much an author interested in human characteristics rather than issues or races, so much a detached observer that her own views never impose themselves upon the reader.

She undoubtedly had her own set of social values, but though they were often at variance with those of the ruthless, money-making Gilded Age, she never preached or advocated any change. Thus we find that her one story which might deserve the term of social criticism, **"Miss McEnders,"** shows the awakening of a moral reformer to the rottenness in her own family.

The literary precepts of the Gilded Age were more of a challenge to her. While the influential Richard Watson Gilder, for example, felt that fiction should be pleasant and avoid the horrifying, the indelicate, or the immoral, Mrs. Chopin wrote in her first novel about murder, drunkenness, and infidelity. Her women particularly were objectionable to the editors. Her very first, Paula Von Stoltz of **"Wiser Than a God,"** refuses the "labor of loving" which a man wants to impose upon her, and becomes instead a famous pianist. In thus opposing the traditional female duties and limitations, she has not a little of what Simone de Beauvoir in *Le Deuxième Sexe* terms the "emancipated woman," that is, a female who insists on the active transcendence of a subject rather than the passive immanence of an object, on an existentialist authenticity obtained through exerting a conscious choice, giving her own laws, and making herself her own destiny. Mildred Orme of **"A Shameful Affair"** is another illustration of this type; she rejects the role of the passive, innocent party who makes no advances in sexual relations and demands instead the responsiblity of an active subject.

The new force which was freed in Kate Chopin through the success of ***Bayou Folk*** is seen particularly in her heroines who live out their strong impulses. She saw and understood all aspects of the female psyche, and her particular interest was woman's awakening to her true nature, whether traditional, emancipated, or a mixture of the two. In **"Regret"** she describes how the middle-aged Mamzelle Aurélie all of a sudden realizes what she has missed by not having children. The heroine of **"Athénaïse"** is an example of the young woman who marries before she is ready; she runs away, but Cazeau, her husband, fetches her back. On the way they pass a "solitary oak-tree, with its seemingly immutable outlines, that had been a landmark for ages," and Cazeau suddenly recalls how his father had recaptured Gabe, a runaway slave, near this spot. Athénaïse runs away again, but only to hurry back to her husband when she realizes that she is bearing his child; as the song comes to the bird, she is now awakened to motherhood and passionate wifehood.

In spite of its "happy ending," this tale is on a deeper level a protest against woman's condition. Athénaïse's "realization of the futility of rebellion against a social and sacred institution" is supported by the story's subtle symbolism. Cazeau's name stands for the *casa* or chateau in which woman lives her hemmed-in existence, and his stern manner and jangling spur stand for the authority which forces her to submission. Athénaïse is indirectly compared to a slave; Gabe then represents the Archangel Gabriel, the herald of pregnancy; and the oak tree represents marriage and motherhood, woman's immutable destiny which makes her the tree of life.

Kate Chopin returned to this subject in ***The Awakening,*** her most profound treatment of the fundamental problem of what it means to be a woman. The novel has much in common with *Madame Bovary* and with Maupassant's "Réveil," a story which relates how Mme. Vasseur, the heroine, is caught in the romantic syndrome of the supposedly great, noble, undivided, transcendent love, and, like the other two heroines, is seduced by a rake after the departure of the more decent young man who has stirred her.

The crucial point is how this event affects the three women. Emma Bovary, of course, continues her self-dramatization, trying to conform to models and gaining little insight into her own nature as she more and more frenetically attempts to escape her dull environment. Mme. Vasseur, on the other hand, perceives that she had never loved the young man except in a dream from which the roué had awakened her, and she returns to a submissive, disappointed respectability with her husband. Edna, meanwhile, has awakened in full to an imperative craving for sex, for independence, and for clarity and self-knowledge; for her, all return to past submission and all continuation of self-delusion is impossible. Instead of blaming the rake as Mme. Vasseur does, she accepts her animalism, feeling neither shame nor remorse. She realizes that sex is largely independent of our volition.

Just as Edna makes no attempt to suppress her sexual desire, she does not hesitate to throw off her traditional duties towards her family. She realizes she is unable to live as the inessential adjunct to man, as the object over which man rules. "I give myself where I choose," she declares when Robert, her young man, suggests he might ask her husband to set her free. What she craves is to be an independent subject, to dictate her own destiny. "I would give up the inessential," she observes. "I would give my money, I would give my life for my children; but I wouldn't give myself." In other words, it is less important for her to live than to have a self, to be able to exert a conscious choice which can bring out her own essence.

Edna thus believes that she can direct her own life. But she comes to acknowledge a responsibility towards her children to spare them the stigma her kind of life would attach to them. Seeing that we are pawns in the hands of procreational nature, and how patriarchal society condemns particularly a freedom-seeking woman who neglects her children, she inevitably finds her power to dictate her own life to be illusory. Wanting her own way at all cost, she chooses the supreme exertion of her freedom: she takes her own life.

Mrs. Pontellier's defeat lies in the fact that she cannot integrate her demands with those of society; her victory is her awakening to consciousness and authenticity. Earlier, she had "wanted to swim far out, where no woman has swum before." Now she swims to her death, thinking of the clanging spurs of an officer who had attracted her, the emblem of male dominance, and of the bees humming among the pinks, the symbol of procreation. Nature and man dictate the life of the woman, and independence is much harder to obtain and much more of a curse for her than for the man, because she is handicapped by biology and because she must justify an untraditional existence against the heaviest possible odds.

The fable **"Emancipation"** suggests that Kate O'Flaherty may have hoped to live an expansive life not unlike that of some of her later heroines, and a friend of hers observed that she might have developed earlier as a writer, had her environment been different. According to all accounts, she was a perfect wife and mother; under the surface, however—and even unknown to herself, as we see in the poem **"The Haunted Chamber"**—she identified deeply with Edna Pontellier. (pp. 24-9)

[**"The Storm"**] is a first-rate short story, and so daring that she never tried to publish it. That she here deals with sex even more unreservedly than Flaubert or Zola is only a minor point compared to the fact that she depicted it as "happy"—not frantic as it is in parts of *Madame Bovary* or destructive as in *Nana,* but as something as natural and beautiful as life itself. There is a cosmic exuberance and a mystic contact with the elements in **"The Storm"** which, together with its frankness, foreshadow D. H. Lawrence.

Another important aspect of this story is that Kate Chopin is able to treat the most crucial of relationships between man and woman entirely without bias. Even in her emancipationist writings there is no misandry and no suggestion that either sex is superior to the other; and now, with the female protest of ***The Awakening*** off her mind and fame within her reach, she shows no slightest trace of being a woman "at war with her lot," as Virginia Woolf expressed it in *A Room of One's Own.* **"The Storm"** is the detached and objective story of a female author who does not write consciously as a woman, who has reached that "freedom" and "peace" which Mrs. Woolf saw as necessary if the genius of an authoress is to be "expressed whole and entire." (pp. 29-30)

In **"Charlie,"** a story written at this time, she can be seen as taking revenge on the males who had killed her creativity when she—in her only example of emasculation—dismembers the father who forbids his daughter to act the role of a man. (p. 30)

Mrs. Chopin's significance lies in her artistry, which already in 1894 was compared to that of Maupassant, and in her daring treatment of vital subjects, in which she was decades ahead of her time.

She took her writing seriously. Not depending on it for a living, she wrote as she pleased, jealously guarding her literary integrity in form and subject. She was a spontaneous storyteller, and she insisted that a tale should write itself "without any perceptible effort on . . . [her] part." She put no word on paper until the story had come to her complete. Then she wrote it down very rapidly. Preferring, in her own words, "the integrity of crudities to artificialities," she made only a few, insignificant changes before offering a story for publication. As a result of her refusal to revise, her stories are occasionally marred by awkward language or improbable coincidences, and though the last sentence of such a story as **"Désirée's Baby"** has a poignancy unsurpassed by Maupassant, it is nevertheless a trick ending.

But what she lost in this way, she gained in freshness of feeling and perception, and she had such an intuitive sense of the artistic that her stories occasionally came to her in a form as finished as that of the French master. Her art is a living thing, as effortless and natural as breathing. Emphasizing character rather than plot, she centers on a small event, takes us right into the story, and develops it logically towards an inevitable conclusion. She achieves her effects through her insight into character, her sense of form, her lucid and precise language, and her light touch. The story **"Regret"** is a perfect illustration of these qualities and of how she could pack a whole drama into a few, unemphatic last lines. It also shows her Gallic simplicity and economy of means, her unobtrusive humor, and the sympathy and intensity she hid behind her restraint and objectivity.

At Fault, her first novel, was written before she was ready for this longer form of fiction. One reason for her writing it was that she had to get her irritation with moral reformers out of her system. This explains in part the artificiality of the plot, the occasionally stilted language, and the woodenness of the central characters. On the other hand, many of the supporting figures—such as the impetuous Grégoire and the worldly Aunt Belindy—are true to life and fully convincing, and a number of scenes are effectively realized.

When Kate Chopin came to ***The Awakening,*** she was in complete command of her art. Form and content are organically fused. The book is a grand orchestration of the symphony of imperative Eros, in which the theme of sex and procreation is played off against that of illusions about love and independence. Hardly a word or a picture is accidental; nothing unessential is included. Man and nature form a continuum of union and solitude, with the sea as the central symbol of Eros and self-assertion. The symbolism of the supporting pairs of lovers is a little too heavy, and certain expressions are mannered, but otherwise the book is a great literary achievement. The author's easy, graceful, and clear style is a perfect vehicle for the unsparing and deeply moving emotional truth. (pp. 31-2)

[Kate Chopin] was the first woman writer in America to accept sex with its profound repercussions as a legitimate subject for serious fiction. In her attitude towards passion, she represented a healthy, matter-of-fact acceptance of the whole of man. She was familiar with the newest developments in science and in world literature, and her aim was to describe—unhampered by tradition and authority—man's immutable impulses. Because she was vigorous, intelligent, and eminently sane, and because her background had made her morally tolerant and socially secure, she could write with a balance and maturity, a warmth and humor not often found in her contemporaries.

Mrs. Chopin was influenced by the feminism of Madame de Staël and George Sand and the realism of Flaubert and Maupassant. Yet she is independent and original. She turns to aspects of the feminine condition which were taboo to the two women and of little interest to the two men, even introducing an existentialist philosophy with foreshadows Simone de Beauvoir. Though she describes many women who are perfectly happy in conventional marriage, she has a number of heroines who demand freedom and an authentic existence. But, as certain of her stories show, she saw at the same time the idea of male supremacy and female submission as so ingrained that women may never achieve emancipation in the very deepest sense. Furthermore, she also looked beyond this emancipation, and there she saw the horror of an unsupported freedom. This, and her awareness of how the woman in particular is a toy in the hands of nature's procreational imperative, lend a note of despair to such a work as ***The Awakening.***

The basic pessimism and the ruthless honesty of this novel unite Kate Chopin more closely with Theodore Dreiser than with any other of the contemporary American writers. These two authors, who both came from Catholic, non-Anglo-Saxon backgrounds, are alike in taking man as the given, the unimprovable. There is a fundamental seriousness and lack of all moralism in ***The Awakening*** and *Sister Carrie* which sets them off from such works as *Maggie: A Girl of the Streets,* Stephen Crane's stereotype seduction story, and *Rose of Dutcher's Coolly,* Hamlin Garland's ethical emancipationist novel. Edna's and Carrie's violations of man's arbitrary code of morals are given without shame or apology; the unillusioned, unidealistic authors present no villains—except the chimeras pursued by their heroines.

Carrie's universality lies in her irresistible fight to get ahead in society, and Dreiser affronted America by glorifying his heroine and letting her succeed in spite of her amorality. Edna, too, has a universal quality in her open-eyed choice to defy illusions and to question the sacredness of morals. Though apparently a loser, she wins an inner victory of knowledge and of authenticity which Carrie—who so often mimics those one step above her on the ladder—can never achieve for all her outer success.

Kate Chopin had no noticeable influence on other American writers. It is doubtful that she was read by Dreiser, for example, even though he started *Sister Carrie* just when ***The Awakening*** was being condemned, or by Ellen Glasgow, who was just beginning to describe unsatisfactory marriages. Had she, like Crane or Norris, been backed by the influential William Dean Howells, or had her novel been put on trial like *Madame Bovary* or *Lady Chatterley's Lover,* she might not only have gained lasting fame, but also have been inspired further to unfold her creative powers.

She was too much of a pioneer to be accepted in her time and place. She had a daring and a vision all her own, a unique combination of realism and pessimism applied to woman's immutable condition. Adverse criticism and early death stopped her from delving as deeply as she could have done into the psychology of her women. But as it is, her best writings are minor masterpieces. They demonstrate an independence and courage, a warm understanding, and more than a touch of artistic genius which entitle them, and their author, to a permanent place in American literature. (pp. 32-3)

Per Seyersted, in an introduction to The Complete Works of Kate Chopin, Vol. I *by Kate Chopin, edited by Per Seyersted, Louisiana State University Press, 1969, pp. 21-33.*

ROBERT D. ARNER (essay date 1970)

[*In the following excerpt, Arner compares the romantic story* "At the 'Cadian Ball" *to the more realistic story* "The Storm," *which was written as a sequel. Arner considers the poetic, realistic rendering of adulterous passion in* "The Storm" *remarkable for its day and unsurpassed by similar treatments in the works of D. H. Lawrence, Ernest Hemingway, and others.*]

Although Kate Chopin began her literary career primarily as a writer of local color stories and sketches, she was soon moving in the direction of a realism more profound than that implied by a simple fidelity to regional idiosyncracies, habits of dress, and speech mannerisms. As early as October, 1894, in a review of Hamlin Garland's *Crumbling Idols* she had publicly rejected "social problems, social environments, local color and the rest of it" as "not of themselves motives to insure the survival of a writer who employs them." She would have agreed with Faulkner that enduring fiction arises only out of the human heart in conflict with itself—the elemental, primitive passions. Yet intention is not always achievement, and eight months earlier in the same year during which she made this statement, her first volume of short stories, ***Bayou Folk,*** was published. The title reveals the local color qualities of the book better than any summary of the contents could. Mrs. Chopin had not yet discovered her individual, artistic voice, and though some of the stories in ***Bayou Folk*** promise better things to come, they are on balance not rewarding reading. Had Kate Chopin written no more than the stories that are in this volume or had she continued to write solely in this vein, she would be today no more than a literary curiosity instead of an important (though badly neglected) minor writer.

The technique Mrs. Chopin seems to have employed to write many of the stories in ***Bayou Folk*** was to superimpose romantic and sentimentally slick situations upon rustic, back-country characters, interspersing a few references to local customs along the way. The dangers and limitations of this sort of procedure are several; besides an obvious insincerity, they include the creation in the reader of the sense that the author is exploiting her material for the sake of "the quaintness of it all," as Larzer Ziff phrased it [see *TCLC,* Vol. 5]. Further, it is a technique which threatens structure, since at any moment the local color aspects of the work are likely to assume dominance at the expense of plot and narrative movement. These are pitfalls into which Mrs. Chopin frequently stumbles, though not as frequently as some of her contemporaries, and they destroy a good deal of the value of her stories for the modern critical reader.

Some of these objections might be raised, for example, against the story entitled **"At the 'Cadian Ball,"** which I have chosen to discuss . . . both because it is fairly typical of Mrs. Chopin's early work and because, four years later, she wrote a sequel to it, **"The Storm,"** which is among the best and most interesting of her tales. In a negative way, then, **"At the 'Cadian Ball"** provides us with a convenient yardstick with which to measure Mrs. Chopin's development away from slickness and local color sentimentalism toward genuine realism. It is the story of Bobinôt, a young Creole who is in love with Calixta, a "little Spanish vixen," and of Alcée Laballiere, a planter who is attracted to his cousin Clarisse (marriage among cousins was common practice in Creole and Acadian Louisiana). (p. 1)

The portraits of Clarisse and Calixta are in the best tradition of local color literature. (p. 2)

According to [the formula for the conventional Southern heroine in past-Civil War fiction], it appears that Calixta's marriage to Bobinôt is a kind of self-inflicted penance for her past behavior; she cannot have Alcée, who is taken from her by a woman who comes with a fabricated story (which, however, has a symbolic appropriateness) about his being needed at home. Since so much of the rest of the story has gone according to convention, the reader easily imagines that Calixta will in time be tamed by marriage and the later responsibilities of being a mother. The only unconventional aspect of the work is the mildly disturbing information that a young girl might take so drastic a step as getting married out of chagrin at being spurned, and even this idea is presented in a context that makes it seem more like poetic justice than like realism. Calixta gets what she deserves for her vixenishness. Had she been a "good" girl, she might have married the prosperous and socially prominent planter, but as it is she must settle for the poorer and less esteemed Bobinôt. Considered by itself and without the information supplied by its sequel, **"At the 'Cadian Ball"** upholds conventional morality and the middle class notion of conjugal love. It says nothing that might offend the general public or be considered a lapse of taste.

The story is conventional in still another way, this time in a fashion that links it to numerous other works closer than itself to the mainstream of American literature. In spurning the full-bodied, full-blooded female Calixta in favor of the more pallid and virginal Clarisse, Alcée Laballiere joins the ranks of other American heroes—in Cooper's, Poe's, Hawthorne's, Melville's, James', Hemingway's, and Faulkner's fiction—who have made the same choice. These characters are typically American, regardless of what their national origins might be, in that they see the woman both as pure maiden and sinister siren and, although invariably attracted to the latter, they just as invariably choose the former. For them woman becomes the embodiment of civilization, the marital union (minus a satisfying sexual relationship) their surest path to salvation from their own baser instincts as well as the ideal of all earthly happiness. Woman stands for hearth, cottage, home, for stability and permanence opposed to the psychological world of the libido where everything is in pieces and all coherence is gone. Alcée projects our national ambivalence toward women and sex, but if this tends to establish his native Americanism (in spite of his French name), it also demonstrates his connection with the heroes of our popular sentimental fiction—our westerns and our detective stories particularly—for whom sexual fulfillment is forbidden and, even (they would have us believe), undesired.

This interpretation of Alcée's choice perhaps turns up unsuspected levels of complexity in what at first appears to be a superficial story, but the fact is that the story remains essentially superficial. Alcée does not choose Clarisse over Calixta for any reasons other than that the convention somehow demands it; no psychological insights into his motives are offered. Neither he nor Mrs. Chopin seem to be aware of any sexual ambivalence on his part. What we have in **"At the 'Cadian Ball"** is a sentimental debasement of a symbolic dichotomy that, in the hands of a Hawthorne or a Melville, was capable of enormous vitality. . . . The prototype of the passionate love story in our literature is Hawthorne's *The Scarlet Letter,* in which adultery takes place before the book ever begins and which is really a novel about the effects of guilt rather than a story about the sin itself.

In such an unhealthy fictional sexual climate, with the painful repressions of Hawthorne on the one hand and the tawdriness of sentimentalism and sensationalism on the other (the Harold Robbins School), it is rare indeed that the reader of American literature gets a breath of fresh air. Even Mrs. Chopin's duly praised ***The Awakening*** resembles *The Scarlet Letter* in one important particular: that its protagonist, Edna Pontellier, is a Presbyterian influenced by, though not obsessed with, a sense of guilt for her sexual adventures. She feels no shame or remorse, Mrs. Chopin tells us, but neither does Hester Prynne. . . . I do not wish to discount, of course, the achievement of Mrs. Chopin's fine novel, which is far more complex than I have indicated and which is significantly different from *The Scarlet Letter* in more ways than it resembles it, but simply to point out that even in this book—perhaps the least inhibited and most honest treatment of heterosexual relationships to be written in America before the twentieth century—sexual fulfillment still carries a price which in important ways has been fixed by the religious and moral establishment.

The heroine of **"The Storm,"** however, which according to a notation on the manuscript in possession of the library of the Missouri Historical Society was written in December of 1898, is not Presbyterian but Roman Catholic, and the difference is decisive. The easy sexual ambience associated with Calixta's Spanish origins comes into play and determines the vast difference between the denouement of the novel and of the story. Mrs. Chopin subtitles **"The Storm," "A Sequel to the 'Cadian Ball,"** but it seems unlikely that she had its plot in mind when she wrote the earlier tale. It is more probable that a rereading of the first story exposed its superficiality and prompted a reconsideration. Mrs. Chopin knew that marriage does not automatically lead to fulfillment and that, in fact, the notion of conjugal love is often inimical to the development and gratification of the female partner. It counsels unions more for social expediency than for love, sanctioning marriage as a necessary outlet for male sexual aggressiveness and as a basis for permanence and stability in society. (pp. 2-3)

The title [**"The Storm"**] has a double reference: first, to a fierce and sudden summer thundershower which, by trapping Bobinôt and his four-year old son in town for an afternoon, is instrumental in brewing an inner tempest—the second storm—in the breasts of Alcée and Calixta and in giving them the opportunity for release. The same storm which imprisons Bobinôt in the village drives Alcée to seek shelter with Calixta, whom he has not seen since the events described in **"At the 'Cadian Ball,"** but for whom he finds his ardor has not cooled. She responds to him, and soon they are in each other's arms. . . .

Few serious American writers, even now, try to describe the physical act of love, and most of those attempts fail for being too literary; one thinks with embarrassment of the scenes in Hemingway's *For Whom the Bell Tolls* and "Fathers and Sons." Adulterous passion is taboo. To quote [Leslie] Fiedler . . . , "Adultery is regarded with horror by the American bourgeois and the classic American novelist alike . . . ; by most of our writers it is not really regarded at all, only ignored at the prompting of a largely unconscious self-censorship." When we reflect that this story was written during the height of the genteel era in American fiction, these passages seem all the more remarkable. What, one wonders, would Howells' twelve-year old maiden have thought of them?

It is not only the matter of these paragraphs which is remarkable, however, but also the manner. Their poetic quality is extraordinary. Mrs. Chopin wishes to capture the transcendent nature of the experience, as is evidenced stylistically by the proliferation of similes and of other figures of speech. The image of the flame, which stands for both life and penetration, is used to underscore the fact that this is a rare union indeed; both male and female are penetrated, both penetrate. Metaphorically, sexes are reversed and finally cease to matter: two have become one. But good poetry should not be too explicit, and Mrs. Chopin shows a fine sense of what should be left out; she truly knows what she is talking about, as Hemingway would have said, and her omissions are filled in by the reader. To say too little would be to be dishonest about a very intense and honest moment; to say too much would be to lend her description a theoretical cast which would reduce it to unreality, a fantasy of the sort that most of the descriptions in *Fanny Hill* are. It is no mean achievement to convey successfully the religious and mystical quality of sexual ecstasy—not to be told that the earth moves under a pair of lovers, but to feel the foundations shaking for ourselves.

There is one final pleasant surprise in store for the modern reader, one final shock to the sensibilities of Howells' hypothetical maiden. When Bobinôt returns home expecting to be scolded because his clothes are muddy, he finds Calixta in a wonderfully happy mood; she treats him royally, and he is pleased and delighted. Alcée, for his part, writes to his wife, who is visiting her parents, informing her that if she wishes she may remain with them longer. Clarisse welcomes the news, for she is secretly repelled by the realities of marriage, especially by sexual intimacy. The last line in the story, as in all good stories, is the punch line: "So the storm passed and everyone was happy." After adultery, they all lived happily ever after! There is no weeping, no wringing of hands, no promising of fresh starts after the event. What Alcée and Calixta have shared really does have a consecration of its own, a consecration which Mrs. Chopin, unlike Hawthorne, accepts. No other so firmly establishes her claim to our attention as a pioneering realist. "To be an artist includes much," Mademoiselle Reisz, the gifted pianist in ***The Awakening*** tells Edna Pontellier; "one must possess many gifts—absolute gifts—which have not been acquired by one's own effort. And, moreover, to succeed, the artist must possess the courageous soul. . . . The soul that dares and defies." She might have been talking about Kate Chopin. (pp. 3-4)

Robert D. Arner, "Kate Chopin's Realism: 'At the 'Cadian Ball' and 'The Storm'," in The Markham Review, *Vol. 2, No. 2, February, 1970, pp. 1-4.*

ROBERT D. ARNER (essay date 1970)

[In the following excerpt, Arner discusses Chopin's early novel At Fault. *He argues that while earlier critics consider the work structurally weak, the central theme, which examines the relationship between the past and the present, is supported by the use of Southern history, racial and class differences, and nature imagery, giving it overall coherence. Arner contends that the novel should not be compared to* The Awakening, *and that it more closely resembles the works of the twentieth-century novelist William Faulkner.]*

In the recent awakening of interest in Kate Chopin's fiction, very little attention has been paid to her first novel, ***At Fault***. . . . Reading it, one discovers not so much adumbrations of ***The Awakening*** as foreshadowing of William Faulkner.

Two tales of love are interwoven in ***At Fault,*** one of which ends happily (though only after much misfortune), the other violently and disastrously. In the first of these plots, David Hosmer, a Northern capitalist, falls in love with Thérese Lafirme, a widowed Louisiana lady. . . . Thérese is on the point of acknowledging her love for him when she learns from his sister, Melicent, that he has previously been married and divorced from a woman who, under the pressures of their disintegrating relationship, had become an alcoholic. Thérese, a Roman Catholic, finds Hosmer's divorce less distressing (she says) than the fact that he has not had the courage to tell her of it himself. . . . Realizing that he cannot hope to win Thérese's hand as things now stand and stung by her interpretation of his behavior, Hosmer inflicts penance on himself by re-marrying his former wife, Fanny Larrimore. . . . One rainy day she runs away from Hosmer, who finds her in a shack owned by an old Negress, Marie Louise, which is perched precariously on a point of land jutting into the raging and swollen Cane River. She is drunk and refuses to leave with her husband. Halfway across the river on the flatboat ferry, fighting the current, Hosmer hears a shriek and turns around to see the cabin . . . slip into the water. In an attempt to save his wife, Hosmer dives into the flooding river but is struck on the head by a floating log. When he finally revives, it is to learn that Fanny has drowned. After a decent lapse of time, he and Thérese, who has had second thoughts on the subjects of cowardice and divorce, are married, though the scar remains on Hosmer's head and, like Hester's scarlet letter, serves as a reminder of his unhappy past. (pp. 142-44)

The second love story centers aroung Grégoire Santien, Thérese's nephew, and Hosmer's sister Melicent. Grégoire falls in love rapidly and passionately, but Melicent, portrayed as a superficial society belle, does not reciprocate, though she finally manages to persuade herself temporarily that she is in love with him. At the same time, glorying in her stoic acceptance of the relentless fate which she romantically imagines pursues her, she recognizes that nothing can come of the affair. . . . The final blow to their deteriorating relationship is delivered when Grégoire kills a man, the half-Indian, half-Negro Jocint, for burning down Hosmer's sawmill; Melicent, appalled by Grégoire's brutality, refuses to have anything further to do with him. . . . [Grégoire] rides off toward Texas, where he is shot and killed in an angry quarrel with a Texas colonel who had called him "Frenchy." Melicent receives the news of his death on a day which has been particularly boring and she welcomes the opportunity to put on mourning since it promises some relief from ennui and a chance to be mysterious about the object of her "sorrow." Melicent is one of the earliest examples of Kate Chopin's fiction of a type and class of women whose shallowness continued to draw her scorn and contempt throughout her career.

These two love stories do not appear to converge thematically, and this is perhaps the chief reason why most unfavorable criticism of the novel has been directed at its structure. To the casual eye, it is likely to seem as though Mrs. Chopin is relying entirely upon the family relationships of the characters to establish connections between the plot and the subplot. In fact, though, it is not merely the simple contrast between Théresé's fortune and her nephew's misfortune which makes the subplot an effective sounding board for the action presented in the main line of the narrative. In terms of the symbolic tensions set up in the book, Grégoire dies because he is dominated by the past, specifically by the Southern racial guilt which provoked the violence of the Civil War; he lives wholly in its shadow. Melicent, in contrast, is a creature of the present, seeking one stimulating experience after the other and never satisfied for long by anything life has to offer. Past and present can, in Grégoire's and Melicent's relationship, effect no union. But Théresé comes in the course of the action to accept the responsibilities and realities of the present, at the same time preserving certain traditions and institutions as a source of stability and time-tested values around which she can organize her life and with which she can give the present moment meaning.

The theme which gives coherence to the novel, then, and which ultimately provides the imaginative framework within which to interpret the marriage of Hosmer and Théresé had to do with the ideas of change and resistance to change. One important manifestation of this theme involves a contrast between an idyllic, pastoral landscape—representing typically order, coherence, tradition, and the past—and the landscape as altered by technology. Mrs. Chopin's description of the Place-du-Bois plantation employs pastoral rhetoric to evoke an image of Louisiana in general and the plantation in particular as an orderly fecund garden untouched by the ravages of the Civil War. . . . (pp. 144-45)

As the owner of the plantation, [Théresé] has brought the land under control and cultivation, so that its orderliness may be taken as a projection of her personality into the world of nature, a metaphoric analogue for her own vision of life. She re-makes the landscape in her own image. The ominous undertones suggested by the wilderness—the sluggish bayou, the untamable river—at the borders of this garden are for the moment forgotten in a celebration of harmony between man and nature. In Théresé's eyes at least, the cultivated ground stands for the viability and the vitality of pre-Civil War agrarianism, for a retreat from the reality of time and history into an imaginative realm where nature is immutable and the old way of life is preserved intact. She gives ground only grudgingly to progress and, when she can help it, not at all. Thus when she builds a new plantation house after financial pressures force her to sell the old one to a railroad company, the house she designs represents her refusal to capitulate entirely to the presence of the present. "In building," says Mrs. Chopin, "she avoided the temptations offered by modern architectural innovations, and clung to the simplicity of large rooms and broad verandas: a style whose merits had stood the test of easy-going and comfort-loving generations." (p. 146)

The simplicity of life in this pastoral setting is directly associated with Théresé's ideas concerning divorce and marriage. Her refusal to admit change or disorder into her external world corresponds to her refusal to acknowledge that moral values and, specifically, the rules governing divorce and marriage may not be the closed and absolute systems she imagines. Altered external conditions would, in fact, argue that inner "realities" must change as well to keep pace with the outer world of reality, and thus in attempting to deny one type of change, Théresé is attempting to deny both. As the cultivated landscape represents stability in the world of nature, so marriage represents social permanence of a kind. (pp. 146-47)

But nature in ***At Fault*** does not represent permanence in the way that Théresé imagines it does. For the term comprehends not only cultivated gardens, but also uncultivated wildernesses, flooding rivers, and for this reason has a more complicated meaning than Théresé is aware of. It embodies the principle of gradual, evolutionary change, the assimilation of alterations forced by the dynamics of geology as by the dynamics of history in the affairs of men. The Cane River, which is constantly encroaching on the land, carving new channels for itself and thus transforming the face of nature, is the master symbol of this type of change. The slow transformation of the landscape, in fact, in a very real way brings about the resolution of the Fanny-David-Théresé triangle, and in a context that leaves little doubt as to what Mrs. Chopin intends the erosion of the land by the river to symbolize. Months before the river floods and sweeps away Marie Louise, Fanny, and the cabin, Théresé pays a visit to the old Negress and insists upon moving the hut away from the water's edge. But Marie Louise reminds her that only a short time before, the cabin was moved to what everyone imagined was a safe distance; yet here the river is again. She will not move anymore. She knows that change, decomposition, and death are part of the natural rhythm of things, and unlike Théresé, who at this point still resists all change, she attempts to live in harmony with total nature. In this way, the novel implies that Théresé's unwillingness to break from the past and her inability to accept the legitimacy of the human need for divorce are in some oblique way connected with the same narrowness of vision that can see only one side of nature, the pastoral, pleasant side. (pp. 147-48)

Théresé's marriage to Hosmer, then, is a union of the past with the present and the future. Symbolically interpreted, it is a wedding of South and North, agrarianism and industrialism, pastoralism and history, tradition and innovation. ***At Fault*** is one of many American novels of this period which depict in their marriage of a Southern and Northern protagonist the binding up of the nation's wounds that Lincoln had hoped to see. The South, as the land of the past, becomes the symbolic repository of human values and ideals and the emblem of an elegant, graceful style of life; the North stands for technological progress and for changes too rapid to be assimilated by a people cut loose entirely from their traditions. Thus to the newly united nation the South supplied order and permanence, the North energy and capital—precisely what Théresé and Hosmer each brings to their marriage. The result is the counterbalance of forces which makes for the same kind of gradual evolutionary change that is fundamental to the rhythms of nature as represented by Marie Louise and Cane River. When Thérésé is ready to accept Hosmer, she is also ready to accept the realities of the present moment and—although the novel does not dramatize this—presumably to move slowly from her agrarianism to Hosmer's industrialism, preserving only what is essential in the past. She can move, in short, from a romantic view of the world, with all that implies so far as attitudes toward the past, toward nature, and toward marriage are concerned, to a realistic one that also sees the past as one of "pain and sin and trouble."

One of the sins lurking in the past is the sin of slavery, and although its black shadow does not exert its influence on the outcome of Thérésé's affair with Hosmer, it is indirectly instrumental in forcing a conclusion to Grégoire's and Melicent's deteriorating romance. We are introduced to the couple as they paddle in a pirogue, the Acadian equivalent of the canoe famous as the scene of greatest intimacy and romantic happiness. But the image turns out to be ironic. We are not in a garden of love paddling down some quiet stream with the moon of June shining over the heads of the lovers, but in a Gothic landscape rich to the point of rottenness. The bayou and the surrounding wilderness are the haunts of alligators, bats, blood-thirsty mosquitoes, and poisonous snakes. (pp. 148-49)

This is not merely an attempt at conventional Gothicism, however, nor simply a scene intended to foreshadow their eventual unhappy destiny. For the two are on a pilgrimage to the grave of Robert McFarlane, formerly the owner of the Place-du-Bois plantation . . . Local lengend has it that McFarlane's ghost "'can't rest' in his grave fur the niggas he's killed.'" Their trip becomes, then, among other things, an odyssey into the Southern past, as the imagery of decay makes clear, and metaphorically the corruption and the savagery of the bayou country are associated with McFarlane's savage brutality and inhumanity. (p. 150)

Although it is too late for the two to visit McFarlane's grave on the day of this first voyage, they do eventually make the journey. . . . Melicent picks a "blood-red" flower growing nearby and places it on the grave. Grégoire, very uncomfortable in the presence of a Southern heritage which for him is a real thing rather than a romantic fancy as it is for Melicent, urges the girl to leave. Although he does not believe in ghosts generally, he harbors a superstitious dread of McFarlane's ghost, perhaps sensing in himself some vague resemblance to McFarlane.

In light of all this talk about a ghost, it can hardly be regarded as a coincidence that the evening on which Grégoire commits the action which separates him once and for all from Melicent, the killing of the half-breed Jocint, is Toussaint's (All Hollows) Eve. McFarlane's ghost is indeed abroad in the land and it materializes as violence and racial murder. Mrs. Chopin remarks pointedly: "The night was so dark, so hushed, that if ever the dead had wished to step from their graves and take a stroll above ground, they could not have found a more fitting hour." Like Hawthorne, Mrs. Chopin is somewhat embarrassed by the idea of having to insist on the reality of spirits; yet the symbolic and historical psychology of the novel demands McFarlane's presence, and so in ambivalent language she summons him. In the woods, she says, "bats were flapping and whirling and darting hither and thither; the gliding serpent making quick rustle amid the dry, crisp leaves. . . . The stage is set for the appearance of Jocint, who, like Jim Bond in *Absalom, Absalom!,* comes as the racial outcast representing the sins of Southern history.

Jocint's reason for wishing to burn Hosmer's sawmill, where he is employed, is perhaps not fully satisfying realistically, but it has a symbolic appropriateness that is obvious. He resents the ritual of daily work at the mill; his heart is in the pine woods. He blames Thérésé for "this intrusive Industry which had come to fire the souls of indolent fathers with a greedy ambition for gain, at the sore expense of revolting youth." . . . Thérésé, who is associated with pastoral and orderly landscapes, is able to effect a compromise with the present as Jocint is not and to bring to the present the order of nature which acts as an antidote to the chaos of rootless, technological society. Her plantation represents the middle ground where nature and technological civilization meet.

Grégoire, who is guarding the mill that night, apprehends Jocint after the fire has started and without a moment's hesitation kills him. The scene that follows, with the roaring inferno of the mill as a backdrop and dark shadows flitting to and fro against the curtain of flame, is little short of apocalyptic. Jocint's father appears to claim his son's body and Mrs. Chopin enlists our sympathies on his side. Grégoire is of course not brought to trial, and in fact is not able to see how his deed merits anything but the thanks of the community; he seemed, says Mrs. Chopin, "utterly blind to the moral aspect of his deed." It was only a half-breed, after all. But Melicent is appalled and refused to speak to Grégoire after the event. She leaves for St. Louis and Grégoire goes into town, where he integrates a saloon at pistol point—an act which he vaguely imagines will cancel out his racial guilt, though he himself thinks that the only person in town good enough to drink with him is the priest. Then he heads for Texas, where he is killed in a quarrel provoked by a Texas colonel who had called him "Frenchy." With this detail, the racial theme of the novel has come full circle from the ghost of old McFarlane pursuing his ghostly slaves to the death of Grégoire, brought on because he resented a slur on his ethnic origins. "Nigger" and "Frenchy" have a lot in common after all, and in one sense at least Grégoire may be said to have slain his brother when he shot Jocint. The spirit of McFarlane stalks victims of all races. Racial guilt drives the white Southerner, Orestes-like, across the South in an effort to escape his past, only to lead him head into it.

Next to this treatment of the past and its pressure on the present, the other themes in ***At Fault*** possess only a passing interest. . . . The most interesting part of the narrative for a reader weaned on William Faulkner's myth of the South is not the union of Thérésé and Hosmer, which is after all conventional enough; it is instead the potentially tragic story of Jocint and Grégoire, two men who could not escape the consequences of Southern history. (pp. 151-53)

Robert D. Arner "Landscape Symbolism in Kate Chopin's 'At Fault'," in Louisiana Studies, *Vol. IX, No. 3, Fall, 1970, pp. 142-53.*

JAMES E. ROCKS (essay date 1972)

[In the following excerpt, Rocks argues that Chopin often reveals her own attitudes through her works, despite the effective use of an objective authorial voice. Rocks also discusses Edna Pontellier's suicide, and concludes that she is a selfish woman who can neither compromise nor control her urge for self-assertion. For other discussions about the significance of Edna Pontellier's suicide, see the excerpts by Per Seyersted (1969), James H. Justus (1978), and Carol P. Christ (1980).]

The kind of authorial objectivity that Henry James advocated in his criticism and demonstrated in his fiction is evident in most of Mrs. Chopin's writing; her early work, like ***At Fault,*** is weakened by shifts of tone and the awkward intrusion of an authorial voice—defects that become less apparent in the short stories she turned to next and that are all but completely absent from her last work, ***The Awakening***. . . . To her the artist must reveal life clearly and completely as it is, without presuming to judge the actions of his characters. Authorial impartiality is an obligation of the artist, for his personal view of reality probably has no special share of truth. However convinced he may be of his own particular capacity to know and understand, the writer must not impose his vision on his reader. The artist must be, above all, the ironist, who can distrust his own view as well as those that contrast with or oppose his own. Mrs. Chopin, as the critics have noted but not sufficiently emphasized, regards an idea or a character from a variety of aspects, never committing herself in any absolute way to the moral rightness or wrongness of the character's behavior. That a particular individual acts in a certain manner is interesting and valuable in itself, and the artist's primary responsibility is to present the character, the action and the context in such a way that they elicit the reader's understanding.

Like any important artist Mrs. Chopin held definite beliefs about the human condition that become clear from a reading of her fiction and that can be formulated into a statement of her unique vision. . . . No degree of authorial objectivity can conceal her notion that the assertion of individual freedom, particularly for the woman, carries with it the assumption of maturity and responsibility, and any reader who misses this dimension of her thought has failed to respond to her ironic vision. In order to portray as impartially as possible the varieties of human experience, Kate Chopin refused to instruct her reader, finding in the fashionable naturalists of the day, like Zola, an overemphasis on thesis, with a resultant tendency to sentimentalism. Her dislike of writers of the Romantic school and some of the local colorists was based on her reaction to these excesses. Particularly amusing, if not annoying, to her were the legions of popular women writers who manufactured plots and emotions and resolved their complications with a happy marriage or the timely death of one or both lovers. In ***At Fault,*** the simple if not witless Fanny at one point takes up "the latest novel of one of those prolific female writers who turn out their unwholesome intellectual sweets so tirelessly, to be devoured by the girls and women of the age." In literature as well as life, Kate Chopin believed (and showed humorously in the very early story, **"Miss Witherwell's Mistake"**), that one must see the world realistically and avoid the falseness and distortion of either the Romantic or the naturalistic view.

In her critical comments Mrs. Chopin defines the artist as an impressionist, not as a copyist, of reality. Employing the term "impression" as she does frequently in her criticism and utilizing the impressionistic technique in her fiction, she shows her awareness of the artist's special view of reality which is not unlike the painter's eye that mixes color, reflects light and sights perspective. Her own best work is a series of impressions, careful of detail and wonderfully evocative, possessing the qualities of the genuine, original and spontaneous that she considered essential to any successful artistic treatment. To achieve the unique and the natural in her own writing, she rarely revised, preferring, as she once wrote, "the integrity of crudities to artificialities." . . . Mrs. Chopin's insistence on originality and spontaneity were doubtless in part reactions against the pervasive traditions of nineteenth-century writing, as was her argument that fiction should not be dominated by plot. In a late piece, **"Elizabeth Stock's One Story,"** she divulges the extent to which the paramount concern for plot can hinder and puzzle the novice writer. In her own case an often rather cavalier attitude toward revision and the ordering of events into a coherent, logical and tightly structured plot at times worked against her talent in the creation of character and setting. Mrs. Chopin's least effective work, from the early ***At Fault*** to many of her later short pieces, tends to be fragmentary and loosely organized. Some of her works are a series of brief, abrupt paragraphs—many only a sentence long—that are seriously lacking in unity and almost totally absent of action. Her most famous work, **"Désirée's Baby,"** with the startling reversal of its conclusion, is, among about a half-dozen excellent short stories, unique for its emphasis on plot. In her best fiction, story, character and setting so perfectly complement one another that the reader must certainly be impressed with Kate Chopin's ability to conceive and execute a story so well. ***The Awakening*** is surely her masterpiece, for it displays her varied talents at their fullest and possesses none of the weaknesses that her belief in impressionism, her occasional indifference to plot and her advocacy of the unusual could give rise to. If she erred on the side of the spontaneous in her manner of composition, it was because she maintained the same attitude toward life as well. (pp. 111-13)

Although Mrs. Chopin is still admired for her evocation of Creole Louisiana—its character and customs and exotic natural setting—she is now recognized as a portrayer of more than merely sectional character types and idiosyncratic beliefs. Her stories can never be read profitably without a consideration of the Creole and Cajun worlds she places them in. But her achievement is far more than simply the meticulous depiction of nineteenth-century Louisiana, among whose interpreters, including Cable and Grace King, she is perhaps the most restrained and least defensive. She did not delineate her former Creole associates simply as curiosities in her fiction, but, rather, as she reveals in **"A Gentleman of Bayou Têche,"** she characterized their strengths and virtues as well as their foibles and pride.

Because Kate Chopin was interested more in the universal than the merely local or topical, she did not concern herself with an historical interpretation of Southern society. . . . Kate Chopin was never indifferent to human suffering but preferred to study it in individual cases rather than as a mass experience; she suggests the plight of the Negro in countless stories and a work like **"La Belle Zoraïde"** describes the general agonies of black slavery in the particular case of one black woman. Since Kate Chopin shared the Southern skepticism toward belief in progress, she did not examine the ideas and movements so much in vogue among writers of the time. Her one story that features a modish liberal thinker, **"Miss McEnders,"** is actually a critique of condescending, uncharitable do-gooders, blind to their own hypocrisy and the evil at their very doorstep. Miss McEnders' attitude of charity exists only as an abstraction, and like most Southerners Kate Chopin had a strong disfavor of abstraction. Her writings assume that man is basically the same now as he has been in the past, despite the disruptions and changes wrought by history.

Because Mrs. Chopin sees the continuity of man's past, she takes as her themes universal human experiences; and because she will not accept absolutist judgments concerning behavior, she treats a variety of viewpoints and sentiments. Her fiction—in individual pieces and as a whole—presents contrasting or opposing ideas, characters and situations and at times creates a kind of dialectic, with each side persuasive and insistent. The subtlety of her craft and her vision is in the tone of irony she imparts to the depiction of any person whose belief or action becomes selfish or overly contentious. Frequently this irony is very fine and offhand (in contrast to the blatant irony of circumstance in the plot reversals of some of her stories), and the reader who is not familiar with a number of her works and who thus has small knowledge of her prevalent themes and attitudes will often miss both the playful and serious irony directed against even her most apparently estimable characters. Because Kate Chopin is an ironist, she gives to her interpretation of the nature, meaning and evaluation of human experience, the continual subject of her exploration into the enigmatic heart of mankind, ample nuance and considerable sophistication.

In all of her fiction she examines the consequences of action and the revelation of new awareness (her principal metaphor is, of course, the adventure of awakening and discovery). Her fiction anticipates that of Joyce, for example, in her use of the technique of the epiphany; most of her stories and the two novels feature moments in which a character becomes aware of the peculiarities of his predicament. These moments are generally painful, but not necessarily debasing, because with the appearance of knowledge ordinarily comes the capacity to change or cope. The one notable exception is, of course, Edna Pontellier in ***The Awakening;*** because she cannot control her desire for self-assertion (and when no one else can help her) she is driven to the ultimately selfish act of suicide. Edna's failure, the only one of such extraordinary proportions in Kate Chopin's fiction, reflects Edna's refusal to compromise, to achieve some sort of center no matter how far from the norm it might be (as it needs must be for the musician Mademoiselle Reisz). (pp. 113-15)

In her fiction Mrs. Chopin portrays the individual's need to respond fully to all aspects of life about him—the physical as well as the spiritual; both body and soul must be given rein to grow freely and in complement to each other. As in **"Two Portraits,"** one the sketch of a saint, who exalts only the soul, and the other that of a sinner, who debases the body, Mrs. Chopin indicates that neither extreme is proper or healthy; or as in **"An Idle Fellow"** or **"A Morning Walk"** she says that man must learn above all to read nature and humankind in order to recognize the harmony of his inner and outer life. In most of her stories she praises the joy of adventure and novelty (her characters frequently journey to New Orleans to discover who they are), but in many of those works she suggests by implication that although it is good to roam it is often better to remain in one's native home. . . . Freedom is no less sacred at home than it is away and the journeying to another place, as in **"The Going Away of Liza"** and **"Caline,"** might bring with it shattered illusions. In **"The Recovery"** a girl regains her eyesight and discovers that darkness was preferable to the bright light that exposes the loss of her youth. In **"Beyond the Bayou,"** one of Kate Chopin's most richly symbolic stories, the old black woman overcomes her fear of the outside and breaks the circle of her confinement to discover a new world. (p. 115)

Experience to Kate Chopin is, then, a mixture of good and evil, happiness and sadness, pleasure and pain; life is as Edna Pontellier learns, "that monster made up of beauty and brutality." . . . [In] many of her stories she describes or implies the physical cruelty and mental anguish that attend man during

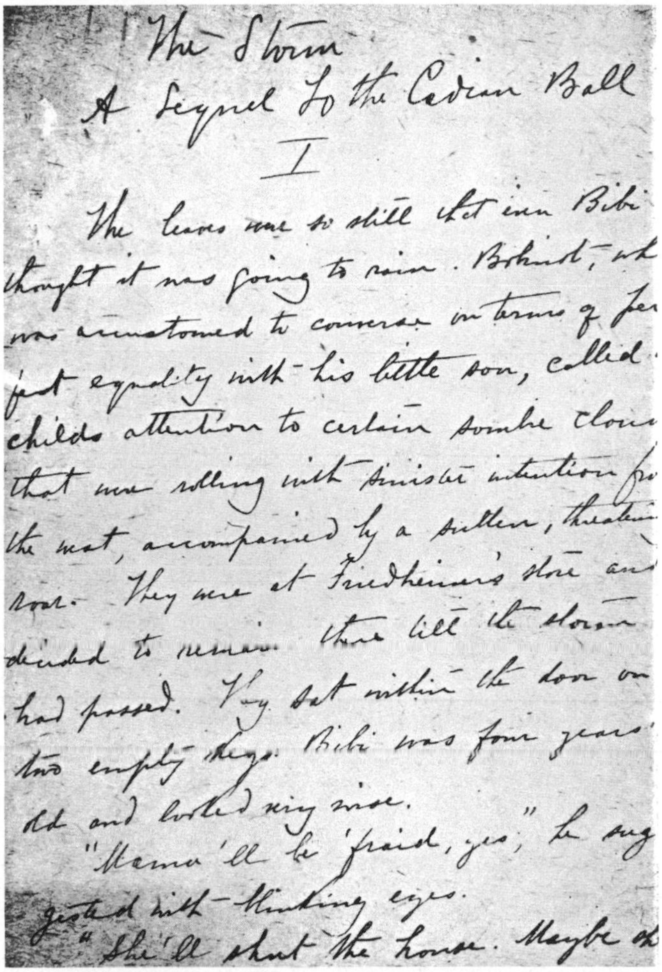
The Storm
A Sequel to the 'Cadian Ball
I
The leaves were so still that even Bibi
thought it was going to rain. Bobinôt, wh
was accustomed to converse on terms of pe
fect equality with his little son, called
child's attention to certain sombre clou
that were rolling with sinister intention fr
the west, accompanied by a sullen, threaten
roar. They were at Friedheimer's store an
decided to remain there till the storm
had passed. They sat within the door on
two empty kegs. Bibi was four years
old and looked very wise.
"Mama'll be 'fraid, yes," he sug
gested with blinking eyes.
"She'll shut the house. Maybe sh

Holograph copy of the first page of Chopin's short story "The Storm."

his life. The passionate behavior of her Creoles gives rise to only one type of the violence she limns; more important is the suffering caused by the conflict between the assertion of the self and the rigid morality of a traditional society. In many of the stories that treat sexual awareness and confusion, among them **"A Shameful Affair," "Regret," "The Unexpected," "Fedora"** and particularly ***The Awakening,*** her characters discover the violent physical and mental effects of repressed desire; only in **"The Storm"** (with the most evocative sexual encounter in all her work) does Mrs. Chopin describe complete and uncomplicated human sexual satisfaction. If sex in her fiction is a cause of profound suffering it is but one example (although perhaps the most apparent) of a need or an experience that can in its intensity warp or destroy an individual. In **"A Wizard from Gettysburg"** a man returns from the war insane; like a youth in Melville's Civil War poetry he has paid a high price for his initiation into experience. In **"Doctor Chevalier's Lie"** a girl dies violently in a brothel, the victim of country ignorance ravaged in its confrontation with city decadence. Mrs. Chopin finds no experience reprehensible so long as it does not harm another; on occasion, however, she advises caution, for any compulsive obsession will inevitably turn upon the individual who holds it. (pp. 116-17)

In Mrs. Chopin's fiction the characters learn the limitations of their own capabilities and rights, which are frequently compromised by prohibiting social codes of behavior. Since Mrs. Chopin is suspicious of most such norms and rules, she allows her characters to test themselves and society; and because she is an honest interpreter of life, she shows them succeeding and failing. For her the pursuit of freedom, her most persistent theme, requires one important consideration: responsibility. Any assertion of the self, won at the expense of others' rights and needs, is not wholly just; likewise, any demands for responsible actions made of another are not completely right. . . . Freedom, as Mrs. Chopin shows often, in such stories as **"A Rude Awakening," "Loka," "Lilacs," "Cavanelle," "Ozème's Holiday"** and **"Polydore,"** demands the fulfillment of duty and trust and necessitates a search for peaceful order; often freedom can be realized more in the denial of the self than in the open abandon of it.

The paradox that out of self-denial comes well-being is a more common situation in Mrs. Chopin's fiction than many readers, particularly those who know only ***The Awakening,*** might realize. Her best works, it must be admitted, rarely feature such an easy contentment, and in the excellent story, **"A Shameful Affair,"** Mildred, like Edna, learns that an awareness of the potential for freedom can bring with it greater understanding of one's imprisonment within the self. Whenever an individual chooses to deny her potential for continued growth and experience in a Kate Chopin story, she must do so only after a consideration of alternative actions, and when she does so she must be allowed to make the choice herself, unencumbered by the pressures of individuals or society. Important stories like **"The Maid of Saint Phillippe," "A Lady of Bayou St. John," "A Respectable Woman"** and **"Athénaïse"** feature strong-willed women who decide independently that they wish to retain what they have. Each story is a tale of renunciation, a patently Romantic theme, and although Mrs. Chopin might suggest, particularly in **"A Lady of Bayou St. John,"** (as she expresses more pointedly in **"Madame Martel's Christmas Eve"**), that such a choice of self-denial may be difficult to serve forever, she is clearly emphasizing in these stories, as in most of those about marriage, that a person's future should be determined, so far as is possible, not by another but by him alone. (pp. 117-18)

All of her writings consider in one way or another the experience of love and the physical and intellectual relations between the sexes; and because her locale is the world of the Creole and the Cajun, known for their passion and pride, her portrayal of love and marriage tends to be forceful. . . . But her best work, although it exposes the cultural origins of her Creole setting, examines marriage in a more universal context. Her attitude toward marriage is essentially traditional—at times, one hesitates to say, even sentimental—and although such excellent works as **"Athénaïse"** and ***The Awakening*** go so far as to question the institution of marriage, particularly for the woman who is not allowed to doubt its sanctity, Mrs. Chopin continually reveals that marriage can be successful and happy and can, as in **"A Mental Suggestion,"** generate the growth of love, but that it exacts compromise and unselfishness if it is to work. . . . In **"A Respectable Woman,"** for example, it can be seen that leaving the spouse might require giving up more than one would gain in another alliance. Although Mrs. Chopin rarely commends conduct that is overly circumspect, she can accept the reasons one might choose to behave safely. And because she understands renunciation, she indicates in several of her finest stories, **"Wiser than a God," "A Lady of Bayou St. John"** and **"A Respectable Woman,"** that the aroused passions can threaten the security of a career or a happy marriage and should be controlled. Because Mrs. Chopin is an ironist she leaves her stories somewhat open-ended, thus giving the reader the sense that carefully adjusted solutions can never be free of future intimidations. Marriage without love or mutual respect is to her, however, clearly immoral; **"The Story of an Hour," "Her Letters"** and **"In Sabine,"** for example, expose graphically the misery of marital discontent. (pp. 118-19)

Some of her short works clearly capitalize on the singular world of Louisiana, but her feeling for nature, her perception of character and her ear for dialect give these most conspicuous examples of local color a definite appeal; and these stories are rarely ever sentimental, a fault of much regional literature at this time. It is fairly obvious, also, that organization was a difficult task for her and that her argument against a too-great emphasis on plot was in part an excuse for this shortcoming of her craft. Her good works do give evidence of an ample imagination, although some rely perhaps too frequently, as critics have been quick to point out, on the use of a sudden and startling ironic reversal. But her sense of dramatic structuring gives to these plot twists from the opening to the conclusion of the story an "inevitableness," as F. L. Pattee said [see excerpt dated 1915]. . . . As a realist and a regionalist she can be compared favorably with other writers of her type and her time; as an ironist she reflects the diverse and sundry truths of her vision in a body of work that, however small, has large historical and literary value. (pp. 119-20)

James E. Rocks, "Kate Chopin's Ironic Vision," in Revue de Louisiane, *Vol. 1, No. 2, Winter, 1972, pp. 110-20.*

PRISCILLA ALLEN (essay date 1977)

[In the following excerpt, Allen attacks as biased previous, male-dominated criticism of The Awakening. *Specifically, Allen contends that critical condemnation of Edna Pontellier is sexist and based on attitudes that preclude the acceptance of woman as a universal symbol of the underdog.]*

Since ***The Awakening*** was so far ahead of its times, it is no wonder that Victorian critics, preoccupied with matters of sex, condemned it. The fact of Edna's adultery blinded them to other aspects of the novel.

What may seem at first strange and anomalous, however, is that modern critics, liberal and enlightened on sexual matters, applaud the novel and urge its reading, but still see no further essentially than their predecessors. (pp. 224-25)

Their overstatement and isolation of Edna's sexual activity causes them to misread. (p. 225)

Eros rules all—on this there is general agreement among these modern critics. They have differences, of course, sometimes depending upon their own critical schema for the book. (p. 226)

In all the schemata, however, the assumption that the book is "about sex" is fundamental.

Modern critics are also surprisingly similar to the turn-of-the-century critics in their judgments of Edna's "failure to her duty" as wife and mother. This is a negative way to approach Edna's real and important actions—to emphasize what she doesn't do instead of focussing on her real accomplishments. The actions are related, of course, in their very opposition: to do one means not to do the other. More important both dramatically and spiritually, however, is that one alternative is negative, passive, and docile while the other is positive, active, and courageous. (p. 227)

While the critics are usually attracted to Edna's sexual activity, their emphasis on the negative aspect of her total struggle ("withdrawal from," "denial of," "neglect of," "restraints") indicates the contradictions they labor under. All of their errors and distortions belong to a particular view of Edna that combines an attraction to or interest in her sexuality with a revulsion before her active strivings. Hence the modern ambivalence: Edna must be both praised and condemned for her sexuality.

Some of the critics make explicit the larger social implications of their judgment of Edna. Arms, for instance, says with hostile tartness: "I suppose that those who look upon the novel as a defense of the New Woman would feel that Mrs. Chopin regards freedom from children as a necessary basis for complete freedom." [see *TCLC,* Vol. 5] (pp. 227-28)

Other critics demonstrate only by implication that they are Edna's antagonists in the "war of the sexes" and as such judge the sexual issue. On one occasion Spangler takes a point of view he attributes to Léonce (but not the Léonce we meet in the novel), the aggrieved husband of the "ruthless" Edna, who must "confront the evidence" that he is "no longer of consequence to his wife." He adds: "For a man who clearly wants nothing more of home than that it should be comfortable, a wife who longs for 'life's delirium' is no minor trial" [see *TCLC,* Vol. 5]. . . . Spangler has not only taken liberties with the text and point of view in constructing a character, but he has generalized his observations for wider application. He is similarly inventive in dealing with Robert. Taking a note perhaps from Wilson's observation that Robert, in avoiding consummation of the love affair, was "an all too honorable young fellow," Spangler opines that his "conventionality" is a "mask to hide a severe deficiency of masculine force." This notion fits in with his earlier assertion that "none of the men in the novel is prepared to cope with Edna." Is the novel about *men* coping with Edna, one might ask, or are Edna's problems with them central?

Even small errors such as Berthoff's that Edna "contemplates divorce" reveal a switched point of view [see Additional Bibliography]. Berthoff interpolates this because he is unconsciously thinking like Robert, who has a "wild dream" of making Edna his wife. (p. 228)

Ordinarily a character's struggle for freedom would touch a responsive chord in all readers. The phenomenon has a universal heart-warming appeal. A success thrills us; a failure in the struggle is tragic. Even slaves who hopelessly revolt are not then castigated for having made a bid for freedom. If anything, their low status makes their attempt all the more poignant. However, these responses do not seem to operate on the critics in the case of ***The Awakening.*** Edna is not accepted as representative of the human spirit simply because she is female. As female she must be dehumanized. It is a universal of our culture that she be designed solely to fit biologic functions, to be sex-partner and mother, mere agent to the needs, sexual and nurturing, of others—the real human beings. The critics' two main concerns about Edna, her sexuality and her neglect of her duties, exemplify this cultural staple. They have not yet seen her as human.

We might begin the process of rescuing ***The Awakening*** by modestly requesting critics to take Edna seriously, even though she is female, as a human being. If her youth, beauty, and sexual accessibility render this feat difficult . . . they may need the artificial aid of imagining Edna as ugly. Let them, though it may shock their sensibilities, switch the physical appurtenances of Mlle. Reisz and Edna for a moment. (They are able to take a Mlle. Reisz seriously—though with a different sort of hostility.) It is an artificial aid, and a temporary one like orthodontia we would hope, but there is another logic to justify it.

Both women are artists, Reisz in music and Edna in painting. It is their seriousness about and sensitivity to art that draw them together. Early in the novel Reisz recognizes the artist in Edna and chooses her as a kindred spirit. . . . Reisz, already firmly established in her independence as a musician—and as a "disagreeable," even "demented," woman, according to various male characters in the novel—acts as Edna's mentor. Edna's feelings for Reisz are at first ambivalent, but her feelings for Reisz's music are not. The power of the music, one of the important metaphors of the novel, cannot be overestimated. (pp. 229-30)

It is Reisz who contributes the wounded bird image (which Spangler finds sentimental), feeling Edna's shoulder blades to see if her wings are strong. The full meaning of this image cannot be appreciated without noting its source. Birds there have been before in the story, birds in cages signifying the spirit bound, wild birds generally signifying freedom from earthbound conditions, but the identification of Edna with a bird and with the possibility of broken wings comes first from her fellow artist, an ugly bird perhaps but with sound wings.

Some critics will object that Edna's art is nothing—a mere extension of the eternal sketching that genteel heroines have indulged in since Jane Austen's day. There are two kinds of answers to this objection. Edna, though she is as modest about her work as Chopin was about hers, continually sells it. She thinks of making her living by it. That fact alone in Business America makes her painting a serious act. Secondly, the quality of her work is not relevant to her need and right to pursue her art. Competence alone does not distinguish the dilettante from the artisan, the amateur from the professional. And for Edna, the impulse to create has all the greater social and public significance for the personal and private obstacles it must overcome. Unlike the drawing of Emma Woodhouse, Edna's drawing is a revolutionary act.

Chopin does not belabor this matter. She gives Edna a skill that she might realistically be imagined to have had and to have had training in. For the rest she is concerned to show Edna's sensuous response to physical reality, the world about her, to her own emotions and yearnings, responses which express her personhood, her precious individuality. Because freedom, individuality, self-expression are not rights to be reserved for gifted artists alone, Chopin shows us that Edna, conventionally brought up, conventionally becoming wife and mother, spontaneously—without contact with blue-stockings or feminist "agitators"—pursues her right to self-expression and cannot feel wicked for doing so. Instead she has a feeling, after setting up her own house, "of having descended in the social scale, with a corresponding sense of having risen in the spiritual." Male critics who delight in Stephen Dedalus' watchwords "silence, exile, and cunning" should applaud Edna's boldness as another triumph of the human spirit. But as we have seen, they do not.

Though critics call him kind, lovable, long-suffering, and so on, Léonce acts as the immediate oppressor of Edna. Her first step towards independence means freedom from his rule, first in his house and then in escape to her own. Chopin explicitly describes the nature of Léonce and dramatizes his oppressiveness in three "nagging" scenes. When we first see them together, he is "looking at his wife as one looks at a valuable piece of personal property." His possessiveness is underscored when we are told "he greatly valued his possessions, chiefly because they were his." In keeping with this quality, he is mainly concerned with making money and showing off his wealth. He is fiercely conventional and supremely insensitive to feelings. He sees his wife's role as caring for him and his children. Not openly forceful in his demands, his most violent act is to leave the dinner table in disgust when he is displeased and go to his club. But he is capable of insidious forms of oppression when he feels, as he seems often to, that Edna's services are not up to the mark, that she has somehow under the surface of her manner detached herself. (pp. 230-31)

Edna's oppression by her children is of a very special sort. Its nature has been confused by critics raising the issue of Edna's neglect. Arms's claim that Chopin "endorses" Léonce's accusations of Edna's neglect is based on a distortion of the text and muddies the water further. (p. 234)

Arms's assertion is based on Chopin's definition of Edna as "not a mother-person." Nowhere, however, does Chopin equate not being a "mother-person" with neglect of children. Almost the opposite is true. She pokes fun at the "mother-persons," who could be seen "fluttering about with extended, protecting wings when any harm, real or imaginary, threatened their precious brood. . . . And she describes in tones of approval the independence of Edna's children. . . . In any case, it is not the physical care of her children that oppresses Edna, for she is remarkably free of that burden. Not only has she a servant who attends them, she has also a mother-in-law who is delighted to take them off her hands for weeks at a time.

There are two explanations for the extremity of the language that Edna uses in "thinking of the children": "the children appeared before her like antagonists who had overcome her; who had overpowered and sought to drag her into the soul's slavery for the rest of her days." One explanation requires that we recapture a historical view of a woman's duties to her children, of her responsibility to their honor and reputation. . . . So far Léonce had put a saving public face on her actions, and through rumors had already reached Mme. Ratignolle about Edna's friendship with Arobin, no irrevocable damage had yet been done. But Edna has reached a turning point in her life; the scene where she assists at the birth of Adèle's child contributes to and culminates in this moment. She must think about her future, which means that she must think also about the future of her children, about her relations with Robert, and so on. (pp. 234-35)

Divorce is not a consideration, for in the 1890s this right had not been recognized generally or won. Though Edna's revolt in itself still has a revolutionary relevance, we must see that as a matter of historical fact her options were different from modern ones. (p. 235)

For her children, she repeats, she is willing to give up "the unessential," but "she would never sacrifice herself for her children." One of the "unessentials" to her children is her being. She has recently visited them and found that they have no need of her; they are perfectly happy with their grandmother. They have need only of her honor and good reputation, which she cannot give them without sacrificing daily her independence and full life. The only way that she can escape her "soul's slavery for the rest of her days" is to die.

It is because she cannot sacrifice herself to the consequences of sexual activity and at the same time is not willing to live without sensuous experience that Edna drowns herself. That is her precise contradiction. . . . (p. 237)

The heroism of Edna is that she is able to pursue her felt needs with so little guilt and that rather than settling for less than a chance to fulfill them she chooses instead to die. For so young a woman, she shows tremendous strength in discovering, defining, and following her natural human needs, despite all the societal pressures on her to conform to a set pattern. ***The Awakening*** is a far more revolutionary novel than any of the critics have realized. What gives it its shock effect today (for it still has that power) and its relevance is that it is a portrait of a woman determined to have full integrity, full personhood—or nothing. (p. 238)

Priscilla Allen, "Old Critics and New: The Treatment of Chopin's 'The Awakening'," in The Authority of Experience: Essays in Feminist Criticism, *edited by Arlyn Diamond and Lee R. Edwards, The University of Massachusetts Press, 1977, pp. 224-38.*

JAMES H. JUSTUS (essay date 1978)

[In the following excerpt, Justus discusses the emotional withdrawal of Edna Pontellier, which he contends is a regression to childhood. He argues that the protagonist is able to escape all personal and social responsibility by her withdrawal and by the final act of suicide. For further discussion of the significance of Pontellier's suicide, see the excerpts by Per Seyersted (1969), James E. Rocks (1972), and Carol P. Christ (1980).]

Despite the recent popularity of ***The Awakening*** among feminist critics, the story of Edna Pontellier is not primarily a study of a woman victimized by an oppressive masculine society; indeed, the continued fascination with this little novel is itself testimony, I think, to Kate Chopin's substantial aesthetic achievement. Its appeal for readers with a sociological orientation is certainly widespread, but to judge not merely from published critical accounts but also from the varied and eclectic reading experiences within the classroom, I am convinced that ***The Awakening*** is a permanent "rediscovery," one which can withstand the vagaries of critical fashion because of its achieved wholeness. Its conceptual ambitiousness and the stylistic restraint by which Chopin renders her theme of the pathology of romanticism are a noteworthy combination, but perhaps its most remarkable achievement is the way in which Chopin's coolly assured psychological insight and technical skill of portraiture merge in the study of one woman.

Although Chopin's decade-long practice of local color fiction doubtless contributes to her success with Edna Pontellier, the protagonist of her novel stands above and apart from such spirited characters as Mildred Orme (**"A Shameful Affair"**), Mrs. Baroda (**"A Respectable Woman"**), and Athénaïse (**"Athénaïse"**). Through these and other characters of the short stories are not merely picturesque (they are not "sweet and lovable" creatures which one reviewer, shocked by ***The Awakening,*** urged Chopin to return to), they do depend upon the special circumstances of race, religion, and custom which American local colorists so rigorously delineated in the latter half of the nineteenth century. Edna transcends the circumstantial exigencies of her time and place in the same way that some of the characters of Edith Wharton transcend their social and cultural boundaries. Like Lily Bart of *The House of Mirth* and Newland Archer of *The Age of Innocence,* Edna Pontellier is a figure beset more by a divided will than by the circumstances of an environing world. For some of Chopin's other female characters who suffer from a radical imbalance, resolution is nearly always achieved in terms of their environing world—and that world's values. The imbalance which haunts Edna is within the self, and the dilemma is resolved in terms of her psychic compulsions. Caught between conflicting urgencies—her need to succumb to her sensuality is countered by an equal need for a freedom that is almost anarchic—Edna never succeeds in creating a new self. The spiritual movement in her story is at best sporadic, halting, impulsive, and at worst regressive and passive.

What is it precisely which Edna Pontellier awakens *to?* It is clear what she awakens *out of:* the life of convention which denies her the full expression of all that is latent within her. The roles she plays in her life are defined not by her but by general circumstances, roles which though not heinous are merely conventional: dutiful wife, loving mother, gracious hostess, dependable friend. But in the course of her emotional and intellectual struggle, her new role—"free woman"—is never satisfactorily realized, and her specific lovers finally become as irrelevant as her friends, husband, and children.

Edna's awakening is neither sudden nor momentous. It begins, in fact, in childhood, during which time, Chopin tells us, Edna "lived her own small life all within herself. At a very early period she had apprehended instinctively the dual life—that outward existence which conforms, the inward life which questions." Significantly, it is not a passionate attachment to Robert Lebrun which first encourages the breakdown of the conforming patterns of her outward life, but *place.* It is setting, that most accentuated element of American local color fiction—setting in its larger sense—which serves that purpose. Grand Isle, a Creole summer resort, is a place of langour, a place of hot sun enveloped by sea breezes from the Gulf, the place of Creole spontaneity and candor. Representing that society, momentarily displaced from a tropically luxuriant Gulf city to an even more tropically luxuriant island, is Adèle Ratignolle, the very epitome of the faithful Creole matron and presumably the one least likely to stimulate discontent within Edna. This "embodiment of every womanly grace and charm" does, however, strike a responsive chord in Edna, who has a "sensuous susceptibility to beauty." But though Adèle, like her sister Creole matrons, is marked by candor of speech, she is also like them, the very soul of fidelity. Attentiveness to husband, children, and home is so much the priority that it leaves no room for what Edna sees as a necessity—the inward life, an identity unconnected to matrimony. If these Creole women are characterized by an "entire absence of prudery" and a total freedom of expression which often embarrass the Kentucky Presbyterian, even Edna recognizes that "inborn and unmistakable" in them is a "lofty chastity" which can not be compromised. (pp. 107-09)

If Adèle Ratignolle is one kind of foil for Edna Pontellier, Mademoiselle Reisz is quite another kind. This "disagreeable little woman, no longer young," with a self-assertive temper and a "disposition to trample upon the rights of others," quarrels with everyone at Grand Isle and is so visibly distressed by its general domestic flavor that one wonders how she can possibly endure so homogenous a watering place. And if Adèle grows wings as a ministering angel, Mademoiselle Reisz knows something about other kinds of wings. After her return to the city, Edna cultivates Mademoiselle Reisz, visiting her, reading Robert's letters, listening to appropriate piano music. At the end of one of these visits, Mademoiselle Reisz puts her arms around Edna and feels her shoulder blades to see if "her wings were strong." "The bird that would soar above the level plain of tradition and prejudice must have strong wings," she says. "It is a sad spectacle to see the weaklings bruised, exhausted, fluttering back to earth." Although Edna professes to be thinking of no "extraordinary flights," the final natural object she sees before her suicide in the Gulf is a "bird with a broken wing . . . beating the air above, reeling, fluttering, circling disabled down, down to the water."

Mademoiselle Reisz is an artist of sorts who lives her own life in modestly bohemian quarters, but despite her credo—"The artist must possess the courageous soul that dares and defies"—she is no more ambitious about her music than Edna is about her painting. Adèle, the sensuously handsome woman, keeps up her music "on account of the children, . . . because she and her husband both [consider] it a means of brightening the home and making it attractive." Unprofessionally, she plays waltzes for general enjoyment; the professional Reisz, awkward, homely, tasteless, plays Chopin primarily for the enjoyment of Edna. As a model for an alternative way of life, Reisz has obvious disadvantages. Chopin's description of her at the piano is clearly meant to suggest a spiritual impoverishment, despite the talent and the courage to think and behave as she pleases. "She sat low at the instrument, and the lines of her body settled into ungraceful curves and angles that gave it an appearance of deformity." Her dust-covered bust of Beethoven, his wizened frame, the shabby artifical violets which she wears in her mousy hair, her Pandarus-like function: these are hardly the marks of one who is successful in the push for complete freedom. She has freedom because she is alone.

For Adèle, complacent satisfaction—never being alone—comes from having no identity beyond her given roles; for Reisz, the ambiguous satisfactions of having her own identity is the result of always being alone. (pp. 109-10)

Edna is caught between the claims of "mother-women" and those of "artist-women," between the sensual aspects of Creole women, who adjust to society by celebrating their procreative powers, and the brittle independence of liberated artists, who resist their culture's sociological limitations with their own kind of creative powers. There is little comfort for Edna in either Madame Ratignolle or Mademoiselle Reisz, despite the fact that between these two she unconsciously vacillates, instinctively seeking a model for her own inchoate longings for an identity lying somewhere unformulated and undefined. There is only herself as she gropes for clarification of what she wants. It is not surprising that Kate Chopin's original title for ***The Awakening*** was "A Solitary Soul." The evidence suggests that the powerful drive toward freedom, to that state where her real identity can be released from the confines of social roles, is the impetus behind Edna's sensual groping and blundering. Neither friends nor lovers can release that identity, and the tragedy within the novel is that even Edna Pontellier, despite her emotional changes, cannot release that identity. (p. 111)

I would suggest that the awakening of Edna Pontellier is in actuality a reawakening; it is not an advance toward a new definition of self but a return to the protective, self-evident identity of childhood. Consider the careful details with which Chopin sketches this process.

On the beach at Grand Isle, the undulating waves of the Gulf remind Edna suddenly of a summer meadow of high grass in Kentucky: "Sometimes I feel this summer as if I were walking through the green meadow again, idly, aimlessly, unthinking and unguided." It is the perfectly ordinary and proper state for childhood: unfocused drift is possible because of the security of childhood. Needless to say, an aimless and unguided drift is not the state appropriate for the willed forging of a new identity. The re-creation of that childhood moment of walking through the high grass of Kentucky triggers also the memory of three unreturned passions: at an early age, a dignified and sad-eyed cavalry officer with a Napoleonic face; some time later, a young Mississippi gentleman already engaged to a young lady on an adjoining plantation; and, after she is a grown woman, a "great tragedian" whose face and figure "haunt her imagination and stir her senses," whose picture under the "cold glass" she kisses passionately. What all three have in common is their remoteness, the safety, we might say, of implausible reciprocity: a father's friend, a neighbor's suitor, an adoring public's stage hero. Each one, Chopin notes, melts "imperceptibly out of her existence," going "the way of dreams." At the age of twenty-eight, these dreams return—and finally in an emotionally destructive way. The charms of romance, the magnetic pull of dreams, are powerful precisely because they are free-floating, impulsive rather than calculating, responding to the heart's desire in whatever shape they may take, and unburdened by the head's responsibility.

If her fancy is mistaken in believing that there was "a sympathy of thought and taste" between her and her husband, the coming of her children is apparently just as disillusioning. Though she loves her two sons, it is an "uneven" love, appreciated better in their absence, which frees her of a "responsibility which she had blindly assumed and for which Fate had not fitted her." The sporadic expressions of her love for them are proportionate to her growing dissatisfaction as wife and mother; pervasive neglect is compensated for by spurts of concentrated attention. When she is most involved in her affair with Alcée Arobin, she lavishes the most intense love on her children. When she confesses her love for Robert openly to Mademoiselle Reisz, she goes to a confectioner's and orders a "huge box of bonbons for the children." After she moves into her pigeon house—an act of impulsive but undifferentiated desire—she goes to visit her children, who are temporarily living with their grandmother in the country—an act of conventional and well-defined responsibility. And though she leaves them "with a wrench and a pang," carrying the sound of their voices with her "like the memory of a delicious song," by the time she reaches the city "the song no longer echoed in her soul."

One can hazard the guess, I think, that Edna is so often unconcerned about her children because she herself is becoming more and more a child. This is not a distorted description of her so-called awakening if we think of childhood as that stage in which dreams are delicious and self-contained whether they come true or not, a period of suspended self-fulfillment when satisfactions are gained at the expense of others, when desires are unanchored and the imagination is free to attach these desires to whatever shapes and forms the fancy dictates, above all, a time—perhaps the only time in human life—when self-indulgence has no costs to threaten its pleasure.

This re-awakening to the self-fulfilling desires of childhood can be measured by the narrative logic of Edna's actions and the internal awareness on the part of Edna and others within the narrative. At one time, after Robert's return from Mexico, Edna herself feels that she has been "childish and unwise" to worry over her lover's reserve. Madame Ratignolle, who as a "mother-woman" should be an authority on the subject, comments on Edna's action in moving out of her husband's house and into the little pigeon house a few blocks away: "In some way you seem to me like a child, Edna. You seem to act without a certain amount of reflection which is necessary in this life." For Edna, of course, that move *is* an impulsive act performed without any great deliberation; but its significance is clear, even to Edna: it is one more step taken "toward relieving herself from obligations," and she equates that relief with her "expansion as an individual." As Chopin puts its, "She began to look with her own eyes, to see and to apprehend the deeper undercurrents of life. No longer was she content to 'feed upon opinions' when her own soul had invited her." From this moment on, she indeed acts upon that formula: the fewer her obligations, the greater her individuality.

Psychologically, Edna does not will herself forward to embrace new experiences attendant upon her sensual and spiritual awakening, but drifts languidly backward, to the realm of romance and dreams. The circumstances of that summer at Grand Isle could not possibly be more propitious. Lazy days of desultory activity, with a husband absent in the city except for weekends, with children attended by a quadroon nurse, and with a devoted swain who entertains her with Creole love songs and stories of enchanted islands, Gulf spirits, and buried pirate treasure. Moreover, this perfect situation is abetted by nature. . . . (pp. 112-14)

It must be admitted that Edna responds rather slowly to these dream-making circumstances. She cries without apparent cause, but does it after midnight on her cottage porch while her husband and children sleep, listening to the hooting of an owl and the mournful lullaby of the sea, responding to an "indescribable oppression, which seemed to generate in some unfamiliar part of her consciousness. . . ." Even her "vague anguish" is romantic, this shadow "passing across her soul's summer day," but her creator disallows her the easy immersion in that romantic moment: "She was just having a good cry all to herself. The mosquitoes made merry over her, biting her firm, round arms and nipping at her bare insteps." Even when Chopin takes another opportunity for authorial comment, it is laced with detachment rather than sympathy: "In short, Mrs. Pontellier was beginning to realize her position in the universe as a human being, and to recognize her relations as an individual to the world within and about her. This may seem like a ponderous weight of wisdom to descend upon the soul of a young woman of twenty-eight—perhaps more wisdom than the Holy Ghost is usually pleased to vouchsafe to any woman." It is certainly more wisdom than Kate Chopin finally allows her protagonist.

If this is the story of the sensual awakening of a woman, two peculiarities of the narrative should be noted: (1) the growth of dissatisfaction in Edna which develops concurrently with her grand love for Robert Lebrun and for her affair with the convenient sexual partner, Alcée Arobin; and (2) her concomitant realization of the fact of aloneness. Her awakening to her own physicality is a response that is, in the usual sense of the terms, neither markedly emotional nor intellectual, but self-sufficient, indulgent, enclosed. Chopin's rather detailed account of Edna's love of music serves as a clue to this self-absorption in its wider aspects.

We are told early on that Edna's response to music is recreative in an almost pictorial manner. . . .

> One piece which that lady played Edna had entitled "Solitude." It was a short, plaintive, minor strain. The name of the piece was something else, but she called it "Solitude." When she heard it there came before her imagination the figure of a man standing beside a desolate rock on the seashore. He was naked. His attitude was one of hopeless resignation as he looked toward a distant-bird winging its flight away from him. . . .

The dreaming self appropriates the initiating music, renames it, and attributes a tangible meaning to the created picture. The picture itself can be seen as a transsexual projection: the naked man is Edna as well as the vaguely identified, wished-for, would-be lover: a kind of redaction of the twenty-eight-swimmers plus one in Walt Whitman's *Song of Myself.*

The ability to imagine pictures when she listens to piano music is the case normally—when, say, Adèle plays in her competent but unprofessional way. When Edna listens to Mademoiselle Reisz, however, something else happens. "Material pictures" refuse to "gather and blaze before her imagination," no pictures of "solitude, of hope, of longing, or of despair" can be summoned. Chopin's description is vivid: the very passions themselves "were aroused within her soul, swaying it, lashing it, as the waves daily beat upon her splendid body. She trembled, she was choking, and the tears blinded her." Whereas "material pictures" safely distance her from the passions when Madame Ratignolle plays, the playing of Mademoiselle Reisz releases the naked passions themselves. The pictorial mode is itself a referent, a cushioned and imaginative one, but in the case of Reisz's playing, the response has no referent, and Edna is at the mercy of her senses.

A more direct, less displaced clue to Edna's growing solipsism also occurs early in the narrative. The circumstances of the setting conspire to make Edna susceptible. . . . For the first time she swims alone. . . . That moment is significant not only because her will blazes for the first time, amazing her husband, but also because the emphasis is on desire as a thing in itself, something to respond to egoistically without the tangible aid of another person, even Robert. The "mystic spirit" allows her the freedom to drift; she blindly follows "whatever impulse moved her, as if she had placed herself in alien hands for direction, and freed her soul of responsibility." The romantic day later on the *Chênière Caminada*—another island in the bay—is a willing bestowal of herself to those "alien hands," manifested magically as an old Acadian in touch with the "mystic spirit abroad" who spins local legends.

The fact of aloneness becomes more and more pronounced in Edna. Her willful behavior puzzles her husband, who seeks advice from the old family doctor. His advice to Léonce is "let your wife alone for a while . . . Don't contradict her. . . ." Léonce does just that—"letting her do as she [likes]." It is advice calculated to annoy Edna's father, who is visiting them: "You are too lenient, too lenient by far, Léonce," he tells him. "Authority, coercion are what is needed. Put your foot down good and hard; the only way to manage a wife." What is interesting here is that both theories—letting her do as she likes and coercing her "good and hard"—sound as much like child-rearing policies as they do wife-managing ones, an equation which will be familiar to students of Victorian domestic culture. But Mr. Pontellier is not a cruel husband—there are no conventionally cruel husbands in Chopin's fiction—and he refrains from chastizing her about the neglect of housekeeping, the cancelling of her Tuesdays at home, and her determination not to attend her sister's wedding ("a wedding is one of the most lamentable spectacles on earth," she tells him), all in the hopes that her behavior is a passing whim. But if "leaving her alone" is a mildly enlightened way to handle Edna Pontellier, it is also appropriate in a poignant and even tragic way. Has she been associating with "pseudointellectual women—super-spiritual superior beings?" the doctor asks Léonce. "That's the trouble," he replies; "she hasn't been associating with any one." This observation is truer than even Edna might perceive. Once her husband leaves for an extended business trip to New York, "a radiant peace settled upon her when she at last found herself alone. . . . she breathed a big, genuine sigh of relief." An unfamiliar but "delicious" feeling comes over her. Chopin's characterization here is as brilliantly acute as the prose is economical. . . . If both the diction and the syntax . . . suggest the picture of a little girl playing house, the implications are more serious. Regression to childhood rather than progress toward a new self-fulfillment is the dominant key. (pp. 114-18)

In Edna's state of dissatisfaction the present Alcée, for all his sexual attractiveness, is no competition for the absent Robert, who seems nearer to her "off there in Mexico" than when he returns; his very absence, nourishing in Edna a "Dreamy, absent look," allows her the frequent luxury of being "alone in a kind of reverie—a sort of stupor." *Dreamy, reverie, stupor,* these words and their analogues pervade ***The Awakening.*** It was George Arms [see *TCLC,* Vol. 5] a few years ago who perceptively observed that for a novel called ***The Awakening,*** much of its action consists of its heroine's sleeping. It is a state which neutralizes any determined struggle to construct a new self, or even to uncover deeper levels of the old one. In a fine touch of characterization, Kate Chopin never allows her protagonist to understand fully what it is she is awakening *to.* . . . If anything, Edna becomes more and more confused. Her earlier life as a wife and mother she describes as a dream out of which she has come; but, once awakened, we are told she likes to "wander alone into strange and unfamiliar places." . . . Which is the dream? To be awakened from a Ratignolle-like domesticity is not to experience "life's delirium," as Edna vaguely anticipates, but to be assailed with "the old ennui" which comes "like something extraneous, independent of volition . . . , overpowering her . . . with a sense of the unattainable." (pp. 118-19)

The one thing which Edna consistently is able to articulate about her awakening, however, is that it means a release from responsibilities. . . . What this means in social terms is that she spends more and more time alone; what it means in psychological terms is that she spends more and more time fashioning an ideal state of romantic self-fulfillment which, practically speaking, requires not even Robert. By the time this conventionally love-sick swain returns from Mexico, avoiding Edna because of their "impossible" love, she has already "resolved never again to belong to another than herself." In Robert's eyes, Léonce Pontellier is an impediment; it means Edna is "not free." His dream, as he calls it several times during their last evening, is to marry her—but that dream is clarly not consonant with Edna's. . . . That is, *she would possess, but she would not be possessed.* It is finally only a mature version of childish self-sufficiency—"I don't want anything but my own way."

Edna's process of awakening is a kind of enlightenment, but it can hardly be called growth. What she discovers does not set her free but binds her even more tightly to a destined end. Moments before her death, she responds again to the seductive murmuring of the sea, which "invit[es] the soul to wander in abysses of solitude." Her final thoughts return not to Robert but to the clanging of the spurs of the cavalry officer, her childish first love, and to the bluegrass meadow of her childhood, with "no beginning and no end," her child-like longing for a state of being stripped of restraints. (pp. 118-20)

It might be useful to remind ourselves that the qualities of craftsmanship which make Kate Chopin's local color stories so memorable are the same ones which distinguish ***The Awakening:*** a sureness of touch in portraiture; an economically evoked sense of place; and a mastery of language (including dialect forms) which renders firmly and precisely both character and setting; and perhaps most important of all, a commendable refusal to match the play of passion and the aroused will of her characters with authorial passion and willfulness. Not even Sarah Orne Jewett, whose work Chopin admired, is so relentlessly detached from the urgencies of her characters.

Finally, behind and controlling ***The Awakening*** there is a quality of vision which sets its author apart from even her literary betters. This little novel is a rough-minded minority report, a demurring gloss on what has often passed in twentieth-century American literature as one of our abiding pieties: that self-knowledge is the threshold to psychic health, the instrument by which the trapped sensibility may be freed. (p. 121)

[Chopin's Edna] learns enough to take only a half-step toward the reshaping of her life. Chopin allows her heroine just enough insight to be able to sense that her real identity is smudged as she plays wife and mother and to begin the search for a satisfying alternative. But that alternative cannot be conceived in terms of maturity but only in the regressive reenactment of the egoism of childhood. Edna is given enough knowledge to destroy herself but not enough to save herself. (p. 122)

James H. Justus, "The Unawakening of Edna Pontellier," in The Southern Literary Journal, *Vol. X, No. 2, Spring, 1978, pp. 107-22.*

CYNTHIA GRIFFIN WOLFF (essay date 1978)

[In the following excerpt, Wolff praises the artistic technique and psychological insight of the short story "Désirée's Baby."]

"Désirée's Baby" remains an enigma. We still tend to admire it and to demonstrate our admiration by selecting it to appear in anthologies; yet the admiration is given somewhat grudgingly—perhaps because we cannot fully comprehend the story. The specifically Southern elements of the story seem significant; however, the nature of their force is not clear. The reversal of the situation that concludes the tale is important (although to a discerning reader it may well be no surprise), but, contrary to Seyersted's remarks [see excerpt dated 1969], the story's full impact patently does not derive from this writer's "trick." And while the story has been accepted as characteristic of Chopin's work, it is in several ways unusual or unique—being the only one of her fictions to touch upon the subject of miscegenation, for example. We might respond to this accumulation of contradictions by assuming that a mistake has been made somewhere along the line—that the tale has been misinterpreted or that it is not really representative of Chopin's fiction. Yet such an assumption would not explain the force of those many years of readers' response; in the end, it would not resolve the persistent enigma of **"Désirée's Baby."** Alternatively, we might try to understand why critics' judgments of the story have been so different, presuming such judgments to be insufficient but not, perhaps, fundamentally incorrect. But more importantly, we must expand our vision of the story in order to see precisely those ways in which it articulates and develops themes that are central to other of Chopin's works. (p. 125)

Chopin construes existence as necessarily uncertain. By definition, then, to live is to be vulnerable; and the artist who would capture the essence of life will turn his attention to those intimate and timeless moments when the comforting illusion of certainty is unbalanced by those forces that may disrupt and destroy. Insofar as Chopin can be said to emulate Maupassant, who stands virtually alone as her avowed literary model, we might say that she strives to look "out upon life through [her] own being and with [her] own eyes"; that she desires no more than to tell us what she sees "in a direct and simple way." Nor is Chopin's vision dissimilar to Maupassant's, for what she sees is the ominous and insistent presence of the margin: the inescapable fact that even our most vital moments must be experienced on the boundary—always threatening to slip away from us into something else, into some dark, undefined contingency. The careful exploration of this bourne is, in some sense, then, the true subject for much of her best fiction.

Certainly it is the core subject of **"Désirée's Baby"**—a story that treats layers of ambiguity and uncertainty with ruthless economy. Indeed, the tale is almost a paradigmatic study of the demarcating limits of human experience, and—since this subject is so typically the center of Chopin's attention—our continuing intuition that this story is a quite appropriate selection to stand as "representative" of her work must be seen as fundamentally correct. (pp. 125-27)

At the most superficial level in **"Désirée's Baby,"** there are distinctions that attend coloration, differences of pigment that carry definitions of social caste and even more damning implications about the "value" of one's "identity." The problem of race is managed quite idiosyncratically in this tale: we have already noted that this is the only one of Chopin's many stories to treat miscegenation directly or explicitly; however, we can be ever more emphatic—this is the only story even to probe the implications of those many hues of skin that were deemed to comprise the "negro" population. Yet from the very beginning Chopin focuses our attention upon this element with inescapable determination: she chooses not to use dialect conversation; she reduces the description of architecture and vegetation to a minimum—leaving only the thematically necessary elements. The result is a tale where the differences between "black" and "white" remain as the only way to locate the events—its only "regional" aspects, if you will—and we cannot avoid attending to them.

Yet for all this artistic direction, Chopin is clearly not primarily interested in dissecting the *social problem* of slavery (as Cable might be); rather, she limits herself almost entirely to the personal and the interior. Thus the dilemma of "color" must ultimately be construed emblematically, with the ironic and unstated fact that human situations can *never* be as clear as "black and white."

In the antebellum South, much private security depended upon the public illusion that whites lived within a safe compound, that a barrier of insurmountable proportions separated them from the unknown horrors of some lesser existence, and that these territorial boundaries were clear and inviolable. The truth, of course, was that this was an uncertain margin, susceptible to a multitude of infractions and destined to prove unstable. At its very beginning, the story reminds us of inevitable change ahead: Désirée is presumed to have been left "by a party of Texans"—pioneers en route to the territory whose slave policies were so bitterly contested when it was annexed that they proved to be a significant precursor to the Civil War that followed. Chopin's touch is light: the implications of this detail may be lost to a modern audience, but they would have loomed mockingly to a reader in 1892, especially a Southern reader.

Even within the supposedly segregated social system there is abundant evidence of violation. "'And the way he cried,'" Désirée remarks proudly of her lusty child; "'Armand heard him the other day as far away as La Blanche's cabin'." . . . What color is La Blanche, we might wonder, and what was Armand's errand in her cabin? "One of La Blanche's little quadroon boys . . . stood fanning the child slowly" . . . , and he becomes a kind of nightmare double (perhaps a half-brother, in fact) for Désirée's baby—a visual clue to the secret of this infant's mixed blood; eventually, his presence provokes the shock of recognition for Désirée. "She looked from her child to the boy who stood beside him, and back again; over and over. 'Ah!' It was a cry that she could not help; which she was not conscious of having uttered". . . . None of the "blacks" is referred to as actually dark-skinned; even the baby's caretaker is a "yellow nurse." . . . (pp. 127-29)

In the end, only Armand's skin is genuinely colored—a "dark, handsome face" . . . momentarily brightened, it would seem, by the happiness of marriage. And if this description gives a literal clue to the denouement of the story's mystery, it is even more effective as an index to character. Armand has crossed that shadowy, demonic boundary between mercy and kindness on the one hand and cruelty on the other. His posture towards the slaves in his possession has always been questionable—his "rule was a strict one . . . and under it his negroes had forgotten how to be gay, as they had been during the old master's easygoing and indulgent lifetime." . . . Little wonder, then, that when his wife's child displeases him, "the very spirit of Satan seemed suddenly to take hold of him." . . . His inhumanity towards Désirée and the servants alike bespeaks an irreversible journey into some benighted region; and the bonfire, by whose light he reads that last, fateful letter, is no more than a visible sign of the triumph of those powers of darkness in his soul. Thus when Désirée exclaims wonderingly, "'my skin is fair. . . . Look at my hand; whiter than yours, Armand'," her comment *may* be relevant to the parentage of each; however, within the context of the story, it figures more reliably as a guide to the boundaries of humane behavior.

Underlying this insistent preoccupation with the literal question of color, then, is Chopin's ironic perception of the tenuous quality of such distinctions: it is simplistic to call "quadroons" and "yellows" "blacks" and "negroes." And if we move from this overt level into the labyrinth of the human soul, we will discover a man who has become lost in the wilderness of his own "blackest" impulses—a master who reverts to tyranny and is possessed by Satan, by the only absolute darkness in the tale. The lesser existence into which Armand sinks stems not from his Negroid parentage, but from a potential for personal evil that he shares with all fellow creatures. . . . (p. 129)

[To] be open to love is to be vulnerable to invasions that we can neither forsee nor fully protect ourselves against. Thus Chopin's rendering of the love between Désirée and Armand is an insistent compression of opposites. Armand is supposed to have fallen in love at first sight. . . . The difference in Armand's life between love and some other force—something equally turbulent but more reckless and cruel—is no more than a hair's breadth or the fluttering of an eye. Linguistically, the two forces cannot be separated at all.

In Désirée's case, the peril of emotional entanglement has different origins; yet if anything, it is even more dangerous. She has been God's gift to her adoptive parents, the child of love as her name implies, helpless and delicate and unable to comprehend anything but love in its purest manifestations. . . . Of the other side of love—of violence and baser passions—she is entirely innocent. In fact, innocence is her most marked characteristic, a kind of childlike, helpless ignorance. . . . The vulnerability of such innocence is captured in her naive questions, in her trusting tendency to turn to her husband who has rejected her, even in the fragility of her garments that were surely intended only for one whose life might be protected from harsh contingencies. When Désirée married, she came to live at her husband's plantation, L'Abri (The Shelter); and such a home seems right, even necessary, for this delicate creature, even though the physical realities of the estate belie its name. . . . However, Désirée must accept this refuge at mere face value: she cannot bring herself to see the ominous possibilities in [the] . . . ancestral trees that portend both life and death.

In the end, Désirée cannot withstand the shock of being forced to acknowledge the contingencies whose existence she has ignored for so long. When Armand's love slips into cruelty, when L'Abri echoes with sibilant mockery, Désirée loses her own tenuous grasp on the balance of life. For her there seems only one choice, one final boundary to cross; and the alternatives are measured by the line between civilization and the patient, hungry bayou that lies just beyond. Madness, murder, death—all these wait to claim the love-child who could not keep her stability in the face of life's inescapable contrarieties. (pp. 130-31)

Much of the effect of this tale derives from the understatement that Chopin employs to render Désirée's annihilation and Armand's inescapable, internal hell. Even more, perhaps, the effect comes from the economy with which she captures the precariousness of the human condition—the persistent shadow-line that threads its way through all of the significant transactions of our lives. This is, perhaps, the most consistent theme in all of Chopin's fictions. We can see it in her choice of subject—preoccupation with marriage that may be either destructive or replenishing, the relationship between mother and child that is both hindering of personal fulfillment and necessary for full womanly development, and the convulsive effects of emergent sexuality. We can see it even more subtlely (but more insistently) in her imagistic patterns. (p. 131)

Read quite independently, **"Désirée's Baby"** may be judged a superb piece of short fiction—an economical, tight psychological drama. However, seen in the more ample context of Chopin's complete work, the story accrues added significance as the most vivid and direct statement of her major concern—the fiction of limits. (p. 133)

Cynthia Griffin Wolff, "Kate Chopin and the Fiction of Limits: 'Désirée's Baby'," in The Southern Literary Journal, *Vol. X, No. 2, Spring, 1978, pp. 123-33.*

CAROL P. CHRIST (essay date 1980)

[An American critic, Christ has contributed articles to such periodicals as Novel *and* Women's Studies, *and her books include*

The Finer Optic: The Aesthetic of Particularity in Victorian Poetry *(1975). In the following excerpt, Christ examines the failure and triumph of Edna Pontellier in terms of social and spiritual quests, a critical position that is similar to that of Per Seyersted (1969).*]

When it was published in 1899, Kate Chopin's story of the awakening of a married woman created a scandal because of its frank treatment of sensuality and suicide. Recently reclaimed as a feminist classic, ***The Awakening*** poses a challenge to critics because of its controversial ending. Is Edna Pontellier's suicide the triumph of a strong woman who chooses to die rather than capitulate to the constricting social mores of her time? Or is it the defeat of a woman too little aware of herself, too weak to face disappointment in her romantic fantasies and to create a life for herself alone? The distinction between spiritual and social quest is the key to resolving this question, I think. Edna's suicide reflects spiritual triumph but social defeat. And the real tragedy of the novel is that spiritual and social quests could not be united in her life. Chopin's novel shows that spiritual awakening without social support can lead to tragedy, and provides convincing testimony that women's quest must be for full spiritual and social liberation.

Edna Pontellier's awakening and search for selfhood is set against the backdrop of two contrasting and, for her, equally unacceptable, images of womanhood: the devoted, voluptuous, mother-woman, Adele Ratignolle, and the eccentric solitary artist, Mademoiselle Reisz. . . . While she may not put it into these words, Edna's quest is for wholeness—for a total sexual and creative life as a woman. Like recent feminists, she implicitly rejects the choice of either a conventional sexual life in a marriage that allows no time for her to express her creativity, or the solitary spinsterhood of a woman who is devoted to her art or career. Like men, she wants both. Her refusal to accept the nineteenth-century choice offered her marks Edna's quest as a particularly modern one.

Edna's awakening is sparked by her friendship with the son of the woman who owned the cottages on Grand Isle where Edna and her family summered. (pp. 27-8)

Robert is more to Edna than the lover of romantic fantasy. He encourages her to learn to swim and thus opens her to the sea in which she discovers the infinity of her soul as well as the sensuality of her body. Their conversations prompt her to think about the meaning of her life, something married women are rarely encouraged to do. He also awakens her to the passions of her body and to the capacity for full sexual experience. (p. 29)

[The] spiritual dimension of the novel is clearly articulated: it concerns Edna's recognition of the nature and potential of her own soul and its relation to the cosmos, "the world about her." This realization seems so simple some might not call it "spiritual." But Chopin clearly intends the reader to compare Edna's awakening to those religious awakenings commonly called conversions, as is evident from her ironic comment, "this may seem like a ponderous weight of wisdom to descend upon the soul of a young woman of twenty-eight—perhaps more wisdom than the Holy Ghost is usually pleased to vouchsafe to any woman." . . . (p. 29)

The sea is the medium of Edna's awakening. Walking by the sea, Edna senses the limitless potential of her soul and begins to question her life. . . . A symbol of infinite and fearful power, the sea is also empowering. . . . Swimming in the ocean is both a physical and spiritual experience; Edna feels control over her body *and* over her soul. Chopin alludes to the rarity of a woman's awakening. . . . Literally Edna is far out in the ocean, but metaphorically her social and spiritual quest carry her far beyond the social conventions that have limited women's sphere. . . . Edna's experience is a classic mystical experience of temporary union with a great power, and the experience provides her with a sense of illumination. (pp. 29-30)

Chopin stresses that to awaken is risky. . . . The element of danger in Edna's experience—a portent of her suicide—is a common feature of mystic experience. Mystical experience shatters an old self, and the mystic who faces nothingness risks becoming lost there—the conventional supports of the self shattered but were lacking the revelation that could lead to the creation of a new self on the other side of nothingness. For a woman the risk is that when the patriarchal definitions of her being are stripped away, she will be faced with radical freedom; she will have no guidelines to tell her how to act. She must have courage, clear-sightedness, and awareness of the consequences of her choices or she may lose herself.

Edna's mystical experience reflects wholeness. She is not transported out of the body into a transcendent world. Instead the experience is extremely physical, even sensual, and in it she finds revealed the power of her body as well as her soul. For her physical, sexual, social, and spiritual awakening occur together.

Edna's awakening starts her on the path of women's social quest, a search for new ways of living in human community. Though not always aware of the consequences of her actions, Edna takes a series of steps, small at first, that move her far beyond the conventional woman's life she had known. Newly aware of the value of her own subjectivity, Edna begins to defy her husband openly. (p. 31)

In his world, which Edna had never directly challenged, there is no room for Edna's new awareness of the value of her own thoughts and feelings. Their first real confrontation occurs at Grand Isle on the night Edna first swims out by herself and feels her passions aroused by Mademoiselle Reisz's piano, Robert's presence, and her own strength. When her husband returns from town late, as he often did, he finds her on the front porch dozing. As usual, he asks her to come in with him, and, as usual, he expects her obedience. When she decides to stay out a bit longer, he orders her in, and she feels "her will had blazed up, stubborn and resistant." . . . This seemingly trivial incident takes on monumental proportions because it is Edna's first direct challenge to the tacit premise of their marriage—his authority.

Back in New Orleans at the end of the summer Edna continues her rebellion. She becomes negligent in her management of the servants. Instead of staying home to receive callers, she goes out for the day. (p. 32)

When she refuses to go on a business trip with him, Pontellier reluctantly decides to let her have her way, and sends his mother for the children, leaving Edna alone. Chopin eloquently depicts what is probably Edna's first adult experience of solitude. . . . Edna sees everything freshly. With Pontellier and his opinions out of the house, she feels free to see with her own eyes and to "experience her own experience." The simple act of deciding which chair she finds comfortable or beautiful has enormous significance—for the first time she is naming her world from her own perspective. (pp. 32-3)

Her confidence in her own powers growing, Edna takes the decisive step of moving out of her husband's home and into a small cottage nearby. This she accomplishes with a small inheritance left by her mother and from the money she makes painting. Like Virginia Woolf after her, Chopin recognizes that women cannot gain freedom to create the world from their own experience until they are freed from emotional and financial dependence on men and from the constant interruptions of household duties and children. Edna's little house, like Woolf's "room of one's own," is a symbol for the psychic emancipation of the female mind. Edna's inheritance from her mother (not her father), like Woolf's 500 pounds a year left by a female relative, also symbolizes women's freedom from male control. Of her new home, Edna remarks, "I know I shall like it, like the feeling of freedom and independence." . . . (pp. 33-4)

With the move into the little house, Edna has taken enormous steps toward her social and spiritual liberation. She has freed herself psychically and financially from a domineering husband; she has begun to develop her artistic talent; she has freely expressed her sexuality. But despite these positive steps, powerful social forces are arrayed against her. There is no one who understands and supports her quest. The two other significant women characters in the book, Mademoiselle Reisz, the eccentric solitary artist, and Madame Ratignolle, the satisfied sensual "mother-woman," sympathize with aspects of Edna's quest, but neither can offer her what she needs—a sympathetic sisterhood or role model for the whole life she seeks. (p. 34)

The male characters in the novel also hold conventional values that prevent them from understanding Edna's quest. Edna's husband at first opposes her newly expressed willfulness and then adopts an attitude of benign tolerance, expecting that she will get over her discontent. Alcée, her lover, though tender and thoughtful, is a conventional ladies' man. Even Robert, whom Edna fancies sympathizes with her awakening, is weak and conventional.

A third force opposing Edna's quest is her own insufficient self-consciousness and dedication in both her art and her life. Though her devotion to her art deepens, Mademoiselle Reisz rightly senses that Edna is not sufficiently dedicated to it to make it her whole life. Edna also lacks self-conscious awareness of the risks she is taking in her life and the consequences she may have to face. Chopin frequently describes Edna *after* her awakening as acting on impulse or drifting through her days as if in a dream. She seems to lack a sense of perspective on her life. One day she is despondent, the next wildly hopeful. Mademoiselle Reisz remarks directly on this quality in Edna when she says, "You seem to act without a certain amount of reflection which is necessary in this life." . . . (p. 35)

Finally there is the unresolved question of the children. They are away with grandparents for the summer, but eventually they must return—their presence challenging Edna's independence and unconventional behavior. In the closed Southern Catholic society of New Orleans in 1899, divorce was not tolerated and knowledge of Edna's scandalous sexual behavior would have made her children social outcasts. Though Edna had said she would not sacrifice herself for her children, she had not considered whether she would be willing to sacrifice their future happiness for her own. (pp. 35-6)

Chopin surrounds Edna's death with contradictory symbols of defeat and rebirth. This makes it difficult to assess the meaning of Edna's final act and accounts for the various readings proposed. There is also the further complication that it is not clear whether Edna's death is consciously chosen suicide or whether it, like much else in Edna's life, is simply drifted into.

Edna's purpose in going to Grand Isle the day she dies is not clear. The day before, she had just witnessed the torture scene of the birth of Madame Ratignolle's child and been reminded to "think of the children." This shocks Edna into a recognition that she cannot avoid the issue of her children indefinitely. When she returns to her little house to discover that Robert has left, she feels "faint" and stays awake all night. When next we see Edna, she is at Grand Isle, the scene of her awakening, telling Victor she has come "for no purpose but to rest." . . . This statement and her request for some fish for her dinner indicate that she probably had not planned suicide when she came to the island. Later, however, Chopin suggests the suicide was contemplated when she says that the night before the children appeared before Edna like antagonists, but "she knew a way to elude them." . . . Still, when Edna goes down to the beach Chopin tells us "she was not thinking of these things." . . . It seems reasonable to conclude that the thought of suicide had crossed Edna's mind the night before, but that she had no firmly conceived plan to take her life when she returned to Grand Isle. Edna was also motivated to return to Grand Isle, the site of her freedom, to reaffirm her commitment to her spiritual and social quests, and apparently followed her impulse to go to the sea without sorting out her purpose.

The last chapter of the book is filled with dual imagery of defeat and rebirth. The key symbol of defeat is the image of the "bird with the broken wing." . . . Moreover, just before the image of the bird with the broken wing appears, the passage about the voice of the sea "seductive, never ceasing, clamoring, murmuring" is repeated, but it concludes simply with a repetition of the warning that the sea invites the soul to "wander in abysses of solitude." . . . The earlier qualification "for a spell" is omitted, and the reader senses that Edna has perhaps lost her soul permanently in the abyss of solitude—the risk that Chopin had hinted at earlier. But this imagery of defeat is followed by extremely positive imagery of rebirth. Edna casts off her clothing and "for the first time in her life she stood naked in the open air, at the mercy of the sun . . . She felt like some new-born creature, opening its eyes in a familiar world that it had never known." . . . Such a passage would not appear in a work whose author intended the reader to see her character as defeated.

In the concluding paragraphs of the novel conflicting imagery abounds. Edna enters the sea and swims far out. She remembers her earlier terror of death, but does not look back. She recalls the blue grass meadow, image of her childhood experience of mystical liberation, and affirms that her husband and children will never possess her body and soul. This imagery seems to confirm the interpretation of her death as a positive act, an affirmation of the spiritual liberation she has known. But then negative images reappear as Edna remembers how Mademoiselle Reisz will sneer at her because she does not have the courage to dare and defy. And her final thoughts are equally conflicting. She thinks first of father and sister—images of censure, of a dog chained to a tree—an image of bondage, of the cavalry officer she once had a crush on—a romantic delusion, but finally of the hum of bees and the musky odor of pinks—images of natural fertility, harmony, and completion.

What is the meaning of the conflicting imagery at the end of the novel? Is Edna a weak-willed woman in the grip of romantic delusions, defeated by her own lack of self-consciousness, as some critics have alleged? Or is she, on the other hand, a feminist heroine who defies convention to return to the scene of her awakening and liberation, and valiantly chooses death rather than a return to a conventional life that would mean psychic and spiritual death?

The interpretation of defeat denies the central event of the novel—Edna's awakening in the sea and the sea's positive meaning for her—and also fails to make sense of the rebirth imagery at the end of the novel. But the interpretation of triumph also ignores an important element of the novel—Edna's lack of full self-consciousness and her weakness, symbolized in the image of the bird with the broken wing. How can the reader resolve this dilemma and provide a satisfactory interpretation of the conclusion of the novel?

I suggest that the clue lies in the distinction between spiritual and social quest. Edna's suicide is a spiritual triumph but a social defeat. In it she states, even if only partially consciously, that no one will possess her body and soul, and affirms her awakening by returning to the sea where it occurred. . . . But Edna's suicide is also social defeat in that by choosing death she admits that she cannot find a way to translate her spiritual awareness of her freedom and infinite possibilities into life and relationships with others. From this standpoint the real tragedy of the novel is that the spiritual and social quests cannot be realized together. This ambiguous and tragic ending seems to reflect Chopin's view that the path to women's liberation is far more difficult and complex than some nineteenth-century feminists had alleged and requires a soul stronger than many women possess. (pp. 36-9)

In my view, Chopin's choice of physical death for her character rather than the alternative of spiritual death by returning to a conventional life reflects Chopin's courageous affirmation of women's awakening. But the weakness of the novel is that Chopin could not envision any person who could give Edna support in her quest nor imagine any alternative for Edna other than spiritual or physical death. (p. 39)

Carol P. Christ, "Spiritual Liberation, Social Defeat: Kate Chopin," in her Diving Deep and Surfacing: Women Writers on Spiritual Quest, *Beacon Press, 1980, pp. 27-40.*

ANNE GOODWYN JONES (essay date 1981)

[In the following excerpt, Jones discusses recurring themes in Chopin's short stories, including: the hypocrisy of social reformers, the effect of sexual repression on individuals and society, and the parallel plight of white women and black slaves.]

The central story in ***At Fault*** concerns Thérèse Lafirme, left at thirty by the death of her husband with the responsibility for a four-thousand-acre plantation. . . . When David Hosmer appears to offer money in exchange for cutting timber from her land, Thérèse at first rejects the invasion of her privacy and then, for business reasons, agrees. The relationship between the healthy, beautiful, and sensible widow and the quiet, grayed, and overly serious man develops through friendship to love. But David's sister Melicent, visiting for the summer, lets slip that her brother has been divorced. Confronted by Thérèse, Hosmer agrees that it was "the act of a coward" . . . to leave his alcoholic wife with only the money to support her habit. He goes back to St. Louis, remarries Fanny Larimore, and takes her away from her seedy hedonistic life to the plantation in Louisiana. . . . She turns again to alcohol; on a trek to get more, she is washed down the river in a storm and drowns. David leaves, and Thérèse continues to run her plantation, taking several months off for trips to Paris and to New Orleans. On a train, the two meet again: both are still in love, and they return to the plantation to marry. (pp. 137-38)

A subplot shows a parallel love affair between the St. Louis girl, Melicent, and a Creole, Thérèse's nephew Grégoire. Grégoire adores Melicent in the old romantic way, and Melicent begins to respond to his advances. But Grégoire murders a man who sets fire to David's sawmill, and Melicent never forgives him. Both leave the plantation; Grégoire is killed far away in a brawl, and Melicent eventually finds herself as an intellectual of sorts.

Chopin's apparent intention in both plots was to demonstrate the pernicious effects of unforgiving and legalistic morality; such righteousness may be more at fault than the sins—whether desertion or murder—it decries. Yet Chopin's novel does not make the point simply or easily. Fanny is carefully developed as the passive product of a pernicious environment, suggesting that Thérèse could be right and that a change of place could help. Thérèse's injunction to David comes as much from apparent sympathy for Fanny's married situation as it does from legalism: "You married a woman of weak character. You furnished her with every means to increase that weakness, and shut her out absolutely from your life and yourself from hers. You left her then as practically without moral support as you have certainly done now, in deserting her. . . . A man owes to his manhood, to face the consequences of his own actions." . . . Chopin seems to imply that the wisdom and tolerance gained from an understanding of life's realities—and not just its moral codes—lead ultimately to true fulfillment and communication. As the story develops this point, it moves each of the four major characters, Thérèse and David, Melicent and Grégoire, from a form of innocence to experience, though only the older couple learns from that experience. Their learning brings happiness as well as wisdom; the resolution to their story shows Thérèse and David joyful and playful, sensual and loving. (pp. 138-39)

Two late stories demonstrate Chopin's hopeful vision of woman in ideal relation to man and to society and her rather gloomy feelings about the possible realization of that vision. **"The Storm"** presents the vision. (p. 141)

Through her entry into the various points of view of those concerned with [the] act of adultery, Chopin asserts the possibility that ***The Awakening*** denied: sex, even outside marriage, can be enjoyed without personal guilt and without at least immediate harm to the others to whom one is emotionally and legally bound. In fact, Chopin implies, freeing sexual passion from conventional restraints puts it into its natural place and therefore frees and enriches the lives of every person in the "community" of the story.

By sharp contrast, **"Charlie,"** written after the psychic devastation of the furor following the publication of ***The Awakening,*** diffuses sexuality into relationships that preclude its performance and moves instead to an examination of socially determined gender roles. **"Charlie,"** the tomboy of widower Laborde's seven daughters, gallops on the levee on a big black horse, cuts her hair short, wears "trouserlets," fishes, shoots, writes poems, invents Tom Sawyer-like fantasies, and idolizes her father. As for him, "in many ways she filled the place of that ideal son he had always hoped for." . . . One day, Charlie, practicing her shooting and, as usual, missing her schooling, accidentally hits Firman Walton in the arm as he emerges from the woods. Walton, who has come to Les Palmiers on business with her father, is charmed by the oldest girl Julia, who is beautiful, dainty, an "angel," and who sits in her dead mother's place at the table. But it is Charlie, not Julia, who falls in love with him.

Though the shooting incident finally convinces her father that Charlie must wear dresses and even be sent away to school to become a lady, he finds it "dismal" to see her in "unfamiliar garb." When she is in New Orleans at school and has determined to become superwomanly, he comes to see her, "hungry for her." . . . They spend a secret day together, buying things, wandering around, and sitting near the lake "feeling like a couple of bees in clover." . . . The narrator says about the father and daughter that "such exceedingly young persons could not be expected to restrict themselves to the conventional order." . . . (pp. 142-43)

Although Charlie fails at dance, music, and painting—the proper "clothing" for a young lady—she succeeds as a poet, winning the school poetry prize. When her father is seriously and permanently injured in an accident at home, Charlie is filled with grief and despair that "she would perhaps never see him again as he had been that day at the lake, robust and beautiful, clasping her with loving arms when he said goodbye in the soft twilight" . . . , and she comes home to help care for him and the plantation. Then Julia announces her engagement to Firman Walton; Charlie feels Julia is a hypocrite, hates her, and calls her "no sister of mine" . . . , clearly expressing her own infatuation with Walton. But her "girlish infatuation which had blinded her was swept away in the torrents of a deeper emotion, and left her a woman." . . . She burns her poems, takes off her mother's engagement ring and gives it to Julia, then tells her father that she has been "climbing a high mountain" and has "seen the new moon." . . . Volunteering to be his (now literally missing) "right hand," she seems likely to marry a local boy, Gus Bradley, whose shyness and plodding unimaginativeness have prevented him from telling her of his long-standing love. Despite his drawbacks, Gus is a responsible, decent man; Charlie throws away her "creams" and dresses, puts on her old riding habit and tomboy manners, and tells him she has always "liked" him and is liking him more and more. She will be free to run the plantation as she chooses. The last line is her father's: "I only wanted to know if you were there." . . . (p. 143)

This story, following as it does both ***The Awakening*** and **"The Storm,"** shows a troubled imagination. Chopin deprives her heroine of both objects of her sexual love. Her father's blood is obviously too close, and Walton chooses the perfect southern lady instead of the unconventional but clearly more intelligent and interesting Charlie. (There is no hint whether Chopin's description of the father-daughter relationship is conscious. There are, however, hints of a rather androgynous love; Charlie is a masculinized girl, and Chopin describes the two using the image of two bees in clover, whereas the conclusion to ***The Awakening*** joins the "male" bees with the "female" pinks.) Though Chopin gives Charlie independence, power, and control, she does so by making her over into a "man"—by giving her not just the internal attributes but the behavior and dress that society deemed masculine, even to guns and spurs. The implications seem to be that sex, love, and independence are mutually exclusive for a woman. She must either become "masculine" and lose her sensual life, or become "feminine" and lose her independence; in fact, to have independence a woman *must* become "male." Given Chopin's work before April, 1900, when she wrote **"Charlie,"** it is a saddening conclusion. (pp. 143-44)

[Publicly] Chopin was fully conscious of the implicit contradictions between lady and artist and made the best of them, largely through irony. More privately, her views on art were, in fact, quite serious. She stood as models Walt Whitman, Guy de Maupassant, Sarah Orne Jewett, and Mary Wilkins Freeman, for very specific reasons. All wrote of "life, not fiction" as she said of Maupassant; all saw the shape and form of writing as essential to meaning. . . . It is no surprise that a woman who found herself in a web of strong traditions would hear the voice of such a writer [as Maupassant] when she looked to her own art and her own most private self.

So strong was Chopin's need and desire to affirm the individual vision that she rejected not just society but social movements, including those whose goals might most nearly resemble her own. ***At Fault*** exposes the reformer's impulse when Thérèse insists that David take back his alcoholic wife. Reform—particularly temperance work—was a realm dominated during the nineteenth century by women. It provided . . . one of the few public arenas in which they could work. Chopin, however, apparently found the independence that such work afforded women not appealing enough to counter her repugnance for its content. In **"Miss McEnders,"** Chopin again details her objections to the "feminine" reforming instinct. (pp. 146-47)

[In this story, she] invokes a code of her own—by implication, a code that includes honesty, self-sufficiency, and experience. There is no hint, however, that Chopin ever thought such values could be gained through social movements.

Nor could they be gained through directly didactic literature. As an artist, Chopin rejected Emile Zola for his "mass of prosaic data, offensive and nauseous description and rampant sentimentality" and for "the disagreeable fact that his design is to instruct us." She argued that it was "unpardonable" for an author to speak through his main character. . . . Chopin disliked Thomas Hardy for the same reason: his characters were, she said, "so plainly constructed with the intention of illustrating the purposes of the author, that they do not for a moment convey an impression of reality." . . . As was the case in so many areas of Chopin's life, she faced an apparent paradox: to argue against moralizing is to presume an ethic of one's own. It is doubtful that she ever resolved this artistic conflict; yet she seems to have held consistently to the belief that the personal vision, whatever it may be, comes first and that "there is far too much gratuitous advice bandied about, regardless of personal aptitude and wholly confusing to the individual point of view." . . . [Thus] Chopin as an artist circumvented as best she could the restrictions placed both by the definition of ladyhood and by the popularity, particularly in the woman writer's tradition, of didacticism.

Chopin's southernness, unlike that of many other writers, took no prominent place in her imagination or her life; at least she did not define herself, as Grace King did, by her region. . . . Nevertheless, granted that Chopin's concerns more centrally had to do with what she saw as the almost immutable and far from regionally limited relationship between woman and man, the symbols she chose to invest her subject with imaginative power come from her southern experience. Hence it is not surprising to find, in **"Athénaïse,"** the clear parallel between the experience of a white woman and that of slaves. (pp. 148-49)

[For] a story whose apparent purpose is to show the stages of a woman's sexual awakening, from repulsion to brotherly asexuality to sensuality, in **"Athénaïse"** Chopin weaves into her fabric the themes of mastery and possession far less explicably than she does in ***The Awakening.*** Though Cazeau has rejected his identification with slavemasters, and though Athénaïse has awakened to her attraction for Cazeau, the final note is a somber, possibly ironic evocation of the parallel to slavery. "A little negro baby was crying somewhere. As Athénaïse withdrew from her husband's embrace, the sound arrested her. 'Listen, Cazeau! How Juliette's baby is crying! Pauvre ti chou, I wonder w'at is the matter with it?.' . . . In **"The Storm,"** Chopin uses the language of possession to describe the act of sex: "he possessed her." . . . And in ***The Awakening,*** the core of the tragedy has to do with the links between possession and sexuality. The cry of that baby will chain Athénaïse, Chopin suggests here, as Cazeau alone could never do. (p. 150)

Other sketches and stories deal more directly with blacks and slavery. **"A Little Free-Mulatto"** tells of the difficulties experienced by a girl whose mixed race permits her no world, no friends—until her family moves to "L'Isle des Mulâtres" where everyone is "just like herself." . . . The problem raised by the sketch, of course, is that happiness for such an alienated person can be found only on an island. **"The Bênitous' Slave"** tells the story of old Uncle Oswald, who searches for and finally finds "his" family, the white people who had owned him before emancipation and with whom he finds happiness by repeating his old role. Hence it can easily be seen as a very conventional apology for slavery. Yet in another sense, the story is about Oswald's persistence in getting what he wants, and about identity, for he feels his very name includes the name of the owner.

An odd sketch, **"A December Day in Dixie,"** tells of the reactions of a man who is on a train going South toward home when a brief snowstorm covers the land. A first-person narrative, the sketch shows not just the narrator but the entire community expressing various kinds of imagination and even insanity because of the snow; the businesslike voice of the traveler's seat mate provides the counterpoint. By the end of the sketch, the snow is melting, and the man goes home to his "dear wife" and to a "southern day." The implication seems to be that the intrusion of an alien, specifically a northern, element into southern life temporarily frees that life; its departure shows the conventions still intact.

"Nég Créol" seems, like **"The Bênitous' Slave,"** to endorse the traditional southern view of slavery, for old Chicot continues to serve the impoverished remnant of his old "family," Mamzelle Aglaé, and when she dies he cries "like a dog in pain" and puts a "little black paw" on her stiff body. Chopin, however, complicates this stereotyping. She tells the story from his point of view, noting that for most people his departure is like the "disappearance from the stage of some petty actor whom the audience does not follow in imagination beyond the wings." Of course, Chopin does precisely what she says most audiences do not—the last line shows him center stage. Moreover, her portrayal of the last Boisduré, Alglaé, is far from attractive; she whines and complains constantly to Chicot, using him both psychologically and economically. It is Chicot who has the intelligence and the loyalty that create character.

Once again, Chopin's use of black people in **"A Dresden Lady in Dixie"** can be seen as stereotyped. In order to cover for the little Cajun girl Agapie, Pa-Jeff, who is black, claims he stole the plantation mistress' Dresden figurine. He does it because, despite Agapie's one act of theft, she has spent days caring for him in his old age. Loyalty and kindness, then, along with the ability to act altruistically without any public reward, are attributed to blacks, providing a clear contrast to Miss McEnders' self-serving righteousness. (pp. 150-51)

In a somewhat confusing story, **"In and Out of Old Natchitoches,"** Chopin follows the fate of a white schoolteacher who refuses to allow a mulatto child into her schoolroom. Chopin dispenses with the mulatto family by sending them to the "Isle des Mulâtres." But the schoolteacher, Mademoiselle Suzanne St. Denys Godolph, is apparently punished for her actions. After she spends some time in New Orleans and develops a relationship with a man named Hector, the very man who had sent the little mulatto to her school comes to claim her for his wife. (He is a "modern" cotton planter, apparently a Creole on the way back up the ladder). One could see this story as Suzanne's punishment for acting like a slaveowner by being herself put into a form of slavery. In any case, again Chopin's sympathies lie, not with the prejudiced whites, but with the freer whites and the mulattoes. (p. 152)

Chopin, then, did concern herself with the South, though she did not identify herself with it. Like other southern women writers, she made connections between blacks and women; like others, she found the Old South an impossible and, in certain senses, an undesirable dream. Most of her work, however, is not regional in concern. . . . Moreover, she saw not just southern, but American experience generally as repressive of great art: American writers might equal the French, she said, "were it not that the limitations imposed upon their art by their environment hamper a full and spontaneous expression." . . . And that environment, as we have seen, was that of the particular southern version of the American experience. For Chopin, then, though the South provided some of her important metaphors, community at its deepest level must have become that community of readers who understood and were in sympathy, of artists in her chosen tradition, and of the few persons who were able to see beyond the mask of her divided self.

That divided self was perhaps best expressed in the conflicts experienced by Edna Pontellier in ***The Awakening,*** and in the psychic fissures expressed by Kate Chopin in her creation of three women who might have been one—Edna, Adèle Ratignolle, and Mademoiselle Reisz. For in her 1899 novel, Chopin drew most clearly the portrait of women, and particularly artists who were women, in the South. (pp. 153-54)

Anne Goodwyn Jones, "Kate Chopin: The Life Behind the Mask," in her Tomorrow Is Another Day: The Woman Writer in the South, 1859-1936, *Louisiana State University Press, 1981, pp. 135-82.*

ELAINE GARDINER (essay date 1982)

[*In the following excerpt, Gardiner examines Chopin's use of contrasts, nature imagery, and cyclical plotting in the short story* "Ripe Figs," *noting that these techniques were common to Chopin's early short stories as well as to the novel* The Awakening.]

One of the most charming pieces Kate Chopin ever wrote occupies only one page of ***The Complete Works. . . .*** **"Ripe Figs"** is not a story except in the most rudimentary sense; it barely qualifies as a sketch. But it charms and seduces the reader with its sensuality and form, and it compels multiple readings. (p. 379)

Part of the charm of this sketch is its brevity and its simplicity of plot and sensibility; part is its delineation of a people and a place, its Local Color atmosphere; and part is its delicate sensory description. **"Ripe Figs"** does not interest solely for these qualities, however, no matter how charmingly achieved. For in its scant three-hundred words, Chopin uses some techniques common to much of her work, techniques which culminate in her masterpiece, ***The Awakening.*** Three of these techniques are her use of contrasts, her use of natural imagery, and her cyclical plotting pattern.

Contrasts abound in ***The Awakening:*** the meadow with the sea, New Orleans with Grand Isle, childhood with adulthood, innocence with experience, Edna with Adelle, Edna with Madame Reisz, Robert with Mr. Pontellier, Robert with Alcee, motherhood with artisthood, confinement with space, waking with sleeping, duty with freedom, and life with death. One could go on, but this list suffices to illustrate the centrality of contrasts in this remarkable novel.

Contrasts are central to **"Ripe Figs"** also: Maman-Nainaine and Babette, youth and age, patience and impatience, innocence and experience, exuberance and staidness, spring and summer, summer and fall, figs and chrysanthemums—and again, I could go on. Without these contrasts, the story would lose rhythm and purpose, for contrasts are at the heart of Chopin's syntax, as well as of her theme. For this is a world of slow yet certain movement and change, not stasis. And yet the ironical beauty of Chopin's use of contrasts here is that they ultimately convey and emphasize continuity and stability. Unlike the contrasts in ***The Awakening,*** where opposites strive for dominance, the contrasts in **"Ripe Figs"** are in happy equilibrium, so that movement and stillness coexist and create the special appeal of the work.

Let me elaborate on a few of the contrasts. Maman-Nainaine and her god-daughter, Babette, are counterpoints. Though their ages are not specified, at least a generation seems to separate them, and the difference is that between youth and maturity. Babette is as "restless as a hummingbird"; Maman-Nainaine is as "patient as the statue of la Madone." Babette "dance[s]" as she goes to check the fig trees and "sing[s]" and "dance[s]" when she discovers they have ripened. Maman-Nainaine is "stately" and has a "placid face" as Babette approaches her with the platter of figs. Babette's is the energy that moves nature along, the "force that through the green fuse drives the flower"; Maman-Nainaine's is the tranquil energy of nature's continuity.

The seasons also contrast—the spring and summer of the story, the fall previewed in the final line, and the winter intimated in the story's movement. The sketch opens in the spring when the figs are "like little hard, green marbles" and closes in the summertime when they are "purple" and "fringed around with their rich, green leaves." But though the actual closing occurs in the summer, the reader is left with a vision of fall—"when the chrysanthemums are in bloom," as Maman-Nainaine entrusts Babette with her message for Tante Frosine. The reader supplies the next seasonal reference, a winter marker of some kind, and the contrasts continue—and with them, movement. The figs and chrysanthemums are emblems of the seasons, markers that signal changes in people's lives, but changes here that are not so much changes as repetitions.

A second technique common to most of Chopin's work is the use of natural images—as emotional correlatives, as symbols, and as structural parameters. This use of natural images accounts, in part, for Chopin's early reputation as a Local Colorist and for her enduring reputation as a masterful evocator of place.

In **"Ripe Figs,"** natural images are paramount. Not only are journeys planned according to when figs ripen and chrysanthemums bloom, but places are defined by what they produce; thus, Bayou-Lafourche, for Maman-Nainaine, is the place "where the sugar cane grows." The story is tightly structured between these natural boundaries, both temporal and spatial. It is these that give such movement as there is to the work. For both Babette and Maman-Nainaine wait on natural changes, one by natural inclination, the other by familial directive. And for this reason, most of the piece describes the progress of nature: ". . . the leaves upon the trees were tender yet, and the figs were like little hard, green marbles"; "warm rains came along and plenty of strong sunshine"; the fig trees have "gnarled, spreading branches"; and the "purple figs" are "fringed around with their rich, green leaves."

This is not yet the rich symbolic imagery which structures ***The Awakening,*** though it does have the same unifying power. The figs and chrysanthemums are important, but other fruits and flowers might serve as well, given the same growing seasons, and they probably do serve Maman-Nainaine at other times.

Without being symbolic, . . . these images are still correlatives for moments of readiness in people's lives. Babette is learning, through Maman-Nainaine's tutelage, to watch and to follow the seasons and nature's changes. "Not that," as the text tells us, "the ripening of the figs had the least thing to do with it," but because "that is the way Maman-Nainaine was." And it is probably the way Babette will be. In her childish exuberance and impatience, she studies the natural processes far more closely than Maman-Nainaine, so closely that for her the ripening of the figs is an excruciatingly slow process. For Maman-Nainaine, the natural process is compressed by her inattention; for Babette, it is extended by her scrutiny. . . . (pp. 380-82)

A final technique of **"Ripe Figs"** that recurs in Chopin's work, most notably in ***The Awakening,*** is the use of a cyclical pattern. Many of Chopin's stories end where they began, albeit not without significant change in the characters or their situations. ***The Awakening*** ends where it began—at Grand Isle, but it is a different Edna who walks into the sea than the Edna who walks up from the sea with Robert in the novel's opening. In **"Ripe Figs,"** the change in Babette is much more subtle, nothing more significant than a couple of months' growth and a sense of observance and expectation rewarded. But the circular pattern of **"Ripe Figs,"** unlike most other Chopin stories with this pattern, is unbroken at the end. For with the ripening of the figs in the summertime begins the next period of waiting, the continuance of the cycle, both of nature and of the characters' lives. Maman-Nainaine will travel to Toussaint in the fall, "when the chrysanthemums are in bloom." The reader finishes the sketch anticipating the movements to follow—movements directed by the seasons, by natural happenings, by the cyclical patterns of these people's lives. These patterns both imitate and anticipate nature's cycle until, with Yeats, we ask: "how can we know the dancer from the dance?" (p. 382)

Elaine Gardiner, "'Ripe Figs': Kate Chopin in Miniature," in Modern Fiction Studies, *Vol. 28, No. 3, Autumn, 1982, pp. 379-82.*

ADDITIONAL BIBLIOGRAPHY

Dyer, Joyce. "The Restive Brute: The Symbolic Presentation of Repression and Sublimation in Kate Chopin's 'Fedora'." *Studies in Short Fiction* 18, No. 3 (Summer 1981): 261-65.

Discussion of the short story 'Fedora.' Dyer considers this brief story one of Chopin's best studies of repression and sublimation.

———. "Gouvernail, Kate Chopin's Sensitive Bachelor." *Southern Literary Journal* 14, No. 1 (Fall 1981): 46-55.

Discussion of the recurring character Gouvernail and of his function in *The Awakening* and other works by Chopin. Dyer contends that since Gouvernail grows increasingly cynical in Chopin's works, he is correctly omitted from her later, "happy ending" stories.

Eaton, Clement. "Breaking a Path for the Liberation of Women in the South." *The Georgia Review* XXVIII, No. 2 (Summer 1974): 187-99.*

Examines the works of women writers who opposed the inequality of men and women through their works. Kate Chopin and her novel *The Awakening* are included in the discussion.

Fletcher, Marie. "The Southern Woman in the Fiction of Kate Chopin." *Louisiana History* VII, No. 2 (Spring 1966): 117-32.

Discussion of Chopin's female characters. Fletcher notes that while Chopin strove to depict realistic characters, her Southern women still adhere in large degree to traditional values, particularly with regard to the proper expression of sexuality.

Gilbert, Sandra M. "The Second Coming of Aphrodite: Kate Chopin's Fantasy of Desire." *The Kenyon Review* V, n.s., No. 3 (Summer 1983): 42-66.

Discussion of *The Awakening* as a feminist fantasy based on the matriarchal myth of Aphrodite/Venus.

Leary, Lewis. "Kate Chopin, Liberationist?" *Southern Literary Journal* III, No. 1 (Fall 1970): 138-44.

Discussion of the feminine and human aspects of Chopin's fiction. Leary discusses Chopin's personal and artistic aims based on evidence provided in Per Seyersted's *Kate Chopin: A Critical Biography* and *The Complete Works of Kate Chopin*.

May, John R. "Local Color in *The Awakening*." *The Southern Review* n.s. VI, No. 4 (October 1970): 1031-40.

Discusses the compatibility of theme, symbolism, and local color in *The Awakening*. May also interprets sexuality in the novel as a universal symbol of freedom.

Ringe, Donald A. "Romantic Imagery in Kate Chopin's *The Awakening*." *American Literature* 43, No. 4 (January 1972): 580-88.

Examines *The Awakening* as a universal, rather than a feminist novel. To support his contention, Ringe refers to the epiphanous experiences of male protagonists in short stories by Chopin, epiphanies which are depicted in much the same way as the revelations of Edna Pontellier in *The Awakening*.

Skaggs, Peggy. "The Boy's Quest in Kate Chopin's 'A Vocation and a Voice'." *American Literature* 51, No. 2 (May 1979): 170-76.

Comparison of *The Awakening* and the short story "A Vocation and a Voice." Skaggs parallels the experiences of Edna Pontellier with those of the boy in the short story, and finds that each gains self-knowledge only after rejecting society's insistence upon sexual repression. Like Donald A. Ringe, Skaggs argues against a feminist reading of *The Awakening*.

Thornton, Lawrence. "*The Awakening:* A Political Romance." *American Literature* 52, No. 1 (March 1980): 50-66.

Comparison of Emma Bovary and Edna Pontellier. Thornton considers the protagonist of Gustave Flaubert's *Madame Bovary* an innocent romantic who is disillusioned by the realities of romance, while Edna Pontellier discovers true freedom only to find that she cannot exercise it without unacceptable consequences.

"Love in Louisiana, Kate Chopin: A Forgotten Southern Novelist." *The Times Literary Supplement*, No. 3580 (October 1970): 1163.

Discussion of local color, love, and passion in Chopin's works.

Zlotnick, Joan. "A Woman's Will: Kate Chopin on Selfhood, Wifehood, and Motherhood." *The Markam Review*, No. 3 (October 1968).

Discusses earlier criticism of Chopin's works. Zlotnick uses Chopin's fiction and diary entries to support the contention that there are affinities between the author and her fictional creations, particularly Edna Pontellier in *The Awakening*, which reveal rebellious tendencies Chopin could not express in her own life.

René Daumal

1908-1944

French novelist, essayist, poet, short-story writer, and dramatist.

Daumal was the author of works characterized by an obsessive spiritual restlessness and by a profound capacity for esoteric scholarship. Believing that art is "knowledge realized in action," he approached writing as primarily a means of expressing his lifelong quest for spiritual enlightenment and liberation, a quest which led him to the study of Sanskrit and the sacred texts of Hinduism. Daumal's two most important works, *La grande beuverie (A Night of Serious Drinking),* and *Le Mont Analogue (Mont Analogue),* describe his rejection of Western values and his subsequent embracement of Eastern philosophy. Daumal's writings are related to those of the Surrealists in that he fully approved of such Surrealist principles as the denial of the existence of external reality and the advocacy of "the Absurd as the purest and most basic form of metaphysical existence." But Daumal was only marginally a Surrealist, for his own idiosyncratic beliefs played as important a role as Surrealist thought in shaping his aesthetic. Moreover, he found certain features of the Surrealist movement unappealing. In particular, his preoccupation with Hinduism and "knowledge of the self," which for him became "the first, last and fundamental object of knowledge," led him to eschew involvement in the types of literary and ideological disputes in which the Surrealists enthusiastically engaged.

Daumal was born at Boulzicourt, in Ardennes. As a young man he attended secondary school at Charleville and then Reims, where he met Roger Gilberte-Lecomte, Roger Vailland, and Robert Meyrat, who comprised a group known as the Simplists. The Simplists dedicated themselves to the principles of Surrealism and to exploring the limits of human consciousness. Together they attempted such phenomena as prearranged meetings in group dreams and experimented with drugs such as hashish and carbon tetrachloride. Daumal's experiences with carbon tetrachloride, which for a time left him near death, provided the inspiration many years later for his essay "Une experience fondamentale," a work in which he described the attainment of a "new state of being" superior in every way to the realm of ordinary awareness and the "passive, backward-looking world of dreams." Roger Shattuck has designated "Une experience fondamentale" as "one of the most authentic and influential texts on extrarational experience written in this century." The Simplists later reemerged as students in Paris, where in 1928 they founded the journal *Le grand jeu.* This magazine was conceived as a challenge by the younger generation to the Surrealist establishment. Its success is attested to by the fact that, soon after its appearance, André Breton, the leader of the Surrealists, invited Daumal to join the Surrealist movement, stating that "he who speaks in this manner, having had the courage to say that he is no longer in control of himself, had no reason to prefer being separated from us." Daumal nonetheless publicly declined Breton's invitation, declaring that, through petty quarreling and controversy over their Communist party affiliation, the Surrealists had lost sight of their goals of social and spiritual liberation. Breton thereupon "expelled" Daumal from the Surrealist movement.

René Daumal

In 1930, following the decline of *Le grand jeu,* Daumal met Alexandre de Salzmann, a disciple of the Russian mystic G. I. Gurdjieff. Salzmann introduced Daumal to Hindu religion and philosophy, an interest that preoccupied him for the rest of his life. In his enthusiasm for Eastern thought, Daumal taught himself Sanskrit and translated many sacred Hindu texts into French. Many of these translations appear in the collection *Bharata: L'origine du théatre, la poesie et la musique en Inde.* In 1936 Daumal's first book, the poetry collection *Le contre-ciel,* appeared. This volume was well received by critics and was awarded the 1936 Jacques Doucet prize for literature. In *Le contre-ciel,* Daumal addressed many themes that recur in his later works, such as the concept of death as a type of Doppelgänger, or "double," and the absurdity of existence. The satire *A Night of Serious Drinking* was the only other work to appear during his lifetime. Daumal died of tuberculosis in 1944, leaving unfinished what later became his most admired work, the novel *Mount Analogue.*

Although Daumal wrote numerous essays on a wide variety of philosophical and religious subjects, including several humorous "'pataphysical" pieces based on Alfred Jarry's absurd "science of imaginary solutions," most critics regard his fictional works *A Night of Serious Drinking* and *Mount Analogue* as his most successful literary achievements. In the first of these, Daumal scathingly denounced the mediocrities and pretensions of French intellectual society. This satire divides society into three groups designated by Daumal as Fidgeters, Fabricators, and Clarificators. The Fidgeters are those who are too aimlessly busy to have time for introspective thought; the Fabricators are the decadent, romantic artists who interpret the world through their own ennervated emotions; and the Clarificators are scientists and philosophers who possess the intellectual superiority to lead society, but who lack spiritual understanding. Daumal's upside-down logic and bizarre twists of plot in this often ironic fantasy imitate the absurdist logic of Jarry and the Surrealists. However, the ending of the tale, which describes the narrator's ascent to a higher, non-dialectical plane of consciousness through the stripping away of all superficialities, clearly reveals the strong undercurrent of Eastern philosophy in Daumal's work. Whereas *A Night of Serious Drinking* concerns those elements of Western society that Daumal rejected, *Mount Analogue* affirms a positive spiritual doctrine. In this work, Daumal attempted to present his own spiritual values in the form of an allegory or myth. Mount Analogue represents the gateway to the invisible world, and though its summit is inaccessible, its base is "accessible to human beings as nature has made them." This description reflects Daumal's own conviction, inspired by the teachings of Gurdjieff, that the key to transcendental knowledge and experience lies in the proper understanding of everyday realities, and in developing a sense of community with others. There is a substratum of Hindu myth in *Mount Analogue* that has led some critics to remark that the book is incomprehensible to readers unfamiliar with Eastern philosophy. However, while many of the episodes in *Mount Analogue* are undoubtedly based on the archetypes of Eastern mythology, and while familiarity with these sources may enhance one's understanding of the novel, most critics find *Mount Analogue* a lucid and amusing work that can be appreciated without reference to an external system of spiritual values.

Although Daumal was a controversial figure in his lifetime, critical reaction to his work in the years since his death has been generally favorable. Critics have consistently praised Daumal for his wit, his profound interest in language, and his scholarship. As Roger Shattuck has pointed out, it was Daumal's determination to learn Sanskrit that "prevented his early attraction to Oriental religion from degenerating into a misinformed cultism." Shattuck adds that "Daumal is one of the few men in this century to have combined Eastern and Western thought into something more valuable than a set of personal eccentricities." Daumal's sincerity and erudition continue to attract new readers to his works today. As interest in the exploration of inner life continues to grow, so has Daumal's stature among readers and critics.

PRINCIPAL WORKS

Le contre-ciel (poetry) 1936
La grande beuverie (satire) 1938
[*A Night of Serious Drinking*, 1979]
Chaque fois que l'aube paraît (essays) 1940; also published as *L'evidence absurde*, 1972
Le Mont Analogue (unfinished novel) 1952
[*Mount Analogue*, 1959]
Essais et Notes (essays) 1953
Poésie noire, poésie blanche (poetry) 1954
René Daumal: Lettres à ses amis (letters) 1958
"The Great Magician" (short story) 1960; published in journal *Evergreen Review*
En Gggarrrde (drama) 1964; published in *The Avante-Garde, Dada and Surrealism: An Anthology of Plays*
Bharata: L'origine du théatre, la poesie et la musique en Inde (essays) 1970
Tu t'es toujours trompé (prose) 1970
Les pouvoir de la parole (essays) 1972
Rasa, or Knowledge of the Self: Essays on Indian Aesthetics and Selected Sanskrit Studies (essays) 1982

A translated selection of Daumal's poetry has appeared in *The Poetry of Surrealism*.

J. TORMA (letter date 1929)

[Torma was a French poet and dramatist. He has been described as an author who "began his literary venture where Rimbaud, Lautrémont, and Jarry had left off." This comment refers to the bizarre, anti-aesthetic nature of Torma's works, which include the drama Le bétrou *and a collection of notes entitled* Euphorismes. *Like Daumal, Torma was influenced by the works of Alfred Jarry and by the latter's concept of 'Pataphysics, a casual ideological doctrine that rejects any religious, scientific, or philosophical explanation of life, as well as recognizing no moral or aesthetic values. In the following excerpt from a letter to Daumal, Torma makes reference to Daumal's article* "'Pataphysics and the Revelation of Laughter," *which was published in the journal* Bifur, *and criticizes Daumal's contention that, as Torma phrases it, "'Pataphysics can be married to mysticism."]*

Don't make excuses for having sent me the number of *Bifur* [in which Daumal had just published an article entitled **"Pataphysics and the Revelation of Laughter."**] *Bifur* is *Bifur*, and you can write on the walls if you feel like it. If you hadn't sent it, I wouldn't have read your essay—and learned that 'Pataphysics can be married to mysticism. That still interests me. (p. 120)

You probably suspect that I don't much appreciate being slapped with the absolute, believing in no other absolute than that of the slap. Isn't this the one and only? Your article annoys me, because everything in it is true. But the tone is missing. Precisely, the word true means nothing here and is a patsy for a pataphysical pat. You're right to speak of chaos. But it's obvious that you believe in it like a kind of God. In spite of all your finesse, dear René, you're on a pilgrim's progress. Let me be malicious. You're playing with the absolute.

Your 'Pataphysics laughs too much. And with a laugh much too comic and cosmic. Putting metaphysics behind 'Pataphysics is like making a belief into a mere facade. When in fact the real nature of 'Pat. is to be a facade which is only a facade, with nothing behind it.

I can't see Dr. Faustroll [the principal character in Alfred Jarry's novel *Exploits and Opinions of Dr. Faustroll, 'Pataphysician*] laughing. I don't have a copy of the book at the moment. But I know what I'm saying—eh?—you write, "Faustroll sneers." You're frightfully out of date. We've passed Mephisto. And evil and a bad conscience, and conscience itself. If Faustroll played at being Mephistophelean it could only be for the pataphysic hell of it. Because Mephistopheleanism is still part of their cookery, as we say. Faustroll is imperturbable. Or not even. He seems natural and isn't natural. Because nature is only a gag neither more nor less interesting than any other.

He doesn't choose. He makes no distinction, he has no preferences. He navigates upside down. But even his navigation doesn't exist. These characters and their adventures aren't real. You can see this in the death and resurrection of Bosse-de-Nage. Still, they aren't imaginary like the heroes of novels and fantastic tales. For in the case of these characters we suppose, at least temporarily and extravagant as the hypothesis may seem, that they could without too much unlikelihood exist. So I see what you're driving at when you say that all defined existence is a scandal. With the One and Co. But why not say—that undefined existence is a scandal, even though the word scandal is unnecessary. Faustroll says: I am God, and he certainly has as much right to say it as God himself. But it's going a bit far—or not far enough—to take him seriously. (pp. 120-21)

J. Torma, in a letter to René Daumal on October 20, 1929, translated by Neal Oxenhandler, in Evergreen Review, *Vol. 4, No. 13, May-June, 1960, pp. 120-21.*

RENÉ DAUMAL (essay date 1941)

[In the following excerpt from an essay on Hindu poetics originally published in Les Cahiers du Sud, *No. 236 (1941), Daumal explains what is in his view the superiority of Eastern to Western concepts of humanity and the universe, a premise on which his most important works are based.]*

One day I saw that all those books had offered me only fragmentary plans of the palace. The first knowledge I acquired, painful and very real, was that of my prison. The first reality I experienced was that of my ignorance, my vanity, my laziness, of everything which bound me to the prison. And when I looked again at the images of the treasures which India, through books and intellect, had sent me, I saw why these messages remain incomprehensible.

We approach those ancient and living truths with our modern European psychic attitudes: there are thus perpetual opacities.

Modern man believes himself adult, complete, having no more to do, until death, than to gain and spend goods (money, vital forces, learning), without these transactions affecting that which calls itself "I." The Hindu regards himself as an entity to complete, a false vision to rectify, a composite of substances to transform, a multiplicity to unify.

We regard knowledge as the specific activity of the intellect. For the Hindu, each of man's activities is seen as a participant in knowledge.

For us, the development of knowledge entails the acquisition, by perceptual and logical apparatus, of new information pertaining to things we can perceive or about which we can hear. In Hindu thought, the development of knowledge entails the perfecting of the apparatus and the organic acquisition of new faculties of understanding.

We say that to know is "to be able" and "to foresee." For the Hindu, it is to become and to transform oneself.

Our experimental method aspires to apply itself to all objects, *except* to the "self," which is rejected in the domains of philosophical speculation and religious faith. For the Hindu, the "self" is the first, last, and fundamental object of knowledge—not only experimental but transformative.

We regard men as equal in *being* and different only in having innate qualities and acquired learning. The Hindu recognizes a hierarchy in the being of men: the master is not only more knowledgeable or more skillful than the student, he *is* essentially more. And it is this that makes possible the uninterrupted transmission of truth.

Finally, for modern man, the acquisition of knowledge is an activity that is separate, independent (or desired to be so) from all others. For the Hindu, it is the transformation of man himself and implies a complete change in his personal expression, in his entire manner of living. (pp. 7-8)

Rene Daumal, "To Approach the Hindu Poetic Art," in his Rasa; or, Knowledge of the Self: Essays on Indian Aesthetics and Selected Sanskrit Studies, *translated by Louise Landes Levi, New Directions, 1982, pp. 7-19.*

ROGER SHATTUCK (essay date 1952)

[An American critic, editor, and translator, Shattuck is an authority on late nineteenth- and twentieth-century French literature. His works include The Banquet Years *(1959),* Marcel Proust *(1974), and* The Craft and Context of Translation *(1961). In the following excerpt from his introduction to* Mount Analogue, *originally published in French in 1952, Shattuck traces the themes of this novel throughout Daumal's life and work.]*

René Daumal's work obliges one to think both in terms of shoes and pocket money, and in terms of the true nature of Western civilization. In all his writing, the world of concrete objects carries its full common sense of pleasure and hardship, of beauty and blight. At the same time his philosophical turn of mind involves him in a real struggle of ideas, one usually carried on by closed minds and obscured by fuzzy words. This struggle pits the 'materialists' with their rational methods against the 'idealists' with their intuitive or spiritual insights. After twenty-five centuries of warfare, the battle lines have lost any orderly array. In recent years Julien Benda and Wyndham Lewis (for the materialists) and Henri Bergson and A. N. Whitehead (for the idealists) have rolled up some powerful as well as noisy artillery. Raising a startlingly clear voice in the din, Daumal proposes something like a modified pacificism. Or rather he tells us all over again that the true battle lies within us and calmly transfers the struggle to the slopes of an interior mountain which we must climb. Most of us find that a harder task than carrying on a rousing battle with an ideological enemy.

There are considerable portions of Daumal's thinking that leave one with the sensation of watching a man climb out of sight on a steep slope. Yet there is no display of superiority or showmanship in his progress; his convictions and his writing are locked together in a profound integrity of purpose. (p. 1)

[***Mount Analogue***] makes no reference to esoteric knowledge; the events it narrates are incredible, yet entirely plausible. The work remained unfinished when he died, but enough had been written to allow us to grasp the whole. . . .

I have set myself the principal task of tracing the themes of ***Mount Analogue*** through Daumal's brief life and long work. (p. 2)

Daumal's work follows Nerval's in its resolve to fuse body and Spirit, speech and sleep, logic and intuition, in order to enter a 'second life'. Nerval, however, prepared himself increasingly to disappear for good into that other world, and finally hung himself in a Paris alley. Daumal, somewhat less afflicted, or blessed, with night vision, resolutely returned to this world, his eyes seeking light again, his mind struggling to tell what he had seen. He was one of the sanest and most wide-awake of men. (p. 3)

The poems, the philosophical and literary essays, the symbolic tales, the letters, all lead back to a *mind*—unquenchable, fearless, full of human sympathy, devoted to seeking and teaching truth. His least polished and most fragmentary works, of which there are many because of the circumstances of his career, give evidence of the scope of his thought and the range of his knowledge. He was entirely at home in philosophy, science, and mathematics. In literature he had absorbed the works of Nerval and Rimbaud and Jarry, three of the most extreme modern visionaries, without losing his perspective on reality and language. (p. 8)

Having cast his mind deep into Indian philosophy, Daumal senses that the reality and meaning of the world can come to us at every moment without our having to rely wholly on extreme situations to wrench us into awareness. Action, as has been pointed out many times, is for Westerners both stimulant and drug. The four stages of Hindu initiation, from the Vedas to the Upinshads, and the complementary disciplines of Yoga and Zen, prepare us not for a career of great exploits to be recalled in old age, but for a life increasingly dedicated to 'the teaching which cuts through illusion'.

Daumal held these several levels of knowledge in place not only by a keen sensibility and intelligence, but also by a sense of ironic perspective on them all—the simple need to laugh finally at the enormous disparity between the particular and the universal, between illusion and truth, between our cross-eyed version of things (by the very fact that we need *two* eyes to see 'straight') and what he facetiously described as the 'objective strabism' inherent in reality. One of his most brilliant demonstrations, called **'The Falsehood of Truth'**, isolates *error* as the principle of creation and existence, for one tiny truth would obliterate the entire universe by its wonder. This advanced cosmic sense of humour has not other name than Jarry's term, pataphysics. (pp. 9-10)

Daumal's waggishness did not prevent him from seeking, seriously, to penetrate the mystery of human thought. Biographical facts reveal the outward circumstances of his search. Daumal's first encounter with the reality of life came not in the usual form of awakening desire, but as an intense and terrifying awareness of death. And when he had conquered this inner threat by learning to control his physical and nervous system, he went on to overcome the temptation of suicide and later the temptation of drugs. And he had to struggle with the temptation to which poets are prone: the tendency to conceive of life and reality entirely through language. ***Mount Analogue,*** in its simplicity of expression and universality of meaning, probably represents Daumal's ultimate reckoning with the problem of language, vehicle and obstacle.

Through these stages of inner struggle, Daumal became increasingly aware of a mode of mental operation which is not new with him or with the age, but which has remained foreign to our activist way of life. He understood very early that the basic act of consciousness is a negation, a dissociation of the *I* from the exterior world of *not-I*. Meaningful perception reduces and refines the *I,* withdraws it from the world into an increasingly strict identity or subjectivity. Then, however, beginning a vibratory rhythm which must follow if self-annihilation is not to result, the pure consciousness expands again into all things, experiences the world subjectively once more, loses itself in the mystery of creation. Baudelaire describes this rhythm of consciousness in the terse words that open *Mon coeur mis à nu:* 'De la vaporisation et de la centralisation du *Moi*. Tout est là' [''The vaporization and the centralization of my *self*. That is the whole of it.'']. Daumal would accept the terms and reverse the order. Centralization or concentration: elimination of everything exterior in order to arrive at the intensity of self-awareness. Vaporization: reassimilation of all the universe in the amplitude of sympathy and action. The alternation of contraction and expansion gives human consciousness its rest and motion, its inner time and space, its own East and West. In contrast to Bergson's intuitive surrender to the object of knowledge, Daumal asserts over and over again in poetry and in discourse the essentially masculine, creative, and revelatory act of *negation,* of dissociating the world from ourselves and from itself in a meaningful dialectic, as when God divided light from darkness, the firmament from the waters. This initial stage of consciousness Daumal called an 'asceticism'; only if this ascetic discipline has been achieved can one attempt the opposite and more tempting movement of fusion with all things.

In 1941 the editor of *Les Cahiers de la Pléiade* asked a number of writers to describe the most significant and crucial experience in their life. Most of the others agreed and then begged off; Daumal, spurred by the example of Milosz' *Epistle to Storge,* produced one of the most authentic and influential texts on extra-rational experience written in this century. In a bare dozen pages Daumal struggles to describe and analyze in rational terms sensations and reflections on the brink of unconsciousness and even death. His youthful experiments with carbon tetrachloride, whose results he has corroborated from other sources, furnish his direct evidence. For nearly twenty years this evidence has left him with the absolute *certainty* (he repeats and underlines the word) of having entered another world. It is not, he insists, the passive backward-looking world of dreams to which he attained, but a realm of superior awareness, which he describes in visual, mathematical, and acoustic detail. Is there, then, more than one kind of unconsciousness? . . . **'A Fundamental Experiment'** ***(Une expérience fondamentale),*** as this essay is called, traces a clear instance of the rhythm of consciousness which I have been describing—first, rigorous consolidation of one's identity as an individual, then expansion into a new realm of direct knowledge by semi-intuitive projection (here, artificially induced by toxic action), and then reconsolidation of one's consciousness by rational scrutiny of one's perceptions. This essay is probably the most appropriate of Daumal's works to read after ***Mont Analogue.***

From his unflinching investigations of the nature of thought and consciousness, Daumal extracted very early the unshakable premises of his philosophy. He rejected any dualistic conception of the universe in favour of a unity of meaning, of existence, and of thought. 'Dialectical materialism, carried to its limit, is not essentially different from absolute idealism or from the Vedanta carried to their limits.' . . . Daumal . . . asserted the convergence of the three great approaches to truth: philosophy (especially Plato's dialectic), the 'initiation' of the occult tradition properly understood, and poetry ('a means of achieving sacred knowledge').

This is the heart of Daumal's thinking, the result of experiments performed back and forth across the threshold of his own consciousness, of a wide ranging knowledge, and of a discipline of mind which usually comes with age and not with youth. Nowhere in his writings does Daumal invoke the doctrines of grace and prayer. He worships no benevolent or anthropomorphic god, nor does he speak of any deity in the Western sense. (His first volume of poems bears the title, ***Counter-Heaven,*** and one of the principal characters in ***Mount Analogue*** is ironically dubbed 'Father Sogol'.) Man achieves inner spiritual progress by his own efforts, by a human discipline that is not a gift of god and can be learned from other men further advanced on the path of knowledge. Teaching and initiation are central to all religions and cultures. Within a system where no truth comes by divine revelation but only by human attainment, the sense of a tradition of knowledge comes to support the entire structure of life. And thus Daumal spoke unflinchingly of a Doctrine, meaning not a narrow set of rituals or dogmas, not art for art's sake in aesthetics, not a fixed philosophical position, but a number of paths leading to the same goal: a higher form of life.

Personally I can follow Daumal this far (and with some misgivings along the way) only because his discipline as a writer kept him out of the swamps of obscurity and false posturing, and because he never deserted for long the everyday world of shoes and pocket money. Even the insufficiencies of language led him back to it. (pp. 10-14)

The insistence that the goal of life is not elsewhere but in life itself, in perfecting life, places Daumal closer to Rabelais (for whom he had great admiration) than to Plotinus. ***La grande beuverie,*** for all the rigour of its dissection of contemporary culture, is a rollicking free-for-all full of word play, pastiche, and self irony. It gives in highly entertaining yet serious form the preliminary negative stage of thought. During the course of this imaginary drunk, Daumal examines, caricatures, and rejects the diversions and delusions of supposedly intelligent people. And yet this furious humour leads to the conclusion that man, rid of his illusions, can attain to a state of maturity.

It should not now seem surprising that at the end of his life Daumal wished to express himself very simply and affirmatively. ***Mount Analogue,*** the work he then proceeded to write, transposes into fiction his own spiritual autobiography. . . . At the time of the book's appearance in France, many reviewers speculated busily over the particular literary genre to which it should be assigned. Most of them settled for the *conte philosophique* [''philosophic story''] in the tradition of Voltaire and Swift, crossed with the marvel tale in the tradition of Cyrano de Bergerac, Poe, and Jules Verne. Daumal himself had said he wanted to do for metaphysics what Verne had done for physics. The critics might have mentioned Bunyan and Blake as well. Though extraneous, this discussion served to indicate the richness of Daumal's story: an adventure tale bordering on science fiction, encompassing poetic and broadly comic passages, leading into spiritual quest, and ending . . . ending in the air. The open ending of ***Mount Analogue*** is only momentarily exasperating; one soon understands that this is the only conclusion that could have kept the book within the domain of literature and at the same time imply a surpassing of any literary form. . . . Daumal's own tongue-in-cheek sub-title turns out to be an accurate designation after all: 'A novel of symbolically authentic non-Euclidean adventures in mountain climbing.'

Mount Analogue is a marvel tale, yet every strand of the story arises out of a perfectly credible psychological situation. At the opening of the story the narrator has published, and forgotten, an article he wrote in half-amused speculation and in which he 'never really believed'. Yet by the irony of human error, that article opens the door to final truth. By a similar irony the only external threat to the expedition comes from some of the original members who betray its goals and form a rival expedition. Even though a spiritual adventure is being related, Daumal comes back several times to the practical and symbolic consideration of money. The unique financial structure of the island of Mount Analogue, far from supporting a material commerce only, derives from and leads back to the highest aspirations of the community. A few unpretentious words . . . repeat the refrain of Daumal's thought: growing up in modern Western civilization obliges us to extinguish certain faculties and to retreat within a pattern of experience that cuts us off from most spiritual knowledge. ***Mount Analogue*** speaks of voyage and liberation in a soft voice that draws one closer to hear.

The most deadly sin, the insidious pride that comes closest to causing the downfall of the expedition, appears in the form of *libido sciendi:* the lust to know. The theme works particularly well, for in the early stages of the story such scientific questions as the curvature of space, high altitude survival, and linguistic shift on the island play a role both in the outward circumstances of the action and in its symbolic ramifications. As time goes on, however, knowledge in the scientific sense becomes meaningless, and each individual finds himself confronted by the single responsibility to advance, in concert with a few companions, toward a snowy peak in a black sky. Early in the story, we are given a picture of the most inhuman of environments: a monastic order corrupted by mutual distrust and denunciation. Later, on the slopes of Mount Analogue, a sense of community emerges as one of the highest forms of knowledge.

The central metaphor of the mountain scarcely needs the justification Daumal gives it in the opening pages. His gifts as a poet allow him to put to vivid use the details of landscape and atmosphere, the dangers and hardships of mountain climbing. The adventures recounted here, symbolic as they may be, never cease to be concerned with frozen toes and heavy packs as well as with the stages of a spiritual quest. There is some mention of a 'higher will' having sway over the island, but a will which confines its acts to preparing the circumstances under which each man will seek his salvation. Thus, the most moving scene in Daumal's novel occurs when Sogol, in a moment of triumph and humility and insight, finds the first 'peradam', a precious stone peculiar to Mount Analogue. In that moment he is reborn and discovers his identity. The later chapters, if written, would probably have described a corresponding transformation in each of the other characters.

I cannot help seeing ***Mount Analogue*** as itself a peradam in the stony fields of literature. The peradam possesses such perfect transparence that it escapes the notice of all except those who are inwardly prepared and outwardly situated to catch sight of its glint. Its discovery and possession give evidence of true election among men and confer inner peace. And the peradam, as we are told in the heading of the uncompleted Chapter V, can curve and uncurve space because of its unique index of refraction. ***Mount Analogue,*** the novel, has the force of a curving and uncurving lens for our minds. Through it, we can glimpse that 'other world' of which Nerval spoke, and Spinoza and Socrates. And yet it is hard to look through it, for so limpid a substance almost escapes one's attention even when it is right under one's eyes. One could conceivably read every word of the book without 'seeing' a thing.

Because of the book's truncated form, one aspect of its 'curvature' comes into full sight only in Daumal's summary of the remaining action. 'Before setting out for the next refuge, one must prepare those coming after to occupy the place one is leaving.' When we reach this passage, we have just been prepared; for ***Mount Analogue*** itself embodies the 'knowledge to be passed on to other seekers'. We have been shown what it is only too human to forget: that between learning and teaching there exists no secure and stationary zone of knowledge. To know means to be learning or to be teaching; there is no middle way. The human mind enjoys no state of passive grace. Yet, beyond a certain point, teaching becomes a very subtle and deceptive undertaking, scarcely to be distinguished from learning. 'Socrates', Daumal writes, 'never teaches anything. He plays the fool, and from time to time tells a legend, assuring us that it's just for his own amusement.' So Daumal, too, with obvious relish, tells us a legend in which we find not doctrine but a sturdy weave of action and reflection, not thoughts only, but men thinking. (pp. 14-17)

Roger Shattuck, in an introduction to Mount Analogue: An Authentic Narrative *by René Daumal, translated by Roger Shattuck, Vincent Stuart Ltd., 1959, pp. 1-18.*

LEON S. ROUDIEZ (essay date 1960)

[*In the following excerpt Roudiez, editor of* The French Review, *discusses* Mount Analogue. *Roudiez compares Daumal's novel to Dante's* Divine Comedy, *but concludes that the most interesting aspect of the novel is what it reveals about the mind of the author.*]

In the translator [Roger Shattuck's] own words, [***Mount Analogue***] by René Daumal is "an adventure tale bordering on science fiction, encompassing poetic and broadly comic passages, leading into spiritual quest." . . .

Undoubtedly, Daumal's novel partakes of science fiction, the imaginary voyage and the philosophical tale. Unlike, however, the tales of Voltaire, that master of the genre, this one is conventionally proper: sex and violence are conspicuously absent. More important, though, is the fact that it leads in the opposite direction from most seventeenth or eighteenth-century imaginary voyages: while the latter stressed common sense and pointed toward a materialistic interpretation of the universe, Daumal rejects both. There must, indeed, have been conscious irony in his using a science-fiction form to emphasize the vanity of scientific knowledge.

Actually **"Mount Analogue"** is symbolic rather than satirical, and its serious pages far outnumber its comic ones. The reader soon realizes that resemblances with most specimens of the above-mentioned genres are superficial: a truer "analogy" might be found with Dante's "Divine Comedy," specifically with the Mount of Purgatory, located in the hemisphere of water as Mount Analogue is in the South Pacific. Daumal's heroes undergo a purifying experience when they approach and begin to climb the mountain which is described as "the bond between Earth and Sky. Its solitary summit reaches the sphere of eternity, and its base spreads out in manifold foothills into the world of mortals."

They realize that the things they had prized most highly are valueless; they are purged of all non-essential considerations, and each one gradually turns inward in order to seek answers to fundamental questions: Who am I? Why? What do I seek? Daumal himself gives no answers—partly because he died before he could finish the novel, mainly because each individual must find them within himself.

Because of the lesson it implies, **"Mount Analogue"** is an obvious antidote to the stories of material success and triumphant technology that are abundantly available. The connoisseur will ponder over questions of philosophical and thematic sources; devotees of Zen Buddhism will be intrigued by the work of an admirer of Hindu philosophy. As a work of art, however, the book has quite a few shortcomings; indeed, the mature reader will be more intrigued by the mind of the author than impressed by his literary accomplishment.

Leon S. Roudiez, "Ascent to Understanding," in The New York Times Book Review, *July 10, 1960, p. 26.*

VERNON HALL, JR. (essay date 1960)

[*In the following excerpt, Hall commends the wit and clarity of Daumal's prose in* Mount Analogue.]

When René Daumal died in 1944, at the age of thirty-six, he left behind him this unfinished tale [**"Mount Analogue"**] a fitting image of his unfinished life. In a certain sense, any poet who died young leaves us speculating as to what he would have produced later, but a Keats could have ten years less of life and still carve his name deeply on the tablet of authentic poets. René Daumal was no Keats. What he had done at his death gave promise, gave hope, but that is all. Perhaps the extravagant tone of the reviews of this book in France owed something to the romantic Chatterton tradition and something to the fact that the reviewers could find in it what they themselves wanted without the embarrassment of having the author's ideas contradict their own.

Daumal's life was, like his novel, a kind of spiritual adventure. . . .

His journalistic and poetic activities were largely subordinate to his search for enlightenment. Thanks to a follower of Gurdjieff, Alexandre de Salzmann (the prototype of Father Sogol), Daumal became convinced that the essential truth lay in the sacred books of India. His belief in the necessity of eliminating everything exterior in order to arrive at intense self-awareness is the controlling principle of **"Mount Analogue."**

In spite of its rather pretentious sub-title, this little philosophical tale, thanks to the wit and clarity of the prose, reads as easily as a superior piece of Science Fiction. Under the leadership of Father Sogol (Logos spelt backward) a group of determined Alpinists sail on the yacht Impossible, reach the mountain they must climb and set up the first camp. At this point, in the middle of a sentence, the novel breaks off, but not before the reader knows that Mount Analogue, stretching from earth to heaven, symbolizes the hard path toward that spiritual insight which can only be obtained by human struggle. He realizes, too, that the struggle demands cooperation between the seekers, since there is no real distinction between teachers and learners.

What there is of this little fable will make most readers regret that the novelist did not live to complete it. . . .

Vernon Hall, Jr., "Posthumous and Symbolic," in New York Herald Tribune Book Review, *August 14, 1960, p. 6.*

DAVID L. NORTON (essay date 1960)

[In the following excerpt, Norton discusses Mount Analogue *as Daumal's allegorical presentation of the spiritual quest.]*

Rene Daumal is certain that truth ultimately is one, and ***Mount Analogue*** is a quest for understanding, not of self, but of the universal essence of things. It rests on the same substratum that supports Yoga, Zen ritual, the experiments of Rimbaud with hashish, and those of Aldoux Huxley with mescalin . . . the conviction that higher states of consciousness are attainable, by extraordinary means.

Mount Analogue is an allegorical marvel tale. It deals with the search for, discovery and ascent of an invisible mountain, the highest on earth, and the supreme symbol of the bond between earth and sky. The nameless narrator of the story is a young literary symbolist who has written an article tracing the outcroppings of the symbol in prophetic literature. He corresponds with "Father" Sogol, ex-novitiate of a heretical order, professor of mountaineering, and amateur physicist, who has established Mount Analogue's existence and location. They carefully recruit a party of eight believers and set out aboard the yacht "Impossible."

The strength of Daumal's book lies in its internal logic. Why Mount Analogue is invisible and not ordinarily approachable is explained both by physical principles and by symbolic necessity, thus achieving a balance which the author maintains throughout. Each difficulty the party encounters along the way is met by "regarding the problem as solved and deducing from the solution all logical consequences," a method which produces results that are fantastic, yet coherent.

Daumal died of tuberculosis in 1944 at the age of thirty-six, leaving the book unfinished. So far as the work is concerned I think this is just as well. In the last chapters, where anticipation gives way to the actual ascent, Daumal appears to grope a bit and his symbols lose their edge. This was predictable. He has led us to expect more than he, or perhaps anyone, could fulfill. By unanimous testimony of those who endorse them, the higher reaches of mystical experience cannot be described in a meaningful way. (p. 96)

David L. Norton, "Return to the Heart's Longing," in The Nation, *Vol. 191, No. 5, August 20, 1960, pp. 95-6.**

LOUISE LANDES LEVI (essay date 1979)

[In the following excerpt from an introduction written in 1979 to a collection of Daumal's essays on Eastern art and philosophy, Levi discusses the influence of mystical studies on Daumal's life and work.]

[René Daumal's] adult life was dedicated to an inner work of the highest rigor and to the completion of his essays, poems, novels, and translations. . . . He mastered Sanskrit and translated a selection of important texts from the *Sahitya-darpana,* the *Chandyoga Upanishad,* the *Bhagavad Gita,* etc. . . .

Daumal did not intend with his study of Sanskrit an institutional process which would result in economic gain or academic position. Rather he pursued the subject as a personal search and research, a "proof," a necessary corollary to his youthful experimentation with carbon tetrachloride and other stimulants (described in his essay **"Le Souvenir determinant,"** 1943, and in an earlier edition of this article **"Une Experience fondamentale"**). His interest in intoxicants, their relation to the inner state and to the origin of language was curtailed, however, by his meeting with Alexandre de Salzmann and his subsequent contact with the Gurdjieff Institute in Paris. "And above all, remember the day when you wanted to throw out everything, no matter how—but a guardian kept watch in your night, he kept watch while you dreamed, he made you touch your flesh, he made you gather your rags—remember your guardian." Daumal continued his studies with the Institute from 1929 until his death, and his writing, particularly his essays on poetics, was deeply colored by his work with this school. (p. 1)

Daumal explored an entire range of literary expression and furthered his knowledge of oriental philosophy and language. The Sanskrit study was, until his death, a major aspect of Daumal's desire to reconstitute, within himself, the Occidental approach to poetic expression and to resuscitate, in an Occidental framework, the essence of sacred art and perception. Daumal sought a poetry which would awaken the poet to his internal reality, not only to the word, tool, and result of that reality. In his essay **"Poetry Black, Poetry White,"** written in 1942, he said, "I will not say 'he' is a white poet and 'he' is a black. This would be to fall from the idea into opinion, discussion and error. I will not even say 'he' has the poetic gift . . . and 'he' not. Do I have it? Often I doubt it and sometimes I believe it absolutely. I am never certain once and for all. Each moment the question is new. Each time the dawn appears the mystery is there in its entirety. But if formerly I was a poet, certainly I was a black poet and if tomorrow I were to be a poet I would like to be a white poet." He formulated a theory of poetic expression in which his researches into the Oriental tradition were brought to bear upon the poetic tradition of the Occidental world. Here an Occidental yoga of poetry is evolved, based not only on the form and content of expression but on a conscious inner process corresponding to an awakened approach to creativity. "White poetry opens the door to one world, that of the only sun, without illusion, real."

Daumal's translation of Sanskrit texts which deal with poetry and composition directly inspired his future work in these areas. In Sanskrit the word is not only a tool of poetic expression, but it is in its esoteric usage the poet's mirror and the mirror of the gods. The Sanskrit alphabet is a sacred formula whose function is, in addition to the complexity of its compositional forms, the direct reflection of the sacred world and its powers. "All recited poems and all chants are, without exception, portions of Vishnu, the great being, reclothed in sonorous form." From the time of Panini (4th century B.C.) Sanskrit was regarded as a perfected vehicle—*samskrta*. It was not subject to development but was considered, by its exponents, to be a direct form of being, in itself an expression of sacred power. Thus, in India, other languages are known as *Prakrtas,* natural tongues which are subject to evolution, but Sanskrit was a fixed expressive form whose potency, exoterically and esoterically, was utilized to develop, record, and reveal man's inner nature. The science of *mantra,* indeed the entire science governing Sanskrit exposition, derives from its unique capacity to create and reflect the state of conscious being. As Daumal states, many of its most revered compositions date from an unrecorded period and are held to be anonymous, or rather, to be the result of a direct process of reception, unrelated to personal authorship.

Daumal's translation work reflects his desire to place this ancient tradition at the service of the European literary intelligence. His translation of Bharata's *Natya Śastra,* considered to be the first written treatise on the arts of poetry, music, and dance, into a vital, living French attest to this deeply felt motive—one which would give to Occidental culture an image of its origin and of an artistic form and formula which existed not to distract but to "awaken"—to awaken man to consciousness of himself. (pp. 2-3)

If the style of the [Daumal's] translations, essays, book reviews, and commentaries appears to be somewhat dry of philosophic comment, it must be remembered that they represent only one aspect of Daumal's creative expression, which was otherwise devoted to fiction, occasional papers, translations (from the English of Hemingway and D. T. Suzuki) and poetry. In all these expressions, however, Daumal's concern was uniquely dedicated to "the power of the word." His life task was consecrated to the silence of the inner world and to the discipline of that void—"one does not know the word by the medium of words but by silence"—and to the relevance of the "word" to the consciousness of man and to the individual, in particular, to the poet whose function is especially related to the phenomena of language, its origin and its creative potential. (p. 3)

[Daumal's] Sanskrit work, as stated, was autodidactic, a product of his unique sensibility and not the product of an academic tradition. Daumal sought within this study proof for the ultimate reality and expression which would indicate, not annihilate, the possibility for man to free himself from the pain of *samsara*—his own ego.

But Daumal's contribution, as shown, was by no means limited to Sanskrit translation, and his other works, two of which have been translated into English, ***Mont Analogue*** . . . and ***La Grande Beuverie*** . . . attest to his humor and his unique approach to the situation of Western man. Nevertheless his Sanskrit study provided both an analytic tool and the structural form for most of his other work, including his poetry, and *La Grande Beuverie* refers directly to this study; beneath its surrealist guise the book is, in fact, an anagram, and the text cannot be followed without at least some knowledge of Daumal's research into the classical traditions and languages of the Orient. (p. 4)

Louise Landes Levi, in an introduction to Rasa; or, Knowledge of the Self: Essays on Indian Aesthetics and Selected Sanskrit Studies *by Rene Daumal, translated by Louise Landes Levi, New Directions, 1982, pp. 1-5.*

MALCOLM BOWIE (essay date 1979)

[*In the following excerpt Bowie reviews* A Night of Serious Drinking, *calling it "intelligent and delightful" and a work of intellectual heroism.*]

[Daumal, a] writer for whom speed and adaptiveness of mind were supreme virtues would have been delighted to learn that the British needed 41 years to bring his ***La grande beuverie*** across the Channel. But it has arrived at last, and should be made welcome as a precious representative of a rare genre: the farce about thinking.

'Philosophy teaches how man thinks he thinks,' says one of Daumal's imaginary sages, 'but drinking shows how he really thinks.' Yet far from mounting a bibulous critique of philosophy, Daumal glories—as did Rabelais, who is resoundingly present in the book—in all that drinking and thinking have in common: both are adventures of consciousness and ways of being obedient to animal appetite; the more you do of either the more you want to do.

Daumal's informing question is 'What are minds capable of?' and the narrative which threads his answers together borrows its simple structure and one of its moral lessons from the drinker's characteristic destiny: mind-flights are followed by plunges into inertia or stupidity, just as sprees are followed by hangovers.

The long, central section of the book contains the spree. It is a brilliant satirical exploration of the world in which paid, professional thinkers do their miserable best. This is a world inhabited by such artisans in thought as Fabricators, Clarificators, Sophers, Scienters, Kirittiks and Logologists. Daumal's Gulliverish narrator discovers that these would-be heroes of the intellect are either stunted stunt-men, virtuosi in the higher pointlessness, or dullards imprisoned within a single conceptual system and thinking the same small thoughts from day to day. Largeness of mind lies in the capacity to exploit a system, exhaust it, discard it and move on.

The mind can do so many things: why be a dung-sweeper in the circus ring when you could be leaping and gliding on the high trapeze? The hangover—the short epilogue is called 'The Cold Light of Day'—sets in as soon as you stop thinking other and new things.

For Daumal's daring young man, then, most thinking that gets done is foolish, and all trapezes are absurdly fragile. Although mental performances can be damaged by circumstantial factors—by the tedium of academic institutions, say, or by the vainglorious delusions of *homo ratiocinans*—a much more serious threat to original invention is intrinsic to acts of thought. This is the threat of 'Ouroborism': words, ideas, arguments are always in danger of 'biting their own tails like the famous worm'. Tautology and circularity are not chance pitfalls that the scrupulous thinker must know about and avoid; they are central both to thinking and to the fabric of the world. Heaven and hell, thirsting and drinking, syllogism and paralogism, sanity and madness are no more than the accidental moulds into which a universal tautologousness flows. But as Daumal's narrative presses towards this culminating vision of entropy, a finer intellectual heroism begins to emerge. The mind can do so many things but all things are the same. What matters in the face of this is the margin, the disputed territory, the suspended moment of uncertainty in which tautology is deferred, in which the thirst-quenching and thirst-creating glass is raised. Inhabit that margin and that moment, he urges: for this is where true thinking happens.

It is extraordinary that a work as intelligent as this, and one that enlists wit and satire in such a variety of unusual causes, should have had to wait so long before gaining, even in France, a more than minimal readership—especially as certain of the dimmer productions of Surrealism have, during the same decades, been sanctified as 'family reading'. But this slowness is perhaps not so extraordinary after all if we heed the austere lesson of Daumal's intellectual gaiety: all thinking that matters is a breaking of bounds, a summons to pleasure, an assumption of risk and, unmistakably, a scandal in the family. (pp. 712-13)

Malcolm Bowie, "Raising the Glass," in The Listener, *Vol. 102, No. 2638, November 22, 1979, pp. 712-13.*

ROBERT RICHMAN (essay date 1980)

[*In the following excerpt Richman discusses* A Night of Serious Drinking, *criticizing what he calls its "cheap side-show of literary styles," and its "bleak" argument.*]

A Night of Serious Drinking, first published in 1938, is only the second book of Daumal's to appear in English; ***Mount Analogue,*** an unfinished parable of a man's climb to spiritual fulfillment, was brought out in the U.S. in the late '60s. . . . Like its predecessor, ***A Night*** describes one man's journey to the spiritually correct life, but the symbolic terrain in this case is an all-night drinking party.

An unnamed narrator begins his trip "thirsting" for something—knowledge, presumably, or truth—and it gets him dead drunk. (This is the first of many ironies.) He falls asleep, and drifts off to a dreamworld where everything that is normally viewed positively has a negative value, and vice-versa. All virtuous human endeavor, for example, is exposed as sham in this new world; the systems of science, philosophy, poetry, and religion (pursued by people called Nibbilists, Scienters, Clarificators, and Pwatts) thwart progress, impede happiness, and waste one's time.

Daumal's sharpest jabs are aimed at the writers in this nether world. To write poetry, "you must feel a particular kind of uneasiness," says the narrator's guide; "you start bellowing until the bellowing brings a word to your throat. You spit it out and write it down. . . . Never think about what you mean to, better still, never mean anything at all, but let whatever wishes to be said, be said through you. . . . Of course, all this happens instinctively." The species known as "kirittiks" (yes) "root out everything published . . . to denounce the least sign of what we term health and to nurse back to sickness any persons who look as though they might forsake it." But false intellectual principles do alleviate the "thirst" for truth; thus our hero finds that he is "able to hold out all this time without a drink."

Ill at east with the postures of rational men, the narrator awakens the next day and proclaims the world "a beautiful place—except for mankind . . . the tiny, cancerous tumor . . . on the universe," which, according to Daumal, shall remain "less than nothing" if it continues to obtain guidance from the philosophical abstractions men have manufactured through the ages. The mature thing to do is forsake the world of theories and abstractions; true salvation, says Daumal, occurs entirely within the individual who sees through the intellectual games that parade as projects for meaning and freedom. Daumal also rejects transcendentalism. To "pursue the business of living" in the real world is centrally important, paradoxically enough, because one can avoid being diverted from spiritual satisfaction only by directly experiencing the insolence of religion, philosophy, and writing.

Daumal's bleak argument is nearly buried, however, in a 120-page mishmosh of satire, symbolism, allegory, irony, poetry, and prose (plus a subject index). It is a cheap sideshow of literary styles and techniques, lacking balance and subtlety, and overstuffed with the author's bad humor—a generally graceless performance. And it all seems deliberate, perversely enough, because in Daumal's vision *all* writing (even Daumal's) is grievously misleading, and the imagination set loose is a damaging distraction too. It is logical, even beautiful, that the book's final, redemptive image is of the imagination winding down, words slowly dissolving, losing their hold over the narrator's mind: "As I speak these words I hear them singing in my head like empty shells . . ."

Rene Daumal sacrifices his book to an idea, and although it is really quite moving, one wonders whether all the pain along the way was worth it. (pp. 40-1)

Robert Richman, "Pwatt's Progress," in The Village Voice, *Vol. XXV, No. 6, February 11, 1980, pp. 40-1.*

MICHAEL WOOD (essay date 1980)

[In the following excerpt Wood discusses the satirical and philosophical elements of A Night of Serious Drinking. *Wood states that Daumal's novel exposes for our inspection the machinery through which religions are created from "needs rewritten as unfulfilled promises."]*

La Grande Beuverie—a less elegant translation would be *The Great Booze*—is a philosophical text in the form of a farce. . . . A group of people—"Whether we were ten or a thousand, no one knew. What is certain is that we were alone"—is seen drinking desperately, in a haze of smoke and excitement. A wise old man smashes a guitar by pronouncing a particular sequence of words. Jokes, dreams, and arguments are exchanged, and a central metaphor begins to emerge. Thirst is a virtue. Those who wish to be drunk at least understand that something is lacking. Delinquent children of Socrates and Rimbaud, they have intuited the extent of their ignorance. The trouble is that there seems to be no way out of this chaotic party. Or rather, the narrator is told, there are exits only into madness, death, and an uncommonly widespread delusion: that of imagining you've escaped when you haven't.

The narrator is taken on a tour of this kingdom of mock escapees, otherwise known as the sick bay, which is a cunningly distorted mirror of our own world, complete with colonies, empires, businesses, railways, and sporting competitions. . . . The sick bay's scientists are described as "failed cannibals." They chop man into a thousand perspectives, and the hero of this realm is a vast cranium suspended over the body and legs of a little cloth doll. His tiny right arm is held up by a wire, and his index finger rests on his temple "in the gesture of one who knows." Above his throne runs a banner bearing the inscription: "I know everything, but I don't understand any of it." The translation, here and throughout the book, is impeccable, and I don't seriously mean to complain even about the sobriety of the title.

Daumal's masters in this genre are Rabelais and Alfred Jarry, but his tone is closer to that of Swift on the subject of the islands of Laputa and Balnibarbi. He doesn't have Swift's malice or invention, though, and there is a good deal of flatness in the book's central section, the visit to the "artificial paradises" of the sick bay. Poets and critics, for instance, appear as Pwatts and Kirittiks (these words are the same in French, where novelists, *romanciers,* become *Ruminssiés,* nicely rendered in this English version as Nibblists), the French Academy is offered as a parody of Olympus, and there is a general air of targets so wide they can't be missed and aren't worth hitting. There is nothing in this section which has the life of the opening scenes of drinking and drunkenness, although there are still one or two remarkable moments. The narrator runs into a friendly character who says he is in the sick bay only to gather material for a book. It is to be called ***La Grande Beuverie,*** and bears a striking resemblance to the work we're reading. The narrator mentions this fellow to an orderly, and comments, "That chap's not ill at all." "They all say that," the orderly replies.

This engaging self-satire mitigates the book's increasing solemnity, and the same note sounds again in a fierce passage on the measures taken by the masters of this mirror world to keep the population down. First they get poets to recommend various brutal forms of suicide. Then other poets sing the praises of opium, hashish, cocaine, and ether. "This was a great success and it has lasted. The manufacturers of drugs and the drug trade are still flourishing, and the volumes of verse which stimulate them are selling like hot cakes." Other men of letters adapted Oriental doctrines and diets and exercises designed to promote "the art of rapidly becoming neurasthenic, neuropathic, cachectic, demineralized, phthisical, and finally a cadaver." None of this is enough, though, and the matter is turned over to the men of power, who quickly invent patriotism and war. Daumal himself had tried suicide, drugs, and was still, at the time of writing, racking himself with Oriental exercises. It is characteristic that he should not think of sparing himself or his practices.

The narrator finally falls through the floor of the sick bay, and finds himself in an empty room littered only with the traces of a party. Daumal wonders aloud whether he should use the literary device of having his character wake from a dream, and plays briefly with the idea that wakefulness in fiction is itself only another layer of sleep. Then all lightness of touch vanishes for good, and the narrator undergoes, in a clanking bit of allegory, a severe stripping down of the self. He burns his chairs, he burns his books, he burns his clothes, and just in time the dawn begins to glimmer at the window, intimating a new life. The wise old man from the first part of the book shows up—in fact, he seems to have been talking the whole time, since the narrator hears him at one point through the floor of the sick bay, "still discoursing down there"—and murmurs a few words of good cheer. "What could be more comforting than to discover that we are less than nothing? It's only by turning ourselves inside out that we shall become something." This sounds like cold comfort, even if it does echo all kinds of conventional religious teaching, and one has the distinct impression of wine being changed into water.

Still, Daumal doesn't expect us simply to believe him. By now we have either caught the bouquet of the true beverage or we haven't. And if we have (and if we haven't), the words don't matter. The wise man, who formerly asserted the power of language over the material world—the smashing of the guitar with words—now points to the complementary fact of language's emptiness. It means nothing unless you make it work. One cannot cure a disease, as Daumal says elsewhere, by reciting a medical treatise. The dictionary won't save us after all.

Daumal was unfailingly lucid, and as Roger Shattuck says [see excerpt above, 1952] never "took cover behind the convenient shrubbery of the 'ineffable.'" But his lucidity was a burden as well as a gift, and his work is haunted by phantoms which seem to have sprung up from language itself. Like that *something* in the wise man's flaccid precept quoted above, where a simple logical contrast (something is the opposite of nothing) is converted into a magical consolation. Or like the "real being" which Daumal, in an essay on "The limits of philosophical language," conjures up out of the sleeves of his vocabulary. No philosophy has its end in itself, he argues. Logic looks toward knowledge, aesthetics toward feeling, ethics toward action. This scheme already seems hopelessly arbitrary and simplified, but I am interested in the *movement* of Daumal's thought here. He now asks what the aim of "general philosophy" is, and all he needs is a word, since his question assumes that it must have an aim, and that the aim must be specifiable. The word he settles on is "being," which he immediately adorns with a fine romance of totality:

> . . . real being [*l'être réel*], which thinks, feels and acts at the same time; which unifies, or should unify these three functions of human life. I say *should unify* because this unity doesn't exist; this being doesn't exist, as long as we need to philosophize. . . .

There is a genuine pathos here, as well as a muddle. Daumal, who wishes to "go beyond language" (*dépasser le discours*), who understands all that language cannot do, does not seem to understand all that language has already done for him in providing him with a name for his philosophical longing and a semblance of reality for his ghostly ideal.

"The philosopher is the cartographer of human life," Daumal says in the same essay. "Discursive philosophy is as necessary to knowledge as a geographical map is to a journey: the great mistake, I repeat, is to believe that in looking at a map one is taking a journey." An even greater mistake is skulking in this argument, one that is astonishingly close to the sick bay delusions of ***La Grande Beuverie:*** that of marking on the map countries which don't exist, or which exist only as names. Daumal, like Gurdjieff, believes the human mind has unused capacities, fabulous riches we have not even begun to exploit. This seems at least plausible, and no doubt we should leave room on the map for these possibilities. But leaving room is quite different from drawing in the possible countries, just as the exploration of an unknown world is quite different from the assumption of a "hidden knowledge" (Daumal's phrase) which awaits the hardy explorer at journey's end. There are more things in heaven and earth than are dreamt of in our philosophy, but it is a sizable step from there to the notion that there is *another* philosophy, possessed by a handful of initiates, which specializes in just those things.

The religion in question here is a religion of man—"all roads lead to man," Daumal says in ***La Grande Beuverie***—but it has the structure of an old theology: our needs are rewritten as unfulfilled promises. What is most attractive about Daumal's ***Le Mont analogue*** is its exposure of this machinery for our inspection. I imagine believers (of almost any kind) may find treasures in the book that I don't; but belief is in no way required for an enjoyment of it.

In his Open Letter Daumal quoted Breton's famous remark about "a certain point" where "life and death, the real and the imaginary, the past and the future, the communicable and the incommunicable, the high and the low cease to be perceived as contradictory." . . . [In] Mount Analogue [Daumal] creates a brilliant image, not for the point, but for the dream of the point. The narrator has published, in the *Revue des Fossiles,* an article on the mythology of mountains, from Mount Sinai to Olympus, from the Himalayas to Golgotha. The "ultimate symbolic mountain," he suggests, must be inaccessible to "ordinary human approaches," which means that earthly mountains, once climbed, lose their "analogical importance." On the other hand, a purely mythical mountain is not much better, since it cannot represent "a way of uniting Earth and Heaven." His conclusion is this:

> For a mountain to play the role of Mount Analogue, its summit must be inaccessible but its base accessible to human beings as nature has made them. It must be unique and it must exist geographically. The door to the invisible must be visible.

The narrator is surprised to receive a letter which takes seriously what he thought of as a "literary fantasy," and calls on his correspondent, one Father Sogol ("a childish anagram, and somewhat pretentious," the owner of this name says), an ex-monk who is currently, among other things, a professor of mountaineering. The two of them combine their fantasies into a single faith—"the very fact that there are now *two of us* changes everything"—and begin to organize an expedition in search of Mount Analogue. Joined by the narrator's wife, they become a group "for which the impossible no longer existed."

Other friends take part in planning the trip, but some drop out when it becomes a reality. Sogol meanwhile, by means of a witty application of the notion of the curvature of space, has figured out how Mount Analogue can exist geographically without ever having been seen. The light bends around it, making it seem not to be there. . . . The mountain is found and the team start the ascent; Daumal's death left them on the lower slopes.

There is a certain amount of sententiousness in the book—"The path to our highest desires often leads through the undesirable"—and, as in ***La Grande Beuverie,*** a good deal of uninspired allegory. But there are also fine touches of visionary realism—when photographs are taken on Mount Analogue, no image appears on the film—and an authentic austerity and humility speak in the following lines, where the explorers wonder what they will be able to offer as payment on the mountain:

> Each one of us kept making his personal inventory, and each one of us felt poorer as the days went on. For no one saw anything around him or in him which really belonged to him. It reached the point where we were just eight beggars, possessing nothing, who each night watched the sun sink toward the horizon.

It is easy to sympathize with the frustration which led Breton and Daumal to dream of a point where logical contraries would collapse into a common reality. "Logic is doubtless unshakable," as Kafka said at the end of *The Trial,* "but it cannot withstand a man who wants to go on living." It is harder to sympathize with Daumal's bland assertion that the notions of abstract and concrete "have no great significance" because "a thing either is or is not." The power of the idea of Mount Analogue was that it *preserved* the notions of abstract and concrete, hypothetical and actual, while asking questions about their relation. If these notions are not significant, all our dreams will come true because there is nothing to stand in their way, and the "method" of Father Sogol (which is to regard a problem as solved and deduce from the solution all the steps he needs to take—hence the implication of inversion in his name) becomes the merest charlatanism. The mountain must remain an invention, a picture of possibly negotiable limits, because it is *as an invention* that we need it. As a location, however spiritual or metaphorical, the mountain can only be a hoax, a trick of words, the dictionary's last laugh. (pp. 41-3)

Michael Wood, "The Great Game," in The New York Review of Books, *Vol. XXVII, No. 6, April 17, 1980, pp. 41-3.*

HILDA NELSON (essay date 1980)

[*In the following excerpt Nelson discusses the close affinity between Daumal and the French poet and prose writer Gérard de Nerval, specifically the similarity of their philosophical ideas.*]

For many years the name of René Daumal and his dedication to penetrating the gates of ivory and entering the universe supplementary to this one has been eclipsed by the writings and presences of the better-known names of surrealists such as André Breton, Louis Aragon, and Paul Eluard. . . .

To be ignored and obscured by more robust writers and presences is, however, hardly uncommon in the annals of literary history. Gérard de Nerval, like so many other "petits romantiques" was also overshadowed by giants such as Balzac, Stendhal, Flaubert, and Baudelaire, and it is only relatively recently that his *contes* and *nouvelles* have gained the recognition they so obviously deserve. (p. 236)

To couple the names of Daumal and Nerval should come as no surprise, for not only do the two men share common fates and attitudes toward life and art but, more importantly, references to Nerval and his works abound in the writings of Daumal. It is not often that one can pair the names of two literary men so intimately and unreservedly as one can with the names of Daumal and Nerval. The only other instance of so obvious a case of "elective affinities" is that of Baudelaire and Poe. The powerful affinity on the part of one writer for another, so apparent in Daumal for Nerval and Baudelaire for Poe, is predicated on the ability and need of the one to project himself *dans la peau de l'autre* ["into the skin of the other"] so spontaneously and completely that they experience the same fears, anguish, and despair, the same metaphysical homelessness, as well as the same fascination for and desire to "nier tout et ne plus concevoir que l'abîme" ["deny everything and think only of the abyss"]. (pp. 236-37)

Both Daumal and Nerval were intensely preoccupied with the nature of reality and the dream, and expressed through their writings the determination to enter the invisible and impalpable world behind the world of appearances. Both saw in the dream "la clef des problèmes métaphysiques" ["the key to metaphysical problems"], a means of liberating man from the human condition. Each was interested in and experimented with extra-sensory perception and the *dédoublement du moi* ["splitting up the self"]. . . . Indeed, Nerval, long before Freud and Jung, sensed that by exploring the unconscious certain dormant forces could be released and that through the dream man could enter into communication with the world behind the world of appearances. Thus man could become a seer, a nocturnal seer, whose dreams were a descent into the dark regions of the self. Nerval develops these concepts in almost all of his writings. . . . (pp. 237-38)

Exploration of the unconscious via the dream and the realization that there exists a correspondence between the internal and the external world, led Nerval to occupy himself with the occult and Oriental theosophies and cosmogonies. By studying the sacred writings of the Orient, which attempted to cut through illusion, Nerval hoped to decipher the underlying significance of the physical world and find a correspondence between the material and the spiritual world, between the macrocosm and the microcosm. It is precisely these endeavors that made such an indelible impression on the young Daumal when he first read the works of Nerval. For Daumal, like his mentor Nerval, strove to find the "point sublime" ["sublime point"], the "vases communicants" ["communicating vessels"], between the world of reality and the world of the dream in the hope of discovering a "nouvel âge d'or" ["new golden age"].

It is primarily *Aurélia,* the work in which Nerval most completely resolves to fuse the world of reality with the world of the dream, that captured the fertile imagination of Daumal. . . . Indeed, it is precisely in *Aurélia* that the narrator succumbs completely to the world of the dream and the *dédoublement du moi*. It is in these series of dreams—that "seconde vie" ["second life"]—, and which make up the greatest part of *Aurélia,* wherein lies the hope that certain and indubitable knowledge of the self and the universe can be gained and which will help the narrator in his long and painful odyssey into the dark regions of the unconscious. . . . (pp. 238-39)

Closely linked to the idea of the dream as a second life, is the idea of the *dédoublement du moi* or double, which plays an equally prominent role in the works of Nerval as well as Daumal. . . . [It] is especially obvious in *Aurélia* where it takes on a personal as well as an artistic dimension. The idea of the double is, of course, closely linked to the problem of the dichotomy of reality and the dream, for to question the nature of reality ultimately resulted in man questioning his very existence, the existence and unity of his ego. In the works of Nerval the notion of the double takes on various meanings and uses. On the one hand, meeting one's double or *férouër* may signify the approach of death. But it can also be understood on a more abstract level: fear of extinction, of *l'anéantissement du moi* which gives rise to the creation of a dual personality with a double destiny. Furthermore, by creating for oneself an *alter ego,* it is possible to free oneself from certain responsibilities, for the double can do things that the *I* cannot permit itself to do and thereby serves as an emotional outlet. (pp. 239-40)

Already at the beginning of *Aurélia* the narrator experiences an instance of the *dédoublement du moi*. Nerval's narrator has just set out on a lonely road in order to follow his *Etoile* "Vers l'Orient." Suddenly he has been stopped and he soon finds himself on a campbed in prison. When the narrator tries to convey to his guards that he has been unjustly imprisoned, he hears a strange voice mingle with the mutterings of the soldiers. Later, when he is being released from prison, he has the strange sensation of seeing his double leave with his friends while *he* remains behind. The narrator eventually realizes that man has a dual nature, one leading toward good, the other toward evil.

The two incidents experienced by the narrator are singled out by Daumal who shares with the narrator the terrible feeling of impotence suffered in the dream. Like Nerval, Daumal is aware that the dream can be troubling as well as illuminating and that these "portes d'ivoir ou de corne" ["portals of ivory or of horn"] that separate our waking life from our second, nocturnal life, can cause us to experience anguish at what we might experience on the other side. (p. 240)

In his allusions to Nerval's various experiences of the *dédoublement du moi* [in the essay **"Nerval, le Nyctalope"** from the collection ***Chacque fois que l'aube paraît***], Daumal narrates how he and his "Phrères Simplistes," as they called themselves, had experienced instances of disassociation. He tells how they had perfected the art of travelling without the aid of that perishable envelope—the body—, and entering into the impalpable and invisible world, that realm where neither space, time, nor disintegration exist. Thus Daumal and a "Phrère" would consent to meet in their dreams at a given time and together walk for hours through the dark streets of the city, eventually to part and return to their respective beds and bodies. . . . The following day, Daumal and his "Phrère" would meet the other "Phrères Simplistes" and recount *their* experiences of the previous night. It is thus understandable that if Daumal could meet in spirit with his "Phrères" and walk with them through the landscapes of the mind, it is not difficult to assume that he could also lose himself with Nerval as the latter traverses the long corridors, or climbs and descends the immense staircases of his own mind.

An instance of the double and the *dédoublement du moi* in the works of Daumal is evident in the legend entitled "Histoire des Hommes-creux et de la Rose-amère" inserted in the pages of his "récit véridique" ["true story"], ***Le Mont Analogue.*** In this tale Mo and Ho are twins who can be told apart only by the medallion they wear: Mo's necklace bears a cross; that of Ho a circle. When the time has come for the father to impart his knowledge to his eldest son, he attempts to resolve the problem by decreeing that whosoever finds and brings back the Bitter-Rose, the flower of discernment, to be found at the summit of the highest peaks, will be named his successor.

Mo sets forth. Soon he sees the Bitter-Rose above him. In his attempt to pluck the flower, he kills a Hollow-Man who lives in the rock, and the Bitter-Rose retreats. Undaunted, Mo returns the next day, but he never completes his quest. He joins the Hollow-Men who, it is said, are the dead or, perhaps, extensions of the living. It is now Ho's turn to seek both Mo and the Bitter-Rose. He discovers Mo in the shape of a hollow and strikes at his head as he had been told to do. Suddenly,

> La forme de Mo devient immobile. Ho fend la glace du sérac, et entre dans la forme de son frère, comme une épée dans son fourreau, comme un pied dans son empreinte. Il joue des coudes et se secoue, et tire ses jambes du moule de glace. Et il s'entend dire des paroles dans une langue qu'il n'a jamais parlé. Il sent qu'il est Ho, et qu'il est Mo en même temps. Tous les souvenirs de Mo sont entrés dans sa mémoire, avec le chemin du pic Troue-les nues, et la demeure de la Rose-amère. ["Mo's form became motionless; Ho opens the ice of the serac and enters his brother's form like a sword fitted into its sheath, a foot into its imprint. He moves his elbows and works himself into place, then draws his legs back out of the mold of ice. And he hears himself saying words in a language he has never spoken. He feels he is Ho, and that he is Mo at the same time. All Mo's memories have entered his mind—the way up Cloudy Head and where the Bitter-Rose has its habitation." (Translated by Roger Shattuck.)].

The most interesting aspect of Daumal's presentation of the double is that it is a synthesis rather than a split or disassociation of the personality. Thus man, as Daumal sees it, once he has found his ideal, can discover his true self and the secrets of the universe; he can become a harmonious whole, a state for which both Daumal and Nerval constantly strove.

Other closely related themes evident in the works of Nerval and Daumal are syncretism, that is, a return to an universal religion common to all, the notion of an universal language—an *Ursprache*—, and totemism, the concept which derives whole tribes or families from an animal, bird, or plant, together with the idea of a mystical relationship with another group or an individual, living or dead. (pp. 241-43)

Daumal, in his essay on Nerval, points out that this phenomenon corresponds to the totemism of primitive groups. Indeed, the use of animals and birds denoting kinship and possessing and imparting wisdom, is evident in almost all primitive myths and folklore, as well as those of the Judeo-Christian world. According to Jung, the bird is a symbol of transcendance and, like other creatures coming from the depths of the ancient Mother Eearth, forms part of the collective unconscious and, as a consequence, recollected during the dream.

The notion of the universality and unity of language, religion, and myth is patently evident in the writings of Daumal. It occurs in Daumal's legend of the Hollow-Men when Ho suddenly finds himself speaking a language he had never spoken before or recollecting the memories of Mo. In his discussion of Nerval, Daumal believes that men have the same concepts, myths, languages, and dreams because everything goes back to an original, elemental source. . . . That is why, explains Daumal, it is possible for him and his "Phrères" to share with Nerval the same ideas and experiences, the same dreams and visions. Thus men, centuries apart, can meet in the "point sublime," Goethe's realm of the Mothers, and live on in the consciousness of others. The continuity of ideas and generations is now fully established and the kinship and mystical relationship Daumal feels for Nerval, becomes clear. (pp. 243-44)

The theme of kinship and the continuity of generations is . . . prominent in *Aurélia*. The narrator's ancestor, the uncle in the guise of a bird, talks to him "de personnes de ma famille vivantes ou mortes en divers temps, comme si elles existaient simultanément" ["of the members of my family, living or dead, in different times as if they existed simultaneously"]. And it is the same uncle who reveals to him that men are immortal and that they will continue to exist in a world where time has come to a standstill. The meaning of the *néant* ["nothingness"] is explained to him and he discovers that it has a different meaning for mortals than it has for the dead. Thus one should not fear the *néant* for it merely signifies modification and continuity in another dimension. Matter, like spirit, will not perish but will be modified. The narrator then has a vision of the continuity of the human race which appears to him as an uninterrupted chain of men and women. . . . The narrator of *Aurélia* now understands that his vision symbolizes the transmigration of souls and that his role on earth is to re-establish the universal harmony of all religions. He now feels that he is in communication with that secret and hidden universe, heretofore closed to him.

In his analysis of Nerval's cosmology, Daumal makes it clear that he does not consider these dreams, visions, or symbols to be those of a madman. They are neither capricious nor fortuitous, and by no means the result of a man's suppressed desires, nor his obsessions with or fear of impotence. Rather, Daumal's intent is to show that Nerval is well acquainted with the *Books of the Dead* of the Egyptians, the *Zohar*, the *Chhândogya Upanishad*, the *Aitareya Upanishad*, the *Prashna Upanishad*, the Tibetan legends concerning *Agarttha*, as well as Kabbala, Gnosticism, and the many other occultist and mystical beliefs that had penetrated France and Germany at the time. To be considered an expert with respect to the *Upanishads* and the *Vedas* by Daumal is exceedingly important since Daumal was himself a scholar of Oriental mysticism and occultism. Daumal recalls the fact that at the beginning of *Aurélia* we discover the narrator in search of his *Etoile*. Indeed, explains Daumal, of the many paths or approaches found in astral space, the one that was to lead Nerval to his *Etoile*, his destiny, corresponds precisely with the astral arteries in Hindu mythology. When the narrator places a talisman on a certain part of the neck of the young man in the sanatorium, this particular point corresponds to the aperture of Brahma, namely, the passage of the solar ray found in the *Upanishads*. . . . In his use of the various elemental creatures such as the *dives, périts, ondines, salamandres, afrites*, etc. so prevalent in the occult world, Daumal considers Nerval to be close to the Hindu tradition. With respect to Nerval's symbolism of the charnel-house of universal history, the harmony of the spheres, the partition of the world, the evolution of the races, the *feu vital* ["essential fire"] and unknown metals, and the ultimate pardon, all, says Daumal, are indications of Nerval's erudition. (pp. 244-46)

Up to this point, the concepts and themes in the writings of Nerval [have] primarily been analysed in terms of Daumal's essays, especially his essay on Nerval. However, the ideas scattered throughout these essays have been set down in ***Le Mont Analogue***. Similar to *Aurélia*, ***Le Mont Analogue*** is a spiritual quest, undertaken by the protagonist, Pierre Sogol, and the narrator, in order to discover certain truths about the self and the universe. . . . It is [the gate of ivory or horn] which leads to the discovery of the world supplementary to this one, the realm where the invisible is made visible and the impalpable is made palpable. It is in search of this world, more real and more lasting, and where men can find peace and solace, that the strange expedition in ***Le Mont Analogue*** is undertaken.

Indeed, the purpose of this extraordinary undertaking is to discover, by boat, the site of a mountain. But the existence of this mountain is hypothetical. Mont Analogue is not of the realm of ordinary experience but, rather, it exists in the universe that is analogical to this one. To reach this mountain several requirements must be fulfilled: "il faut que son sommet soit inaccessible, mais sa base accessible" ["it is necessary that its summit be inaccessible, but its base accessible"]. The second requirement is that it must be unique and it must exist geographically, for only then can the door to the invisible be made visible. The machinery to discover the mountain that will unite Heaven and Earth, the imaginary and the real, is set in motion when the narrator receives a letter from Pierre Sogol, the initiator of the spiritual voyage. It is only after he has met Sogol that the narrator discovers a sense of non-belonging to the exterior world, the world of every day reality. It is the *chameleon law*, the law of adaptability, to which the narrator has just been initiated. It is a simple response to the stimuli of one's environment, that is, it is an animal response to one's environment, a response civilized man has completely forgotten, for he is now only able to respond intellectually.

But to make this expedition possible more people are needed. In order to convince others of the existence of this analogical mountain, Sogol uses perhaps the finest example of pataphysical reasoning that would have warmed the heart of its inventor, Alfred Jarry. By using an orator's trick he gives to each individual present the erroneous impression that he, each individual, alone has not yet been initiated, and, who, then, eager to belong to the majority, becomes easily convinced. Then, after having ruled out several hypotheses, Sogol concludes that Mont Analogue can exist in any region of the surface of the earth. If it has not been located heretofore, it is because its location is impervious to eyesight and to approach, except at certain times and under certain conditions. Furthermore, Mont Analogue has gone unnoticed because of curved space. Due to gravity, space is curved or warped and thus it is possible to miss the mountain. But with Sogol at the helm and with the proper attitude, the region of Mont Analogue can be and, indeed, is finally penetrated.

Once they have reached the base of Mont Analogue, the travellers discover that the *chameleon law* is again making itself felt. For instance, conventional words, words used in the world of every day experience, are no longer applicable on Mont Analogue. They also discover that all authority is in the hands of the mountain guides and that this authority is based on the number of *péradams* a man has managed to accumulate. A *péradam* is a true crystal and found primarily as one begins to ascend the higher slopes of Mont Analogue. Only rarely is it discovered on the lower slopes, and it is revealed only to those who seek it with sincerity and a true need. It is not by accident that it is Sogol who is the first to discover a *péradam* before he has even begun his journey to the summit.

Another discovery the travellers make during their ascent is the importance of the continuity of generations, for one generation always prepares the way for the next one. One caravan of climbers leaves behind a few men to help the next group prepare camp; only then can they continue their own ascent. In his *Postface* to ***Le Mont Analogue*** Daumal explains this procedure in greater detail which testifies to the importance he attributed to it. One of the basic laws on Mont Analogue is that one can only reach the summit after one has prepared the various encampments for those that follow. (pp. 246-49)

The concept of the continuity of generations in, indeed, an essential part of Oriental thought and we have seen to what extent both Nerval and Daumal made use of it in their works. Besides serving as an intellectual and artistic device, the concept plays an equally important role in the psychic life of the two men: their fear of and obsession with death and suicide and their urgent need for a belief in immortality. Furthermore, each man believed that for man's personal and collective salvation, it is necessary for each generation to prepare the next generation for the difficult voyage of life. Only through careful preparation can the new generation discern for itself the true from the false and the hollow, and thereby create for itself a more authentic existence. By ridding himself of the many layers of Western civilization, especially its heritage of eighteenth century enlightenment, basic, elemental, and total man, could once more come to the fore. Only then could man liberate himself from the limitations of time and space and from fear of the *néant* [''void'']. For ultimately, Daumal and Nerval were committed to the liberation of total man, physical as well as spiritual.

In order to accomplish the liberation of total man, Daumal, like Nerval, was concerned with the discovery of the paths or approaches that lead to certain truths about man and nature. In an essay entitled **''De l'attitude critique devant la Poésie,''** published in *Cahiers du Sud,* Daumal attempts to show that poetry, far from being a vague and ephemerous pastime for a few dilettantes, can, indeed, lead man to live once more in harmony with the universe and, by extension, with himself.

The first approach or path which can contribute to man's discovery of the self and the universe is Philosophy which Daumal conceived as an amalgam of two complementary disciplines, namely the dialectical method of the West, that is, Plato, Hegel, and Marx, and the disciplines and teachings of the Orient, especially that of Budda. The combination of these two ways of viewing the universe and man is essential to man's liberation and rehabilitation, for Western philosophy has, unfortunately, imposed an order upon man that conceives him as having a dual nature and, likewise, attributes this duality to the universe. This view of man, Daumal believes, has contributed considerably to Western man's sense of anguish and imprisonment. The Orient, on the other hand, by viewing man and the universe as a unified whole, has spared man this terrible conflict between the spiritual and the material. The second path, the occult, is closely related to the theosophies and cosmogonies of the Orient and, as such, can equally contribute to man's liberation. The third approach is Poetry. By combining poetry with Philosophy and the Occult, Daumal, like the Illuminists and the Platonists before them, sees the poet once again as a seer and prophet, divinely inspired and, like the magician of ancient times, able to reveal to man the world behind the world of appearances.

We can thus see to what extent the writings of Daumal are a repository for certain approaches to truth and, as such, serve future generations as a guide in their own ascent to the summit of Mont Analogue. Likewise, the writings of Nerval are also paths by which he, as well as future generations—Daumal included—can achieve liberation and salvation. (pp. 249-50)

Hilda Nelson, ''Gérard De Nerval and René Daumal, Two Nyctalopes,'' in Nineteenth-Century French Studies, *Vol. VIII, Nos. 3 & 4, Spring & Summer, 1980, pp. 236-51.**

ADDITIONAL BIBLIOGRAPHY

Review of *A Night of Serious Drinking,* by René Daumal. *Choice* 17, No. 1 (March 1980): 79.

Brief review that describes *A Night of Serious Drinking* as a Rabelaisian tour-de-force with an atmosphere reminiscent of the works of William Burroughs and Lewis Carroll.

Fremantle, Anne. Review of *Mount Analogue,* by René Daumal. *Commonweal* LXXIII, No. 11 (9 December 1960): 282.

Review that compares *Mount Analogue* to *Pilgrim's Progress* and other works portraying a spiritual quest.

Penland, Patrick R. Review of *Mount Analogue,* by René Daumal. *Library Journal* 85, No. 14 (August 1960): 2812.

Review in which the critic states that *Mount Analogue* addresses themes common to many works of mainstream twentieth-century American fiction. He states that ''to recommend this book only to a science fiction audience would be an injustice.''

Sturrock, John. ''Fidgeters and Fabricators.'' *The Observer* (16 December 1979): 39.

Review of *A Night of Serious Drinking.* Sturrock calls Daumal ''a clear and amusing writer,'' but ''too scathingly dismissive of conventional thought to win one over to him.''

(Henry) Havelock Ellis

1859-1939

English essayist, critic, novelist, poet, autobiographer, editor, and translator.

Courtesy of Prints and Photographs Division, Library of Congress

Described by H. L. Mencken as "the most civilized Englishman of his generation," Ellis is regarded as one of the foremost pioneers in the study of human sexuality. His best-known work, the seven-volume *Studies in the Psychology of Sex,* presents hundreds of case histories that frankly reveal sexual behavior as practiced by a cross section of individuals in the nineteenth and early twentieth centuries. Throughout his psychological works, Ellis emphasized the normality rather than the abnormality of various sexual functions and practices, thereby becoming greatly responsible for the change in British and American attitudes toward such hitherto forbidden areas of sexuality as homosexuality, masturbation, and female sexual responsiveness. A prolific and versatile writer, Ellis also contributed significantly to English letters both as the editor of the highly respected Mermaid Series, containing works by Elizabethan and Jacobean dramatists, and as a discerning critic of world literature.

Born in Croyden, Surrey, Ellis was the son of middle-class parents. His father, a merchant sea captain, was away from home for long periods of time, leaving Ellis's mother, a devout evangelical who held strict Victorian values, responsible for rearing and educating her son and four daughters. In his candid autobiography *My Life,* Ellis states that his mother rarely showed physical affection, but that when she did, it was of a most unusual nature. He vividly recalls how his mother once playfully held his sister's urine-soaked diaper in his face and two occasions when, while walking through a park, his mother stopped and urinated, knowing full-well that Ellis could see and hear her. In his autobiography, Ellis discloses that it was probably his relationship with his mother that instilled in him what he called "the germ of perversion" that was the eventual source of his own deviant means of sexual fulfillment: urolagnia, or sexual arousal most readily achieved while watching a woman urinate. Most critics agree that these childhood incidents, coupled with the staid Victorian beliefs that dominated Ellis's early life, inspired, to a certain extent, his studies of human sexuality.

At the age of sixteen, Ellis set sail with his father on a trip around the world, but disembarked in Australia to take a position teaching school, an experience that was recorded much later in his only novel, *Kanga Creek: An Australian Idyll.* During his four years in Australia's isolated bush country, Ellis experienced several slight romantic encounters that revealed his lack of sexual education. Puzzled by his maturing sexual needs, which had been stifled by Victorian prudishness, he was unable to fully comprehend his physical desires or to express them in romantic situations. Also a source of stress for the adolescent Ellis was the frequency of his nocturnal emissions which, according to his account in *My Life,* were never accompanied by erotic stimulation or orgasmic response. For twelve years he recorded these occurrences, and he later incorporated his personal chronicle as an anonymous case history in *Studies in the Psychology of Sex*. It was during this troubled time that Ellis began to read the works of philosopher and physician James Hinton, whose free-thinking attitudes toward science and life effected a kind of mystical conversion in Ellis. Thereafter, Ellis decided to dedicate his life to the study and explication of human sexuality so that the "mysteries" of sex might be understood by others. In 1879 Ellis returned to England, and during the following year he began the first of his seven years of medical studies at St. Thomas's Hospital in London. This period marked the beginning of Ellis's growing interest in several intellectual areas, including science, philosophy, sociology, anthropology, and literature. It was also during this time that he met and fell in love with the well-known South African novelist Olive Schreiner, whose feminist ideas greatly influenced Ellis. Although their love affair ended because of his peculiar sexual needs, the two remained devoted friends until Schreiner's death in 1920.

In order to support his medical studies, Ellis contributed articles on a variety of subjects to several magazines. One of his most notable early contributions was a critical essay written in 1883 on the works of Thomas Hardy. Biographer Vincent Brome has described Ellis's "The Novels of Thomas Hardy" as "the first long literary essay based not only upon a meticulous reading of Hardy's works, but an Easter spent in Dorset where

Ellis steeped himself in the atmosphere of Egdon Heath." The essay drew a letter from Hardy himself, who appreciated Ellis's thorough critical method in discussing his works. Critics agree that Ellis's subsequent literary criticism, collected in *The New Spirit, Affirmations, Views and Reviews,* and *From Rousseau to Proust,* is characterized by his scientific approach to literature; like the French critic Hippolyte Taine, he believed that the appropriate way to assess literature was to understand the author's biographical and environmental background. Recognized for his insightful literary criticism, Ellis was eventually called upon to edit the works of many foreign authors, most importantly the dramas of Henrik Ibsen. In addition, he was asked to edit the Mermaid Series, which introduced the unexpurgated works of the great Elizabethan and Jacobean dramatists to English readers. Many critics believe that the sexual openness of these dramas held a natural appeal for Ellis. It was while working on this project that he met the English poet and literary critic Arthur Symons, who was also editing several volumes of the Mermaid Series, and who became his lifelong friend. During the 1880s they travelled together to Paris where they met many literary figures, including Paul Verlaine, Stéphane Mallarmé, Joris-Karl Huysmans, and Rémy de Gourmont. At this time Ellis was also involved with the Fellowship of the New Life, a reformist group whose number included several prominent literary figures, among them Bernard Shaw and Edward Carpenter. Eventually the group split, creating a new faction: the socialist Fabian Society.

At the Fellowship of the New Life, Ellis met Edith Lees, who became his wife in 1891. According to biographers, their twenty-five-year marriage was one of profound love, but also one filled with emotional pain caused by their unconventional lifestyle. For most of their marriage Ellis and Lees lived apart, and although they professed "openness" in marriage, each was hurt by the other's extramarital affairs. Their separations and undemanding attitudes, however, allowed Ellis to devote his time to his voluminous studies and enabled Lees to pursue her own writing career. In addition, Lees traveled abroad and throughout England on behalf of her shy husband, lecturing on Ellis's many studies. She also detailed for him her own lesbian affairs, which appear as a case study in his work on homosexuality, *Sexual Inversion.* Although Ellis became a qualified physician, he rarely practiced medicine, choosing instead to follow his wide-ranging interests and to devote his time to research and writing. Living a long and healthy life, he collected and cataloged a vast amount of encyclopedic information that eventually found its way into his works. He died in 1939.

Ellis's first volume of his famous *Studies in the Psychology of Sex* is *Sexual Inversion,* a lengthy work based on thirty-three case histories and a study that some critics refer to as an "apology" for homosexuality. It was the first work on sexuality that did not discuss sexual deviance in terms of the criminal mind or the mentally ill. Concerned with the congenital possibilities of homosexuality, Ellis posited that its social acceptance can be argued by the prevalence of homosexuality in the animal world and by its cultural relativism: seemingly, homosexuality can be accounted for in all societies, past and present. This first volume was distributed by George Bedborough, secretary of the Legitimation League, a group that advocated freedom of sexual variety and the legitimation of children born out of wedlock. On May 31, 1898, in an attempt to disband the Legitimation League, the police arrested Bedborough for selling *Sexual Inversion,* which was deemed obscene literature. Although there was a sound defense for the work as a scientific study, Bedborough was intimidated into pleading guilty to the charge, and Ellis chose to remain aloof from the proceedings, working on his next volume, *The Evolution of Modesty, the Phenomenon of Sexual Periodicity, Auto-Erotism.* Ellis contracted to have this latter work published in the United States as Volume I of *Studies in the Psychology of Sex,* and he revised *Sexual Inversion* to appear as Volume II. With *The Evolution of Modesty, the Phenomena of Sexual Periodicity, Auto-Erotism,* Ellis dispelled many of the myths that surrounded the bugbear of Victorianism—masturbation. He was one of the first researchers to maintain that masturbation did not lead to serious illness, that it was performed by individuals of all ages, and that it was a frequent practice among women. Paul Robinson observes that Ellis's studies concerning female masturbation "served to undermine the nineteenth-century belief that women lacked sexual feelings." In this work, Ellis again employed case histories, and, as in all of his seven volumes of *Studies in the Psychology of Sex,* he relied on first-person accounts by the subjects involved to add credibility to his discussions.

Despite their somewhat infamous beginning, *Studies in the Psychology of Sex* continued to be published over several years without incident. In the other volumes of *Studies,* Ellis sought to enlighten individuals about both physiological and psychological aspects of human sexuality. He disclosed that sexual growth was developmental and that childhood experiences were to some extent responsible for adult sexuality. Ellis also candidly discussed such social concerns as birth control, eugenics, prostitution, sex education, and the institution of marriage. Furthermore, he openly considered male and female sexual responsiveness and concluded, in accordance with Sigmund Freud's theories, that impotence or frigidity is psychological in nature. Since Freud and Ellis developed their psychological sexual theories at virtually the same time, critics often contrast the two psychologists. A major difference between Ellis and Freud was their approach to studying sexuality; while Freud's works concentrate on abnormal sexual behavior, Ellis contends that all sexual behavior is relative, and therefore normal. Commentators suggest that Freud used a scientific method in his studies, suggesting motives and treatment for certain deviant actions, whereas Ellis gathered information and discussed his findings in a philosophical, rather than scientific, manner. Although Freud has more than eclipsed Ellis with his psychoanalytic theories of sexuality, critics agree that Ellis was also a vital contributor to modern sexual studies. As such, he has been recognized by contemporary sexual researchers, including Alfred Charles Kinsey, William H. Masters, and Virginia E. Johnson.

Although Ellis contributed works in a variety of genres, he is best known today for his taboo-breaking *Studies in the Psychology of Sex*. In light of the fact that the turn of the century gave way to freer attitudes regarding sex, some early critics maintained that Ellis's *Studies* dated quickly, while others cited changing sexual attitudes as directly attributable to Ellis's work. Regarding this controversy, Ellis stated: "My work, I knew, must in the nature of it be always crumbling and everyday grow a little more out of date. I have myself had to rewrite parts of it. Nevertheless, I felt that my satisfaction was justified. I had not created a work of art. But I had done mankind a service which mankind needed . . .". Critics unanimously agree with

Ellis on this point, and today he is regarded as one of the most influential pathfinders in the study of human sexuality.

(See also *Contemporary Authors*, Vol. 109.)

PRINCIPAL WORKS

The Criminal (nonfiction) 1890
The New Spirit (criticism) 1890
The Nationalization of Health (essays) 1892
Man and Woman: A Study of Human Secondary Sexual Characters (nonfiction) 1894
Mescal: A New Artificial Paradise (essay) 1897
**Studies in the Psychology of Sex: Sexual Inversion, Vol. I* (nonfiction) 1897
Affirmations (criticism) 1898
***Studies in the Psychology of Sex: The Evolution of Modesty, the Phenomena of Sexual Periodicity, Auto-Erotism, Vol. II* (nonfiction) 1899
The Nineteenth Century: A Dialogue in Utopia (essays) 1900
Studies in the Psychology of Sex: The Analysis of the Sexual Impulse, Love and Pain, the Sexual Impulse in Women, Vol. III (nonfiction) 1903
A Study of British Genius (nonfiction) 1904
Studies in the Psychology of Sex: Sexual Selection in Man: Touch, Smell, Hearing, Vision, Vol. IV (nonfiction) 1905
Studies in the Psychology of Sex: Erotic Symbolism, the Mechanism of Detumescence, the Psychic State in Pregnancy, Vol. V (nonfiction) 1906
The Soul of Spain (essay) 1908
Studies in the Psychology of Sex: Sex in Relation to Society, Vol. VI (nonfiction) 1910
The World of Dreams (essays) 1911
The Task of Social Hygiene (nonfiction) 1912
Impressions and Comments, first series (diary and criticism) 1914
Essays in War-Time (essays) 1917
The Philosophy of Conflict, and Other Essays in War-Time (essays) 1919
Impressions and Comments, second series (diary and criticism) 1921
Kanga Creek: An Australian Idyll (novel) 1922
Little Essays of Love and Virtue (essays) 1922
The Dance of Life (essays) 1923
Impressions and Comments, third series (diary and criticism) 1924
Sonnets, with Folk Songs from the Spanish [translator] (poetry) 1925
Studies in the Psychology of Sex: Eonism and Other Supplementary Studies, Vol. VII (nonfiction) 1928
The Art of Life: Gleanings from the Works of Havelock Ellis (essays, criticism, and nonfiction) 1929
Fountain of Life: Being the Impressions and Comments of Havelock Ellis (diary and criticism) 1930
More Essays of Love and Virtue (essays) 1931
Views and Reviews: A Selection of Uncollected Articles (essays and criticism) 1932
From Rousseau to Proust (criticism) 1934
My Confessional: Questions of Our Day (essays and criticism) 1934
My Life (autobiography) 1939
From Marlowe to Shaw: The Studies, 1876-1936, in English Literature (criticism) 1950
Sex and Marriage (nonfiction) 1951
The Unpublished Letters of Havelock Ellis to Joseph Ishill (letters) 1954

*This work was revised and renumbered in 1901 as *Studies in the Psychology of Sex: Sexual Inversion, Vol. II.*

**This work was revised and renumbered in 1900 as *Studies in the Psychology of Sex: The Evolution of Modesty, the Phenomena of Sexual Periodicity, Auto-Erotism, Vol. I.*

THOMAS HARDY (letter date 1883)

[*Hardy is considered one of the greatest novelists in English literature. His work resembles that of earlier Victorian novelists in technique, while in subject matter it daringly violated literary traditions of the age. In contrast to the Victorian ideal of progress, Hardy depicted human existence as a tragedy determined by powers beyond the individual's command, in particular the external pressures of society and the internal compulsions of character. His desire to reveal the underlying forces directing the lives of his characters led him to realistically examine love and sexuality in his fiction, a practice that often offended his readers and endangered his literary reputation. In 1883, in* The Westminster Review, *Ellis wrote one of the earliest critiques of Hardy's works, defending and praising the novelist's realistic examination of human sexuality. In the following excerpt, Hardy expresses his appreciation for Ellis's laudatory appraisal.*]

My Dear Sir,

I have read with great interest your article [**"Thomas Hardy's Novels"**] in the "Westminster", and can inadequately express by letter my sense of your generous treatment of the subject. I consider the essay a remarkable paper in many ways, and can truly say that the writing itself, with its charm of style, and variety of allusion, occupied my mind when first reading it far more than the fact that my own unmethodical books were its subject-matter. If novelists were a little less in the dark about the appearance of their own works what productions they might bring forth, but they are much in the position of the man inside the hobby-horse at a Christmas masque, and have no consciousness of the absurdity of its trot, at times, in the spectator's eyes.

However, I cannot complain of any invidious remarks thereon in my case. The keen appreciativeness which the article discloses sets me thinking, as I mentioned above, of the writer; it is an appreciativeness which, having the novelist's work as a skeleton to build upon, seems in many cases to create the beauties it fancies it perceives in that work. "The prosperity of a jest lies in the ear of him" etc.; and the truism is not a whit less forcible when applied to a novel.

As to certain conditions and peculiarities you notice in the stories, I may mention that many are the result of temporary accidents connected with the time of their production, rather than of deliberate choice. By-the-by, I think that in speaking of men of the Wilhelm Meister and Daniel Deronda class as being my favourite heroes, you are only saying in another way that these men are the modern man—the type to which the great mass of educated modern men of ordinary capacity are assimilating more or less.

I hope to read some more of your critical writings in the future, and believe I shall discover them without a mark.

Thomas Hardy, in a letter to Havelock Ellis on April 29, 1883, in From Marlowe to Shaw: The Studies, 1876-1936, in English Literature of Havelock Ellis *by Havelock Ellis, edited by John Gawsworth, Williams and Norgate Ltd., 1950, p. 7.*

THE SPECTATOR (essay date 1890)

[*In the following excerpt taken from an early review, Ellis's* The New Spirit *is harshly criticized for contributing to moral decay through its bold scientific approach to the problems of society.*]

Mr. Havelock Ellis,—if "Mr." be the proper title, of which we have considerable doubt,—has not very well defined to himself what it is that he really wishes to praise under the name of "the New Spirit" [in his **"The New Spirit"**]. Scientific audacity is, no doubt, a great part of it; distaste and even hatred for conventionalism is another great part of it; a strong desire for strong emotions is a third great part of it; a profound belief that the new attitude to be taken by women in affairs is to introduce a far-reaching and a wholesome revolution into the social spirit of the age, is a fourth element of considerable potency in the book; and perhaps the fifth may be a hesitating impression that an age of Socialism is at hand. But these various elements are very vaguely delineated and very much confused, and when we lay the book down, we feel that the only thing we can certainly say about it is, that the "New Spirit" is to bring with it a return to moral chaos with hardly any guiding principle at all. Perhaps the nearest thing to a definition of "the New Spirit," is to say that it is the spirit which is common to Diderot, Heine, Walt Whitman, Ibsen, and Tolstoi; and as that which is common to three at least of these writers is chiefly an enthusiastic immodesty, we may safely assert that a very potent element in "the New Spirit" is to be what Havelock Ellis would call a "frank paganism," and what we should have described by a much less agreeable phrase. Never to be ashamed of facts, is the only very coherent exhortation running through the book. The five writers we have named are studied and described with a good deal of force, and apparently after a very conscientious study of them, though of the two best known to the present writer, Heine and Whitman, we should say that the criticism is quite inadequate, and that the author is so delighted to detect the disappearance in them of shame, that every fault is forgiven so soon as that "note" of "the New Spirit" is perceived. It certainly does seem to be remarkable that what is expected from the emancipation of women, is something like the exclusion of modesty from amongst the rank of human virtues. Havelock Ellis seems to ground his view of this side of woman's activity on her very great superiority to man in the arts of practical organisation. He admits, and even contends for, the superiority of man in the ideal region, in all that is called genius; but genius he treats as possibly a morbid growth. . . . And on the ground that women are asserted to be stronger in "the lower, that is, the more important nervous centres," it is assumed that they can and will face the facts of life more audaciously than men, and that they will help men in getting rid of that conventional insincerity which ignores the unlovely parts of human life, and beautifies its general aspect at the cost of injurious social figments, which men have not the courage to expose. At all events, the only coherent constituent of "the New Spirit" which this book professes to set forth, is a vehement hatred, amounting to a passion, against conventional unveracities, and a determination that they should be swept away. To which we reply, that by all means they should be swept away, but not by ignoring and destroying the truths of which most social conventions are the low-water mark, but by bringing the conscience of society to the point at which these truths shall be fully realised, and at which their drift shall not be allowed to dwindle to a mere pretence. (pp. 441-42)

The real teaching of this book is the old Antinomianism, a teaching which, we venture to say, would be as fatal to the veracities of which Havelock Ellis wishes to be the prophet, as it is to the spiritual subjugation of the passions, and the dominion of the higher affections,—the affections which are grounded in reverence and pledged to constancy,—over the lower elements of man's nature. Nothing can really plead effectually the cause of veracity, which is not born of the conscience. Without the conscience veracity is non-existent, and with the conscience, that to which you are bound to be true is the law to which the conscience bears witness. Havelock Ellis says that "the charm of Jesus can never pass away when it is rightly apprehended." If his book means what it appears to say in every chapter, the "charm" of Jesus excites in him a mere swelling wave of emotion towards one who had "permanently expanded the bounds of individuality." That was not our Lord's claim for himself. He claimed for himself that he was one with the righteousness of God, and could help the race to purify itself at the same flame. We cannot imagine anything of which it could be more necessary for human nature, so taught, to purge itself, than the "New Spirit" of Havelock Ellis. (p. 443)

A review of "The New Spirit," in The Spectator, *Vol. 64, No. 3222, March 29, 1890, pp. 441-43.*

HAVELOCK ELLIS (essay date 1897)

[*In the following excerpt from the general preface to his* Studies in the Psychology of Sex, *published in 1897, Ellis recalls the origin of his work in sexual psychology and explains the necessity for openly investigating an element of human nature that had long been suppressed.*]

The origin of these ***Studies*** dates from many years back. As a youth I was faced, as others are, by the problem of sex. Living partly in an Australian city where the ways of life were plainly seen, partly in the solitude of the bush, I was free both to contemplate and to meditate many things. A resolve slowly grew up within me: one main part of my life-work should be to make clear the problems of sex.

That was more than twenty years ago. Since then I can honestly say that in all that I have done that resolve has never been very far from my thoughts. I have always been slowly working up to this central problem; and in a book published some three years ago—***Man and Woman: a Study of Human Secondary Sexual Characters***—I put forward what was, in my own eyes, an introduction to the study of the primary questions of sexual psychology.

Now that I have at length reached the time for beginning to publish my results, these results scarcely seem to me large. As a youth, I had hoped to settle problems for those who came after; now I am quietly content if I do little more than state them. For even that, I now think, is much; it is at least the half of knowledge. In this particular field the evil of ignorance is magnified by our efforts to suppress that which never can be suppressed, though in the effort of suppression it may become perverted. I have at least tried to find out what are the facts, among normal people as well as among abnormal people; for, while it seems to me that the physician's training is necessary in order to ascertain the facts, the physician for the most part only obtains the abnormal facts, which alone bring little light. I have tried to get at the facts, and, having got at the facts, to look them simply and squarely in the face. If I cannot perhaps turn the lock myself, I bring the key which can alone in the end rightly open the door: the key of sincerity. That is my one panacea: sincerity.

I know that many of my friends, people on whose side I, too, am to be found, retort with another word: reticence. It is a mistake, they say, to try to uncover these things; leave the sexual instincts alone, to grow up and develop in the shy solitude they love, and they will be sure to grow up and develop wholesomely. But, as a matter of fact, that is precisely what we can not and will not ever allow them to do. There are very few middle-aged men and women who can clearly recall the facts of their lives and tell you in all honesty that their sexual instincts have developed easily and wholesomely throughout. And it should not be difficult to see why this is so. Let my friends try to transfer their feelings and theories from the reproductive region to, let us say, the nutritive region, the only other which can be compared to it for importance. Suppose that eating and drinking was never spoken of openly, save in veiled or poetic language, and that no one ever ate food publicly, because it was considered immoral and immodest to reveal the mysteries of this natural function. We know what would occur. A considerable proportion of the community, more especially the more youthful members, possessed by an instinctive and legitimate curiosity, would concentrate their thoughts on the subject. They would have so many problems to puzzle over: How often ought I to eat? What ought I to eat? Is it wrong to eat fruit, which I like? Ought I to eat grass, which I don't like? Instinct notwithstanding, we may be quite sure that only a small minority would succeed in eating reasonably and wholesomely. The sexual secrecy of life is even more disastrous than such a nutritive secrecy would be; partly because we expend such a wealth of moral energy in directing or misdirecting it, partly because the sexual impulse normally develops at the same time as the intellectual impulse, not in the early years of life, when wholesome instinctive habits might be formed. And there is always some ignorant and foolish friend who is prepared still further to muddle things: Eat a meal every other day! Eat twelve meals a day! Never eat fruit! Always eat grass! The advice emphatically given in sexual matters is usually not less absurd than this. When, however, the matter is fully open, the problems of food are not indeed wholly solved, but everyone is enabled by the experience of his fellows to reach some sort of situation suited to his own case. And when the rigid secrecy is once swept away a sane and natural reticence becomes for the first time possible. (pp. xxvii-xxix)

It is perhaps a mistake to show so plainly at the outset that I approach what may seem only a psychological question not without moral fervour. But I do not wish any mistake to be made. I regard sex as the central problem of life. And now that the problem of religion has practically been settled, and that the problem of labor has at least been placed on a practical foundation, the question of sex—with the racial questions that rest on it—stands before the coming generations as the chief problem for solution. Sex lies at the root of life, and we can never learn to reverence life until we know how to understand sex.—So, at least, it seems to me. (p. xxx)

Havelock Ellis, in a preface to his Studies in the Psychology of Sex, Vol. I, Part 1, *Random House, 1940, pp. xxvii-xxx.*

BERNARD SHAW (letter date 1898)

[*Shaw is generally considered the greatest and best-known dramatist to write in the English language since Shakespeare. Following the example of Henrik Ibsen, he succeeded in revolutionizing the English stage, disposing of the romantic conventions and devices of the "well-made play," and instituting the theater of ideas, grounded in realism. During the late nineteenth century, Shaw was also a prominent literary, art, and music critic. As Samuel Hynes has noted, Shaw was driven by a rage to better the world. A Fabian socialist, he wrote criticism that is often concerned with the humanitarian and political intent of the work under discussion. The following excerpt is taken from a letter Shaw wrote to Henry Seymour, editor of the magazine* The Adult, *shortly after publisher George Bedborough was prosecuted for distributing Ellis's* Studies in the Psychology of Sex. *Shaw protests against the foolishness of such a prosecution and praises the integrity of Ellis and his work.*]

The prosecution of Mr Bedborough for selling Mr. Havelock Ellis's book [***Studies in the Psychology of Sex***] is a masterpiece of police stupidity and magisterial ignorance. I have read the book carefully; and I have no hesitation in saying that its publication was more urgently needed in England than any other recent treatise with which I am acquainted. Until it appeared there was no authoritative scientific book on its subject within reach of Englishmen and Englishwomen who cannot read French or German. At the same time Englishmen and Englishwomen are paying rates and taxes for the enforcement of the most abominably superstitious penal laws directed against the morbid idiosyncrasy with which the book deals. It is almost invariably assumed by ignorant people that this idiosyncrasy is necessarily associated with the most atrocious depravity of character; and this notion, for which there appears to be absolutely no foundation, is held to justify the infliction of penalties compared to which the punishment of a man who batters his wife almost to death is a trifle. (p. 57)

In Germany and France the free circulation of such works as the one of Mr. Havelock Ellis's now in question has done a good deal to make the public in those countries understand that decency and sympathy are as necessary in dealing with sexual as with any other subjects. In England we still repudiate decency and sympathy, and make virtues of blackguardism and ferocity.

However, I am glad to see, by the names of your [Free Press Defence] committee, that a stand is going to be made at last for the right to speak and write truthfully and carefully on a subject which every rascal and hypocrite in the country is free to treat falsely and recklessly. It is fortunate that the police have been silly enough to select for their attack a writer whose character stands so high as that of Mr. Havelock Ellis; and I have no doubt that if we do our duty in the matter the prosecution, by ignominiously failing, will end by doing more good than harm. (p. 58)

Bernard Shaw, in a letter to Henry Seymour, in August, 1898, in his Collected Letters: 1898-1910, *edited by Dan H. Laurence, Dodd, Mead & Company, 1972, pp. 57-8.*

SIGMUND FREUD (letter date 1899)

[*An Austrian neurologist, Freud was the father of psychoanalysis. The general framework of psychoanalytic thought, explained in his seminal work* The Interpretation of Dreams *(1900), encompasses both normal and abnormal behavior and is founded on the tenet that all behavior is motivated by antecedent causes. Freud's interrelated theories on the unconscious (primitive impulses and repressed thoughts), the libido hypothesis (sexual energy that follows a predetermined course), the structure of personality (id, superego, ego), and human psychosexual development (sequential stages of sexual development) have been widely used in the treatment of psychopathology utilizing four main analytic techniques: free association, dream analysis, interpretation, and transference. Although Freud was sometimes harshly criticized for his innovative theories, especially for such ideas as infantile sexuality and the Oedipus and Electra complexes, he was for the most part greatly respected as a thinker and teacher. In addition, Freudianism has had significant influence on various schools of philosophy, on religious and political ideas, and on artistic endeavors such as surrealism in art, atonal music, and stream of consciousness in literature. Thus, along with such important thinkers as Karl Marx, Friedrich Nietzsche, and Albert Einstein, Freud is considered one of the most important influences on modern thought. Freud and Ellis were both pioneers in the field of sexual psychology, establishing much of their thought concurrently, although not always in accord. While Freud's theories defined some aspects of human sexuality as pathological, Ellis chose to work from the premise that all sexual conduct is normal. As leaders in their field, each was aware of the other's work, and each held the other in high esteem. In the following excerpt, Freud comments on Ellis's writings on hysteria.]*

A pleasing thing which I meant to write to you about yesterday is something from—Gibraltar, from Mr. Havelock Ellis, an author who concerns himself with the subject of sex and is obviously a highly intelligent man, as his paper in the *Alienist and Neurologist* (October, 1898), which deals with the connection between hysteria and sexual life, begins with Plato and ends with Freud. He gives a good deal of credit to the latter, and writes a very intelligent appreciation of *Studies on Hysteria* and later publications. . . . At the end he retracts some of his praise. But something remains, and the good impression is not entirely obliterated. . . . (pp. 271-72)

Sigmund Freud, in a letter to Wilhelm Fliess on January 3, 1899, in his The Origins of Psycho-Analysis: Letters to Wilhelm Fliess, Drafts, and Notes, 1887-1902, *Marie Bonaparte, Anna Freud, and Ernst Kris, eds., translated by Eric Mosbacher and James Strachey, Basic Books, Inc., Publishers, 1954, pp. 270-72.*

JOYCE KILMER (essay date 1912)

[*Kilmer, an American poet and critic, is best known for his popular, sentimental poem* "Trees." *In the following excerpt from a sarcastic review of* The Task of Social Hygiene, *he dismisses Ellis's book as the product of a writer driven by the latest, trendiest fads in social thought.*]

We have so many American Shakespeares and American Brownings and American Dickenses that it is pleasant to find, for once, the English counterpart of an American author. Mr. Havelock Ellis is the English James Huneker. And just as the American Browning is inferior in philosophy and technique to his European predecessor, so Mr. Ellis falls below Mr. Huneker. The resemblance is a matter of method. That brilliant impressionism which Mr. Huneker applies to art and letters Mr. Ellis applies to pathology, sociology, and ethics. Both write entertainingly, both are attracted by the new and the bizarre. But Mr. Huneker knows something about art and letters.

"Whatever is new, is right," may be considered Mr. Ellis's motto, if we may accuse him of so old-fashioned a thing as a motto. That the theories which he advocates [in **"The Task of Social Hygiene"**] are at variance with each other does not in the least discourage this picturesque enthusiast. . . . For instance, Mr. Ellis, like every student of social problems, finds himself confronted by the lamentable fact of the falling birth-rate. That Mr. Ellis hails this fact with extraordinary delight, calling it a proof of a high state of civilization, that he actually holds up for admiration "a state of general well-being in which the births barely replaced the deaths," must not be taken as a proof that he is deliberately fantastic. He is trying with attractive earnestness to live up to the modern creed, which is simply "I believe in modernity." There is something rather pathetic about this spectacle. Here is a man of education and some standing, a man who has lived and read and traveled, and who, nevertheless, is so obsessed by this sentimental modern superstition that he deliberately puts away history, logic, and common sense. On a previous page, in a momentary lapse into old-fashioned reasonableness, he has stated the obvious truth, using Germany and England as examples, that a high grade of physical and nervous stability accompanies fertility; and that in the large cities, where the birth-rate is nearly always lower than in the country, the population "inevitably loses its stamina, its reserves of vital energy." But the dreadful conscience of the Modern pricks Mr. Ellis, and he hastens to forget what he has just written, and to rejoice in the spread of sterility, quoting with approval the ghastly remark of an unnamed member of the French Societé d'Anthropologie on the steady decline of his nation's birth-rate, "There is nothing to be done, except to applaud!"

Books like **"The Task of Social Hygiene"** are entertaining and should be harmless to readers over fifteen. But the trouble is that not all people will give Mr. Ellis his due. He is an artist, and should be so regarded. He collects the latest fashions—"Votes for Women," "Eugenics," and the rest—and describes them as vividly and charmingly as he described, in earlier days, the people and cities of Spain. But some of the people who share with him his enthusiasm for things new and strange insist on regarding him not as a brilliant journalist but as a scientist, a writer of textbooks, a serious teacher. . . .

Mr. Ellis's paganism (tremblingly we write the word) is of a particularly interesting variety. Recently we have learned, from specialists in the subject, a few of the things that Paganism (the capital letter is important) means. Paganism is Liberty, Mysticism, High Mindedness, Health, Beauty, Love—there are few pleasant things that Paganism is not. The trouble is that certain writers have attempted to give their paganism greater prestige by claiming that it is the paganism of classic Greece—by tracing the ancestry of Mr. Edward Carpenter through Pater to Homer, and doing other similar genealogical feats. Mr. Havelock Ellis, it is pleasant to note, is above this sort of thing. He is an admirer of Ellen Key—of course—but he does not call her a Pythoness or a Bacchante. He has no sentimental affection for classic Greece. Instead he states quite frankly where, as a reformer of the world, his sympathies lie. His admiration goes out to "the late Greek world under the Roman Empire." "At that time," says Mr. Ellis, (speaking without a suspicion of irony,) "the soul was being turned in on itself to discover new and joyous secrets; the secret of the love of nature, the secret of mystic religion, and not least, the secret of romantic love." In another place Mr. Ellis praises Ovid, not as a poet, but as "the pioneer of a chivalrous attitude toward women," and he speaks of the "refinements and courtesies which he sets forth in such charming detail."

This is refreshing; it is very manly and straightforward of Mr. Ellis. We have suspected that some contemporary "pagans" were drawn more to the decadence of the Empire than to its classical period, but our timid suggestions to this effect have not been received with enthusiasm. And here, at last, comes Mr. Ellis, who has no hesitation in holding up for the admiration of his fellow-pagans "the late Greek world under the Roman Empire!"

Fascinating in style and substance as all **"The Task of Social Hygiene"** is, and this is said seriously, for Mr. Ellis writes well, and his subjects are interesting—it is to the chapter on Eugenics that the reader will turn most eagerly, and which he will read with most pleasure. With characteristic humor, Mr. Ellis gives to this division the paradoxical title, "Eugenics and Love."

Of course, Mr. Ellis is heartily in favor of Eugenics. Who is not? Does any one say "Children shall not be born well"? It is by no means a new science. Even before Francis Galton, a certain philosopher noted that if the fathers ate sour grapes, the teeth of the children would be set on edge. And that the sins of the fathers are visited upon the children was known in the days of Moses. A Eugenic programme, some centuries old, consists in the attempt to keep the fathers from sin. The new Eugenist wishes to keep the sinner from fatherhood. And not only the sinners (forgive the archaic term!) are to be restrained from marriage, but the invalid, the mentally or physically deficient—all, in fact, who are not almost perfect. It is a splendid idea. No more destructive unions like those which produced the consumptive Keats and Stevenson, the lame Byron and Scott! Would Robert Browning marry this bed-ridden invalid? Put him in jail, and take Miss Barrett to the Segregated Colony!

It is, we repeat, a splendid idea. But like many beautiful modern schemes it is sentimental, visionary, and impracticable. You can by hammering into a man's head certain crude facts about sin and its consequences to himself and his family make him lead a decent life. This really has been done once or twice in the history of the world. But reams of law and armies of police cannot keep men from begetting children. Nor will the members of any community ever be so blindly bigoted, so fanatical, so degenerate, as to take on themselves the hideous task of condemning their fellowmen to sterility because of some slight physical or mental imperfection.

But Mr. Ellis is not to be condemned with the causes he advocates. There must be some one to tell us about new and picturesque movements, and Mr. Ellis is eminently fitted for the work. He has a graceful style, and he is amiably enthusiastic. He has written a very entertaining book.

Joyce Kilmer, "The Happy Eugenists," in The New York Times Book Review, *November 17, 1912, p. 672.*

H. L. MENCKEN (essay date 1912)

[From the era of World War I until the early years of the Great Depression, Mencken was one of the most influential figures in American letters. His strongly individualistic, irreverent outlook on life and his vigorous, invective-charged writing style helped establish the iconoclastic spirit of the Jazz Age and significantly shaped the direction of American literature. As a social and literary critic—the roles for which he is best known—Mencken was the scourge of evangelical Christianity, public service organizations, literary censorship, boosterism, provincialism, democracy, all advocates of personal or social improvement, and every other facet of American life that he perceived as humbug. In his literary criticism, Mencken encouraged American writers to shun the anglophilic, moralistic bent of the nineteenth century and to practice realism, an artistic call-to-arms that is most fully developed in his essay "Puritanism As a Literary Force," *one of the seminal essays of modern literary criticism. A man who was widely renowned or feared during his lifetime as a would-be destroyer of established American values, Mencken once wrote: "All of my work, barring a few obvious burlesques, is based upon three fundamental ideas. 1. That knowledge is better than ignorance; 2. That it is better to tell the truth than to lie; and 3. That it is better to be free than to be a slave." Mencken called Ellis "the most civilized Englishman of his generation" (see excerpt dated 1921), and he wrote several favorable reviews of Ellis's writings. In the following excerpt, Mencken offers a succinct overview of Ellis's works.]*

Ellis is one of the most learned and clear-minded Englishmen of our time. A psychiatrist, a psychologist and a sociologist of very high rank, he is also a charming writer and a sound critic. He is the editor of the invaluable Contemporary Science Series, and has himself contributed several volumes to it. He is one of the editors of the excellent Mermaid Series of old English dramatists. He was one of the first Englishmen to write intelligently about Ibsen. His book on the causes and processes of dreams is the best in any language. Saving only Sir Francis Galton, he has made a more valuable contribution to the statistical study of genius than any other man. His great monograph on **"Man and Woman"** is the starting point of every current discussion of secondary sexual differences.

But above and beyond all these works are his six volumes of **"Studies in the Psychology of Sex."** Here we have the labor of years, the labor of a scientific Hercules. Every pertinent fact and observation, in whatever language, is set down, weighed, appraised. The abysmal delvings of Germans and Russians, the gay flights of Frenchmen and Italians, the tedious figurings of Englishmen and Americans, even the views and traditions of Arabs and Chinese, are put in order, compared, digested, studied. And to all this staggering welter of material, to all this homeric accumulation of data, Ellis brings the path-finding faculty of a trained and penetrating mind. He has that supreme sort of common sense which is the mother and father of genuine science. He discerns the general fact in the Alpine rubbish heap of special facts. The result is a magnificent contribution to human knowledge—a contribution not immediately assimilable, of course, by the folk at Christendom, but one that they must eventually get down, in the sugar-coated pills of lesser sages, if they are ever to shake off their abominable doctrine that the only decent way to discuss the most important of all the facts of life is by silly indirection and with nasty giggles. (pp. 153-54)

H. L. Mencken, "A Visit to a Short Story Factory," in The Smart Set, *Vol. XXXVIII, No. 4, December, 1912, pp. 151-58.**

MRS. HAVELOCK ELLIS [EDITH LEES ELLIS] (essay date 1918)

[A novelist, essayist, and lecturer, Edith Lees Ellis was one of the most important influences on Ellis's life and work. Although their unconventional marriage brought them as much pain as happiness (for the most part they lived separately and had other lovers), each was devoted to the other in spirit. On behalf of the shy, reticent Ellis, Edith traveled throughout Europe and America, lecturing on such social issues as eugenics, birth control, and sex education, concerns that Ellis championed in his written works. In the following excerpt, she offers an interesting personal glimpse of her husband and his work.]

There are some personalities one always sees in imagination in certain surroundings which have been created by some great painter. . . . A series of pictures Havelock Ellis instinctively loves is that of St. Jerome in his study. In them he has unconsciously seen an image of the student within himself. In that little cell open to the air and the sun, the peaceful philosopher ponders over the great secrets in nature and in books. A tame lion lies at St. Jerome's feet, just as a fox and a snake in the wilds of Cornwall have remained at Havelock Ellis's side unafraid of one so absorbed in his thoughts. For both, domesticity has been reduced to the simplest expression. The whole universe, in thoughts, in dreams and books, in science and in art seems to lie before one who, from a boy to a mature man, is bent on fitting the right keys into secret locks. The ordinary ambitions and hopes of men have little meaning for him. Trivialities, and averages, and even malicious gossip, leave him undisturbed. He is an unraveller of mysteries as well as an organiser of practical issues. He is a hermit and yet an iconoclast. He is a lover of mankind and at the same time a withdrawer from their haunts. If, like a St. Bernard dog, he could express himself in his daily human life, through wagging a tail or lashing it, or barking and growling in turn, while keeping his written words for his more adequate expression, social life would not have such terrors for him as now.

Edward Carpenter once laughingly said of him that he reminded him of a snail cautiously peeping from his shell, and a social sound or a rough touch sends him immediately out of sight into his own world of observation into which no one dare intrude. Olive Schreiner, again, described him as between a Christ and a faun; his aloofness from and yet nearness to human beings makes this image true. From his book of ***Impressions and Comments,*** we can gather the diverse conclusions that, with this temperament, he has come to during his life of fifty-five years. Such subjects as Bathing, Streams and Children, Solitude, Gods and Flowers, reveal the poet and the artist upon which the man of science is founded. Those who know Havelock Ellis best realise that the sensitiveness and tenderness and deep intuitions of a woman, added to the virile intellectualism of a man, with glimmerings of the fantastic fear and also the wisdom of a child, dip and dodge in all his life-work around problems which are so deep, subtle, and many-sided that most of us shrink from approaching them at all. A *fighter* for truth, in the militaristic sense he is not—only one of her careful and observant sentinels. By nature a poet, by education a scientist, the dreaming and probing consequent on this dual individuality have produced a man of unusual serenity and understanding, a man of sentiment, yet free from sentimentality. He is at once a poised idealist and an accurate statistician—a man whose written words must inevitably lead others to deeds for the good of the race.

To women he owes the best that is in him and to them he has paid back his debt. His understanding of the primitive and complex in their natures is a little bewildering even to those of us who think we know ourselves. The parasite, the doll, the rebel, the angel, the idiot, and the over-woman must all acknowledge that this man has somehow surprised many secrets which women themselves, as yet, scarcely realise. . . . Havelock Ellis's attitude to sex and to woman is the attitude of the future man to the future woman. (pp. 558-60)

It was a vivid realisation that the universe is a living *whole,* and that there is a oneness beneath all apparent contradictions that made Havelock Ellis know, in a flash, that the infinitely great and the finitely small are locks and keys in a scheme greater than any human brain can conceive. He became in a moment a man of faith, a faith involving no intellectual beliefs, and far removed from all creeds and superstitions. He has never lost that vision. It lies at the background of his six books on the ***Psychology of Sex,*** and is at the root of his studies of the Abnormal, the Criminal, the Man of Genius. It brings light to his serious face when looking at pictures or listening to music. It is behind the holiday mood which enables him to realise the soul of Spain and the colour and charm of Morocco. It has enabled him to see the Angel with the flaming sword behind those revelations of the intimacies and crudities of the sexual life which to many only suggest disorder or dirt. We find it in embryo in his early book ***The New Spirit,*** and in more diverse and elaborate detail in the book of ***Impressions and Comments.*** (pp. 560-61)

"What you oppose you assist," is one of this forerunner's favourite sayings. He has realised that life is a force like a spiral: that is, that it is a series of expansions and resistances. There must be both or there is a lack of real energy. To have a perfect whole there must be inconsistencies. "Life, even in the plant," he says in ***Impressions and Comments,*** "is a tension of opposing forces. Whatever is vital is contradictory, and if of two views we wish to find out which is the richer and the more fruitful, we ought perhaps to ask ourselves which embodies the more contradictions." In other paragraphs of ***Impressions, Little Things, Apples and Pears,*** and other apparently insignificant subjects, the universality of his outlook is shown in what appears to him to be the delicate intonations of human life. The whole book is a sort of diary of his own mental atmosphere and personal impressions and not, as in many of his sex and criminal studies, a retrospect of those men and views of his age which make many footnotes essential. (pp. 562-63)

With Edward Carpenter, Olive Schreiner, and James Hinton, Havelock Ellis sees the significance of Love as a fine art, rather than as a frenzied episode or as a mere primitive egotism. He has the faith of the forerunner when he analyses and seeks to understand what Lecky calls the "most mournful and the most awful figure in history." He knows that the cure, alike for the puritan and the prodigal, lies in the evolution of the greater love which knows neither repression nor excess. In this wider and deeper and more joyous love is the richer life of the world. The true lover, combining spontaneity with spiritual order, is the rarest and sweetest product of evolution. The policeman, even the eugenic policeman, is only a makeshift. Why men like Havelock Ellis accentuate the need for eugenic education is not because they build their faith on any system of defence against race degeneracy, but because they realise that it is better to try to purify the race by prevention of evils than to spend incalculable time in eliminating the products of the excess of freedom. (p. 563)

Havelock Ellis sees as a forerunner, an onlooker, a mystic and a Spartan. Love and Art are his keys to the Universe. In love he hears music and in music the rhythm of life and love and death in one. Statistics are valuable to him only as notes to the musician. Facts are useful to him as words are to the poet, and ethics essential as colour to the artist, who knows how to use notes, words, and colour to interpret spiritual realities. For spiritual realities are what we are all seeking. It is a sort of jealousy we feel toward a forerunner which makes us crucify him or try to blow out his torch before he can hand it on to another. The true forerunner, however, can always die smiling—for he sees. (p. 564)

Mrs. Havelock Ellis [Edith Lees Ellis], "Havelock Ellis," in The Bookman, *New York, Vol. XLVII, No. 5, July, 1918, pp. 558-64.*

H. L. MENCKEN (essay date 1921)

[*In the following excerpt from a discussion of* Impressions and Comments, *Mencken states that "Havelock Ellis is undoubtedly the most civilized Englishman of his generation," one of the most often-quoted tributes to Ellis. Mencken's review of* Impressions and Comments *originally appeared in 1921.*]

If the test of the personal culture of a man be the degree of his freedom from the banal ideas and childish emotions which move the great masses of men, then Havelock Ellis is undoubtedly the most civilized Englishman of his generation. He is a man of the soundest and widest learning, but it is not his positive learning that gives him distinction; it is his profound and implacable skepticism, his penetrating eye for the transient, the disingenuous, and the shoddy. So unconditioned a skepticism, it must be plain, is not an English habit. The average Englishman of science, though he may challenge the Continentals within his speciality, is only too apt to sink to the level of a politician, a green grocer, or a suburban clergyman outside it. . . . The late war uncovered this weakness in a wholesale manner. The English *Gelehrten,* as a class, not only stood by their country; they also stood by the Hon. David Lloyd George, the *Daily Mail,* and the mob in Trafalgar Square. Unluckily, the asinine manifestations ensuing—for instance, the "proofs" of the eminent Oxford philologist that the Germans had never contributed anything to philology—are not to be described with good grace by an American, for they were far surpassed on this side of the water. England at least had Ellis, with Bertrand Russell, Wilfrid Scawen Blunt, and a few others in the background. We had, on that plane, no one.

Ellis, it seems to me, stood above all the rest, and precisely because his dissent from the prevailing imbecilities was quite devoid of emotion and had nothing in it of brummagen moral purpose. Too many of the heretics of the time were simply orthodox witch-hunters off on an unaccustomed tangent. In their disorderly indignation they matched the regular professors; it was only in the objects of their ranting that they differed. But Ellis kept his head throughout. An Englishman of the oldest native stock, an unapologetic lover of English scenes and English ways, an unshaken believer in the essential soundness and high historical destiny of his people, he simply stood aside from the current clown-show and waited in patience for sense and decency to be restored. His **"Impressions and Comments,"** the record of his war-time reflections, is not without its note of melancholy; it was hard to look on without depression. But for the man of genuine culture there were at least some resources remaining within himself, and what gives this volume its chief value is its picture of how such a man made use of them. Ellis, facing the mob unleashed, turned to concerns and ideas beyond its comprehension—to the humanism that stands above all such sordid conflicts. There is something almost of Renaissance dignity in his chronicle of his speculations. The man that emerges is not a mere scholar immured in a cell, but a man of the world superior to his race and his time—a philosopher viewing the childish passion of lesser men disdainfully and yet not too remote to understand it, and even to see in it a certain cosmic use. A fine air blows through the book. It takes the reader into the company of one whose mind is a rich library and whose manner is that of a gentleman. He is the complete anti-Kipling. In him the Huxleian tradition comes to full flower.

His discourse ranges from Beethoven to Comstockery and from Spanish architecture to the charm of the English village. The extent of the man's knowledge is really quite appalling. His primary work in the world has been that of a psychologist, and in particular he has brought a great erudition and an extraordinarily sound judgment to the vexatious problems of the psychology of sex, but that professional concern, extending over so many years, has not prevented him from entering a dozen other domains of speculation, nor has it dulled his sensitiveness to beauty nor his capacity to evoke it. His writing was never better than in this volume. His style, especially towards the end, takes on a sort of glowing clarity. It is English that is as transparent as a crystal, and yet it is English that is full of fine colors and cadences. There could be no better investiture for the questionings and conclusions of so original, so curious, so learned, and, above all, so sound and hearty a man. (pp. 189-92)

H. L. Mencken, "Five Men at Random: Havelock Ellis," in his Prejudices, third series, *Alfred A. Knopf, 1922, pp. 189-92.*

ARTHUR SYMONS (essay date 1922)

[*While Symons initially gained notoriety as an English decadent of the 1890s, he eventually established himself as one of the most important critics of the modern era. As a member of the iconoclastic generation of fin de siècle aesthetes that included Aubrey Beardsley and Oscar Wilde, Symons wholeheartedly assumed the role of the world-weary cosmopolite and sensation hunter, com-*

Ellis as a young man. Mary Evans Picture Library.

posing verses in which he attempted to depict the bohemian world of the modern artist. He was also a gifted linguist whose sensitive translations from Paul Verlaine and Stéphane Mallarmé provided English poets with an introduction to the poetry of the French Symbolists. However, it was as a critic that Symons made his most important contribution to literature. His The Symbolist Movement in Literature *(1899) provided his English contemporaries with an appropriate vocabulary with which to define their new aesthetic—one that communicated their concern with dreamlike states, imagination, and a reality that exists beyond the boundaries of the senses. Symons also discerned that the concept of the symbol as a vehicle by which a "hitherto unknown reality was suddenly revealed" could become the basis for the entire modern aesthetic. A proper use of the symbol "would flash upon you the soul of that which can be apprehended only by the soul—the finer sense of things unseen, the deeper meaning of things evident." This anticipated and influenced James Joyce's concept of an artistic "epiphany," T. S. Eliot's "moment in time," and laid the foundation for much of modern poetic theory. Ellis met Symons when the latter edited the fourth and fifth volumes of the Mermaid series, and the two formed a friendship that spanned thirty-five years. Together, in 1890, they entered the café life of Paris, meeting such prominent French literary figures as Paul Verlaine, Stéphane Mallarmé, Joris-Karl Huysmans, and Rémy de Gourmont. In the following excerpt, Symons offers a balanced discussion of Ellis's* Affirmations. *For another discussion of this work, see the excerpt by Desmond MacCarthy (1939).*]

Havelock Ellis occupies a curious position among contemporary writers; he is not quite a man of letters nor entirely a man of science, and he has many of the merits, as well as certain of the faults, of both. Criticism, to him, is a branch of anthropology; but then, to him, anthropology means much more than it means to most people. It means, in short, the whole art, science and fact of life; and to this great problem, life as expressed in literature, he comes with an equipment of culture which few other critics of the day can boast of. He shows himself in **"Affirmations"** and in **"The New Spirit,"** a cautious student of the literature of most times and nations; and in these books and in scattered essays, a student also of painting and of music, a traveler and an observer. Caring chiefly to consider literature on that side which seems to appeal most intimately to the present, he is as conscious of tradition as the most conservative of critics, and it is almost a prejudice with him to be entirely without prejudice. (p. 81)

[**"Affirmations"**] contains five essays, on Nietzsche, Casanova, Zola, Huysmans and **"St. Francis and Others."** The last is a kind of epilogue, perhaps the best piece of writing in the book, a summing-up of many questions, scarcely in any sense literary; the others are not merely, as the preface might lead us to imagine, excuses for discussion, essays round about writers, but minute and elaborate studies of Nietzsche the philosopher, Casanova the memoir-writer, Zola the novelist, and Huysmans the artist in prose. They are more than this, if you like; but they are never less. And they have that fine, in England that rare, quality of being essays about literature which are not, in the bad sense, literary. There is little excuse for writing any more books merely about books (except as handbooks and histories of literature, which have their educational value). What must always be worth writing about is literature in its relation to general ideas and in its relation to life. There we have a chance of making something which, in its turn, shall be literature; or, if not literature, at least a useful and entertaining branch of anthropology.

The study of Zola, though it contains some good passages, is the least interesting and the least novel of these essays. In Huysmans, Ellis has a more congenial subject, and his analysis of that singularly instructive career reminds one of those "essays in contemporary psychology" which Bourget wrote with so learned an insight into the soul of literature before attempting his vague, tedious and irrelevant incursions into the souls of people in society. It is a study of the whole origin and tendencies of the art of Huysmans, in which a subject discussed in one of those very essays of Bourget, the essay on Baudelaire, is taken up and carried further: the much misunderstood question of decadence in art. In Casanova, Ellis has a still more congenial subject, and his essay on Casanova will delight every reasonable reader of the most entertaining memoirs in the world, and duly scandalize every one who has been foolishly scandalized by Casanova. No writer before Ellis has ever done anything like justice to Casanova. Even the Goncourts, in their studies of the eighteenth century, but rarely refer to him; John Addington Symons mentions him slightingly in introducing the inconceivably inferior Carlo Gozzi; even now there are people who think the memoirs were written by Stendhal, as there are people who think Shakespeare's plays were written by Bacon; and for the most part, serious persons are as shy of referring to Casanova as if he were a pornographic writer for private subscribers only. Ellis, therefore, comes forward almost as a discoverer; and he comes forward declaring with justifiable confidence that here is "one of the great autobiographical revelations which the ages have left us, with Augustine's, Cellini's, Rousseau's, of its own kind supreme." It is scarcely too much to say that his essay is more than a statement, it is a proof, of the supremacy of Casanova; and it is in one of those apparent paradoxes which, carefully considered, are full of fundamental truth, that he reminds us of the particular service—that "athletics of the emotions"—which we can derive from the particular quality of these memoirs.

In what might be called objective qualities the essay on Nietzsche is no doubt the most valuable of Ellis's essays. It is a subtle interpretation, at once statement and commentary, of a philosopher of our day.

There remains the final paper on **"St. Francis and Others,"** and here Ellis sums up, with an admirable serenity, an absolute freedom from those ideals which at one time threatened to absorb him, his general conclusions on the questions of progress, civilization and the arts of life. (pp. 81-2)

Arthur Symons, "An Appreciation of Havelock Ellis," in The Double Dealer, *Vol. III, No. 14, February, 1922, pp. 78-83.*

CHRISTOPHER MORLEY (essay date 1924)

[*Morley was a popular American novelist, journalist, and literary critic. Throughout his long career he worked on the editorial staffs of several newspapers and magazines, including the New York* Evening Post, Ladies' Home Journal, *and, for nearly twenty years,* The Saturday Review of Literature. *In the following excerpt, Morley discusses Ellis's* The Dance of Life, *agreeing with Ellis's perception of "the primitive sensibility of the dance as the germ of all thought, all morals." For further discussion of Ellis as a philosopher, see the excerpts by Mark Van Doren (1924), Van Wyck Brooks (1928), Charles Angoff (1935), and Desmond MacCarthy (1939).*]

After reading **"The Dance of Life"** once, I thought: how agreeable to sit down and write copiously about it. After reading it twice, a more decent humility prevails. To "review" Mr. Ellis's fertile and fructuating book would be as impossible as to review life itself. For it speaks to those interior questionings and honesties where the happiest wisdom is silence. Yet, for an action to be comely (Mr. Ellis somewhere suggests) it need only be fitting to its particular relationships at its particular moment. The relation that has grown up between this book and myself is such that I would feel cowardly not to testify. And perhaps the man who has crowned his old age by this noble résumé of a life's thinkings would find no impropriety in a salute from a young ignoramus desperately but sincerely groping for those liberations of spirit that help to make life artful. It is by its echo in young and undisciplined hearts that Mr. Ellis's book will prove its virtue. (p. 797)

The dance of life! I have feared that to modern connotation Mr. Ellis's title may sound misleading: for the word *dance* has acquired slipshod and rowdy suggestions. The rhythms and measures he divines are more majestic and more obscure, more truly jocund yet also more tranquil, than those our mind is wont to image. . . . When I remember the perfected charm and gusto of that jolly sport, whether indoors or on green lawns or damp riverside meadows, I realize what Mr. Ellis means when he suggests the primitive sensibility of the dance as the germ of all thought, all morals. So I beg for faith in the instinct of the true artist. That is sufficient for me: I am a solifidian.

But all advances in thought, as Mr. Ellis summons many testimonies to prove, are assisted by fictions. And this book itself, so full of brave encouragement, is, I daresay, fictive enough. For though he urges us to believe that perhaps the art-instinct is the *primum mobile* of the spirit world (just as some one element may be fundamental in all matter), yet we know ourselves too well to be over-hopeful. Is there any sensitive person who has not found himself continually hampered and thwarted in his justest impulses, calloused by the friction of competing hopes, crazed by the tragedy of needless and meaningless hastes and bickerings, thus tottering an errant course rather than proceeding with the clear sobriety of art? Civilization, though it often extorts our reluctant admiration, yet is also maddening. I have seen a New York taxi-driver spinning his cab round a crowded corner, unconsciously roll his eyes with just the bewildered frenzy of a dog that isn't yet quite certain whether to bite or not. I have ridden in suburban electric trains where the continual crashing of metal doors, jarring of windows, jolting of starts and stops, racing of belated passengers to leap aboard at every station, all combined in a hullabaloo so shocking that unless one retired into a secret core of indifference one would surely go insane. Only too well we know our lives to be absurd and unwholesome; and we seek passionately, impossibly, to be made significant and whole.

These contradictions and paradoxes of life as we know it, Mr. Ellis patiently and generously considers. With the occasional sprinkle of bitterness that is palatable in philosophy, with the nicest simplicity of manner, and (more important still) with an eye cleansed by feasting on the wideness of Time and Space, he takes us through the four great arts that are most urgent to our condition: the art of Thinking, the art of Writing, the art of Religion, the art of Morals. Ever since I first encountered the book, I have wished there were some way of making it compulsory study for parsons. For though it gives little consolation to Churches, it has profound energy for those who esteem religion as the noblest form of aesthetic.

The fiery particle will not be put off with quibble or evasion. It is, it *is* important and needful that one should at least try to live life as an art, that it should be exempt from pitiable hagglings and cowardly surrenders. And Ellis's special charm, perhaps, is that he keeps rediscovering to us those most precious of all secrets—our own thoughts, those we buried, forgot, or fled from in dismay. The notions we were a little leery of, that we folded neatly and hid under a stone while we went bathing in the clear swift stream of life, we here find again and recognize as the most important. His pages on the essential unity of science and art, for example. He insists that they are homoiousian (a word he does not use, but I do, for I love a good rollicking pedantry now and then). Those passages are the richest delight to anyone who has been privileged to guess the imaginative poetical spirit that irradiates all genuine scientific inquiry. Everywhere he is on the side of the angels; and while he says very little that is novel or startling to any alert thinker, yet he says quite enough to galvanize many a merchant in intellectual hand-me-down and shoddy. And his substance is charmingly organized and thought out. The chapter on literary art is truism to any intuitive lover of language; yet how admirably and winningly put. Always we find him taking the cudgel against stultifying rule and rigidity, the picayune pettifogging spirit that would construe the text of life as a proofreader corrects galley slips. In the **"Art of Morals,"** for instance, how eloquently he buttresses every artist's contention (sure to be misunderstood, of course) that to the philosopher there is no such thing as "morality," as vulgarly apprehended; for morality ceases to exist when it becomes conscious. Morality, of course, is merely what is mannerly and customary: and Mr. Ellis frankly would have us all as "immoral" as Jesus was.

What, then, if we try to lay penpoint upon it, is the cardinal bearing of this great book? I think it is this, that each of us (if capable of thought at all; and he excellently insists that not all are so capable) is an artist creating his own truth from the phenomena life gives him. The kingdom of heaven is within us indeed, and each must be his own Buddha, his own Christ, his own Leonardo. This dark and pricklesome necessity surely does not imply any relaxing of our imperilled responsibility, rather an all the more stringent devotion to our little ember of artistic conscience. Out of these fantastic intractable materials that life has poured about us we must compose our picture as best we may—like prisoners of war carving cunning toys of corncobs and peanut shells and chewing gum. Time—which is, I suppose, the canvas we paint on, the clay we knead—flows fast and faster—so fast, sometimes, we dimly suspect ourselves very close to the place it comes from. Every instant is an emergency, and we are apprenticed to the art of living before we know enough to have any choice. As so often on railroads, the brakeman doesn't call out the names of the stations until after the train has started. By the time we learn where we are going—it sounds very like Nothingness?—it is too late to cancel the ticket.

Any man who writes as plainly as Mr. Ellis of the real issues of life, is certain of a few sniffs and hoots. But he helps us towards the only task worth while, the only task that can bring us peace—the attempt to deal not as hucksters, but as poets, with the rough, blazing, infinitely precious fragments of life. He helps us to face the exquisite riddle with greater piety and courage, and to turn our necessity to glorious gain. Perhaps it is not inappropriate to say of his book, as he says of Lange's "History of Materialism" that so moved him years ago, "it can never be forgotten by any one who read it in youth." (pp. 798-801)

Christopher Morley, "The Creative Life," in The Yale Review, *Vol. XIII, No. 4, July, 1924, pp. 797-801.*

MARK VAN DOREN (essay date 1924)

[*Van Doren, the younger brother of Carl Van Doren, was one of America's most prolific and diverse writers of the twentieth century. His work includes poetry (for which he won the Pulitzer Prize in 1939), novels, short stories, drama, criticism, social commentary, and the editing of a number of popular anthologies. He wrote accomplished studies of Shakespeare, John Dryden, Nathaniel Hawthorne, and Henry David Thoreau, and served as the literary editor and film critic for* The Nation *during the 1920s and 1930s. Van Doren's criticism is aimed at the general reader, rather than the scholar or specialist, and is noted for its lively perception and varied topics of discussion. Like his poetry and fiction, his criticism consistently examines the inner, idealistic life of the individual. In the following excerpt, Van Doren discusses the mature and profound vision of life Ellis presents in his* Impressions and Comments, third series. *For further discussions of Ellis as a philosopher, see the excerpts by Christopher Morley (1924), Van Wyck Brooks (1928), Charles Angoff (1935), and Desmond MacCarthy (1939).*]

Havelock Ellis is only sixty-five years old, but throughout the third and final series of his **"Comments and Impressions"** . . . he speaks like one who believes that he is done. Death has begun to be something that he can love; a feather from her soft wing has touched his eyes, the scythe has pricked him and left him bleeding, and he is not sorry. He thinks of Prospero, "the man who has finally grasped the whole universe in his vision, as an evanescent mist, and stands serenely on the last foothold and ultimate outlook of the world," and he is content with such wise company at the close of a long day spent without rest yet without haste. The author of **"The New Spirit," "Man and Woman," "Studies in the Psychology of Sex,"** and **"The Dance of Life"** rises quietly from profound labors along the darker edges of man's mind and walks free upon an earth which he now sees for the first time, perhaps, in its complete and shining beauty.

The quality of his present vision he has himself defined in a magnificent passage describing the final phase of any great artist's genius—Rodin, Michelangelo, Titian, Rembrandt, Turner, and Shakespeare are in his mind. . . . It is the soul of his universe that Mr. Ellis is asking us to see in this last but surely not yet finished phase—the soul behind all natural things, the soul one glimpse of which "converted" him to a very special kind of religion years ago. It shows itself clearly to him now as he goes on holidays of the spirit along the Cornish cliffs or through the vineyards of the South. It is manifest in sun and spray, in the green oncoming wave, in the music of Bach, in the aeroplane which takes him once to France, in the twisted, vigorous vine, in the metaphysics of obscenity. It reconciles for him the most stubborn of all opposites—"the diversity of the world" and "its inability to accept its own diversity." It saves him from the romanticism "which lies in seeking after a beauty the world cannot hold and in failing to see the beauty it really holds." But in particular it glows for him through all the rich memories of books and men which leisure now allows to return. If he is the ripest commentator on human life today it is because he knows and remembers more pertinent things than any other man, and because these things are grown not only into his mind but also, apparently, into his body; so that to observe for him is to reflect, and to reflect is to feel truth spreading like a warm dye through nerve and sinew and bone.

It is to be hoped that Mr. Ellis will write many more books, and incidentally that he will continue as here to chastise the age into which—unfortunately, he thinks—he was born. "I am sometimes called 'modern,'" he remarks, "and there is nothing that I less desire to be called. The only modern things that I care for are those that are as old as the dawn or the rainbow or at least as the wild rose."

Mark Van Doren, "First Glance," in The Nation, *Vol. CXIX, No. 3101, December 10, 1924, p. 640.*

ISAAC GOLDBERG (essay date 1926)

[*As a critic, Goldberg's principal interests were the theater and Spanish-American literature. His* Studies in Spanish-American Literature *(1920) and* Brazilian Literature *(1922) are credited with introducing two neglected national groups of writers to English-language readers. In the following excerpt from his* Havelock Ellis: A Biographical and Critical Survey, *Goldberg provides an early survey of Ellis's works.*]

[***The Criminal***] together with ***The Nationalisation of Health***, . . . may be looked upon as forming a biological pendant to the psychological and spiritual implications of ***The New Spirit.*** These books, indeed, are what we might call Ellis's "new body." ***The Criminal*** . . . was done in the way of a *tour de force*. ***The Nationalisation of Health*** grew somewhat more logically out of Ellis's medical experiences. In these appears for the first time, the Ellis of the case method and the statistical table. After ***The New Spirit,*** statistics and cases would be among the things least expected from this seeming visionary. Yet his imaginative flights are based on just such solid investigation; the eagle weighs heavier than the air through which it soars. He may quote Homer in the original Greek; he may interest himself in the artistic strivings of the criminal type; yet throughout is a sanative balance of art and science, a healing humaneness and Humanism. The conclusions which Ellis reached have become common property, although our attitude toward the criminal is still vindictive rather than curative. (p. 140)

The Nationalisation of Health is similarly preoccupied with the technology of social improvement, studying this time not the abnormal but the so-called normal element of society. Here Ellis speaks out of a recent medical experience in London, in large manufacturing towns and in rural districts. The young mystic of ***The New Spirit*** is no deliquescent dilettante of the exotic and the esoteric. He knows that trees, though they lift their crowns heavenward, are rooted in the soil. He complains, indeed, in his Preface, that "we postpone laying the foundations of our social structure in order to elaborate its pinnacles," whereas (in the Conclusion) "Under no national system can training of the mind be placed before the life of the body."

"The fate of man," reads the epigraph of the book, too optimistically, "is in his own hands." Yet that fate may be altered, given a new direction, a finer impetus. Recent investigations into the phenomena of heredity and environment, indeed, have invested those biological terms with a new, a fairly Ellisian unity. They are not, it seems, different and implacable entities but rather different and amenable aspects. They represent a fate that is largely, if not wholly, in man's own hands. The outlook of the book, as of all the man's work, is distinctly, though not polemically, international. Ellis's conception of democracy itself, indeed, appears as one of "international self-realisation." (pp. 141-42)

The early books of Ellis seem to follow, consciously or intuitively, a definite plan. ***The New Spirit*** states an attitude toward the universe, studying its exemplification in a selected number of personalities. ***The Criminal*** and ***The Nationalisation of Health*** provide for that spirit a sound biological foundation, a perfect social background. In ***Man And Woman*** . . . we have the first definite sexual study by Ellis, though certainly not the first intimation of Ellis's interest in the subject. Man and woman thus emerge from the potential paradise of the mind and body. (p. 143)

The importance of ***Man And Woman,*** aside from its investigation into the structural differences between the sexes and the consequent difference of response to stimuli, lies in its unwillingness to accept the conventional distinctions. Men and women, it seems, are more alike than we have been taught to consider them. Many of the differences that are supposed to be rooted in sex are really sourced in social history and attitude. (pp. 143-44)

Affirmations, virtually, is a ripened continuation of ***The New Spirit.*** In it Ellis, studying Nietzsche, Casanova, Zola, Huysmans, St. Francis and others, reveals five aspects of the complex but harmonious personality that is himself. That the same man should be able to feel an unforced interest in men so disparate is obvious testimony of what I may call a certain spiritual versatility. Eclecticism is a word that too often has denoted a refined superficiality; yet in the deeper sense, Ellis is, precisely, an eclectic who inclines rather to skepticism than to syncretism. His selection becomes, thereby, not a meaningless mosaic of mannerisms, but the harmonious pattern of a significant soul. In the end, of course, nothing matters; until that end, however, nothing becomes almost synonymous with everything. ***Affirmations,*** as much as a book about the men whose names adorn its chapters, is a book about Havelock Ellis. "Our own affirmations are always the best." In that simple line from his Preface is implicit almost a program of creative eclecticism. In the studies that follow it becomes explicit. Each of the studies, moreover, comes in the nature of a pioneer offering. That on Nietzsche . . . was virtually the first to introduce the great figure to English readers; it remains one of the most balanced treatments of a great, if unbalanced, mind. The Casanova is almost astounding in its grasp of an antipodal nature. Not only is it one of the great essays on the "Chevalier"; it is one of the sagest essays that our contemporary letters may boast,—an appreciation fairly classical for its depth of insight and firm grace of expression, transcending its subject and embodying a principle of life. The Zola and Huysmans essays are each, in a different sense, incomplete. They consider these men at a time when the relation between them was closer than it appears in the light of Huysmans's later work. The essay on Zola is based chiefly on Ellis's reflections during the translation of *Germinal;* at the time he knew little about the man's labors and felt no special interest in him. Huysmans, on the contrary, he knew thoroughly and studied deeply on the basis of everything the man had published up to the date of the essay. "But if I had waited till his death," Ellis has told me lately, "I should never have written it, for his later development and writings do not interest me at all." And if St. Francis closes a book that Nietzsche opens, that, too, is as it should be when human strivings are viewed from above the conflict of petty terminologies. For St. Francis could be hard, and the creator of the Superman bore his cross to the grave. The saint had come to asceticism over the path of license; the sinner, born of religious forbears, had traced the same path from the opposite direction. The same path, not divergent roads. (pp. 169-71)

In ***The Nineteenth Century,*** Ellis seems, at the opening of the twentieth, to be taking counsel with himself. In the dialogue that fills the small book he is both voices. Looking backward, as Bellamy did in a famous book, Ellis is in reality looking forward; or, looking downward from the height of his aspirations to the level of our clumsy reality. The sub-title of the book is ***An Utopian Retrospect,*** yet the implied Utopia of Ellis is a solid and rational polity. It is, in essence, a Utopia of the higher activities, rather than of economic necessities, the conquest of which it assumes. It is, as from its definition of philosophy it would have to be, undogmatic, if on occasion ironic with overtones of contempt. (p. 183)

Noticeable in the book . . . is Ellis's deep admiration for architecture as the cradle of the other arts. "No better proof exists of the death of art than the inability to make vital buildings." Twenty-three years later he begins the chapter on the Art of Dancing, in ***The Dance of Life,*** with the statement that "Dancing and building are the two primary and essential arts. The art of dancing stands at the source of all the arts that express themselves in the human person. The art of building, or architecture, is the beginning of all the arts that lie outside the person; and in the end they unite." In Ellis, indeed, all things in the end unite. Architecture has been called frozen music. May we not, in a very literal sense, consider the body as a dance which is itself living architecture? Toward such a view Ellis, in ***The Nineteenth Century,*** seems clearly inclined, for "the human body is itself the supreme achievement of Nature in overcoming all those difficulties with which the builder is confronted."

It is in this book, too, that occurs the phrase *the supreme art, the art of living.* "Is it not strange that even then, when the race had already existed for many thousand years, the most elementary of all truths, that for living things the art of living must ever be the supreme art, had never been grasped?" If I seem to dwell upon this central phase of Ellis's labors, it is because I feel that in the year 2000, as some other Ellis sets down his Utopian retrospect, he will still have need of repeating those words. (pp. 185-86)

A Study of British Genius brings us back to the Ellis of charts and figures,—the statistician with a soul. Though genius itself may be an incommensurable, mysterious accident, yet it has its commensurable aspects. It was Ellis's purpose to analyze the geographical source and the psychological and anthropological characters of genius; this, combing carefully through the National Dictionary of Biography, he meant to do in a manner that would be scientifically systematic, yet at the same time devoid of an elaborate apparatus that would possess only deceptive value. He appreciates the labors of those who have studied genius as a manifestation of insanity, as he appreciates the investigations of those who, like the pioneer Francis Galton, ignored the psychiatric and even psychological aspects of genius, centering their attention upon the anthropological and statistical sides. (p. 187)

Besides being the most impersonal of his books, and the one which involved most labor in the writing, [***A Study of British Genius***] was the first attempt to study genius in a strictly biological spirit, on an objective foundation. (p. 188)

In ***The Soul of Spain*** Ellis studies that country as an individualist among the nations, through its representative figures and its representative regions. The materialistic aspects of the subject are set aside—what we might call the "body" of Spain—and the attention focussed upon spiritual values. Ellis, interested in those energies directed "not chiefly towards comfort or towards gain, but towards the more fundamental facts of human existence," recognizes chiefly those qualities with which he himself profoundly sympathizes. As Keyserling, in that remarkable work, *The Travel-Diary of a Philosopher,* travels through the world, so Ellis travels through Spain; so Ellis, more exactly speaking has travelled through life itself. (p. 189)

The Soul of Spain, though for Ellis it is an excursion into the specialty of others, is none the less a highly appreciated addition to the library of Iberiana. It is a series of essays rather than a unified volume, yet it has a true unity that lies, not in the nation written about, but in the man writing.

To this period belongs a magazine article which, like that on the color sense in literature, stands out for its experiments in a new field, as a pioneer effort. Coincidentally, it deals likewise with the color sense chiefly. ***Mescal: A New Artificial Paradise,*** in the *Contemporary Review,* January, 1898, treats of a certain cactus eaten by the Kiowa Indians of New Mexico,—then known as *Anhelonium Lewinii,* or mescal button. Becoming interested in the drug from American accounts of its effects, Ellis performed upon himself the first experiment, outside of America, in an attempt to describe its vision-producing efficacy. The results, which he recorded as the drug was working on him, he has transcribed from these original notes, together with those of an artist friend and two poets—one of them William Butler Yeats—who had been induced to make similar experiments upon themselves. Results vary with the personal constitution. The normal individual acquires an intoxication that Ellis describes as chiefly "a saturnalia of the specific senses, and above all, an orgy of vision." (pp. 192-93)

The ***Studies in the Psychology of Sex*** are the central work of an artist of life upon life and its central function. They synthesize the man. They contain, as they are the product of, Ellis the poet, the physician, the lover as artist, the biologist, the statistician, the pioneer, the social seer and the philosophical anarchist,—the freely functioning individual who is the flower of all social striving, if society is to be anything more than a coffin of conformity. (pp. 195-96)

[Ellis's ***The World of Dreams***], though belonging to the introspective type of dream book in which division Freud's epoch-making volume also takes its place, is built upon purely personal lines; it does not, moreover, accept without qualification the findings of the great Viennese Jew. Indeed, Ellis's interest has been centered upon the normal dream, which he regards as one of the clues to that greater dream called life. (p. 212)

From ***The World of Dreams,*** which is not so much a treatise as a personal record upon which is built a series of observations and speculations, it appears that Ellis regards the Freudian interpretations as being often sound, though with a marked tendency to the far-fetched assumptions of most pioneer geniuses. To Ellis the wish-type of dreaming is undoubtedly a type, but only one of many. Closely related to such a type, yet quite distinct from it, he considers the contrast-dream, in which we may dream things quite alien to our real desires. The Freudian explanation of such dreams is familiar to the student. Ellis's explanation is that they are vestigial impulses within us that might, under altered circumstances, have inclined us in a different direction entirely. All things thus would seem possible to the personality. Perhaps a wish is but a chemical majority? At any rate, here Ellis does not see evidences of released repression, but relics of a choice that once was more possible than now. So, too, indicating that the same dream may proceed from diverse causes, Ellis instances the dream of eating; this may derive from genuine hunger, in which it is an emotional dream, representing wish-fulfillment of the Freudian type, or it may derive from actually being too full of food, in which case it is an intellectual dream picturing a theory to account for the sensation of fulness. (pp. 214-15)

The significance of the dream book to Ellis's life lies in the parallel that it draws between the two worlds of waking and sleeping,—in the blending of two provinces commonly held to be sharply divided. Without establishing a poetic identity between the two states, I may summarize the case somewhat in this manner: Far more than we imagine, we reason while we dream; far more than we imagine, we dream while we reason. (p. 215)

With relation to psycho-analysis the most important statement of Ellis appears in ***The Philosophy of Conflict,*** in his essay on ***Psycho-Analysis in Relation to Sex.*** Though Ellis was not absolutely the first in England to call attention to Freud, his very first volume of the ***Studies in the Psychology of Sex*** was the first book to contain a full exposition in English of the views set forth in the studies in hysteria by Breuer and Freud. Ellis was, indeed, prepared for the reaction of these writers against the prudery of Charcot. A year before the appearance of their book he had, in ***Man and Woman,*** himself expressed the opinion that "the part played by the sexual emotions in hysteria was underestimated." From this time, as Ellis has recorded, there began between him and Freud an "exchange of publications and occasionally letters." Freud found in the Englishman's ***Studies*** more than one helpful suggestion in the development of his doctrines, "suggestions which I had not myself been inclined to carry to an extreme or dogmatic form." In this way Freud, by the histories of normal persons in the third volume of the ***Studies,*** was encouraged to "follow up the task he had already begun of pushing back the sexual origins of neuroses to an ever earlier age, and especially to extend this early origin so as to cover not only neurotic but ordinary individuals, an extension of pivotal importance, for it led to the Freudian doctrine becoming, instead of a mere clue to psychopathology, an alleged principle of universal psychological validity." (pp. 217-18)

The Task of Social Hygiene, following within a year upon ***The World of Dreams,*** reveals a tight grip upon reality that might not have been suspected by the casual reader of the earlier book. Ellis is constantly surprising one with this sound practicality. His *Utopias* rise from firm foundations. His conception of social hygiene includes, as his very first book foreshadowed, all those things that may better be accomplished by social effort to the end that a finer type of individual may be bred. (p. 220)

The Task of Social Hygiene, which does not seem to be so well known as it should be, is really, as are in another sense the ***Studies,*** a prose corollary of the later, poetic ***Dance of Life.*** The one deals with the techniques of life as the other with its arts; the one was written primarily by Ellis the Socialist and the other by Ellis the Individualist; the one represents Collectivism at its soundest, the other beautifully exemplifies Ellis's "reasonable anarchy." (p. 223)

The ***Impressions And Comments,*** though formally dated just before the war and brought to completion in 1923, were really begun [during Ellis's] . . . distant Australian days. In themselves they form a spiritual diary,—perhaps rather an ideary,—couched in intensely personal terms, in a language that flutters at times between poetry and prose, suggesting at the best moments a very music of thought and feeling. Indeed, if one looks for the more intimate aspects of Ellis, expressed in language that attains a maximum of power with a seeming minimum of effort,—that is rich without being lavish, that is a perfect medium for the inner life it portrays,—one should go to the ***Impressions And Comments.*** These are not books to study, date by date, in chronological order. They may be opened anywhere. Their least quality is a rare intellectual honesty, which is but the beginning of wisdom. Though time and again Ellis returns to questions that have occupied him since loneliness and Nature taught him meditation, always he adds a novelty that transforms the material. He has the Midas-touch that makes not gold but beauty. As time goes on, he sees the world less and less as an accretion of facts, as a laboratory of Truth, as an arena of the intellect; it becomes a harmony of emotions, a universal Beauty. (pp. 224-25)

It is in ***The Dance of Life*** that Ellis concentrates the essence of his living. One may regard it as the complement to his ***Studies in the Psychology of Sex.*** In the ***Studies,*** the roots of life; in the ***Dance,*** the flower. In the ***Studies,*** the body; in the ***Dance,*** the soul. Yet these are no more separable entities than are root and blossom, body and breath.

The Dance of Life is a symphonic volume, written by the youngster of the poems, by the hero of ***Kanga Creek,*** after a lifetime spent in the service of life. It is the fulfillment of every impulse that throbbed in the teacher's veins as he stamped through the Australian bush declaiming verses to love, stirred by the promptings that he but half understood. Not only is it a spiritual summary of Ellis's career; it is an intellectual stocktaking of contemporary civilization. Its very title is a profound affirmation, a paean that drowns out the echoes of the medieval Dance of Death.

Life is a dance and the dance is the symbol of life. With Ellis it is as he says of Hippias, who was in the line of "those whose supreme ideal is totality of existence." That, too, is the ideal of Ellis, and the ***Dance*** is, in one aspect, an attempt to suggest that totality of existence. Out of the findings of the specialists, who slice the world apart into their various provinces, Ellis tries to reintegrate our spiritual universe. You must not be surprised to find that, in so doing, he quotes liberally from others and makes use of their results. (pp. 235-36)

Life, to Ellis, is an art which may be subdivided into component arts. Those he considers after his luminous introduction are—and this list reads strangely, no doubt—The Art of Dancing, The Art of Thinking, The Art of Writing, The Art of Religion and The Art of Morals. Whereupon follows a conclusion in which an attempt is made to measure the mode of that life which is art. (p. 237)

In dancing, Ellis beholds the very rhythm of existence; it preceded the other arts. "To dance is to take part in the cosmic control of the world." (p. 238)

The important principle underlying the chapter on the Art of Thinking is that *science is art*. Quoting Keyserling, Ellis agrees that "The thinker works with laws of thought and scientific facts in just the same sense as the musical composer with tones. He must find accords, he must think out sequences, he must set the part in a necessary relation to the whole. But for that he needs art." This is a profound statement; at bottom, man is everywhere the artist, and the application of his personality to his material—an inevitable conjunction—produces what we call art. (pp. 238-39)

The Art of Writing, to me, is one of Ellis's most enjoyable productions. He is, as one might have guessed, deeply aware of the important rôle played by the unconscious in all creative endeavor; the fetich of "progress" does not mislead him; he knows that when we take on the new we lose some good in the old; he does not waste weary moments over grammatical peccadilloes; indeed, he is of the opinion that there seems to be no more pronounced mark of decadence of a people and its literature than a servile and rigid

> subserviency to rule. It can only make for ossification, for anchylosis, for petrification, all the milestones on the road of death. In every age of democratic plebeianism, where each man thinks he is as good a writer as the others, and takes his laws from the others, having no laws of his own nature, it is down this steep path that men, in a flock, inevitably run.
>
> (pp. 239-40)

In the chapter on The Art of Religion occurs that important biographical account in which Ellis traces the period of his emotional and intellectual expansion. "One must win one's own place in the spiritual world painfully and alone. There is no other way of salvation. The Promised Land always lies on the other side of a wilderness."

Ellis's Art of Morals is as different from the current acceptation of morality as is his art of religion from the corpses of doctrine that lie buried in church and synagogue and his art of writing from the jerking skeletons that are galvanized into the semblance of life by lists of precepts. To him life is an art and the moralist is the critic of that art. The conception goes back to the Greeks, among whom the good and the beautiful were identical. (p. 240)

Ellis's Conclusion finds that the attempt to apply measurement to civilization is a failure. "That is, indeed, only another way of saying that civilization, the whole manifold web of life, is an art." We cannot, however, he points out toward the end, afford to do without the sane and wholesome persons who are so well balanced that they can adjust themselves to the conditions of every civilization as it arises and carry it on to its finest issue. Here, indeed, we have the great artists of Life, and Ellis himself answers to such a requirement. Emerson would have called him one of the world's representative men; on second thought, because of his preëminence and that of men like him, I would call them *unrepresentative* men, the breeding of which cannot be superintended by rule but by Nature herself. (p. 241)

Isaac Goldberg, in his Havelock Ellis: A Biographical and Critical Survey, *Simon and Schuster, 1926, 359 p.*

VAN WYCK BROOKS (essay date 1928)

[An American critic and biographer, Brooks is noted chiefly for his biographical and critical studies of such writers as Mark Twain, Henry James, and Ralph Waldo Emerson, and for his influential commentary on the history of American literature. His career can be neatly divided into two distinct periods: the first, from 1908 to 1925, dealt primarily with the negative impact of European Puritanism on the development of artistic genius in America. Brooks argued that the puritan conscience in the United States, carried over from Europe, produced an unhealthy dichotomy in American writers and resulted in a literature split between stark realism and what he called "vaporous idealism." During this early period, Brooks believed that America had no culture of its own, and that American literature relied almost exclusively on its European heritage. After 1925, and his study on Emerson, Brooks radically altered his view of American lit-

erary history. He began to see much in America's past as unique and artistically valuable, and he called for a return in literary endeavors to the positive values of Emerson, as opposed to the modern pessimism of such writers as T. S. Eliot and James Joyce. Despite the radical difference in these two critical approaches, one element remains constant throughout Brooks's career, namely his concern with the reciprocal relationship between the writer and society. In the following excerpt, originally published in The New Republic *in August 1928, Brooks pays tribute to Ellis as a man whose thought has matured from that of an "austere scientist" to that of a philosopher of the universe. For further discussion of Ellis as a philosopher, see the excerpts by Christopher Morley (1924), Mark Van Doren (1924), Charles Angoff (1935) and Desmond MacCarthy (1939).*]

With every new work that he publishes, Havelock Ellis seems to approach more and more closely than any other living Englishman the type of the Renaissance scholar, a Leonardo with less inventiveness, with an infinitely smaller range of practical faculty, but with an almost equal spread of horizon. Known first as an austere scientist in a very limited realm, he has developed into a philosopher, one of the wisest and most poetic of contemporary speculators on life in general, a physician of the soul who has done more than any of his countrymen in our day to heal the disease from which the modern soul suffers. (p. 287)

He had contributed a few articles to the magazines, but his real literary career began in 1890 with the publication of **"The New Spirit,"** a sort of outgrowth of the Fellowship of the New Life, a little society which he formed with Thomas Davidson, Percival Chubb and one or two others, the object of which was the cultivation of character through the subordination of material things to spiritual, the seed of the subsequently formed Fabian Society. He edited several volumes for the Camelot Series and undertook the editorship of the Mermaid Series of Elizabethan Dramatists . . . ; and presently he became general editor of the Contemporary Science Series which was to deal with the various social and politico-economical problems of the day, the most recent researches in the knowledge of man, the past and present experience of the race and the nature of its environment. To this he contributed **"The Criminal"** and various translations of foreign works, followed by **"Man and Woman,"** the first of his works dealing specifically with the sexual question. The publication of the **"Studies in the Psychology of Sex"** involved him in a judicial prosecution that reverberates to this day, and he was unable to publish the series in England. But it was this series that brought him his international fame and made him a world authority on what he has called, with some justification, the central fact of life. (pp. 289-90)

From this time onward his mind took a wider and wider sweep. There were digressions during which he indulged his love of travel, especially in Spain, his love of literature, celebrated most adequately, perhaps, in **"Affirmations,"** his general attitude to the immediate past, expressed in **"The Nineteenth Century,"** his **"Study of British Genius," "The Task of Social Hygiene"** and **"The World of Dreams,"** culminating in the three series of **"Impressions and Comments,"** dealing with almost every aspect of human thought and behavior, and **"The Dance of Life,"** that very beautiful work which sums up his conclusions on man and the universe. "Autumn Leaves" is the title which Mr. Peterson [see Additional Bibliography] gives to these later writings, the ripe harvest of his long life. At the end, he was to have the richest flowering of all. "Today, at sixty-nine," says Mr. Peterson, "he is living out a beautiful old age, much beloved, active, carefree, understood, a sage who realizes that he has come into his own. . . . Fifty years ago, under the grim shea-oaks beside Sparkes Creek, he passed beyond the dilemmas and antitheses which have enfeebled the modern mind. He passed from an alien world to the World as Beauty, as a Living Whole, which no doctrine of mechanism or logical analysis can destroy. Since then he has walked his serene path alone, not so much an eclectic who puts things imperfectly together as a mystic who cannot see things apart; not so much a descendant of Goethe as a more articulate Blake, who has blended the fires within his soul and made his work a genuine marriage of Heaven and Hell." Certainly the most mature and appealing of modern English men of letters. (pp. 290-91)

Van Wyck Brooks, "A Leonardo of Our Day," in The New Republic Anthology: 1915-1935, *edited by Groff Conklin, Dodge Publishing Company, 1936, pp. 287-91.*

V. S. PRITCHETT (essay date 1931)

[*Pritchett is a highly esteemed English novelist, short story writer, and critic. Considered one of the modern masters of the short story, his work in this genre is a subtle blend of realistic detail and psychological revelation. Pritchett is also considered one of the world's most respected and well-read literary critics. He writes in the conversational tone of the familiar essay, a method by which he approaches literature from the viewpoint of a lettered but not overly scholarly reader. A twentieth-century successor to such early nineteenth-century essayist-critics as William Hazlitt and Charles Lamb, Pritchett employs much the same critical method: his own experience, judgment, and sense of literary art are emphasized, rather than a codified critical doctrine derived from a school of psychological or philosophical speculation. His criticism is often described as fair, reliable, and insightful. In the following excerpt, Pritchett favorably reviews* More Essays of Love and Virtue.]

The customs of the young generation are the blasphemies of the old, and the law is always in the hands of the old. . . . [The] young are struggling to put new life into an order deadened by "moral" over-capitalisation. What are they to do? Is it to be the old process of waiting for the old to die?

There is a course that will ease the unusual strain between us and our children's grandparents—that is, the education of the old. Such an education is intended in Dr. Havelock Ellis's latest book of essays [***More Essays of Love and Virtue***]. The pioneer, in what is freezingly called Social Hygiene, he has suffered the customary baptism of ridicule and hatred, and now, made perfect in cunning by long experience, comes forward as the mediator. Cursed with their own solemnity, the young cannot have things all their own way. It is possible, Dr. Ellis thinks, "that there may be limits to the consciousness it is desirable for us to possess in youth of the processes going on with us and of the direction in which we are moving." Nothing is certainly more stultifying to the young (nor more comical in them too) than a knowledge of the end, than learning how to die when they have only just begun living. It is possible to be young and old many times in a lifetime.

Though in this book he is treating of extremely controversial subjects—subjects, that is to say, on which the young and old minds differ most—Dr. Ellis lifts them on to a plane of unruffled examination and reflection. He can go to the heart of the dispute in matters relating to the new mother, eugenics, the renovation of the family, obscurity and sex, and can skillfully disarm the opponents. (p. 671)

Before the old-minded cry out, however, at the inevitable changes in convention, they might consider this essay on the Renovation of the Family. A Russian critic who divided women into two main groups, the monandric and polyandric, found that in the Soviet the monandric, one-man women who bring up their families, are much more numerous and more gifted for public life under modern conditions than the polyandric type which Communist life has been supposed to favour. The fact is no less illuminating for Dr. Ellis's shrewd amusement with the fact that the critic's investigators were all women, who notoriously are hard on their polyandric fellows.

It is in the revaluation of obscenity that the disagreement between young and old is chiefly remarkable. . . . Dr. Ellis compares the obscenity-hunters of this century with the witchfinders of the seventeenth. The witch-illusion disappeared when people ceased to be afraid of it; and we know now that there is an enormous amount of morbid, terrified illusion in the belief that the body and its functions are things of shame. But Dr. Ellis must be read for his careful examination of these matters for he has the true Socratic dignity and shrewdness. (pp. 671, 673)

V. S. Pritchett, in a review of "More Essays of Love and Virtue," in The Fortnightly Review, *n.s. Vol. 130, No. 779, November, 1931, pp. 671, 673.*

BERTRAND RUSSELL (essay date 1933)

[A respected and prolific author, Russell was an English philosopher and mathematician known for his support of humanistic concerns. Two of his early works, Principles of Mathematics *(1903) and* Principia Mathematica *(1910-13), written with Alfred North Whitehead, are considered classics of mathematical logic. His philosophical approach to all his endeavors discounts idealism and asserts a progressive application of his "logical atomism," a process whereby individual facts are logically analyzed. Russell's humanistic beliefs often centered around support of unorthodox social concerns, including free love, undisciplined education, and the eradication of nuclear weapons. His staunch pacifism during World War I led to a six-month imprisonment and began a history of political and social activism which culminated when, at the age of eighty-nine, he was again jailed for his active participation in an unruly demonstration advocating unilateral nuclear disarmament. After the incident Russell stated: "What I want is some assurance before I die that the human race will be allowed to continue." Regarding Russell, biographer Alan Wood states: "He started by asking questions about mathematics and religion and philosophy, and went on to question accepted ideas about war and politics and sex and education, setting the minds of men on the march, so that the world could never be quite the same as if he had not lived." In recognition of his contributions in a number of literary genres, Russell was awarded the Nobel Prize in literature in 1950. In the following excerpt, Russell discusses* Psychology of Sex, *referring to the work as "an epitome of the seven volumes of Havelock Ellis's original studies . . ."]*

When many years ago Havelock Ellis wrote his ***Studies in the Psychology of Sex*** he was doing a daring thing. In spite of the complete sanity of his outlook and the truly scientific spirit of his investigations, the work was greeted with an outcry, and for a long time parts of it were banned in England. To this day Dean Inge, in praising the author for his other works, mentions that one in a tone of regret, and in public libraries, such as the Bodleian, it is not available to readers except with the Librarian's written permission. But although there still are backwaters where the old taboos linger, their power has been enormously diminished. Havelock Ellis was a pioneer. Consider that he welcomed psycho-analysis at its birth as a promising infant, while in this book he may be almost said to write its biography. His attitude towards psycho-analysis, as he says himself, "has from the first been sympathetic, though never that of a partisan"; he is suspicious of sweeping theories concerning the Oedipus complex and the rest of the gods of Freud's Valhalla, but he admits everything for which there is definite evidence.

Havelock Ellis's most notable quality is a kindly sanity. Almost all writers on sex have some axe to grind; they want to prove that people hate their fathers, or love their mothers, or ought to know all about sex at the age of three, or ought to know nothing about sex till the age of twenty-one. Some wish to prove that sex covers the whole of life; others that it is nothing but an unimportant and temporary aberration from which well-regulated persons are immune. Havelock Ellis holds none of these theories: on each subject in turn he knows what is to be known, and draws the conclusions of a sensible, unprejudiced person who likes people to be happy. (p. 325)

[***Psychology of Sex***] is in some sense an epitome of the seven volumes of Havelock Ellis's original studies, but it has not by any means the literary defects that one associates with an epitome. It is well written and pleasant to read; it contains most of what the ordinary man or woman should know of what is in the earlier volumes, except the case histories, which are interesting and illuminating, and, moreover, consoling to all who are not completely normal. In Victorian days it was assumed that there was a certain fixed pattern of behaviour, very rigidly defined, from which only a few degenerates departed even in the smallest particular. This we now know to have been an opinion due to the wilful ignorance of that age on a subject of the gravest importance. It is a great mistake to suppose, as some people still do, that it is only medical men who need to have a knowledge of sex psychology. (In actual fact, as Havelock Ellis points out, many of them have very little.) Every man or woman entering upon marriage is liable to come to grief, or at any rate to have times of poignant suffering, through ignorance. In modern civilised life immediate successful consummation is probably the exception rather than the rule, but most young people do not know this, and are consequently led to imagine dreadful things.

It is, I suppose, useless to hope that Bishops and Members of Parliament will read this book. If, however, by some miracle, any one of them should come across it, I hope he will read Chapter V. The statute book in England, though not in most Continental countries, is disfigured by mediaeval penalties for acts which only appear as crimes to men sunk in mediaeval superstition. The tendency of legislation during the last fifty years has been to give superstition in this respect more scope for its persecuting instincts rather than less. (pp. 325-26)

Few books on the subject of sex can be so confidently recommended to all and sundry as this truly admirable volume. It does not, like some books, over-emphasise the purely physical, nor, like some others, suppose that complete sublimation is likely to be wholly successful. Its views on marriage are sane, and even somewhat conservative. But what above all recommends the book is its universal charity, resulting from the attempt at an understanding at once sympathetic and scientific. (p. 326)

Bertrand Russell, "Havelock Ellis on Sex," in The New Statesman & Nation, *n.s. Vol. V, No. 108, March 18, 1933, pp. 325-26.*

CHARLES ANGOFF (essay date 1935)

[A Russian-born American novelist, journalist, and critic, Angoff worked as managing editor of The American Mercury *from 1931 to 1934, succeeding H. L. Mencken as editor in 1934. He has written several volumes of literary criticism, including the two-volume* A Literary History of the American People *(1931) and a revealing work about his former editor,* H. L. Mencken: A Portrait from Memory *(1956). However, Angoff is best known for his autobiographical novels, which are praised for their accurate depiction of Jewish life in America. In the following excerpt, Angoff disagrees with those critics who praise Ellis for his philosophical and critical studies of life and literature. While Angoff credits Ellis with important contributions to the knowledge of human sexuality, he belittles his contribution to philosophical studies, concluding that Ellis is "a great scientist but a third-rate philosopher." For contrasting views of Ellis's stature as a philosopher, see the excerpts by Christopher Morley (1924), Mark Van Doren (1924), Van Wyck Brooks (1928), and Desmond MacCarthy (1939).]*

They who have read Mr. Ellis's previous non-scientific writings, especially **"Affirmations"** and the three volumes of **"Impressions and Comments,"** will not find much that is really new in the present book [**"My Confessional"**]; but novices might well buy it, for it forms a really excellent introduction to the ideas and style of one of the most influential men of our age. My own first encounter with the man's body of thought was in 1923, when **"The Dance of Life"** was published. It seemed that everybody in the United States was reading it and being impressed by its "clarity, profundity, and wisdom." I read the book very carefully, and found it singularly vague, irrelevant, and unilluminating. Then—spurred on by one critic's exuberant claim that Ellis was "undoubtedly the most civilized Englishman of his generation" [see H. L. Mencken excerpt dated 1921]—I read most of his other books, and a large number of his articles. The man grew on me, as the saying goes. I could feel only the highest respect for one who had the courage, insight, learning, and industry to produce the monumental six volume series of **"Studies in the Psychology of Sex"** in the dark years 1897-1910. I also liked **"The Nationalization of Health," "A Study of British Genius,"** and **"The Task of Social Hygiene."** But his other books, especially the aforementioned **"Affirmations," "Impressions and Comments,"** and **"The Dance of Life"** left me dissatisfied. I was puzzled, because these were the very books which were read the most widely and praised the most highly, and by people who at the time had reputations for discrimination.

Now that I have read his latest book I am more convinced than ever that Mr. Ellis is one of those unfortunate men who have written the most about the subjects they are least competent to discuss, and who have been praised extravagantly for the wrong things. He is first and foremost a physician and psychologist, specializing in the history and treatment of sex problems, and he had said all he had to say in 1910, when the last volume of his **"Studies in the Psychology of Sex"** appeared. All his books since then have been either repetitions of ideas first stated in this series, or, what has been far more frequent, collections of immature and hollow ideas expressed in suave but distressingly lifeless prose. I do not wish to belittle his really great contributions to the science of sex. I only wish to place him more accurately in the realm of general thought. In short, he is a great scientist but a third-rate philosopher. Some of his meditations, in fact, come perilously close to the meditations of Arthur Brisbane and Walter Lippmann. (pp. 118-19)

It has been said of Ellis that he "belongs in the line of Goethe," that he is full of "godless mysticism," that he is an analyst, a synthesist, and a universalist. Is he all of these things? Is he any one of these things? I have grave doubts. His wisdom consists largely of kindly expressed banalities, . . . and his analysis of world affairs is almost wholly made up of well-intentioned ignorance. He who says that the proletariat will soon disappear from England and the United States doesn't know what he is talking about. If there is one thing on which all economists agree, it is that the proletariat all over the world is increasing, through the subjection of the middle classes. And what supernal insight is there in the remark that war will not be abolished until the world organizes an international police force? This is Sunday-school prattle. Nowhere in all his books does Mr. Ellis show that he fully understands how wars come about, how strong the economic element is, and how foolish it is to speak of the brotherhood of nations before economic rivalries are disposed of.

The world owes a great deal to Mr. Ellis for helping free the basic functions of the human body and mind from the shackles of ecclesiasticism and savage morality, but that does not give him the right to assume so Olympian an attitude toward the struggles of all of us to obtain the modicum of physical comfort, without which all the fine writing about Love and the Dance is so much guff. "To see the World as Beauty," says Mr. Ellis, "is the whole End of Living." But how can the world seem beautiful to a hungry man as he looks helplessly upon his starving and bedraggled wife and children?

In the every-day world of struggling for one's daily bread and butter, as I have tried to show, Mr. Ellis is completely lost. He is also lost in the realm of the arts, which is somewhat strange, for he has spent many years of his long life in the study of literature, painting, music, and dancing. He was one of the original sponsors of nudism, which every honest physician and psychologist knows is a quackery. And he has praised lavishly such dubious people as Samuel D. Schmalhausen, Count Keyserling, Ortega y Gasset, Nicholas Berdyaeff, James Hinton, Benedetto Croce, and Benjamin de Casseres. (pp. 119-20)

No one can doubt that Mr. Ellis will live long in the memory of mankind for his heroic championship of sense, decency, and beauty in sexual matters. For that he deserves our deep and abiding respect, perhaps as much as does Sigmund Freud. But let us not dim his real glory by praising him for something he is not. He is not a philosopher, in the large and immemorial sense of that honorable word. He is a great medical and psychological scientist. That God did not also make him a philosopher is no reason why his admirers should. (p. 120)

Charles Angoff, "Havelock Ellis," in American Mercury, *Vol. XXXIV, No. 133, January, 1935, pp. 118-20.*

C.E.M. JOAD (essay date 1936)

[Joad was an English philosopher and the author of three dozen books, most of which address questions of ethics, religion, and human nature. He became popular and widely-known in England during World War II through his participation in the B.B.C. panel-show "Brains Trust." Through the radio program and his written works, Joad espoused his own philosophy based on rationalism, pacifism, and distrust of much of modern science for its role in industrializing and standardizing society. In the following excerpt from a review of Questions of Our Day, *Joad praises Ellis as one of the most important influences on twentieth-century thought and as a masterful writer. He finds, however,*

that despite its graceful style, Questions of Our Day *evidences few new ideas in Ellis's philosophical development.*]

Men like Shaw, Wells and Ellis have been the mental opticians of an age. Looking at the world through spectacles which these men have tinted for them, the present generation is apt to see everything in their colours and to dismiss as platitudes what their fathers denounced as heresies. It is, indeed, the Nemesis which waits upon those who tell the truth for the first time, that after a time we should think we have always known what they told us. We have the grace sometimes to canonise the announcer, but in the literary, no less than in the Christian, world it is only the safe men who become canons, and a decline in influence only too often accompanies a rise in eminence.

These observations are naturally suggested by a consideration of Havelock Ellis's latest book [***Questions of Our Day***], coupled with the reception of his recently published ***My Confessional.***

The present book consists of a hundred short pieces, each of about eight hundred words in length. Too long for aphorisms, too short for essays, they belong, so far as their form is concerned, to the category of what the popular press knows as "leaderettes." The occasion of their writing is in the majority of cases the receipt of a letter from an enquirer to which the piece is written in answer. . . . As he ranges from subject to subject, it is by the enormous scope of the book, and, by consequence, of the versatility of a writer who can take sex and education, marriage and the cinema, art and cookery, philosophy and euthanasia, mob hysteria and the inferiority complex, Keyserling and kissing among the Japanese in his stride, that the reader is chiefly impressed.

On all these subjects Havelock Ellis writes with wisdom and charm. He is never heavy-handed, never didactic, never boring; there is, I fancy, no living writer who, in the strict sense of the word, is so pre-eminently "readable." Like most of the great stylists, he gives the impression that to write is the easiest thing in the world. You have only, it seems, to put pen to paper and good style naturally results. It is partly, I suspect, the effect of this easy, natural manner of writing that enables Havelock Ellis to give the impression that, whatever his subject, he is sufficiently the master of it to afford to be at play with it. Yet as one reads these mellow, melodious pages, it is impossible to avoid asking oneself what has become of the rebel of thirty years ago. When such a variety of subjects is treated, it is no doubt unreasonable to expect distinctive doctrines to appear. But Havelock Ellis is a great man, a pioneer and prophet to the generation now coming to middle age, and one has a right to look to him for some word of light and leading in these difficult times. Light there may be—the diffused mellow light shed by the vision of a very old man, who has climbed to a position above the melée, and looks down upon mankind and its struggles with the kindly interest of an entomologist regarding an ant heap. . . . The familiar Ellis doctrines are restated. People are very mixed, and what is one man's meat is another man's poison. Therefore, you cannot lay down rules for other people. Life, in fact, is an art, an art that one must practise for oneself, and cannot learn from others. (The real trouble, of course, is that one has to give public performances while one is still learning.) The exercise of authority, therefore, is at best a nuisance, at worst an outrage. We must not, however, encourage the publication of such a work as *The Brown Book* of the Hitler terror, for fear of arousing in others the emotions we deplore in the Nazis. No metaphysical doctrine should command belief, for there are no absolute truths. The golden rule, in fact, in thought as in conduct, is that there is no golden rule. So much we have known these many years. We learnt it first from Montaigne, an author to whom Havelock Ellis frequently refers, and Ellis has himself since retaught it. But in this latest book he has added little to his teaching.

C.E.M. Joad, "Havelock Ellis's Obiter Dicta," in The New Statesman & Nation, *n.s. Vol. XI, No. 264, March 14, 1936, p. 403.*

JOSEPH WOOD KRUTCH (essay date 1936)

[*Krutch is widely regarded as one of America's most respected literary and drama critics. A conservative and idealistic thinker, he was a consistent proponent of human dignity and of the preeminence of literary art. His literary criticism is characterized by such concerns: in* The Modern Temper *(1929) he argued that because scientific thought has denied human worth, tragedy had become obsolete, and in* The Measure of Man *(1954) he attacked modern culture for depriving people of the sense of individual responsibility necessary for making important decisions in an increasingly complex age. In the following excerpt, Krutch discusses Ellis's humane approach to the study of human sexuality.*]

It was of course primarily as educator that [Havelock Ellis] played his role. Despite a certain amount of original investigation, he was above all else a scholar, and the [**"Studies in the Psychology of Sex"**] are based chiefly upon published work which Ellis disinterred from the pages of a thousand learned journals as well as from innumerable books, many of which were exceedingly obscure. His work was to coordinate, to compare, and above all else to present to a general public a body of esoteric and forbidden knowledge. He might, indeed, put in a claim to that often bestowed title "the last of the Victorians," for his enterprise was in one of the great Victorian traditions—that, namely, of Lecky and Westermarck and Spencer and Frazer, each of whom was inspired by the typical late Victorian conviction that man was to be saved by availing himself of the knowledge which specialists had acquired in fragments and from which it was the business of such as they to deduce various usable conclusions.

The difference was merely that Ellis selected the last subject to be opened for discussion, that he proposed to apply to the study of sex that method of dispassionate inquiry which even those who ostensibly championed its universal applicability hardly wished to see employed in the exploration of a field surrounded by taboos which were the most difficult to exorcise because they had remained the least completely rationalized. Perhaps the greatest of his achievements was just that he was able ultimately to establish the assumption that knowledge about sex was not essentially different from knowledge about anthropology or politics or the social sciences.

The very limitations now most often cited against his work were virtues for the moment and for the purpose. He is descriptive, empirical, eclectic, and, to a certain extent, literary. In his anxiety to collect every scrap of relevant testimony his tendency is to be so far from rigidly critical that certain topics are treated almost after the manner of a commonplace book and that even the often valuable case histories are neither controlled nor critically evaluated. It is also perfectly true that he proposed no psychological or neurological system, that he seems often to do no more than to take testimony and record opinions. But the very fact that the influence of even such a system builder as Freud was relatively slight is fortunate rather than unfortunate. It would have been a calamity if the first great attempt to survey the field had been limited in its scope by the premature adoption of too fixed a method or too sure a conviction. And Ellis had what was much more important for the success of his enterprise—a spirit essentially humane. The atmosphere of the **"Studies"** does not repel as the atmosphere of Krafft-Ebing or even of much of Freud's writing repels by its suggestion of the hospital and the laboratory. He was not writing primarily for the clinical practitioner. He was not primarily concerned with the sexually ill. He was simply accustoming the general public as well as lawyers and doctors and teachers to the idea that a rational attitude toward sex was one of the essential conditions of a good life.

He had, indeed, only three leading ideas. The first was the premise, already referred to, that sex might be investigated and discussed in precisely the same spirit as any other subject of large human concern. The other two were equally simple. One was that we had better find out what men and women actually felt and desired and did before we classified as "perverse" or "abnormal" any feeling or desire or act; that our notions of what is "normal" ought, in other words, to be not a priori but empirical. The third was that man's capacity to love sexually could and should be valued, developed, and educated precisely as his capacity to think, to play, to create, or to exercise any other of the functions of a human being was valued and developed and educated—not of course in isolation or without regard to social consequences but as part of normal existence.

These three ideas, continually reiterated, give to the **"Studies"** such unity as they have. They seem, of course, now obvious almost to the point of fatuity—so obvious, indeed, that it is not easy to believe they were ever totally rejected. (pp. 386-87)

Joseph Wood Krutch, "Homage to Havelock Ellis," in The Nation, *Vol. CXLII, No. 3690, March 25, 1936, pp. 386-87.*

KARL MENNINGER (essay date 1939)

[Menninger is an American psychiatrist who, in 1919, with his father Charles and his brother William, founded the now world-famous Menninger Foundation and Clinic, a psychiatric research center for the treatment of mental illness. In the following excerpt, Menninger offers his opinion of Ellis's scientific studies of sex and compares the methods of Sigmund Freud and Ellis. For further comparisons of Freud's and Ellis's works, see the excerpts by Mary M. Colum (1939), Bernard DeVoto (1939), and Phyllis Grosskurth (1980).]

As a thoughtful boy of sixteen Ellis dedicated himself to the study of sex at the period in life when other youths are solving their adolescent struggles by indulgence in political and religious fervor or by ostentatious rebellions against custom and social orthodoxy. He pursued this idea with scientific detachment and with unfaltering courage in the face of bitter and slanderous opposition, indifferent alike to applause and praise on the one hand and abuse and criticism on the other. Substantially, Ellis did three things. In the first place, he made a careful, thorough, and honest collection of data relating to a phase of biology which the hypocrisy and prudery of medical science had, until Ellis, caused to be ignored for the most part. In the second place, he evolved and advocated a hedonistic philosophy of life tempered if not determined by the sane, scientific attitude toward sex which his studies engendered. In the third place, he presented his scientific findings and philosophical beliefs to the world with that artistic combination of directness and delicacy which made them acceptable to non-scientific readers.

It is inevitable that Havelock Ellis should be compared with Freud. Like Freud, Ellis was scientist, physician, psychiatrist, psychologist, philosopher, and essayist. Like Freud, he bravely but modestly stuck to his principles in the face of persecution. Like Freud, he was vastly and widely misunderstood. Like Freud, he recognized the importance of sex. While Ellis was saying that sex was the center of life, Freud was saying that the sex instinct should be called the life instinct. Freud has acknowledged his indebtedness to Ellis for several ideas and terms. But their ways parted, for Freud is primarily a clinician, and this Ellis never was. While Freud worked with patients, Ellis worked with ideas. Both had the ideal scientific attitude, but of the two only Freud used the traditional scientific method. Even Ellis's celebrated **"Studies in the Psychology of Sex"** was chiefly a collection of data. They had no practical applications, no therapeutic usefulness. Freud looked at the same data not in large collections but in individual instances, and asked, "Why should these things exist in this person? Why does he feel or act as he does?" And then he proceeded to find out. What Freud did was to explain the why and the how of the facts which Ellis tabulated. On the other hand, while the work of Ellis supplied no means for understanding or relieving the individual, it formed the basis for a philosophy of life which benefited and enlightened the entire world, and thus prepared the way for Freud's work with individuals.

It seems extraordinary today that the leading British medical journal, the *Lancet,* refused to review a scientific study of homosexuality by a medical man (Ellis) and explained this in an editorial entitled The Question of Indecent Literature, claiming that it had not been published under the proper auspices. To this Ellis made reply that none of the medical publishers whom he had approached were interested in the publication of such a book. By others than the medical press the first volume was called "a wicked, bawdy, scandalous, and obscene book." (p. 103)

How does it come about that some individuals, such as Ellis and Freud, can have so completely escaped those psychological fetters which bind all of us? The answer is not easy to give. This much one can say, however, that there certainly was in Ellis a highly developed sensitiveness to the principles of dialectics, to the recognition of truth in the opposite. Early in his life he wrote that there were few questions about which, after a study of both sides, he did not come to a conclusion "totally opposite to the orthodox one which I have always been taught to believe true." Discussing this further, Ellis said that he felt sure that he was not actuated by any spirit of perversity, but on the contrary was frequently "convicted" in spite of himself and "made miserable." To one psychoanalytically oriented this accidental substitution of the word "convicted" when he obviously meant to write "convinced" suggests how strongly determined this attitude was by emotional factors. It is significant that Ellis, who led a most idealistic sexual life, should have written the world's greatest treatise on the abnormalities of sex. Olive Schreiner once wrote that Ellis was like a cross between a Christ and a faun. But all this does not explain him; it only indicates that it was out of vast internal contradictions that there grew an outer life characterized by a magnificent unity of purpose and spirit. (pp. 103-04)

Karl Menninger, "Havelock Ellis—1859-1939," in The Nation, *Vol. 149, No. 4, July 22, 1939, pp. 103-04.*

DESMOND MacCARTHY (essay date 1939)

[*MacCarthy was one of the foremost English literary and drama critics of the twentieth century. He served for many years on the staff of the* New Statesman *and edited* Life and Letters. *Among his many essay collections* The Court Theatre 1904-1907: A Commentary and a Criticism *(1907), which is a detailed account of a season when the Court Theatre was dominated by Harley Granville-Barker and Bernard Shaw, is especially valued. According to his critics, MacCarthy brought to his work a wide range of reading, serious and sensitive judgment, an interest in the works of new writers, and high critical standards. In the following excerpt, MacCarthy discusses the achievements of Ellis as an iconoclast in the study of human sexuality and as an important critic of life and literature, commenting specifically on* Affirmations. *For another discussion of this work, see the excerpt by Arthur Symons (1922); for further discussions of Ellis as a philosopher, see the excerpts by Christopher Morley (1924), Mark Van Doren (1924), Van Wyck Brooks (1928), and Charles Angoff (1935).*]

Havelock Ellis became the first notable English writer to discuss sex openly and with detachment, and it is largely due to him that now fewer people knock their lives to pieces in the stuffy darkness of compulsory sex-ignorance. . . .

Havelock Ellis will be remembered primarily as a great taboo-breaker—one of their rescuers—by English-speaking peoples. But he was also an analytical reader of the first order, though he was first and foremost interested in what he called the Art of Living. He was far too rational to be a complete rationalist, and too sensitively aware of poetic values to be a pure hedonist. He was wise, and he was an individualist, aware of the many-sidedness of things. He held that the Art of Life always must allow for the personal equation. He was fond of comparing this Art to that of Dancing. It was a continual adaptation of instinctive movements to a pattern and rhythm dictated by a man's times, his inheritance, his race, his country. I am told he found his own deepest responses to life reflected in Blake. Self-suppression was a phrase which summed up for him a great part of the meaning of life, and that necessarily included the expression of the social side of man; though I don't think he agreed with the Communist philosophy that only the Social Self really counts. I should very much like to have read his comments on Caudwell's remarkable book, *Illusion and Reality*. . . . (p. 139)

Certainly, as a critic, what he looked for in books was the expression of the author's individuality. He called one of his most remarkable books ***Affirmations.*** The first question he asked himself as a critic was "What does this writer affirm?" The next, "How did he come to affirm precisely that?" His statement of a writer's "message" was always trenchant and clear, his psychological analysis of the man extremely acute, and the estimate of the value of his contribution impartial. What moved him most in literature was the sincere expression of preferences and beliefs, and the energy which springs from sincerity. Yet he distinguished more surely than any other English critic I can think of between the importance of the work and the value of the man himself who achieved it. Havelock Ellis, though he was endowed with the aloof curiosity of a man of science, was also extremely sympathetic by nature; and his sympathy with human weakness enabled him to see that it was often through pain and failure due to congenital weakness that a writer discovered what proved important to mankind. An original work was by no means always the product of a great man; often rather it was born of an inadequacy—Rousseau, Proust, are examples. "It is the miracle of genius—even from of old vaguely apprehended—that through an incomplete, defective, if not infantile instrument, the voice of wisdom is heard"—to quote from almost his last book, ***From Rousseau to Proust*** . . . , one of the best and most interesting of English books on French literature.

Thus it was that though Havelock Ellis's criticism was that of a man with an enthusiastic response to great achievements, it had none of the faults of the hero-worshipper. His deep concern for the good of humanity made him comparatively indifferent to works of unoriginal perfection, since they did not contribute importantly to the Art of Life. Only in the other arts (he often discussed painting, architecture, music) were his estimates ever "aesthetic," and even then he constantly sought the sociological or psychological interest behind his own impressions. This habit made his notes of travel—his book on Spain for example—often particularly interesting. Lastly, though having "affirmations" of his own, the keynote of his criticism, and, I suspect, of his nature, was an absence of hostility towards those whose conclusions negated them. (pp. 139-40)

Desmond MacCarthy, "Havelock Ellis," in The New Statesman & Nation, *n.s. Vol. XVIII, No. 439, July 22, 1939, pp. 139-40.*

MARY M. COLUM (essay date 1939)

[*Colum, who contributed criticism regularly to such publications as* The New Republic *and* The Saturday Review, *was called "the best woman critic in America" by William Rose Benét in 1933. Others, however, have noted that Colum sometimes allowed personal prejudice to color her critical judgment. In the following excerpt, she compares the approaches to the study of sexuality of Sigmund Freud and Ellis and assesses Ellis's autobiography* My Life. *For other discussions of* My Life, *see the excerpts by Graham Greene (1951), Alan Hull Walton (1967), and Malcolm Muggeridge (1967); for further comparisons of Freud's and Ellis's work, see the excerpts by Karl Menninger (1939), Bernard DeVoto (1939), and Phyllis Grosskurth (1980).*]

That everything relating to sex can now be discussed freely is owing largely to the work of these two investigators [Sigmund Freud and Havelock Ellis]; that the homosexual has the right to live and be regarded with more or less tolerance is owing more to Havelock Ellis than to any other writer. That women in Anglo-Saxon countries have a vote, that they have made considerable progress toward social equality with men are, more than is commonly realized, owing to Ellis' writing, as for something like half a century he was outstanding amongst those who advocated complete social equality of men and women. To him and to Freud is owing the modern attitude toward insanity, the increasing tendency to regard it as a disease like any other disease. Ellis, more than Freud, perhaps, was inclined to believe that, fundamentally, there was not much difference between criminals and the insane. What the world owes both these men is very great.

In spite of the resemblance between their general conclusions and psychological attitudes, the two, at bottom, were so different in temperament, in mental and emotional equipment, that it is difficult to think of them in the same terms. Though both were medical men, outside that they had divergent trainings. In his chosen work, Havelock Ellis was self-trained; Freud had worked with most of the great men of his time in the psychological field, beginning with Charcot.

There is, besides, no doubt but that Freud was the greater man. He was more single-minded; he had more natural sincerity—for sincerity is a gift of the gods, like beauty or talent, and no one can be sincere simply by desiring to be. Freud could not write a line that did not convey a mental directness, a combined sincerity of thought and emotion; no matter how mentally sincere Havelock Ellis was, his literary style arouses doubts of his integral emotional sincerity. It was doubtless true that Freud was arrogant and intolerant of disagreement, but single-minded people who have worked against fearful odds to put over what they believe to be the truth are likely to be intolerant. Freud was persecuted at the end as in the beginning, and died an exile from the land of his birth and the city identified with his work.

The early prejudice against Havelock Ellis dissipated; his life work was a success; and in his old age, as he writes in the preface to his autobiography, "the precious, unsought balms of love and devotion, almost of worship, poured on my head." He left his autobiography, ***My Life,*** which he considered the most "perdurable piece of work" he was likely to leave behind. His chief effort in life, he tells us, was to help others, and he wanted his autobiography to be a help to people in their problems. To be of such help, it would have to be, he decided, a real spiritual biography.

In all literature, according to him, there are only three genuine and first-class autobiographies: Rousseau's *Confessions,* Saint Augustine's, Casanova's *Memoirs*. These are genuinely intimate accounts of the writers' lives and temperaments, and Rousseau's *Confessions* are, for Havelock Ellis, a model of their kind. Indeed, we get the impression of a very Rousseauan personality in ***My Life***—Rousseauan in its neuroticism, in its extreme sympathy with women, in its self-centeredness, its reserves and lack of reserves. But Ellis had even more of a sentimental attitude toward himself than Jean Jacques had. He was of a seafaring ancestry, and this fact drew out romantic notions about himself. . . . (pp. 258-59)

Unlike Rousseau, he does not, on the whole, find many undesirable qualities in himself. Even though he unconsciously discloses his egoism and his sanctimoniousness, he seems to have been a very kindly and affectionate person, one without worldliness, without ambition in the vulgar sense, but with a conviction that he had a great life's work to do. . . .

The bulk of ***My Life*** is taken up with accounts of his relationship to his wife, Edith, who died in 1916. Havelock Ellis and his wife set out to solve a problem which may, in actual fact, be insoluble except for a few exceptional persons. They wanted to have a union that would not exclude intimate friendships with members of the other sex. It was a period of experiments of this sort. Ellis and his wife were to live together and yet be as independent as possible. They started with the belief, stronger on his side than on hers, that a relationship between a man and a woman was their own private affair and did not need the sanctification of church or law unless there were children—and they agreed that in their case there were not to be any. Later, they were legally married, each deciding to contribute equally to joint expenses and to have at times separate residences so as to preserve the freshness and interest of their relationship. As Joseph Wood Krutch notes in his book on the drama, Havelock Ellis' influence was the sanction for the Bohemianism of a generation ago and the literature that came out of it. (p. 259)

While it is possible that the revelations in ***My Life*** will be a help to some people, it seems to me the help will be in the direction of a conviction that any old prosy marital relationship is better than this experimental stuff. As shown in this book, the relationship between Ellis and his wife seems to have been very neurotic; there is in it a strained emotionalism that is not very different from what is in that half-mad book of Strindberg's on his relations with women. Some of what is recorded is of a triviality that passes belief—accounts of the time he got his wife's breakfast and bath; how he exclaimed, "My baby!" when she twisted her foot. Then there are interminable sentimental letters conveying over and over again the same protestations of devotion and neurotic concern. These two were, if not ardently devoted to each other, at least obsessed with each other. After her death, Havelock Ellis settled down in tranquillity with a lady named Françoise, in a relationship which he describes as a "beautiful and prolonged episode." However, he tells us nothing more about it; it might be a help if he informed us whether those recurrent friendships with women which had so upset his wife had ceased in his more mature relationship with Françoise. (p. 260)

Mary M. Colum, "Literary Pioneers and Re-creators," in Forum and Century, *Vol. CII, No. 6, December, 1939, pp. 258-63.**

BERNARD DeVOTO (essay date 1939)

[*An editor of* The Saturday Review of Literature *and longtime contributor to* Harper's Magazine, *DeVoto was a highly controversial literary critic and historian. A man whose thought enraged much of America's literary establishment during the 1930s and 1940s, he was frequently motivated by anger at authors he considered ignorant of American life and history. As a critic, he admired mastery of form and psychological subtlety in literature. His own work is characterized by its scholarly thoroughness and by its vigorous, infectious style. In the following excerpt from the October 1939 issue of* Harper's, *DeVoto lavishly praises Ellis's pioneering work in the study of human sexuality, but he notes that Ellis's works are not psychological studies relating behavior to motive or necessity. Rather, he believes that Ellis's major work,* Studies in the Psychology of Sex, *is more aptly characterized as an anthropological or encyclopedic study of the subject, and that it remained for Sigmund Freud to study the psychological aspects of sex. For further comparisons of Freud's and Ellis's work, see the excerpts by Mary M. Colum (1939), Karl Menninger (1939), and Phyllis Grosskurth (1980).*]

One cannot undertake hopefully to determine what a great man has done. What he thinks it was is likely to be wrong and what is generally accepted about it is almost certain to be wrong. The title of Ellis's great work was a misnomer. He called it ***Studies in the Psychology of Sex,*** but it wasn't that. It was studies in the anthropology of sex, it was the world's first scientific encyclopedia of sexual information—and it was of course, incidentally to its purpose, the first charter of sexual inquiry and a vindication of the mind's decencies. He went out to determine what the facts were, the tabooed facts, the facts forbidden recognition by church and state and by resistances much stronger than either, the "real natural facts of sex apart from all would-be moralistic or sentimental notions." It is an astonishing thing that no such effort, on a useful scale, had ever been made in all the world's history before Ellis undertook it toward the beginning of the last decade of the nineteenth century. He carried it through to the end he had envisioned, opposed as savagely as any enemy of an established religion, attacked as unscrupulously as any enemy of an established government, vilified in a grotesque and obscene furor that was diagnostic of the conditions he wanted to clear up. And the book that embodied his findings is a great book, a monument in the advance of thought, of science, of (if the word may still be spoken with grave lips) civilization. It is great not only in what it revealed but in what it accomplished. A book that has altered the substance of things and produced a probably permanent effect on mankind.

But it is not a psychology of sex. Ellis's illimitable energy was expended almost altogether in determining facts of behavior and had little concern with relating them to motive or necessity. He had few theorems, few hypotheses, and such as he had were superficial and optimistic and tended to be mystical. Follow him only a little way beyond what the Ubangi do and what the church fathers said and how such people or such others behave on such occasions—and you get either into an anarchy abhorrent to science where no law operates, not even probability, or into a dewy vision colored with the century's most illusory hope, where things happen as if by the flowers' will and where a freer, finer, godlike race is on its way to mastery. His social achievement was to force recognition on a willfully reluctant world, and his scientific achievement was to describe the previously unstated. It remained for others to open up the psychology of sex, to dig beneath description to causes, to reveal the dynamism in the facts that were static for Ellis. There is a brave serenity in Sigmund Freud's mind too, but in the knowledge that supports it you do not find the hopefulness that is inseparable from Ellis.

Furthermore, though the great work has had an undeniably immense effect on society, one cannot be sure just what that effect is. The past fifty years have seen changes in society's understanding of sex, its attitudes toward sex, and even its sexual practices. Yet those changes are almost unappraisable, since no one can be quite sure, for all their vividness, just what they consist of, nor quite sure, for all their explosiveness, just how far they have gone, nor quite sure, for all their extent, just whom they affect. It is equally impossible to appraise the part played in these revolutionary changes by any single force, such as Ellis's research, of the great composite that effected them. Foremost in time, exhaustive in scope, a work of genius, his book was a principal equation in the intellectual foci; it has influenced, directly and by the most innumerable and circuitous indirections, millions of people who never heard of it, who could not understand it, but who think and act and perhaps feel otherwise than they would have done if it had not been written. But there is no way of telling how great a part it plays in those altered thoughts and actions; no one can assign a value to that *x*. (pp. 81-3)

Mankind, however, seems no nearer than it was to the inner peace and outward mastery that Ellis believed in. Calvary is no longer degraded by the irrelevant execution of two thieves; but for the generality of mankind the way of the flesh remains what, for the generality of mankind, it has always been, a way of the cross. The ultimate traveler from Mars who is to pass judgment on human affairs will note that much, and will be unemotionally aware of other reactions as well. For all freedoms are stern, and every person of mature years has friends for whom this one has been disastrous. It has destroyed many lives by imposing on them one further choice which they were not strong enough to survive. From Mars, Ellis and the movement in which he was so conspicuous must sometimes look like one further item in the paralysis of the social will. The strength of conventions, prejudices, and intolerance is that they protect the weak by making up their minds and determining their behavior from without. Some men might have been better workmen or thinkers if they had not undertaken to decide their sexual conduct for themselves. A society might be better armed against disintegration if it could conserve the forces which enlightenment dissipates. It was the strength of the old-time religion, however false, that it simplified the duty of man. It was the strength of the old-time morality, however unenlightened, whatever lives it maimed, that it was taken for granted. Enlightenment has increased the complexity of individual choice. It has forced a primitive animal already overburdened by his own civilization to live, as Freud says, that much more beyond his psychological means. Sexual enlightenment has not been Micawber's half-crown that makes all the difference, but it is clearly an unallocated farthing in the sum that has produced bankruptcy.

Precisely there one identifies Ellis's limitation. It was a limitation of his time that it did not recognize the limitations of its material, the limitations of the human race. One thinks of him (in fading afternoon) as a crusader riding eastward out of the Victorian sunset, a last champion of his century's hope. To learn, to know, to declare, to let the light and air in would be enough! The fetid mass of irrationalities which he uncovered would yield to reason; turn it over often enough in open air and the spores of fear and failure must be killed. What was wrong was not the nature of man, which must be sound by all the criteria that could be recognized, but man's ignorance and the institutions which his ignorance had enabled his fears and cruelties to build. But there was an older affirmation—that in much wisdom is much grief and he that increaseth knowledge increaseth sorrow.

As Ellis came downstage in triumph there entered quietly from an upper wing the unobtrusive figure of Dr. Freud. He has only a small place in Ellis's page: Ellis welcomed and praised him but seems either not to have fully understood or not to have been much interested in what he was about. But it was that unobtrusive figure who revealed the linkages in the facts which Ellis had so magnificently assembled and who began to make clear what was behind them. The world which Freud opened up was far more desperate than any Ellis had ventured into, and the race proved to be far more limited, far more beset by forces beyond its control. To let the light and the air heal as much as they could, to let knowledge arm reason to the uttermost, yes—but Freud uncovered bounds beyond which healing cannot go and reason has no force. The goal of the freedom in which Ellis believed was apocalyptic: freedom as power in itself, freedom as invincible. Freud's was a humbler, sterner, sadder freedom: freedom for man to grapple with reality liberated from unconscious forces within himself. Ellis's was a freedom of hope; Freud's of fortitude. Ellis's turned Prospero alone and unconquerable toward the stars. Freud's merely gave Prospero weapons which he might use against the Caliban with whom he must live forever on his seagirt isle. Freud revealed the irreducible, the immutable, the insoluble, which for Ellis had always been the insubstantial fabric of illusion—and with that revelation the nineteenth century ended in the psychology of sex, and the twentieth came in. (pp. 84-6)

Bernard DeVoto, "Meditation in Fading Sunlight," in his Minority Report, *Little, Brown and Company, 1940, pp. 80-7.*

WILLIAM RALPH INGE (essay date 1939)

[An Anglican prelate, scholar, and essayist, Inge was the Dean of London's St. Paul's Cathedral for twenty-three years. In addition to his clerical duties, he contributed weekly articles to the Evening Standard, *gaining recognition as a modern critic of so-*

cial, political, and religious concerns. Inge's criticism of topical issues was candid, incisive, and generally so pessimistic that newspapers dubbed him "the Gloomy Dean." However, in responding to his sobriquet Inge stated: "I have tried only to face reality, to be honest, and to refuse to be foolishly optimistic." Many of his essays and articles are collected in Outspoken Essays *(1919) and* Lay Thoughts of a Dean *(1926). In the following excerpt from an essay originally published in a July 1939 issue of the* Evening Standard, *Inge provides a general appraisal of Ellis's importance.*]

As a classical scholar, I have several books on my shelves which would be confiscated by the police if they were written in English instead of in Greek or Latin. I do not think they do me any harm. But I must confess that I burnt the first two volumes of the ***Psychology of Sex*** as being too unwholesome. An abridged edition, with much less offensive matter, is now procurable.

However, this is no reproach to Ellis, whose book helped to promote a more rational attitude to abnormalities which for many centuries had been ferociously punished as crimes. Superstition and the story of the fate of Sodom and Gomorrah had something to do with the horror which vented itself in extreme severity. (p. 244)

One of Ellis's earlier books is called ***The Task of Social Hygiene.*** Social hygiene, he says, is more radical and more scientific than social reform. It must complete the work which the reforms of the nineteenth century began. Social reform accepts the stream of life as it finds it, and while working to cleanse the banks of the stream makes no attempt to purify the stream itself.

We may mark four stages in the movement of the nineteenth century. First came the effort to make our towns clean and sanitary. Then factory legislation. Then education, and lastly the effort to guard the child before school age, and to bestow due care on the future mother. All these are environmental; there can be no radical cure of social evils until the State acknowledges its responsibility for the intrinsic quality of its citizens.

This means of course that Ellis was an enthusiastic eugenist. He was an early disciple of that great man, Sir Francis Galton, and, like his master, realized that it is useless to try to legislate in advance of public opinion. Ellis however is much less cautious than Galton, who was always moderate, almost conservative. But he accepted the view that the task of the eugenist is to educate public opinion. It is a slow and disheartening labour. In some ways there has been a distinct falling back since Ellis's earlier books. In fact, the whole trend of thought since the Great War has been reactionary.

Ellis finds that war is the worst enemy of civilization. He examines the subject from every side, and can find nothing to say in favour of this, the supreme curse of the human race. He goes rather further than some would be willing to follow him when he thinks that unregulated increase of population is the chief cause of war. That it is one cause is obvious; and indeed the dictatorships deliberately discourage family limitation on the ground that the State needs more food for powder, and that what they call natural expansion of numbers is a justification for the wish of the militant State to dispossess its more pacific or more prudent neighbours of their territory.

Some of our younger eugenists have partly given way to this argument, and agitate for a higher birthrate at home. Ellis sternly discourages this concession to militarism. He would deliberately prefer a smaller population of higher quality, and he sees that what is called negative eugenics is the only way of preventing a gradual deterioration of our national stock. Nature is more important than nurture, and quality is much more important than quantity.

On almost every question in which science and common sense are ranged against tradition and prejudice, Ellis is found on the right side. He hates and despises the fashionable anti-intellectualism, and is perfectly fearless in following wherever reason leads the way. His influence will take time to soak in, and perhaps the forces of inertia and reaction will be always too strong for his reforms to be adopted; but I know no man in our time who has done more to batter down antiquated prejudice and stupid obscurantism.

He would like to see all doctors Civil Servants, all hospitals nationalized, and private medical practice abolished. Things seem to be moving in this direction. The Ministry of Health ought, he thinks, to be one of the chief Government offices, with very wide powers. But he is never tired of insisting that those who cry out for "more births" really mean "more deaths," for unregulated increase soon reaches its limits.

There are other sides to his rich and widely sympathetic mind. He was a great traveller, and his favourite countries were France and Spain. He loved to look upon life as an art—even a kind of ritual dance, and he found that the French understand the art of living much better than we do. The life of the average Englishman is not artistic. "Like a sailor on shore, we maintain our equilibrium by rolling heavily from side to side." French civilization has a grace and poise which we cannot emulate.

But the land that he loved best was Spain. In his beautiful book, ***The Soul of Spain,*** he interprets to us, as none had done before, that strange country of fire and ice, of mysticism and cruelty, of loyalty and anarchism. We should not have expected him to feel any sympathy with the reactionary Catholic Church in the Peninsula; but he loved the Mass as celebrated in Spain, in which he found a solemn dramatic exhibition, "the initiation of the individual into the spiritual life of the world." (pp. 244-48)

William Ralph Inge, "Havelock Ellis," in his A Pacifist in Trouble, *Putnam, 1939, pp. 243-48.*

OSCAR CARGILL (essay date 1941)

[*An American educator, historian, and literary critic, Cargill edited critical editions of the works of such major American authors as Henry James, Walt Whitman, Frank Norris, and Thomas Wolfe. In the following excerpt, Cargill offers a balanced survey of Ellis's major works and discusses the influence of Ellis's life and work on the moral thinking of the American people.*]

[Ellis] made a long visit to Paris with [his] friend, Arthur Symons, before publishing his first book, ***The New Spirit***. . . . This visit led to meetings with the French Decadents whom Symons admired—Mallarmé, Huysmans, Verlaine, Moréas—and to a lasting attachment to one of them, Rémy de Gourmont, as omnivorous a reader as Ellis himself in the varied fields of literature, anthropology, psychology, and sex. Out of this visit and friendship grew Ellis' lasting interest in Naturalistic and Decadent French literature which he, with Swinburne, Wilde, Symons, and Dowson, helped to make a vogue in England. There is no sign of this in ***The New Spirit,*** however, with its five studies of Diderot, Heine, Whitman, Ibsen, and Tolstoi. This book is one of ecstatic hero-worship and mysticism: "To pronounce the names of such men is of the nature of an act of worship." Defining religion as "the sum of the unfettered expansive impulses of our being" (surely one of the most extraordinary definitions of religion ever given, though the prompting of Whitman is clear enough), Havelock Ellis discovers that religion is the driving force of all his heroes:

> . . . It is strange: men seek to be, or seem, atheists, agnostics, cynics, pessimists; at the core of all these things lurks religion. We may find it in Diderot's mighty enthusiasm, in Heine's passionate cries, in Ibsen's gigantic faith in the future, in Whitman's not less gigantic faith in the present. . . .

The total effect of this is to deny the possibility of being irreligious, and to suggest that unqualified strong emotion—no matter what its character, provided that it is sufficiently unfettered and expansive—is itself somehow sacred and to be respected. This heresy would not be worthy of belaboring if it did not reappear so frequently in the author's later work. The extraordinarily popular book ***The Dance of Life*** . . . is permeated with it. Here it is argued that all the creative activity of man, including his literature and his religion, is rhythmical, like the dance, which Ellis uses effectively to symbolize what for him is the rhythm of the universe. The reader may inquire what harm lurks in so pretty a conceit. The answer is, none if properly understood, but the tendency of man is to take all figures of speech too literally. To identify religion, which must be either the highest intellectual and spiritual exercise of man or nothing, with primitive urges, frenzies, ecstasies, rhythms, orgasms, deliriums, into which the (perhaps futile) effort to achieve self-abnegation and rapture may break over, is as mistaken as to assume that the waste products in the manufacture of radium are every whit the equivalent of radium itself. Scepticism is more logical than this, and on the whole has done less harm in the world.

About a year after the publication of ***The New Spirit,*** in December, 1891, Ellis was married to Miss Edith Lees, a former secretary of the New Life Association, a fanciful outcropping from the first Fabian group, the Progressive Association. Mrs. Ellis, a novelist and essayist legitimately bent upon a career of her own, was apparently responsible for the form of this union, which she described as the "Semi-Detached Marriage." Husband and wife had separate residences, outside friendships, and diversified interests, but appeared to maintain a strong affection for each other as long as Mrs. Ellis lived. This illusion was shattered, however, by Ellis himself in his autobiography, ***My Life*** . . . , a book which whittled the sage down to a small man more effectively than all the hostile criticism ever directed at him. The union appears to have been of the sort properly reported under abnormal attachments in ***The Studies in the Psychology of Sex,*** without either respect or affection to grace it. One other lamentable lack in Ellis' life was children, for the psychologist, so earnestly bent on knowing all aspects of sex, could never report authoritatively on that culminating experience, parenthood, which (say what you will) crowns all relationships. (Where, in the ***Studies in the Psychology of Sex,*** is there any mention of the simple fact that children are sometimes born as a result of sexual union and have to be cared for?) In passing, it seems proper to remark that literarious people generally are better reporters on marital miscues and irregular conduct than they are good counsellors, for if not neurotic themselves, their very genius denies them the average relationship. Ellis, himself, is far better at satirizing unfortunate situations and wrong-headed attitudes in sex relationships than he is at developing a program of happy conduct. This is well illustrated in ***Man and Woman*** . . . , in which Ellis, comparing the sexes, successfully maintains that many of the differences are not biological, but merely superstitions, grounded in the traditional attitudes of society. Yet, in the end, he admits the "conservatism of Nature" a more imponderable thing than the "conservatism of man," and allows that his investigation has merely shown us "in what state of mind we ought to approach the whole problem." It is a negative victory.

Even less than Freud, is Havelock Ellis a laboratory scientist. His method is synthetic: he has read the letters or listened to the verbal accounts of hundreds of people about their sex life, has absorbed the reports of anthropologists and the conjectures of psychologists, and has meditated the whole to produce the bulk of the ***Studies in the Psychology of Sex.*** Yet Professor Parshley, by no means an easily satisfied critic, has approved of the method as sufficiently "scientific." Whether one should go as far as Dr. Parshley and affirm that the ***Studies*** are "in each case an orderly, documented, intelligible and illuminating picture that affords at once a clear understanding of the phenomena in question and a firm basis for determining future action, whether personal or social" seems highly dubious. It would be wiser to regard Havelock Ellis as an extraordinarily capable compiler who has arranged a great mass of chaotic material so that genuinely scientific work on it could be begun—that is, as soon as the physiologists and zoologists are ready to recapture that field (plainly theirs) which the psychologists have usurped. It should be pointed out, however, that Ellis, in his very character of compiler, has been more willing to consider the evidence of science outside his field than has Freud. For example, while restating Freud's theory of childhood sexuality, Ellis imposes a cavil by citing Matsumato's proof that hormonic activity begins at puberty. In the end science may reject less of Ellis than of Freud, for this reason, though Ellis is much less the original thinker. Ellis had a share, however, in developing the ideas of auto-eroticism and of narcissism before they were exploited by psychoanalysis, and it is claimed for him, on the basis of his essay on Casanova, that he anticipated Freud in describing the creation of literature as a form of sublimated sex activity.

Parshley is amused that Ellis should consider the ***Studies*** too "cold and dry" to interest the "non-scientific frivolous reader." He points out that, not only has the subject matter a fascination of its own, but "unfortunately" the author has "underestimated his charm of style, which is far from being 'cold and dry.'" Indeed, as early as the publication of ***The New Spirit*** Ellis showed himself a master of prose style. The man wrote so much better than the average critic that few reviewers have had the temerity to analyze his thought. It is doubtful, with all our tendency to truckle, if any British author has had such uniformly favorable American reviews. We have taken up Ellis and coddled him, as the English do occasionally one of our authors. Yet the reviews say but one thing, "how exquisite the style." Supple, sinuous, and effective it surely is: there are no better-written passages in contemporary English than some of those in the series of ***Impressions and Comments*** . . . and in that superb little volume, ***The Soul of Spain*** . . . , which first sent Gertrude Stein, Waldo Frank, and Ernest Hemingway down into the Iberian peninsula. Our favorite passages in these purely literary books are those on Milton's love of olives and the Spaniard's love of noise. How one could say better what Ellis says in these we cannot conceive. Yet Ellis' mastery of style not only has given him immunity from criticism, but has lent seductiveness to whatever he has said. He and Freud had a pervasiveness, one from style and the other from image, almost unrivalled in the early 'twenties.

Although he clung to his early Fabian belief in "advancement," hence was not like Freud on this score, Ellis shared the Vienna master's hostility towards social morality and authority. This is more often implicit in his work than explicit, for example:

> . . . We cannot have too much temptation in the world. Without contact with temptation, virtue is worthless, and even meaningless. To face temptation and reject it may be to fortify life; to face and accept temptation may be to enrich life. . . .

It is but a step from this to argue that vice should be condoned, since it is plainly put into the world for a good purpose. Youthful America was half prepared to accept this dogma, if we are to believe G. Stanley Hall; further, our youngsters were carelessly eager to accept temptation as a way of enriching life. Those who had read Boccaccio had doubtless forgotten his ironical treatment of this ethic, or were too naïve to suspect the irony.

It was the naïveté of the generation which read Ellis (a fault which could hardly be charged to him, even if he shared it) that made him a dangerous writer and books like the inexpensive ***Little Essays of Love and Virtue*** incendiary volumes. This particularly popular book was prepared with the hope that it might "come into the hands of young people, youths and girls in the period of adolescence," who Ellis thought should decide "whether the book is suitable to be placed in the hands of older people." ***Little Essays,*** like Ellen Key's *The Century of the Child,* frankly makes its appeal to the Younger Generation by arraying it against its elders. "The world is not dying for lack of parents." The nineteenth century is depicted as building up a "harsh tyranny" of "duties," "reticences," and "subserviences." The United States, as a result, is more given to "solitary sexual indulgence" than any other nation. Jung and Freud are cited to win conviction that other and worse punishments are impending for the continent. "It is passion, more passion and fuller, that we need." While there is an admirable treatment of what Ellis terms "the play function of sex" in the book, and an altogether proper insistency on eugenics and a single standard (not of morals, but of freedom) for men and women, the approach to the subject and the emphasis are all wrong. The flattery of youth and the conviction of righteousness given them by the volume reveal an irresponsibility and immaturity hardly consistent with Ellis' reputation as "a thinker." In the last analysis, whatever Ellis may have contributed to "science," it is plain that he is one of the chief exponents of the *laissez-faire* morality which was to sweep America between 1915 and 1930. (pp. 619-24)

Oscar Cargill, "The Freudians," in his Intellectual America: Ideas on the March, *The Macmillan Company, 1941, pp. 537-763.**

GRAHAM GREENE (essay date 1951)

[Greene, an English man of letters, is generally considered the most important contemporary Catholic novelist. In his major works, he explores the problems of spiritually and socially alienated individuals living in the corrupt and corrupting societies of the twentieth century. Formerly a book reviewer at The Spectator, *Greene is also deemed an excellent film critic, a respected biographer, and a shrewd literary critic with a taste for the works of undeservedly neglected authors. In the following discussion of Ellis's* My Life, *Greene takes a harsh view of Ellis and his unconventional marriage. For other discussions of* My Life, *see the excerpts by Mary M. Colum (1939), Alan Hull Walton (1967), and Malcolm Muggeridge (1967). Greene's essay was originally published in his collection* The Lost Childhood, and Other Essays *in 1951.*]

[In ***My Life,***] which is at times crude and conceited, at others perceptive and tender, Havelock Ellis tells the story of an 'advanced' marriage. That is really the whole subject—there are chapters on his family and his childhood, on his experiences in Australia as a young school-teacher buried in a bush station and first conceiving his career in sexology, but these are only introductory to his meeting with Edith Lees, the secretary of the New Fellowship, and their long unhappy theoretical marriage. The background is already period: an odd charm hangs around the Fabian Society, around anarchists, feminism, what Ellis himself calls in an admirable phrase, 'that high-strung ethical tension': it is necessary to be reminded that encased in those years were real people, muddled and earnest and tortured.

This is an extraordinarily intimate autobiography, far too intimate to be suitable for general reading. (p. 366)

After a time [the Ellises] ceased to live as man and wife, though a kind of passionate tenderness always remained like a buoy to mark the position of a wreck. In London, Ellis had a flat of his own, and in the country they lived in two adjoining cottages (the middle-aged man, when his wife was ill, lay with one ear glued to the intervening wall). All the while Mrs. Ellis was being driven to the last breakdown of health and sanity by the remorseless Moloch theories that love was free, jealousy ignoble, possession an indignity. She couldn't always keep it up. 'Oh: Havelock, don't feel you don't want me. I let myself drift into thinking you only want Amy and not me. . . . All I feel I want in the world is to get into your arms and be told you want me to live.' This towards the end of her life, for the miracle was that their love was never killed by the theory—it was only tortured. On his side he never relented: he would write coolly, tenderly back about the spring flowers, and his work was never interrupted: the sexology studies continued to appear, full of case histories and invincible ignorance. And yet, between this ageing man with his fake prophet's air—rather like a Santa Claus at Selfridge's—and the woman haunted by extending loneliness and suspicion, so much love remained that one mourns at the thought of what was lost to them because they had not been born into the Christian tradition. (pp. 367-68)

Graham Greene, "Invincible Ignorance," in his Collected Essays, *The Viking Press, 1969, pp. 366-368.*

JOHN STEWART COLLIS (essay date 1959)

[In the following excerpt from his Havelock Ellis, Artist of Life: A Study of His Life and Work, *Collis provides an overview of the seven volumes that comprise Ellis's* Studies in the Psychology of Sex.]

H.E. always held that science had begun at the wrong end. It began with the stars and not for a long time did it work its way towards man himself. In his Dialogue about the Nineteenth Century there is a passage on the curious fact that great expensive observatories were built for the minute study of the stars while it was yet considered almost morally wrong to study the laws of human life. "They knew all about the laws of what they called gravitation, but they thought it impure to ascertain the laws by which human beings are attracted to one another and repelled.'' If only science could have started from the right end we might be in better shape today, he felt.

It was this which he sought to remedy in his seven volumes on the Psychology of Sex. ''Now that the problem of religion has been practically settled,'' he said, in his characteristic manner, ''and that the problem of labour has at least been placed on a practical foundation, the question of sex stands before us as the chief problem.'' He did not hope to solve it, but he felt that if he could succeed in stating it we would have at least half of knowledge. For the trouble about ignorance here is that it leads to the attempt to suppress what cannot be suppressed, but can be perverted. In other civilizations the sexual instinct could often grow up and develop wholesomely. In our modern civilization we do not allow it to develop wholesomely. H.E. mentions the creditable attempt of the Catholic Church to ventilate the subject in the *De Matrimonio* of Sanchez. In this the sexual life of man was set out in an admirable spirit of objectivity and even scientific accuracy. But it was paraded in its relationship to sin: we learn what is a lawful sin, and what is a mortal sin. But today we need the same spirit and temper applied from a different standpoint. Now we want to know what is normal and abnormal in relation to physiology and psychology. We want to know what is lawful to man as a child of Nature rather than as a child of sin. We want to know what is a venial sin against Nature, and what is a mortal sin against Nature—though this sort of ruling was easier for the theologians.

It may surprise some readers—as it certainly surprised me until I examined what was in the books—that seven volumes calling for half a life-time's labour would be necessary on this theme. It may seem a curious comment upon modern civilization. I think it is. And no one who is not a psychiatrist or doctor can possibly feel called upon to read all the books. But the genuine scientist and investigator does his job thoroughly: he ventilates the subject in all its aspects, he covers the whole ground. Then whatever aspect is a problem to any given person can be studied in these pages coolly set forth in the manner of a natural historian, and, as it happens here and is unlikely ever to happen again, by an artist in words. (pp. 105-06)

Volume I deals with ***The Evolution of Modesty, The Phenomenon of Sexual Periodicity, and Auto-Erotism.*** He opens a window onto a wide field in relation to modesty; its different aspects according to race and era; its base of fear in children and animals; its place in courtship as a necessary foundation for audacities. We are then shown how important it is to grasp the fact of sexual periodicity, so that men can understand the deep-rooted phenomenon of women's menstruation and all that it implies, and women the cycles in men; and it is pointed out that just as there is a seasonal periodicity in rapes and outbreaks among prisoners and a seasonal curve in suicide and insanity, so in earlier times the annual sexual rhythm, being less inhibited and thus more obviously pronounced, compelled the Church to license seasonal erotic orgies and festivals such as the Feast of Fools. Finally, in this volume, we come to auto-erotism and learn how much more this field covers than masturbation, a vast area of normal life more or less infused by auto-erotic phenomena. This chapter, going so fully into the subject, has brought enlightenment and liberation to the guilt-darkened victims of the nineteenth century. Regarding Freud's over-well known idea that everything could be traced to sex, it might be useful to give the view of Havelock Ellis: ''The sexual impulse is not, as some have imagined, the sole root of the most massive human emotions, the most brilliant human aptitudes—of sympathy, of art, of religion. In the complex human organism, where all the parts are so many-fibred and so closely interwoven, no great manifestation can be reduced to a single source. But it largely enters into and moulds all these emotions and aptitudes, and that by virtue of its two most peculiar characteristics: it is, in the first place, the deepest and most volcanic of human impulses, and, in the second place—unlike the only other human impulse with which it can be compared, the nutritive impulse—it can to a large extent be transmuted into a new force capable of the strangest and most various uses.''

Volume II—that is, the Volume I of the Bedborough Trial—deals, as we know, with ***Sexual Inversion.*** This means the sexual instinct turned by inborn constitutional abnormality towards persons of the same sex—in some cases turned so strongly that H.E. is able to quote a woman as declaring, ''I cannot conceive a sadder fate than to be a woman—an average woman reduced to the necessity of loving a man!'' In this volume H.E. gives a formidable historical survey of men and women who have been inverts, many of them being persons of exceptional intellect and high character and moral leadership; and it is a survey which also includes homosexuality among birds, dogs, rams, bulls, white rats, cockchafers, monkeys, and pigeons. He devotes chapters exclusively to the authorities on the subject; to the theory of it, the treatment of it, and the attitude of society to it (in many cases what worries the invert is not conscience nor police but the attitude of the world). In most of his volumes he includes fascinating case histories and appendices, and here we have accounts of ''Homosexuality Among Tramps'' and ''The School Friendship of Girls.'' It is unquestionably one of the most important of these ***Studies,*** and after fifty years has already begun to effect legislation.

The third volume is called ***The Analysis of the Sexual Impulse, Love and Pain, The Sexual Impulse in Women.*** In this he deals with some of the most essential fundamental problems. Analysis is called for, he insists, for ''unless we understand the exact process which is being worked out beneath the shifting and multifold phenomena presented to us we can never hope to grasp in their true relations any of the normal or abnormal manifestations of this instinct.'' In his study of Love and Pain he discusses the sources of those aberrations which are called sadism and masochism, aspects often expressed in the impulse to strangle, the desire to whip or be whipped, not to mention biting. He points out how Pain and not Cruelty is the essential element in sadism and masochism, and how these desires (and actions) are linked with normal and fundamental aspects of the sex impulse, and in elementary forms are found to be normal and in some degree present at some point in sex development—for their threads are subtly woven in and out of the whole psychological process of sex and not easily reduced to simplicity. Finally, while the sexual impulse in men is fairly obvious and well understood, he shows how in women it is even more important and a good deal more obscure in terms of qualitative difference.

Since love, seen in the broad biological aspect, is only in a limited extent a response to beauty, H.E. makes clear in Volume IV that to a greater extent beauty is simply a name for the complex of stimuli which most adequately arouses love—through touch, smell, hearing, and, above all, vision. Thus in Volume IV, called ***Sexual Selection in Man*** he examines this aspect of his Study and goes into its many ramifications, exploring the significance of the skin as the mother of all the senses; the place of the bath and the history of cleanliness; the origins of the kiss, its relation to biting, and its expression even among snails, birds, and dogs; the story of sound, including that of the voice, in the rhythm of sexual selection; the primitiveness of smell, the differentiation of odours, the influence of perfumes; and the primacy of vision in all this machinery through the appeal of beauty, the allure of adornment, the attraction of stature, the use of mirrors in feeding the lust of the eyes, and the magnetism of movement in the mystery of the dance.

Volume V treats of ***Erotic Symbolism, The Mechanism of Detumescence, The Psychic State of Pregnancy.*** In the first he reveals how sexual symbolism gives us the key that makes perversions intelligible; in the second he carefully and fully studies "the one physiological act in which two individuals are lifted out of all ends that centre in self and become the instrument of those higher forces which fashion the species; and in the third he comes to the psychic state of the woman who thus occupies the supreme position when she can perform the everlasting miracle which all the romance of love and all the cunning devices of tumescence and detumescence have been invented to make manifest.

Lastly in Volume VI—for I do not consider it necessary to summarize Volume VII with ***Eonism and other Supplementary Studies***—we come to ***Sex in Relation to Society.*** It is a very long book. It has been read more, I think, than the other studies, for its matter is of such universal importance and interest. It deals with the mother and her child; with sexual education and with nakedness; with the valuation of purely sexual love; with the function of chastity; with the problem of sexual abstinence; with prostitution; with the conquest of the venereal diseases; with sexual morality; with marriage; with the art of love; and with the science of procreation. I content myself with a list. I close with what are almost his own closing words. "We have now at last reached the point from which we started, the moment of conception, and the child again lies in its mother's womb. There remains no more to be said. The divine cycle is completed." (pp. 106-10)

John Stewart Collis, in his Havelock Ellis, Artist of Life: A Study of His Life and Work, *William Sloane Associates, 1959, 233 p.*

ALAN HULL WALTON (essay date 1967)

[*In his introduction to Ellis's* My Life, *from which the following excerpt is taken, Walton provides a general appreciation of Ellis as one of the most modern thinkers of the early twentieth century. He credits Ellis with contributing published work in a diversity of areas and also provides background information on Ellis's life and work. For other discussions of* My Life, *see the excerpts by Mary M. Colum (1939), Graham Greene (1951), and Malcolm Muggeridge (1967).*]

Ellis was . . . one of the original and pioneer figures in a small, but elect, and infinitely influential group leading modern civilised thought; all of them living and writing within the past eighty years, though not in every case personally known to each other. The names of the other luminaries in this magnificent terrestrial galaxy are: William James, Sir J. G. Frazer, F.W.H. Myers, Sir Arthur Eddington, Sir James Jeans, Albert Einstein, Bernard Shaw, Sigmund Freud, C. G. Jung, Albert Schweitzer, Sir Julian Huxley, Aldous Huxley, and Pierre Teilhard de Chardin. Omit a single name from this list, and the present state of knowledge and understanding—not to mention human standards and conditions—could not be as they are.

It seems a pity that Havelock Ellis should be remembered today almost solely because of his magnum opus, the ***Studies in the Psychology of Sex*** (together with its derivative works); for, as we shall see, he was blessed with such superlative gifts that he was able to cast his net unbelievably wide, leaving valuable contributions not only in the fields of anthropology and sociology, but equally as frequently in the domains of literature and literary criticism. This situation perhaps arose because his first sexological work (though by no means his first book) to be published was the subject of a prosecution on the grounds of criminal obscenity. The book in question was the first (now the second) volume of the famous ***Studies.*** It was called ***Sexual Inversion,*** and was the first serious and detailed scientific study of homosexuality to be written in the English language. It still remains one of the most important; and has certainly not become faded and dulled with age, as has the work of Krafft-Ebing and many of Ellis's European contemporaries. In this, of course, lies one of the hall-marks of genius—that a man's work is written virtually for all time, despite the fact that an occasional interpretation may later (and only possibly) be superseded. For despite the posturings and declamations of a number of psychiatrists and latter-day investigators, none of whom are even a patch on Ellis, I find much of his work in this field remarkably lacking in 'datedness'. (pp. xxi-xxii)

In the long run I think it will be found that Ellis has contributed more to the understanding of sex, and to its necessary rehabilitation after the insanities and shame of the nineteenth-century period of oppression and distortion, than either Freud or Kinsey—inestimable as are the contributions of these undoubted giants. Kinsey, of necessity, dealt only with the strictly observable facts of human sexual behaviour. And Freud dispensed with the religious approach to life, reducing everything to a level of interpretation which can only be called material (although his system may be said to contain a demonology peculiar to itself). Ellis, on the contrary, though certainly no churchman, understood the things of the spirit, and spiritual values, with a rare profundity—as readers of his autobiography will be quick to realise—just as he equally understood the physical and the psychological, with a wide and total perception, and with the firm grasp of the trained scientist. Nevertheless, it has been suggested by one rather fashionable literary man that he aped Freud and the Freudian method. Nothing could be further from the truth; for he was free from all those artificial and impersonal attitudes so dear to the psychoanalyst and the father-confessor. He was a born confident, unravelling the troubles and difficulties of his friends quite naturally, and apparently simply, through the medium of his wide learning and his exceptional gifts of human understanding, allied with the most sensitive intuition and the rarest delicacy of soul. Psychoanalysis can destroy and reshape personality from the rubble of destruction, but Ellis's gifts do not destroy: they cleanse, consolidate, and integrate. There is a vast difference between the two methods; and Ellis's method—most likely not realised by him—was that of the saints. . . . One of those who talked to him in this intimate way has said: "When, suddenly, he looked at you, knowing that he could help, the revelation was of the utmost kindness, and his smile made his face one of the most expressive I have ever known."

Today all the important, all the seemingly vital jobs, tend to be done by specialists—even by 'specialised' specialists. And I think it would be true to say that many of us are not altogether happy about this. We don't like the complete specialist, because all too frequently he can't see the wood for the trees; and we know that, in any case, he certainly hasn't got all the answers—is, in fact, debarred from them by the mere fact of his specialised specialisation.

Havelock Ellis was a specialist, but of a totally different kind. He didn't specialise in a single subject, or a subdivision of a subject; on the contrary he specialised in many things, of which sex and its aspects were only a few. He was a specialist in life itself. And his wide knowledge in other fields contributed vastly to his understanding of sex and its psychic mechanisms.

His published work . . . covers an astonishingly wide area—anthropology, sociology, psychology, the study of sex in almost all its manifestations, travel, art, religion, literary criticism, poetry, editing, drama, translation (including fiction), and some very worthwhile column-work in the daily press. His erudition was amazing. At an early age he inaugurated the famous *Mermaid Series* of unexpurgated reprints of Elizabethan and Restoration dramatists, editing the volumes himself, and writing some of the Introductions (he persuaded Swinburne to write the General Introduction to the set). Then he conceived the idea of the almost monumental, and once very important, *Contemporary Science Series,* editing each volume, and personally translating some of them with exceptional skill. In ***Affirmations,*** a volume of literary essays, he introduced Huysmans and Ibsen to English readers. His travel book, ***The Soul of Spain,*** is a gem. So is his Australian idyll, ***Kanga Creek.*** Then we have the philosophical ***Dance of Life;*** and the collections of literary studies, ***From Rousseau to Proust,*** and ***From Marlowe to Shaw;*** not to mention the intimate journals, published in three volumes, under the title of ***Impressions and Comments,*** and worthy to take their place alongside the best in this genre of literature. His masterly translation of Zola's *Germinal* is still available in the Everyman edition; and his collected newspaper columns were reprinted in a series of volumes which include ***My Confessional*** and ***Questions of Our Day.*** (pp. xxii-xxiv)

As a mastery of literary grace and style Ellis has few equals, and certainly no superiors in his own language. As a vehicle for his rare learning and insight such prose is unique and magnificent to the point of miracle, proclaiming not only a scientist of unusual sensitivity, but also the poet, the artist, and the seer.

With regard to his basic method of work when dealing with scientific subjects, Ellis has left us his own description, commencing with the genesis of this method:

> My demand to make literature, as apart from reading it, I can scarcely trace the beginning of. At an early age I would buy penny notebooks, some of which I still possess, and in these I entered . . . the record of the occurrences of my life that chiefly interested me, together with . . . extracts from . . . passages which struck me. These notebooks slowly became more elaborate. I began to index them and to co-ordinate the quoted passages under a few headings. In fact the literary methods I later followed were already growing up slowly and spontaneously, without the slightest stimulus or assistance from outside, at the age of ten. By the age of twelve I had prepared a little book for publication. It was called ***The Precious Stones of the Bible.*** It contained nothing original but was an orderly compilation of all the facts on the subject I could bring together from the small supply of books at my disposition. . . . When I look back now at that little book I seem to see in it the germ of my later books, I mean those of more scientific character; then, as now, it was my desire to accumulate with an open mind all the information I could acquire and present it in a fair, orderly, and attractive way, though I could not then, as I have since learned to do, in that act create afresh a form that my own spirit had moulded.
>
> (pp. xxiv-xxv)

Such seems to have been the method he utilised when writing his autobiography [***My Life***], collecting and arranging all the facts in pertinent order and relatedness and making comparisons; but with this difference—that he was able to apply to this book the increasingly beautiful and artistic method which is apparent in his purely literary work.

Havelock always held that there were few really great autobiographies in the world. In fact he believed that few people were capable of writing this kind of book. The volumes in this category which drew his respect and admiration can be counted on the fingers of one hand. They are: *The Confessions* of St. Augustine, the autobiography of Benvenuto Cellini, the *Mémoires* of Casanova, the *Confessions* of Rousseau, and the *Monsieur Nicolas* of Restif de la Bretonne. (p. xxvi)

And although his own life was certainly totally different and very far removed from those of his masters in this field, I do not think it would be too much to say that he was very much their equal in his own autobiography. If, at times, he may seem either reticent or reserved, we may say the same of the others. Even Restif, out-spoken though he is, never goes into clinical detail concerning certain private and intimate events. Yet he leaves us in no doubt as to what he means, delineating his images by inference rather than in the crudity of bold and gaudy strokes. This, of course, is true art; and it is the way which Ellis follows—for the very good reason that a literal and surgical description of intimate events can only distort their spiritual and psychic implications, and distort even more than any distorting-mirror could possibly misrepresent the visual images of such events. Language, being purely relative, this might be said to be true of any situation; but it seems to me that it is infinitely more true when we come to the still vexed question of sexual episodes. Perhaps this is one of the reasons why the *whole* truth can only be told by the sensitive and reticent artist (whether in words or in paint)—by the true poet, rather than the mere writer. And, of course, Ellis was a poet, even in his prose. (pp. xxvi-xxvii)

[With Ellis, all] his characters live, breathe, and pulsate with the most fascinating verisimilitude. The genius of the famous ***Studies,*** and of the critical essays, has been transferred, not only whole, but transfigured, to the pages of ***My Life.*** And these considerations become even more valuable and important when we think of the people he knew: Verlaine, Huysmans, Rémy de Gourmont, Hack Tuke, Edward Carpenter, Madame Darmesteter, Rodin, Henri de Regnier, and Arthur Symons—not to mention innumerable others. . . .

On the other hand Ellis was a little reticent about the names of one or two of the women he loved. Understandably so, when it is realised that they were still living at the time he wrote. Amy, for example, was the daughter of Dr. Barker Smith, one of his close friends. But he does not mention her surname in his text. Margaret Sanger, the great American pioneer of contraception, is another of those women whose identity is kept in the background. And so is *La Douce,* the tantalisingly attractive, intelligent and mysterious woman who occupies the closing pages of his narrative. *La Douce,* whom Havelock sometimes lovingly called 'Naiad', just as she referred to him as 'Faun', is still with us, and has contributed the *Foreword* to the present volume. She is, to use her pen-name, Françoise Delisle (an anagram on 'de Ellis'); a literary woman in her own right, and virtually, if not in actual fact, the second Mrs. Havelock Ellis. There is no doubt but that Françoise was the greatest, the last, and by far the longest love of Havelock's life. I have a copy of the final letter he wrote her, written for delivery after his death, and it is one of the most moving tributes of man to woman which I have ever read. In fact I doubt if Ellis would have reached the great age which he did without the love, the care, and the devotedness of this miraculous creature. (pp. xxvii-xxviii)

Ellis believed there were few really great biographies in the world, and that these can be counted almost on the fingers of one hand. I believe, moreover, that the unprejudiced reader will find in this volume one more of these great biographies—the ultimate work and the unvarnished confessions of another of those rare and luminous individuals who only occasionally grace our human scene—and a book which can do much to lighten life's way for every reader blessed with a little insight and understanding. (p. xxxi)

Alan Hull Walton, in an introduction to My Life *by Havelock Ellis, William Spearman, 1967, pp. xxi-xxxi.*

Ellis in his later years. Mary Evans Picture Library.

MALCOLM MUGGERIDGE (essay date 1967)

[*An English man of letters, Muggeridge has long had a reputation as an iconoclast. A socialist and outspoken atheist during the 1930s, he later eschewed socialism and embraced Christianity during the 1960s. His conversion, however, did nothing to mitigate his stinging satire. Organized religion, contraception, abortion, heart transplants, pornography, public education, and egalitarianism have all been the objects of his wrath. In the following excerpt from a sarcastic review written shortly after* My Life *was reissued, Muggeridge disparages Ellis's importance as a scientist on the grounds that Ellis was himself too strange a man to serve as a reliable guide for others.*]

There are few things more repulsive than picturesque old men. If ever I find myself cultivating a venerable white beard and hair to match I shall know that the end has come. The thought is put in my mind by looking at the picture of Havelock Ellis on the dust-jacket of his autobiography, first published in 1940 and now re-issued. To be vain about youthful good looks is permissible, though still not edifying; one remembers with distaste all the high-table camp talk about Rupert Brooke's good looks (for instance, Lytton Strachey's high-pitched 'Rupert is *en beauté* tonight' on catching a glimpse of him at a theatre) among Cambridge homosexuals. But to be vain amidst the foliage of old age is disgusting, and betokens an obsessive narcissism.

Ellis was a classic example. His body, he indicates in ***My Life,*** gave off sweet smells; 'my mother when she kissed me used often to say that my cheeks were scented, and my wife, who has frequently made the same remark, has also said that my cast-off shirts have a distinct odour of cedar.' His head, he writes, passed for being 'noble', his eyes for being bright and beautiful; 'Olive Schreiner said once of my nude form that it was like that of Christ in the carpenter's shop in Holman Hunt's *Shadow of the Cross*'. On another occasion Olive Schreiner compared him to the 'eager, bright-eyed satyr in Rubens's picture, *Silenus*'. A 'dear friend loves to call me "Faun", and Edward Carpenter, with the quiet twinkle of his luminous eyes, once said to me: "He is the god Pan."'

Faun or Pan or Christ, or all three at once, Ellis clearly had a great and abiding passion for himself. He works lovingly over his limbs, features and organs, only leaving out the genitals, one feels, because they were too sacred in his eyes to be included even in this auto-erotic survey. Nothing clouded the serenity of his relationship with himself; they never, as it were, spoke a cross word to one another—he and himself. It was a perfect marriage, and if there were occasional infidelities—with his wife Edith, with Olive Schreiner, with 'Amy' who turns out to have been the daughter of his friend Dr Baker Smith, with Margaret Sanger, the early American contraception evangelist, and with Françoise Delisle the companion of his last years, actually a French woman named Françoise Lafitte-Cyon—his only true love and dear companion was himself.

With so narcissistic a temperament Ellis was bound to find his relations with women—to put it mildly—unusual and delicate. Alan Hull Walton, in his introduction to this new edition of ***My Life,*** insists that Ellis was neither impotent nor homosexual. We must take his word for it, though none of the relationships with women described in ***My Life*** can be considered as normal, or, in the accepted sense, sexually satisfying. His wife turned out to be a lesbian, and after their marriage soon reverted to lesbian practices. In the end the poor woman went off her head, becoming, except in occasional lucid moments, fiercely hostile towards Ellis. Olive Schreiner, with whom he was according to his own account in love, was clearly a passionate woman (Ellis called her 'lion' and she him 'my soul's wifie'), but their indulgence in sensuality together, such as it was, can scarcely have been, from her point of view, up to scratch. Some idea of how it went is perhaps conveyed by the following bizarre incident:

> I see her at her rooms at Hastings where I had come to spend the week-end with her, bringing at her desire my student's microscope, for she wished to observe living spermatozoa, which there was no difficulty in obtaining to place under the cover glass for her inspection, and I see her interest in their vigorous mobility.

This is not, I should suppose, quite what Antony and Cleopatra were up to. . . .

However one looks at it, Ellis was by way of being a sexual oddity, and to that extent, one might have supposed, ill-equipped to be a guide, philosopher and friend in this particular field. Yet he, along with Krafft-Ebing and other maestros, prepared the way for—in Alan Hull Walton's words—'undoubted giants' like Freud and Kinsey, and the so-called Sexual Revolution of our time. His ***Studies in the Psychology of Sex*** has been, and for all I know still may be, highly regarded; I well remember as a smutty adolescent scouring its footnotes for juvenile erotica, and seeing it displayed, along with treatises in a like vein, in what used to be known as 'rubber shops'. In a sense, indeed, he emerges from the pages of ***My Life*** as a true prophet, embodying, as he did, the narcissism, the self-love tapering off into impotence, of the sex-obsessed times which lay ahead.

Malcolm Muggeridge, "The Prophet of Sex," in New Statesman, *Vol. 73, No. 1887, May 12, 1967, p. 653.*

EDWARD M. BRECHER (essay date 1969)

[In his study The Sex Researchers, *Brecher examines the lives and works of those individuals who, from the turn-of-the-century to the present, have contributed to the study of sex. Of these researchers, he concludes that Ellis "presented concepts of individual and cultural relativism which underlie almost all significant sex research today." In the following excerpt from that study, Brecher discusses* Studies in the Psychology of Sex, *noting many of Ellis's physiological and psychological findings that have been supported by other researchers, notably Alfred Charles Kinsey, William H. Masters, and Virginia E. Johnson.]*

The panorama of human sexuality which emerges from [Ellis's ***Studies in the Psychology of Sex***] startlingly anticipates many of the findings of Kinsey, Masters and Johnson, and other recent researchers. Let me cite just a few examples. (p. 37)

Human sexuality is far from a simple phenomenon. In some respects it is mammalian, shared with the other mammals. In some respects it is molded by historical influences. In many respects it is influenced by cultural expectations—the particular customs and beliefs prevailing in the community at the time. Adult sexuality is very profoundly influenced (here Ellis agrees with Freud) by parental attitudes and by early childhood training and experiences. Social class and economic and educational status also play their roles. Underlying all of these influences are the inherited anatomical structure of the body and the physiological functioning of the body at each moment. And all of these factors together fall short of providing an exhaustive explanation.

These themes recur over and over again in subsequent sex research. They illustrate also another significant aspect of Ellis's ***Studies***—their primary emphasis on *normal* human sexuality. The ***Studies*** cover almost all of the generally recognized variations in sexual behavior—male and female homosexuality, sadism, masochism, exhibitionism, voyeurism, fetishism, incest, satyriasis, nymphomania, transvestism, and zoophilia, to mention only a few. Ellis exhibited a sympathetic understanding of even those variations which his contemporaries deemed most repellent.

When writing of incest, for example, he could recall that on his return from Australia, after an absence of four years, he formed with his sister Louie "an intimate friendship which at first was touched by sexual emotion. This could not have happened if the long absence during which she grew into womanhood had not destroyed that familiarity which inhibits the development of sexual interest. This little experience . . . enabled me to understand from personal knowledge how it is that, as a rule, sexual emotion fails to spring up between close relatives or people living together from before puberty, and under what circumstances—by no means of such rare occurrence as is usually believed—it may spring up. I was thereby enabled in later years to give clear precision to my conception of the psychological foundation of exogamy." In addition, of course, Ellis's personal touch of urolagnia, and his familiarity with Edith's lesbianism, enabled him to understand from the inside a broad range of similar deviations—and to appreciate how they can in some cases enrich rather than impoverish experience. But his primary emphasis was on "normal" human sexuality, with the term "normal" very broadly defined. As he explained in his ***Studies:***

> It is a very remarkable fact that, although for many years past serious attempts have been made to elucidate the psychology of human perversions, little or no endeavor has been made to study the development of the normal sexual emotions. Nearly every writer seems either to take for granted that he and his readers are so familiar with the facts of normal sex psychology that any detailed statement is altogether uncalled for, or else he is content to write a few fragmentary remarks. . . . Yet it is unreasonable to take normal phenomena for granted here as in any other region of science.

Everybody is not like you and your friends and neighbors. This, as we have seen, was the central theme of many of Ellis's ***Studies.*** But a second theme, of almost equal importance, weaves through the volumes in counterpoint to the first: *Even your friends and neighbors may not be as much like you as you suppose.* As Ellis himself expressed it: "So far from the facts of normal sex development, sex emotions, and sex needs being uniform and constant . . . the range of variation within fairly normal limits is immense, and it is impossible to meet with two individuals whose records are nearly identical."

Many of his examples might well be the cases of the man and woman next door. There was the American woman, for example, "a devout church-goer, [who] had never allowed herself to entertain sexual thoughts referring to men." Yet "she masturbated every morning when standing before the mirror by rubbing against a key in the mirror-drawer. A man never excited her passions, but the sight of a key in any bureau-drawer aroused erotic desires."

There was also the ardent sex reformer, devoting her life to denunciations of masturbation, prostitution, and other sexual activities, whose whole life was shattered when she discovered in her forties that the harmless little game she so often played with herself was in fact the masturbating act which she so loathingly described in her public speeches and writings. (pp. 38-9)

There was also the minister of the gospel, aged fifty-seven, who informed Ellis: "My whole nature goes out to some persons, and they thrill and stir me so that I have an emission while sitting by them with no thought of sex, only the gladness of soul found its way out thus, and a glow of health suffused the whole body."

At the other extreme, Ellis could cite cases of both men and women who had reached middle age without any sexual arousal or experience whatever. He himself was not too far from this end of the scale, at least until middle age.

This enormous variation in sexuality among people who in other respects seem to be quite like us and our friends and neighbors is most clearly visible in the scores of detailed case histories—Ellis called them "histories of sexual development"—which fill hundreds of pages of the ***Studies.*** Ellis collected these histories in many ways. Some were provided by his friends and mistresses; indeed, his wife's history up to the date of her marriage is included. . . . Many were the histories of men and women who came to him for help in distress, and many more came from readers of his early volumes who wrote to Ellis, received replies, and thereafter engaged in frank correspondence with him over periods of years or even decades.

These histories were not included in the ***Studies*** to make theoretical points, or to illustrate specific phenomena. Rather, they present the ebb and flow of human sexuality as it actually occurs, from early childhood to old age, including wishes, desires, and fantasies as well as actual experiences. Many are tragedies; a few have comic overtones. Just as reading Ellis's **"Evolution of Modesty"** has awakened countless readers to the enormous variations in sexuality from one culture to another and from one historic era to another, so reading Ellis's case histories has alerted many (myself among them) to the enormous variations within a single culture during a single era—a culture and an era which are not so very unlike our own. Ellis's "histories of sexual development" probably influenced Freud and perhaps enabled Freud to correct a major error in his early theories. (pp. 40-1)

Ellis "histories of sexual development" illustrate another point which Ellis repeatedly stressed: the absence of any objective boundary between the normal and the abnormal. "The majority of sexual perversions, including even those that are most repulsive," Ellis taught, "are but exaggerations of instincts and emotions that are germinal in normal human emotions."

Ellis was essentially a naturalist, observing human sexuality rather than judging it—much as another scientist might observe the behavior of gall wasps, hamsters, or chimpanzees. The heterosexual and the homosexual, the celibate and the libertine, the sadist, the masochist, and the fetishist, the lovers of excrement and of corpses—Ellis saw them all as variant expressions of a common human impulse. Few men before him achieved that scientific objectivity. Most contemporary sex research . . . shares his naturalistic perspective.

Ellis was also a crusader, concerned to introduce reforms in the sexual education of children, in adult attitudes toward sex, and in attitudes toward sexual variations. Having described things objectively as they really are, he went on to draw ethical conclusions. The whole body of his work is richly infused with a sense of human values, and on issue after issue he fought for a realization of those values.

It could not have been otherwise. For in the course of his research, Ellis uncovered in all its poignancy the tragic waste resulting from sexual ignorance and sexual repression. He saw the bachelors and the spinsters, the blighted love affairs and the unfulfilled marriages. He saw the sufferings of the damned imposed by a callous society upon masturbators, adulterers, homosexuals. He saw with an emotional directness arising out of his own personal experience the blight which follows when the normal emotional responses of love and affection are divorced from the "evils" of "lust"—that is, from physiological response. And his studies persuaded him—as most serious students of sex are today persuaded—that this waste and these tragedies are avoidable. Hence he threw himself wholeheartedly into movements for sexual freedom and sexual reform.

He urged, for example, that sexual manifestations during infancy and childhood should be accepted casually, as a routine matter of course. He argued for the frank sexual education of both boys and girls from an early age. He favored greater freedom of sexual experimentation during adolescence, and "trial marriage" as a prelude to actual marriage. He demanded equal rights—including equal sexual rights—for women, greater freedom of divorce, a repeal of the laws banning contraception. And he stated with clarity the legal principles which should govern homosexual and other variant behavior. . . . (pp. 44-5)

Ellis's ability to combine a highly objective naturalism in his scientific study of sex with a deeply committed fervor for sexual reform has also characterized many of his successors. (p. 45)

And Ellis in his last years . . . delighted that the Victorianism against which he had so long battled was beginning to fade. "I cannot see now a girl walking along the street," he wrote in old age, "with her free air, her unswathed limbs, her gay and scanty raiment, without being conscious of a thrill of joy that in my youth was unknown. I can today feel in London as in earlier days I scarcely could even in Paris, that I am among people who are growing to be gracious and human."

No man alive or dead contributed more to that change than Havelock Ellis himself. (pp. 48-9)

Edward M. Brecher, "The First of the Yea-Sayers: Henry Havelock Ellis (1859-1939)," in his The Sex Researchers, *Little, Brown and Company, 1969, pp. 3-49.*

DEREK STANFORD (essay date 1970)

[In the following excerpt, Stanford examines Ellis's literary criticism, which concentrated on the biographical background ("heredity and environment") of an author. He maintains that Ellis's scientific training influenced his criticism, allowing him "to get at the motive forces at work in the man." For a more in-depth discussion of Ellis's literary criticism, see the excerpt by Tom Gibbons (1972).]

Ellis's first essays in literary criticism had been written and published while he was still a medical student, and the trend and regimen of thought which his training accustomed him to was carried over into the field of literary examination. Appreciative as he was of the style and content of a book, it is always the man he seeks beyond the image of the author. Nor is his interest here focused solely on the *intellectual* aspect of the person. Instead, he seeks to trace his features in the records of childhood, youth, and adulthood; in his conduct as son, lover, husband and father. Can one locate some temperamental essence?—it is this which Ellis wishes to know.

Perhaps, then, we may describe him as a critic whose twin keys are those of heredity and environment; and where Sainte-Beuve might resort to the diaries and letters of the author and his circle, the gossip of cliques and *salons*, Ellis would more likely turn to the ramifications of a family tree and to every scrap of knowledge concerning his forebears. In Ellis's criticism, physical and temperamental traits, ancestral details and place of birth with conditions and locations of up-bringing abound. The head of Verlaine (half cenobite, half satyr), the gray Ardennes countryside where he was reared; the Norman-Norse inheritance in Remy de Gourmont; Zola's explosive energy derived from the racial compound of French, Greek and Italian blood; Casanova's freak exuberance, product of his Hispanic-Venetian parentage—these are but a few of the guiding images which we encounter in Ellis's criticism.

Unlike so many writers of the 'nineties, these of Ellis make for naturalness and health. The notion of masks, which Wilde and Yeats sponsored, offered a good argument for artificiality and affectation. Ellis distinguished between two types of literary expression: 'the literature that is all art' and 'the literature of life', choosing only to write, at any length, upon the latter. From this one might guess rightly that it was contents and outlook which called forth his focussing attention. Literature he saw as something contributing to sanity—something which strengthened what was authentic. In the preface to his book ***The New Spirit,*** he spoke of the constituent essays as 'a bundle of sphygmographic tracings'—apt metaphor for one concerned with cultural health!—and spoke of the critic's engagement with the author of power or talent in terms which suggested those later employed in 'An Open Letter to Biographers'. 'Whenever,' he declared, 'a great literary personality comes before us . . . it is our business to discover or divine its fundamental instincts; we ought to do this with the same austerity and keen-eyed penetration as, if we were wise, we should exercise in choosing the comrades of our daily life. He poses well in public; he has said these brave words on the platform; he has written those rows of eloquent books—but what (one asks oneself) is all that to me? I want to get at the motive forces at work in the man; to know what his intimate companions thought of him; how he acted in the affairs of everyday, and in the great crises of his life; the fashion of his face and form, the tone of his voice. How he desired to appear is of little importance. I can perhaps learn all that is important from a single involuntary glance, or one glance into his eyes.'

This is a model *declaration of intention* and serves to distinguish Ellis as a critic from those of both his decade and the present. Unlike him, the aesthete of the day was concerned with his author in terms of that author's literary pose. Whether he posed ill or well was the question that interested the aesthetic critic most (as one sees from such books as Wilde's *Intentions* and Ross's *Masques and Phrases*). To this position Ellis made reply that 'how he [the author] desired to appear is of little importance'. In distinction to those aesthetic critics who took art to be the *precious surface* of an author, Ellis proclaimed his desire to 'get at the motive forces at work in the man'.

This declaration sets Ellis apart from the American New Critics of the 'thirties, or our own Dr Leavis today, whose motto might well be 'not the singer but the song', 'The text's the thing' is what they both affirm; but for Ellis the text may be a starting point, a shaft down into the essential man. Ellis's concern with this 'essential man' determines his slant as a critic, which is that of the biographer. And the biographical angle which fascinates him most pertains to a physiological and psychological assessment of his subject.

Aristotle tells us that if we wish to understand the nature of a thing we shall attain this information best by looking at its origins; and no critic of the 'nineties, within essay-length limits, has better practised this procedure.

Ellis's concern as a biographer with 'the influences, physical and moral, which surround the period of [his subject's] conception, the welfare of his pre-natal life, whether he was born naturally and in due season' and his belief that 'the fate of all of us is in large measure scaled at the moment we leave the womb', naturally establishes a link between sexology and criticism. It is a connection we find maintained, with liberal unpedantic application, in most of the essays in ***The New Spirit*** and ***Affirmations*** and even more so in those papers (many written much earlier) which were finally gathered together in his chief book on French literature ***From Rousseau to Proust***. . . . (pp. 137-39)

The relationship between sexology and criticism posited by Ellis leads him to espouse what we today should term 'the new morality'. In his essay **'Concerning Jude the Obscure'** (first published in *The Savoy,* no. 6, October 1896) he remarks that 'the great novelists of the present century who have chiefly occupied themselves with the problem of passion and the movements of women's hearts . . . have all shown a reverent faith in what we call Nature as opposed to Society; they have all regarded the impulses and the duties of love in women as independent of social regulation, which may or may not impede the free play of passion and natural morality'.

The basis of our new permissive morality, Ellis sees as rooted in a concept of Nature as distinct from Society. This is how he states the opposition between these two ideas. 'On the one side . . . we have Nature and her unconsciousness of all but essential law, on the other the laws framed merely as social expedients without a base in the heart of things, and merely expressing the triumph of the majority over the individual. . . . This conflict reaches its highest point around women.' 'True or falsely,' Ellis continues, 'woman has always been for man the supreme priestess . . . of Nature'—a statement which, in the context of the debate, carries forward the 'nineties Cult of Woman to the point where it gives rise to 'the new morality' we have with us today.

Considering Ellis's close connection, through his friend Arthur Symons, with the *literati* of the 'nineties, it is in fact surprising that his vast sexological knowledge did not make a deeper impression on them. (pp. 139-40)

It is particularly in the field of literary symbolism that one might expect to find the influence of Ellis's sexological thought. In the field of sex Ellis had early realized that 'every fetish is a symbol' and that 'the number of objects . . . which may acquire special erotic significance is practically infinite'. Ellis had dealt comprehensively with the factor of 'Erotic Symbolism' in volume V of his ***Studies in the Psychology of Sex*** . . . and with 'Symbolism in Dreams' in his book ***The World of Dreams***. . . . The ideas he expounded in these volumes were most likely present to him, embryonically, in earlier years; but no reflection of them seems apparent in either Symons or Yeats—

the two British authors of the 'nineties consciously concerned with Symbolist theory. How different, for example, might Yeats' collection *The Rose* have been had the poem considered the sexological symbolism of that flower! Indeed, it is not perhaps too great a claim to suggest that the weakness of the Symbolist Movement was related to its exponents' all but total lack of scientific knowledge. Alone of the men of the 'nineties, Ellis possessed, to a high degress, the anthropological intelligence. Those amateur dabblings in alchemy, astrology, and the occult—which certain partisans of Symbolism professed—were no efficient substitute for his. The Irish contingent could possibly claim some folk-lore studies to bear out their arcane logic; but, for the most part, the Symbolists in Britain were subjective doodling obscurantists, idly indulging in weak dreams of escape.

If Ellis's influence on the sphere of contemporary poetry was nil, in the field of fiction it was not much larger. Two volumes of his ***Studies in the Psychology of Sex*** had appeared by 1899. This was preceded by ***Man and Woman: A Study of Human Secondary Sexual Characteristics*** . . . , intended, Ellis tells us, 'as an introduction to my later and more extensive work'. 'Before entering on that great task,' he continues, 'dealing with the primary sexual functions on their psychic side, it was necessary to clear the ground—entangled and over-grown by many weeds—for the presentation of the secondary and, as I term them, tertiary sexual characters. That had never been undertaken before on a comprehensive basis and in a critical spirit.' The image of woman in the fiction of the 'nineties is less sentimental, more objectively observed than in that of the six, say, previous decades; yet, even so, one feels, time and time again, a defective knowledge on the author's part. Just how widely Ellis's ideas and information were defused among the *literati* of the 'nineties it would be hard to say. One can only conjecture: not enough. (pp. 140-41)

Derek Stanford, "Havelock Ellis: 'Huysmans'," in his Critics of the 'Nineties, *John Baker, 1970, pp. 134-71.*

TOM GIBBONS (essay date 1972)

[In the following excerpt, Gibbons offers an overview of Ellis's literary criticism, emphasizing that Ellis applied the same scientific approach to his literary criticism that he did to his studies of human sexuality. Gibbons's essay was originally a lecture delivered at the University of Nottingham on 22 November 1972. For another discussion of Ellis's critical methods, see the excerpt by Derek Stanford (1970).]

In 1890 Ellis published his first two original books, ***The Criminal*** and ***The New Spirit. The New Spirit,*** a series of essays on such literary figures as Diderot, Heine, Whitman, Tolstoy and Ibsen, provoked considerable hostility when it appeared. Said *The Dundee Advertiser,* for example: 'We only refer to this unpleasant compilation of cool impudence and effrontery to warn readers against it'. . . . For the moment I merely note some of the ways in which it seems typical of its day and age. Firstly, it is highly optimistic: Ellis attributes the dawn of a new era to the concept of evolution, which has 'penetrated every department of organic science, especially where it touches man'. Secondly, it preaches a highly eclectic form of religious mysticism, and this is accompanied by a transcendental view of the arts which appears to derive from Schopenhauer and has much in common with that of the French Symbolists: art is said to have the power of conveying directly to the soul of the spectator a supernatural world of spiritual reality which cannot be put into words by philosophers. Thirdly, ***The New Spirit*** hints at a new form of socialist State led by a new aristocracy. Fourthly, and much less obviously, its whole critical approach is heavily influenced by the investigations into hereditary genius carried out by Francis Galton. Ellis's critical essays are strongly biographical and show a marked interest in the personalities of artistic men of genius as revealed by their works. The work is 'explained' psychologically as the product of a particular temperament, and the temperament itself is then 'explained' anthropologically as the product of a particular ancestry and geography.

Writing much later, in 1919, Ellis denied that he was ever a disciple of Lombroso. 'I was merely an outsider who enjoyed the spectacle', he said. Whether or not this is strictly true, he certainly played an important part in creating the 'spectacle' to which he refers, and certainly helped to pave the way for the public outcries against 'decadent' literature and 'degenerate' artists which darkened the English cultural scene between 1895 and 1914. In 1889 he had published **'A Note on Paul Bourget'** . . . and translated in full the French critic's 'theory of decadence'. This so-called theory, which relates decadence in literary style to decadence in the social order, has played a considerable part in the line of English 'reactionary' cultural criticism which leads from Matthew Arnold *via* Nietzsche, A. R. Orage and T. E. Hulme down to T. S. Eliot. (As will be remembered, Eliot's *For Lancelot Andrewes* is actually subtitled 'Essays in Style and Order'.) Now, in the same year as ***The New Spirit,*** Ellis published his book on ***The Criminal.*** In this work, which shows a strong interest in Lombroso's ideas, Ellis refers to the Decadent poet Verlaine as 'an interesting example of the man of genius who is also distinctly a criminal'. In 1891 he published his own translation of Lombroso's book *The Man of Genius,* which contains a chapter on the French Decadents under the heading of 'Literary and Artistic Mattoids', and which makes the overall claim that 'the signs of degeneration are found more frequently in men of genius than even in the insane'. A similar interest underlies Ellis's investigations into the ancestry of contemporary English writers in his essay on **'The Ancestry of Genius'**. . . . (pp. 128-29)

During 1896 Ellis contributed to most of the eight issues of [Arthur] Symons' famous but short-lived periodical *The Savoy,* later publishing several of these essays in his volume of ***Affirmations***. . . . In this second major collection of critical essays he wrote on Zola, Nietzsche, Huysmans, and (a rather surprising pair of companions) Casanova and St. Francis. . . . [The] essays on Nietzsche and Huysmans are the first full-scale studies of these important European authors to have been published in England, and draw attention to two interesting developments in Ellis's critical approach to literature. Firstly, in the preface to ***Affirmations,*** we see him distinguishing between the literature of art, which cannot be discussed at all, and the literature of life, whose content can be discussed and morally evaluated as he himself discusses and evaluates it in this book. In making this distinction Ellis seems to be avoiding the *impasse* he had created in ***The New Spirit*** when he presented literature and the arts as something essentially supernatural which cannot be talked about in everyday language. Secondly, in his essays on Casanova and Zola we find him modifying his psychological approach to artistic genius by introducing what would now be called a theory of 'sublimation'. In his essay on Casanova he states that 'A certain degree of continence—I do not mean merely in the region of sex but in the other fields of human action also—is needed as a breeding-ground for the dreams and images of desire to develop into the perfected visions of art'. In his essay on Zola he finds the basis of Zola's fictional methods in the deprivations which the novelist suffered as a child. (p. 130)

Ellis's critical essays are generally disguised as a scientist's bland investigations into the psychology of artistic genius in men of letters. The disguise is extremely thin, however, and *The Dundee Advertiser* was by no means the only one to penetrate it. As Ellis freely admitted later, his essays are also a means of presenting his own *avant-garde* views on literature and society, and especially on such matters as sexual morality and censorship. He uses his essays to support whatever seems to him to foster individual unity of being, and to oppose whatever seems to him to prevent the achievement of this unity. In particular he opposes puritanical Christianity, literary censorship, and commercialism.

What he supports he usually calls 'classicism', and the immediate ancestor of his classicism is in fact the Hellenism of Swinburne, especially as this is expressed in Swinburne's poem 'The Last Oracle'. In this poem, it will be remembered, Swinburne seeks to persuade us that the whole world has been made to 'moan with hymns of wrath and wrong' since the life-affirming chant of well-adjusted Hellenes was supplanted by the life-denying wail of guilt-ridden Christians.

Swinburne however had not realized that the latest discoveries of modern science might be called in to re-habilitate his Hellenic ideals. It was therefore John Addington Symonds, who had learned this primary lesson of the evolutionary age, who was singled out by Ellis in 1885 as representing 'whatever is best' in the criticism of the day. (p. 132)

In his review of Edward Carpenter's *Towards Democracy* . . . Ellis makes clearer what he had intended by [his] 'Hellenic conception of the whole'. 'Mr. Carpenter', he says, 'has a profound sense of the mystery and significance of the body: he cannot see any salvation for man till he is able to enter into pure and frank relation with his own body. . . .' A similar enthusiasm for authors who oppose a dualistic concept of flesh and spirit is apparent in a selection of Heine's prose writings which Ellis published in 1887. In the introduction to this selection Ellis praises the Hellenic ideals of Heine. (p. 133)

The introduction to Ellis's selection from Heine is one of the essays included in ***The New Spirit***. . . . In the introduction to this book Ellis enthusiastically prophesies that a major renascence of the human spirit will be brought about particularly by the development of modern science, which is in accord with what he calls 'the true Greek spirit'. The five authors discussed in the chapters which follow are presented as liberators of the human spirit, who embody the various stages of this classical renascence as it has been evolving during the previous hundred years.

Of the various writers and artists discussed by Ellis in ***The New Spirit,*** it is the painter Millet and the poet Whitman whose works come closest to fulfilling the ideals of this coming classical renascence:

> Millet and Whitman have . . . made the most earnest, thorough, and successful attempts of modern times to bring the Greek spirit into art. . . . It is not by the smooth nudities of a Bouguereau or a Leighton that we reach Hellenism. The Greek spirit is the simple, natural, beautiful interpretation of the life of the artist's own age and people under his own sky, as shown especially in the human body.

This classical paganism, with its fundamental belief in the identity of flesh and spirit, is according to Ellis most fully expressed in Whitman's attitude towards sexual relationships. Turning the tables on his puritanical readers, Ellis implies that it is Christian ideals about sex which are *im*moral, while Whitman's are exactly the reverse. . . . (pp. 133-34)

In ***Affirmations,*** which was published eight years after ***The New Spirit,*** Ellis makes a very similar point with regard to Nietzsche. Passing lightly over Nietzsche's concepts of master-morality and the Superman, Ellis presents him in the main as one who 'desired to detach the "bad conscience" from the things that are merely wicked traditionally, and to attach it to the things that are anti-natural, anti-instinctive, anti-sensuous'. (p. 134)

The Hellenistic dissatisfaction with 19th-century culture which Ellis shares with Nietzsche has led him to an increasing preference for the classical 18th century, as he states in his essay on Casanova in ***Affirmations.*** The 18th century was one in which Christianity seemed to be decaying, and in which the 'Tolerant paganism of classic days' was asserting itself robustly in England.

'Decadence', so often regarded during the period as the antithesis of classicism, was not discussed by Ellis in any detail until his essay on Huysmans in ***Affirmations.*** In this essay he discusses three main types of decadence: social, artistic, and religious, finding little to complain of in the first two, and rather more to complain of in the last. Concerned that so many of his contemporaries should have totally rejected the natural world for the supernatural, Ellis contrasts this form of 'decadence' with his own classical paganism:

> Pagan art and its clear serenity, science, rationalism, the bright, rough vigour of the sun and the sea, the adorable mystery of common life and commonplace human love . . . make up the spirit that in any age we call 'classic'.
>
> Thus what we call classic corresponds on the spiritual side to the love of natural things, and what we call decadent to the research for the things which seem to lie beyond Nature.

The present time, says Ellis, is one in which a reaction against 'The classic party of Nature . . . has attained a certain ascendancy'. Confident that his contemporaries will eventually return to Nature, he tolerantly advises them to 'be drunken with mediaevalism, occultism, spiritualism, theosophy, and even, if you will, protestantism—the cup that cheers, possibly, but surely not inebriates—for the satisfaction that comes of all these is good while it lasts'.

In his Hellenistic campaign to free the sexual instinct, Ellis understandably complained that contemporary English authors were not free to discuss the sexual aspects of human experience. In his early **'A Note on Paul Bourget'** he compares the restricted subject-matter of contemporary English fiction unfavourably with the freer subject-matter of French and Russian fiction. 'We are not likely to see in England . . .', he says, 'any successful union of the French and English novel, because our great English novelists have not touched the facts of life with the same frankness and boldness, and their conception of normal life is unduly restricted'.

Ellis's earliest major literary article was a long and detailed survey of Thomas Hardy's novels which appeared in *The Westminster Review* for April 1883. In this he had particularly praised Hardy for the realistic way in which his heroines were depicted. For the heroines of conventional Victorian fiction, said Ellis, sexual passion is always vanquished by considerations of morality. Hardy's women, however, are 'creatures . . . made up of more or less untamed instincts for both love and admiration, who can never help some degree of response when the satisfaction of those instincts lies open to them'. (pp. 134-35)

Ellis's attack upon the evasiveness of Victorian fiction is pressed home in his essay on Zola, which also appeared in *The Savoy* and was later reprinted in ***Affirmations.*** 'All our great poets and novelists from Chaucer to Fielding', writes Ellis, 'wrote sincerely and heroically concerning the great facts of life'. In the 19th century, however, literary exploration has given way to commercial exploration, with the result that contemporary English literature has become parochial and infantile. . . . (p. 136)

Zola is praised by Ellis for having extended the range of literary language and the range of the novelist's subject-matter. Zola, he says, has restored to the novel its freedom to deal with the 'central functions of life' which is essential to great literature. He concedes that Zola has to some extent 'missed the restraint of well-balanced art' in his treatment of these functions, but defends him against charges of morbid and obsessive interest in these matters by claiming that there are far worse cases in literature. The authors who have been most obsessed by sex and excretion, he says, 'have been clerics, the conventional representatives of the Almighty'. In these respects, Zola has 'by no means come up with Father Rabelais and Dean Swift and the Rev. Laurence Sterne'. These remarks are almost certainly intended as a rejoinder to Max Nordau, who was currently encouraging the literary censorship which Ellis opposed by teaching the British public that 'M. Zola is affected by coprolalia to a very high degree', and that the fact of Zola's being 'a sexual psychopath is betrayed on every page of his novels'.

Hellenistic nostalgia for pagan simplicity during the 19th century goes hand in hand with disdain for industrialization and commercialism, and it is for these topics that Ellis reserves his sharpest and least ambiguous tone. In the introduction to ***The New Spirit*** he complains that 'The fanatical commercialism that has filled so much of our century made art impossible', but he takes comfort from the fact that England is losing her commercial supremacy. 'There will soon be no reason', he notes with satisfaction, 'why the coarse products of a great part of the earth should be sent all the way to a small northern country to be returned in a more or less ugly and adulterate manufactured condition'.

These attitudes are intensified and elaborated in ***Affirmations,*** which has as a dominant motif the ideal of 'fine living' from which men are barred by the material and mechanical 'triumphs' of the Victorian era. (pp. 136-37)

Ellis's critique of Victorian commercialism was continued and extended in ***The Nineteenth Century: A Dialogue in Utopia***. . . . Provoked by the frequently expressed view that the century just ended was 'the most wonderful century that up to then the world had seen', he expressed his disapproval more directly and polemically than hitherto.

It was commercialism, according to Ellis, which underlay both the follies of the 19th century and the self-deceptions by which it sought to conceal them. Commercialism was taken to be civilization itself. . . . (pp. 137-38)

The same commercialism which underlay imperialism, arrogant nationalism and military violence was also responsible for the spread of journalism, of mass-produced opinion, and consequently of the herd-instinct. . . . Commercialism, finally, was responsible for the spread of ugliness and the decay of literature, architecture, and the arts. . . . (p. 138)

The Nineteenth Century is in the form of a dialogue between two men who are looking back on Victorian society from a period in the remote future. This narrative technique produces an effect of distance which re-inforces the prevailing tone of coolly detached irony. Tone and technique together bespeak Ellis's evolutionary confidence that the future belongs to Hellenism, and that 19th-century sexual repression, literary censorship and commercialism will wither away.

'To-day', wrote Ellis in 1890, '. . . we stand . . . at the beginning of a new era . . .', and there is little doubt that he speaks here for most of his young contemporaries in the age of evolutionism. Yeats's account of the 'tragic generation' of the *fin-de-siècle* is extremely persuasive, but we should probably remember that its author was dedicated to the fashioning of public myths out of personal experiences. Large numbers of Ellis's contemporaries saw themselves not as a 'tragic generation' but as heralds of a new age which would sweep away their own 'effete and degenerating culture' as Ellis calls it in ***The New Spirit,*** their 'spiritually barren and exhausted age' as he calls it in ***Affirmations.***

Seen from the point of view of the history of literature and literary criticism, Ellis is undeniably a figure of major importance, especially as an innovator and an introducer of new ideas from the Continent. He wrote the first full-length introductions in English to the work of Nietzsche and Huysmans, edited the first collection of Ibsen's plays, and launched Bourget's 'theory of decadence' upon its English career. He also drew early attention to the work of such Russian authors as Turgenev, Gogol and Dostoievsky, and of such Scandinavian authors as Brandes and Björnson. Employing his own seminal ideas, together with those of Bourget and possibly Freud, he attempted to introduce the methods of psychology into literary criticism. Employing the ideas of Galton and Lombroso, he attempted to introduce the methods of anthropology. In the face of hysterical hostility he defended and discussed the work of authors like Zola, Hardy and Tolstoy, describing these men as moral and religious teachers at a time when Zola's English publisher had recently been prosecuted and when Nordau had persuaded many intelligent people that they were degenerates to a man.

Looked at more widely, from the point of view of the history of ideas, Ellis is interesting and important in two main ways. Firstly, he reflects the new world-view which had been brought about by evolutionary theories of history and by the sheer growth of scientific and historical information during the late 19th century. Ellis inhabits a conceptual world so different from that of Matthew Arnold, for example, that a 20th-century reader of ***The New Spirit*** will find it difficult to remember that the second series of Arnold's *Essays in Criticism* had been published no more than two years before it appeared.

Secondly, Ellis displays three important characteristics of late 19th-century and early 20th-century thinking about the future of mankind. The first is his keen interest in the factors necessary to produce a new race of men of genius. The second is his attempt to formulate a unified view of man and the universe to replace that of a Christianity regarded by many of his generation as no longer tenable. In making this attempt at a new synthesis, Ellis relies upon biological assumptions. 'We know at last', he writes in ***The New Spirit*** about mankind's future progress, 'that it must be among our chief ethical rules to see that we build the lofty structure of human society on the sure and simple foundations of man's organism'. For Ellis, man is an organism which possesses three basic instincts: the sexual instinct, the artistic instinct, and the instinct for religious mysticism. It is the satisfaction of these instincts which constitutes wholeness, according to Ellis, and his criticism is always directed against the things which in his view prevent the achievement of this wholeness.

The third important characteristic is his use of modern science and the latest literature to rehabilitate thoroughly traditional ideals, such as those of Hellenism. Like many of his contemporaries, Ellis looked not forwards but *backwards* in time to find an adequate image of the human perfection to which evolution was supposed to be leading.

As a pioneer in the application of psychology to literary criticism Ellis paved the way for I. A. Richards, C. K. Ogden, and those who applied Freud's theories to literature. As an apologist of 'the whole man alive', opposing both Manichaeism itself and Manichaean restrictions upon the subject-matter of literature, he stands at the beginning of a movement which finds its fullest expression in the work of D. H. Lawrence. As a critic of commercialized culture, in his rejection of 19th-century literature in favour of 18th-century literature, and in his preference for the classical over the romantic and decadent, he anticipated much that was to appear some years later in far more doctrinaire and aggressive forms in the literary and social criticism of the so-called 'reactionary' critics such as T. E. Hulme, Alfred Orage, and T. S. Eliot. (pp. 138-40)

Tom Gibbons, "The New Hellenism: Havelock Ellis As a Literary Critic," in Renaissance and Modern Studies, *Vol. XVII, 1973, pp. 122-40.*

PAUL ROBINSON (essay date 1973)

[*In the following excerpt, which originally appeared in the Winter 1973 issue of* Salmagundi, *Robinson discusses Ellis's modern ideas in the area of human sexuality, specifically focusing on the first two volumes of his* Studies in the Psychology of Sex: Sexual Inversion, *which discusses homosexuality, and* The Evolution of Modesty, the Phenomena of Sexual Periodicity, Auto-Erotism, *which discusses masturbation.*]

Sexual Inversion, the first volume of the ***Studies*** to appear, serves as an admirable introduction to Ellis's modernist convictions. Although cast in the form of a scientific treatise, the book was in essence an apology for homosexuality—a classic example of Ellis's lifelong effort to broaden the spectrum of acceptable sexual behavior. The choice of language, the analogies, the case histories, and the explicit theoretical structure of the book all served to create an impression of homosexuality as an innocuous departure from the sexual norm, and one not without its advantages for society. Thus while the book may not have been a completely satisfying analytic treatment of the subject, its moral stance was magnificently consistent.

The opening chapter of ***Sexual Inversion,*** though seemingly devoid of theoretical interest, found Ellis indulging in two characteristically modern techniques of sexual persuasion: the argument from animal behavior (used so effectively a half-century later by Alfred Kinsey) and the argument from cultural relativism. Ellis simply noted that homosexuality had been observed among several animal species, particularly among birds, and that it existed in nearly all known human societies. He also suggested that homosexual behavior was regarded with "considerable indifference" by most non-Western peoples, and that even within Europe the lower classes showed little repugnance to it—observations transparently intended to cast doubt on the notion that homosexuality was "unnatural."

At the expressly theoretical level Ellis made three principal contentions in ***Sexual Inversion.*** Undoubtedly the most important of these was his insistence on the congenital nature of inversion. Homosexuals, he argued, were born to their particular sexual orientation, and apparent cases of acquired inversion revealed, under careful scrutiny, merely the retarded emergence of an innate disposition. In support of this claim, Ellis cited the frequent occurrence of homosexuality within the same family, as well as the tendency of many inverts to manifest their sexual preferences very early in life, "without previous attraction to the opposite sex." (pp. 4-5)

By arguing that homosexuality was invariably congenital, Ellis intended to undermine any suggestion that inversion might be considered a vice, a form of behavior willfully indulged out of either boredom or sheer perversity. Moral censure and legal prohibition were thus out of the question. At the same time, the congenital theory also set Ellis at odds with the Freudians, and with the generally antisomatic tendencies of much early-twentieth-century psychology. With Freud the notion of acquired inversion obtained a new lease on life, now no longer in the overtly moralistic form preferred by nineteenth-century thinkers, but translated into the ethically neutral language of psychoanalysis. According to Freudian theory, homosexuality (or, more precisely, male homosexuality) originated in an unsuccessful resolution of the Oedipus complex: a boy became excessively attached to his mother, ultimately identified with her (rather than with his father), and then sought in male sexual objects substitute selves whom he might love as he had been loved by his mother. Ellis doubted that this psychic mechanism could be demonstrated in the histories of more than a few inverts, and in any case the Freudian analysis ignored the indisputably hereditary character of inversion, as well as the fact that many young homosexuals felt attracted to their own sex long before the Oedipal crisis came to a head. He was prepared to acknowledge that the homosexual boy was often passionately fond of his mother, but this attachment, he believed, was not so much Oedipal as it was a reflection of the "community of tastes" the inverted boy naturally shared with his mother. Needless to say, Ellis took a dim view of all psychoanalytic claims about curing homosexuality. In fact, it was precisely the exaggerated therapeutic ambitions of the Freudians that inspired his critique. His case histories had convinced him that inversion was a permanent state of affairs, and indeed that the vast majority of homosexuals had no desire to be "cured."

I have placed "cured" in quotes because Ellis himself did so. It was a major contention of ***Sexual Inversion***—second in importance only to Ellis's insistence on the congenital nature of inversion—that homosexuality could not properly be considered a disease. Here again Ellis was taking issue with Krafft-Ebing, who had characterized inversion (or at least congenital inversion) as "a functional sign of degeneration," implying thereby that it was but one manifestation of some more general process of deterioration. To be sure, Krafft-Ebing sometimes intended "degeneration" to carry the neutral evolutionary sense of "fallen away from the genus." For the most part, however, he was happy to surround homosexuality with an aura of sickness, and the terminology of "degeneration" served that purpose admirably.

Ellis, by way of contrast, struggled to devise a language that avoided any suggestion of pathology. Thus he preferred to call homosexuality an "abnormality"—emphasizing that he used the word in a purely statistical sense—or, more frequently, an "anomaly," a label that, to my ears at least, is nearly devoid of pejorative overtones. On other occasions he termed inversion a "sport" or variation. He also proposed an ingenious analogy, borrowed from John Addington Symonds, that was obviously meant to subvert the pathological conception of homosexuality. Inversion, he argued, ought to be compared to color-blindness. . . . No sooner had Ellis submitted this analogy than he withdrew it in favor of an even more generous one. Color-blindness still implied some sort of deficiency. He therefore suggested instead a comparison with "color-hearing," the ability, that is, to associate sounds with particular colors. In terms of this final analogy, inversion appeared less a defect than a special talent.

At stake in this question of pathology was the very serious matter of whether homosexuals could function effectively in their nonsexual capacities. The theory of degeneration distinctly implied that they couldn't. Ellis, however, not only denied this implication, but sought to reverse its effect by repeatedly associating inversion with artistic and intellectual excellence. No fewer than thirty pages of ***Sexual Inversion*** were devoted to homosexuals "of exceptional ability," and Ellis also reported that over half of his case studies revealed unusual "artistic aptitudes." His tactic in this instance may have been ill-advised—to me it betrays something of the patronizing attitude that feminists have come to call "pedestalism"—but his intentions were clearly consistent with the larger apologetic purposes of the book. Far from being degenerates, homosexuals turned out to be responsible for some of civilization's finest achievements. (pp. 5-7)

At the heart of ***Sexual Inversion*** stood Ellis's case histories—the biographies of thirty-three men, taking up, in the final edition, over one hundred pages of text. Most of these histories were presented in the first person, and they served Ellis's polemical objectives even more effectively than did the explicit theoretical apparatus of the book. If Ellis were not so transparently honest, one might suspect him of having manufactured these autobiographies expressly to confute the popular image of homosexuality. He conceded that his sample was hardly random. All his cases were British or American, and many of them were solicited from his literary and scientific acquaintances. Most important, almost none of the accounts was obtained because the individual in question had come into conflict with the law or had sought psychiatric help. One might say that just as Krafft-Ebing's or Freud's case histories exhibited a pathological bias, Ellis's histories were biased in the direction of health.

No reader of ***Sexual Inversion*** could possibly have considered Ellis's homosexuals degenerate—in Krafft-Ebing's sense of the term. For one thing, they wrote too well. Almost without exception their life histories were set forth in lucid, graceful prose. Most of these men also had pursued remarkably successful careers as physicians, teachers, men of letters, and artists. Characteristically they claimed to be of sound heredity and to enjoy general good health. They had little to say about their families, thereby eliminating even the possibility of a Freudian interpretation of their sexual orientation, and not uncommonly they themselves articulated Ellis's congenital explanation of homosexuality. Most of them also denied that they were in any obvious sense effeminate, and although Ellis professed to be unconvinced, he joined them in rejecting "the vulgar error which confuses the typical invert with the painted and petticoated creatures who appear in police-courts from time to time." Neither were these men misogynists. On the contrary, the majority of them claimed to value female companionship highly. (pp. 9-10)

Perhaps most important of all, the autobiographies revealed the deeply emotional character of the inverts' sexual attachments. Repeatedly these men insisted that their relationships were as intense, as gratifying, and even as durable as any heterosexual romance. Ellis did not accept this—or any other—claim of his correspondents uncritically. But his occasional dissent or qualification only lent an aura of judiciousness to his presentation, making the book all the more effective as a piece of sexual criticism.

Indeed, ***Sexual Inversion*** could be counted a complete polemical success were it not for Ellis's weak treatment of female homosexuality. The book dealt primarily with male inversion, and it is no doubt significant that even in matters of sexual deviation the masculine variant received the earliest and most elaborate examination. In ***Sexual Inversion*** women were confined to a single chapter, and although Ellis stated that homosexuality was just as common among women as men, he presented only six case histories. Even more bothersome than this disparity in the extent of his treatment was his apparent lack of interest in reconstructing the popular image of lesbianism. He was, for example, as emphatic about the mannishness of the typical female invert as he had been reserved about the effeminacy of the male invert. Ellis's views on women and female sexuality were in general ambiguous, and I think the unequal treatment meted out to male and female homosexuals reflected this larger difficulty in his thinking.

What Ellis had achieved for homosexuality in ***Sexual Inversion*** he sought to do for masturbation in ***Auto-Erotism,*** which appeared in 1899 as part of the second volume of the ***Studies in the Psychology of Sex.*** The essay effectively defused what had become the most cherished anxiety of Victorian sexual ideology: the belief that masturbation invariably led to serious illness, even to insanity. The *locus classicus* of this doctrine was William Acton's *Functions and Disorders of the Reproductive Organs,* an enormously influential work first published in 1857. (pp. 10-11)

In ***Auto-Erotism*** Ellis took direct issue with this doctrine, and, as in the case of ***Sexual Inversion,*** his argument symbolized a major shift in opinion among early-twentieth-century sexual authorities. There was, he insisted, simply no evidence linking masturbation with any serious mental or physical disorder. The supposition of such a connection was in fact incompatible with "the enormous prevalence of masturbation." Ellis even argued that masturbation could be a legitimate source of mental relaxation. And he solidified his case, as he had done with homosexuality, by citing evidence of masturbation among animals, as well as among "nearly every race of which we have any intimate knowledge."

More interesting than this direct assault on Victorian orthodoxy, and more revealing of Ellis's polemical subtlety, were his efforts to relate masturbation to a variety of activities and experiences that even nineteenth-century theorists considered relatively innocent. Thus he argued that masturbation was but one manifestation of a general psychosexual syndrome, for which he coined the term autoerotism. Under this rubric he included, alongside masturbation itself, such disparate phenomena as erotic dreams, daytime fantasies, narcissism, and hysteria, all of which, he suggested, involved "spontaneous sexual emotion generated in the absence of an external stimulus." The grouping was significant, as Ellis's definition implied, precisely because each of these phenomena, except, of course, masturbation, was more or less involuntary. Indeed, Ellis claimed that the "typical" manifestation of autoerotism was the occurrence of orgasm during sleep, and to separate masturbation from such an obviously spontaneous sexual experience was, in his mind, to create "a special and arbitrary subdivision of the field." Thus by means of an inference that might be called innocence by association, masturbation was transformed from a malignant vice into a benign inevitability. Moreover, throughout the essay Ellis seemed preoccupied with the purely conceptual matter of establishing the boundaries and internal contours of his new sexual category. This concern lent the argument a curiously abstract tone, which at once disguised and abetted Ellis's polemical intentions. Under closer scrutiny his category turns out to be rather flimsy. It does not represent a particularly useful or cogent grouping of psychosexual phenomena. Yet by creating a mood of dispassionate inquiry, even the essay's intellectual pretensions contributed to its critical effect.

Perhaps the most subtle feature of ***Auto-Erotism*** was Ellis's insinuation that autoerotic phenomena were especially common in women. Most of the examples he discussed involved female subjects, and he explicitly stated that adult masturbation was considerably more frequent in women than in men. In one sense this contention served to undermine the nineteenth-century belief that women lacked sexual feelings. But in a paradoxical fashion the argument also drew upon that very prejudice for its emotional effect. Masturbation was robbed of its viciousness when it turned out to be no less prevalent among supposedly chaste middle-aged ladies than among sex-crazed adolescent boys. (pp. 12-13)

I have begun by discussing Ellis's views on homosexuality and masturbation primarily because they offer an instructive introduction to his modernist tendencies. One cannot, however, do justice to Ellis as a theorist simply by rehearsing, in serial fashion, his opinions on the major sexual questions of the day. This might convey something of the breadth of his interests—and he obviously entertained the ambition to treat human sexuality in its totality—but it would fail to give an adequate impression of the conceptual unity that informed his survey. Admittedly, in any comparison with a major theoretical intelligence such as Freud, Ellis is apt to appear somewhat ramshackle and eclectic. His style of argument was rather leisurely, and his organizational principles often opaque. Still, his sexual writings were bound together by a number of grand themes, which, though lacking the sharp contours of Freud's unifying doctrines, clearly reflected his intention to examine human sexuality in a systematic, theoretical fashion.

Among the most important of these recurring themes were the notions of tumescence and detumescence. Understood literally, these terms described the vascular congestion and decongestion that accompany orgasm. But Ellis also employed the concepts to signify the entire process of sexual arousal and release. In this larger sense, tumescence designated the "accumulation" of sexual energy during arousal, and detumescence the "discharge" of that energy at the moment of climax. For Ellis this essential sexual process was comparable to any physical event in which energy was stored up and expended:

> Tumescence is the piling on of the fuel; detumescence is the leaping out of the devouring flame whence is lighted the torch of life to be handed from generation to generation. The whole process is . . . exactly analogous to that by which a pile is driven into the earth by the raising and then the letting go of a heavy weight which falls on the head of the pile. In tumescence the organism is slowly wound up and force accumulated; in the act of detumescence the accumulated force is let go and by its liberation the sperm-bearing instrument is driven home.

I need hardly point out that this conception of the sexual process bears a striking resemblance to Freud's libido theory. Indeed, it was no accident that of all Freud's doctrines, only his hypothesis of a libidinal economy claimed Ellis's unqualified enthusiasm. The sexual energy postulated by Ellis was, like Freud's libido, extremely malleable. It could assume apparently nonsexual guises (as in sublimation), and it could combine with, or itself be reinforced by, other forms of human energy—attributes of considerable theoretical significance. In effect, both Freud and Ellis treated human sexuality according to the model of a closed phenomenon in women was the clitoral erection, and Ellis implied that if women's sexual sensitivity were confined to the clitoris, their responses would probably exhibit the same direct, uncomplicated character found in men. But "behind" the clitoris was the "much more extensive mechanism" of the vagina and the womb, both of which demanded satisfaction. Ellis by no means accepted the Freudian doctrine that adult female sexuality was exclusively vaginal. In fact, he ridiculed the idea, suggesting it could have been conceived only by someone who lacked any direct knowledge of women's sexual experiences. But although the clitoris remained for him the chief focus of sexual pleasure in women, the involvement of the intricate and in a sense distant internal organs meant that arousal was more difficult and, above all, slower in the female than in the male. Here then was an important organic foundation of courtship.

Ellis also claimed that female sexuality was more massive and more diffuse than male sexuality. By this he meant simply that a larger portion of the female body participated in sexual arousal. Ellis was among the architects of the theory of erogenous (or erogenic) zones—the notion that certain parts of the body, notably its entrances and exits, function as special centers of sexual responsiveness. In its Freudian guise this theory was to become a standard component of modern sexual doctrine. Curiously, Ellis seemed to consider these erogenous zones uniquely feminine. Erotic sensitivity in men, he suggested, was limited to the penis, "the point at which, in the male body, all voluptuous sensation is concentrated, the only normal masculine center of sex." Indeed, he would not even allow that the scrotum might be sexually responsive. In women, by way of contrast, several nongenital areas, above all the breasts, participated in sexual excitement, and this greater diffusion of sexual sensitivity meant, once again, that arousal for the woman was a slower and more elaborate process than for the man.

In Ellis's mind it followed from the greater diffusion of female sexuality that sex necessarily figured more prominently in the psychology of women than in that of men. That is to say, he believed that women were, to a greater extent than men, sexual beings. "In a certain sense," he wrote, in a particularly unfortunate turn of phrase, "their brains are in their wombs." No doubt Ellis felt he was doing women a service in thus asserting their innate sexual expertise. He was in effect seeking to refute the Victorian doctrine of woman's asexuality by transforming her into the supreme representative of sex. Yet nothing reveals more dramatically the perils that the sexual revolution held in store for women: the revolutionaries threatened to convert them into sexual objects, creatures so preoccupied with their sexual needs as to be incapable of functioning in any other capacity.

Ellis also maintained that female sexuality was essentially passive. Men were propulsive, women receptive. In sexual relations the woman was the "instrument" from which the man "evoked" music. Here Ellis was in complete accord with his Victorian predecessors, a rather surprising state of affairs in view of his sharp break with nineteenth-century tradition on almost all other sexual matters. In Ellis's defense I should point out that he considered female passivity only apparent, intended, through a policy of studied delay, to increase sexual desire both in the woman herself and in her partner. He also acknowledged that neither the vagina nor the womb was an entirely inert sexual organ: during intercourse the vagina to a certain extent drew the penis into itself, and the muscular action of the womb had a similar effect on the semen. But these matters were only lightly touched on in the ***Studies,*** while the natural sexual passivity of women received constant reiteration.

In Ellis's opinion female passivity was so basic to the organization of human sexual life that it had given rise to a universal character trait among women: modesty. Modesty was thus for him no mere refinement of civilization, but an almost instinctual component of feminine psychology, "an inevitable by-product of . . . the naturally defensive attitude of the female." Not surprisingly, Ellis's insistence on the innate sexual passivity and modesty of women seriously prejudiced his thinking about their proper place in the larger order of things, and to a certain extent he must share with Freud intellectual responsibility for what Kate Millett has called the sexual counterrevolution.

In sum, courtship—the conscious pursuit of tumescence—was made necessary, in Ellis's view, by the complex, diffuse, and essentially passive nature of female sexuality. We may now consider Ellis's notion of the contents of courtship—those procedures that succeeded in bringing the female to tumescence in the face of her organic resistance. Needless to say, the responsibilities of courtship fell largely to the male. In sexual relations, as in life as a whole, Ellis seemed to imply, biology had assigned man the more creative role. To a certain extent the male fulfilled his responsibilities simply by following his instincts. Thus in keeping with traditional sexual opinion, Ellis held that the forcefulness of the male's pursuit would normally overcome the female's biological inhibitions. Her own modest reactions merely prolonged the chase until tumescence had been achieved, at which point she naturally surrendered herself to the man. Ellis even made the improbable claim that women were never attracted to men by their beauty, but only by their physical vigor, which alone promised the "primary quality of sexual energy which a woman demands of a man in the sexual embrace." As a sexual allurement beauty was an exclusively feminine attribute.

Ellis struck a more modern note when he argued that the male's natural aggressiveness ought to be tempered by a considerate attention to the woman's sexual needs. Since women were slow to arousal, it followed that sexual intercourse should be preceded by extensive foreplay, during which the man, while remaining the active agent, assumed an essentially gentle, coaxing attitude. Normal foreplay, Ellis suggested, might even include cunnilingus, a practice Krafft-Ebing had condemned as a masochistic perversion. He also recommended *coitus reservatus*—prolonged intercourse in which the man held back his own orgasm, thereby allowing the woman to achieve repeated climaxes. Ellis found it difficult to reconcile this new emphasis on considerateness with the traditional need for masculine aggression. He simply stated that the proper balance of both attitudes was essential to "the art of love."

We recognize in Ellis's plea for the sexual rights of women an important component of modern sexual consciousness. Ellis's long chapter on "The Art of Love" in the sixth volume of the ***Studies*** was in a sense the prototype for the countless how-to-do-it sexual manuals published over the last half-century. Moreover, this attempt to reorganize sexual relations in terms of the peculiarities of female sexuality represented an important historical advance. At the same time, we can regret that Ellis did not successfully eliminate the masculine bias of traditional sexual wisdom. There was an almost sinister note of manipulation in his exposition of the art of love, and it can be argued that the male's newfound solicitousness was in some ways even more demeaning to women than the simple neglect to which their sexuality had been subjected in the nineteenth century. (pp. 14-21)

Paul Robinson, "Havelock Ellis," in his The Modernization of Sex: Havelock Ellis, Alfred Kinsey, William Masters, and Virginia Johnson, *Harper & Row, Publishers, 1976, pp. 1-41.*

A.O.J. COCKSHUT (essay date 1977)

[In the following excerpt, originally published in 1977, Cockshut discusses the spiritual element behind Ellis's enthusiasm for sexual ideology.]

The most surprising, and the most significant, feature of Havelock Ellis's sexual theory is its intense religious earnestness. A man who spent thirty years in the composition of books of sexual case-histories might be expected to lose some of his early idealistic excitement. Ellis never did; he was one of those rare men who never became familiar with the everyday. He was the sort of man for whom every dawn and every sunset is as wonderful as if it were the first or the last he had ever seen. And so it was with sex. Ellis writes at times in the style of an imprisoned troubadour sighing for a momentary glimpse of a *princesse lontaine,* or like Rudel in Browning's *Rudel to the Lady of Tripoli*. But—and it is a fundamental and astonishing difference—he writes thus of the *function* of sex, not of an idealized person. The ordinary veneer of familiarity about the facts of the matter, which most people develop in adolescence or in early adult life, was never found in him. Aspects which become to most people trivial or shameful or simply uninteresting never became so to him. His first involuntary daytime emission he called 'natural and beautiful'. He was affected all his life by what he called 'urolagnia'—that is, he experienced sexual pleasure from urination, and intense sexual stimulation from the sight or the idea of a woman urinating. He wrote lyrically of this last as a subject for serious art, and was of the opinion that a masterpiece of Rembrandt, which originally had this subject, had been spoilt by overpainting due to false notions of decency. Here he reminds us for a moment of Sterne; but the contrast is more important than the similarity. There is nothing titillating in Ellis's treatment of this subject, so long as his account is read in the spirit in which it was written. Strange as it must seem to many, he finds something inspiring, almost holy here.

Ellis's chief complaint against the early Victorians (and previous ages too) was that they denied intense sexual sensation to women. Inclined usually to condemn wrong views gently, he was moved for once to something like indignation when he quoted earlier writers who said that it was a vile aspersion to ascribe sexual feelings to women, or maintained that an orgasm was, in a woman, a sign of a lascivious personality.

Ellis's deep respect for female sexuality was put to a test very much sharper than most men have to endure. His wife was an active and extremely passionate lesbian. Ellis took a vicarious emphatic joy:

> In what the special beauty of that night lay it was not for her to tell, or for me to ask, only to divine, but I know that she always recalled the anniversary of it as one of the sacred days of her life.

The word 'sacred' here is especially characteristic of this whole school of thought. How easy it would be to present the situation either in terms of broad farce or of morbid psychology. Ellis does not so much reject such interpretations as remain sublimely oblivious to them. Here, paradoxically, we can see an element of continuity. The early Victorians had idealized women's power of love, believing it to be far stronger and purer than men's. Ellis idealizes women for having more exquisite sexual sensations. The idea that men pay for their superior strength by a certain moral coarsening remains the same in these two very different guises.

It would seem that Ellis's tenderness about women was different from the normal male kind, springing as that does from an awareness of difference, of polarity. Ellis's tenderness was much more due to identification. He felt the woman in himself. Or rather, it might be truer to say that he felt both male and female sexuality as a wonderful, inspiring *continuum,* in which differences of gender were secondary. Hence his quite unusual degree of interest in his own body and its functions; hence also his power of empathy with the raptures of a lesbian wife.

Like many other seminal minds—and Ellis was perhaps more influential than any other Englishman has ever been in changing moral attitudes on sexual questions—he was suggestive rather than dogmatic and open to many different interpretations. His own sexual emotions were so unusual that if his influence had been confined to those capable of feeling just as he did, it would have been slight. Rather, his influence was pervasive in developing a general sympathy in the respectable public for *all* kinds of sexual abnormality and every misfortune consequent upon the weakness of the will to restrain impulse. There was only one proviso; all aberrations and all weaknesses must be such as to touch the heart.

Yeats gives the following most instructive account of the reception of the news that Oscar Wilde had been sent to prison for homosexual practices:

> 'Wilde will never lift his head again,' said the art critic, Gleeson White, 'for he has against him all men of infamous life.' When the verdict was announced the harlots in the street outside danced upon the pavement.

Plenty of evidence could be adduced to show that Yeats (and White) were substantially correct about public feeling. That is to say, many respectable men of the world, both bachelors and fathers of families, resorted to prostitutes. They felt themselves justified in regarding homosexuals with horror and contempt. Ellis, probably more than anyone else, was responsible for a gradual change in sentiment, so that resort to prostitutes, being a commercial transaction devoid of all respect and tenderness, would be regarded as more shameful than any sexual practice which could make any claim, however tenuous, to the name of love.

The dancing harlots and their clients would probably have justified their sense of moral superiority by some concept of 'natural' and 'unnatural'. A later generation, influenced by Ellis and others, might retort that homosexuality, too, was natural, in that it corresponded to some people's natural impulse. Prostitution, on the other hand, was unnatural, being a commercial exploitation, and being, above all, joyless. Homosexuality here is merely an illustration, a useful one because of the exceptional horror which it excited. It serves as a type of all sexual abnormalities capable of arousing tenderness. Ellis, himself not homosexual in the least, was yet influenced in all his theorizing by the fact that his urolagnia was a much rarer deviation from the accepted norm, and one that most people would have considered as strange (or perhaps repellent).

There remains the difficult question, what kind of religious feeling was it that issued in Ellis's genuine expression of awe, his pervading sense of the sacredness of sexual topics? Ellis seems to have been a 'nature mystic' of the non-religious kind. He was the kind of person who could lose the sense of himself and feel completely merged into a natural scene, as he describes in the part of his autobiography which deals with his time in Australia. From one point of view, Ellis was a revivalist of a very old religion, the religion of phallic worship, conceived as an expression of the deepest forces of nature.

But this is not the whole story. He is also fond of transferring Christian theological terms into his rhetoric of sexual joy. Nor is this entirely empty rhetoric. When he tells us of the bitterness and the glory of being married to a lesbian, he is very much in earnest when he speaks of the path of Calvary; and he goes on 'as all Christendom has testified, that path of Calvary is not the path of failure.' (pp. 143-46)

In all this, of course, Ellis is the forerunner of Lawrence, who makes an exactly similar application of the spiritual resources of Christian earnestness to the dark gods of the flesh. But there is also, as we shall see, a profound difference. For Ellis sex is polymorphous; the traditional sense of polarity between male and female blurred, almost lost. Lawrence restored and intensified it, and so regarded as perverse and soul-destroying many things that Ellis was prepared to tolerate. . . . What concerns us here is . . . the *cult* of Lawrence as a purveyor of sexual freedom. It is easy to show that those most enthusiastic in the cult are generally far from agreeing with what Lawrence actually said. The so-called 'permissive' sexual ethic of much post-war fiction tends to claim Lawrence as its standard-bearer, because of his great talents. Actually, that ethic is rather a conflation of some aspects of Lawrence (often minor and rather uncharacteristic ones) with the teachings of Grant Allen and Havelock Ellis. The fact that in some respects these two last preach incompatible doctrines, and that each is incompatible in some ways with Lawrence is seldom noticed. Grant Allen's cheerful hedonism, plus Ellis's tolerance of the unusual, added to the intense pseudo-religious earnestness of both Ellis and Lawrence—this is the mixture often presented to us in publishers' blurbs as the acme of modernity. In reality the ideas are all from sixty to ninety years old.

Or rather, what was new in these ideas was sixty to ninety years old. But much more than was realized, some parts of Ellis's teaching was very traditional. In part, of course, this was simply because, despite his dreamy prose style, he was in many ways a sensible man; and there are certain traditional insights which can never be discarded without a flight into unreality. But there was one very important respect in which Ellis did not either invent anything new or repeat traditional wisdom. He was more influenced than he knew by the very men of his father's or grandfather's generation against whom he supposed himself to be in rebellion. He thought and wrote of sex always with maximum earnestness. He did not allow much for the play of mood and fancy, and for the lewd, light-hearted aspects of love. Now it is arguable that the early Victorians whom, in this, he imitated were themselves aberrant from the traditional wisdom of the race. It is a hard saying for ordinary human nature, whether the subject is religion, politics, literature, sex or anything else, that *no* allowance must ever be made for play of mood, for recreation, for frivolity. He was thus responsible (in part and unwittingly) for a new kind of pharisaism based on a ponderous sexual seriousness. The 'holier than thou' attitude of the new scribes and pharisees of the dark gods has been a tiresome feature of the 'Lawrence' cult. And, as we have seen, the Lawrence cult has only a tenuous relation to what Lawrence wrote, and is derived, in essentials, from the doctrines of Ellis. (pp. 146-47)

A.O.J. Cockshut, "The Optimists," in his Man and Woman: A Study of Love and the Novel 1740-1940, *1977. Reprint by Oxford University Press, New York, 1978, pp. 136-60.**

JEFFREY WEEKS (essay date 1977)

[*In the following excerpt, Weeks summarizes Ellis's contribution as a pioneering reformer of the public attitude toward sex.*]

Ellis once advised Margaret Sanger to follow a middle road in challenging authority. It was a middle road that Ellis travelled in his advocacy of sex reform, and as a result many of his views have now become commonplace. Unlike his near contemporary Sigmund Freud, he left behind no clear theoretical heritage, no school of devoted followers, no sustained effort to found a new science of sexology as Freud attempted to found a science of psychoanalysis. The content of Ellis's major work, ***Studies in the Psychology of Sex,*** now seems empirically dated and theoretically weak compared to the imaginative flights of a Freud.

Nevertheless, an analysis of Ellis's work does reveal a great deal about the nature, strengths and weaknesses of the pathmakers in sexual frankness. For he attempted to sum up and give coherence to the various reforming attitudes that were in the air. In his writings we can see the effort needed to break out of the Victorian taboos; and the scars that the struggle left behind.

In the first place it is important to recognise Ellis's role as an *ideologist*. The purpose of his works was to change attitudes and to create a new view of the role of sex in individual lives and in society. He set out to rationalise sexual theory, and in doing so helped lay down the foundations of a 'liberal' ideology of sex. The essence of this was a greater toleration of sexual variations; a desire to relax the rigid moral code; and an emphasis on the 'joys of sex'. Its weakness was its inability to ask *why* societies have continued to control sexuality and persecute sexual minorities throughout the ages; and as a result its eventual absorption into capitalist value structures.

Secondly, and perhaps his most real and lasting achievement, he was a pioneer in bringing together and categorising information on the different types of sexual experience. Even this, to us apparently elementary task, shocked his contemporaries. It was, however, an essential preliminary to any rational study of sexuality. From it stemmed two central strands in his approach: the acceptance of the (now largely discredited) view of the biological roots of sexual variations—particularly homosexuality; and the use of evidence from other cultures to underline his argument that morals were not unchanging or unchangeable, but were in constant evolution. The ***Studies*** are a pot-pourri of details about the enormous variety of sexual experiences through different times and climes.

Thirdly, he recognised that the question of the social roles of the two sexes was of paramount importance in the new century, particularly because of the influence of the women's movement. He therefore attempted to suggest guidelines for more humane and equal sexual and social relations and behaviour. The particular form these guidelines took now seem among the most reactionary aspects of his work—particularly his view of woman's role—and reveal clearly the ways in which he was trapped within the stereotyped images that he inherited. And yet, for a long period, his preoccupations were shared by all progressive tendencies, including revolutionary socialists. Marxism in its great period rarely ventured to work out a materialist theory of sexuality, but relied on the most advanced bourgeois theories. This left a yawning gap in socialist notions of sexuality which has continued to this day, and which has allowed all sorts of backward ideas to rush in.

But to grasp fully Ellis's impact we must also look at the way he was viewed by his contemporaries. Margaret Sanger spoke of the tremendous sense of excitement she felt when she first encountered Ellis [see Additional Bibliography], and this seems to have been a common response. Conservative leaders of the women's movement shunned his overt support in case his reputation damaged the cause, while radicals such as Stella Browne, Emma Goldman and Margaret Sanger saw him as a giant who:

> beyond any other person, has been able to clarify the question of sex and free it from the smudginess connected with it from the beginning of Christianity, raise it from the dark cellar, set it on a higher plain.

Ellis provided a rationale for sex reform which, inadequate as it now appears, was a major achievement for his time. It is this which justifies placing Ellis as one of the pioneer sexual enlighteners of the twentieth century. (pp. 180-82)

Jeffrey Weeks, "Havelock Ellis and the Politics of Sex Reform," in his Socialism and the New Life: The Personal and Sexual Politics of Edward Carpenter and Havelock Ellis *by Sheila Rowbotham and Jeffrey Weeks, Pluto Press, 1977, pp. 139-86.*

VINCENT BROME (essay date 1979)

[*In the following excerpt from his biographical work* Havelock Ellis: Philosopher of Sex, *Brome offers a balanced assessment of Ellis as a psychologist, literary critic, and philosopher.*]

If it was characteristic of Havelock Ellis's creed that he reconciled opposing disciplines in the sweep of his vision, bringing science into mysticism and art into science, it never gave much satisfaction to rigorously analytical minds. Yet Ellis's language occasionally rose to those heights where it breaks through rational resistance, and a sense of communion with mystical realities momentarily defeats rational doubt. Ernest Jones remarked of ***Little Essays of Love and Virtue*** that it was 'a book to read and enjoy, not to criticise'. The quality of his spirit sometimes disarmed his worst critics.

Ellis developed that spirit of renaissance humanism which, first confined to re-interpretation of classical antiquities, grew deeper and richer as its boundaries extended. Like the renaissance humanists he pressed forward from man in society to the individual dominating society, but he went beyond that to the inner problems of man knowing himself. The romantic streak which ran through much of his thinking was re-affirmed by his scientific optimism but the new enlightenment of which he was clearly a part has only achieved partial realization. One classification always broke down with Ellis. There was an echo to every statement made about him.

Dr Kinsey pays frequent tribute to Ellis in his studies but rightly says, 'The monumental work of Havelock Ellis and of Freud . . . did not involve a general survey of persons . . .' without 'sexual problems which would lead them to professional sources for help. . . .'

But he remained a pioneer and it was pointless to complain that he lacked modern methods. In his day his approach was original enough, and similarities remained between his own work and Dr Kinsey's.

As a psychologist he had the scientific attitude but lacked the subtleties of the scientific method. He brilliantly charted a whole continent of sexual behaviour but did not sufficiently investigate motive. Freud not merely worked for years unravelling the tangled skeins of his patients' thoughts, conscious and unconscious; he saw that they could hopelessly deceive themselves, he took little at its face value and detected unconscious patterns far below the surface.

Ellis had all the evidence. He wrestled with it for years. He identified the widespread permeation of sex in many unexpected areas, he apprehended infantile sexuality, religious sexuality and the element of sexual sublimation in art; but his theories were vague. He could not convincingly explain what he found. Freud could and did. His insight was of a different order. As a psychologist Freud succeeded where Ellis failed, but Ellis's benign influence was—in Victorian England—more persuasive than Freud's. He brought to the problems of human relationships a compassion which not merely marked him out in the cold world of science, but won the sympathetic hearing of people hostile to his beliefs. His books were strewn with findings on many basic human problems, and he established a rationale for sex reform which was a major achievement in his time. He stands as the leading English pioneer in the modernization of sex, and the renovation of the relations between the sexes, but women's liberation has now entered new conceptual fields which he would find dubious. The feminist movement today regards Ellis's ***Sex in Relation to Society*** as very old-fashioned with its admission of monogamy and the family as the best *social* basis for relations between the sexes. As for his lofty protestations about love, they consider them extravagantly romantic. Women's liberation would also take exception to his biologically based role prescription in which man is dominant and the woman submissive. Characteristically, a woman's passivity had, in Ellis's credo, to be aroused by a man, and the idea that a woman could herself assume the role of the man and take the sexual initiative would be alien to him. True fulfilment in a woman meant having at least one child in her lifetime and the responsibilities of the family were social and not individual. Each sex was clearly differentiated for Havelock Ellis and in the perfectly balanced society each would fulfil the different biological drives of its own nature, opening the way to the good and just community. Modern feminists find much of this unacceptable and when Ellis spoke of pregnancy as a woman's destiny which lifts her 'above the level of ordinary humanity to become the casket of an inestimable jewel', he simply incites them to ribaldry. However, as Jeffrey Weeks has said in his study of Havelock Ellis: 'Ellis's views on marriage and motherhood found their realisation in the idea of family allowances, the state supporting the family in the interests of healthy childhood and social stability.' Moreover, in Western societies generally family patterns not only fulfil the implications of Ellis's much more traditional thinking, but the majority of women appear to sympathize with his outlook. (pp. 252-53)

As a mystic he did not undergo the austere discipline described by Aldous Huxley. There was no first, second and third stage of annihilation leading to the incandescent core of contemplative life. Equally, the spirit informing the Cloud of Unknowing was not his. At first sight, his was a form of mysticism open to anyone. It had much in common with pantheism and he was most lost at the lyrical heart of life when the beauties of nature—the sound of the sea from a cliff-top, a bank of flowers on a summer day—worked magic with his senses.

His was not Brahmanic pantheism nor Buddhistic nihilism, both of which, rejecting the unreality of the apparent world, had something approaching contempt for the human personality. Neither was it Neoplatonic. The assumption that reason is capable of mapping all phenomena, except that of God, which being beyond reason must be assigned to the realms of mysticism, did not appeal to him. He was not Neoplatonic, because Neoplatonism too scorned the world of the senses. Even Plotinus was ashamed of the prison of his body, disliked naming his parents and in contradiction to Ellis said that moments of ecstatic union were so rare that 'I myself have realised it but three times as yet. . . .'

The literature of mysticism is full of irritating terms like The One and the Many, the Self and Not Self, and the Absolute Union. Ellis made little play with such jargon but there were many sources which had something in common with his own outlook. Sufism amongst the ninth-century Mohammedans of Persia delighted in a natural pantheism, where mystic awareness of all things heightened the intensity of being alive.

His mysticism did not in fact completely fit anywhere. The creeds of Meister Eckhart, John of the Cross, Henry More or Boehme, did not correspond; his feet remained too firmly on the ground for such thinkers. Always the whole man, Ellis reconciled, without any marked sense of effort, materialism and mysticism, and it was the essence of his creed that one could not exist without the balance of the other.

In this way he achieved a common-sense mysticism peculiar to twentieth-century man. Certainly it offered to those who shared his temperament an escape from everyday life, but many amongst his disciples were incapable of sustaining the self-sufficiency which it demanded. Modern psychology might speak of substitute gratifications, but Ellis believed that his mysticism brought him nearer to what he regarded as the heart of living. He was too much of a scholar not to know that mysticism derived from the Greek—to shut the eyes—but he insisted that his eyes were fully open.

As a literary critic, ***The New Spirit, Affirmations*** and ***From Rousseau to Proust,*** contained some good criticism in that particular school inspired by Taine. It was essentially a sane, down-to-earth, school. Taine, in constant intercourse with men like Renan, Sainte-Beuve, Gaultier and Flaubert—all regarded highly by Ellis—set out to study man in one of his pathological crises. He loved to abstract and classify as Ellis did, and if his positivist philosophy was too despairing for Ellis, and his condemnation of mankind too wholesale, he had the same preoccupation with the study of man. Ellis—who had read Taine extensively—was influenced by him in his early and middle years, which led him to follow a similar approach to literary criticism in the ***New Spirit*** and ***Affirmations.*** Taine believed that each great writer was a product of his race, environment and time. Whereas history had once been a frame to criticism, criticism, in his work, tended to become the frame, each writer epitomizing a certain epoch. In just such a manner, Ellis explained the ***New Spirit*** through selected persons, and his ***Affirmations*** through Nietzsche, Casanova, Zola, Huysmans, and St Francis.

Taine combined the roles of artist, *litterateur,* scientist and philosopher, and perfected a style which delighted in bold, highly coloured themes. Ellis matched most of these elements, but his style was distinguished in a different way. His ***Essay on the Art of Writing*** was a salutary experience in a world of literary criticism fast retreating into places unintelligible to the average reader. He even brought science into literary criticism when he wrote ***The Colour Sense in Literature,*** analysing the literary significance of colour in the work of different poets; psychology was invoked to analyse Proust; ethnography grammatical usage.

He regarded Croce as the most instructive literary critic of the time and believed with him that 'there are no objective standards of judgment', that 'we cannot approach a work of art with our laws and categories.' We had to comprehend the artist's own values, and only then were we fit to pronounce on his work—a complete contradiction of the intentional fallacy of today.

If literary criticism, in Ellis's day, had not fully explored those psychological subtleties which distinguished Richards, *Principles of Literary Criticism,* and the schools represented by Eliot, Leavis and Lionel Trilling might consider his simplicities naïve, in a sense he was a pioneer of the psychological approach. But his criticism today would be regarded as *belles lettres.*

Amongst his idolaters there were many who spoke with reverence of his poetry. The impulse to song seems to have died in modern poetry, and so many academic niceties have revolutionized verbal music that, once again, Ellis's work would appear absurd beside that of T. S. Eliot or Ezra Pound. Following every precept of his own critical creed, even when judged within his own period, values and form, his talents are not best represented by the sonnets he wrote in his lifetime. His poetry is a private poetry in a sense very different from Eliot's meaning of the term. It does not easily survive publication.

As a philosopher he merged something of Spinoza, Herbert Spencer, Rousseau, Bergson and Jules de Gaultier with the little-known Castillian writer José Rodó. 'For Gaultier, the world is a spectacle', he wrote. 'It is only in Art that the solution of Life's problems can be found. Life is always immoral and unjust. It is Art alone which, rising above the categories of Morality, justifies the pains and griefs of Life. . . .' To see the world as beauty. . . . Could that be considered a philosophy?

It is clear that Ellis's philosophy did not fall into any category common to academic philosophy. It was not rationalist, positivist or analytical; terms like methodology would have irritated him, and the finer reaches of linguistic analysis remained for him, barren. Indeed, Ellis's philosophy, as with his religion, risked the charge that it was no philosophy at all. Plainly he invited this. He believed that every man who had reached that stage of development in which he enjoyed 'the philosophic emotion' would find 'his own philosophy. . . .'.

As unsophisticated a statement as ever encouraged donnish disdain. What followed was worse if one were a professor of philosophy. 'To be the serene spectator of the Absurdity of the world, to be at the same time the strenuous worker in the Rationalisation of the world—that is the function of the complete Man. But it remains a very difficult task, the supreme task in the Art of Living.'

In the last analysis Ellis's credo was best understood when personified in that type of human being which he considered ideal. But there a difficulty arose. Painfully creating around himself the contemplative life of the scholar, enriched by many friends and lovers, Ellis appeared to believe that his own capacities for love and aesthetic experience could be realized in large numbers of others. But Havelock Ellis was a rare human being. (pp. 253-56)

Vincent Brome, in his Havelock Ellis, Philosopher of Sex: A Biography, *Routledge & Kegan Paul, 1979, 271 p.*

PHYLLIS GROSSKURTH (essay date 1980)

[*In the following excerpt from her* Havelock Ellis: A Biography, *Grosskurth discusses Ellis's study of homosexuality,* Sexual Inversion. *In addition, she provides a perceptive comparison of Ellis and Sigmund Freud. For other comparisons of Freud's and Ellis's work, see the excerpts by Karl Menninger (1939), Mary M. Colum (1939), and Bernard DeVoto (1939).*]

Sexual Inversion was an unprecedented book. Never before had homosexuality been treated so soberly, so comprehensively, so sympathetically. To read it today is to read the voice of common sense and compassion; to read it then was, for the great majority, to be affronted by a deliberate incitement to vice of the most degrading kind.

Ellis's aim was to dispel myth, to puncture prejudice, and to present as factual a report of the real situation as possible. The first sentence of the book marks his consistent view of the subject: "Sexual inversion, as here understood, means sexual instinct turned by inborn constitutional abnormality towards persons of the same sex." Ellis was not the first to proclaim the organic nature of inversion, but he was the first person to write a book in English which treated homosexuality as neither a disease nor a crime. That such sexual proclivity is not determined by suggestion, accident, or historical conditioning is apparent, he argues, from the fact that it is widespread among animals and that there is abundant evidence of its prevalence among various nations at all periods of history. The incidence of relatives sharing the same propensities, Ellis also sees as firm evidence of the inherited character of inversion. . . . Most people regarded homosexuality (a word rejected by Ellis because it could cover experiences arising out of temporary circumstances) as manifestations of the criminal or the insane, but Ellis stresses that none of his cases has been charged with a misdemeanour (although many had contemplated suicide) nor are they degenerates, but are frequently found among the most cultivated members of the community. (p. 185)

The persuasiveness of his argument is based on his thirty-three case-histories. Credibility is created by the first-person narratives, but it would be simplistic to conclude—as Ellis does—that these people are emotionally healthy simply because of their own avowals. Unfortunately, no copy of the questionnaire he used has come to light, but as most of the histories cover certain aspects of temperament and experience, it is reasonable to make a fair guess as to what information was asked for: data about parents, siblings, and education; relatives who had been inverts; first sexual experience; masturbation; erotic dreams; preferred form of sexual activity; responses to opposite sex; avocations; favourite colour; ability to whistle; and attitude towards their anomaly. Some few of the subjects were known to Ellis personally, but most of them had been supplied by Symonds, Carpenter, and—the American cases Dr. J. G. Kiernan of Chicago. There was no attempt to do a sampling on a representative cross-section of different levels of society—most of them seemed to be members of the upper middle class—and Ellis appeared unaware of the limitations of his restricted selection. His theoretical assumption seemed to be that if a sufficient number of cases was amassed, the evidence would speak for itself. Nor is there any adequate statistical basis for his surmise that the incidence of homosexuality among the general population was between two and five per cent. The enigmatic "A correspondent" who is frequently cited is to be distrusted as an elliptical mode of persuasion. It was a hit-or-miss method, but it is questionable whether a more sophisticated mode of sampling such as Kinsey's (and even his far more ambitious method came under criticism for some of these same reasons) could have yielded the evidence Ellis was seeking—because he was seeking support for something he already believed: namely, the congenital nature of inversion and the fact that the invert was leading a furtive, often tragic existence because of the guilt imposed upon him by collective prejudice. Ellis's book, then, was fundamentally a polemic, a plea for greater tolerance, and the forces of current morality were quite right in recognizing the revolutionary nature of its proposals, all the more dangerous because they were couched in straightforward, simple language appropriate to the natural acceptance of what was currently regarded as a highly unnatural phenomenon. (pp. 186-87)

It is not happy reading. Dean Inge threw his volume into the fire [see excerpt above, 1939]. Marie Stopes described it as "like breathing a bag of soot; it made me feel choked and dirty for three months." Even Margaret Sanger was later to read these accounts and recoil in disgust from the long sequence of abnormal behaviour, but it is difficult to understand the lack of sympathetic understanding for those whose lives were crippled by remorse and undefined longing. Towards these unfortunate people Ellis's attitude strikes a reasonable balance: he describes, he explains, but he never launches into impassioned rhetoric or sentimentality. A note of romanticism does unfortunately creep in when he quotes from "Z" (Symonds) with his high-flown talk about altruistic "comradeship." I have a suspicion that the form which the sexuality of the cases assumes is perhaps manipulated slightly to give the impression of harmless and innocent caresses. Also, a reader could not fail to take note of the fact that many of these inverts did not practise masturbation, that nineteenth-century bugbear to which was attributed all manner of dire results.

Ellis was more indebted to the method and attitude of Krafft-Ebing's *Psychopathia Sexualis* than he acknowledged. He, too, addressed his book exclusively to doctors and lawyers. The information he required from his case-histories was much the same. Like Krafft-Ebing, Ellis was convinced of the hereditary basis of inversion; one's parents were one's fate, experience was simply a confirmation rather than an education of sexual patterning. The fundamental difference between them lay in Krafft Ebing's rather inconsistent view that inversion could and should be cured by hypnotism or suggestion. Above all, they differed on their attitude towards inverts. For Krafft-Ebing they were virtually pariahs, "step-children of nature," whereas Ellis was the first heterosexual investigator to grant them dignity as complete human beings.

His treatment of lesbianism is a good deal more uncertain, its tentative tone the inevitable result of insufficient evidence. He ventured the speculation that female inversion was probably far more common than in males but was not regarded as a social evil because men tended to view it with amused condescension. He presents only six case-histories; one of them—History XXXVI—obviously represents Edith, who has found that "repression leads to morbidity and hysteria. She has suffered much from neurasthenia at various periods, but under appropriate treatment it has slowly diminished. The inverted instinct is too deeply rooted to eradicate, but it is well under control." He finds significant differences between the male and the female invert. The male is depicted as resisting stereotypes, with a tendency perhaps to mild neurosis, yet by and large appearing and acting like most "normal" males; but the female emerges as someone distinctly nervy, boyish in appearance, with a deep voice, able to whistle, capable of deep-enduring attachments—someone, in fact, rather like Edith.

In the final edition of ***Sexual Inversion*** (1915) Ellis had to take into account later theories and investigations subsequent to the first edition. Magnus Hirschfeld's massively documented *Die Homosexualität* (1914) he acknowledges as the authority in its field. Hirschfeld, as a practising homosexual, was only too happy to find his cases supporting the invert's usual self-defence; and Ellis was grateful to have Hirschfeld's evidence to buttress his own case. Freud and the Freudians, however, presented an unwelcome and divisive strand in the movement towards a general acceptance by medical authorities of the congenital nature of inversion. In *Three Essays on the Theory of Sexuality* (1905) Freud enunciated his theory, subject to later refinements, of homosexuality as a manifestation of diverted sexual development. According to Freud, inverts have never recovered from an initial intense love for their mothers; and unable to move on to a re-directed love for the opposite sex, in a narcissistic turn-about seek another male to love as their mothers loved them. Ellis totally rejected the theory of the Oedipus complex. In his literal way, he took the nomenclature in an absolutely descriptive sense. He found it ludicrous to assign incestuous interpretations to the vague, unlocalized feelings of small children. While Ellis admits that inverts often have a rather over-developed attachment to their mothers, this he attributes to a shared community of tastes involving the sort of trust they cannot find in the outside world. While he will grant that the psychic mechanism may in some cases correspond to the process described by Freud, Ellis asserts categorically: "any theory of the etiology of homosexuality which leaves out of account the hereditary factor in inversion cannot be admitted." Ellis is particularly disturbed by the assumption held by some of Freud's followers that psychoanalysis could "cure" the invert; while he will concede that morbid fears, suspicions, and irritabilities might be modified (actually Freud's own position), he rejects utterly the attempt to re-direct an organic inborn temperament. . . . More important, Ellis ignores entirely the different evidence on which he and Freud based their conclusions. Ellis liked to think he was investigating the healthy, while Freud was confining himself to the pathological. But Ellis had no way of knowing the relative emotional health of his subjects. There was a large element of the naïve in his outlook, and he tended to accept the obvious, practical, British commonsensical appearance of things. A dream could be explained, for instance, by what one ate before retiring or the way one was lying; he never questioned the "why" of the particular content of a dream. Freud's theories were derived from intensive contact with the psyches of his patients, Ellis's from devised questionnaires.

Freud was later to object that Ellis avoided "decisions"—that is, committing himself to certain positions (perhaps the Freudian!) about the dynamics of the psyche. But in this book he spoke out more clearly, more directly, more responsibly than he was ever to do again. "When I review the cases I have brought forward," he concluded, "and the mental history of inverts I have known, I am inclined to say that if we can enable an invert to be healthy, self-restrained and self-respecting, we have often done better than to convert him into the mere feeble simulacrum of a normal man." From his pages the invert emerges as a mutation, an anomaly, a "sport," to be compared perhaps with those who possess colour-hearing, which, after all, may be regarded as a sort of talent, so that it is possible to assume that the invert is not only an acceptable member of society but a talented one. But if Ellis presumed to make such "decisions," it was to be expected that the forces of outraged convention would combine to enforce their demolition. (pp. 187-90)

Phyllis Grosskurth, in her Havelock Ellis: A Biography, *Alfred A. Knopf, 1980, 492 p.*

ADDITIONAL BIBLIOGRAPHY

Alcorn, John. "Butler: The New Spirit." In his *The Nature Novel from Hardy to Lawrence,* pp. 25-41. New York: Columbia University Press, 1977.*

Discusses Ellis's *The New Spirit* as belonging to the early twentieth-century's "naturist" literature, a form in which the critic also places works by Thomas Hardy and D. H. Lawrence. Alcorn states that in the naturist realm, "biology replaces theology as the source both of psychic health and moral authority."

Bernstein, Herman. "Havelock Ellis." In his *Celebrities of Our Time: Interviews,* pp. 136-42. New York: Joseph Lauren, 1924.

Interesting 1912 interview with Ellis. Ellis discusses the women's movement in England, the influence of Friedrich Nietzsche and Leo Tolstoy on life and literature, and offers a brief commentary on American literature.

Birth Control Review: Special Havelock Ellis Issue XI, No. 2 (February 1927): 37-62.

Appreciations of Ellis's work in the field of sex psychology and birth control by several doctors and critics. A brief statement by Sigmund Freud and comments by Houston Peterson and Isaac Goldberg are included.

Calder-Marshall, Arthur. *The Sage of Sex: A Life of Havelock Ellis.* New York: G. P. Putnam's Sons, 1959, 292 p.

Biography that offers a candid discussion of Ellis's own sexual activities and their relationship to his studies of human sexuality.

———. "Havelock Ellis and Company: 'Lewd, Scandalous, and Obscene'." *Encounter* XXXVII, No. 6 (December 1971): 8-23.

Biography and criticism. This essay is primarily concerned with the trial of George Bedborough, the distributor of Ellis's *Sexual Inversion,* who was indicted for distributing an obscene book.

Cerf, Bennett. In his *At Random: The Reminiscences of Bennett Cerf,* pp. 112-15. New York: Random House, 1977.*

Brief reminiscence of Cerf's meeting with Ellis in 1936.

Craig, Alec. "The Injustice of the Law." In his *The Banned Books of England,* pp. 123-49. London: George Allen & Unwin, 1937.*

Provides historical background and gives circumstances that led to the banning in England of Ellis's *Sexual Inversion.*

———. "Havelock Ellis." In his *Above All Liberties,* pp. 44-74. London: George Allen & Unwin, 1942.

General overview of Ellis's life and works.

Delisle, Françoise. *Friendship's Odyssey.* London: William Heinemann, 1946, 495 p.

Autobiography of Ellis's longtime companion Françoise Delisle. The second part of this work vividly and candidly chronicles Delisle's twenty-year relationship with Ellis.

Ernst, Morris L. Foreword to *Studies in the Psychology of Sex, Vol. I,* by Havelock Ellis, pp. v-viii. New York: Random House, 1936.

Discusses Ellis's social and scientific contributions in the field of human sexuality.

Fradkin, Betty McGinnis. "Havelock Ellis and Olive Schreiner's 'Gregory Rose'." *The Texas Quarterly* XXI, No. 3 (Autumn 1978): 145-53.

Speculates that Ellis had a latent desire to be a woman. Fradkin's original thesis is based on information drawn from the unpublished correspondence of Olive Schreiner and Ellis.

Gawsworth, John. Foreword to *From Marlowe to Shaw: The Studies, 1876-1936, in English Literature,* pp. 9-12. London: William and Norgate, 1950.

Explains how Gawsworth came to edit *From Marlowe to Shaw.* In 1938 Gawsworth was asked by Ellis, who was at the time seriously ill, to dispose of his personal library, at which time Gawsworth proposed that Ellis assemble several of his uncollected essays to form a companion piece to *From Rousseau to Proust.*

Gingrich, Arnold. "The Synthetic Art: An Exposition of the Aesthetic of Havelock Ellis." *The Open Court* XXXIX, No. 6 (June 1925): 338-49.

Examination of Ellis's conceptions of art and aesthetics by the founding editor of *Esquire.*

Green, H. M. "The Novel." In his *A History of Australian Literature: Pure and Applied, Vol. I,* pp. 648-76. Sydney: Angus and Robertson, 1961.*

Brief accolade for Ellis's only novel, *Kanga Creek: An Australian Idyll.*

Hogben, Lancelot. "Havelock Ellis." In his *Dangerous Thoughts,* pp. 181-93. New York: W. W. Norton & Co., 1940.

Criticism of Ellis's works from a sociological viewpoint.

Ishill, Joseph. Introduction to *The Unpublished Letters of Havelock Ellis to Joseph Ishill*, by Havelock Ellis, pp. xi-xxviii. Berkeley Heights, N.J.: Privately printed, 1954.

Critical survey of Ellis's works, written in 1929 by Ellis's friend.

Mencken, H. L. "A Nietzschean, a Swedenborgian, and Other Queer Fowl." *The Smart Set* XV, No. 2 (June 1913): 145-52.*

Discusses Ellis's essay collection *The Task of Social Hygiene*. Mencken focuses primarily on the essay "Immorality and the Law."

———. "Havelock Ellis." In his *The Bathtub Hoax, and Other Blasts and Bravos from the "Chicago Tribune,"* edited by Robert McHugh, pp. 145-50. New York: Alfred A. Knopf, 1958.

General appreciation of Ellis, written in 1926.

Peterson, Houston. *Havelock Ellis: Philosopher of Love*. Boston: Houghton Mifflin Co., 1928, 432 p.

Thorough biography up to 1928. Peterson's work has been called by Van Wyck Brooks "the first really adequate account we have had of the gracious being who has ripened so beautifully in the late autumn of his life."

Quennell, Peter. "Change Was in the Air—and He Helped to Put It There." *The New York Times Book Review* (22 March 1959): 7.

Review of John Stewart Collis's *Havelock Ellis: Artist of Life*. Quennell discusses Ellis's personal life and offers general criticism of his work.

Sanger, Margaret. "Havelock Ellis." In her *Margaret Sanger: An Autobiography*, pp. 133-41. New York: W. W. Norton, 1938.

Reminiscences by birth-control advocate Margaret Sanger, who recalls her first meeting with Ellis and the long friendship that developed between the two.

Schreiner, Olive. *The Letters of Olive Schreiner, 1876-1929*. Edited by S. C. Cronwright-Schreiner. Boston: Little, Brown, and Co., 1924, 410 p.*

Chronicles Schreiner's relationship with Ellis from its beginning in 1884 until her death in 1920.

Symonds, John Addington. Letter to Havelock Ellis. In his *The Letters of John Addington Symonds, Vol. III*, edited by Herbert M. Schueller and Robert L. Peters, pp. 458-59. Detroit: Wayne State University Press, 1969.

Letter written in 1890, praising Ellis's *The New Spirit*. Symonds collaborated with Ellis on an early edition of *Sexual Inversion*, but died before the work was completed. Worried that Symonds's name might be damaged by the publication of a work about homosexuality, his literary executor asked that Symonds's name be removed from the title page, and that all of his contributions to the work be deleted. Furthermore, to halt the distribution of the Symonds's version of *Sexual Inversion*, Symonds's estate purchased all the existing copies and had them destroyed. Ellis then rewrote a new edition of the work, which was published in 1897.

"A Havelock Ellis Anthology." *The Times Literary Supplement*, No. 1425 (23 May 1929): 414.

Review of *The Art of Life: Gleanings from the Works of Havelock Ellis*. This essay provides general criticism of Ellis's works and praises the collection under consideration.

Watkins, E. I. "Havelock Ellis: To the Unknown God." In his *Men and Tendencies*, pp. 111-24. 1937. Reprint. Freeport, N.Y.: Books for Libraries Press, 1968.

Lengthy examination of Ellis's non-religious ethic. Watkins believes that "Ellis has rejected not the true God but a more or less anthropomorphic and in any case finite conception of God falsely supposed to be the God of Christian theism."

F(rancis) Scott (Key) Fitzgerald

1896-1940

American novelist, short story writer, essayist, screenwriter, and dramatist.

The following entry presents criticism of Fitzgerald's novel *The Great Gatsby*. For a complete discussion of Fitzgerald's career, see *TCLC,* Volumes 1 and 6.

Courtesy of Prints and Photographs Division, Library of Congress

Considered the finest achievement of Fitzgerald's literary career, *The Great Gatsby* is widely recognized as a classic of American literature. Like most of his best-known works, Fitzgerald's masterwork examines the Jazz-Age generation's search for the elusive American dream of wealth and happiness and scrutinizes the consequences of that generation's adherence to false values. In *The Great Gatsby,* Fitzgerald employed a first-person narrator, Nick Carraway, to tell the story of Jay Gatsby, a farmer's son turned racketeer, whose ill-gotten wealth is acquired solely to gain acceptance into the sophisticated, moneyed world of the woman he loves, Daisy Fay Buchanan. Gatsby's romantic illusions about the power of money to buy respectability and the love of Daisy—the "golden girl" of his dreams—are skillfully and ironically interwoven with episodes that depict what Fitzgerald viewed as the callousness and moral irresponsibility of the affluent American society of the 1920s. Set amid the glamour and the raucousness of that decade, Gatsby's tragic quest and violent end foretell the collapse of an era and the onset of disillusionment with the American dream.

In 1923, after achieving popular and financial success with his first two novels, *This Side of Paradise* and *The Beautiful and Damned,* Fitzgerald wrote to his editor Maxwell E. Perkins and declared: "I want to write something new—something extraordinary and beautiful and simple and intricately patterned." The work, which he had already begun when he wrote Perkins, was *The Great Gatsby*. However, financial difficulties delayed the completion of Fitzgerald's new novel; his extravagant lifestyle, coupled with the miserable failure of his drama *The Vegetable; or, From President to Postman,* necessitated that he write himself out of debt through the quick sale of several magazine stories. Although the writing of *Gatsby* was interrupted by work on these short stories (which Fitzgerald referred to as "all trash"), many critics observe that the stories he wrote during this period—specifically "Winter Dreams," "The Sensible Thing," and "Absolution"—served to test and refine the themes and motifs he later used in *The Great Gatsby*. It was not until 1925, while living in France, that Fitzgerald finished his "intricately patterned" novel, a work which he hoped would make him financially solvent once and for all. Despite the fact that *The Great Gatsby* gained the respect of many prominent American writers, reviews of the novel were mixed and did not spur the sales needed to achieve popular or financial success. Some early critics faulted Fitzgerald for his inability to handle tragedy within the novel, while others believed that *The Great Gatsby* was merely a commercial vehicle written to appeal to Hollywood moviemakers. Fitzgerald himself attributed the novel's failure to what he considered its lack of an important female character, as well as its poor title. (*The Great Gatsby* was conceived as the book's title by Perkins. Fitzgerald reluctantly acquiesced to his editor's choice after arguing long and unsuccessfully for such titles as "Gold-Hatted Gatsby," "Among the Ash-Heaps and Millionaires," "Under the Red, White and Blue," and "Trimalchio in West Egg.") Unfortunately for Fitzgerald, the publication of *The Great Gatsby* marked the beginning of his decline in popularity. Afterward, though he continued to write short stories and screenplays, he wrote only two other novels: *Tender Is the Night,* a strong though technically flawed autobiographical work that was another commercial disappointment, and *The Last Tycoon,* an unfinished work that many critics believe would have approached the current literary status of *The Great Gatsby,* had it been completed.

At the time of his death in 1940, much of Fitzgerald's fiction, including *The Great Gatsby,* was forgotten or unread. However, a growing Fitzgerald revival, begun in the 1950s, has led to the publication of numerous editions of his novels and stories. Today, *The Great Gatsby* is the subject of many and diverse critical assessments and reappraisals that have elevated the novel to its current prominent position in American literature. Critics agree that one of the major reasons for *The Great Gatsby*'s high literary reputation is the work's finely crafted structure. Sustained by the use of a first-person narrator, the novel exhibits a controlled and detached point of view that distinguishes it from the extremely subjective style of Fitzgerald's earlier works. Many commentators maintain that this advanced narrative technique was greatly influenced by Joseph Conrad, whose works Fitzgerald had studied, and whose narrator in *Lord Jim* and *Heart of Darkness* is often compared to Nick Carraway. Similar to Conrad's narrator Marlow, Nick offers only a tentative, often ambiguous view of a complex world. In this respect, Nick's reliability as interpreter of the story's characters and action is one of the major points of contention among critics of *The Great Gatsby*. While some critics affirm R. W. Stallman's assessment that "the moral rectitude of Nick is but the mask of hypocrisy," others agree with Frederick J. Hoffman's comment that "Carraway was not only interested in the fundamental decencies . . . he was also firmly disposed to judge the people around him with reference to them." Although these opposing views regarding *Gatsby*'s narrator elicit different interpretations of the work, most critics observe that Fitzgerald made brilliant use of his narrator. In addition to the finely honed narrative structure of *The Great Gatsby*, the work relies on a concentrated prose style, a profound understanding of the characters, and an abundance of images and symbolic elements, all of which serve to form the very intricate patterns Fitzgerald had hoped to achieve.

Critics concur that *The Great Gatsby* rises above being a mere chronicle of a past American era, and most believe that the novel's continued popularity demonstrates modern America's fascination with the American dream. James E. Miller, Jr., has written that "although *The Great Gatsby* is deeply rooted in the 1920s, and at the same time appears to provide a commentary on American character and the American dream, it is still something more—something reaching out beyond its time and beyond its place. In short, the novel embodies and expresses the simple, basic human desire and yearning, universal in nature, to snatch something precious from the ceaseless flux of days and years and preserve it outside the ravages of time." It is this universality of the novel's themes that has allowed *The Great Gatsby* to survive and attain a place among the classics of American literature.

(See also *Contemporary Authors*, Vol. 110; *Dictionary of Literary Biography*, Vol. 4: *American Writers in Paris, 1920-1939;* Vol. 9: *American Novelists, 1910-1945; Dictionary of Literary Biography Yearbook: 1981; Dictionary of Literary Biography Documentary Series*, Vol. 1; and *Authors in the News*, Vol. 1.)

EDMUND WILSON (letter date 1925)

[*Wilson, considered America's foremost man of letters in the twentieth century, wrote widely on cultural, historical, and literary matters, authoring several seminal critical studies. He is often credited with bringing an international perspective to American letters through his widely read discussions of European literature. Perhaps Wilson's greatest contributions to American literature were his tireless promotion of writers of the 1920s, 1930s, and 1940s, and his essays introducing the best of modern literature to the general reader. Wilson and Fitzgerald were close friends from the time of their university days at Princeton. Fitzgerald considered his former college literary editor his "intellectual conscience," and through his first three novels and ill-fated drama he looked to Wilson for advice and discipline. In the following excerpt from a letter to Fitzgerald, Wilson comments on the "brilliance" of* The Great Gatsby *and notes the superiority of the novel's literary style to that of Fitzgerald's earlier works.*]

[***The Great Gatsby***] is undoubtedly in some ways the best thing you have done—the best planned, the best sustained, the best written. In fact, it amounts to a complete new departure in your work. The only bad feature of it is that the characters are mostly so unpleasant in themselves that the story becomes rather a bitter dose before one has finished with it. However, the fact that you are able to get away with it is the proof of its brilliance. It is full of all sorts of happy touches—in fact, all the touches are happy—there is not a hole in it anywhere. I congratulate you—you have succeeded here in doing most of the things that people have always scolded you for not doing. I wish, in your next, you would handle a more sympathetic theme. (Not that I don't admire Gatsby and see the point of the whole thing, but you will admit that it keeps us inside the hyena cage.) (p. 121)

I particularly enjoyed the man who takes the oculist's advertisement for the eyes of God. (p. 122)

Edmund Wilson, in a letter to F. Scott Fitzgerald on April 11, 1925, in his Letters on Literature and Politics: 1912-1972, *edited by Elena Wilson, Farrar, Straus and Giroux, 1977, pp. 121-22.*

F. SCOTT FITZGERALD (letter date 1925)

[*In the following excerpt from a letter to his friend and former schoolmate Edmund Wilson, Fitzgerald comments on the major flaw of* The Great Gatsby. *For further discussion of* Gatsby *by its author, see the excerpt dated (1934).*]

Thanks for your letter about the book. I was awfully happy that you liked it and that you approved of the design. The worst fault in it, I think is a BIG FAULT: I gave no account (and had no feeling about or knowledge of) the emotional relations between Gatsby and Daisy from the time of their reunion to the catastrophe. However the lack is so astutely concealed by the retrospect of Gatsby's past and by blankets of excellent prose that no one has noticed it—though everyone has felt the lack and called it by another name. Mencken said (in a most enthusiastic letter received today) that the only fault was that the central story was trivial and a sort of anecdote (that is because he has forgotten his admiration for Conrad and adjusted himself to the sprawling novel) and I felt that what he really missed was the lack of any emotional backbone at the very height of it.

Without making any invidious comparisons between Class A and Class C, if my novel is an anecdote, so is *The Brothers Karamazoff*. From one angle the latter could be reduced into a detective story. However the letters from you and Mencken have compensated me for the fact that of all the reviews, even the most enthusiastic, not one had the slightest idea what the book was about. . . . (p. 105)

F. Scott Fitzgerald, in a letter to Edmund Wilson in 1925, in Twentieth Century Interpretations of "The Great Gatsby": A Collection of Critical Essays, *edited by Ernest H. Lockridge, Prentice-Hall, Inc., 1968, pp. 105-06.*

H. L. MENCKEN (essay date 1925)

[*From the era of World War I until the early years of the Great Depression, Mencken was one of the most influential figures in American letters. His strongly individualistic, irreverent outlook on life and his vigorous, invective-charged writing style helped establish the iconoclastic spirit of the Jazz Age and significantly shaped the direction of American literature. As a social and literary critic—the roles for which he is best known—Mencken was the scourge of evangelical Christianity, public service organizations, literary censorship, boosterism, provincialism, democracy, all advocates of personal or social improvement, and every other facet of American life that he perceived as humbug. In his literary criticism, Mencken encouraged American writers to shun the anglophilic, moralistic bent of the nineteenth century and to practice realism, an artistic call-to-arms that is most fully developed in his essay* "Puritanism As a Literary Force," *one of the seminal essays of modern literary criticism. Mencken favorably reviewed Fitzgerald's novels and short story collections as they appeared during the 1920s, and published several of Fitzgerald's stories in* The Smart Set, *a literary magazine he coedited with George Jean Nathan from 1914 to 1923. In the following excerpt from a review published in the Baltimore* Evening Sun *in 1925, Mencken discusses the marked improvement of Fitzgerald's literary style in* The Great Gatsby, *yet calls the underlying plot a mere "glorified anecdote." This opinion had been expressed by Mencken several weeks before the composition of his* Evening Sun *review in a letter written to Fitzgerald, whose comments on Mencken's judgment appeared in turn, in a letter to Edmund Wilson (1925).*]

Scott Fitzgerald's new novel, ***The Great Gatsby,*** is in form no more than a glorified anecdote, and not too probable at that. The scene is the Long Island that hangs precariously on the edges of the New York city ash dumps—the Long Island of gaudy villas and bawdy house parties. The theme is the old one of a romantic and preposterous love—the ancient *fidelis ad urrum* motif reduced to a macabre humor. The principal personage is a bounder typical of those parts—a fellow who seems to know everyone and yet remains unknown to all—a young man with a great deal of mysterious money, the tastes of a movie actor and, under it all, the simple sentimentality of a somewhat sclerotic fat woman. (p. 89)

This story is obviously unimportant, and though, as I shall show, it has its place in the Fitzgerald canon, it is certainly not to be put on the same shelf, with, say, ***This Side of Paradise.*** What ails it, fundamentally, is the plain fact that it is simply a story—that Fitzgerald seems to be far more interested in maintaining its suspense than in getting under the skins of its people. It is not that they are false; it is that they are taken too much for granted. Only Gatsby himself genuinely lives and breathes. The rest are mere marionettes—often astonishingly lifelike, but nevertheless not quite alive.

What gives the story distinction is something quite different from the management of the action or the handling of the characters; it is the charm and beauty of the writing. In Fitzgerald's first days it seemed almost unimaginable that he could ever show such qualities. His writing, then, was extraordinarily slipshod—at times almost illiterate. He seemed to be devoid of any feeling for the color and savor of words. He could see people clearly and he could devise capital situations, but as writer qua writer he was apparently little more than a bright college boy. The critics of the Republic were not slow to discern the fact. They praised ***This Side of Paradise*** as a story, as a social document, but they were almost unanimous in denouncing it as a piece of writing.

It is vastly to Fitzgerald's credit that he appears to have taken their caveats seriously and pondered them to good effect. In ***The Great Gatsby*** the highly agreeable fruits of that pondering are visible. The story, for all its basic triviality, has a fine texture, a careful and brilliant finish. The obvious phrase is simply not in it. The sentences roll along smoothly, sparklingly, variously. There is evidence in every line of hard and intelligent effort. It is a quite new Fitzgerald who emerges from this little book and the qualities that he shows are dignified and solid. ***This Side of Paradise,*** after all, might have been merely a lucky accident. But ***The Great Gatsby,*** a far inferior story at bottom, is plainly the product of a sound and stable talent, conjured into being by hard work.

I make much of this improvement because it is of an order not often witnessed in American writers, and seldom indeed in those who start off with a popular success. The usual progression, indeed, is in the opposite direction. (pp. 90-1)

There is certainly no sign of petering out in Fitzgerald. After his first experimenting he plainly sat himself down calmly to consider his deficiencies. They were many and serious. He was, first of all, too facile. He could write entertainingly without giving thought to form and organization. He was, secondly, somewhat amateurish. The materials and methods of his craft, I venture, rather puzzled him. He used them ineptly. His books showed brilliancy in conception, but they were crude and even ignorant in detail. They suggested, only too often, the improvisations of a pianist playing furiously by ear but unable to read notes.

These are the defects that he has now got rid of. ***The Great Gatsby,*** I seem to recall, was announced a long while ago. It was probably several years on the stocks. It shows on every page the results of that laborious effort. . . . There are pages so artfully contrived that one can no more imagine improvising them than one can imagine improvising a fugue. They are full of little delicacies, charming turns of phrase, penetrating second thoughts. In other words, they are easy and excellent reading—which is what always comes out of hard writing.

Thus Fitzgerald, the stylist, arises to challenge Fitzgerald, the social historian, but I doubt that the latter ever quite succumbs to the former. The thing that chiefly interests the basic Fitzgerald is still the florid show of modern American life—and especially the devil's dance that goes on at the top. He is unconcerned about the sweatings and sufferings of the nether herd: what engrosses him is the high carnival of those who have too much money to spend and too much time for the spending of it. Their idiotic pursuit of sensation, their almost incredible stupidity and triviality, their glittering swinishness—these are the things that go into his notebook.

In ***The Great Gatsby,*** though he does not go below the surface, he depicts this rattle and hullabaloo with great gusto and, I believe, with sharp accuracy. The Long Island he sets before us is no fanciful Alsatia; it actually exists. More, it is worth any social historian's study, for its influence upon the rest of the country is immense and profound. What is vogue among the profiteers of Manhattan and their harlots today is imitated by the flappers of the Bible Belt country clubs weeks after next. The whole tone of American society, once so highly formalized and so suspicious of change, is now taken largely from frail ladies who were slinging hash a year ago.

Fitzgerald showed the end products of the new dispensation in ***This Side of Paradise.*** In ***The Beautiful and Damned*** he cut a bit lower. In ***The Great Gatsby*** he comes near the bottom. Social leader and jailbird, grand lady and kept woman, are here almost indistinguishable. We are in an atmosphere grown increasingly levantine. The Paris of the Second Empire pales to a sort of snobbish chautauqua; the New York of Ward McAllister becomes the scene of a convention of Gold Star Mothers. (pp. 91-2)

H. L. Mencken, "'The Great Gatsby'," in F. Scott Fitzgerald: The Man and His Work, *edited by Alfred Kazin, Macmillan/Collier, 1962, pp. 89-92.*

GERTRUDE STEIN (letter date 1925)

[*An American novelist, poet, critic, and dramatist, Stein has been described as the mother of modern literature. She was an outstanding force both as a daring experimentalist and as a patron of avant-garde artists and writers. Through her various linguistic experiments, she moved toward increasing abstraction in her work, mirroring the movement in the pictorial arts from impressionism to abstract representation. Her desire to reduce language and description to their essence created a fragmenting effect in her writing that foreshadowed the fragmentation of our modern era and the corresponding interest in the individual—the part instead of the whole. During the 1920s, Stein's Paris home became a center of intellectual stimulation for scores of writers, including Fitzgerald and Ernest Hemingway—American expatriates whom Stein called the "lost generation." In the following excerpt from a letter to Fitzgerald, Stein favorably assesses* The Great Gatsby. *Fitzgerald's dedicatory note, which Stein praises, reads: "Once Again to Zelda."*]

Here we are and have read your book [***The Great Gatsby***] and it is a good book. I like the melody of your dedication and it shows that you have a background of beauty and tenderness and that is a comfort. The next good thing is that you write naturally in sentences and that too is a comfort. You write naturally in sentences and one can read all of them and that among other things is a comfort. You are creating the contemporary world much as Thackeray did his in *Pendennis* and *Vanity Fair* and this isn't a bad compliment. You make a modern world and a modern orgy strangely enough it was never done until you did it in ***This Side of Paradise.*** My belief in ***This Side of Paradise*** was alright. This is as good a book and different and older and that is what one does, one does not get better but different and older and that is always a pleasure.

Gertrude Stein, in a letter to F. Scott Fitzgerald on May 22, 1925, in The Crack-Up *by F. Scott Fitzgerald, edited by Edmund Wilson, New Directions, 1945, p. 308.*

JOHN M. KENNY, JR. (essay date 1925)

[*In the following excerpt, Kenny harshly criticizes* The Great Gatsby, *suggesting that Fitzgerald wrote the novel not as an enduring literary work, but with the hope that it would be adapted and produced as a film.*]

Taken alone, ***The Great Gatsby*** is a mediocre novel. In the light of [Fitzgerald's] former books, it marks an important stepping-stone toward a literary excellence which Scott Fitzgerald ought some day to achieve.

The Great Gatsby wasn't great at all—just a sordid, cheap, little crook whose gawdy palace on the Sound with its Saturday night parties, his glittering motor cars, speed boats, and hydroplanes, and his tawdry friends would classify him as what is called, in the Broadway vernacular, "a butter and egg man." For Fitzgerald he provides a convenient, if hackneyed, background upon which to weave his tale. Throughout the first half of the book the author shadows his leading character in mystery, but when in the latter part he unfolds his life story we fail to find the brains, the cleverness, and the glamor that countless melodramatic writers have taught us to expect of these romantic crooks.

The other characters in the book are of flimsy material, and when the author sets a real warm human emotion in their frail bodies the strain is too great, and they are left a smoking sacrifice on the altar of Fitzgerald's development of character insight. One feels he might better have pictured the unnatural types one has been taught to expect from him.

It is not beyond probability that Mr. Fitzgerald may have had one eye cocked on the movie lots while writing this last novel. The movie type of wild Bacchanalian revel, with the drunken ladies in the swimming-pool and garden fêtes that just drip expensiveness, are done to perfection—and who knows but that they will offer some soulful Hollywood director a chance to display his art? But for a writer in whom there is the spark at least of real distinction to be so palpably under suspicion of catering to Hollywood is a grievous thing.

John M. Kenny, Jr., in a review of "The Great Gatsby," in Commonweal, *Vol. II, No. 4, June 3, 1925, p. 110.*

T. S. ELIOT (letter date 1925)

[*Perhaps the most influential poet and critic of the first half of the twentieth century, Eliot is closely identified with many of the qualities denoted by the term Modernism: experimentation, formal complexity, artistic and intellectual eclecticism, and a classicist view of the artist working at an emotional distance from his or her creation. He introduced a number of terms and concepts that strongly affected critical thought in his lifetime, among them the idea that poets must be conscious of the living tradition of literature in order for their work to have artistic and spiritual validity. In general, Eliot upheld values of traditionalism and discipline, and in 1928 he annexed Christian theology to his overall conservative world-view. Of his criticism, he stated: "It is a by-product of my private poetry-workshop: or a prolongation of the thinking that went into the formation of my verse." In the following excerpt, Eliot offers Fitzgerald his highest praise for* The Great Gatsby. *Although Eliot stated that he "should like to write more fully . . . about such a remarkable book," he apparently failed to do so.*]

The Great Gatsby with your charming and overpowering inscription arrived the very morning that I was leaving in some haste for a sea voyage advised by my doctor. I therefore left it behind and only read it on my return a few days ago. I have, however, now read it three times. I am not in the least influenced by your remark about myself when I say that it has interested and excited me more than any new novel I have seen, either English or American, for a number of years.

When I have time I should like to write to you more fully and tell you exactly why it seems to me such a remarkable book. In fact it seems to me to be the first step that American fiction has taken since Henry James. . . .

T. S. Eliot, in a letter to F. Scott Fitzgerald on December 31, 1925, in The Crack-Up *by F. Scott Fitzgerald, edited by Edmund Wilson, New Directions, 1945, p. 310.*

REBECCA WEST (essay date 1931)

[*West is considered one of the foremost English novelists and critics to write during the twentieth century. Born Cecily Isabel Fairfield, she began her career as an actress—taking the name Rebecca West from the emancipated heroine of Henrik Ibsen's drama* Rosmersholm*—and as a book reviewer for* The Freewoman. *Her early criticism was noted for its militantly feminist*

THE GREAT GATSBY

BY

F. SCOTT FITZGERALD

Then wear the gold hat, if that will move her;
If you can bounce high, bounce for her too,
Till she cry "Lover, gold-hatted, high-bouncing lover,
I must have you!"
—THOMAS PARKE D'INVILLIERS.

NEW YORK
CHARLES SCRIBNER'S SONS
1925

Title page of the first edition of F. Scott Fitzgerald's The Great Gatsby. *Copyright 1925 Charles Scribner's Sons. Copyright renewed 1953 Scott Fitzgerald Lanahan. Reprinted with the permission of Charles Scribner's Sons.*

stance and its reflection of West's Fabian socialist concerns. Her first novel, The Return of the Soldier *(1918), evidences a concern that entered into much of her later work: the psychology of the individual. West's literary criticism is noted for its wit, its aversion to cant, and its perceptiveness. Of her own work, West has commented: "I have always written in order to discover the truth for my own use, on the one hand, and on the other hand to earn money for myself and my family, and in this department of my work I hope I have honoured the truth I had already discovered. I have like most women written only a quarter of what I might have written, owing to my family responsibilities. I dislike heartily the literary philosophy and practice of my time, which I think has lagged behind in the past and has little relevance to the present, and it distresses me that so much contemporary work is dominated by the ideas (particularly the political and religious ideas) of the late eighteenth or nineteenth century, and those misunderstood." In the following excerpt from an essay written in 1929 (but slightly revised for inclusion in her book* Ending in Earnest*), West comments on the undeserved obscurity to which* The Great Gatsby *had been relegated by the late 1920s.*]

So many books are published nowadays that works deserving of a considerable measure of survival are swamped almost immediately and sink into the region of the forgotten. It shocked me to see that when Arnold Rothstein was shot and the newspapers were publishing all the information about him they could find, not one journalist mentioned that he had obviously served Mr. Scott Fitzgerald as model for Meyer Wolfsheim in ***The Great Gatsby***. Yet ***The Great Gatsby*** was surely a remarkable novel. For one thing it gave a superbly imaginative vision of the gaunt outskirts of New York, where the same force that makes the city sends up sporadic buildings, but does not form them or the life they house into civilized patterns as it does in the city. The prodigiousness of the garage proprietor and his wife, and their complete irrelevance to anything but violence, linger in my mind as vividly as when I read it; and so does the damnation of Daisy and her husband and her friends when they drift into this world of violence because they are incapable of doing anything in their own. This novel has not been superseded in the common mind by better books: merely by other books. (pp. 1-2)

Rebecca West, "Rescued from Excess," in her Ending in Earnest: A Literary Log, *Doubleday, Doran & Company, Inc., 1931, pp. 1-5.**

F. SCOTT FITZGERALD (essay date 1934)

[*In the following excerpt from his introduction to the 1934 edition of* The Great Gatsby, *Fitzgerald discusses early criticism of the work and assesses* Gatsby *as an "honest book."*]

I'd like to communicate to such of them who read [***The Great Gatsby***] a healthy cynicism toward contemporary reviews. Without undue vanity one can permit oneself a suit of chain mail in any profession. Your pride is all you have, and if you let it be tampered with by a man who has a dozen prides to tamper with before lunch, you are promising yourself a lot of disappointments that a hard-boiled professional has learned to spare himself. (pp. 155-56)

[***The Great Gatsby***] is a case in point. Because the pages weren't loaded with big names of big things and the subject not concerned with farmers (who were the heroes of the moment), there was easy judgment exercised that had nothing to do with criticism but was simply an attempt on the part of men who had few chances of self-expression to express themselves. How anyone could take up the responsibility of being a novelist without a sharp and concise attitude about life is a puzzle to me. How a critic could assume a point of view which included twelve variant aspects of the social scene in a few hours seems something too dinosaurean to loom over the awful loneliness of a young author.

To circle nearer to this book, one woman, who could hardly have written a coherent letter in English, described it as a book that one read only as one goes to the movies around the corner. That type of criticism is what a lot of young writers are being greeted with, instead of any appreciation of the world of imagination in which they (the writers) have been trying, with greater or lesser success, to live—the world that Mencken made stable in the days when he was watching over us.

Now that this book is being reissued, the author would like to say that never before did one try to keep his artistic conscience as pure as during the ten months put into doing it. Reading it over one can see how it could have been improved—yet without feeling guilty of any discrepancy from the truth, as far as I saw it; truth or rather the *equivalent* of the truth, the attempt at honesty of imagination. I had just reread Conrad's preface to *The Nigger*, and I had recently been kidded half haywire by critics who felt that my material was such as to preclude all dealing with mature persons in a mature world. But, my God! it was my material, and it was all I had to deal with.

What I cut out of it both physically and emotionally would make another novel!

I think it is an honest book, that is to say, that one used none of one's virtuosity to get an effect, and, to boast again, one soft-pedalled the emtoinal side to avoid the tears leaking from the socket of the left eye, or the large false face peering around the corner of a character's head.

If there is a clear conscience, a book can survive—at least in one's feelings about it. On the contrary, if one has a guilty conscience, one reads what one wants to hear out of reviews. In addition, if one is young and willing to learn, almost all reviews have a value, even the ones that seem unfair. (pp. 156-57)

F. Scott Fitzgerald, "Introduction to 'The Great Gatsby'," in F. Scott Fitzgerald: In His Own Time, a Miscellany, *edited by Matthew J. Bruccoli and Jackson R. Bryer, The Kent State University Press, 1971, pp. 155-57.*

ALFRED KAZIN (essay date 1942)

[A highly respected American literary critic, Kazin is best known for his essay collections The Inmost Leaf *(1955) and* Contemporaries *(1962), and particularly for* On Native Grounds *(1942), a study of American prose writing since the era of William Dean Howells. Having studied the works of "the critics who were the best writers—from Sainte-Beuve and Matthew Arnold to Edmund Wilson and Van Wyck Brooks" as an aid to his own critical understanding, Kazin has found that "criticism focussed many—if by no means all—of my own urges as a writer: to show literature as a deed in human history, and to find in each writer the uniqueness of the gift, of the essential vision, through which I hoped to penetrate into the mystery and sacredness of the individual soul." In the following excerpt, Kazin states that it was Fitzgerald's tremendous understanding of the character Gatsby that enabled him to depict so skillfully his tragedy and, even more consequentially, the illusory nature of the American dream.]*

Fitzgerald always saw life as glamour, even though he could pierce that glamour to write one of the most moving of American tragedies in ***The Great Gatsby.*** Something of a child always, with a child's sudden and unexpected wisdom, he could play with the subtle agonies of the leisure class as with a brilliant toy; and the glamour always remained there, even when it was touched with death. In one sense, as a magazine writer once put it, his books were "prose movies," and nothing was more characteristic of his mind than his final obsession with Hollywood. In the same way much of his writing always hovered on the verge of fantasy and shimmered with all the colors of the world. Just as the world swam through his senses without being defined by him, so he could catch all its lights and tones in his prismatic style without having to understand them too consciously. What saved his style from extravagance was Fitzgerald's special grace, his pride in his craft; but it was the style of a man profoundly absorbed in the romance of glamour, the style of a craftsman for whom life was a fairy world to the end.

To understand this absorption on Fitzgerald's part is to understand the achievement of ***The Great Gatsby,*** the work by which his name will always live. In most of his other work he merely gave shallow reports on the pleasures and self-doubts of his class, glittered with its glitter. He tended to think of his art as a well-oiled machine, and he trusted to luck. Rather like Stephen Crane, whom he so much resembled in spirit, the only thing he could be sure of was his special gift, his way of transfusing everything with words, the consciousness of craft; and like Crane he made it serve for knowledge. But like Crane in another respect, he was one of those writers who make their work out of a conflict that would paralyze others—out of their tragic moodiness, their troubled, intuitive, and curiously half-conscious penetration of the things before them. And it is this moodiness at the pitch of genius that lights up ***The Great Gatsby.*** For Fitzgerald was supremely a part of the world he there described, weary of it but not removed from it, and his achievement was of a kind possible only to one who so belonged to it. No revolutionary writer could have written it, or even hinted at its inexpressible poignance; no one, perhaps, who was even too consciously skeptical of the wealth and power Jay Gatsby thought would make him happy. But for Fitzgerald the tragedy unfolded there, the tragedy that has become for so many one of the great revelations of what it has meant to be an American at all, was possible only because it was so profound a burst of self-understanding.

To have approached Gatsby from the outside would have meant a sacrifice of Gatsby himself—a knowledge of everything in Gatsby's world save Gatsby. But the tragedy here is pure confession, a supplication complete in the human note it strikes. Fitzgerald could sound the depths of Gatsby's life because he himself could not conceive any other. Out of his own weariness and fascination with damnation he caught Gatsby's damnation, caught it as only someone so profoundly attentive to Gatsby's dream could have pierced to the self-lie behind it. The book has no real scale; it does not rest on any commanding vision, nor is it in any sense a major tragedy. But it is a great flooding moment, a moment's intimation and penetration; and as Gatsby's disillusion becomes felt at the end it strikes like a chime through the mind. It was as if Fitzgerald, the playboy moving with increasing despair through this tinsel world of Gatsby's, had reached that perfect moment, before the break of darkness and death, when the mind does really and absolutely know itself—a moment when only those who have lived by Gatsby's great illusion, lived by the tinsel and the glamour, can feel the terrible force of self-betrayal. This was the playboy's rare apotheosis, and one all the more moving precisely because all of Gatsby's life was summed up in it, precisely because his decline and death gave a meaning to his life that it had not in itself possessed.

Here was the chagrin, the waste of the American success story in the twenties: here, in a story that was a moment's revelation. Yet think, Fitzgerald seems to say to us, of how little Gatsby wanted at bottom—not to understand society, but to ape it; not to compel the world, but to live in it. His own dream of wealth meant nothing in itself; he merely wanted to buy back the happiness he had lost—Daisy, now the rich man's wife—when he had gone away to war. So the great Gatsby house at West Egg glittered with all the lights of the twenties, and there were always parties, and always Gatsby's supplicating hand, reaching out to make out of glamour what he had lost by the cruelty of chance. (pp. 320-22)

Alfred Kazin, "Into the Thirties: All the Lost Generations," in his On Native Grounds: An Interpretation of Modern American Prose Literature, *Reynal & Hitchcock, 1942, pp. 312-62.**

WILLIAM TROY (essay date 1945)

[In the following excerpt, Troy commends The Great Gatsby *for Fitzgerald's skillful employment of a narrator who is a spectator*

to the action discussed in the novel, a technical device similarly used in works by Joseph Conrad and Henry James. He further indicates that Gatsby *is essentially the story of the narrator's moral development from "deluded youth to maturity."*]

Not until ***The Great Gatsby*** did Fitzgerald hit upon something like Mr. Eliot's "objective correlative" for the intermingled feeling of personal insufficiency and disillusionment with the world out of which he had unsuccessfully tried to write a novel.

Here is a remarkable instance of the manner in which adoption of a special form or technique can profoundly modify and define a writer's whole attitude toward his world. In the earlier books author and hero tended to melt into one because there was no internal principle of differentiation by which they might be separated; they respired in the same climate, emotional and moral; they were tarred with the same brush. But in ***Gatsby*** is achieved a dissociation, by which Fitzgerald was able to isolate one part of himself, the spectatorial or aesthetic, and also the more intelligent and responsible, in the person of the ordinary but quite sensible narrator, from another part of himself, the dream-ridden romantic adolescent from St. Paul and Princeton, in the person of the legendary Jay Gatsby. It is this which makes the latter one of the few truly mythological creations in our recent literature—for what is mythology but this same process of projected wish-fulfillment carried out on a larger scale and by the whole consciousness of a race? Indeed, before we are quite through with him, Gatsby becomes much more than a mere exorcizing of whatever false elements of the American dream Fitzgerald felt within himself: he becomes a symbol of America itself, dedicated to "the service of a vast, vulgar and meretricious beauty."

Not mythology, however, but a technical device which had been brought to high development by James and Conrad before him, made this dissociation possible for Fitzgerald. The device of the intelligent but sympathetic observer situated at the center of the tale, as James never ceases to demonstrate in the Prefaces, makes for some of the most priceless values in fiction—economy, suspense, intensity. And these values ***The Great Gatsby*** possesses to a rare degree. But the same device imposes on the novelist the necessity of tracing through in the observer or narrator himself some sort of growth in general moral perception, which will constitute in effect *his* story. Here, for example, insofar as the book is Gatsby's story it is a story of failure—the prolongation of the adolescent incapacity to distinguish between dream and reality, between the terms demanded of life and the terms offered. But insofar as it is the narrator's story it is a successful transcendence of a particularly bitter and harrowing set of experiences, localized in the sinister, distorted, El Greco-like Long Island atmosphere of the later 'Twenties, into a world of restored sanity and calm, symbolized by the bracing winter nights of the Middle Western prairies. . . . By reason of its enforced perspective the book takes on the pattern and the meaning of a Grail-romance—or of the initiation ritual on which it is based. Perhaps this will seem a far-fetched suggestion to make about a work so obviously modern in every respect; and it is unlikely that Fitzgerald had any such model in mind. But like *Billy Budd, The Red Badge of Courage,* or *A Lost Lady*—to mention only a few American stories of similar length with which it may be compared—it is a record of the strenuous passage from deluded youth to maturity. (pp. 56-8)

William Troy, "Scott Fitzgerald—The Authority of Failure," in Accent, *Vol. 6, No. 1, Autumn, 1945, pp. 56-60.*

FREDERICK J. HOFFMAN (essay date 1951)

[*In the following excerpt, Hoffman maintains that it is Nick Carraway, the narrator of* The Great Gatsby, *who makes the story a success by providing the reader with a moral base from which to judge characters and their actions. He also contends that the work was the culmination of Fitzgerald's literary development, and particularly praises Fitzgerald's technical expertise in narration, symbolism, and imagery. For further discussion of the narrator's role in* The Great Gatsby, *see the excerpts by R. W. Stallman (1955), David O'Rourke (1982), and Colin S. Cass (1983).*]

The Great Gatsby . . . is F. Scott Fitzgerald's artistic center: to it all of the promise of his earlier fiction leads; to it the later work was always to be referred—by critics and by Fitzgerald himself, as the "line," the core of his achievement and art. Fitzgerald had succeeded in that novel against great odds; he had taken hold of materials that in their very richness might have defeated a score of more ambitious but less capable artists. He had, in short, brought into clear focus all of the preoccupations and experiences less capably treated in his earlier novels; and he never treated them so well again. (p. 120)

The time Fitzgerald spent in the writing of ***The Great Gatsby*** was also devoted to a careful examination of his weaknesses and a consolidation of whatever formal gains he had made since the beginning. He had, as he said, not only to find the most suitable approach to his materials but also to justify these materials to himself. . . . (p. 123)

One of his happiest decisions was to present ***The Great Gatsby*** through the mind and eye of a narrator only partially committed to participating in and judging its world. Nick Carraway is a key to the novel's considerable success. Carraway was not only interested in the fundamental decencies ("I am one of the few honest people that I have ever known."); he was also firmly disposed to judge the people around him with reference to them. It is important also that Carraway should have come from the Midwest—both the geographical and the moral Midwest. For Saint Paul had been a point of moral return for Fitzgerald from the beginning of his adult career; the young men and women of many of his short stories pass through Chicago—almost always ignorant of it, whether it be Dreiser's Chicago or any other's—on "the way back." Carraway had decided not to return after World War I, because the Midwest "now seemed like the ragged edge of the universe," but he brought his reserve and his country suspicions to the bond business and to the "small eyesore" of a house at West Egg. Everything that Carraway had was small-scale and unpretentious: his house "squeezed between two huge places that rented for twelve or fifteen thousand a season," his car, his cook who "muttered Finnish wisdom to herself" over the stove, his mind. The effect of all this upon the narrative is to reduce its materials to scale, and to make its frightening confusion and litter comprehensible and measurable.

It is in this way that we learn to know the almost fabulous Gatsby, with the full and honest advantage of Carraway's reductive and orderly judgment. What Edith Wharton had said of Gatsby is true [see *TCLC* Vol. 6]: Gatsby is not given in abundant and exhaustive detail, but continuously evoked and suggested, with a remarkable economy of effect which is a tribute to Carraway's tidy mind and Fitzgerald's sense of form. Gatsby needs just that sort of gradual and speculative construction; as his person and his mind slowly come into our attention, it is with Carraway's anxious concern over the truth of him that we receive him. What is at the beginning a grotesque and shabbily ostentatious world is thus continuously being reduced to the scale of observation entrusted to Fitzgerald's narrator.

Beyond that, and to enforce it, there is the symbolic organization given the novel's detail. Here again, the great progress made in the development of Fitzgerald's art is obvious. The Valley of Ashes which literally intervenes between Manhattan and the "two Eggs"; the symptomatically brooding eyes of Doctor T. J. Eckleburg, the valley's tutelary deity; the green light at the end of the Buchanan dock; the El Greco scene near the close of the novel; a Midwesterner's self-consciously distorted image of his despair over the amoral callousness of the world of Gatsby's parties—these are a major symbolic means of bringing chaos within the scope of an ordered view. They might have seemed only factitiously effective were it not that they are accompanied throughout by a most skillful power of evocation. Through it a few details are made to serve a large purpose—as in [the] description of the apartment where Tom Buchanan keeps his mistress on their trips to New York. In its portrayal of vulgar and crowded taste reside implications of the violence to come. . . . (pp. 123-25)

Similarly, in sharp, brief images, Fitzgerald achieves the *multum in parvo* effect of great fictional art; Wolfsheim "began to eat with ferocious delicacy"; the Buchanans "drifted here and there unrestfully wherever people played polo and were rich together"; Gatsby's cream-colored car was "bright with nickel, swollen here and there in its monstrous length with triumphant hat-boxes and supper-boxes and tool-boxes, and terraced with a labyrinth of windshields that mirrored a dozen suns"; the grateful surprise of "Owl-Eyes" in Gatsby's library over the fact that the books were real served to increase his admiration for his host: "The fella's a regular Belasco. It's a triumph. What thoroughness! What realism! Knew when to stop, too—didn't cut the pages. . . ."

As we are led to Gatsby through the mind and moral sense of Carraway, so we are asked to view his death as Carraway has viewed it. The world of Gatsby's West Egg estate has collapsed as soon as there is any risk of its being challenged by the real world. . . . Nick Carraway is left, not only to see to Gatsby's decent burial but to make something of his strange story. Coming back for one last time, before his return to "the bored, sprawling, swollen towns beyond the Ohio," he takes up the romantic illusion where Gatsby's death has left it, and tries to bring away from West Egg a final reconstruction of its meaning. He has not only fully accepted Gatsby as the only person of his New York experience who is secure in his judgment; he has gone beyond that, to associate Gatsby with American tradition: the Dutch sailors' eyes who had first seen Long Island as "a fresh, green breast of the new world" are its beginning; the mansion of James J. Hill is a symbol of its gross opportunity; the figure of Dan Cody, whose magic influence has changed drab James Gatz into Jay Gatsby, represents the beginning of decadence; and Gatsby himself, to look at him through Carraway's eyes, is a tragic victim of its final exhaustion. . . . (pp. 125-26)

Frederick J. Hoffman, "The American Novel between Wars," in his The Modern Novel in America: 1900-1950, *Henry Regnery Company, 1951, pp. 89-130.**

TOM BURNAM (essay date 1952)

[*In the following excerpt, Burnam maintains that the symbolism in* The Great Gatsby *reveals a theme often overlooked by critics; he proposes that the work overtly addresses the inability to recapture the past, while, less obviously, Fitzgerald expressed a need to restore order in a chaotic world. Burnam discusses the narrator of* Gatsby, *whom he believes vacillates between Nick Carraway and Fitzgerald himself, and the symbols which support his reading of the work.*]

It is . . . possible to read ***The Great Gatsby*** and remain content with a single symbol: the green light (which, as a student once informed me, ought legally to be red) at the end of Daisy's dock. To those who do not feel a need to inquire further, the light obviously stands for what Nick Carraway says it stands for: "the orgiastic future that year by year recedes before us." True, even the most pragmatic reader may wish to add that the green light might also represent to Gatsby a projection of his wishes: a signal to go ahead, to "beat on . . . against the current," to attempt so desperately with his "unbroken series of successful gestures" the recapturing of that past which he can never attain.

But there is still more in ***The Great Gatsby*** than a protagonist, a plot, and a green light. Many elements in the story, perhaps, will puzzle the practical-minded, for on the level of simple narrative they cannot be accounted for. What does one make, for example, of the faded blue eyes of Dr.T. J. Eckleburg, those staring, vacant, yet somewhat terrible eyes so much more than an abandoned signboard; of the ash heap and its "ash-grey men, who move dimly and already crumbling through the powdery air" over which the eyes brood changelessly; of George Wilson's despairing mutter as he gazes at the eyes, "You may fool me, but you can't fool God!"

And there is the matter, too, of the odd scene in which Nick and Jordan Baker discuss Jordan's carelessness with automobiles. One could easily find structural reasons for such a conversation between Nick and Daisy, or Gatsby and Daisy, for it is Daisy who runs down Myrtle Wilson. But why emphasize *Jordan*'s inability to handle an automobile safely? I believe the answers to this question and the others I have posed are concerned with a more complex organization than is commonly assumed, an organization of symbols the whole meaning of which was not entirely clear to Fitzgerald himself. For Fitzgerald-as-Fitzgerald and Fitzgerald-as-Carraway, the gleeman of the Gatsby saga, are not the same, though both appear alternately throughout the novel, intertwining like the threads in a fabric whose sheen depends not only on the materials out of which it is made but on the light in which it is viewed.

It seems to me a very interesting fact that the overt theme of ***The Great Gatsby*** has little to do, actually, with the novel's use of symbol. It is indeed likely, as a matter of fact, that the subdominant motif—which I hope soon to expose—very often overshadows what Fitzgerald apparently intended to be his principal theme. Of course, it is true that in making its point about the paradoxical futility of an attempt to recapture the past, ***The Great Gatsby*** obviously also says much more; one measure of its greatness is the complex and ironic quality of Gatsby's attempt to beat against the current. For he—and he alone, barring Carraway—survives sound and whole in character, uncorrupted by the corruption which surrounded him, which was indeed responsible for him; from his attempt at the childishly impossible he emerges with dignity and maturity. Yet no major work of fiction with which I am acquainted reserves its symbols for the subtheme; the more one thinks about ***The Great Gatsby,*** the more one comes to believe that F. Scott Fitzgerald may not have entirely realized what he was doing.

I think it is evident that not even the most skilful novelist could make us quite accept a young bond salesman of Nick Carraway's background and experience (even one who was "rather literary in college") as capable of composing the wonderful description in chapter iii of Gatsby's parties, or the passage later on in the same chapter beginning "I began to like New York," or managing to contrive that unique and poignant apostrophe to the "hundred pairs of golden and silver slippers" which "shuffled the shining dust . . . while fresh faces drifted here and there like rose petals blown by the sad horns around the floor." In other words, Nick as Nick is one thing and Fitzgerald as himself is another—something, incidentally, which Fitzgerald tacitly admits in a letter presently to be quoted. Thus the novel may very well involve not merely the theme which Nick presents in his own character, but also another which may be called, for lack of a better name, the "Fitzgerald theme." And it is toward the latter, I believe, that almost all the symbolism in ***The Great Gatsby*** is directed.

Nick Carraway, as Nick, could very well point everything he said toward the magnificent and at the same time sordid spectacle, Gatsby; could praise in Gatsby "something gorgeous . . . some heightened sensitivity to the promises of life" and rub out the obscene word some prowling urchin has scrawled on the white steps of the dead Gatsby's deserted mansion. But F. Scott Fitzgerald is the one who introduces, I think unconsciously, a fascinating examination of certain values only peripherally related to Gatsby's rise, his dream, and his physical downfall. And, if we turn to this other area, this non-Carraway thematic possibility, we see at once that ***The Great Gatsby*** is not, like *Lord Jim,* a study of illusion and integrity, but of carelessness. Our "second" theme—perhaps the more important regardless of Fitzgerald's original intention—becomes a commentary on the nature and values, or lack of them, of the reckless ones.

We know that the critics were not alone in sensing a certain lack in ***The Great Gatsby.*** Fitzgerald himself felt it, was uncomfortable about it, tried to explain it away even though there is evidence that he always regarded ***Gatsby*** as his greatest piece of work. No one agreed, however, about what the lack was. Fitzgerald could not define it consistently; in a letter to John Peale Bishop postmarked August 9, 1925, he calls ***The Great Gatsby*** "blurred and patchy" and adds: "I never at any one time saw him clear myself—for he started out as one man I knew and then changed into myself [n.b.!]—the amalgam was never complete in my mind." In a letter written the same year to Edmund Wilson, however, he shifts his ground [see excerpt above, 1925]: "The worst fault in [***The Great Gatsby***] I think is a BIG FAULT: I gave no account (and had no feeling about or knowledge of) the emotional relations between Gatsby and Daisy from the time of their reunion to the catastrophe." And then he goes on to make a particularly significant remark if we keep in mind the distinction between Nick Carraway and Scott Fitzgerald: "However the lack is so astutely concealed by the retrospect of Gatsby's past *and by blankets of excellent prose* [my italics] that no one has noticed it—though everyone has felt the lack and called it by another name." Later in the same letter Fitzgerald calls this "BIG FAULT" by still a different, though cognate, term: ". . . the lack of any emotional backbone at the very height of it [i.e., the Gatsby story]."

Now, all of this self-analysis, it seems to me, misses the point. The "lack" is there, all right, and Fitzgerald strikes at least a glancing blow when he speaks of the "blankets of excellent prose"—Fitzgerald prose, please note, not Nick Carraway prose; for in the letter to Wilson, Fitzgerald is clearly speaking as author and craftsman. But, still, he misses; for it is doubtful that the "emotional relations" between Gatsby and Daisy *need* any more explaining than they get in the novel. . . . Certainly one must assume that, if the novel means anything, it cannot concern itself with the love of Jay Gatsby, boy financier, for the pretty wife of Tom Buchanan, football hero. In other words, the point of the Carraway theme, at least, has everything to do with precisely the emptiness of the Gatsby-Daisy "emotional relations"—those same emotional relations which Fitzgerald seemed to feel, I think quite wrongly, it was a "BIG FAULT" not to elaborate upon. That Daisy exists both in, and as, an emotional vacuum into which Gatsby, being Gatsby, could attempt to pour only the most obvious and contrived cheap-novel sentimentalism has everything to do with the ironic quality of his final defeat at her hands. And the novel would be the worse, I believe, for the very thing the author says it needs: an exegesis of this vacuum and Gatsby's response to it. Fitzgerald's instinct for craftsmanship, we may be thankful, operated before his analysis as critic.

No, it is not the details of Gatsby's later love for Daisy; nor is it that Gatsby turns into Fitzgerald, though this is closer; nor yet is it (as, says Fitzgerald, Mencken thought [see excerpt above, 1925]) that the central story is "a sort of anecdote"—none of these things is responsible for that feeling of something missing which many readers have experienced but that none seems able to account for. As a matter of fact, what is really "missing" in ***The Great Gatsby*** is not so much a specific element in plot or even theme; the *sense* of something missing comes, rather, from the inherent confusion of themes, the duality of symbol-structure of which Fitzgerald seems to have been unaware. The book, great as it is, still falls short of its possibilities because its energies are spent in two directions. If ***The Great Gatsby*** revealed to us only its protagonist, it would be incomparable. Revealing, as it does, perhaps a little too much of the person who created it, it becomes somewhat less sharp, less pointed, more diffused in its effect. (pp. 7-10)

It is commonplace to cite chapter, verse, and semicolon to support the view that Fitzgerald's tragedy was that he had not been born to wealth. . . . Yet to say that Fitzgerald wanted money, and to stop there, seems to me to say nothing. What did he seek that money could, he thought, provide? Or, perhaps more accurately, what did he think the rich possessed, because of their money, that he wanted so badly?

The answer, I believe, is that he wanted order. Fitzgerald, like Mark Twain, saw around him only chaos. And, again like Mark Twain, he tried to find an ordered cosmos in his own terms. Twain plunged himself into a machine-world where *B* always follows *A,* as a lever on a typesetter always responds to the cam which actuates it. Fitzgerald seemed to think he could discover in that magic world of the rich "safe and proud above the hot struggles of the poor" the sanctuary he seems always to have sought. Like "Manley Halliday" in Budd Schulberg's *The Disenchanted,* Fitzgerald had "a strong sense of pattern." The list which Gatsby's father shows to Nick Carraway is not so important for what the old man thinks it represents, that his son "was bound to get ahead," though this is a part of the Carraway theme. Rather, in its boyish effort to reduce the world to terms in the Chaucerian sense of "boundaries," the "schedule" imposes on the haphazard circumstances of life a purpose and a discipline, just as Fitzgerald the man attempts in his novel the same sort of thing.

Many elements now seem to fall into place. The conversation about carelessness between Jordan Baker and Nick assumes a different stature, and in the thin red circle which Gatsby's blood traces in his swimming pool "like the leg of transit" we can see a meaning: the end-and-beginning within which lies, at least, something else than *khaos,* the mother of all disaster. "It is not what Gatsby was," a student of mine once wrote, "but what had hold of him that was his downfall." "What had hold of him"—and of F. Scott Fitzgerald himself—was the dream that all share who seek to impose some kind of order on a cluttered universe. The meaning Gatsby sought—the "order," if you will—was Daisy; when the betrayal came, his dream disintegrated. . . . (pp. 11-12)

Lionel Trilling thinks that Jay Gatsby "is to be thought of as standing for America itself." Perhaps; everyone is Everyman, in a sense, and Gatsby can stand for America as conveniently as he can stand for himself. But it seems to me that the true significance of ***The Great Gatsby*** is both more personal and more specific. The "spiritual horror" which Mr. Trilling finds in the novel he ascribes to "the evocation of New York in the heat of summer, the party in the Washington Heights flat, the terrible 'valley of ashes' seen like a corner of the Inferno from the Long Island Railroad . . . Gatsby's tremendous, incoherent parties . . . the huge, sordid and ever-observant eyes of the oculist's advertising sign." This we may accept; but summer heat and ashes and oculists' signs are horrible not per se but *per causam.* The cause of the horror is, in ***The Great Gatsby,*** the terrifying contrast between the Buchanans, Jordan Baker, the obscene barflies who descend in formless swarms on Gatsby's house, all symbolized by the gritty disorganized ash heaps with their crumbling men, and the solid ordered structure so paradoxically built on sand (or ashes) which Gatsby's great dream lends to his life. And over it all brood the eyes of Dr. Eckleburg, symbols—of what? Of the eyes of God, as Wilson, whose own world disintegrates with the death of Myrtle calls them? As a symbol of Gatsby's dream, which like the eyes is pretty shabby after all and scarcely founded on the "hard rocks" Carraway admires. Or—and I think this most likely—do not the eyes in spite of everything they survey, perhaps even because of it, serve both as a focus and an undeviating base a single point of reference in the midst of monstrous disorder?

> It was all very careless and confused [says Nick]. They were careless people, Tom and Daisy—they smashed up things and creatures and then retreated back into their money or their vast carelessness, or whatever it was that kept them together, and let other people clean up the mess they had made.

Here Fitzgerald nearly calls his turn—yet he misses again. For Tom and Daisy retreat "back into their money *or* their vast carelessness." And in the implication of the phrase we see that Fitzgerald was himself unready to give up his old warm world; that Jay Gatsby was not the only one to pay a high price for living too long with a single dream. (p. 12)

Tom Burnam, "The Eyes of Dr. Eckleburg: A Reexamination of 'The Great Gatsby'," in College English, *Vol. 14, No. 1, October, 1952, pp. 7-12.*

MALCOLM COWLEY (essay date 1953)

[*Cowley has made several valuable contributions to contemporary letters with his editions of important American authors (Nathaniel Hawthorne, Walt Whitman, Ernest Hemingway, William Faulkner, F. Scott Fitzgerald), his writings as a literary critic for* The New Republic, *and, above all, for his chronicles and criticism of modern American literature. Cowley's literary criticism does not attempt a systematic philosophical view of life and art, nor is it representative of a neatly defined school of critical thought, but rather focuses on works—particularly those of "lost generation" writers—that he believes personal experience has qualified him to explicate and that he considers worthy of public appreciation. The critical approach Cowley follows is undogmatic and is characterized by a willingness to view a work from whatever perspective—social, historical, aesthetic—that the work itself seems to demand for its illumination. In the following excerpt, Cowley presents a general discussion of* The Great Gatsby.]

There is a moment in any real author's career when he suddenly becomes capable of doing his best work. He has found a fable that expresses his central truth and everything falls into place around it, so that his whole experience of life is available for use in his fiction. Something like that happened to Fitzgerald when he invented the story of Jimmy Gatz, otherwise known as Jay Gatsby, and it explains the amazing richness and scope of a very short novel.

To put facts on record, ***The Great Gatsby*** is a book of about fifty thousand words, a small structure built of nine chapters like big blocks. The fifth chapter—Gatsby's meeting with Daisy Buchanan—is the center of the narrative, as is proper; the seventh chapter is the climax. Each chapter consists of one or more dramatic scenes, sometimes with intervening passages of straight narration. The "scenic" method is one that Fitzgerald probably learned from Edith Wharton, who in turn learned it from Henry James; at any rate the book is technically in the Jamesian tradition (and Daisy Buchanan is named for James's heroine, Daisy Miller).

Part of the tradition is the device of having the story told by a single observer, who stands somewhat apart from the action and whose vision "frames" it for the reader. In this case the observer plays a special role. Although Nick Carraway doesn't save or ruin Gatsby, his personality in itself provides an essential comment on all the other characters. Nick stands for the older values that prevailed in the Middle West before the First World War. His family isn't tremendously rich, like the Buchanans, but it has a long established and sufficient fortune, so that Nick is the only person in the book who hasn't been corrupted by seeking or spending money. He is so certain of his own values that he hesitates to criticize others, but when he does pass judgment—on Gatsby, on Jordan Baker, on the Buchanans—he speaks as if for ages to come.

All the other characters belong to their own brief era of confused and dissolving standards, but they are affected by the era in different fashions. Each of them, we note on reading the book a second time, represents some particular variety of moral failure; Lionel Trilling says that they are "treated as if they were ideographs," a true observation; but the treatment does not detract from their reality as persons. Tom Buchanan is wealth brutalized by selfishness and arrogance; he looks for a mistress in the valley of ashes and finds an ignorant woman, Myrtle Wilson, whose raw vitality is like his own. Daisy Buchanan is the spirit of wealth and offers a continual promise "that she had done gay, exciting things just a while since and that there were gay, exciting things hovering in the next hour"; but it is a false promise, since at heart she is as self-centered as Tom and even colder. Jordan Baker apparently lives by the old standards, but she uses them only as a subterfuge. Aware of her own cowardice and dishonesty, she feels "safer on a plane where any divergence from a code would be thought impossible.''

All these, except Myrtle Wilson, are East Egg people, that is, they are part of a community where wealth takes the form of solid possessions. Set against them are the West Egg people, whose wealth is fluid income that might cease overnight. The West Egg people, with Gatsby as their archetype and tragic hero, have worked furiously to rise in the world, but they will never reach East Egg for all the money they spend; at most they can sit at the water's edge and look across the bay at the green light that shines and promises at the end of the Buchanans' dock. The symbolism of place has a great part in Fitzgerald's novel, as has that of motorcars. The characters are visibly represented by the cars they drive: Nick has a conservative old Dodge, the Buchanans, too rich for ostentation, have an ''easy-going blue coupé,'' while Gatsby's car is ''a rich cream color, bright with nickel, swollen here and there in its monstrous length with triumphant hat-boxes and supper-boxes and tool-boxes, and terraced with a labyrinth of wind-shields that mirrored a dozen suns''—it is West Egg on wheels. When Daisy drives through the valley of ashes in Gatsby's car, she causes the two deaths that end the story.

The symbols are not synthetic or contrived, like those in so many recent novels; they are images that Fitzgerald instinctively found to represent his characters and their destiny. When he says, ''Daisy took her face in her hands as if feeling its lovely shape,'' he is watching her act the charade of her self-love. When he says, ''Tom would drift on forever seeking, a little wistfully, for the dramatic turbulence of some irrecoverable football game,'' he suggests the one appealing side of Tom's nature. He is so familiar with the characters and their background, so absorbed in their fate, that the book has an admirable unity of texture; we can open it to any page and find another of the touches that illuminate the story. We end by feeling that ***Gatsby*** has a double virtue. Except for *The Sun Also Rises* it is the best picture we possess of the age in which it was written and it also achieves a sort of moral permanence. (pp. xviii-xx)

Malcolm Cowley, ''Introduction: The Romance of Money,'' in Three Novels: The Great Gatsby, Tender Is the Night, The Last Tycoon *by F. Scott Fitzgerald, Charles Scribner's Sons, 1953, pp. ix-xx.*

DOUGLAS TAYLOR (essay date 1953)

[*In the following excerpt, Taylor addresses mythic aspects of* The Great Gatsby *and suggests that Jay Gatsby represents a Christ-figure within the novel. For an opposing view, see the excerpt by E. C. Bufkin (1969-70).*]

Few critics dispute the superbness of Scott Fitzgerald's achievement in ***The Great Gatsby.*** In precision of workmanship, elegance of prose style, and control of dramatic point of view, it represents to my mind Fitzgerald's genius at its sustained best. No other novel of the period, with the exception of *The Sun Also Rises,* can be said to have succeeded so perfectly in transforming the mind and manners of its time into something artistically worthy of the intense moral and social conditions which produced them. The features of the book which stand out most strongly in one's mind—the swirling, sideshow anonymity of Gatsby's Long-Island parties, the huge, ominous eyes of the oculist's sign brooding perpetually over the hot, desolate ''valley of ashes,'' the shrill, oppressive atmosphere of Myrtle Wilson's flat, the brutal, cowardly truculence of Tom Buchanan, the poignant dream and pathetic bad taste of Gatsby himself—concentrate a multiple image of an America that had lost its standards and its sense of the moral fitness of things, and had given itself over to a self-deceiving myth that would some day come apart like wet cardboard.

The book is so very good that one is tempted occasionally to go along with the assumption that some influence, other than his own moral growth, operated to aid his imagination in organizing and disciplining his thought and feeling as maturely as it did. Nevertheless, the use of a dramatic narrator to unify a series of swift and intensive scenes was a technique ideally adapted to a talent of Fitzgerald's kind, for, aside from the advantages of compositional compactness, such a method allowed his imagination to project in the form and subject of the novel a conception which enabled him to externalize and to exploit simultaneously from within and without both sides of a nature that was split between sentiment and self-criticism. Gatsby and Nick Carraway unquestionably are coextensive with his own feelings about each side of this nature, and are developed within a context of insights which control their precise moral and creative meanings through a bifocal view that manipulates at once the attitudes of intimacy and detachment with a distinctness that is never blurred. (p. 30)

This sense of ''double vision'' informs both the general organization of ***Gatsby*** and the arrangement of its smallest thematic details, and, at one point very early in the narrative, Fitzgerald seems to have imbedded in a casual reflection of Nick Carraway's an image which not only emphasizes this double view and represents what may be Fitzgerald's own evaluation of one of the major defects of his earlier novels, but offers a possible esthetic justification for the novel's form as well. It is when Nick, having settled at West Egg and looking forward to the long, quiet days of summer, decides to revive a somewhat neglected habit of reading, doing so with the feeling that ''. . . I was going to bring back all such things into my life and become again that most limited of all specialists, the 'well-rounded man.' This isn't just an epigram—*life is much more successfully looked at from a single window, after all.*'' Invariably, Nick's experience will demonstrate both an aspect of his nature and the bifocal continuity of the book itself, as when he pauses wistfully amidst the busy loneliness of the New York evening to watch a thick congestion of crowded taxicabs moving toward the theatre district, and notes how ''Forms leaned together in the taxis as they waited, and voices sang, and there was laughter from unheard jokes, and lighted cigarettes made unintelligible circles inside. Imagining that I, too, was hurrying toward gayety and sharing their intimate excitement, I wished them well.'' The fine control of language in this passage, with its precise use of detail that mingles several qualities of sensation in a swift interplay of mood, feeling, and idea, the tonal proportions of the colloquial rhythms of the first sentence that evoke and lengthen, through its strong liquid properties, the extent of Nick's longing for the warmth and attachment the experience suggests, the sudden withdrawal and running-away of the emotion expressed in the half-nostalgic, half-ironic ''I wished them well,'' indicates the degree to which Fitzgerald's imagination had matured along with the sense of poetic artistry which could compress and modulate variations of action, character, and atmosphere in words that could feel through to the essential quality of a situation and reproduce its most accurate overtones. (p. 31)

In Nick Carraway, Fitzgerald conceived a figure who was to function as a center of moral and compositional activity which fused both the dramatic action and the values it implied. His character, though literally credible, can be regarded as a kind of choric voice, a man who embodies the moral conscience of his race, ". . . a guide, a pathfinder, an original settler," who ". . . wanted the world to be . . . at a sort of moral attention forever," but never forgets that ". . . a sense of the fundamental decencies is parcelled out unequally at birth." The very form and larger idea of the novel allows for this possibility, and throughout the narrative, such a relation to the action is suggested both by the nature of his detached moral involvement and by the pitch and timbre of a diction that compels one to have an instinctive faith in his point of view. (pp. 31-2)

Inasmuch as Nick Carraway's point of view represents the significant moral force of ***Gatsby,*** one is led inevitably to recognize the nature of Jay Gatsby's "incorruptible dream" through the continuous series of moral and emotional insights which reflect Nick's understanding of the importance of the values involved. In spite of the pathetically naive assumptions which lie behind Gatsby's vision of life, Nick chooses ultimately to commit himself to the beliefs it fosters, because, seen against the callous, destructive charm of Daisy and Tom Buchanan's world, it becomes, to his mind, not the gaudy, unsplendid show-piece which attracts the vagrant and the vulgar, but a creative dream of intense magic and passion of purpose that flows from an innate fineness of heart and feeling. It is the worth and dignity of which the human will and imagination is capable traduced by a specious conviction, inarguably American in character, that the noblest intensities of existence are available if the objects with which they are ostensibly synonymous can be possessed. . . . [Gatsby's] personal tragedy is his failure to understand the complex quality of the mind and motives which go into [Daisy's] fine-seeming world of wealth, for he is captivated by the delightful, exquisitely ordered surface without discerning the behind-the-doors ruthlessness, the years of infinite duplicity and subterfuge that a shrewd, self-preoccupied class has practiced to preserve the power and well-being such a surface implies. Only after the accident, when his vision starts to come to pieces like one of those toy clocks won at carnivals, and he has ". . . lost the old warm world, paid a high price for living too long with a single dream," does he probably sense how very different the very rich are. (pp. 33-4)

In developing the implications of his theme, Fitzgerald seems to have further enriched their quality by uniting them—perhaps unconsciously—with a level of social-anagogic meaning that is at once actual and ironic in its dimensions. With frequent scriptural analogies which, though only general in outline, evoke echoes of the Last Supper, the Week of the Passion, and the Crucifixion, as well as numerous other Biblical accounts, Gatsby and the recurring symbols of the novel are given a quality of profane divineness which points ironically toward the idea of a land and people whose actual deification of its aggressive faith in its vision of life has become a formidable secular dogma. The statement that ". . . Jay Gatsby of West Egg, Long Island, sprang from his Platonic conception of himself," that "He was a son of God—a phrase which, if it means anything, means just that—and he must be about His Father's business, the service of a vast, vulgar, and meretricious beauty," confirms one's feeling that Fitzgerald had in mind the thought of the "self-formed" nation that has made "the American dream" a pageantry and "the success story" an ideal, a nation which is withdrawing progressively from the social, moral, and political reality that surrounds and affects its daily actions into a specious but comforting public image of itself which every popular feature of its cultural life has helped to create and is compelled to maintain. Thus, Gatsby, overtly identified with the figure of Christ, can be regarded as morally and poetically interchangeable with the spirit of a land that believes its destiny to transcend both natural and human limitations, and which, like Simon Magus (Acts 8: 9-24), the sorcerer of Samaria who bewitched the people into thinking he had the power of God, and with whom Fitzgerald seems to have crossed the Christ-image to reinforce the irony of his meaning, is convinced its wealth can buy the mystery of the Holy Ghost.

To realize this aspect of his theme and to engage it cogently with the national drama it signifies, Fitzgerald developed the general character of Gatsby's experience to correspond with that of the life and agony of Christ. From the moment he boards Dan Cody's yacht on Lake Superior until his burial and subsequent resurrection in the wonder of the "Dutch sailors' eyes," the movement of his life follows the triadic rhythm of both Christian and pre-Christian myth: purpose, passion, pain, or insight: Denying his parents, his symbolic rebirth aboard the yacht, coinciding with the phrase "His Father's business," parallels Christ's action at the Temple (Luke 2: 46-49), where he disclaims Joseph and Mary, saying "'I must be about My Father's business,'" while Gatsby's travel with Dan Cody, his almost genuflective feeling for Daisy, his blue, purposive parties that spin out like cotton-candy the fluff and faith of a "Universe of ineffable gaudiness" suggest respectively, and by profane contrast, Christ's temptation on the Mountain (Luke 4: 4-8), when Satan let Him look on "all the kingdoms of the world in a moment of time," His passionate visionary love of man, and His itinerant dissemination of an incorruptible, unpretentious faith that offered another kind of mystery and achievement. Moreover, the rapid unfolding of crucial scenes which lead up to Gatsby's burial—the furtive, unquiet indefiniteness of his reunion with Daisy, the ridding of his house of partygoers, her deliberate words at the luncheon that betray their liaison to Tom, the struggle, or *agon,* between the two men in the suite at the Plaza, Daisy's cowardly, conspiratorial behavior following the accident, Tom's vicious report to Wilson which results in Gatsby's death, the trial, denial, and flight of Daisy, of Wolfsheim, of Klipspringer, of the multitude of hangers-on who lived gainfully on his dream's outer edges—have their sacred equivalents in the accounts in the Gospels of the Passion, the Last Supper, and the Crucifixion, which relate variously Christ's precariousness and distress in His final week of life. . . . The scriptural analogy is made complete when Gatsby's father, like the titular Joseph, arrives to bury his son, and by the sudden appearance at the funeral of "Owl-Eyes," whose metonymic name points poetically to the grotesque omniscience of the oculist's sign—the novel's fantastic image of the commercialized desolation of the American spirit—, and whose presence corporealizes the symbol of Gatsby's spiritual Father. . . . In the final pages, Nick's reflective identification of Gatsby with the Dutch sailors and the American past can be viewed, in a sense, as a resurrection, for it evokes and gives a transient lyric body to the memory of a dead dream that lies ". . . somewhere back in that vast obscurity beyond the city, where the dark fields of the republic rolled on under the night," reincarnating him in a past he tried so desperately to revive, and uniting its quality with the idea of a nation which persists wistfully and religiously in its belief in the inexhaustible fullness of its native possibilities.

If this hasty and somewhat superficial analogic reading of ***Gatsby*** is considered as a possible approach to its larger moral content, then Gatsby's death, as Christ's, can be understood as a symbolic enactment of the concept of the mythic Scapegoat-Hero, but its dramatization in a context which runs against its positive religious implications of rejuvenescence and redemption turns its meaning into one of ironic nullification and defeat. (pp. 34-6)

As Yeats and Eliot and Joyce had seized on ancient dignities to gather flux into an "artifice of eternity," so Fitzgerald has used myth in ***The Great Gatsby*** in a less monumental fashion to alchemize the anarchy of modern life into a unity and permanence. Whatever one may think of the moral beliefs such a device assumes, the manipulation particularly of the novel's climax in ritual terms to dignity a tragic but otherwise commonplace homicide seems to me an extremely effective method for representing, by contrast with the vital social-religious solidarity of antiquity, the contemporary break-up, decline, and disappearance of that intense, imperative kind of spiritual awareness which unifies with its commonly-held hierarchy of values and attachments every layer of a social-cultural complex, and which combines conscience and imagination in the feelings and ideas it projects into the forms and ceremony of religious belief. It is the dramatic postulation of such an awareness which generates in proportion to the degree of its absence in modern Amerian life the ironic moral interplay between the values associated with the symbolic quality of Gatsby's death and the actual remoteness or exclusion of these same values from the moral habits which the American national mind takes for granted. (pp. 37-8)

[In ***The Great Gatsby,***] Fitzgerald achieved a unity and completeness of artistic expression which, in range and depth of general import, gives an encompassing and enduring force to the multiplicity of American moral and social experience. In doing so, he revealed not a romantic limitation of insight, as Mr. Mizener [see Additional Bibliography] seems to think, in committing Nick Carraway—and himself—to Gatsby's point of view, but rather a discipline and sureness of mind which led him to sense somehow that Jay Gatsby was at once larger and more significant in the issues he dramatized than the literalness concentrated in his "capacity for wonder."

In elucidating above what seemed to me to be the social-anagogic undertones of ***Gatsby,*** I have attempted to bring into relief a somewhat different set of relations inhering in its content without wishing either to dislocate too severely its superb coördination of thought and feeling or to give the impression of stretching it over a perverse procrustean bed of meaning. Neither has it been my object to claim for such a view an oracular exactness it cannot have, nor to suggest that the relations indicated were to any real extent a defined or consciously controlled part of Fitzgerald's intention. If, as is apparently the case, Fitzgerald was unaware of his theme's connections with religious myth, it does not inevitably mean that these same connections may not have functioned within the deeper ethical folds of his imagination as a quiet archetypal modifier of the known quality of his feelings about his subject.

Over and above this suggested archetypal mode of imagination, however, Fitzgerald, though probably having little more than conversational familiarity with the great anthropological works of his day, with Harrison or Frazer or Jung, assumedly would have had a very natural and fluent understanding of the Bible owing to the early religious training of his Irish-Catholic background, and it is this powerful imaginative influence, as well as the moral atmosphere of which it was a part, that can be said to have contributed largely to the formation of the quality of mind which, as Mr. Mizener has pointed out, makes his ". . . basic feeling for experience . . . a religious one." It is represented with greater dramatic force in the extended irony of ***Gatsby,*** but it is more or less present in everything he wrote. (p. 39)

Douglas Taylor, "'The Great Gatsby': Style and Myth," in The University of Kansas City Review, *Vol. XX, No. 1, Autumn, 1953, pp. 30-40.*

R. W. STALLMAN (essay date 1955)

[An American educator, biographer, critic, and editor, Stallman is considered a leading scholar of the life and works of Stephen Crane. In the following excerpt, he disagrees with critics who maintain that the narrator of The Great Gatsby *acts as the author's moral voice, utilizing themes and symbols from the novel to support his argument. In addition, he examines the use of time in* The Great Gatsby. *For further discussions of* Gatsby's *narrator, see the excerpts by Frederick H. Hoffman (1951), David O'Rourke (1982), and Colin S. Cass (1983).]*

A year before ***The Great Gatsby*** saw print Fitzgerald's best friend had written him off as an irresponsible artist incapable of knowing what to do with the rare jewels that somehow fell into his lap. "I want to write something new," Fitzgerald told Maxwell Perkins, "—something extraordinary and beautiful and simple and intricately patterned." And new and extraordinary and beautiful and simple it is. But what transforms the novel into greatness is its intricately patterned idea. It is the idea of a myth-hero—the hero as a modern Icarus—who impersonates an Epoch while belonging to Space and Time. Gatsby belongs not exclusively to one epoch of American civilization but rather to all history inasmuch as all history repeats in cycle form what Gatsby represents—America itself. Gatsby transcends reality and time. His confused time-world results from the confused morality of the epoch he inhabits, "The Age of Confusion." Fitzgerald read Oswald Spengler's *The Decline of the West* the same summer he was writing ***The Great Gatsby,*** and the influence of Spengler's mixed perspectives of history is manifested in Fitzgerald's conception of a hero who confuses the past with the present and whose time-world is wrenched from the logic of time.

A "son of God" born out of his own "Platonic conception of himself," Gatsby goes "about His Father's business, the service of vast, vulgar, and meretricious beauty." The incredible Gatsby!—"liable at the whim of an impersonal government to be blown anywhere about the world." Smiling at Nick Carraway, Gatsby's smile metaphysically embraces "the whole eternal world." He resides only particularly at West Egg, for he exists simultaneously on two planes: the mythic or the impersonal *and* the human, the immaterial *and* the real. Through Nick, the narrator, the Inconceivable Gatsby is seen from the human point of view, but his universal genius is also viewed astronomically as it were from Cosmic Eyes Above. The province of his history extends from fabulous San Francisco (the city of his professed beginnings), eastward from the Golden Gate to the "clam-flats" of Lake Superior, the shores of Michigan, the peninsula of Long Island Sound, and down to the West Indies and the Barbary Coast; in Europe it extends similarly from one seaboard to the other; from England and France eastward to little Montenegro on the Adriatic. The incredible Gatsby has been three times around the continent, and he has lived in all the capitals of Europe like a rajah—"a turbaned 'character' leaking sawdust at every pore as he pursued a tiger through the Bois de Boulogne." Gatsby's world begins in the "Age of Confusion" and, crossing seas of antiquity, it romps

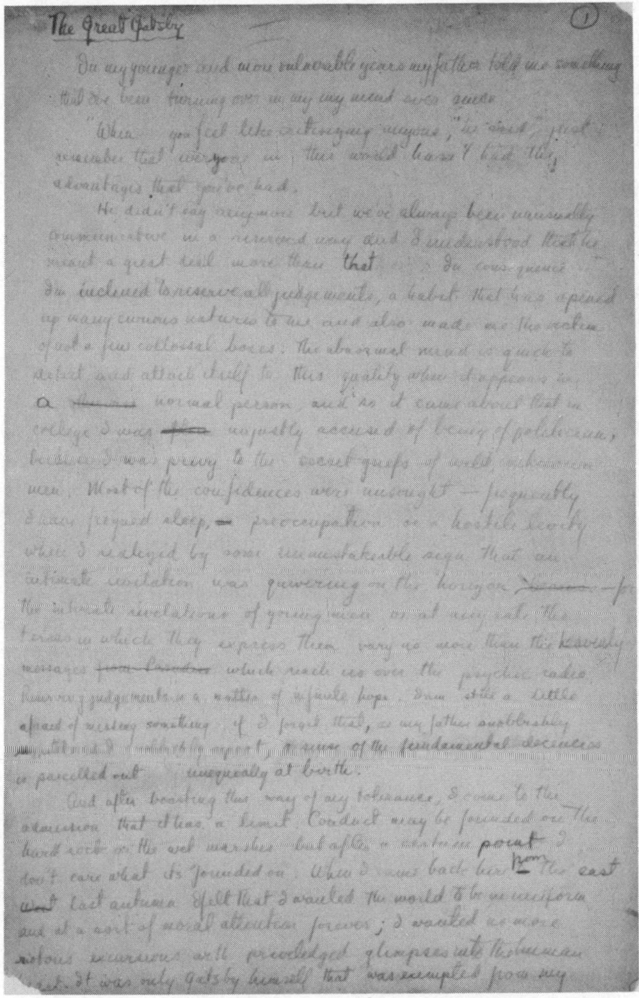

The Great Gatsby (1)

In my younger and more vulnerable years my father told me something that I've been turning over in my mind ever since.

"When you feel like criticizing anyone," he said, "just remember that all the people in this world haven't had the advantages that you've had."

He didn't say any more but we've always been unusually communicative in a reserved way and I understood that he meant a great deal more than that. In consequence I'm inclined to reserve all judgements, a habit that has opened up many curious natures to me and also made me the victim of not a few collossal bores. The abnormal mind is quick to detect and attach itself to this quality when it appears in a normal person, and so it came about that in college I was unjustly accused of being a politician, because I was privy to the secret griefs of wild unknown men. Most of the confidences were unsought — frequently I have feigned sleep, preoccupation or a hostile levity when I realized by some unmistakable sign that an intimate revelation was quivering on the horizon — for the intimate revelations of young men or at least the terms in which they express them vary no more than the heavenly messages which reach us over the psychic radio. Reserving judgements is a matter of infinite hope. I am still a little afraid of missing something if I forget that, as my father snobbishly suggested and I snobbishly repeat, a sense of the fundamental decencies is parcelled out unequally at birth.

And after boasting this way of my tolerance, I come to the admission that it has a limit. Conduct may be founded on the hard rock or the wet marshes but after a certain point I don't care what it's founded on. When I came back from the East last autumn I felt that I wanted the world to be in uniform and at a sort of moral attention forever; I wanted no more riotous excursions with privileged glimpses into the human heart. It was only Gatsby himself that was exempted from my

Holograph copy of the first page of F. Scott Fitzgerald's The Great Gatsby. *Copyright 1925 Charles Scribner's Sons. Copyright renewed 1953 Scott Fitzgerald Lanahan. Reprinted with the permission of Charles Scribner's Sons.*

("like the mind of God") from the Jazz Age to the Age of Reason through the Restoration to the Dark Ages of the Holy Grail and, finally, back to the Roman realms of Petronius wherein Gatsby as Trimalchio ends his career. It is no accident that Gatsby fears time; for Trimalchio (his prototype in Petronius's *Satyricon*) kept a trumpeter to announce constantly how much of his lifetime was gone and ordered a broken urn to be carved with a horologe in its center "so that anyone looking to see the time must willy-nilly read my name." (pp. 2-3)

The Gatsby world is wrenched into confusion and disorder by Gatsby's two-way dream—into the past and into the future. "In the meantime / In between time"—what remains is the hole in time. As Gatsby cannot tell past from future, the present is the same for him as one or the other—*now* being for him the tomorrow he hopes to possess or the yesterday he hopes to recapture. It is his moral disruption that accounts for the disruption of time in the Gatsby world. Gatsby's confused time-sense equates with his moral ambivalence. In ***The Great Gatsby*** moral ambivalence correlates with the confused time-theme of the novel and has its corollary in Fitzgerald's Conradian technique of symbolism that is itself ambivalent. The parallel to the divided selfhood of Gatsby is provided by the narrator, by the divided selfhood of the morally ambivalent Nick. Gatsby cannot distinguish time now from time past and future, nor right from wrong, whereas Nick is morally ambivalent not because he does not know right from wrong but rather because he is false to himself, a hypocrite. The Middle West is shown up for what it is by the person who best represents it, Nick Carraway. . . . Nick is the window of our viewpoint of Gatsby's romantic dream, the romantic being placed thus within a framework of cynical realism. Nick's character is determined thus by his function in the novel. Fitzgerald's method is hinted at in Nick's remark that "life is much more successfully looked at from a single window, after all." But Fitzgerald has placed us before a very deceptive piece of glass, an almost opaque and certainly a very complicated frame of reference. The very events of that summer of Nick's initiation into Eastern life elude analysis because of Nick's deliberate omissions and ambiguities in rendering his account of it. His facts resist reduction to simple certitude. Whether Nick is engaged to the girl back in the West, for instance, or whether Nick possessed Jordan (as Gatsby possessed Daisy) are questions difficult to answer because the truth is camouflaged. That Nick did possess Jordan can only be inferred, but even Jordan's accusation is ambiguous in its inferences: "Nevertheless, *you did throw me over*. . . . I don't give a damn about you now, but it was a new experience for me, and I felt a little dizzy for a while."

In his affair with Jordan, Nick is (he admits) only "half in love with her." Gatsby tells Nick his life-history "at a time of confusion, when I had reached the point of believing everything and nothing about him." The ambivalence of Nick's divided selfhood arises from his fear of committing himself to life by more than halves, and consequently he is drawn simultaneously in two directions: towards the Jordan side of his nature and towards its opposite in Gatsby. (pp. 4-5)

It has been said that ***The Great Gatsby*** is a "kind of tragic pastoral, with the East the exemplar of urban sophistication and culture and corruption, and the West . . . the exemplar of simple virtue." Mr. Mizener [see *TCLC,* Vol. 1] tells us that Fitzgerald thought of the West as the exemplar of simple virtue, but what Fitzgerald presumably thought differs considerably from what he renders in his novel. What he wrote into his novel was a criticism of the West, as well as a criticism of the East. Not only is Western morality criticized in ***The Great Gatsby,*** but Fitzgerald presents not a single character to exemplify it. Every one of his Middle Westerners is dishonest. The only true exemplar of Christian morality is the insignificant Greek, Michaelis, and he is an Easterner. The moral rectitude of Nick is but the mask of hypocrisy. As for the Middle West, it is as narrow in outlook as Nick with his "provincial squeamishness," and it is hardened furthermore by its medieval-like "interminable inquisitions," which spare only the children and the very old. The East is not the sole exemplar of sophistication; for out West we get the pseudo-sophisticated and snobbish cliques of college youths matching their social registers: "Are you going to the Ordays'? the Herseys'? the Schultzes'?" Their holiday gayeties faintly echo the hollow celebrations of Gatsby. Nor is the West exempted from corruption. Gatsby's gangster business is carried on not only out East but also out West.

In the temporal sense as in the moral, the West is as dead as its Eastern analogy, West Egg—that "wasteland" of Eastern life. Even the farmland characteristic by which the West is known transposes itself to the East: "a valley of ashes—a fantastic farm where ashes grow like wheat into . . . grotesque gardens." West Egg—in Gatsby's house and Nick's equally defunct Castle Rackrent—represents the negation of life; whereas East Egg represents the affirmation of life—in the dynamic Buchanans and their equally dynamic house and lawn. Like everything else in the novel, both these eggs are blunted at their contact end. They are defective, not complete wholes—"not perfect ovals—like the egg in the Columbus story, they are both crushed flat at the contact end—but their physical resemblance must be a source of perpetual wonder to the gulls that fly overhead." Nick tells us that they are dissimilar in every particular except shape and size, but he does not define their dissimilarity. One difference between Nick's West Egg and Tom's East Egg is symbolized by what Nick deals in—bonds—and what Tom deals in—stocks. Tom trades on stocks, which fluctuate by the minute; and East Egg throbs with life. West Egg, the dead egg, is thus named so as to identify it with the Middle West where the flux of time is defunct or fixed, not flowing in rain but frozen in snow. Mr. Gatz refuses to ship the body of his son back West because Gatsby "rose up to his position in the East." Nothing in the Golden West is golden except the coaches of the Chicago, Milwaukee & St. Paul railway, and they are a murky yellow. Nobody goes West except Nick. And even when he is in the East, the rising sun "threw my shadow westward." The West, as in classical literature, figures as the land of the unliving, and that is what Nick retreats to.

They are all of them confused Middle-Western-Easterners, and the story that Nick narrates of his summer of Eastern life is a nine-reel Eastern-Western love story documenting the Decline of the West. "I see now that this has been a story of the West, after all. . . ." And isn't it also a story about Nick, after all? The Nick story is inseparable from the Gatsby story, the one twining around the other to provide parallelisms to it. His matriculating at the Probity Trust is (as he says) like graduating backward into a second prep-school, and so Nick is put backward in time while simultaneously going forward—as a bond salesman dealing in futures. Nick thus provides analogy with Gatsby who, in his futuristic dream to repeat the past, is similarly drawn simultaneously forward and backward in time. Clocktime jumps back momentarily when Daisy asks him how long ago it was that they last met and Gatsby—reckoning by the future—answers: "'Five years *next* November.' The automatic quality of Gatsby's answer set us all back at least another minute." Gatsby has set back the clock five years in that imaginary minute, and it is this contingency that Gatsby recognizes when he admits to Nick that his scheme to meet Daisy again has been all "a terrible, terrible mistake." His so-called ancestral home at West Egg is a confused mélange of contradictory cultures and epochs, and his personal failure is symbolized by this "huge incoherent failure of a house"—the failure of Gatsby's own confused and incoherent life since five years ago when his dream possessed him. This "unprecedented place" represents his own quest to fix time, and Daisy is appalled by it because of its incoherence. Here the impossible has been achieved—time rearranged, history fixed. So Gatsby took over the house of a man who was as crazy as Gatsby about reinstating the past, a man who went into immediate decline when his unretarded neighbors obstructed his antiquarian program to have their cottages thatched with straw. It was like turning the clock back.

Nick presents himself on the first page of his story in the figure of a defunct arch-priest at the confessional-box, a prig with holier-than-thou airs who has rejected all further "riotous excursions with privileged glimpses into the human heart." His summer excursion into the riotous heart of the East he now repudiates, now that he has failed at facing into life, and nettled by it he lumps his own failure with that of all the others, rationalizing that as Middle Westerners "we possessed some deficiency in common which made us subtly unadaptable to Eastern life." His initiation has ended with his retreat back home, a retreat back to the clean, hard, limited world of the West where life is conveniently regulated by the moral straight-jacket of the Simple Virtues. "When I came back from the East last autumn I felt that I wanted the world to be in uniform and at a sort of moral attention forever." So Nick on the rebound proposes to save the world by regimenting it, by policing it morally. That Nick is to be seen as the moral center of the book, as one critic proposes, that his character "can be regarded as a kind of choric voice, a man who embodies the moral conscience of his race" [see excerpt above by Taylor, 1953], is a notion possible only to the duped reader who has been beguiled by the deceptive flow of Nick's words to take them at their face-value. At the center of the book what is there but a moral and temporal hole? Not Nick but Time is the true moralist. Fitzgerald has contrived that first page of ***The Great Gatsby*** as a front to the whole book. Here is Nick as arch-prig all dressed up in a morally hard-boiled starched shirt of provincial squeamishness and boasted tolerance, the hypocrite! His boasted tolerance, as we come to see *through* his protective mask, is in fact intolerance, and his rugged morality but polished manners. His proposal to regiment the world amounts to a negation of faith in humanity and of faith in life itself, and it masks his own spiritual bankruptcy. No moral vision can radiate from Nick's closed heart. The moral uniform he would clothe the world in smothers the riotous heart, it denies life and challenges it at its very godhead. And that is what Gatsby, after all, incarnates—the life-giving force.

Only one thing betrays Nick, and that is his ragged lawn at Castle Rackrent; what his "irregular lawn" signifies is that Nick himself is not as morally regular as he pretends. He professes a detestation of anything messy or disorderly, yet his own lawn is never trimmed except when Gatsby has his gardener repair it. He detests careless people, yet he himself is careless; he detests bad drivers, yet he himself is a bad driver—a bad sport. And Gatsby, because his life is confused and disordered, has the same passion for order and restraint as Nick. When his parties get out of hand, Gatsby grows more correct as the hilarity mounts. Nick's morality amounts to the restraint of keeping up appearances; he is a stickler for the punctilios of correct form and decent conduct. Because "I wanted to leave things in order," Nick pays a courtesy call on Jordan before leaving for the West. His leaving things in order amounts to his shaking hands with her after having thrown her over, that being the decent thing to do! (pp. 5-7)

The Great Gatsby is clocked on fast time, and not only is time speeded up but also space. "It was nine o'clock—almost immediately afterward I looked at my watch and found it was ten." The fall of the earth into the sun is averted by Tom's injected "wait a minute," and that theoretical pause defines what is for him an impossibility, a contradiction of his dynamic forward nature. Gatsby, that "overwound clock," cannot wait even for Daisy: "I can't wait all day." No Wasting Time was one of his resolves when as a boy he plotted how to mend the clock to make the most of time, but his time-schedule ironically he recorded on the fly-leaf of *Hopalong* Cassidy! Time cannot stop Gatsby; he cannot be arrested, though a frantic policeman attempts to arrest him, only to apologize for not recognizing who the great Gatsby really is. "Excuse me!" The rushing time-flow of the novel gets arrested only momentarily here and there, as when Myrtle peers out of her garage window and "one emotion after another crept into her face like objects in a slowly developing picture." And space (only in McKee's photographs is space fixed) leaps likewise its boundaries. "The lawn started at the beach and ran toward the front door for a quarter of a mile [as though the lawn were Tom himself as Yale football-end racing for the goal line], *jumping over sun-dials* and brick walls and burning gardens—finally it reached the house drifting up the side in bright vines as though from the momentum of its run." So *fresh* is this grass that it climbs impertinently into Buchanan's house, and "just as things grow in fast movies," so the leaves burst hurriedly on the Buchanan trees. On the broiling afternoon of the crack-up the confused time witnesses a silver curse of moon hovering "already in the western sky." This breach in nature exemplifies the book's theme of the breach in time, and a parallel sign of nature's disorder is the premature moon shining in the afternoon sky at Gatsby's July party, a wafer of a moon. The sunset glows upon Buchanan's porch, but there are four prematurely lighted candles. "'Why candles?' objected Daisy, frowning. She snapped them out with her fingers." Daisy thereby identifies herself with Day, in opposition to Night. "I always watch for the longest day of the year and then miss it." She misses it because one season overlaps with another; summer, advancing before its appointed time, is already here (two weeks before June 21st). It is as though the stage props for Act II prematurely appeared for Act I. (pp. 12-13)

Space and time—which formerly only the gods controlled—are conquered today by the tin chariots that hurl us at the rate of a century a minute towards the green light of the future. Our ailing machines pause in flight only long enough to get reconditioned—at garages to get repaired, at house-parties to get uplifted, or at drug-stores to get refueled: "You can buy anything at a drug-store nowadays." A garage is our temple of worship, our spiritual machines resting here for repair. Here to minister to our needs is the archpriest of commotion, an anonymity named George B. Wilson, and here—conferring in secret—is the priestess of power and pressure and combustion. She is the Jazz Age goddess not of fecundity but of dynamo-energy, a woman with "no facet or gleam of beauty," but of such panting vitality that she seems "as if the nerves of her body were continually smouldering." Out of the temple we race towards the green light, down the roadway which recedes year by year before us. It is Nick's birthday and also it is the last day of summer, this day of the crack-up, "I was thirty. Before me stretched the portentous, menacing road of a new decade."

Time as the roadway has its parallel symbol in time as the current: "So we beat on, boats against the current, borne back ceaselessly into the past." Time-in-flux figures as rain, and time-fixed as symbolized by pools. Goddard's scientific idea (as Tom reports it) is that the white race is going to be "utterly submerged." Destiny by water conditions Gatsby's life from beginning to end. He meets death while floating in a pool, the swimming pool not before used all summer; Daisy he meets as he steps from a pool of rainwater, and as it rains then so it rains at his funeral. At every landing point in his incredible history his life juts upon water. Even his house belongs to the sea, in the persistent rumor that he lives not in a house but in a boat, "a boat that looked like a house and was moved secretly up and down the Long Island shore." "Blessed are the dead that the rain falls on"—*blessed* because the mess and refuse of their lives is washed away.

That Gatsby has connections of a supernatural order is evidenced by the yellow car he drives, that Chariot of the Sun. Bright with nickel and many layers of glass surrounding "a sort of green conservatory," it is "terraced with a labyrinth of wind-shields that mirrored a dozen suns." Thus it resembles the sun. But also—being green and terraced—it resembles the earth. As it is "swollen here and there in its monstrous length with triumphant hat-boxes and supper-boxes and tool-boxes," it bulges out into space. As tricky a contraption as any Daedalus ever conceived! A rolling hot-house as it were, Gatsby's car serves as the conservatory for his dream-flower—Daisy. (Its three-noted horn links it also with Daisy, for she wears a three-cornered hat.) Green, the color of its upholstery, symbolizes the future (as in the green light that flickers on the Buchanan dock across the bay from Gatsby); but green is also the symbol of excitements, desires unfulfilled, expectations or hopes. (pp. 13-14)

Night and day (darkness and sunlight) are juxtaposed in every section of the novel, almost in every episode excepting the terminal one which depicts sunless scenes of rain and snow and night; and as the novel ends in night, so it begins with night descending upon the setting sun. East and West, though Nick pretends to make discriminations, are alike in their dread of night. In the West an evening is "hurried from phase to phase toward its close, in a continually disappointed anticipation or else *in sheer nervous dread of the moment itself*." Thus time now eludes them all, and night is denied. (p. 15)

Gatsby incarnates the power of dream and illusion, the recurrent cycles of youth's capacity for wonder by which new worlds have been conquered since the beginning of civilization—the dream of a conquest of space-and-time, the illusions which reality deflates, the power of youth and faith in hope. (As Fitzgerald puts it, there are the winged and the wingless.) Gatsby, winged upwards by his "heightened sensitivity to the promises of life," transcends "what foul dust floated in the wake of his dreams," and his sun-thoughts soar beyond the sun, beyond Daisy, "beyond everything. He had thrown himself into it with a creative passion, adding to it all the time, decking it out with every bright feather that drifted his way." Like Icarus, Gatsby soars against the tyranny of space-and-time by which we are imprisoned, only to be tragically destroyed by his own invention.

Day opposes night, and consequently throughout the novel white dominates its opposite. The futuristic green light that Gatsby prays to promises the day—Daisy. When Gatsby first knew her she drove a white roadster and wore a white dress; in the opening scene of the book she and Jordan wore white dresses; both Gatsby and Nick wear white flannels; Buchanan's red and white mansion stands amidst the white palaces of fashionable East Egg; Nick's books on banking shine in red and gold over the "white chasms of Wall Street. Out in the Middle West everything is white. Here in their homeland night is camouflaged by Christmas lights and holiday gayeties, bright snow contradicting the darkness. Nick's Middle West is represented as a long frosty dark-winter, whitened not by the sun (Daisy is out East!) but rather by the snow that keeps time frozen in.

That wintry night-world of the West—Nick's West differs from Gatsby's—is what Nick retreats to after his experience of life out East, and what he retreats from is that El Greco night-world of the East. The night-vignette Nick paints of the East as a drunken woman carried on a stretcher is an image symbolic not only of the East but also of the West, for it signifies the plight of all these Middle Western Easterners (or Eastern Middle Westerners): their isolation, their loneliness, their anonymity. Four nameless men carry the nameless woman, her hand dangling over the stretcher and sparkling "cold with jewels." Gravely the men turn in at a house—the wrong house. "But no one knows the woman's name, and no one cares." Everyone's identity overlaps with another's because everyone is without identity, isolated and anonymous and alone. "I found myself," says Nick at the end, "on Gatsby's side, and alone." Gatsby's loneliness is proverbial, and Nick diagnoses what ails everyone in his confessing to that "haunting loneliness" he feels in himself and in others.

On Nick's last night in the East the moonlight discloses an obscene word some boy has chalked on the white steps of Gatsby's house, and Nick erases it. Nick performs the same service for the romantic Gatsby as the youth in *Madame Bovary* performs for that self-deluded romanticist, Emma Bovary, over whose grave a young boy kneels as in a ritual of dedication. (pp. 15-16)

R. W. Stallman, "Gatsby and the Hole in Time," in Modern Fiction Studies, *Vol. I, No. 4, November, 1955, pp. 2-16.*

RICHARD CHASE (essay date 1957)

[*An American critic and educator, Chase is widely recognized for his scholarship in the field of American literature. In his most important work,* The American Novel and Its Tradition *(1957), he delineated the romantic characteristics of the American novel, which he believed differentiate it from its more realistic predecessor, the European novel. Chase has also written extensively on the works of Emily Dickinson, Herman Melville, and Walt Whitman. In the following excerpt, he maintains that in the figure of Jay Gatsby, Fitzgerald presented an American version of the archetypal hero of European legend. Chase further asserts that the novel's uniqueness is achieved through the realistic and distinctively American social situation in which Fitzgerald places his hero, Gatsby.*]

The special charm of ***Gatsby*** rests in its odd combination of romance with a realistic picture of raw power—the raw power of the money that has made a plutocracy and the raw power the self-protective conventions of this plutocracy assume when they close in a united front against an intruder.

Gatsby gives us an unforgettable, even though rather sketchy, sense of the 1920's and what the people were like who lived in them. We know what the people were like because we are shown the publicly recognized gestures and attitudes by which they declare themselves as belonging to a certain ambiance at a certain time. Their manners (perhaps one should say their mannered lack of manners) are a clearly minted currency as readily negotiable as the money they all have such a lot of. At the same time the hero who comes to his spectacular grief is not only a man of the 1920's but a figure of legend. No one can doubt that the legend engaged the imagination of the author more deeply than the society in which the legend is played out. (p. 162)

The story of Jay Gatsby is in origin an archetype of European legend and it is fascinating to observe how, in Fitzgerald's hands, this legend is modified and in some ways fundamentally changed in accordance with American ideas.

The European (perhaps universal) archetype has been memorably described, in relation to the novel, by Mr. [Lionel] Trilling himself. In his Introduction to *The Princess Casamassima,* Mr. Trilling refers to the legend of "the Young Man from the Provinces" which finds expression in certain great novels, such as Stendhal's *The Red and the Black,* Dickens's *Great Expectations,* and Balzac's *Père Goriot*. The young hero of the legend is likely to come from obscure or mean beginnings. There is some mystery about his birth; perhaps he is really a foundling prince. He is "equipped with poverty, pride and intelligence" and he passes through a series of adventures which resemble the "tests" that confront the would-be knight in Arthurian legend. He has an enormous sense of his own destiny. The purpose of his quest is to "enter life," which he does by launching a campaign to conquer and subdue to his own purposes the great world that regards him as an insignificant outsider. "He is concerned to know how the political and social world are run and enjoyed," as Mr. Trilling writes; "he wants a share of power and pleasure and in consequence he takes real risks, often of his life."

At this point one begins to see how much and how little Gatsby belongs to the tradition of the Young Man from the Provinces. He has the necessary obscure beginning, born Gatz somewhere in the Middle West. He has come to the more socially advanced East and made his way to a position of wealth and influence. He is more or less a mythic figure; he seems to have sprung from "a Platonic conception of himself" rather than from any real place; he is rumored to be the nephew of the Kaiser; he pretends to be an Oxford man and to have lived like a young rajah in all the capitals of Europe; he has committed himself "to the following of a grail." A good deal of this legendary build-up is comic in tone and satiric in intent. But Arthur Mizener, Fitzgerald's biographer [see *TCLC,* Vol. 1], is correct in saying that the ironies of ***The Great Gatsby*** are never allowed to destroy the credence and respect given by the author to the legend of his hero. The life and death of Gatsby inevitably call to the mind of Nick Carroway, the narrator, the ideal meaning of America itself. Gatsby somehow invokes the poetic appeal of the frontier and his pursuit of the ideal recalls once again the "transitory enchanted moment when man must first have held his breath in the presence of this continent, compelled into an aesthetic contemplation he neither understood nor desired, face to face for the last time in history with something commensurate to his capacity for wonder."

These concluding lines are so impassioned and impressive, even if a little overopulent in the Conradian manner, that we feel the whole book has been driving toward this moment of ecstatic contemplation, toward this final moment of transcendence. What, at the end, has been affirmed? Apparently it is not the "power and pleasure" derived from knowing and mastering "the political and social world." At the end of *Père Goriot* what is affirmed by Eugene Rastignac's challenge to Paris *is* this "power and pleasure." And whereas it is true that Julien Sorel in *The Red and the Black* seeks an ideal transcendence, in the manner of many French heroes, from those of Racine to those of Malraux, his field of operations is social to a far greater degree than Gatsby's is ever shown to be.

Gatsby does not seek to understand and master society as an end; and we have to take it on faith that he has understood and mastered it at all—was he *really* a bootlegger and a dealer in dubious stocks? Of course he was, but neither he nor his author nor his author's narrator, himself a bond salesman, shows any interest in these activities. Nor has Gatsby's shadowy battle with the world been, as it is for his European counterparts, a process of education and disillusion. *He* does not pass from innocence to experience—if anything it is the other way around, the youth who climbed aboard the millionaire's yacht being more worldly than the man who gazes longingly at the green light across the bay. (pp. 162-65)

No one seems to know what T. S. Eliot meant when he wrote Fitzgerald that ***Gatsby*** was the first step forward the American novel had made since Henry James [see excerpt above, 1925]. The statement seems meaningful, however, if we compare ***Gatsby*** with James's only novel of similar theme, *The American*. Christopher Newman is a more relaxed, less willful, and less self-destined figure than Gatsby, but he comes of a similarly legendary America, makes a great deal of money, and vainly pursues a woman who is the flower of a high world forever closed to him. James, however, is content with his pleasure in the odd angularities of the legend of the successful American. And he sends Newman home, baffled and saddened by his rejection but not mortally hurt. It is a part of the fate of both Newman and Gatsby that they have information with which they could avenge themselves on their highly placed antagonists and that out of magnanimity they both refuse to do so.

But Fitzgerald has made more of the legend. For whereas Newman remains an odd though appealing stick of a man Gatsby has a tragic recklessness about him, an inescapably vivid and memorable destiny. He has something of that almost divine insanity we find in Hamlet or Julien Sorel or Don Quixote. Fitzgerald's great feat was to have opened out this possibility and to have made his American hero act in a drama where none had acted before. For although there had been reckless and doomed semilegendary heroes in American fiction, none had been made to play his part in a realistically presented *social* situation. Fitzgerald opened out the possibility, but scarcely more. It was not in him to emulate except for a brilliant moment the greatest art. (pp. 166-67)

Richard Chase, "Three Novels of Manners," in his The American Novel and Its Tradition, *Anchor Books, 1957, pp. 157-84.**

E. C. BUFKIN (essay date 1969-70)

[*In the following excerpt, Bufkin examines Fitzgerald's use of "characters as doubles" in* The Great Gatsby. *He believes that Fitzgerald was influenced by Joseph Conrad's employment of this technical device which parallels characters and scenes, and he posits that the character Myrtle Wilson is the double of Jay Gatsby, citing their similar personality features and experiences.*]

The eminence of ***The Great Gatsby,*** its unstinting popularity with readers, and its undiminishing attraction for critic and scholar attest superbly to Fitzgerald's successful actualization of his purpose. Rereadings and reexaminations of this work continue to discover in it fine examples of artistry and craftsmanship.

One aspect of the novel heretofore given incidental mention but little relevant treatment is the pattern that makes Myrtle Wilson, through parallels, the double of Gatsby. This pattern is an important yet still neglected one in the "system of carefully plotted interior parallels and cross references" in ***Gatsby*** noted by John W. Aldridge, and I believe that, for several reasons, it deserves further attention. Once marked, it acts as a corrective to such unpersuasive readings (or rather overreadings) as that by Douglas Taylor [see excerpt above, 1953], who endeavors to impose upon the copious richness actually *within* the novel a so-called mythic pattern that ingeniously presents Jay Gatsby as an allegoric jazz-age Christ. Further, it illustrates that, most likely from Conrad, Fitzgerald learned use of the paralleling of scenes and of characters as doubles, a thematic-structural device equally important in ***Gatsby*** as Marlovian first-person narrator and rearranged chronology. And finally the parallel of Gatsby and Myrtle as doubles reveals niceties of structural detail that are illustrative of Fitzgerald's mastery of control and distancing, which averted the easily obtained effects of sentimentalizing the character of Gatsby.

The word *double* as used in literary criticism, Albert J. Guerard has pointed out, is "embarrassingly vague." He finds that the double exists in many forms. Principally pertinent to my use of the idea—or technique—is Guerard's observation that a minor character may be a major character's double by reenacting the major character's traumatic experience. Gatsby and Myrtle, sharing many features, are, I suggest, doubles in this sense; and various duplications occur in the novel that establish and strengthen these two characters' identification as such. The strategy is not only to make the reader see Myrtle, in Aldridge's words, as an actor "in a dumb show caricaturing Gatsby's tragedy," but to make him see Gatsby more objectively as one who, though he was "worth the whole damn bunch put together," was yet a "poor son-of-a bitch."

Details of age, conduct, and social standing proclaim the doubles. Gatsby is "a year or two over thirty," and Myrtle is "in the middle thirties." Just as Gatsby is a mysterious figure who leads a secret or hidden life, so Myrtle is, according to her husband who should know, "a deep one," who leads a secret life as paramour of Tom Buchanan. Both Gatsby and Myrtle are victims and are socially inferior to Nick, Daisy and Tom Buchanan, and Jordan Baker. Tom calls Gatsby "Mr. Nobody from Nowhere" (a social as well as professional, or business, epithet), and this identification, or lack of it, is applicable to Myrtle.

Far more important, however, is their relationship to the Buchanans, those other two-of-a-kind. Gatsby is engaged, above all, in a romantic quest for a beau ideal—"the king's daughter, the golden girl," Daisy; as quester he is playing the same role as Myrtle. Her quest is for Tom, the rich man. Although Myrtle's quest is to her as romantic and as idealized as Gatsby's is to him, its squalor and its frankness create an obvious surface contrast to his. Yet this contrast of superficial dissimilarities tellingly and pointedly signalizes basic *sameness,* which is less readily perceived. Both Gatsby and Myrtle, as Aldridge has mentioned, are "given vitality by a dream that is far larger than any possibility of fulfillment." Gatsby, as he tells Tom, intends to take Daisy away and marry her, to lead her to the marriage that is the logical continuation and culmination of the courtship—and the physical relationship—begun with her in Louisville and interrupted by his war service in Europe. Myrtle,as her sister Catherine tells Nick, intends, likewise, to marry Tom, who is (she says) going to divorce Daisy. This marriage too would follow—logically, according to Myrtle's mode of thinking—a sexual relationship that is seen against a background of war; in this case, it is the domestic strife between Myrtle and her husband who mistreats her and locks her up. This restriction of freedom, keeping Myrtle from Tom, is itself paralleled in the situation of Gatsby, who was kept on in England after the war by some official "complication or misunderstanding" and was consequently for a longer while not free to return to Daisy.

Naively, both Gatsby and Myrtle see their quests as only elegant and sublime. Each, according to them, is motivated and championed by genuine love. Proud Myrtle fancies herself vastly superior to her husband George ("he wasn't fit to lick my shoe"); and, as her sister confides to Nick, Tom is her first real "sweetie." Gallant Gatsby states that Tom is unworthy of Daisy and confesses to Nick that he has never singleheartedly loved anybody but Daisy, the "first 'nice' girl he had ever known."

The unrealistic outlook of these two social innocents, Gatsby and Myrtle, is emphasized in the origin of the affairs of both. Each pair of lovers—Gatsby and Daisy, Tom and Myrtle—is brought together by chance, by sheer accident, and each is immediately attracted by the other's material or physical qualities. Gatsby meets Daisy while he is a young officer at Camp Taylor in Louisville; Myrtle first encounters Tom in a train. "He [Tom] had on a dress suit and patent leather shoes," Myrtle says, "and I couldn't keep my eyes off him. . . ." This report echoes what Jordan Baker says of seeing Gatsby with Daisy for the first time: "The officer [Gatsby] looked at Daisy while she was speaking, in a way that every young girl wants to be looked at some time, and because it seemed romantic to me I have remembered the incident ever since." Gatsby, says Nick, "knew that he was in Daisy's house [in Louisville] by a colossal accident," yet like Myrtle he is dauntless in the attempt to build a life on chance. Full of overtones, "colossal accident" refers, ironically, to both the initiation of these affairs and their termination: one "colossal accident" is to end not only the relationships of Myrtle and Gatsby with Tom and Daisy but their lives also. The forces of society and money as well as the force of character predetermine the failure of the two unrealistic questers.

The purpose of this particular paralleling is, clearly, to keep a moral perspective dramatically before the reader. Gatsby's goal is actually no more admirable, despite the ensplendored vision he takes of it, than Myrtle's. Daisy is no more worthy than Tom, and Gatsby's thinking her so does not make her so; thus the materiality and carnality of Myrtle's quest act as a moral balance to Gatsby's. Nick's report of Gatsby's report of his affair with Daisy could describe equally well Myrtle's affair with Tom: "He took what he could get, ravenously and unscrupulously—eventually he took Daisy one still October night, took her because he had no real right to touch her hand." Myrtle is thus Gatsby's double in another way. She represents Gatsby unadorned—his instinctual, unrefined, consciously repressed self; and her doubling presence in the novel places him quite outside the tradition of Christ-like heroes and directly in a line that runs from Rastignac and Julien Sorel to Joe Lampton in *Room at the Top*.

One should note further how, in a brief scene in Chapter IV, Myrtle as double functions exactly to this same purpose, providing structural instead of narrative comment on Gatsby. The technique is Conradian in that the reader's response is never allowed to become simplistic or to remain static; his sympathetic admiration of Gatsby is constantly tempered with impartial judgment. Gatsby has just told Nick, while they are riding in his "gorgeous car," a fantastic story about his life because "I don't want you to get a wrong idea of me from all these stories you hear." Then as they travel along, "the valley of ashes opened out on both sides of us," says Nick, "and I had a glimpse of Mrs. Wilson straining at the garage pump with panting vitality. . . ." The juxtaposition here creates a grim comic irony: Nick listens to pretentious Gatsby and sees Gatsby's double; what-is impinges upon what-is-said-to-be, both pumping.

Fitzgerald, going further, has underscored the parallel of the yearnings of the doubles Gatsby and Myrtle toward an illusory higher world by use of duplication of symbolic pose and gesture. During the scene on the night when Nick first sees him, Gatsby stretches out his arms in the direction of the Buchanans' home across the bay from which shines a green light (itself an ironic symbol). Myrtle, fleeing to Tom whom she mistakenly believes to be in Gatsby's car, which she has been closely watching for all afternoon, rushes out into the "gathering darkness" with outstretched, gesticulating arms, "waving her hands." Importantly, Michaelis, who saw and reports the scene, says that the car, when it struck Myrtle, had appeared to him to be "light green." Color thus connects questers as well as house and car as images of Daisy and Tom, their goals.

Even in their deaths the parallel of Gatsby and Myrtle is sustained. Both are destroyed, of course, through their association with the "careless" Buchanans, who "[smash] up things and creatures," as Nick says. Tom of the "cruel body" crushes Gatsby spiritually and metaphorically; after coming up against him in the scene in the Plaza Hotel in New York, Gatsby is, as Nick later recapitulates, "broken up like glass against Tom's hard malice"—against Tom's ethically wrong behavior. Discussion of Daisy is the link between that scene and its parallel. In their New York apartment Tom also breaks, actually, Myrtle's nose; that scene, coming earlier, thus not only parallels but foreshadows. (pp. 517-22)

After being struck down by Daisy, Myrtle kneels in the dust, her blood dropping onto it. Gatsby, shot floating on water, drips blood into it. The parallel is as exact as the related elemental contrasts that compose it: man-woman, water-dust. And there is continuation of parallel in the removal of bodies. Myrtle as corpse lies in the garage, in the valley of ashes, viewed by curious passers-by; Gatsby as corpse lies in his mansion by the bay, grotesque counterpart of garage, where prying youngsters come to look in.

Toward the end of the novel, Gatsby's father shows Nick "a ragged old copy of a book called *Hopalong Cassidy,*" on the last fly-leaf of which is written an itemized two-part list of self-improvements; this list had been composed long ago by the young James Gatz in the attempt to become better than he was and in the determination "to get ahead." The "SCHEDULE" includes "Dumbbell exercise and wallscaling" and "Practice elocution, poise and how to attain it"; the "GENERAL RESOLVES" includes "No more smokeing or chewing," "Bath every other day," "Read one improving book or magazine per week," and "Be better to parents." The placing of this list causes it to create at first, in this context, an effect of pathos and to elicit admiration for the ambitious boy. But by reference to a parallel that has occurred earlier on, the effect is altered. Myrtle, also attempting to rise, to make herself more appealing and more attractive than she actually is, spouts a list of self-improvements: "I'm going to make a list of all the things I've got to get. A massage and a wave, and a collar for the dog, and one of those cute little ash-trays where you touch a spring, and a wreath with a black silk bow for mother's grave that'll last all summer. I got to write down a list so I won't forget all the things I got to do." . . . The urge to improvement is beyond question commendable; but, even bedecked and disciplined, Myrtle and Gatsby—the one buying dogs and displaying cosmopolitan magazines and "an over-enlarged photograph" of a "stout old lady" in a bonnet, who is her mother; the other buying palaces and displaying "real" books and a "large photograph of an elderly man in yachting costume," who is Dan Cody, his surrogate father—these doubles remain flamboyant and tawdry failures. Going beyond the merely minor role of a character to illustrate promiscuous Tom's philandering and whoring, Myrtle exists in the novel as a major instrument that continually mirrors for the reader the real nature, the basically unattractive essence, of Gatsby himself.

For the two are, at bottom, alike; and if Gatsby is, as Nick suggests, a knight ("he found that he had committed himself to the following of a grail"), then Myrtle is a courtesan in a cosmopolitan court of love. (pp. 522-23)

The crucial Myrtle-Gatsby parallel is that which concerns their common determination to attach themselves, at last, to their lovers. Myrtle, at the garage, has decided to leave George for Tom, and Gatsby, at the Plaza, has decided to take Daisy away from Tom. It is a master stroke of plotting that arranges events so that one action and one agent destroy the doubles, Myrtle and Gatsby. Actually, it becomes evident, one set of doubles kills the other. Daisy as driver of Gatsby's car now doubles for Tom, and when she kills Myrtle she simultaneously kills Gatsby. Thus Myrtle now emerges as a "ghastly harbinger of death," which Otto Rank identifies as one of the double's great roles. The coming of Gatsby's own actual death, thus anticipated and already vicariously enacted by his double, is merely a matter of time, and it is fitting that the murderer of Gatsby—Myrtle's husband George—be sent to finish the working out of the symmetrical plot by Daisy's double, her husband Tom.

The compactness and constriction of ***The Great Gatsby*** required the use of such an economical technical device as the parallel-double. It must very likely have come to Fitzgerald from Conrad. But its effects, not the least of which is dramatic intensity, must have derived from Henry James. Myrtle, a double-figure in Fitzgerald's splendid carpet, functions as a source of Jamesian operative irony, indicating not only Gatsby's basic nature but (that possible other case) what, without "his Platonic conception of himself," he might have remained and so not "turned out all right at the end." "If he'd of lived," his father proudly says, "he'd of been a great man." As Gatsby's double, as the vulgar suppressed self, Myrtle is an image of the road not taken by Gatsby. The ironic contrast between the doubles finally redounds to Gatsby's favor, of course, or else Fitzgerald's novel would have failed. Because of his "heightened sensitivity to the promises of life" and his "creative passion," Gatsby *does* "get ahead." After scaling walls and attaining poise at last, he transcends, to a peculiar eminence, the primitively impassioned and lurid cheapness that keeps Myrtle forever earthbound, kneeling in dust. She, then, is the device by which, through paralleling and doubling, we can accurately align our vision of Gatsby; by which, without exaggeration, we can truly gauge and evaluate his greatness. (p. 524)

E. C. Bufkin, "A Pattern of Parallel and Double: The Function of Myrtle in 'The Great Gatsby'," in Modern Fiction Studies, *Vol. XV, No. 4, Winter, 1969-70, pp. 517-24.*

BARRY GROSS (essay date 1970)

[*In the following excerpt, Gross discusses* The Great Gatsby *as one of the great tragic works of American literature. He believes that the long-lasting appeal of* Gatsby *lies, in part, in the American reader's willing responsiveness to the novel's tragic hero.*]

The Great Gatsby and the twenties are still, of course, inseparable. Published in 1925, the exact middle, the exact peak of the decade, the novel has become a cultural document. Without intending to, Fitzgerald wrote a love song to and a threnody for a time. Like Janus, he looked back and forward simultaneously, back to all the dreams that had impossibly come true, ahead to all the nightmares that were surely to come.

Yet, hand it to a college freshman who knows nothing about the twenties and he knows precisely what the novel is about. Unlike most critics, whose ***Great Gatsby*** is rarely the ***Great Gatsby*** one reads, he responds to it as it was meant to be responded to. Of all the responses to the novel Fitzgerald had heard, he thought that of Roger Burlingame, an editor at Scribners, best described "whatever unifying emotion the book has." Mr. Burlingame said the novel made him "want to be back somewhere so much."

But where? If the emotion the novel elicits is nostalgia, then today's college freshman cannot possibly feel anything akin to what Mr. Burlingame might have felt. The novel *does* elicit a nostalgic response, but not the sort of nostalgia we usually think of. It is not nostalgia for a time or a place. It is nostalgia for an attitude.

Listening to Gatsby, Nick Carraway is reminded of an elusive rhythm, a fragment of lost words, something heard somewhere a long time ago. Listening to Nick, so are we. We are reminded of an attitude toward life that we still stubbornly hold to despite the world's refusal to confirm it. We are reminded of heroism.

The Great Gatsby satisfies very basic needs that few contemporary novels can satisfy. It satisfies our need to see ourselves writ large. It satisfies our need to remember our infinite capacities. It satisfies our need to confirm our stubborn faiths in the ideals of courage and honor and love and responsibility. Like Gatsby's smile, the novel concentrates on us with an irresistible prejudice in our favor, believes in us as we would like to believe in ourselves, assures us that it has the impression of us that, at our best, we hope to convey. (pp. 331-32)

The Great Gatsby was an act of faith, an act of courage. At three o'clock in the morning [Fitzgerald] saw the dark night of the soul, but he also saw something else. He saw things as they were, what Lionel Trilling calls the condition, the field of tragedy, but he also saw things as they should be. It is this tension between realism and idealism, between knowledge and faith that lies behind all great tragedy. It is this tension that cannot be resolved, that can only be accepted, that Keats, his favorite poet, called negative capability, that Fitzgerald came to call the wise and tragic sense of life.

Fitzgerald gave it a peculiarly American twist. To those who would insist that America cannot, by definition, produce tragedy, Fitzgerald provided proof that it could. In the past such affirmation in the face of defeat was the prerogative of great men alone. Before him only Melville had succeeded in elevating an American to tragic height. But Ahab achieves the tragic height of a Macbeth, not of an Oedipus or a Hamlet or a Don Quixote. In ***The Great Gatsby,*** Fitzgerald was able to endow *two good* men with the wise and tragic sense of life.

He did not regard the attainment of such a perception as a mark of greatness. He regarded it as a necessity for any life at all. Without it, life would be an extinction up an alley. With it, life would at least be a journey, a journey of hope. The hope would, in the end, be dashed. The attempt to control one's destiny is foredoomed. But that really is no matter. Still the journey must be undertaken. Still the attempt must be made.

That is what ***The Great Gatsby*** is about and that is why we continue to cherish it. Our contemporaries tell us ours is an anti-heroic, anti-tragic age, but we do not really believe them. We persist in believing, despite all proofs to the contrary, the

Gal 20—Fitzgerald's Trimalchio—46725—12-14-31E ("Rot-Gut") Ferret and the De Jongs and Ernest Lilly—they came to gamble, and when Ferret wandered into the garden it meant he was cleaned out and Associated Traction would have to fluctuate profitably next day.

A man named Klipspringer was there so often and so long that he became known as "the boarder"—I doubt if he had any other home. Of theatrical people there were Gus Waize and Horace O'Donavan and Lester Myer and George Duckweed and Francis Bull. Also from New York were the Chromes and the Backhyssons and the Dennickers and Russel Betty and the Corrigans and the Kellehers and the Dewars and the Scullys and S. W. Belcher and the Smirkes and the young Quinns, divorced now, and Henry L. Palmetto, who killed himself by jumping in front of a subway train in Times Square.

Benny McClenahan arrived always with four girls. They were never quite the same ones in physical person, but they were so identical with one another that it inevitably seemed they had been there before. I have forgotten their names—Jaqueline, I think, or else Consuela, or Gloria or Judy or June, and their last names were either the melodious names of flowers and months or the sterner ones of the great American capitalists whose cousins, if pressed, they would confess themselves to be.

In addition to all these I can remember that the Ascott-Jones came there at least once and the Cockrell girls and young Brewer, who had his nose shot off in the war, and Mr. Albrucksburger and Miss Haag, his fiancée and Ardita Fitz-Peters and Mr. P. Jewett, once head of the American Legion, and Miss Claudia Hip, with a man reputed to be her chauffeur, and a prince of something, whom we called Duke, and whose name, if I ever knew it, I have forgotten.

All these people came to Gatsby's house in the summer.

At nine o'clock, one morning late in July, Gatsby's gorgeous car lurched up the rocky drive to my door and gave out a burst of melody from its three-noted horn. It was the first time he had called on me, though I had gone to two of his parties, mounted in his hydroplane, and, at his polite invitation, made frequent use of his beach.

"Hello, old sport," he said, "you're having lunch with me in the city to-day, and I thought you might like to ride up now."

That formal caution that enveloped his every word was less perceptible in the daytime—as he stood balancing on the dashboard of his car he seemed very natural, after all. His body had about it that American resourcefulness of movement—a characteristic that is due, I suppose, to the absence of heavy lifting work in youth and, even more, to the formless grace of our nervous, sporadic games.

"I suppose you've seen my car?"

I'd seen it. Everybody had seen it. It was a rich cream color, bright with nickel, swollen here and there in its monstrous length with triumphant hat-boxes and supper-boxes and tool-boxes, and terraced with a labyrinth of wind shields that mirrored a dozen suns.

"Handsomest car in New York," he informed me. "I know it's pretty gay, but what's the use of riding around in a big hearse?"

Sitting down behind many layers of glass in a sort of green leather conservatory, we started to town.

"I've got a favor to ask you, old sport," he said, "and I want to inquire one thing before I begin."

"All right."

"Have you ever had what's known as an affaire de cœur?"

"Why—never a very serious one."

"Never?" he insisted.

"Never."

He patted the knee of his caramel-colored suit.

"Very well," he decided; "I'll have to begin in a different way. Let me ask you this: What's your opinion of me, anyhow?"

A little overwhelmed I began the generalized evasions which that question deserves.

"Be frank, old sport," he urged me.

But I didn't know what I thought of him yet, and so as a facetious substitute I passed on to him, as well as I could remember, the various sinister accusations that had flavored conversation in his halls.

"I'll tell you God's truth." His right hand suddenly ordered divine retribution to stand by. "I am the son of some wealthy people in the Middle West—all dead now. I was brought up in America but educated at Oxford, because all my ancestors have been educated there for many years. It's a sort of tradition."

He looked at me sideways—and I know why Jordan Baker had believed he was lying. He hurried the phrase "educated at Oxford," or swallowed it, or choked on it, as though it had bothered him be-

Galley proof of F. Scott Fitzgerald's The Great Gatsby *with corrections by Fitzgerald. The galley heading* (Fitzgerald's Trimalchio) *reflects the rejected title for the book,* Trimalchio in West Egg. *Copyright 1925 Charles Scribner's Sons. Copyright renewed 1953 Scott Fitzgerald Lanahan. Reprinted with the permission of Charles Scribner's Sons.*

opposite. That is why we go out of our way to honor the hero and extol him when we think we recognize him, whether his name is John Kennedy or Martin Luther King or Che Guevara.

We are Nick Carraway, grown a little solemn with the feel of those long winters of our discontent, grown a little complacent from having been raised in the house of our security. Cautious, politic, wise, meant to swell a rout or two, but not Prince Hamlet. Yet we yearn to acknowledge our Hamlet, not just the Hamlet out there but the Hamlet in us. If Gatsby is the *great* Gatsby, it is because Nick thinks he is. (pp. 333-34)

Disillusioned and lonely, Nick finally meets Gatsby, who clearly represents everything Nick has been taught to scorn, to disapprove of. Gatsby's house is a huge and incoherent eyesore. His tastes run to pink suits and flashy cars. His parties follow the rules of the most vulgar amusement park. He is rumored to be a criminal, a killer.

Yet, against all logic, Nick finds himself attracted to Gatsby. He listens to Gatsby's preposterous autobiography with first incredulity, then fascination, and finally belief. He wants to believe Gatsby, wants to believe that this elegant roughneck, this proprietor of the elaborate roadhouse next door, is a person of consequence. And when Jordan tells Nick about Gatsby's five-year love for Daisy, Nick's beliefs are confirmed. Gatsby comes alive to him because Nick wants him to. Gatsby is the antidote to Nick's interior rules which keep him at a standstill, to his fear of involvement which keeps him from living.

Contrary to all his principles, he allows himself to become involved, allows himself to be used as a Pandarus to Gatsby's Troilus and Daisy's Cressida. But it is really Nick who uses Gatsby. He uses him as a model. There are only, Nick realizes, the pursued, the pursuing, the busy, and the tired. Gatsby is all of these and possessed by intense life. Nick is none of these and possessed by a fear of life. He overcomes his repulsion at life's inexhaustible variety long enough to commit himself to Jordan Baker.

But Nick discovers, as James Baldwin puts it, that connections *willed* into existence can never become organic. Gatsby has thrown himself into his dream of Daisy with a colossal vitality, a creative passion that Nick cannot begin to approximate. Unlike Nick's, Gatsby's commitment is not to a woman but to a vision. That is why, although Daisy is corrupt, Gatsby's dream of her is not. (pp. 335-36)

But to understand why Gatsby's dream of Daisy is incorruptible, we must go back to the night Gatsby saw that the blocks of the sidewalk really formed a ladder that mounted to a secret place above the trees. He knew he could climb to it and once there suck on the pap of life, drink down the milk of wonder. He also knew he could climb to it only if he climbed alone, only if he devoted all his energies, all his commitments to getting there. Such a climb could not be made half-heartedly.

But there was Daisy standing beside him, breathless, immediate. He knew that once he kissed her his mind would never romp again like the mind of God. Daisy could not be won by halves either. He must choose between the stars and a mortal flower. Against all logic, he weds his unutterable visions to her perishable breath and the incarnation is complete forever.

His commitment is to his Platonic conception of himself. To this he is faithful to the end. Gatsby's greatness resides in this vigil, in his protection of an internal flame. His vision comes from an inner light which he sustains and follows. He looks at life from a single window, an isolation that insures his purity. (pp. 336-37)

This is the greatness of the visionary and, as such, is inimitable. Nick cannot *be* Gatsby because he cannot *choose* to have a vision. And even if he could, he would not. The total commitment to an impossible dream is, of course, insane and very dangerous. Nick is too sensible to ever want to pay the price for living too long with a single dream. As an ideal, Gatsby is unapproachable. He can only be wondered at, not emulated.

Nevertheless, he is an ideal we need to recognize and affirm. For Gatsby represents nothing less than wonder itself, the heightened sensitivity to the promises of life, the extraordinary gift for hope, the romantic readiness that makes life something more than an extinction up an alley, that makes life a journey. Gatsby is one with the Dutch sailor whose boat was similarly propelled against the current by a fidelity to an impossible dream. (pp. 337-38)

Gatsby's morality may be nothing more than a chivalrous reflex, nothing more than what H. L. Mencken called it, the sentimentality of a sclerotic fat woman [see excerpt above, 1925]. But it is a morality nevertheless and in lieu of any other. In this too Gatsby atones for the world's failure, its failure to provide standards in terms of which human behavior may be measured and judged. Gatsby's moral response has to do with that Platonic conception of himself, with those ineffable dreams that permit him to transcend a brutal and materialistic world. In Gatsby Nick finds the connection between ideality and morality, between the capacity for wonder and the capacity for responsibility. The price for living too long with a single dream *is* too high. But the price for living too long without one is even higher, not to the physical but to the spiritual life.

Although Nick must disapprove of Gatsby from beginning to end, he is able to recognize and affirm what Gatsby represents. In that recognition and affirmation lie Nick's heroism. He is able to affirm Gatsby in words when he tells him he is worth the whole damn bunch put together. He is able to affirm him in gestures when he erases the obscene word scrawled on Gatsby's steps. He is able to affirm him in deeds when he commits himself to and assumes responsibility for the dead Gatsby, when he invests his intense personal interest to which everyone is entitled at the end.

More important even, he is able, finally, to assume responsibility for himself. He left the Midwest without confronting the girl he was fleeing but before he leaves the East he confronts Jordan Baker. No longer able to lie to himself and call it honor, he admits his dishonesty and carelessness. He has learned not to be like the Buchanans who smash up things and people and then retreat back into their vast carelessness, leaving other people to clean up the mess they make. He has learned not to trust some obliging sea to sweep his refuse away. (pp. 338-39)

He wants, he says, no more riotous excursions with privileged glimpses into the human heart. He wants, he says, the world to be in uniform and at a sort of moral attention forever. He is no longer interested, he says, in the abortive sorrows and shortwinded elations of men.

But the only sort of moral order the world can create is the order of the inquisition which spares only children and the very old. The only order that is liberating is the one each man must create for himself. The riotous excursions are, at least, excursions, and not extinctions up an alley. The abortive sorrows and shortwinded elations of the human heart are what makes it beat.

In the final analysis, Nick knows all that. In telling Gatsby's story and his own, he does create an order, he does affirm the sorrows and elations of the heart. He becomes, in earnest, the guide, the pathfinder he fancied himself to be when he first arrived at West Egg. He captures the elusive rhythm, remembers the lost words, communicates the incommunicable something heard somewhere a long time ago.

Gatsby is the hero we need to acknowledge and affirm, but the hero we dare not be. Nick, who is, like us, within and without, simultaneously repelled and enchanted by the inexhaustible variety of life, is the hero we can and must become. (pp. 339-40)

Barry Gross, "'Our Gatsby, Our Nick'," in The Centennial Review, *Vol. XIV, No. 3, Summer, 1970, pp. 331-40.*

JAMES E. MILLER, JR. (essay date 1975)

[*In the following excerpt, Miller examines* The Great Gatsby *as a "powerful embodiment" of the corrupted era in which it was written—the Jazz Age—and as a commentary on the elusive American dream and the desire to transcend time. In his discussion, Miller also provides a revealing character analysis of Jay Gatsby. For further discussion of* Gatsby *and the American Dream, see the excerpt by Alfred Kazin (1942); for additional comments by Miller on this novel, see* TCLC, *Vol. I.*]

Although ***The Great Gatsby*** conveys much of its meaning obliquely through its imagery, it still is filled with what Henry James called "solidity of specification" and what T. S. Eliot named "a solid atmosphere." Although ***The Great Gatsby*** is much more than a book about the 1920's, it remains solidly based in the era and place that gave it birth. But it is not only based there: it also provides, in some sense, a commentary on the times.

The 1920's saw the enshrinement of business as the religion of America, and at the same time saw some of the most pervasive business and governmental corruption the country had ever experienced. (p. 191)

Fitzgerald's novel is a more powerful embodiment of the spirit of the times than the collected works of Sinclair Lewis, perhaps because Fitzgerald *dramatised* while Lewis *stated*. The corruption of the 1920's saturates ***The Great Gatsby.*** Gatsby's "greatness" is constructed in part on illegal activities that are never fully and clearly defined—bootlegging in a string of drug stores? the handling of bonds from governmental bribes? big-time gambling and gangster war-fare? No matter. Our imagination improves on the withheld reality (as in James's *Turn of the Screw* and *The Ambassadors*). Even the narrator Nick Carraway is infected with the "business ethic" of the time as he pursues his career as a bond salesman and confesses: "I bought a dozen volumes on banking and credit and investment securities, and they stood on my shelf in red and gold like new money from the mint, promising to unfold the shining secrets that only Midas and Morgan and Maecenas knew."

Tom Buchanan comes from the world of established wealth, which, though contemptuous of the blatant kinds of corruption represented by Gatsby and his associates, itself indulges quietly and discreetly in bribery, blackmail, and manipulation (preferably legal) to maintain and consolidate its power. It is a world that has lines into the more obviously corrupt world, as witness Tom's friend Walter Chase, a one-time associate of Gatsby, who is willing to spy on Gatsby for Tom (and no doubt for a price). In many ways Tom Buchanan is the most sinister character in ***The Great Gatsby,*** as he seems to typify the American business man (man of power) who remains the perpetual adolescent intellectually. . . . Tom is presented as circling around an idea that might provide the means for the application of his brute strength and financial power—racial suppression: "Civilization's going to pieces . . . I've gotten to be a terrible pessimist about things. Have you read 'The Rise of the Colored Empires' by this man Goddard? . . . The idea is if we don't look out the white race will be—will be utterly submerged. It's all scientific stuff; it's been proved."

If Tom Buchanan appears sinister in all his respectability, Jordan Baker appears pathetic in her petty cheating at golf. But her corruption cannot be dismissed as minor, as it suggests the contagiousness of the 1920's disease (the disease is not, of course, confined to the 1920's, but it reached epidemic levels in that age). In a few swift strokes, Fitzgerald through Nick reveals her character and her world. "When we were on a house-party together up in Warwick, she left a borrowed car out in the rain with the top down, and then lied about it—and suddenly I remembered the story about her that had eluded me that night at Daisy's. At her first big golf tournament there was a row that nearly reached the newspapers—a suggestion that she had moved her ball from a bad lie in the semifinal round. The thing approached the proportions of a scandal—then died away. A caddy retracted his statement, and the only other witness admitted that he might have been mistaken." It is not surprising that, given her allies in the world of the rich, the unpleasant incident would be "fixed." But the point revealed in the novel is that however easily a cheating episode can be hushed-up, a debased spirit cannot so quickly be mended or fixed. Jordan Baker remains what she is, a product of the pervasive corruption of the period: she will cheat her way through life.

Meyer Wolfsheim is the most clear-cut figure of 1920's gangsterdom. He lurks in the shadows behind Gatsby throughout, and when he emerges briefly in the restaurant scene in New York to have lunch with Gatsby and Nick, we glimpse something of his career in his short and sweet tale of the "night they shot Rosy Rosenthal." . . . Later, Gatsby tells Nick: "Meyer Wolfsheim? . . . he's a gambler. . . . He's the man who fixed the World's Series back in 1919."

Although the foreground of ***The Great Gatsby*** is largely filled with the super-sophisticated life of the rich and pleasure-bound figures of the jazz age, the "roaring twenties," not far in the background are the Rosy Rosenthals, the Meyer Wolfsheims, the Walter Chases, in violent pursuit of money and the good, easy life. The two worlds share in common the universal desire for the right "business gonnegtion," and the reader may be sure that at the edges, where the two worlds meet in the shadows, such "gonnegtions" are negotiated and consummated continually.

Gatsby's own "corrupted innocence" lies at the heart of the meaning of the novel. And although he is quite obviously a figure of the 1920's, he is also something more. Although ***The Great Gatsby*** is deeply rooted in its time, it is considerably more than a revelation of life in the jazz age. It transcends its time to reveal something about America, American character, and the American dream. Tom Buchanan and the others exploit the American "business ethic" (or "gangster ethic") for their own sordid advantage. But Gatsby is as much victim as exploiter. From the moment that we (with Nick) first set eyes on him, we sense that he is vulnerable in his innocence in some way that all the others are not. He is standing outside in the dark night, looking over the waters from West Egg to East Egg: ". . . he stretched out his arms toward the dark water in a curious way, and, far as I was from him, I could have sworn he was trembling. Involuntarily I glanced seaward—and distinguished nothing except a single green light, minute and far away, that might have been the end of a dock. When I looked once more for Gatsby he had vanished, and I was alone again in the unquiet darkness."

Trembling? Perhaps Gatsby is the only character (except Nick) capable of *trembling* in the "unquiet darkness" of the novel. Surely he is the only character in pursuit of something transcendent and worthy of his own submission. And it is his tragedy that his vision of transcendence comes to focus on an object that is enchanting on the surface, rotten at the core.

To trace the origins of Gatsby's dream means beginning near the end of the novel and zig-zagging back and forth in order to piece together the broken pieces of his life. For example, it is only in the last chapter that we encounter (through his father come East for the funeral) Gatsby as a boy. And in that mid-western boyhood we discover the roots of Gatsby's transcendent vision. Gatsby's father shows Nick a tattered copy of an old *Hopalong Cassidy* book, and there on the flyleaf are the resolutions that the boy James Gatz made for his self-improvement and "getting ahead." (pp. 192-95)

From Gatsby's boyhood we must jump to his young manhood . . . for our next glimpse of the development of the dream. We learn only the bare outline of his life on Dan Cody's yacht, encountered on Lake Superior. It was at this time that Gatsby began the remaking of himself, beginning with the change of name from James Gatz to Jay Gatsby: "The truth was that Jay Gatsby of West Egg, Long Island, sprang from his Platonic conception of himself. He was a son of God—a phrase which, if it means anything, means just that—and he must be about his Father's business, the service of a vast, vulgar, and meretricious beauty. So he invented just the sort of Jay Gatsby that a seventeen-year-old boy would be likely to invent, and to this conception he was faithful to the end." Thus, even before the encounter with Daisy, the dream appears unworthy of the dedication of the dreamer, and curiously at odds with his astonishing innocence. The adventure on the Cody yacht concludes with Gatsby as victim (cheated of the money left him by his rich patron).

The next transformation in Gatsby takes place on his initial encounter, as a young officer in the army, with Daisy Fay in Louisville, and for this event we have only fragmentary accounts in scattered chapters. But from these it is clear that the vague, inchoate dream alights on Daisy, and romantically transfigures her into a creature of Gatsby's imagination. . . . (p. 196)

Gatsby's re-encounter with Daisy is, of course, the action represented in the foreground of the novel as constructed, but the fate of Gatsby's dream is not so fully delineated. We must speculate with Nick as to Gatsby's feelings and insights: "There must have been moments even that afternoon [their first rendezvous after five years] when Daisy tumbled short of his [Gatsby's] dreams—not through her own fault, but because of the colossal vitality of his illusions. It had gone beyond her, beyond everything. He had thrown himself into it with a creative passion, adding to it all the time, decking it out with every bright feather that drifted his way. No amount of fire or freshness can challenge what a man will store up in his ghostly heart."

In the confrontation scene between Gatsby and Tom, in the New York hotel room, when Tom reveals to Daisy what his spies have learned about Gatsby's activities, Gatsby appears to lose control as he begins to talk excitedly and irrationally, "defending his name against accusations that had not been made." At this critical turning point, we are told that "only the dead dream fought on as the afternoon slipped away, trying to touch what was no longer tangible, struggling unhappily, undespairingly, toward that lost voice across the room." Was the dream dead or dying for Gatsby at this point? Although he plays out the role he has assigned himself in relation to Daisy, there are hints that he might have developed some self-awareness. But there is suggestion too that he preserved his illusion intact. When Nick leaves him standing outside the Buchanan house, after Daisy has killed Myrtle Wilson with Gatsby's car, and after we have just glimpsed (with Nick) the cosy, conspiratorial scene of Tom and Daisy at a kitchen table holding cold fried chicken and bottles of ale—Gatsby appears to be devoted to the "sacredness of the vigil." But does he sense, on some level of consciousness, what Nick tells us and we know to be true—that he is "watching over nothing"?

The complexity of Gatsby's illusion, and his own complicated feelings about it, are suggested in a number of astounding remarks that he drops in off-hand manner in casual conversation. For example, as Nick at one point (before the New York confrontation scene) is trying to find the right description for Daisy's voice, Gatsby says: "Her voice is full of money," and Nick is overwhelmed with the aptness of the metaphor. In another instance, after the confrontation scene, as Nick and Gatsby are discussing the relation of Tom and Daisy, Gatsby suddenly says: "In any case, . . . it was just personal." And Nick asks the reader: "What could you make of that, except to suspect some intensity in his conception of the affair that couldn't be measured?"

It is no doubt this immeasurable and indefinable "intensity" of Gatsby's dream that induces Nick to call out to him, on their last meeting (when Gatsby is still waiting for the call from Daisy that will never come): "You're worth the whole damn bunch put together." Nick adds: "I've always been glad I said that. It was the only compliment I ever gave him, because I disapproved of him from beginning to end. First he nodded politely, and then his face broke into that radiant and understanding smile . . ." And as Nick senses something of Gatsby's embryonic awareness, he remembers his first encounters with Gatsby at his big parties: "The lawn and drive had been crowded with the faces of those who guessed at his corruption—and he had stood on those steps, concealing his incorruptible dream as he waved them goodby." At Gatsby's death, we must again speculate with Nick as to the extent of Gatsby's self-knowledge: "I have an idea that Gatsby himself didn't believe it [the call from Daisy] would come, and perhaps he no longer cared. If that was true he must have felt that he had lost the old warm world, paid a high price for living too long with a single dream." But whatever the extent of Gatsby's final insight, Nick's judgment remains clear from the moment it is presented on the second page of the novel: "No—Gatsby turned out all right at the end; it is what preyed on Gatsby, what foul dust floated in the wake of his dreams that temporarily closed out my interest in the abortive sorrows and short-winded elations of men."

How can it be that Gatsby, surrounded by so much corruption, can remain innocent? We know something of the sordidness of the sources of his fortune, and we witness the moral shallowness of Daisy, about whom he has spun the gossamer foundations of his fantastic and colossal dream. We cannot even be sure that he has, in the face of defeat, achieved that kind of self-knowledge that would render his fate genuinely tragic. We can only speculate, as Nick speculates, on what he has learned in his obsessive pursuit of so unworthy an object. But Nick's judgment is clear in Gatsby's defense, and after all is said—it is only Nick's Gatsby that we come to know in the novel. But even as Nick asserts Gatsby's worth above all the others, he is compelled to add that he "disapproved of him from beginning to end." It is the moral awareness that Nick achieves in the progress of the action of the novel that enables him, in spite of Gatsby's "corruption," to affirm that he came out all right in the end. His ambivalent moral judgment is not unlike that of Owl-Eyes, the party guest who earlier was startled to find the books in Gatsby's library real. He is the only one of the multitudinous party-goers to attend Gatsby's funeral, and he says the final word at the graveside: "The poor son-of-a-bitch." . . . It is moral sympathy for a victim whose innocence transcended his corruption. (pp. 197-99)

Although ***The Great Gatsby*** is deeply rooted in the 1920's, and at the same time appears to provide a commentary on American character and the American dream, it is still something more—something reaching out beyond its time and beyond its place. In short, the novel embodies and expresses the simple, basic human desire and yearning, universal in nature, to snatch something precious from the ceaseless flux and flow of days and years and preserve it outside the ravages of time. This is obviously a theme that is not confined to the 1920's or to America. Although it may not win the designation of "archetypal," it is hard to imagine a time when human beings did not feel it deeply.

The Great Gatsby is a novel relentlessly devoted to the present, set, as it is, in its total action in the summer of 1922. But it is a novel that is haunted by the past—Gatsby's and America's—and it is the past which reaches into and shapes the present. Gatsby himself embodies in a grotesque way the desire to transcend time. When Nick repeats to him a truism, "You can't repeat the past," he astonishingly replies: "Can't repeat the past? . . . Why of course you can!" To Gatsby time appears as submissive to his will as wealth or power: "He looked around him wildly, as if the past were lurking here in the shadow of his house, just out of reach of his hand." And he cries out: "I'm going to fix everything just the way it was before." Gatsby's desire is not peculiarly American, but his stupendous self-assurance that he can recreate the past may well derive from the dark underside of the American dream. But time will run out on Gatsby, as it has on the American dream—and as it does on all human dreams and desires and aspirations.

It is this theme, more feeling than statement, that is evoked by the lyric style of ***The Great Gatsby.*** Throughout the novel, Nick responds in a deeply personal way to the events he witnesses, translating them into feelings that lie so deep as to defy precision of language. For example, at the end of Chapter VI, after Gatsby has tried to explain Daisy's meaning for him and the absolute necessity of recovering that lost past, Nick muses:

> Through all he said, even through his appalling sentimentality, I was reminded of something—an elusive rhythm, a fragment of lost words, that I had heard somewhere a long time ago. For a moment a phrase tried to take shape in my mouth and my lips parted like a dumb man's, as though there was more struggling upon them than a wisp of startled air. But they made no sound, and what I had almost remembered was uncommunicable forever.

"An elusive rhythm, a fragment of lost words"—we feel with Nick a sense of loss of the past that cannot be articulated. This sense of loss becomes acute and central in the closing lines of the novel, as Nick meditates on Gatsby's abortive dream: "He had come a long way to this blue lawn, and his dream must have seemed so close that he could hardly fail to grasp it. He did not know that it was already behind him, somewhere back in that vast obscurity beyond the city, where the dark fields of the republic rolled on under the night." Nick has come to realize that Gatsby's dream was lost before it was even dreamed, as the American dream itself had been frittered away, squandered in the past. But Nick's last thoughts move away from Gatsby to himself—and to "us"—as he meditates on time, and present, past, and future: "Gatsby believed in the green light, the orgiastic future that year by year recedes before us. It eluded us then, but that's no matter—tomorrow we will run faster, stretch out our arms farther . . . And one fine morning—" Nick here breaks off, the vision intercepted before it is launched, and speaks his last words on Gatsby's, his, the American, the human predicament: "So we beat on, boats against the current, borne back ceaselessly into the past."

With these closing words we find that we ourselves have become participants in the novel's meaning, as the action has broadened out to include us all. It is impossible to respond to those final words without being thrown back into one's own past, in painful memory of those momentous events of purely personal meaning that have slipped away to be lost forever. We are all Gatsbys yearning to recreate the past; we are all Nick Carraways lyrically regretting the rush of time swiftly past our grasp. And as we close the book and look about us, touched by an "elusive rhythm, a fragment of lost words," we may feel something of the impulse of the protagonist at the end of *The Waste Land*—to gather fragments to shore up against our ruin. (pp. 200-02)

James E. Miller, Jr., "Fitzgerald's 'Gatsby': The World As Ash Heap," in The Twenties: Fiction, Poetry, Drama, *edited by Warren French, Everett/Edwards, Inc., 1975, pp. 181-202.*

EDWIN MOSES (essay date 1977)

[*In the following excerpt, Moses posits that the inevitable tragedy within* The Great Gatsby, *following the pattern of classical tragedy, results from Jay Gatsby's disturbance of the natural balance of ascribed social relationships.*]

I'd like to suggest . . . that a lot of ***Gatsby***'s power stems from the sense of tragic inevitability which Fitzgerald develops in the very first chapter.

The aspect of tragedy I'm concerned with here is nemesis: the inevitable, convulsive righting of a balance in nature which the tragic hero has disturbed. When Macbeth listens to the witches and kills the king, when Lear listens to the voice of senility and divides his kingdom, they cause a breakdown in the natural order which can only be—and ultimately must be—repaired by their deaths. When Gatsby determines to steal Daisy away from Tom, he similarly rends the fabric of things, here defined in social terms, and the outcome is the same. Because the law he breaks is petty and arbitrary, the object he hopes to attain by breaking it frivolous, his fate is simultaneously tragic and ironic—but it's inevitable nevertheless, and Gatsby *himself* looms large enough to make it matter. (pp. 51-2)

The fundamental natural law in the world of ***The Great Gatsby*** is that the relationship between self and environment—physical setting as symbol and embodiment of social milieu—is integral. Jake Barnes is the same man anywhere, but the Buchanans depend for their identity on the East Egg estate and all that it implies. So when Gatsby attempts to break down that relationship by leaving his own milieu and luring Daisy from hers, he looses chaos into the world and invites nemesis. In Shakespeare the commonest agent of nemesis is military action; here it is social action. Because the people in this world depend for their sense of self on what others think of them, the Buchanans can destroy Gatsby simply by denying him the identity he has so desperately struggled to develop. Tom's affair with Myrtle, drawing him away from his proper sphere in East Egg into a tawdry apartment in the city, has jarred the natural order even before Gatsby arrives. By the end of the first chapter it will be clear that Gatsby will strain it to the breaking point, and thereby bring about his tragic ending.

Fitzgerald goes to great lengths to establish the essential link between the Buchanans and the place they inhabit. It's true that they "drift unrestfully" and that Nick doesn't believe this last move of theirs is permanent, but always they drift where "people [are] rich together," so whether or not they stay on this particular estate, it remains their emblem—it forms and identifies them. To begin with, Tom's lawn behaves very much like Tom: it "*r*[*uns*] toward the front door" and "*jump*[*s*] over sun-dials," like a football player, and then "*drift*[*s*]," . . . like this particular ex-football player. Fitzgerald further links Tom and the house by introducing him at the end of a sentence *about* the house: "The front was broken by a line of French windows, glowing now with reflected gold and wide open to the warm windy afternoon, and Tom Buchanan in riding clothes was standing with his legs apart on the front porch." . . . And the first words of his which Fitzgerald reports are not "How are you?" which would imply an interest in Nick, but rather "I've got a nice place here." The focus of his attention is all outward, on the things he owns: regarding Nick apparently as a kind of machine for admiration, he "turn[s him] around by one arm" and aims him at the Italian garden, the roses, the motor-boat. It's not "Love me, love my roses," but rather "Admire my property, admire me." For all his money and power, Tom still needs this sort of support from Nick. The main point here, though, is that this method of presenting Tom and his property instills very strongly the feeling that he's part of the place; that the elaborate house and grounds represent and form the man. They're in no essential way separable.

Daisy's characteristic place is the inside of the house. In *The Sun Also Rises* Hemingway introduces Brett in a four-word sentence—"With them was Brett," repeated to reveal her impact on Jake—which isolates and focuses attention on her as an individual. But Fitzgerald presents Daisy, as he does Tom, as part of a setting: "The only completely stationary object in the room was an enormous couch on which two young women were buoyed up as though upon an anchored balloon." . . . And: "Then there was a boom as Tom Buchanan shut the rear windows and the caught wind died out about the room, and the curtains and the rugs and the two young women ballooned slowly to the floor." . . . Fitzgerald's descriptions of Daisy and the place, even more than with Tom, overlap at a number of points. The place: glowing French windows, bright rosy-colored space, windows gleaming white, rippling breeze. Daisy: white dress rippling in the breeze, bright eyes and mouth, glowing face. She belongs to this place; she can't exist apart from it. And she can't exist in a human vacuum either: her identity as much as Tom's is formed by the response of other people. Her first coherent remark, which she makes with regard to the citizenry of Chicago, is "Do they miss me?" This is a version of the central question of her existence—"How do they respond to me?"—and so Nick's jokingly hyperbolic reply is appropriate to the occasion. In this world the perceived depends on the perceiver for its being.

Having established the laws and necessities that his people live by, Fitzgerald introduces the forces which will threaten that order and so will have to be exorcised: Myrtle Wilson and Gatsby. His introduction of Gatsby into the scene is brilliant, a masterpiece of economy:

> "You live in West Egg," Jordan remarked contemptuously. "I know somebody there."
>
> "I don't know a single—"
>
> "You must know Gatsby."
>
> "Gatsby?" demanded Daisy. "What Gatsby?"
>
> Before I could reply that he was my neighbor dinner was announced; wedging his tense arm imperatively under mine, Tom Buchanan compelled me from the room. . . .

This anticipates the climax of the chapter, in which Nick sees Gatsby standing alone in the darkness. And it suggests the form of nemesis which will overtake Gatsby. Ultimately the Buchanans will deny him the identity—Jay Gatsby, rich socialite, worthy squire to Daisy—that he's been striving so desperately to establish; now Tom denies him even his identity as Jay Gatsby, Nick Carraway's neighbor. By refusing to respond to him in any way, these people (excluding Nick) in effect declare his non-existence—and in Fitzgerald's world they're in a position to make such a declaration stick. (pp. 53-5)

By reiterating the Buchanans' restlessness Fitzgerald has revealed the potential instability of their world, and now Myrtle Wilson's telephonic invasion suggests that a crisis is imminent. (The heavy emphasis on Tom's great power makes it seem likely—but not inevitable, at this point—that the victims of the resulting catastrophe will be not the defenders of the red-and-white Georgian castle, but the invaders.) The great significance of setting, and the degree to which the characters are part of the setting, imparts considerable importance to physical movement: if one is a fixture in a given physical and social environment, his abrupt departure is naturally disruptive. When Tom leaves the room to answer the phone, and Daisy, after some chatter even more frivolous and irrelevant than usual, gets up and follows him, the result is a tense tableau: the room, all of a sudden, is noticeably empty. Fitzgerald heightens the tension by clever manipulation of point of view. Nick up to this point has observed and speculated, but outwardly at least has maintained a fair degree of detachment. So his response to the present events—his "instinct . . . to telephone immediately for the police," and his attempt "to look pleasantly interested and a little deaf" . . .—inevitably electrifies the atmosphere.

Fitzgerald introduces his major characters in reverse order, in terms of their ultimate importance: Tom, Daisy, Gatsby. At the point when he appears in person, at the end of the first chapter, Gatsby has no obvious connection with the people and events that have come before. But the part he will play in the Buchanans' lives is implicit in Fitzgerald's selection and presentation of detail. To begin with, Fitzgerald has been careful to establish that Tom and Daisy are essentially two of a kind. Tom is a willful and domineering man who gets what he wants with money and muscles; Daisy, his feminine counterpart, dominates with the face, the smile, the "low, thrilling voice." . . . Tom's restlessness is revealed by his affair with Myrtle Wilson; Daisy's, explicitly, by her conversation ("God, I'm sophisticated") with Nick. The difference is that Tom's random power and willfulness has borne fruit, so to speak, whereas Daisy's for the moment has not. Given all this, the logic of the situation simply demands another man: Daisy's lover-to-be is the x-factor required to balance the equation. And the way that Gatsby's name has been spotted into the conversation at the dinner party . . . reveals Gatsby as the missing man. Fitzgerald has manipulated the elements in this scene so skillfully that during a first reading and without benefit of title one could deduce Gatsby's place in the story.

The final question is how Gatsby's role is revealed as inevitably tragic. I've stressed the integral and inviolable relationship between people and their characteristic place. So if Tom and Daisy are people of the opulent light, Gatsby is a creature of the "unquiet darkness" in which Nick first sees him, physically separated from that light (and from the green light at the end of the dock) by a tremendous symbolic barrier, the bay that separates West from East Egg. Thus Gatsby is revealed as inevitably a part of but inevitably alienated from that scene toward which he yearns. He appears alone—an invariable characteristic of the tragic hero is that he is or becomes isolated—and the last and highly charged words of the chapter are that "when I looked once more for Gatsby he had vanished. . . ." Darkness is Gatsby's element, his characteristic place, in which he cannot bear to stay but to which he must return. The natural order of things is stronger than he is: nemesis overtakes him, and he vanishes at the end of the novel as at the end of the chapter. The pattern of the whole is implicit in the part.

That Fitzgerald believed in this created world as real was essential—otherwise the novel would have revealed itself as a cynical potboiler—but we as readers need not believe in it in that sense to feel its power. We can be cynical about the inevitability of anything in the world of our own experience, and yet find the unfolding of the tragic design in Fitzgerald's world profoundly reassuring. We need faith in this at least, I think: that in "a little world made cunningly" man the image-maker can transcend the chaos we feel around us. Fitzgerald never managed to create order in his own life, but he did in ***The Great Gatsby,*** and for that we should be deeply grateful. (pp. 55-7)

Edwin Moses, "Tragic Inevitability in 'The Great Gatsby'," in CLA Journal, *Vol. XXI, No. 1, September, 1977, pp. 51-7.*

KEATH FRASER (essay date 1979)

[In the following excerpt, Fraser discusses the ambiguity of Nick Carraway's sexuality in The Great Gatsby. *In this unusual examination he asserts that a study of Fitzgerald's original manuscript and a careful reading of the finished work reveals Nick's homosexual tendencies.]*

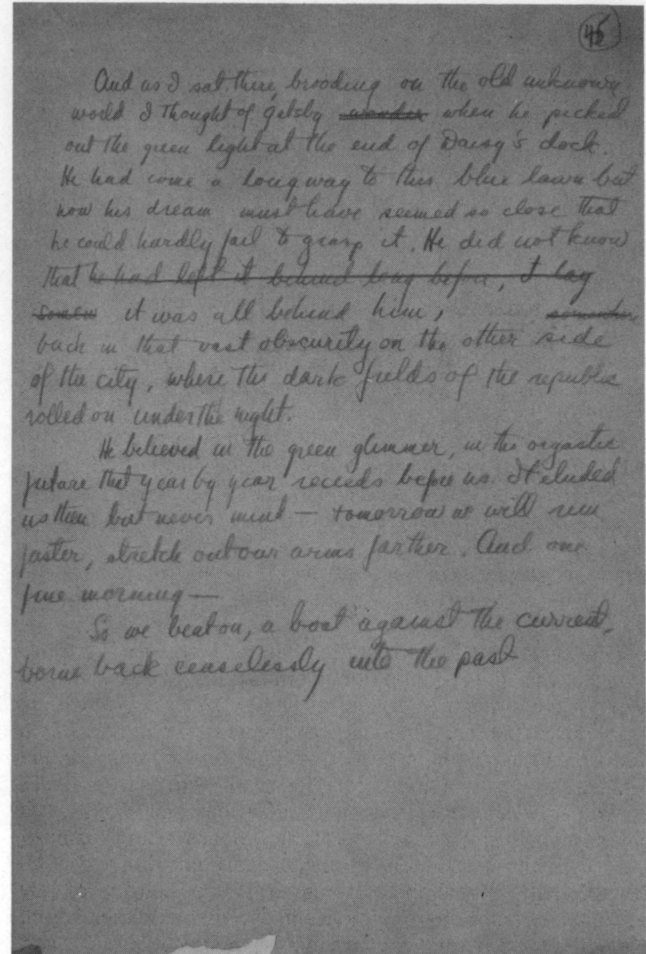

45

And as I sat there brooding on the old unknown world I thought of Gatsby when he picked out the green light at the end of Daisy's dock. He had come a long way to this blue lawn but now his dream must have seemed so close that he could hardly fail to grasp it. He did not know that ~~he had left it behind long before, it lay~~ it was all behind him, back in that vast obscurity on the other side of the city, where the dark fields of the republic rolled on under the night.

He believed in the green glimmer, in the orgastic future that year by year recedes before us. It eluded us then but never mind—tomorrow we will run faster, stretch out our arms farther. And one fine morning—

So we beat on, a boat against the current, borne back ceaselessly into the past

Holograph copy of the last page of F. Scott Fitzgerald's The Great Gatsby. *Copyright 1925 Charles Scribner's Sons. Copyright renewed 1953 Scott Fitzgerald Lanahan. Reprinted with the permission of Charles Scribner's Sons.*

"Gonnegtions" are of course important in ***The Great Gatsby,*** for without them Gatsby's rumoured association with crime, and its particular dialect, would not ring as true. The presence of Wolfsheim serves to connect Gatsby with the underworld from which his riches are hatched and his plans to marry Daisy made possible. "Gonnegtions" are Gatsby's dream, and also Nick's. What Gatsby of West Egg is seeking, by means of the lucrative business afforded by the underworld portrayed in Wolfsheim, is a con*egg*tion with Daisy Fay of East Egg. In this light, Gatsby's "Platonic conception of himself" is enriched by what I take to be Fitzgerald's allusion to Plato's parable in *The Symposium* about the origin of love. In *The Symposium* Aristophanes is made to tell how Zeus, angered at the behaviour of the three circular shapes constituting the orginal sexes, decides to cut each in half: like eggs, says Plato, sliced in half by a hair. Yearning ever since to be reunited with himself, man has sought to couple with his other half. According to Plato, the resultant halves of the original hermaphrodite became heterosexual men and women; halves of the original female, lesbian women; while fragments of the first male turned into men who have devoted their lives (honourably in Plato's eyes) to the intimacy of boys and other men ("it requires," says Plato, "the compulsion of convention to overcome their natural disinclination to marriage and procreation''). If ***The Great Gatsby*** is a love story, and it is, it is one aware of this complex sexuality of antiquity. As we shall see, it is not only to *The Symposium* that we must turn for confirmation of the novel's peculiar and hitherto unnoticed sexuality—the theme of what follows—but also to *The Satyricon* of Petronius.

Here and there in Fitzgerald's novel inklings of depravity turn reader into voyeur. One never quite knows, for example, how to read the last page of Chapter 2, a scene which follows the dissolute party in Myrtle Wilson's apartment, when Nick Carraway follows Mr. McKee out to the elevator. Descending, McKee suggests Nick have lunch with him some day—anywhere—and the elevator boy snaps: ''Keep your hands off the lever.'' . . . Apologetic, McKee says he was unaware he was touching it. The narrator says he would be glad to go. Where they go is to McKee's bedroom: ''. . . I was standing beside his bed and he was sitting up between the sheets, clad in his underwear, with a great portfolio in his hands.'' Then some more of the narrator's ellipses between what we presume are titles of photographs taken by McKee are followed by Nick's abrupt removal to ''the cold lower level'' of Pennsylvania Station where he lies waiting for the morning train. It is an odd scene because Nick never goes to lunch with McKee and McKee never reappears. Odder still is the fact that Nick joins McKee in his apartment when no invitation, apart from the one to lunch, is spoken, and no rapport between the two men at Myrtle's party is established—except for Nick's having wiped a spot of dried lather from McKee's cheekbone when McKee has dozed off in a chair.

What I am about to suggest is that the quality of concealment in ***The Great Gatsby*** is adroit enough to have caused us to read over scenes we are intended to read through. Is there in the novel a cultivated ambiguity, such as that of the McKee episode, which flirts with, but never answers the question of Nick Carraway's sexuality, because Nick refuses to tell us the whole truth about himself? What is recoverable of Fitzgerald's earliest intentions, in Bruccoli's edition of ***The Great Gatsby: A Facsimile of the Manuscript*** (1973) [see Additional Bibliography], may help to cloud the issue more than clear it up. Deleted from the novel we now have are words, phrases, and sentences of a section which, in the manuscript, follows directly from what now is the conclusion of Chapter 2—that is, the scene in McKee's bedroom. (In the final version of the novel this section, which concludes with the second epigraph quoted above, is removed to become the conclusion to Chapter 3, the account of Gatsby's first party.) More willing in the ***Facsimile,*** it would seem, to acknowledge the ambiguous nature of the bedroom scene, Fitzgerald pauses to compound the mystery by conceding that ''a false impression'' . . . has been given by virtue of the fact that the few events discussed thus far in the story appear to have occupied all of Nick's time. Fitzgerald's original intention, if it can be rescued from pencilled-out lines in the manuscript, was to suggest that these events, in Nick's words, ''were merely incidents sandwiched in between other incidents that interested me or fascinated just as much—in fact the man I balled around with most all summer doesn't appear in this story at all.'' . . . This revelation is cancelled out in favour of the more concealed phrase, ''my own affairs''—which became the phrase we now have, ''my personal affairs.'' . . . It may be merely coincidental that McKee, who never reappears, and the man Nick says he ''balled around with most''—but who is hushed up—appear at the same stage of the original novel, when Fitzgerald is in the process of establishing the character of his narrator. Yet sexual implications, even in the muted final version, are not lost on us, and in the manuscript do serve to challenge our accepted reading of Nick's sexuality.

In this section of the ***Facsimile*** Nick goes on to mention a brief affair with a girl from the accounting department of the Probity Trust company he works for in New York. The reason for his letting ''the affair blow quietly away,'' in the manuscript, is the same offered in the final version—because, according to Nick, the girl's brother ''began throwing mean looks in my direction.'' . . . What is perhaps revealing are Nick's original words, the words Fitzgerald began to use, then scratched out and buried beneath the curious reason Nick offers for his escape from this girl. The words he starts to use, to explain the breakup, are ''but her brother began *favoring me with . . .*'' (my emphasis). . . . With what? It seems a peculiar phrase to start explaining the reason for leaving this brother's sister. Does the rewritten version lead us away from a more honest confession? Probity Trust—Nick's company—tends to affirm those qualities which Nick would have us believe are his—honesty, conscientiousness, uprightness—and yet one is left wondering whether Nick is telling us the whole truth about abandoning the girl, indeed the whole truth for abandoning any girl, especially the one out West. As for his dropping Jordan Baker, we have tended to believe him when he calls Jordan ''incurably dishonest,'' . . . and because of this seldom have we believed Jordan when she, in turn, claims Nick to have been less than honest and straightforward in his relationship with her.

In view of what has been presented so far it may not be too soon to suggest that what Nick might in part be concealing, even escaping from, is what the narrator of **''The Rich Boy''** (agreed to be among Fitzgerald's finest short stories, and written immediately after ***The Great Gatsby***) calls ''abnormality.'' Perhaps we have taken Nick too much at his word—without trying to read through such a scene as the one in McKee's bedroom with the whole of Nick's character in view. Conceivably, his penetrating self-analysis on the opening page of the novel has lulled us into accepting his own protestation of being ''normal.''

He appears to begin his story in a way calculated to disarm his reader, encouraging him ''to reserve all judgments.'' . . . By suggesting that he himself has refrained from criticizing others—by following his father's advice—Nick may be pleading his own case with us. ''The abnormal mind,'' he observes, ''is quick to detect and attach itself to this quality when it appears in a normal person, and so it came about that in college I was unjustly accused of being a politician, because I was privy to the secret griefs of wild, unknown men.'' Such men, alongside Nick, are categorized by him as ''abnormal'' because they are attracted to him. And so when ''an intimate revelation was quivering on the horizon'' he has tried to appear tolerant, yet disinterested: ''for the intimate revelations of young men, or at least the terms in which they express them, are usually plagiaristic and marred by obvious suppressions.'' The choice of words and phrases is peculiar. Why, for example, are such intimate revelations—flawed as they are by plagiarism and suppression—''abnormal''? Presumably, because such revelations are offered by ''unknown'' men, and are therefore gauche and indiscreet. But rather than perceiving these as a ''normal'' hazard for a man as attractive to other men as Nick boasts he is, he condemns them as belonging to those who were born with rather less than their share of ''the fundamental decencies.'' . . . Mainly because of his disarming admission of snobbery, we have always been convinced of Nick's own fundamental decencies—indeed doubtful if there is another narrator in modern literature more trustworthy than he. Yet in *The Satyricon* there is a narrator who is almost certainly as much a model for Fitzgerald's character as Conrad's trusty and frequently mentioned Marlow. (pp. 330-33)

Still of little interest to scholars is the way Fitzgerald handles sexuality in his writings. The truly great artists, according to Virginia Woolf, are androgynous in mind, and Leslie Fiedler, in passing, has noted this interesting quality in Fitzgerald (it is a quality Fiedler is reluctant to admire): "In Fitzgerald's world, the distinction between sexes is fluid and shifting, precisely because he has transposed the mythic roles and values of male and female, remaking Clarissa in Lovelace's image, Lovelace in Clarissa's. With no difficulty at all and only a minimum of rewriting, the boy Francis, who was to be a center of vision in *The World's Fair,* becomes the girl Rosemary as that proposed novel turned into ***Tender is the Night.*** Thematically, archetypally even such chief male protagonists as Gatsby and Dick Diver are females" [see *TCLC,* Vol. 1]. Fitzgerald himself, of course, acknowledged that "I am half feminine—at least my mind is. . . . Even my feminine characters are feminine Scott Fitzgeralds." This last sentence could be put another way: his masculine characters are masculine Scott Fitzgeralds, which is to say they are no less feminine than his own "half feminine" mind. At the party in Myrtle Wilson's flat, for example, Nick, looking out the window, makes an admission which is generally read as a comment on the tension created by the technique which critics have admired in the novel: Fitzgerald's ability to observe as well as to participate. "I was within and without, simultaneously enchanted and repelled by the inexhaustible variety of life." . . . It has never been read as a suggestion of the narrator's epicene nature. (p. 334)

Throughout the novel Nick holds the masculine forms of Gatsby and Tom in sharp contrast. For him, Gatsby's form seems preferable to Tom's, yet it is Tom's masculinity which captures Nick's attention in so convincing a manner that critics of the novel, in identifying the grander theme of the American dream, have perceived in Tom the cruel and palpable foil to Gatsby's idealism and illusion. For Nick the "gorgeous" Gatsby fails to come "alive" until Jordan Baker explains to him that Gatsby's house was deliberately chosen by its owner to be across the bay from Daisy's own house in East Egg. Then, says Nick, "He came alive to me, delivered suddenly from the womb of his purposeless splendor." . . . In contrast to the insuperably *physical* purpose in the novel of Tom Buchanan, Gatsby and his purpose seem clearly metaphysical, springing agilely from that "Platonic conception of himself." . . . Imagery associated with Gatsby suggests solipsism, sexlessness. It is otherwise with Tom: "Not even the effeminate swank of his riding clothes," Nick observes, "could hide the enormous power of that body—he seemed to fill those glistening boots until he strained the top lacing, and you could see a great pack of muscle shifting when his shoulder moved under his thin coat. It was a body capable of enormous leverage—a cruel body." . . . (p. 335)

Here is a body of rather more interest to Nick than the one he courts in Jordan Baker. In fact, it fascinates him. As the novel progresses Tom's body comes to represent, far more than Gatsby's corruption and criminal associates do, the threat and evil force of the book. "Making a short deft movement, Tom Buchanan broke her nose with his open hand." . . . The nose, of course, is Myrtle's. Myrtle's husband, on the other hand, suffers Tom's cruelty in a more subtle and central way, reaching its culmination on the fatal day Nick lunches with the Buchanans. The day is blisteringly hot. On his way to lunch Nick comments to himself, "That any one should care in this heat whose flushed lips he kissed, whose head made damp the pajama pocket over his heart!" Upon entering Tom's house he records what he overhears: "'The master's body!' roared the butler into the mouthpiece. 'I'm sorry, madame, but we can't furnish it—it's far too hot to touch this noon!'." . . . Nick then adds: "What he really said was: 'Yes . . . Yes . . . I'll see'." . . . In fact the caller is Myrtle's husband, hard up for cash, hoping Tom will sell him the car on which Wilson hopes to make enough profit to take his wife away. What Nick purports to hear first is an illusion, yet it is an illusion artistically contrived to make the scene which follows between Tom and Wilson at the garage all the more adroit with respect to the underlying competition between the two rivals for Myrtle Wilson's favours. More particularly, it causes us to examine Nick's own narration of the scene.

> "Let's have some gas!" cried Tom roughly. "What do you think we stopped for—to admire the view?"
>
> "I'm sick," said Wilson without moving. "Been sick all day."
>
> "What's the matter?"
>
> "I'm all run down."
>
> "Well, shall I help myself?" Tom demanded. "You sounded well enough on the phone."
>
> With an effort Wilson left the shade and support of the doorway and, breathing hard, unscrewed the cap of the tank. In the sunlight his face was green.
>
> "I didn't mean to interrupt your lunch," he said. "But I need money pretty bad, and I was wondering what you were going to do with your old car."
>
> "How do you like this one?" inquired Tom. "I bought it last week."
>
> "It's a nice yellow one," said Wilson, as he strained at the handle.
>
> "Like to buy it?"
>
> "Big chance," Wilson smiled faintly. "No, but I could make some money on the other."
>
> "What do you want money for, all of a sudden?"
>
> "I've been here too long. I want to get away. My wife and I want to go West." . . .
>
> (pp. 335-36)

I want to suggest that this scene, like the McKee scene, is easily passed over, and that the sexual undertow adrift in the particular images which link Wilson and Tom has been carefully set up by Fitzgerald to contrast the two male rivals. We recall that three chapters earlier Nick has admired the incomparable form of Gatsby's car—the one Tom now is driving—"swollen here and there," observes Nick, "in its monstrous length." . . . In ***The Great Gatsby*** it is worth remembering that the car is a symbol of masculinity, and the women (Jordan and Daisy) who drive cars do so badly, upsetting, even killing people. In the same chapter that Nick draws our attention to Gatsby's proud possession, he also glimpses "Mrs. Wilson straining at the garage pump with panting vitality as we went by.'' . . . The scene above, with Tom and Wilson, seems therefore suggestive in the images it chooses to repeat. There is the elongated car driven by the potent Tom; and in the pump yet another phallic image, at which Wilson strains with rather less vitality than his wife, who has thrown him over for Tom. (p. 336)

[If] Jordan Baker, for example, is a ''type'' she is one whose ''typical'' qualities are significant in our appreciation of why Nick Carraway is attracted to them. As a champion athlete she, like Tom, is at home in the world of men. In addition, according to Nick, she has a ''hard, jaunty body,'' . . . a body ''like a young cadet.'' . . . She is, moreover, androgynously named; and her name—for someone as impressed by the shapes of cars as Nick—''combines two automobile makes'' (according to one scholar), ''the sporty Jordan and the conservative Baker electric.'' The car metaphor is dually important in the novel, for not only does it connect Tom and Wilson—a connection leading to Myrtle's death as well as Gatsby's—but it also connects Nick and Jordan soon after they meet, and . . . when they part. . . . (p. 339)

Just why they part is not clear, though to Jordan it is evident that their incompatibility derives from duplicity on Nick's part. Nick, it seems, always has been ''half'' attracted to women (''I wasn't actually in love, but I felt a sort of tender curiosity''). . . . (p. 340)

The critical problem is thus simple: is the novel plainly weak in those parts, for example Nick's relationship with McKee, his affair with Jordan, which remain shady and ambiguous; or do we give Fitzgerald the benefit of the doubt and look for other, perhaps deeper reasons to explain his apparent shortcomings in the novel? What ***The Great Gatsby*** seems about in part, and where it derives its suggestiveness and energy, lies in what is not accounted for, what is undisclosed. The whole of Gatsby's affair with the underworld is the obvious example of this theme and its expression. But an important statement of the theme is also, one feels, Nick's ''protestation of being average and honest and open''—to put into his mouth the narrator's words in **''The Rich Boy.''** It is not unreasonable to suppose that Nick's readiness to declare his cardinal virtue to be honesty, is deliberately intended to mislead us. This declaration tempts us into accepting everything he tells us as the whole truth, though my evidence so far is intended to suggest that the oblique or metaphoric power of the novel prevents a simple reading of the way Nick looks at the world and at himself. In any effort to understand Gatsby, there are connections (''gonnegtions'') that need to be made about the storyteller himself, but which we have traditionally ignored because we have always trusted Nick as average, honest, and above board.

What, then, is he hiding? An uncertain sexuality becomes an unavoidable conclusion. He is no longer simultaneously enchanted and repelled by the double vision from the window in Myrtle Wilson's New York apartment, nor is he, upon his return to the West, that ''well-rounded man'' he had hoped to become when ''life is much more successfully looked at from a single window.'' . . . His return to the West is not a solution, but a desire to escape the indecent ambiguities of conduct, ''founded'' on either ''hard rock'' or else ''wet marshes.'' . . . No longer tolerant of the excesses of others, Nick reaffirms his own Puritanical heritage with an extreme desire to see ''the world . . . in uniform and at a sort of moral attention forever.'' . . . His return is not to the girl he left behind, for he does not seem naturally inclined, in Plato's words, to marriage and procreation, and only in an oblique way is he prepared to acknowledge his own ambivalent sexuality by the association Fitzgerald allows him through the important classical echo of Petronius. (Nick, we remember, confesses his having been ''rather literary'' at college, and his allusion to ''the shining secrets that only Midas and Morgan and Maecenas knew'' . . . is his way of introducing himself and us to the ''bond business.'')

Persuasive evidence of the theme of impotence and bisexuality in ***The Great Gatsby*** is discoverable in *The Satyricon* of Petronius, to which Fitzgerald was so sufficiently drawn that at different times he wished to call his novel after one of its characters. *Trimalchio* and *Trimalchio in West Egg* were the working titles which strongly guided Fitzgerald's composition of ***The Great Gatsby*** (a title which never satisfied him). Trimalchio, of course, is the name of the wealthy and vulgar host who throws the garish party in the chapter of *The Satyricon* called the ''Cene Trimalchionis.'' What is crucial to my own discussions is not so much Trimalchio, which is what Nick calls Gatsby in the novel, as the narrator of *The Satyricon,* who attends Trimalchio's party, and whose name is Encolpios. Encolpios, who has in some way offended the fertility god, Priapus, provides what plot survives in *The Satyricon* by journeying, so scholars believe, from Marseilles east to Italy, and quite likely to the centre of the empire, Rome. Encolpios—and his name may well derive from the Greek word, *kolpos,* which, among several definitions, means vagina and womb—is a sort of Odysseus in quest of love: he is certainly a conscious parody of Odysseus, but an Odysseus both impotent and bisexual.

Now Nick (or Dud, as Fitzgerald conceived him) fails with women as Encolpios does, though not for lack of trying. Mistaken by Wolfsheim for another man who is looking for a ''gonnegtion,'' Nick, like Gatsby, is nevertheless seeking a connection with women. Interestingly, the ''gon'' of ''gonnegtion'' is the Greek root for seed (*goné*), and one wonders, in light of Fitzgerald's subtle and conscious use of names, whether Carraway, which after all is a seed, isn't seeking ''egg'' in the same sense that he is portrayed as a ''bond'' salesman looking for business connections—from which he also flees, incidentally, rather than become tainted with the seediness (the pun seems suitable) of easy money proffered by the likes of Gatsby . . . and Wolfsheim. There is nothing as blatantly ambivalent about Nick Carraway's sexuality as there is about that of Encolpios. Yet Fitzgerald's narrator, not unlike Petronius's, does describe in his own odyssey a parody, a parody of the American dream which rises to the poetic height we have come in ***The Great Gatsby*** to accept as its most indigenous quality. In Fiedler's words, ''Fitzgerald's young men go east . . . in quest . . . of . . . an absolute America; a happy ending complete with new car, big house, money, and the girl.'' That Gatsby and Nick *both* fail to win the girl is an interesting comment upon the subtlety of the novel. For if we begin to read through the novel with the problem of sexuality in mind, then the normal critical interpretations which focus mainly on Gatsby are seen to be too straightforward. These interpretations fail to recognize that the corruption of the novel originates not merely in Gatsby's shady business connections, but also in Nick Carraway's disingenuous sexuality. This sexuality, when peered at beside the bright and ethereal sexuality of Gatsby, or the dark and cruel sexuality of Tom, may well shed more light on why, in the novel's concluding words, ''the orgiastic future . . . year by year recedes before us,'' . . . and why the dud-like and impotent pursuit of that future diminishes the American dream of attaining what Anson Hunter in **"The Rich Boy"** tries over and over to get—the girl. (pp. 341-43)

Keath Fraser, "Another Reading of 'The Great Gatsby'," in English Studies in Canada, *Vol. V, No. 3, Fall, 1979, pp. 330-43.*

ROBERT EMMET LONG (essay date 1979)

[*Long is the author of* The Achieving of The Great Gatsby: F. Scott Fitzgerald, 1920-1925, *a thorough examination of Fitzgerald's literary apprenticeship and the influences that led to his masterwork. Also discussed are the manuscript versions of the novel, which reveal its various stages of development. In the following excerpt, Long finds that* Gatsby *is patterned after the traditional fairytale.*]

In its vision of modern emptiness, ***The Great Gatsby*** is a key document of the twenties, so much so that had it not been written the twenties would actually seem diminished. It is as vivid today (and as "surprising") as when it was written, and has an intense life. Gatsby's vividness has been reinforced on so many different levels of myth and folklore that it is difficult to say which most controls his conception. The woodchopper's son, the young man from the provinces come to the great city, Dick Whittington, Horatio Alger—all stand in the background of his conception. But perhaps as importantly as from any other source, Gatsby comes from the fairy tale; for if the novel has, in Henry James's phrase "the imagination of disaster," it also has the imagination of enchantment. There is a sentence in the manuscript, but not included in the book, that reveals Gatsby. It occurs when he is among Daisy's circle at Louisville. "He was a nobody with an irrevealable past," Fitzgerald comments, "and under the invisible cloak of a uniform he had wandered into a palace." With its palaces and invisible cloaks, Gatsby's imagination has a fairy-tale quality. Almost instinctively, he regards Daisy Fay as a princess, a girl in a white palace, and the spell of the fairy tale, too, marks his ascendency from his midwestern farm to his own palace of a kind at West Egg. Gatsby becomes a kind of fairy-tale prince in disguise, is deprived of his princehood while retaining his princehood in essence, the consciousness of a noble inheritance, of an inner sovereignty belonging to a prince, even though he wears a shepherd's garments.

Fitzgerald refers to Long Island by name very rarely in the novel; it seems disembodied as well as real and is a region of wonder. Carraway's recall of his adolescence at the end is, too, part of the child's perception of life as wonder, as in the fairy tale. And there is a strong demarcation in the novel between good and evil; the Buchanans' world, and the Wilsons', seem somehow bewitched by evil forces, which are beyond containment or control. The evocative energies of the fairy tale help to account, I think, for the helplessness one feels before the enchanted horror of the world Fitzgerald creates in the novel, a world in which the good prince is put to death, and the dark prince reigns. Other American novelists before Fitzgerald drew from the fairy tale; Henry James did so in *The Portrait of a Lady* and other novels. But Fitzgerald is alone in the twenties in drawing from the resources of the fairy tale to create his age, to touch the depths of its irrationality, and at the same time to create one of the most memorable characters in the American fiction of the 1920s.

Since World War II there have been novels published in America that have some claims to seriousness, and yet after one has read them one can hardly remember their characters. Compare with these the power of dramatic projection in ***The Great Gatsby,*** the way in which Jay Gatsby lives in one's imagination, refusing to be dislodged. Such enduring life is the mark of exceptional achievement, can only be the result of a creative conception of astonishing depth and power, which ***The Great Gatsby*** continues to give the impression of being. (pp. 183-84)

Robert Emmet Long, in his The Achieving of "The Great Gatsby:" F. Scott Fitzgerald, 1920-1925, *Bucknell University Press, 1979, 226 p.*

ANDRÉ LE VOT (essay date 1979)

[*In the following excerpt from his* F. Scott Fitzgerald: A Biography, *originally published in France in 1979, Le Vot provides a thematic examination of* The Great Gatsby *and a detailed analysis of the skillful use of color through which Fitzgerald implied the novel's themes.*]

[In his works, Fitzgerald] sometimes identified himself with a prestigious double, found himself by disavowing a mutilating, humiliating lineage, asserted that he was a self-made man in the true sense of the term: the son of his works, who had broken loose from his moorings, burned his ships and striven to outdo himself. At other times Fitzgerald tried to dispel his worst fears by miring his character in impotence and renunciation.

In ***Gatsby,*** these two antithetical and heretofore alternating attitudes are juxtaposed, confronting each other in a dialectical relationship. No lonter does the author identify with one or the other, shifting with the wind from fair to stormy. For the first time he is not speaking in his own name, in reaction to the events of the moment. He is detached, looking down from above, so distant from his immediate preoccupations that they become mere landmarks in a panorama that embraces his whole era, that stretches to the very horizons of America's history. Fitzgerald does not do this topically and anecdotally, as he did in ***The Beautiful and Damned,*** in which he thought he was meaningfully addressing the problems of his generation, but serenely and objectively, abandoning the half-truths of social realism to reach the symbolic truth of a global vision.

This vision relies for its effectiveness on a coexistence of contrasts, on their simultaneous operation. To register this new depth of field, this dual aim missing from his earlier work, Fitzgerald had to stretch his own limits, to venture into unexplored novelistic terrain. And there he built an intricate palace of echoes and mirrors, a meticulous architectonic complex, all in trompe l'oeil that traps, refracts, fragments, reconstructs a reality in which he is invisible, but which reflects better than all his autobiographical writing the heart of the problems he and his generation faced.

He begins by creating a fundamental split between the character who is watching and judging and the one who dreams and acts. The first task is assigned to Nick Carraway, his narrator. Nick, newly arrived from his native Midwest in the spring of 1922, is skeptical, seemingly blasé but, at bottom, incurably romantic. He is fascinated by New York life and dreams of making his fortune. As an underpaid stockbroker, he comes into contact with the tremendously rich Buchanans, his cousin Daisy and her husband, Tom, whom Nick knew at Yale. They live in a posh mansion in East Egg, Long Island. Nick has rented a rundown cottage across the bay, in West Egg, where he is invited to the wild parties of his flamboyant neighbor, the enigmatic Jay Gatsby. This early experience in the world of the rich excites his caustic wit, toward the Buchanans, especially the proud and brutal Tom, and toward Gatsby, whose absurd lies and pathetic man-of-the-world pose Nick penetrates.

Thus is defined, in the book's first three chapters, the psychology of the man who will recount that summer's events. He has an objective observer's unflagging curiosity and a humorist's quick perception of the ridiculous. He sees himself as detached, cultivated, unprejudiced. In short, he presents a picture of a man with a sense of proportion and prides himself on a faintly amused tolerance for other people's follies. He makes a point of obeying the rules of propriety and is driven by his social inferiority to maintain a constant vigilance. The secrets he discovers or that are entrusted to him confirm his notion of his own importance and moral superiority.

These, however, are mere appearances. This flattering self-portrait is soon wiped away by Nick's constant lack of assurance and his immaturity. His true nature emerges as the story unfolds. Irresolute, timid, manipulated by those around him, he is a Middle Western cousin of those young people of good family who wander through nineteenth-century novels in search of an identity without ever really learning about love. Incapable of realizing his dreams or of loving wholeheartedly, he tries to give substance to his deepest aspirations by living vicariously. In Gatsby he finds a man who, despite his social sins, is richly endowed with all the qualities Nick lacks: creative imagination, tenacity, boldness, passion. Through Gatsby he will achieve a kind of grandiose romantic destiny that his withered soul and middle-class pretensions could never otherwise reach. In Gatsby, whom he'd have invented had he been a novelist, he recognizes the hero he wished to be and never will be. His sense of his own life is submerged, his potentialities flower, the superman's adventure becomes his own.

This identification is similar in many ways to what a reader or movie viewer feels, with the difference that Nick never suspends his critical judgment. Faithful to his character, he maintains his conventional moralist's reserve as long as he can. "Gatsby," he says, represents "everything for which I have an unaffected scorn." He is won over to him only after a long and reluctant revision of his values. What is ridiculous about the man, his affected manner of speaking, his dandyish clothes, his ostentatious acts, all irritate and wound Nick's sense of reserve and sobriety, but they are informed with a dignity that commands respect.

In any case, these are only questions of manners. Nick finds it more difficult to accept the fact that Gatsby is an unscrupulous gangster, the alarming Wolfsheim's right arm. The narrator's respect for the proprieties has not prepared him to associate mystical flights of love with an outlaw's criminal behavior. Yet when he reaches his moral maturity, he takes Gatsby's side. The corrupt means Gatsby uses to achieve his ends have not altered his fundamental integrity, his spiritual intactness. His means reflect the corruption of the times; they are the only ones available to an indigent cavalier seeking his fortune. True corruption, Nick discovered, lies in the hearts of those who despise Gatsby, especially in Tom's.

The complete reversal of Nick's attitude toward Gatsby, from an amused disdain that Tom could share to a wholehearted, militant identification that blames Tom and those like him for his hero's death, this cross-current of judgments and feelings, provided Fitzgerald's talent with a broad compass that he exploited to the fullest. The whole gamut of comic effects comes into operation as the gap between subject and object narrows. Seen from a distance, when Gatsby is simply a ridiculous stranger, he is treated as a caricature. But when Nick shares his feelings, trying to keep his emotions under control, the humor is tender and compassionate, which still allows the narrator to stand off a bit. And when this reserve becomes impossible to maintain, when the subject identifies with the object of his interest and Nick, so to speak, blends with Gatsby, becomes Gatsby—for it is Nick alone, speaking with Gatsby's voice, who tells Gatsby's love story—the tone changes completely. What was at first grotesque is now sublime, mocking rejection has become passionate loyalty, ironic understatement has changed to lyric hyperbole. From then on, Fitzgerald brought to bear all the resources of his evocative and iridescent prose. Here again, the situation lends itself admirably to stylistic variations, modulations of tone, from fervor to nostalgia.

Fitzgerald had already experimented with these various modes in a fragmented, isolated way. In ***Gatsby,*** for the first time, inspired by his subject, he found a simple, effective technique for joining them, combining them within a single narrative, setting the changes in his narrator to them like the movements of a piece of music. More generally speaking, two modes, satiric and lyric, dominate the book, expressing its two major themes, which contrast with and complement each other. The first records the failure and inadequacies of an unsatisfied, disquiet, disoriented society in search of something in which to invest its unused energy, a society unable to realize its eagerness to live intensely without disorder and violence. Tom, Daisy, Myrtle, Wolfsheim and, in the background, the people who crowd into Gatsby's parties, embody this new world-weariness. The book's second theme celebrates a vision that transfigures the world and gives meaning and direction to these disappointed hopes and unsatisfied yearnings. His conversion accomplished, Nick exalts Gatsby's creative imagination, his "extraordinary gift for hope, a romantic readiness such as I have never found in any other person and which it is not likely I shall ever find again."

Something of the disorganized sterility of Fitzgerald's own recent history is in these scenes of manners. And it is the revival of his creative power, the liberation of his imagination that he was celebrating in exalting a hero who, despite his weaknesses, embodied that power and freedom: "There was something gorgeous about him, some heightened sensitivity to the promises of life, as if he were related to one of those intricate machines that register earthquakes ten thousand miles away."

The aim that emerges from the opposition of two forms of reality, two modes of expression, is not merely abstract or didactic. It is woven into a web of existence that is in itself profoundly meaningful and functional; its extraordinary poetic richness modulates, accompanies, deepens the writer's purpose.

Light and color were used to maximum effect in creating these secret atmospheres that are more climates of the soul than of places or events. Among these, as distinct in their natures and connotations as any other natural duality, the colors yellow and blue are the most significant; it is they that best reflect the fundamental duality of Fitzgerald's imaginary world. They are usually linked in such a way that their contrast underlines the nature of a given situation or moment. Their conjunction seems to be the sign of a fleeting instant of harmony and beauty, whereas their dissociation suggests disorder or latent conflict. There is nothing pat or preestablished about the effects they engender. Blue can be cold or tender or sentimental, yellow ardent or powerful or destructive, and these are just some of the associations that seem obvious. But their "meaning" is never frozen into an allegorical hierarchy. Glowing within a constellation of other symbols, a color can serve as a leitmotiv. For example, Gatsby, whose innermost nature is stamped by the influence of the moon, of water, of night, is associated with blue, the blue of the grass in his lawns and of his servants' uniforms. But the image he shows the world, a false one, is deliberately given a golden, sunlit gleam, as in is luxurious yellow automobile. Tom Buchanan is subject to no such ambiguity: he is determinedly sunny, aggressively sure of his power, a sturdy, straw-haired man of thirty who is first seen in the book standing booted and solid before his French windows as they glint with the gold of the setting sun. Fitzgerald's use of color could be purely descriptive, but rarely did he fail to aim at another reality beneath the surface. If there is one area in Fitzgerald's work in which realism is no more than a facade, it is in his use of color and light.

The story's realistic background is merely a prop. Blue is, of course, the color of water, the sky, twilight; whiskey, wheat and straw are golden. But these colors are concurrently literary qualities that draw the deep meaning of their relationships not only from this individual artist's imagination, but also from the collective imagination of a country, a history. (pp. 142-46)

Close to this type of usage is the synesthesia by which a color in ***Gatsby*** is not only seen but felt, touched, tasted, savored in its density and weight. The specific density of yellow is as well a moral factor here as a physical one. In the heroic days of the pioneer settlements west of the Alleghenies, farmers who found it too difficult and costly to haul their crops over the mountains converted their grain into alcohol, which was lighter and less bulky; the alcohol was easily exchanged for gold, or replaced gold in local barter arrangements. Metamorphoses of yellow, its conversion from one form to another, the concentration of its substance that transforms its nature and distorts its original meaning: here we have a new and central metaphor in Fitzgerald's imagination.

The process is clearly perceived in the vegetable kingdom: in it, yellow appears as a ripening and perversion of green. The shoot eventually becomes grain, what is juicy becomes dry, what is flexible hardens from vegetable to semimineral. A bluish sprout turns green, then, as though by combustion, goes yellow. Temporally, blue and green are the colors of growth, yellow that of fructification. On the one hand we have a fluid *span of time,* on the other an *instant,* intense and concentrated. Yellow is a point of culmination, a state, a substance, whereas blue and green are merely hope, surge, change. Realization of green's promise implies loss of substance—sap—and the dynamic and creative thrust of growth. Potentialities shrink in the transmutation; this is an immense reduction of dream to experience.

And experience, the actual series of events, tastes of ashes and death. For wheat's fate is to be reduced to flour, just as a mineral crumbles into dust. Vegetation's opposite is parodied in the Valley of Ashes, on the road from West Egg to New York, which sits like a gigantic memento mori, a Dantesque spectacle of nature ravaged and reduced to dust, a "desolate area of land. This is a valley of ashes—a fantastic farm where ashes grow like wheat into ridges and hills and grotesque gardens; where ashes take the forms of houses and chimneys and rising smoke and, finally, with a transcendent effort, of men who move dimly and already crumbling through the powdery air."

Gatsby's whole story and, behind it, that of a grand dream gone awry center on this symbol of contemporary America and its companion vision, on the book's last page, of a Long Island imagined in its primitive splendor, as the first navigators must have seen it. . . . (p. 147)

A new world's green freshness, the green light shining in the night: symbols of hope gone dry in the sun's heat. When wheat is ripe, its stalk, deprived of sap, goes to straw. Straw is sterile, inflammable, dangerous. When Nick takes the train to see the Buchanans on the hottest day of the year, his presence foretells the sun's victory, the conflagration that will disperse the book's characters; "the straw seats hovered on the edge of combustion." He and Gatsby wear straw hats when they go to visit Daisy, an admirable touch in a story that generally ignores men's headgear; nothing else could quite so well have connected the desiccating powers of gold and straw. A quatrain in the epigraph defines Gatsby's relationship with Daisy as that of a "gold-hatted, high-bouncing lover," and Fitzgerald had briefly considered calling his novel *Gold-Hatted Gatsby*. The iconographic and symbolic nature of the detail is reinforced a few pages farther on when women's hats are seen as helmets of metallic thread. A fairy-tale touch is introduced in Gatsby's remark that Daisy's voice is golden; the remark is immediately linked to fable by Nick's evocation of the musical clinking of gold, his vision of a princess in a white palace, "the king's daughter, the golden girl."

These few touches are enough to call up a legendary background. The two rivals, Buchanan and Gatsby, are competing in a tournament, and when they switch cars, it is meaningful because the machins then designate their drivers' real natures. Tom, the knight of the sun, the "sturdy, straw-haired man," takes the wheel of Gatsby's yellow car while Jay, the straw-hatted schlemiel, appropriately drives his adversary's blue convertible coupe. (p. 148)

Almost always, the juxtaposition of blue and yellow signals a state of balance and euphoria. The girls in yellow, for example, sound the trumpets of happiness in Gatsby's blue gardens. (p. 151)

This special image of juxtaposed blue and gold occurs again and again in flashes of gold on windows in the blue twilight. What is important here is the relationship of values rather than specific differences in pigmentation. Blue's tendency . . . is to darken, yellow's to brighten. Even when the two related colors pull away from each other, the blue toward a dull black and the yellow toward shining white, as they do in ***Tender Is the Night,*** the effects of their association are unchanged. The verb "to bloom," frequently used in conjunction with them, reveals the secret nature of colors that glow only at night, against a shadowy background, but are dried and withered by sunlight. This is why it is important to see yellow, the sun's prevailing color, apart from the sun's other two attributes, its heat and light. It reaches all its varnished intensity, its gleaming clarity, only when it is shielded from the light around it, contrasted with dark blue or displayed like a jewel against the velvety blackness of night. Daytime yellow is intolerably strident.

Removed from this night-colored casket, which demarcates it and serves as a foil for it, yellow glares, grows hostile. Its light burns and cracks what it touches, becomes the color of disintegration and chaos. It is beneficial only at a distance. A spectator must also stand off from it, in creative shadow; if he nears the light, it bursts into flame. The tyranny of the senses overwhelms the fervor of contemplation. But if proper precautions are taken, then yellow, resplendent in the darkness, becomes the emblem of a mystical vision. In **"Absolution"** Fitzgerald came closest to formulating an aesthetic—even an ethic—of yellow, merging it with the festival spirit, but carefully distinguishing its sacred and profane aspects. He speaks in the voice of the priest urging Rudolph to visit an amusement park:

> Go to one at night and stand a little way off from it in a dark place—under dark trees. You'll see a big wheel made of lights turning in the air . . . and everything will twinkle. But it won't remind you of anything, you see. It will all just hang out there in the night like a colored balloon—like a big yellow lantern on a pole."
>
> Father Schwartz frowned as he suddenly thought of something. "But don't get up close," he warned Rudolph, "because if you do you'll only feel the heat and the sweat and the life."

This may have been the lesson Gatsby learns. Hadn't Nick told him that his brilliantly lighted house resembled a fairground? At his parties he always remains aloof from his guests, never joining in their games, their dancing; he stands alone in the moonlight on the top step of the marble stairs leading to his door. This separation in space reflects a distancing in time as well. Removed from the present, he lives in memory a love reduced to its essence, for it too is sheltered from "the heat and the sweat and the life."

A whole connotative system is thus erected in climates and seasons of the spirit. A thorough study could bring out the isomorphism of yellow, the sun, heat, dryness and shrillness, for example, in contrast with their opposites, blue, the moon, coolness, moisture and depth. The qualities of day and night, of dawn and dusk, summer and winter are subject to the attraction of these magnetic poles dissociated from their alternation in time, making their influence felt not only in clock and calendar time but in interior space. In the last resort, the countless elements in these two constellations can only be identified by what is most immediately visible in them, the yellowness or blueness of their brightest stars, which thus take on the status of ultimate, indivisible meanings, of the grand, antithetical system that pervades Fitzgerald's universe. Finally, yellow and blue become primary elements, essential qualities toward which gravitate the material and spiritual principles on which the specific character of Fitzgerald's work is based. They can rightly be considered the monads of his imaginary cosmos. (pp. 151-52)

André Le Vot, in his F. Scott Fitzgerald: A Biography, *translated by William Byron, Doubleday & Company, Inc., 1983, 393 p.*

JEFFREY STEINBRINK (essay date 1980)

[In the following excerpt, Steinbrink discusses Fitzgerald's artistic intent in The Great Gatsby, *which he believes attempts to reconcile the past and present while maintaining hope for the future.]*

Fitzgerald wrote the bulk of ***The Great Gatsby*** in 1924, when he was twenty-eight. It might be described as an attempt to explore the relationship between the past and the present in the hope of discovering a sense of balance between giddiness and despair capable of sustaining a man without delusion as he enters life's long decline. It is many other things as well, of course, but among its main concerns is how to face "the promise of . . . loneliness . . . , a thinning briefcase of enthusiasm, thinning hair" as we drive "on toward death through the cooling twilight." ***The Great Gatsby*** exhorts those of us who would be reconciled with the future to see the past truly, to acknowledge its irrecoverability, and to chasten our expectations in view of our slight stature in the world of time and our ever-diminishing store of vitality.

We are brought to this understanding, however, only when we realize and accept the unlikelihood of regeneration or renewal in an entropic universe. Repeatedly in ***The Great Gatsby*** Fitzgerald allows us (and perhaps himself as well) to entertain the hope that it is possible to make a "fresh start"—to undo the calamities of the past or to relive its quintessential moments. The geographic dislocation of all the important characters in the novel is in itself suggestive of this hope; each, like Fitzgerald himself, is a midwesterner gone east, a descendant of the pioneers trying to reverse the flow of history. (p. 159)

The notion that the flow of history can be arrested, perhaps even reversed, recurs in ***The Great Gatsby*** as a consequence of the universal human capacity for regret and the concomitant tendency to wish for something better. Nick Carraway has come East not simply to learn the bond business, but because his wartime experiences have left him restless in his midwestern hometown and because he wishes to make a clean break in his relationship with a woman whom he likes but has no intention of marrying. The predominant traits of Nick's character—patience, honesty, and levelheadedness—derive from his sure senses of history and social position, and yet in the chronology of the story he is first to succumb to the idea that life is subject to continual renewal. . . . The fresh start Nick seeks in the East represents not so much a rejection of his heritage as a declaration of its inadequacy to satisfy the rather ambiguous yearnings of the post-war generation. Stimulated by his contact with the teeming city and the novelty of his circumstances of West Egg, Nick gives in to a most compelling illusion. "I had that familiar conviction," he says, "that life was beginning over again with the summer." . . . (p. 160)

Tom and Daisy Buchanan, their marriage in pieces, have similarly come East, determined to settle after several years of "drift[ing] here and there unrestfully wherever people played polo and were rich together." . . . "'I'd be a God damned fool to live anywhere else,'" says Tom, whose foolishness is hardly a consequence of geography. Tom is a classic manifestation of entropic theory in human form. Nick describes him as "one of those men who reach such an acute limited excellence at twenty-one that everything afterward savors of anti-climax." . . . Tom's single consolation may well be his muddled perception that he is not alone in his fall. "'Civilization,'" he says, "'[is] going to pieces'." . . . Daisy lives with a perpetual illusion of recreation, transparent even to herself; she supposes that the meaning of life can be restored or revived by proper superficial ministrations, as rhinestones are added to an old gown. Thus she instigates senseless and enervating trips to the city, speaks thrillingly of dismal and mundane topics, and is charmed by Jay Gatsby's devotion without fully comprehending its meaning.

Even Jordan Baker, hard, cool, and perhaps the most resolutely cynical of Fitzgerald's characters, gives lip service to the regeneration myth. To Daisy's theatrical but heartfelt question, "'What'll we do with ourselves this afternoon . . . , and the day after that, and the next thirty years?''' Jordan responds, '''Don't be morbid. . . . Life starts all over again when it gets crisp in the fall'.'' . . . Her remark neatly complements Nick's earlier acknowledgement of a sense of rebirth with the coming of summer, but Nick discovers (as Jordan apparently does not) that while these illusions may give momentary comfort, to surrender to the myth of rejuvenation is to deny both the nature of reality and the chance for a modicum of contentment. Jordan, of course, surrender to nothing and so is unlikely to be much affected by her misconceptions.

The same cannot be said of the Great Gatsby himself. Like Nick, Daisy, Tom, and Jordan, Gatsby has emigrated from the heart of the continent to establish himself in the East, and like them he is anxious to believe that the possibilities of life do not diminish with time; unlike them, however, he adopts the myth of regeneration as the single sustaining principle of his existence. Gatsby's past is punctuated by a series of seeming fresh starts: As a young boy he jotted Franklinesque resolutions in his copy of *Hopalong Cassidy,* proving to his father's satisfaction that he '''was bound to get ahead.''' As a seventeen-year-old combing the beaches of Lake Superior he readied himself for the future by fashioning a wholly new identity. As a protegé of Dan Cody he acquired the experience which began turning his romantic musings into hard realities. As an army officer he assumed a manner in keeping with the deference paid him by society and took Daisy Fay as a kind of emotional hostage. After the war he did what he thought necessary to become what he had let Daisy believe he was, and to ransom her back.

Gatsby's accomplishments are a credit to his energy, enthusiasm, and singlemindedness, his sheer determination at all costs to stem the flow of history's current. ''There was something gorgeous about him,'' Nick says, ''some heightened sensitivity to the promises of life . . .—it was an extraordinary gift for hope, a romantic readiness such as I have never found in any other person and which it is not likely I shall ever find again.'' . . . His gift for hope, as it turns out, is Gatsby's curse as well as his blessing, since it insulates him from the rational and experiential restraints which might otherwise temper the intensity of his ambition. Having managed so well at apparent self-creation and recreation, he allows his sensitivity to life's promises to blur into a belief in its limitless possibilities; ultimately he longs to conquer the passage of time itself. History is a very real force to Gatsby—in fact, almost a tangible commodity—and his patient, arduous assault upon it sometimes seems likely to succeed. (pp. 160-62)

The act of self-generation, a marvelous exercise of will in the face of the force of history, established the terms of Gatsby's life and set the tone of his subsequent behavior. He learned early that detachment, disingenuousness, chicanery, and nerve often rendered even the most imposing circumstances malleable; especially under the protective mantle of his army lieutenancy he found himself capable of taking from the world almost anything he wanted, virtually without penalty. In taking Daisy, however, he allowed his detachment to slip, and once more he entered the world of time—of human ties, memories, and decay. (p. 162)

His affair with Daisy becomes the definitive circumstance of Gatsby's past. In a sense it is the *only* circumstance, all others—his experiences in the war, his five-months' study at Oxford, his ''gonnegtion'' with Meyer Wolfsheim, his lavish Long Island parties—seeming to him significant or relevant only insofar as they related to his regaining her love. Gatsby realizes the intensity of his commitment to this past only when he returns from the war to visit Louisville, Daisy's hometown, after she has wed Tom Buchanan. He finds amid the familiar walks and houses no vestige of the happiness he had known there and he understands that his memories lie buried in time as well as space. . . . That this longing persists, undiminished, is suggested by Gatsby's striking a similar attitude when Nick first sees him, peering across the bay toward Daisy's green light, five years later. (p. 163)

Because he believes in the myth of regeneration and misapprehends the nature of history in an entropic cosmos, Gatsby becomes a victim of his past. He tells Nick that he has drifted about since the war '''trying to forget something very sad that happened to me long ago',''' . . . but in truth he has not only kept alive his memory of losing Daisy but devoted all his energies to getting her back. As his sympathy for his extraordinary neighbor grows Nick comes gradually to appreciate the scope and sincerity of Gatsby's single passion. ''He talked a lot about the past,'' Nick says, ''and I gathered that he wanted to recover something, some idea of himself perhaps, that had gone into loving Daisy. His life had been confused and disordered since then, but if he could once return to a certain starting place and go over it all slowly, he could find out what that thing was.'' . . . To ''return to a certain starting place'' is precisely Gatsby's ambition—to fight back through time and make a fresh start in order to ''correct'' history and suspend the steady dissipation of the universe. (pp. 163-64)

Although this truth comes to Nick slowly as the threads of the story gradually unravel in his hands he is nevertheless awe-struck by the proportions of Gatsby's ambition, the quality of his hope, and the degree of his confusion. ''He wanted nothing less of Daisy,'' Nick marvels, ''than that she should go to Tom and say: 'I never loved you.' After she had obliterated four years with that sentence they could decide upon the more practical measures to be taken. One of them was that, after she was free, they were to go back to Louisville and be married from her house—just as if it were five years ago.'' . . . The custodian of common sense and of historical consciousness, Nick urges moderation. '''I wouldn't ask too much of her,''' he says. '''You can't repeat the past.''' '''Can't repeat the past?''' Gatsby cries incredulously. '''Why of course you can . . . ! I'm going to fix everything just the way it was before. . . . She'll see'.'' . . . Here, then, is an open acknowledgement of Gatsby's presumption—of his ''greatness'' and his error. He will ''fix'' the past just as Wolfsheim fixed the 1919 World Series, by manipulating people and circumstances to suit his necessities. Gatsby, says [David W.] Noble, ''would bring Daisy back to 1917. He would obliterate her marriage and her motherhood. He would restore her virginity.'' It is the supreme test of his Platonic will and of his faith in the human capacity for renewal, a test which he can only fail.

The scene of that failure is the confrontation between Gatsby and Tom Buchanan which takes place in a Plaza Hotel suite on a hot August afternoon. There Gatsby, who assures Daisy that her unhappy relationship with Tom is '''all over now,''' insists that '''It doesn't matter any more. Tell him the truth,''' he urges, '''—that you never loved him—and it's all wiped out forever'.'' . . . Here, however, the irreversibility of human experience asserts itself as Tom—brutish and self-indulgent and sure of his instincts—breaks Daisy's spirit of rebellion by showing that it rests on a lie. '''Oh, you want too much!''' she cries to Gatsby. '''I love you now—isn't that enough? I can't help what's past . . . I did love him once but I loved you too'.'' . . .

That Daisy "can't help what's past" marks the end of Gatsby's hopes for the future, since it is precisely that help which he had expected of her. Nick, who is as prepared to accept Daisy's limitations as Gatsby is determined to deny them, observes that after her admission ". . . only the dead dream fought on as the afternoon slipped away, trying to touch what was no longer tangible. . . ." . . . (pp. 164-65)

Gatsby's dream, the exercise of his Platonic will, obscures his vision of the world as it is and clouds his understanding of the historical process. It becomes Nick's responsibility, in telling Gatsby's story, to see that process truly and to reconcile to it the events of the summer of 1922. He is, in fact, driven toward this integrative view of past and present both by his penchant for honesty and by a sense of the connectedness of time which is part of his inheritance as a Carraway. Unlike Gatsby, Nick accepts the circumstance of being rooted in space and time, acknowledging both the limitations and the reassurances which those roots provide. Speaking of his home at the end of the book—no longer "the ragged edge of the universe" but "my Middle West"—Nick says, "I am part of that, a little solemn with the feel of those long winters, a little complacent from growing up in the Carraway house in a city where dwellings are still called through decades by a family's name." . . . (p. 167)

Nick returns to that home after Gatsby's death, reversing the tendency toward eastern migration with which the story began and indicating an intention to take up life where he had left it—to reenter the flow of his own personal history rather than resist it. In doing so he seems to many to be admitting defeat and withdrawing from the uncertainties of the present into the security of the past. Having had his glimpse of life's futility, proponents of this reading assert, Nick shrinks from further involvement and seeks a kind of non-life near the ancestral hearth. Finally to regard Nick in this way, however, seems to place him ultimately in the camp of the Buchanans, whose relationship with the world at large has deteriorated to a series of retreats, escapes, and evasions. Nick has neither the callousness nor the moral opacity to behave with the vast carelessness of Tom and Daisy, and to reduce him to their stature is to deny the genuine sympathy, even love, with which he tells Gatsby's story.

The telling of that story itself is perhaps the best evidence that Nick refuses simply to withdraw from the experiences of the summer but seeks rather to learn from them. Certainly his capacity for optimism—together with his adolescent restlessness—has been greatly diminished by his having been so privileged a witness of Gatsby's fall. He returns to Minnesota a somber, sadder, and more modest man than he left. And yet for him to retire from life altogether would amount to an ultimate repudiation of Gatsby and his fragile, fated dream. Nick is determined, rather, to demonstrate Gatsby's greatness as well as his monumental foolishness, and in telling the story to examine the interplay of vision and restraint, of timeless imagination and historical reality, in the hope of striking a proper balance between the two. He sees that it is the tension between the incessant diminution of energy in an entropic universe and the perennial thrust of human expectations which gives life meaning.

It is on this note of accommodation, of very modest dreams in light of the sobering realities of history, that ***The Great Gatsby*** ends. Looking simultaneously back over the story he has told and forward to the future, Nick acknowledges with gratitude man's gift for hope while he accepts with equanimity the disillusionment which that gift often precipitates:

> Gatsby believed in the green light, the orgiastic future that year by year recedes before us. It eluded us then, but that's no matter—tomorrow we will run faster, stretch our arms farther. . . . And one fine morning—
>
> So we beat on, boats against the current, borne back ceaselessly into the past. . . .

And so we must, apparently, for according to Fitzgerald man lives successfully only in a state of equilibrium between resistance to the current and surrender to its flow. He must accommodate the lessons of his past to his visions of the future, giving it to neither, in order to stand poised for happiness or disappointment in the present. (pp. 167-68)

Jeffrey Steinbrink, "'Boats against the Current': Mortality and the Myth of Renewal in 'The Great Gatsby'," in Twentieth Century Literature, *Vol. 26, No. 2, Summer, 1980, pp. 157-70.*

WARREN BENNETT (essay date 1980)

[*In the following excerpt, Bennett discusses Fitzgerald's use of eye imagery in* The Great Gatsby. *He maintains that the novel's pattern of ocular imagery was prefigured in several of Fitzgerald's earlier works and that this imagery was later refined and employed as an important aspect of* Gatsby.]

The billboard advertisement of Doctor T. J. Eckleburg in Fitzgerald's ***The Great Gatsby*** and its emphasis on Eckleburg's eyes has been the subject of a prodigious amount of interpre-

Dust jacket of the first edition of F. Scott Fitzgerald's The Great Gatsby. *Copyright 1925 Charles Scribner's Sons. Copyright renewed 1953 Scott Fitzgerald Lanahan. Reprinted with the permission of Charles Scribner's Sons.*

tation and commentary. Eckleburg is discussed variously as a god, or an anti-god; the commercial deity of a decadent society; or more profoundly, "the evil of the human condition overseen and modified by conscience." Another approach to Eckleburg has been to suggest a secondary source for his presence in the novel, thereby extending the range into such works as T. S. Eliot's *The Waste Land,* Harold Bell Wright's novel *The Eyes of the World,* or *The Goncourt Journals* for 1861. This scholarship has yielded valuable insights, but in concentrating on Eckleburg's eyes, other significant eye imagery has been neglected, and no one has studied Fitzgerald's own work as a possible source of either the Eckleburg image or other ocular imagery.

The purpose here is twofold: to demonstrate a pattern of ocular imagery in ***The Great Gatsby*** and to show that this imagery had its genesis in Fitzgerald's earlier work. The pattern includes a complex of ocular imagery surrounding Jay Gatsby, the spectacle complex of Owl Eyes and Ewing Klipspringer, as well as the vortical image of T. J. Eckleburg. (p. 207)

[**"Absolution"**] . . . was part of the "mid-west-19th-century-Catholic plot, which may be designated the *Ur-Gatsby.*" The main character, Fitzgerald said,

> was perhaps created on the image of some forgotten farm type of Minnesota that I have known and forgotten, and associated at the same moment with some sense of romance . . . a story of mine, called **"Absolution"** . . . was intended to be a picture of his early life, but . . . I cut it because I preferred to preserve the sense of mystery.

The story, therefore, is particularly important in prefiguring the complex of ocular imagery surrounding Jay Gatsby.

The "forgotten farm type" is Rudolph Miller, later to become James Gatz, alias Jay Gatsby. Rudolph is a "beautiful, intense little boy of eleven," with "two enormous, staccato eyes, lit with gleaming points of cobalt light;" "eyes like blue stones, and lashes that sprayed open from them like flower-petals." . . . We learn that when Rudolph's eyes are "half-closed" they manifest that moment when Rudolph has become transformed into a different personality, his double, Blatchford Sarnemington. (p. 208)

This is the childish phase of the mind that Nick Carraway will describe as capable of romping "like the mind of God"; . . . the most "grotesque and fantastic conceits haunted him in his bed at night. A universe of ineffable gaudiness spun itself out in his brain . . .". . . . The ritual of the half-closed eyes will then lead to James Gatz's "SCHEDULE," on the back cover of *Hopalong Cassidy,* and from there to Gatz's metamorphosis into "Jay Gatsby," his "Platonic conception of himself" as the "son of God . . . about His Father's business, the service of a vast, vulgar, and meretricious beauty." . . . That the beautiful eyes of this intense little boy . . . had some conscious or unconscious influence on Fitzgerald while working on ***Gatsby*** seems evident in three narrative situations where Gatsby's eyes function as the point of contact for the magnetic-emotional relationship that exists between Gatsby and Daisy.

The first narrative situation involves Jordan telling Nick how Daisy met Gatsby. Jordan says, "The officer looked at Daisy while she was speaking, in a way that every young girl wants to be looked at sometime." . . . Whatever the unstated charm of Gatsby's personality, his magnetism is exercised through his eyes, and it is great enough to change Daisy's life. . . . (pp. 208-09)

In the second narrative situation, four years later, the magnetic power of Gatsby's eyes is still capable of drawing Daisy to him. Gatsby meets Daisy again in Nick's eyesore of a house and stands with his head resting against a "defunct mantelpiece clock." From this position his "distraught eyes stared down at Daisy." . . . Nick is made uncomfortable by the silent tension of this visual-emotional communication and leaves the house. When Nick returns, "Daisy's face [is] smeared with tears" while Gatsby "smile[s] like a weather man, like an ecstatic patron of recurrent light"—a simile that seems more than coincidentally reminiscent of Rudolph Miller's eyes "lit with gleaming points of cobalt light."

The emotional relationship between Gatsby and Daisy in this scene is again taken for granted by Fitzgerald, but amplification of the meeting is possible by looking at two similar scenes, one in **"The Diamond as Big as the Ritz,"** . . . and one in **"The Sensible Thing."** . . . (pp. 210-11)

In **"The Diamond as Big as the Ritz"** the hero, John Unger, meets Kismine, the heroine, and their eyes are used as such a direct means of communication that Fitzgerald puts their messages in quotation marks as dialogue. (p. 211)

In **"The Sensible Thing"** one of a "cluster of stories related to the novel [***Gatsby***], in which Fitzgerald is testing or salvaging material," . . . eyes are again significant in the reunion of George Kelly with Jonquil Cary. . . . The George-Jonquil scene prefigures the reunion scene between Gatsby and Daisy. In the Gatsby-Daisy reunion, Gatsby's "distraught eyes stared down at Daisy," . . . and Daisy's response, "sitting, frightened but graceful, on the edge of a stiff chair," . . . is as ambivalent as Jonquil's [staring at George, which could mean] "everything or nothing." But again, a curious thing happens. When Nick returns from his walk, Gatsby and Daisy are "sitting at either end of the couch, looking at each other as if some question had been asked, or was in the air, and every vestige of embarrassment was gone." . . . The essential dialogue that establishes relationship in both **"The Sensible Thing"** and ***Gatsby,*** is the dialogue of the eyes.

This dialogue function of the eyes in the magnetic-emotional relationship is most explicitly revealed in a third narrative situation, the confrontation scene between Gatsby and Tom. After a brief clandestine affair with Daisy, Gatsby goes to the Buchanan house. Daisy becomes increasingly threatened and confused during lunch, but ironically complains about the weather, saying it's hot. Until this decisive moment Daisy has been almost as convinced as Gatsby that he really is a son of God. He dominated the weather at their reunion (it "stopped raining" . . . and now he is waiting to usher in "all the promises of life." . . . (pp. 211-12)

The scene is the zenith of their relationship; yet it takes place silently when their eyes meet in space. Gatsby's eyes assure Daisy that she will always gleam "like silver, safe and proud above the hot struggles of the poor." . . . Daisy's eyes respond with the message that she loves him, and Tom Buchanan "saw."

The confrontation between Gatsby and Tom is then delayed until they are in a New York hotel room. Gatsby breaks up "like glass" . . . under Tom's hard malice, and Daisy's "frightened eyes told that whatever intentions, whatever courage she had had, were definitely gone." . . . (p. 212)

Such a patterned sequential use of eye imagery suggests that Fitzgerald's mind was so fixed on the ocular imagery established in the Ur-Gatsby/**"Absolution"** material that he unconsciously continued to use it as the primary communication in the Gatsby-Daisy relationship. Fitzgerald's desire to write something intricately patterned, which would also be a "consciously artistic achievement," . . . probably accounts for the extension of the Gatsby imagery to what could be called the transmutation of Rudolph Miller/James Gatz into the characters of Owl Eyes and Ewing Klipspringer, both of whom are part of the spectacle imagery complex.

Whatever the symbolic intention of these characters in the imagery pattern of the novel, it seems clear that the spectacles, and perhaps the characters, had their genesis in ***This Side of Paradise***. . . . [At] Princeton, Amory makes friends with Tom D'Invilliers, "'that awful highbrow . . .' who signed the passionate love-poems in the *Lit*," . . . but he admires from a distance a god of the class, Dick Humbird, "the magnificent, exquisite Humbird." . . . Both D'Invilliers and Humbird wear spectacles. (pp. 212-13)

The spectacles as a sign that a person is wiser and shrewder than his contemporaries, although that person keeps his cleverness carefully concealed, seems at least partially relevant to Owl Eyes. But it is uncertain that D'Invilliers and Humbird, as characters, prefigure either Owl Eyes or Klipspringer; it is more probable that Owl Eyes and Klipspringer are foreshadowed by two other characters in ***This Side of Paradise***, Mr. Ferrenby and Garvin, who appear in a section of the final chapter, titled "The Big Man With Goggles."

As Amory is walking to Princeton, he is given a ride by a millionaire, Mr. Ferrenby, who is "large and begoggled and imposing" . . . ; his companion, Garvin, is a "little man" . . . whose goggles give him an "owl-like look." . . . The goggles, of course, accent the eyes, and they are another form of spectacle, but the significance of these characters in relation to Owl Eyes and Klipspringer involves other parallels.

Mr. Ferrenby is a large "middle-aged" man . . . as Owl Eyes is a "stout, middle-aged man." . . . Mr. Ferrenby is "inclined to stare . . . as if speculating steadily but hopelessly some baffling hirsute problem" . . . as Owl Eyes is "staring with unsteady concentration at the shelves of books." . . . Mr. Ferrenby's chief characteristic is a "great confidence in himself." . . . Owl Eyes also exudes confidence when he says, ". . . you needn't bother to ascertain [the reality of the books]. I ascertained." . . . (pp. 213-14)

There are similar parallels between Garvin and Ewing Klipspringer. Garvin is an "artificial growth" . . . on Ferrenby as Klipspringer is "the boarder" . . . at Gatsby's. Garvin is described as a "lower secretarial type," one of those who "consecrate . . . their lives to second-hand mannerisms." . . . Klipspringer is a "slightly worn" . . . young man, and if not a lower secretary, he is at least Gatsby's resident piano player, whose musical talents are just as second-rate as Garvin's mannerisms. Garvin is treated with disdain by both Ferrenby and Amory. He is interrupted in mid-sentence by Ferrenby: "'the human stomach—' he began; but the big man interrupted rather impatiently;" and interrupted in mid-word by Amory: "If you took all the money . . . and divided it up in equ——" "Oh, shut up!" Amory says. . . . Klipspringer is likewise treated with disdain by Gatsby: "I'm all out of prac——," Klipspringer says; "'Don't talk so much, old sport,' commanded Gatsby. 'Play!'." . . . Both Garvin and Klipspringer are physically affected by domination: Garvin's eyes "twitched nervously," . . . and Klipspringer has a "spasm of embarrassment." . . . There is, however, an important difference between Ferrenby-Garvin and Owl Eyes-Klipspringer. Garvin is linked to Ferrenby as a companion, but Klipspringer is linked, not to Owl Eyes—other than the spectacle imagery—but to Gatsby.

These parallels and the prefigurations seem to demonstrate the "consciously artistic achievement" which Fitzgerald attempted in ***The Great Gatsby.*** The Rudolph Miller/Jay Gatsby eye imagery was almost certainly present in the novel from the beginning, then extended to include spectacles and the characters of Owl Eyes and Klipspringer. But the full expression of the imagery pattern, which is the vortical image of Doctor T. J. Eckleburg, was not realized in Fitzgerald's mind until the summer of 1924 [when he became fascinated by the imagery pictured on a proposed Scribner dust jacket.] (pp. 214-15)

This is an image that is a ghostly apparition that appears overlooking some scene that involves contradiction: tragedy, sexual guilt, or ideals and disillusionment. There are four such scenes in Fitzgerald's earlier work that are of particular significance in the way they prefigure the ghostly apparition of Eckleburg: two in ***This Side of Paradise*** and two in ***The Beautiful and Damned.***

In ***This Side of Paradise,*** the chapter "Under the Arc-Light," we are told that "tragedy's emerald eyes glared suddenly at Amory over the edge of June." . . . Amory and Alec Connage have gone with a crowd in two automobiles to New York in quest of adventure. On the way back, about twelve o'clock, they are stopped on the road by an "old crone" in a kimono. Amory and Alec leap to the scene of the accident and "Under the full light of a roadside arc-light lay a form, face downward in a widening circle of blood." . . . They turn the form over: it is Dick Humbird, the god of the class who has "cold eyes behind tortoise-rimmed spectacles." . . . This accident may prefigure the death of Myrtle Wilson in ***Gatsby.***

The primary prefiguration, however, lies in the ghostly apparition of "tragedy's emerald eyes . . . over the edge of June"—associated as these eyes are with the tortoise-rimmed spectacles of Humbird. Tragedy's emerald eyes will put on the god's spectacles in ***The Great Gatsby*** and become "the eyes of Doctor T. J. Eckleburg, which had just emerged, pale and enormous, from the dissolving night"; and George Wilson, Myrtle's husband, will stare at them and say, "God sees everything." . . . (p. 217)

The second scene in ***This Side of Paradise*** prefiguring the Eckleburg apparition also involves the cold eyes of Dick Humbird. After Humbird's death, Amory and Fred Sloane are having a wild night with two girls, Axia Marlowe and Phoebe Column, that they have picked up from the Garden show. In the section called "The Devil," they go to the girls' apartment. Axia is sexually responsive to Amory and there was "a minute while temptation crept over him like a warm wind, and his imagination turned to fire." . . . [Later] emotions of sexual temptation and guilt [manifest] themselves in the ghostly apparition of the spectacled face of the magnificent Humbird. The apparition is symbolic of what Amory later refers to as the paradox of sex and beauty. . . . Amory's quest for beauty is, of course, Gatsby's quest, and the apparition of the spectacled face of Humbird in the alley becomes the paradoxical T. J. Eckleburg in a "valley of ashes," brooding over the adulterous guilt of Tom Buchanan and Myrtle Wilson.

The employment of the ghostly apparition in relation to adultery is extended in ***Gatsby*** to include the phenomenon of sexual jealousy. When Tom Buchanan, Nick, and Jordan Baker are on their way to New York, following Gatsby and Daisy, they stop for gas at George Wilson's garage.

> Over the ashheaps the giant eyes of Doctor T. J. Eckleburg kept their vigil, but I perceived, after a moment, that other eyes were regarding us with a peculiar intensity from less than twenty feet away.
>
> In one of the windows over the garage the curtains had been moved aside a little, and Myrtle Wilson was peering down at the car. . . . I realized that her eyes, wide with jealous terror, were fixed not on Tom, but on Jordan Baker, whom she took to be his wife. . . .
>
> (pp. 217-19)

This use of the apparition of eyes in terms of adultery, jealousy, and terror is prefigured in Fitzgerald's second novel, ***The Beautiful and Damned.*** Anthony Patch has been having an adulterous affair with Dorothy Raycroft. One night, in desperate jealous fear, Dot calls Anthony at his army camp and threatens suicide. Anthony goes to her, but he must do so without a pass. On the way back he is caught and sent to the guardhouse. The prisoners, working on the camp roads, are suggestive of the ash-gray men of the valley of ashes in ***Gatsby,*** who "swarm up with leaden spades and stir up an impenetrable cloud:" . . . "The heat of the day had changed, somehow, until it was a burnished darkness crushing down upon a devastated land." Anthony experiences his body as "something phantasmal, something almost absurdly unreal." . . .

> Then one afternoon in the second week he had a feeling that two eyes were watching him from a place a few feet beyond one of the guards. This aroused him to a sort of terror. He turned his back on the eyes and shovelled feverishly, until it became necessary for him to face about and go for more gravel. Then they entered his vision again, and his already taut nerves tightened up to the breaking-point. The eyes were leering at him. . . .

These ghostly apparitions of eyes—whether tragedy's, Humbird's or Dot's—do not account, however, for the concreteness of Eckleburg as a billboard advertisement. This aspect of Eckleburg is prefigured in a much different kind of scene in ***The Beautiful and Damned*** and involves a more complex disillusionment with ideals, life, and society.

In the chapter "Symposium," Anthony and Gloria are hosting a party. Gloria goes to her bedroom to lie down, but she is frightened by the ghostly figure of a guest, Joe Hull, standing in her doorway. When he leaves, she flees to the nearby train station intending to go to New York. Anthony follows her and is followed by Dick Caramel, a writer, and Maury Noble (an elaborated parallel of Dick Humbird). . . . (p. 219)

Maury climbs to the roof of a shed and from there, "outlined as a shadowy and fantastic gargoyle" . . . launches into a monologue about his experiences and final disillusionment.

Several of the ideas that Maury expresses are either restated in ***Gatsby*** or subtly woven into the fabric of characters and events. For example, Maury's statement that "In this republic I saw the black [race] beginning to mingle with the white" . . . is almost literally transferred to Tom Buchanan when he says, "The idea is if we don't look out the white race will be—will be utterly submerged." . . . Maury says, "the beauty of succulent illusions fell away from me. The fibre of my mind coarsened and my eyes grew miserably keen." . . . Gatsby arrived at the same disillusionment when he "looked up at an unfamiliar sky through frightening leaves and shivered as he found what a grotesque thing a rose is." . . .

The major significance of the Maury Noble scene to T. J. Eckleburg, however, is in a statement Maury makes about billboards, coupled with the description of Maury himself:

> "It must be for such occasions as this," he began softly, his words having the effect of floating down from an immense height and settling softly upon his auditors, "that the righteous of the land decorate the railroads with bill-boards asserting in red and yellow that 'Jesus Christ is God,' placing them appropriately enough, next to announcements that 'Gunter's Whiskey is Good.'" . . .
>
> Only Maury Noble remained awake, seated upon the station roof, his eyes wide open and fixed with fatigued intensity upon the distant nucleus of morning. He was wondering at the unreality of ideas, at the fading radiance of existence. . . .

Maury's "righteous of the land" become in ***Gatsby*** a "wild wag of an oculist." . . . The billboards to which Maury refers decorate the railroads. Eckleburg is located where the "motor road hastily joins the railroad." . . . Maury's billboard asserts, "Jesus Christ is God." George Wilson looks at the eyes of Eckleburg and asserts, "God sees everything." . . . (p. 220)

Perkins wrote Fitzgerald, 20 November 1924 [see *TCLC*, Vol. 6], ". . . all these things, the whole pathetic episode, you have given a place in time and space, for with the help of T. J. Eckleberg . . . you have imparted a sort of sense of eternity." . . . The significance of Eckleburg is not in his presence as an isolated symbol, but in his presence as the full expression of a pattern of imagery that includes both the ocular imagery of Jay Gatsby and the spectacle imagery of Owl Eyes and Klipspringer. In addition, the various worlds of Fitzgerald's fiction are worlds that are consciously and unconsciously connected, and future studies of the meaning of the ocular imagery pattern in ***The Great Gatsby*** may find important clues in Fitzgerald's earlier use of such imagery. (p. 221)

Warren Bennett, "Prefigurations of Gatsby, Eckleburg, Owl Eyes, and Klipspringer," in Fitzgerald/Hemingway Annual: 1979, *edited by Matthew J. Bruccoli and Richard Layman, Gale Research Company, 1980, pp. 207-23.**

DAVID O'ROURKE (essay date 1982)

[In the following excerpt, O'Rourke maintains that Nick Carraway is an unreliable narrator and as such presents a distorted account of Gatsby's story. O'Rourke further observes that Gatsby does not remain a static figure throughout the novel—as Nick would have readers believe—but rather, that Gatsby was ready to rebuild his life despite his shattered illusions. For further discussions of Nick Carraway as narrator of The Great Gatsby, *see the excerpts by Frederick J. Hoffman (1951), R. W. Stallman (1955), and Colin S. Cass (1983).]*

Critics interested in the role of Nick Carraway as narrator in ***The Great Gatsby*** may be divided into two rather broad groups. The majority position is the traditional one: Nick is considered quite reliable, basically honest, and ultimately changed by his contact with Gatsby. A variation of this interpretation has Carraway stumbling to his conclusion, thereby accounting for a number of discrepancies in his narration; in short, Nick progresses from innocence to experience before finally locating a moral vision. Against this position may be found a small number of critics who hold that Nick is quite unreliable: a sentimentalist at least, and possibly dishonest and immoral. Hence, ***The Great Gatsby*** is either a deceptively tricky novel, or one that is artistically flawed in both character and structure. Both camps seem to agree on one point: the character of Gatsby remains static throughout the book; at the end he is still waiting for Daisy's telephone call, clutching, as it were, to his quixotic dream. The critical controversy merits a brief return to the text as our final understanding of Gatsby is almost entirely dependent upon the reliability of Carraway's narration.

To begin with, Nick is not very intelligent. He draws attention to this fact by stating that Jordan Baker avoids "clever, shrewd men," and then admits to being "slow-thinking" himself. Secondly, it is generally accepted that Nick has at least a minor problem with honesty. He lies to himself, and consequently the reader, about his relationship with a girl back home; he is challenged by Jordan, "I thought you were rather an honest, straightforward person;" . . . and, after Gatsby's death, he praises Catherine's character for lying to a judge. It would be incorrect to call Carraway a compulsive liar, but a mistake not to be wary of any further inconsistencies. In addition, it might be noticed that, while Nick has his two Midwestern feet firmly on the ground, his mind is not totally averse to a little sentimentality. Gatsby becomes his romantic hero by the end of the 1922 summer and is portrayed as such, sometimes to an embarrassing extent, throughout the course of Nick's memoir. Lines such as, "Gatsby, who represented everything for which I have an unaffected scorn," . . . are ultimately quite humorous in view of Carraway's beside-himself tendency to cheerlead. (pp. 57-8)

It would be naive to expect a slow-thinking, sentimental, and occasionally dishonest narrator to be totally reliable. When an element of distortion is added, the challenge of perception becomes prodigious. Carraway is particularly susceptible to alcohol in ***The Great Gatsby.*** On the afternoon of Myrtle's party, he states, "I sat down discreetly in the living-room and read a chapter of *Simon Called Peter*—either it was terrible stuff or the whiskey distorted things, because it didn't make any sense to me." . . . A couple of weeks later at Gatsby's party, he notes, "I had taken two finger-bowls of champagne, and the scene had changed before my eyes into something significant, elemental, and profound." . . . But whiskey and champagne are not the only agents of distortion in ***The Great Gatsby.*** The East, in particular the two Eggs, is an "enchanted wood," a "magical country"; indeed, it has the authenticity of Universal Studios. The houses tend to be re-creations and the people actors and actresses playing either self-conceived, as in the case of Gatsby, or socially-determined roles. In addition, Gatsby is a producer, a "regular Belasco," . . . and perhaps prefiguration of Monroe Stahr. He attempts to re-create the past by conjuring what he imagines to be Louisville-type parties on the lot of his property. Curiously, Daisy finds even these too realistic, preferring the twice-removed gestures of "the moving-picture director and his Star." . . .

For all these obstacles, the reliability of Nick's narration is quite surprising. His "slow-thinking" is channeled into caution, his dishonesty is rare and ultimately acknowledged, and his break with Jordan signals an astute, if slow to crystallize, moral sense. He has never had much difficulty seeing through the artifices of the East, perhaps because Tom and Daisy are such splendid examples of its opulence. His tendency to an almost cinematic sentimentality is, however, never quite held in check; this leads to a misrepresentation of one of the most crucial scenes in the novel:

> If that was true he must have felt that he had lost the old warm world, paid a high price for living too long with a single dream. He must have looked up at an unfamiliar sky through frightening leaves and shivered as he found what a grotesque thing a rose is and how raw the sunlight was upon the scarcely created grass. A new world, material without being real, where poor ghosts, breathing dreams like air, drifted fortuitously about . . . like that ashen, fantastic figure gliding toward him through the amorphous trees. . . .
>
> (p. 58)

The description is melodramatic; that Gatsby would actually find leaves "frightening" and a rose "grotesque" is unlikely. In fact, Nick's projection of what his hero "must have felt" before death does not at all correspond to Gatsby's movements of the day. For a man who has been broken by a dream, Gatsby has had a good breakfast with Nick, puts on his bathing suit at two o'clock, and goes to his garage for a pneumatic mattress. He uses the pool for the first time all summer, a summer which has been marked by his obsession with an illusory dream. If anything, this suggests adjustment and redirection—the pool, a baptism to life. Referring to Daisy's telephone call, Nick states, "I have an idea that Gatsby himself didn't believe it would come, and perhaps he no longer cared." . . . The fact that Nick himself had earlier in the afternoon tried to get Gatsby on the phone four times—only to discover that the line was being "kept open for long distance from Detroit" . . .—subtracts from the profundity of this observation. By afternoon, Gatsby was in no way expecting to hear from Daisy.

The character of Gatsby does not remain "static" throughout the course of the summer's events; it is only Nick's conception of him that does. This is evident in the symbolic portrayal of Gatsby's own house. It is first described as "a factual imitation of some Hotel de Ville in Normandy, with a tower on one side;" . . . in short, it is a palace, a castle out of a fairy tale. A couple of days before Gatsby's reunion with Daisy, the mansion is "blazing" the peninsula with light; Gatsby is outside, "glancing into some of the rooms," . . . savoring his dream at its peak. But, after his contact with Daisy, the "enchantment" of the house begins to dissipate. Before a couple of weeks have passed, the mansion has lost its imaginative quality altogether, reflecting instead Gatsby's actual state: secretive and criminal. After Gatsby's ridiculous vigil before the altar of Daisy, after she has kept him waiting until four o'clock in the morning before turning out the light, Gatsby returns to his house to do a mental inventory with Nick. Carraway first observes, "There was an inexplicable amount of dust everywhere, and the rooms were musty, as though they hadn't been aired for many days." . . . They throw open the French windows of the drawing room, and Gatsby tells the true story of his past, relating the history of his love for Daisy. Nick notes,

"It was dawn now on Long Island and we went about opening the rest of the windows downstairs, filling the house with grey-turning, gold-turning light." . . . The vacuity of his dream slowly "dawns" upon Gatsby; by noon, he has dismissed any last straws of hope and has once again begun to take charge of his life.

As narrator, Nick is in the tradition of Bartleby's employer: a good enough fellow, prudent, slightly obtuse but, nevertheless, willing to help if he can. As Bartleby remains an enigma for his employer, so the East remains for Carraway "distorted beyond my eyes' power of correction." . . . The employer is blinded by the categories of the rational mind, whereas Carraway is distracted by an aptitude for sentimentality. Fortunately, Nick does not walk away completely empty-handed, and this is why the "Marlowe method" works so well. Nick's rejection of Jordan (and all that she represents) is surely a healthy sign, and one that cannot be dismissed as easily as a number of commentators have attempted. Still, Carraway ultimately misses the moral of his summer with Gatsby: one can neither go back in time, nor succeed in re-creating the past. Nick's return to the Midwest is not only a geographical retreat, but an attempted escape into an idyllic past. The sentimentality of his reminiscences stops just short of making angels in the snow: "That's my Middle West—not the wheat or the prairies or the lost Swede towns, but the thrilling returning trains of my youth, and the street lamps and sleigh bells in the frosty dark and the shadows of holly wreaths thrown by lighted windows on the snow." . . . Nick's attempt at re-creating the past—the memoir of the summer of 1922—is likewise doomed to failure. In detective-like fashion, he doggedly puts the pieces together, but finally succeeds in resurrecting only a shell of the events. In both is life and memoir, Nick glosses over Gatsby's final alternative to retreat—to make a stand, and adjust—suggesting a not very optimistic future ahead. So Nick beats on, boat against the current, being "borne back ceaselessly into the past." (pp. 59-60)

David O'Rourke, "Nick Carraway As Narrator in 'The Great Gatsby'," in The International Fiction Review, *Vol. 9, No. 1, Winter, 1982, pp. 57-60.*

COLIN S. CASS (essay date 1983)

[In the following excerpt, Cass provides a balanced assessment of one of the most controversial elements of The Great Gatsby: *Nick Carraway's reliability as narrator. For further discussions regarding Fitzgerald's narrator, see the excerpts by Frederick J. Hoffman (1951), R. W. Stallman (1955), and David O'Rourke (1982).]*

Matthew Bruccoli once remarked that by accommodating Gatsby, Nick Carraway acts as pimp for his cousin, Daisy Buchanan. Certain other scholars have called Nick a pander, and there is considerable evidence to support this view. Nevertheless, it must be carefully interpreted, for it can have disastrous thematic implications, leading, as it does, directly to the question of Nick's reliability as narrator. It is quite possible that Nick is guilty as charged, that Fitzgerald knew what he was doing, and at the same time that the proper inferences to draw from Nick's guilt are mainly technical rather than thematic.

"Pimping" may be too strong a word for what Nick does, since it connotes sexual trafficking for profit. It's true that Nick doesn't profit from his involvement, yet all the principal characters recognize the unsavory side of the transaction. For this reason Gatsby approaches Nick, who sees himself as "one of the few honest people that I have ever known," . . . not directly as neighbor to neighbor, but indirectly through Jordan. She, unlike Nick, is "incurably dishonest" . . . and tainted by the scandal of having moved her ball during a golf tournament, a fact that Gatsby apparently knows, since he is quick to tell Nick that "Miss Baker's a great sportswoman, you know, and she'd never do anything that wasn't all right." . . . Gatsby, knowing what will be discussed when Nick has tea with Jordan, regards it as a "big request," . . . about which he is hesitant because, as Jordan later explains, "He thought you might be offended." . . . After Nick agrees to play the go-between, Gatsby offers to pay for the service: "It wouldn't take up much of your time and you might pick up a nice bit of money. It happens to be a rather confidential sort of thing." . . . Nick refuses this offer because it "was obviously and tactlessly for a service to be rendered," yet Nick pointedly excludes Tom when he invites Daisy: "'Don't bring Tom,' I warned her." Daisy herself recognizes the oddness of the situation: "'Are you in love with me,' she said low in my ear, 'or why did I have to come alone?'." . . . Once the lovers have been brought together, Nick, more like a pander than a host, decorously absents himself. And after the meeting has been brought about, Gatsby reiterates his offer to pay: "Do you mean you've been thinking over what I proposed the other night?" . . . In short, everyone realizes that there is, or could seem to be, a dirty side to these arrangements.

The implications of this reading are very serious. . . . R. W. Stallman [see excerpt above, 1955], who rather boisterously calls Nick a hypocrite several times, also observes that "Though Nick disbelieves in it, he nevertheless arranges for the reunion of the lovers whom time has divorced, and thereby he involves himself, Honest Nick, in the adulterous affair and shares the responsibility for its consequences."

If a sound case can be made for Nick as hypocrite, then his narrative becomes unreliable, especially as a vehicle of Fitzgerald's moral thinking, and ***The Great Gatsby*** turns into a very cynical book indeed. (pp. 314-15)

But several circumstances of this "pimping" should cause doubts. One is that, since Nick does not profit in any financial way, the usual motive for a pimp is absent. What, then, *is* Nick's motive? (p. 315)

The truth is that convincing explanations of Nick's action are lacking. He has no particular reason to ingratiate himself to his vulgar neighbor, a virtual stranger who, among other things, "represented everything for which I have an unaffected scorn." . . . A more plausible motive is that Nick wants to please Jordan. He does have some romantic interest in her: "I wasn't actually in love, but I felt a sort of tender curiosity." . . . Yet a man who prides himself on his integrity is not likely to compromise it very much for a dishonest woman he pursues with so little ardor and relinquishes so soon.

Among motives, the best of a poor lot is that Nick would play the go-between for Daisy's sake. Fitzgerald in Chapters One and Two gives Nick a good look at Tom's affair with Myrtle, as well as Daisy's unhappiness about it. Incidentally, Nick's response is hardly characteristic of someone about to begin a little pandering: "my own instinct," he says, "was to telephone immediately for the police," . . . and again, ". . . I was confused and a little disgusted as I drove away. It seemed to me that the thing for Daisy to do was to rush out of the house, child in arms. . . ." . . . As for Daisy, she has "an absolutely perfect reputation" and perhaps "never went in for amour at all." . . . These considerations let Jordan feel that ". . . Daisy ought to have something in her life." . . . Possibly Nick acts in order to help Daisy get what she will like, it being no more than what Tom is getting for himself. The trouble here is that such a shoddy judgment goes straight to the heart of the book, for the narrator who begins by asking for a world at moral attention proves capable of judging that two wrongs can make a right, or that to clean up one Buchanan mess he should help make another.

The lack of a strong motive for Nick also leads to other questions. In Chapter Three Gatsby succeeds in establishing, via Jordan, a means of communication with Daisy. Why does Nick need to be involved? As if to disarm this question, Fitzgerald has Nick ask it himself: "I don't like mysteries and I don't understand why you [Gatsby] won't come out frankly and tell me what you want. Why has it all got to come through Miss Baker?" Gatsby doesn't answer, but Fitzgerald forces the subject forward again when Nick sees Jordan:

> Something worried me.
>
> "Why didn't he ask you to arrange a meeting?"
>
> "He wants her to see his house," she explained. "And your house is right next door."
>
> "Oh!"
>
> "I think he half expected her to wander into one of his parties, some night," went on Jordan, "but she never did. Then he began asking people casually if they knew her, and I was the first one he found. It was that night he sent for me at his dance, and you should have heard the elaborate way he worked up to it. Of course, I immediately suggested a luncheon in New York—and I thought he'd go mad:
>
> "'I don't want to do anything out of the way!' he kept saying, 'I want to see her right next door.'
>
> "When I said you were a particular friend of Tom's, he started to abandon the whole idea." . . .
>
> (pp. 316-17)

Despite Fitzgerald's efforts to make these arrangements believable, Nick really need not be involved in the clandestine and adulterous reunion, and his presence would not normally be welcome. As Jordan recounts it, Gatsby's reasoning about this reunion is unconvincing. For the small advantage of immediately showing Daisy his house, Gatsby submits to the potentially great disadvantage of relying on a stranger—one who could well take the part either of the honorable lady (his relative) or the injured husband (his "particular friend"), or who might protest on behalf of his own moral position. And although Gatsby says he doesn't "want to do anything out of the way," his scruple is virtually meaningless, since the reunion itself will be irregular, no matter where it is accomplished, as Daisy herself sees as soon as Tom is excluded. In other words, to the lack of a clear motive for Nick in this pandering, we must add a similar lack of motive for Gatsby in *asking* him to pander. Seen critically, the whole action is rather implausible.

And, as a matter of fact, so are a number of other important events in ***The Great Gatsby.*** In Chapter Two, would Tom Buchanan force his wife's relative off a commuter train in order to introduce his mistress? Once reunited, would Gatsby and Daisy insist that Nick accompany them on their tour of Gatsby's house—bedrooms, closets, and all? What are the odds that Nick would be present at Gatsby's on the one afternoon when Tom, Sloane and the lady happen by on horseback? If the lovers had chosen Daisy's luncheon as the time to confront Tom, would they be likely to invite Jordan and Nick? Aren't the arrangements for the trips to and from New York City rather contrived? If Tom's suspicions have been aroused at lunch, why would he choose that time to try out Gatsby's car? It is also a remarkable coincidence that Gatsby's car needs gas, that Tom stops at Wilson's station just in time to learn that he is losing his mistress as well as his wife, that conversation at the gas pump turns promptly to the identity of the eventual murder car, that Myrtle looks out the window, making her own fatal misidentifications, and that Nick notices her doing so. Although no single improbability is too much to accept, the accumulation, added to the already shaky justifications for going to New York in the first place, forces an obvious conclusion upon us. Fitzgerald has run up against technical problems with his plot. . . . (pp. 317-18)

Other contrivances are also needed to get everyone back from the city. Tom must send Daisy ahead with Gatsby. The others must dawdle at the Plaza to give the lovers a good start. The lovers must now use Gatsby's car. And Daisy must decide that driving a powerful, unfamiliar car out of New York City will calm her nerves. Myrtle, who had been locked upstairs by Wilson, must now be downstairs and unlocked, for she will have to notice the returning car (conveniently misidentified, and no longer driven by Tom) in time to decide to rush at it. It will have to go fast enough to kill her, but not so fast that she cannot intercept it. On the way home, Tom must forget to drop Nick off in West Egg. At Tom's front door, Nick's disgust must finally catch up with him so that rather than going inside or being driven home, he can find Gatsby in the garden and then observe the conspiratorial Buchanans through the pantry window. The next day, Gatsby's chauffeur and other servants need to ignore gunshots on the grounds so that Nick can be present when the bodies are discovered.

I see only one explanation for such implausibilities. Fitzgerald must resort to them so that the main events in the plot will befall as he imagined them, and so that Nick, his first-person narrator, will have first-hand knowledge about the key scenes in somebody else's love affair. Although ***The Great Gatsby*** is a splendid novel, critics give it too much credit when they write as if every word is freighted with the author's meaning. We can not afford to be so ingenuous about the actual process of concocting a fiction. (p. 318)

Once the existence of these technical difficulties is recognized, Fitzgerald's efforts to conceal them also become obvious. One way to make the reader overlook implausibilities is to teach him to trust the narrator. Repeatedly, therefore, Nick protests his honesty. He calls himself "one of the few honest people that I have ever known." . . . Jordan says she likes him because "I hate careless people," . . . the implication being that Nick is not careless. (pp. 318-19)

Furthermore, Nick is constantly made to account for his information, thus defending against the deadliest objection to a first-person narrative, that the narrator could not know all that he reports. Indeed, the first page of the novel is devoted substantially to this matter: ". . . I'm inclined to reserve judgments, a habit that has opened up many curious natures to me," Nick says. . . . (p. 319)

Much of Nick's information comes to him either because someone forces it on him, ostensibly against his will, or because he cannot politely extricate himself from situations Fitzgerald actually needs to have him observe. Notice how Fitzgerald forestalls the reader's protest that Tom would never introduce Nick to his mistress:

> Though I was curious to see her, I had no desire to meet her—but I did. I went up to New York with Tom on the train one afternoon, and when we stopped by the ashheaps he jumped to his feet and, taking hold of my elbow, literally forced me from the car.
>
> "We're getting off," he insisted. "I want you to meet my girl." . . .

The result of Tom's characteristic assertiveness is, Fitzgerald hopes, that the reader will never think to object either that this is the last thing Tom would want to do, or that an adult like Nick could not very easily be "forced" off a train if he seriously opposed the idea.

Once Fitzgerald has maneuvered Nick into the scenes he must witness, Nick is constantly but unsuccessfully trying to leave, as if to reassure the reader that Nick himself sees how unlikely his presence is. (pp. 319-20)

The reader's response to improbable material will, in first-person narration, depend not only on the general trustworthiness of the narrator, but also on how the narrator himself responds to such material. One tactic is to make him seem at least as sceptical as the reader. We have seen Fitzgerald using this ploy already, when he makes Nick sound hostile to Gatsby's indirection ("Why has it all got to come through Miss Baker?") and then stubbornly return to the point himself when he confronts Jordan ("Why didn't he ask you to arrange a meeting?"). Fitzgerald handles the implausibility of Nick's being invited to the showdown in much the same intrepid fashion:

> He was calling up at Daisy's request—would I come to lunch at her house tomorrow? Miss Baker would be there. Half an hour later Daisy herself telephoned and seemed relieved to find that I was coming. Something was up. And yet I couldn't believe that they would choose this occasion for a scene—especially for the rather harrowing scene that Gatsby had outlined in the garden. . . .

The arrangement *is* rather unbelievable, yet by letting Nick say that first, Fitzgerald hopes to win our uncritical assent to an implausibility which, because of his narrative convention, he is compelled to foist on us. Quite the same tactic is at work when Jordan admits that Gatsby hesitated because Nick might be offended, or when Nick refuses Gatsby's offer of payment as too obviously for a service to be rendered. Objections at these points would be well founded, since he ought to be offended, and the service is rendered. Fitzgerald therefore hopes to discharge these objections in advance so that they will not accidentally go off and ruin his plot.

There is one more device an author can employ, provided he doesn't abuse it, and in relation to Nick's pandering, this last tactic is crucial. If the author has created a sufficiently strong sense of his narrator's reliability, then he can risk letting the narrator draw a conclusion that the unguided reader would probably not draw from the same facts. In short, the narrator can bluff. When Jordan relays Gatsby's tainted request that Nick play the pander for his married relative, Nick's response is neither righteous indignation on the one hand, nor worldly complicity on the other, but astonishment that so little is asked of him:

> "He wants to know," continued Jordan, "if you'll invite Daisy to your house some afternoon and then let him come over."
>
> The modesty of the demand shook me. He had waited five years and bought a mansion where he dispensed starlight to casual moths—so that he could "come over" some afternoon to a stranger's garden.
>
> "Did I have to know all this before he could ask such a little thing?" . . .

Considered with Fitzgerald's technical problems in mind, this response is entirely predictable. If Nick had refused on moral grounds, he would have excluded himself from the book's central scene. And if he had agreed with a worldly tolerance for waywardness in others, then he would have denied himself the right to the sweeping moral pronouncements that the book begins and ends on. Fitzgerald's only choice is to make Nick seem temporarily to have missed the point. For the plot's sake Nick must cooperate, but for the theme's sake he must not appear to cooperate with anything he recognizes as seriously immoral. Furthermore, the author does all he can to distract us from the moral ramifications of what does amount to pandering. Jordan, for instance, abets Nick in his technically necessary underestimate of the situation: "You're just supposed to invite her to tea." . . . Nick's light joking when Daisy asks why she had to come alone—"That's the secret of Castle Rackrent" . . .—serves the same purpose. It underplays the moral significance of the action, not because Fitzgerald thinks the action has no moral significance, and surely not because he wants readers to begin doubting the integrity of his narrator, but because his first-person narrative created a technical problem he could not plot his way out of. The critic who draws thematic inferences from material so obviously necessitated by the author's technical dilemma is like the listener who finds musical significance in the scratches on his records.

Also germane to a discussion of Nick's pandering is the pander metaphor in the Dutch-sailors paragraph:

> And as the moon rose higher the inessential houses began to melt away until gradually I became aware of the old island here that flowered once for Dutch sailors' eyes—a fresh, green breast of the new world. Its vanished trees, the trees that had made way for Gatsby's house, had one pandered in whispers to the last and greatest of all human dreams; for a transitory enchanted moment man must have held his breath in the presence of this continent, compelled into an aesthetic contemplation he neither understood nor desired, face to face for the last time in history with something commensurate to his capacity for wonder. . . .

As several commentators have said, Fitzgerald means the relationship between the sailors and the new world to be analogous to the Gatsby-Daisy relationship. The sailors come with an almost boundless human capacity for wonder, and for the last time in history there is, in an unexplored continent, something big enough to satisfy it. The continent flowers for the Dutch sailors, and the subsequent history of America is the wilting of the flower, the failure of reality to sustain their romantic expectations. Likewise, Gatsby invests his enormous capacity for wonder in a real Daisy who, like the new world, flowers for Gatsby. . . . The rest of that story is, of course, the disillusioning of Gatsby, who watches Daisy, the incarnation of his vision of love, as she tumbles short of his dreams.

Although this much is clear, the Dutch-sailors paragraph becomes critically troublesome if we reflect that pandering always involves three parties. In the paragraph all three are unambiguously identified: the man (Dutch sailors), the woman (fresh green breast of the new world), and the pander (trees that pandered in whispers). But because Fitzgerald has emphasized the parallel between Gatsby-Daisy and sailors-new world, he naturally provokes the question, Who, if anyone, is the pander in the Gatsby-Daisy story? Who, in other words, is analogous to the trees? Who else *can* it be but Nick, particularly when other evidence already points in his direction?

This reasoning seems to prove that Fitzgerald wants Nick recognized as a pander after all, but the matter is not simple, and at heart it is entirely a question of authorial intention. There are three possibilities. The first and least likely is that Fitzgerald intended flatly to contradict himself, as he would do by implying in one place that Nick is a pander, then by denying it in another. Either the affirmation or the denial is probably true, but both cannot be.

The second possibility is the affirmative one, that Nick is a pander and the Dutch-sailors passage proves it. The objection to this argument is that the authority of one scrap of indirect and metaphoric evidence must be used to overrule all the contrary evidence of Fitzgerald's efforts to avoid giving this impression of his narrator. Moreover, there is no assurance that the three-part analogy had to have been completed in Fitzgerald's mind: Gatsby can remain parallel to the Dutch sailors, as Fitzgerald probably intended, but it doesn't follow that there must have been a go-between in both affairs. Still another question is how exactly Fitzgerald understood the word "pandered." Given the masculine and feminine imagery in the Dutch sailors passage, the word seems appropriate, even inspired, and yet in **"The Freshest Boy,"** written three years after ***The Great Gatsby,*** Fitzgerald says "pandered" where he seems to mean "catered": "The institutions which pandered to the factory workers were the ones patronized by the boys—a movie house, a quick-lunch wagon on wheels known as the Dog and the Bostonian Candy Kitchen." Here the connotations of sexual trafficking are completely incongruous, and the misused word should give us pause before we erect too much theory upon it in ***Gatsby.***

Finally, there is the negative possibility, to which I subscribe: that although the exigencies of first-person narrating make Nick do the work of a pander, and although the Dutch sailors passage appears to confirm his role by analogy, Fitzgerald nevertheless intends that the reader should not regard Nick as a pander. Fitzgerald's attempts to establish the reliability of his narrator; the technical necessity of doing so in order to conceal unavoidable implausibilities; and the transparent difficulties he had with his plot and narrative convention have been examined. Moreover, his tactics are consistent with what we would expect. Fitzgerald, who once said of himself, ". . . I guess I am too much a moralist at heart, and really want to preach at people in some acceptable form . . . ," needs to protect his narrator's moral position. That is not to say that Nick must be perfect. His success depends, indeed, on his seeming a believable human with normal faults. Yet to praise Gatsby and denounce the East, Nick must be an upright man, not a liar, a hypocrite, or a pander. As for the Dutch sailors passage, had it occurred to Fitzgerald that his word "pandered" was going to remind anyone that Nick might be called a pimp, I believe he would have taken steps to prevent this reading, which is, by most other indications, contrary to his intention. (pp. 321-24)

Colin S. Cass, "'Pandered in Whispers': Narrative in 'The Great Gatsby'," in College Literature, *Vol. X, No. 3, Fall, 1983, pp. 314-26.*

ADDITIONAL BIBLIOGRAPHY

Babb, Howard S. "*The Great Gatsby* and the Grotesque." *Criticism* V, No. 4 (Fall 1963): 336-48.

Details and discusses grotesque elements in *The Great Gatsby.* Babb maintains that it is Fitzgerald's intermingling of the "oddly humorous with the terrifying" that makes *Gatsby* a powerful study of society.

Barbour, Brian M. "*The Great Gatsby* and the American Past." *The Southern Review* n.s. IX, Part 1 (Spring 1973): 288-99.

Posits that *The Great Gatsby* is in fact a story about the conflict of two American dreams: the Franklinian Dream, or the acquisition of wealth based on the ideas of Benjamin Franklin, and the Emersonian dream, or moral and spiritual freedom based on the thought of Ralph Waldo Emerson.

Bicknell, John W. "The Waste Land of F. Scott Fitzgerald." *The Virginia Quarterly* 30, No. 3 (Summer 1954): 556-72.*

Considers parallels between *The Great Gatsby* and T. S. Eliot's *The Waste Land,* noting that each pessimistically renders "symbols and images of waste, desolation, and futility." This essay also discusses Fitzgerald's novels *Tender Is the Night* and *The Last Tycoon.*

Bruccoli, Matthew J. Introduction to *The Great Gatsby: A Facsimile of the Manuscript,* by F. Scott Fitzgerald, pp. xiii-xxxv. Washington, D.C.: Microcard Edition Books, 1973.

Provides interesting background information on the genesis of *The Great Gatsby* and details the progressive changes of the work from manuscript to unrevised and revised galley proofs. Bruccoli is also the editor of the *Fitzgerald/Hemingway Annual,* which presents criticism and bibliographical updates on the works of Fitzgerald and Ernest Hemingway, and the author of *Some Sort of Epic Grandeur: The Life of F. Scott Fitzgerald.*

Callahan, John F. *The Illusions of a Nation: Myth and History in the Novels of F. Scott Fitzgerald.* Chicago: University of Illinois Press, 1972, 221 p.

Comprehensive study of history, myth, and personality in Fitzgerald's novels that includes a lengthy chapter on *The Great Gatsby.*

Carlisle, E. Fred. "The Triple Vision of Nick Carraway." *Modern Fiction Studies* XI, No. 4 (Winter 1965-66): 351-60.

Posits that Nick Carraway, the narrator of *The Great Gatsby,* functions within the story on three levels: 1. as a detached moralist, 2. as a partially detached, limited participant in the story's action, and 3. as a full participant in the action of the story as one of its characters. Carlisle also believes that *Gatsby* is the story not only of Jay Gatsby, but also of Carraway, who matures from innocence to self-awareness.

Elmore, A. E. "Nick Carraway's Self-Introduction." *Fitzgerald/Hemingway Annual: 1971,* edited by Matthew J. Bruccoli and C. E. Frazer Clark, Jr., pp. 130-47. Washington, D.C.: Microcard Editions, 1971.

General discussion of Fitzgerald's narrative technique in *The Great Gatsby.*

Emmitt, Robert J. "Love, Death, and Resurrection in *The Great Gatsby.*" *Aeolian Harps: Essays in Literature in Honor of Maurice Browning Cramer,* edited by Donna G. Fricke and Douglas C. Fricke, pp. 273-89. Bowling Green, Ohio: Bowling Green University Press, 1976.

Proposes that *The Great Gatsby* employs mythological treatments of love, death, and rebirth, similar to those discussed in *The Golden Bough* by Sir James Frazer and *From Ritual to Romance* by Jessie L. Weston. Emmitt notes that these two works were mentioned by T. S. Eliot as inspirational sources for his *The Waste Land,* a work which Fitzgerald knew well.

Fahey, William A. *F. Scott Fitzgerald and the American Dream.* New York: Thomas Y. Crowell Co., 1973, 177 p.

Biographical and critical work that focuses on Fitzgerald's quest for the American dream in his life and in his works.

Fetterley, Judith. "*The Great Gatsby:* Fitzgerald's *droit de seigneur.*" In her *The Resisting Reader: A Feminist Approach to American Fiction,* pp. 72-100. Bloomington: Indiana University Press, 1978.

Feminist reading of *The Great Gatsby.* Fetterley views *Gatsby* as "another American 'love' story centered in hostility to women and the concomitant strategy of the scapegoat."

Godden, Richard. "*The Great Gatsby:* Glamor on the Turn." *Journal of American Studies* 16, No. 3 (December 1982): 343-71.

Discusses Jay Gatsby's sophisticated role-playing as a dramatic act so obvious that it is reminiscent of Bertolt Brecht's epic theater, in which the actor (in this case Gatsby) may comment on the play itself, detaching the viewer from the artificial character role. Godden details instances in which it appears that Gatsby is commenting on his own character.

Graham, Sheilah. *The Real F. Scott Fitzgerald: Thirty-Five Years Later.* New York: Grosset & Dunlop, 1976, 287 p.

Personal, forthright account of the last three and a half years of Fitzgerald's life, written by his lover and companion Sheilah Graham in an attempt to correct what she believes are misconceptions about Fitzgerald and their relationship. Graham discusses Fitzgerald's alcoholism, his marriage to Zelda Sayre, his career, and their affair. Graham is also the author of *Beloved Infidel,* a work about her relationship with Fitzgerald.

Harvey, W. J. "Themes and Texture in *The Great Gatsby.*" In *Twentieth Century Interpretations of "The Great Gatsby,"* edited by Ernest H. Lockridge, pp. 99-100. Englewood Cliffs, N.J.: Prentice-Hall, 1968.

Informative discussion of the use of language in *The Great Gatsby.*

Johnson, Christiane. "*The Great Gatsby:* The Final Vision." *Fitzgerald/Hemingway Annual: 1976,* edited by Matthew J. Bruccoli, pp. 109-15. Englewood, Colo.: Information Handling Services, 1978.

Examines the concluding passage of *The Great Gatsby* in which America's early beginnings are discussed. Johnson believes that it is this final vision of America that gives the novel its mythical dimensions.

Kazin, Alfred, ed. *F. Scott Fitzgerald: The Man and His Work.* New York: Collier Books, 1962, 221 p.

Collection of critical essays on Fitzgerald and his work; includes criticism by Gertrude Stein, John Peale Bishop, Edmund Wilson, and T. S. Eliot.

Langman, F. H. "Style and Shape in *The Great Gatsby.*" *Southern Review* VI, No. 1 (March 1973): 48-67.

Detailed analysis of language in *The Great Gatsby.* Langman believes that it is *Gatsby*'s prose that gives the novel its evocative power.

Lisca, Peter. "Nick Carraway and the Imagery of Disorder." *Twentieth Century Literature* 13, No. 1 (April 1967): 18-28.

Maintains that most critical discussions of *Gatsby* have placed too much emphasis on Nick Carraway's moral viewpoint in the novel, and in so doing, have obscured the technical brilliance of the work.

Minter, David L. "Dreams, Design, and Interpretation in *The Great Gatsby.*" In *Twentieth Century Interpretations of "The Great Gatsby": A Collection of Critical Essays,* edited by Ernest H. Lockridge, pp. 82-9. Englewood Cliffs, N.J.: Prentice-Hall, 1968.

Examines Jay Gatsby as a builder and dreamer of a "new world," and of Nick Carraway as the novel's narrator and witness to Gatsby's actions.

Mizener, Arthur. *The Far Side of Paradise: A Biography of F. Scott Fitzgerald.* Rev. ed. Boston: Houghton Mifflin Co., 1965, 416 p.

First comprehensive biography of Fitzgerald.

Mulford, Carla. "Fitzgerald, Perkins, and *The Great Gatsby.*" *The Journal of Narrative Technique* 12, No. 3 (Fall 1982): 210-20.

Discusses revisions of *The Great Gatsby* by Fitzgerald and his editor, Maxwell Perkins, as revealing important developments in the novel's overall structure.

Quirk, Tom. "Fitzgerald and Cather: *The Great Gatsby.*" *American Literature* 54, No. 4 (December 1982): 576-91.*

Examines the literary influence of Willa Cather on Fitzgerald, linking her novels *My Ántonia* and *Alexander's Bridge* with *Gatsby.*

Scott, Robert Ian. "A Sense of Loss: Entropy vs. Ecology in *The Great Gatsby.*" *Queen's Quarterly* 82, No. 4 (Winter 1975): 559-71.

Analyzes the "corrupting effects of time and wealth" on the various sets of human relationships in *The Great Gatsby.*

Stallman, Robert Wooster. "Conrad and *The Great Gatsby.*" *Twentieth Century Literature* 1, No. 1 (April 1955): 5-12.*

Determines that *Gatsby* owes more to Joseph Conrad's work than its first-person narrative structure. Stallman believes that a careful assessment of *Gatsby*'s plot, characterizations, and imagery reveals an even closer link with Conrad's work. For additional criticism of *The Great Gatsby* by Stallman, see excerpt above, 1955.

Stern, Milton R. *The Golden Moment: The Novels of F. Scott Fitzgerald.* Chicago: University of Illinois Press, 1970, 462 p.

Focuses on the "autobiographical impulse" in Fitzgerald's novels.

Tanselle, G. Thomas, and Bryer, Jackson H. "*The Great Gatsby:* A Study in Literary Reputation." *New Mexico Quarterly* XXXIII, No. 4 (Winter 1963-64): 409-25.

Informative survey of criticism about *The Great Gatsby,* from the earliest reviews through the explosion of *Gatsby* criticism in the 1950s.

Trilling, Lionel. "F. Scott Fitzgerald." *The Liberal Imagination: Essays on Literature and Society,* pp. 236-46. Garden City, N.Y.: Anchor Books, 1953.

General criticism of Fitzgerald with special critical attention to *The Great Gatsby.* Of the novel, Trilling writes: "*The Great Gatsby* . . . is still as fresh as when it first appeared; it has even gained in weight and relevance, which can be said of very few American books of its time."

Watts, Emily Stipes. "Crooked Money and Easy Money." *The Businessman in American Literature,* pp. 55-63. Athens: University of Georgia Press, 1982.*

Examines Jay Gatsby's illegal business connections and describes *The Great Gatsby* as "the best known of the crooked-money novels."

Stefan (Anton) George

1861-1933

(Also wrote under pseudonym of Edmund Delorme) German poet, translator, and essayist.

George is considered to have been the foremost representative in Germany of the late nineteenth-century European movement away from literary Naturalism and toward the ideology and stylistic tenets of Symbolism. Influenced by the French poets Charles Baudelaire, Paul Verlaine, and especially by the poet and Symbolist theoretician Stéphane Mallarmé, George sought to reinvest German poetry with the formal beauty represented by the works of Johann Wolfgang von Goethe. His own poetry was often of an unsurpassed technical excellence. In keeping with Mallarmé's Symbolist precepts, George endeavored to create mood, rather than to recreate events or objects. He also translated into German the works of Baudelaire, Mallarmé, Gabriele D'Annunzio, Algernon Swinburne, and William Shakespeare, as well as the works of many lesser-known French, Italian, Dutch, Danish, and Polish poets who exemplified the Symbolist credo of "art for art's sake" to which he subscribed.

Courtesy of the German Information Center

George was the son of a prosperous Rhineland wine merchant. His parents encouraged his early intellectual development by sending him at age thirteen to the Ludwig-Georg Gymnasium, a noted secondary school. George studied there for six years, mastering Greek and Latin as well as a number of modern European languages. But instead of entering a university after graduating from the gymnasium, George began to travel, visiting Switzerland, Italy, Spain, England, and France. In Paris he met Mallarmé, whose poetry and hermetic way of life greatly influenced him. In the poem "Franken" ("Frankish Lands"), which appeared in the collection *Der siebente Ring (The Seventh Ring),* George later paid eloquent tribute to the country where he realized new possibilities of artistic expression. In Symbolism he found the precision of form and devotion to beauty that he felt were lacking in the German fin-de-siècle movement of literary Naturalism. In addition, Mallarmé's famous Tuesday evening gatherings of writers and artists inspired George to assemble his own coterie, later known as the *Georgekreis* ("George circle"). He sought, however, not to establish an intellectual forum of equals, but rather to set up a series of master and disciple relationships, with himself as undisputed master. George attempted to enlist the poetic prodigy Hugo von Hofmannsthal, who was then in his teens, as his first disciple. Hofmannsthal may have misunderstood George's impassioned pleas for devotion; in any case, Hofmannsthal's father intervened and demanded that George leave his son alone. In later years the two established a guardedly cordial relationship, marred for George by the fact that Hofmannsthal would not adopt the worshipful attitude expected of *Georgekreis* members. George's circle of followers included poets, editors, translators, artists, literary critics, and literary historians, among them Karl Wolfskehl, Carl August Klein, Friedrich Gundelfinger (renamed Gundolf by George), and Klaus von Stauffenberg, who in 1944 was the agent of the unsuccessful attempt to assassinate Adolf Hitler with a briefcase bomb. Until late in his life George maintained no permanent residence, but lived alternately with various of his disciples in Germany and Switzerland. In 1892 George founded the periodical *Blätter für die Kunst,* which served as the principal organ for disseminating what George termed his "new art." It contained George's poetry and that of other *Georgekreis* members, translations of Symbolist poets, and essays promulgating Symbolism as a literary mode. George believed that adherence to his poetic precepts would bring about a renaissance in German—and, by extension, European—culture, which would in turn lead to widespread spiritual renewal. He instituted new methods of orthography, including his own idiosyncratic system of spelling, capitalization, and punctuation, as well as a new and simplified typeface (which closely resembled his own handwriting). He also established strict poetic rules: for example, no rhyme could be used more than once. This led to the revival of many archaic words and occasionally to the invention of new ones in order to provide a yet unused rhyme.

A central event in George's life was his meeting with Maximilian Kronberger late in 1901. George saw in the thirteen-year-old boy, whom he called Maximin, the incarnation of the ideal of advanced spiritual and intellectual development that he thought his "new art" would bring about. Maximin's death at sixteen inspired what critics regard as George's most beautiful and purely lyrical poetry, contained for the most part in the collection *The Seventh Ring*. In the years following the boy's death, Maximin became for George not just a poetic inspiration and the symbol of a new age, but the god of the "neue Reich"—the new empire of intellect that George believed was forthcoming in Germany. At this time George abandoned the role of master for that of chief prophet and interpreter of this new German god of youth. His final volumes of poetry were almost meaningless to readers unaware of Maximin's significance to George. In these final works, *Der Stern des Bundes (The Star of the Covenant)* and *Das Neue Reich (The Kingdom Come),* George preached the divinity of Maximin and prescribed the behavior required of his followers. Despite their obscure nature, aspects of these poems—the cult of youth, the espousal of German nationalism, and the call for devotion to an absolute leader—were taken up by the emergent National Socialist party. George was offered a prominent position among the artists and writers nurtured by the Nazi regime. His response was to leave Germany for Switzerland, where he spent the rest of his life.

Critics generally examine George's career chronologically, finding that such an approach reveals not only his growth and development as a lyric poet, but also the course of his private spiritual quest, which began with his dream of a rebirth of the soul in this life through the arts, and which culminated in his fixation upon Maximin as the god of a new era of spiritual and artistic fulfillment. George's first three volumes of poetry—*Hymnen (Odes), Pilgerfahrten (Pilgrimages),* and *Algabal*—first appeared in privately printed editions and were later published as a single volume. Ulrich K. Goldsmith writes that the appearance of *Odes* marked "the beginning of the 'new poetry' and the eclipse of naturalism, according to George's tenets." The poems of *Pilgrimages* present George questioning his poetic vocation and searching for his own poetic creed. In *Algabal* George examined the soul of the modern artist, cast as the decadent Roman boy-emperor Heliogabalus, or Algabal. This work has been cited as an example of pure aestheticism in German literature, closely related in theme to the contemporaneous works *The Picture of Dorian Gray* by Oscar Wilde and *À Rebours* by Joris-Karl Huysmans. In his first three volumes of poetry, George explored his initial reaction to French Symbolism. Still seeking his own poetic style, he professed austerity and precision as the ideal modes of poetic expression, but often wrote instead in a highly ornamental style. The poem "Die Spange" ("The Link") in *Pilgrimages* is often interpreted as an explanation of this dichotomy: he speaks of being unable to obtain the "iron" necessary to fashion the "firm smooth band" of a clasp or link, and therefore has it made instead of ornamental gold studded with gems. This has been seen as a reflection of George's conviction that the debased state of the German language made it impossible for him to express himself in a pure and simple way. George's next volume of poetry was entitled *Die Bücher der Hirten- und Preisgedichte, der Sagen und Sänge und der Hängenden Garten (The Books of Ecologues and Eulogies, of Legends and Lays, and the Hanging Gardens).* It is divided into three sections, each devoted to a different culture: ancient Greece, medieval Europe, and the Orient. In the poems of each section George examines the soul of the poet as it would be expressed in that time and place. Many of the poems in *The Book of Ecologues and Eulogies* question whether the acquisition of worldly goods and the love of a woman are the proper goals of a poet.

The publication of *Das Jahr der Seele (The Year of the Soul)* marked a turning point in George's personal life and in his career. The first of his works to be made generally available outside of the *Georgekreis,* critics agree that *The Year of the Soul* is the product of George's artistic maturity and contains his most technically accomplished poems. E. K. Bennett has noted that *The Year of the Soul* has always been "the most popular and the most quoted" of George's works. Gerhard Masur finds that this volume "remains one of the most delicate manifestations of lyrical inspiration in the German language; for many it represents the purest expression of George's genius." Divided into three sections, *The Year of the Soul* traces the poet's emotional and spiritual growth through three seasons: from autumn ("Nach der lese") through winter ("Waller im Schnee") to a new way of life in summer ("Sieg des Sommers"). Critics theorize that George's year of the soul has no spring because he has not experienced the complete spiritual renewal appropriate to that season of rebirth. Many of the poems in *The Year of the Soul* are cast in dialogue form, but in his preface George warned that "seldom are the I and the You so much the same soul as in this book." In *The Year of the Soul* George rejected relationships with women as inadequate for poetic inspiration and presents male companionship as the ideal. Goldsmith writes that "with the emergence of this male friendship there comes immediately a new release of creative power which takes the form of pedagogic guidance." This tendency to impart instruction became more pronounced in George's final volumes of poetry. *The Seventh Ring* begins with poems defending George's poetic vision and his growing admiration for German tradition and for male beauty. This collection also contains many "Lieder," or songs: short, intense lyrical verses of love and devotion to Maximin. Increasingly in the middle and final sections of *The Seventh Ring* are found poems which argue for Maximin's deification. George's last works, *The Star of the Covenant* and *The Kingdom Come,* contain poems which establish doctrine to be followed by the members of the *Georgekreis* who accepted the myth of Maximin as a god embodying divine forces of youth, beauty, and power.

George's critical reputation has long been entangled with the controversies surrounding his life. He expressed contempt for the general public and for years was well known only within his circle of disciples, who produced adulatory assessments of George's work but little real criticism. His career suffered most when the Nazis appropriated his poetry of a "new Reich" in an attempt to present George as the prophet of nazism. Some critics still maintain that George's final poetic works, hailing an invincible, godlike German youth, are indeed welcoming paeans to Nazism. Some commentators theorize that George rejected the proffered ties with the Nazi party because he was too egoistical to accept a subordinate role in any regime. However, members of the *Georgekreis*—who produced most of the biographical material available on George—have argued that George was never a proponent of any aspect of nazism, either in spirit or in fact. They cite his self-imposed exile to Switzerland, the many Jewish *Georgekreis* members, and George's lifelong conviction that poetry should shun any social or political questions, as evidence that George was unaware that his poetry of a spiritual empire would be applied to a political one.

The greatest part of George's activity as a poet, essayist, and translator was devoted to the renewal of German poetry. In introducing the doctrines of Symbolism to his national literature he played an important role in the growth of this movement and the waning of literary Naturalism. While his influence, both as a poet and a personality, may have effected less than the spiritual renewal he had hoped to bring about, George's own work may be said to have attained his ideal of a spiritually motivated art of high aesthetic purity.

(See also *TCLC,* Vol. 2 and *Contemporary Authors,* Vol. 104.)

***PRINCIPAL WORKS**

Hymnen (poetry) 1890
[*Odes* published in *The Works of Stefan George,* 1949]
Charles Baudelaires Blumen des Bösen [translator] (poetry) 1891
Pilgerfahrten (poetry) 1891
[*Pilgrimages* published in *The Works of Stefan George,* 1949]
Algabal (poetry) 1892
[*Algabal* published in *The Works of Stefan George,* 1949]
Die Bücher der Hirten- und Preisgedichte, der Sagen und Sänge und der Hängenden Garten (poetry) 1895
[*The Books of Ecologues and Eulogies, of Legends and Lays, and of the Hanging Gardens* published in *The Works of Stefan George,* 1949]
Das Jahr der Seele (poetry) 1897
[*The Year of the Soul* published in *The Works of Stefan George,* 1949]
Der Teppich des Lebens und die Lieder von Traum und Tod (poetry) 1900
[*The Tapestry of Life, The Songs of Dream and Death* published in *The Works of Stefan George,* 1949]
Die Fibel: Auswahl erste Verse (poetry and essays) 1901
Tage und Taten (notes and sketches) 1903
["Days and Deeds," 1951; published in journal *University of Kansas City Review*]
Maximin: Ein Gedenckbuch (poetry) 1906
Der Siebente Ring (poetry) 1907
[*The Seventh Ring* published in *The Works of Stefan George,* 1949]
Dante, Stellen aus der Göttlichen Komödie [translator] (poetry) 1909
Shakespeare, Sonnette [translator] (poetry) 1909
Der Stern des Bundes (poetry) 1914
[*The Star of the Covenant* published in *The Works of Stefan George,* 1949]
Gesamte—Ausgabe der Werke. 18 vols. (poetry, essays, and dramas) 1927-34
Das Neue Reich (poetry) 1928
[*The Kingdom Come* published in *The Works of Stefan George,* 1949]
Briefwechsel zwischen George und Hofmannsthal (letters) 1938
The Works of Stefan George (poetry) 1949; also published as *The Works of Stefan George* [revised edition], 1974

*The first publication dates of the majority of George's works refer to privately printed editions.

TAYLOR STARCK (essay date 1919)

[In the following excerpt, Starck places George within the ranks of German neo-Romantics who revolted against the realism predominant during the previous fifty years of German literature. Starck discusses George's poetic principles, in particular his devotion to the doctrine of art for art's sake.]

In recent years the most powerful literary tendency that has been making itself felt is the revulsion against the realism of the last half century. The development of the Irish school of romanticists has had an important influence and the growth of the little theaters in this country is intimately connected with the revival of romanticism. Germany, too, has a large group of neo-romanticists who have been deluging the literary market with fantastic tales and tenuous dramatic productions. But none of these has outlined so careful a program or insisted with such vigor upon the acceptance of his principles as Stefan George, the Rhinelander. Born in 1869, he has the most vigorous years of his life already behind him, and yet it is but little more than a decade since Richard Meyer directed the attention of the public to his work. To speak of a public is rather to exaggerate the number of his readers. They are still relatively few and the seven or eight collections of his verse by their very outward aspect—binding, paper, and printing—appeal only to the select class which he wanted to reach. Indeed the poet is himself responsible for the scant attention which has been paid to him. With Olympian aloofness he wished to speak only to those whom he admitted to his guild and keep all others at a safe distance. Again and again he expresses his contempt for the mob, which, of course, includes the grubbing literary critic with his insatiate greed for unearthing sources and discovering "influences." To be sure, this pose, for thus it must be called, does not proceed from sheer scorn of the masses as such, but because he feels that the socialistic and collectivist tendencies of the day are of their very nature inimical to individual artistic creation. . . . The poet must grow and develop far from the noisy babble of the world marts—*ein Talent bildet sich im Stillen;* the merest suggestion of professionalism in literature is a withering influence for delicate poetical growths. (pp. 1-2)

It was such considerations that impelled George and his disciples to gather behind closed doors and withhold their productions from the baneful influences of shallow literary critics. The meagre output of the school was published only for their own enjoyment in the privately printed *Blätter für die Kunst.* . . . (p. 2)

As far as the form of his work is concerned [George] shows an intimate relationship with the French Parnassians. Like them he strove to regain the polished form which had been lost through the centrifugal forces at work in the naturalistic productions; like them he was unalterably opposed to unchecked subjectivism, slipshod or repeated rimes and all looseness in poetic form. The ending of the line seems to have engaged his attention particularly and nowhere in German literature has such a variety of riming syllables been used. He goes to the extreme of maintaining that a rime once used loses its value for the poet and should seldom or never be repeated. The inevitable result of such an exacting rule was that innumerable obsolete words had to be resuscitated and curious compounds invented to satisfy the demands of the rime. He went to the extent of composing in Middle High German for practice in strict metrical form. But even then George found it impossible to obey to the letter the rules which he had himself formulated. The metrical forms in his poems show far less variety, the four line stanza of four or five feet riming *abab* or *abba* being the favorite. His most recent volume consists largely of poems in unrimed lines of five feet, mostly iambic pentameters. Whatever may be the deficiencies of his work through over-artificiality it cannot be gainsaid that he has enriched poetic diction by his revival of obsolete and Middle High German words.

Equally severe is he in his dicta respecting the content of the individual poem and the forms of poetic writing. A poem should be abstracted from the world of daily endeavor, free from theories of life and problems of state and society; it should be simple and clear and present objectively one single picture without the reflections and personal opinions of the poet. Wherever George has consistently adhered to this principle he has succeeded in creating lyrics of the greatest delicacy, particularly in his nature poems. . . . But this relentless application of the principle *L'art pour l'art,* this complete withdrawal into the rarified atmosphere of superworldly observation; the excessive condensation of the sentence attained through an inordinate use of genitive phrase; coupled with the demands made upon the reader's attention by a text almost bare of capitals and marks of punctuation—all this tends rather to obscurity than the limpid clearness for which the poet strove.

Not only did George draw narrow boundaries within which the lyric poem must revolve, but he also restricts poetry almost entirely to the lyric category. With the novel, especially the novel of the realistic type, he has no patience; "litterarische Reportage, Berichtsserstatterei" ["literary reportage, newspaperwork"] he scornfully calls it. Toward the drama he maintains a more conciliatory attitude, but believes the stage of the present day to be barren of poetic productions. The drama has reached a point where, in his estimation, the dramatists are chewing their cud, existing on that which has been handed down through the generations and that they are writing for a theater with a tremendous machinery demanding plays written expressly for it. . . . It is the disuse into which verse has fallen in dramatic writing that is largely responsible for this condition. . . . And so he sees the hopes for a rebirth of the drama founded upon a restoration of the verse to its old place. To build the foundations for this new drama, for the drama receives furtherance rather through the coöperation of a group of poets with the same ideals than individual effort, he inaugurated a *Bühne der Blätter für die Kunst.* The object of this dramatic society was to give amateur performances in private houses in which particular attention should be paid to simplicity of grouping, aesthetic movements and to recitation. . . . George lays great stress upon this last point because the mannerisms arising from the stereotyped stage recitation have made all oral performances of poetry unrhythmical. (pp. 3-5)

George feels that it is his mission to recreate the world in a poetic sense, to develop a new power of joyous artistic contemplation. (p. 5)

A careful study might reveal a strong Nietzschean strain in George's work; and indeed it is in one sense essentially that of a romanticist. The ever recurring *Sehnsucht nach der Sehnsucht,* the insistence on the unity of the arts, the glorification of night and sorrow; all this recalls to us the early romanticists. The list of his translations, which includes Rossetti, shows strong leanings toward this school and it is no mere accident that he, like Novalis and the Schlegels, is an ardent Roman Catholic. But, on the other hand, the avoidance of multiplicity of detail, the preference of classic outlines to the wild confusedness of a Brentano makes us hesitate before assigning him to his place. (p. 6)

Taylor Starck, "Stefan George and the Reform of the German Lyric," in Modern Language Notes, *Vol. XXXIV, No. 1, January, 1919, pp. 1-7.*

ARTHUR BURKHARD (essay date 1934)

[In appraising George's place in modern German poetry, Burkhard finds little similarity between George and either the literary Naturalists or the neo-Romantics. Burkhard believes that the peculiar quality of George is exemplified by what he terms the pure reason found in his poems. Burkhard compares George with the German poet and dramatist August Platen, who modeled his satiric plays on the classic Greek drama and whose poetry is characterized by an attempt to achieve perfection of form.]

Stefan George, who died last December in Locarno, was commonly esteemed the high priest of modern German poetry. He lived apart from the world; he kept himself aloof from everything mundane. His poetry is so far removed in spirit and purpose from "Volksdichtung" ["poetry of the people"] that it seems a singular misapprehension of his real nature to designate him, as press dispatches did at his death, the prophet of the Third Reich, the poet laureate of Nazi Germany and the ancestor and herald of Hitlerism. The title rather than the content of his latest collection of verse, **"Das Neue Reich" ["The Kingdom Come"],** published in 1928, apparently encouraged these inappropriate designations. The Stefan George who turned into superbly polished German verse such dissimilar works as Baudelaire's "Fleurs du Mal," Dante's "Divina Comoedia" and Shakspere's sonnets, and who produced during the last forty years approximately a dozen volumes of profoundly original poems in solemn, stately measures, impresses the discriminating observer as a priest and prince among German poets rather than as a national prophet or political propagandist. Even one of his most loyal disciples is content to proclaim him simply "Dichter, Herrscher, Meister" ["poet, lord, master"]. (p. 49)

His significance [among modern German poets] is particular rather than general. His artistic principles and his self-conscious poetry derive from his aristocratic nature. As he desires only to evoke and stimulate moods by means of words, he neither observes nor describes things or events. Nor does he report or moralize. Without interest in providing entertainment or instruction, he assembles no information and makes no comment on conditions. He indulges neither in protest nor complaint. He spurns the masses, deigning to speak neither to the proletariat nor the bourgeoisie. Addressed to no one in particular, his verses invite no reply. Purely personal in form and expression and impersonal in effect, they make no application of general principles to any specific problems of humanity. Much as he differs in all these respects from the naturalistic writers who were in favor during his early period, Stefan George is scarcely less unlike the neo-romantic poets who enjoyed a later vogue. He resembles the neo-romanticists in his esteem for men noble both by birth and character, in his sympathy for the unhappy and lonely man on a throne—Ludwig II or Heliogabalus, Nietzsche or Leo XIII—rather than for the starving and exploited workman. His cult of beauty inspired him, even as it did neo-romantic writers, to create verses less ethical than aesthetic, less moral than beautiful, less good than fine. Yet he differs from them decidedly in his staunch refusal to depict the spiritual states of an individual or to reflect personal emotional disturbance in his poetry. Behind emotion and above it in all the works of Stefan George sits enthroned triumphant reason. The clear, cool mind of the poet controls and refines emotion, purging it of all purely subjective elements, so that the form and content of the final version of his poems appear impersonal and apply as universal.

The peculiar quality of Stefan George becomes apparent from a comparison with his most celebrated German contemporary, Rainer Maria Rilke. Rilke is, like George, too comprehensive as a poet and a personality to remain a part of any merely temporary literary movement; moreover he impresses many as a more appealing person and a much more approachable and human poet. Compared with Rilke's verses, the poems of Stefan George appear less pictorial than plastic, less musical or melodious than architectonic and monumental. The very titles of his different collections, which have been recently assembled in a sumptuous "Gesamtausgabe" ["complete edition"], stand firm like marble columns, simply but completely fashioned and which unite to form together the spacious, well-ordered porch of a symmetrical temple—solid in structure, substantial in composition, pure in design—where only the consecrated gather in a spirit of religious devotion when they wish to worship at the sacred altar of beauty. (pp. 51-2)

Within [George's collections of poetry] the verses are arranged according to a regular system determined by the principles of balance and proportion that are rather severely applied. As we may well expect from such an expert master of form—sensitive to the color of vowels and the character of consonants, adept at alliteration and assonance, final and medial rhyme—the individual poems are all carefully, fastidiously composed. Compact, compressed, pregnant with content, rarified, refined, reduced to the very essence, they appear timeless and cosmic, making the impression of the typical and universal, the absolute and eternal. The inspiration may derive from actual experience but all trace of the personal source has been banished forever from the poem in its final form. Independent of time and space, superior to any individual or temporal character, the poems are symbolical in significance and become almost mythical. Fashioned by artistic law, the language has also severed all connection with the organic life of the speech employed by ordinary men. The poems, composed of such material and in this form, are cut off from human contacts and live a life alone and above, like a chiselled statue of marble or a precious bit of handicraft, carved of ivory or modelled in gold.

Perhaps Stefan George would have preferred to mould all his masterpieces from baser metal, had he been able to procure the desired cool, smooth, firm effect of a strip of solid steel, but he was often forced by sheer necessity to resort to the brilliance of precious gems and rich gold—or how else is one to interpret **"Die Spange" ["The Link"],** one of the simplest and most revealing of his symbolical poems?—

Ich wollte sie aus kühlem eisen
Und wie ein glatter fester streif,
Doch war im schacht auf allen gleisen
So kein metall zum gusse reif.

Nun aber soll sie also sein:
Wie eine große fremde dolde
Geformt aus feuerrotem golde
Und reichem blitzendem gestein.

[I wanted it of coolest iron
And fashioned like a firm smooth band.
Yet all the mountain's shafts were barren,
Had no such metal for the mold.

Different now it shall be made.
Like a great and wondrous cluster:
Of gold which is as red as fire,
Of richest sparkling precious stones.
(Translated by Ulrich K. Goldsmith)]

Certain it is that Stefan George's poems are now simple, severe, chaste, austere; now decorated, splendid, festive, regal. His heroes are now devout priests and primitive ascetics, now cruel neurotics or luxurious supermen. He is, himself, at once Catholic and Pagan, modern German and ancient Greek, national and cosmopolitan; in his own words, both the one and the other, the beginning and the end: "Ich bin der Eine und bin Beide . . . Ich bin ein end und ein beginn."

This comprehensive quality in Stefan George's character that made him attempt to embrace the culture of the ages in his treatment of the classical, mediaeval and oriental tradition in his **"Bücher der Hirten und Preisgedichte, der Sagen und Sänge und der hängenden Gärten,"** is matched by his cosmopolitanism. (pp. 52-3)

Stefan George celebrates in his poetry the victory over passion and even over renunciation. He reverses the customary artistic procedure, for with him the purpose of poetry is no longer the expression of feeling by means of art. Feeling is reduced in his verses to a position of secondary importance; it remains merely a means of expression, while expression itself, art, has become the poet's ultimate aim and purpose. In poems resulting from this practice there is no place for impulsiveness or spontaneity, doubts or scruples, action or passion. In them, emotional expansiveness appears unbecoming, conventional love, if not unnatural, at least unseemly. They voice no instinct or urge, give expression to no unrest or desire, indulge in no sentimentality or longing. Scrupulously avoiding expression of emotional unrestraint, they possess neither youth nor warmth. In consequence, they impress most people as calm and formal, measured and reserved, solemn and ceremonial. . . . Poems composed of such stanzas are not callow ventures during a noisily exultant poetic spring. The product of plan and discipline, allowed to mellow to autumnal maturity, they appear meditative and moderate, collected and controlled, classic and contained. . . . (p. 54)

The poems are all purposely far removed from the spirit of the present day and intentionally deprived of every realistic indication of a recollected environment. Ancient Hellas is preferred to modern Europe and Sparta to Athens, but usually the preference is the less specific one of South to North. . . . The atmosphere pervading the scene is always mild and tempered but also always unfamiliar and remote. Instead of the fresh fields of the radiant out-of-doors, the author constructs an unnatural garden, like a bit of still life, without the warmth of spring and without a breath of air. . . . But whether the natural scene is the background for a highly cultivated society . . . , or a virginal landscape for a primitive state of civilization . . . , it has always been so constructed that it represents a condition that nowhere ever actually existed. The landscape, like the language and the people in these poems, is stylized into a pattern that bears the stamp of Stefan George, the "St. G. Schrift." Nature, like life, is forced to conform to his tradition, to become not of one place nor or our time but for every place and for all time.

Although Stefan George departs to the land of his heart's desire and moves in a sphere suspended above sordid reality, he does not merely dwell in an imaginary realm of dreams nor while his time idly away as he basks in the ideal world of beautiful illusion. He may seem to be like Platen, whom he resembles in other respects also, in this removal from his time and country, but he feels that in his own case this aloofness is not simply a flight from self, an escape from responsibility, a desertion of the colors and a shirking of duty. He remains, on the contrary, at the undisturbed centre of the universe, serene and superior, as he observes the concentric rings of human emotion ebb away from him to break against the distant shore, but he reserves the right to comment on them in a spirit of philosophic calm. . . . He is not only a priest who preserves the sacred rituals of the past as he hopes for better times to come, but also a seer and sage who peers with unclouded eyes into the future, a prophet and a law-giver who has established a liturgy for the elect. . . . (pp. 54-6)

There is a hard, unyielding quality in the poetry and in the person of Stefan George that will long endure the attacks of time. . . . This sculptural sureness and monumental immobility are the product of a dominating and indomitable will. His will is strong, his goal is high, his thought is clear, his spirit deep. He follows his lofty and sublime ideal, unfalteringly and unflinchingly. . . . One can comprehend his impatient scorn of clumsy contemporaries who consider him only an anointed prince and condemn him as an empty poseur. . . . For he cannot be disposed of as a mere counter of syllables, a dainty rhymster, a cold, unfeeling formalist. He is not simply a modern Platen, much as he resembles him in his virtues and his faults, his subtleties and refinements of feeling, his pomp and festive splendor, his linguistic and metrical perfection, his worship of the divinity of form to an extent that makes his sober and sedate, august and earnest measures seem very much mannered.

Stefan George is of the chosen, confident of his right to rule. He wraps his priestly robes about him, but he does not lie down to pleasant dreams. He feeds the sacrificial fires in the temple of art, convinced of the nobility and aristocracy of his sacred office, content to represent the poet as priest. To such a master of form and expression in poetry, posterity will surely not refuse the rewards he so often celebrates in his verse and so abundantly deserves. . . . (pp. 56-7)

Arthur Burkhard, "Stefan George, 1868-1933," in The German Quarterly, *Vol. VII, No. 2, March, 1934, pp. 49-57.*

A. N. RAYBOULD (essay date 1935)

[*In his essay "Stefan George and the Germany of To-Day," Raybould identifies George as the prophet of nazism but explores the likelihood that such was not George's intention. The critic believes that, in writing the nationalistic poetry of* The Star of the Covenant *and* The Kingdom Come, *George saw himself as a prophet of a new age, led by youth "rich in action, and victorious in strength, moving in order, rhythm and harmony." Yet Raybould finds it doubtful that George ever regarded National Socialism as the fulfillment of his ideal. Eric Bentley (1944) similarly disclaims any connection between George and the Nazi party.*]

Stefan George, the idol of a select literary clique, the poet who lived apart from the crowd in an aristocratic atmosphere of his own creating, was really the prophet of the Germany that we have before our eyes to-day. George severed himself, in his art and otherwise, from all the later traditions of his country, as Germany to-day is breaking away from all those traditions which expressed her former life. As his country is scorning the old systems of thought and philosophy, so George scorned them in his day, choosing to stand alone and to forge new and strange weapons of form to defend his novelty of thought—perhaps to veil its thinness—as Germany to-day is forging new weapons of discipline to defend a new movement, perhaps to veil the weakness of the philosophy that lies behind this movement.

Stefan George is generally considered the most remarkable poet of modern Germany. His place as a poet is almost undisputed, but his political influence is not so generally acknowledged. This influence lay in his appeal to youth, in his belief in a new humanity and in the power of youth to build up a new world on the ashes of the old. He called to youth, and youth responded, inspired by new faith in themselves, in their power to break the fetters forged by their forbears, and in the strength of youth to go out to something absolutely new. This new romanticism is the mainspring of the National Socialist movement, which is essentially a youth movement, and of which Stefan George was the prophet. (p. 729)

Stefan George lived to see the National Socialist revolution, but whether he regarded it as the fulfilment of his ideal is doubtful. The poet dreams, the world acts. George's idea of hierarchical service could hardly find a place in the world as it is to-day. In Germany as elsewhere it is the masses who throw weight into the scale. He denied to the masses the right of superior knowledge, claiming this as the privilege of the few, and advocating the need of an intellectual *élite*. George's appeal was always to the few rather than to the many, and to the leaders rather than to the followers. And yet, strange paradox, his call has been heard by the many.

Stefan George had an exalted idea of the poet's mission. He believed this mission to be that of prophet and law-giver. Personally his ambition was to sound a clarion for all to hear and to become in the highest sense a national poet. ***Der Stern des Bundes*** and ***Das Neue Reich*** are written to this end. In these he gave his message in accents sufficiently clear and strong, but the question arises: Was the message worthy of the form in which it was clothed? A certain lack of philosophic thought, of clear outlook, and of grasp on life may strike the reader. The national lyric is a new venture; can it stand without being buttressed by old truths? George's lyrics, though objective and non-personal, are not cold. The beauty of the form even lends to them a white fire of intensity, but is it a fire capable of scattering sparks to kindle future fires? He forged a language of steel and gold in which to give his message, but will the inner voice within the metal ring true with the passage of time? His apparent denial of everything was perhaps but a prelude to an affirmation of higher possibilities, but were such possibilities based on realities which endure? He dreamt of a new melody of human life as he dreamt of new melodies of lyric form. He saw a new order rising, rich in action, and victorious in strength, moving in order, rhythm and harmony. This dream has been seized, acted upon, popularised, but can it be made lasting or real? He is the prophet of a certain phase of thought prevalent everywhere, but more definitely prevalent in Germany, a phase insisting on the fight for race and blood, on the doing away with Christian ideals, and the elimination of all elements alien to national cult. Stefan George believed in his own race, believed in their capacity for order, discipline and force, and in their ultimate survival, as the survival of the fittest, the new generation, "*das junge Geschlecht*" ["the young generation"]. . . . Strange that a poet who was accused of worshipping beauty merely for beauty's sake should have been led by political dreams. Dreams and visions come and go, but the poet's art, if it is art, remains for ever. (pp. 730-31)

George as an artist was a conscientious worker, perpetually striving after greater perfection of form. Each successive volume marked a step forward on the upward ladder. From the tender beauty of the ***Hymnen*** and the ***Pilgerfahrten*** in 1891 he rose to the passion and glow of ***Algabal*** in 1892. In his ***Ruch der Hirten*** the form is marked by an ascent to a primitive religiosity, and in the sequence of his subsequent creations the discipline of form always follows the discipline of thought. In the ***Jahr der Seele*** and in ***Das Neue Reich*** form and thought go hand in hand towards the expression of prophetic vision. Here his words are chosen as stones in an architectural structure, each chosen and cut with a view to supporting the whole. Like the early hymns of the Christian Church, George's lyrics are objective, non-personal, non-individualistic. He was the first to present the echo of these hymns in German, and to show the possibility of their Germanising. This alone gives an idea of the widening of the language under his hand. He tuned German till he made it give forth monumental sounds. But those who care for the ordinary German lyrics, for such poets as Lenau, Eichendorf, Heine, will have difficulty in appreciating George. He has no affinity with the nineteenth century romantic poets, unless perhaps with Novalis and Hölderlin, in whose poetry sound is made to accord not so much with individual feeling, as with soul upheavals expressed by word and tone. Like theirs, George's poems play in those realms that lie between the individual soul and the visible world. He has nothing of the simplicity of form to be found in Goethe's lyrics, and nothing of the clear outlook of Goethe's classic poems. Nothing is further from George than the classicism of Goethe and Schiller.

Stefan George's rhythms are peculiar, exotic, in a certain sense archaic, resembling early and long forgotten forms of poetry; they are difficult to read because he introduced a new orthography (now largely adopted), and they are difficult to the ear because of the necessary intonation, and yet the beauty of his verse can be best appreciated only when it is read aloud, in the manner of psalmody, as he intended. These difficulties have given rise to much fault finding, not lessened by the difficulty of getting at the poet's thought. It may be an axiom that beauty is simple, but the simplest is often the hardest to understand, and the monumental simplicity after which George strives comes under this category. The beauty of his verse may be superficially apparent to the superficial reader, it can really only appeal to those who have time and patience to study it. And in this case, it is sometimes asked if the message repays the search for it. (pp. 733-34)

A. N. Raybould, "Stefan George and the Germany of To-Day," in Contemporary Review, *Vol. CXLVII, June, 1935, pp. 729-34.*

E. M. FORSTER (essay date 1943)

[*Forster was a prominent English novelist, critic, and essayist, whose works reflect his liberal humanism. His most celebrated novel,* A Passage to India *(1924), is a complex examination of personal relationships amid the conflicts of the modern world. Although some of Forster's critical essays are considered naive in their literary assessments, his discussion of fictional techniques in his* Aspects of the Novel *(1927) is regarded as a minor classic in literary criticism. In the following excerpt, originally published in 1943 and reprinted in his* Two Cheers for Democracy *(1951), Forster discusses the reactions to World War II offered by the works of André Gide and George. Forster suggests that Gide's reactions are those of a humanist, George's of an authoritarian. Forster finds it to George's credit that he rejected proferred ties with the Nazi party.*]

Two modern writers of European reputation, the Frenchman André Gide and the German Stefan George, offer contrasted reaction to the present chaos. I will begin with Gide. . . .

He is a humanist. The humanist has four leading characteristics—curiosity, a free mind, belief in good taste, and belief in the human race—and all four are present in Gide. (p. 228)

He is not cynical about the human race. And consequently—for it is a consequence—he has no class prejudice and no colour prejudice. It remember so well the last time I met him: it was in an international congress of writers at Paris in the 'thirties, and he had to make a speech. A tall, willowy figure, he undulated on the platform above the vast audience, rather full of airs and graces and inclined to watch his own effects. Then he forgot himself and remembered the human race and made a magnificent oration. His thesis was that the individual will never develop his individuality until he forms part of a world society. As his thought soared, his style became fluid, and sentimentality passed into affection. He denied that humanity would cease to be interesting if it ceased to be miserable, and imagined a social state where happiness will be accessible to all, and where men, because they are happy, will be great. At that time the menace of Fascism was already darkening our doorways, and it seemed to us, as we listened to Gide, that here was a light which the darkness could not put out. It is not easy, in a few words, to give a picture of a very complicated individual; let me anyhow make it clear that he reacts to the European tragedy as a humanist, that the four characteristics of humanism are curiosity, a free mind, belief in good taste, and belief in the human race, and that he has been prepared to suffer for his beliefs: they have not been just for the study and the cloister; and consequently men honour him.

Now there are other reactions to the European tragedy besides humanism. Let us turn to Stefan George and see what he did in the face of the approaching darkness—George, a fine lyric poet, a sincere man of high ideals and of an iron will. He died exactly ten years ago, in 1933, after the establishment of Hitler's power. He was born in a very different Germany, in 1868. Well educated, and versed in European culture, he thought of his country as one among many, and owed a special debt, in his early poems, to France. By nature he was a recluse. He wrote for a small circle of friends and was accepted by them as their chief. Then he had an intense personal experience which exalted his poetry but did not improve his judgment, and as a result of that experience the circle of friends hardened into a cult, and George almost assumed the airs of a priest. Domineering and humourless, he trained his young disciples and began to send them out into the world. He taught them to despise the common man and to despise women, to prefer instinct to brains, and to believe in good birth, and in state organisation. A friend of mine who attended the University of Heidelberg used to see these disciples of George in the streets, 'almost dancing, tall, graceful and athletic, with their heads thrown back, as if they were trying to avoid the sight of common humanity.' It seemed like the coming of a new aristocracy, and George himself was a natural aristocrat, just as Gide is a natural democrat. He was an exceptional person, highly gifted as a poet, a lofty idealist with something of a prophet's grandeur. He knew it, and he made the mistake of thinking that when a person is exceptional he ought to be a leader. The idea of leadership, so seductive and so pernicious both for the leaders and the led, invaded this fine artist. The swastika was stamped on the covers of his latest books, his poems spoke of a Fuehrer and a New Reich, and he found a cure for the evils of his age not in humanism, like Gide, but in authority. That was his reaction to the approaching European tragedy: authoritarianism.

The Nazis were not slow to take him up. From their point of view he was one of them. The National Socialists, it has been well said, have a peculiar gift for adopting and defiling ideas that have been of real value in their time, and they did not spare Stefan George. They patronised him and he had the misery of seeing his work exploited by cads—the greatest misery which a fastidious writer can undergo. He saw his ideals put into practice by Hitler, and it was more than he could stand. Doctor Goebbels wrote to him—no doubt with Hitler's approval—and offered him high honours as a poet in the gangster state. To his glory, he never answered the letter. Germany had become intolerable, and in 1933 he went away to Switzerland to die. That is his end—a sad end but a dignified one. The poet whom the Nazis claim as their own could not stand their foulness and preferred to die in exile.

Creative writers are always greater than the causes that they represent, and I have not interpreted either Gide or George to you in this brief summary of their respective attitudes. I have, for instance, conveyed nothing of the quality of their emotion or their style, nor is it possible to do so except by quotations. But they neatly illustrate two contrasted reactions in this age of misery: the humanist's reaction, and the authoritarian's. (pp. 229-31)

E. M. Forster, "Gide and George," in his Two Cheers for Democracy, *Harcourt Brace Jovanovich, 1951, pp. 228-31.**

ERIC BENTLEY (essay date 1944)

[Bentley is considered one of the most erudite and innovative critics of the modern theater. He was responsible for introducing Bertolt Brecht, Luigi Pirandello, and other European playwrights to America through his studies, translations, and stage adaptations of their plays. In the following excerpt, originally published in 1944, Bentley discounts the attempts to include George among the Nazis, finding that George's "neue Reich" was an empire of the mind. The attempts to annex George as the poet and prophet of the Third Reich, Bentley maintains, can be attributed primarily to statements made about George by members of his circle who found favor with the Nazi party. A. N. Raybould (1935), similarly concludes that George never intended his spiritually motivated poetry to be applied to a political purpose.]

Early in 1889 Friedrich Nietzsche, hitherto the greatest mind in Europe, left Turin, a mental corpse. Just at this time there entered Turin a young German who was to continue Nietzsche's work, though as yet he did not know it. This was Stefan George, who had already written not a little, planned much more, and published nothing. He took up Nietzsche's idea of an élite and formed his Circle (*Georgekreis*). . . .

The influence of Nietzsche was of course felt at this time in many directions, but the influence he exerted on George was purely in the direction of Heroic Vitalism. For the same social and psychological forces were at work in the George Circle as in Carlyle and Nietzsche. George is characterized by the same ambivalence, that is, just like Carlyle and Nietzsche, he has a Nazi side and a liberal side, and thus becomes a subject of endless partisan controversy. (p. 194)

On the one hand, George transferred the Nietzschean philosophy to the spiritual plane, and the tone of George Circle writings is much more lofty and remote from worldly affairs. On the other hand, it is the boast of Georgeans that George put into effect what Nietzsche merely thought. For George actually brought together such a group of believers in Heroic Vitalism as Nietzsche had often dreamed of, and the superman who was never more than a glimmer for Nietzsche was for the Circle incarnate in the boy they called Maximin. Furthermore George wrote specifically of the heroic rebirth of Germany after the First World War. (p. 195)

The pattern of the George movement is sinister, for is not George a sort of a literary Hitler, with Nietzsche as his Houston Chamberlain, Maximin as his Horst Wessel, and [Friedrich] Gundolf as his [Alfred] Rosenberg? The subject is worth investigating since George is a first-rate poet, and a poet peculiarly of our time. In that he bases his work not upon an accepted system of values but upon a subjective myth, in that he inclines more to nuance than to irony, in that he has more virtuosity than imagination, in that, like Richard Strauss, he prefers splendid orchestration to Mozartian integration, George is the greatest of all decadents. In his mastery and presentation of one small tract of experience, in his superb control over the dialectic of the short poem, he is the greatest of minor poets. If he is also one of the most meretricious of minor prophets, he nonetheless achieves through his prophetic pose the quality which of all moral and aesthetic qualities is most remote from the present age: grandeur. (pp. 195-96)

In the late 'eighties and early 'nineties, he learned a lesson from each major European country. England, which he knew as much from his friendship in Germany with Cyril Scott as from his two visits to London, made him feel the value of a national culture as against the hitherto municipal culture of Germany. France brought him into contact with many modern poets. . . . Spain, it is said, filled him with a longing for leadership.

This longing is the mainspring of George's career. . . . D. H. Lawrence, vainly seeking equality in love, concluded in despair that equality was undesirable, and that lordship and slavery were the terms of human relationship. A spiritual son of Nietzsche, George reached this conclusion without preliminaries. *Herrschaft und Dienst* (lordship and service), these were the prime necessities of the spirit. George was not imbued with mere lust for power. His urge to lead was ambivalent. It carried with it the urge toward abasement before a greater leader.

If George's life was a pursuit of incarnate deity, it was also a flight, a long flight from the middle-class home and the philistine, commercial society to which it belonged. Reverse the values of *Kleinbürgertum* ["the lesser bourgeoisie"] and you will have the values of Nietzsche and George. Seeking refinement, nobility, and religion, Nietzsche and George were of necessity very lonely men. They yearned for stronger bonds than the love of women. They yearned to lead men and to be led.

George was a supreme egotist. As a boy he sketched a language of his own and a kingdom. As a man he established himself as a literary dictator. (pp. 197-98)

George's life from 1898 to 1919 has with some reason been identified with his magazine *Die Blätter für die Kunst,* which appeared in twelve series between those dates. The George Circle was his little world, and the record is one of the exits and entrances of the members. A list of them is not uninformative. It contains many nonentities, several conscientious scholars, one brilliant critic. [Friedrich] Wolters' pretence [in his *Stefan George und die Blätter fur die Kunst: Deutsche Geistesgeschichte seit 1890*] that their history is "the intellectual history of Germany" is, of course, monstrous, but it shows how the group thought of itself. The Circle was a closed one. Among German contemporaries, the only important poet whom they were ever interested in, aside from the Master, was Hugo von Hofmannsthal who at first was a leading contributor to the

Blätter but later refused to be domineered by George, and quit. (p. 199)

What was George's attitude to the events of 1914-33? Progressively he and his friends shifted away from their aestheticism. In fact they claimed never to have been aesthetes but to have avoided both Zola's naturalism and Wilde's aestheticism in their obvious superiority to both. That they avoided naturalism is obvious. That they avoided aestheticism has to be argued by reference to their *Männerbund*. [In a footnote, the critic defines the term as "male league," and adds "German youth organizations, sometimes boy-scoutish, sometimes aesthetic, sometimes fascistic, are a social phenomenon of first-rate importance."] The aesthete is devoted to abstract Beauty, to art for its own sake; George is devoted to manhood, to art for *his own* sake. Art for Art's sake was a religion, but George's religion was different, a strange compound of *Calamus* and *Thus Spake Zarathustra,* a religion of man and, specifically, of Maximin, man, artist, hero, and god.

Sometimes Wolters writes as if George were a social poet, an anti-democratic political leader. George himself never wrote on politics, but Wolters, Gundolf, and the others were merely their master's mouthpiece in their frequent sallies against the "modern idols" of technological progress, feminism, the masses, and permanent peace. This Georgean philosophy is not that of Hitler and Rosenberg, for it has little to say of race; many of the Circle (Wolfskehl, Morwitz, Gundolf, Kantorowicz) were Jews; so were many friends of the movement such as Georg Simmel. If Rosenberg's key term is Race, George's is the Hero. If Hitler's most individual contribution in *Mein Kampf* is his analysis of propaganda and mass politics, George's attitude is contempt for all such concerns. It is true that he combines a hatred of the masses *qua* mob with a love of them *qua* Volk, but his love of the German Volk, while no Christian charity, was not always exclusive or bloodthirsty.

> *Erzvater grub, erzmutter molk*
> *Das schicksal nährend für ein ganzes volk.*
>
> ["The patriarch delved, the matriarch did her milking, fostering destiny itself for a whole people" (**"Urlandschaft"** in ***Teppich des Lebens***).]

This is regional love of soil, not political love of nation.

But sometimes George was closer to politics. The Messianic Hope of Germany, the expectation of a national awakening out of the spirit of youth, Hölderlin's vision of a German Hellas, which we have seen to lie at the root of Nietzsche's faith, was also the dominant image of George's life after the death of Kronberger. (pp. 202-03)

What were the relations of Stefan George and the Nazis? The question has been much discussed, and Germanophobes have gone too far. . . . The truth is not easy to come by. There are stories, contradicted by many non-Nazis, that George not only ignored the overtures of Goebbels and Rust, who offered him money and a laureateship, but swore he would never live in Germany after 1933 nor would he be buried there. Another story is that George insulted Goebbels by having a reply sent to him by Morwitz, a Jew. Morwitz says he told the German government that George "did not wish to discuss the boundaries between art and politics."

What did the Nazis say? One of them, Hans Naumann, dedicated the sixth edition of his book on modern German poetry (1933) to Our Leaders, i.e., Hitler and George. Both, he says, are of German peasant stock, both without wife or kinsfolk, both have the same ideal of race and leadership, both have developed organically in their literary productions, both live for others. Gottfried Benn, sometimes accounted the ablest Nazi man of letters, confirmed Naumann at a writers' conference. A book was written by one Margarete Klein who elaborated the theme. But evidently we have false ideas about Nazi unanimity, for the same year—1938—which produced Miss Klein's book produced a denunciation of George by another Nazi named Hans Rössner. Rössner correctly observed that the *Georgekreis* was not Nazi in that (1) George did not understand the philosophy of race; (2) George did not understand the role of woman as creator. (pp. 205-06)

Rössner made some points which help us to a summing-up from our different standpoint. George, he says, was not the founder of a new humanism, but the last relic of an old order. He was a nineteenth-century decadent who by his strength of will gathered round him the parasites of the West—Jews. Rössner is not hard on George's homosexuality except in so far as it implies misogyny. . . . [Rössner] demonstrates that for all their anti-democratic realism the *Georgekreis* are interested in Napoleon and other heroes only as an influence upon "intellectual history."

This is acute, true, and crucial. George is not any sort of a politician; his interest is centered in the intellect and the individual. . . . Stefan George's New Empire is of the mind, and any impression we may have to the contrary is due either to George's occasional inconsistency, to the richness in suggestion of his verse which is relevant on so many planes of reality, or to statements of other members of the Circle. (p. 206)

Many of Stefan George's beliefs and attitudes are Carlyle and Nietzsche over again. The total rejection of the bourgeois world, the desire to recruit a new class of leaders, the worship of heroic life as exemplified in certain epochs of the past—these are familiar traits. But whereas we see Carlyle groping after Heroic Vitalism and Nietzsche defiantly brandishing it, we find George taking it up in a tired, melancholy, and bitter way. He is an Heroic Vitalist of a later generation.

One of the special symptoms of George's Heroic Vitalism is the peculiar twist he gives to the Bohemianism which was already the culture pattern of the artist, especially in France and Germany. George's Bohemianism is not gay but austere, not carefree but deliberate, not disreputable but pretentious. Previous Bohemianism was a frivolous protest against Puritan propriety; George's Bohemianism was quasi-religious. (p. 207)

In studies of George one reads of two cults: the cult of technique and the cult of the self. Their meaning is interlocked. That technique, the least secret of things, should become a cult is a symptom of decadence in art and nihilism in culture. The modern world is rejected, external nature is regarded as alien and hostile now that the gods have fled from thence, the poet is alone. How can he find value and meaning in life? Paradoxically he does it by surrendering to the disvalued, alien, external world. He abandons himself to sensations, and by so doing claims to restore value and meaning to the world. Such is aestheticism, the basis of the cult of technique.

The cult of the self—the phrase is that of the French reactionary, Maurice Barrès—is its inevitable complement. The poet, in his enormous superiority, in his immoralist espousal of good and evil alike, in his unique capacity to feel sensations and create values, is "the most powerful man in the world." He therefore believes in himself. As one critic put it: the difference between George and Jesus, when they call on men to leave all and follow them, is this: Jesus points with one hand to himself, with the other to heaven; George points with one hand to himself, and with the other to himself. (p. 208)

George was an outsider. His sexual constitution, reinforced by his position as an artist, made him so. He called on his disciples to leave house and home. He hated the mores. . . . His hatred of bourgeois life is at the root of his linguistic theory and practice. He hated nineteenth-century speech, and *a fortiori* its imitations by the naturalists. Therefore he invented an entire language of his own; loved to speak and read foreign languages which did not for him have everyday associations; finally, forged an hieratic German of his own at the opposite pole from colloquialism. In the era of monopoly capital he not only repudiated capitalist civilization and "escaped" to a dream-world, he constructed a model of capitalist civilization in the cultural sphere. As a supermagnate and dictator of culture, he established himself as the monopolist of poetry; all the other poets and schools were decried or, worse, ignored. (pp. 208-09)

Yet Stefan George is Nietzsche simplified and distorted. Not only is he a smaller mind but a much less flexible one. Some of Nietzsche's vitalistic philosophy is taken over, but the pragmatic attitude to truth gives place in George to an Hellenic cult of the Whole and to an Hellenic assumption of fixed and eternal verities. George came of Catholic stock and appealed to Catholic words and symbols much as Carlyle appealed to Presbyterian words and symbols. As with Carlyle the result is contradiction. On the one hand George keeps up an appearance of austere and orthodox virtue. On the other he follows Carlyle, Baudelaire, and Nietzsche into diabolism, as for instance in a poem called ***Der Täter,*** where the man of action expresses his contempt for those who have never looked their brother over with a view to stabbing him, and in ***Der Gehenkte,*** where the criminal is found to be the prerequisite of virtue and culture. At this point the ascetic George is not far from the voluptuary, D'Annunzio, or from the aesthetic diabolism of intellectual fascists generally.

Catholicism, Hellenism, nobility, pride, egotism, Bohemianism, illiberalism, homosexuality, diabolism—the mind and art of George is a strange compound. In its wilful inconsistencies, its arrogant gestures, and its anti-social attitudes, it bears witness to the failure of nerve in European culture which weakened the intelligentsia and postponed or undermined democracy. The George Circle is one of the many cultured groups which have developed reactionary tendencies at a time when reaction threatens their very existence. One need not seek a theoretical refutation of their position. The hero with the folkish banner swept them away and thereby closed a curious chapter in cultural history. (p. 209)

Eric Bentley, "Stefan George and His Circle," in his The Cult of Superman: A Study of Heroism in Carlyle and Nietzsche, with Notes on Other Hero-Worshippers of Modern Times, *Peter Smith, 1969, pp. 194-209.*

D. J. ENRIGHT (essay date 1948)

[Enright is an English poet, novelist, and critic who has lived abroad, teaching English literature at the universities of Egypt, Japan, Berlin, Thailand, and Singapore, for more than twenty years. His poetry is noted for its conversational style and frequently displays empathy with the victims of betrayal. In the following excerpt, Enright finds that George's poetic genius achieved its full scope only in the poems contained in the collection The Year of the Soul. *In his other works, Enright maintains, George's concern with spreading a "message" interfered with full artistic expression.]*

What is strange about the case of Stefan George is that a poet so obviously possessing the qualities and abilities of a considerable poetic genius should yet have produced so little work that is undeniably great poetry. The more closely we study George's work the more conscious we become of a particular failure at the very heart of his canon. The poet, assuming the functions of priest, prophet and reformer simultaneously, took upon himself the utterance of a 'message' which developed at a different rate from his poetry; the 'philosophy' and the 'poetry' could not be geared together—the former was always attempting to lead in a direction where the latter could not follow, and as a consequence both failed to fulfil themselves. Except, that is, in a handful of poems where his *poetic* genius, at any rate, achieved its full scope—poems most of which come from the volume ***Das Jahr der Seele*** **('The Year of the Soul'),** published in 1897. The present article is an attempt to elucidate this failure by considering two of George's volumes, ***The Year of the Soul*** and ***Die Bücher der Hirten- und Preisgedichte, der Sagen und Sänge, und der hängenden Gärten*** **('The Books of Shepherds' Songs and Songs of Praise, of Legends and Lays, and of the Hanging Gardens'),** which appeared two years earlier, in 1895. For in these two volumes we see George wavering between the kind of poetry for which he was naturally gifted and the kind of ethical-philosophical prophetism in which he was ambitious.

In his preface to the ***Books of Shepherd's Songs*** George says:

> . . . von unsren drei grossen bildungswelten ist
> hier nicht mehr enthalten als in einigen von uns
> noch eben lebt
>
> (Of our three great formative civilizations nothing more is included here than still lives on in some of us).

The emphasis may be supposed to lie on the word *einigen*—'some of us'—for in the poems which follow there is not any protracted attempt to persuade us that these *Bildungswelten* ["images of worlds"] (Greek, Mediaeval and Oreintal) or, rather, the qualities of spirit produced and fostered by these worlds, can and should be re-created in the inhabitants of the modern age. Their appeal is, consciously I think, to a small minority. The various qualities of spirit and character and the 'atmosphere' of life as it was, or as the poet supposed it to have been, in these three formative or cultural civilizations are presented in this book, and the cultivated reader (the actual or potential Georgean) is left to enjoy that with which he is supposed to have an innate sympathy.

Concerning each of the three sections of the volume, [Friedrich] Gundolf tells us [in his study *George*], it is essential to understand that what is happening is 'keine Auffrischung des Vergangenen, sondern Vergegenwärtigung eines Ewigen'—not a revival of the past, but a presentation or realization of something eternal. . . . Here are experiences which can be lived by us: yes, but we have to be convinced that these experiences are worth living. Gundolf's method of proof is by praise; or by a species of quasi-philosophical eloquence which only serves to lead us away from the poetry. . . . (pp. 242-43)

In some of the poems of the first section we find the qualities and experience of the Disciple expounded and extolled without any reference to the qualities and nature of the God: in, for instance, ***Auszug der Erstlinge,*** which deals with the 'Departure of the Firstborn', chosen by fate (or the gods) to leave their homes and fulfil some high, redeeming function, to travel towards some undesignated goal. . . . [What] George wishes to do is to re-create in us the experience of 'being chosen by the gods', 'being dedicated', with the consequent experience of 'sacrifice'—here the sacrifice of mean, comfortable home-pleasures in the service of the gods and of the People. But in ***Geheimopfer*** the sacrifice is more drastic—the sacrifice not of comfort and safety and petty happiness, but of life itself; yet even this is made gladly. . . . But is this kind of evocation appropriate to the aims which George was becoming more and more conscious of? Naturally enough, George does not wish to present Greek life without the 'dark gods'—the Dionysus without whom there can be no Apollo—but I feel that in this poem the dark gods are being whitewashed in a way that makes them less, rather than more, relevant to a modern, sick, society. The effect of the short panting lines with their regular, piston-like beat and the drawn-out sigh in the longer final line—more suggestive, perhaps, of some mild sexual orgy than of deliberate blood-sacrifice—is to 'prettify' the experience, to take the sting out of it, to rob it of what might have been a salutary terror in the face of the unknown God. (pp. 244-45)

Geheimopfer manages to be both ineffectual and distasteful. Style and matter are somehow at odds; we cannot say that one is more mature than the other, but only that their conjunction is unhappy. . . . George's appeals, George's approach, are too slick: he is on nodding terms with the unknown god before he has even come face to face with him, and we cannot be very deeply impressed by a contact with the ancient deities, with 'vanished divinity', which has apparently been established at such little cost and with so little effort.

One of the best of the Hellenic poems is ***Der Ringer;*** this neat little character-sketch of a wrestler is certainly a fine piece of reportage; it puts our contemporary English 'Reporter Poets' to shame. . . . But is it more than reportage? It does not need to be more in order to reach a high poetic standard, but it must be more if it is to sustain Gundolf's profound exegesis—to sustain, that is to say, the considerable weight of the George Circle and all that this stood for. Yet the qualities of character and the particular kind of spiritual distinction which we are meant to admire in the Wrestler are cold, unappetizing and, worst of all, unhelpful. We admire the poet's skill in sculping his hero: but we would hardly care to meet the hero outside the stadium. This is one of the points perhaps—and there are several of them—at which the poet's path and the path of National Socialism intersect; but we have to remember that if those paths meet, they meet only to divide again and to travel in very different directions.

With a certain change of emphasis, the same kind of criticism must be brought against the second section of the book, the Mediaeval World. Gundolf's enthusiasm finds rather tactless expression when he tells us that the Parsifal legend even in Wolfram's epic is not so real, vital and operative as in these poems of George's. We cannot help but suspect a modern poet of some kind of bogusness whose poetry contrives to be more mediaeval than the Middle Ages, to out-Wolfram Wolfram. And what we find in the ***Legends and Lays*** is not the pure essence of religion and chivalry but a weakened, diluted and even sentimentalized eclecticism: Pre-Raphaelite knights, but no real blood; the mild temptation in the dim chapel, but not the fearful struggle with the fiend; an urbane renunciation of the world, but none of the stringencies of mediaeval mysticism. The poet's concern is overwhelmingly with the Squire, the Novice, the Disciple, the Devotee—Capetanakis rightly remarked, 'no one has ever depicted so temptingly as George the bliss of the disciple whose only aim in life is to serve the master' [see *TCLC,* Vol. 2]—and the Divinity who inspires all this service is a dim, vague figure hidden away in the background. The great theme is *Dedication:* but we may feel that dedication is a meaningless conception once it is separated from its object. Where does George's 'Pfad der Ehre' lead? Presumably to the Holy Grail—but only *presumably,* because, for George, to travel loyally and courageously and altruistically is apparently more important than to arrive at a worthy conclusion.

Hence it is not surprising that occasionally there is a disturbing air of religiosity about the poems: incense mixed a little too heavily with the smoke of battle. And occasionally the idea of the 'brotherhood of warriors' is tainted with preciosity, with a slightly repellent sentimentality: as in the poem called ***Der Waffengefährte*** **('The Brother-in-Arms')**—in which, by the way, Gundolf claims to find the apotheosis of *Mannentreue* (a word which can hardly be translated into English: 'fraternal loyalty' or 'soldierly fidelity', a superior kind of *Kameradschaft*). . . . ***Sporenwache*** is the title and subject of another poem: the Vigil of the Spurs—the young squire, preparing for the accolade, must *renounce* and *dedicate* . . . It is this narrow aspect of the Middle Ages, this element taken out of its context, that appeals so strongly to George. (pp. 245-47)

The poet's vision of the Orient, which comprises the third section of the book, is similarly eclectic: the perfumes without the dust, the beautiful bodies but not the starving beggars. But in this hot, glamorous eastern atmosphere . . . George the prophet is content to take a siesta while George the poet, by himself for once, achieves poems of considerable beauty. The reader is left to enjoy himself, almost completely, and hence we can read most of this section without that feeling of being continually on the defensive, of continually resenting the tone of cold superiority in which George's verse is often enunciated. Here is a good example of the kind of writing which we shall meet, on a higher level, in George's next book—**'Du lehnest wider eine silberweide'**—the captured scene, the transfixed gestures, the mild and impersonal melancholy, the little story that neither has nor requires a point. . . . (p. 248)

The Year of the Soul, I believe, is George's greatest poetic success; it contains that part of his work which will undoubtedly survive long after the George Circle and the traditions of the Master have been forgotten. It may be regarded as significant that this volume occupies the central position in the chronological list of George's works. . . . [A] literary-critical evaluation of ***The Year of the Soul*** will be in accordance with its chronological position: the poet is already at the height of his poetic powers but he is not yet absolutely sure of his *mission,* and thus we are spared that cold, imperious, distant didacticism—distant and cold because the poet is too proud to resort to persuasiveness—and that assured consciousness of superiority which mar much of his later work.

The 'place' of ***The Year of the Soul*** is a northern park; the 'time' changes from autumn to winter and then to summer; the 'action' consists largely of a dialogue between two people—an *I* and a *You*—but often the dialogue approaches soliloquy and it seems that what we are overhearing is the self-communings of the poet during the changing seasons of creative power. George says in his preface: 'selten sind so sehr wie in diesem buch Ich und Du dieselbe seele'—'I and You are rarely so much the same soul as in this book'; but this prose statement is more precise and definite on this point than are the poems.

Each poem, at any rate, stands in its own right, many of them apparently 'pure' impressions, similar to the images from the ***Book of the Hanging Gardens;*** but here endowed with a far greater vitality—with the power of leaving their frames and moving into the mind and heart of the reader. . . . It is possible that, as Prof. Bowra suggests . . . :

> The poems are a symbolical presentation of a crisis in the poet's life. He passes from the aftermath of the harvest in autumn through the sterility of winter to new life in summer [see *TCLC,* Vol. 2].

But the symbolism is not underlined; the poet has not interposed his personal feelings—whether of self-pity or of satisfied weariness—between the autumn vision and the reader. The vision is allowed to achieve its *own* feeling, to communicate its *own* message; and the vision is that 'the park they say is dead' is very far from dead, and the message is the sense of illumination which the vision leaves with us, the gift of an increased awareness of the natural scene and a heightened enjoyment of living—in its simplest aspect, an unpretentious but cogent assurance that life *is* worth living. Without that assurance, no philosophy can help us very much—and we find it more easily in George's humble nondescript Park than in his hushed mediaeval chapel or his Hellenic arena. (pp. 249-50)

Such poetry cannot be said to be evocative of more than it says; it does not carry out the spiritual exploration for which Rilke's mobile quivering line is so apt—it simply does not attempt that kind of thing. Each word snaps into place in the line, each line snaps into place in the stanza, all the stanzas are bound tightly together into the poem. There is no vagueness and little mystery, no very obvious emotion and little ratiocination: but there is precision and clarity—above all, a keen apprehension of the small detail, whether of sight, sound or smell, which will crystallize the whole scene. This art is the apotheosis of confidence: the poet does not waver, doubt, stumble, hesitate or retrace his steps. . . . The picture is complete when George inscribes the last word of the last line of a poem; a statement has been made, not a question asked and answered. This seems to me an art of a limited kind—especially when we compare it with Rilke's work—but not so narrow that we can afford to neglect the fine achievement of George's best poetry. (p. 251)

The peculiar success of these poems lies in the fact that for once—and not, alas, for long—what is seen is the meaning of what is shown; idea and appearance are identical; spiritual and physical are at one; technique and subject-matter cannot be distinguished. The interpreter is starved for material, and the literary critic comes into his own.

Prof. Bowra speaks of the 'melancholy' of ***The Year of the Soul,*** which, he considers, 'is partly that of a man who feels himself imprisoned in his own personality, and needs an outlet, a wider field for his energies.' Again, it seems to me that this estimate of ***The Year*** is based on a higher opinion of George's later volumes than mine, on an acceptance of these books as the genuine apotheosis of his work; the admirer of ***The Seventh Ring*** and ***The Star of the Covenant*** and ***The New Empire,*** looking back on ***The Year,*** is bound to find it limited and even 'minor'. Quite probably George himself felt that in this volume he was making little headway with the momentous task of spiritual regeneration of which he was becoming increasingly conscious; but I believe that ***The Year of the Soul*** offered George a greater outlet and a wider field for his *poetic* energies than any other volume. As for the melancholy of this book—one has to use that word to describe the prevalent tone of the poems—it is a quiet, impersonal kind of melancholy, the pensiveness of a man who for a time has *escaped* from the prison of his own personality. Above all, if the melancholy of the book is 'autumnal', it is the melancholy of an autumn that has brought home a good harvest and is already thinking of the spring to follow.

But there is one element of Georgeanism, important to any study of the poetry as 'cult', which we must notice in this book. And that is the poet's recognition of his alone-ness: the *I* is aware that it has not yet found a fitting and worthy *You.* Here we have the beginnings of the Master's yearning for a Disciple. In the present collection of poems this yearning is present only as conscious 'loneliness', a human desire for friends and a true sympathy of spirits—but later we find it growing more extreme and less 'human', until it even degenerates into self-pity carefully disguised under a vast assumption of priestly superiority.

The shift from this gentle melancholy loneliness to a colder, harder aloofness—the attitude not of a man who lacks friends but of a man who desires only followers—is prognosticated in the poem which begins:

> Des sehers wort ist wenigen gemeinsam
>
> (The word of seers is not for common sharing).

In the volumes which follow [***The Tapestry of Life (Der Teppich des Lebens), The Seventh Ring (Der Siebente Ring),*** and ***Star of the Covenant (Der Stern des Bundes)***], we find George in unmistakable fashion deserting poetry to expound a message which—though it never attains to clarity—seems to be comprised of a mixture of philosophy, social reform and dim political desiderations, with a religious veneer. . . . The final volume, ***The New Empire (Das Neue Reich . . .),*** claims victory for George and his disciples. . . . But, resident in the tone and quality of the poems of this and the previous volume, we find *not* a proof of victory but a recognition of defeat. Georgeanism, as cult and message, has not justified the terrible sacrifice of poetic talent which it entailed. (pp. 252-53)

George's poetry is 'mysticism': an uneasy partnership of poetry and philosophy in which neither comes to maturity. (pp. 253-54)

D. J. Enright, "The Case of Stefan George," in Scrutiny, *Vol. XV, No. 4, December, 1948, pp. 242-54.*

E. K. BENNETT (essay date 1954)

[Bennett's Stefan George, *the first book-length study of George in English, provides a more balanced assessment of the poet and his works than earlier studies written by* George-kreis *members whose adulation of the "master" hampered any real criticism of his works. In the following excerpt from that study, Bennett supplies a chronological survey of the poet's life and career, finding that the poems of George's middle period, contained in the volumes* The Year of the Soul, The Tapestry of Life, *and* The Seventh Ring, *represent "the height of George's poetic achievement."]*

When George turned his attention to the writing of poetry in the later eighties of the [nineteenth] century, the great lyric impulse in German poetry coming from Goethe had reached its end, stung to death by the irony of Heine. The tradition of 'Gefühlslyrik'—the immediate expression of feeling—still continued, but its practitioners were minor poets whose sentimentalities merely reiterated themes and emotions which the earlier poets had exhausted. (p. 20)

It was . . . George's visit to Paris in 1889, his meeting with the Symbolist poet Albert de Saint Paul, and through him his acquaintance with the group of Symbolist poets of whom Mallarmé was the centre, which determined for George the type of poem he was to write, and evoked in him a conscious acceptance of their methods. 'A conscious acceptance'; for it is with George, in whom all is deliberate, not merely the question of an influence unconsciously imbibed, but of a decision taken. Unpremeditatedness, whether in song or in life itself, is not a characteristic of George. Indeed a deliberate reaction against the all too unpremeditated or not sufficiently premeditated poetry of his German contemporaries was part of his own poetic impulse—if impulse be the right name for something in which the functioning of the will played so important a part. But the methods of the French Symbolists were not accepted without certain modifications on the part of George, so that in a comparison of his poems with those of his French contemporaries it will be seen that there was no question of slavish imitation. (pp. 20-1)

Disgusted with the civilization of his own country he turned to France, and found there 'en France dulce Terre' ['in France sweet land'] the things which were dear to him, signalizing by name the writers Villiers de l'Isle Adam, Verlaine and Mallarmé. When his first slight volume of poems entitled ***Hymnen*** appeared, his adherence to the principles and methods of the French Symbolists was apparent, while the underlying principles of poetry in accordance with which he was to work were set forth in the early numbers of *Die Blaïter für die Kunst*. . . . The first number contains the following announcement of policy:

> The name of this publication announces already in part what its aims are: to serve art, especially poetry and letters, whilst excluding all that has reference to the state and society.
>
> It desires an art of the mind—an art for art's sake. Therefore it stands in contrast to that outmoded and second-rate school which had its origin in a mistaken conception of reality; it cannot, further, concern itself with world reforms and dreams of happiness for all in which at present the source of all that is new is seen; these may be very beautiful but they belong to spheres other than that of poetry.
>
> We consider it a merit that we do not begin with precepts, but with actual works of poetry which will illustrate our intentions and from which later the rules may be derived.

It is thus from the outset an art of the mind which is demanded, one in which it is essential, in the reader as well as the poet, that the mind should co-operate. This requirement is fulfilled by the poetry of George: the mind of the reader must be at work if he is to derive any satisfaction from it. But this does not mean that poetry must be the expression of thought. George writes: 'A poem is not the reproduction of a thought, but of a mood [*stimmung*]'; and again: 'We do not desire the invention of stories but the reproduction of moods; not reflection but presentation; not entertainment but impression'. This principle is maintained consistently in all George's poems, even in the hortatory poems in the later volumes. (pp. 22-3)

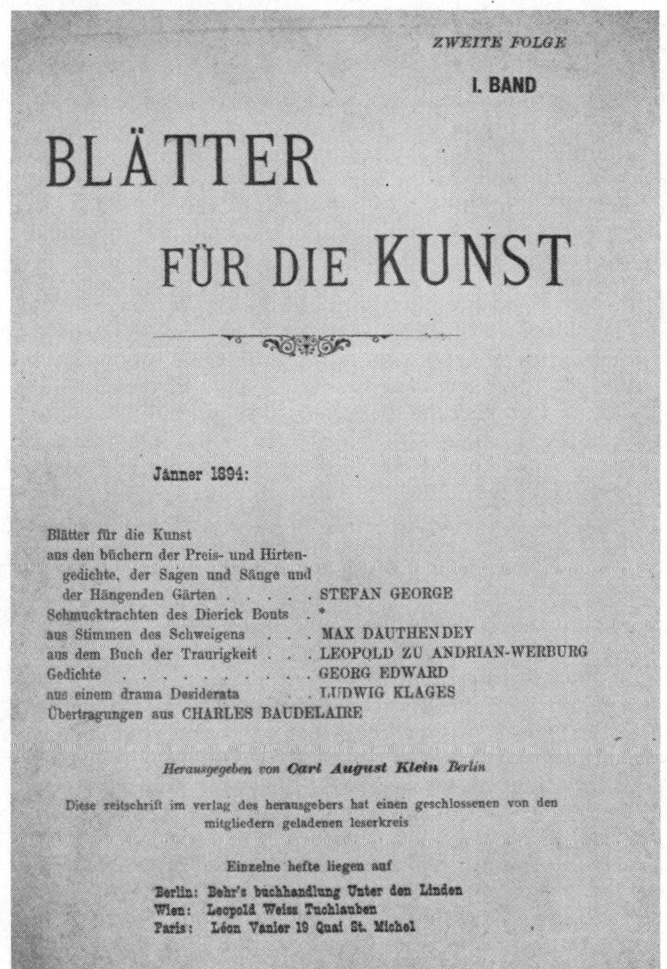

ZWEITE FOLGE

I. BAND

BLÄTTER

FÜR DIE KUNST

Jänner 1894:

Blätter für die Kunst aus den büchern der Preis- und Hirtengedichte, der Sagen und Sänge und der Hängenden Gärten	STEFAN GEORGE
Schmucktrachten des Dierick Bouts .	*
aus Stimmen des Schweigens . . .	MAX DAUTHENDEY
aus dem Buch der Traurigkeit . . .	LEOPOLD ZU ANDRIAN-WERBURG
Gedichte	GEORG EDWARD
aus einem drama Desiderata . . .	LUDWIG KLAGES
Übertragungen aus CHARLES BAUDELAIRE	

Herausgegeben von ***Carl August Klein*** *Berlin*

Diese zeitschrift im verlag des herausgebers hat einen geschlossenen von den mitgliedern geladenen leserkreis

Einzelne hefte liegen auf

Berlin: Behr's buchhandlung Unter den Linden
Wien: Leopold Weiss Tuchlauben
Paris: Léon Vanier 19 Quai St. Michel

Title page of an issue of George's journal Blätter für die Kunst.

George writes almost exclusively symbolical poems, and in the earlier volume where the presentation of a 'Stimmung' (*un état d'âme*) is primarily his aim, the basic significance of the poem is easily revealed by the appositeness of the symbol chosen. Thus ***Die Spange*** at the end of ***Pilgerfahrten*** and ***Vogelschau*** at the end of ***Algabal,*** by their place in the order of poems, hint at once at some significance with regard to the poet's situation. In ***Das Jahr der Seele*** the poem which begins 'Die blume, die ich mir am fenster hege' ['the flower that I tend at my window'] sheds its material significance and reveals its emotional message on a first reading; even in the last volume, ***Das Neue Reich,*** the poem ***Das Lied*** is manifestly beneath its legendary narrative a statement of the poet's lot on earth. But not all of George's poems yield up their symbolical meaning so readily. It may perhaps be legitimately assumed that such poems have in their composition a more conscious effort of the will, a greater attention to the elements of form and the deliberate choice of words than the poems which are the direct expression of feeling, and such poems as come, so to speak, surging up unhampered from the subconscious. . . .

From all that has been said it will be apparent that George was a very self-conscious and deliberate poet, in whom the elements of will and intention were manifestly at work in the process of composition. He took upon himself the rôle of poet and in the light of his conception and conviction of what it should be, he played his rôle with conscientiousness and unremitting attention. But it was his very awareness of himself as *il fabbro* ['the artificer'] which aroused a feeling of hostility to his poetry—strengthened by the recognition of a similar principle in the conduct of his life—a feeling which expressed itself in such disapproving terms as 'mannered', 'artificial' and 'unnatural' by the general public. (p. 30)

In the growing uncertainty and questioning of values in the second half of the nineteenth century art became a moral problem which found expression in the writings of various investigators into the nature of society, notably in the works of Tolstoi. In Germany the dramatist and critic Paul Ernst found it necessary to assign to art an ethical function as a means of educating 'das Volk' ['the people'] before he could with a quietened conscience devote himself to literature as a profession. Ten years later in the early writings of Thomas Mann the dubiety of art became one of the main themes. For Stefan George however no such problem arose. But the unquestioned acceptance of aestheticism with him is made possible by the assimilation to it of two essentially ethical ideas, the ideas of dedication (*Weihe*) and discipline (*Zucht*). These are the controlling forces to which all the poetry of George is subject; and they manifestly imply a sense of responsibility in the practice of his art, which may be implicit in many poets but is rarely so explicitly revealed as in George. The first poem in the early ***Hymnen*** is entitled ***Weihe.*** Thus the theme is announced from the beginning, and in some of the other early poems its importance is illustrated by references to another element, *Leidenschaft* (passion), which, since it is inimical to the poet's absolute dedication to his art is represented as an invasion of the sanctuary of poetry by the emotions of ordinary life. The expression of *Zucht* in the world of art is crystallized in the idea of form, that is to say in the unremitting effort of the poet to achieve perfection of form. (p. 31)

[It] may be maintained with some justification that the poems of the middle period (***Das Jahr der Seele, Der Teppich des Lebens,*** and ***Der Siebente Ring***) are the height of George's poetic achievement. The poems in the later volumes, notably in ***Der Stern des Bundes*** and to a considerable extent in ***Das Neue Reich,*** are markedly different in form and subject matter from the earlier ones; and the change which has taken place in the poetry reflects the change in the spiritual life of the poet himself, so that here in the more conventional sense the word development is apposite. That development reveals George in the earlier stages as a seeker for illumination, for a significance to life; finding it in his middle period, or rather having it revealed to him; and then using that illumination to survey the world of European civilization at the beginning of the century and pass judgment upon it. Given the nature of the subject matter in ***Der Stern des Bundes*** it is only to be expected that poetry will set aside her more traditional charms and adopt a severer and harsher mode of expression. (pp. 32-3)

Die Fibel with its immature beginnings being left aside, the first volume in which the determining and permanent literary influences upon George are operative is the one which includes ***Hymnen; Pilgerfahrten; Algabal*** . . . , the three parts of which had been published separately before [in privately distributed editions of one hundred volumes each]. It may be noted that the tripartite arrangement within the volumes is common to several of the later collections.

The first group, ***Hymnen,*** are in the manner of the French Symbolists, more markedly so indeed than the poems in any succeeding volume. The poet seeks to give in each of the poems a presentation (*Darstellung*) of a transitory aspect of his inner life (*état d'âme*) by means of symbols which take the form in many of the poems of aspects of landscape—narrowly circumscribed aspects such as of a terrace with vases; a corner of a park with a fountain; a stretch of sea shore. All are evoked and suggested, not carried out in detail; but with a very noticeable and already masterly employment of colour, which continues indeed throughout the early volumes, as does the ability to make skilful use of vowel sounds to produce a musical effect. . . . The first poem, ***Weihe,*** represents the inner preparation of the poet for the coming of Inspiration (*die herrin*) which consecrates him to his function as a poet. (p. 33)

The group ends with a poem called ***Die Gärten schliessen;*** and the next group, ***Pilgerfahrten,*** is prepared for by the last line: 'Pilger mit der hand am stabe' ['Pilgrim with a staff in his hand']. The situation is given in the *Aufschrift* ['epigraph'] to the next group: George as a pilgrim setting forth in his search for illumination. Endowed with his gift of poetry, feeling himself a dedicated being, but disturbed by the allurements of life to which from time to time he yields, he proceeds upon his solitary way; and the remainder of this volume and the two succeeding ones show him seeking and proving, yielding at times to passion, to melancholy and despair, and communicating in symbolical form his inner experiences. ***Pilgerfahrten*** shows us more of the conflict between the dedicated poet and those emotional disturbances which militate against the carrying out of his sacred function: his fallings away from his high calling through misgiving, world-weariness, through ignoble contact with the life of the crowd. There are poems of admonition to himself; poems in which he conjures up the journeys of his childhood; one in which the meaninglessness of all growth is symbolized in the attitude of a woman as she looks down upon the flowers in her garden. . . . (p. 34)

Algabal [the third group of poems] reveals an aspect of George's poetry which is confined to this particular volume and owes much to certain tendencies and movements in French poetry in the second half of the century, namely to that which is usually stigmatized as *Décadentisme* and attributed to Baudelaire, Rimbaud and above all to Huysmans: an attitude of mind which has its essential source in the dissatisfaction of the poets of the time with the materialistic, scientific civilization which the nineteenth century brought with it. The particular reaction to the civilization of the age which finds expression in *Décadentisme* is only one of many others; all of which, however, are basically a rejection of it. The *Décadents* go further than the Parnassians and Symbolists, for they reject the life of nature altogether and seek to set up in its place an artificial life in which they cultivate a mode of existence which draws its values from artificiality. . . . These are the ideas which are put into practice by the hero of the ***Algabal*** poems, the Late Roman Emperor Heliogabalus, and they represent in extreme form the ideas of George—exaggerated, over-coloured, the idea of artificiality forced almost into a caricature of itself.

In the spiritual pilgrimage of George to which each volume of poems bears witness, ***Algabal*** represents the stage in which artificiality is glorified and a complete abandonment to it is essayed and tested as a possible solution in the search for a satisfying mode of life. George, like Huysmans, rejected it, but in the working out of the problems of his own being in terms of the emperor-priest he created a work of richness of colouring, rhetorical splendour and a certain outmoded beauty. The identification of George with Algabal is of course not complete. It is not so much with the perverse and cruel tyrant, which according to history he was, but with one who was both priest and emperor and thus set aside by his position from the ordinary life of man—in that sense 'dedicated' as George felt himself to be as a poet. (pp. 36-7)

This collection of poems is unlike much of the early works of George in so far as the poet has made a coherent symbol for himself in the person of Algabal and lived through a certain phase of experience in his imagined hero. The same pattern recurs, though less definitely,and with an unnamed hero in ***Die Hängenden Gärten.*** But this phase of experience is now over—a solution has been tried but has proved inadequate; new experiences must be sought and put to the test. At the end of ***Algabal*** stands the poem ***Vogelschau***—'Weisse schwalben sah ich fliegen' (white swallows I saw flying); it represents a turning away from the exotic, from the world of 'Unnatur' ['unnaturalness'], symbolized in underground palaces and gardens, from the artificiality of a realm constructed entirely by the hand of man in defiance of nature. . . . This poem forms the transition from the atmosphere of the world of Algabal to one in which there prevails a more tonic and astringent air, which gives the atmosphere for the next collection: ***Das Buch der Hirten.***

The poems of this collection have as their setting the Greece of the idylls, not the heroic Greece but the every-day pastoral, bucolic life. The second collection, ***Das Buch der Sagen und Sänge,*** has the Middle Ages for its setting; the third, ***Das Buch der Hängenden Gärten,*** the Orient. In none of the collections is there any attempt at an archaeological reconstruction of a past age. The civilizations chosen are symbols of states of mind of the poet—stages in his search for illumination of the significance of life. Each one represents an attitude to life, of which the figures which appear in the poems are representatives; and the poems in all these books are concerned with imaginary figures. These may well be projections of the poet's inner life, but each poem considered individually and apart from its setting still remains a self-contained evocation of a person, a mood, a situation, thus carrying out the principle announced in *Die Blätter für die Kunst* that the aim of poetry was presentation, not reflection, the transformation of the poetical idea into a concrete form. In no one of the poems appears a character vouched for by history; but the figures, though imaginary, are nevertheless typical of a situation or of the period of which they are representative. In this collection appears clearly for the first time the very marked habit of the later George to present characters, which interest not so much by their individual qualities as by their existence as types, so that a certain statue-like quality is common to most of them.

The contrast between ***Algabal***—George's most colourful and brilliant achievement so far—and ***Das Buch der Hirten*** could not be greater. From the violent exoticism of the earlier work he passes to an atmosphere of cool serenity, and the colours are correspondingly subdued to pastel shades; from the rejection of nature and the febrile determination to create an artificial world, to the acceptance of the ordinary life of nature, and to the picture of a life lived in accordance with it. . . . Here are no passions at work, but a calm following of that which seems to be the natural order of man's life, though the presentation is tinged by a certain melancholy, which is indeed apparent in all the early volumes. . . . Nothing here excites or distresses intensely—everything has the calm and simplicity of figures on a frieze: the music of the verse is very subdued and solemnly moving; its metrical form the long unrhymed line.

The periods chosen in these collections are, as has been said, symbols of states of mind of the poet. Thus though they are successively investigated and presented, they exist also contemporaneously. In turning away from bucolic Greece, George is not rejecting it as he had rejected the world of Algabal. No single period symbolizes his whole ideal of life; it is in the combination of the three that this consists.

It has been said that George's ideal of life lies in the synthesis of the three elements of which man is compounded: 'Geist, Seele und Leib' (spirit, soul and body); though in his later works more importance is assigned to 'Leib'. The terms as used by George defy an exact definition but it may roughly be said that 'Geist' represents the living in accordance with ones destiny; 'Seele' the elements of enthusiasm, devotion and loyalty; 'Leib' the recognition of the body and the sensuous life. In passing from ***Das Buch der Hirten*** to ***Das Buch der Sagen und Sänge*** we find ourselves again in a world—the world of the Middle Ages—which seemed to George at this time to have produced a harmonized and unified life, just as the Greece of the earlier collection had done, but of a different kind. Again we have poems presenting characteristic figures of a period—for George it is largely the period of chivalry and song, with religious devotion as an integral element of it. . . . Again there is no attempt at antiquarian resuscitation of a past age. George lets his imagination wander through mediaeval times and identifies aspects of his own inner life with certain figures, certain characteristic situations. The theme of dedication and passion in conflict recurs once or twice: in ***Der Ritter der sich verschlief,*** and more markedly in ***Sporenwache,*** in which for a moment the youth forgets his religious dedication during the vigil and the picture of a maiden he had once seen passes before his thoughts.

The beautiful youth in heroic pose or in heroic function is one of the characteristic figures which appears in all these early collections. It is central with George, for it is the symbol at this stage of 'das schöne Leben' ['the beautiful life']; it occurs again in ***Der Teppich des Lebens*** and ultimately transcends even the symbolical and becomes the realization of 'das schöne Leben' in the ideal figure of Maximin in ***Der Siebente Ring*** and ***Der Stern des Bundes.***

The poems of the next collection: ***Die Hängenden Gärten*** are more akin to the poems of ***Algabal,*** though without their violence and cult of artificiality. After the bucolic world of the shepherds and the heroic world of the Middle Ages, the world of this oriental ruler is assayed as a symbol of the sensuous life. Thus after the life of the spirit and the life of soul, the life of the body is examined as a possible mode from which satisfaction may be obtained. As in ***Algabal*** a certain vague succession of events, hinted at rather than stated, forms the string upon which the poems are threaded, so in this collection there is a central figure, though he is not named. Ruler and priest, he neglects his functions as such for love; half of his country is overrun by the enemy; he goes as a minstrel slave to the court of another ruler; gives this up, too, from an inner dissatisfaction and a sense of the valuelessness of all activity. In the last poem but one, he is seen looking back upon all he has lost. He hears voices from the stream—the last poem, ***Stimmen im Strome,***—which call to him and promise him recovery, refuge and peace. But even this may not bring satisfaction. Beyond it is annihilation, dissolution, absorption into the elements. This poem with its floating, swaying music (largely due to the frequent use of present participles) represents this in symbolical form in the voices of the water nymphs who draw him down to the pleasures of their life beneath the waves, promising him ultimate bliss in his dissolution and transformation into the waves themselves.

In so far as the three worlds represented in the three books are spirit, soul and body, at the end of the third book the synthesis of the three has not been achieved, though no one of the three has been rejected. It is no doubt logical that the end of the book which is symbolical of 'Leib' should be dissolution, since that is the end of the body and all that pertains thereto. A comparison between the last poems in each of the three collections reveals a positive note only in the second one, which represents 'Seele' in the hymn to the Virgin ***Lilie der Aue.*** The last poem in ***Das Buch der Hirten*** is called ***Das Ende des Siegers*** and suggests that the hero in the last resort will be overcome. Wounded by the monster which escapes him, with a wound that will not heal, he ends in pitiable decay. It would seem therefore that in so far as no synthesis has yet been brought about between the claims of spirit, soul and body, the most positive and enduring value is that offered by 'Seele'. The conflict 'Weihe-Leidenschaft' which appears in the earlier collections fades out with ***Das Buch der Hängenden Gärten.***

The next volume establishes a connection with the earlier ones by its very title. The poet still upon his 'Pilgerfahrten', after essaying all these modes of experience, having rejected some and turned aside from the exclusive acceptance of any, turns back to his own soul and holds communion with himself in the park-like landscape of ***Das Jahr der Seele.*** The settings of the earlier collection had been drawn from the historical past or the exotic or the artificially imaginative. Here the background is nature, but nature moulded and controlled by the hand of man and almost in its particular form created by it. The background is to a great extent revealed by suggestion rather than by direct description; but with the colours, the atmosphere, the feel of Autumn, Winter and Summer as much conditioning the 'Stimmungen' of the 'ich' and 'du' ['I' and 'you'] of the poems as conditioned by them. What belongs to nature exclusively and is not the effect of the hand of man is primarily the ordered procession of the seasons, and even from this Spring has been omitted. (pp. 38-42)

The tendency to see George as a figure of masterfulness, of complete self-possession, to which the later volumes lend some evidence has been extended to cover the whole of his life. This is a simplification of his personality which is not justified. Up to and including ***Das Jahr der Seele*** there is a continuous reference in the poems to states of mind which are far from indicating such a convinced attitude of self-possession. As has been suggested, all these earlier collections express a seeking and proving of possible modes of life, and in all of them there are poems which are the expressions of uncertainty, misgiving, doubt and even of world-weariness and despair, so that on the whole it may be said that a sense of melancholy prevails, not least in ***Das Jahr der Seele*** and in ***Traurige Tänze.*** It is only from ***Der Teppich des Lebens*** onwards that the personality of George, as revealed in his poetry, presents the appearance under which he is generally envisaged, and emerges as that of one whose attitude to life is a positive one: masterful, autocratic, even dictatorial.

For the poems included in ***Der Teppich des Lebens*** . . . , above all in the poems of the *Vorspiel* ['prelude'], announce the illumination, the promise of fulfilment, the attainment of which had been the aspiration recorded in all the earlier poems. The *Vorspiel* is also in a more inward sense a prelude—a prelude to the revelation of Maximin, which forms the core of the following volume: ***Der Siebente Ring, Der Teppich des Lebens*** has again a tripartite division; *Vorspiel; Teppich des Lebens; Lieder von Traum und Tod.* With this volume a new idea enters George's poetry—the idea of a *message.* The idea of a *mission* had been implicit in his poetry from the beginning; now it becomes more explicit, fortified by the message. In the *Vorspiel,* it is as yet a message delivered to him by the Angel; but in the later volumes it will become a message which he himself is called to deliver to his country and his generation. In the twenty-four poems which make up the *Vorspiel* the ideal of life which is to be his is announced by the Angel to him, and the various tentative modes represented in the earlier volumes coalesce and are crystallized in the ideal of 'das schöne leben', which is henceforth to determine his thinking. (pp. 45-6)

Already in these poems of the *Vorspiel* appears the prophetic idea of a new community of race and people. The poet is to take up his place among those leaders and rulers in the world of the spirit whose influence has spread over centuries. He feels his mission as a leader in that world confirmed; and he conceives of history as the sum of these great and heroic personalities—of whom he himself is one—who are the vital factors in the development of mankind. The *Vorspiel* is the central manifesto of George's doctrine of life.

The actual *Teppich des Lebens* forms the second part of the collection and is introduced by the poem ***Der Teppich (The Tapestry).*** This explains the title of the volume. The poems are to give pictures of characteristic figures which make up the pattern of life, illuminate aspects of it and declare its significance. They are individual figures, but all presented with a simplicity, abstractness and sometimes allusiveness which make them rather types and symbols than differentiated individuals, and with a general tendency to see them heroically as figures taken from a primitive form of life. All the poems are in the same form as those of the *Vorspiel.* They include such poems as ***Urlandschaft***—a picture of a primaeval landscape into which man makes his irruption; ***Der Freund der Fluren***—the gardener tending his plants; ***Der Jünger***—the disciple; ***Die Fremde***—the strange woman who comes to the village, creates disturbance there by her allurements, and disappears leaving behind only the child which she has borne there. Characteristic figures are represented already in ***Das Buch der Hirten*** and ***Das Buch der Sagen und Sänge*** with their settings of antiquity or the Middle Ages. George's method here is not new to him, but it has received confirmation from the message of the Angel. It continues throughout the later volumes. Such poems may be described, making use of George's own title for a number of poems in this collection, *Standbilder—Standbilder der Menschheit (Statues of the human race);* heroically seen, sometimes presenting in rather abstract fashion typical aspects of life, and calculated to stimulate a sense of human greatness and pride, though not all represent admirable aspects of human life.

The next volume, ***Der Siebente Ring,*** which did not appear until eight years later, is considerably larger than any of the others and is of primary importance, for it embodies the ideas enunciated in the *Vorspiel* of ***Der Teppich des Lebens,*** embodies in fact in the person of Maximin 'das schöne leben', whose messenger had visited George in the earlier volume. It is divided into seven parts, and the fourth, the central one, entitled *Maximin,* is the core of the work, anticipated in the first three parts, and reflected upon those that follow it. It is in this volume that George appears not only as the poet with a message, but also as the seer; and thus the thought content of his poems acquires increasing importance. George himself in the opening poem entitled ***Das Zeitgedicht*** anticipates the surprise which his contemporaries will feel when faced with the change in his poetry and in the poet himself; that he whom they formerly blamed for his aesthetic withdrawal from life (whilst they themselves rushed into it with uproar and hideous greed); he whose inner struggles and torments they had failed to recognize—that he should have exchanged his pipings for the brazen notes of the trumpet. Where they see change however there is in reality continuation, for it may be that all beauty, strength and greatness will arise tomorrow from the calm flutings of a youth.

Zeitgedichte are poems which attack contemporary social and political abuses and prevailing attitudes of mind which are felt to be evil. They are nothing new in German literature. . . . [The *Zeitgedichte*] of George are basically concerned with heroic judgments passed on the actual conditions of civilization. . . . This part of the volume, however, and the following one (*Gestalten*) stand somewhat apart from the poems which form the core of the book: the third, fourth, fifth and sixth parts—*Gezeiten (Tides); Maximin; Traumdunkel* and *Lieder*. In these is celebrated the achievement, the manifestation of 'das schöne Leben' in the person of Maximin, the beautiful, gifted youth who is deified by George.

It is this deification of Maximin that constitutes the stumbling block for many an appreciative reader of George's poetry; and indeed the various subtle and metaphysical interpretations of the poet's cult of Maximin, offered by disciples, seem almost calculated to make things worse. For Maximin emerges not merely as a symbol of the godhead, but as the god himself. . . . (pp. 47-9)

In the division *Gezeiten,* in which the human intercourse between George and Maximin finds expression, George's poetic quality is at its finest, and some of this quality flows over into the songs in the latter part of the volume, awakening sympathy and tenderness for a grief which was manifestly so deeply and poignantly felt. But this has reference primarily to Maximin the human being; with Maximin the god, the attempt is made to surround him with all the attendant circumstance of a godhead who triumphs over death and remains a living being in the minds of his worshippers. And the reader remains fundamentally unmoved. It is unlikely that many, outside of George's own circle, will feel able to accept Maximin as a religious revelation, even though they may accept him as a poetic inspiration. They may rather regard all the religious paraphernalia as a sign of the urgent need of George's generation to find a substitute for the gods who had disappeared. . . . In the last volumes of his poetry [George] judges, reproves, warns, admonishes and foresees imminent destruction. Thus in ***Der Stern des Bundes*** . . . and ***Das Neue Reich*** . . . , the last two volumes, the spirit of the *Zeitgedichte* and the spirit of the Maximin poems combine to form a unity of inspiration.

In the poems of ***Der Stern des Bundes*** it is the voice of the poet-seer, poet-prophet which prevails. Where in the *Zeitgedichte* the evils of contemporary civilization are denounced implicitly by reference to figures who stand in contrast to it, in the later volume the attack is more direct. Raising his voice as the seer, George warns against the degeneracy of modern times, castigates the weaknesses and falseness of democracy, refutes the belief in a fallacious prosperity, pours scorn upon materialism and the falsely optimistic idea of progress based upon it, deplores the absence of heroism, and foresees still greater evils to come. It is the voice of one crying in the wilderness that the day of judgment is at hand. The message continues to be expressed in abstract, symbolic terms—no reference is made to concrete instances, no names are mentioned to be held up to obloquy, no place is named. Often the setting seems to be suggested by classical themes or borrowed from the Bible. Through this world of symbols the figure of George passes, proclaiming the wrath to come, the destruction which is now inevitable. (p. 51)

George's *oeuvre* is grandly planned and carried out on the grand scale. But something is felt to be lacking in it. A walled city, it is laid out—like one of those German towns of the Renaissance which were planned with geometrical precision by some autocratic prince of the age—with gardens, open places, fountains and palaces, a temple surmounting all. About its streets goes one in singing robes extolling, acclaiming, admonishing, warning. We hear his voice but we rarely see him. The inhabitants stand in noble and heroic attitudes. But they neither move nor speak. For they are the sons not of Prometheus but of a Pygmalion to whom no divine boon has been granted. In fact they are statues, and one is the statue of a god. (p. 57)

E. K. Bennett, in his Stefan George, *Bowes & Bowes, 1954, 63 p.*

M. BOULBY (essay date 1957)

[*In the following excerpt, Boulby finds that* Algabal *expresses George's Nietzschean response to the decadent themes of the French Symbolists. While admitting that the French Symbolist poets were a great influence upon George, Boulby interprets* Algabal *as an expression of the artist's struggle to overcome decadence through the power of the will—which is also, he believes, the theme of Friedrich Nietzsche's* Der Wille zur Macht (The Will to Power).]

[***Algabal***] has an interesting historical position in German literature, appearing as it did in the year both of the triumph of *Die Weber* and of the founding of *Die Blätter für die Kunst,* and being by far the most striking work of George's youth; a detailed study of it reveals a remarkable similarity between its problems and those which occupied Nietzsche at the end of his career and particularly in *Der Wille zur Macht*.

The predominant influence of the French symbolist poets upon George—especially of Baudelaire upon ***Algabal***—is undeniable. It is uncertain what George knew and had read of Nietzsche when he composed this work, but it may well not have been a great deal. By 1892, of course, Nietzsche was already famous, and his ideas were contributing decisively to the disintegration of the so-called naturalist movement. (p. 72)

[Nietzsche] conceives of the superman-artist as the conqueror of decadence, who triumphs through will-power, who achieves formal mastery, and who in his art—or otherwise stated, the small part of the world he is able to organize for himself—establishes the rule of simple, iron law. But in *Der Wille zur Macht* this second conception of the artist detaches itself only loosely from the first, for the reason that the first is contained within the second; it is the incessant struggle of the will to master decadence which, in Nietzsche's view, creates the true artist, and thus almost all the discussions of the artist in *Der Wille zur Macht* concern themselves, one way or another, with this very tension and its implications, a version of the celebrated contrast between Dionysiac and Apolline.

It is therefore interesting to discover that the root experience in ***Algabal*** is something of this kind. George's Heliogabalus is, of course, a symbol of the artist par excellence. . . . It is certainly true that the major source of ***Algabal*** is the decadence, the cult of artificiality and of *l'art pour l'art* prevalent among the French writers of the age; Huysmans' remarkable novel, *A Rebours,* concerned as it is with the life of an aesthete apart from the world in an exotically decorated cellar, bears a strong similarity to George's work, and especially to the first section, 'Im Unterreich'. But George has added to this decadent world something of his own, the quality of will. It is always pointed out that George rejected mere aestheticism, but it is often overlooked that the essential subject-matter of this whole work is the struggle of the artist's will with the degenerating forces of decadence. (pp. 74-5)

The essence of decadence, according to Nietzsche, was lack of will, surrender to stimuli and impulses. The fundamental characteristic of Algabal is, however, Will itself. In 'Im Unterreich' the four poems which describe the underground palaces depict a world which is the creation of a ruthless individual will . . . , an unnatural artificial world which has only one master. . . . The creation of this perfectly ordered world provides Algabal with a refuge from the senseless world outside, and gives him the strength to live. The final poem of 'Im Unterreich' describes it as an unnatural world of death, a garden created by Algabal alone, which needs neither air nor warmth; a garden of sombre, volcanic colours. . . . It seems right to see in the black flower a symbol . . . of the culmination of artifice, the final achievement of the will in this direction. Algabal's will-power, however, serves another purpose besides this purpose of construction. It is the strength which enables him to struggle against and successfully resist the temptations of life, of the senses, of his decadent impulses. (p. 75)

George's Algabal is also the embodiment of the acceptance of Fate. *Amor Fati!*—this also was an essential corner-stone of Nietzsche's thought. (p. 76)

The people suffer the fate of his tyranny; he himself however suffers a yet harsher fate. . . . It is not fitting for those who are born to the purple to complain, whatever fate may afflict them. All is inevitable, so Algabal fears no Ides of March. As a boy he understood his peculiar destiny. . . .

It is his fate to have power, but also to find suffering everywhere. All love is imperfect and disappoints him; omens perhaps deceive him, prophecies may be false; all that remains is to accept one's fate and not wish it to be otherwise, but to act upon it. . . . (p. 77)

A tyrant of creative will-power, living under an inexorable destiny whose executor he is, Algabal becomes a supreme example of individualism. He demands for himself the strange, the exotic, the novel . . . , and every subtlety of sensation and experience. He longs to create the black flower, the final perfection of artifice. He will share his power and his experiences with no one else. The holy image of the god in the inner sanctum is for his eyes alone. He is a jealous tyrant and above all he is jealous of his own untouchability, his own perfection. Around him is a zone of silence. (pp. 77-8)

Already this narcissism may most convincingly be seen as a symptom of decadence, and certainly not as an aspect of individualistic dignity. Two of Algabal's most pronounced characteristics are his 'purity' and '*naïveté*'. It is to be remembered that the historical Heliogabalus was scarcely more than a boy, and Algabal therefore lacks real worldly experience, is fundamentally immature and childish in his vanity and introspection. His purity and *naïveté* are, however, an elaborate sophistication *à la* Baudelaire; Algabal's decadent luxury and artifice are his destiny, and in the acceptance of this he remains in his own eyes and those of the poet pure and immaculate, and also chaste; George is here subscribing to one of the most prominent cults of nineteenth-century 'decadent' literature. (p. 78)

It is absurd to attempt to deny or discount, as [Friedrich] Gundolf largely does, the presence of decadence, in the French sense, in ***Algabal.*** Algabal has the qualities of the contemporary French decadent, in the tradition of the 'Romantic agony'. These qualities are also those which Nietzsche, with Wagner in mind, ascribes to the artist in general in *Der Wille zur Macht*. Algabal is sensual and excitable to a high degree and susceptible to every kind of erotic and sadistic stimulus. The aestheticism of Algabal's strange underworld is as undeniable a part of the decadent tradition as is the sensuality of the Emperor's orgies, in one of which the revellers are eventually suffocated under a rain of roses, and as is the death-longing which persuades the tyrant to poison two lovers in their blissful sleep. . . . But throughout the work the Emperor's individualism, though often sorely weakened, preserves its integrity. Algabal's will never gives up the struggle to be the supreme master, and unlike Huysman's hero, George's is never quite submerged. Algabal can almost stand apart from his own decadence and decadent experiences; he watches the orgy, it seems, rather than takes part in it, until by an act of cruel power he brings it to its morbid close. . . . Gundolf sees in the decadent and quasi-Dionysiac elements in Algabal's world merely a threat to the tyrant's individuality. . . . But these elements are certainly more than just a threat; they are one pole of Algabal's nature, just as they were of George's at this time. The other pole is will and, above all, will-to-form. George's primary impulse as a poet was will-to-form, and form not only in art, but also in personality and life; it is will on which Algabal's uncanny art is based, and it is this art which enables him to live in an outside world which is devoid of meaning. Here we have the basic similarity between the Nietzschean tension—between will-to-power and decadent nihilism—and that of George after his visits to France. It is what Nietzsche calls 'Wille zur Meisterschaft' which gives Algabal the power to be an artist, the power to detach himself and stand aside, the strength to remain immaculate and 'pure' in the midst of orgy. . . . (p. 79)

The final poem in ***Algabal*** is entitled **'Vogelschau'.** It is a poem which looks out from Algabal's world towards something new. It has been taken by most critics as heralding the abandonment of this world and George's victory over decadence. The conflict, however, in the heart of the work itself, has never been clearly elucidated. . . . The conflict in ***Algabal*** is close to that in *Der Wille zur Macht;* it is the struggle out of decadence through the will to artistic creation and to form, the struggle towards form in art and form in life; the antithesis between the artist of decadence and the artist of will is the root experience which George has expressed in ***Algabal,*** just as it is the root conflict in Nietzsche's last analysis of the problem of the modern artist. It is therefore not surprising that George was in later years directly influenced by Nietzsche for his reaction to decadence had been always Nietzschean in kind. (p. 80)

M. Boulby, ''Nietzsche's Problem of the Artist and George's 'Algabal','' in The Modern Language Review, *Vol. LII, No. 1, January, 1957, pp. 72-80.**

ULRICH K. GOLDSMITH (essay date 1959)

[*In his* Stefan George: A Study of His Early Work, *Goldsmith examines the development of George's career through the ''Max-*

imin'' poems in The Seventh Ring. *In the following excerpt, Goldsmith explores the influence of the French Symbolists on George, and compares many opinions shared by George and Mallarmé about the role of the poet as a leader and creator. Goldsmith characterizes* The Year of the Soul *as the last of George's volumes of purely lyrical poetry and finds that this volume contains some of the poet's finest and most appealing work.*]

The relationship between Stefan George and the French symbolists, including Mallarmé, has been investigated by various critics. Many parallels in the motifs and in the use of imagery have been demonstrated. Furthermore, certain aspects in the personal lives and attitudes of Mallarmé and George have been emphasized. For the present study, individual details in the work and traits of resemblance in the lives of the two poets are not so important as, first, the degree of affinity that exists in their general attitude to the poet's task and, second, the points in which George essentially differed from the French master.

George, like Mallarmé, believed in the supreme creative power of the word and hence in the special position and mission of the poet. He recognized that if the Absolute can be made real through verbal expression, the poet assumes a divine role, that is, the part of the creator himself. Mallarmé, in fact, arrives at that extreme position, where the self is the ultimate creative authority, whence his periods of ''impuissance'' are unresolved, perplexing paradoxes. George's position is essentially the same, although he expressly recognizes and respects those subterranean forces that can set limits to the poet-creator. In **''Das Wort''** (first published in 1919) he speaks of the ''gray Norn'' to which the poet has to go to find the name for the inventions or visions of his dream (*''wunder von ferne oder traum''*). If the Norn does not give the poet the name, the dream cannot be transformed into reality. . . . (pp. 33-4)

George, like Mallarmé, experienced the loneliness of the artist and found a partial answer in surrounding himself with a select circle of disciples, though here already George differs from his French master, because the systematic education which his proselytes underwent reached far beyond the more informal relationships within Mallarmé's circle.

George's loneliness was, like Mallarmé's, accompanied or even caused by a lack of sympathy for the masses. Hence his poetry was never intended to be especially intelligible or pleasing to them. Both men devoted themselves expressly to wresting some of the words of general usage from their common contexts and to give them new meaning. Archaic or rare words were deliberately revived to enhance the subtlety and preciousness of their poetry. But there is a clear difference in purpose between the two poets. Mallarmé's later poetry, for example *Un Coup de Dés,* shows an increasing obscurity of meaning, as he endowed his words and symbols with private esoteric connotations and invented his own syntax. . . . George, on the other hand, while admiring the mystery in Mallarmé's work, never went to such an extreme in his own. While he felt it to be his task to give new freshness and beauty to the German language, he did not transform it into a code intelligible only to himself. Some of his word choices are unusual or precious, his syntax is often difficult and his style compressed. He expects the reader to exert himself mentally. Yet, with very few exceptions, he does not play with ambiguities and obscurities. The Frenchman was guided by esthetic considerations only, as he exhausted the ultimate possibilities of his native tongue, which offered itself as a very refined and supple medium. George made it his task to re-structure and cultivate a language that lacked musicality and rhythmic discipline. He consciously accepted the historic responsibility for a renascence in German poetry, when his French friends persuaded him to go back to Germany. His native instinct for leadership responded. Thus, naturally, he was filled with burning hope for recognition. The fact that his work at first seemed inaccessible by virtue of its originality does not mean that the poet was indifferent to its reception. His refusal to lower his standards and to make concessions to public taste constitutes George's integrity, even though his fear of any contact with vulgarity takes exaggerated forms. The contrast between the two poets becomes particularly clear when George's violent opposition to his contemporaries and their work is compared with Mallarmé's conciliatory and tolerant attitude towards rival currents in French literature. . . . George wanted to exert an influence on the world. If his life and work, during the decade following his visit to France, show the marks of isolation from society, these marks are deceptive. The isolation was not entirely voluntary. One may consider his opposition to certain trends and people unjustified, but it is incorrect to say that he deliberately planned to establish a reputation of exclusiveness for himself. When he returned to Germany, there simply was no market for the ''new poetry''. The very limited and private first editions of his works during the decade are explained neither by a desire to remain unknown nor as a kind of advertisement through secrecy. Rather, the reason for his course of action was simple necessity: he was unknown; so his very unusual work was unacceptable to any of the commercial publishing houses. His own resources allowed him to print only very small editions. Besides, he had a distinct and justified distaste for the inartistic typography and bindings used in the book trade generally at that time. The same observations apply to the publication of *Blätter für die Kunst*. (pp. 34-5)

Up to and including ***Das Jahr der Seele*** . . . , George's poetry, with a few notable exceptions (e.g., **''Manuel''** and **''Die Aufnahme in den Orden''**), is purely lyrical and free from the didactic element of the later work, but, beyond the wrestling with personal problems and the expression of rare moods in rare words, there is the poet's constant striving to become fit for his greater mission. The first five books are the record of George's pilgrimage in search of kindred souls, of friends, of an audience. He did not merely dream of the return of the poet's, of man's soul to a Platonic Eden—like Mallarmé. The goal of his ultimate striving was a rebirth of the soul in *this* life, with the help of art. For this purpose the *Blätter für die Kunst* were founded in 1892. George realized that Symbolism, in its other-worldly aspects, had led men like Mallarmé into a dead end from which it was impossible to re-establish contact with the vital forces of society. No matter in what light George's method may appear today, he considered it his task to influence the world in which he lived and to reassert the poet's prestige as a leader of his nation. (pp. 35-7)

So far as George's relations with France are concerned, his later development is not in contradiction to the period when he was still under the impact of symbolism, because he was intent upon developing his own position from the outset. . . . He happened to feel at home with the symbolists and sympathized with their attempt at finding an answer to the problem in a cultivation of pure art. The fact that his own solution later was a considerable modification of theirs is a different matter, and ought not to prevent the recognition of the decadent elements of symbolism in George. (p. 38)

[The] poetry which George wrote during and after his first Paris visit bears unmistakably the impact of the French experience. Nevertheless, only very few poems can be said to be imitations, in spirit and form, of Baudelaire or his successors. The main outcome of the contact with France lies in the increasing mastery of poetic forms and in the use of symbolistic techniques, and generally in the fact that he was greatly encouraged by the high regard in which his French friends held the Poet's calling. Otherwise, as far as the content of his poetry is concerned, the new work is not essentially different from that which preceded the journey to France. Stefan George continued to struggle with his own problems in his own way. (pp. 38-9)

Das Jahr der Seele is George's fifth book, and perhaps, his best known. It contains some of his finest and most appealing lyrical poetry. Here the poet developed to perfection the technique of using nature symbols to render moods of the soul—*"Seelenzustände," "états d'âme"*—in admirably concise form. . . . Similar to the French symbolists, George insists that the full intent of the poet is realized, when his words create the suggested mood of a poem in the listener or reader. The actual "event" of the poem consists in this process of evocation. As he says in the *Blätter für die Kunst:* "The poem is the highest, the final expression of an event: not the rendering of a thought but a mood." In this process, biographical details, although they may have been contributing causes originally, would hinder rather than help the reader in his attempt to enter into the mood of the poem itself. The actual event "has, through art, undergone such a transformation that it has become unimportant to the artist himself, and for anyone else the knowledge of it would be confusing rather than enlightening." Yet, for a full understanding of ***Das Jahr der Seele*** as part of the poet's total work, facts from his life which explain the genesis of this work must not be ignored. The most important question in this connection is: to whom does the poet refer in ***Das Jahr der Seele,*** when he uses *"Du"* and *"Wir"*? He says in the preface: "Seldom are the I and the You so much the same soul as in this book." (pp. 71-2)

The central tension of these poems consists in the varying degrees of sympathetic accord between two souls: poet and woman. The latter is not necessarily one woman; she is woman in general, as George had experienced her up to the time of writing. (p. 72)

How are the soul's varying moods and situations recorded? The manner in which inward experiences are told in the book shows a far subtler use of nature symbols than would be found in the work of, let us say, a romantic poet who wants to tell of his rejection by his lady. There, nature's varying aspects would serve as illustrations of what went on in the poet's life. Here, however, the natural phenomena serve as symbols in the creation of an inward, psychological landscape. The poet cannot ever be said to be in idyllic harmony with nature, so that she would willingly yield the symbols which he requires for his own sovereign purposes. How unsympathetic George's attitude toward nature was has been observed by various people who knew him. . . . Between the poet and nature there is a tension as between antagonists. For George there lurked behind the more pleasant natural phenomena a demonic, primordial force, the chaos, which might break through at any moment to destroy beauty and form. It is the "Other" (*"das Andere"*) against which the creative spirit of God or man pits itself to wrest from it a cosmos. George states this attitude expressly in the famous lines from **"Der Templer"** in ***Der Siebente Ring*** where nature's chaotic forces are seen as submitting to the creative mind only if he can compel "the great nurturing mother" to do the work he demands. . . . But expressions of this conception can be discerned in George's work long before ***Der Siebente Ring*** and before ***Das Jahr der Seele.*** Ominous forces are felt to be at work in the singeing atmosphere of **"Nachmittag"** in the ***Hymnen***. . . . [In ***Algabal***] Algabal's subterranean realm springs from the desire to be independent from natural forces. In the **"Traurige Tänze",** at the end of ***Das Jahr der Seele,*** the poet states his determination to pursue his own course in defiance of nature's forces even while the elements are storming in upon him, as if to take revenge for long neglect. . . . The very presence of demonic forces in the poet himself made him aware of them in nature and challenged him to tame and harness them.

In ***Das Jahr der Seele*** this tension between the artist and nature becomes symbolical for the tension between the two souls of poet and woman, except that, while he can make nature yield her symbols, he is gradually led to reject woman as inadequate for the needs of the creative genius. It is significant that the soul's adventures in the **"Jahr"** take place, most of the time, not in a wild forest, but in a *tamed* landscape, a park. (pp. 72-4)

In the first section of the book, the **"Jahr der Seele"** in the narrower sense, three seasons of the year, autumn, winter, and summer, under the titles *"Nach der Lese"*, *"Waller im Schnee"*, and *"Sieg des Sommers"* ["after the harvest," "pilgrims in the snow," and "triumph of summer"], furnish the material from which the soul's experiences are fashioned.

The woman who accompanies the poet in autumn and winter (she is never described; only the effect of her personality on the poet is conveyed) is not, he knows for certain, the ideal SHE from whom he has been looking for so long, but she brings temporary alleviation of his loneliness. . . . (p. 74)

As they become "pilgrims in the snow" both of them feel the cold and comfortless winter air which has come to dominate their companionship. . . . It is becoming clear why the relationship must be broken off. Woman is too close to the chaotic spirit of nature (which the poet wants to dominate). He despairs of wresting her secret from her. They have nothing in common. He has nothing to thank her for, which he would have, if she would only let *him* comfort *her* in her melancholy. . . . That means that woman has no understanding at all of the great honor which he bestows on her as he reveals to her his secret wishes and needs. . . . The subtle selfishness of the man, in fact a certain revengefulness, emerges in the poem **"Die blume die ich mir am fenster hege".** This flower saddens him by drooping its head as if it were to die—and this in spite of all his good care! . . . It is a very accomplished poem, although difficult to interpret. One may consider the flower a symbol of disappointed love in the poet rather than of the beloved herself. (pp. 75-6)

The poems in **"Nach der Lese"** and **"Waller im Schnee",** most of them artistic masterpieces, convey a deep sense of failure, although the author makes it clear that he considers his failure merely a station in the pilgrim's progress toward greater experience. The new, more hopeful season is announced in the last winter poem, as the poet crosses the thawing waters of the river by boat and sees a "brother" waiting on the opposite bank. . . . Surprisingly enough, the season that follows now is summer. A possible explanation is that the complete renewal of the soul, for which alone spring would be the fitting symbol, has not yet arrived. It does not belong in this book. In **"Sieg des Sommers"** the poet announces merely a harmonious interlude of new life. (p. 76)

With the emergence of this male friendship there comes immediately a new release of creative power which takes the form of pedagogic guidance. Hints of the pedagogical talent of the poet had previously appeared in the poems of personal characterization, apostrophe, and advice. . . . The number of poems of this sort is increased in the ***Jahr;*** the whole middle section of the book consists of personal apostrophes and occasional poems. But even in the summer cycle of the ***Jahr*** proper, precisely at the moment of the appearance of the "brother", the pedagogical tendency becomes evident, which eventually led him to write the "State" poetry of ***Der Stern des Bundes.***

All the motifs of the inner story of the two souls which has just been sketched are found again in the third and last section of the book, the *"Traurige Tänze"*, though here all exterior details are excluded and the poet proceeds entirely by means of an inner dialogue. The "sad dances" take place within the soul and the I and the You are indeed identical. In mysterious and alluring rhythms the experiences of the three seasons are evoked by means of allusion and recollection, or by translation into other "corresponding" terms of experience. Even though, in this section too, the more reassuring motif of approaching happiness can be found, the predominant note is sad dejection. The solitary poet's concern with his creative powers recurs in the first part of this section and is expressed with inescapable magic in the poem **"Dies leid und diese last."** . . .

The second part of the *"Tänze"* renders the soul's aforementioned fright in the face of the changing seasons and of the underground forces of nature. (p. 77)

For the poet, the woman who would not let herself be fashioned into what he wanted her to be becomes inadequate as a companion. His creative forces seek the male Eros as a more inspiring guide to creative work as he wants to perform it. The pedagogue who was later to found an informal Academy for young men, on the Platonic pattern, renounces woman as too bound up with primitive natural forces. It would be wrong to say that because he was a rejected lover he made the best of it and turned in another direction. Probably his imagination or his subconscious mind directed and manipulated his experiences so that he should arrive on the path where he felt he could be most creative and true to himself. All the suffering and heartbreak of the "year of the soul": he wanted it or needed it. (p. 80)

During the victorious summer season, spent in the "brother's" company, the poet is beginning to strike a stronger note of life affirmation than he has ever been able to find before. It seems that with the new form of friendship he hopes at last to find himself and to sing "songs as he would wish to sing them." . . . He discovers that he has a message for the youth of his country and he wishes to pass on the lesson he has learned, namely that happiness consists in the enjoyment of the here and now. Filled with this feeling of *Diesseitigkeit,* he censors those who, in their quest for the ideal, can never reconcile their dreams with reality. . . . (p. 81)

This censure of romantic idealism marks the parting of the ways between Stefan George and Mallarmé. From now on it was to be his constant endeavour to make the "kisses" of dream and reality coincide and to communicate to others his mastery of the here and now. His poetry ceases at this point to be purely lyrical, since it no longer confines itself to a search for beautiful expression of personal experiences but becomes the vehicle of the poet's emerging sense of moral responsibility as a leader of youth. In the anticipation of this new and to him more fruitful phase of his life the poet ends the book with the praise of a new liberating breeze . . . , in a poem which leads over to the next cycle of poems, soon to rise "from the often painful oppression of the year of the soul". (pp. 81-2)

During the first phases of his quest, from the ***Hymnen*** to ***Das Jahr der Seele,*** in which a physical companion was the immediate objective, he experienced the inadequacy of human companionship. Woman is renounced altogether, and the fruitfulness of the male Eros is only hinted at as a hope for the future. The poet's resigned acceptance of solitude produced the melancholy of ***Das Jahr der Seele.*** (p. 84)

George's rise to intellectual and artistic eminence from 1890 until the first World War is unique in the history of literature; no other modern European poet has been able or has even endeavored to create for himself deliberately a position of intellectual leadership. His success is largely explained by the fact that he was possessed by the urge to rule. As a young man he had to determine whether to yield to this urge and become a man of action in the world of business or politics, or whether to become a poet. Power, in the practical, political sense of the word, was a temptation to him; he said once: "If, at the age of twenty, I had had 20,000 soldiers, I would have routed all the potentates of Europe." He overcame this temptation because he realized that worldly power was transitory, while spiritual authority, resting on the magic power of the Word, could surpass all earthly dominions. Hence, with the zeal of a prophet and reformer, who feels challenged by the corruption of his age, he wanted to create his own spiritual "state". (pp. 120-21)

Ulrich K. Goldsmith, in his Stefan George: A Study of His Early Work, *University of Colorado Press, 1959, 172 p.*

MICHAEL M. METZGER AND ERIKA A. METZGER (essay date 1972)

[*The Metzgers's* Stefan George *is a chronological examination of George's life and poetic career. The book includes a thorough bibliography of works about George in both German and English. The following excerpt summarizes George's lifelong efforts to bring about a renewal of German poetry and to create "a modern, 'spiritual' art which would continue the tradition" of the French Symbolists.*]

"I am an end and a beginning." These words from ***Der Stern des Bundes*** define the poet's capacity to embrace all extremes of earthly existence. As self-appraisal, they have also been aptly cited as an index of Stefan George's place in the development of lyrical poetry in Germany. To accord with the sequence of George's career as a poet, however, this formulation would have to be reversed, for his role in influencing the main trends of this development precedes the time in which he perpetuated the tradition of the classical idealism of Goethe and Hölderlin. This apparent later "conservatism" of form on George's part, his attempt to express values alien to the disillusioned *Weltanschauung* of modern man, has led to his consistent exclusion, on the critics' part, from the ranks of truly "modern" poets, to a denial even of his relevance to the major literary movements of his time and ours. Thus, Hugo Friedrich groups George with "heirs and late classical authors of a centuries-old lyrical style," and Hans Magnus Enzensberger considers him too far removed from the "world language" (*Welts-*

prache) of lyrical evolution in the past century for inclusion in his *Museum of Modern Poetry*.

Especially in the light of Enzensberger's working definition of modern poetry as "poetry after Whitman and Baudelaire, after Rimbaud and Mallarmé," such judgments distort the truth, useful as they may be in defining their author's intentions. Choosing to see only the latest phase of Stefan George's creative life, such historians ignore the fact that the greater part of his activity as a poet, translator, and critic was devoted to the "renewal" of German poetry, to the creation of a modern, "spiritual" art which would continue the tradition which, as George himself acknowledged, was founded by Baudelaire and the "masters," Verlaine and Mallarmé. These opinions, still widely held, were pronounced almost a decade ago. Lately, a wider awareness of Stefan George's significance to the literary scene of his time outside his immediate circle is becoming apparent, as evidenced by Manfred Durzak's recent study of George's influence on Expressionist writers, such as Ernst Stadler, Georg Heym, Carl Sternheim, Ernst Blass, Gottfried Benn, Fritz von Unruh, and Reinhard Goering.

Stefan George was a modern poet through more than an accident of birth. In his life and art he sought answers to the same questions which had occupied Baudelaire and Mallarmé: the existential problems of the creative spirit in an adversary relationship to the axioms of the empiric universe. This opposition is engendered by the individual's perception of another, transcendent dimension of reality which can only be expressed symbolically. Through the magic of words, the poet can create an esthetically, and ultimately morally, felicitous "antiuniverse." Because of the hermetic quality of the poet's relationship to language, the contours of this "antiuniverse" are even more idiosyncratic and private than comparable writings of the German Romantics, which, for all their visionary nature, still had archetypal analogues in folk songs and legends. It is the tension between an intensely perceived subjective world and an apparently ephemeral objective reality, with the poet consciously opting for the former, which constitutes the watershed between the "traditional" and the "modern."

Stefan George's development as a poet can be seen in terms of a lifelong attempt to resolve this polarity. Conditioned, at least in part, by his upbringing in the Catholic faith and by a strong affinity for Platonic idealism, George was, from the very outset, at odds with the extremes of nihilism implicit in the poetry of Baudelaire and Rimbaud, for whom the synthetic order of the work of art represented the only rescue from the chaos of existence. This nihilism seemed to dictate the poet's flight into a solipsistic world of hermetic symbols. In ***Hymnen, Pilgèrfahrten*** and especially in ***Algabal,*** the possible joys, but also the certainly present terrors, of such an escape from confrontation with existence are pondered, and the solipsistic alternative rejected.

The "three books" convey the insight that men in other and earlier cultures were better able to endure the trials of human existence through knowledge of their inclusion in a divinely ordained order, their unquestioning commitment to their fates. The rationalistically ordained alienation between perceiving mind and empiric matter had not yet been inflicted upon them. In ***Das Jahr der Seele*** and ***Der Teppich des Lebens,*** George's conviction emerges that this alienation, through which man has become, in his own eyes, merely a mechanically and biologically determined element of the universe, is not *necessarily* in the nature of things, is not an inescapable curse of modern existence. Rather, the individual can be reconciled in his existence to the universe of "objective reality." This can occur through his understanding of the transcendent interrelation of all phenomena, that the universe is the physical extension of a higher, spiritual realm, man's fate the symbolic expression of an ultimately inscrutable providence, analogous to divine will. Thus, George commits himself to the essentially religious world view, theologically unorthodox as his synthesis of pantheistic ideas might be.

This new intellectual and spiritual constellation put Stefan George into opposition with the "modern" insights about human existence and the hopelessness of its alienation. In contrast to the esthetic, subjective order which the Symbolists had created in their poetry, George had seemingly found a moral, objective order, to which his art was thenceforth to be subordinated. Formal perfectionism, exciting variety of rhythms, rhymes, and moods, continued to characterize his poems; but in ***Der Siebente Ring, Der Stern des Bundes,*** and ***Das Neue Reich,*** these elements no longer served the search for a subjectively satisfying order, but the proclamation of a hopefully redemptive perception. A poet whose beginnings had associated him closely with the significant trends of contemporary European poetry, George now became a "vatic" poet, a "seer" and idealistic interpreter of a high principle of will in the world in the tradition of Goethe, Hölderlin, and Nietzsche.

To his mind, George had achieved the synthesizing harmony between the subjective and objective perception of reality which contemporary and younger poets were still seeking, either in an embrace of pure feeling, as with the Expressionists, or, in the case of later poets, in an attempt to integrate material reality, the language and concerns of the present, into their poetry. This certainty in the midst of uncertainty, this absoluteness in the face of a general insight into the relativity of all things, obviously served to isolate George in his time. These qualities explain much of the vehemence in the controversy his name is still capable of arousing. The apparent assurance he had in the rightness of his views, George's fatalism as to whether he would ever be understood is expressed in the last lines of a poem from ***Das Neue Reich:***

> You had a vision fair and new,
> But time grew old, no man now lives,
> If e'er he'll come, you do not know,
>
> He who can see this vision too. . . .

Whether or not we can see and share Stefan George's vision of the world and his times, his works bear witness to the unremitting striving of a man of unique poetic and intellectual powers to find a higher meaning in his existence and ours. (pp. 189-91)

Michael M. Metzger and Erika A. Metzger, in their Stefan George, *Twayne Publishers, Inc., 1972, 208 p.*

SUZANNE NALBANTIAN (essay date 1977)

[*In the following excerpt, Nalbantian discusses the depiction of the soul as a symbol of spiritual barrenness in George's* The Year of the Soul.]

The collection of poems most pertinent in terms of crystallizing metonymies of the soul at the turn of the century is Stefan George's ***Das Jahr der Seele***. . . . Here it is not a question of detecting the actual use of the word since the entire set of poems alludes to the various movements and designations of the soul. The sense of the soul is derived from contexts evoking unfulfilled love, lack of communication, sterile human relationships, abuse of sensitivity and a general pervasive mood of emptiness pervading the earthly scene. Reconciled as the speaker and his addressee are to the emptiness of their metaphysical state, they engage in a mock drama of life, gesturing to each other in a cold, dispassionate manner. Having no illusion, they fail to suffer the consequences of disillusion. The sequence of poems captures the soul in various phases of its decline and inactivity.

Many commentators have noted the exclusion of the season of spring in the tracing of the passage of the soul through the metaphoric states of autumn (*Nach der Lese*), winter (*Waller im Schnee*) and summer (*Sieg des Sommers*). (pp. 87-8)

Rather than spring, the winter of the soul is its most valid characterization and becomes its metonymy. The key poem central to the unravelling of the significance of the soul is **'Wo die strahlen schnell verschleissen'** which concludes the section ***Waller im Schnee***. . . .

> Wo die strahlen schnell verschleissen
> Leichentuch der kahlen auen
> Wasser sich in furchen stauen
> In den sümpfen schmelzend gleissen.
>
> Und zum strom vereinigt laufen:
> Türm ich für erinnerungen
> Spröder freuden die zerspringen
> Uno für dich den scheiterhaufen
>
> Weg den schritt vom brande lenkend
> Greif ich in dem boot die ruder-
> Drüben an dem strand ein bruder
> Winkt das frohe banner schwenkend.
>
> Tauwind fährt in ungestümen
> Stössen über brache schollen.
> Mit den welken seelen sollen
> Sich die pfade neu beblümen. . . .

> When the shining rays swiftly strike a shroud of bare pastures, water in the furrows does stand and in the flashing softened swamps does shine. And by the dashing united rivers, I evoke for memories brittle joys which are cracking, and for you the funeral pyres. My step guided away from the blaze, I grasp the oars in the boat—yonder on the shore a brother waving the blithe banner, flags. The dewy thawing wind travels in tumult, thrusting itself over fallow lands. With the withered soul shall the paths be reflowered.

The 'withered souls' or 'welken seelen' are intrinsic to the general image of the wasteland which is the principle landscape of the poem. The soul is in contact with those aspects which represent barrenness of the human condition as made manifest in the images relating to emptiness, frost and stagnation. For example, in the first stanza there is reference to the bare pastures ('die kahlen auen') and to stagnant swamps ('Wasser sich in furchen stauen / In den sümpfen schmelzend gleissen'). Ironically, the attempt at thawing the ice and removing the barrier of frost is undermined by the condition at the end of the poem which describes the perpetual reflowing of the plains with souls of a withered condition.

Interpreted as an ironic love poem, even the memories which are described as brittle ('sproder freuden') are effaced as the soul attempts a withdrawal from the scene of love. The reference to the winking brother in the third stanza suggests the universality of the soul's state. The refurbishing of the plain with new withered souls points to the endless cycle of dying souls. The thawing of the snow does not provide an accompanying revival and blossoming of soul.

Of the climates used as correlatives of the soul's condition, winter then is most characteristic. The souls are most often withering on waste plains of discontent. The opening poem of *Nach der Lese* in fact points to the ironic gathering of the dead and decaying flowers before the advent of frost which represents its ultimate condition. In the place of outright reference to states of soul through specific uses of the word, the landscapes both of the wasteland or more especially of the familiar dead park ('der totgesagte Park') opening the collection are the trigger for the soul's designation. In fact, in the opening poem, the poet invites the reader to witness the dying of the soul as he beckons him into the dead park to gather the dead and fading souls:

'Komm in den totgesagten Park und schau . . .'

Elsewhere, as in the poem **'In freien viereck mit den gelben steinen'**, additional aspects of the soul's condition are conveyed in the further characterization of the park scene which includes empty stone, fountains, and dead birch branches. The scene is still and silent under the shadow of the moon. . . . Thematically, the poem deals with unfulfilled love in which the souls cloistered in the dead park engaged in meaningless parley. At the centre of the park is the basalt cavity which is the receptacle of the dead souls when talking ceases and mere vestiges of past intercourse remain as fragments or shadows. The aura of silence reigns, suggested by the frigid winter stillness: 'in tiefer kalter winterlicher stille.'

Finally, aside from the key images of wasteland, dead parks and withering flowers which closely mirror the soul's state, there is a particular gesture which graphically conveys the soul and its emptiness. Empty hands raised into empty spaces and blank eyes peering out from blank faces appear in the poem **'Die blume die ich mir am fenster hege.'** . . . The mood results from having severed all relations with life, symbolized in the cutting of the stem of the already fading and ailing flower. Devoid of spiritual essence, the physical is all that remains, and its constituents in terms of eyes and hands spell its empty substance.

The characterization of dead souls in dry months is not peculiar to George. It is strikingly present in other major poets of the time in the passage from the nineteenth to the twentieth century: Hofmannsthal, Rilke and T. S. Eliot. (pp. 88-90)

Suzanne Nalbantian, "The Post-Symbolists: The Winter of the Soul," in her The Symbol of the Soul from Hölderlin to Yeats: A Study in Metonymy, *Columbia University Press, 1977, pp. 86-99.**

PETER VIERECK (essay date 1982)

[In the following excerpt, Viereck provides a technical study of the method he calls "transplanting"—a rigorously faithful translation which remains as true as possible to the original source—which he used to render poems of Georg Heym and Stefan George into English.]

Transplanting does not mean "free" translation in the slovenly sense; it means rigorously faithful translation (faithful to sound, rhythm, feeling as well as meaning) plus something else: context. A moved plant dies unless its roots are moved along with it. Historical context and psychological context are the roots and the soil of a poem. . . .

A technical problem: two-syllable rhymes are particularly crucial to the esthetic strategy of Georg Heym and Stefan George. The richness of the resultant sonorousness almost justifies all the nuisances of an inflected language. English, having shed its noun and verb endings, has very few such feminine rhymes; to keep using the same few is not sonorous but soporific. Hence the English ear accepts reasonably close assonance or consonance in feminine but not masculine rhymes; here Wilfred Owen's slant rhymes sometimes serve as model. What really matters—what is sought in these pages—is the connotational message of the original, the sonorous bisyllabic connotation, even if expressed via different vowels or consonants. . . . (p. 87)

A free-verse translation of rhyme (or a rhymed translation of free verse) is not a living transplanting. When the foreign author intends free verse, he uses it, and it must be translated into English free verse; when not, not. This holds true for functional organic rhyme, not mere artificial or mechanical clicks; fortunately Heym and George are not guilty of the latter, an abuse which—endemic in much pre-1914 English poetry—justifies free verse, in the same way that tyranny justifies revolt.

The intention of these two poets is betrayed unless their monosyllable rhymes are mostly translated with strict fidelity to consonants and vowels; the connotation of mellifluous pairing is often more meaningful than the literal meaning. This point can be proved by a specific example: in George's **"The Anti-Christ"** the human voice rhymes faithfully (with the connotation of good faith); the anti-Christ's voice uses false rhymes (with the connotation of bad faith); this contrast—a free verse translation would lose it—is the real meaning of this very great lyric.

Less of a technical problem are German metrics; German and English—like Russian—are strongly accented iambic-pentameter literatures, in contrast with the unstressed and often caesura'd hexameters of French and Polish, whose ripples—to us—seem more elusive than quicksilver. The transplanter's main concern has been to convey in English the lavish suggestiveness of George's rhythms and the onomatopoeia of Heym's (after Heym's style change of late 1911 when he broke with George's stately lilt: the younger poet's declaration of independence from his father figure, a break concealed behind something so seemingly trivial as enjambed line endings).

Enjambing is used far more sparingly by George than by most German and English poets of the pentameter tradition. And when he does move unpausingly to a new line, this is often his "body language" for a mood of conflict and change: the serene hysteria of a willed nervous tic. The transplanter must cultivate a particularly sensitive ear for the varied tempo of George's varying pauses, whether slowed up by long vowels, speeded by short ones, or made subsurface-resonant by voiced or nasalized consonants: three alternatives whose emotional equivalents in English often require a change of consonant or vowel. An obvious example (most are subtler): the German 'd' and 'v' are less voiced at the end of syllables than in English, yet not entirely equivalent to an English 't' and 'f'. Sometimes it rings truer to substitute an English 'k' sound as a closer equivalent of the emotion connoted by hovering between voiced and unvoiced.

All such detailed little unofficial "rules"—these examples are merely the start—the transplanter must keep in mind. He must also keep in mind the need to violate all rules whenever the total esthetic effect overrides the separate details.

Generalizations require concrete examples. To savor the "lavish suggestiveness" of George's vowel music (cited above), read *aloud* these two lines from his ***Hymnen*** (. . . , his first book); note that his invented script omits capital letters for nouns and omits most commas):

Dann rauschen alle stauden in akkorden
Und werden lorbeer tee und aloe.

The rest of this teen-age exercise is juvenilia so uninterestingly derivative from Mallarmé (whose salon was then the shrine of George's pilgrimage to Paris) as to be better left untranslated. But the exceptions, these two pentameters, cry out for scrutiny. Adhering to the original meter but leaving the meaning merely literal, we get:

Then all the bushes sough in chords of music
And change to laurel, tea, and aloe-fragrance.

But here the reader must search not in his dictionary but in his ear and among his associations for the real meaning. The landscape is that of the gorgeous East, and "aloe" in German has not two but three syllables (Al-o-e); hence the word's flowing sound, each of the last two vowels being an entire syllable. The middle of each key word echoes a preceding word, progressing from the "au" of "rauschen", echoed in "Stauden," to the "d" of "Stauden," echoed in "Akkorden". Next, the "or" of "Akkorden" echoes onward in the "or" of "Lorbeer," concluding with the "ee" of "Tee" melting dawdlingly into the final "e" of "Aloe".

The effect is that of a sultry southwind, blowing vowel-pollen from blossom to blossom, a cross-fertilization of androgenous ambiguity, where every "bush" is the vegetable kingdom's erogenous zone (forgive if rich purple verse infects us into purple prose). "Lavish" indeed! A heavy-calorie dessert-diet. But the magic soon becomes overrich, overripe, as George himself soon recognized; this early, lush, unaustere George is a far cry from the brutal unadorned intensity emerging in **"Das Zeitgedicht,"** a poem typical of that midway turning-point book, ***Der Siebente Ring*** (***The Seventh Ring*** . . .):

Ich euch gewissen, ich euch stimme dringe
Durch euren unmut der verwirft und flucht.

In our inadequate English (again, the rest of this overpedagogic poem is being left untranslated):

I your conscience, I your voice am piercing
Right through your gloom that casts away and curses.

By the time of ***Der Stern des Bundes*** (***The Star of the Covenant*** . . .) all overmusical "decadence" gets repudiated in three lines of concealed self-hatred, rejecting his own *Jugendstil* (i.e., *art nouveau*) origins:

Und alle jugend sollt ihr sklaven nennen
Die heut mit weichen klängen sich betäubt
Mit rosenketten überm abgrund tändelt.

In our English:

But you shall label all the young ones lackeys
Who drug themselves on mushy music now,
Who skirt with chains of roses the abyss.

At this point an outsider might bellow: "Hey, what the hell is going on here?" What kind of new self is this self-invented poseur now inventing? What mask (of anti-effete effeteness) is becoming man, heroic man? The answer is simply this: having first made the German language a ripe and flowing Italian, George by 1913 has made it a taut and monosyllabic English; in no case is this cosmopolitan Hellenizing Rhinelander (whose earlier signature was not Stefan but Étienne) ever really writing German (in the narrow sense of "German," the sense of—in their different ways—Schiller, Uhland, Dehmel). His Latinate style and his Anglo-Saxon style each has its beauty, and both are represented in these pages.

Relying on an ear continuously steeped for decades in both languages, the transplanter can only convey these two phases of George (and their synthesis in his one perfect poem, **"Final Song,"** published 1928) by weighing the emotional and associational impact of every separate vowel-clang and consonant-hammer and every separate syllable-hum—and then weighing the Gestalt of every arching configuration that reshapes and sometimes contradicts all letters, all syllables. (pp. 88-91)

[After the Gleaning]
[Nach der Lese]

We're striding up and down the lane of beeches,
Their leaves aglitter, almost to the portal
And see across the field beyond the hedges
The almond tree a second time in petal.

We seek out benches where the sun still lingers,
Where no strange voices put our trance to flight;
In revery we're linked by twining fingers;
We savor long mild lethargies of light.

We're grateful for the hints of rays that glisten
From treetops down to us in weightless flood;
We look up only now and then to listen
When back to earth the ripened apples thud.

[from ***Das Jahr der Seele,*** 1897, 1899]

(p. 95)

This autumn lyric of 1897 is a selfsufficient ivory tower, so "unsullied" by social concerns ("strange voices") that it achieves a unique perfection. But a narrow one. It is the German equivalent of William Butler Yeats's "Innisfree"; together they are the German and Anglo-Irish equivalents of the French symbolism that George imbibed directly in Paris from Mallarmé, and Yeats indirectly from middlemen like Arthur Symons. George and Yeats are both being (as was then the *décadent* fashion) weary. But vigorously weary. The vigor guarantied that the *fin de siècle* mood would not last; a second stage followed.

In the second stage, above all in ***The Star of the Covenant,*** 1913-14, certain social realities (never economic but an elitist socialization of aesthetics) did matter to George. They mattered in the same way to Yeats when he, too, entered the twentieth century. What was the Irish Abbey Theater but a socialization of aesthetics? Both poets were always busy being self-invented aristocrats, scorners of any middle-class age of industry and any liberal age of reason. Not always but temporarily, both were also—in their middle period—doing something else: reaching out to their nation's supposedly unspoilt roots, Irish or German, even while retaining a French-influenced cosmopolitanism. Their second stage is glibly called "nationalist" by their approving nationalist countrymen, but the word misleads if it connotes the soapboxing political chauvinism of the day. The misunderstanding between poet and countrymen was mutual. Result: a final third state of disillusionment with their social concerns, their impractical hope of regenerating a nation not through politics but through beauty.

Both needed a specific human symbol for their more general ideal of a regenerating beauty: a symbol to be virtually deified in the tradition of Dante's Beatrice. The Maud Gonne of Germany's Yeats was the Munich boy Maximin—this after the woman George had loved, Ida Coblenz, deserted the temple he was building for her. Though both knew and were influenced by Oscar Wilde and were influenced by Nietzsche, Yeats and George never met, never corresponded, never influenced each other. The independent parallel development of their lives and styles is so uncanny that it merits a separate book, especially if one happens to agree with the transplanter's opinion that they are the greatest modern renewers of their respective languages.

Their ultimate scorn for their respective societies (Yeats's for "the seeming needs of my fool-driven land," George's for bourgeois democrats and Nazis alike) led both back to the *l'art pour l'art* of their youth. Back with a difference. Their return used a new diction, far removed from the *fin de siècle* lushness they had shared in the 1890s. In the last poem of his last book, George returned to an ivory tower poetry as "pure" as that of **"After The Gleaning"** but—the "but" is crucial—with that simpler, more vigorous style of his second, socially engaged period. The temporary departure of George and Yeats from art's sake can be justified entirely in terms of art's sake: because better written. Even though it failed, their departure from art's sake, their reaching out toward their national roots, honed their diction into a stronger, more artistic tool.

After a lifetime of experimenting with pace and resonance, with every more rigorous rhythm control, there comes a time when everything—quite suddenly—falls into place in the just-rightness of a single line, a single phrase. With Yeats the line is "Targeted, trod like spring"; with George "Greifbar im glanz, der Gott." Independently attained, this example of uncanny parallel includes an identical scansion and wrench of accent, identical mood of lofty transfiguration, even identical alliteration (between first and fourth syllables, both accented). It is as if, in the very core of both languages, lurked one identical ultimate rhythm, toward which all poetry has been groping and which, like the grail, is found only after a life of selfdiscipline, of secular asceticism. The word "earned" comes to mind; after such a lifetime of suffering for craftsmanship, both poets earned the right to say (again parallel passages but with George always "striding"): "I am blest by everything, / Everything I look upon is blest" and "Durchs offne feld kam ich geschritten . . . / Mein ganzes leben seh ich als ein glück." ("Through the holy field I came striding . . . / My whole life I look upon as blest").

So much for broader background, but at this point the context again narrows to **"After The Gleaning,"** the most flawless as well as most representative poem of George's first stage and the fourth poem in his book ***The Year of the Soul,*** a book privately printed for his circle in 1897 and publicly in 1899. In the poem and in most of the book, the rhythms tend to be stately, the consonants resonantly voiced, the vowels deep (compare the vowels and consonants of Yeats's "bee-loud glade" in "Innisfree"), the syllables sonorous, with slow end-stopped lines favored over quick run-overs. It is the style Heym first slavishly imitated, then angrily purged from his own work.

What of the Englishing of this style and this poem? No problem keeping enough rhymes feminine or keeping the triple-el alliteration of line 8; no problem with the echoing undertones and resonating phonemes, the pacing solemnity, the languors of *Yellow Book* and "Innisfree." But, among many fidelities, some dubious liberties have as usual been ventured. In the last line, why expand "on the ground" ("auf den boden") into "back to earth"? "Back" adds new implications of tomb, womb, and entropy; the transplanter could justify them (on grounds that "Boden" sounds both earth-motherly and ominous) but not very convincingly; so he won't try. In line eight the German dative ending "-en" gives a loitering slowdown effect ("langen milden leuchten") that is lost in the uninflected English monosyllables; but fortunately, even in English, the lingering voiced consonants, "ng," "m," and "d," do give our ear the slow-flow effect that is so crucial to the line, to the poem, and to the whole book. It is an effect that George, like Yeats in that period, found in the Rossetti and Dowson poems they both were then—temporarily—steeped in.

In all the George poems of the 1890s and early 1900s, "striding" ("schreiten") is the key verb (see line one of **"After The Gleaning"**): key in meter, sound, mood as well as meaning. As used by the poet, the verb connotes a robe-trailing priest-king, watched by awe-struck acolytes and striding majestically down the marble steps of a Greek (no, late Hellenistic, not really Greek) temple. At its best the mood connotes a dignity ("Würde" is a second key word of George) genuinely impressive, an effect never fully achieved in German literature before, though strained after in the Venice sonnets of Platen. And yet, and yet (George begets yets): after too many marble steps and too many static George poems about his self-appointed divine dignity—"O never change a garb of dignity" intones another George poem—the irreverent American transplanter can only add: O for a banana peel! (pp. 96-8)

The **"After The Gleaning"** sample here transplanted uses the "stride" effect at its restrained best and cannot be faulted. But overusing the effect leads George to spoil, for example, his brilliant Dante translations by infelicitously translating "entrate" as "stride" ("durchschreite") in the "All hope abandon, you who enter here" passage. The result, as with George's equally brilliant Shakespeare and Baudelaire translations, sounds more like George than like his apotheosized Dante. . . .

Line four contains the most evocative image in the entire [***Year of the Soul***]: "The almond tree a second time in petal." The first stanza's interaction of painting and music (a pre-Raphaelite portrait of lovers in a garden plus the "drowsy numbness" and "rich to die" music of the Keats of 1819) culminates with a sigh of inevitability in the fruit-fall of the final line: "When back to earth the ripened apples thud." Perhaps no other autumn lyric in world literature so gracefully incarnates Shakespeare's "ripeness is all." (p. 99)

Peter Viereck, "On Transplanting into New Gardens: Georg Heym and Stefan George," in The Literary Review, *Vol. 26, No. 1, Fall, 1982, pp. 87-101.**

ADDITIONAL BIBLIOGRAPHY

Antosik, Stanley J. "The Spiritual Kingdom of Stefan George: The Kingdom Gained, the Kingdom Lost." In his *The Question of Elites: An Essay on the Cultural Elitism of Nietzsche, George, and Hesse,* pp. 80-134. Bern: Peter Land, 1978.

Examines the development of the circle of followers who regarded George as a spiritual and cultural master and who, George believed, constituted an intellectual elite. The second section of the chapter devoted to George discusses the gradual waning of his dream for spiritual renewal of German culture in the 1920s, as he realised that "there could be no place for something like the Georgean movement in the Third Reich."

Andrews, Wayne. "The Gospel According to Stefan George." In his *Siegfried's Curse: The German Journey from Nietzsche to Hesse,* pp. 171-97. New York: Atheneum, 1972.

Extremely sarcastic account of George's life and career. Andrews characterizes George as "an interesting if not an extraordinary poet" and George's followers as "minor" and "second- and third-rate" in their fields.

Bithel, Jethro. "Stefan George—The Man." *German Life and Letters* n.s. IX, No. 1 (October 1955): 47-55.

Discusses the major biographical studies of George: Friedrich Gundolf's *George* (1924), Friedrich Wolters's *Stefan George und die Blätter für die Kunst* (1930), Ernst Morwitz's *Die Dichtung Stefan George* (1934), Robert Boehringer's *Ewigen Augenblick* (1945) and *Mein Bild von Stefan George* (1951), Edgar Salin's *Um Stefan George* (1948), and Claude David's *Stefan George: Son oeuvre poétique* (1952). None of these works are available in English and much of this review article consists of untranslated quotes.

Breugelmans, Rene. "Alienation: the Destiny of Modern Literature? Oscar Wilde and Stefan George." *Mosaic* 2, No. 1 (Fall 1968): 18-28.*

Compares George's and Wilde's shared beliefs in the concept of art for art's sake, in the sovereignity of the artist, and in rejecting any intrusion of contemporary social issues into art.

Curtius, E. R. "Stefan George in Conversation" and "George, Hofmannsthal, and Calderon." In his *Essays in European Literature,* translated by Michael Kowal, pp. 107-28, 142-68. Princeton: Princeton University Press, 1973.*

Personal recollection of social encounters with George, interspersed with some historical retrospective of his life and career. Curtius found that contrary to George's reputation as austere and unapproachable, he was—at least in the years 1906 and 1907—relaxed and affable in company. The second essay cited compares George's and Hofmannsthal's poetic use of the literary and linguistic traditions of France, Italy, and Spain.

Enright, D. J. "Stefan George, Friedrich Gundolf and the Maximin Myth." *German Life and Letters* n.s. V, No. 3 (April 1952): 176-83.

Explores the significance of Maximin in George's life and in his poetry. While the boy's death was seen by George as confirmation of his deity, and therefore an event almost to be welcomed, George's unhappiness at losing a beloved friend is also evident in the poems of *The Seventh Ring.*

Franklin, Ursula. "The Quest for the Black Flower: Baudelairean and Mallarméan Inspirations in Stefan George's *Algabal.*" *Comparative Literature Studies* XVI, No. 2 (June 1979): 131-40.

Traces "the figure of the decadent prince and his artificial anti-nature" as an image of the poet's isolation from materialistic society in the works of Charles Baudelaire, Stéphane Mallarmé, and George.

Gide, André. Journal entry for 7 April 1908. In his *The Journals of André Gide, Vol. 1: 1889-1913,* translated by Justin O'Brien, pp. 229-30. New York: Alfred A. Knopf, 1949.

Mentions meeting George, "whom I have long wanted to know and whose work I admire each time I manage to understand it." Gide describes George's appearance and manner ("an evident awareness of his evident superiority") in detail.

Goldsmith, Ulrich K. "Stefan George and the Theatre." *PMLA* LXVI, No. 2 (March 1951): 85-95.

Traces George's interest in the theater from *Manuel* and *Phraortes,* two dramatic fragments that he wrote as a student. At various times in his career, George alternately condemned the theater as an unnecessary form of artistic expression or called for explicit reforms in both the art of acting and writing plays. Goldsmith finds this duality indicative of "an outstanding character trait in George: he wanted either to rule a sphere of activity or to have nothing to do with it."

Gsteiger, Manfred. "Expectation and Resignation: Stefan George's Place in German and in European Symbolist Literature." In *The Symbolist Movement in the Literature of European Languages,* edited by Anna Balakian, pp. 255-267. Budapest: Akadémiai Kiadó, 1982.

Finds that even though *The Year of the Soul* was the last of George's strictly Symbolist poetic works, George's "Symbolist beginnings were not . . . merely an episode; they form the basis for his whole writing, and are the key to an understanding of his work." George's introduction of Symbolism to German literature "gave German poetic tradition new life."

Masur, Gerhard. "The Self-Enchanted: The Crisis in Poetry." In his *Prophets of Yesterday: Studies in European Culture 1890-1914,* pp. 106-58. New York: Macmillan, 1961.*

Examines George's dissatisfaction with the state of fin-de-siècle German poetry and his efforts toward its renewal, including the founding of the periodical *Blätter für die Kunst* and the application of severe, formal standards to poetry.

Morwitz, Ernst. "Stefan George." In *Stefan George: Poems,* by Stefan George, translated by Carol North Valhope and Ernst Morwitz, pp. 9-36. New York: Pantheon Books, 1943.

Chronologically arranged biographical and critical study.

Norwood, Eugene. "Stefan George's Translation of Shakespeare's Sonnets." *Monatschefte* XLIV, No. 1 (January 1952): 217-24.

Establishes George as the first translator of Shakespeare's sonnets into German to most closely reproduce the sound and form of the original works.

Oswald, Victor A., Jr. "The Historical Context of Stefan George's *Algabal.*" *The Germanic Review* XXIII, No. 3 (October 1948): 193-205.

Examination of the historical sources about the emperor Heliogabalus. Oswald attempts to determine which of these sources may have been available to George when he wrote *Algabal.*

Rilke, Rainer Maria. Letter to Friedrich von Oppeln-Brownikowski. In his *Selected Letters of Rainer Maria Rilke, 1902-1926,* translated by R.F.C. Hull, p. 130. London: Macmillan, 1947.

Letter of 29 May 1907. Rilke writes "I admire the poetry of Stefan George" and calls an earlier meeting with George "one of my most cherished memories."

Rosenfeld, Paul. "The Nazis and Stefan George." *The New Republic* 103, No. 18 (28 October 1940): 581-84.

Explains the widespread misconception that the poems of *The Seventh Ring,* predicting the coming of a "New Reich embodying highest spiritual values," actually hailed the advent of nazism.

Scott, Cyril. "Reminiscences of Stefan George." *German Life and Letters* XII, No. 3 (April 1959): 186-90.

Personal recollection of George. Scott theorizes that poor English translations of George's poetry and repugnance for his homosexuality may have contributed to his lack of recognition in English-speaking countries.

Stirck, S. D. "Stefan George and the 'New Empire'." *German Life and Letters* II, No. 3 (April 1938): 175-87.

Summation of some contemporary German critical assessments of George. Stirck finds George to be possibly the most controversial figure in German literature because of the political interpretations applied to his final works.

Valhope, Carol North, and Morwitz, Ernst. "Method and Purpose of the Translation." In *Stefan George: Poems,* by Stefan George, translated by Carol North Valhope and Ernst Morwitz, pp. 252-54. New York: Pantheon Books, 1943.

Explication of the goal, method, and purpose of translation of a selection of George's poems. The Morwitz's translations are critically examined by Hermann J. Weigand (see Additional Bibliography), who praises their translations for resolving many obscurities and misconceptions common to interpretations of George's texts.

Viereck, Peter. "Stefan George, Perilous Prophet." *The Antioch Review* XI, No. 1 (March 1949): 111-16.

Examines the place in George's life and works of nationalism, hero-worship, and the enlistment of a cult of youthful followers—elements which were exploited by the Nazis in establishing their own doctrines and in attempting to enlist George as the poet laureate of their party.

Weigand, Hermann J. Review of *Stefan George: Poems,* by Stefan George, translated by Carol North Valhope and Ernst Morwitz. *Journal of English and German Philology* XLII (1944): 141-49.

Characterizes George's poetry as "the key to Germany's most significant cultural movement of the last half century," and finds the translations in *Stefan George: Poems* were governed not by a desire to interpret the way George would have written in English, but to accurately reproduce the original meaning of his poems. Though Weigand finds that the translators often fail to do this, he regards their work as an invaluable first step in making George's works accessible to English-language readers.

Knut Hamsun

1859-1952

(Pseudonym of Knut Pederson; also wrote under pseudonym of Knut Pedersen Hamsund) Norwegian novelist, essayist, dramatist, autobiographer, short story writer, and poet.

The Granger Collection, New York

Hamsun is widely considered to be Norway's greatest novelist. Highly praised during his lifetime by such eminent contemporaries as Thomas Mann and André Gide, he received the 1920 Nobel Prize in Literature on the merits of one of his most famous novels, *Markens Grøde (Growth of the Soil)*. In this novel, and in many others, Hamsun depicted the daily activities of simple, hardworking farmers and small-town folk, demonstrating his admiration for the strong, spiritually independent individual as well as his deep affection for the beauty of the Norwegian countryside. A source of national pride during most of his life, Hamsun fell out of popular favor during and after World War II because of his pro-Nazi activities, and it was not until several years after his death that widespread interest was revived in the man and his work.

Born Knut Pedersen, he was raised in Nordland, a scenic region above the Arctic Circle where his impoverished parents worked the family farm "Hamsund." Although poorly educated, the boy decided at an early age to become a writer, and as an adolescent he worked at a wide variety of low-paying jobs in Christiania (Oslo) to support himself during his literary apprenticeship. By age nineteen he had published three unsuccessful books and several newspaper articles, some of them written under the name of Knut Pedersen Hamsund. (A printer's error later resulted in the name Hamsun, which the author adopted). Disappointed in his attempts to be accepted by a major publisher and frustrated in his efforts to raise money for a university education, Hamsun twice emigrated to the midwestern United States during the 1880s, supporting himself by working as a journalist, farmhand, streetcar conductor, and lecturer on world literature. Failing to achieve any success in America, he returned to Norway and in 1889 published the essay collection *Fra det Amerikas aandsliv (The Cultural Life of Modern America)*, his first work to attract critical attention in Scandinavia. An attack on the shallowness of American thought and literature and on the nation's growing materialistic spirit, *The Cultural Life of Modern America* was followed a year later by *Sult (Hunger)*, a novel that many critics consider Hamsun's masterpiece.

Autobiographical in many respects, *Hunger* details the thoughts of a starving would-be writer who is driven by a demonic "hunger" to practice his craft in spite of the niggardly fees paid him for his articles. Unlike much of the Norwegian literature of the era, *Hunger* is devoid of any overt social message, reflecting Hamsun's acceptance of despair, hardship, and struggle as unavoidable complements to joy, and reflecting as well his unique literary theory. Expounded in a series of lectures delivered soon after the appearance of *Hunger*, Hamsun's theory called for a radically new type of literature devoted to the psychology of the individual. From his readings in the works of Fedor Dostoevski and several pre-Freudian theorists, Hamsun believed that the individual is motivated by psychological processes too intricate to be conveyed through traditional literary techniques. His answer, as evidenced in *Hunger*, was an impressionistic technique similar to the stream of consciousness style developed later by James Joyce. In addition to calling for a literature concerned with the inner life, Hamsun lectured against contemporary Norwegian literature's preoccupation with effecting social change, attacking in particular the works of Henrik Ibsen—once while Ibsen himself sat glowering in the front row of the lecture hall. In spite of the furor caused by Hamsun's assault on many of Norway's leading writers, these lectures brought Hamsun nationwide attention and markedly influenced turn-of-the-century Norwegian literature (Ibsen's *The Master Builder*, a drama concerning a psychologically beseiged genius, is believed by some critics to have been a response to Hamsun's polemics), while the success of *Hunger* brought Hamsun the financial security he had long sought, enabling him to devote all of his time and skill to writing.

The works written by Hamsun from 1890 until the end of his career are often divided into two overlapping periods. During the first, which lasted until approximately 1913, Hamsun wrote what many critics believe to be his finest works; in addition to *Hunger*, these include the novels *Mysterier (Mysteries)*, *Pan, af løitnant Thomas Glahns papirer (Pan)*, and *Victoria: En kaerligheds historie (Victoria)*. These, like *Hunger* and the other novels of Hamsun's early career, reflect the influence of Friedrich Nietzsche in their concern with social outsiders who live according to their own nonconformist values and who make no appeal for the understanding or sympathy of the "common herd." In *Mysteries,* life in a quiet Norwegian coastal town is disrupted when an eccentric stranger, Johan Nagel, suddenly appears in the village and then, a few weeks later, disappears just as abruptly. Through Nagel, Hamsun revealed his admiration of the young, amoral *Übermensch* ("overman" or "superman") as well as his contempt for politicians and the infirm elderly. In *Pan* the protagonist is again a wanderer, this time a hunter who lives alone with his dog in a hut in the forest. *Pan* has been a favorite of many critics, including Gide, who "found in it, very plausibly set forth, the unacknowledged relationships between our opinions, our thoughts, even our religious convictions, and the physiological state of our being, as in Dostoyevsky's Raskolnikov, but perhaps with even more subtlety and in a quite unexpected, deeply personal way." *Pan* is marked by a new emphasis in Hamsun's fiction, as here for the first time the natural beauty of northern Norway is displayed and extolled. *Victoria* tells of a lowly writer's ill-starred love for the aristocratic woman of the novel's title. Of this work, considered one of the most beautiful love stories in modern European literature, John Updike has written that the moral "seems to be 'There's always a catch somewhere,' or 'God has fashioned [love] of many kinds and seen it endure or perish.' Such an inconclusive conclusion, a standoff, well caps this eerily static love story, whose characters, though immersed in bookish circumstances, proudly reject the dynamism of characters."

With *Børn av tiden (Children of the Age)* in 1913, Hamsun's novels began to portray the lives of multiple characters, rather than the relative few of the early works, while the style of the novels changed from the earlier impressionism to a fairly conventional third-person form. *Children of the Age* and its companion volume *Segelfoss by (Segelfoss Town)* are social satires that depict the development of a tightly-knit, self-supporting farming community into a bustling, materialistic town. In these and in many of his later novels, Hamsun expressed his deep contempt for urban society, which he regarded as a social sickness leading to the conditions he had come to loathe in American cities: self-centeredness, low cultural standards, contempt for individuality, and gullible subservience to an essentially corrupt intellectual and political elite. Hamsun now held up as his ideal the pioneer-farmer, who through self-reliance and hard work carves a homestead out of the wilderness, working in harmony with nature rather than despoiling it. Himself the owner of a farm in southern Norway, Hamsun came to consider himself as much a farmer as a writer, seeing the soil and its husbandry as a source of physical, psychological, and spiritual nourishment. His Nobel Prize-winning novel *Growth of the Soil* concerns the life of a rugged, uncomplaining farmer to whom working the land and enjoying its yield form a sufficient and fulfilling purpose in life. Written in a grand, lyrical style reminiscent of the Old Testament, *Growth of the Soil* has received praise for the natural beauty it describes as well as unfavorable criticism for its occasionally brutal naturalistic elements, such as its frank, impassive account of a mother's strangling of her deformed newborn daughter. Critics consider the other most notable works of Hamsun's later career to be *Landstrykere (Vagabonds), August (August),* and *Men livet lever (The Road Leads On),* a trilogy of sardonically humorous novels concerning the life of August, a wandering musician, inventor, and liar. A man whose unconventional ideas and persuasive speech upset the *status quo* in every village at which he stops, August was the last major character created by Hamsun during his long career. He wrote little during the 1930s, though by that time he was renowned throughout Europe as a literary master. His reputation plunged, however, when in 1940 he welcomed the invading Nazis into Norway, writing: "Norwegians! Throw away your rifles and return home. The Germans are fighting for us and all neutrals." Hamsun was arrested in 1945 after the fall of Vidkun Quisling's collaborationist government and charged with treason, but because of his age and allegedly unbalanced mental state he was judged not responsible for his actions, then heavily fined and released. His memoirs of the wartime and postwar era, *Paa gjengrodde stier (On Overgrown Paths),* are considered a convincing rebuttal to the charges made against his mental stability. Hamsun stopped writing after completing *On Overgrown Paths,* and died three years later.

Remarking on the difficulty of dispassionately appraising Hamsun's work, Thomas Mann—who was himself initially drawn to and later repelled by Hamsun's thought—wrote that "there is something bewildering in the phenomenon of healthy sophistication and sophisticated health that Hamsun magically portrays; in the organically resolved conflict between his democratic modernity and his internationalism, the perfected progressiveness of his artistry and his aristocratic closeness to the earth and to nature, which is the source of all the antisocial, antipolitical, antiliterary, antidemocratic, and antihumane attacks and demonstrations of will that the world has had to put up with from him." And from 1940 until the mid-1960s, much of the criticism written on Hamsun's work tended to focus on the author's controversial social and political beliefs and on their reflection in his fiction. Some critics, notably Leo Lowenthal, have traced a totalitarian bent throughout Hamsun's canon, citing as evidence Hamsun's anti-intellectualism, his contempt for democracy, his primitivism, and his glorification of youth and power. One critic, writing anonymously in a 1940 issue of *The New Republic,* dismissed a contemporary English translation of *Den sidste Glaede: Skildringer (Look Back on Happiness)* as "Nazi-Nordic moonshine at its dullest"—this though the novel was originally published in 1912. Critics have traced many of the controversial aspects of Hamsun's thought to the influence of Arthur Schopenhauer, August Strindberg, and Nietzsche, whose philosophies are reflected in Hamsun's pessimism and exaltation of the amoral individual, as well as his recurrent expression of disdain for women and for Great Britain.

Although the question of Hamsun's totalitarian tendencies continues to be discussed, in recent years English and American critics have focused on more traditional thematic and technical aspects of Hamsun's works, a critical trend occasioned perhaps by the passage of time and the ongoing retranslation and reissuing of Hamsun's major novels, begun during the mid-1960s. Hamsun is today highly praised for his skill at characterization and setting, as well as for the effective experimental technique of his early novels. Cited by the German critic Paul Fechter as "the first of the great twentieth-century modernists," Hamsun has been called Norway's greatest literary figure after Ibsen, and acknowledged as a major influence on the work of many of the twentieth-century's most prominent writers.

(See also *TCLC,* Vol. 2 and *Contemporary Authors,* Vol. 104.)

PRINCIPAL WORKS

Fra det moderne Amerikas aandsliv (essays) 1889
[*The Cultural Life of Modern America,* 1969]

Sult (novel) 1890
[*Hunger,* 1899]
Mysterier (novel) 1892
[*Mysteries,* 1927]
Ny Jord (novel) 1893
[*Shallow Soil,* 1914]
Redaktør Lynge (novel) 1893
Pan, af Løitnant Thomas Glahns papirer (novel) 1894
[*Pan,* 1920]
Ved rigets port: Forspil (drama) 1895
Livets spil (drama) 1896
Siesta (short stories) 1897
Aftenrøde (drama) 1898
Victoria: En kaerligheds historie (novel) 1898
[*Victoria,* 1923]
Munken Vendt (drama) 1902
Dronning Tamara (drama) 1904
Svaermere (novel) 1904
[*Dreamers,* 1921; also published as *Mothwise,* 1921]
Under høstsjernen (novel) 1906
[*Under the Autumn Star,* published in *Wanderers,* 1922; also published in *The Wanderer,* 1975]
Benoni (novel) 1908
Rosa: Af student Parelius' papirer (novel) 1908
[*Rosa,* 1926]
En vandrer spiller med sordin (novel) 1909
[*A Wanderer Plays on Muted Strings,* published in *Wanderers,* 1922; also published in *The Wanderer,* 1975]
Livet ivold (drama) 1910
[*In the Grip of Life,* 1924]
Den sidste Glaede: Skildringer (novel) 1912
[*Look Back on Happiness,* 1940]
Børn av tiden (novel) 1913
[*Children of the Age,* 1924]
Segelfoss by (novel) 1915
[*Segelfoss Town,* 1925]
Markens Grøde (novel) 1917
[*Growth of the Soil,* 1920]
Konerne ved vandposten (novel) 1920
[*The Women at the Pump,* 1928]
Siste kapitel (novel) 1923
[*Chapter the Last,* 1929]
Landstrykere (novel) 1927
[*Vagabonds,* 1930; also published as *Wayfarers,* 1980]
August (novel) 1930
[*August,* 1931]
Men livet lever (novel) 1933
[*The Road Leads On,* 1934]
Ringen sluttet (novel) 1936
[*The Ring Is Closed,* 1937]
Paa gjengrodde stier (memoirs) 1949
[*On Overgrown Paths,* 1967]

FREDERIC TABER COOPER (essay date 1914)

[*An American educator, biographer, and editor, Cooper served for many years as literary critic at* The Bookman, *a popular early twentieth-century literary magazine. In the following excerpt from a review of several books by various authors, Cooper turns from an appraisal of H. A. Mitchell Keays's novel* Mrs. Brand *to offer lukewarm praise for Hamsun's* Shallow Soil.]

Murder and suicide and a woman hovering on the brink of dishonour would be a fairly adequate definition of the book we have just been discussing; and suicide and dishonour are also leading ingredients of the volume next in order, ***Shallow Soil,*** translated from the Norwegian of Knut Hamsun. Yet to put the chief emphasis on this aspect of the volume would be to do it serious injustice. The author's main intent is to satirise existing social conditions in Norway, where it would seem,—at least if we are to accept the vivid and diverting picture that he draws,—that the younger literary and artistic circles are taken, both by themselves and by others, with a most portentous seriousness, while the merchant class, the real backbone of the country, is held up to contempt and ridicule, and tolerated only so long as it good-naturedly pays for extravagant suppers and other social diversions of impecunious poets and journalists. Even a reader with no personal experience of Norwegian life feels instinctively that the author's special brand of satire verges upon broad caricature, and at times one suspects that this whole picture of a Scandinavian Bohemia is a *roman à clef,* in which more than one portrait has been drawn with a certain amount of personal animosity. Unless we make allowance for exaggeration, it becomes impossible to understand how the delicate plants of literature and art could have put forth such a flourishing growth from such exceedingly shallow intellectual soil. Nevertheless, there are just a few unforgettable things in this volume. . . . The book is sadly uneven, but there are moments in it of monumental bigness. (p. 326)

Frederic Taber Cooper, "The Accustomed Manner and Some Recent Novels," in The Bookman, *New York, Vol. XXXIX, No. 3, May, 1914, pp. 320-28.**

EDWIN BJÖRKMAN (essay date 1920)

[*Björkman was a Swedish-American novelist and critic who, through his translations, introduced American readers to the works of such major Scandinavian authors as August Strindberg, Bjørnstjerne Bjørnson, and Georg Brandes. In the following excerpt from his introduction to* Hunger, *Björkman offers a survey of Hamsun's career to-date.*]

Since the death of Ibsen and Strindberg, Hamsun is undoubtedly the foremost creative writer of the Scandinavian countries. Those approaching most nearly to his position are probably Selma Lagerlöf in Sweden and Henrik Pontoppidan in Denmark. Both these, however, seem to have less than he of that width of outlook, validity of interpretation and authority of tone that made the greater masters what they were. (p. iii)

[One] might expect him to prove a man of the masses, full of keen social consciousness. Instead, he must be classed as an individualistic romanticist and a highly subjective aristocrat, whose foremost passion in life is violent, defiant deviation from everything average and ordinary. He fears and flouts the dominance of the many, and his heroes, who are nothing but slightly varied images of himself, are invariably marked by an originality of speech and action that brings them close to, if not across, the borderline of the eccentric.

In all the literature known to me, there is no writer who appears more ruthlessly and fearlessly himself, and the self thus presented to us is as paradoxical and rebellious as it is poetic and picturesque. (pp. iii-iv)

The Northland, with its glaring lights and black shadows, its unearthly joys and abysmal despairs, is present and dominant in every line that Hamsun ever wrote. In that country his best tales and dramas are laid. By that country his heroes are stamped wherever they roam. Out of that country they draw their principal claims to probability. Only in that country do they seem quite at home. Today we know, however, that the pathological case represents nothing but an extension of perfectly normal tendencies. In the same way we know that the miraculous atmosphere of the Northland serves merely to develop and emphasize traits that lie slumbering in men and women everywhere. And on this basis the fantastic figures created by Hamsun relate themselves to ordinary humanity as the microscopic enlargement of a cross section to the living tissues. What we see is true in everything but proportion.

The artist and the vagabond seem equally to have been in the blood of Hamsun from the very start. Apprenticed to a shoemaker, he used his scant savings to arrange for the private printing of a long poem and a short novel produced at the age of eighteen, when he was still signing himself Knud Pedersen Hamsund. This done, he abruptly quit his apprenticeship and entered on that period of restless roving through trades and continents which lasted until his first real artistic achievement with **"Hunger,"** in 1888-90. It has often been noted that practically every one of Hamsun's heroes is of the same age as he was then, and that their creator takes particular pain to accentuate this fact. It is almost as if, during those days of feverish literary struggle, he had risen to heights where he saw things so clearly that no subsequent experience could add anything but occasional details.

Before he reached those heights, he had tried life as coal-heaver and school teacher, as road-mender and surveyor's attendant, as farm hand and streetcar conductor, as lecturer and free-lance journalist, as tourist and emigrant. . . . [While in America,] he failed utterly to establish any sympathetic contact between himself and the new world, and his first book after his return in 1888 was a volume of studies named **"The Spiritual Life of Modern America,"** which a prominent Norwegian critic once described as "a masterpiece of distorted criticism." But I own a copy of this book, the fly-leaf of which bears the following inscription in the author's autograph:

"A youthful work. It has ceased to represent my opinion of America. May 28, 1903. Knut Hamsun."

In its original form, **"Hunger"** was merely a sketch, and as such it appeared in 1888 in a Danish literary periodical, "New Earth." It attracted immediate widespread attention to the author, both on account of its unusual theme and striking form. It was a new kind of realism that had nothing to do with photographic reproduction of details. It was a professedly psychological study that had about as much in common with the old-fashioned conceptions of man's mental activities as the delirious utterances of a fever patient. It was life, but presented in the impressionistic temper of a Gauguin or Cezanne. (pp. v-vii)

It was followed two years later by **"Mysteries,"** which pretends to be a novel, but which may be better described as a delightfully irresponsible and defiantly subjective roaming through any highway or byway of life or letters that happened to take the author's fancy at the moment of writing. Some one has said of that book that in its abrupt swingings from laughter to tears, from irreverence to awe, from the ridiculous to the sublime, one finds the spirits of Dostoyevski and Mark Twain blended.

The novels **"Editor Lynge"** and **"New Earth,"** both published in 1893, were social studies of Christiania's Bohemia and chiefly characterized by their violent attacks on the men and women exercising the profession which Hamsun had just made his own. Then came **"Pan"** in 1894, and the real Hamsun, the Hamsun who ever since has moved logically and with increasing authority to **"The Growth of the Soil,"** stood finally revealed. It is a novel of the Northland, almost without a plot, and having its chief interest in a primitively spontaneous man's reactions to a nature so overwhelming that it makes mere purposeless existence seem a sufficient end in itself. . . . It is a wonderful paean to untamed nature and to the forces let loose by it within the soul of man.

Like most of the great writers over there, Hamsun has not confined himself to one poetic mood or form, but has tried all of them. From the line of novels culminating in **"Pan,"** he turned suddenly to the drama, and in 1895 appeared his first play, **"At the Gates of the Kingdom."** It was the opening drama of a trilogy and was followed by **"The Game of Life"** in 1896 and **"Sunset Glow"** in 1898. The first play is laid in Christiania, the second in the Northland, and the third in Christiania again. The hero of all three is Ivar Kareno, a student and thinker who is first presented to us at the age of 29, then at 39, and finally at 50. . . . Hamsun's ironical humor and whimsical manner of expression do more than the plot itself to knit the plays into an organic unit, and several of the characters are delightfully drawn, particularly the two women who play the greatest part in Kareno's life: his wife Eline, and Teresita, who is one more of his many feminine embodiments of the passionate and changeable Northland nature. Any attempt to give a political tendency to the trilogy must be held wasted. Characteristically, Kareno is a sort of Nietzschean rebel against the victorious majority, and Hamsun's seemingly cynical conclusions stress man's capacity for action rather than the purposes toward which that capacity may be directed.

Of three subsequent plays, [**"Vendt the Monk," "Queen Tamara,"** and **"At the Mercy of Life,"**], the first mentioned is by far the most remarkable. It is a verse drama in eight acts, centred about one of Hamsun's most typical vagabond heroes. The monk Vendt has much in common with Peer Gynt without being in any way an imitation or a duplicate. He is a dreamer in revolt against the world's alleged injustice, a rebel against the very powers that invisibly move the universe, and a passionate lover of life who in the end accepts it as a joyful battle and then dreams of the long peace to come. The vigor and charm of the verse proved a surprise to the critics when the play was published, as Hamsun until then had given no proof of any poetic gift in the narrower sense.

From 1897 to 1912 Hamsun produced a series of volumes that simply marked a further development of the tendencies shown in his first novels. . . . (pp. vii-x)

The later part of this output seemed to indicate a lack of development, a failure to open up new vistas, that caused many to fear that the principal contributions of Hamsun already lay behind him. Then appeared in 1913 a big novel, **"Children of the Time,"** which in many ways struck a new note, although led up to by **"Rosa"** and **"Benoni."** The horizon is now wider, the picture broader. There is still a central figure, and still he possesses many of the old Hamsun traits, but he has crossed the meridian at last and become an observer rather than a fighter and doer. Nor is he the central figure to the same extent as Lieutenant Glahn in **"Pan"** or Kareno in the trilogy. The life pictured is the life of a certain spot of ground—Segelfoss manor, and later the town of Segelfoss—rather than that of one or two isolated individuals. One might almost say that Hamsun's vision has become social at last, were it not for his continued accentuation of the irreconcilable conflict between the individual and the group.

"Segelfoss Town" in 1915 and **"The Growth of the Soil"** —the title ought to be "The Earth's Increase"—in 1918 continue along the path Hamsun entered by **"Children of the Time."** The scene is laid in his beloved Northland, but the old primitive life is going—going even in the outlying districts, where the pioneers are already breaking ground for new permanent settlements. Business of a modern type has arrived, and much of the quiet humor displayed in these the latest and maturest of Hamsun's works springs from the spectacle of its influence on the natives, whose hands used always to be in their pockets, and whose credulity in face of the improbable was only surpassed by their unwillingness to believe anything reasonable. Still the life he pictures is largely primitive, with nature as man's chief antagonist, and to us of the crowded cities it brings a charm of novelty rarely found in books today. With it goes an understanding of human nature which is no less deep-reaching because it is apt to find expression in whimsical or flagrantly paradoxical forms.

Hamsun has just celebrated his sixtieth birthday anniversary. . . . There is every reason to expect from him works that may not only equal but surpass the best of his production so far. But even if such expectations should prove false, the body of his work already accomplished is such, both in quantity and quality, that he must perforce be placed in the very front rank of the world's living writers. To the English-speaking world he has so far been made known only through the casual publication at long intervals of a few of his books: **"Hunger," "Victoria"** and **"Shallow Soil"** (rendered in the list above as **"New Earth"**). . . . [The American and English publics] may safely look to Hamsun as a thinker as well as a poet and laughing dreamer, provided they realize from the start that his thinking is suggestive rather than conclusive, and that he never meant it to be anything else. (pp. xi-xiii)

Edwin Björkman, in an introduction to Hunger *by Knut Hamsun, translated by George Egerton, Alfred A. Knopf, 1920, pp. iii-xiii.*

KATHERINE MANSFIELD (essay date 1920)

[*Mansfield was an important pioneer in stream-of-consciousness literature and one of the first English authors whose fiction depends upon incident rather than plot, a development which significantly influenced the modern short story form. Throughout 1919 and 1920, Mansfield conducted a weekly book-review column in* The Athenaeum, *a magazine edited at the time by her husband, John Middleton Murry. In the following excerpt from one of her* Athenaeum *reviews, published in issue No. 4702, June 11, 1920, Mansfield praises* Growth of the Soil.]

It is difficult to account for the fact that **'Growth of the Soil,'** the latest novel by the famous Norwegian writer, is only the second of his works to be translated into English. Knut Hamsun is no longer young; he has fulfilled his early promise and his reputation is assured, and yet, except for **'Shallow Soil,'** which was published some years ago, we have had nothing but the echo of his fame to feed upon. Perhaps this is not wholly lamentable. How often we find ourselves wishing that we had the books of some writer we treasure to read for the first time, and if the novel before us is typical of Knut Hamsun's work—as we have every reason to believe it is—there is a feast before us. (pp. 211-12)

If **'Growth of the Soil'** can be said to have any plot at all—any story—it is the very ancient one of man's attempt to live in fellowship with Nature. It is a trite saying when we are faced with a book which does renew for us the wonder and the thrill of that attempt that never was there a time when its message was more needed. But solitude is no cure for sorrow, and virgin country will not make anyone forget the desolation he has seen. Such a life is only possible for a man like the hero, Isak, a man who has known no other and can imagine none. Nevertheless, there remains in the hearts of nearly all of us an infinite delight in reading of how the track was made, the bush felled, the log hut built, so snug and warm with its great chimney and little door, and of how there were animals to be driven to the long pastures, goats and sheep and a red and white cow. In the opening chapter of **'Growth of the Soil,'** Knut Hamsun gives us the picture of an immense wild landscape, and there is a track running through it, and we spy a man walking towards the north carrying a sack. . . . The man is Isak. It is extraordinary, how, while we follow him in his search for the land he wants, the author gives us the man. His slowness and simplicity, his immense strength and determination, even his external appearance, short, sturdy, with a red beard sticking out, and a frown that is not anger, are as familiar as if we had known him in our childhood. It is, indeed, very much as though we were allowed to hold him by the hand and go with him everywhere. The place is found; the hut is built, and a woman called Inger comes from over the hills and lives with him. Gradually, but deeply and largely, their life grows and expands. We are taken into it and nothing is allowed to escape us, and just as we accepted Isak so everything seems to fall into place without question. **'Growth of the Soil'** is one of those few novels in which we seem to escape from ourselves and to take an invisible part. We suddenly find to our joy that we are walking into the book as Alice walked into the looking-glass and the author's country is ours. It is wonderfully rich, satisfying country, and of all those who dwell in it, gathered round the figures of Isak and Inger, there is not one who does not live. At the end Isak is an old man and his life is ebbing, but the glow, the warmth of the book seems to linger. We feel, as we feel with all great novels, that nothing is over. (pp. 212-13)

Katherine Mansfield, "A Norwegian Novel," in her Novels and Novelists, *edited by J. Middleton Murry, Alfred A. Knopf, 1930, pp. 211-13.*

JOSEF WIEHR (essay date 1921-22)

[*In the following excerpt, Wiehr divides Hamsun's career into three periods and discusses the characteristics of theme and character in each of the three phases.*]

The life-work of Knut Hamsun comprises three periods. The first extends to and includes ***Munken Vendt.*** This drama constitutes the culmination and summing up of all those tendencies which characterize the earlier part of the author's career. The typical hero of this group of works is the young man of thirty who is at odds with existence in general and with society and its standards and values in particular, and who violently rebels against existing conditions. There is a great deal of similarity in the psychological make-up and even in the external circumstances and experiences of these individuals. They are without home or definite place in society, the conventions and restrictions of which they disregard, chiefly because their lack of polish, resulting from social contact, makes adjustment impossible for them, although they try to persuade themselves and us that social intercourse is insincere and built upon sheer humbug and sham. A mania for complete independence is also common to them, the price they pay for it is isolation and failure. They are ardent and constant lovers, but not one of them wins the woman of his affections. The most precious factors in their emotional lives are the admirations and the longings which they cherish, and the memories which, with them, never fade. The inner life, not outward reality, is for this type of chief, in fact, of sole importance. But the outside world, nevertheless, exercises a very strong influence upon them. Being one and all sensitive to a high degree of irritability, they respond violently to all outside impressions; the reaction is often wholly out of proportion to the external cause.

These young men are governed by impulses of a very irrational and compelling nature. The inhibitions of the normal individual do not exist for them, though regret frequently follows almost immediately upon their erratic conduct. It results from the fact that, in spite of all outward disdain, they cannot dispense with social contact. Since they are entirely governed by impulses, originating from the ever changing environmental influences, the permanent in their personalities, i.e., character, is often obscured to such a degree that it seems to be lacking. As a matter of fact, all the individuals of this type are really possessed of very strong will-power, which, however, is not directed to the attainment of those ends which are generally recognized as desirable. Because they neglect to strive for worldly success, sacrificing it for the sake of their independence, and, due to the great variety of external influences and impressions, behave in a very inconsistent and often contradictory manner, they appear weak and vacillating to the superficial observer.

They ignore all moral questions and acknowledge no moral obligations, but their lofty pride and self-respect protect them against debasement; they do not even allow themselves the same latitude which they accord to others, whose transgressions of various kinds they view with a great deal of indulgence. Their ideal is the intellectual and ethical aristocrat, the man who stands above all laws imposed by society upon its members, precisely because he is governed by superior insight and ethical principles far more exacting than those commonly subscribed to by the rest of mankind. This does, however, not preclude violations of accepted moral standards.

In its attitude towards humanity, this type is highly individualistic and anti-social. Indifference to, if not contempt for, all cultural values of the present age is characteristic of it. Real grandeur and genuine beauty and culture are not to be found in our times according to these iconoclasts. The ruling spirit of the age, that of democracy, is inimical to true culture, they hold, and the leaders of the masses are destitute of originality, nobility, and greatness. Democracy they regard with disgust, because of its real or supposed tendency to reduce all men to a common level, which, of necessity, spells mediocrity. Hence the contempt of Hamsun's favorite type for the masses. There has been an intimate connection between the rise of democracy and industrialism. The organized industrial laborer is the chief exponent of democracy; this is the main reason for the unfavorable verdict pronounced upon our modern economic development; that it has physical and moral decline in its wake is another.

In their efforts to escape from the disconcerting turmoil of life, Hamsun's heroes seek to achieve the closest communion with nature in its more primitive state. Their love of nature, as well as their other characteristics, they share with the author, who has remained ever loyal to it, though his attitude towards it has undergone a certain change. All the earlier works of Hamsun are highly subjective and full of personal elements; Hamsun has depicted himself in them from many different angles. That is one of the reasons why he, almost without exception, chose a man for the central figure, though he has drawn a number of women characters in the first group of his works with great care and in detail. He is fond of two opposite types: one, proud, disdainful, and coquettish; the other, simple, naive, and self-effacing. His heroes are usually attracted by two women of such divergent character. The poems of Hamsun, which were published in collected form two years after ***Munken Vendt,*** belong in the very nature of the case to the first period, during which they originated. Although few in number, they cover a wide range of emotional experiences and indicate a progressive emancipation of the poet's own self from external influences that have caused him torment.

The productions of the next ten years, which may be said to constitute the second period, are of a somewhat heterogeneous character. A change in the attitude of the author towards life becomes manifest in ***Svaermere,*** which must be grouped with ***Benoni*** and ***Rosa.*** While not objective in the strict sense of the word, the personal elements have disappeared, no note of revolt is struck, and the lives of the main characters do not end in failures. ***Under Høststjaernen*** and ***En Vanderer spiller med Sordin*** belong together because of their contents; but in the former, the main theme is the hopeless infatuation of a man in his forties, in the latter, it is the tragic fate of Lovise Falkenberg. This is the only instance where Hamsun deals with the emotional experiences of a woman who has been married for years, in all other cases he depicts only the spring time of love. To be sure, Adelheid Holmsen might be included here, but the author does, in this instance, barely touch the surface of things. An element common to the two novels mentioned above is the praise of the simple life led by the tillers of the soil. Nature is extolled as the great consoler as before, but treated more objectively. It exercises, however, the same mystic influence upon the author as previously.

Livet ivold deals with city life, and if we accept the musician Fredriksen's estimate of it, we need not wonder that Hamsun dislikes, if not detests it. There are some splendid passages in ***Ny Jord*** referring to the toilers of the city, which seemed to contain the promise of a more elaborate treatment of this subject by Hamsun, but probably because of his aversion to industrialism, which dominates to a large extent the lives of the humble and poor in the city, he has not made it the theme of any of his works. Only three of his novels and three plays have their settings in the city at all. Most of Hamsun's productions belong to the category of *Heimatkunst* [*folk art*]. (pp. 120-23)

In ***Den siste Glaede*** the personal element is once more of paramount importance. While the author calmly accepts his own lot, he cannot forbear to wield his cudgel against certain tendencies of the time which seem to him of a most harmful nature. The tone of regret over the decline of his powers so pronounced in this narrative certainly did not prepare the world for his achievements during the sixth decade of his life, which comprises the third and, in most respects, the greatest period of his activity.

The four great novels which he produced since 1912 have the feature in common that the personal element is not brought in directly. Although the pictures here presented are strongly tinged by the author's point of view and accompanied by copious comment, they afford a fair insight into the present-day life in

Nordland; the same may be said of several works of the preceding period, they deal, however, with conditions of two generations ago.

We may well apply to these novels Zola's definition: "*Une oeuvre d'art est un coin de la nature vu à travers un tempérament*" ["A work of art is a corner of nature seen through a temperament"]. But the "temperament," i.e., the individuality of the author, the personal equation, is, in the case of Hamsun, a weighty factor, for which large allowances must be made.

Børn av Tiden presents the decline and fall of an aristocrat of the old school, who is submerged by the tide of progress; the sequel shows the deterioration of a once so simple community under the influence of advancing industrialism, while in ***Markens Grøde*** the author extols the heroism of the pioneer. In these works there is a didactic purpose, but in ***Konerne ved Vandposten,*** Hamsun was contented to portray life as he sees it; although comment by the author is not lacking, the reader is called upon to formulate his own conclusions.

Knut Hamsun has dealt more than any other novelist with the people and the conditions in *Nordland,* for which he harbors a deep affection because of the comparative absence of civilization, the naïveté and simplicity of the people, and the plainness of their lives. In point of time, he limits himself almost wholly to the present and recent past. Only in ***Munken Vendt*** he dates the events earlier than the middle of the nineteenth century. ***Dronning Tamara*** does, of course, not figure here. His early tenets he has changed but little, only his attitude towards existing conditions has become more tolerant. The classes which he dislikes most are the intellectuals, authors and artists included—the emancipated woman and the bureaucracy really come also under this head—the old, backward peasant stock, and the very antipode of it, the industrial laborer. Why he should find fault with the peasant, who tenaciously clings to the old, time-honored mode of life, is not quite apparent, considering Hamsun's general attitude. But on the one hand, he hates stagnation, it is better that we should move, even if we are headed in the wrong direction; the fulness of life consists for him in the maximum of action. On the other hand, the peasant has really become infected by modern conditions and has lost many of his old virtues, while he firmly adheres to his old faults and vices, and "stagnation" is for Hamsun almost a synonym for "death."

His aversion to industrialism results from his anti-democratic spirit and the conviction that the industrial life impairs the stamina of the people. Democracy and industrialism are perhaps nowhere more highly developed than in England and the United States, and this fact accounts largely for Hamsun's antipathy against all things English or American. As in other matters, there has been no change in his views. He has not abandoned any of his convictions, and if to-day he stands on a pedestal, it is not because he has compromised or made any concessions. Intellectual and cultural pursuits seem to him worthless, in part, because the things striven for are in themselves without real value, in part, because the actual attainments are mediocre. Intellectualism is for him, moreover, inimical to the highest possible development of the individual. He derides it in spite of his admiration for culture and his longing for poetic beauty.

Since he claims that the past was far greater than the present is, it may seem strange that he never attempted the treatment of a great historical character. But this would have involved the absorption and utilization of a great deal of material already in existence and produced by others, a task which might well seem superfluous to him. His fertile imagination and the life about him afforded him more interesting and valuable themes, for in spite of his romanticism, Hamsun is intensely devoted to the realities of the present day.

He has produced a large number of highly original and interesting figures, but not a single great man or woman, for even Isac cannot be reckoned as great. Judged from the esthetic point of view, to be sure, he is of monumental proportions, and he strongly appeals to our sympathy in spite of the humble simplicity of his life.

Various critics maintain that Hamsun was greatly influenced, especially in regard to style, by a number of foreign authors. Dostojewsky, Mark Twain, and Bret Hart are the ones most frequently mentioned, but no exact investigation of this question has yet been made. There is one troublesome feature to be taken into account. The style of Hamsun constitutes in its perfection probably the greatest charm of his works, and it is always well attuned to the theme. And what a difference there is in the style, let us say, of ***Pan*** and ***Victoria*** as compared with that of ***Markens Grøde*** and ***Konerne ved Vandposten.*** The time element does not account for it, for it is almost as great in works that stand in close proximity to each other. There is, surely, a wide gap between the style of ***Markens Grøde*** and the novels which immediately preceded and followed this splendid prose epic.

Maurice Francis Egan writes in the August number of the American-Scandinavian Review for the year 1921: "It is regretable that translations from Scandinavian literature or history are not so popularly read as they might be. This is because they lack what the average American demands in all his books—cheerfulness, a touch of humor, and a lesson which will teach him to be more contented with life. (pp. 123-26)

"Our taste is eclectic. *Shores Acres* and *Way Down East* appeal to us when Strindberg and Hauptmann and Ibsen rather bore us; but given any foreign novel or drama with intense human interest, which carries with it the triumph of a moral idea, and to a man we will read it with pleasure."

It is just this absence of "the triumph of a moral idea" which will stand most in the way of any popularity of Hamsun's works with the great majority of American readers. For him, morals are "the least human element in man," and he is more attracted by the sinner than by the saint, because of the seemingly larger store of energy and vitality usually manifested in the former. His views in regard to sexual questions would particularly offend American readers. It must, however, be remembered that Hamsun unconditionally condemns all frivolity, licentiousness, and perversity—not really on moral grounds, but because they result in racial deterioration. While he does not admit it, he, in the last analysis, finds morals essential to the good of the race. In his tolerance towards offences resulting from strong, healthy, and normal appetites, he goes, however, very far.

Hamsun's attitude towards Christianity is in itself even more objectionable, but it will give less offence, since it is not as manifest on every page of his works as his lack of morals. Radical utterances are virtually confined to ***Sult,*** where their force is lessened by the irresponsibility of the character in question, to ***Munken Vendt,*** and a number of the poems. The shafts aimed at Reverend L. Lassen, it should be remembered, are directed not at the minister of the Gospel, but at the official of the state. (p. 126)

The clergy of the state church find themselves in the awkward position resulting from dual allegiance, and it is not at all surprising that with many of them the temporal affairs usurp the lion's share of their time and attention. The whole system has been criticised by some of the foremost authors of modern Norway. As usual, Hamsun presents only isolated facts and figures without really entering upon the problem. He has penetrated a little more deeply into it than ordinarily in his portrayal of the bureaucracy of the country, but here, too, the picture of the situation is far from complete. (p. 127)

It has been charged against Hamsun that his ideas are not constructive. While perfectly true, this criticism is, in a manner, ill-advised. Hamsun makes no secret of it that in his opinion there are already too many "constructive ideas" in this world, why should he augment their number? His program is, moreover, so simple that it requires no elaborate constructive ideas. Work to the full extent of your capacity at some productive task, seeking your joy in its performance, perpetuate your kind, keep close to nature, regard life as a loan conferred upon you, as a boon to which you have no claim whatsoever, bear its vicissitudes bravely and manfully, preserve at all hazards the dignity of your own soul, and meet death fearlessly in the conviction that it is a beneficent provision of nature, that is the whole gospel which he has tried to preach.

The return to a simpler mode of life, that of the tiller of the soil, seems to him the remedy for the present ills of humanity. But people will not and cannot follow the road which he points out. Only upheavals and catastrophes of inconceivable magnitude could bring about the conditions which Hamsun extols as the only sane and natural ones. (pp. 127-28)

But did Hamsun desire to point out the way to all the nations of the globe, or did he address his exhortations to the smaller circle of which he himself is a member? Hamsun's own fellow countrymen, more particularly the people of *Norland,* and, in a general way, all the so-called backward nations, are in a much better position to follow his advice than the millions that populate the countries leading the world in industries. As has been stated before, much of Hamsun's art is *Heimatkunst.*

In the end, there is no cause for pessimism. As Hamsun says in his latest novel: "Things go on just the same, all of them and some of them, indeed, go well. What is best of all, we do not know." He has spoken many a harsh word and has fought obstinately for his ideas and convictions, but he is aware of the relativity of the truths which he proclaims. (pp. 128-29)

Josef Wiehr, "Knut Hamsun: His Personality and His Outlook upon Life," in Smith College Studies in Modern Languages Special Issue: Knut Hamsun, *Vol. III, Nos. 1 & 2, October, 1921-January, 1922, pp. 1-130.*

REBECCA WEST (essay date 1922)

[*West is considered one of the foremost English novelists and critics to write during the twentieth century. Born Cecily Isabel Fairfield, she began her career as an actress—taking the name Rebecca West from the emancipated heroine of Henrik Ibsen's drama* Rosmersholm*—and as a book reviewer for* The Freewoman. *Her early criticism was noted for its militantly feminist stance and its reflection of West's Fabian socialist concerns. Her first novel,* The Return of the Soldier *(1918), evidences a concern that entered into much of her later work: the psychology of the individual. West's greatest works include* The Meaning of Treason *(1947), which analyzes the motives of Britain's wartime traitors—notably, William Joyce ("Lord Haw-Haw")—and* Black Lamb and Grey Falcon *(1942), a record of the author's 1937 journey through Yugoslavia. West's literary criticism is noted for its wit, aversion to cant, and perceptiveness. In the following excerpt from a highly favorable review of* The Wanderers, *West compares and contrasts Hamsun's thought and technique with that of Anatole France.*]

In ***Wanderers*** Knut Hamsun has made such an extension of our knowledge of the relationship between men and women as Anatole France made in *Le Lys Rouge* or *Histoire Comique*. There is, of course, the extremest difference in personality and literary environment. One thinks of M. France as sitting down to some glossy, tidied desk and faced by a vase of bright fresh flowers, writing with pains and yet with ease, whereas one feels that Knut Hamsun writes profusely but against a handicap of physical inaptitude, that as likely as not he upsets a bottle of ink on the carpet for each novel he writes. M. France's characters, dismissed to liberty in the finish of their story, would go elegantly whatever their sorrows might have been, to lunch at Armenonville; Knut Hamsun's characters, similarly liberated, would choose to take a walk (the female doubtless clad in one of those Scandinavian tartan skirts) among the dark pillars of a fir forest and listen to the soughing of its branches in the winter wind that sends the geese flying south. But they both have the same interest in the relationship between men and women that springs from something in them quite embarrassingly ordinary, but which is turned into something quite extraordinary by their contempt (suave on M. France's part, bickering and guffawing on Hamsun's) for the respectable, and the romantic, points of view, and by their hunger for some beauty that will survive the touch of their own irony. This takes both of them strange journeys, reports of which are not acceptable to the common man; for to those who wish to be assured that life is not a mockery of those who have to live it, it is nearly as necessary to believe that the relationship between men and women is fundamentally benign, as to others to believe that death is the portal of a kinder world. The truths, bleak as anything in Ecclesiastes, which lie behind *Le Lys Rouge* and *Histoire Comique* make the reader resent the wit and sensuous loveliness that decoyed him into contact with this intolerable view of destiny. Yet these books endure because of their beauty, which is above all pleasantness. ***Wanderers,*** too, will make its enemies, for it is a sad book which aches like regret itself. But it will endure, because it also has that beauty. (p. 97)

This is, in its way, as wise a book as ***Growth of the Soil,*** though it is not so tremendous. It has that same special quality of sagacity about development. Knut Hamsun knows that people change, which is a fact of life that many quite great authors ignore; even among the creations of Balzac one is sometimes disturbed by an unnatural fixity of character which withstands the passage of decades. Hamsun knows also how they change. He can tell how this or that soul will weather, just as if he were a man and they different sorts of stone. He is one of the wisest of the great Europeans. (p. 98)

Rebecca West, in a review of "Wanderers," in New Statesman, *Vol. XIX, No. 472, April 29, 1922, pp. 97-8.*

EDWIN MUIR (essay date 1923)

[*Muir was a distinguished Scottish novelist, poet, critic, and translator. With his wife Willa, he translated works by various German authors unfamiliar to the English-speaking world, including Gerhart Hauptmann, Hermann Broch, and, most notably, Franz Kafka. Throughout his career, Muir was intrigued by psychoanalytic theory, particularly Freud's analyses of dreams and Jung's theories of archetypal imagery, both of which he often utilized in his work. In his critical writings, Muir was more concerned with the general philosophical issues raised by works of art—such as the nature of time or society—than with the particulars of the work itself, such as style or characterization. In the following excerpt from his review of* Victoria, *Muir examines similarities between Hamsun's works and those of Robert Burns and Thomas Hardy, judging Hamsun to be Hardy's successor as a master of characterization and for his understanding of human nature.*]

There is probably no one writing at present who has a more assured status as a great writer than Knut Hamsun. He is the imaginative artist of the present day who gives the fullest and most satisfying sense of natural power, of an imaginative empire over life, easy, unembarrassed, without inhibition, flowing spontaneously into a form which, defined and harmonious to an unusual degree, yet has the appearance of a natural growth, a natural happening. No one, while appearing so casual, secures so infallibly all the virtues, and more, which artistic deliberation sets out to achieve. Of peasant birth, with a training as far removed as possible from the systematic and the academic, he possesses a power which in its quality is not unlike that of another peasant whose culture was picked up in an unusual way, Burns: the power of speaking in such a voice that what he says seems at the same time to be literature and nature. Like Burns, too, he is by the combined force of unregenerate human nature and of imagination invigoratingly free from inhibitions and prejudices; and his temper, more fundamentally if less obviously emancipated than that of any other writer of our day, is emancipated not by virtue of an intellectual conquest, but by that of his original nature and the attitude to the world which is given in it. There is no sense of tension in his liberty. To read him is to be given a free outlook on the world in the most delightful and the most fundamental way: through the imagination and, as it were, by the operation of nature herself. Spontaneity and form are united in him in a perfection which belongs only to those whose natural power is mighty, and yet whose nature has been neither distorted nor driven in upon itself. There are few writers who are at once so unembarrassed before life and who find so much beauty in life. Before nature Hamsun is a piece of nature; before humanity, even in those aspects of it which astonish or distress the greatest and the smallest writers, he is a piece of human nature. And being so organically knit to his subjectmatter, which is the earth and mankind upon it, he is most objective where he is most subjective, and in expressing himself seems to express all that unregenerate human nature which is so well-known to him.

"Victoria" is not one of his greatest novels, but it has on every page the mark of a great writer, and is one of those minor exercises which, in the sureness and ease with which everything is accomplished, sometimes give a more vivid sense of the power behind them than greater works do. It has a curious resemblance to **"Pan."** As there, the treatment is lyrical, episodic, and, one would say, were it not for the solidity of the touch, impressionistic. In both stories there is a hero with an infusion of nature so strong that it gives him a shade of coarseness (this coarseness one also enjoys), and a heroine who, in the degree of her femininity, can only be compared with those of Mr. Thomas Hardy. **"Pan"** was the tragedy of the man; **"Victoria"** is that of the woman; and the two novels might be regarded as variations on the same theme, or as complementary. It would be hard to render justice to the delicacy with which the story is managed, or to the truth which, without a disfiguring touch, shines through it. **"Victoria"** is one of the most exquisite of Hamsun's novels. If it has a fault it is that the ease of its movements seems at times to be too easy; the author could have weighted some of the scenes more than he has done; he might have sustained his imagination in a single episode longer than he has seen fit. The defect of the book, rich in smaller compensations, is that it is designed too deliberately to please, even to enchant. Hamsun piles one delightful episode upon another, always terminating them before there is any danger of our getting tired; and that is a method which, while it maintains the reader's pleasure continuously, is not serious enough to produce the emotion of great art. The book, then, is exquisite in the best and in the worst sense, rather than great. Nevertheless it contains, in spite of its shortness, half a dozen great scenes, scenes as good as Hamsun has ever written, and several characters who, sketched with a touch, with less than a touch, have a reality that is final and unmistakable. Hamsun's characterization is more economical than that of any except the very greatest writers; he has not to describe, he has, one almost believes, merely to name a character for him to stand before our eyes. With women he is best of all, and no one in modern times except Mr. Thomas Hardy equals him in the portrayal of them. Victoria and Camilla, both of them merely sketched, give that sense of a truth existing in them beyond the reach of observation or analysis which, like the creations of the highest imagination in poetry, has a touch of the occult. This gift of occult imagination, this final understanding of human nature, Hamsun has, now that Mr. Thomas Hardy has ceased to create, alone among living writers.

Edwin Muir, "A Great Writer," in The Freeman, *Vol. VII, No. 178, August 8, 1923, p. 522.*

HUGH WALPOLE (essay date 1927)

[*Walpole was among England's most popular novelists during the three decades preceding World War II. His skill at describing settings, his gift for conceiving interesting plots, his adherence to traditional novel forms in an age of experimentation, and his accessibility as a lecturer and public figure contributed to his wide readership in the United Kingdom and North America. In the following excerpt, Walpole uses a review of* Mysteries *as a springboard from which to express his dissatisfaction with many of Hamsun's works. Tracing the weaknesses of Hamsun's novels to the author's nihilistic world view, Walpole cites Hamsun's self-absorbed contempt for life as the central flaw in his literary theory.*]

Knut Hamsun is for most English and American writers the author of one book, and that book, of course, is **"Growth of the Soil."**

It stands out, indeed, in a curiously isolated position from the rest of his work; at any rate, as we know it. Were it not for **"Growth of the Soil"** one would say that Hamsun is among the ablest modern Scandinavian writers, but that nothing of his that we have seen gives him claims to genius. In these other works Hamsun's world is modern, morbid, introspective, tortured; his characters in books like **"Segelfoss Town"** and **"Shallow Soil"** have natures half fairy and half demonic, they appear and disappear murmuring incantations, malevolent like gnomes, shaggy like bears, and even when he clothes them in the strong, straight bodies of Scandinavian peasants they are liable at any moment to surrender inhumanly to some spell that is only half visible to ourselves. The truth is that in these other books Hamsun is saturated with himself; they tell us stories of other human beings, but never as emphatically as they recount his own moods; one can see him surrendering to his own creations for a moment and then suddenly caught by some mental disturbance that he gives us superimposed upon his story.

This is only to say that he has the modern novelist's malady of self-absorption. With the exception of his one great book, it seems to be impossible for him to conceive of some one more powerful than himself; Tolstoy's self-abnegation to Anna, Stendhal's to his Duchess, Flaubert's to Emma Bovary, Balzac's to Cousine Bette—this divine rising above self cannot be counted among the triumphs of the modern novel.

And this leads us in Hamsun's novels again and again to ask ourselves whether his personal company is worth our while; pleasant companion he is not, he would probably not wish to be, he has all that contempt for his reader that is common to the intellectual novelist of our period. He has also, let it in fairness be added, moods of contempt for himself, but here, as again with his contemporaries, he excuses himself by blaming life, which, of course, seems to him a misshapen, bungling confusion of futile effort. In novels like **"Segelfoss"** and **"Shallow Soil,"** however, it is his object to create a world outside himself; in novels like **"Pan," "Victoria"** and this book, **"Mysteries,"** he is a creator only of his own moods. In **"Segelfoss"** at least he did give us a world that was in a way external to himself, a world half Hans Andersen and half Dostoievsky. Its background is its principal charm; you feel that here every prospect pleases and only man is vile, and man is vile in a kind of infantile way; as though he were born cretin and it would have been better for everybody had he been strangled at birth. Behind these misshapen creatures the little fishing town, with its glittering bay, its twisted houses, its shops for odds and ends, its clear, sunny air, fresh winds and sparkling sun, is tempting and idyllic. Its serenity is forever clouded by the works of the devil, but the devil is half-hearted, as though he were an old man broken in years, with rheumatics and lumbago, bored with his evil deeds and wanting to be left alone. The beautiful heroines of these stories are always simple and innocent, like Faust's Marguerite; they are not led to heaven by a choir of angels simply because Hamsun doesn't believe in a heaven, and so they pass away in a kind of neurasthenic nostalgia.

Drama is forever beginning in these novels and is forever checked; that is only to say once again that they belong to our modern period. How, as one reads one clever modern novelist after another, does one long for some persistent action, not of necessity physical; the action of "The Golden Bowl" suffices. The later stories of Henry James offer a good parallel here, the spiritual action in these books may be on its physical side very slight, but on the spiritual side it is exceedingly active and never relaxed for an instant; the souls of Kate Croy, Maggie Verver, the Prince and the others are in mortal danger, and, if we believe in souls, we await with an almost passionate anxiety to know whether they will be rescued from the dragon or not. But, then, James in that is old-fashioned; reason for life was given to him by just that belief, and it is the trouble with the novels of Hamsun, Mr. Aldous Huxley, Mr. Sherwood Anderson and the rest that there is no reason for life, human beings are caught in a trap set by a malicious child who in an idle moment had nothing better to do.

Hamsun's case is the more interesting because in **"Growth of the Soil"** he touched quite another world. I don't know how he regards that book; it may be that like other authors he is exasperated by the constant public preference for one of his works over all the others, but one does ask oneself continually why, having once lived in such an air, he has apparently abandoned it for the rest of his days. In that great book his two characters move forever upward through a stern, unrelenting but marvelously beautiful landscape; there is nothing sentimental or weak in their progress; he asks us neither to pity nor applaud them; he offers them no mitigation and never for an instant intrudes upon their inevitable history his own personality. He has there, too, what all the great novelists have, a complete universe to which they belong; this universe transcends them so that it is true in one degree or another of all human effort, and we can apply their history to our own experience. Reading that book, we do not ask for any justification of life or whether there is another that follows it; after our experience of it our own lives are richer and more exciting.

This book **"Mysteries"** is apparently an early work belonging to the period of **"Pan"** and **"Victoria."** The hero is a dark uncertain figure entering the little town for no apparent reason, plunging at the end into the sea apparently from personal pique. He is a man whose life is mysterious simply because we are not told enough about it. If your hero knocks a man down on one page, gives a poor old woman some money on another and kisses a girl against her will on a third, these events are not of necessity mysterious, but become so if the novelist does not trouble to give us his psychological links. It is very easy for the novelist to say that the reader is stupid and should understand more than he is told; the reader is only too ready, nay eager, to understand, but if the novelist is lazy and expects the reader to be flattered by that laziness he is demanding too much. Hamsun would deny, of course, that he is lazy; his own psychological states are very clear to himself, or at any rate are clear at flashing moments; but he has created a figure who is definitely concerned with a certain sequence of events, and that sequence is either the novelist's own or it is not. It is of no use because he is on a morning out of temper with the world that his hero should also be out of temper, having on the page that he wrote yesterday been engaged quite happily in the pursuit of a lady, on the purchase of a ship or the beginning of an interesting journey. (pp. 1, 6)

What it comes to is that behind Hamsun's hero there has not been enough creative passion. This does not mean that in the book itself there are not scenes of great creative vigor; there is one scene toward the beginning of the novel which describes the bullying of a poor and defenseless man by a brutal and stupid one, which is tremendous in its power. This seems to be the prelude to a development of passionate feeling, but it leads to nothing. And it may be the author's exact purpose that it should lead to nothing; then in that case the very absence of consequence should itself be a consequence, but there is simply an idle withdrawal of the author from all participation in the affair.

What is really absent from the heart of this book and from the heart, I fancy, of very much modern fiction, English and American, can be better explained by comparison. It has happened that just before and just after the reading of this book I enjoyed once again the adventure of two old-fashioned but very fine romances; I say romances deliberately because they are romantic in their conception, their use of coincidence and their poetry. One of these was the "Smoke" of Turgenev, the other "The Woodlanders" of Thomas Hardy. . . . Many pages of "Smoke" are devoted to the most tiresome irony, and Turgenev lashes with almost hysterical scorn puppets who are never worth his anger. There is nothing in anything of Hamsun's so impossibly unreal as these pages of Turgenev's; they are contemporary pages like the files of old newspapers or the yellow pages of books resurrected from a forgotten drawer.

In "The Woodlanders" too there is a naïveté and innocence of which Hamsun in spite of his Hans Andersen interludes would disdain to be guilty. . . . When we think of Turgenev's amateur polemics and Hardy's innocent constructions Hamsun seems a grown man beside them. Why is it then that Turgenev and Hardy remain of gigantic stature and Hamsun, save in this one great book, is a mere man among men? There are perhaps many reasons, but I believe the principal one to be that both Turgenev and Hardy in their greater books are caught up into a passionate creation and at their finest moments are carried beyond all consciousness of themselves as deliberate artists away into regions far greater than their own human ones. The passionate love of the man and woman in "Smoke," the dumb and beautifully unconscious endurance of Marty South and Winterbourne in "The Woodlanders," arrive not through the taking of infinite pains nor through the personal reaction against life of their authors, but rather from an overwhelming unanalyzed consciousness of and sympathy with human nature at its most real.

We can disregard all the simplicities in Hardy because Marty South and Tess and Jude and Bathsheba Everdene are created with a fiery passion, but the figures in **"Pan"** and **"Victoria"** and **"Mysteries"** are reflections of Hamsun's own personal moods; remove Hamsun and they do not exist. But Tess and Jude were before Hardy came.

On the other hand, it would be foolish to pretend that the modern collections of autobiographical tempers presented as novels are not of value and interest, only you cannot have it both ways; if we are to have tea with Mr. Hamsun we shall have an interesting afternoon, because Mr. Hamsun is an interesting man, but his energetic and discontented presence will hinder our meeting anybody else; it will be a tête à tête.

And after all there is **"Growth of the Soil."** (p. 6)

Hugh Walpole, "Tete-a-Tete with Knut Hamsun," in New York Herald Tribune Books, *May 22, 1927, pp. 1, 6.*

CLIFTON P. FADIMAN (essay date 1929)

[*Fadiman became one of the most prominent American literary critics during the 1930s with his insightful and often caustic book reviews for* The Nation *and* The New Yorker *magazines. He also reached a sizeable audience through his work as a radio talk-show host from 1938 to 1948. In the following review, Fadiman favorably discusses* Chapter the Last, *comparing it to Thomas Mann's novel* The Magic Mountain, *which was published two years earlier.*]

The reader of Knut Hamsun's most recent production will notice at once that its setting and, to a degree, its theme are those of Thomas Mann's masterpiece, *The Magic Mountain*. With the exception of the peasant-hero (Hamsun's latest modification of his Isak of ***Growth of the Soil***) all the characters are either patients or officials in a large mountain sanitarium; and both Mann and Hamsun are interested in observing the effects of physical and mental disease on the human soul. Here the resemblance ends; for Mann is endeavoring to shadow forth the whole temper of pre-war Europe and also to interpret a complicated metaphysic of Time; whereas Hamsun's book is much simpler and less ambitious, though not less successful. He reverts in ***Chapter the Last*** to one of his favorite themes: the opposition between the peasant-soul and the citizen-soul, an opposition which, with him, always ends in the defeat of the latter in favor of what is direct and primitive. In this novel we watch the gradual change in the temperament of a superficially cultivated young business-woman as she turns inevitably to the good brute of the neighboring *saeter*. The story is enriched by a number of remarkable character-studies of her fellow patients—all doomed, Hamsun would imply, not merely by their illnesses but by their turning away from the simplicities of the soil and the elements.

Chapter the Last is rather more loosely constructed than any of Hamsun's previous narratives; but the qualities of large humanity, shrewd humor and profound perception are here in the degree to which he has accustomed us. At this date there is little more to be said about one who is so indubitably a great writer than he cannot sink below the level of almost continuous beauty and honesty. The least chapter in this relatively unpretentious novel puts to shame almost all contemporary American writing.

Clifton P. Fadiman, in a review of "Chapter the Last," in The Bookman, *New York, Vol. LXX, No. 3, November, 1929, p. 312.*

HENRY MILLER (letter date 1934)

[*An American novelist, essayist, and critic, Miller was one of the most controversial authors of the twentieth century. The ribaldry and eroticism of such works as* Tropic of Cancer *(1935) and* Tropic of Capricorn *(1939) made him perhaps the most censored major writer of all time. Many of Miller's best known works are autobiographical and describe the author's quest for truth and freedom as well as his rejection of modern civilization. Miller called himself "a holy old Untouchable" and wrote, according to Kenneth Rexroth, for those "to whom the values, the achievements, and the classics of the dominant civilization are meaningless and absurd." In the following excerpt from a letter to Anaïs Nin, Miller praises* Mysteries *and encourages his friend to read the novel. Miller himself read and reread the book many times during his life, and stated: "Hamsun, as I have often said, is one of the authors who vitally affected me* as writer. *None of his books intrigued me as much as* Mysteries." *For further remarks by Miller on* Mysteries, *see the excerpt dated 1971.*]

[Riding] the subway, I reread ***Mysteries*** which I am holding for you. It swept me off my feet again. And what resemblances there are between Hamsun and myself! *His* dreams, his crazy stories, his buffoonishness! It's a *deceptive* book! If you were to pick it up all by yourself and *skim* thru it, you would probably say it was *trash*. But, believe me, it isn't. And you *can't*, or *mustn't* skim it through. He *was* and still remains one of my idols. I wanted to get ***Wanderers*** for you but this is equally representative—if not quite so poetic. But all his force, his passion, his whimsicality, are here. You ought to adore it. (pp. 131-32)

Henry Miller, in a letter to Anaïs Nin on March 26, 1934, in his Letters to Anaïs Nin, *edited by Gunther Stuhlmann, G. P. Putnam's Sons, 1965, pp. 131-32.*

ALRIK GUSTAFSON (essay date 1939)

[*In the following excerpt, Gustafson closely examines* Growth of the Soil.]

[***Growth of the Soil***] appeared in the fall of 1917; and its instantaneous success, in Norway, and in translated form in nearly every country in the world, has demonstrated that Hamsun was not wrong when he referred to it, even while it was in the process of becoming, as "something good . . . big in its plan" and "a great work . . . which should be a challenge to my generation." It was all of this; and today by almost unanimous critical consent it is admitted to be the greatest of Hamsun's novels. One is reminded, as one reads Hamsun's words about his great novel, of certain prophetic words written by one of the great masters of English poetry—"One day I shall write a book which the world will not willingly let die." And when one has read the great Norwegian prose epic ***Growth of the Soil,*** one feels that to link Hamsun thus with Milton is not to do an injustice to the great master of the English poetic epic of more than two centuries and a half ago.

And yet what a difference between *Paradise Lost* and ***Growth of the Soil***! . . . . Milton, in whose genius is magnificently merged the double artistic tradition of the Middle Ages and the Renaissance, works out a poetic tapestry of rich and intricate pattern—colorful, musical, everywhere instinct with the weight of whole civilizations of culture. Hamsun, the modern child of a more primitive artistic tradition, writes simply, with a strangely effective laconic terseness: his manner bare, firm, almost stolid in its refusal to indulge in rhetorical poetic flights. . . . Milton sings of angels and archangels, of the succession of hierarchies culminating in the Godhead—too often, perhaps, forgetting to keep Adam, and *his* tragedy, at the center of the poet's picture, too often forsaking the solid things of the earth for the magic music of the spheres. Hamsun, on the other hand, remains ever firmly on earth: mysteries enough his Isak comes upon, but they are not garbed in the imagery of a long ecclesiastical tradition. . . . Milton boldly and solemnly announces his theme in the opening lines of his epic. Hamsun, less bold, less formal, *insinuates* his theme, quietly, simply, usually in a loose, fragmentary form, into the very fabric of his story. . . . Milton approaches his ethical problem largely in terms of a traditional theology. Hamsun, scarcely less interested in the problem of evil, approaches the moral issue free of any traditional preconceptions either as to the nature of evil or the way of salvation. . . .

Everywhere does one find such contrasts as these between *Paradise Lost* and ***Growth of the Soil;*** and the contrasts, it might be said, represent the difference between a world of form and idea still steeped in a mass of literary and ecclesiastical traditions and a modern world in which the artistic spirit has been permitted to move more easily, more freely, less weighed down by ideas and forms encased in a world of tradition. (pp. 199-200)

The purely artistic triumph that Hamsun attains in his novel lies largely, perhaps, in his ability to reduce life to its simplest, most elemental forms, disdaining completely certain romantic techniques of story-telling often employed by even the best of novelists. Hardy, for example, in *The Return of the Native,* must make central in his story of an otherwise essentially rural Egdon Heath the mysteriously exotic character of Eustacia Vye. With Hamsun in ***Growth of the Soil*** there is nothing of this kind. His central characters, Isak and Inger, are simple souls, and neither of them, we are assured, is beautiful to look upon. . . . The events of the story are as unassuming as the characters—unassuming, and yet basic, for they treat with a direct, laconic simplicity of such natural phenomena as birth and growth and death, of human mating, of man earning his bread by the sweat of his brow. And with an unerring sense of the appropriate, Hamsun no more seeks to surround these fundamental functions of life with the sentimental trumpery of the average novelist than he tries to make Inger beautiful or Isak handsome.

Out of such material as this it is that Hamsun's theme gradually emerges: man has all he needs when he is at work close to the soil—the so-called "values of civilization" being in reality merely will-o'-the-wisps that man pursues always at his own risk. . . . The wilderness has all, yes—food and clothing and shelter in plenty for those who will work . . . and so much more, even, for those who work and are sometimes fain to dream. (pp. 201-02)

It may be significant . . . in considering those forces which led Hamsun to the conclusions reached in ***Growth of the Soil,*** that the pages of this novel were penned in the heart of the War years. Nowhere in the novel does one come upon any specific evidences to justify the supposition that Hamsun was reacting against an over-developed civilization which had made possible the fearful carnage of the World War, and no other evidence, so far as I know, has been turned up to prove the point. Still one is prone to suspect that such evidence is to be found, probably hidden away in some Norwegian provincial newspaper files from these years. In any event, it seems difficult to believe that Hamsun was not aware of the arguments against a modern war implicit in the general thesis of ***Growth of the Soil.*** The problem treated in ***Growth of the Soil*** is a universal problem, everywhere and at all times present; and so Hamsun sees no necessity of narrowing his argument or its application to any particular time or place. It is simply a story of *man*—not *a* man—at work with nature; it relates the epic struggle between the eternal processes of nature and an encroaching modern industrial civilization. The World War—being peculiarly destructive because a modern industry provided the belligerent nations with weapons never previously known in the history of warfare—must have seemed peculiarly horrible and futile to the man who, in the healthy rural isolation of Nordland, was composing ***Growth of the Soil*** in the years 1916 and 1917.

One need not read beyond the first chapter of the novel to see that Hamsun intended his story to be universal in its appeal and in its application; and all the succeeding chapters confirm this first impression, culminating ultimately in the magnificently conceived simplicity and power of the final paragraphs of the last chapter. . . . How inevitably the elevated, universal tone of this closing scene turns the reader's memory back to the first scene in the novel—Isak, alone at first, struggling through the wilderness, plodding across the far-stretching, seemingly interminable hills . . . seeking, seeking. . . . It is significant that we do not even know his name at first—"The *man* comes walking to the north." A *worker* he is—"a born carrier of loads. . . ." Neither in time nor in space is he localized—merely "a lumbering barge of a man *in the forest. . . .*" What matters it where he struggles? or in what period of time? He is the eternal symbol of the Worker, the eternal Sower—in all generations, in all climes, "a ghost risen out of the past to point the future, a man from the earliest days of cultivation, a settler in the wilds, nine hundred years old and, withal, a man of the day."

A symbol, yes. . . . Yet what a warmly *human* symbol this "barge of a man" is: strong as an ox, stubbornly persistent in his work, nearly always triumphant in his generation-long struggle with nature, almost a superman in a primitive world of heavy daily tasks this Isak is. And still so naïvely human in his innermost self. Hamsun never seems to tire, in depicting Isak's early years with Inger, to throw a roguish, kindly searchlight upon Isak's little vanities, especially his childish delight at words or looks of praise from Inger when he has performed some particularly praiseworthy task. . . . Perhaps the most riotously roguish bit of humor that Hamsun creates at Isak's expense is his description of Isak's demonstration of the new mowing-machine that he had bought secretly down in the village and had quietly transported to the neighborhood of Sellanraa. (pp. 203-06)

Kindly is all of this humor, with no note of cutting satire in it; for Hamsun loves his Isak and the simple folk at Sellanraa farm as he has loved none of his other creations. And this humor of Hamsun's—in the early parts of the novel so bantering, so sly, so robustly roguish—ultimately comes to reveal another, profounder side, as does all great, abiding humor. When we get more deeply into the story of Isak and Inger, we find Hamsun's roguish spirit blending almost imperceptibly into that phase of all great humor which we call pathos—a profound, warmly human pathos in Hamsun, capable of a rich, understanding sympathy toward his chief characters in the hour of their trials.

Much as some critics have made of certain of the undeniably great passages in ***Growth of the Soil,*** particularly those passages which lend a tone of dignified epic elevation to the story of Sellanraa farm, I have never felt that such passages are Hamsun's greatest creative achievement in the novel. More beautiful, I feel, is Hamsun's treatment of a couple of episodes in the novel which center their attention on the relation between man and woman, Isak and Inger, during moments of deep inner strain and violent potential conflict. At no other point in ***Growth of the Soil,*** or for that matter in none of Hamsun's novels, do we come upon a more mellow, understanding, profoundly sympathetic Hamsun—nor a Hamsun who is a more delicately sensitive *artist*. (p. 207)

A mellow, all-embracing human sympathy, ready to forgive and to forget, incapable of bearing a grudge or passing a final judgment—this is the impressive moral stature to which Isak attains in his quiet, simple, lumbering way. There is nothing of false heroics here, nothing of the cheap, or the theatrical—only a man who believes in the existence of right and wrong, but who does not believe that wrong should be long remembered or brooded over, for nature herself will seek a balance between good and evil and provide at the last any judgment upon man or beast which a sin against nature might perchance incur.

And it is in the spirit of Isak's wise and healthy humanity that Hamsun's own final words of judgment fall upon all of the weak and wayward characters in the novel: first, upon the only momentarily wayward Inger; and then upon the others—upon Brede Olson, the misfit settler at Breidablik; upon "the imperishable Oline," sneaking old busybody; and upon Eleseus and Barbro, two of the children of the original settlers who had become contaminated by life "in the town." . . . There are really only two characters in the novel for whom Hamsun has no sympathy: first, Fru Heyerdahl, the feminist, who busies herself much more with "advanced ideas" than with the obvious and immediate duties of parenthood; and secondly, Andresen, the petty merchant-adventurer, who in his small way gambles on an industrial development and fails miserably. They represent the canker of civilization in its most unhealthy, its least defensible forms; and as such they come in for Hamsun's most withering irony whenever they appear in the pages of the novel.

Some words about Hamsun's style in ***Growth of the Soil.*** Its mark is a direct, laconic simplicity; its tone is one of simple epic elevation. Hamsun attains here the heroic manner without ever resorting to the traditional literary means. At no point in the novel does he employ any of the rhetorical tricks which usually accompany the "epic manner." His style is short, clipped, markedly epigrammatic, without ever stooping to the merely banal or to the commonplace. It is idiomatic in the best sense of the word—in the sense that Hazlitt defines the idiomatic in his essay "On Familiar Style." Hamsun has on occasion indulged in a brutally exaggerated realism reminiscent of some of the prose of Strindberg—whom, by the way, he admires greatly. But there is none of this in ***Growth of the Soil.*** Nor is there in this novel anything of the posed, stilted, dress-shirt manner which Scandinavian authors, particularly lyric poets, so frequently affect. And yet Hamsun somehow achieves "the grand manner" in the sum total effect of ***Growth of the Soil.*** Impossible is it for the reader to forget the subtly dignified tone of epic elevation attained in the opening and closing scenes of ***Growth of the Soil,*** a tone gained largely by a marvelously appropriate simplicity of phrase; and scores of other passages in the novel are in their way equally effective.

The secret of this stylistic triumph is that Hamsun never loses sight of the particular world in which his story moves. It is a simple, natural, instinctive world—alone by itself, for the most part, in the great *Almenning*. The people in this world are not complex, sophisticated, "civilized"; they go about their simple tasks, performing their daily round of duties, untroubled by those introspective moods that eat at the roots of will and character among more cultured classes. They know the phenomena of birth and growth and death as the everyday phenomena that they are—not artificially, as "objects of analysis." Hamsun keeps all of this constantly in mind, and he fits his style to this instinctive, primitive world of Sellanraa farm. The simple, direct, laconic idiom that he adopts as the primary pattern of his style in ***Growth of the Soil*** is one which exactly duplicates the thought patterns of the simple folk he is depicting; and, unlike other great novelists who have written of the peasant, Hamsun maintains the idiom with a marvelous consistency throughout his novel. In the straightforward matter-of-factness of this idiom—an idiom that deviates neither into extreme brutality of phrase nor into sentimental idyllicism of word choice—Hamsun has created an appropriateness of style in the so-called "peasant novel" which is perhaps unique in world literature.

That Hamsun's simple, straightforward prose has, however, a poetry of its own should be sufficiently apparent to any discerning reader of ***Growth of the Soil.*** It falls, of course, into that species of poetry to which Wordsworth has given the name "the poetry of common life." Hamsun, indeed, goes even a step further at times than did Wordsworth in actual practice; for he insists upon presenting certain imaginative responses of his peasant characters in the half-formed, fragmentary, only partially articulate lyric manner characteristic of actual peasant thought patterns and peasant speech. Sivert's experience by the river's side one evening, as he caught up the notes of the mating ducks, is a case in point—"A sound had floated through him, a sweetness, and kept him standing there with a delicate, thin recollection of something wild and splendid, something he had known before, and forgotten again." Here there is no effort to analyze, to probe, to get beyond the *actual quality* of Sivert's own half-articulate response—"a delicate, thin recollection of *something* wild and splendid, *something* he had known before, and forgotten again." The experience is one for Sivert to wonder at, to be thankful for, not to talk of or to theorize about. And Hamsun, the author, is no more concerned with theorizing about this experience than is Sivert himself. Hamsun simply *records* the experience, as it had formed itself with a fleeting, formless suddenness in Sivert's consciousness during that marvelous evening hour in the woods at the river's side.

Not always, however, is Hamsun's style in ***Growth of the Soil*** lyric in the delicate, mystery-filled sense that we find it in the passage when Sivert experiences his sudden glimpse of other-worldly loveliness in consequence of his hearing the musical notes of two mating ducks. Isak and Inger and Sivert have only occasional moments of such rare, inexplicable spiritual content. For the most part their feet are planted firmly on the ground, their concerns, physical and mental, are immediate and of the earth earthy. It is therefore the heavy labors of man and the solid produce of the soil that Hamsun comes to sing most frequently in ***Growth of the Soil:*** Isak at work in the fields; Inger among her pots and pans or busy in the cow shed; the marvelous growth of corn at Sellanraa farm; and the vegetables, especially the lowly potato—to Hamsun no mean subject for poetry of a kind!

> What was that about potatoes? Were they just a thing from foreign parts, like coffee; a luxury, an extra? Oh, the potato is a lordly fruit; drought or downpour, it grows and grows all the same. It laughs at the weather, and will stand anything; only deal kindly with it, and it yields fifteen-fold again. Not the blood of a grape, but the flesh of a chestnut, to be boiled or roasted, used in every way. A man may lack corn to make bread, but give him potatoes and he will not starve. Roast them in the embers, and there is supper; boil them in water, and there's a breakfast ready. As for meat, it's little is needed beside. Potatoes can be served with what you please; a dish of milk, a herring, is enough. The rich eat them with butter; poor folk manage with a tiny pinch of salt. Isak could make a feast of them on Sundays, with a mess of cream from Goldenhorn's milk. Poor despised potato—a blessed thing!

Here is a prose poem on a subject that would have warmed Wordsworth's heart. And yet I am not sure that Wordsworth would have approved of the *manner* in which the paragraph is conceived; for its robust aggressiveness of temper, at once roguish and serious, leaves little occasion for casting over the subject that "certain coloring of the imagination" which Wordsworth felt was essential even in poems dealing with lowly, concrete subjects. Hamsun is here, perhaps, more in the tradition of Whitman than of Wordsworth.

The potato, being useful, is a blessing unto man; and therefore it is an appropriate subject for poetry. Likewise is work—the ceaseless labor of man in loving cooperation with a reasonably fertile and kindly nature. Isak, brute of a worker that he is, becomes in consequence the most poetic of all of the conceptions that Hamsun introduces into his novel. Isak is no dreamer, no gambler—merely a man of stubbornly persistent herculean labors, wresting from the soil what the soil is ready to yield to one who instinctively understands her, loves her, works with her. It is Geissler who is the dreamer, his son the gambler; and both of them are failures. . . . (pp. 209-12)

Isak is "one of the two-and-thirty thousand" who count constructively in the marvelous processes of nature because he takes up life on life's own terms, instinctively divining the pace that nature sets, and adjusts his willing labors to the tempo and scale which a great and kindly nature intimates to him as he works upon her surface. And as he works he transforms some of nature's features, but he never defaces her, never makes her barren, as does the "lightning" at times—for nature is after all the Great Mother, who gives out a rich, abundant life if only man knows how to find his way to her and use her well.

Such is Hamsun's arresting message to an over-industrialized modern civilization. The message comes to us most strongly in the closing pages of the novel—and appropriately at the close, having, as it were, grown naturally and organically out of the impressively simple story of Isak and Inger and Sellanraa farm which has preceded. Hamsun was to write other novels in later years, some of them not without a strong note of decadence, even of partial cynicism; but in none of these later novels does he renounce that faith in man at work close to the soil which is the noble central burden of ***Growth of the Soil.*** (pp. 213-14)

Alrik Gustafson, "Hamsun's 'Growth of the Soil'," in The American Scandinavian Review, *Vol. XXVII, No. 3, September, 1939, pp. 199-214.*

MAXWELL GEISMAR (essay date 1940)

[*Geismar is considered one of America's most prominent historical and social critics. Although he often openly confessed that literature is more than historical documentation, Geismar's own critical method suggests that social patterns and the weight of history, more than any other phenomenon, affect the shape and content of all art. Geismar's major enterprise—a multi-volume history of the American novel from 1860 to 1940—clearly demonstrates his fascination with the impact of external forces on literature. His praise of such writers as Ernest Hemingway, John Dos Passos, and John Steinbeck, and his criticism of others, such as Henry James and the post-World War II writers, depends almost exclusively on how these artists were affected by and responded to the conditions in their particular societies. Many of Geismar's contemporaries, and many scholars today, have criticized his inability to see art as anything beyond social documentation. In the following excerpt from a favorable review of* Look Back on Happiness, *Geismar notes the tension in Hamsun's work between the author's desire to shun the "common herd" and his desire to enlighten its members, and between his insight and his prejudice.*]

Perhaps the most notable Scandinavian writer of our day, Knut Hamsun is certainly the most perplexing. Embodying in himself all the discontents of modern civilization, he adds to these, it almost seems, the timeless conflicts of the race. Shoemaker, teacher, farm hand, vagabond, he sought through Faustian experience the answers which philosophy cannot give. A Norwegian Nietzsche, despising the common man he describes so well, disappointed and still restless, he retired to his native forests. Here, a self-imposed pariah, a voice from the northern wilderness, his lofty jeremiads invoking doom and destruction upon modern civilization, he sees in the splendors of Rousseau's natural man our only salvation. But his spirit fleeing, as if cursed, from this very primitive glory he proclaims, he still remains, confuting all racial doctrines, as the eternal wandering Nordic Jew.

Creating such dilemmas, each new work of his translated has its special interest, and **"Look Back on Happiness"** is no exception. Both arrogant and humble in its tone, filled with tempestuous conflicts portrayed in icy language, in these pages Hamsun's hatred of humanity vying with his passion to save us, and his insight stumbling over his prejudices, **"Look Back on Happiness"** is a fascinating study in the follies of maturity. The narrator-hero of the story, the curious "I" of Hamsun's work who is half a tragic chorus on man's frailty and half the embodiment of this frailty, is an established literary man bitter over his own success. Wealthy and famous, acknowledged as a master (as Hamsun was by such other artists as Gide, Gorki, Wells and Thomas Mann) and indeed acknowledging himself as a master, this acidulous hero finds in his old age not tolerance but increasing hatred, not certainty but the growing perception of his own errors, not peace but the sword of spiritual dissension. If he, like Hamsun, once stood questioning before the mystery of life, now before the secret of the grave he fulminates!

Illuminating this complex and raging personage is that fine economy of craft which generally marks Scandinavian work, and in the case of Hamsun and Sillanpaa reaches its high peak. The novel itself is centered around a Norwegian village hostelry, a sort of Grand Hotel of the soil, to which come a variety of disturbed souls. . . . This group has its heroine—a certain Ingeborg Torsen who is not only unhappy herself but the cause of unhappiness in others. Alluring but frustrating, reckless but virginal, Ingeborg, the modern literary lady, attracts all contiguous males—the sullen Solem, the unsuspecting apostle of Switzerland upon whom Solem takes a grim revenge, an impecunious actor, among others, and lastly and very strangely the narrator of the novel himself. . . .

Portraying himself . . . as absurd, grotesque, even obscene, the narrator gives his story a power that is brutal and unashamed. In one sense **"Look Back on Happiness"** is a sort of horror tale, without murder or crime, indeed with hardly any physical action, that pure horror of the spirit for which all else is the mere symbol. And achieving at the end Ingeborg's happiness at the cost of his own, the narrator finds in his renunciation little of our conventional sublimity. To Hamsun he that gives is also cursed. Alone, the dissenting voice, the narrator wanders off once again, not the broken angel seeking his lost paradise, but an ingenious and perhaps evil Lucifer almost planning to destroy it.

In **"The Ring Is Closed"** Hamsun, taking for himself this same wanderer's role, claimed a final objectivity. Though **"Look Back on Happiness"** is a less solid work, and not comparable again to **"Hunger,"** it may be closer to the truth of Hamsun himself. For him there will be no objectivity, nor balance, nor final peace. The young rebel is the ancient Ishmaelite. The answer of the grave will also be inadequate, his soul immortally indignant, his perturbed spirit mocking at that last illusion of death.

Maxwell Geismar, "Hamsun, Norwegian Nietzsche," in New York Herald Tribune Books, *April 7, 1940, p. 6.*

KNUT HAMSUN (interview date 1949)

[Captured by the Allies at the end of World War II, Hamsun was subjected to psychiatric tests to determine if he was mentally stable at the time of his collaboration with the Nazis. During the course of Hamsun's examination, one analyst said to his subject: "I take it for granted that in the course of your life you have analyzed yourself thoroughly. As far as I can see, you have always been aggressive. Another impression is that you are sensitive and vulnerable. Is that correct? And which other qualities do you possess? Are you suspicious? Egoistic or generous? Jealous? Do you possess any characteristic sense of righteousness? Logician? Emotional or cold nature?" Hamsun replied as follows.]

I have only analysed myself in one way, in that in my books I have created several hundred different characters. Each of them is developed out of myself, with faults or perfections as is the case with fictitious characters. The so-called naturalistic period in literature wrote of people with principal qualities. It had no use for a finely integrated psychology, the people possessed a particular disposition that determined their actions. Dostoyevskij and many others taught us all something about man. I believe that right from the beginning of my production there is no person with any such straightforward principal quality. They are all without so-called character, they are all split and complex, not good, not bad, but both, subtly differentiated in their natures, changing in their actions. And thus no doubt I am myself. It is altogether possible that I am aggressive, that perhaps I have something of all the qualities which you, Sir, suggest—sensitive, suspicious, egoistical, generous, jealous, overrighteous, logical, emotional and cold—all these qualities are human. But I do not think that in myself I see the predominance of any one of them. To that which constitutes me also belongs the genius which has enabled me to write my books. But I cannot analyse it. Brandes called it divine madness.

Knut Hamsun, in an extract from "The Three Hamsuns: The Changing Attitude in Recent Criticism,"

Hamsun appears in court during his trial for wartime collaboration with the Nazis. From On Overgrown Paths *by Knut Hamsun, translated by Carl E. Anderson. Paul S. Eriksson, Publisher.*

in Scandinavian Studies, *Vol. 32, No. 3, August, 1960, p. 139.*

LEO LOWENTHAL (essay date 1957)

[*In the following excerpt, Lowenthal attempts to demonstrate that "there is, in all (Hamsun's) novels, an anticipation of the Nazi ideology. He rejects modern, urban, industrial society with its frustrations and responsibilities. His solution is a flight to nature in the form of submission to forces beyond human control, with which he combines admiration of 'blood, race, and soil.'" For a contrasting opinion, see the excerpt by Harald Naess (1967), who refutes Lowenthal's charges.*]

At his best the modern writer, like all writers, keeps alive the hopes of the individual and the ideal of his self-realization in society; even the defeats he portrays are meaningful within this context. At his worst, however, he can fall victim to an irrational escape into the arms of authoritarianism. Knut Hamsun was this kind of writer. In the twenties and thirties his work not only enjoyed an excellent international literary reputation but also was regarded—even by liberals and socialists—as politically above reproach. However, in his act of joining Quisling's party during the Second World War, he expressed in practice the authoritarian themes and moods that had long been implicit in his novels: the pagan awe of unlimited and unintelligible forces of nature, the mystique of blood and race, hatred of the working class and of clerks, the blind submission to authority, the abrogation of individual responsibility, anti-intellectualism, and spiteful distrust of urban middle-class life in general. (p. 190)

The image of nature in Hamsun's novels has little in common with earlier conceptions of nature as a source of directives for human conduct. It lacks the critical element that made Rousseau's naturalism, for example, a progressive political and cultural force in the eighteenth century. Since the Renaissance man had seen himself able, at least potentially, to conquer some of nature's forces. This attitude reflected his faith in the unlimited potential of reason and, specifically, his hope for political and social reconstruction.

In Hamsun, submission to nature functions as an escape from the burden of social responsibility. This passive attitude in part explains why Hamsun's heroes are able to profess sentimental pity for the unsheltered animal, the tree in the wind, or for the withering foliage. In the fate of nature's children, they see a reflection of their own helplessness. To be a victim in the world of men is a threat to dignity. There is a certain solace, on the other hand, in being a victim of majestic natural forces for which man cannot be expected to be personally accountable.

Paradoxically, this new type of submission to nature is closely related to political submission. The yearning for surrender to nature as it appears in Hamsun's novels not only glorifies the awareness of individual weakness but at the same time exalts reverence for superior power in general. (p. 192)

In the analysis that follows, an effort will be made to show that the sentimental conceptions of nature and peasant in Hamsun's novels anticipate an intrinsic part of those political ideologies that forge the concepts of leader, social coercion and soil into a tool of brutality.

At first sight, Hamsun does not seem qualified to represent the emergence of a typically modern European authoritarian ethos. (It is noteworthy, however, that it was in Germany that Hamsun obtained his greatest response from the very beginning.) Coming from a small country that, unlike the larger nations, has primary economic interests in agriculture and fishing, Hamsun might be expected to portray themes different from those of writers in highly industrialized nations. But, in fact, it is just this disparity between Norwegian conditions and the situation of the larger and industrially more advanced countries that makes Hamsun's picture of his society so reassuring at first glance and so foreboding upon closer analysis.

Hamsun's first novel, ***Hunger,*** written in autobiographical form and published in 1890, states the themes that are almost endlessly repeated in the later novels: abandonment of any participation in public life, submission to the stream of incomprehensible and incalculable forces, distrust of the intellect, flight from the city and escape to nature. (pp- 193-94)

One of Hamsun's figures once replied to an apologist for the city:

> You have your home in the city, it is true, and you have decorated it with trinkets and pictures and books; but you have a wife and a maid and hundreds of expenses. In waking and sleeping you must struggle with things, and you never have peace. I have peace. Keep your spiritual goods and the books and art and newspapers, keep your coffee houses and your whiskey which always makes me sick. Here I can roam about the woods, and I feel fine. If you put intellectual problems to me and try to drive me into a corner, I merely reply that God is the source, and that men are in truth only specks and threads in the universe. Even you have gone no further.

The motif of peace is rare in Hamsun's writing; its use here as the key to the blessings of rustic life could perhaps be interpreted as a legitimate protest against urban conditions. When, however, a protest in the name of a seemingly higher idea becomes a wholesale condemnation of civilization, when it does not discriminate between marketplace manipulation and family life, between the newspaper and artistic creations, between anxious restlessness and emotional pleasure, between the futility of mere distraction and the earnestness of serious reading—all of which Hamsun spurns with equal rancor—then we are not dealing with alert social criticism, but with anti-intellectual resentment. Hamsun in the same breath ridicules the cheap pictures on the wall and jeers at the intellect. The final outcome of such impotent resentment is the surrender to brute power. (p. 195)

The philosophy of liberalism did not encompass the idea that the whole world had come within man's power. Subject and object were opposed in the forms of active man and conquerable nature. Nature was raw material and man the unrealized potential; man realized himself in its conquest. Social relationships were implicit in this interaction; the knowledge of nature was won through communication of man with man, and nature was transformed by organized societal enterprise. The relationship toward which Hamsun's ideas tend is of a totally different kind. Nature is no longer looked upon as an object for scientific and practical control; instead Hamsun's hero consecrates his life in rapt surrender to nature and even in mystical identification. . . . (pp. 197-98)

To Hamsun, nature means peace, but a peace which has lost its spontaneity and its will to know and to control. It is a peace based on submission to every arbitrary power, a pantheism which offers an escape from the gloomy framework of history.

Nature comes to mean the solace of the unchangeable and the all-pervasive:

> . . . he lost himself, was carried away and wrapt in the frenzy of sunshine . . . He was in a mysterious state, filled with psychic pleasure; every nerve in him was awake; he had music in his blood, felt akin to all nature, to the sun and the mountains and everything else, felt surrounded by a whisper of his own ego-sense from trees and tufts and blades of grass.

The hero avoids asking any embarrassing questions about the rest of mankind. He shows concern only for his own fate. There is even a hint that nature is his private property and that his enjoyment of it is a kind of personal possession. Paragraph after paragraph of exalted description communicates neither observation nor knowledge, but only a desire for personal omnipotence and for pantheistic possession of the world by emotional immersion:

> The sky all open and clean; I stared into that clear sea, and it seemed as if I were lying face to face with the uttermost depth of the world; my heart beating tensely against it, and at home there.

The timelessness of such pantheism gives the illusion of an immediate, complete possession of the entire world, a possession that at the same time cuts off historical progress. Gone is the optimistic dualism of liberalistic philosophy which always maintained close contact with history, considered the transitoriness of the human situation, and often gave birth to a conception of the future, Utopian to be sure, in which a final stasis of perfection might be reached.

Hamsun's identification with the whole of nature can be consummated with no exertion and with no fear of disillusionment. What the Utopians had envisioned as a potential unity of man and nature comes to be proclaimed as already realized: the meaning of man's life is to be found in natural factors such as blood and soil. When such a myth is consciously used in the interests of a power apparatus, as it was under fascism, men are told that their inevitable and irrevocable share of nature is their "race" and their nation. (pp. 198-99)

[For Kant,] the sublimity of nature and the experience of man's helplessness before it are counterbalanced by the concept of nature as subordinate in the face of humanity. It is man's own knowledge and imagination which creates the conception of the grandiosity in nature that dwarfs him. In the end, the rational faculties of man are of a higher order than the elemental force of nature, and they allow him to see it as sublime, instead of simply terrifying. . . . Thus for Kant, nature is not to console man for frustrations, but to stimulate his moral and intellectual development.

In Hamsun, the relation of man to nature takes on an entirely different cast.

> I stood in the shelter of an overhanging rock, thinking many things; my soul was tense. Heaven knows, I thought to myself, what it is I am watching here, and why the sea should open before my eyes. Maybe I am seeing now the inner brain of earth, how things are at work there, boiling and foaming.

The locus of knowledge has become nature itself, mysterious and beyond man's capacities to know. Hamsun's questions are framed so they cannot be answered; his tired individuals seek to silence themselves as quickly as possible. They really have nothing to say, and they welcome the storm that can roar loudly enough to drown out their own silence. The relationship of man to nature as seen by Kant is reversed; for Hamsun the storm serves as an occasion for increasing the individual's awareness of his own insignificance. . . . Anxiety enters as a component of Hamsun's pantheism. Kant's pride in human autonomy is replaced by a sentimental uneasiness that is announced in every thunderstorm and that is subsequently ramified as a jumble of mawkish sympathies for both natural objects and spiritual difficulties. Hamsun's nature world foreshadows the affinity of brutality and sentimentality, a well-known phenomenon in Nazi Germany. (pp. 199-201)

When Hamsun speaks of the forces of nature to which man should subject himself, it is, as we have noted, mostly of the woods and the sea. But when he speaks of man himself, as he should be, he leaves these unspoiled provinces behind and speaks foremost of farming. Hamsun's emphasis is not upon the social conditions of the farm; rather, he is again involved in constructing the myth which demands the necessity of man's submission to nature. The peasant tunes himself to forces stronger than himself, and that is supposed to be the lesson he can teach us. In addition vigorous youth and women are portrayed as truly obedient to nature's forces. Hamsun gives us, in fact, a gallery of unheroic heroes, whose qualities are primarily those of subjection and discipline.

Hamsun's peasants are not individuals; they are aspects of nature, and his apparent admiration of them is not a love of man, but a reverence for the domination of nature over its inhabitants.

> His [the peasant's] life was spent in this work and that, according to the season; from the fields to the woods, and back to the fields again.

This sentence is typical. The peasant himself is not characterized; he is presented only as a natural phenomenon that comes and goes like the blossoming and withering of the leaves in the forest. That is precisely the identity which Hamsun seeks, an identity established by nature, not by man. . . . (p. 203)

As contrasted with the emptiness of urban existence, the concreteness of the peasant's world seems to comprise the meaning of life itself:

> He did not feel poor and forlorn, as he really was; why, all the stones he had cleared looked just like a crowd of people around him, he was personally related to every stone, they were acquaintances every one, he had conquered them and got them out of the ground.

The authoritarian state did not have to invent the idea of man's roots as being in blood and soil, nor devise the manipulation of this slogan as a solace for want. "We will not be any happier if we eat more bacon," says Hamsun's peasant in defending life on Norwegian soil against a life outside that might mean greater material success; the worst fate is

> . . . to be torn up by the roots from our own barren soil and transplanted into richer . . .

If we accept this belief, we do not scorn the hardest labor, for we know "where we really do belong."

> It is a good thing to belong to one's class, otherwise one becomes an upstart and gets one's originality frittered away.

A good thing if you are a peasant, that is. Hamsun's eulogy of the peasant, apparently undertaken in the spirit of social critique, ends up as a sermon on temperance, humility, privation. The message is to keep one's roots where they are, even though the soil may be very poor indeed.

As we might expect, Hamsun combines his cult of the hero and that of natural forces with praise for the vigor of youth *per se*. In comparison with this vigor, the restrained wisdom of maturity counts for little; the demand of youth for power is natural obedience to the "law of life." (pp. 205-06)

Along with the peasant, the vagabond receives affectionate treatment in every period of Hamsun's career. August, his favorite, longs "to shoot the knife out of the hand of a man who was trying to make off with his wallet" because that would be a thrill for the "children of the age" in their dreary existence. As a matter of fact, Hamsun seems fascinated by such brutal mischief. . . . In this pseudo-romantic flirting with a nuisance crime, he ridicules the "unheroic" spirit of urban efficiency ("no thunderbolt ever falls"); he cries for "gigantic demi-gods" and blunders into a political program of violence:

> The great terrorist is greatest, the dimension, the immense lever which can raise worlds.

The peasant with his roots in the soil and the bohemian vagabond with no ties to anything may seem mutually exclusive idols. Still, Hamsun's ability to sympathize with such apparently opposite types has a certain logic; their common denominator is the rejection of organized urban culture, in favor of the application of raw, unmediated "natural" force. Incidentally, it was the socially uprooted literati (the "armed bohemians," as they have been called) who performed the spadework of German fascism, playing up the cult of the hero and the maintenance of one's roots in the soil.

In Hamsun, the function of such marginal figures as the vagabond is emphatically different from that in the literature thus far discussed. From Cervantes through Ibsen, marginal characters have stood outside society and criticized it in the name of freedom and self-determination. In Hamsun, however, such figures serve as coquettish expression of his veneration of brutality and power.

The endorsement of violence and mischief seems to be a far cry from the theme of passive surrender to nature. But the connection between violence and passivity becomes unequivocal in Hamsun's treatment of the relation between the sexes. In his novels there is a conspicuous absence of genuine yearning for love. When one of his characters is seized by a strong passion, it is quickly transformed into sado-masochistic torment of himself or of the partner. This is as true of the desperate ecstasy of the hero in ***Hunger,*** or of the literally speechless and unexpressed affair between the main characters in ***Victoria,*** as of the mutual hatred of the partners in ***Pan.*** The hero of ***Mysteries*** enjoys telling his beloved the most frightening and brutal stories; the hero of ***Pan*** shoots his dog and sends the corpse as a farewell gift to the beloved from whom he has become estranged. (pp. 207-08)

Whatever is distinctly human and spiritual is forgotten. Love, which for Cervantes and Shakespeare appeared as the key phenomenon in the autonomous development of modern man, becomes reduced in Hamsun to a bawdy jeer at free will. Hamsun belittles Ibsen's women, and thumbs his nose at Ibsen himself for his description of Nora (in *A Doll's House*):

> I know a sage, and he wrote of woman. Wrote of woman, in thirty volumes of uniform theatre poetry: I counted the volumes once in a big bookcase. And at last he wrote of the woman who left her own children to go in search of—the wonderful! But what, then, were the children? Oh, it was comical: a wanderer laughs at anything so comical.

Woman attains fulfillment of her destiny when she limits her functions to those of a housewife and a mother. This enshrinement of biological function leads Hamsun to bitter hatred for any emancipation, intellectuality, or political reforms that women might desire and finally, in an attack on actresses, to utter contempt for the "modern woman." . . . The ideal peasant woman, wife of the ideal peasant in ***Growth of the Soil,*** unpleasant in appearance and not always faithful, has a meaningful existence as a housewife and mother. . . . This theme is constantly reiterated: woman receives her true consecration as a mother. . . . (pp. 210-11)

In such idealization of fertility, biology takes precedence over the conventions of middle-class morality; as in the case of Inger, sexual vicissitudes are blinked—indeed are condoned—provided the end or denouement is that of producing children. This was also a stock in trade of the Nazi ideology, which reduced womanhood to a biological function. (p. 211)

The idolatry of nature is set up against "a world where cheating goes on in the dark." The composition of this rejected world is quite apparent. It is, in brief, an inventory of modern urban society that Hamsun condemns—industry, public officials, the natural sciences, the teaching profession, the coffee house, the corporation, and countries under liberal governments—as well as the city, the intellectuals, the workers and platforms of social reform; these are all surveyed in the novels and dismissed as hateful. Significant, for example, are his contemptuous remarks on Gladstone, and his rejection of "the modern type, a man of our time," who believes "all the Jew and the Yankee have taught him." He has warm words of praise for Sweden because she is oriented toward Germany, not toward Switzerland, and he tells the English that they "will someday be whipped to death by the healthy destiny of Germany."

Numerous are his attacks on Switzerland—not just coincidentally the model of democratic experimentation. In one of his novels, a man plans to build a comfortable home for his family in the "Swiss fashion." He is taken to task by Hamsun for believing he can learn something

> . . . from a miserable little people up in the Alps, a people that throughout its history has never been or done anything worth speaking of.

These attacks are typical of a romanticizing primitivism anticipating in literature the sneering propaganda of the middle-European authoritarian parties against "effeminacy" and the "morass" of the big cities. When Hamsun assumes the posture of social critic, he focuses his attention only on superficial, secondary aspects of industrial society. Everything the inquiring mind finds of interest and of crucial importance—including consideration for mutual help—is flattened out, or swept away with an imperious gesture. Not accidentally, a chief butt of his ridicule are the manufacturers of consumer goods, whom he epitomizes in those who seem most readily to lend themselves to caricature, such as producers of canned goods, candies and herring-meal. (pp. 212-13)

For Hamsun, intellectuals and public officials exemplify middle-class triviality. The work of the journalist, the teacher and the historian find no favor in his eyes. Scientists are represented as having wrought a permanent injury against man; science is an empty mechanism, an incomprehensible hodge-podge of data. . . . [Hamsun attacks] the "sons of clerks," the "official residence," and the "garden of the commonplace" where everything is decided "on account of age, length of service, and school learning." (p. 213)

Now—as we see the clerk, the bureaucrat, the intellectual portrayed as sickly, decadent, impotent—there emerges by implication the counter-image of the self-assured, vigorous, tough Nordic hero. Those who do not display these virtues are summarily disqualified.

Contempt for factory workers and for workers' movements permeates Hamsun's novels. (p. 214)

The competitive interwovenness of urban lower strata appears as a threat to the "heroic" *status quo*—life on the soil. . . .

For Hamsun the struggle for an increase in material welfare is merely vulgar. Whatever rational justifications such claims may have is no concern of his. He engages in a variety of attacks on "the proletariat's strong and blind craving for food," on "the roar of the masses," who unfortunately have learned from "mechanical reading and writing" how beautiful it is to "live by others' labor." But worst of all are the destructive tendencies that are bound up with the workingman's "worldly greed."

> They [the masses] want to roar and turn things upside down, and when it comes to a pinch even their own leaders can't hold them in. The whole thing's crashing, let it crash!

Here indeed we are face to face with the nihilistic furor of the authoritarian mentality. (p. 215)

[The] loss of faith by Europeans in their rationalistic daydreams, wherein their power had seemed to grow without bonds, was given respectability by the anti-liberal literati's devaluation of reason. Hamsun's anti-intellectualism soon became apparent in his attacks on earlier nineteenth-century writers. One of his heroes calls Maupassant "crude and soulless," Tolstoi "a fool in philosophy" who talks "twaddle," and Ibsen a "little writing oddity" who has brought shame upon his country, a land which has engendered nothing but "peace conferences, the skiing spirit, and Ibsen so far." In 1892, Hamsun already contributed to the authoritarian *Führer* cult—which jeers at the moral anxieties and compulsions of the intellectual, while arrogantly exalting the morally insensate body-beautiful ideal of the racial hero—when he joined his contempt for one of Ibsen's more remarkable sayings with an alleged physical weakness of the playwright:

> The great poet produces a pursed-lips expression, braces his chicken breast to the utmost, and delivers himself of the following words: "To make poetry is to summon oneself to the Day of Judgment."

(pp. 216-17)

Hamsun's mythology throws new light on his misanthropic contempt. His exalted picture of life stands side by side with the image of crawling and creeping man, in the same way that authoritarian propaganda later combined ostensibly lofty notions with expressions of vulgar misanthropy. A metaphysics of the miserableness of man is mobilized against the idea of human progress. Every desire for a more rational organization of society becomes incongruous. (p. 219)

Behind Hamsun's bitter responses to contemporary civilization lies the cold and nihilistic negation of the very image of man on the road to freedom. His characters are not truly individuals but irrelevant particles in an ahuman process forever beyond their control. Both as an artist and as a political partisan, he was unequal to the challenge of the great heritage of libertarian thought in the West. (pp. 219-20)

Leo Lowenthal, "Knut Hamsun," in his Literature and the Image of Man: Sociological Studies of the European Drama and Novel, 1600-1900, *The Beacon Press, 1957, pp. 190-220.*

ISAAC BASHEVIS SINGER (essay date 1967)

[A Polish-born American novelist, short story writer, children's author, and translator, Singer is widely held to be the foremost living writer of Yiddish literature. Awarding Singer the Nobel Prize for Literature in 1978, the Swedish Academy cited him for "his impassioned narrative art which, with roots in a Polish-Jewish cultural tradition, brings universal human conditions to life." Among his best-known works are the novels The Slave *(1962) and* Shosha *(1978). In the following excerpt from his introduction to* Hunger, *Singer, who considered Hamsun to be a major influence on his own work, offers a general study of Hamsun's career and critical reputation.]*

Writers who are truly original do not set out to fabricate new forms of expression, or to invent themes merely for the sake of appearing new. They attain their originality through extraordinary sincerity, by daring to give everything of themselves, their most secret thoughts and idiosyncrasies. Knut Hamsun's genius is totally a product of self-searching and introspection. This became immediately apparent in his first novel, ***Hunger***. People do not love alike; neither do they starve alike. It is interesting to note that although ***Hunger*** was published during a time of social upheaval and revolutionary propaganda, none of the reformers seized upon it as support for their claims and demands. Those who are so fond of stressing the poverty of the masses detected in this work an almost inimical element. Knut Hamsun took the basic human experience of hunger and made it such a highly individualistic sensation that everything common dropped away from it. In this sense, he went even further than Dostoevsky. There is a strong resemblance between Hamsun's hero in ***Hunger*** and Dostoevsky's Raskolnikov in *Crime and Punishment*. Both suffer extreme need. Both are literary neophytes. Both are highly nervous, virtually bordering on madness. Both are spiritual aristocrats. I nearly said Nietzscheans, although Nietzsche was still a student when Dostoevsky wrote his classic.

But, for all their similarity, the two heroes are fundamentally different. Raskolnikov is a man deeply rooted in Russia and matters Russian. Dostoevsky gave a thorough picture of Raskolnikov's mother, of his sister and her groom, of Raskolnikov's friend Rasumihin, along with a whole array of true Russian types and characters. Dostoevsky portrayed the society that produced a Raskolnikov. In Hamsun's work we see the city of Christiania; we feel its physical and spiritual climate; Hamsun mentions names of streets and buildings, but at the same time the reader realizes that the hero is as far removed from his surroundings as if he were in a foreign land. His hunger can be said to be entirely antisocial. He is starving, not because he cannot find a job in the city or on the farm, but mainly because he is obstinately determined to live from his writing although he is just a beginner. He is hungry both for bread and for inspiration. He is lonely, not because he cannot make friends, but because he has no patience for others. He suffers the shame of those who must rise above their fellow creatures or perish.

It is characteristic that when Raskolnikov reminds the investigating prosecutor of the possibility of his escaping from Russia, the prosecutor points out that people like Raskolnikov do not escape. Raskolnikov is tied to Russia. Hamsun's hero, on the other hand, ends by signing on as a crewman on a freighter bound for the seven seas. (Hamsun himself visited America twice in the 1880's and worked as a farmhand in North Dakota and as a streetcar conductor in Chicago. He even wrote a book at that time, ***The Cultural Life of Modern America,*** in which he sharply vilified this country. In later years he recanted his views.) Raskolnikov is finally redeemed by entering upon a term of penal servitude in Siberia accompanied by his beloved, Sonia, and in a spirit of religious resurrection. Hamsun's hero is, in substance, a suicide, although he does not actually kill himself. Raskolnikov seeks a reckoning with God, while Hamsun's heroes wrangle with fate. In a sense, the hero of ***Hunger*** wages a hunger strike against destiny. He seems to say: "Either give me inspiration or I'll take my life and frustrate your schemes. . . ." But destiny neither provides him with the inspiration nor allows him to die. He is constantly saved by some temporary deliverance. An editor prints an article or a sketch and the hero is paid a few kroner. Then the ordeal begins all over again. . . .

The suicidal character of Hamsun's hero—all the heroes of his earlier novels are one and the same person—comes out in his masterpiece, ***Pan.*** Lieutenant Glahn in ***Pan*** is as lonely as the hero of ***Hunger.*** Glahn has settled somewhere in a hamlet at the edge of a forest in northern Norway without any practical purpose—simply to be alone. (pp. v-viii)

Fictional heroes who are estranged from their environment seldom emerge lifelike. With most writers, such heroes are mere shadows, or, at best, symbols. But Hamsun is able to portray both the environment and the alienation, the soil and the extirpation. His heroes have roots even though they cannot be seen. The reader never knows precisely how they have become what they are, but their existence is real all the same. Hamsun's favorite hero is a young man in his late twenties or early thirties, rash, good-natured, with no plans for the future, always anticipating some happy chance, yet at the same time resigned and melancholy. While Dostoevsky's heroes beat their breasts and seek solutions for themselves and for mankind, Hamsun's hero is frivolous in word and deed. He speaks to people as he would to a dog or to himself.

Hamsun is less popular in the United States than in Europe, but European writers know that he is the father of the modern school of literature in his every aspect—his subjectiveness, his fragmentariness, his use of flashbacks, his lyricism. The whole modern school of fiction in the twentieth century stems from Hamsun, just as Russian literature in the nineteenth century "came out of Gogol's greatcoat." . . . This writer was enchanted with Hamsun's prose for years. Hamsun was perhaps the first to show how childish the so-called grownups are. His heroes are all children—as romantic as children, as irrational, and often as savage. Hamsun discovered even before Freud did that love and sex are a child's game. . . .

Hamsun belonged to that select group of writers who not only interested a reader but virtually hypnotized him. (pp. viii-x)

There were a number of reasons why Hamsun's star waned, as the saying goes. To begin with, he lived too long. It would have been better for him artistically had he flared and gone out, as Byron did. But Hamsun lived past ninety and wrote almost to the very end. It may sound like a paradox, but the novel that won him the Nobel Prize, ***Growth of the Soil,*** marked the beginning of his literary decline. Hamsun himself had grown disgusted with Hamsunism. He attempted to become an epical rather than a lyric writer. He was only partly successful in ***Growth of the Soil.*** Everything that followed, ***The Women at the Well, The Wanderers,*** and other subsequent works, were uneven blends of stale romanticism and meager naturalism. Hamsun's literary output of the twenties disappointed his admirers and probably him as well.

The second reason was the violent social changes brought about by the two world wars. Hamsun was not the writer for champions of social justice. They sensed within him the eternal pessimist, the scoffer and profaner. During World War II, the eighty-year-old Hamsun was guilty of a most tragic mistake. Nazi critics read into Hamsun, as they had into Nietzsche, support for their ideologies, and Hamsun deceived himself into thinking that Nazism would spell the end of the left-wing radicalism which repelled him. The Knut Hamsun who had kept aloof of the masses and social reformers allowed himself to be taken in by Nazi demagogues. (pp. x-xi)

But the literary and political errors of his later years cannot erase Hamsun's colossal role in the literature of the twentieth century, even though he actually wrote his best works in the nineteenth century: [***Hunger, Mysteries, Editor Lynge, Pan,*** and ***Victoria***]. . . . (In the intervening years, he published a number of plays.) His novels ***Benoni*** and ***Rosa*** . . . were nothing more than variations of ***Pan.*** (p. xi)

Was Knut Hamsun's career nothing more than a great literary quirk? Far from it! All that is genuine has roots. Hamsun was deeply rooted in his country and in Scandinavian culture. But, like many other masters, he was a man before his time. His skepticism, or perhaps it could be called Pyrrhonism—doubting even the doubts—belonged to a later era. To Hamsun, man was nothing but a chain of moods that kept constantly changing, often without a trace of consistency. Man was, therefore, as strong as his weakest mood. The hero of ***Hunger*** doubted the existence of God, yet he prayed to Him. He loved, but he belittled this love and all that it stood for. He strove for artistic revelation, yet wasn't really serious in his approach to art. Doubt, not only the philosophical but the mundane, found in Hamsun its narrator par excellence.

Because he was responsible for a whole school of writing, Hamsun cannot appear as fresh today as he did when he literally stunned Europe with his content and his style. But it can be positively stated that none of his disciples has surpassed him. This is particularly true of his two classics, ***Hunger*** and ***Pan.*** . . . It is not Hamsun's fault, as it wasn't Byron's, that he inspired a virtual chorus of imitators who muddled his literary achievements. It is almost axiomatic that the more original a writer is, the more he is mimicked. Both Byron and Hamsun transformed skepticism into art. Both expressed the futility of a life that is blind, of a hope without faith, of a fight without purpose.

Both were masters at portraying the abyss of the human emotions. (pp. xi-xii)

Isaac Bashevis Singer, "Knut Hamsun, Artist of Skepticism," in Hunger *by Knut Hamsun, translated by Robert Bly, Farrar, Straus and Giroux, 1967, pp. v-xii.*

ROBERT BLY (essay date 1967)

[*An American poet and translator, Bly is considered an important influence on contemporary American poetry. A leader in the movement called Deep Imagism, he holds that human intellect forms a barrier between inner and outer realities, and that the poet must create art "which disregards the conscious and the intellectual structure of the mind entirely and by the use of images . . . bring forward another reality from* inward *experience." In 1958 Bly became the founding editor of the Fifties Press (later the Sixties Press, Seventies Press, and now, the Eighties Press), which currently publishes* The Eighties *(formerly* The Fifties, The Sixties, *and* The Seventies*), a periodical devoted to modern American poetry and to the translated works of little-known European and South American poets. Himself a translator of the novel* Hunger *into English, Bly closely examines Hamsun's first major work, in the following excerpt.*]

One reason ***Hunger*** is powerful is that it compresses into a few months ten years of genuine and desperate life. Hamsun's ten years of starvation and physical labor were, in their effect, like Dostoevsky's term in the Siberian prison: the experience drove him harshly into himself, intensified his imagination, and made him more than just a "writer." It forced him to be inward. . . . Antonio Machado, the Spanish poet, said that the writer should listen to himself, and "ought to overtake by surprise some of the phrases of his inward conversations with himself, distinguishing the living voice from the dead echoes." Hamsun realized all this: in his preface to ***The Cultural Life of Modern America,*** he said, "Truth telling does not involve seeing both sides or objectivity; truth telling is unselfish inwardness" (*uegennyttige Subjectivitet*).

In ***Hunger,*** Hamsun was participating in a general turn toward inwardness in European thought at the end of the nineteenth century: Kierkegaard took part in that movement also, as did the Danish novelist Jens Peter Jacobsen, whose work Rilke loved so much. Like Jacobsen and Kierkegaard, Hamsun turned inward with great determination. ***Hunger*** was prepared for by hour after hour, year after year of keeping watch on the moods rising and falling in his mind. An idea or an impulse rises above the horizon like a moon: Hamsun watches its whole course carefully, like an inward astronomer, convinced we have been too casual in watching the movements of the "heavenly bodies" or demonic bodies inside.

He watches with immense care. Our better novelists show vividly how their characters' thoughts make, over a half-hour period, curious loops and unexpected turns. But Hamsun is able to draw such a map for a *minute* of his character's time. He has a magnifying glass on his eye, like a jeweler's. The reader is constantly astounded by the precise detail with which we come to know the character's intelligence, and also by the intensity of that intelligence.

How few books there are today in which a genius is the main character! Fewer and fewer, as serious novelists more and more tend to put people of lower intelligence than themselves into books, so that the readers will feel at home. Hamsun disdains such a practice. To have the hero of your work the most intelligent person you can imagine is more a Greek than a Christian idea. The Greeks liked heroes with great strength of personality and vigorous intelligence. ***Hunger*** shares with the ancient tragedies and much ancient poetry another Greek quality—a curious joyfulness. It's odd to suggest that a book named ***Hunger*** is essentially a joyful book, but it is true. The mood of the prose is delight: a delight in watching the intelligence, particularly the tendency of the intelligence to *play,* even in deep crisis.

Hunger shocked many readers, and still does, because Hamsun does not resort to rhetoric or hysteria when he catches sight of demonic impulses. The more orthodox Western attitude toward the demonic, in which both Billy Graham and William Burroughs in differing ways are trapped, responds to anything demonic with hysteria. Hamsun watches a cruel impulse come forward—for example, the desire to save face that ends his character's conversation with the street whore in Part Three—and he neither becomes moralistic like the orthodox religionist nor does he lick his lips hungrily as the de Sade disciples do, but rather looks at the impulse calmly, even affectionately. His calmness, like that of the old Zen teacher, suggests that all this hysteria about the impulses is senseless and unintelligent: the essence of right life is this—when you are hungry, eat; when you are tired, sleep. The book then is morally at odds with a great deal of Western literature, and it is incompatible with most European moral literature. ***Hunger*** blew much moralistic work of the time, like Ibsen's, apart. (pp. xiii-xv)

The swiftness and pungency of the prose [of ***Hunger***] astounded everyone. It made Norwegian seem like a young language. . . . [The] United States probably contributed something to the newness of the style. The Norwegian novelist Sigurd Hoel said he thought the excitability, the constant slang, and the sarcasm of American talk had a lot to do with ***Hunger***'s style. In Norwegian, the sentences are abrupt, swift, and graceful, curiously like the best of Hemingway. Some thirty years later, Hemingway's short and pungent sentences startled American readers used to the long sentences of Dickens and Henry James.

We notice that ***Hunger*** has one other quality that reminds us of a Hemingway novel: it is not a book of social protest. It is not a cry against a society that will allow the kind of poverty we see throughout the book. The reason in Hamsun's case is simple. He does not have faith enough in the middle class even to make a proposal to it. By contrast, Zola actually trusted the middle class even as he attacked it: he thought that if an injustice was pointed out clearly, the middle class would correct it. Hamsun's experience with the middle class as a youth had taught him, as similar experiences taught W. C. Fields, that the bourgeoisie could not be trusted. As an adult, he saw it as the killer of the impulsive and exuberant life he believed in. (pp. xix-xx)

One interesting faith runs through all of ***Hunger***—a curious, almost superstitious faith in the unconscious. The main character listens a great deal "with his antennae." He senses the woman in black under the street lamp is linked to him even before he talks to her. He is sure the word "Cisler" is a sign to him from "higher powers." He obeys his impulses instantly, showing an unusually open avenue between his unconscious and his consciousness, no matter if it is an impulse to bite his own finger (which pulls him out of a serious daze), or the impulse to hire a taxi and drive off to a nonexistent address, or the impulse to speak to strangers. He takes great delight in obeying these impulses.

The main character of ***Hunger*** feels no pity for himself, and we do not, because there is a sense throughout the entire novel that his starvation was somehow planned by his unconscious—that somehow his unconscious has chosen this suffering as a way for some part of him to get well. The hero of ***Hunger*** obeys the unconscious, and remains in hunger, despite suffering, until he has lived through what he must, or learned what he had to. What seems to us catastrophe, his spirit experiences as secret victory. His anarchic inability to support himself is experienced by his spirit as obedience. What seems to the careless observer a series of sordid collapses appears to his spirit as a series of ascetic exultations, in each of which some tiny filaments holding the personality to its past shell are separated. His obedience to the unconscious, even at the cost of physical suffering, is the right thing; it is the road of genius and of learning. His painful starvation has called up an immense reserve of healing power that had been lying concealed in the psyche. (pp. xxi-xxii)

When Hamsun's hero has lived through what he must, and has learned what he must, his unconscious loses interest in his hungering and allows him to take a job on the ship, and the book ends. By that time, he has been changed. The hero realizes this on the ship at the end. As he looks back toward Christiania, "where the windows shone with such brightness," he understands that he is now set apart, that he will never be a part of the comfortable domestic life of Europe. Hamsun of course was not his character, and it cannot be said that he himself became wise. (p. xxii)

Robert Bly, "The Art of 'Hunger'," in Hunger *by Knut Hamsun, translated by Robert Bly, Farrar, Straus and Giroux, 1967, pp. xiii-xxii.*

HARALD NAESS (essay date 1967)

[The author of several articles on Hamsun's work (see Additional Bibliography), Naess offers evidence, in the following excerpt, that "Hamsun's social philosophy should be measured, not by his attitudes to Germany, a country barely mentioned in his literary production, but rather by the image of America, which was always one of his major themes." The essay from which the following excerpt is taken was written, in part, to defend Hamsun from such critics as Leo Lowenthal (1957), who, "by pointing out similarities in (The Cultural Life of Modern America) *and in the scandalous wartime articles, and by reinforcing their theories with selected quotations from his other journalism and creative writing, . . . try to prove that Hamsun was always a Nazi."]*

It is rumored that Hamsun's book ***Fra det moderne Amerikas Aandsliv (From the Intellectual Life of Modern America)*** will soon appear in English translation. Hamsun himself never wanted this early work republished, claiming its style was "frightfully poor and childish." Strictly as a guide to the American cultural sense of the 1880's the book is probably worthless; on the other hand, it is both delightful reading and an important document for students of Hamsun's thought and literary style. (p. 305)

Hamsun called his book a thesis, a scholarly account of American conditions, and since his personal impressions were so limited one would conclude that he relied heavily on printed sources. He probably read Kristofer Janson's *Amerikanske forholde (American Conditions)* from 1881, and it is clear that Sir Lepel Griffin's devastating account *The Great Republic* (or rather a shorter version in the *Fortnightly Review*) had been a favored inspiration; at other times his arguments echo the thinking of Matthew Arnold and Herbert Spencer. Hamsun himself claimed he had no written sources available at the time of writing, which fits well with a story of how he barged into the Copenhagen Public Library, asked for books on America, and received a Scandinavian encyclopedia which he studied eagerly. (p. 310)

Though Hamsun wrote a brilliant style, illustrating his points with amusing examples, his book on America consists for the most part of trivial observations, comments on the speed and restlessness, the ignorance of conditions in foreign countries, the excessive patriotism, the vulgarity of taste, the tendencies to violent behavior, the significance of churchgoing, etc. Georg Brandes remarked that using Hamsun's method it would be possible to write the same book about any country in the world. Of great interest, however, are the sections on American writing and certain basic social theories which underlie most of Hamsun's later authorship and which are here expressed for the first time.

In his book Hamsun used the Haymarket Square riot and the following trial to illustrate the arbitrariness of legal practices and the power of public opinion in the United States. Hamsun was not himself an anarchist, but he had friends with anarchist sympathies, and, as an artist, he approved of their philosophy which resembled his own literary program in being avant-garde and strongly individualistic. On the other hand he was opposed to all ideas of equality: Whoever wishes to look for Nazi ideology in Hamsun's book will find it most easily in his treatment of underprivileged groups in America, the Indians, the negroes, the women. The statements about the negro are the most tactless; here Hamsun's language approaches the worst abusive slang of the poor white. But then it is also from their level he views the problem: the while laborer fearing competition and reacting to the eating habits and sexual vigor of his black comrade.

Hamsun's attitude to the negro later changed, but not the attitude to women. His women characters from Laura (1878) to Bridget (1949) are all ridden by social ambitions which ruin their relationship to the man they love. It was not until his stay in America that Hamsun developed fully his idea of the modern Eve, impertinent, childless, well educated, with more time for her hobbies than for her husband, yet for all that neurotic and dissatisfied. Already in his first articles from America he described her in great detail; in his book on America he made her responsible for a number of ills, among them the deplorable state of American art: America's art was led by its women, just as Germany's literature was led by its women and laid waste by them. In all this Hamsun viewed the American woman not so much as an individual with human rights, rather as an aesthetic object. He considered her more attractive than any other woman in the world, but also prudish and cold and quite unable to set off the general lack of beauty and grace he found in America and which gradually turned him away from democracy and made him an aristocrat. Hamsun's view of life was the view of an aesthete. To him the ideal society was one which displayed a special harmony resulting from mutual confidence, tolerance and graceful customs among its members. Such harmony existed only where each person knew his proper state and behaved accordingly. The dissatisfaction and disrespect Hamsun had encountered among women and negroes in the United States typified that country's lack of culture or lack of nobility. He saw it also in the primitive curiosity of most Americans, their habit of never thanking the hostess after meals (the Scandinavian *takk for maten*) and their disrespectful *how do you do,* a "shout thrown after people in the street." To Americans, Hamsun claimed, all symbols of respect were empty forms. (pp. 311-12)

In 1918 he headed his article **"Bonde" (Farmer)** with the monition: "Take your daughter home from the city!", and a Danish author who had written him for advice was told: "You and I should not live on poetry and emptiness, we should play a part as human beings, marry and have children, build homes and till the soil." This new insight into the importance of farming and manual work in general also influenced Hamsun's view of America. It was a gradual process. In his articles on the tourist trade before and after World War I he still attacked the "lords and ladies from Yankeelands all over the world," and the United States were made responsible for Germany's defeat. In an interview from 1918 he referred to his stay in America as "wasted years, years full of bitter disappointment." On the other hand he must have realized that if tourism was typically American, then love of home, family, good neighbors and hard work was no less so. Toward the end of the twenties Hamsun's opinion of America, therefore, was colored less by his hatred of the tourist trade than by his respect for a young and vigorous nation which had outgrown some of the ugly features in Hamsun's sketch of 1889. America had advanced in culture during those forty years, and so in a sense had Hamsun. "Cultured" is the word which best describes the article **"Festina Lente"** written in 1928. In it he expressed his gratitude for what he had learned from Americans; he also praised their generosity, which he found typical, and their high respect for all honest labor. He was impressed with their intellectual scene and considered the American novel to be the most refreshing and most original in the world. However, Hamsun was not primarily interested in knowing whether Americans enjoyed the right kind of equality or a satisfactory cultural life. On this occasion he asked about their contentment and peace of mind, and he found there was little of it among them. Their rush and restlessness, which Hamsun had described forty years earlier in his book about America, had increased rather than diminished since then. The orientals, on the other hand, were content with their lives; they smiled at the impetuous ways of the occidentals and lowered their heads in contemplation. Americans, Hamsun claimed, could do no better than study the wisdom of the East.

"Festina Lente" is friendly criticism. Hamsun knew he could not make America responsible for all the agitation of modern times. Life had become restless also in Europe, even in Norway; industry came because all people wanted it. Hamsun's warning, therefore, goes out, not to America alone, but to the Western World as a whole.

There is a special relationship between Hamsun's "journalism" and his strictly "creative" writing. Impressions and opinions which Hamsun rushed to print in Norway's daily papers later appeared in his books as constructive ideas based on profound and responsible thinking. There is for instance the article from 1915 about unmarried mothers who killed their newborn babies ("hang them! . . . hang the first hundred!") and the treatment of this subject in ***Growth of the Soil,*** where sympathy and irony blend into a bitter humanity which distinguished Hamsun's later writing and which even applied to the problems Hamsun gathered under the designation "America." Various nations have received such symbolic treatment in Hamsun's work. England represented decadence and record hunting, Russia resignation and contemplation, Switzerland the tourist trade, Germany youthful vigor. America stood for these and other qualities, actually for the whole modern world as it is reflected in Hamsun's novels. The novels show the poet's attempt to come to terms with his times. Normally he failed, not necessarily because he was backward, but because he was a pessimist by temperament and a man of no compromise. Nevertheless, there was a development in Hamsun's relationship to his times. In his journalism it appeared as an orientation toward Hitler's Germany, in his creative writing as a reconciliation with America, a reconciliation due in part, no doubt, to the resignation of old age, but also to new knowledge.

Three questions always recur in Hamsun's discussion of the New World: the respectability of manual labor, the value of technical progress, and the rhythm of life in the United States.

The hero doesn't work in Hamsun's early novels; his time is taken up with women, philosophizing, and dreams of the future. That Hamsun himself reacted against this sort of individualism is seen from his novel ***Shallow Soil*** . . . , in which he portrays the artists as useless scroungers, while their opponents, the businessmen, hold the author's sympathy. ***Shallow Soil*** is not a great novel, but important in the history of Hamsun's works, since it shows the first signs of a democratic process which gradually brought Hamsun's characters down to earth. The early hero's theorizing is taken over by some local eccentric, and the aristocratic artist-heroes themselves are replaced, first by businessmen and gentlemen farmers, later by shopkeepers and smallholders. Hamsun at first was reluctant to give up the good family background of his farmer protagonists. He said of Nils Dreng: "He had certain personal notions of honor, inherited through many generations. A boy from a large farm behaved different than a boy from a small holding." But already in ***Growth of the Soil*** nothing is known of Isak's relatives, and in ***Vagabonds*** it is explicitly said of Ezra that his people were paupers.

Isak Sellanraa in ***Growth of the Soil*** is a chosen man; the gods send their servant Geisler to him and give him success because he is so hardworking and so faithful to the soil. . . . The young man with no assets but his ambition and will to work hard who sets up a new home for himself and his family resembles nothing so much as an early immigrant to the States. Isak Sellanraa is referred to as "the margrave," but he is neither a German junker nor a Norwegian *Odal* farmer; rather he is like one of the tenant farmers from Norway that Bjørnson met in North Dakota: "They have as much of the world's most fertile land each of these tenant farmers as the most prosperous of our big farmers in Norway." Hamsun did not mention these new rich farmers in his book on America; he probably knew they played a smaller part in reality than in the world of the poets. The average American farmers round the turn of the century were "somewhat footloose in their attachment to the soil as well as somewhat hasty and shiftless in its cultivation." Nevertheless Jefferson's independent farmer ideal lived on among the Americans. Agriculture should be their natural occupation, and they should be small farmers because the small farm would best develop the economic and political independence of its owner and produce in him a fruitful community spirit. Hamsun's Ezra is such a farmer. He enjoys the fruits of his industry in a happy homelife. But he is also an important man in his district, somewhat lonely perhaps, and not really popular with his neighbors. Still, he is the person who deals out his provisions and saves the parish from starvation, and he is a courageous man who defends his family with the axe when his rights are infringed upon. Hamsun, then, had come to realize that "certain personal notions of honor" could be developed also in a pauper's son, and this realization must have changed his attitude to "the pariah caste from all over the world" which inhabited America.

At the same time that Hamsun shaped his character Ezra, President Hoover spoke of America's "rugged individualism" and

Grant Wood showed in his American Gothic a self-will and a fanaticism of a kind which is rarely found even in Hamsun's sternest aristocrats. Hamsun had no knowledge or understanding of such tough and stubborn yeomen when he wrote his book on America, but he used them—often with added humor—in his later pictures of Norwegian farm life. They are the pioneers Isak, Axel (***Growth of the Soil***), Daniel (***Chapter the Last***), and Ezra. Their inexhaustible industry, their independence and natural conservatism were inspired by an idealism which was typically American and became typical of Hamsun. Full of disappointment over having to work as a farm laborer in America, Hamsun had written to a friend: "But then it is not a *shame* to work here, as it is in Norway." Strangely, it was to take him thirty years to overcome that shame.

The pioneer farmer Ezra, for all his love of the soil, is a man of somewhat limited imagination. He scorns the idea of spruce planting which Hamsun himself conducted on a grand scale at Nørholm—and the reader is never told that he understood—as Hamsun did—the usefulness of a tractor. Hamsun was a mechanics-minded person. His characters appear in strange costumes, invent curious machines, and engage in fantastic undertakings. There are Happolati's electrical hymnbook in ***Hunger*** (first mentioned in the four articles from America), the mechanical forest saw in ***With Muted Strings*** (Hamsun's own invention), and Isak's ingenious goat feeder in ***Growth of the Soil.*** Growing up in the busy coastal villages of *Nordland* (Hamarøy, Tranøy, Kjerringøy), Hamsun was nurtured in the spirit of enterprise and did not at first judge technical inventions morally; but gradually he came to view them as good or bad according to whether they produced good or bad activities. Whatever helped the farmer without disrupting the old order was praised; whatever led to the formation of the country town and advanced modern civilization was condemned. These opinions Hamsun developed in his social novels after the turn of the century, describing the progress of civilization as a disease in several stages. First industry arrives in the countryside. Then workers, trade unions, banks and money economy, and with it general dissatisfaction and moral decline. Finally Hamsun gathers the victims in a sanatorium where they wait for the end. . . . In ***Chapter the Last*** the poet presents the pneumonia, tuberculosis, and syphilis of the patients at the sanatorium, as well as their sadism, homosexuality, impotence, and procuration. The little light toward the end where Leonard Magnus, the suicide, decides to go back to life and his responsibilities, is not enough to change the impression of ***Chapter the Last*** as being Hamsun's gloomiest novel. Hamsun's last novels, which all describe the life of homecoming emigrants, were written in a different style. They still show modern civilization as an infectious disease; yet here, where the poet attacks the very root of the evil, America, the tone seems more positive. The feeling of something conciliatory in the style of these "American" novels is explained . . . most of all by the character who dominates the action in ***Vagabonds, August,*** and ***The Road Leads On.***

August is one of Hamsun's greatest figures. The trilogy about him occupies one fifth of Hamsun's literary production, his life is not only more completely illuminated than that of other Hamsun characters, but also commented on by Edevart, his friend, and by Edevart's sister and brother Pauline and Joakim as well as by Ezra and others. . . . August has a number of qualities which, while they are common among ordinary men in all countries, are often singled out as being typically American. There is, for instance, his belief in all manufactured goods, synthetic products of all types, and everything which is large. August's gold teeth, his propaganda for preserves, verandas with colored glass, red mail boxes, door bells, his Christmas tree farm, and giant sheep ranch are the expressions of an imagination which could well be Norwegian. But when August carries out his dreams, he is driven by a pioneer instinct which is better termed American. Thus the people of Polden have some difficulty making out how August, who is such a wonderful liar, can also be a hard worker. American is also August's violence: people are known to carry guns in other civilized countries, but this man shoots or stabs without warning. His vehemence is frightening even to friends. . . . American above all is August's unusual energy. His projects, however, are not based upon sound thinking and thorough investigations, but are the results of a sudden inspiration. August's activity often resembles a nervous disorder, like that "restless racing around" which Hamsun associated with America.

Time and again August is described as being sterile, which no doubt means that nothing of what he does is constructive, just as the development he symbolizes only leads to nothingness. However, August is not only sterile and useless, but a danger for all people with whom he gets into contact. From the girl with the lion mane he had received "a reminder," "a disease of 2½ years' duration." The doctor keeps him quarantined at Polden, but at Segelfoss he courts Cornelia with his disgusting old man's love which is really what destroys him in the end: the witch warns him, and when he persists she plunges him into the abyss. August's disease is an image of the world's disease. Hamsun enumerates the symptoms: August is a liar, ruthless, unreliable; he has no weight; he is without depth; he drags his roots behind him; and Hamsun concludes: "This single individual had it in his power to corrupt both town and countryside." (pp. 315-22)

Really August is Hamsun's Peer Gynt. Hamsun had attempted to shape him before, in ***The Monk Vendt,*** but he lacked then both the dignity and humility which is asked of the person who has to sit in judgment over his self. August is tried and sentenced over and over again through the three volumes. Apparently it is of the greatest importance to the poet that this gad-about receives full justice. And while August has little reason to feel happy about the final verdict "he was ignorant and therefore innocent," he should be pleased with the judge's wonderful humor and understanding, with the spirit of humanity which colors the whole case against him. (p. 323)

[In ***The Ring Is Closed,*** Abel Brodersen, just back from America,] does not fit into the well-regulated life of his little home town and reacts against the snobbery of the upper classes and the well-to-do. In this place all people value each other according to dress; a man's suit will tell if he is normal, prosperous, permanently employed. Abel spends some of his inheritance on clothes, but it is against his nature somehow to keep clean and tidy; soon he is left with nothing but a common laborer's shirt and pants. Abel's indifference resembles that of another emigrant, Edevart, in the August trilogy. They have both been disappointed in love; they have lost their hope and ambition and have become restless during many years abroad. . . .

The reader who claims this is all caused by America may well find support in ***August,*** but not in ***The Ring Is Closed.*** Abel replies to Olga's question: "You mean when did I begin to develop? A long time ago, I'm afraid. Way back in childhood. I was so utterly lacking in all chances—and so it all began." Actually it is a constitutional flaw, a special refinement of character, which slowly deforms the personalities of both Edevart and Abel. Where they differ is in their attitude to America. Edevart no longer thinks of his farm in Dakota where he toiled for three years, but Abel misses his days in Kentucky—there he had found a pace which suited his temperament. He had become restless, and his life in foreign lands matured him. (p. 324)

Abel's memories of his life in Kentucky are rather vivid when one considers that Hamsun had never visited the South. There is no doubt that he was inspired by images of the South in modern American writing. On the other hand he may himself have seen something resembling southern decadence in his Irish work-mates at Dalrymple's farm—after the harvest period was over, when they drank and gambled and squandered their money with no thoughts of the future. The character Evans in the autobiographical account **"On the Prairie"** has a lot in common with Abel and his friend Lawrence, and the story of how they made corn mush and afterwards fried it in slices to get bread, is first mentioned in Hamsun's account of his Madelia days. All in all, much of Abel's life is based upon Hamsun's memories of his own experiences; there is, also in this respect, a close relationship between author and character which may serve well to protect Abel against the critics' attacks on his personality. It has been said of ***The Ring Is Closed*** that it shows the Hamsun protagonist at the end of a long downward career; the romantic hero has here degenerated into an animal with whom no reader can identify and whom no author would want to make the bearer of his message. But there are many excuses for Abel Brodersen. His childhood years as the only son of an old, miserly lighthouse attendant and his alcoholic wife turns him into a lonely person and one badly in need of friendship. He is a faithful friend, and even where he is betrayed and, in turn, himself betrays, he manages to preserve his integrity. (pp. 325-26)

Hamsun's social writing did not develop properly until after the turn of the century; one might say it began with the new Norway in 1905. In that year Hamsun published his impressions from a journey to Turkey in which, as often as the occasion justified it, he showed his contempt for business, emancipated women, and socialists. He also found it interesting to contrast the East and the West. . . . (p. 327)

Hamsun's novels during the next thirty years contained his further speculations over these questions. New people entered into the picture, Isak and Ezra with their steel plows, and August who was too busy to keep track of Sundays and Mondays. The greatest change came with Abel, in that he—who had so few demands and of work only did what was strictly necessary—was not a Turk, but an American. Hamsun's new interest in the South owed a lot to the works of the young American novelists, whom he admired, but it should also be kept in mind that even during his years in the States Hamsun had praised the leisurely life of southern aristocrats. In his sketches from Abel's home, poverty-stricken Green Ridge in Kentucky, Hamsun seems to indicate that America's many poor whites may long have practiced the eastern philosophy he recommended so strongly in **"Festina Lente."** This realization affected his opinion of America's restless rhythm, as well as his general view of America's role in the modern world. In his final judgment America is colossal, a land of infinite possibilities.

Before he appeared in court to answer for his pro-German stand during World War II, Hamsun was examined by the psychiatrist Professor Gabriel Langfeldt. To him he described himself, as well as his many hundred characters, in the following manner: "They are all split and complex, not good, not bad, but both, subtly differentiated in their natures, changing in their actions" [see excerpt above, 1949]. With his portraits of Ezra, August, and Abel, Hamsun presented an apologia not only for himself, but, symbolically, also for modern times, for America, which he thereby admitted to be a land of greater contrasts than he had been willing to allow forty years earlier. (pp. 327-28)

Harald Naess, "Knut Hamsun and America," in Scandinavian Studies, *Vol. 39, No. 4, November, 1967, pp. 305-28.*

STANLEY KAUFFMANN (essay date 1969)

[Kauffmann is one of America's most well-known contemporary film and theater critics. A contributor of reviews to several magazines, he is currently the film critic of The New Republic. *Although the theater and cinema are of primary concern to Kauffmann as a critic, he is also knowledgable in the field of world literature. In the following excerpt, Kauffmann discusses* Victoria *and its complementary relationship to the earlier novel* Pan.]

Hunger is not only the best of the Hamsun I have read (five books), it seems to me a masterpiece. The newly republished work ***Victoria,*** which is a short novel like ***Hunger*** and ***Pan*** and which has been put into adequate English by Oliver Stallybrass, is marked strongly with the fierce, fantastic, mordant Hamsun flavor.

"I hope to have my new book ready by the end of the month," Hamsun wrote his German publisher about ***Victoria*** in September 1898, "a kind of 'pendant' to ***Pan***. . . ." So a word first about ***Pan.*** In 1855 Lieutenant Glahn, a young gentleman, spends the summer in a hut in the northern forests, living on the game he hunts. He falls in love with Edvarda, the daughter of a merchant in the nearest town, and she with him, but in a sequence of prismatic modulations, pride intervenes. At summer's end when he leaves, she asks for his hunting dog. He shoots the dog and sends the body to her. In an epilogue set in India some years later, a hunting companion who is jealous of Glahn's attentions to a girl, shoots him and passes it off as an accident. Pan, the god of forests and, one might say, of the pleasure-principle, has finally crushed Glahn, a lover circumscribed by pride, against the rocks of reality. The retribution that he carried within him, that had been in him long before he met Edvarda, has finally flowered.

In ***Victoria,*** which is set on the same mountainous coast of Norway, the social status of the two lovers is reversed and intensified. Johannes, the miller's son, falls in love with Victoria, the daughter of the castle, when they are both children, and he is treated with friendly condescension. He goes off to a university, writes poems, which get published, and a "major work." (Its description suggests ***Hunger.***) When Johannes returns, Victoria confesses her love for him yet becomes engaged to a young lieutenant. The latter is killed in a hunting accident, and Victoria tells Johannes that she now wants him. But with timing as unlucky as in the last scene of *Romeo and Juliet,* he has just become engaged to another girl. The book ends with Victoria's death, soon after, and with her voice from the grave—a long letter in which she tells Johannes that she accepted the lieutenant in order to save her bankrupt father. The grinding machineries of life—once again—seem to have little relation to the feelings of people living within them.

Recounted thus, ***Victoria*** may sound like the scenario of a 19th-century ballet. Several matters make the novel quite otherwise.

First, there is Hamsun's power of construction. The shape of the book is spare, in contrast with its ripe content; there is not one scene too many, and there are plenty of interstices for our imaginations to fill. Second, there is, familiar in Hamsun, a power of wild fantasy—interwoven scenes in which Johannes uses the vocabulary of experience to compose private rhapsodies. But, most of all, there is Hamsun's scathing view of beauty even while he adores it, a love of the ideal and also a sense of its ludicrousness. (p. 28)

As a "pendant" to ***Pan,*** this novel is related in more than status inversion. It also reuses such matters as the forest setting, the tendons of fantasy, a gala party as a focal point, and a hunting accident. Love as ecstasy, love as acid, is again the theme. But it is a weaker work than ***Pan. Victoria*** keeps redeeming itself from peasant-and-princess romance by its *conviction* of romance, but mainly by the harsh intrusion of mortality and the intimations of the twentieth century. The emphasis in ***Pan*** is quite the reverse, and so no redemption is necessary. It starts with wild solitude, it drinks solitude like a lifesaving draught. (All through the Hamsun that I know, solitude—not loneliness—recurs as a kind of blessing.) Love appears later and touches to life both the heart and the cruelty of Glahn. The effect is more immediately engaging, the antinomies are more tense.

Still, lesser though it is, ***Victoria*** is very much better than it promises to be. It is one of those late 19th-century artworks that face the results of the individualist revolution of the early 19th century. And in its sense of the increasing anachronism of class barriers—individualism would automatically make this so, quite apart from political change—it relates closely to much of Strindberg. . . . Even in this minor novel, Hamsun, the peasants' tyrannized son, has a great deal in common with the author of *Miss Julie* and *The Son of A Maidservant*. (p. 43)

Stanley Kauffmann, "Stanley Kauffmann on Norway's Forgotten Giant," in The New Republic, *Vol. 160, No. 5, February 1, 1969, pp. 28, 42-3.*

CARLA WAAL (essay date 1971)

[*In the following excerpt, Waal discusses Hamsun's dramas, a subject that has remained largely unexamined by other critics.*]

Winner of the Nobel Prize for literature in 1920, Hamsun is best known for novels such as [***Hunger (Sult), Pan,*** and ***Growth of the Soil (Markens grøde)***]. . . . (p. 75)

That Hamsun was also a playwright is not as well known, since he usually spoke disparagingly of dramatic literature and even more so of the theatrical profession. . . . Despite his scornful remarks, Hamsun must have felt an attraction to the dramatic form; between the years of 1895 and 1910 he finished six plays.

During Hamsun's formative years, the plays of Henrik Ibsen dominated Norwegian theatrical life and earned international respect as significant literary works. Hamsun, the young rebel, proclaimed himself an explorer of new literary territory and relentlessly criticized Ibsen for what he called dry, mechanical, and puzzling plays. Ibsen's influence was not easy to escape, however, and Hamsun began by using much the same style and structure one finds in *An Enemy of the People* or *Ghosts*. His first three plays, with their prose dialogue and contemporary settings, present the life of a philosopher at the ages of twenty-nine, thirty-nine, and fifty. They were published and first produced between 1895 and 1898. ***At the Gate of the Kingdom (Ved rigets port),*** the first play, introduces the scholar Ivar Kareno as a stubborn champion of unorthodox ideas. (pp. 75-6)

Since Kareno proclaims his philosophy with vigor, it is difficult to ignore. Opposed to the liberal, humanistic views of the majority, he speaks scornfully of the masses and theorizes along Nietzschean lines. Kareno's arrogant and intolerant view of society was used many years later as evidence of Hamsun's lifetime admiration for Germanic culture and predisposition to Naziism. Theatre critics never took the philosophy very seriously; they suggested that one should disregard the content and emphasize the courageous independence of Kareno's stand. Viewed as a heroic idealist, Kareno symbolizes the honest individualist standing alone against the established leaders of society. He also embodies Hamsun's provocative ideas about the supremacy of youthful vigor. In the first play of the trilogy a university professor represents the successful, petty, and inflexible older generation; ironically in the final play Kareno himself becomes pathetic proof of the cowardice and shallowness of age.

Although the philosophical issues are intimately related to the marital conflict, the personal crisis is more dramatically effective than the ideological debate. Kareno is at first self-centered and unappreciative of his wife; by the time he naïvely offers to do anything to keep her, she no longer cares for him. Elina, the fun-loving girl from the country, is one of several characters in Hamsun's works who become corrupted after moving to the city; it is no surprise in the second play of the trilogy to see that she has become shameless and hard.

The first and third plays of the trilogy are conventional in structure and realistic in detail, taking place in a parlor, with a series of visitors coming to call amid the bustle of domestic routine. Conversation proceeds in a straightforward, clear fashion, with occasional touches of wit and irony. The middle play of the trilogy is more subtle and impressionistic, suggesting that the playwright was developing a new style. If he had continued in that direction, Hamsun might have stood beside his idol Strindberg as one of the innovators of modern drama.

In ***The Game of Life (Livets spil),*** the philosopher is working as a tutor in North Norway, teaching the sons of the merchant Oterman. Kareno hopes to finish a book culminating his life's work, but is unable to concentrate because of his infatuation with Oterman's attractive daughter Teresita. (p. 76)

Several elements of this play contribute to its originality and the impression that its style has elements of expressionism. Teresita, the unhappy and taunting heroine, is partly responsible; her self-contradiction, her unreasonable actions, and the imagery of her speech seem to bare the workings of the subconscious. She describes her emotions in metaphors such as a red cock and a large green flower, and speaks of the man she loves as the moon and as an island. There is also a character in the play who functions as an obvious symbol. He is an old man who appears often, waiting to deliver a message to which no one will listen. It is he who accidentally shoots Teresita, and at the final curtain he stands alone—his name is "Justice." Although it may slow the action, Act III is especially effective in creating a dream-like mood of horror and decay. It takes place in the public square on a winter day; the scene is dark except for the moon and the Northern lights glowing in the sky. Hamsun manipulated the crowd skillfully, showing the arrival of a dreaded epidemic. As people become ill, a mood of hysteria builds up and reactions vary from the singing of a foolish drunken man to the stringent exhortations of a salesman of religious tracts. . . .

If life is a "game," as the title suggests, it is a senseless and cruel game; even Teresita, who has tried to play with the lives of her admirers, becomes a helpless pawn in the hands of the "blind animal" called Justice. With the fierceness of passions and the variety of human frailties displayed in ***Game of Life,*** it is not surprising that the play caused a protest in conservative circles when first produced in Norway. Perhaps in the violence and confusion of the ending, critics ignored Kareno's final brief speech. "Wise Nemesis," he says, as though accepting the punishment for his weakness—for having humbled himself at Teresita's feet, when he should have stayed in his magical tower—awaiting insights and visions. (p. 77)

Sunset [*Aftenrøde*] is similar to ***At the Gate of the Kingdom,*** not only in style but in the cast of characters who enter and leave the Karenos' parlor. Now they are twenty years older than when they were introduced, and the years have made them foolish, hypocritical, and cautious. Each has learned the art of compromise, but Kareno does not accept this new mode of action until he has vacillated and broken promises several times during the course of the play. When he finally justifies his softened views by saying that he has become "mature," his most ardent young admirer tries to assassinate him—just as Kareno himself had once written should be done with leaders who betray their cause. Despite his rationalizing, desires for prestige, luxury, and revenge over his youthful rival Jerven appear to be the true causes of Kareno's capitulation.

As with other plays in the trilogy, the title of ***Sunset*** is a major symbol, for Kareno has reached the twilight or "sunset" of his life. At the final curtain he settles down to tell Elina's illegitimate daughter a fairy tale about "a man who would never give in."

Hamsun's next dramatic work was a complete departure from the trilogy in setting, style, and magnitude. Over a period of almost four years Hamsun struggled to write a dramatic poem built around some of the dream characters from ***Pan.*** The epic composition, which was originally planned to be the first part of a trilogy, grew to be eight acts long, and the trilogy was never continued. From the start, Hamsun realized that this play could not be successful on the stage. . . . The drama surprised the public in 1902, for it was different from anything Hamsun had written previously.

The loosely structured plot covers many years in the life of Munken [Friar] Vendt, a vagabond hero who experiences extremes of wealth and poverty—sometimes a preacher, sometimes a thief, and finally a shoemaker. . . . There are some of the same elements one finds in certain of Hamsun's novels: the ambitious merchant representing power and greed; the aristocratic heroine ambivalent in her affections; the rebellious and isolated hero at odds with society; and romance a frustrating duel between two proud individuals.

An obvious comment to be made on ***Munken Vendt*** is that the play and its hero are reminiscent of *Peer Gynt,* the only play by Ibsen which Hamsun admired. Some critics have interpreted both dramas as combining a romantic depiction of life among country folk with considerations of deep ethical and religious ideas. The same verse form is used in each play. Both heroes are charming, deceitful adventurers. Although they both evade responsibility and escape from their pursuers, Vendt reflects more deeply than Peer and maintains his consciously defiant philosophy without apology. Peer is loved generously by the patient Solveig, but Munken Vendt's love does not show him such forgiveness and trust. (pp. 77-9)

Hamsun's next dramatic work, ***Queen Tamara (Dronning Tamara),*** was published in 1903 and produced in January, 1904. It is the only prose play he placed in a remote historical setting. While traveling in Russia and the Middle East several years earlier, Hamsun heard of a queen who ruled in the Caucasus from 1184-1212 and noted the ruins of Christian churches from that period. Having also written a narrative about his trip, Hamsun here constructed a unified and intense series of events in the court of the Christian queen. (p. 79)

The simple prose style and open, almost blunt, dialogue in this play make each character easy to understand. In fact the clear-cut conflicts and frank confessions bring the play close to melodrama. Tamara is the most interesting character—childishly impetuous, accustomed to exercising her royal prerogative, yet dependent on the counsel of a zealous old priest. Her tender recollections of the early days of her marriage, her aroused vanity and exhilaration over the courtesy of the captured Khan, and her quick forgiveness of Prince Giorgi's treachery are evidence that she longs for a submissive feminine role. Mildness and generosity are her other dominant traits: probably natural goodness rather than the teachings of Christianity leads her to show tolerance far beyond the customs of that primitive society. (pp. 79-80)

Hamsun's last play was ***In the Grip of Life (Livet ivold . . .),*** a four-act prose drama with a modern setting. It was written for the Russian public, partly to earn royalties but also because Hamsun felt that only the Russians knew how to produce his plays. Critics have described this play as "Russian" and have said that Hamsun here proved himself to be a "Scandinavian Chekhov." ***In the Grip of Life*** was a success at the Moscow Art Theatre and has reportedly been performed more often than any other of Hamsun's plays.

All events of this tragicomedy take place on the seventieth birthday of "Old" Gihle, who is cheerfully unaware of the tensions of the evening. The focus of interest is his wife Juliane, who is bewildered and desperate about losing her lover Blumenschøn, even though he is crippled and greedy. (pp. 80-1)

Juliane evokes little sympathy. Having married for financial security, she still demands the audience and the romance she enjoyed as a stage star. Unable to accept the fact that she has changed, she is obsessed with a craving for admirers. Hamsun probably created this merciless portrait to illustrate his conviction that the way of life of professional theatre artists leads to degradation.

In the Grip of Life presents a bitter picture. If one understands these people to be in its "grip," then life must be malicious and meaningless. Like others of Hamsun's works, the play may also have been depicting the foolishness and disappointments of age, when pleasure and achievement come to an end. The strong servant from South America symbolizes Juliane's final defeat and shame. She had laughingly predicted that her last lover would be a Negro; now she accepts the fulfillment of that prediction.

At the Norwegian premiere in 1910 applause following the final curtain had to compete with the ardent blowing of a whistle by one patron; when asked why he was causing a disturbance, he said because the action of the play was so unmotivated! Although that protester's judgment may be deserved, Hamsun at least painted a full psychological portrait of the leading character. The production was criticized on several counts: because it had failed to sustain attention, because the brutal picture of humanity was merciless, and because the characters evoked no pity. While the macabre humor and witty dialogue revealed his brilliance, ***In the Grip of Life,*** to quote one critic, "does not add any new leaf to the author's laurel wreath."

The leaves in Hamsun's laurel wreath represent his novels, but the plays also deserve attention in a total study of his authorship for several reasons. First, they had a degree of theatrical effectiveness, as evidenced by the success of certain productions, especially in Germany and Russia. If Hamsun had established a satisfactory working relationship with an innovative company of Scandinavian actors, he might have been stimulated to further efforts as a playwright. Some of the characterizations are memorable for their vividness and individuality; his desperately unhappy heroines like Teresita and Juliane provided especially rewarding roles for interpretation on stage. Second, the content of the plays and Hamsun's attitude toward theatre have been material for serious psychological study. They were analyzed with great interest after World War II when Hamsun was being examined as a psychiatric patient prior to his trial as a war criminal. Finally, an acquaintance with the plays leads to deeper understanding and appreciation of Hamsun's novels. In comparison the plays are found to convey less often the mystical beauty of the Norwegian landscape, subtle lyricism, probing of the unconscious, and the agonizing awkwardness of social situations. There are, however, similar character types, as well as specific characters who appear in both plays and novels, such as Bondesen, Munken Vendt, and Iselin. Moreover, there are comparable problems of isolation, unrequited love, and the struggle to develop a philosophy. Studying the plays and novels together gives insight into a creative artist's growth and achievement.

Although he admired Strindberg's genius, Hamsun did not venture with the Swedish playwright into new dramatic territory. Hamsun did not believe the theatre could do justice to intimate psychological portraits, tense silent encounters, and unexpected transitions between dream and reality. Instead he concentrated his creative genius in the novel form. In his novels can be found certain passages that have greater theatrical potential than any of the scenes in his plays. (pp. 81-2)

Carla Waal, "The Plays of Knut Hamsun," in The Quarterly Journal of Speech, *Vol. LVII, No. 1, February, 1971, pp. 75-82.*

HENRY MILLER (essay date 1971)

[*In the following excerpt, Miller discusses* Mysteries, *a novel he had praised and recommended to Anaïs Nin many years earlier (1934). Miller reveals that his longstanding interest in Hamsun's second novel lies in the work's reflection of many of the struggles in his own early career and notes that when reading* Mysteries, *"I always feel as though I am reading another version of my own life."*]

From the way I have marked up this new translation of the book, it would seem as if I had never read it before; yet this must be the seventh or eighth time I have done so. Though it is not the greatest book ever written, it is closer to me than any other book I have read. Hamsun is the author I deliberately tried to imitate, obviously without success. I am not alone in this fatuous worship of Hamsun. He seems to have been to those of my generation what Dickens was to the readers of his time. We read everything he wrote and panted for more. . . .

Reading this book, I always feel as though I am reading another version of my own life. And, just as I forget whole chunks of my life because they are too painful to remember, so I forget blocs of **"Mysteries"** from one reading to the next.

One never knows for sure what motivates Herr Nagel's behavior (I call him "Herr" because that is how it was given in the earlier translation and because "Mister" does not suit him at all). He arrives from nowhere in a little town without a name, and there for a brief spell he plays at being God. We know no more about him at the end than at the beginning of the book—and that is what makes this tragic romance so absolutely delicious. Way back before his time he was already the adorable, incomprehensible anti-hero, an artist, one feels certain, who has chosen life as his medium.

One of the most noticeable features of this novel is Nagel's scorn and contempt, his positive loathing, for the bourgeoisie. It was in this same atmosphere that I grew up, rebelled and finally became a writer. (p. 1)

The people with whom one grew up, what did one have in common with them? Nothing, really; absolutely nothing. The authors one read were one's true friends; the musicians likewise. For the intelligent, sensitive individual the problem was the same all over the world. How to gain attention, how to be listened to seriously, how to negate the stupid activities of the politicians. He struck such a true note, Hamsun—one identified with him immediately. They were not only romances, his novels, they were often rhapsodies. He was also a master of discord.

And then the characters. Where else but in Hamsun would one expect to find a Martha Gude? Or "Minutten," called "The Midget" in this translation. (Minutten seems so much better to me. There may be a thousand midgets but only one Minutten.) And what a diabolical little monster he is! We have only to mention Dagny Kielland, the pastor's daughter, and the circle is complete. I said a while back that Nagel came on the scene playing God. What medley of roles he plays just vis-à-vis these three characters! The clown, the buffoon, the lover, the con man, the fixer, the patron, the phony detective, the intellectual, the artist, the enchanter. The madness of it all is created right before your eyes. Now you see it, now you don't. What stupid discussions during the typical Nordic drinking parties! And always the road leading to the parsonage, be it high noon, midnight or 3 in the morning. What love scenes and aborted love scenes in the depth of the forest! Creating the sorrow and suffering all by himself. And we don't want it to end. We enjoy every tragic moment of this hopeless love affair. It becomes our very own.

And if, according to psychologists, Herr Nagel must be regarded as a masochist, what a glorious masochist he is! Who would not rather be that particular masochist than a famous psychologist? I am even more curious than the publishers as to how this present generation will take the book. I notice that Hermann Hesse's work has made a strong appeal to the young; perhaps Hamsun will too. He should be right up their street, since he too was a dropout, a wanderer, an outcast, an everlasting rebel and an eternal foe of the establishment.

The thing about Hamsun is, of course, that he knew how to create music out of his misery. He had none of the 999 escapes open to the young today. His only escape was in and through nature. Were he alive today he might denounce the young as bitterly as he did the bourgeoisie of his day or the so-called great men of his day. Even in his crazy rantings about the great, the very great and the men of genius, there is such profound common sense. Above all, one feels his scorn and contempt for his own country, even for their great men, of which he admitted the existence of only one. (pp. 1, 30)

For all the bitterness, the madness, the hatred, the scorn, and the vilification let loose in this book, one must never forget that Hamsun was first and foremost a lover of nature, a loner, a poet of despair. He makes one laugh at the most unexpected moments—perhaps even in the midst of a passionate love scene—and sometimes for the wrong reasons. He can turn things upside down in the twinkling of an eye. Indeed, often he seems trying to come undone, to wriggle out of his own skin. But however mordant his humor, however biting his recriminations, one feels and knows that here is a man who loves, who loves love and who is doomed never to find a true and proper mate. He is definitely what one might call an aristocrat of the spirit.

How grateful I am that I ran across his work early in life, that I think as much (or more) of him today than when I first read him. (p. 30)

Henry Miller, "'We Read Everything He Wrote and Panted for More'," in The New York Times Book Review, *August 22, 1971, pp. 1, 30.*

ERICH HELLER (essay date 1980)

[Heller, the author of several critical studies of the works of Thomas Mann and Franz Kafka, reexamines the unlikely alliance of the highly respected Hamsun with the Nazi ideology, in the following discussion of Hamsun's greatest novels.]

Hamsun, who outraged the vast majority of his fellow Norwegians by publicly applauding the power that occupied his country in April 1940—he was, we should remember, 81 years old at the time—not once in his novels expressed sentiments as vicious as the anti-Semitism voiced by Pound's *Cantos,* attitudes no less vicious for being conveyed in meters and rhythms that reputedly have significantly enriched the poetic possibilities of the English language. On the contrary, in ***Wayfarers*** . . . Hamsun has lavished great imaginative affection on the Jew Papst, the good-natured, kind-hearted, and humorously fraudulent itinerant, peddling watches that certainly could not compete with the astronomical predictability of his appearing, boisterous and melancholy, at every village fair throughout the region.

Melancholy and boisterous, good-natured and fraudulent—such play on the contradictoriness of a character who nonetheless emerges as a perfectly convincing person suggests the particular quality of Hamsun's art and, therefore, his cast of mind and, therefore, some of the causes of his downfall. I shall come back to this.

The best of his many novels evoke in a highly sophisticated manner—this is the irresistible charm of the paradox that Hamsun embodies—the complex primitivity of life lived in the villages and small towns (such as the Segelfoss of his novels) on the islands and along the fjords of Norway; and if, as in the first work that spectacularly initiated his career, ***Hunger*** . . . , the scene is a city as large as Oslo (called Christiania at the time), the action—or what in more conventional novels would be the action—takes place entirely within the one character who is the story's protagonist and narrator. Yet this "inwardness" needs explaining. When Hamsun, one year before ***Hunger***—before, that is, he had established his reputation—published his determinedly biased book on America, ***The Cultural Life of Modern America*** . . . , he prefaced it with a sentence, intended no doubt simply as an apology, but remarkable for the reverberations it set off in its aphoristic succinctness: "Truth is neither two-sided nor objective; truth is precisely disinterested subjectivity."

The word "subjectivity" never had been used in this way. ***Hunger,*** by being the book it is, was to define Hamsun's meaning. For it is precisely through this subjectivity that Christiania, in its "objective" facticity (even the names of its streets and squares are factually correct) comes to life as intensely as cities hardly ever do in the naturalist literature of the epoch. Certainly the Christiania of ***Hunger*** is a fact verifiable by anyone who knows the city. Yet it is a fact of the poet's soul, just as is Baudelaire's Paris and Rilke's too (in *The Notebooks of Malte Laurids Brigge*), or Kafka's Prague (and the America he imagined in his first novel), or T. S. Eliot's London, the "Unreal City" of *The Waste Land*. If Kierkegaard had written novels, they would possess this concrete inwardness.

Indeed, Hamsun's ***Hunger*** vigorously attacks our senses with Christiania's sights, sounds, and smells. For days on end, after closing the book, we feel that we have actually met its shopkeepers, pawnbrokers, policemen, and prostitutes; climbed staircases to deserted addresses on streets given by name, trying to find a long-neglected friend who may help us, desperately hungry as we are, to some food; or we sit on a bench at the harbor, watching the ships on the mother-of-pearl-colored sea. At the same time all this is piercingly unreal, not in the manner of an evanescent dream, but by virtue of an absurd enhancement of the real as occurs in nightmares or hallucinatory states induced by exhaustion. After Hamsun, only Kafka, who was an avid and admiring reader of his, had the power of effecting such metamorphoses; and certainly Kafka could have said of Prague (did he not actually say it?) what Hamsun says of Christiania right at the beginning of ***Hunger:*** "All this happened while I was walking around starving in Christiania—that strange city no one escapes from until it has left its mark on him." (pp. 29-30)

Never before had hunger, physical hunger, been explored with such elaborate intensity and pursued to the ultimate fantasies and derangements it causes in the mind; and never before had it been so true to say of a man starving in a big city that he had only himself to blame for his starvation. A novel called ***Hunger,*** published in 1890, by its very title certainly would have raised expectations that Hamsun was bound to disappoint. His hero's misfortune is not due to cruel social circumstances but is a matter of free choice, if there can be free choices in Hamsun's universe of preordained and irrevocable destinies. Choice lies only in the acceptance of fate. There is no rebellion in ***Hunger,*** most certainly no protest against society—that hazy entity that performs for sociologically minded modern people the same function that ether did for pre-Einsteinian physicists. It is all more like a hunger strike against God. In extreme moments of near-fainting, this hungry man does curse, but he curses—the curse. "When nothing helped, no matter how hard I tried, . . . I shouted and roared threats up to the sky, shrieked God's name hoarsely and savagely, and curled my fingers like claws." What is the curse? It is his knowing that he is meant to be a writer and nothing else, and nobody's sharing this knowledge with him. Nobody? With regard to Hamsun himself, thousands of readers, after they have been enslaved for hours by his ability to transform hunger into a work of art, see him become what he was sure he was all the time, an artist. Although Hamsun's hungry man, like Kafka's hunger artist, is, in his own way, an allegorical figure, Hamsun's is more successful in practicing his art: he survives. Survivors, resilient and competent men and women, always have commanded Kafka's respect. Perhaps Hamsun gave him more cause for admiration than the author of ***Hunger*** could possibly have known. . . .

When in February 1952 he died at Nörholm, where he had built his house with the study, the "Dichterhaus," separate from it (a neat symbol of the separation of art from his life), he was 93, a deaf and almost blind man, a survivor of himself, deeply at odds with his own people, prosecuted for high treason in its law courts, and almost forgotten as a writer. (p. 30)

[***Mysteries, Pan,*** or ***Victoria***]. . . . Here was the poet of changelessness whose every character was conceived by his imagination as if to reveal the ingrained mendacity of all manifestos that aimed at changing human beings by engineering a change of social circumstances. (Ibsen once sat in the front row of the hall when the young lecturer Hamsun assailed the dramatist-reformer's beliefs—and perhaps made him write *The Master Builder* afterward.) Here was the creator of the truest, tenderest, and, in their verbal restraint, most sensuous love scenes in modern literature, and the artist who knew how to play most captivatingly on the muted strings of language. How did he avoid being repelled by that loud-mouthed, cheap painter who killed millions of people because they did not fit his cheap notion of what the picture of mankind ought to look like? (pp. 30-1)

In ***The Growth of the Soil*** Hamsun said of an old peasant that his age was 900 years, that he had been resurrected from the remote past and yet pointed toward the future, a man from the time when the first plough furrowed the soil, and yet a man of today. When Hamsun was in his 80s, Hitler unbelievably succeeded in making him believe that he, the leader, had come to lead the insurrection against the lettered, clever, and hollow men.

Many of Hamsun's fellow Norwegians sought in America an easier and more lucrative life than their homeland offered them. Their numbers swelled in the 1880s. "Dragging their torn roots behind them," as Hamsun says in ***Wayfarers,*** they are shown again and again in his novels. Before he and the world knew he really was a writer, he himself might have settled in America. He tried twice. (p. 32)

In the summer of 1888 he left America, sailed to Copenhagen, ready magisterially to pronounce on the culture of the new continent. ***The Cultural Life of Modern America*** is a witty, eloquent, amusing, and, more often than not, wrong-headed book. He might have been warned by what he himself said in print about Mark Twain's *The Innocents Abroad:* that it was marred by the author's rather superficial acquaintance with European traditions, the inadequacy of his aesthetic perception, his provincial nationalism, and the all too blatant intrusion of his political persuasion. The persuasion was, of course, radical-democratic.

Although Hamsun's own political or quasipolitical convictions made themselves heard at least as loudly in his book on America, it certainly could not be said of them that they were democratic. They were rather Nietzschean in their intellectual-aristocratic bearing, and radical only in their aversion to the tyranny wielded by the masses over the works of the mind, to the naive religiousness and the numbing of the tragic sense through the optimism of the therapeutic popular pedagogues. It is, certainly, Walt Whitman's "marvelous naiveté" that has won "a couple of followers" for his mediocre "tabular poetry, those impossible inventories of people, states, housewares, tools, and articles of clothing"; and it is Emerson's preachiness that made this "Aesop of the American mob of moralists" the supplier of "mottoes for their most ingenuous, goody-goody books." Later in his life Hamsun recanted his harsh pronouncements on America, called the book "my youthful sin" and its views "lopsided," and opposed its re-publication. Yet many passages of it are magnified projections of his abiding belief that "we become more and more civilized and lose in spirit." After 1889 and 1890, the years in which ***America*** and ***Hunger*** were published, Hamsun's biography is that of a more and more successful novelist and—at least outwardly—secure family man until in old age catastrophe overtook him. (pp. 32-3)

The mob of moralists. . . . One of the ***Wayfarers*** episodes that is bound to haunt the reader's mind for a long time is the dying of Skipper Skaaro, one of the more powerful men of the fjords, owner of the vessel "Seagull," and notorious womanizer. He hires the girls of the village for good money to stack the catches of herring in the hold of the ship. The prettier women he would then invite to his cabin. One day he invited Ane Maria, a married woman, but as it turned out in the end, his end, invited her not insistently enough. When she played coy and fussy, he angrily left her. This was his undoing, for the passionate and emotionally unstable Ane Maria felt rejected by this and was determined to have her revenge. A little later, on a Sunday, after having put on her best finery, she lured Skaaro to [a] bog near her village. . . . Hamsun unflinchingly describes his slow sinking, his futile pleas for help, her resolution to let him perish, her turning away from the bog, pretending to call rescuers, but only in order to watch secretly the final moments of his being sucked in by this fiendish piece of nature; and Hamsun's description is so detached as to avoid any possible identification of his own moral feelings with the victim's desperate outcry against the "diabolical evil." When a year and a half later, as once again the "dark days of autumn set in," she was plagued by her conscience and gave herself up, "there was a kind of pride, of hauteur about Ane Maria"—very different from the somnambulating Lady Macbeth's immersion in her guilty nightmare, or Raskolnikov's longing for atonement. It is neither incommensurate with Hamsun's genius to evoke such comparisons nor irrelevant to the large question of how imaginations differ with regard to their moral textures. That Hamsun, whatever his advanced age may have contributed to his failure, was, despite his aristocratic stance, so renitently indifferent to the abysmal words and deeds; so blind to the glaring deceptions of that German seducer of the masses; and—no doubt because of his own love of the earth—so willing to believe in the false prophet's prophecies of the blood and the soil while he at the same time cunningly manipulated all the available technologies, is surely related to an imagination capable of maintaining its moral composure in describing Ane Maria's "pride and hauteur." . . . Indeed, August's "It cannot be otherwise" is very close to his maker's sense of life. (pp. 33-4)

Hamsun's quite extraordinary last work, ***On Overgrown Paths***—it appeared one year before his death—is a strange collection of moving memories, expiring poetic perceptions, and disquieting descriptions of the poet's agonized life as a patient in an asylum for the insane (Ezra Pound comes instantly to mind), as an inmate in a home for old people, and as an accused before a tribunal that, after long hesitations and delays, found him guilty and made him poor by ordering him to pay a vast sum of money (collaborators had to make amends for Germany's extortions). From this last book Hamsun emerges as an obstinate and stubbornly misguided Norwegian patriot. He had believed in Hitler's assurances that his country would play an important role in the Germanic empire to come. Sometimes he sounds as if he looked forward to a Norway that would be as triumphant in the world as Kirsten Flagstad was in its opera houses; or, had he felt less defeated, he might have added: as his novels were in the literary world. . . . "Midsummer 1948" is the date of the last line of ***On Overgrown Paths:*** "Today the Supreme Court upheld the sentence and I stop writing." Halfway through the book he had said: "God bless everything that is not merely idle talk. Silence, too, is blessed by God." It should be engraved on the tombstone standing above the silence of a great writer. (p. 34)

Erich Heller, "The Triumph and Defeat of Knut Hamsun: Norway's Great Novelist," in The New Republic, *Vol. 183, Nos. 5 & 6, August 2 & 9, 1980, pp. 28-34.*

DOLORES BUTTRY (essay date 1982)

[The author of several articles on the work of Jean-Jacques Rousseau and Hamsun, Buttry is currently at work on a book concerning Hamsun's attitude towards art and the artist. In the following excerpt from her study of the short story "Hemmelig Ve," *she offers evidence that the work "may be considered an early expression of Knut Hamsun's ambivalent feelings toward artistic activity."]*

The Norwegian writer Knut Hamsun is known for his Rousseauian opposition to technological progress and city life and for his paeans to the beauty of nature and the joys and virtues of country life; one of those odes to elemental man—***Markens grøde (Growth of the Soil)***—won Hamsun the Nobel Prize for literature in 1920. Scandinavianists also honor in the great Norwegian a master of style, a veritable prose poet, as well as a pioneer of the psychological novel. No critic has ever considered the detractor of "civilization" to be deeply concerned with *Künstlerproblematik;* but the fact remains that Hamsun was, as a conscious artist, quite familiar with the dilemma of the artist, and his preoccupation with the artist's suffering is evident in ***Sult (Hunger), Mysterier (Mysteries), Pan, Victoria*** and many other works. The subject of this essay is a little pearl of narrative fiction which may be interpreted as an allegorical description of the spiritual no-man's-land which is the natural habitat of the creative artist.

"Hemmelig Ve" ("Secret Suffering") is one of the stories published in 1897 in the collection entitled ***Siesta.*** It may be considered an early expression of Knut Hamsun's ambivalent feelings toward artistic activity. The story is a first-person narrative in which the author relates how he was pursued and tormented over the years by a stranger. Four meetings of the two characters are described and these encounters have several significant characteristics: they occur in different countries and over many years. Thus, the universal and permanent nature of the struggle is symbolized. There is an eerie sense of both intimacy and animosity in the two personalities. The author's nemesis seems to know all about him and after the overt violence of the first meeting, during which the nemesis physically attacks the author, we find in the three subsequent encounters an obsession on the part of the author with humiliating and showing his indifference to his persecutor. The omniscience of the nemesis and the attitude of the two characters toward each other represents the internal nature of the struggle.

The story is a striking verbalization of Knut Hamsun's antagonism toward the artistic activity forced on him by his very nature. The duel between the two personalities must be interpreted symbolically. The author's nemesis, who turns up everywhere and seems to know everything about his prey, may be understood as the subconscious, the irrational self, the mind. We will call him the creative self. The narrator represents his opposite number, the rational self, the active man. Let us call him the practical self; the practical self is simultaneously attracted to and intimidated by the creative self. To a far greater extent than many other artists, Knut Hamsun was consciously aware of the dichotomy between the active man and the introspective artist. Hamsun's love of the simple, practical life is well-known. He always decried art and regretted that he was not a simple farmer. He wrote numerous letters to the Norwegian Authors' Union complaining about being addressed as "Forfatteren hr."—"author." . . . He was driven to create in spite of himself. It was not within his power to *choose* to retire to his farm and stop writing. His antagonism to art shows through in his story. The narrator thinks he understands the stranger at the end of the tale: he theorizes that the stranger tried to goad him into turning him over to the police; the stranger had probably committed a crime which weighed heavily on him, and desired to be caught. The subconscious insight of Hamsun was that art deprived the artist of peace and happiness, thrust open the locked doors of the irrational, damaged the individual's ability to harmonize with others in family and society, and should be punished for this debilitation wrought upon the practical self. The sadistic and masochistic traits of the story **"Hemmelig Ve"** surely are the subconscious expressions of Knut Hamsun's love-hate relationship to his muse.

The background situation of the first visitation already indicates a discrepancy between the will and the ability to engage in artistic activity. The narrator remembers that at the time he first came into contact with the stranger he was sitting alone in his room trying to copy music; this activity was a great strain to him because he could not read music. The very first sentence of the story informs us that the narrator has now been exposed to the persecuting stranger for the fourth time. The threatening aspect of the stranger is made clear: "He stalks me everywhere; I'm never safe from him because he turns up and meets me face to face in the most out-of-the-way places." The first encounter occurs when the stranger appears in the narrator's room in Copenhagen and suggests a drive to Tivoli that evening. The narrator declines but then reconsiders: "I first said no—I really don't know why I said no right away—but a moment later I decided to go along." . . . The natural reflex action of refusal was the healthy response; the drive turns out to be disastrous. After sinister and inexplicable attempts to frighten the narrator, the stranger attacks him with a nail, a corkscrew, or like instrument, producing a wound which left a permanent scar: "To this very day I have a reminder on my neck of that evening." . . . Although the narrator was able to pull the rope signalling the coachman to stop, the driver didn't notice anything of the tension between his two passengers.

The contrast between the two men is apparent. The first visitation is heralded by the stranger's knock at the door. The narrator remembers it as "light, very muted, as from a woman's hand." . . . The description of the man who enters confirms this impression of femininity: "A man of about thirty, pale, with dark eyes, narrow shoulders, conspicuously narrow shoulders." . . . The stranger is the opposite of the practical man of action.

The attitude of the narrator toward the stranger changes during the course of the story: after the amazement and hostility which the attack of the first encounter aroused in him, by the time he sees his nemesis for the second time—on a train in Germany a few years after the first meeting—his feelings have changed from hostility to curiosity. (pp. 1-3)

The assumption that both men are two facets of a single personality receives support in numerous ways. When the stranger seeks out the narrator for the first time, he says he came to "greet you as a countryman and old acquaintance." . . . The first and last meetings take place in the room of the narrator. The first time, in Copenhagen, the stranger knocks at the door. The fourth time, in Oslo, the narrator returns to his room to find the stranger already there, waiting for him. The stranger seems to know the narrator thoroughly; during the third encounter, in a gambling casino in New York, the stranger ascertains that the narrator is being cheated by the establishment. Furthermore, when the narrator enters the train compartment for the second confrontation, he ascertains "The compartment was empty. There were no others but he himself in there." . . . It is almost as if the stranger did not exist—the compartment is "empty" although he is in it. Either the stranger is a figment of the narrator's imagination, or he is a part of his own personality. Later the narrator admits that "I deliberately behaved as if I were alone in the compartment." . . . (pp. 3-4)

There is a reciprocal urge to humiliate. During the course of the train ride, all the while ignoring the presence of the narrator, the stranger takes out some sharp rusty objects which seem to be picklocks, and files them until they are shiny—then he lays them on the outstretched legs of his companion. The latter shows his contempt by refusing to acknowledge the presence of the stranger. Once again, another person comes across the scene—this time the train conductor—and, like the coachman years before, doesn't notice anything out of the ordinary.

What is the significance of these duels and encounters? The continual sparring, the mutual disdain, expresses well the incompatibility of the creative and active spheres. That the stranger is a symbol for the creative self—or the subconscious, if you will—is evident. We have noted his feminine characteristics, which indicate distance from a life of action. When the narrator saw the stranger in the train years after the first meeting, he noticed that "he hadn't aged in the least since I last saw him." . . . The stranger represents the imaginary world—so he always appears the same. The only difference the narrator notices is that while he was elegantly dressed the first time he saw him, the second time he appears shabbily dressed. Perhaps this is because art had to attract the narrator at first—but years later he had tasted of the price, and while the stranger is still "this interesting person," he doesn't appear as attractive or as well-off as before.

Already at the first meeting the narrator had noticed the ambiguous nature of the intruder: "I only remember that his words were often such that they could be understood in several ways, that there was something behind them and that the man himself made a mysterious impression on me." . . . (p. 4)

The creative self is threatening because it is allied with the irrational and because it infringes on the functioning of the practical self. At the first encounter, during the cab ride, the cab is closed and the narrator says that even though it is dark he sees the stranger well and sees what he is doing—namely, staring at him and dangling the rope. The rational character is aware of the threat of the irrational. Then the stranger asks, "You aren't afraid, are you?" . . . The threatening aspect of the creative self is clear. Why is the creative self threatening? Why does the stranger attack the narrator physically, draw blood, and leave a scar? Art does violence to life. Art draws its raw material from the real life of the artist, and the act of observing and expressing, the introspection of the artist detracts from his ability to function well in real life. He gives his blood and acquires scars. The creative self depends on the rational man and on his experiences for its subject matter. Therefore, during the third encounter in the casino, the stranger "followed my bets with more interest than he paid to his own." . . . The creative self watches the practical self closely and draws from it.

When the stranger yells across the gaming table to the narrator, "Don't you see they're cheating you?" he is representing the superior insight of the subconscious. Indeed, although the creative self uses the practical self as a source of raw material, it also has the key to impenetrable secrets. The creative self filed the rusty picklocks until they were sharp and shiny, and although he studiously avoids speaking to the narrator in the train, he does not try to conceal the nature of the instruments: "He turned these iron instruments over in his hands as if he were already picking a lock with them; he also tried to open his own suitcase with a couple of them. It was literally as if he intentionally wanted to show me what they should be used for." . . . Art unlocks many secrets; the subconscious provides symbols capable of conveying insight. The creative self attempts to initiate the practical self into the secrets. The narrator has acquired an inkling of the purpose of art. And yet, his deep distrust of art surfaces a moment later: "Watch out! I thought to myself; he is mocking you by being so obvious and open about it. There's something behind it, he is trying to lure you to something!" . . . The practical self is suspicious and on his guard—he has experienced before how the creative self can harm him. He therefore behaves in the compartment as if he were alone—he tries to ignore the creative impulse. The stranger in the train never even looks at the narrator, and the latter does his best to reciprocate the contempt: "I was preoccupied with just one thought: to return his deep contempt." . . . The creative self despises the imperceptive practical self and the practical self suspects the arrogant creative self. During the last meeting in the narrator's room, the mutual belittling continues, but the stranger has the last word. The narrator admits, "He got the better of me again. This person was always superior to me." . . . Art is suspect, even dangerous. The narrator is amazed that when the conductor comes, the stranger makes no attempt to conceal the picklocks—on the contrary: "It was as if he had waited for this opportunity to put his dangerous things on display." . . . The picklocks are dangerous—the practical, rational self is more comfortable when the locks to the subconscious are securely closed.

The practical self is never safe from the intrusion of the irrational—in various foreign countries and even in his own room he is importuned by the creative self. He is never safe from him, and he never knows when he will be subjected to him. He resents the continual intrusion. At the gaming table in New York the presence of the stranger, who pays so much attention to the narrator's bets, irritates and frustrates the latter: "If this person came again and butted into my affairs I would complain to the croupier." . . . The creative artist is subjected to periods of inspiration, even when these are unwelcome intrusions: the artist may unburden himself of a joyous overflow or attempt to free himself from a nightmare.

Eventually the artist must reconcile himself to the tyranny of the creative self. At the end of the story the narrator says: "Recently I have learned to think of him without resentment; he interests me very much; I am waiting to meet him again." . . . The artist learns to accept his schizophrenic predicament and waits for the next visitation of his muse. The creative self, the pale man with the black eyes, has been understood by the narrator, the artist. . . . (pp. 5-6)

It is highly significant that the characters in the story other than the two protagonists are oblivious to the struggle which takes place under their noses. The coachman took no notice of the physical attack and the conductor ignored the many picklocks which the stranger noisily dropped all over the floor of the compartment. The ordinary human being is not aware of or attracted to picklocks which lead to repressed and unwelcome secrets. The means of penetrating into the dark recesses of the mind have no lure for the ordinary person; nor would that person be aware of the struggle being so violently waged between the creative self and the practical self on the battlefield of the artist's mind. The artist must wage that battle alone and without aid or understanding; that is his "secret suffering." (pp. 6-7)

Dolores Buttry, "'Secret Suffering': Knut Hamsun's Allegory of the Creative Artist," in Studies in Short Fiction, *Vol. 19, No. 1, Winter, 1982, pp. 1-7.*

JOHN UPDIKE (essay date 1983)

[*Considered a perceptive observer of the human condition and an extraordinary stylist, Updike is one of America's most distinguished men of letters. Best known for such novels as* Rabbit Run *(1960),* Rabbit Redux *(1971), and* Rabbit Is Rich *(1981), he is a chronicler of life in Protestant, middle-class America. Against this setting and in concurrence with his interpretation of the thought of Søren Kierkegaard and of Karl Barth, Updike presents people searching for meaning in their lives while facing the painful awareness of their mortality and basic powerlessness. A contributor of literary reviews to various periodicals, he has frequently written the "Books" column in* The New Yorker *since 1955. In the following excerpt (originally published in a slightly different form in* The New Yorker, *Vol. LIV, No. 36, October 23, 1978), Updike discusses* The Women at the Pump, *which was retranslated into English and republished in 1978. The critic also briefly examines* The Cultural Life of Modern America, *terming it an "ill-tempered" and "ill-considered" work. Since 1967 Updike has reviewed several of Farrar, Straus & Giroux's translations of Hamsun's novels (see Additional Bibliography).*]

This panoramic novel of a nameless coastal town [***The Women at the Pump***] was originally published in 1920, when Hamsun was sixty-one and somewhere near the middle of his long literary career. It was in 1920 that he received the Nobel Prize. Even at this distance, Hamsun strikes us as less and more than a master like Mann or Ibsen; he was, like Byron, a phenomenon. His rise to fame, his irascible diffidence, his impact upon European literature, the enduring energy of his prose were all phenomenal. In ***The Women at the Pump,*** Hamsun sought to broaden his piercing talent, to turn to steady illumination the lightning flashes of his youthful work. The author was ready to settle down and tell us all about "things in a small town."

> Ah, that little anthill! Everyone busy with his own affairs, crossing each other's path, elbowing each other aside, sometimes even trampling on each other. That's the way it is, sometimes they even trample on each other . . .

The cast of ants is genially spread before us, from the town magnate, C. A. Johnsen, a shipowner and Double Consul, down to Olaus of the Meadow, the abusive town drunk; at the center of the novel stands one-legged Oliver Andersen, whom an accident at sea has mutilated in a mysterious way that, as his wife, Petra, keeps having babies, keeps the town women gossipping around the pump. . . . It is typical of Hamsun to have his hero apparently commit murder and to make so little of it. Making little, in the tradition of Viking stoicism, was his curious genius as a truth-teller but, on the broad social canvas he here proposes to fill, something of a fault. Our would-be naïve interest in the characters and their interwoven lives is considerably discouraged by the author's frequent disavowals of significance, his impatient darting from one thread to another, and his urge to scold his own creations. (pp. 429-30)

"One is saddled with the world one creates, as all creators are." Hamsun wrote this of Oliver, but he must have thought of himself. He is saddled with this fictional fabric but chafes under it; he sighs, snorts, and bucks. His characters talk, in his opinion, "claptrap and bunkum, sentimentality and bombast," and his maimed hero, "one of the jellyfishes that lay breathing in mortal stupidity and nothingness by the edge of the quay," no sooner has a few ideas than the author tells us, "They flashed into his head and were not worth much." Crises dissipate, mysteries remain, and the kind of tough forgivingness with which the townspeople view one another lends even the most dramatic events a tinge of the inconsequential. Of course, that is Hamsun's point, embodied in his unmanned, rascally, but indomitable hero: life goes on. (pp. 430-31)

The contemporary reader—beset, as the world of print sinks deeper into the twilight behind the television console, by panicked claims that each new book is urgent, exhaustive, or the latest thing—might enjoy this volume for its example of an author so fully, even arrogantly, at ease with his audience. Though Hamsun must have had the plot's major turns in mind, the first half, especially, of the novel gives the impression that he sat down at his desk each day with little more than a trust that something entertaining would happen on the page. As he maunders and meanders, he never looks behind him, confident that his readers are following. His wandering gradually takes him through six or so town households, but not before his central device—the appearance of both brown-eyed and blue-eyed babies in the impotent Oliver's family—has worn quite thin. On the other hand, the self-deceiving manner in which Oliver prostitutes his wife and takes a father's pleasure in the fruits of her infidelities is portrayed with a beautiful tact and believableness.

Only the Russians can match Hamsun's feel for the inconsistencies of the human soul, its quantum jumps through the rather irrelevant circumstances of life. As in all his fiction, small inanimate things—registered letters, a sack of eiderdown—animate the human landscape, and pantheistic bliss surges through the remissions of coping. . . . [Oliver's] town seems to have no parson—at least, none figures as a character—and its people are mostly irreligious; yet God clings to Hamsun's vocabulary, as the one term for expressing his reverence before creation and his love of the non-human. Love among human beings he instinctively perceives as mutual vexation. Though there are many women in the book, and a number of them sharply seen, none are shown in love. . . . Women in their nesting, not their mating, aspects evoke tender images from Hamsun:

> She was not knee-deep in calculations; she was a natural girl like the rest, Nature herself directed her tactics. . . . There was nothing incomprehensible in this, any more than a hen among the flower beds is incomprehensible.

But, so unexpected is the image, the hen among the flower beds is revealed as just that—incomprehensible. The rises and falls, advancements and setbacks, matches and maneuvers of the characters are embedded in an underlying mystery, that of existence itself. It is as if the actors in an Ibsen play, with their politics and posturing, were taken off the resounding stage, out of the sheltering proscenium arch, and set beneath an exhilarating, dwarfing sky. (pp. 431-32)

As [Hamsun's] American publishers plan their next volumes, they might consider turning momentarily from the later fiction and giving us some of his earlier theoretical writing, particularly his 1890 manifesto, **"From the Unconscious Life of the Mind,"** and his famous, contentious dissertations upon his esteemed contemporaries. His lecture series ***The Cultural Life of Modern America,*** which was printed as his first book, in 1889, has, I discover, been translated into English and published in this country. . . . The volume, based upon Hamsun's two Midwestern sojourns in the 1880s, tells us what many foreigners have volunteered to tell Americans: we are crude, money-mad, chauvinistic, corrupt, and inane. Hamsun's account of theatre in the United States as he knew it is a hilarious and probably not unjust descriptive flight; elsewhere, he fulminates against "African half-apes" whose freedom has turned America into a "mulatto stud-farm," wistfully looks forward to "the mighty revolts of individual geniuses who suddenly thrust mankind forward for several generations," protests the tyranny in the United States of women and of Boston, demolishes Whitman by quoting his worst poetry, and dissects Emerson with some spirit and shrewdness. According to Hamsun, Emerson has "that happy faculty of a writer or a speaker of being able to *say things*" but leaves us with only "a lapful of things said." Emerson's major failings are "his undeveloped *psychological* sense and thereafter his overdeveloped *moral* sense." Reverse the proportions, and you have Hamsun, just as you have Hamsun's positive aesthetic program in this negative criticism: "He has no eye for the slight stirrings of the psyche, the delicate manifestations of will and instinct, all that subtle life of nameless shadings." These shadings, these stirrings were to be the substance of the novel ***Hunger*** . . . , which launched Hamsun's comet. But in these ill-tempered and ill-considered lectures, as in ***The Women at the Pump*** thirty years later, he shows the magisterial ability to keep talking—however busily he appears otherwise engaged—about himself. (p. 433)

John Updike, "Saddled with the World," in his Hugging the Shore: Essays and Criticism, *Alfred A. Knopf, 1983, pp. 429-33.*

ADDITIONAL BIBLIOGRAPHY

Buttry, Dolores. "Music and the Musician in the Works of Knut Hamsun." *Scandinavian Studies* 53, No. 2 (Spring 1981): 171-82.
Examines "the importance of music to Hamsun and its constant coupling with the experience of cosmic unity experienced in nature," and presents "a portrait in broad strokes of the musician in Hamsun's works."

Downs, Brian W. "Kinck and Hamsun." In his *Modern Norwegian Literature: 1860-1918,* pp. 165-88. Cambridge: Cambridge University Press, 1966.*
An informative survey of Hamsun's career.

Eddy, Beverley D. "Hamsun's *Victoria* and Munch's *Livsfrisen:* Variations on a Theme." *Scandinavian Studies* 48, No. 2 (Spring 1976): 156-68.*
Examines thematic similarities between Hamsun's novel *Victoria* and painter Edvard Munch's *Livsfrisen.* Eddy perceives the works as reflections of "a simultaneous but independent development from Naturalism and Impressionism. This parallel development can be traced through the long careers of both artists; it is particularly interesting in *Victoria* and *Livsfrisen,* however, because both works may be considered experiments with trite, outdated forms and a conscious break with certain aspects of their own earlier works."

Knaplund, Paul. "Knut Hamsun: Triumph and Tragedy." *Modern Age* 9, No. 2 (Spring 1965): 165-74.
A biographical essay that focuses on Hamsun's hatred of England and on his pro-German sympathies.

Lovett, Robert Morss. *"Growth of the Soil."* In his *Preface to Fiction: A Discussion of Great Modern Novels,* pp. 41-52. Chicago: Thomas S. Rockwell Co., Publishers, 1931.
A close, thematic discussion of *Growth of the Soil.*

McFarlane, J. W. "The Whisper of the Blood: A Study of Knut Hamsun's Early Novels." *PMLA* LXXI, No. 4 (September 1956): 563-94.
A close examination of *Hunger, Mysteries, Pan,* and *Victoria.*

Naess, Harald S. "The Three Hamsuns: The Changing Attitude in Recent Criticism." *Scandinavian Studies* 32, No. 3 (August 1960): 129-39.
Examines trends in the critical reception of Hamsun's works. Naess divides Hamsun's career into three periods, beginning with "his receiving the Nobel Prize, then [continuing] with World War II and his prosecution for collaboration with the enemy, and [ending] with a period in which his last book, his death, and the centenary of his birth form the outstanding events."

———. "A Strange Meeting and Hamsun's *Mysterier.*" *Scandinavian Studies* 36, No. 1 (February 1964): 48-58.
Offers evidence that the episode of the "young and mysterious woman" in *Mysteries* describes Hamsun's brief romantic relationship with the English writer and translator George Egerton (Mary Chavelita Dunne).

Popperwell, Ronald G. "Interrelatedness in Hamsun's *Mysterier.*" *Scandinavian Studies* 38, No. 4 (November 1966): 295-301.
A study offering evidence that in *Mysteries* "society is presented almost as a biological organism, implicitly atavistic in character, and made up of interrelated and interdependent organisms, of which some are strong and aggressive and others weak and submissive. Together they form a cohesive whole in which the normal concerns of the realistic novel play little part."

Slochower, Harry. "The Imaginative Metaphor: Paul Gauguin, Knut Hamsun, D. H. Lawrence." In his *No Voice Is Wholly Lost . . . ,* pp. 132-46. New York: Creative Age Press, 1945.*
Discusses *Pan, Growth of the Soil, The Ring Is Closed,* and *Look Back on Happiness* as expressions of Hamsun's preference of the natural world over the industrial, and of his knowledge that an increasingly industrial society is unavoidable.

Updike, John. "Knut Hamsun." In his *Picked-Up Pieces,* pp. 141-53. New York: Alfred A. Knopf, 1976.
Reviews recent translations of *Hunger, On Overgrown Paths, Mysteries,* and *Victoria.* Of *Hunger* and *On Overgrown Paths* Updike writes that the two books, written sixty years apart, "are beautiful in the same way. They are laconic, brutal, joyous, and not quite formless." The critic judges *Mysteries* to be lacking in

the "weird jubilation" of *Hunger*, and concludes of *Victoria* that the novel's moral "seems to be 'There's always a catch somewhere,' or 'God has fashioned [love] of many kinds and seen it endure or perish.' Such an inconclusive conclusion, a standoff, well caps this eerily static love story, whose characters, though immersed in bookish circumstances, proudly reject the dynamism of characters."

———. "A Primal Modern." In his *Hugging the Shore: Essays and Criticism*, pp. 424-29. New York: Alfred A. Knopf, 1983.

Discusses a recent translation of *The Wanderer* (*Under the Autumn Star* and *On Muted Strings*).

Van Marken, Amy. "One of Knut Hamsun's Female Main Characters, Julie d'Espard." *Scandinavica* 13, No. 2 (November 1974): 107-15.

Discusses the central role of Julie d'Espard in *Chapter the Last*.

Frances Ellen Watkins Harper

1825-1911

American poet, novelist, essayist, and short story writer.

Harper was a celebrated orator, social activist, and one of the most popular black poets of her era. Her works are considered transitional, mediating between the subject matter and viewpoints of pre- and post-Civil War black writers: while she wrote against slavery, she also broke away from the purely propagandistic mode of the antislavery poet and became one of the first black writers to focus on national and universal problems. In her novel *Iola Leroy; or, Shadows Uplifted,* published in 1892, Harper countered the negative stereotypes of black Americans that pervaded contemporary fiction with educated, highly principled black protagonists who foreshadowed the characters created by twentieth-century writers.

Born to free parents in Baltimore, Harper was orphaned when she was three years old, and was subsequently raised by an aunt and uncle. She attended her uncle's school for free children and was influenced by his strong beliefs in discipline and hard work, and by his association with such abolitionists as William Lloyd Garrison. At age thirteen Harper was sent away to earn her own living, and found a job caring for the children of a bookseller. Although she was being trained as a seamstress, Harper demonstrated a desire for knowledge and a skill for writing that were recognized by the bookseller's wife, who allowed Harper access to the family library. During this period Harper composed poems with religious and moral themes, some of which were reprinted in newspapers and in a now-lost volume called *Autumn Leaves* or *Forest Leaves*. The desire to live in a free state induced Harper to move to Ohio, where, in about 1850, she began teaching domestic science at Columbus Union Seminary. Later she taught elementary school in Little York, Pennsylvania, and it was there that she first witnessed the passage of runaway slaves along the Underground Railroad. Incensed when her home state of Maryland passed a law in 1853 forbidding black citizens to enter the state under the threat of enslavement, Harper sought ways to actively participate in the antislavery movement. Boston abolitionists eager to display exemplary black speakers encouraged Harper to become an elocutionist, and after the success of her maiden lecture, entitled "The Education and Elevation of the Colored Race," she accepted an invitation to become a regular speaker for the Anti-Slavery Society of Maine. A strong, pleasant voice, attractive appearance, and reserved manner helped to make Harper a sought-after lecturer on the East coast. Although she spoke without notes, Harper often quoted from her own poetry during these lectures, which both enhanced her presentation and encouraged the sale of her *Poems on Miscellaneous Subjects,* published in 1854. Harper routinely contributed money to the Underground Railroad and other causes and sent letters and provisions to the imprisoned John Brown, a man she considered a martyr. During the last two weeks of Brown's life, as he awaited execution, Harper lived with his wife in order to lend moral support.

After her marriage in 1860, Harper gave up travelling, but when her husband died four years later she resumed her lecture tours. With the conclusion of the Civil War and the enforcement of the Emancipation Proclamation, her speeches shifted to Reconstruction themes stressing the divisive effects of racism as well as the need for temperance, domestic morality, and education for black Americans. Ignoring the advice of friends, and despite failing health and dwindling financial resources, Harper continued to speak before black and racially mixed audiences—often without a fee—throughout the still-dangerous South. Until the end of her career she remained active in such religious and social organizations as the Women's Christian Temperance Union and the American Woman Suffrage Association. She died at age 85 in Philadelphia.

Like Paul Laurence Dunbar, Harper was extremely popular with both black and white audiences. Most critics believe that her popularity as an orator was largely responsible for the favorable reception of her first book, *Poems on Miscellaneous Subjects,* which sold well enough to be reissued several times. Imitative of the works of Henry Wadsworth Longfellow and John Greenleaf Whittier, the poems in the volume are primarily antislavery narratives. Although Harper believed that black writers "must write less of issues that are particular and more of feelings that are general," most of her poetry nevertheless conforms to a propagandistic intent. Two such recurring themes of the collection, the plight of black families destroyed by slavery and the sometimes ennobling relief of death, are represented most effectively in "The Slave Mother." The poem portrays the dilemma of an escaped slave who knows that her capture is inevitable and decides to drown her infant rather than allow it to be raised in servitude. While the poem has been praised as a poignant and effective ballad, its heavy-handed and intrusive didacticism is jarring to modern readers. J. Saunders Redding, for example, has commented that Harper "was apt to gush with pathetic sentimentality." However, Jean Wagner has indicated that in order to fairly judge Harper's work critics must remember that in the nineteenth century deliberate sentimentality was frequently employed to gain audience sympathy.

In addition to her abolitionist poetry, Harper wrote many poems patterned after biblical stories. In early poems like "Saved by Faith," Harper depicted God as a merciful being who offers solace for human suffering. Joan R. Sherman finds this type of poem moving but contends that "her alliance to a dynamic warrior God" is poetically more interesting. Poems of the latter type call for justice on earth rather than the reward of an afterlife and often contain situations analogous to contemporary events: in "Ethiopia" God intervenes to free black people from bondage, while "The Martyr of Alabama" invokes a "militant redeemer." Sherman considers Harper's post-Civil War poems more intelligent and objective than her early works and notes that, despite an often militant urgency, they still maintain a conciliatory tone.

Moses: A Story of the Nile and *Sketches of Southern Life* are considered Harper's best works, though they are not as well known as *Poems on Miscellaneous Subjects*. Published fifteen years after her first collection, *Moses* chronicles the Hebrew patriarch's life, stressing the personal sacrifices he made in order to free the Israelites. Most critics consider this a non-racial work, but the poem's emphasis on leadership and self-sacrifice is consistent with Harper's often-stated hopes for black leadership and unity. The skillful use of metrically uneven blank verse and the portrayal of Moses' complex emotions and strong personality, however, depart drastically from the mechanical meter and sentimental subjects of her earlier poems. Like *Moses, Sketches of Southern Life* has been praised for its ingenuity and unity. The collection is unified by the narrators Aunt Chloe and Uncle Jacob, who describe common situations in the lives of Southern black Americans and comment on their political and social position. In her personification of these characters, Harper introduced a colloquial, though non-dialect, idiom that realistically represented the speech of her characters and helped temper the intrusive nature of Harper's didactic intent. While most critics agree with Redding that the racy, colloquial language of *Sketches of Southern Life* foreshadowed the dialect speech that Dunbar perfected, Kenny J. Williams finds Harper's method a more skillful and realistic presentation of black speech patterns and ironic humor than that of Dunbar, for Dunbar often utilized unrealistically pathetic or comic elements in his dialect poems. However, Jean Wagner disagrees completely, concluding that this early attempt to reproduce black speech was unsuccessful and noting that Harper's "language and humor are far from being authentically of the people."

In addition to her poetry, Harper published short stories and the novel *Iola Leroy*. Although her stories were artistically weak, "The Two Offers" is historically significant as the first short story known to have been published by a black American. While her short stories went virtually unnoticed in her lifetime, her novel *Iola Leroy* received favorable attention. Contemporary critics praised the work, observing that Harper's portrayal of the events from pre- to postwar years "derives added interest from being written from an inside view by one of the race." Modern critics, however, consider the work a melodramatic and sentimental treatment of light-skinned blacks who sacrifice themselves to help other black people and forego the comfortable lives possible if they were to pass as white. But the novel is considered more important for its positive portrayal of black characters than as an example of distinguished literary art. Hugh M. Gloster, for example, who believes that the novel is idealistic but unrealistic, nevertheless concludes that the work is significant because Harper countered the derogatory stereotypes of black people common in American fiction with well-mannered, educated characters of high moral convictions. Robert Bone also recognized *Iola Leroy* as a transitional work that "combines elements of abolitionism with incipient attacks on caste," making it one of the last works before a new generation of black writers began to advocate active resistance and violence.

Known primarily as an orator and social activist, Harper saw in artistic creation a means for expressing her political and ethical ideas. Today considered a minor poet of the abolitionist era, Harper and her works possess historic rather than artistic significance. Sherman expressed Harper's importance as a transitional black writer whose "ballads on issues of national concern represent a unique and significant movement by a black poet, a breaking away from exclusively racial protest themes."

(See also *Contemporary Authors*, Vol. 111.)

PRINCIPAL WORKS

**Poems on Miscellaneous Subjects* (poetry and essays) 1854
"The Two Offers" (short story) 1859; published in journal *Anglo-African Magazine*
Moses: A Story of the Nile (poetry and essay) 1869
Poems (poetry) 1871
Sketches of Southern Life (poetry) 1891
Iola Leroy; or, Shadows Uplifted (novel) 1892
Poems (poetry) 1900

*This work was published in at least twenty editions during Harper's lifetime, with various additions made throughout its publishing history.

W. L. G. [WILLIAM LLOYD GARRISON] (essay date 1854)

[Garrison, an American abolitionist and civil libertarian, founded the antislavery journal Liberator *and was cofounder of the American Anti-Slavery Society. The following excerpt from his introduction to the first edition of Harper's* Poems on Miscellaneous Subjects, *originally published in 1854, implies that the works should not be judged by overly strict standards, but rather as the works of a deserving apprentice poet. While he believes that Harper demonstrates talent, he also suggests that she needs encouragement and cultivation.]*

There are half a million free colored persons in our country. These are not admitted to equal rights and privileges with the whites. As a body, their means of education are extremely limited; they are oppressed on every hand; they are confined to the performance of the most menial acts; consequently, it is not surprising that their intellectual, moral and social advancement is not more rapid. Nay, it is surprising, in view of the injustice meted out to them, that they have done so well.

Many bright examples of intelligence, talent, genius and piety might be cited among their ranks, and these are constantly multiplying.

Every indication of ability, on the part of any of their number, is deserving of special encouragement. Whatever is attempted in poetry or prose, in art or science, in professional or mechanical life, should be viewed with a friendly eye, and criticised in a lenient spirit. To measure them by the same standard as we measure the productions of the favored white inhabitants of the land would be manifestly unjust. The varying circumstances and conditions of life are to be taken strictly into account.

Hence, in reviewing the following [***Poems on Miscellaneous Subjects***], the critic will remember that they are written by one young in years, and identified in complexion and destiny with a depressed and outcast race, and who has had to contend with a thousand disadvantages from earliest life. They certainly are very creditable to her, both in a literary and moral point of view, and indicate the possession of a talent which, if carefully cultivated and properly encouraged, cannot fail to secure for herself a poetic reputation, and to deepen the interest already so extensively felt in the liberation and enfranchisement of the entire colored race. (pp. 3-4)

W.L.G. [William Lloyd Garrison], in a preface to Poems on Miscellaneous Subjects *by Frances Ellen Watkins, Merrihew & Thompson, Printers, 1857, pp. 3-4.*

PHEBE A. HANAFORD (essay date 1882)

[In the following excerpt, Hanaford, an American poet and biographer, characterizes Harper as an eloquent lecturer.]

Frances E. W. Harper is one of the most eloquent women lecturers in the country. As one listens to her clear, plaintive, melodious voice, and follows the flow of her musical speech in her logical presentation of truth, he can but be charmed with her oratory and rhetoric, and forgets that she is of the race once enslaved in our land. She is one of the colored women of whom white women may be proud, and to whom the abolitionists can point and declare that a race which could show such women never ought to have been held in bondage. She lectures on temperance, equal rights, and religious themes, and has shown herself able in the use of the pen. (p. 326)

Phebe A. Hanaford, "Women Lecturers," in her Daughters of America; or, Women of the Century, *B. B. Russell, 1882, pp. 305-30.**

WILLIAM STILL (essay date 1893)

[Still's chapter on Harper in his The Underground Railroad *(1871; see Additional Bibliography) is considered the primary source of biographical information on the poet. In the following excerpt taken from Still's introduction to* Iola Leroy, *he emphasizes the social and moral concerns that he believes inform Harper's "entertaining and instructive" novel.]*

I confess when I first learned that Mrs. Harper was about to write "a story" on some features of the Anglo-African race, growing out of what was once popularly known as the "peculiar institution," I had my doubts about the matter. Indeed it was far from being easy for me to think that she was as fortunate as she might have been in selecting a subject which would afford her the best opportunity for bringing out a work of merit and lasting worth to the race—such a work as some of her personal friends have long desired to see from her graphic pen. (p. 1)

And now I am prepared to most fully indorse her story [**"Iola Leroy, or Shadows Uplifted"**]. I doubt whether she could, if she had tried ever so much, have hit upon a subject so well adapted to reach a large number of her friends and the public with both entertaining and instructive matter as successfully as she has done in this volume.

The grand and ennobling sentiments which have characterized all her utterances in laboring for the elevation of the oppressed will not be found missing in this book.

The previous books from her pen, which have been so very widely circulated and admired, North and South—**"Forest Leaves," "Miscellaneous Poems," "Moses, a Story of the Nile," "Poems,"** and **"Sketches of Southern Life"** (five in number)—these, I predict, will be by far eclipsed by this last effort, which will, in all probability, be the crowning effort of her long and valuable services in the cause of humanity. (pp. 2-3)

[Being] widely known not only amongst her own race but likewise by the reformers, laboring for the salvation of the intemperate and others equally unfortunate, there is little room to doubt that the book will be in great demand and will meet with warm congratulations from a goodly number outside of the author's social connections.

Doubtless the thousands of colored Sunday-schools in the South, in casting about for an interesting, moral story-book, full of practical lessons, will not be content to be without **"Iola Leory, or Shadows Uplifted."** (p. 3)

William Still, in an introduction to Iola Leroy; or, Shadows Uplifted *by Frances E. W. Harper, second edition, James H. Earle, Publisher, 1893, pp. 1-3.*

G. F. RICHINGS (essay date 1896)

[Richings, a black American historian, provides a brief laudatory review of Iola Leroy *in the following excerpt from his* Evidences of Progress among Colored People *(1896). Richings contends that works such as* Iola Leroy *will help overcome racial prejudice in America.]*

Mrs. Frances Ellen Watkins Harper . . . has been a writer of ability for many years. . . . The literary effort of her life is the beautiful story, entitled, **"Iola Leroy; or, The Shadows Uplifted."**

This book is indeed a gem and should be read by every one. I am confident if such books written by Colored writers could be read by the leading White people of our country, much good might be done in breaking down the awful prejudice which now exists. Her book received many very fine press comments from the leading White papers of this country; for want of space I can only give one:

> The story of **"Iola Leroy"** is well worth reading. The plot is natural and the characters are to be found in everyday life. The dialogue is exceedingly clever, full of pathos, humor, and authentic. The plot covers periods before, during, and after the war, and gives abundant opportunity for changing scenes and dramatic effects. Mrs. Harper has never written to better effect nor with a more worthy object in view.

The book will greatly increase her popularity as a writer and prove vastly beneficial to the cause of her brethren.

(pp. 415-16)

G. F. Richings, "Prominent Colored Women," in his Evidences of Progress among Colored People, *AFRO-AM Press, 1969, pp. 411-28.**

[W. E. BURGHARDT Du BOIS] (essay date 1911)

[An American educator and man of letters, Du Bois is considered one of the most outstanding figures in twentieth-century black American history and literature. Concerned throughout his life with the plight of black Americans, Du Bois rejected the accommodationist theories of Booker T. Washington—who stressed the importance for black students of industrial education rather than political action—and promoted the radical cause of immediate equality and full citizenship for black Americans. A founder of the National Association for the Advancement of Colored People (NAACP), he edited that organization's periodical The Crisis *from 1910 to 1934. His best-known book,* The Souls of Black Folk *(1903), is considered a landmark work in the history of black American self-awareness. In the following excerpt from a* Crisis *editorial written shortly after Harper's death, Du Bois offers a laudatory appraisal of Harper's importance as a figure in black American literature.]*

[Frances Harper's] active life, beginning with her first published book of poems, covered over sixty years of stirring history, from the Compromise of 1850 down to Mr. Taft's inaugural address. She was associated with all the great leaders of the abolition cause and has lectured to hundreds of audiences throughout the land.

It is, however, for her attempts to forward literature among colored people that Frances Harper deserves most to be remembered. She was not a great singer, but she had some sense of song; she was not a great writer, but she wrote much worth reading. She was, above all, sincere. She took her writing soberly and earnestly; she gave her life to it, and it gave her fair support. She was a worthy member of that dynasty, beginning with dark Phyllis in 1773 and coming on down past David Walker, Wells Brown, Neil, Whitman and Williams, down to Dunbar, Chesnutt and Braithwaite of our day. (pp. 20-1)

[W. E. Burghardt Du Bois], "Writers," in The Crisis, *Vol. 1, No. 6, April, 1911, pp. 20-1.**

BENJAMIN BRAWLEY (essay date 1917)

[Along with Alain Locke and Sterling Brown, Brawley is considered one of the most influential critics of Harlem Renaissance literature. An educator, historian, and clergyman, Brawley is the author of textbooks on English literature and drama for use at black universities. Most of his literary contributions are concerned with black writers and artists, and with black history. In the following excerpt, Brawley briefly discusses Harper's influences and praises her as one of the few significant black American writers to appear in the era between Phillis Wheatley and Paul Laurence Dunbar.]

With the exception of a few noteworthy individuals, conscious literary effort on the part of the Negro in America is, of course, a matter of comparatively recent years. Decades before Emancipation, however, there were those who yearned toward poetry as a means of artistic expression, and sought in this form to give vent to their groping, their striving, and their sorrow. Handicapped as they were, scores of these black bards must forever remain unknown. . . . At least three persons, however, in the long period between Phillis Wheatley and Paul Dunbar, deserve not wholly to pass unnoticed. These were George Moses Horton, Mrs. Frances Ellen Watkins Harper, and Albery A. Whitman. Each one of these poets had faults and even severe limitations as an artist. Each one had also, however, a spark of the divine fire that occasionally even kindled a flame. (p. 384)

In 1854 appeared the first edition of ***Poems on Miscellaneous Subjects,*** by Frances Ellen Watkins, commonly known as Mrs. Frances E. W. Harper, who was for many years before the public and who is even now remembered by many friends. Mrs. Harper was a woman of strong personality and could read her poems to advantage. Her verse was very popular, not less than ten thousand copies of her booklets being sold. It was decidedly lacking in technique, however, and much in the style of Mrs. Hemans. ***The Death of the Old Sea King,*** for instance, is in the ballad style cultivated by this poet and Longfellow; but it is not a well-sustained effort. Mrs. Harper was best when most simple, as when in writing of children she said:

I almost think the angels
  Who tend life's garden fair,
Drop down the sweet white blossoms
  That bloom around us here.

The secret of her popularity is to be seen in such lines as [those in] ***Bury me in a Free Land.*** . . . (pp. 386-87)

Benjamin Brawley, "Three Negro Poets: Horton, Mrs. Harper, and Whitman," in The Journal of Negro History, *Vol. II, No. 4, October, 1917, pp. 384-92.**

J. SAUNDERS REDDING (essay date 1939)

[In To Make a Poet Black *(1939), Redding provided a scholarly appraisal of black poetry, including a historical overview as well as biographical information about individual poets. In the following excerpt from that work, Redding discusses* Poems on Miscellaneous Subjects *as a product of the propagandist school of antislavery poetry. While Harper's later works encompass broader concerns, Redding considers them weaker, more maudlin poems. Like Vernon Loggins (1931) and Joan R. Sherman (1974), Redding finds the "racy" colloquial language of* Sketches of Southern Life *authentic, anticipating James Weldon Johnson's use of black idiom while avoiding the comical or pathetic dialect of Paul Laurence Dunbar. Jean Wagner (1963) disagrees, finding the language transitional but not authentic. Redding concludes that most of the poems, probably written to be recited, suffer from metrical difficulties when read.]*

In 1854, while Douglass was climbing in importance as the spokesman and ideal of the Negro race, there appeared in Philadelphia a thin volume called ***Poems on Miscellaneous Subjects,*** by Frances Ellen Watkins. The title is significant, for it indicates a different trend in the creative urge of the Negro. Except for Jupiter Hammon and Phillis Wheatley, Negro writers up to this time were interested mainly in the one theme of slavery and in the one purpose of bringing about freedom. The treatment of their material was doctrinal, definitely conditioned to the ends of propaganda. A willful (and perhaps necessary) monopticism had blinded them to other treatment and to the possibilities in other subjects. It remained for Miss Watkins, with the implications in the title of her volume, to attempt a redirection. (pp. 38-9)

In 1861 Mrs. Harper (Frances Ellen Watkins) wrote to Thomas Hamilton, the editor of the *Anglo-African,* a monthly journal that had been established the year before: "If our talents are to be recognized we must write less of issues that are particular and more of feelings that are general. We are blessed with hearts and brains that compass more than ourselves in our present plight. . . . We must look to the future which, God willing, will be better than the present or the past, and delve into the heart of the world." (p. 39)

To what degree Frances Ellen Watkins followed her own advice can be judged from her writings. In one sense she was a trail blazer, hacking, however ineffectually, at the dense forest of propaganda and striving to "write less of issues that were particular and more of feelings that were general." But she was seriously limited by the nature and method of her appeal. Immensely popular as a reader ("elocutionist"), the demands of her audience for the sentimental treatment of the old subjects sometimes overwhelmed her. On the occasions when she was free "to delve into the heart of the world" she was apt to gush with pathetic sentimentality over such subjects as wronged innocence, the evils of strong drink, and the blessed state of childhood.

Poems on Miscellaneous Subjects was published when Miss Watkins was twenty-nine years old. It is evident from the poems in this volume that she had not thought out the artistic creed later indited to Thomas Hamilton. Her topics are slavery and religion, and these first poems mark her as a full-fledged member of the propagandist group. (p. 40)

At first she was sometimes tense and stormy, as in **"Bury Me In a Free Land."** . . . After ***Moses*** Miss Watkins tended more frequently to the maudlin. Her later volumes show her of larger compass but of less strength than does the first. Though she held conventional views on most of the social evils of the day, at her best she attacked them in a straightforward manner. (pp. 40-1)

Miss Watkins wrote a great many sentimental ballads in obvious imitation of the ballads which appeared with monotonous regularity in *Godey's Lady's Book* and other popular monthlies. The ballad form was well suited to some of her material and was an excellent elocutionary pattern. Even now the recitation of the piece **"The Dying Bondman"** has not lost its effectiveness. (p. 41)

Practically all the social evils from the double standard of sex morality to corruption in politics were lashed with the scourge of her resentment. Her treatment of these topics never varied: she traced the effects of the evil upon some innocent—a young and dying girl, as in **"A Little Child Shall Lead Them,"** or a virtuous woman, as in **"The Double Standard,"** or a sainted mother, as in **"Nothing and Something."** But her treating these evils at all entitles her to respect and gratitude as one who created other aims and provided new channels for the creative energies of Negro writers.

In some of Miss Watkins's verse one thing more is to be noted especially. In the volume called ***Sketches of Southern Life*** the language she puts in the mouths of Negro characters has a fine racy, colloquial tang. In these poems she managed to hurdle a barrier by which Dunbar was later to feel himself tripped. The language is not dialect. She retained the speech patterns of Negro dialect, thereby giving herself greater emotional scope (had she wished or had the power to use it) than the humorous and the pathetic to which it is generally acknowledged dialect limits one. In all of her verse Miss Watkins attempted to suit her language to her theme. In ***Moses*** she gives her language a certain solemnity and elevation of tone. In her pieces on slavery she employs short, teethy, angry monosyllables. Her use of dialectal patterns was no accident. She anticipated James Weldon Johnson.

Miss Watkins's prose is less commendable than her poetry, though here, too, she made a departure by trying the short story form. Her prose is frankly propagandic. The novel ***Iola Leroy; or, Shadows Uplifted,*** published in 1893, was written in "the hope to awaken in the hearts of our countrymen a stronger sense of justice and a more Christlike humanity in behalf of those whom the fortunes of war threw homeless, ignorant, and poor, upon the threshold of a new era." It is a poor thing as a novel, or even as a piece of prose, too obviously forced and overwritten, and too sensational to lift it from the plane of the possible to the probable. Her short stories, two of which were published in the *Anglo-African,* were no better in kind. Her knowledge of slave life and of slave character was obviously secondhand, and the judgments she utters on life and character are conventional and trite. As a writer of prose Miss Watkins is to be remembered rather for what she attempted than for what she accomplished.

In general Miss Watkins was less confined than any of her contemporaries. Her poetry can be grouped under four heads—religious poems, traditional lyrics of love and death, antislavery poems, and poems of social reform, of which the antislavery group is not the largest. Her poetry was not unduly warped by hatred. . . . [She] gave to some of her pieces a lightness of touch that was sadly lacking in most of the heavy-footed writing of her race. A great deal of her poetry was written to be recited, and this led her into errors of metrical construction which, missed when the poems are spoken, show up painfully on the printed page. In all but her long, religious narrative, ***Moses,*** simplicity of thought and expression is the keynote.

She was the first Negro woman poet to stand boldly forth and glory in her pride of race, but she was not too vindicative. Her ambition to be the pivot upon which Negro writers were to turn to other aims, to compass more than themselves in their racial plight, was not accomplished. But before her death in 1911, the movement of which she had been the first champion had a brief and brilliant revival. (pp. 42-4)

J. Saunders Redding, "Let Freedom Ring," in his To Make a Poet Black, *McGrath Publishing Company, 1968, pp. 19-48.**

HUGH M. GLOSTER (essay date 1948)

[*Gloster, editor of several anthologies of black writers, discusses* Iola Leroy *in the following excerpt from his* Negro Voices in American Fiction. *While the Reconstruction focus makes the novel transitional, Gloster charges that Harper's work is almost wholly based on William Wells Brown's novel* Clotelle *(1853). Even though her characters counter then-popular derogatory stereotypes, Gloster believes that they are depicted in a sentimental, idealistic manner. For a similar assessment of the novel, see the excerpt by Robert Bone (1965).*]

Both in the time of its publication and in the nature of its contents Frances Ellen Watkins Harper's ***Iola Leroy, or Shadows Uplifted*** . . . is a transitional novel. Appearing eight years before the turn of the century and treating both the ante- and post-bellum period, it was the first published novel by an American Negro after the Civil War and the first to treat the era of Reconstruction.

There is little question about the source of ***Iola Leroy:*** it is almost wholly the product of reading [William Wells] Brown's *Clotelle*. Like *Clotelle*, ***Iola Leroy*** is a study of the color line, the principal characters being either white or light enough to pass. (p. 30)

In ***Iola Leroy*** Mrs. Harper—who before the Civil War was the best-known Negro writer of Abolitionist verse as well as the author of **"The Two Offers"**—helped to establish the precedent of developing well-mannered, educated colored characters to offset the stock figures of the plantation tradition. The novel suggests that near-whites should cast their lot with the minority group. Frankly admitting the propagandistic nature of her work, Mrs. Harper writes in a note on the last page of the book:

> From threads of fact and fiction I have woven a story whose mission will not be in vain if it awaken in the hearts of our countrymen a stronger sense of justice and a more Christlike humanity in behalf of those whom the fortunes of war threw, homeless, ignorant and poor, upon the threshold of a new era. . . .

In the attempt to prepare a novel that would inspire justice among whites and emulation among blacks, Mrs. Harper handles characters and situations with sentiment and idealism rather than with objectivity and realism. Nevertheless, ***Iola Leroy*** is historically significant as an attempt to counteract stereotypes and as a transitional novel showing the shift from the slavery background to the Reconstruction setting. (p. 31)

Hugh M. Gloster, "Negro Fiction to World War I," in his Negro Voices in American Fiction, *The University of North Carolina Press, 1948, pp. 23-100.**

JEAN WAGNER (essay date 1963)

[*A French author and critic, Wagner has written on the works of black and Southern writers of the United States, with a particular interest in the fiction of Flannery O'Connor. A student of American slang and dialects, Wagner is the author of the critical anthology* Black Poets of the United States *(1963). Translated into English in 1973, the collection of critical essays is regarded as one of the most authoritative and innovative tools available for the study of black American poets and poetry. In the following excerpt from that work, Wagner finds most of Harper's early works too sentimental for modern tastes, and believes that* Sketches of Southern Life *remains interesting because of Harper's evocation of the characters Aunt Chloe and Uncle Jacob. Noting the innovative use of black idiom in the poems, Wagner nonetheless judges the speech inauthentic and contends that Paul Laurence Dunbar is the poet who first captured the essence of Southern black dialect. For further discussion of the use of black idiom in this collection, see the excerpts by Vernon Loggins (1931), J. Saunders Redding (1939), and Joan R. Sherman (1974).*]

Frances Ellen Watkins Harper . . . was perhaps the best-known black abolitionist writer of the [nineteenth century]. She is said to have sold more than fifty thousand copies of her first two volumes of poetry during the tours she undertook to preach against slavery. Her first collection, ***Poems on Miscellaneous Subjects*** . . . , shows the influence of Longfellow. Almost always she wrote narrative verse, and her aim clearly is to move the reader, to tears if possible, over the slave's wretched lot. There is, for example, the child torn from his mother (**"The Slave Mother," "The Slave Auction"**), or the wife fearful for her husband on the eve of his taking flight (**"The Fugitive's Wife"**), or again the heroic slave who, for refusing to give away the companions with whom he had conspired, is flogged until he dies. Anxious that the lesson might not sink in deeply enough, the writer often intervenes at the end of her story to underline the moral and to appeal to the kindly feelings of her readers. Today this tearful sentimentality wearies us. In contrast, some pieces included in a later volume, ***Sketches of Southern Life*** . . . , can still arouse a certain interest because of the characters evoked. The author's Aunt Chloe and Uncle Jacob actually constitute one of the first attempts at a rapprochement between black poetry and black people. But her language and her humor are far from being authentically of the people, who will not find their first true poet before the arrival of Dunbar. (pp. 22-3)

Jean Wagner, "Introduction: The Origins of Black Poetry," in his Black Poets of the United States: From Paul Laurence Dunbar to Langston Hughes, *translated by Kenneth Douglas, University of Illinois Press, 1973, pp. 16-36.**

ROBERT BONE (essay date 1965)

[*Bone, an American critic and educator, is the author of the critical histories* The Negro Novel in America, *from which the following excerpt is taken, and* Down Home: A History of Afro-American Short Fiction from Its Beginnings to the End of the Harlem Renaissance *(1975). A student of Afro-American, English, and American literature, Bone has said of himself: "A white man and critic of black literature, I try to demonstrate by the quality of my work that scholarship is not the same as identity." Bone calls* Iola Leroy *a work which, because of its treatment of the Reconstruction, falls between abolitionist works and the belligerent works of younger novelists of the 1890s. For a similar discussion of the novel, see the excerpt by Hugh M. Gloster (1948).*]

[***Iola Leroy*** by Frances E. W. Harper] is a transitional work which combines elements of Abolitionism with incipient attacks on caste. With its setting in the Civil War and Reconstruction periods, ***Iola Leroy*** lacks the urgency of the other protest novels of the 1890's. The explanation is not far to seek: Mrs. Harper was one of the foremost Abolitionist poets of the 1850's, but she was sixty-seven years old when ***Iola Leroy*** was published. She was separated from the other novelists of this period by a full generation; her social consciousness, formed during the Abolitionist struggle, did not encompass the post-Reconstruction repression. (pp. 31-2)

Robert Bone, "Novels of the Talented Tenth," in his The Negro Novel in America, *revised edition, Yale University Press, 1965, pp. 29-50.**

KENNY J. WILLIAMS (essay date 1970)

[*Williams's* They Also Spoke *is considered a standard work in the critical history of black writing in America. In the following excerpt from that work, Williams surveys Harper's poetry and concludes that although* Poems on Miscellaneous Subjects *is self-consciously didactic, it is Harper's single greatest contribution to American letters.*]

[Francis Ellen Watkins Harper's] ***Poems on Miscellaneous Subjects,*** first issued in 1854, went through several editions. In 1857 she added to the collection, and by 1871 it was published as the "twentieth edition." It seems apparent from the letters of the day that she distributed this book during her many lectures in order to gain additional funds for her work in the anti-slavery movement. Such widespread distribution may well explain her popularity as a poet during the period. A large number of the poems which appear in ***Poems on Miscellaneous Subjects*** are narrative; however, there are a few lyrics included. Just as Wheatley demonstrated great fidelity to Pope, her literary model, so Harper demonstrated an equally faithful fidelity to Longfellow, her selected literary mentor. She also published two collections simply entitled ***Poems.*** One appeared in 1871 and included short verse which had not been included in her first volume. The other appeared in 1900 and contained what she considered to be her best work.

Moses: A Story of the Nile represents her most ambitious and her most symbolic work. Published before 1869, it never mentions the Negro's position in America nor the problems which immediately occurred as a result of the Emancipation Proclamation; yet it is quite obvious that the poem is an attempt to use the story of Moses very much as the poets of the spirituals had done in order to emphasize the need for a racial leader. The poem begins as a dramatic one; however, the narrative element soon becomes dominant. . . . The effectiveness of the poem is considerably heightened by the symbolic interpretation of Moses' contribution to and for the freedom of his people.

Perhaps of all of her work ***Sketches of Southern Life,*** which first appeared in 1872 and subsequently in 1888 and 1896, is the most original. While much of her poetry tends to be didactic and to use characters only as a means for getting a ''message'' to the reader, in ***Sketches of Southern Life*** Harper is far more subtle. The work consists of a series of poems which are unified through two characters: Aunt Chloe and Uncle Jacob. Both of these characters are similar to some of Dunbar's in the sense that they capture the essence of primitive life in America. Yet, Aunt Chloe, who tends to comment on the major issues of the day, and Uncle Jacob, who is the more mystical of the two, do not use dialect. In this respect Harper anticipates James Weldon Johnson who also rejected dialect in favor of what he was later to define as the ''Negro idiom.''

The more consciously anti-slavery poems appear in her first volume. Two poems appear entitled **"The Slave Mother."** In one a mother laments as her child is taken away and is given to a slave trader. In the other a fugitive mother kills her baby when she senses that she is to be recaptured and sent back into slavery. Both are effective anti-slavery ballads because they concentrate upon the very emotional relationship between mother and child; however, both are somewhat marred by the author's own deliberate intrusion as she comments on the action. **"The Fugitive's Wife"** recounts the terror and agonizing despair of a female slave whose husband is planning to make a run toward freedom. The experiences of a slave who had heard of a plot to escape but who had elected to be beaten to death rather than reveal the secrets of his fellow slaves is simply told in **"The Tennessee Hero."** In all of these poems Harper is able to penetrate the feelings of a people haunted and broken by the chains of slavery. Unlike the typical abolitionist she does this without becoming mawkishly sentimental. In each poem she builds her case by letting each tragic example of the effects of slavery serve as an indication of the broken bodies and broken spirits which resulted because of slavery's inhumanity to man. In **"The Slave Auction,"** for example, she presents the impact of human sales upon families and concludes the poem by pointing out the terror of such sales. (pp. 120-23)

Mrs. Harper's faith in the eventual solution of human problems is perhaps best exemplified by **"The Present Age"** which, though one of her later poems, is most reminiscent of Longfellow. (p. 125)

In **"A Grain of Sand"** is demonstrated Harper's characteristic of finding a lesson or a moral in everything around her. . . . **"Truth"** also shows her ability to find a moral lesson from ordinary objects; at the same time the poem also indicates her attempt to vary her stanza pattern by shifting from the trochaic rhythmic structure of **"A Grain of Sand"** to the more common iambic tetrameter. As is frequently typical in didactic poetry of this name, the poet permits an image—in this case the image of the rock and the seed—to occupy the bulk of the work; then in the last stanza the meaning of the image is revealed. (pp. 127-28)

Occasionally Frances Harper used the ballad meter with varying degrees of success. In the ballad of **"Vashti"** she was able to adhere more strictly to the form; however, in **"The Dying Bondman"** she tells the story of a dying slave with the simplicity which is characteristic of her anti-slavery poems. This is one of the few poems in which she does not insert her own comments. Both of these ballads are indicative of her strong interest in contemporary problems. Long a supporter of women's rights, Harper tells in **"Vashti"** the story of a young woman who dared to disobey her husband who was also her king. In both ballads the central characters are intent upon gaining freedom. (pp. 130-31)

When she died in 1911, Frances Ellen Watkins Harper had lived and worked through the last days of slavery, through the Civil War, through Reconstruction with all of its attendant problems, and on into the twentieth century. She was essentially optimistic in the Longfellow tradition, but her optimism was not totally unjustified. She had seen progress being made, and as a popular lecturer and poet she had played an important role in that progress. If her poetry appears too moralistic for the modern temperament, it must be remembered that didactic poetry was at one time the most popular poetic type. If she appears too concerned about the contemporary problems of her day, it must be remembered that she belonged to a poetic tradition which maintained that poetry was not a form separate from the ordinary materials and concerns of everyday life. She was a woman who believed in causes. When the Civil War was over and abolitionism was no longer relevant, she turned her attention to women's rights and to the Women's Christian Temperance Union. She did not wholly ignore the problems of the freedmen, but she felt—as did others then—that these problems were well on the way to being solved. Her greatest contribution, however, remains in the area of anti-slavery literature, and when she wrote **"Bury Me In a Free Land,"** she had no doubt that America would one day be a completely free country. (pp. 134-35)

Kenny J. Williams, ''And the Poets Came Forth: Tendencies in Nineteenth-Century Negro Poetry,'' in her They Also Spoke: An Essay on Negro Literature in America, 1787-1930, *Townsend Press, 1970, pp. 115-52.**

JOAN R. SHERMAN (essay date 1974)

[Sherman, a literary historian whose works have appeared in several journals and periodicals, is the author of Invisible Poets: Afro-Americans of the Nineteenth Century, *from which the following excerpt is taken. While Sherman finds that the poems in Harper's early collections may seem maudlin to modern readers, she nonetheless believes that Harper is of great importance because she was a black poet who broke away from purely racial protest themes to treat other national issues. Sherman agrees with critics who find wit and irony in the discourses of Aunt Chloe in*

Sketches of Southern Life, *and she considers later uses of dialect by other black writers to be refinements of Harper's pioneering method. For other discussions of the use of black idiom in Harper's works, see the excerpts by Robert T. Kerlin (1923), Vernon Loggins (1931), J. Saunders Redding (1939) and Jean Wagner (1963).*]

Mrs. Harper's verse is frankly propagandist, a metrical extension of her life dedicated to the welfare of others. She believed in art for humanity's sake. . . . (p. 67)

Her poems were "songs to thrill the hearts of men / With more abundant life," "anthems of love and duty" for children, and songs of "bright and restful mansions" for the "poor and aged" (**"Songs for the People,"** 1894). Except for ***Moses*** . . . and ***Sketches of Southern Life,*** . . . Mrs. Harper's lyric and narrative poetry varies little in form, language, or poetic technique.

Her numerous religious poems embrace both New and Old Testament ideologies and imagery, honoring their respective God heroes, a gentle Redeemer and a fiery Jehovah. The former brings "comfort, peace and rest," "changes hearts of stone / To tenderness and love" through grace, and offers a "crown of life" hereafter to all who trust in him. This God of light and mercy appears in several early poems like **"That Blessed Hope"** and **"Saved by Faith,"** . . . in poems of the middle years when, following the loss of her husband in 1864, Mrs. Harper seems preoccupied with death (twelve of the twenty-six selections in ***Poems*** . . . concern dying or life after death), and in the 1890's the same God of love dominates some two dozen poems such as **"The Refiner's Gold," "The Sparrow's Fall," "The Resurrection of Jesus,"** and **"Renewal of Strength."** Mrs. Harper's fervid commitment to Christian virtues and her faith in a "gloryland" are moving, but poetically more interesting is her allegiance to a dynamic warrior God who "hath bathed his sword in judgement," who thunders in "whirlwinds of wrath" or swoops with a "bath of blood and fire" to redress injustice in *this* world. It is the God of the Israelites who will free her people, as in **"Ethiopia."** . . . In poems like [**"Lines," "Retribution,"** and **"The Martyr of Alabama"**], Mrs. Harper invokes the God of Moses not only as a militant redeemer, but also as the scourge of men and nations who "trample on His children." She wrote to John Brown in prison in 1859: "God writes national judgements on national sins." Thus when men of Cleveland returned a young fugitive girl to slavery to "preserve the union," Mrs. Harper prophesied the coming chaos in one of her best poems, **"To the Union Savers of Cleveland."** . . . Mrs. Harper seldom shows such righteous indignation as gives power to this poem, and even less often is she bitter or cynical. However, these emotions do invigorate such poems as **"The Bible Defense of Slavery,"** . . . **"The Dismissal of Tyng,"** . . . and **"A Fairer Hope, A Brighter Morn"** . . . in which the poet denounces white "prophets of evil" who weave phantom fears of miscegenation out of their own guilt in order to oppress the race they formerly enslaved.

In many other poems on racial themes, such as **"Eliza Harris"** . . . and **"The Slave Auction,"** . . . Mrs. Harper describes the anguish of slave mothers, the heroism of black men, and the suffering of fugitives and captives. As in most abolitionist verse, emotions of fear, pain, and pity are generic, like the situations, detached from both poet and poetry. Without Mrs. Harper's dramatic recitations they remain superficial, sentimental period pieces. On the other hand, when the poet speaks in her own voice, as in **"Bury Me in a Free Land,"** . . . true passion is felt, and the poem succeeds. . . . More objective and intellectual than the abolitionist verses are Mrs. Harper's postwar appeals for freedmen's rights. Although often militantly urgent in tone, they express conciliatory sentiments. **"Words for the Hour"** . . . is addressed to "Men of the North." . . . **"An Appeal to the American People"** . . . reminds white Americans of the black soldiers' heroism, chides them for ignoring these "offerings of our blood," and appeals to their manhood, Christian principles, and honor to see justice done in the nation. There are no suggestions of black separatism in these poems; rather, the poet optimistically envisions racial brotherhood and national progress. . . . (pp. 67-70)

As black and white work together for mutual betterment, their souls must be pure and their hearts consecrated to Christian morality and social welfare. In some three dozen "reform" ballads Mrs. Harper weeps for families ruined by King Alcohol, and she gushes over innocent children and helpless women threatened or ruined by a sinful world. Her lecture audiences were captivated by these catalogues of human frailty which now seem maudlin. Nevertheless, such ballads on issues of national concern represent a unique and significant movement by a black poet, a breaking away from exclusively racial protest themes to write "more of feelings that are general . . . and delve into the heart of the world." . . . In **"The Drunkard's Child"** . . . a boy dies of neglect in his besotted father's arms. A ruined bride, mother, and child regain happiness through "the gospel and the pledge" in **"Signing the Pledge"** . . . ; a dozen unsuspecting people are destroyed by drink in the melodramatic **"Nothing and Something"** . . . ; and a typical father repents at the sight of his child's empty Christmas stocking in **"The Ragged Stocking."** . . . Mrs. Harper was also an outspoken champion of women's rights. In **"A Double Standard"** . . . a deceived young girl speaks:

Crime has no sex and yet today
  I wear the brand of shame;
Whilst he amid the gay and proud
  Still bears an honored name.

. . . . .

No golden weights can turn the scale
  Of Justice in His sight;
And what is wrong in woman's life
  In man's cannot be right.

Other oppressed women are victims of economic injustice, as in **"Died of Starvation"** . . . , or martyrs to man's pride like Vashti, Queen of Persia. Occasionally Mrs. Harper projects her own moral and spiritual strength into biblical heroines, creating appealing individuals, warm, courageous, loving women who transcend the cause they espouse. In poems like [**"Rizpah, the Daughter of Ai," "Ruth and Naomi," "Mary at the Feet of Christ,"** and **"Vashti"**] . . . emotions tied to specific crises are conveyed in simple, direct language, giving the poems a vibrant immediacy as well as lasting human validity.

Most of Mrs. Harper's religious, racial, and reform verse resembles the typical nineteenth-century work in Rufus W. Griswold's *Female Poets of America* (1848, 1873), possessing by today's standards more cultural and historical than aesthetic value. Generally her diction and rhymes are pedestrian; the meters are mechanical and frequently dependent on oral delivery for regularity, and the sentiments, however genuine, lack concreteness and control. However, Mrs. Harper attains notable artistic success with ***Moses: A Story of the Nile*** . . . and the Aunt Chloe poems in ***Sketches of Southern Life***. . . . ***Moses,*** a forty-page narrative in blank verse recounting the career of

Israel's leader, was no doubt inspired by the Emancipation and Lincoln's death. Through a dramatic dialogue of Moses and Charmian, the poet describes Moses' departure from the Pharaoh's court. Then her narrative moves briskly through the Old Testament story to Moses' death. Mrs. Harper handles the blank verse skillfully, bringing the biblical events to life with vivid imagery. . . . In grisly detail, the ten plagues descend on Egypt: "every fountain, well and pool / Was red with blood, and lips, all parched with thirst, / Shrank back in horror from the crimson draughts / "; frogs "crowded into Pharaoh's bed, and hopped / Into his trays of bread, and slumbered in his / Ovens and his pans." . . . The poem's elevated diction, concrete imagery, and formal meter harmoniously blend to magnify the noble adventure of Moses' life and the mysterious grandeur of his death. Mrs. Harper maintains the pace of her long narrative and its tone of reverent admiration with scarcely a pause for moralizing. ***Moses*** is Mrs. Harper's most original poem and one of considerable power.

She shows a similar talent for matching technique and subject in the charming series of poems which make up most of ***Sketches of Southern Life***. . . . Aunt Chloe, the narrator, is a wise, practical ex-slave who discusses the war and Reconstruction with earthy good humor, as Uncle Jacob, a saintly optimist, counsels prayer, "faith and courage." These poems are unique in Mrs. Harper's canon for their wit and irony; the colloquial expressions of Aunt Chloe's discourse form a new idiom in black poetry which ripens into the dialect verse of Campbell, Davis, and Dunbar in the last decades of the century. . . . The Aunt Chloe series is successful because a consistent, personalized language and references to everyday objects give authenticity to the subjects while directly communicating the freedmen's varying attitudes of self-mockery, growing self-respect, and optimism without sentimentality. Serious issues sketched with a light touch are rare in Mrs. Harper's work, and it is unfortunate that Aunt Chloe's fresh and lively observations were not enlarged.

Mrs. Harper wrote a great quantity of poetry during half a century, all of it in moments snatched from her public life as lecturer and reformer. Possibly ***Moses*** and ***Sketches*** were composed during her brief marriage, only four years out of eighty-seven that might be called leisure time. Her race protest and reform verse, combined with her lectures, were effective propaganda; she takes honors as well for the originality and harmony of poetic form and language in ***Moses*** and the innovative monologues of Aunt Chloe. In short, Mrs. Harper's total output is the most valuable single poetic record we have of the mind and heart of the race whose fortunes shaped the tumultuous years of her career, 1850-1900. (pp. 70-4)

Joan R. Sherman, "Frances Ellen Watkins Harper," in her Invisible Poets: Afro-Americans of the Nineteenth Century, *University of Illinois Press, 1974, pp. 62-74.*

EUGENE B. REDMOND (essay date 1976)

[*In the following excerpt, Redmond discusses the most characteristic themes of Harper's work.*]

Critics generally agree that Mrs. Harper's poetry is not original or brilliant. But she is exciting and comes through with powerful flashes of imagery and statement. Her models are Mrs. Hemans, Whittier, and Longfellow, and so we find an overwhelming influence from the ballad. In reading her poetry in public, Mrs. Harper was able to appeal to what [James Weldon] Johnson (*God's Trombones*) called a "highly developed sense of sound" in Afro-Americans. . . . She apparently knew her limitations, for [William H.] Robinson tells us [see Additional Bibliography] that her popularity

> . . . was not due to the conventional notion of poetic excellence, Mrs. Harper was fully aware of her limitations in that kind of poetry, it was due more to the sentimental, emotion-freighted popularity which she had given the lines with her disarmingly dramatic voice and gestures and sighs and tears.
>
> (p. 76)

Up until the Civil War, Mrs. Harper's favorite themes were slavery, its harshness, and the hypocrisies of America. She is careful to place graphic details where they will get the greatest result, especially when the poems are read aloud. An example of this is found in **"The Slave Mother."** . . . A similar play on the emotions is seen in such poems as **"Bury Me in a Free Land," "Songs for the People," "Double Standard"** (with its stirrings of feminism), and **"The Slave Auction."** A woman is not solely responsible for her "fall," she suggests in **"A Double Standard,"** adding:

And what is wrong in a woman's life
In man's cannot be right.

Highly readable and less academic in her use of poetic techniques and vocabularies, Mrs. Harper is nevertheless quite indebted to the Bible for much of her imagery and moral message. And she is able to merge and modify the folk and religious forms in such a poem as **"Truth,"** in which she opens with a debt to the spirituals:

A rock, for ages, stern and high,
Stood frowning 'gainst the earth and sky,
And never bowed his haughty crest
When angry storms around him prest.
Morn, springing from the arms of night,
Had often bathed his brow with light,
And kissed the shadows from his face
With tender love and gentle grace.

Several religious songs are suggested here; but she also loves to return to the theme of women, as she does in **"A Double Standard"** and **"The Slave Mother."** In the ballad **"Vashti"** she tells of the heroine who dared to disobey her dictator-husband. The strength and determination of womanhood is expressed in the last two stanzas:

She heard again the King's command,
And left her high estate;
Strong in her earnest womanhood,
She calmly met her fate,

And left the palace of the King
Proud of her spotless name—
A woman who could bend to grief
But would not bow to shame.

Certainly a comprehensive biographical-critical study of Mrs. Harper is long overdue. (pp. 76-7)

Eugene B. Redmond, "African Voices in Eclipse(?): Imitation and Agitation (1746-1865)," in his Drumvoices, the Mission of Afro-American Poetry: A Critical History, *Anchor Press, 1976, pp. 43-84.**

PATRICIA LIGGINS HILL (essay date 1981)

[*In the following excerpt from one of the longest and most detailed essays yet written on Harper's career, Hill offers a thematic discussion of Harper's poetry.*]

Very little has been written about Frances Watkins Harper, the major black female literary figure and "the most popular nineteenth-century poet before Dunbar." As a poet and a public lecturer for various social reform causes, the Abolitionist Movement, the Underground Railroad, the Women's Suffrage Movement, and the Women's Christian Temperance Union, Harper has been hailed as "the Bronze Muse" of the antebellum period. She has been described by S. Elizabeth Frazier as "having attracted more attention by her poetic productions than any Negro woman since Phyllis Wheatley."

Harper's popularity, unlike Phyllis Wheatley's however, is not based on conventional notions of poetic excellence. In her handling of poetic forms and her major subject matter—race (abolition in particular), religion, and women's rights—she is considered generally to be less a technician than either of her contemporary abolitionist poets, James Whitfield and George Moses Horton. According to Benjamin Brawley [see excerpt above, 1917], Harper's earlier poems, especially ***Poems on Miscellaneous Subjects*** . . . and ***Poems*** . . . , in which she relies primarily on the ballad stanza and rhymed tetrameter, reveal the heavy influences of Henry Wadsworth Longfellow, John Greenleaf Whittier, and Felicia Dorothea Hemans. With the exception of ***Moses: A Story of the Nile*** . . . and ***Sketches of Southern Life*** . . . , Harper's poetry varies little in form, language, and poetic technique.

Harper's fame as a poet, instead, rests on her excellent skills in oral poetry delivery. Her oratorical talents have been attested to by her contemporaries and modern critics alike. . . . As Gloria Hull in "Black Women Poets from Wheatley to Walker" has astutely observed, Harper's

> popularity stemmed from the fact that she took her poetry to the people just as did the young black poets of the 1960's and 70's. As a widely traveling lecturer of the Anti-Slavery Society, who spoke to packed churches and meeting halls, giving dramatic readings of her abolitionist poems which were so effective that she sold over fifty thousand copies—an unheard figure—of her first two books.

Indeed, there are similarities between Frances Harper's poetry and the verse of the new black poets—Imamu Baraka (LeRoi Jones), Madhubuti (Don L. Lee), Nikki Giovanni, Lalia Mannan (Sonia Sanchez), and others. Just as these latter-day poets base their oral protest poetry primarily on direct imagery, simple diction, and the rhythmic language of the street to reach the masses of black people, Harper relies on vivid, striking imagery, simplistic language, and the musical quality and form of the ballad to appeal to large masses of people, black and white, for her social protest. Moreover, she, like the new black poets, embraces an "art for people's sake" aesthetic, rather than a Western Caucasian aesthetic assumption, "an art for art's sake" principle. In her poem **"Songs for the People"** which is her closest statement on aesthetics, Harper makes this point clear. . . . Clearly, in this poem and in her other works, Harper assumes the stance of a poet-priestess whose "pure and strong" songs serve to uplift the oppressed in particular and humanity as a whole. The corpus of her poetry indicates that she, like the new black poets, however, is primarily concerned with uplifting the masses of black people. According to William Still the question as to how Harper could best serve her race lay at the very core of her literary and professional career. . . . She answers this question early in her career when she writes to Still in 1853 that she has decided to devote her life to the liberation of her people. As she expresses to him, "It may be that God Himself has written upon both my heart and brain a commissary to use time, talent, and energy in the cause of freedom." . . . This intrinsic concern for black liberation led her to envision herself as a race-builder, the black shepherd who will provide leadership for her flock of sheep (the black masses). In her February 1870 letter to Still, Harper states, "I am standing with my race on the threshhold of a new era . . . and yet today, with my limited and fragmented knowledge, I may help my race forward a little. Some of our people remind me of sheep without a shepherd." . . . (p. 60)

Harper's poetry is essentially a product of this vision. In this regard, she focuses the majority of her poems on abolition and postwar appeals for freedmen's rights, suffrage, and racial equality. Even her major religious poetry such as ***Moses: A Story of the Nile*** reflects her concern for the liberation of blacks. Also, as a race-architect, Harper undertakes the black woman's cause and women's rights as a whole. As Larsen Scruggs points out, Harper reminds the Southern freedwomen who had been victims of physical abuse that "they had rights which all men should regard and that a free people could be a moral people only when the women were respected." Thus, in several of her poems she champions the cause of women's rights and stresses the important roles that women must play in the black liberation struggle.

The major theme of Harper's abolitionist poems is the evils of slavery. Even though she was born free in Baltimore, Maryland, in 1825, and was educated in the North in Pennsylvania and Ohio, she identifies readily with the brutalities of the Southern slavery system. As Linda Riggins makes clear, because Harper herself was orphaned at the age of three and was in constant contact with slaves while working in the Underground Railroad, she "easily identifies with the emotional loss accompanying the break up of a family" [see excerpt above, 1972]. Consequently, most of her abolitionist verse deals with the tragic impact of the slavery system upon the black nuclear family.

In **"The Slave Auction"** from ***Poems*** . . . , for instance, Harper uses harsh, graphic imagery to bring attention to this tragic emotional loss. In this poem, she portrays the anguish of the slave mothers who are standing defenselessly watching their children sold away. . . . She concludes her poem by insisting that only those who are slaves themselves can fully understand the deep sense of loss. . . . (pp. 60-1)

Again, using emotionally charged language and imagery, Harper depicts the break up of the black slave family in two other abolitionist poems, **"The Slave Mother I"** and **"The Fugitive's Wife"** from ***Poems on Miscellaneous Subjects.*** **"The Slave Mother I,"** . . . which is very similar to **"The Slave Auction,"** tells of a mother's parting from her son who is to be sold to a slave trader. . . .

In **"The Fugitive's Wife,"** . . . Harper varies her theme slightly. This poem depicts the agony of a slave woman whose husband is planning to escape. Even though she is suffering because he must leave her, she encourages him to escape to freedom. . . .

Unlike **"The Fugitive's Wife,"** the slave woman in Harper's **"Eliza Harris"** . . . shares the fortune of not being totally separated from her family. In this poem, which Vernon Loggins postulates the ballad influence of both Longfellow and Whittier [see excerpt above, 1931], the poet tells of the experiences of Harriet Beecher Stowe's character Eliza who escapes to the North with bloodhounds at her heels. . . . However, Harper portrays in another poem, **"Slave Mother II,"** . . . the ill fate of a slave mother who attempts to escape with her children. In this ballad, the poet reflects a theme that was prevalent in the nineteenth-century slave narratives—that death is preferable to slavery. . . .

Harper repeats the "death is preferable to slavery" theme in **"The Tennessee Hero."** . . . As she relates in the introduction to the poem, this work tells of a black male slave who "heard his comrades plotting to obtain their liberty and, rather than betray them, he received 750 lashes and died." . . .

Indeed, to Harper, the worst evil that has befallen the black race is that of slavery. In one of her best abolitionist poems, **"Bury Me in A Free Land,"** . . . in which her own poetic voice is clearly heard, she expresses that the worst fate that she could suffer would be to be buried in a land of slaves. . . . (p. 61)

Harper's abolitionist poems only marked the beginning of her struggle for black liberation. Her postwar appeals for freedmen's rights can be found in her many lectures, her novel ***Iola Le Roy,*** . . . and her several volumes of poems, [***Moses: A Story of the Nile, Poems, Sketches of Southern Life, The Martyr of Alabama and Other Poems, The Sparrow's Fall and Other Poems, Atlanta Offering Poems, Poems,*** and ***Light Beyond the Darkness***]. . . . Her post-Civil War literature stems primarily from her extensive travels throughout the country. . . . She observed the violations of voting privileges, the lack of education and educational facilities, and the physical abuse of black people. . . . (pp. 61-2)

These concerns are reflected in her postwar poetry. For instance, in **"Word for the Hour,"** she appeals to the "Men of the North" to help to uplift the Southern black in terms of education and voting rights. . . .

In **"An Appeal to the American People,"** . . . Harper calls on white America to improve the conditions of the black soldiers who fought side by side with the white infantry during the Civil War. . . .

The continued physical abuse of blacks also lies heavily on Harper's mind. In another poem, **"The Martyr of Alabama,"** . . . she protests the actual death of Tim Thompson, a black Alabama boy, who was killed because he refused to dance for some Southern white males. . . . The poet uses vivid, descriptive imagery to unfold this horrifying event. . . .

Even though Harper realizes the wrongs and crimes committed by white Americans to blacks, she advocates interracial brotherhood, rather than black separatism as the solution to the black liberation problem. Her poem, **"The Present Age,"** . . . expresses her optimism for racial equality. . . .

Much of Harper's optimism about the black liberation struggle stems from her strong religious beliefs in Christian brotherhood and social equality. In this respect, her major religious poems deal also with the black liberation cause. One such poem is ***Moses,*** . . . a forty-page blank verse narrative on this religious leader's life and death, which Joan R. Sherman considers to be Harper's best poem and one of considerable power [see excerpt above, 1974]. This work was obviously inspired by the Emancipation and the death of Abraham Lincoln. As Still has observed, Harper frequently praises Moses and compares black people to the Israelites in bondage. . . . In addition, in her April 19, 1869, correspondence to him, Harper compares Moses to Lincoln. . . .

Just as Harper believes that Lincoln has been summoned by God to free her people, she portrays Moses, in this moving poem, as the great Liberator of the Israelites. . . .

The God of Moses is evoked again by Harper in **"Retribution."** He appears as the scourge of men and nations who "trample on his children." (p. 62)

On the whole, Frances Harper's postwar appeals for freedmen's rights are more effective than her abolitionist verse. Essentially, the former are less emotional, more objective than the latter. For instance, in ***Moses*** there is less moralizing than in her earlier verse. In addition, such poems as **"An Appeal to American People"** and **"The Present Age"** give a more balanced, optimistic view of the race problem than her early poems.

Besides her strong religious convictions in Christian brotherhood and social equality, Harper draws much of her optimism about the race problem from her postwar tour of the South. . . .

Harper's Southern experiences convinced her that her social purpose concerning women must be two-fold: on the one hand, she must champion the cause of women's rights, while on the other hand, she must appeal to the women of both races, black and white, to become actively involved in the uplifting of the black race. After her 1867-1871 Southern tour, Harper spent a substantial portion of the last forty years of her life attempting to accomplish this purpose. Harper championed the women's rights cause as a lecturer and member of the National Association of Colored Women and the National Council of Women in the United States. In the latter organization, May Wright Sewall, Susan B. Anthony, and Harper were the most active members. On February 22, 1891, for example, Harper delivered an eloquent, moving speech, **"Our Duty to Dependent Races,"** in which she represented the black race, not as a dependent race, "but as a member of the body politic who asks simple justice under the law, the protection of human life, education and complete citizenship." . . . Throughout her discourse, she urged also black and white women to improve the social/political status of the black race as well as their own social conditions.

These passionate pleas are apparent in Harper's poetry as well. Above all, her women's poetry stresses that woman/womanhood must be respected by man and society as a whole. In her poem, **"A Double Standard,"** . . . which Eugene Redmond observes has "the stirrings of feminism," Harper makes the point clear. Her protagonist, a seduced woman, scorns society for excusing the male's social behavior in the affairs of love while holding the female responsible for hers. . . . She insists, in her concluding stanza, that the same moral standards which apply to woman should apply to man. . . .

The "respect for womanhood" theme is also evident in Harper's **"Vashti."** . . . In this poem, her biblical heroine Vashti, Queen of Persia, falls victim to her husband's male pride. Her tyrant-husband commands her to unveil her face which, in return, will bring shame to her womanhood. Harper projects her own moral strength and courage into Vashti, who decides instead to give up her throne rather than shame herself and all other Persian women as well. (p. 63)

While such poems as **"Vashti"** and **"A Double Standard"** help to advance the women's rights cause, other poems point out the significant roles that Harper feels both black and white women must play in the black liberation struggle. Her Aunt Chloe poems from ***Sketches of Southern Life,*** which form a new idiom in black poetry that ripens into the dialect verse of Campbell, Davis, and Dunbar, emphasize Harper's views on how the black woman can best serve her race during the antebellum period.

As with Vashti, Harper projects her own moral strength, courage, and social/political statements into Aunt Chloe, her charming, witty black protagonist, who has survived slavery and the separation from her two sons, and who has dedicated the remainder of her life to race-building during the Reconstruction era. In this regard, Aunt Chloe functions much like Harper herself: she exhorts the freedmen to gain education, to be independent, responsible, voting citizens, and to build strong black communities based on mutual cooperation and Christian morality.

In order to serve as an inspiration for other blacks in her small Southern town community to obtain their education, Aunt Chloe teaches herself to read. . . .

Besides emphasizing the need for the Southern blacks to obtain an education, Aunt Chloe appeals to the freedmen to become responsible, voting citizens. In **"The Deliverance,"** . . . she chides several of the black males for selling their votes. She reveals that some of them sold their votes for "three sticks of candy," while others such as David Rand "sold out for flour and sugar / The sugar was mixed with sand." Yet, Aunt Chloe is quick to point out that the David Rands are exceptions to the rule. . . . She makes clear that most of the freedmen understood "their freedom cost too much / For them to fool away their votes / For profit or for pleasure." However, until more freedmen vote responsibly, Aunt Chloe maintains that black female activists like herself must continue to intervene in the political process on behalf of the race. . . .

Above all, Aunt Chloe stresses that black males and females must work together for the betterment of the race. In **"Church Building,"** . . . for example, she tells that her male confidante and companion, Uncle Jacob, advises the black community after Emancipation "all to come together / And build a meeting place." The church is eventually built because the people "pinched and scratched and spared / A little here and there."

While, in the Aunt Chloe poems, Harper emphasizes how the black woman can help uplift her race, she addresses white American women in her poem **"An Appeal to My Countrywomen"** . . . to help advance the black freedom cause. She reminds them that while they are praying for "the sad-eyed Armenian[s], the exile[s] of Russia" and others who are suffering throughout the world, black men and women are suffering in this country. . . . In order to persuade them to take up the black liberation cause, Harper appeals to them as women, sisters, and mothers. First of all, she asks them to pity men who are the ones who cause wars. . . . Then, she calls them as sisters of black women to have compassion for and to identify with the freedwomen who are still suffering throughout the South. . . . And, finally, Harper appeals to their motherhood, insisting that they pray not only for the black race but also for their own sons who must pay for their fathers' sins. . . . (p. 64)

There are feminist overtones in her women's poetry as a whole. In this poem, Harper appeals to white females to form a bond of sisterhood with black females to help to correct the social ills of white males. And, in the Aunt Chloe series, the protagonist and other black women radicals are seen rectifying the political mistakes committed by black males. In addition, her poem **"A Double Standard"** establishes her clearly as the first black feminist poet. However, these poems, like Harper's other works, are essentially a product of her concern for social equality. In **"A Double Standard,"** she wishes simply for males and females to be judged on equal terms, by the same moral standards. Furthermore, her intention in such poems as the Aunt Chloe series and **"An Appeal to My Countrywomen"** is to draw from women the leadership qualities and talents necessary to insure the rights of the freedmen. As an example, in **"The Deliverance,"** she champions the black suffrage rather than women's suffrage cause. This poem, like her other works, reveals that her major concern remains that of black race-building. In this regard, Harper effectively uses both her black and feminine consciousness and her special literary talents as a black female artist to accomplish this end. (pp. 64-5)

For her poetic and other literary achievements, Frances Watkins Harper deserves honor as a major healer and race-builder of nineteenth-century America. Her own words express the contributions she has made to black America and to America as a whole. In her essay **"Our Greatest Want",** she declares:

> We [black people] need men and women whose hearts are the homes of a high and lofty enthusiasm and a noble devotion to the cause of emancipation, who are ready and willing to lay time, talent and money on the altar of universal freedom.

No words more aptly describe Harper who devoted unselfishly most of her adult life and literary talents for this cause. Her numerous poems and other works attest to this complete devotion. Her abolitionist verse and postwar appeals for freedmen's rights are effective propaganda: these "songs stir like a battle cry / Wherever they are sung." Her poem ***Moses,*** that has rhythms which liberate the minds and spirits of her readers, audiences, and her people as a whole, is the most natural and original verse that she produced. And her Aunt Chloe poems, which put her a century ahead of other black feminist poets, have a colloquial naturalness of speech and truth to black characterization achieved by no other poet before Dunbar. In essence, as Sherman makes clear, Harper's total output "is the most valuable single poetic record we have of the race whose fortunes shaped the tumultuous years of her career, 1850-1900" [see excerpt above, 1974]. . . .

However, in spite of Harper's literary achievements, she is relatively unknown today. Like many other black literary artists and race-builders, her deeds and achievements, for the most part, have been forgotten. Soon after her death in 1911, her volumes of poetry disappeared from print and only occasional mention of her works appears in major black literature anthologies.

Whatever may be the reason for her present obscurity, Frances Watkins Harper and her poetry deserve serious literary/critical attention. As the editor of *Crisis* reminds us: "It is however for her serious attempts to forward literature among colored people that Frances Harper deserves to be remembered. She was a worthy member of that dynasty beginning with dark Phyllis in 1773 . . ." [see excerpt above, 1911]. Like Wheatley, Harper, the Black Muse of her age, has made significant contributions to black poetry. As the "Bronze Muse," an early black social protest poet, and the major black female poet of the nineteenth century, Harper has helped to lay a sound aesthetic foundation upon which much of contemporary black poetry is based. (p. 65)

Patricia Liggins Hill, "'Let Me Make the Songs for the People': A Study of Frances Watkins Harper's Poetry," in Black American Literature Forum, *Vol. 15, No. 2, Summer, 1981, pp. 60-5.*

ADDITIONAL BIBLIOGRAPHY

Barksdale, Richard, and Kinnamon, Keneth. "The Struggle Against Slavery and Racism, 1800-1860: Frances Watkins Harper." In their *Black Writers of America: A Comprehensive Anthology*, pp. 224-25. New York: Macmillan, 1972.

Brief assessment of Harper as a mediocre poet and inferior prose writer whose exposure as a lecturer led to success as a writer.

Brown, Hallie Q. "Frances E. W. Harper." In her *Homespun Heroines and Other Women of Distinction*, pp. 97-103. 1926. Reprint. Freeport, N.Y.: Books for Libraries Press, 1971.

Biographical sketch focusing on Harper's career as an orator and her work with the Underground Railroad.

Dannett, Sylvia G. L. "Freedom Lectures." In her *Profiles of Negro Womanhood: Volume I, 1619-1900*, pp. 94-109. New York: M. W. Lads, 1964.

Biography and critical comment. Dannett's laudatory remarks about Harper's poetry and the novel *Iola Leroy* are secondary concerns in the essay.

Majors, M. A. "Frances E. W. Harper." In his *Noted Negro Women: Their Triumphs and Activities*, pp. 23-7. Chicago: Donohue & Henneberry, 1893.

Laudatory remarks about Harper's character and career. Majors cites supporting information from book entries and journal reviews on the oratorical and literary career of Harper and on her qualities of high morality and civic consciousness.

Montgomery, Janey Weinhold. "Analysis of Selected Speeches from 1851 to 1875" and "Conclusions." In her *A Comparative Analysis of the Rhetoric of Two Negro Women Orators—Sojourner Truth and Frances E. Watkins Harper*, pp. 46-92, 92-4. Hays: Fort Hays Kansas State College, 1968.*

Examines the significance of voice, subject, audience, and other factors in Harper's lectures. Montgomery closely compares the oratory techniques of Harper and Sojourner Truth.

O'Connor, Lillian. "Transitional Speakers: In Ohio, Frances Watkins." In her *Pioneer Women Orators*, pp. 93-4. New York: Columbia University Press, 1954.*

Mentions Harper as among the first women orators before the Civil War.

Robinson, William H., Jr. "Frances E. W. Harper." In his *Early Black American Poets: Selections with Biographical and Critical Introductions*, pp. 26-38. Dubuque: Wm. C. Brown, 1969.

Selections of Harper's poetry, with a short biographical introduction to her life and works.

Still, William. "Frances Ellen Watkins Harper." In his *The Underground Railroad*, pp. 755-80. 1871. Reprint. New York: Arno Press and The New York Times, 1968.*

Biographical essay. Still, a contemporary and personal friend, is considered the authoritative biographical source on Harper. He includes excerpts of letters written to him by Harper and newspaper reviews of her lectures.

Whiteman, Maxwell. Introduction to *Poems on Miscellaneous Subjects*, by Frances Ellen Watkins. 1857. Reprint. Philadelphia: Historic Publications, 1969.

Bibliography of works and principal sources of biographical and bibliographic information.

Alfred Jarry

1873-1907

French dramatist, novelist, short story writer, essayist, critic, and poet.

Despite the brevity of his literary career, Jarry exercised a profound influence on the development of twentieth-century drama. His masterpiece, *Ubu Roi,* a scatological farce that caused a riot at its premier in 1896, is now generally considered the prototype for the modern Theater of the Absurd. In creating the memorable ''Père Ubu''—a comic but appalling embodiment of malice and greed whom Cyril Connolly wryly christened ''the Santa Claus of the Atomic Age''—Jarry sought to free the theater from the artificial restrictions imposed upon it by the nineteenth-century demand for realism, and to restore to it some of the simplicity and vigor of classical Greek drama. However, Jarry's dramaturgical innovations were largely overlooked and misunderstood by critics preoccupied with his play's more superficially shocking aspects. Consequently, at the time of Jarry's death a few years later, his works and ideas were nearly forgotten. Interest in his work was revived, however, with the advent of Dadaism and Surrealism in the early twentieth century. Today Jarry is recognized as one of the great liberating influences in modern literature.

The Granger Collection, New York

Jarry was born in Laval, Mayenne, near Brittany. His father was a traveling salesman for a wool factory, and his mother was the daughter of a Brittany judge. Jarry, a brilliant student though an unregenerate troublemaker, attended the Lycée at Rennes from 1888 to 1891. While there, he encountered an obese and unpopular physics professor, Monsieur Hébert, whom the students had nicknamed ''Père Heb'' or ''Ebé,'' and who had already been the subject of numerous mocking schoolboy narratives. Jarry soon organized a performance of one of these satirical productions. The play in question, composed by several students and subsequently lost, was called *Les Polonais* (''The Poles''), with Père Heb depicted as the King of Poland. In later years Jarry rewrote and transformed *Les Polonais* into *Ubu Roi.*

At school, Jarry excelled in the sciences as well as Greek and Latin, and works such as *Gestes et opinions du Dr. Faustroll, pataphysicien (Exploits and Opinions of Dr. Faustroll, Pataphysician)* reflect the diligence with which he kept himself informed of the latest scientific developments throughout his lifetime. In 1891 Jarry went to Paris to attend the Lycée Henri IV and to prepare for the difficult entrance exams for the École Normale. While there, he studied theories of comedy and laughter with Henri Bergson and developed his interests in the Symbolist movement in French literature, heraldry, anarchism, and the occult. In 1893 Jarry met Marcel Schwob, a prominent Symbolist writer and the editor of *L'écho de Paris.* Schwob introduced Jarry into Parisian literary circles, and soon he was welcome at various literary gatherings where he met Stéphane Mallarmé, Rémy de Gourmont, Albert Samain, and Pierre Louÿs, as well as other influential Symbolist writers. Jarry's bizarre attire and studied eccentricities brought him instant notoriety in the cafés and salons of Paris. A man who was known to keep owls and chameleons, he would appear in public wearing a long black cape, a cyclist's uniform, or perhaps a paper shirt with a tie painted on, and carrying a loaded revolver that he would occasionally fire for dramatic effect. In April of 1893 his poetry and prose began appearing in *L'écho de Paris,* and he was awarded both of that paper's literary prizes for the best work by a young author. Thus encouraged, Jarry abandoned his plan of attending the École Normale in favor of a career in letters. He began collaborating with Rémy de Gourmont on the production of an art review entitled *L'ymagier,* which was devoted to the presentation of popular and religious woodcuts. After quarreling with Gourmont, he continued on his own with a review of the same nature entitled *Perhinderion.* This elaborate publication exhausted the modest inheritance Jarry had received upon the death of his parents, and he was thereafter forced to support himself with his writing. He also received financial help from his friend Alfred Vallette, editor of the *Mercure de France,* and Vallette's wife, Rachilde, who later became Jarry's biographer.

In his lifetime, Jarry was as famous for his deliberate nonconformity as he was for his ideas on art. Following the premier of *Ubu Roi,* Jarry began to adopt the pompous paraphrastic speech of his creation, and to employ the royal ''we'' in conversation. His friends addressed him as ''Père Ubu.'' As Roger Shattuck has observed, Jarry was seeking, through such eccentric behavior, to break down the barriers between imagination and reality, and to ''force his life into a mold closer to literary fiction than biological survival.'' In order to sustain this hallucinatory quality in his day to day life, Jarry abandoned himself to the use of alcohol, drinking ether when he could not afford absinthe. Against all reason, Jarry lived his life in self-destructive compliance with his aesthetic. In 1903 the *Revue blanche,* for which Jarry had written the weekly column ''Gestes,'' folded. With his only reliable source of income gone, Jarry gradually succumbed to malnutrition and poverty. He died in 1907 from tubercular meningitis complicated by his alcoholism.

In creating Ubu, Jarry deliberately set out to undermine the concept of realistic theater. *Ubu Roi, Ubu cocu (Ubu Cuckolded)* and *Ubu enchaîné (Ubu Enchained)* are Symbolist dramas in the sense that linear chronology and the convention of the well-made plot are abandoned, and the action of the play is instead allowed to unfold in the manner of an hallucination. Nor are Ubu and his retinue realistic characters. Their physical grotesqueness and peculiar inhumanity, which Jarry wished to reinforce through the use of masks, suggest to critics that they are intended to serve as representations of malign subconscious forces. Jarry also advocated the use of a curtainless stage with only a painted backdrop for scenery; cardboard props, such as cutout horses hung around the actors' necks for equestrian scenes; and a special mechanical tone of voice for the actors. Jarry's hope was that these devices would make the action of the plays seem as remote from reality as possible. Jarry's early critics generally failed to appreciate this approach to theater. Many were too incensed over his use of vulgarity in the plays' dialogues to take any note of their other merits. Others merely failed to see any point at all to the antics in the plays. Some critics today speculate that the hostile reception given *Ubu Roi* is the principal reason why Jarry's later *Ubu* dramas, *Ubu Cuckolded* and *Ubu Enchained,* do not possess the same finished form and comic quality as their predecessor. They believe that Jarry became disillusioned with writing for the theater after 1896, and thereafter reserved his best literary efforts for his fiction.

Jarry's other writings, from *Les minutes de sable mémorial* to *Dr. Faustroll,* reflect both the coarseness of Ubu and the lyricism of the Symbolists. Critics today often disagree, as they did in Jarry's lifetime, concerning his intentions in incorporating such disparate modes of expression into the same works. Some argue that the technique reflects his underlying nihilism; others, such as Roger Shattuck, believe that it reveals a positive side to Jarry's dark vision. Shattuck explains that although Jarry created in Ubu ''a one-man demolition squad twenty years before Dada, he incorporated this figure into works that go on to broach transcendental values. A single facet of his works does not represent Jarry as an author and fails to show his desperate effort to create and destroy simultaneously: to transform.'' This inextricable mingling of nihilism and idealism is one of the factors responsible for the lack of consensus among critics seeking the ultimate merit of Jarry's works. Jarry's occasional obscurity in works such as *L'amour absolu,* and his peculiar logic, manifested most dramatically in his discussions of pataphysical phenomena in *Dr. Faustroll,* have also contributed to the critical controversy.

Dr. Faustroll is Jarry's most influential work apart from his *Ubu* dramas. Jarry found his inspiration for writing the novel in the stories of H. G. Wells and Jules Verne. The amazing events described in *Dr. Faustroll* are related by Jarry with such careful attention to scientific detail that the narrative soon begins to take on a disconcerting air of reality. In this work, Jarry also defined ''pataphysics'' for the first time. This ''science of imaginary solutions'' as Jarry explained it, enables Faustroll to build a time machine, to sail in a sieve, and to calculate the surface area of God. Pataphysics is Jarry's most ingenious device, and many modern writers, such as Boris Vian and Eugene Ionesco, have acknowledged the influence of Jarry's absurd ''science'' on their works.

When Jarry died in 1907 his place in literature was far from assured, and his name was already fading from memory. He remained in obscurity until the 1920s when Antonin Artaud's dramatic theories revived interest in his works. In 1927 Artaud honored Jarry as the inspiration for his own Theater of Cruelty by founding the Théâtre Alfred Jarry in Paris. In 1949 Vian and Ionesco also paid a unique tribute to Jarry: in recognition of Jarry's invention of pataphysics, they instituted the Collège du Pataphysique (''College of Pataphysics''), declaring that it ''refused to serve any purpose, refused to save mankind, or what is even more unusual, the world.'' Despite such assertions, the College's official publications, such as *Les Cahiers du Collège de Pataphysique (The Notebooks of the College of Pataphysics),* have consistently been among the best available sources of criticism on Jarry, and its members have made many valuable contributions to Jarry scholarship. Today an increasing number of critics consider Jarry as important an author as Charles Baudelaire and Arthur Rimbaud, and the study of his writings has accelerated in recent years. As critical controversies surrounding Jarry's works are more closely examined, readers may more fully comprehend his ''daring and enigmatic'' works, written, as Linda Klieger Stillman has pointed out, ''at a critical moment in the history of man and of literature: the inauguration of what we now call the modern age.''

(See also *TCLC,* Vol. 2, and *Contemporary Authors,* Vol. 104.)

PRINCIPAL WORKS

Les minutes de sable mémorial (drama, prose, and poetry) 1894
César-antéchrist [first publication] (drama) 1895; published in the journal *Mercure de France*
[*Caesar-Antichrist,* 1971]
''De l'inutilité du théâtre au théâtre'' (essay) 1896; published in the journal *Mercure de France*
[''Of the Futility of the 'Theatrical' in the Theater'' published in *Selected Works of Alfred Jarry,* 1965]
Ubu Roi (drama) 1896
[*Ubu Roi,* 1951; also published as *King Turd,* 1953; *King Ubu* in *Modern French Theatre,* 1964; and *Ubu Rex,* 1969]
Les jours et les nuits: Roman d'un déserter (novel) 1897
[*Days and Nights: Journal of a Deserter* (partial translation) published in *Selected Works of Alfred Jarry,* 1965]
L'amour en visites (short stories) 1898
L'amour absolu (novel) 1899
Ubu enchaîné (drama) 1900
[*King Turd Enslaved* published in *King Turd,* 1953; also published as *Ubu Enchained* in *The Ubu Plays,* 1968]
Messaline (novel) 1901
[*The Garden of Priapus,* 1936; also published as *Messalina* (partial translation) in *Selected Works of Alfred Jarry,* 1965]
Le surmâle (novel) 1902
[*The Supermale,* 1968]

Gestes et opinions du Dr. Faustroll, pataphysicien (novel) 1911
[*Exploits and Opinions of Dr. Faustroll, Pataphysician* published in *Selected Works of Alfred Jarry,* 1965]
**Ubu cocu* [first publication] (drama) 1944
[*Turd Cuckolded* published in *King Turd,* 1953; also published as *Ubu Cuckolded* in *The Ubu Plays,* 1968]
Oeuvres complètes. 8 vols. (dramas, novels, short stories, essays, criticism, and poetry) 1948
King Turd (dramas) 1953
Selected Works of Alfred Jarry (dramas, essays, poetry, and novels) 1965
The Ubu Plays (dramas) 1968

*This work was written in 1897 or 1898.

ALFRED JARRY (letter date 1896)

[*In the following excerpt from a letter to Lugné-Pöe, the director of the first production of* Ubu Roi, *Jarry outlines his conception of how the work should be presented on stage.*]

I am writing beforehand to ask you to give some thought to a project which I would like to submit to you and which I hope may interest you. Since ***Ubu Roi,*** which you liked, is a complete story in itself, I could, if you liked, simplify it somewhat, and then we would have something which could not fail to be funny: you yourself found it funny when you read it without bias one way or the other.

It would be interesting, I think, to produce this (at no cost, incidentally) in the following manner:

1) Mask for the principal character, Ubu; I could get this for you, if necessary. And, in any case, I believe that you yourself have been studying the whole question of masks in the theater.

2) A cardboard horse's head which he would hang round his neck, as they did on the medieval English stage, for the only two equestrian scenes; all these details fit in with the mood of the play, since my intention was, in any case, to write a puppet play.

3) One single stage-set or, better still, a plain backdrop, thus avoiding the raising and dropping of the curtain during the single act. A formally dressed individual would walk on stage, just as he does in puppet shows, and hang up a placard indicating where the next scene takes place. (By the way, I am absolutely convinced that a descriptive placard has far more "suggestive" power than any stage scenery. No scenery, no array of walkers-on could really evoke "the Polish Army marching across the Ukraine.")

4) The abolition of crowds which usually put on a terrible collective performance and are an insult to the intelligence. So, just a single soldier in the army parade scene, and just one in the scuffle when Ubu says "What a slaughter, what a mob, etc. . . ."

5) Choice of a special "accent," or, better still, a special "voice" for the principal character.

6) Costumes as divorced as far as possible from local color or chronology (which will thus help to give the impression of something eternal): modern costumes, preferably, since the satire is modern, and shoddy ones, too, to make the play even more wretched and horrible. (pp. 67-8)

I have not forgotten that this is no more than a suggestion for you to ponder at your leisure, and I have only discussed ***Ubu Roi*** with you because it has the advantage of being the sort of play that most of the public will appreciate. (p. 68)

Alfred Jarry, in a letter to Lugné-Pöe on January 8, 1896, translated by Simon Watson Taylor, in his Selected Works of Alfred Jarry, *edited by Roger Shattuck and Simon Watson Taylor, Grove Press, Inc., 1965, pp. 67-8.*

ALFRED JARRY (essay date 1896)

[*In the following excerpt from his essay* "Of the Futility of the 'Theatrical' in the Theater" *(originally published as* "De'l' inutilitié du théâtre au théâtre" *in* Mereure de France, *1896), Jarry outlines his ideas on the proper techniques and functions of a modern theater.*]

I think the question of whether the theater should adapt itself to the public, or the public to the theater, has been settled once and for all. The public only understood, or looked as if they understood, the tragedies and comedies of ancient Greece because they were based on universally known fables which, anyway, were explained over and over again in every play and, as often as not, hinted at by a character in the prologue. Just as nowadays they go to hear the plays of Molière and Racine at the Comédie Française because they are always being played, even though they certainly don't really understand them. The theater has not yet won the freedom to eject forcibly any member of the audience who doesn't understand, or to comb out the potential hecklers and hooligans from the auditorium during each interval. But we can content ourselves with the established truth that if people do fight in the theater it will be a work of popularization they are fighting over, one that is not in the least original and is therefore more readily accessible than the original. An original work will, at least on the first night, be greeted by a public that remains bemused and, consequently, dumb.

But first nights are attended by those capable of understanding!

If we want to lower ourselves to the level of the public there are two things we can do for them—and which *are* done for them. The first is to give them characters who think as they do (a Siamese or Chinese ambassador seeing *The Miser* would bet anything that the miser would be outwitted and his money box stolen), and whom they understand perfectly. When this is the case they receive two impressions; firstly they think that they must themselves by very witty, as they laugh at what they take to be witty writing—and this never fails to happen to Monsieur Donnay's audiences. Secondly they get the impression that they are participating in the creation of the play, which relieves them of the effort of anticipating what is going to happen. The other thing we can do for them is give them a commonplace sort of plot—write about things that happen all the time to the common man, because the fact is that Shakespeare, Michelangelo, or Leonardo da Vinci are somewhat bulky; their diameter is a bit difficult to traverse because genius, intelligence, and even talent are larger than life and so inaccessible to most people.

If, in the whole universe, there are five hundred people who, compared with infinite mediocrity, have a touch of Shakespeare and Leonardo in them, is it not only fair to grant these five hundred healthy minds the same thing that is lavished on Monsieur Donnay's audiences—the relief of not seeing on the stage what they don't understand; the *active* pleasure of participating in the creation of the play and of anticipation?

What follows is a list of a few things which are particularly horrifying and incomprehensible to the five hundred, and which clutter up the stage to no purpose; first and foremost, the *decor* and the *actors*.

Decor is a hybrid, neither natural nor artificial. If it were exactly like nature it would be a superfluous duplication. . . . (We shall consider the use of nature as decor later.) It is not artificial, in the sense that it is not, for the five hundred, the embodiment of the outside world as the playwright has seen and re-created it.

And in any case it would be dangerous for the poet to impose on a public of artists the decor that he himself would conceive. In any written work there is a hidden meaning, and anyone who knows how to read sees that aspect of it that makes sense for him. He recognizes the eternal and invisible river and calls it *Anna Perenna*. But there is hardly anyone for whom a painted backdrop has two meanings, as it is far more arduous to extract the quality from a quality than the quality from a quantity. Every spectator has a right to see a play in a decor which does not clash with his own view of it. For the general public, on the other hand, any "artistic" decor will do, as the masses do not understand anything by themselves, but wait to be told how to see things.

There are two sorts of decor: indoor and outdoor. Both are supposed to represent either rooms or the countryside. We shall not revert to the question, which has been settled once and for all, of the stupidity of *trompe l'œil* ["deceive the eye (with illusion of reality)"]. Let us state that the said *trompe l'œil* is aimed at people who only see things roughly, that is to say, who do not see at all: it scandalizes those who see nature in an intelligent and selective way, as it presents them with a caricature of it by someone who lacks all understanding. Zeuxis is supposed to have deceived some birds with his stone grapes, and Titian's virtuosity hoodwinked an innkeeper.

Decor by someone who cannot paint is nearer to abstract decor, as it gives only essentials. In the same way simplified decor picks out only relevant aspects.

We tried *heraldic* decors, where a single shade is used to represent a whole scene or act, with the characters poised harmonically *passant* against the heraldic field. This is a bit puerile, as the said color can only establish itself against a colorless background (but it is also more accurate, since we have to take into account the prevailing red-green color blindness, as well as other idiosyncrasies of perception). A colorless background can be achieved simply, and in a way which is symbolically accurate, by an unpainted backdrop or the reverse side of a set. Each spectator can then conjure up for himself the background he requires, or, better still, if the author knew what he was about, the spectator can imagine, by a process of exosmosis, that what he sees on the stage is the real decor. The placard brought in to mark each change in scene saves the onlooker from being regularly reminded of base "reality" through a constant substitution of conventional sets which he really only sees properly at the moment the scene is being shifted.

In the conditions we are advocating, each piece of scenery needed for a special purpose—a window to be opened, for instance, or a door to be broken down—becomes a prop and can be brought in like a table or a torch.

The actor adapts his face to that of the character. He should adapt his whole body in the same way. The play of his features, his expressions, etc., are caused by various contractions and extensions of the muscles of his face. No one has realized that the muscles remain the same under the make-believe, made-up face, and that Mounet and Hamlet do not have the same zygomatics, even though in anatomical terms we think that they are the same man. Or else people say that the difference is negligible. The actor should use a mask to envelop his head, thus replacing it by the effigy of the CHARACTER. His mask should not follow the masks in the Greek theater to indicate simply tears or laughter, but should indicate the nature of the character: the Miser, the Waverer, the Covetous Man accumulating crimes. . . .

And if the eternal nature of the character is embodied in the mask, we can learn from the kaleidoscope, and particularly the gyroscope, a simple means of *illuminating*, one by one or several at a time, the critical moments.

With the old-style actor, masked only in a thinly applied make-up, each facial expression is raised to a power by color and particularly by relief, and then to cubes and higher powers by LIGHTING. (pp. 69-72)

By slow nodding and lateral movements of his head the actor can displace the shadows over the whole surface of his mask. And experience has shown that the six main positions (and the same number in profile, though these are less clear) suffice for every expression. We shall not cite any examples, as they vary according to the nature of the mask, and because everyone who knows how to watch a puppet show will have been able to observe this for himself.

They are simple expressions, and therefore universal. Present-day mime makes the great mistake of using conventional mime language, which is tiring and incomprehensible. An example of this convention is the hand describing a vertical ellipse around the face, and a kiss being implanted on this hand to suggest a beautiful woman—and love. An example of universal gesture is the marionette displaying its bewilderment by starting back violently and hitting its head against a flat.

Behind all these accidentals there remains the essential expression, and the finest thing in many scenes is the impassivity of the mask, which remains the same whether the words it emits are grave or gay. This can only be compared with the solid structure of the skeleton, deep down under its surrounding animal flesh; its tragicomic qualities have always been acknowledged.

It goes without saying that the actor must have a special *voice*, the voice that is appropriate to the part, as if the cavity forming the mouth of the mask were incapable of uttering anything other than what the mask would say, if the muscles of its lips could move. And it is better for them not to move, and that the whole play should be spoken in a monotone.

And we have also said that the actor must take on the body appropriate to the part. (pp. 73-4)

Alfred Jarry, "Of the Futility of the 'Theatrical' in the Theater," translated by Barbara Wright, in his Selected Works of Alfred Jarry, *edited by Roger Shattuck and Simon Watson Taylor, Grove Press, Inc., 1965, pp. 67-8.*

W. B. YEATS (essay date 1926)

[In the following excerpt from Yeats's The Trembling of the Veil *(1926), the poet describes his and the audience's reactions to the first performance of* Ubu Roi.*]*

I go to the first performance of Alfred Jarry's ***Ubu Roi,*** at the Théâtre de L'Oeuvre, with the Rhymer who had been so attractive to the girl in the bicycling costume. The audience shake their fists at one another, and the Rhymer whispers to me, 'There are often duels after these performances', and he explains to me what is happening on the stage. The players are supposed to be dolls, toys, marionettes, and now they are all hopping like wooden frogs, and I can see for myself that the chief personage, who is some kind of King, carries for sceptre a brush of the kind that we use to clean a closet. Feeling bound to support the most spirited party, we have shouted for the play, but that night at the Hôtel Corneille I am very sad, for comedy, objectivity, has displayed its growing power once more. I say: 'After Stéphane Mallarmé, after Paul Verlaine, after Gustave Moreau, after Puvis de Chavannes, after our own verse, after all our subtle colour and nervous rhythm, after the faint mixed tints of Conder, what more is possible? After us the Savage God.' (pp. 348-49)

W. B. Yeats, "The Trembling of the Veil," in his Autobiographies, *Macmillan, 1955, pp. 107-382.**

Drawing by Jarry for the cover of the program for Ubu Roi *as performed by his Theatre des Pantins in 1898. In the scene depicted, Father Ubu is giving the order to advance. Reprinted courtesy of Grove Press, Inc.*

HERMAN SCHNURER (essay date 1932)

[In the following excerpt, Schnurer notes that he fails to find any artistic merit in Ubu Roi, *referring to it as nothing more than a schoolboy's outburst.]*

It was at the time when Mallarmé, in all seriousness, published a book entitled *Divagations;* when literary societies bore names like the *Hirsutes,* and the *Zutists;* when obscurity had become a great quality in writing; and when stringing the public—*épater le bourgeois*—was the greatest sport of all. (p. 350)

It was then, in 1896, that Alfred Jarry's play, ***Ubu Roi,*** was produced at the Théâtre de l'Oeuvre. Lugné-Poe, a high-minded director, was fond of innovations and of experiments. He was partial to symbolic pieces and to foreign ones (Ibsen, Shaw Maeterlink); at times he took a chance on a play that was simply bizarre. Such was this ***Ubu Roi.*** Some critics took it seriously and read all sorts of profound ideas into it. There is always a crew of inspired initiates who rant and rave over what they understand least: that is the exclamatory school of criticism. These gentlemen wrote about the symbolic significance of Papa Ubu, one-time Ubu Rex, potentate of Poland. To them, the figure was synonymous with bureaucratic greed, vanity, and imbecility. The curious thing about it all is that this derived Ubu, the creature of the critics, became a type, like Flaubert's *Homais,* like Monnier's *Monsieur Prudhomme,* like Sinclair Lewis' *Babbitt.* Through no fault of Jarry's, this shadow developed a tenacious life and is in very flourishing health today.

Now the original farce is innocent of anything like a coherent piece of satire. It is literally a school boy's elucubration; it was born in a provincial high school. To us, it is interesting chiefly because of the light it throws on the conduct of Jarry after the performance of the piece. Papa Ubu, the hero (?), is an enormously fat creature who waddles around the stage with a pear-shaped cardboard mask over his entire head. His favorite pastime is assassinating his many enemies by means of "the chariot of phynances". (Don't try to understand.) He delivers himself of horrific oaths and of all the bad words which delight adolescents on a rampage; the first utterance that greets the spectator is Colonel Cambronne's expression of Waterloo fame. From time to time Ubu issues a solemn official statement worthy of immortality:

> A great country, Poland. If there were no Poland, there would be no Poles.

The whole effect of the show was to shock, to startle, to mystify. Jarry suddenly found himself in the public eye, befriended by unusual men (Mirbeau, Paul Fort, Guillaume Apollinaire, etc.) and dubbed with a reputation which never left him; or, more exactly, with a reputation which he never wanted to leave: thenceforth he was *un fumiste.* Ask a Frenchman what that means and he will shrug his shoulders: a grown-up man, whose grave and solemn pursuit, whose only pursuit in life, is the perpetration of literary pranks, is not easy to describe.

"His antics, his smallest actions, everything in him, was literary," says Apollinaire with a great deal of shrewdness. Jarry belongs to that odd class of men whose conduct is subordinated to their æsthetics. André Maurois speaks of Flaubert's notion of the real writer: a person to whom experience has no meaning except as a happening to write about. That, precisely, is the constant thought in Somerset Maugham's character, the novelist Ashendon. One could multiply these examples. As a matter of fact, in the case of a Byron, of a Jarry, there is even more than the subordination of conduct to a literary conception; their very conduct is literary, to use Apollinaire's accurate phrase. (pp. 350-51)

Each man to his speciality. Byron took to melodrama and Jarry to mystification. (p. 352)

Herman Schnurer, "Alfred Jarry," in The Sewanee Review, *Vol. XL, No. 3, Summer, 1932, pp. 350-53.*

MAURICE NADEAU (essay date 1945)

[In the following excerpt, Nadeau comments on Jarry's two prototypical characters, Père Ubu and Dr. Faustroll, and praises Jarry for his use of humor. This work was originally published in France in 1945 as Histoire du Surréalisme.]

Jarry, confusing in a perpetual hallucination his own existence with that of Père Ubu, identifying himself with his creation in every detail, to the point of forgetting his civil status, signifies the eruption into life of humor, the supreme value of "those who know": that humor which he managed to exude with even his last breath. Ubu, "admirable creation for which I would give all Shakespeare and a Rabelais" (Breton), is the bourgeois of his time, and still more of ours. He coagulates in himself the cowardice, the ferocity, the cynicism, the disdain for the mind and its values, the omnipotence of *la gidouille* (the belly). He is the prototype of a class of tyrants and parasites the extent of whose misdeeds Jarry, dead too soon, was unable to contemplate.

The answer to Père Ubu is Docteur Faustroll, *savant pataphysicien,* imperturbable logician, carrying to their ultimate consequences the "speculations" of the geometricians, physicists, and philosophers, and quite at ease in a world grown utterly absurd. For even more than the types created, it is the atmosphere of Jarry's work which is unique and inimitable. Humor is the fourth dimension of this world, without it futile and unlivable. It seems to sum up Jarry's testament. A secret conquered at the cost of long suffering, humor is the answer of superior minds to this world in which they feel themselves alien. More than a natural secretion, as it has too often been regarded, humor manifests, on the contrary, the heroic attitude of those who are unwilling to compromise. It is as far from the famous "romantic irony" that considers with a detached expression and from a supraterrestrial world the unimportant events of this one, as from the cubist and futurist fantasies, diversions of esthetes or bohemians who still imagine they have a part to play. Jarry never played a part, any more than he lived his life. He made himself another life, a marginal one which he fulfilled perfectly. (pp. 72-3)

Maurice Nadeau, "The 'Stimulators' of Surrealism," in his The History of Surrealism, *translated by Richard Howard, The Macmillan Company, 1965, pp. 69-78.**

DAVID I. GROSSVOGEL (essay date 1958)

[Grossvogel, one of Jarry's harshest critics, states that Ubu Roi *was a dramatic failure because the only device Jarry was capable of using to provoke laughter was shock.]*

Withal, ***Ubu Roi***'s "Merdre!" which unexpectedly rang up the curtain at the Œuvre one evening in December 1896, was a brief but correct summation of a particular climate, and as such it echoed in time and space beyond the sensitive ears of first-nighters. Limiting the word's implications to the actual performance, it might be of more than sociological interest to speculate why it so affected the audience represented by its official critic, Francisque Sarcey, who walked out before the end of the performance.

This audience was willing to credit a stage world whose visible aspects, intensified by the living actor, allowed identification until the moment of comedy, that is to say, until one of its aspects was so demeaned or distorted as to be no longer a suitable projection of the spectator who then conveniently effected in laughter his withdrawal, signifying his understanding that the stage world was actually a fraud. As the curtain rose on ***Ubu Roi,*** the spectators may have had time to catch a preliminary glimpse of repellent masks disguising the human lure. Jarry himself, in a ten-minute allocution before the start of the play, had given fair warning. . . . But the spectators took this warning to be part of a sham ritual acceptable only while it was not taken seriously. Jarry's little elephants perched on shelves encouraged such disbelief and strengthened the onlooker's refusal to acknowledge his own implication in the experiment.

However, it is doubtful whether the audience apprehended the masks in the short time allowed Gémier, who, as Ubu, immediately flung out the opening word. This word, though known to the spectators, was unacknowledged by the decorous part which they had lent temporarily to the ritual. Although it remains to be determined how much of its impact Jarry actually wished translated into laughter, laughter alone would have signified the successful absorption of the shock after the disturbance; in a comedy played according to the usual rules, this disturbance would have been wholly artificial. The fact that the audience could not re-establish its accustomed status through laughter shows that Ubu's initial intrusion did not conform to the standard contract. The spurious surface and the game were immediately forgotten: there was a genuine assailant on stage.

To overwhelm the fiction on stage is not the function of comedy since such overwhelming would have the effect of awakening the spectator upon whom the assault might have been effected harmlessly: the spectator's sensitive reality is now in question. In view of Jarry's procedure, one might ask whether he actually intended ***Ubu Roi*** to be funny. Jarry himself seems to have been one of the first victims of the Ubu myth, making his Catulle Mendès' opinions about the play by stating, in his **"Questions de théâtre":** . . . "I wanted [. . .] this mirror [. . .] of man's eternal imbecility [. . .] Truly, there is nothing that might lead one to expect a funny play." Doubt might be entertained further when considering the tragic effects of the assumption of Ubu's personality by Jarry. Originally, however, the play *was* meant to be funny: it had started out, some ten years before its performance at the Œuvre, as a school boy's spoof against a certain physics and chemistry professor called Hébert, whose nickname, Le Père Hébé, was corrupted into the less perishable form vouchsafed to the hero. Satire cannot succeed if its victim is not shown in such a way as to enable the onlooker to assert by laughter his own superiority over the victim's simulacre. Whatever changes were made subsequently would hardly appear to encourage serious contemplation of a play that tells the story of an incredibly coarse, covetous, and cruel hero who, abetted by the ambitions of a wife whose moral ugliness is very much like his own, becomes king of Poland through a staccato series of improbable murders, battles, assaults, and diverse outrages, only to be routed with as little concern and ending his career on the open seas, headed back for France. As a matter of fact, Jarry's original intentions are confirmed by a letter which he wrote in 1894 to Lugné-Poë, who entertained somewhat different ideas about the play [see excerpt above, 1894]. In regard to the staging of his farce, Jarry outlined a number of suggestions with the aid of which he hoped that "we would have something whose comic effect would be assured." The intent was certainly there.

In the same letter to Lugné-Poë, Jarry sets forth specific aspects of his dramatic vision. In summary form, his six main paragraphs call for a suggestive stage stripped down to a few essential symbols—masks, rudimentary sets, token individuals for crowds—as well as an "accent" or "special voice" for the protagonist and modern clothes as distant as possible from local color. These indications are early evidence of his concern to keep his stage world akin to that of puppets. The allocution introducing ***Ubu Roi*** (the play was indeed a puppet show in its original form, ***Les Polonais***) merely repeats the idea. In an essay significantly called **"De l'inutilité du théâtre au théâtre"** [see excerpt above, 1896], Jarry suggests the replacement of the actor's fallible structure by masks. . . . The play of artificial lighting *(la rampe)* upon planes of the skillfully moved mask would provide the mask with its own gamut of expressions. The author then refers again to that dramatic superman, *Guignol,* to show how, contrary to conventional, imitative pantomime, such masks could achieve "universal gestures." It is interesting to note that Jarry's indications never go beyond the plastic and that he seems not to have realized that all drama but superficial comedy relies on an essential stylization that demands more than just the token assistance of masks.

In none of this does the actor play a part except as skilled clockwork. It is curious to hear Jarry compare him at the end of his article to the "skeleton hidden under the animal flesh and whose tragicomic value has been recognized in every age." For, as a matter of fact, the skeleton can have tragicomic value only if it suggests a man, whereas Jarry wishes to invert this suggestion by having a man do no more than actuate a mask. Hollow surfaces are indeed the areas upon which laughter assays the human want—but only *after* the delusion that had given reality to those surfaces. And similarly, Bergson's suggestion of something mechanical grafted upon the human, demands that the human allusion point up the humorous discrepancy. Jarry would appear to suggest a far greater depersonalization, one whereby puppets would not draw their life from a suggestion of the human, but wherein puppets would be true anti-people requiring the most precise machinery available—a man for the present. When the incongruous adventures of Ubu and his crew are once again resumed in ***Ubu sur la Butte*** . . . , Guignol himself introduces the action and clearly defines the nature of its participants. However, in a genuine *Guignol,* the dummy is granted evanescent life by the naïve onlooker, while Jarry, by use of the mask, has not only destroyed such evanescent realism but has also established, through his brutal implication of the audience, the reality of the human beneath the mask.

The failure of the dramatist Jarry, otherwise a perceptive theorist of the stage, comes from overlooking the fact that the stage is only half of the theater. The public, that important other half, he ignored, or at best, regarded with the utmost contempt. . . . Still, in the pendant **"Questions de théâtre,"** Jarry had written about ***Ubu Roi:*** "I wanted the stage to be before the public, once the curtain was up, like that mirror in the tales of Madame Leprince de Beaumont, where the one who is vice-ridden sees himself with the horns of a bull or the body of a dragon according to the exaggeration of his vices." The "one who is vice-ridden" here referred to *knew* that the reflected image was his because he was before a mirror and a mirror has only one reality, that of the one looking into it. In order for the stage to be "mirror" the spectator must first credit the figure on stage as his own projection. He obviously cannot afford the intromission of laughter which is merely a way of rejecting the reflection whenever it grows critical. And should even the spectator recognize in the reflection an existing aspect, he would operate the mechanism of comedy by recognizing *someone else.*

But even Jarry had to grant the existence of a public and its theatrical autonomy: "Art and the understanding of the crowd being so incompatible, we might have erred, we allow, in attacking the crowd directly in ***Ubu Roi;*** the crowd was angered because it understood only too well, no matter what it might say" (**"Questions de théâtre"**). That denial of comprehension had been made by Jarry, not by the spectator. In serious speculations, he is forced to acknowledge the autonomy of the audience, as when he refers to token sets that must be recreated by the viewer, the "character" who must be apprehended intellectually, etc.; but he limits his world audience to an aggregate of five hundred qualified participants. Whatever acknowledgment he makes, the terms of the acknowledgment are his.

In the chapter devoted to Ubu's creator, André Breton (*Anthologie de l'humour noir,* 1940) offers an insight into the nature of Jarry's dramatic contempt: "Literature, starting with Jarry, moves forward dangerously, upon ground that is mined. The author compels recognition of himself beyond his work." He then quotes from Freud to construe these writings as the author's instinctual projection. His surmising that there was no Ubu *creation* to which Jarry might have fallen sway, but that the character *was* Jarry, seems probable after the reminiscences of observers like Rachilde and Gide. In this light, the image of the hateful mirror can be understood to reflect especially Jarry's own aggressiveness. Even such symbolistic works as ***César-Antéchrist*** . . . , that apocalyptic projection of the Platonic soul in which Ubu again symbolizes the lowest order, or ***Les Minutes de sable mémorial*** . . . , bear the characteristic mark of Jarry's destructive satire though no hostile public could be aimed at here: the very esotericism of these works presumes the five hundred elect admitted by the author.

Furthermore, the image of Ubu upon which Jarry conferred moral utilitarianism after Ubu's fall from grace, making it the "mirror" of a degraded bourgeoisie, simply does not exist. Ubu exhibits gusto in mayhem and delight in slaughter; he constantly asserts his egocentricity, as in ***Ubu sur la Butte*** when surrounding Russian hordes cannot prevent him from eating and drinking heartily. In the same play he is superbly truculent and does not waste time in self-pity, even when led off at the end: "Good Lord, where will I hide? What will become of Mère Ubu? Adieu, Mère Ubu, you are ugly indeed today, is it because we are having people over?" Such traits hardly fit the description which Jarry himself gave of Ubu in his **"Questions de théâtre"** or his **"Paralipomènes d'Ubu"** . . . when he characterized Ubu as a quintessence of all that is cowardly, vile and stupid. Rather, the character evinces healthy sadism and a general egocentrism reminiscent of that which the numerous anecdotes spun about and around Jarry himself suggest. It will be noted, moreover, that in ***Ubu enchaîné*** . . . , the hero even becomes a moralizing voice after he has voluntarily chosen slavery in truculent avowal of his past misdeeds: his symbolically egocentric jail is a world of which the "free men" deliberately attempt to deprive him. This is the play wherein he has been sent as a galley slave to the Turkish sultan, only to be recognized as the sultan's dangerous and long lost brother who must be dispatched promptly, once again, upon the open seas.

It is hard to see Jarry's plays as anything beyond more or less felicitous formalizations of the author's personality—an effort at self-projection which he carried on throughout most of his life, according to the accounts of his intimates. Such self-projection into the drama invalidates another part of it, for it points to an exclusive concept of laughter—if laughter there is indeed—limited to the single device of shock. It has been noted that shock, within certain limits, might be a trigger of laughter. However, Jarry relied too exclusively on this single trick, jeopardizing the very mirth he appears to have sought and, incidentally, availing himself of only a handful of the many Farce modes. Contrasted with the contemporaneous *Champignol* and *Boubouroche*, ***Ubu Roi*** is striking especially by the paucity of means through which it sets about to achieve laughter. Debased but indestructible, his specialized creatures suffer the restrictions and the unwieldiness of automata. Little given to psychic motion, they and their world lack sensual appeal—that of color, physical suggestion, or spectacle—which characterizes those other worlds, the circus, the comic opera, etc., in which shells are not credited either, though their attributes never exclude a modicum of the senses. This is, instead, the world of Jarry, one in which sexual union is unavailing; it is that of his symbolistic ***Haldernablou*** (in ***Les Minutes de sable mémorial*** . . .) whose title is interestingly derived from the juxtaposed names of the sadistic mysoginist, Duke Haldern, and that of his page Ablou. (pp. 20-8)

Jarry's stage figures, from which all blood and all pain have been removed, walk their staccato course through a series of incidents owing little to their own psychic configuration and never truly affecting them. As the spectator notices quite soon that these personages are well-armored—that they are in fact only armor—his pleasure must be restricted to the Platonic contemplation of their blow-dealing. The fare is similar to that provided, in slightly different worlds, for Wilde's or Guitry's spectators. The puppets' aggressiveness is absorbed and enlarged by the thoroughly ill-tempered and abusive language that they hurl at each other. The exchange of vituperation has been carried out with such gusto in ***Ubu Roi*** that it frequently reveals the poet and has conferred upon Jarry distant kinship with Rabelais. Still, it is damning to hear Ubu come to life so clearly in anecdotes narrated about Jarry by Rachilde, Jacques-Henry Lévesque, and so many others, through the simple expedient of a clipped, incisive phrase using the regal plural and an occasional archaism. (pp. 28-9)

How distant the Rabelais kinship actually is, can be readily ascertained by reading both men's ***Pantagruel***. . . . Jarry's homonymous play copies faithfully incidents such as Panurge's discussion with Pantagruel about the advisability of marriage, or Panurge's comportment aboard ship during and after the storm, but in so doing it robs them of their savour and life. ***Ubu enchaîné*** is similarly vapid, giving point to Mère Ubu's remark about her husband having seemingly "forgotten the word." Plays like ***Le Moutardier du pape*** . . . and ***Par la taille*** . . . remain equally listless even though the aggressive tone endures. It is not easy to understand Gide's estimate of the Ubu dialogue inserted in ***Les Minutes de sable mémorial*** as "an extraordinary, incomparable, and perfect masterpiece" (*Mercure de France*, 1946). The insistence on aggressive epithet and the remorseless egomania dull the sting which they were originally intended to deliver and require increasing indulgence to represent anything like laughter-laden revelations.

Idle criticism finds little difficulty in ascribing meaning to works already resplendent with the spotlight of notoriety and so ***Ubu Roi*** has come to be a "timeless, placeless" endeavor that "shamelessly displays what civilization tries hard to hide, and *that* is more than lavatory brushes and schoolboy swearing, it is an aspect of truth" (Barbara Wright in her introduction to the Gaberbocchus edition of ***Ubu Roi***, 1951). But if this were an aspect of truth, as Jarry himself intimated—albeit belatedly—the audience would have turned its laughter to comprehension and assimilation. As it is, the truth apparently lay in the revelation of a rather pathetic figure, a Wizard of Oz amplifying his own fractious voice through the sound-box of what were to have been masks larger than life. (pp. 29-30)

David I. Grossvogel, "Les enfants terribles: Jarry, Apollinaire, Cocteau," in his The Self-Conscious Stage in Modern French Drama, *Columbia University Press, 1958, pp. 19-67.**

JOHN UPDIKE (essay date 1965)

[*Considered a perceptive observer of the human condition and an extraordinary stylist, Updike is one of America's most distinguished men of letters. Best known for such novels as* Rabbit Run *(1960),* Rabbit Redux *(1971), and* Rabbit Is Rich *(1981), he is a chronicler of life in Protestant, middle-class America. Against this setting and in concurrence with his interpretation of the thought of Søren Kierkegaard and of Karl Barth, Updike presents people searching for meaning in their lives while facing the painful awareness of their mortality and basic powerlessness. A contributor of literary reviews to various periodicals, he has frequently written the "Books" column in* The New Yorker *since 1955. In the following excerpt, Updike expresses his dislike for certain characteristic features of Jarry's writings, most notably his "repellent sense of inhumanity" and the "arbitrary cruelty" of certain episodes in* Ubu *and* Dr. Faustroll. *However, Updike also expresses the opinion that "Jarry's life, as a defiant gesture, matters more than his works." In Updike's view, "compared to Jarry, most of today's so-called Black Humorists seem merely exadmen working off their grudges in sloppy travesties of a society whose tame creatures they remain still."*]

[There] is little life in Jarry's writings. "I imitate nothing," he once said, and his works more resemble graffiti, cartoons, technical treatises, and verbal games than novels and plays seeking to portray human life in action. He achieved fame in 1896 with **"Ubu Roi,"** which was derived from school-boy skits perpetrated against an incompetent science teacher in the lycée at Rennes. Its first word is a modified obscenity, and its hurly-burly of schoolboy cruelty and Shakespeare parody (a monstrously simplified Falstaff murderously ascends to the throne of a nonexistent Poland) does not make very good reading now. . . . **"Ubu Roi"**—whose first performance occasioned a riot in the audience and left a young spectator from Ireland, William Butler Yeats, to conclude momentously in his journal, "After us the Savage God"—now in its bare text wears the sadness of a faded program, a testament to vanished fireworks. **"Selected Works of Alfred Jarry"** begins with several sequels to **"Ubu Roi,"** in which Jarry exercises a more mature wit and allegorizes his instinctive anarchism with scenes such as Ubu flushing his conscience down the toilet. But the liberating outrageousness of such farce is dimly felt; rather, one feels suffocated by a stunted sensibility and an arbitrary cruelty. As with the currently admired school of neo-pornography (e.g., "Last Exit to Brooklyn"), the author's participation appears suspiciously enthusiastic. . . . [A] repellent note of inhumanity, of frenzy, runs through Jarry's fiction as uncontrolled hyperbole. The novel **"Messalina"** is not meant to be absurd, but at the height of applause in a great stadium we are told that "the sound of Messalina smacking her lips dominated the uproar." (pp. 222, 224)

Purple is too pale a word for such passages. Jarry's non-fiction is better controlled: his remarks on dramaturgical science, calling for a theatre of "man-sized marionettes," are—though exasperated in tone—cogent. His scientific and blasphemous essays show demonic ingenuity and humor. After reading H. G. Wells' "The Time Machine," Jarry, with a relentless wealth of engineering detail, set down plans for one, consisting of an ebony bicycle frame mounted on three gyroscopes aligned with the three planes of Euclidean space. In **"The Passion Considered as an Uphill Bicycle Race,"** the Cross becomes a bicycle "constructed of two tubes soldered together at right angles"—"and it is worth mentioning in this connection that Jesus rode lying flat on his back in order to reduce his air resistance." Jarry's mad hyperbolism veers close to profundity. (pp. 224, 226)

Although **"Selected Works of Alfred Jarry"** contains only a few chapters of what Professor Shattuck elsewhere calls "the best of his novels," **"Les Jours et Les Nuits,"** and omits entirely "the most difficult and personal of all his texts," **"L'Amour Absolu,"** it includes *in toto* his exasperating "neo-scientific novel" entitled **"Exploits and Opinions of Doctor Faustroll, Pataphysician."** (p. 226)

Though it contains some good metaphors and jokes, the tale is top-heavy with personal allusions and pseudo-science, clotted with obscurities, and darkened by Jarry's infantile cruelty. (p. 227)

How can one judge Jarry? Apollinaire expressed the hope that his weird works "will be the foundation of a new realism which will perhaps not be inferior to that so poetic and learned realism of ancient Greece." Gabriel Brunet explained him by saying, "Every man is capable of showing his contempt for the cruelty and stupidity of the universe by making his own life a poem of incoherence and absurdity." I think the second estimate more plausible; Jarry's life, as a defiant gesture, matters more than his works, which are largely pranks and propaganda of a rarefied sort. Compared to Jarry, most of today's so-called Black Humorists seem merely ex-admen working off their grudges in sloppy travesties of a society whose tame creatures they remain still. Though we cannot grant him the comprehensive sanity and the reverent submission to reality that produce lasting art, we must admire his soldier's courage and his fanatic's will. (pp. 227-28)

John Updike, "Death's Heads," in The New Yorker, *Vol. XLI, No. 33, October 2, 1965, pp. 216-28.**

MANUEL L. GROSSMAN (essay date 1967)

[In the following excerpt, Grossman outlines the specific correspondences between Jarry's ideas on theater and the evolution of the Theater of the Absurd. For another discussion of Jarry's influence on modern drama, see the excerpt by George Wellwarth in TCLC, *Vol. 2.]*

Although critics have pointed to the significance of Alfred Jarry in the development of the theatre of the absurd, they have not provided a detailed account of the relationship between Jarry's ideas and the tenets of the newer form. (p. 473)

According to Martin Esslin [see *TCLC,* Vol. 2], the man who first coined the phrase, the theatre of the absurd is based upon a highly specialized definition of the word "absurd."

> Absurd originally means "out of harmony," in a musical context. Hence its dictionary definition: "out of harmony with reason or propriety; incongruous, unreasonable, illogical." In common usage in the English-speaking world, "absurd" may simply mean "ridiculous." But this is not the sense in which it is used when we speak of the Theatre of the Absurd. In an essay on Kafka, Ionesco defined his understanding of the term as follows: "Absurd is that which is devoid of purpose . . . cut off from his religious, metaphysical, and transcendental roots, man is lost; all his actions became senseless, absurd, useless.

Esslin distinguishes between dramatists such as Anouilh, Giraudoux, Salacrou, Sartre, and Camus and those of the absurd theatre. Although these playwrights also express "the senselessness of life," they do so in such a way as to "present their sense of the irrationality of the human condition in the form of highly lucid and logically constructed reasoning. . . ." With the absurdists it is an entirely different story. "The Theatre of the Absurd strives to express its sense of the senselessness of the human condition and the inadequacy of the rational approach by the open abandonment of rational devices and discursive thought . . . it merely *presents* it in being—that is, in terms of concrete stage images of the absurdity of existence."

Esslin's comments convey something of the sense of kinship which exists between the world created by Jarry's theatre and the world of the absurdists. The idea of "concrete stage images of the absurdity of existence" is reminiscent of Jarry's theatre. This is particularly true in the case of the ***Ubu*** cycle which contains such elements as a mass slaughter of the so-called pillars of society (***Ubu Roi***), a scientist who treats his instruments as if they were living beings ***(Ubu cocu),*** a disobedience drill in which the soldier who is least obedient to orders is given the most praise, and a dictator who when finally brought to trial gloriously confesses to all of his bloody crimes (***Ubu enchaîné***). Jarry may have himself thrown down the banner which the absurdists chose to follow when he stated that "relating comprehensible things only serves to deaden the spirit and falsify the memory, whereas the absurd exercises the spirit and makes the memory work."

Moreover, Jarry's philosophy of pataphysics served to underscore many of the principles of absurdity. The tenets of pataphysics were first advanced in the ***Gestes et opinions du Docteur Faustroll, pataphysicien,*** a novel which was published after Jarry's death in 1911. As "the science of the particular," pataphysics questions some of the premises of the scientific method. (pp. 473-74)

The definition of pataphysics, as Jarry expressed it, is based on the idea of "imaginary solutions." "DEFINITION. *Pataphysics is the science of imaginary solutions which symbolically attributes the properties of objects, described by their virtuality, to their lineaments.*" In his essay "What is Pataphysics?'' Roger Shattuck offers a detailed explanation of the concept of ''imaginary solutions.''

> In the realm of the particular, every event arises from an infinite number of causes. All solutions, therefore, to particular problems, all attributions of cause and effect, are based on arbitrary choice, another term for scientific imagination. Gravity as curvature of space or as electro-magnetic attraction—does it make any difference which solution we accept? Understanding either of them entails a large exercise of scientific imagination. Science must elect the solution that fits the facts—travel of light or fall of an apple.

Richard Coe connected pataphysics with the idea underlying the philosophy of the absurd. ''For Pataphysics,'' claimed Coe, ''all things are equal. The 'scientific' and the 'nonsensical' weigh alike in the scale of eternity, since both are arbitrary, both are absurd.'' ''Above all,'' he continues, ''Pataphysics incarnates, through its very absurdity, the practical philosophy of the absurd.'' After defining pataphysics, Martin Esslin concurs as to its instrumental role in the development of the absurdist philosophy.

> In effect, [pataphysics is] the definition of a subjectivist and expressionist approach that exactly anticipates the tendency of the Theatre of the Absurd to express psychological states by objectifying them on the stage. And so Jarry . . . must be regarded as one of the originators of the concepts on which a good deal of contemporary art, and not only in [*sic*] literature and the theatre is based.

Perhaps even more revealing, the world created in Eugene Ionesco's plays closely parallels Jarry's concept of pataphysics. Jacques Guicharnaud, the author of *Modern French Theatre*, has pointed out many of the similarities.

> The revolutionary aspect of his plays [Ionesco's], denying the traditional flow of action and traditional concept of characters, plus the often incoherent or disconnected appearance that results makes them seem like parodies of the real world. Here fantasy is not a door opened onto a beyond; it is the source of a farcical universe parallel to traditional reality.

Guicharnaud used the very language of Jarry's pataphysics to describe Ionesco's theatre. ''Ionesco creates a universe parallel to ours which, presented with the greatest objectivity and in terms of realism, enjoys the same right to exist as our world.''

Ionesco's personal life has also reinforced his connection with Jarry. He has been a member of the erstwhile College of Pataphysics. In this capacity he recently gave a talk on a B.B.C. program in which he examined ''The Pataphysics of the Theatre.'' He began this curious talk with a characteristically Jarryesque line, ''Reality is the only unreality.''

Another way in which Jarry's theatre may have anticipated the theatre of the absurd was in its tendency to break down the distinction between comedy and tragedy. According to Robert W. Corrigan, editor of *Comedy: Meaning and Form,* this tendency has become increasingly dominant among contemporary exponents of the theatre of the absurd. (pp. 475-76)

Although ***Ubu Roi*** was presented in 1896 as a ''comédie dramatique,'' Jarry was particularly disturbed when he realized that the audience had interpreted it strictly as a comedy. After the performance, he lectured the audience who had found ***Ubu Roi*** a droll play. He proposed that the masks alone should have been enough of an indication that this was a comedy only in the same sense that the ''macabre English clown or the dance of death'' is a comedy. He went on to mock those who found Père Ubu's dialogue humorous. According to Jarry, Père Ubu's vicious remarks should not have been interpreted as ''des mots d'esprit,'' [''witticisms''], as various ''ubucules'' had interpreted them, but rather as ''stupid phrases'' which justifiably evoked the retorts ''Quel sot homme! . . . quel triste imbecile'' [''What a stupid man! . . . what a wretched imbecile''] and other suitable epithets from Mère Ubu.

Moreover, Jarry informed the audience that he and Lugné-Poe, the director of the production, had at first seriously considered ***Ubu Roi*** ''en tragique.'' (p. 476)

In a recent book entitled *La Comédie,* Pierre Voltz sums up the form of comedy which is expressed in Jarry's theatre. Referring to it as the ''comedy of the absurd,'' he proposes that this type of comedy arises from the absurdity of Ubu's behavior, which is ''cruelly and irrefutably logical'' while at

Woodcut by Jarry titled ''Veritable portrait of Monsieur Ubu'' from the first edition of Ubu Roi *by Alfred Jarry (1896). Reprinted courtesy of Grove Press, Inc.*

the same time the actions of a purely instinctual being. It is a variation on this type of comedy which the exponents of the theatre of the absurd have perfected. This is particularly true of Eugene Ionesco and Samuel Beckett, the two principal spokesmen of the movement.

Ionesco and Beckett, like Jarry before them, have attempted to evoke an atmosphere of the absurd through the comic techniques of the popular theatre. Although Beckett explores the images of the circus and the music hall, and Ionesco is more preoccupied with the conventions of the Punch and Judy theatre, both playwrights, following Jarry's lead, make use of the "comedy of the absurd." (pp. 476-77)

Manuel L. Grossman, "Alfred Jarry and the Theatre of the Absurd," in Educational Theatre Journal, *Vol. XIX, No. 4, December, 1967, pp. 473-77.*

SIMON WATSON TAYLOR (essay date 1968)

[*Taylor, a noted Jarry scholar, outlines the critical reception that Jarry's works have received. Taylor explains his belief that much of the critical confusion over Jarry's intentions has been the result of identifying Jarry with Ubu and "separating Ubu from the spiritual source that motivated him—pataphysics." For other discussions regarding pataphysics, see the excerpts by Barbara Wright (1977) and Christopher Innes (1981.)*]

Les Minutes de Sable Mémorial is essential to an understanding of all Jarry's later work, since within a framework of ultra-symbolism (almost a *reductio ad absurdum* of symbolist preoccupations with the ambiguity of meaning and the magic of sound) the author carefully introduces and blends the subtle intrusion of the concept of pataphysics and the gross intrusion of Monsieur Ubu. At this stage, pataphysics is defined only allusively . . . and didactically in the introductory conversation between Professor Achras, collector of polyhedrons, and his uninvited guest. . . . Jarry gives a hint of the dual frame of reference within which he intends to develop the Science, in the following brief exchange from the same scene:

> ACHRAS: Oh but it's like this—fancy even thinking of moving in like that on people. It's a manifest imposture.
>
> UBU: A magnificent posture! Exactly Sir, for once in your life you've spoken the truth.

In other words, the manifest imposture of Ubu is equivalent to, and inseparable from, the magnificent posture of pataphysics.

Between 1894 and 1898 Jarry worked steadily on the development of this Universal Science which was to supersede what he summed up succinctly in a later text as "la Science avec une grande Scie" (*scie* is a slang expression for anything tedious), and his original concept of a theoretical exposition of pataphysics gave way to the more grandiose scheme of a Rabelaisian narrative, not only incorporating this theoretical apparatus, but applying it to the literary, artistic and scientific achievements of his era, within the context of a journey undertaken by the hero from one highly symbolic (and symbolist) island to another, and through the supplementary universe called Ethernity. This densely allusive "neo-scientific novel" (Jarry's own sub-title) describes the ***Gestes et Opinions du Docteur Faustroll, Pataphysicien.***

The misunderstandings about Jarry's intentions that pursued him during his life, and continued to haunt him long after his death, resulted from the arbitrary separation, in the mind of the reader, the critic, the playgoer, of the person of Ubu, the Master of Phynances, from the spiritual nutrition of the force that motivated him—pataphysics, the "science of imaginary solutions", which "will examine the laws governing exceptions, and will explain the universe supplementary to this one".

The confusion began with the first performance of ***Ubu Roi*** in 1896, when the only general consensus of opinion among those who watched the play or read the critics' reviews was that it was the most scandalous event in the French theatre since the tumultuous premiere of Hugo's *Hernani* in 1830, when the rearguard supporters of classicism fought it out in the aisles of the theatre with the advocates of the new romanticism. (p. 1132)

Jarry's death in 1907 made it clear how little impact his ideas had made on most of his contemporaries, even on the writers who had been closest to him and had aided him most vigorously during his short, precarious existence. Vallette's tribute to him, two weeks after his death, in the pages of the *Mercure de France,* was not untypical: "He was endowed with ingenuity rather than with imagination", and "One has the impression that with all his gifts Alfred Jarry might have left behind him a more significant body of work". An exception must be made for Apollinaire, who had known Jarry since 1900 (it was Jarry who introduced him to the Douanier Rousseau in 1907). Apollinaire's article on Jarry, "Feu Alfred Jarry", published in 1909 in the review *Les Marges,* was a shrewd assessment:

> There are no terms to describe accurately this particular liveliness of feeling in which lyricism becomes satirical, in which satire, focusing upon reality, goes so far beyond its objective as to destroy it and at the same time soars so high that it is scarcely attainable by poetry, while triviality emerges here as perfect discernment and, through some inexplicable phenomenon, becomes necessary.

And when ***Faustroll*** was published reluctantly, in 1911 . . . Apollinaire was one of the few critics to deign to notice it at all. He hailed it as "the most important publication of 1911".

After that, silence until 1918, when André Breton, then a medical student aged twenty-two, wrote an essay on Jarry which showed a surprising knowledge of the details of his life and work. . . . This important article, which first appeared in the review *Les Ecrits Nouveaux* in 1919, and was reprinted in 1924 in *Les Pas Perdus,* was a harbinger of the importance that the Surrealists were to attach to Jarry as a predecessor of their movement. But the Freudian inclinations of surrealist ideology tended to entrap Jarry fatally in the meshes of psychoanalytic theory, as in Breton's introduction to Jarry in his *Anthologie de l'humour noir* (1940), and to a ludicrous extent in Marcel Jean and Arpad Mezei's *Genèse de le pensée moderne* (1950); and the Surrealists' fascinated reverence for the concept of the *poète maudit* led them to refurbish the endless and often apocryphal legends about Jarry's behaviour—the folk-lore of absinthe bottle, revolver, bicycle and fishing rod—while neglecting the more profound aspects of the man who created Ubu and invented pataphysics.

The systematic, scholarly and disinterested study of Jarry's work may be said to have started in 1947, with the publication by Maurice Saillet in the review *Fontaine* of an essay, "Sur la Route de Narcisse (Jarry et la Peur de l'Amour)", in which he analysed the essential factor of introversion in Jarry's highly visual imagination. Two years later Saillet became one of the founding members of a "Collège de Pataphysique". . . .

The review [of the Collège de Pataphysique] has been absolutely invaluable . . . in terms of the inspired exegesis of Jarry, and the patient discovery, interpretation and publication of unknown or rare texts by him. One must be grateful to the Collège for having effectively removed this highly complex and many-faceted genius, whose life was as extraordinary as his writing, from the hands of the ill-informed and shallow-minded commentators who knew nothing of Jarry but Ubu, misunderstood the nature of Ubu, and then identified Jarry with the results of their misconceptions. (p. 1133)

Simon Watson Taylor, "Alfred Jarry: The Magnificent Pataphysical Posture," in The Times Literary Supplement, *No. 3475, October 3, 1968, pp. 1132-33.*

BRIAN E. RAINEY (essay date 1969)

[Rainey describes the cultural and social climate in France during the 1890s in order to demonstrate that Jarry and his works were reflections of that era.]

Jarry ranks as one of the most remarkable characters of the *fin de siècle* period: he is chief among those who made Paris famous as the centre of eccentric artists. . . . Jarry is a curious Gallic mixture of gravity and lightheartedness. The literary Ubu is like this too; we laugh at his impossible shape and his actions, yet we are aware of a more serious vein. In this way, Jarry is a man of his time, for it seems as if this attribute was part of the *fin de siècle* spirit. (p. 34)

When we examine the literary Ubu more closely, this mingling of the serious and the comic becomes clear; Ubu is at once a commentary on and a revolt against the world in which Jarry lived. All the elements . . . are there: anarchy—Ubu wishes to destroy everything, to be King over a non-existent people. The desire for money is there—Ubu kills off all the nobles by means of his financial hook. Corruption and cowardice are the order of the day. Ubu once consults his conscience—which he keeps conveniently in a box—as to whether he should kill a man whose house he has just taken over. When the conscience tells him that the man is harmless and helpless, Ubu says "Good, we'll kill him then—back in the box, conscience." Jarry left us in no doubt as to the serious intent of Ubu. He felt it necessary to address the first-night audience before the play, telling them that they were free to see in Ubu as many allusions as they wanted, or purely a simple puppet. We know that he had already used puppets, and what he really wanted from the actor was the performance of a live puppet with mask and assumed voice, so that the actor's personality did not show through. Accordingly, the decor should be plain and placards should be brought on to the stage.

Indeed we see in Jarry much of what will be in the future Brechtian, a sort of early *Verfremdungstechnik* ["alienation effect"]. If anything else is needed to give a feeling of universality to Ubu it is in Jarry's concluding statement of the Introduction: "Quant à l'action qui va commencer, elle se passe en Pologne, c'est-à-dire Nulle Part" ["Concerning the performance that is about to begin, it takes place in Poland, that is to say Nowhere"]. Nowhere for Jarry means everywhere, and first of all the country that one is in. For this reason, Ubu speaks French, though Jarry hastens to add that his vices are not exclusively French. Ubu has achieved real universality; there is no more need for us to say whether he has been plagiarised, or whether he resembles the Rabelaisian Panurge or the Shakespearean Falstaff.

However, Jarry was to be disappointed by the reception accorded ***Ubu Roi,*** and in his ***Questions de Théâtre,*** a post mortem, he complains of the public's lack of understanding. He had intended that Ubu should be a sort of exaggerating mirror in which the spectator should see his own vices enlarged. The public of the day were willing to accept in a more or less blasé manner a few deaths caused by anarchist attacks, a few hundred ordinary people ruined by one or two men's desire for money, but put this on a larger and absurd scale, where Ubu invents a disembraining machine which will execute hordes of people or where he kills all the nobles of Poland to get their money, and the audience protests at the absurdity but does not understand. It cannot be denied that Ubu wears the outer trappings of the comic—his fat ridiculous person, his speech, his cowardice, his pomposity—but Ubu is really a thoroughly evil Lord of Misrule, the wicked alter ego: that alter ego which, according to Catulle Mendès, is composed of "eternal human imbecility, eternal lust, eternal gluttony, the vileness of instinct magnified into tyranny." Viewed in this light, ***Ubu Roi*** cannot be seen to be a comedy; it is rather a sort of didactic tragedy in which Ubu is to be pitied and feared rather than laughed at.

But we must not limit ourselves only to ***Ubu Roi;*** in ***Ubu Cocu,*** Père Ubu is what Jarry calls "l'anarchiste parfait" ["the perfect anarchist"] and we see him, "a very porcupine hunched up against humanity." With his servants the Palotins he continues his work of impaling and disembraining, consulting at times his conscience, which he keeps in a case covered with spider's webs. The theme of the whole thing is "Craignez et redoutez le maître des Phynances" ["Fear and dread the master of Phynances"].

In ***Ubu Enchaîné,*** we are tempted at the beginning to believe that Père Ubu has reformed. He does not use the "mot d'Ubu" ["Ubu word," i.e. *merdre*] and he declares his intention of becoming a slave. However, as we read on, we discover that the so-called free-men are men who use their freedom only to be able to disobey and since they always do disobey, they are no longer free. Slavery is thus a state of security for Ubu. He knows very well that the free men will want to be in it; when they ask to be made slaves, he is once more master.

There is nothing which Ubu holds sacred; he seeks to destroy everything and is blackly nihilistic in his actions. "Cornegidouille," says Ubu, "we shall never have demolished everything if we don't destroy the ruins too! The only way I see of doing that is to put up fine new buildings instead." Jarry and Ubu were the demolition experts, it was not for them to do the building. All Jarry could do was build up for himself a new reality, a world of hallucination, the realm which is reached by the science of 'Pataphysics, which he defined, in true M. Hébert terms, as "the science of imaginary solutions, which symbolically attributes the properties of objects, described by their virtuality, to their lineaments." Obviously it is not given us all to attain this realm, but we can benefit from Jarry's revolt. Those who saw him purely as an eccentric or madman, and who looked on Ubu as a gross vulgar buffoon were in error. "We notice," says Ubu in ***Ubu Enchaîné,*** "that what makes children laugh often inspires fear in grown-ups." Ubu is a picture of society which may well inspire this fear. (pp. 35-6)

Brian E. Rainey, "Alfred Jarry and Ubu: The 'Fin de Siecle' in France," in Wascana Review, *Vol. 4, No. 1, 1969, pp. 28-36.*

BARBARA WRIGHT (essay date 1977)

[*Wright discusses Jarry's novel* Dr. Faustroll *as the antithesis and the complement to the nihilism of the* Ubu *plays. She interprets the concept of pataphysics as Jarry's affirmation that "the virtual or imaginary nature of things as glimpsed by the heightened vision of poetry or science or love can be seized as real." For more discussion of the nature of Ubu's relationship to pataphysics, see the excerpts by Simon Watson Taylor (1968) and Christopher Innes (1981).*]

It was in [***Gestes et opinions du Docteur Faustroll, pataphysicien***] that Jarry elaborated his "science" of Pataphysics, the science that lies behind all his thinking. Among other "formal definitions" of Pataphysics, we have:

> Pataphysics is the science of the realm beyond metaphysics; or, Pataphysics lies as far beyond metaphysics as metaphysics lies beyond physics—in one direction or another.
>
> Pataphysics is the science of the particular, of laws governing exceptions.
>
> Pataphysics is the science of imaginary solutions.
>
> For Pataphysics, all things are equal.
>
> (pp. v-vi)

The Supermale does not talk in so many words about Pataphysics, but the whole book is imbued with that science. The key word in the first definition of Pataphysics that I quoted is "beyond," and the essence of the Supermale is that he goes beyond everything hitherto imaginable. He is also very much the "particular," the "exception," and as for an "imaginary solution" . . . The book was published in 1902, but Jarry set it in 1920, a date very much in the future for him—so much in the future, in fact, that he didn't live to see it. ***The Supermale,*** like ***Faustroll,*** brings together most of the elements of Jarry's manifold talents and interests: poetry, classical learning, science, fantasy, imagination, comedy, and humor. It even reflects his hobbies—Elson's skill with a revolver, and the very idea of a bicycle as an inanimate hero—but more importantly, as with ***Faustroll, The Supermale*** is obsessed with the potentialities of man and what he considers to be his limitations; with the idea of extending frontiers, pushing the possible to the limits of the imaginable, discovering what might be done by will power to liberate and control the energy of the universe.

André Marcueil is one of a long line of Jarry's heroes with whom he identified himself—supermen so superior to ordinary mortals that they become God. In ***Faustroll*** ("Jarry's spiritual autobiography") Dr. Faustroll is a man-god who survives his own death. In the ***Amour Absolu,*** whose hero is called Emmanuel Dieu, "Jarry makes himself God"; in ***César Antéchrist*** he asserts that one has to be God in order to be a man, and in the ***Amour en Visites*** he writes: "man must amuse himself in the image of his creator. God has amused himself savagely ever since he has been God, only he isn't going to amuse himself much longer, because I am here. A good God always dethrones another God." (pp. vi-vii)

[Jarry's] megalomania was a mask for a great deal of misery, but his works have already guaranteed him that "worthy celebrity" that Catulle Mendès predicted for him eighty years ago. (p. vii)

Barbara Wright, in an introduction to The Supermale (Le surmâle) *by Alfred Jarry, translated by Ralph Gladstone and Barbara Wright, New Directions, 1977, pp. iii-vii.*

KEITH S. BEAUMONT (essay date 1979)

[*In the following excerpt, Beaumont examines Jarry's novels and concludes that they are united by three fundamental principles: a sustained hostility to all forms of realism; a tendency to regard language as the sole reality; and a tendency to treat all forms of literature, as well as life itself, as a sustained and elaborate game.*]

To the general reading public, Jarry is known largely or even exclusively as the author of ***Ubu Roi.*** Yet ***Ubu Roi*** represents only one element in a large and varied output, which includes other plays, a small but important body of writings on the theatre, a volume of verse, half-a-dozen musical comedies and farces, a vast collection of journalistic articles and reviews and, most important of all, a total of seven novels. Though none of these achieved much success in his lifetime—few were published in more than a couple of hundred copies, and most were greeted even by his friends with baffled incomprehension—they have attracted growing interest in the last 30-40 years. Amidst a diversity of forms and techniques, these novels point the way forward to more recent literary theory and practice (including the work of some of the "New Novelists"). More significantly, they end by calling into question not only the nature, but the very existence of the novel itself. For Jarry's novels raise the question of the relationship between "truth" and "fiction", between reality and imagination and, even more fundamentally, between reality and language itself.

Jarry's career as a novelist spans the years 1896/7 to 1903/4. Although the roots of his early work lie in the Symbolist movement, he quickly moved beyond its limited horizons and almost sacramental attitude towards literature. . . . He did however retain two features of Symbolism which reinforced inherent tendencies of his own mind and character—its fundamentally individualistic and egotistic view of the world, and its belief in the primacy of imagination. Not only do all of his fictional "heroes" contain a good deal of his own personality and ideas, but almost all his novels affirm in one form or another the primacy (if not always the triumph) of the individual self and of the imagination over "the world".

His first novel, ***Les Jours et les Nuits, roman d'un déserteur,*** was published by the Mercure de France. . . . It contains, in a dense and erudite style, both a savage satire upon army life (based on his own experiences as a conscript), and an account of the spiritual quest of its hero, Sengle (derived, via Rutebeuf, from the Latin *singulum*), for the achievement of a spiritual identity with his lost "double". The main character however remains shadowy, and both characterisation and plot are intentionally fragmentary. The novel contains numerous digressions and philosophical discourses, and the text includes also poems and the accounts of several dreams or experiences of hallucination. For Sengle is a would-be "deserter" not only from the army, but also from what Jarry likes to call "l'Extérieur", who attempts to achieve a fusion of dream and waking consciousness, or of night and day, in a continuum of hallucinatory awareness—a theme which looks forward to the ambitions of the Surrealists. . . . Yet the precise status of such ideas remains ambiguous, and Jarry's tone is frequently . . . a tantalizingly uncertain mixture of apparent seriousness and spoofing. Equally characteristic is his account of Sengle's attempts to recapture and relive his own past, which is strangely reminiscent of the most cherished themes of Proust (with whom he shares a common intellectual narcissism, in the form of an obsession with the "self", with time, and with their own past and especially childhood). One passage at least in ***Les Jours et les Nuits*** reads in fact almost like an anticipated parody of parts of *Le Temps retrouvé*. (pp. 80-1)

Jarry's next novel, ***L'Amour en visites*** . . . , could not appear more different. It has been seen as a piece of hack-writing, an exploitation of the popular *veine grivoise* perpetrated solely for financial gain. Yet those who bought the book and read it in this spirit were sorely deceived, and none more so than the semi-literate publisher of pornography, Pierre Fort, who accepted it on the basis of the first few chapters. It is a motley collection of chapters increasingly disparate in character. The first seven recount, with an abundance of racy and colourful narrative and rapid exchanges of dialogue, episodes in the life of the book's hero, Lucien. They reveal Jarry's ability to turn his hand successfully to conventional and popular styles of writing. The last four chapters move away from this style first to allegory, then to poetic drama, and finally to scatological farce in the account of Mère Ubu's secret tryst with her lover in the latrines!

Gestes et opinions du docteur Faustroll, pataphysicien, completed in 1898 but not published integrally until four years after his death, in 1911, is the densest, most complex and, at first sight, most bewildering of his works. Though he sub-titled it "roman néo-scientifique", it has few of the traditional attributes of a novel. In it, the thin narrative thread provided by Faustroll's imaginary navigation between a series of "islands", each of which represents the particular imaginative universe of a writer, artist or musician, tenuously links together such diverse elements as the reproduction of legal documents, descriptive tableaux and passages of (pseudo-) scientific analysis and philosophico-metaphysical speculation. In this almost encyclopaedic work, Jarry has attempted to create a synthesis of his views in the fields of literature, art, science and philosophy, all of which meet in the principles of his pataphysics, the "science of the particular" and "science of imaginary solutions", whose spirit is admirably summed up by Dr. Faustroll himself.

Dieu est le point tangent de zéro et de l'infini.

La Pataphysique est la science . . .

. . . .

FIN

Alfred Jarry

Ce livre ne sera publié intégralement que quand l'auteur aura acquis assez d'expérience pour en savourer toutes les beautés.

A. J.

Holograph copy of the final page of the manuscript of Jarry's Faustroll. *Reprinted courtesy of Grove Press, Inc.*

Faustroll was followed by ***L'Amour absolu,*** Jarry's emotionally most highly-charged novel, which appeared, at the author's expense. . . . Together with ***Faustroll,*** this is the most difficult of his works to characterize by reference to conventional literary forms. Though Jarry calls it a "novel", it has no plot or characters in any hitherto accepted sense of the terms, and might equally appropriately be called a "prose poem". Its structure is cyclical, the whole of the action taking place within the mind of its hero, Emmanuel Dieu (in this respect, the novel looks forward to the work of a novelist such as Claude Simon). However, Emmanuel has not a single, but a multiple identity: he is at one and the same time God and man, the Son of God, the Holy Spirit, son, husband and lover of Miriam (or Varia), who is simultaneously his mistress, wife and mother, and the Virgin (the Mother of God). This complex relationship hints at an explanation of the title of the novel: for this love is "absolute" not only in a mystical sense, but in that of a fusion of different kinds of love—the love of the child for its mother, the incestuous love of the adolescent son for that same mother, and the love of "God"—in the person of Emmanuel Dieu—for his wife and mistress from all eternity. At the centre of the book however is Emmanuel's passionate relationship with his mother, the account of which curiously combines elements of near-farce with moments of dramatic intensity. But the theme of incestuous love merges progressively with that of death, a theme which comes to dominate the novel, no doubt reflecting something of Jarry's own private obsessions. Quite apart from the fascinating biographical insights which ***L'Amour absolu*** offers us, however, it is a remarkable work for other, more purely literary reasons. It contains a wealth of rich and compelling images—imagery of light and darkness, of imprisonment, of death, images drawn from Classical and Norse mythology, from Christian sources, from mediaeval folklore, from Rabelais and *The Thousand and One Nights,* and from other sources. Its fifteen short chapters are made up of single-sentence paragraphs, many of which have the terseness and lapidary quality of verse. And it encompasses a vast range of emotional registers from whimsical or ribald humour through nostalgia and tender evocation to the pathetic and the intensely passionate. All of these features give to ***L'Amour absolu*** something of the richness and density of poetry, and make of it the most intense and moving of Jarry's creations.

The two novels which followed appear radically different yet again. ***Messaline, roman de l'ancienne Rome*** . . . and ***Le Surmâle, roman moderne*** . . . stand together like the two halves of a diptych. The first goes back for its subject to the first century A.D.; the second is set in the technological world of the year 1920. Both novels centre around the theme of sexual exploits, not to say "performance"—the one female, the other male. And both are far more conventional in form and style than any of Jarry's previous novels: each tells a "story", introduces a set of recognizable "characters", and evokes a more-or-less realistic background to the events related.

The events related in ***Messaline*** are drawn mainly from the Roman historian Tacitus, supplemented by Juvenal and other Classical authors. The novel describes the frenzied passion of the Empress Messalina, wife of Claudius, her debauchery and corruption of the whole Imperial court, and her eventual death at the hands of a tribune on the orders of a belatedly-enlightened Claudius. As a background to these events, it presents a vivid and memorable portrait of 1st century Rome, stressing its cruelty and barbarity, its corruption and venality, its preoccupation with religious cults and beliefs, and the universal obsession with sexual indulgence. Read on this level ***Messaline*** is on the whole an impressive novel, containing moments of intense drama and a wealth of powerful imagery. ***Le Surmâle,*** on the other hand, moves away from this dramatic intensity towards fantasy and even farce. Where ***Messaline*** reveals Jarry's knowledge of the Classical world, it testifies to his fascination with the technological wonders of the 20th century and to his admiration for what was then known as the "scientific novel". It reveals also his love of sport, in which human endurance is tested to the limits, and particularly of cycling (he was himself a fanatical cyclist).

The plot of the novel is a deceptively simple one. It opens with the startling assertions of its hero, André Marcueil, that "l'amour est un acte sans importance, puisqu'on peut le faire indéfiniment" ["the act of love is without importance, since one can perform it indefinitely"], and that "les forces humaines n'ont pas de limites" ["human energy has no limits"]. These apparently extravagant claims are subsequently put to the test, and proven, by Marcueil in two episodes. The first is the "Course des dix mille milles", in which a five-man cycling team from America, strapped to a tandem, attempts to race a specially designed locomotive over a distance of 10,000 miles from Paris to Siberia and back, at speeds of over 300 kilometres an hour, sustained only by the miraculous "Perpetual-Motion-Food" whose basis is a mixture of alcohol and strychnine—only to be beaten to the finishing post by a mysterious lone cyclist who is none other than Marcueil himself! The second episode consists of the attempt by Marcueil and Ellen Elson to break the record of "l'Indien tant célébré par Théophraste, Pline et Athénée" referred to by Jarry's favorite author, Rabelais, who "le faisait [i.e. made love] en un jour soixante-dix fois et plus" ["could do it more than seventy times a day"]—a task in which they succeed by making love no fewer than 82 times in the space of 24 hours! ***Le Surmâle*** appears therefore as a rollicking tale of alternately fantastic, dramatic, spectacular, passionate and—with the death of its hero—tragic events. Its language is simple, characterisation is clear-cut, with a panoply of secondary characters and an abundance of lively dialogue, and authorial standpoint is that of the conventional omniscient narrator who analyses the hidden motives of his characters and moralizes upon their actions.

La Dragonne, Jarry's last, uncompleted novel, is different in character yet again. It is a work heterogeneous in the extreme: the first part contains a cleverly satirical portrait of small-town provincial life, set in the mountains of Savoy, written in a style which, though underscored by irony, conforms wholly to the conventions of 19th century descriptive realism; the second consists mainly of a long, self-contained episode entitled "La Bataille de Morsang"; while the third part is a nostalgic, sentimental, and all too often maudlin and falsely "poetic" account (parts of it were in fact probably written by his sister Charlotte after his death) of its hero's rediscovery of his own past. This is the most straightforwardly autobiographical of Jarry's works, in which he draws freely upon his own experiences of these years and, in the last part of the novel, upon his own boyhood memories in order to supplement the deficiencies of the narrative. Though its chief interest is biographical, it does contain a number of scenes remarkable for other reasons, most notably "La Bataille de Morsang" which, together with the episode of the cycle-race in ***Le Surmâle,*** provides an outstanding example of what might be called Jarry's "fantastic realism". It recounts its hero's savage revenge upon the army in which he had been intended to serve and upon his fiancée who had abandoned him to become the regimental whore. By a brilliant piece of military strategy, described with a wealth of precise tactical and ballistic details (almost every one of which, taken individually, is totally plausible), he succeeds in causing a whole regiment to annihilate itself! The action takes on a symbolic dimension also: for the hero's revenge upon the army, together with his associated ritual murder of the representatives of womankind, authority and even God, constitute a projection of Jarry himself into absolute terms—the expression of a dream of the total destruction of Society, and a "revenge" upon existence itself.

These seven novels appear, then, widely and wildly disparate. They encompass a range of styles from the idiosyncratically poetic to the satirically realistic, and from the tenderly evocative to the ribald and farcical, often within the same work. They range from the eschewal of "character" and "plot" to the apparent reversal of this trend in the novels from ***Messaline*** onwards. While the contempt for the conventions of realism manifested in the early novels contrasts with the partly or wholly realistic and even naturalistic vein of the later ones. On a thematic plane, the novels range from the rejection of the external world in favour of the inner world of the imagination and of the past, to the apparent glorification of the material world and the technological marvels of the future. Finally, where some seem to be pitched at a level beyond the total comprehension of all but a tiny minority at most, others appear to show a growing awareness of the needs of a wider public. And in ***Le Surmâle,*** on the surface the most immediately accessible and most readable of all his novels, Jarry seems at last to have given the general public of his day what it wanted—pandering to its superstitious belief in the wonders of "science", catering to its love of the spectacular, providing a reassuringly moral *dénouement* in Marcueil's apparent punishment (albeit by means of an accident) for his *hubris* and, stylistically, responding positively to Rachilde's challenge to "écrire comme tout le monde" ["write like everyone else"].

What, if any, common features therefore can be found? It is true that a number of themes recur—the expression of Jarry's persistent misogyny (though the apparently lyrical evocation of love in ***Le Surmâle*** would seem to contradict this), his obsession with death, and his frequent association of the themes of love and death. Certain patterns of imagery also recur from one novel to another, for example the imagery of light and darkness used to represent differing states of consciousness in ***Les Jours et les Nuits, L'Amour absolu*** and ***La Dragonne.*** But these are relatively superficial links. On a much deeper level, all of Jarry's novels are united by three fundamental principles: a sustained hostility to all forms of "realism"; a tendency to regard language as the sole "reality"; and a tendency to treat all forms of literature, as life itself, as a sustained and elaborate "game".

Jarry's hostility to realism runs through all his work (despite occasional appearances to the contrary), manifesting itself in a variety of ways. In his theoretical pronouncements, it takes the form of an open expression of contempt for all forms of "realism" or "naturalism", with their exclusive concern for the particular, or for the historically or socially confined—the converse of which can be seen in his preoccupation with the figure of Ubu, in whom he saw an authentic creation of "myth", or an eternal archetype. It takes the form, in his poetry and in such novels as ***Les Jours et les Nuits*** and ***L'Amour absolu,*** of the exploitation and projection of elements of his own private imaginative universe. It can be seen also in the farcical world—which is neither completely "real" nor yet completely "false"—of his musical comedies, from which the universe of ***Gestes et opinions du docteur Faustroll, pataphysicien*** is not far removed. While in other novels, such as ***Messaline*** and ***Le Surmâle,*** it takes the form of the subtle *undermining* of apparent "realism" from within. For, despite appearances, ***Messaline*** is very far from being a historical novel (Jarry in fact shares the prejudice of the whole Symbolist generation against history, refusing to see in the past any fundamental uniqueness). History serves here merely as a *décor* and a pretext, and at the centre of the novel is not Rome of the 1st century A.D., nor even the Empress Messalina, but the insatiable and irresistible force of sexuality itself—associated with violence and cruelty, with the theme of death and, most important of all, with the theme of religious aspiration. For the sexual drama of ***Messaline*** is one enacted ultimately, through a profusion of symbols too numerous to list here having both religious and erotic connotations, by "the gods" themselves. The novel thus presents, in reality, a purely symbolic and mythical drama. But at the same time, the historicity of the work is undermined also by the inclusion of a number of strangely incongruous elements which end by shattering the credibility of the world which it creates. This is achieved above all through the introduction of the character of "Valérius l'Asiatique", to whom Jarry not only chooses to attribute certain of his own personal traits, but of whom he makes a native of China—both a historically impossible, and a caricatural figure as well, for he is made to appear as the embodiment of the popular 19th century image of a Chinese mandarin! The incident (reminiscent of the wilful sabotage occasionally practised by a novelist such as Robbe-Grillet) serves to remind us that we are after all dealing with a "fiction". While in ***Le Surmâle,*** to the alert and critical reader (but how many were there among Jarry's contemporaries?), the repeated insertion into the narrative of incongruous details (the "death" and "resuscitation" of the cyclist Jewey Jacobs, or the "death" of Ellen Elson which turns out merely to have been a fainting fit) as well as the frequent sudden and unexpected changes of tone (from lyrical tenderness to farce to pathos and back to farce again) have an even more devastating effect. Behind the facade of realism, whose conventions Jarry is here spoofing just as surely as he satirizes those of the *vaudeville* and *roman feuilleton* in ***L'Amour en visites, Le Surmâle*** is in fact one of his most secret works, whose true subject is the cancelling out of its own imaginary world by itself.

In his systematic opposition to all forms of realism and his championing of all forms of imaginative deformation and expression, Jarry is in line not only with the most outstanding artists of his own time—the Nabis (with whom he was closely associated in the mid-1890's), Gauguin (idol of the Symbolists), Cézanne and a number of the founders of Cubism—but with the dominant trend of modern art as a whole. At the same time, his cultivation of the extravagantly imaginary makes of him a precursor of such latter-day admirers (and fellow "pataphysicians") as Raymond Queneau and Boris Vian. But Jarry is not just a lover of the fantastic or richly imaginative for its own sake. He goes far beyond the Symbolists' view of the imagination as the sole source of æsthetic value to assert or to imply, paradoxically, that it is the source of "truth" itself. It is important to grasp that Faustroll's "visits" are to a series of imaginary worlds not only of the arts and literature, but of science, theology and metaphysics as well. For behind this feature of Jarry's work lies the view that "reality" itself—or what we *take* to be reality—is, in large measure at least, a product of "imagination". This belief—or this intuition—forms a cornerstone of his pataphysics, the "science of imaginary solutions" which, by placing all such creations of the imagination on the same plane, "legitimizes" and accepts them all.

Secondly, the creation of multiple levels of meaning or interpretation is a feature not only of ***Messaline*** and ***Le Surmâle*** but, in different ways, of the whole of Jarry's work. And it is a creation which begins with the potential polysemy of *words* themselves. In the appropriately entitled "Linteau" or preface to his first published volume, ***Les Minutes de sable mémorial*** . . .—whose title is itself a gem of polysemy—, Jarry formulated the ambition (in which the inspiration of Mallarmé can be seen) to "suggérer au lieu de dire, *faire dans la route des phrases un carrefour de tous les mots*" ["suggest rather than say, *to make in the route of sentences a crossroads of all words*"]. It is an ambition which informs almost the whole of his work. It can be seen in the deliberately facile puns of his "Théâtre mirlitonesque" and the more sophisticated word-play and linguistic distortion of ***La Chandelle verte,*** whose ultimate function, beyond the creation of humorous effects, is the very destruction of accepted meanings, and thereby of accepted views of the world. On a more constructive plane, it can be seen in the obvious polysemy of the title and sub-title of ***Les Jours et les Nuits,*** where the terms "day" and "night" create at least three different levels of meaning in the text, upon which the novel unfolds simultaneously. The same is true of ***L'Amour absolu,*** where, in addition to the title, such terms as *fils, époux, mere* and *épouse* create a similar multiplicity of levels of meaning which make of Emmanuel Dieu simultaneously a condemned man awaiting execution at the coming dawn, the Son of God reliving the story of his Passion, and simply a man (perhaps the novelist himself) "qui rêve assis près de sa lampe" ["who dreams sitting by his lamp"].

A third development also takes place in Jarry's work. To borrow the terminology of Saussurian linguistics, *signifier* tends to detach itself from *signified*—language tends to break away from any reference to a "real" world to assume an existence of its own. A shining example is provided by the character of "Valérius l'Asiatique", where it is the *word* "Asiatic" (doubtless referring originally to Asia Minor) which has inspired the wholly fanciful portrait which Jarry has created. Another, from the same novel, is the episode of the mysterious objects named *murrhins,* undoubtedly chosen on account of their name, through which Jarry establishes, by phonetic association, a link with *la myrrhe* and hence with *la mort* (an association which occurs in ***L'Amour absolu*** also). In ***Le Surmâle,*** an example is provided by Marcueil's reappearance, at the start of the lovemaking marathon, as "the Indian"—not the native of the Indian sub-continent referred to by Rabelais and the Classical authors he quotes, but the popular stereotype of the North American "redskin" inspired by the novels of Fenimore Cooper. Whilst in ***Faustroll,*** a further brilliant example is to be found in the good doctor's discovery of "ethernity" which, thanks to the suggestive possibilities of the name, he is able to subject to a physiochemical analysis! The result is that, not only does the text tend to dissociate itself from "reality" to become an independent and autonomous imaginative creation, but it tends to become an independent and autonomous *linguistic* creation also. Language tends to create its *own* reality. Thus the text of ***L'Amour absolu,*** which constitutes "la création de son [i.e. Emmanuel's] *désir",* becomes (in large part at least) a self-contained imaginative, and therefore linguistic, creation, without reference to any other "world" than that of the novel itself. In ***Messaline,*** Jarry creates a complex network of symbols which end by "signifying" nothing but themselves and each other, as in an intricate game of mirrors. Whilst in ***Les Jours et les Nuits,*** in the chapter entitled "Les Propos des assassins" (where *assassins* is to be understood in relation to its etymology in *hashish*) he has created a remarkable piece of writing which proceeds entirely by phonetic and semantic association. As Jarry himself summed up the situation, firstly in ***César-Antéchrist*** . . . , and then in a lapidary phrase in one of his "Speculations": "Le signe seul existe . . . provisoire" ["the sign alone exists . . . provisionally"], and "Il n'y a que la lettre qui soit littérature" ["Only the letter is literature"].

None of this, however, is the result of mere perversity or of a mere literary quirk. Reflections on the nature and status of language (together with an interest in other systems of "signs") run through Jarry's work, and form an important part of the subject-matter of the articles in ***La Chandelle verte.*** Behind his incessant word-play and verbal clowning lies a particular view of the nature of language, a deep-seated intuition that all "reality" is, at bottom, not just a product of imagination but, more precisely and more profoundly, a *linguistic* reality—an assemblage of ideas, of forms, of structures which resolve, ultimately, into mere words.

The extraordinary variety in the character of Jarry's novels itself hints at a third and final element of his outlook. It suggests, firstly, an interest in formal experimentation as an end in itself. But, even more important, it suggests a detachment from the whole "art" of novel-writing, an attitude which sees all literary forms as mere conventions, as the (arbitrary) rules in an elaborate game. Nowhere is this tendency more in evidence than in ***Le Surmâle.*** Not only is sexual activity implicitly portrayed here (as in ***Messaline***), through its association with the notion of record-breaking, as a form of "sport", but a series of detailed parallels in structure, in events and in imagery between the episode of the cycle-race and that of Marcueil's and Ellen's love-making make of the latter even more clearly every bit as much of a sport or game as the former. And to make matters even clearer, the notion of "game" is referred to explicitly several times in the text itself. Through the inclusion of a profusion of literary, historical and mythological allusions and quotations, moreover, the adventures of Jarry's "supermale" are made to sum up and to parody all the legendary supermen of the past, present and future, as well as the forms and traditions of a whole literature of love.

Equally telling is the theme of disguise or of masks—present not only in Marcueil's "Indian" (which is itself the subject of a private joke) but also in his adoption of at least four other roles or disguises, and embodied in the character of Ellen Elson as well. The idea is implicit also in Jarry's identification with Faustroll (who, in his combination of erudition and impish humour, represents his creator far more truly and fundamentally than that other *persona,* Ubu). Like Marcueil, Jarry too in his writing adopts a series of different masks or disguises and, chameleon-like, moves in and out of all forms and styles as of all philosophical and moral viewpoints with ease. This essentially "ludic" conception of literature, latent in all of his novels as in his poetry and theatre also, forms part of a broader attitude towards life as a whole which is admirably manifested in ***La Chandelle verte*** and which is embodied in his philosophy of pataphysics—an attitude of detachment from all things, and a tendency to regard all ideas and activities as mere conventions, or as rules in a vast and intricate "game". (pp. 81-90)

Keith S. Beaumont, "Alfred Jarry, Novelist," in Australian Journal of French Studies, *Vol. XVI, Part I, January-April, 1979, pp. 80-90.*

CHRISTOPHER INNES (essay date 1981)

[Innes discusses the failure of Ubu Roi *as conventional satire, but commends it as the prototype of modern anti-realistic theater. Innes states that Jarry's* Ubu *plays are, in effect, illustrations of the theory of pataphysics. For a different view of the relationship of the* Ubu *cycle to the concept of pataphysics, see the excerpt by Barbara Wright (1977). For further confirmation of Innes's arguments, see the excerpt by Simon Watson Taylor (1968).]*

Elements of symbolist staging have become an accepted part of the modern theatre's technical repertoire. . . . But most of the general concepts of symbolist drama have dated badly because their viewpoint was basically conventional. Their choice of subject matter tended toward traditional legend and artificial medievalism, while the religious aspect of their work remained within the socially accepted limits of catholicism and their attempts to explore the subconscious appear facile in the light of Freud and Jung. Yet out of this context comes one of the key works of modern drama which has had a decisive influence on avant garde theatre, Alfred Jarry's ***Ubu*** trilogy, and it is no accident that ***Ubu roi*** . . . was originally conceived as a puppet play and first performed by Lugné-Poe's Théâtre de l'Oeuvre, where the same year Jarry had played the role of the Old Man of the Mountains in Lugné-Poe's symbolist production of *Peer Gynt.* At the same time the more obvious superficial aspects of the play, the scatological obscenity, the deliberate crudeness of dialogue and presentation, the grotesque farce, all make a statement that is fundamentally opposed to symbolist principles, as W. B. Yeats, whose French was too limited to understand any of Jarry's deeper intentions, was quick to see [see excerpt above, 1926]. . . . (p. 21)

[The] initial reactions to the play concentrated on those elements designed to insult the audience's sensibilities: the flouting of moral taboos, the anarchic attack on social institutions or the provocative parody of all the turn-of-the-century thematic and stylistic expectations of serious drama. What primarily came across was the deliberate childishness of plot and characterisation. On this level the monstrous figure of Ubu seems to sum up Jarry's intentions, a grotesquely ugly embodiment of our most despicable instincts, whose involvement in any situation reveals his own amoral and anti-social qualities in all the participants, exposing the rapacity, avarice, self-serving treachery and ingratitude, conceit, cowardice and simple greed that he epitomises to be at the root of all human activities, and particularly those that are conventionally valued as honourable, heroic, altruistic, patriotic, idealistic or in any way socially respected. Thus Ubu reduces kingship to gorging oneself on sausages and wearing an immense hat, economic competition to a kicking, struggling race, social reform to slaughter motivated solely by envious cupidity, battle royal to boastful brawling, or religious faith to fearful superstition manipulated by the unscrupulous for their own benefit. In other words, a figure symbolising all that bourgeois morality condemns is claimed to be representative of the real basis of bourgeois society, which then stands condemned by its own principles.

To attack society on the basis of hypocrisy, even when it aroused vehement indignation on the part of 'right-minded' critics, as with *A Doll's House* or *Ghosts* or Strindberg's naturalistic dramas, was intellectually acceptable. But here the style of presentation undermined the satiric commentary. The characters, 'depersonalised' by masks and grotesque costumes or represented by life-size dressmaker's dummies (there were forty of these, outnumbering the actors), lacked any of the psychological depth associated with serious drama. Their motivations are inconsistent, their inner natures openly expressed in the simplest terms—so removing any suspicion that they might have a three-dimensional core of individuality. And their lines were delivered in an artificial singsong voice with exaggerated articulation. Similarly, instead of a setting which either documented a specific social environment naturalistically, or even served as a symbolic projection of emotional states, Jarry's scene, with its centrepiece of a marble fireplace incongruously set in a landscape where tropical foliage arbitrarily mixed with arctic snow, was explicitly 'supposed to represent Nowhere'. This had a poetry of its own, related both to a primitive like Gaugin and to the later surrealists, but the overall effect hardly corresponded to conventional notions of the poetic. The execution was crude, like Ubu's mask which was obviously cardboard, or the costumes which were deliberately 'shoddy'. The plot is equally paltry. (pp. 22-3)

In his epigraph to the play Jarry refers to Shakespeare, singled out undoubtedly because the romantics had elevated him to practically divine status as the proponent of heroic individualism, and the action is clearly a farrago of Shakespearean situations: the bloody murder of a good king and the flight of his son from *Macbeth,* the father's ghost and Fortinbras leading a revolt against the palace from *Hamlet,* Buckingham whose reward for helping a usurper is refused from *Richard III* and the bear from *The Winter's Tale*. At first sight this seems no more than frivolity, literary parody without a point. But it ties in with Jarry's rejection of art as 'a stuffed crocodile' and gains thematic relevance in the context of his exploration of 'the power of the base appetites', since Shakespeare can be seen as representing the ideals of western culture which are thus shown to be fake. If ***Ubu roi*** undermines the very concept of man's nobility by treating as ludicrous the images that were held up to every schoolboy as models of human as well as dramatic excellence (remembering that Jarry was still at school when he wrote the first version of the play), reducing heroic actions to burlesque and fine sentiments to pastiche, the other plays in the trilogy attack equally basic aspects of 'civilised man'. ***Ubu Cuckolded*** (***Ubu cocu*** . . .) dismisses the moral nature of the individual, with Ubu flushing the toilet on the shapeless figure of his conscience, which he carries around in a suitcase and only consults to discover if the innocent are helpless enough to be victimised without personal danger; while ***Ubu Enchained*** (***Ubu enchaîné*** . . .) discredits the notion of individuality *per se*. Here it is the national motto of 'liberty, equality, fraternity' itself that is under attack with 'free men' being drilled in 'blind and unwavering indiscipline', demonstrating their liberty by such consistent disobedience that they can be controlled by simply being ordered to do the opposite of what is required. Individualism is presented as such rigid conformity that paradoxically the only possibility of asserting free will, which by definition must be the opposite of orthodoxy, lies in following orders, and Ubu decides to become a slave. He progressively 'promotes' himself to lower and lower forms of servitude, from a domineering servant to a serf who can be whipped, from a gaoler to a galley-slave. Finally, since the whole population emulates him, storming the prisons to win the deepest dungeons for themselves, stealing his fetters and rushing to the Turkish galleys in a wild competition for the most absolute form of 'freedom', Ubu is left with no one to act as his master or gaoler, and determines that 'from now on I shall be the slave of my Strumpot', or base instincts and physical appetites, which is indeed the point at which liberty (to indulge one's desires) and slavery (to one's 'lower' nature) become inseparable.

This attack on the fundamental concepts of western civilisation is accompanied by the satiric denigration of everything bourgeois, ranging from snobbery and artistic salons to rent-collection and academic pedantry. But the satire is curiously unfocussed, and the constant descent into nonsense undermines any conventionally serious point Jarry might be making. The nihilism is so anarchic that it discredits itself—and the surprising thing is that recent commentators, like the critics in that first audience who at least had the justification that the uproar prevented any of the play's subtler aspects from coming across, continue to see the primary intention of ***Ubu roi*** in purely negative protest and shock effect. If this were its real value, Artaud would hardly have named his theatre after Jarry.

As Jarry's friend Apollinaire pointed out, his satire 'operates upon reality in such a way that it totally destroys its object and rises completely above it', becoming a form of poetic vision in which the comprehensiveness of the negation itself becomes creative. The ***Ubu*** plays in fact are exercises in Jarry's theory of 'pataphysics', a 'science of imaginary solutions'. This bears much the same relationship to science, the rational way of analysing and describing the world, as Jarry's anti-theatre does to conventional drama. Its premise is that what we perceive as our world is no more than a mental construct, and that therefore there is no true distinction between perception and hallucination. What has the status of reality is simply whatever exerts the most powerful hold on the imagination, and in Jarry's view the accepted laws of physics, being based on observed norms, are 'correlations of . . . accidental data which, reduced to the status of unexceptional exceptions, possess no longer even the virtue of originality'. Obviously these are imaginatively inferior to 'the laws governing exceptions', and pataphysics deals with the particular instead of the general. It also works on the principle of the identity of opposites, defines external form as essence in a true symbolist way, and so becomes a way of describing 'a universe which can be—and perhaps should be—envisaged in the place of the traditional one'. It is in this sense that the staging for ***Ubu roi*** should be understood, a contradictory synthesis of incongruities, liberating the imagination by the unusual juxtaposition of everyday objects and simultaneously offering an alternative universe in which anything is possible. . . . (pp. 23-5)

However, Jarry's intention is not simply to present his audience with a surrogate reality, but to force each spectator to imagine his own; and all the elements in this comedy of total warfare, quite apart from their thematic significance, can be seen as hallucinatory techniques. Beneath the crudely insulting and childishly simple surface is a sophisticated manipulation of vision. The inversion of norms, exaggeration and oversimplification undermine our everyday frame of reference, as do the fusion of the inflated and prosaic or the tone of grandiose banality. The scatological obscenity and gratuitous violence are shock effects to make normal reactions seem obsessive or inappropriate. Thus try as we may to apply socially approved feelings to Jarry's mass demolition of characters, who are literally chopped to mincemeat, torn to pieces, stuffed into sewers, impaled or exploded, we can only find the violence and death funny. Such extreme and wholesale slaughter discredits or deadens conventional responses—particularly if there is no relation between cause and effect, as when one character is chopped in two and both halves continue to function as before, or another's hair is set on fire and his only comment is 'what a night, I've got hair ache'. Similarly, the distortions of perspective in the setting overload the audience's capacity to rationalise the picture presented to them, as does the syllogistic logic demonstrating the identity of opposites (which is particularly obvious in ***Ubu Enchained***) or the transformations and multiplications of characters (like Achras and Rebontier in ***Ubu Cuckolded*** who have a crocodile and monkey as their doubles, while the crocodile, whistling like a steam engine, is defined as a snake).

Where Rimbaud had advocated a 'reasoned derangement of the senses' for the poet, Jarry applies it to the audience, and one of his lighter, non-dramatic essays on **'The surface area of God'** provides a clear example of his working method. Logical thought patterns form the wall which must be breached before any level of visionary experience can be evoked, so the weight of satiric humour is brought to bear against the structures of rationalism themselves. Here the rational tools for analysing the physical world—geometry, algebraic equations, symbolic logic—are used to define the dimensions of an abstract symbol, and the resulting confusion of categories has a curious double effect. The scientific approach, with its careful mathematical framework of premise, postulate, demonstration, corollary and definition is made to appear ludicrous, empty pedantry. Paradoxically it also gives an impression of solidity and intellectual coherence to an imaginary construct. In a similar way the conclusion that 'God is the tangential point between zero and infinity' both presents a thesis that a theologian might accept and (punningly) denies the very existence of God. It is precisely the 'reasoned' nature of this 'derangement' which makes it so effective, and the same paradoxical irrationality characterises Jarry's plays. Habitual assumptions about reality and socially learned responses are called into question, cutting the ground from under our mental feet. At the same time our imagination is challenged, both by the extravagance of the dramatic world and by the self-parodying theatricality of the presentation, where single characters stand for a whole army, but puppet qualities and unnatural voices exaggerate their symbolic nature into artificiality, or where placards announce changes of scene, but without any of the unobtrusiveness of Shakespearean staging, being carried in by a man in full evening dress who trots across the stage on the points of his toes to underline the irrelevance of specifying place in a setting that is 'Nowhere'. As Jarry put it in the epigraph to ***Ubu Enchained:*** 'We shall not have succeeded in demolishing everything unless we demolish the ruins as well. But the only way I can see of doing that is to use them to put up a lot of fine, well-designed buildings.' The 'ruins' stand for traditional concepts, the nationalisms and rationalisms of post-industrial society, and these can only be effectively abolished by restructuring the bricks into alternate visions. Hence the extra letter in Ubu's notorious opening expletive, which gives an example of Jarry's method in miniature. Transforming 'merde' into 'merdre' makes the familiar strange, the scatologically shocking becomes simultaneously hallucinatory, and (in one of Jarry's typical puns) a fundamental aspect of reality is subtly distorted to challenge and liberate the spectator's imagination.

Jarry's approach is too confused, his techniques, drawn from *grand guignol* puppet theatre, symbolist abstraction and Shakespeare, too diversified for the full impact of his drama to be realised. On the one hand his intention is satiric protest, confronting the public 'like the exaggerating mirror in the stories of Madame Leprince de Beaumont, in which the depraved saw themselves with dragons' bodies, or bulls' horns, or whatever corresponded to their particular vice'. On the other he is trying to create 'an ABSTRACT theatre', with masks replacing the psychological portrayal of an individual by 'the effigy of the CHARACTER' and 'universal gesture' achieving 'essential expression'. The contradictions are too extreme. Ubu is not only an antisocial force capable of devastating the bourgeois *Weltanschauung,* a wish-fulfilment figure destructive to the point of self-destruction—hence Jarry's own identification with his character, signing himself 'Ubu' and speaking in a Ubuesque 'special voice' that reduced the semantic content of his words to nonsense by giving equal weight to each syllable. Ubu also epitomises the qualities of the bourgeoisie, whom Jarry despised. Negative and positive elements are superimposed, self-cancelling. As a result his plays had little immediate effect. After the initial shock, Jarry's work rapidly became accepted as 'art'. . . . [When] Gémier played the role again in 1908 it was 'before a completely calm, one might almost say indifferent audience . . . neither amused, nor scandalised, nor surprised'. The performance was prefaced by an academic lecture appraising Jarry's literary significance, the effect was judged

Drawing of Jarry by Picasso from the 1923 edition of Doctor Faustroll. *Reprinted courtesy of Grove Press, Inc.*

to be 'very spiritual' and Gémier planned to found a 'Théâtre Ubu', creating new plays around Jarry's characters. The most dispiriting thing for an artist who aims to *épater les bourgeois* [''shock the bourgeoisie''] is the capacity of society to absorb irritants, like an oyster seeing dirt thrown into the works only as a potential pearl, and by the 1920s the academic industry had made Jarry's anarchism harmlessly respectable with pedantic essays such as 'Brahma and Ubu, or the historical spirit'. But his true significance lies in the appeal to the irrational and (through the elements of deliberate naivety and the primitive, child's convention in stage presentation) pre-social level of the mind, which was picked up by Artaud and by the 'College of Pataphysics'. . . . (pp. 26-9)

Christopher Innes, ''Dreams, Archetypes, and the Irrational,'' in his Holy Theatre: Ritual and the Avant Garde, *Cambridge University Press, 1981, pp. 18-58.**

IHAB HASSAN (essay date 1982)

[*Hassan is an American critic and the author of numerous studies devoted to important figures and trends in modern literature. In the following excerpt from* The Dismemberment of Orpheus, *Hassan discusses Jarry's nihilism and attempts to demonstrate that he was influenced by the Marquis de Sade. Hassan argues that Jarry saw a person as both God and machine, and equated humanity's apotheosis with its dehumanization.*]

The avant-garde, in the technical literary sense, comes into being with 'Pataphysics, Futurism, Dadaism, and Surrealism. Sade, Lautréamont, Rimbaud, a whole century of Romantic metaphor, countless years of human error, and man's search for the Absolute—all these prepare its way. In a larger sense, the avant-garde merely follows the logic of Western history. Yet following or leading, its spirit creates those vanishing forms that intrude upon us still, demanding a reckoning. (p. 48)

Alfred Jarry . . . invents 'Pataphysics. He also dedicates his life to a career that denies both art and life. In his world, paradox and triviality rule the waning day. He believes the soul is a tic, and love a form of perpetual motion. He ends as a prophet of otherness, standing beside himself, Ubuesque. He also ends as a humorist of the infinite. André Breton notes, in his *Anthologie de l'humour noir,* that the distinction between art and life explodes with Jarry who carries revolvers, discharging them freely into the world, and so unites himself to its facts. The explosion of each bullet seems a note in his laughter. (p. 49)

''His life,'' [Roger] Shattuck writes, ''and his work united in a single threat to the equilibrium of human nature.''

It is more than a threat; Jarry perfects the act, the art, of human denaturalization. He carries Romantic self-assertion, beyond alienation of the Self, to the limits of self-dissolution. This is implicit in Sade whose presence lurks in Jarry's science fantasy, ***Le Surmâle***. . . . The hero of that work, André Marcueil, lives on Perpetual Motion Food; races a train across Asia, riding on his vélo; copulates indefinitely under experimental conditions; and with sheer brain energy, overwhelms an 11,000-volt machine designed to inspire love. At the end, the machine ''falls in love'' with Marcueil as they ''embrace'' in a shower of sparks and destruction. Jarry asks the central question: ''Who are you, Man?'' And he answers: both God and Machine. The dehumanization of man, we see, is also his apotheosis. It is no wonder that to young André Gide, Jarry seems to speak with the voice of a nutcracker.

In converting man into machine and life into artifice, Jarry obeys the Absurd, and therein lies his freedom. The principle of universal convertibility, on which 'Pataphysics is founded, also denies fixed valence and discrete identity. Fact is equivalent to dream, past to present, reason to madness, space to time, and self to other. There are no limits, no contradictions. Parody, paradox, and hallucination are techniques of veracity. Humor depends on the continual reversal of terms. Style takes the form of radical ambiguity. As Jarry himself puts it: ''. . . the relation of the verbal sentence to every meaning that can be found in it is constant . . . ;'' from which Shattuck concludes: ''All interpretations are on a par, are equivalent. . . . A text means all things equivocally . . . writing is a slip of the tongue.'' The silence of Jarry is precise and consistent.

But what, precisely, is the science of 'Pataphysics, of which Ubu is a Doctor? In ***Gestes et opinions du docteur Faustroll,*** 1911, Jarry explains:

> 'Pataphysics is the science of the realm beyond metaphysics. . . . It will study the laws which govern exceptions and will explain the universe supplementary to this one. . . .
>
> Definition: 'Pataphysics is the science of imaginary solutions, which symbolically attributes the properties of objects, described by their virtuality, to their lineaments.

In short, 'Pataphysics is the science of Nonsense. It assumes the absolute futility of thought. It implies both equivalence and reduction, and functions as a parodic myth. In that ''myth,'' God is the shortest distance between zero and infinity, as Dr. Faustroll claims. Dr. Faustroll babbles on, and his monkey, Bosse-de-Nage (Bottom-Face), punctuates his master's learning with scatological events, crying always: ''Ha, ha.'' The science has a gay and desperate side. We can understand why it inspired a number of free spirits to found, in 1949, a Collège de 'Pataphysique.

Like Sade, Beckett, or Burroughs, Jarry suffers from a reductive rage; he belittles our world. At times, there is something almost sacramental about his peculiar nihilism. But the ferocity of his deadpan humor betrays his animus against the condition of man. Great-souled, Jarry's person is small; and he dwells in burrows or caves. A misanthropist, he gallantly evades the complications of love. The little we know about his sexual life suggests that he feels horror for woman, *mater generatrix*. The world's body remains alien to him, and the ''adipose tissue'' of motherhood is ''odious because it has a function—it produces *milk*.'' The most famous expression of Ubu remains ''Shitter''! Reduction leads finally to waste; this is the essential joke of life.

The literary joke, however, is more ample, and its form rather more cunning. (pp. 50-2)

The horror of ***Ubu Roi*** is that it happens Everywhere; actually, its setting is Poland which, as Jarry pedantically explains, is Nowhere. The action is childish, cruel, bestial, funny, and absurd; the hero is gross, deadly, stupid, rapacious, and wholly without scruples. Ignoble as he may be, Ubu endures, a brutish Everyman who resembles us all *because* he is nature, a canny union of id and ugly ego. His concerns are three: ''physique,'' by which he means matter, ''phynance,'' by which he means money and status, and ''merdre,'' which subsumes all his concerns. Ubu is the all-gut gutless wonder, the bulging monument of bourgeois clichés, the end of history. He embodies the banality. He poisons his guests with a dirty broom, murders his master, the King of Poland, to usurp his throne, massacres the nobility to empty their coffers, and flees from the battlefield. The play which begins arbitrarily with obscenity must end, as Père and Mère Ubu make their way to France, with nonsense. "Ah, gentlemen!" Père Ubu says, "however beautiful it [France] may be, it can never equal Poland. If there weren't any Poland, there wouldn't be any Poles!" Existence is farce. Yet the play grimly denounces the corruptions of man and society, and its humor explodes in violence and sudden death. At bottom, ***Ubu Roi*** is an assault on the audience, on the reality they think to possess. Its proper coda is "The Song of Disembraining" in which we are all Rentiers of Reality". . . . (pp. 52-3)

But the assault of the play is also on language. Ubu speaks his own debased argot, mispronouncing words and making up others of his own: "merdre," "oneille," etc. The speeches are brief, truculent, jocular, and entirely otiose. It is as if language were constantly searching for its lowest common denominator in slang, obscenities, oaths, expletives, and clichés. Elegance is banished and poetry appears fleetingly in the form of rude popular ditties. Words express nothing, change nothing. The action of the play is an outrage, neither comic nor tragic, its structure is that of chaos disguised as slapstick; its style denies its own powers. Jarry parodies himself in Ubu, and parodies art in his writings. Once, in "real life," he fires his revolver at a sculptor and then exclaims: "N'est-ce pas que c'était beau comme littérature?" ["Wasn't that as beautiful as literature"]. The expression remains with him throughout his career, a clarion of contempt.

Jarry's contempt for art, however, is not simple. He admires Maeterlinck, for instance, and some aspects of the Symbolist aesthetic. He requires simplicity of design in the theatre, heraldic decors, masks and costumes that represent "effigies of character," a particular statement of the universal. He requires stylization, as in a marionette show or a Japanese play. He insists on a theatre for elite audiences, a theatre of *action* in which the elite participate in the genuine act of creation—let the masses copulate! In such a theatre, the proper applause is silence. Speaking of ***Ubu Roi,*** Jarry says: "It is not surprising that the public should have been aghast at the sight of its ignoble other-self, which it had never before been shown completely." The work of art, then, is an act of vicarious creation for the elect; for the rest, it is only insult and affront.

With time, however, even the act of creation loses its special authority. Jarry's parody deepens; his art becomes more gratuitous. ***Almanach du Père Ubu*** . . . , is pastiche, a collection of dates, figures, tables, drawings, letters, catalogues, necrologies, etc. In ***Ubu enchaîné*** . . . , the destructive spirit consumes itself: Ubu chooses self-enslavement, slaughtering everyone who stands between him and his aim. *"Cornegidouille!"* he exclaims, ". . . we will not have demolished all if we do not demolish also the ruins!" Nonsense attains its apocalyptic end. Why not ask for a toothpick on one's deathbed?

Alfred Jarry believes that the mind functions after death, and that its dreams are all we ever know of paradise. We do not see the dreams of that mind in his work; we only see the splattered brain. . . . Like Sade, like Lautréamont, Jarry carries his revolt against life to the seat of consciousness, and substitutes his dream for what men call reality. Like them, he strikes in the crotch. Laughingly, he crushes love into a bloody thing; the blood itself turns into excrement. This "sublime debauchee" is also a master of modernity. "With Alfred Jarry," Apollinaire writes in "The New Spirit and the Poets," ". . . we have seen laughter rise from the lower regions where it was writhing, to furnish the poet with a totally new lyricism." (pp. 53-5)

Ihab Hassan, "Interlude: From 'Pataphysics to Surrealism'," in his The Dismemberment of Orpheus: Toward a Postmodern Literature, *second edition, The University of Wisconsin Press, 1982, pp. 48-79.**

LINDA KLIEGER STILLMAN (essay date 1983)

[Stillman is a specialist in French literature and the author of critical studies of the works of Arthur Adamov, Jean-Paul Sartre, and Roland Barthes. In the following excerpt from her book-length study of Jarry and his works, Stillman examines Jarry's writings from a psychoanalytic perspective, concluding that they reveal a pattern of narcissism that is "eerily predictive of modern consciousness."]

[It] is no accident that mirroring, doubling, repetition, and displacement inform Jarry's novels, taken individually or intertexually. A decentered pluralism of psychic self-theatricalizations has become the hallmark of the modern psyche. With the help of psychoanalytic discourse Jarry's texts become clearly intelligible and they are eerily predictive of modern consciousness. Psychoanalysis explains the symbolic relations which structure the Subject; and the dominant "psychological disposition" of modern Western culture—according to social historian Christopher Lasch and analysts Otto Kernberg and Heinz Kohut—is narcissism. Jarry's self-theatricalization into a multiplicity of doubles tragically renders material a madness which marks the particular pathology of the modern era.

Narcissism, in its various manifestations throughout Jarry's texts, exceeds mere rhetorical posturing around the image of self-engrossment or of the infolding of language itself. His writings concretize, with astonishing lucidity, the delirious fragmentation of man and, correlatively, of his discourse. The essential fragmentation of this textual universe, however, in Jarry's case, mimes what was probably the primal splitting of pathological narcissism. The most insistent narrative patterns and dramatic characterizations in the fiction trace biographemes such as the absent father, the mother's devaluation of the father, and the exaggerated role of the son in the mother's defense system. Add to these the probability of guilt regarding the death of his infant brother. His avowed need to be special, unique, or, to quote him, "precious," acts as a nodal point for a range of isolating and terrifying narcissistic fantasies. Perpetual-Motion-Food nourishes a pathologically grandiose self and assures its omnipotence. . . . The Supermale's sexual and athletic exploits, because of their very automatism and absence of pleasure, aim at neutralizing or forestalling the chronic threat of fragmentation that precedes the full-blown psychosis. Marcueil typifies the narcissistic male: his arrogant and exploitive behavior toward women derives from an unconscious projection of hostility against the imago of the mother.

Obsessively freighted with metaphors of the Double, seemingly endless stratification of perverse sexual penchants, and reliance on "primary process" thinking (rejecting linear causality in favor of symbolism and magic), works such as ***Days and Nights*** and ***The Supermale*** afford Jarry the therapeutic opportunity to act out the pathological characterology with which he invests his literary counterparts. He projected his intrapsychic aggression and anxiety upon incarnations of his fundamental personality organization. This tendency to "primitivize" thought leads from Ubu's stilted diction to the obsessional use of neologisms. Symptomatic of the narcissist's inner void, "Ubu-speak" is the diction of a robot, never sincerely jealous, sad, angry, and who cannot cry. Ubu transposes this personality in yet another way: "People may appear [to the narcissist] either to have some potential food inside, which the patient has to extract, or to be already emptied and therefore valueless. His attitude toward others is either deprecatory—he has extracted all he needs and tosses them aside—or fearful—others may attack, exploit, and force him to submit to them." His greed, destructiveness, and intense ambition are all characteristic of the narcissist. Likewise, Sengle's antisocial behavior [in ***Days and Nights***], Haldern's sadistic and open physical violence toward the object of his sexual exploits [in ***Haldernablou***], and Emmanuel God's "self-concept of the hungry wolf" [in ***Absolute Love***]. Emmanuel God's oral-sadistic fantasy relates to his identification of his eyes with sharp-fanged wolves. Generally, the most basic mother-infant interactions reside in the domain of the visual. Often aggressively cathected, the visual takes the place of failed physical contact (oral or tactile) or even of the mother's closeness. Narcissism goes hand in hand with a hypercathected visual sense, as Faustroll's visit to the Isle of Her [in ***Dr. Faustroll***] illustrates. There, the water's immobile surface is "like a mirror" and its sovereign is a Cyclops. In front of this giant male's frontal eye hangs a two-sided mirror. His extraordinary sight easily penetrates ultraviolet "things." This therapeutic activation of the grandiose self corresponds to Kohut's "mirror transference" in which the child seeks to retain a degree of archaic narcissism, on the one hand, by attributing perfection and strength to a grandiose self and, on the other hand, by relegating all imperfection to the external world. The narcissist attempts to reestablish the stage when the mother's gaze—reflecting the child's exhibitionism or other aspects of maternal participation in her child's narcissistic pleasure—confirms the individual's self-esteem. (pp. 139-42)

As Jarry's texts (especially ***The Supermale***) demonstrate, narcissistic sexual desire—to take one example of the dynamics of this division—is fundamentally masochistic: "the subject fantasizes an ecstatic death as the result of being attacked by an alien self" (cf. the Love-Inspiring Machine animated by Marcueil's own strength). An equally sumptuous occurrence of autoerotic activity portrays Sengle kissing the lips of Valens: "The plaster mouth became flesh and red in order to drink the libation of Sengle's soul [. . .]. And after the instant of redness, the lips turned green and adhered, completely cold, to Sengle's blackened lips." . . . This reverse alchemical symbolism (proceeding from red to green to black) mimics the narcissistic regression at work in the novel.

Jarry evokes a similar image when he declares his wish to be so hideous that his presence would cause women to abort in the streets or give birth to Siamese twins joined at the forehead. Such desires betoken the symptoms of narcissistic rage that permeate his life and his art. Often, the precariously omnipotent characters swing from experiences of inner devastation to grandiose potentiality and infinite freedom. Their need for homage and adoration (in the cases of, for example, Haldern and Emmanuel God), their exploitive and at times parasitic relationships with others (Ubu above all), give rise to defensive fantasies of grandeur and inflated self-concepts, evidence of developmental arrest. (pp. 142-43)

In retrospect, Jarry's writings seem to express particularly well the pathology which governs the fundamental personality configuration of the modern age. (p. 145)

Linda Klieger Stillman, in her Alfred Jarry, *Twayne, 1983, 166 p.*

ADDITIONAL BIBLIOGRAPHY

Bierman, James H. "The Antichrist Ubu." *Comparative Drama* 9, No. 3 (Fall 1975): 226-47.

Examines *Ubu Roi* in its original context as part three of Jarry's *Caesar-Antichrist*. Bierman contends that Jarry's interest in esoteric symbolism was more profound than is commonly recognized, and that symbols from the tarot, the cabbala, and heraldry are all integral to a complete understanding of *Ubu Roi*.

Humphries, John Jefferson. "The Machine as Metaphor: Jarry's *Pompe à Merdre*." *Romantic Review* LXXIII, No. 3 (May 1982): 346-54.

Explores Jarry's fascination with machinery. Humphries argues that Jarry saw the machine as a perfect metaphor for language.

Spingler, Michael K. "From the Actor to Ubu: Jarry's Theatre of the Double." *Modern Drama* XVI, No. 1 (June 1973): 1-10.

Examines Jarry's conception of the actor's function in modern drama.

Stillman, Linda Klieger. "Physics and Pataphysics: The Source of *Faustroll*." *The Kentucky Romance Quarterly* XXVI, No. 1 (1979): 81-92.

Explores Jarry's use of genuine scientific research as a starting point for the descriptions of fantasy phenomena in *Dr. Faustroll*.

Styan, J. L. "Jarry, Precursor of Surrealism in France: *Ubu Roi* (1896)." In his *Modern Drama in Theory and Practice: Symbolism, Surrealism and the Absurd, Vol. 2*, pp. 45-50. Cambridge: Cambridge University Press, 1981.

On the relationship of *Ubu Roi* to the modern movement in the theater. Styan examines Jarry's influence on Guillaume Apollinaire, André Breton, and Jean Cocteau.

Taylor, Simon Watson. Introduction to *The Ubu Plays*, by Alfred Jarry, translated by Cyril Connoly and Simon Watson Taylor, pp. 11-16. London: Methuen & Co., 1968.

History of the writing, publication, and production of the *Ubu* cycle.

White, Kenneth S. *Savage Comedy: Structures of Humor*. Edited by Kenneth S. White. Amsterdam: Editions Rodopi N.V., 1978, 63 p.

Scattered references to Jarry in this study of the manner in which certain twentieth-century dramas reflect the notion of a savage and malevolent cosmos.

York, Ruth B. "*Ubu* Revisited: The Reprise of 1922." *The French Review* XXXV, No. 3 (February 1962): 408-11.

Details of the production and the critical response to Lugné-Pöe's production of *Ubu Roi* at the Theatre de L'Oeuvre in 1922. Excerpts from the critic's reviews and from Lugné-Pöe's notes are in French and are not translated.

Ring(gold Wilmer) Lardner

1885-1933

(Also wrote under pseudonym of James Clarkson) American short story writer, journalist, dramatist, autobiographer, essayist, and poet.

Lardner is considered one of the most accomplished humorists and satirists in American literature. Best known for such frequently anthologized short stories as "The Golden Honeymoon," "Champion," "Some Like Them Cold," and "Haircut," he drew upon his background as a small-town Midwesterner and experience as a sportswriter to render his amusing, biting fiction in the idiom of the semieducated, middle-class American "boob." Praised during his lifetime by H. L. Mencken and other major critics as a formidable satiric adversary of American provincialism, Lardner has since been recognized as a master storyteller in the tradition of Mark Twain and Sherwood Anderson. Like the works of these classic American authors, Lardner's writings reflect both the humorous nostalgia as well as the deep bitterness of his personal life.

The Granger Collection, New York

Born into a wealthy family in the town of Niles, Michigan, Lardner was raised and privately educated in the genteel environs of his parents' estate, where he developed a strong interest in baseball, music, and drama. After his family suffered a severe financial setback in 1901, he worked unsuccessfully at a variety of jobs in Niles and in nearby Chicago. One position that he held and apparently found particularly harrowing was that of the sole bookkeeper, bill collector, and meter inspector for the Niles Gas Company, an ill-paying, discouraging experience that was later described in his story "The Maysville Minstrel." Leaving the gas company in 1905, Lardner wrote the lyrics and music for his first published work—the Niles American minstrel group's musical comedy *Zanzibar*—and, shortly thereafter, began work as a reporter for the South Bend, Indiana *Times*. During the next few years he developed into a highly respected sportswriter, leaving South Bend and working for several Chicago newspapers. Travelling with the White Sox and the Cubs, Lardner came to understand the humor, quirks, and concerns of the individual ballplayers, becoming their friend and confidant. His first attempts to incorporate the players' breezy, slang-filled language into fiction appeared in "In the Wake of the News," a widely read daily column that he wrote for the *Chicago Tribune* from 1913 to 1919. During this time *The Saturday Evening Post* carried a series of Lardner's stories that described the adventures of a semiliterate bush-league pitcher named Jack Keefe. In these epistolary "busher" stories, which evidence Lardner's approaching maturity as a yarn-spinning storyteller as well as his thorough knowledge of the average rookie's struggles to reach the major leagues, the bellicose Keefe offers his "idears" on life, baseball, and—most importantly—his own greatness, in a progression of comically misspelled letters to his long-suffering friend, Al Blanchard. The stories were collected and published as *You Know Me Al: A Busher's Letters* in 1916, by which time Lardner was an established contributor of fiction to such popular magazines as *Redbook, McClure's,* and *The Saturday Evening Post*. The stories he wrote for these periodicals, which were later collected in *Gullible's Travels, Etc.* and *Own Your Own Home,* humorously portray the lives of affable, middle-class Midwesterners who strive to attain the status and material pleasures of highbrow society, only to make ludicrous fools of themselves. During World War I, Lardner served as a war correspondent for *Collier's,* recounting his overseas experiences in that magazine and in *My Four Weeks in France*. He also put Jack Keefe in a military uniform for the stories collected in *Treat 'Em Rough: Letters from Jack the Kaiser Killer* and *The Real Dope,* which marked Keefe's last appearance in Lardner's fiction.

The Real Dope was published in 1919, a watershed year in Lardner's life. It was the year he ended his career as a variety columnist and sportswriter for the *Chicago Tribune* and moved to the East, where he hoped to establish himself as a successful writer of Broadway musicals. His decision to leave sportswriting was prompted and augmented by his deep disillusionment over certain developments and events in professional sports. One key development in baseball was the introduction of the "jackrabbit," or live, ball (a close relative of the modern hardball), which completely changed the nature of the game, ushering in the era of Babe Ruth and other homerun hitters who could win or lose games by a single swing of the bat. This new emphasis, in turn, changed the nature of the average baseball fan, who became interested primarily in the results of games rather than the fairness and skill with which they were played. To Lardner, baseball—long noted for its low-scoring games as well as the speed, skill, and versatility of the players—was becoming increasingly dominated by a collection of highly paid, hamfisted strongmen who were being cheered on by a demanding, loutish audience. In addition Lardner was, like many Americans, stunned by the 1919 "Black Sox Scandal," which resulted when a group of mobsters bribed eight members of the heavily favored Chicago White Sox to lose the World Series to the Cincinnati Reds. Lardner considered the entire affair to be not only a disgrace to the game he had so long enjoyed, but a personal betrayal as well, for he was on friendly terms with several of the players—one of whom, shortly before evidence of wrongdoing was verified, lied to Lardner about his involvement. According to his son, screenwriter Ring Lardner, Jr., the "Black Sox Scandal" as well as the 1926 Jack Dempsey-Gene Tunney heavyweight boxing match—the famous "long-count" fight, which was believed by many to be tainted by scandal—convinced Lardner that if anything in life could be "fixed," it probably was. Ironically, the result of his disenchantment was that during the decade that is today known as the "Golden Age of Sports" he wrote few empathetic or successful stories about athletes. Lardner's stories, which had always contained varying degrees of satire in addition to their humor, became increasingly satiric. During this period he wrote his most accomplished works.

Lardner settled in Great Neck, Long Island, where he was a neighbor of F. Scott Fitzgerald, Groucho Marx, George M. Cohan, and other Jazz-Age writers and show business people. He had been completely unsuccessful in interesting Broadway producers in his sketches for musicals when, in 1923, his friend Fitzgerald directed the attention of editor Maxwell E. Perkins of Charles Scribner's Sons to the short story "The Golden Honeymoon" and suggested that Scribner's publish a collection of Lardner's best stories. Perkins, who, through his work with such major authors as Fitzgerald, Ernest Hemingway, and Thomas Wolfe, came to be known as one of America's most perceptive and respected editors, was highly impressed with Lardner's story, a wistful and gently humorous account of an elderly couple's unexpectedly eventful anniversary trip to Florida. With Lardner's approval he gathered what Fitzgerald considered Lardner's ten most significant stories (including "Champion," "Some Like Them Cold," "Alibi Ike," and "The Golden Honeymoon"), persuaded Lardner to write a humorous, explanatory preface to each story, and published the resulting collection as *How to Write Short Stories (with Samples)* in 1924. Immediately popular, *How to Write Short Stories* was Lardner's first book to appear under the imprint of a major publisher; as a result his fiction, for the first time, came under the scrutiny of America's most influential critics, who praised Lardner as a master of satire and—with Sinclair Lewis and Mencken—as an important voice in the then-raging cultural war against American provincialism. While noting with approval what George Whicher termed Lardner's "ability to report with seeming unconsciousness the appalling mediocrity and vanity of the middle-class soul," some critics expressed the hope that Lardner would turn from short fiction to write a novel. Concluding his largely favorable review of *How to Write Short Stories,* Edmund Wilson asked, "Will Mr. Lardner, then, write his *Huckleberry Finn*? Has he already told all he knows?" Throughout the 1920s, Perkins and Fitzgerald also urged Lardner to devote his skill to writing a novel, but he continued to work in the shorter forms. Apart from his stories, he did publish some short nonsense plays that are considered superb examples of their genre. But as critics unanimously agree, the short story was his métier, and with the appearance of *The Love Nest, and Other Stories* in 1926 he reached the height of his fame. In addition to such works as "A Day with Conrad Green," "Zone of Quiet," "Mr. and Mrs. Fix-it," and "The Love Nest"—stories that are considered among Lardner's very best—the collection contains what is today regarded as a masterpiece of satiric short fiction, "Haircut." Narrated in the blithe, first-person ramblings of a talkative village barber, "Haircut" tells of the heavy-handed antics of a small-town practical joker, of the respect accorded him by the townsfolk for being such a "card," and of his violent death in a dubious hunting "accident." Upon reading the story, Perkins wrote to Lardner to say, "I read 'Haircut' . . . and I can't shake it out of my mind;—in fact the impression it made has deepened with time. There's not a man alive who could have done better, that's certain." Renowned for his short stories, Lardner finally achieved long-sought success in the theater with the musical comedy *June Moon,* based on his story "Some Like Them Cold." (His only other production, *Elmer the Great,* folded shortly after its opening.) But in spite of Lardner's success, the production of *June Moon* and the publication of the short story omnibus *Round Up,* both in 1929, marked the end of his greatest creative period.

Throughout much of his career Lardner had struggled unsuccessfully with alcoholism, depression, and insomnia, and during the mid-1920s he had discovered that he suffered from tuberculosis, as well. He was frequently hospitalized for these maladies during the early 1930s, although during this time he still managed to write a large number of stories and articles. The most intriguing of these was a series of magazine essays on the state of public radio programming which, to the puzzlement of his readers and critics, was heatedly attacked by the noted satirist for what he considered the pornographic lyrics of certain popular songs as well as the prurient humor of radio comedians. Lardner published what Hemingway called "those pitiful dying radio censorship pieces" monthly in *The New Yorker* from June 1932 until August 1933. A month after the final installment appeared, Lardner died of a heart attack.

Since the time *How to Write Short Stories* was published, Lardner has been recognized as a masterful humorist and satirist, with critics of his day especially amused that members of the American "booboisie" avidly read his stories while failing to perceive his mockery of their speech and values. A few months before Lardner's death, Clifton Fadiman posited that there was more to Lardner's satire than critics had previously seen, writing: "The special force of Ring Lardner's work springs from a single fact: he just doesn't like people. Except Swift, no writer has gone farther on hatred alone. I believe he hates himself; more certainly he hates his characters; and most clearly of all, his characters hate each other. Out of this integral-triune repulsion is born his icy satiric power." Fadiman's "triangle of hate" theory, embraced by Wilson and Maxwell Geismar, dominated criticism of Lardner's works until recent years. Such stories as "The Golden Honeymoon," "The Love Nest," "Ex Parte," and "Who Dealt?"—works that are concerned with the foibles of married life in suburban America—were viewed as misanthropic denunciations of the institution of marriage, while the early "busher" stories and the boxing story "Champion" were found to evidence Lardner's contempt for professional athletes. In the character of welterweight boxer Michael (''Midge'') Kelly of ''Champion,'' Lardner created what Forrest L. Ingram called ''one of the most despicable characters in American fiction.'' But though considered one of Lardner's bitterest, albeit flawed, stories, ''Champion'' is perceived by the author's most recent critics as a work indicative of a concern that runs throughout Lardner's canon: his disillusionment with the values and morals of America's Jazz-Age culture. Jonathan Yardley has argued that having been raised in a highly protective home and in a slow-paced small town, and having spent the formative years of his career travelling—as Fitzgerald described it—''in the company of a few dozen illiterates playing a boy's game,'' Lardner retained throughout his life the provincial values of trust, fairness, mannerliness, and scorn for pretense. Likewise, he registered the provincial's unfailing shock when these values were violated; hence his contempt for self-centered bullies like Midge Kelly, for liars like Kelly's public-relations man, and for gullible dupes like the ''champion's'' admirers. Hence, also, his marked change in attitude toward professional sports after the ''Black Sox Scandal,'' and his writing of what critics have termed his ''puritanical'' *New Yorker* radio columns. Such critics as Yardley and Ring Lardner, Jr. have also noted that Lardner's bitterness was probably deeply rooted in the troubles of his personal life, such as his alcoholism, depression, and sleeplessness, as well as his longtime lack of success as a professional playwright and his continuous struggle to earn enough money to support himself, his wife, and his four sons amid the extravagant Long Island society that has been accurately described by Fitzgerald in *The Great Gatsby*. In spite of the extreme bitterness of many of Lardner's stories, modern critics tend to agree with Yardley's belief that Lardner's middle-class readers laughed at his characters in recognition, not in ignorance or derision, and that Lardner ''understood that it is the fate of most of us to struggle toward insubstantial goals and to fail even in that, and he was amused in a sad and pensive way by what he saw from that Olympian peak he occupied, but he watched with compassion rather than contempt, dismay rather than distaste.''

Although most of Lardner's many short stories are unknown by today's readers, and though his work has never attracted a particularly large body of criticism, his most famous stories have been widely praised and his technique widely imitated. J. D. Salinger, Mark Harris, and Hemingway have acknowledged Lardner's influence, while evidence strongly suggests that in his novel *Tender Is the Night* Fitzgerald portrayed his friend in the character Abe North, a tall, would-be songwriter who possesses Lardner's sad, deepset eyes and a serious drinking problem. (Another inebriated character in Fitzgerald's fiction bears a nickname given Lardner by Chicago ballplayers during his sportswriting days—''Owl Eyes,'' in *The Great Gatsby*.) Sherwood Anderson has called Lardner a natural storyteller and such noted authors as Virginia Woolf, J. M. Barrie, Thomas Wolfe, and Dorothy Parker have deeply admired his work. With a brief reference to Wilson's early review of *How to Write Short Stories,* Elizabeth Evans has summarized the current critical view of Lardner, calling him ''a spokesman of the twenties'' who ''showed how many people lived, bearing and displaying their foibles, pettiness, misguided ambition, misplaced values. He was a superb humorist, an effective satirist, and a gifted short story writer. His *Huckleberry Finn* did not come, but readers are much in his debt for a great deal of entertainment and some excellent writing.''

(See also *TCLC,* Vol. 2; *Contemporary Authors,* Vol. 104; *Dictionary of Literary Biography,* Vol. 11: *American Humorists, 1800-1950;* and Vol. 25: *American Newspaper Journalists: 1901-1925.*)

PRINCIPAL WORKS

Zanzibar (drama) 1905
Bib Ballads (verse) 1915
You Know Me Al: A Busher's Letters (short stories) 1916
Gullible's Travels, Etc. (short stories) 1917
My Four Weeks in France (sketches) 1918
Treat 'Em Rough: Letters from Jack the Kaiser Killer (short stories) 1918
Own Your Own Home (short stories) 1919
The Real Dope (short stories) 1919
The Young Immigrunts (sketch) 1920
The Big Town: How I and the Mrs. Go to New York to See Life and Get Katie a Husband (short stories) 1921
Symptoms of Being Thirty-Five (sketch) 1921
Say It with Oil: A Few Remarks about Wives (sketch) 1923
How to Write Short Stories (with Samples) (short stories) 1924
What of It? (short stories, sketches, and dramas) 1925
The Love Nest, and Other Stories (short stories) 1926
The Story of a Wonder Man (autobiography) 1927
Elmer the Great [with George M. Cohan] (drama) 1928
June Moon [with George S. Kaufman] (drama) 1929
Round Up (short stories) 1929; also published as *The Collected Short Stories of Ring Lardner,* 1941
Lose with a Smile (short stories) 1933
Some Champions: Sketches and Fiction (essays and short stories) 1976

***THE NEW YORK TIMES* (essay date 1918)**

[*In the following excerpt an anonymous critic favorably reviews* My Four Weeks in France.]

''My Four Weeks in France'' is a diary of Ring Lardner's trip done in his best vein, and will be welcomed by all those who have become familiar with **''You Know Me, Al''** and his other stories which are among the most popular humorous stories of the day. . . .

Our impression is that there have been few Americans so thoroughly glad to get back to their country as Mr. Lardner or more utterly unfitted for the hardships of a soldier's life, his one experience in a borrowed uniform having ''fed him up,'' as the English say.

''We managed the puttees in thirty-five minutes,'' he says. ''It is said that a man working alone can do them in an hour, provided he is experienced. It's no wonder regular correspondents and British officers are obliged to wear canes. The wonder is they don't use crutches.''

''Soldiers Tell of Life at the Front,'' in The New York Times, *Section 5, August 25, 1918, p. 316.**

ROBERT C. BENCHLEY (essay date 1923)

[*An essayist, actor, screenwriter, and radio personality, Benchley was one of the most popular American humorists of the early twentieth century. A writer who portrayed his entire life as a series of frustrations and humiliations, he has been described by Wolcott Gibbs as "by far the most brilliant and consistent of the school, originating with (Stephen) Leacock, who performed such dizzy miracles with parody, non sequitur, garbled reference, and all the other materials of off-center wit." During his career Benchley wrote humorous reviews and essays for the New York* World, Life, The Bookman, *and* The New Yorker. *In the following excerpted review of Lardner's* "Say It with Oil," *a story published in a volume with Nina Wilcox Putnam's* "Say It with Bricks," *Benchley offers lukewarm praise, stating that it reads like the formula humor regularly suggested by editors of popular magazines, in this case John Siddall of* The American Magazine. *(In an unexcerpted portion of this essay, Benchley writes of the deadly effects that result when humorists subordinate their talent to the demands of magazine editors, likening the humorists to hapless victims who are eventually "found dead in the woods.")*]

In pointing to Ring Lardner's **"Say It With Oil"** (reprinted from "The American Magazine" in a Siamese volume with Nina Wilcox Putnam's "Say It With Bricks") we do not even remotely imply that Mr. Lardner will ever be found dead in the woods as a humorist because of having been seized by a magazine editor. Even magazine editors can't kill Mr. Lardner. His reply to Mrs. Putnam's synthetic attack on husbands has more laughs in it than you will find in the collected works of any other humorist. But it does in the main show that the idea was Editor Siddall's. It does show that Mr. Lardner didn't care an awful lot about doing it, and that he was glad when it was done and in the mail. It is a typical magazine editor's idea, and the fact that Mr. Lardner got some laughs into it doesn't make it any better. There are plenty of things that Ring Lardner ought to be doing, without spending his time trying to rewrite something that editors have been suggesting to funny men for hundreds of years. (p. 457)

Robert C. Benchley, "The Fate of the Funny Men," in The Bookman, *New York, Vol. LVII, No. 4, June, 1923, pp. 455-57.**

THOMAS BOYD (essay date 1924)

[*Boyd was an American novelist and biographer who is best known for his novel* Through the Wheat *(1923), a depiction of life on the Western Front during World War I that has been compared, in its realism and power, to Stephen Crane's* The Red Badge of Courage *(1895). In addition to his novels, Boyd wrote several biographies of major figures in early American history. He was also a newspaperman for several years in St. Paul, Minnesota, where he associated with a literary colony of realistic writers whose number included Sinclair Lewis and F. Scott Fitzgerald, among others. In the following excerpt, Boyd favorably reviews Lardner's* How to Write Short Stories.]

Why we laugh is of little moment so long as we do laugh, but the cause of our contemplative mood is, perhaps, of more importance. For laughter is a nervous reaction whereas contemplation employs the mind. Therefore, it would be of greater interest to discover why we are silent and thoughtful after we have read Ring Lardner's recently published volume than to seek out the reason for our mirth.

Each Sunday Mr. Lardner amuses millions of people; critics have praised the accuracy of his American vernacular, the sharpness of his satire, and the spontaneity of his humor. But scant attention has been given the bearing these qualities have upon his stories. (p. 601)

By itself, his practised illiteracy is unimportant except as it contributes to the wealth of Americanisms. But in clothing his stories this vernacular creates a perfect style, less melodious than Moore's, less colorful than Cabell's, less conscious than Doughty's, yet fully as agreeable and perhaps not so tiresome as that of the last two named. For Mr. Lardner takes his characters from the great mass in which he, himself, is rooted. Each is a sharp separate entity to him, not representative of a type but of humanity. He understands his people as Galsworthy understands the English upper middle class. And instead of their minds' becoming his the condition is reversed and the flow and stem of those curious, misspelled, misapplied words round out his creations marvelously. Thus he is enabled to write such a story as **"The Golden Honeymoon"** in which every word, every abbreviation is a revelation of this old man—past seventy—who goes south for the winter with his wife. It is a simple and unique story, having a complete existence in itself. A lifetime is summed up in those few pages which would be barren if written in any other way; those short sentences, added as though they were afterthoughts; that record, so minutely kept, of the arrival and departure of the train; and the confession, "I used to pitch a pretty fair shoe myself, but ain't done much of it in the last twenty years."

Then there is **"Some Like Them Cold"** with its boastful beginning and the sure tapering down to the end, enshadowing abandoned hopes and dulled desires. Not literally, it tells of a man and a girl on a treadmill, seeking to rise from it, but being drawn more firmly to it in their attempt to escape. It evokes a greater feeling of the uncertainty of existence and of active sympathy than all of Charlie Chaplin's pathetic shoes.

Save one, all of the stories [in ***How to Write Short Stories***] are amusing. That is **"The Champion"** and it reads as if it had been born under a cloud of indignation. Like Arthur Morrison's "Mean Streets" it strikes too rudely upon the senses. It is veracious enough, but that very honesty results in a lack of verisimilitude at the close. This objection may be only the posture of "seeing life steadily and whole" over again but yet, as in O'Neill's "All God's Chillun", the raw stuff of the study is so offensive to inherent prejudice that a sense of drama is bound to follow even if the author, toward the end, had his characters throwing custard pies. But **"Horseshoes", "A Frame Up", "The Facts", "Alibi Ike"** and, assuredly, **"Some Like Them Cold"** are for laughter as they are being read; though they leave you silent and thoughtful long after the merriment is gone. (pp. 601-02)

Thomas Boyd, "Lardner Tells Some New Ones," in The Bookman, *New York, Vol. LIX, No. 5, July, 1924, pp. 601-02.*

SHERWOOD ANDERSON (essay date 1926)

[*Anderson was one of the most original and influential early twentieth-century American writers. He was among the first American authors to explore the effects of the unconscious upon human life. Anderson's "hunger to see beneath the surface of lives" was best expressed in the collection of bittersweet short stories* Winesburg, Ohio *(1919). This, his most important book, exhibits the author's characteristically simple, unornamented prose style and his personal vision, which combined a sense of wonder at the potential beauty of life with despair over its tragic aspects. Anderson's style and outlook were influential in shaping the writings of Ernest Hemingway, William Faulkner, Thomas Wolfe, John*

HOW TO WRITE SHORT STORIES

[WITH SAMPLES]

BY

RING W. LARDNER

NEW YORK · LONDON

CHARLES SCRIBNER'S SONS

MCMXXIV

Title page of the first edition of Ring W. Lardner's How to Write Short Stories. *Copyright 1924 Charles Scribner's Sons. Copyright renewed 1952 Ellis A. Lardner. Reprinted with the permission of Charles Scribner's Sons.*

Steinbeck, and other American authors. Much of Anderson's own writing was influenced by the work of D. H. Lawrence, Gertrude Stein, and his close friend Theodore Dreiser. In the following excerpt, Anderson praises Lardner as a sensitive, perceptive writer who is comparable to Mark Twain. Anderson was struck by what he perceived as Lardner's shyness, a characteristic discussed further in the essay "Meeting Ring Lardner" *(see Additional Bibliography).*]

When it comes to our Mr. Ring Lardner, here is something else again. Here is another word fellow, one who cares about the words of our American speech and who is perhaps doing more than any other American to give new force to the words of our everyday life.

There is something I think I understand about Mr. Ring Lardner. The truth is that I believe there is something the matter with him and I have a fancy I know what it is. He is afraid of the highbrows. They scare him to death. I wonder why. For it is true that there is often, in a paragraph of his, more understanding of life, more human sympathy, more salty wisdom than in hundreds of pages of, say Mr. Sinclair Lewis's dreary prose—and I am sure Mr. Lewis would not hesitate to outface any highbrow in his lair.

I said that I thought I knew what was the matter with Mr. Ring Lardner. He comes from out in my country, from just such another town as the one in which I spent my own boyhood, and I remember certain shy lads of my own town who always made it a point to consort mostly with the town toughs—and for a reason. There was in them something extremely sensitive that did not want to be hurt. Even to mention the fact that there was in such a one a real love of life, a quick sharp stinging hunger for beauty would have sent a blush of shame to his cheeks. He was intent upon covering up, concealing from everyone, at any cost, the shy hungry child he was carrying about within himself.

And I always see our Mr. Ring Lardner as such a fellow. He is covering up, sticking to the gang, keeping out of sight. And that is all right too, if in secret and in his suburban home he is really using his talent for sympathetic understanding of life, if in secret he is being another Mark Twain and working in secret on his own *Huckleberry Finn*. Mark Twain wrote and was proclaimed for writing his *Innocents Abroad, Following the Equator, Roughing It*, etc., etc., and was during his lifetime most widely recognized for such secondary work. And Mark Twain was just such another shy lad, bluffed by the highbrows—and even the glorious Mark had no more sensitive understanding of the fellow in the street, in the hooch joint, the ballpark and the city suburb than our Mr. Ring Lardner. (pp. 50-1)

Sherwood Anderson, "Four American Impressions," in his Sherwood Anderson's Notebook, *Boni & Liveright, 1926, pp. 47-58.**

H. L. MENCKEN (essay date 1926)

[*From the era of World War I until the early years of the Great Depression, Mencken was one of the most influential figures in American letters. His strongly individualistic, irreverent outlook on life and his vigorous, invective-charged writing style helped establish the iconoclastic spirit of the Jazz Age and significantly shaped the direction of American literature. As a social and literary critic—the roles for which he is best known—Mencken was the scourge of evangelical Christianity, public service organizations, literary censorship, boosterism, provincialism, democracy, all advocates of personal or social improvement, and every other facet of American life that he perceived as humbug. In his literary criticism, Mencken encouraged American writers to shun the anglophilic, moralistic bent of the nineteenth century and to practice realism, an artistic call-to-arms that is most fully developed in his essay* "Puritanism As a Literary Force," *one of the seminal essays in modern literary criticism. An enthusiastic admirer of Lardner's stories because of their mockery of the species "boobus Americanus," Mencken favorably reviewed several of Lardner's collections in the pages of* The American Mercury *and the* Chicago Sunday Tribune. *In the following excerpt from an essay that combines his reviews of* How to Write Short Stories *and* The Love Nest, and Other Stories, *Mencken praises Lardner's skill at capturing the speech of the common American, while lamenting that Lardner's works—because of their close identification with a specific era in American history—will soon be dated.*]

A few years ago a young college professor, eager to make a name for himself, brought out a laborious "critical" edition of "Sam Slick," by Judge Thomas C. Haliburton, eighty-seven years after its first publication. It turned out to be quite unreadable—a dreadful series of archaic jocosities about varieties of *Homo americanus* long perished and forgotten, in a dialect now intelligible only to paleophilologists. Sometimes I have a fear that the same fate awaits Ring Lardner. . . . His stories, it seems to me, are superbly adroit and amusing; no other contemporary American, sober or gay, writes better. But I doubt that they last: our grandchildren will wonder what they are about. It is not only, or even mainly, that the dialect that fills them will pass, though that fact is obviously a serious handicap in itself. It is principally that the people they depict will pass, that Lardner's Low Down Americans—his incomparable baseball players, pugs, song-writers, Elks, small-town Rotarians and golf caddies—are flitting figures of a transient civilization, and doomed to be as puzzling and soporific, in the year 2000, as Haliburton's Yankee clock peddler is to-day.

The fact—if I may assume it to be a fact—is certain not to be set against Lardner's account; on the contrary, it is, in its way, highly complimentary to him. For he has deliberately applied himself, not to the anatomizing of the general human soul, but to the meticulous histological study of a few salient individuals of his time and nation, and he has done it with such subtle and penetrating skill that one must belong to his time and nation to follow him. I doubt that anyone who is not familiar with professional ball players, intimately and at first hand, will ever comprehend the full merit of the amazing sketches in **"You Know Me, Al"**; I doubt that anyone who has not given close and deliberate attention to the American vulgate will ever realize how magnificently Lardner handles it. He has had more imitators, I suppose, than any other living American writer, but has he any actual rivals? If so, I have yet to hear of them. They all try to write the speech of the streets as adeptly and as amusingly as he writes it, and they all fall short of him; the next best is miles and miles behind him. And they are all inferior in observation, in sense of character, in shrewdness and insight. His studies, to be sure, are never very profound; he makes no attempt to get at the primary springs of human motive; all his people share the same amiable stupidity, the same transparent vanity, the same shallow swinishness; they are all human Fords in bad repair, and alike at bottom. But if he thus confines himself to the surface, it yet remains a fact that his investigations on that surface are extraordinarily alert, ingenious and brilliant—that the character he finally sets before us, however roughly articulated as to bones, is so astoundingly realistic as to epidermis that the effect is indistinguishable from that of life itself. The old man in **"The Golden Honeymoon"** is not merely well done; he is perfect. And so is the girl in **"Some Like Them Cold."** And so, even, is the idiotic Frank X. Farrell in **"Alibi Ike"**—an extravagant grotesque and yet quite real from glabella to calcaneus.

Lardner knows more about the management of the short story than all of its professors. His stories are built very carefully, and yet they seem to be wholly spontaneous, and even formless. He has grasped the primary fact that no conceivable ingenuity can save a story that fails to show a recognizable and interesting character; he knows that a good character sketch is always a good story, no matter what its structure. Perhaps he gets less attention than he ought to get, even among the anti-academic critics, because his people are all lowly boors. For your reviewer of books, like every other sort of American, is always vastly impressed by fashionable pretensions. He belongs to the white collar class of labor, and shares its prejudices. . . . Lardner, so to speak, hits such critics under the belt. He not only fills his stories with people who read the tabloids, say "Shake hands with my friend," and buy diamond rings on the instalment plan; he also shows them having a good time in the world, and quite devoid of inferiority complexes. They amuse him sardonically, but he does not pity them. A fatal error! The moron, perhaps, has a place in fiction, as in life, but he is not to be treated too easily and casually. It must be shown that he suffers tragically because he cannot abandon the plow to write poetry, or the sample-case to study for opera. Lardner is more realistic. If his typical hero has a secret sorrow it is that he is too old to take up osteopathy and too much in dread of his wife to venture into bootlegging.

Of late a sharply acrid flavor has got into Lardner's buffoonery. His baseball players and fifth-rate pugilists, beginning in his first stories as harmless jackasses, gradually convert themselves into loathsome scoundrels. The same change shows itself in Sinclair Lewis; it is difficult, even for an American, to contemplate the American without yielding to something hard to distinguish from moral indignation. Turn, for example, to the sketches in the volume called **"The Love Nest."** The first tells the story of a cinema queen married to a magnate of the films. On the surface she seems to be nothing but a noodle, but underneath there is a sewer; the woman is such a pig that she makes one shudder. Again, he investigates another familiar type: the village practical joker. The fellow in one form or other, has been laughed at since the days of Aristophanes. But here is a mercilessly realistic examination of his dung-hill humor, and of its effects upon decent people. A third figure is a successful theatrical manager: he turns out to have the professional competence of a chiropractor and the honor of a Prohibition agent. A fourth is a writer of popular songs: stealing other men's ideas has become so fixed a habit with him that he comes to believe that he has an actual right to them. A fourth is a trained nurse—but I spare you this dreadful nurse. The rest are bores of the homicidal type. One gets the effect, communing with the whole gang, of visiting a museum of anatomy. They are as shocking as what one encounters there—but in every detail they are as unmistakably real.

Lardner conceals his new savagery, of course, beneath his old humor. It does not flag. No man writing among us has greater skill at the more extravagant varieties of jocosity. He sees startling and revelatory likeness between immensely disparate things, and he is full of pawky observations and bizarre comments. Two baseball-players are palavering, and one of them, Young Jake, is boasting of his conquests during Spring practice below the Potomac. "Down South ain't here!" replies the other. "Those dames in some of those swamps, they lose their head when they see a man with shoes on!" The two proceed to the discussion of a third imbecile, guilty of some obscure tort. "Why," inquires Young Jake, "didn't you break his nose or bust him in the chin?" "His nose was already broke," replied the other, "and he didn't have no chin." Such wise cracks seem easy to devise. Broadway diverts itself by manufacturing them. They constitute the substance of half the town shows. But in those made by Lardner there is something far more than mere facile humor: they are all rigidly in character, and they illuminate that character. Few American novelists, great or small, have character more firmly in hand. Lardner does not see situations; he sees people. And what people! They are all as revolting as so many Methodist evangelists, and they are all as thoroughly American. (pp. 49-56)

H. L. Mencken, "Four Makers of Tales," in his Prejudices, fifth series *Alfred A. Knopf, 1926, pp. 34-63.**

J. BROOKS ATKINSON (essay date 1928)

[*As drama critic for* The New York Times *from 1925 to 1960, Atkinson was one of the most influential reviewers in America.*

In the following review of Elmer the Great*—a dramatic comedy based on Lardner's short story* "Hurry Kane"*—Atkinson praises Lardner's skill as a writer of entertaining dialogue and hails the play as "farce entertainment in an original vein."*]

Sometimes the great braggart pitcher in **"Elmer the Great"** is happy; sometimes he is blue. For Ring Lardner, author of the baseball comedy that is now at the Lyceum, has stirred bits of farce, drama and melodrama into a strange medley of unrelated entertainment; as a playwright he is neither supercilious nor subtle. But the half genius who stands as the hero of his comedy is an immensely amusing creation, and perhaps a satire on the whole buoyant American spirit as well. . . .

As every one knows who has read Mr. Lardner's baseball burlesques, Elmer Kane has not only a "fast ball," but a swelled head. When he is in the pitcher's box he makes no mistakes. But when he is swaggering around among mere human beings, with a chip on his shoulder, he is "sassy, ignorant and misfortunate," as one of his team-mates complains.

In **"Elmer the Great"** Mr. Lardner has left him with all the ridiculous absurdities that make for broad and sardonic farce, and left him also with a prodigious appetite that at breakfast encompasses ham, potatoes, pancakes, apple pie, doughnuts, gingerbread, coffee and a glass of milk. In fact, late in the baseball season Elmer goes up before Judge Landis on charges of eating during the game. The "empires," as Elmer calls them, suspect him of putting lard on the ball.

In a tautly constructed first act Mr. Lardner shows how Elmer leaves Gentryville, Ind., to join a New York ball club. Then his troubles, and Mr. Lardner's, begin in earnest. For the plot of this rambling comedy concerns a gambler's scheme for bribing the New York players to throw their chance for the league pennant. During one of his evenings in Chicago the thick-headed Elmer has gambled away more than his first season's salary; and to involve him even more thoroughly the gamblers trick his Indiana sweetheart into signing a fake letter. Dramatically, it is a labored device, none too happily executed in the second act. . . .

For the rest Mr. Lardner has cut capers at random and written a great many capital lines of dialogue. There are good baseball scenes at the Florida training quarters, where Elmer's indomitable temperament yields rich comedy. There is a crisp and stirring scene in the St. Louis clubhouse where Elmer's frantic dealings with the gamblers nearly cost him his uniform. And there is an imposing conclusion, in which Elmer now one of the great world heroes, swells out his chest more ridiculously than ever. Mr. Lardner's craftsmanship does not join the various parts of his piece smoothly. But the broad characterization and the strong baseball flavor keep **"Elmer the Great"** generally interesting. . . .

Those who had come to **"Elmer the Great"** with the keenest expectations were no doubt disappointed. For all that, it yielded farce entertainment in an original vein.

J. Brooks Atkinson, "Elmer, the Twirler," in The New York Times, *September 25, 1928, p. 29.*

GEORGE JEAN NATHAN (essay date 1929)

[*Nathan has been called the most learned and influential drama critic the United States has yet produced. During the early decades of the twentieth century, he was greatly responsible for shifting the emphasis of the American theater from light entertainment to serious drama and for introducing audiences and producers to the work of Eugene O'Neill, Henrik Ibsen, and Bernard Shaw, among others. Nathan was a contributing editor to H. L. Mencken's magazine* The American Mercury *and coeditor of* The Smart Set. *With Mencken, Nathan belonged to an iconoclastic school of American critics who attacked the vulgarity of accepted ideas and sought to bring a new level of sophistication to American culture, which they found provincial and backward. Throughout his career, Nathan shared with Mencken a gift for stinging invective and verbal adroitness, as well as total confidence in his own judgments. In the following excerpt from a favorable review of* June Moon, *Nathan praises Lardner for his adept comic writing and his ability to effectively define his characters through dialogue.*]

The theatre that aims at amusement alone—which isn't such a bad aim after all—is represented pretty well at its best in Ring Lardner's and George S. Kaufman's **"June Moon,"** as funny a spiel as has come this way in some time. As a play, the exhibition is something less than no great shakes, but as a laugh brewery it tickles the critical ribs in a very benign fashion. Based roughly on Lardner's excellent short story **"Some Like Them Cold,"** it goes after the spectator's horselaughs with both fists—and does it get them? After a prologue that is flat, it opens fire and it doesn't let up until the last curtain falls.

Lardner is generally praised for his gift of recording the common speech with a jocose exactness. But in the praise there is often overlooked his even greater talent, to wit, the quick stamping of character by means of a discriminating analysis of the content of such speech as the particular character would think in it and use it. It is a talent that even George Ade never possessed in his slang day, for Ade's characters' speech issued from their mouths rather than, as in Lardner's case, from their intrinsic natures. There is hardly a character in **"June Moon,"** for instance, that doesn't become immediately recognizable for what he afterwards fully proves himself to be the moment he opens his lips and says his first say. In his play as in his stories, Lardner pictures character not so much by act as by speech, not so much by physical identification as by verbal. And I am not certain, for all the critical eloquence often issued to the contrary and for all that is written about introspection, psychic development and incisive external description, that this isn't at times a pretty good method. (pp. 502-03)

"The public be damned," "Let him who is without sin cast the first stone" and "She hit me first" each provides a more eloquent analysis of its spokesman's character than any ten thousand words of description that might be written of him. "You know me, Al," is a snapshot of a man revelatory of his nature, character and very look.

As you hear Lardner's dialogue you promptly recognize and know intimately, even with your eyes closed, the men who speak it. You can see their faces, their clothes, their each future act, their very souls. The common notion that Lardner is simply a phonograph is silliness glorified. He is a sharp observer and creator of character who masks his high proficiency in that greatest misgiving and hobgoblin of professorial criticism: low humor. (p. 503)

George Jean Nathan, "One Ring Circus," in American Mercury, *Vol. XVIII, No. 72, December, 1929, pp. 502-03.*

CONSTANCE ROURKE (essay date 1931)

[*Rourke was a pioneer in the field of American cultural history. Her reputation was established by her* American Humor: A Study of the National Character *(1931), which is still widely studied. The work advances Rourke's opposition to such critics as Van Wyck Brooks and T. S. Eliot, who asserted that America had no cultural traditions other than those it had imported from Europe. Rourke theorized that an American cultural tradition indeed exists, and that it is based on humor. The findings presented in* American Humor, *and in Rourke's later* The Roots of American Culture *(1942), were a major factor in leading Brooks and other critics to reassess and revise their previously held opinions of America as a cultural wasteland. In the following excerpt from* American Humor, *Rourke examines Lardner's technique and places it in the tradition of the nineteenth-century Yankee storyteller.*]

After the long sway of the mechanized short story Lardner has turned back to prime materials in their old and sprawling personal form. His mimicry, like that of [Sinclair] Lewis, is in the native tradition, close and truthful, yet with a leaning toward large rhythms and typical effects. He commands verbiage in the old style, jargon and the American delight in jargon, and the flattest Yankee manner. "Maysville was a town of five thousand inhabitants, and its gas company served eight hundred homes, offices, and stores." He even uses the favored mode of comic misspelling in the monologue which goes back to the almanacs and was perfected by Artemus Ward. "Well he swang and zowie away went the ball pretty near 8 inches distants wile the head of the club broke off clean and saled 50 yds down the course."

Like the characters of the early comic tales, his people are nomads. They have just moved into a neighborhood and are soon to move away; they lack backgrounds, they are only seen in pairs or trios, seen without families often, or with only a boresome friend. Old couples out of their native habitats sun their bones among other old couples just as homeless along the curbs or in the parks of Florida winter resorts. Even those tales which have to do with a group are projected against a void, or against some transitory scene like a hotel, a train, a baseball park. Here indeed are familiar subjects, familiar turns of story-telling, with intensifications of mood and a considerable difference in the effect of final character and the sense of character. The earlier wanderers of comedy were always foot-loose. These, their descendants, are continually netted by circumstance, by baseball contracts, importunate hostesses, or old age. Their orbit is far smaller; and the colored, the local background of an earlier time is gone: none of the interwoven look and feeling of place belongs to them, as it belonged to the comic figures of an earlier time. That process of amalgamation which has seemed a determined purpose of the comic sense might have wreaked its worst upon them. These people might be a final product of a humor that had worn away idiosyncrasies, taking with it all the edged elements of character. They are American; they are nothing but American, and essential to all parts of the country. That is the single outcome; that is the triumph too of Lardner's portrayal.

All his stories turn on humor; practical jokes make the substance of many situations as in an earlier day, but in the end the brutality which underlies them is exposed. That innocence which once was made a strong strain in American portrayals is seen uncombined with shrewdness and revealed as abysmal stupidity. At times the old comic ferocity appears, as in ***Hair Cut;*** but this has grown several-sided and in the end more human, for it is subjected by understatement to a withering blast of feeling. Lardner has pushed the monologue or the brief comic tale to an ultimate revelation by a series of negations; his tie is with that Yankee art which gained its effects by negation and a pervasive underlying theme. Derision becomes an outward shell covering a multitude of submerged emotions, rage, fear, bewilderment, an awkward love; the blank formula takes on intensity; emotion is still inarticulate, as earlier under the comic sway, but it surges toward the surface. (pp. 292-94)

Constance Rourke, "Round Up," in her American Humor: A Study of the National Character, *Harcourt Brace Jovanovich, 1931, pp. 266-304.**

RING LARDNER (letter date 1933)

[*On August 24, 1933, Lardner wrote a letter to Wilma Seavey, who had earlier written to him as the result of an argument with her fiancé, Paul Ogden, over Lardner's attitude toward his characters. In the following excerpt, Lardner records his only direct comment on the question of his hating his characters.*]

Dear Miss Seavey: . . .

I don't suppose any author either hates or loves all his characters. I try to write about people as real as possible, and some of them are naturally more likeable than others. In regard to your argument, I think the decision should be awarded to you, because I cannot remember ever having felt any bitterness or hatred toward the characters I have written about.

Ring Lardner, in a letter to Miss Seavey on August 24, 1933, in his Letters from Ring, *edited by Clifford M. Caruthers, Walden Press, 1979, p. 296.*

HEYWOOD BROUN (essay date 1933)

[*Broun was a highly respected American sportswriter, critic, essayist, and fiction writer who gained a wide audience through the syndicated daily columns he wrote for various newspapers from 1912 until his death in 1939. He wrote the following appraisal, in which he finds Lardner to be more a satirist than a humorist, shortly after Lardner's death.*]

[Lardner was] a significant commentator who expressed the life of America in the language and from the point of view of a baseball reporter . . . .

I can not resist the temptation of pointing out that Ring Lardner was saying in effect that what is true of a short-stop or a rookie outfielder may be true of a very considerable section of the human race.

He interpreted life shrewdly by dealing with it in terms of the individuals he knew best. . . .

Somewhat after the manner of Twain, Lardner had such a fierce impatience with so many things and men and theories that he had to sneak up on them through the waving grass of the light and laughing touch. But certainly he was pained, and would be now, to have anybody think that **'The Champion'** was a funny story. Some critics have hailed this particular story as his masterpiece. I can not agree at all. To me it marks one of his failures. The sawed-off shotgun shows too visibly above the rushes. . . .

[Lardner] had a passion for the thing called style.

His few criticisms of other authors were chiefly directed against the people who seemed to him sloppy writers. He couldn't endure the work of Theodore Dreiser.

There, again, remains meat for debating societies in the years to come. The Dreiser canvas is undeniably much larger. But the Lardnerian brush stroke is incomparably more skilful. Let posterity fight it out.

And, speaking of Dreiser, I think there is one discovery Ring Lardner never made. He knew he was an artist and a stylist, altho he would have been burned at the stake before saying so, but I doubt that he ever realized that he was in some essential way a proletarian artist. I mean he dealt with subtleties of emotion in such a way that even the vast army of simple-minded magazine readers took him to their heart as one of their own.

Heywood Broun, "Ring Lardner—Interpreter of Life," in Literary Digest, *Vol. 116, No. 16, October 14, 1933, p. 19.*

ERNEST HEMINGWAY (essay date 1934)

[Hemingway was one of the most influential and well known American novelists of the twentieth century. Critics generally regard his distinctive writing style—terse, lucid, and unornamented—as his greatest contribution to literature. Hemingway's style grew out of his early newspaper writing and was deeply influenced by the work of Gertrude Stein, Sherwood Anderson, and Ezra Pound. With F. Scott Fitzgerald, e. e. cummings, and John Dos Passos, Hemingway was part of a group of disillusioned American writers who lived in Paris during the 1920s and were collectively known as the "lost generation." Hemingway's early writings (in particular the short story "My Old Man"*) were influenced by Lardner's works, although in later years Hemingway denied that Lardner had ever been more than a marginal influence. (Hemingway, in fact, distanced himself in a like manner from all his influences.) In the following excerpt he disparages the realism of Lardner's stories, claiming that Lardner's aversion to employing profane language greatly lessened the authenticity of his work—especially his sports stories. Hemingway wrote* "Defense of Dirty Words," *excerpted below, while on a fishing trip in the Caribbean, hence the reference to his sunburned skin. He also refers to Westbrook Pegler, who was a conservative newspaper columnist, and to W. O. McGeehan, who was sports editor of the* New York Herald Tribune.]

What seems to have gotten under what used to be our skin before it peeled was a statement by Mr. Pegler that "Ring Lardner never wrote a dirty scene or line or even a dirty word, although he produced some pieces dealing with acts of misconduct by very unpleasant characters." . . .

Ring Lardner has not been dead long enough for anyone more interested in literature than in the personality of his friends to criticise him with the impartial scalpel of the post-mortem examiner. But when it is done, and it will take a finely ground and disinterested scalpel to post him properly, for there were many places which Battle Creek, Michigan and Chicago made difficult to dissect, it will be stated that what kept Ring Lardner from being a great writer was the very thing for which Mr. Pegler praises him in his column.

It was not that he did not care for the human race, any writer would need the breadth of love of an Aimee MacPherson to embrace all classes of it, but he felt superior to the part of it that he knew best. And I am a little afraid that Mr. Pegler is morally superior to it too.

Take the matter of dirty words. I doubt if a day has passed in my life in which I have not heard what Mr. Pegler calls dirty words used. Therefore how could a writer truly record any entire day and not use dirty words?

On certain days and in certain places I have heard almost no sentences which did not contain at least one of the words which both the Latin races and ourselves use in times of stress. The principal one of these words is that uttered by General Cambronne at the battle of Waterloo.

It was a single word and it was spoken instead of that classic phrase "The old guard dies but never surrenders." The general said, "Merde." But that is a word Ring Lardner would not write in English, nor I take it, in admiration for his purity of speech, would Mr. Pegler. And no true idea of war can be conveyed without using the true words, nor can any true pictures of professional sport be given without using the words.

It is true that writing in a daily paper or in a magazine Mr. Lardner was restricted in his use of words. But when a writer publishes a book, he can use whatever words he finds are necessary to the accurate presentation of the people he is writing about if he and his publishers will take the risk. . . .

Mr. Lardner and Mr. Pegler are both pros. They write for money. Or rather Mr. Lardner did and Mr. Pegler does. But, with the late W. O. McGeehan, they are intellectuals. Otherwise why would they feel superior to other pros because they make their money with their hands? The only way I could explain the late McGeehan's attitude toward prize-fighters was that he felt his particularly offensive brand of superiority toward preliminary fighters because he made more money pounding a typewriter than they did pounding each other; while he hated the headliners because they made more than he. (p. 19)

It certainly is an amusing sport, the cauliflower industry, where nothing's comic-er than walking on the heels. Somebody else's heels. Mr. McGeehan showed us how comic and contemptible it all was. I never knew him but they all said he was a Prince.

Ring Lardner was a Prince too, who with never a dirty word wrote of these who make it with their hands in the nightly tragic somewhere of their combat, distorting the language that they speak into a very comic diction, so there's no tragedy ever, because there is no truth. . . .

No writer can write anything that is truly great when he feels superior to the people he is writing about, no matter how much compassion he may have. Ring Lardner wrote two fine stories. One, **"Some Like Them Cold"** was about someone that he was sorry for, and in his sorrow, forgot to be superior. The other was **"The Golden Honeymoon"** in which he wrote about people that he truly admired. (p. 158B)

When he was in that hospital that he headed No Visitors in those pitiful dying radio censorship pieces that he wrote in the *New Yorker*, Max Perkins of Scribners wrote and asked if I would autograph a book for him. It was some book of mine that was coming out and he said Ring had asked him a couple of times about when it would be out. I wrote in it, "To Ring Lardner from his early imitator and always admirer, Ernest Hemingway" and that still goes. There was plenty to admire. But I wish he had felt differently, for the sake of American writing, about certain things and I am sorry if it is too soon after he is dead to speak about him as a writer without confusing it with what a good fellow he was. It is a compliment to pay of course. But certain compliments are seldom well received. (p. 158D)

Ernest Hemingway, "Defense of Dirty Words: A Cuban Letter," in Esquire, *Vol. II, No. 4, September, 1934, pp. 19, 158B, 158D.*

MAXWELL E. PERKINS (letter date 1934)

[Associated with Charles Scribner's Sons from 1910 until his death in 1947, Perkins is considered to have been one of the greatest

editors of twentieth-century American literature. Gifted with shrewdness, sensitivity, patience, and a single-minded devotion to his profession, he discovered and maintained long editor-author relationships with such eminent writers as F. Scott Fitzgerald, Ernest Hemingway, and Thomas Wolfe, among many others. Having read Hemingway's appraisal of Lardner's skill (see the excerpt dated 1934), Perkins wrote to Hemingway and offered the following candid opinion of Lardner's work.]

Ring was not, strictly speaking, a great writer. The truth is he never regarded himself seriously as a writer. He always thought of himself as a newspaperman, anyhow. He had a sort of provincial scorn of literary people. If he had written much more, he would have been a great writer perhaps, but whatever it was that prevented him from writing more was the thing that prevented him from being a great writer. But he was a great man, and one of immense latent talent which got itself partly expressed. I guess Scott would think much the same way about it. (p. 96)

Maxwell E. Perkins, "Maxwell E. Perkins Letter to Ernest Hemingway on November 28, 1934," in his Editor to Author: The Letters of Maxwell E. Perkins, *edited by John Hall Wheelock, Charles Scribner's Sons, 1979, pp. 95-8.*

JAMES T. FARRELL (essay date 1945)

[*Farrell was an American novelist, short story writer, and critic who is best known for his Studs Lonigan trilogy, a series of novels that examines the life of a lower middle-class Chicagoan. Influenced primarily by the author's own Irish-Catholic upbringing in Chicago's rough South Side, and by the writings of Theodore Dreiser, Marcel Proust, and James Joyce, Farrell's fiction is a Naturalistic, angry portrait of urban life. His literature explores—from a compassionate, moralistic viewpoint—the problems spawned of poverty, circumstance, and spiritual sterility. Farrell has written: "I am concerned in my fiction with the patterns of American destinies and with presenting the manner in which they unfold in our times. My approach to my material can be suggested by a motto of Spinoza which I have quoted on more than one occasion: 'Not to weep or laugh, but to understand.'" In the following excerpt, Farrell discusses Lardner's characters and their self-obsessed, empty lives. The critic perceives Lardner's attitude toward the human condition as one of pity rather than hatred, a view of Lardner held also by Jonathan Yardley (1977) and V. S. Pritchett (1977).*]

Ring Lardner began his career in fiction most unpretentiously with ***You Know Me Al*** and other baseball stories. These pieces are lighter, gayer than his later work. He took the heroes of the sports pages and showed that they were made of anything but the cloth of heroism. Some of them were eccentric Yahoos; others were boasting braggarts, irascible and childish in their vanity. Later he scored the same points with greater melancholy, with increased scorn. His most important work is contained in the collection of his stories, ***Round Up;*** this book has attained both a wide popular audience and a high critical praise. It is well worth discussing now, more than a decade after Lardner's death.

The first trait that strikes you about most of Lardner's characters is their intense competitiveness. When they are not engaging in some highly competitive business or sport, they are amusing themselves with a cutthroat game of bridge or golf. And they exhibit this same intensity in their social climbing and in the contempt they feel for anyone not exactly like themselves. Almost all of them have the same social standards: they are busy not only keeping up with, but getting ahead of, the Joneses—with the Joneses, that is, whose names appear on the society pages.

They are so competitive, in fact, that they can scarcely play a game of solitaire, or even a solitary round of golf, without cheating themselves. Their bragging is generally calculated to prove how clever they are—how good at checkers, prize-fighting, baseball, golf, or bridge; how well traveled they are; how many rich people they have met; how well they dance—in short, with how much envy the world should regard them.

We really see, however, that these people do not fit the images they present to the world. For one thing, they are among the most banal characters in all modern American fiction; in fact, I doubt if any other American writer of this century has so skillfully and so extensively used banality as did Ring Lardner. Besides being banal, these characters are ignorant, too, but this is not their major deficiency; if it were, the spectacle they present would be less depressing. Chiefly, they are bores: they interrupt card games, conversations, amusements, in order to indulge their seemingly endless interest in themselves. But even their love of monologues is not the fundamental quality about them. Rather it is their moral code—if such it may be described.

In general, whenever a Lardner character performs an act of kindness, is sympathetic or generous to someone else, he or she is taken advantage of; in this world the decent person is a sucker. Likewise, if any of these characters dares give vent to a genuine feeling—a feeling that is delicate, expressive, unsmothered in the dreary and sometimes vicious sentimentality which passes for feeling in this world—he is regarded as a comic.

Here is a world in which the principle of *caveat emptor* applies recurrently in social relationships, in human relationships of love, friendship or family. Thus the satire of Ring Lardner reveals the working out of the mechanisms of American civilization. By depicting, in terms of social life, an extension of the competitive system, Lardner reveals certain consequences of the rise of American economy and American civilization. He tells us what many comfortable, successful, and even rich and famous people are like as human beings—documenting the terrible or dreary cost of success in terms of what happens to the human personality.

Lardner's characters are the "rugged individualists" of the baseball diamond, the prize ring, Broadway, the golf links, the card table or the Pullman car; the terrible irony emerging from his stories is that here they are these rugged individualists, doing what they claim they want to do—enjoying the fruits of money, fame, prestige, buying the comforts available to American wealth—here they are, alike as rubber stamps. Their main desire is to be a better rubber stamp than the next person. And they are so proud of themselves! They expect to be liked, admired, envied, because they are precisely what they are. As is usually the case in satire, vices are paraded for virtues; here social vices strut, eager for praise and applause.

The meaning of Ring Lardner's stories can, I believe, be made more concrete if we contrast two of them—**"A Caddy's Diary"** and **"Golden Honeymoon."** In the first of these we meet the youngest character of ***Round Up,*** a sixteen-year-old caddy at a golf club, the members of which are the best (that is, the richest) people of a characteristic small town. The boy keeps a diary, hoping that he will thereby learn to write, and make money as a writer. He has also acquired the ambition to make an easy living as a golf pro.

The prosperous golfers at the club are all pretty much the same. They all have the same passion to win and to appear better players than they are. The boy becomes popular—earning big tips—by catering to their vanities and by helping them conceal their real scores. The pretty lady whom he admires is no different from the rest; she allows him to cheat for her so that, in competition with another woman, she may win a dress she doesn't need. The richest man in town does likewise, in order to win a prize of nine golf balls instead of six. One of the club members becomes unpopular when he absconds with eight thousand dollars of his bank's money. But the caddy wonders if it is any sillier to cheat for eight thousand dollars than for a dress or three golf balls. He concludes—establishing one of Lardner's major points—that "these people have got a lot of nerve to pan Mr. Crane" (the absconder) "and call him a sucker for doing what he done, it seems to me like eight thousand dollars . . . is a pretty fair reward compared with what some of these people sell their soul for, and I would like to tell them about it."

The caddy speaks for Ring Lardner. In his days as a working sports writer and newspaper humorist he saw people doing just these things. He told of it with barbed humor, with gaiety, and later with the most mordant irony of any writer of his generation. This story also establishes the meanings of the Lardner world in another sense, for it shows the ideals and habits of this world operationally: its standards influencing the younger generation, pointing out to youth a way to success and ease.

The caddy has a sincerity that most of Lardner's adults lack—otherwise he would never have posed the moral question he did—but he is destined to lose that sincerity and become like the adults. Thus, we can interpret this story as describing more or less how a Lardner character gets that way.

Contrasted with this boy are the old couple of **"Golden Honeymoon."** This story stands at the other boundary of the Ring Lardner world, so to speak, revealing what has happened to the oldest protagonist of ***Round Up.*** After fifty-two years of marriage, the old man describes, in monologue, the couple's golden honeymoon trip to Florida. This is a very funny story. And yet, under its affectionate humor, we are troubled by a sense of emptiness and futility. Lardner's ear for speech has recorded accurately the sound of an old man reciting time tables, telling us when the trains arrived at and departed from a succession of railroad stations on the way to Florida. We see an old man so drained of inner life, of feelings, of curiosity, that the time table itself has become highly meaningful.

In Florida we learn, as if we were listening to the recitation of more time tables, that the couple stayed in a rooming house and how they met the man who had years ago been a rival for "Mother's" hand. Flashes of a jealousy, dead for fifty-two years, occur as the two old men play checkers, horseshoes, "five hundred," and vie as to the cafeterias at which they eat and the excellence of the States in which they live. The narrator feels that he is the better man when he wins at checkers, and offers involved explanations as to why he lost at cards and horseshoes. His petulance finally breaks up the foursome and ends the amusements which were all the two old couples had in common.

The story ends with a recitation of time tables on the return trip. What underscores the impression of emptiness is that now it makes no difference who was the better man in the rivalry for Mother's hand. The winner and the loser are no different from each other; had their roles been reversed fifty-two years ago, they would still be the same as we see them in their old age. **"The Golden Honeymoon"** thus closes the cycle of experience whose beginning was described in **"A Caddy's Diary."**

Others have written satire with more pretension, or with a greater surface scope; but to my mind no other American writer has achieved Lardner's mastery of satire. His knife was sharper; it cut more deeply—so deeply, in fact, that these people who seem so dreary, so banal, so self-centered, often emerge for us as yearning, unhappy creatures who are lost, deprived and vaguely unsatisfied.

There is a singular contradiction in nearly all these people. Living an intense social life, they are antisocial. They can never really establish human relationships with one another. Seemingly always together, they are alone, unable to reach across a world bounded by their own skins. They are continually talking to establish a public image of themselves, as if they were filled with some ungratified yearning, some hole in their spirits which must forever be a vacuum. They are singularly repressed. They do not know how to be friends, they do not know how to love one another. Their loves are framed in the language of the popular songs, and as quickly die. Often, underneath the sentimental image of love, a cancer exists, as

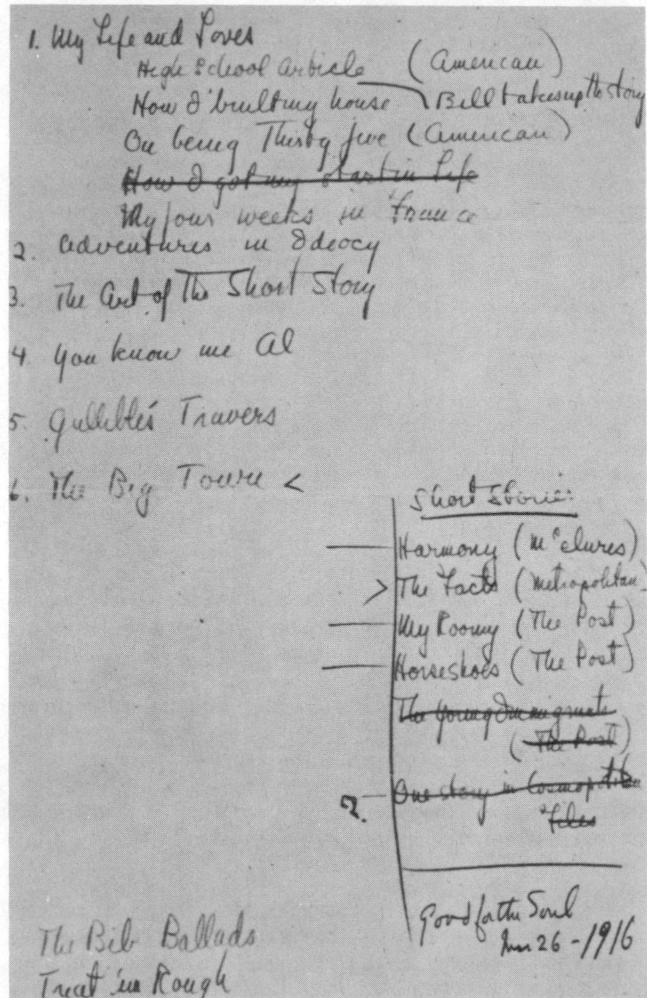
1. My Life and Loves
High School Article (American)
How I built my house } Bill takes up the story
On being Thirty five (American)
~~How I got my start in life~~
My four weeks in France
2. Adventures in Idiocy
3. The Art of the Short Story
4. You know me Al
5. Gullible's Travels
6. The Big Town <
Short Stories:
Harmony (McClures)
The Facts (Metropolitan)
My Roomy (The Post)
Horseshoes (The Post)
~~The young immigrunts (The Post)~~
? ~~One story in Cosmopolitan~~ "files"
Good for the Soul
Jan 26 - 1916
The Bib Ballads
Treat 'em Rough

Fitzgerald's list for Maxwell Perkins of Lardner's works that could be collected in a uniform edition. The notation in the lower right-hand corner is by Perkins. By permission of Harold Ober Associates, Inc.

in **"The Love Nest."** Bored with themselves, they bore one another, and then, with renewed energy, with restored lung power, they plunge forth again into another dreary card game, another dull vacation, another empty, even pitiful, little escapade.

Now and then there escapes from one of these people a cry of frustration, a cry which at least verges on agony and loneliness. Such is the last letter of the girl in one of the most masterful of these stories, **"Some Like Them Cold."** Her correspondent has bragged, encouraged her, led her on, and then tells her coldly that he is to marry another girl. (pp. 31-6)

We know that she is probably destined to go through the same disappointment again, that she is lonely and frustrated, that she cannot admit a defeat which has so hurt her. We know that her disappointment will leave a lasting scar of bitterness.

Here we see the significance of these characters trying to create fantastic public images of themselves. Here is the pathos of emptiness. And it is this pathos which deepens the stories of Ring Lardner, which gives a melancholy overtone of humanity to his cold and objective portraits of all these dullards, these child egomaniacs, these trivial "regular fellows." This is the essence of his writing—writing which has won for itself an enduring place in contemporary American fiction. (p. 36)

James T. Farrell, "Ring Lardner's 'Round Up'," in his The League of Frightened Philistines and Other Papers, *The Vanguard Press, 1945, pp. 31-6.*

CLEANTH BROOKS AND ROBERT PENN WARREN (essay date 1959)

[Brooks and Warren are considered among the most prominent practitioners of the New Criticism, an influential movement in American letters which paralleled a critical movement in England led by I. A. Richards, T. S. Eliot, and William Empson. Although the various New Critics—whose number also included John Crowe Ransom, Allen Tate, and R. P. Blackmur—did not subscribe to a single set of principles, all believed that a work of literature had to be examined as an object in itself through a process of close analysis of symbol, image, and metaphor. For the New Critics, a literary work was not a manifestation of ethics, sociology, or psychology, and could not be evaluated in the general terms of any nonliterary discipline. The criticism of Brooks and Warren strongly influenced critical writing and the teaching of literature in the United States during the 1940s and 1950s. In the following excerpt from their jointly written textbook Understanding Fiction, *Brooks and Warren closely examine and interpret Lardner's most widely reprinted short story,* "Haircut." *Theirs is considered the standard reading of Lardner's story. For a reading of this story that directly contradicts the interpretation of Brooks and Warren, see the excerpt by Charles E. May (1973).]*

The main action [in **"Haircut"**] is the story of the "card," the practical joker. He has no shred of human perception or feeling, and his jokes are, naturally, brutal and stupid, only a way of inflating his own ego. In the end, one of his jokes backfires, and we have the moral satisfaction of seeing the biter bit, the joker caught in the destructive consequences of a joke whose destructive nature for other people he could never have understood or cared about. Assuming that the card is adequately characterized, that the setting of the small town is adequately rendered for us, and that the plot is logically worked out, we might still feel that this main action, taken by itself, is somewhat over-simple and predictable, even too moralistic and too obviously an illustration of brutal arrogance being paid off. Anyway, it would seem that Ring Lardner must have felt some dissatisfaction with a naked presentation of the main action, such as we might have if it were told on the author's own responsibility; for he provides a narrator, the barber, who gives us his version of the business.

The use of the narrator does make the story seem less bare and simple, but, of course, complication for the mere sake of complication would scarcely justify itself. What positive values is Ring Lardner aiming at in the use of the barber? To answer this we may well begin by asking another question: What is the barber like? More specifically, what is his attitude toward the story he tells?

The barber, we quickly discover, admires the card, and thinks that life is pretty dull around town now that the card is gone. The barber has accepted the card at his own evaluation, has vicariously participated in the brutal jokes, and is, therefore, a kind of accomplice. So we have a deepening of the originally simple action—a sense that brutality and evil thrive by a kind of connivance on the part of those who do not directly participate in it, a sense of the spreading ripples of complicity always around the evil act.

There is, also, another kind of deepening, not in content this time but in the way of presentation. Let us suppose that the narrator of the story had merely told us about people like the barber, people who had some tacit complicity with the card's jokes, and that he himself, the narrator, found such people reprehensible. Given this treatment, we would find ourselves in immediate agreement with his attitude. There would be no shock of the collision between the narrator's attitude and our own. But as things actually stand, there is a shock of collision between the narrator's attitude and our own, a growing need to reassess things and repudiate his attitude. In other words, Lardner has used an inverted and ironical method. The narrator does not represent the author's view, nor our own. The barber is put there to belie, as it were, the meaning of the story, and by so doing to heighten our own feelings—even to irritate us to a fuller awareness of what is at stake in the story.

If the story were told directly, or told by a narrator whose attitudes were congenial with our own, we should be inclined to say: Of course, the card is a brute, a louse, and got just what he deserved. But we might say it too quickly, too easily, and we might be inclined to dismiss the whole business. As it is, we are compelled, in a greater or lesser degree, to take issue with the barber, and in taking issue we are drawn more deeply into the story. (pp. 145-46)

Cleanth Brooks and Robert Penn Warren, "Ring Lardner: 'Haircut'," in their Understanding Fiction, *second edition, Appleton-Century-Crofts, 1959, pp. 136-50.*

HOWARD W. WEBB, JR. (essay date 1960)

[Webb is considered one of the most astute commentators on Lardner's works. In the following excerpt, he traces the development of Lardner's distinctive use of language as a vehicle for characterization.]

Ring Lardner was not a mere journalist nor a literary comedian. He was a literary artist, sensitive to the world in which he lived and to the problems involved in transferring that world to the realm of fiction. He once denied that he was a satirist: "I just listen," he said. The statement was one of his finest ironies, for central to his art was his distinctive style, the Lardner idiom. This was not a transcription but a stylization of what H. L. Mencken has called "common American": a skillful blending of malapropisms, slang, confused pronoun and verb forms, mispronunciations, misspellings and rhetorical effects that describes socially and psychologically the characters who use it. Its essential function is to create and simultaneously to ridicule these characters. Lardner did not suddenly invent this style; he developed it over a period of some years. More than any other element of his work, it became his trade mark, and through it he has continued to exert an influence upon American writers.

Like most Americans, Lardner began to listen, and to learn the fundamentals of his language, in the home of his parents in Niles, Michigan. Here, too, the idiom, which was rooted in the Lardners' social status, began to develop. The house in which Lardner grew up, the youngest son of wealthy and indulgent parents, may serve as both symbol and explanation of his childhood position and experience. Standing on a bluff overlooking the wooded bank of the St. Joseph River, it was surrounded by an immense yard enclosed by a rail fence. Behind this fence, Lardner spent much of his early life. Until he was eight, he was not allowed to leave the yard except in the company of the family or a servant; until he was twelve, he did not attend public school, being educated by his mother, who gave him a good background in English composition and literature, and later by a private tutor. His education and his semi-isolation produced in Lardner an unusual sensitivity to "incorrect" language, a quality undoubtedly heightened because it was shared by his mother and by his sister and brother, who were his constant companions. These four found such language comic and made it a prime medium of family humor. Thus, the rude elements of the idiom were at first a shared means of rendering, however unconsciously, a social judgment: the taunt of aristocrats at the grammatical inelegancies of the lower class. (pp. 482-83)

Not until he had observed and listened to professional baseball players did Lardner have the material which enabled him to organize and give creative direction to what had originally been family fun. For five of his eight years as a sports writer, from 1908 to 1913, he spent "about ninety nights per annum in lower berths" as he followed one major-league team or another from spring training to the end of the season. In these years he acquired an intimate knowledge of the eccentric world of the ball players. (p. 483)

Within this world, their way of life was as special and circumscribed as Lardner's had been in the years he spent behind the rail fence. Within this world, the vernacular was not a deviation but the norm; the language the players used constituted part of a pattern which included the way they ate, the clothes they wore and certain eccentric forms of behavior, both on and off the diamond.

The milieu of major-league baseball, then, provided Lardner with a means of centering, for purposes of literary creation, his sensitivity to language differences and his talent for verbal mimicry. Put into the mouth or made to flow from the pen of a ball player, the idiom was immediately identified with a particular way of life; in effect, a character was already partially created.

As a sports writer, however, Lardner had little occasion to do more than write his daily stories. (p. 485)

Not until June, 1913, when he was employed by the *Chicago Daily Tribune* to conduct its daily sports column, "In the Wake of the News," did Lardner have a forum where he might experiment creatively with the idiom. This he did at once. On June 11, 1913, nine days after his by-line had first headed the column, the initial installment of "a novel" [**"The Pennant Pursuit"**] was sandwiched between a limp wisecrack and some strained verse. . . . [Ten] chapters related how, in the course of one season, Verne Dalton, having succeeded in his "studys," rose from college ball player to World Series hero, incidentally making a tidy fortune and marrying "the daughter of a New York millionair."

With **"The Pennant Pursuit"** Lardner began to fashion the idiom into a literary device. In this "novel" it retained, as it always did, a measure of the social attitude in which it had had its source, but it had moved beyond the aristocratic taunt and the family joke. The function of the idiom in these ten chapters is not merely to laugh at the lower class nor to tell a story but to create a character. With the words "strod" and "jymnaseium," attention is focused not on the hero of the tale but on the Copy-Boy author, who is revealed through his narrative as a disciple of Horatio Alger and the Frank Merriwell stories, with very little knowledge of either the fundamentals of language or the profession of baseball. Furthermore, the medium of this portrait is irony. Behind the language and hero-image of the Copy Boy, giving these elements their edge and meaning, was the amused awareness of Ring Lardner.

The function of this ironic portrait was to satirize the sports fan, and, in so doing, it made the criticism of human behavior that is basic to much of Lardner's work. The fans in the second decade of the century were inclined to endow sports, and particularly baseball, with high ideals and to expend upon them much emotion; and there was a tendency to transfer both ideals and emotion from the sports to the personalities of the players. A stereotype of the professional athlete was thus created, an image of a friendly, colorful, able competitor who loved his work and knew his way around. Like most stereotypes, this one had little resemblance to the reality it purported to define. Lardner, with his intimate knowledge of the professionals, was fully aware of the unreality of this image, and the Copy Boy's novel was in effect his condemnation of the stereotype. More generally and more importantly, it was a condemnation of the person who engaged in such degrading self-deception. (pp. 486-87)

On September 28, 1913, a piece entitled **"The First Game,"** purporting to be a New York player's account of the opening game of the 1913 World Series between the Giants and the Athletics, occupied almost the entire column. Since the first game of the Series that year was not played until October seventh, Lardner's intention was obvious. Even more pointed were the by-line, "By a Athlete," and the footnote which asserted that the author was "Unassisted." (p. 487)

Like the earlier piece, **"The First Game"** portrays a character in terms of language and attitudes; again the medium is irony, and again the function of the portrait is to criticize the ball-player stereotype and those who worship at this shrine. An understanding of this criticism, however, depended upon a knowledge of the norm Lardner had established in earlier columns. Lacking this knowledge, the reader would be interested only in the personality of the narrator, which can be comprehended without any reference to Lardner's immediate satiric purpose. The reason for this is that **"The First Game"** renders not one judgment but two. In addition to its comment on the stereotype, it also carries a condemnation of the nameless narrator, who represents one instance of the reality which the stereotype failed to define. Significantly, the criticism of this figure is the same one Lardner made of the Copy Boy and of all the worshipping fans. The narrator's entire account is a fabric of fraud: the belittling of umpires and other players, the bragging, the transparent excuses, the remarks about the "doll in the box back o' our bench." All these details reveal the anonymous athlete of **"The First Game"** engaged in degrading self-deception.

This piece, then, represented a further advance. Moving beyond a criticism of the stereotype, Lardner had created an original and independent character. This was, as a comparison of **"The First Game"** with **"The Pennant Pursuit"** indicates, largely the result of a more imaginative use of the idiom. In the earlier selection the Copy Boy communicates in written form; he is striving to be literary, and the idiom as it appears in his story consists primarily of errors in spelling and punctuation. The humor is essentially orthographic, like that of Artemus Ward. On the other hand, the narrator of **"The First Game"** is more like Sut Lovingood. He tells his story orally, and the idiom as it appears in his tale represents the actual speech of a ball player. And he is talking about himself, about his own behavior in his own special world. In **"The First Game"** there is a distinct correlation between the narrator, the narration and the language in which the narration is set forth. (pp. 488-89)

In general, the "Wake" columns between October, 1913 and March, 1914 show Lardner using the idiom with increasing frequency, facility and imagination. Sometime during these months he wrote his first short story, **"A Busher's Letters Home."** In this story, and in the five others which compose ***You Know Me Al,*** Lardner brought the idiom to maturity. Here it is more stylized and more imaginatively employed than ever before, and here one can see how central, indeed, how essential, it was to Lardner's art.

There is first the matter of plot. In much of the baseball fiction that was contemporary with **"A Busher's Letters Home,"** plot was the dominant feature. For example, in [Arthur Chapman's] "The Pink Sox Scout" a clever young woman gets a busher pitcher under contract and sells him to a major-league team. . . . In Lardner's story nothing in Jack Keefe's movement from the minors to the majors and back to the minors inherently commands the reader's attention. The plot, the rise and fall of a rookie, is simple and antiquated. It exists largely as a vehicle for the idiom.

The idiom's importance is further indicated by the setting of the story, or, more properly, by the relationship between idiom and setting. In **"A Busher's Letters Home"** Jack Keefe is placed squarely within the world of professional baseball. A brash young rookie, not yet "city broke" (in spite of his insistence that "I seen enough of city life not to be scared of the high buildings"), he owns but one "suit of cloths" and eats with his knife. . . . At night, after a game, Jack has leisure time to fill; but instead of seeking contacts with the world outside baseball, he remains with the other players, touring the town ("I come over to Frisco last night with some of the boys and we took in the sights") or playing cards in a hotel room. These details are all vivid and vital to the story, but what makes the world of Jack Keefe ultimately convincing and true is the language in which it is reported, the idiom. Without this, the details would be merely the observations of an outsider looking in.

Even the method of narration appears to have been at least partially determined by the idiom. When it is rendered in written rather than oral form, the idiom has a greater comic potential; thus, as the title indicates, the story is told through a series of letters which Jack Keefe writes to his friend Al. The effect of the epistolary device is to combine orthographic humor, like that of **"The Pennant Pursuit,"** with the humor of a personal and professional vernacular, like that of **"The First Game."** (pp. 489-91)

Finally, it must be recognized that the idiom calls attention and gives point to the attitudes expressed and the situations described. Its essential function is to create and simultaneously to satirize a character. What Jack says is not alone important, nor is the way in which he says it of chief significance. Rather, what makes the "busher" stories memorable is *how* Jack says *what* he says. This relationship between form and substance is subtly and effectively exhibited in a passage which contrasts Jack Keefe with the great Christy Mathewson, whom Lardner considered both a great pitcher and a fine man:

> After the game was over I says to him [Mathewson] Where is that there fade a way I heard so much a bout and he says O I did not have to use none of my regular stuff against your club and I says Well you would have to use all you got if I was working against you and he says Yes if you worked like you done Sunday I would have to do some pitching or they would not never finish the game. Then I says a bout me haveing a sore arm Sunday and he says I wisht I had a sore arm like yourn and a little sence with it and was your age and I would not never loose a game so you see Al he has heard a bout me and is jellus because he has not got my stuff but they cant every body expect to have the stuff that I got or ½ as much stuff. This smart alex Mcgraw was trying to kid me to-day and says Why did not I make friends with Mathewson and let him learn me some thing a bout pitching and I says Mathewson could not learn me nothing and he says I guess thats right and I guess they is not nobody could learn you nothing a bout nothing and if you was to stay in the league 20 years probily you would not be no better then you are now so you see he had to add mit that I am good . . .

The key sentences are: "he has heard a bout me and is jellus because he has not got my stuff but they cant every body expect to have the stuff that I got or ½ as much stuff." and "Mathewson could not learn me nothing." Throughout the passage, and particularly in these phrases, Jack's coarse, assertive manner is complemented and emphasized by his coarse, ungrammatical language. In both tenor and terms he is revealed as another figure who engages in degrading self-deception.

As Lardner had listened and, with increasing aesthetic insight, recorded what he heard, his artistry had grown and his idiom had matured. In later stories he would use the idiom in new ways, to indicate various levels of social stratification or to characterize an unusual personality, and sometimes abandon it altogether; but in the stories collected in ***You Know Me Al,*** he had for the first time synthesized his awareness of language differences, his knowledge of the world of professional baseball and his criticism of the stereotype. In doing this he had created his generic character, a figure who is far more than a joke or a bit of journalistic satire. And the means of creation was the Lardner idiom, which has endured. (pp. 491-92)

Howard W. Webb, Jr., "The Development of a Style: The Lardner Idiom," in American Quarterly, *Vol. XII, No. 4, Winter, 1960, pp. 482-92.*

CHARLES E. MAY (essay date 1973)

[*In the following excerpt, May offers an unconventional interpretation of* "Haircut," *perceiving it as, to a great degree, an indictment of the reader's sense of self-righteous satisfaction at the fate of the unsympathetic Jim Kendall. This view contrasts with the reading of this story by Cleanth Brooks and Robert Penn Warren (1959).*]

Reader response to the anthologist's favorite Ring Lardner short story, **"Haircut,"** has largely been determined by Brooks and Warren's early discussion in *Understanding Fiction* . . . : "We have the moral satisfaction of seeing the biter bit, the joker caught in the destructive consequences of a joke whose destructive nature for other people he could never have understood or cared about" [see excerpt dated 1959]. . . . In addition to making this rather simple moral judgment, the critics, of course, point out that the barber-narrator's acceptance of Jim Kendall's jokes deepens the action so that we have, as Brooks and Warren suggest, "a sense that brutality and evil thrive by a kind of connivance on the part of those who do not directly participate in it, a sense of the spreading ripples of complicity always around the evil act."

However, such a reading ignores the act in the story which is more evil than Jim's jokes; that is, Jim's "accidental death." Perhaps because the killer is a half-wit, readers have felt that no one is guilty. But I believe that Lardner's satire is even more savage than we have heretofore thought. I suggest that his attack is not just on the practical joker and a small town's obtuse moral sense, but even more on the reader's willingness to approve of the extreme penalty for Jim as his just deserts for his practical jokes. The reader becomes as morally implicated in the death as the barber and the townspeople by accepting what was obviously their use of the idiot Paul to rid themselves of a troublemaker and prankster that they hated and feared.

Many clues in the story suggest that the townspeople are neither so delighted with Jim's jokes as the barber implies, nor that the barber himself is as obtuse as we would like to believe. But the reader is so busy feeling superior to the barber, so busy making fun of him and feeling appalled at Jim's jokes that he fails to sense the horror of the murder and the town's willing acceptance of it. For example, that Jim has his own special chair in the barber shop and that if anyone was sitting in it, "why they'd get up when Jim came in and give it to him"; that when he is making fun of Milt Sheppard's Adam's apple, Milt would have to "force a smile"; that when Jim fails in his efforts with Julie, Hod Meyers "had the nerve" to kid him about it—all this should be sufficient to indicate that Jim is not so much admired as he is feared. The barber's final comment—"It probably served Jim right, what he got"—has at least as much emphasis as his "we miss him around here."

Moreover, several details in the story suggest that the barber and the townspeople are more sympathetic with Julie's dilemma than with Jim's pranks and that the barber doesn't think that Paul is such an idiot after all. For example, when telling about Jim's calling Paul crazy or cuckoo, the barber says, "Only poor Paul ain't crazy, but just silly." He also has been told by the doctor that the boy was getting better, "that they was times when he was as bright and sensible as anybody else." Nor is the barber so insensitive and crude that he fails to recognize and understand Julie's love for the doctor: "I felt sorry for her and so did most other people." Moreover, the barber can well imagine the doctor's response and dilemma when he learns about the joke Jim plays on Julie: "It's a cinch Doc went up in the air and swore he'd make Jim suffer. But it was a kind of delicate thing, because if it got out that he had beat Jim up, Julie was bound to hear of it and then she'd know that Doc knew and of course knowin' that he knew would make it worse for her than ever. He was goin' to do somethin', but it took a lot of figurin'."

And finally, the barber knows that the doctor told Paul that "anybody that would do a thing like that ought not to be let live." Such clues surely indicate that the barber is neither so crude that he applauds Jim's joke on Julie, nor so stupid that he thinks Jim's death was "a plain case of accidental shootin'." "Poor Paul" is nothing more than a pawn, encouraged by the doctor and abetted by the town. Brooks and Warren are surely right, that there is a sense in the story of "spreading ripples of complicity always around the evil act"; but the evil lies in something more than Jim's jokes, and the complicity is more than just the barber's apparent sanction of them. The whole town, by its acceptance of "accidental shootin'," is implicated in the crime; and the reader becomes implicated by his willingness to accept Jim's death as a fate he "richly deserves."

The barber says at the end that "Jim was a sucker to leave a new beginner have his gun. . . ." But the biggest sucker of all is the reader who, by allowing himself to be taken in by Lardner's control of the story and thus feel so morally superior to the barber, becomes an accomplice to the most evil act of all.

Charles E. May, "Lardner's 'Haircut'," in The Explicator, *Vol. XXXI, No. 9, May, 1973, Item 69.*

RING LARDNER, JR. (essay date 1976)

[*One of Ring Lardner's four sons, the critic is himself a distinguished screenwriter who is perhaps best known for his screenplay for the 1970 antiwar film* "M.A.S.H." *During the 1950s Ring Lardner, Jr. was blacklisted as one of the "Hollywood Ten," a group of screenwriters who refused to cooperate with the Red-hunting House Un-American Activities Committee. In the following excerpt from his* The Lardners: My Family Remembered, *Lardner posits that his father's alcoholism—not a personal philosophy of misanthropy—was at the root of his bitterness, and that the self-deprecating mockery found in some of his work was aimed not at himself, but at deflating the pretentiousness of high-brow critics.*]

Perhaps the severest strain on the critical mind is to accept a writer who appears not to take his work seriously, and accordingly it fantasizes that his levity masks a hatred of the world and himself. (p. 157)

In 1933, six months before Ring's actual death, Clifton Fadiman came up with the revelation that Miss Spooldripper represented the compulsive need for "ironical self-castigation" of a writer who had "gone farther on hatred alone" than anyone since Swift. . . . I believe he hates himself; more certainly he hates his characters; and most clearly of all his characters hate each other" [see *TCLC*, Vol. 2]. (pp. 157-58)

Thirty years later in his introduction to ***The Ring Lardner Reader,*** Maxwell Geismar wondered why Ring "insisted on describing his own best work in curious terms of disparagement" and found that "the self-depreciating strain in Lardner's work from the beginning . . . had become a kind of self-loathing.'' In *Ring Lardner and the Portrait of Folly,* published in 1972, Geismar's reading between the lines had grown more assured:

> These curious prefaces to the stories [in ***How to Write Short Stories***] are an ironical and farcical statement of Lardner's true feelings about himself, his career, his work. He wasn't just kidding; rather their morbid humor allowed him to confess his true state of mind. That ''wolf at the door,'' which represented Lardner's constant fear of not being able to make enough money to maintain his family's standard of living—a standard he himself insisted on for his wife and children—led him to some dark reflections on his own writing career, to wish he had never been born.

The ordinary reader, of course, read the same prefaces and found no such hidden significance. He just thought they were funny, or perhaps not so funny, depending on his taste. But he had no doubt about the intention behind them. Which brings us pretty close to the difference between a reader and a critic. The former may have invoked his unalienable right not to read scholarly introductions, but he had skimmed enough of them to know whom Ring was kidding. The parodies were directed not inward at the author himself but at the heavy-handed academic types, the literary essayists and authors of prefaces. They were thus an integral part of Ring's work as a whole, in which the main target was always pretense and pomposity.

Literary critics and historians, whose lethal occupation is the dissection of living prose, had trouble with Ring from the start. For one thing, their preferred pattern for an artist of any stature is that his talent be recognized initially by a few critical pioneers, who then proceed to their secondary function of elevating the general public to an appreciation of his merits. Sometimes, however, popular acclaim comes first, and the critics, gradually, reluctantly, have to accept the prior judgment of the common people. So it was with Dickens and Twain, with Chaplin and Gershwin, and so it was with Ring, in whose case the reluctance lasted more than a decade.

He was not an easy man for the arbiters of American literature to take to their bosoms. He wrote for, and managed to please, the conspicuously nonintellectual readers of the popular magazines. His stories dealt with ballplayers and other denizens of the lower depths of American culture. They made people laugh rather than think and they were written in a version of English without literary precedent. (pp. 158-59)

Of course some of his stories expose their principal characters so devastatingly the reader who went no further might suspect the author of misanthropy. But his tolerance and even affection for other characters he invented are equally obvious. As often happened, Dorothy Parker said it better in a few words than her fellow critics did in paragraphs when she wrote of ''his strange, bitter pity'' [see excerpt dated 1929].

It is also true there was a mordant side to his nature that developed with physical illness into periods of melancholy. The fact that he sought and failed to find release in alcohol has led to speculation about the roots of the despair that presumably provoked the addiction. But my empirical research into this particular disease leads me to believe that it is more likely to be the cause of depression than the result of it. The alcoholic is dismayed by his failure to conquer the addiction and he takes to drink to relieve his dismay, but the end result is that he increases it instead. In Ring's case the vicious circle was aggravated by his staunchly Protestant conscience.

Although he never kept copies of his stories, he did get reviews of his books, and later of his plays, from a clipping service. I never actually caught him at it, but I'm quite sure he read them in the privacy of his workroom. And he gradually came to realize he had made a name for himself in American literature. As an increasing body of critics followed the lead of F.P.A., H. L. Mencken, Burton Rascoe and Gilbert Seldes in recognizing his special quality, he responded by writing parodies of literary criticism. But that was just a defensive reaction, a necessary façade for a man whose work was a continuous indictment of people who took themselves too seriously. He knew perfectly well how good he was and better than anyone what an effort it was, especially in the later years, to live up to it. (pp. 159-60)

Ring Lardner, Jr., in his The Lardners: My Family Remembered, *Harper & Row, Publishers, 1976, 371 p.*

JONATHAN YARDLEY (essay date 1977)

[Yardley is the author of the definitive biography of Lardner. In the following excerpt from that work, Yardley offers a survey of Lardner's career, remarking that Lardner viewed humanity ''with compassion rather than contempt, dismay rather than distaste.'' For similar discussions of this point, see the excerpts by James T. Farrell (1945) and V. S. Pritchett (1977).]

[The] saga of Jack Keefe encompassed three books and a large handful of uncollected short stories. ***You Know Me Al*** is unquestionably the best of the lot, written as it was when Ring's enthusiasm for his subject was at its peak. ***Treat 'Em Rough*** is trivial, of interest now only to Lardner scholars, and not of much interest to them. ***The Real Dope*** contains enough good moments to compensate for its overall flatness. Of the loose odds and ends, the two best—**''Call for Mr. Keefe!''** and **''Along Came Ruth''**—are now available in the 1976 collection, ***Some Champions.***

You Know Me Al is not a novel but it comes close to having the form of one. In the letters Jack Keefe writes to ''Friend Al'' back home in Bedford, Indiana, Ring tells the loosely structured tale of an incredibly brash rookie who joins the White Sox, fails in his initial major-league test, is sold to the minors, returns and pitches well, marries a gold-digging shrew, and ends the season as a reasonably well established big-league performer. It was, at the time of its publication, the first book to treat baseball and the men who played it as the subjects of literate fiction, and ever since it has suffered under the handicap of being dismissed, or condescended to, as a ''baseball novel.'' It is indeed that, but it is also much more: Jack Keefe is one of the great ''originals'' in American fiction, and the language with which he writes his friend is an expression of the vernacular that has had a lasting effect on the way American writers describe American talk.

Jack Keefe may be a bit larger than life, but not much. From his very first appearance, his character was firmly set; Ring allowed no significant deviations from it. Jack is pigheaded, cocky, gullible, selfish, sentimental, naïve, stubborn, self-deceiving—and talented. He is a fountain of alibis, mangled axioms and witless repartee. He is a terrible tightwad, but at the bargaining table Charles Comiskey routinely takes him to the cleaners. He fancies himself a great lover, and in the course of his rookie season manages to propose to three equally horrible women, finally landing the dreadful Florrie. He has a great natural talent but—and here we have what Ring hated most—he abuses it; he allows himself to get "hog fat" and he makes no effort to learn the refinements and subtleties of the pitcher's trade; as Christy Mathewson tells him, when he complains of having a sore arm, "I wisht I had a sore arm like yourn and a little sence with it." (pp. 164-65)

The baseball in ***You Know Me Al*** is notable for the accuracy and sensitivity with which Ring, through Jack, reported it. John Lardner, who in his very different way was almost as successful and influential a sports writer as his father, wrote in his introduction to a 1960 edition of the book: "Its broader values to one side, there has never been a sounder baseball book. . . . [I]f you stop to pick over the accounts of ball games, you see that each detail is correct in relation to place, weather, time of year, and the hitting, pitching, or fielding idiosyncracies of a hundred players. . . . I have never read a piece of baseball fiction, besides this one, in which there was no technical mistake." Even allowing for filial pride, that is an accurate assessment.

It was when Ring took Jack away from the baseball diamond that he ran into trouble. The stories in ***Treat 'Em Rough*** and ***The Real Dope*** were written not out of Ring's own experience and observations, but out of a desire to meet the demands of the market. In 1918 and 1919, when they were published, the market wanted war stories with a strong dose of patriotism; the trouble was that Ring hated war, had no real sense of what was going on in Europe, and agreed with Dr. Johnson about patriotism. In ***Treat 'Em Rough*** Jack enlists and reports to Al from Camp Grant, in Illinois, that "I am out of baseball now and in the big game," but Ring was merely going through the motions in suggesting that Jack was doing something noble. Jack's adventures include barracks scrapes, an inexplicable promotion to corporal, a flirtation, and assignment to Camp Logan, Texas, where he awaits transfer to Europe.

He gets there in ***The Real Dope,*** which picks up a bit because Ring had at least seen the European front and had an idea, albeit a foggy one, of what was happening over there. Jack tells Al that his letters will contain "the real dope that I seen myself," but it is Jack himself, in the book's too obvious title, who is the real dope. He is determined to win the war single-handedly, but when he finally does see "action" the enemy turns out to be a member of his own company. The device of most of the episodes is a practical joke played on Jack by one soldier or another, with the consequence that the stories are formula work, but there are some fine Lardner touches. . . . (pp. 168-69)

Purely in terms of Ring's later work and his literary reputation, the most important work of the period after the busher stories is ***Gullible's Travels*** and, more specifically, the title story itself. It was here that Ring truly established himself as a satirist of middle-class suburban life. He had, to be sure, taken on the subject in 1915 with the four ***Own Your Own Home*** stories, but they are now rather difficult to read because of the proliferation of misspellings, abbreviations and colloquialisms. In the ***Gullible*** stories, Ring used the same themes but explored them with more subtlety, satiric skill and stylistic sureness. His subjects, as they would be for the rest of his career, were acquisitiveness, social pretentiousness, domestic discord, the frailty of human relationships.

The stories are more accessible than those in ***Own Your Own Home*** because the form is conversational rather than epistolary. Whereas Fred Gross told about his housebuilding misadventures and his wife's efforts to establish herself in suburban society in the form of letters to his brother, Charley, these are monologues by Joe Gullible, delivered to a friend named Edgar. The device freed Ring from the obstacles created by semiliterate writing; by using the spoken word, he was able to use the vernacular without misspellings and abbreviations, with the result that the stories move more swiftly.

Joe Gullible and his wife, "the Missus," live on the South Side of Chicago, but they have their eyes on moving in more exalted company; they have caught what Joe calls "the society bacillus." (p. 184)

It is in the long title story . . . that Ring's talents as a social satirist bloomed. (p. 185)

It is a superb short story. Joe and the Missus are lively characters, Joe with his snappy humor and sly self-awareness, the Missus with puppish earnestness—and both of them with their halting yet abundant affection for each other. The Palm Beach scenes are expertly done—Ring had made plenty of mental notes during his vacation there earlier in 1916—and there are many fine incidental moments, such as a casual conversation between Joe and another traveler on the southbound train. The dialogue is clipped, sharp and true. Most of all, however, there is a particular and unusual gentleness to the story. Ring clearly loved these two silly but good people, and there is not a trace of malice in his satire. He understood the normal human longings that made them want to advance in "society"; he also understood that what they thought was better was really not any good at all, and the point of the story is to try to teach them this lesson. They do not, of course, learn it quite well enough, and the last story in the book finds them once again trying to crash the gates of what they perceive to be the elite, but he does not condemn them for having trouble in giving up their little dreams.

Too many critics with too many political axes to grind have seized upon Ring's social satire as a manifestation of his so-called "bitterness," of his alleged "hatred" for ordinary mankind. There were indeed things in life that he hated, but mankind was not one of them. He understood that it is the fate of most of us to struggle toward insubstantial goals and to fail even in that, and he was amused in a sad and pensive way by what he saw from that Olympian peak he occupied, but he watched with compassion rather than contempt, dismay rather than distaste.

Nothing else in this period quite matches ***Gullible,*** but for its light-hearted charm, **"Alibi Ike"** is memorable. (pp. 187-88)

The story is neither complicated nor profound; it is genial and professional, and neither attribute should be underestimated. (p. 188)

Leaving aside its other qualities—Ring's carefully reproduced baseball talk, his seemingly offhanded reporting of minute details of the game, his creation of a fine cast of characters—**"Alibi Ike"** is notable simply as an example of his craftsmanship, his ability to write for the commercial short-story market without lowering his own standards. **"Alibi Ike"** was written as an entertainment, because that is what the *Saturday Evening Post* promised its readers. That magazine, like its less successful competitors, was the nation's evening amusement. It provided a diversion from the troubles of the day just ended, and it demanded a high degree of competence from its contributors; whether their stories offered romance, drama, escape or humor, they were expected to engage the reader's immediate interest and hold it throughout. What is remarkable about Ring is that he met this requirement and went it one better: in his most successful stories he transcended mere entertainment. In some he created a small, real world; **"Alibi Ike"** is one of these. In others he created larger-than-life characters; Elliot, the brutally violent ballplayer of **"My Roomy,"** is one. In still others he satirized pretensions of one sort or another; **"The Facts,"** slick though it is, makes some telling points about a family of overwhelming self-righteousness and the hypocritical young man who wants to marry into it. (pp. 188-89)

Ring in these first-person stories was the mouthpiece for his characters. The statement is not derisive, for it took extraordinary skill to be able to distinguish the subtleties of the way these people talked and thought, and then to turn them into effective fiction; it also required Ring's controlling intelligence to determine what went in and what stayed out, what was emphasized and what was underplayed. But Ring himself stayed in the background, performing what was essentially the role of a creative editor. When he moved more into the foreground, in the third-person stories, he was less sure of himself.

"Champion" is one of the earliest of these—it was published in October, 1916—and it proves the point. It caused quite a shock when it first appeared because it was a tough exercise in debunking, as opposed to demythologizing. The subject was a boxer named Midge Kelley, and . . . the first paragraph set the stage with quick precision:

> Midge Kelly scored his first knockout when he was seventeen. The knockee was his brother Connie, three years his junior and a cripple. The purse was a half dollar given to the younger Kelly by a lady whose electric had just missed bumping his soul from his frail little body.

The immediate reaction of readers was that Ring was telling the blunt, brutal truth about boxing, and indeed that may have been what Ring thought he was doing. But a closer examination of that paragraph reveals the flimsiness of the devices on which he was hanging his tale. Only the first of the three sentences, in point of fact, can accurately be called "tough." The other two are larded with melodrama, with easy tugs at the heartstrings: the crippled boy in "his frail little body." Such images are employed throughout the story. (pp. 189-90)

There can be no doubt that Ring was genuinely angered by the moral corruption that pervaded boxing—he often wrote about the stark differences between appearance and reality in the ring and the seedy enterprises constructed around it—yet the self-righteous tone of **"Champion"** is wholly unlike Ring. So, too, is the simplistic melodrama. The explanation probably lies in the discomfort Ring felt with a structure that required him to describe things rather than to let them describe themselves. **"Champion"** could well have been a splendid story had Ring told it through the eyes of Wallie Adams, Midge's manager, whose cynical description of Midge provides the raw material for an equally cynical reporter. . . . (p. 190)

Any writer as topical as Ring is going to produce some period pieces, and Ring wrote his share. But **"Champion"** is not one because of what its people wear or how they talk. It is one because of the curious naïveté that is the soft underbelly of its purportedly tough talk. Ring seemed to think that if his boxer punched out such embarrassingly obvious targets as a crippled kid brother and a trembling young wife, the story would be an effective portrait of callousness. **"Champion"** is actually so out of character for Ring that it is as if he had written "Abie's Irish Rose." (p. 191)

Ring's fascination with nonsense took a form most recognizable to his later readers in a couple of plays published in the "Wake" in December, 1918. One was **"La Bovina,"** the other **"La Maledizione di Pudelaggio,"** a "Yuletide Opera in Two Acts." (p. 198)

By comparison with Ring's truly superb nonsense plays of the twenties, **"I Gaspiri"** and **"Cora, or Fun at a Spa,"** these are relatively amateurish efforts; the inspired zaniness of those future efforts was still taking shape in Ring's mind. But considered within the context of a six-days-a-week newspaper column, they are seen in a very different light. Other newspaper columnists may have been as consistently funny as Ring, though that is debatable; but none has ever been as consistently ingenious, as full of surprises and inventions. (p. 199)

"The Young Immigrunts" was intended as a parody of *The Young Visiters,* which had caused quite a stir because it was purported to be the work of an obviously precocious nine-year-old English girl, Daisy Ashford. Ring did not believe the claim, notwithstanding an impressive amount of documentation to prove it, and he found the book a sitting duck for a spoof. To write it as he wished to, however, required a certain juggling of young Lardners, as described by Ring Lardner, Jr.: ". . . Ring, wanting to tell the story from a child's standpoint and still have the sales value of his own name on the book, transferred me to the car and John to the train so the work could be credited to 'Ring W. Lardner, Jr.—With a Preface by the Father.'" Ring wrote that preface with the appearance of a straight face, but any reader could see through the disguise, even though some apparently did not. (p. 221)

Since *The Young Visiters* has vanished from whatever niche it once occupied in our literary consciousness, it is fortunate that **"The Young Immigrunts"** is so successful purely as humor that it can be read with utter ignorance of the original. . . . Ring showed his mastery of childish language while embellishing it with pure Lardner: "I may as well exclaim to the reader that John is 7 and Jimmie is 5 and I am 4 and David is almost nothing as yet you might say and tho I was named for my father they call me Bill thank God." The story is simply an account of the journey as seen by Bill, relying for its humor principally on his characterization of his father, his eccentric spellings and his child's-eye view. . . . (p. 222)

No other book of Ring's, ***You Know Me Al*** included, has the coherence of vision *and* structure that ***The Big Town*** has. He did better writing elsewhere, and told funnier stories, and had more penetrating perceptions—but for overall quality and unity this has a strong claim to being his best book. Its characters are lively and memorable, not the caricatures that would become all too common in Ring's later fiction. The depiction of the lures awaiting unsuspecting country suckers in the big city is knowing, and the portrayal of the Finches' struggles to avoid utter capitulation to temptation is funny but sympathetic. Perhaps, however, what is most important for readers more than a half-century later is that the book still reads easily and well; there are, to be sure, some dated references, but they would be roadblocks only for the most insistently literal-minded. The city has changed and so has the country, but the clash between the one and the other still goes on; the story Ring tells here of how one couple conducts its own little struggle is an enduring delight, and for the reader coming to it for the first time, a welcome surprise.

Contemporary caricature of Lardner. Courtesy of Prints and Photographs Division, Library of Congress.

Ring had turned thirty-five on March 6, 1920, but it took him more than a year to get around to celebrating the occasion as he was wont to do, in print. He did so with a magazine piece, published in the May, 1921, issue of *American* magazine, and printed as a book that August under the title ***Symptoms of Being 35.*** He marked the passage of the years with a touch of nostalgia, the usual amount of humor at his own expense, and nine "gen. symptoms of 35 and vicinity as I have found them." The nostalgia took the form of reminiscences about buying beer as a teenager in Niles, and the self-mockery had a familiar note: "When a guy is named Ring W. and is expected to split their sides when ever somebody asks if your middle name is Worm which is an average of 35 times per annum over a period of 35 annums, why it can't help from telling on you." The best part of the piece, however, remains the symptoms, which are a touch anachronistic but still easily recognizable. (pp. 234-35)

[The] short story **"Some Like Them Cold"** was far and away the best of his fiction. Published by the *Saturday Evening Post* on October 1, 1921, it is told in the epistolary form, the letter writers being Charles F. Lewis, a would-be songwriter trying to cut a swath in New York, and Mabelle Gillespie, a young woman he has met at the LaSalle Street Station in Chicago, shortly before his departure. (p. 247)

The self-portraits that Charles and Mabelle paint are absolutely devastating. Each letter adds a few more touches of oil to the canvas, so that eventually a young man who had seemed amiable and naïve turns out to be gullible and ignorant, and a young woman who had seemed hopeful and sympathetic is shown to be conniving and contemptible. Each of them, in the end, is living a lie: his is that he can make a success out of songwriting and his marriage to a venal shrew, hers that she has found a new suitor or, for that matter, that she has the charm, intelligence, personality and beauty to attract any suitor, any time.

Not much of the milk of human kindness dripped from Ring's pen in the composition of this story; still, it is not the work of a "hater," but of a writer looking at two particularly unappealing subjects with a cold, honest eye. Underlying the story, too, is the unrealized wish that if these two people were not so hopelessly vain and self-deluding, they might find each other and some measure of happiness; but it is precisely because they are merely human, with all the possibilities of failure that implies, that they cannot make what is probably the most promising connection available to either one of them.

Further proof of the humane if uncompromising vision that guided Ring's craft is another story published during this period. **"The Golden Honeymoon"** was written while Ring and Ellis were at the West Florida resort of Belleair in the spring of 1922. (p. 249)

In 1933 the young Clifton Fadiman, a book reviewer still making his reputation, celebrated Ring in the *Nation* as the ultimate in literary hatred and pounced on **"The Golden Honeymoon"** as a case in point: ". . . it is one of the most smashing indictments of a 'happy marriage' ever written, composed with a fury so gelid as to hide completely the bitter passion seething beneath every line. Under the level of homey sentiment lies a terrific contempt for this quarrelsome, vain, literal old couple who for fifty years have disliked life and each other without ever having had the courage or the imagination to face the reality of their own meanness" [see *TCLC,* Vol. 2]. Fadiman was indeed young, so his failure to comprehend the modus vivendi of a long and reasonably successful marriage was pardonable. Ring understood, doubtless from watching the old folks of St. Pete from his perch at nearby Belleair, the unwritten rules that permitted these people to have their minor spats and running arguments while maintaining a foundation of affection and mutual understanding. If the story is not, as Ray Long thought it was, purely "human interest writing," it is still much closer to that in its respect for two people who have managed to muddle through a half-century together than it is to the venomous vision that Fadiman discerned. (pp. 250-51)

Ring's most important work in the months before the publication of ***How to Write Short Stories*** was published in what was, for him, a most unlikely place, the *Chicago Literary Times,* edited by Ben Hecht; it appeared there in February, 1924, and five months later it was also published in the *Transatlantic Review,* then under the acting editorship of Ernest Hemingway. In the latter it was introduced by Hemingway in an unsigned editorial as an antidote to the pretensions of Dada and its leading spokesman, Tristan Tzara: ". . . what profound admiration we have for Americans who really do know French and how tired we get of others who pretend to and how very much better dadas the American dadas, who do not know they are dadas . . . are than the French and the Roumanians who know it so well." The piece was a nonsense play called **"I Gaspiri (The Upholsterers)."** . . . (pp. 269-70)

Ring wrote many other nonsense plays in the years to come, the best of them being **"Cora, or Fun at a Spa"** and **"Taxidea Americana,"** but **"I Gaspiri"** is eminently representative—which is to say that it is a dazzling collection of verbal and visual non-sequiturs, all of them wildly comical. The plays do not submit to rational analysis for the simple reason that they are antirational. Though they were often seized upon as Dada or surrealism, they were not consciously written to conform to any literary movement or passing fancy. They were simply the direct products of Ring's invention, the final summations of all the nonsense he had seen in the world around him. They stand firmly enough on their own unique merits; they do not need to be encumbered with the weight of any literary "school," for the only one they belong to is their own—Ring's. (p. 272)

Ring made a great splash with the publication in *Liberty* (where [his brother] Rex was fiction editor) of what remains his most famous story, **"Haircut."** Max Perkins, after reading it, wrote him that "I can't shake it out of my mind. . . . There's not a man alive who could have done better, that's certain," and readers around the country agreed. The story—is there a reader anywhere over the age of thirty who does not know?—consists of a monologue by a small-town barber who, as he tends to a customer, slowly unfolds the story of a local dolt, Jim Kendall, whose penchant for cruel practical jokes ultimately leads to the dissolution of a promising romance, and in an act of vengeance, his own death. The story's enormous impact at the time of its publication and its subsequent appearance in countless anthologies are explained by its conciseness, its tone and the skill with which it was constructed. Ring did not waste a word in telling it, and he told it exactly right: the barber's droning talk, his mindless laughter as he recalls Kendall's jokes, his unemotional reaction to a gruesome story—all create the mood of the tale while at the same time delivering a terse, harsh commentary on small-town mores. The last two paragraphs are small classics, containing as they do worlds of insight into both the barber and the small town's life-must-go-on indifference to what has happened. . . . (pp. 287-88)

Both **"Zone of Quiet"** and **"The Love Nest"** were important departures for Ring because they marked a turn away from first-person narration to third-person. . . . The trouble was that he only occasionally was able to avoid the problems he had encountered when he wrote **"Champion"**—basic among them a tendency to be too obvious in theme and exposition—even though the period from 1925 to 1930 was his most prolific as a writer of fiction. With the exception of **"I Can't Breathe"** and **"Insomnia,"** all his most durable work was done by the time he had finished **"Haircut"**; it is scarcely mere happenstance that both of those stories are told in the first person. (pp. 291-92)

Nine stories from this period were collected under the title ***The Love Nest*** and published by Scribner's in March, 1926; besides the title story, they were **"Haircut," "Zone of Quiet," "Women," "A Day with Conrad Green," "Reunion," "Rhythm," "Mr. and Mrs. Fix-It"** and **"Who Dealt?"** Of the ones not already discussed, the best is the last, and it is told in the first person. It is not so much a narration as one long gurgle by a brand-new bride who, playing bridge with her husband, Tom, and his friends Arthur and Helen . . . , babbles her way into the kind of self-revelation that is Ring's fictional art at its finest. (p. 293)

The "autobiography" [***The Story of a Wonder Man***] is not among Ring's more important books, but it has a distinct zany charm and enough genuinely funny episodes to remain entertaining. A fair amount of Ring's work that has received more scholarly and/or critical attention is actually of less merit, but it is probable that the book's overall tone of deliberate silliness has scared some serious readers away from it. (p. 307)

Of the sixteen new stories [collected in ***Round Up***], only **"I Can't Breathe"** deserves to be ranked with Ring's best; the rest are professional, for Ring was always that, and entertaining, but they are the work of a writer who was working solely for money and consciously or unconsciously was reverting to material that had served him well in the past. **"The Maysville Minstrel,"** for example, uses the device of the cruel practical joke, one dating back to his earliest fiction. **"Mr. Frisbie"** is a variation on one of the ***How to Write Short Stories*** pieces, **"A Caddy's Diary"**; both are about rich people who habitually cheat at trivial games, both are narrated by caddies. **"Hurry Kane,"** as already noted, employs a trick of plot that was used better in **"A Frame-Up." "Travelogue"** is a refinement of an uncollected story, **"Tour Y-10"**—and, it certainly must be added, a great improvement on it.

In addition to repetition there is a strong element of obviousness in these later stories. That had been a problem with Ring's third-person fiction from the start, for he was never able to master the art of exposition when he assumed an omniscient stance, but in these stories the obviousness covers not just incidental moments of character development but plot itself. (p. 331)

The stories [collected in ***Lose with a Smile***] consist of a correspondence between Danny Warner, a marginal Brooklyn outfielder, and Jessie Graham, his girl friend in Centralia, Illinois. They have much the same sunny nostalgia as the autobiographical pieces; they are amusing and diverting; they are written with Ring's customary professionalism and command of his material. They are derivative of much of his own work—notably ***You Know Me Al*, "Some Like Them Cold"** and ***June Moon***—but not so much that they are incapable of standing on their own merits. Minor though it is, the book can be viewed as a summation of much of Ring's career, and in that respect it is much like William Faulkner's *The Reivers*—another exercise in amiable nostalgia which, though short of the writer's best work, somehow typifies it. (p. 360)

[Ring] suggested to Harold Ross [of *The New Yorker*] that he do a radio column and Ross quickly accepted. The first of the pieces was published on June 18, 1932, and the last on August 26, 1933. There are twenty-five of them in all, an impressive number, and many of them are Ring at or near his best. They include his bizarre campaign against "pornography," but they also contain the best parody he ever wrote and a number of revealing disclosures about himself. Most of the names of performers and the call letters of stations are obviously now out of date—that is why Max Perkins thought a collection of the pieces would be impractical—but the quality of the writing and thinking is high. Overall, they show Ring as a person concerned with questions of taste, artistic quality and slick sentimentality. He was a close listener and a lively writer. (p. 363)

[Ring] never completely let go of the campaign [against "pornography"], and he certainly never admitted defeat. He referred to himself whimsically as "this red-hot crusader against immorality," but to him the crusade itself was a serious business. He really did believe that the lyrics of popular songs had the power to corrupt, and he believed that the radio censors should be vigorously at work. He was both old-fashioned and

Middle Western, and he held strongly to the conservatism and prudery he had learned as a boy. The postwar upheaval in sexual attitudes and behavior touched him only to the extent that he became all the more conservative, all the more priggish. (p. 367)

[**"Odds Bodkins"**] appeared in *The New Yorker* of October 7, 1933, and it is the last piece of nonfiction Ring wrote. It almost certainly was composed in the last month of his life. The subject of the parody was a New York columnist named O. O. McIntyre, long since deservedly forgotten, who came from Gallipolis, Ohio, but had acquired and embellished all the affectations of the urban sophisticate. To readers in the more than five hundred newspapers that took the column, McIntyre described his life in breathlessly self-serving terms, painting a portrait of New York that bore no resemblance to reality but that made him seem, to small-town rubes from coast to coast, the very epitome of big-city wit and fashion. It is not in the least bit necessary to have read a single one of his columns in order to appreciate how devastating and funny Ring's parody was—and still is. . . . (p. 379)

That Ring could have written a piece as clever and amusing as this in the physical condition he by now was in is a tribute to his courageous determination to keep his spirits, and those of others, as high as possible. Certainly he had his times of depression; they were more frequent and of greater duration as his illness worsened and his physical pain intensified; sometimes he sat by himself, sobbing, his face in his hands. Yet the very existence of **"Odds Bodkins,"** and the radio pieces, and the stories that were published posthumously, is the most striking evidence available to rebut the widespread assumption that he was willing himself toward death in the final years, that his alleged disgust with mankind and himself had produced in him a suicidal urge. All these pieces—not to mention all the letters he wrote to cheer people up, and the love he gave his family and friends—are proof positive that to the very end his dominant urge was to survive and to create, even if he knew that the pain of survival was great and that most of the writing he did was but a pale reflection of what he had once been able to do. (p. 381)

Ring made people laugh, and he still does. Jack Keefe, that true American original, is a great comic character; so is the "wise boob," whether he takes the name of Joe Gullible or Tom Finch or Fred Gross—or Ring Lardner. The nonsense plays have lost none of their wild humor and never will, for they are timeless. Ring's humor is as American as his language: wisecracking, sardonic, earthy, self-mocking. He helped teach us not only to laugh at ourselves but to laugh at that which is unique in us, to delight in our very American-ness.

In doing that, he helped us to see ourselves. He was a writer of manners, and the manners he described were those of a society markedly different from that in the novels of Edith Wharton and Henry James. He wrote about the manners of the bleachers and the clubhouse, the mezzanine and the dressing room, the barbershop and the beauty parlor, the Pullman car and the touring car, the kitchen and the diner, the bridge table and the bowling alley. He watched us get rich, and he showed us how foolish we often looked as we threw our new money after idle and inane pleasures and possessions; if he had been truly bitter or misanthropic or hateful, he never would have succeeded in making us laugh at ourselves so heartily.

He wrote so perceptively and accurately about what he saw because he was a great journalist. This, in the end, is the singular accomplishment of his life. Ring came into the profession when it was held in far too much disdain even to be considered a "profession"; it was a line of work pursued by coarse people who had a coarse talent for putting words together in a speedy way. He was one of the very first people to bring creativity and felicity of style to the press. He set an example that was eagerly followed by younger writers. His aristocratic manner and confident bearing gave the lie to the argument that journalists were by their very nature guttersnipes. The quality of his writing and the doggedness with which he kept it so high proved that good prose and journalism were not mutually exclusive. So, too, he showed that in newspapers one could do serious work and be respected for it.

In assessing him, moreover, the work of his life must not be stressed at the expense of his life itself. Marc Connelly, in a letter to Ellis, got somewhere close to the point when he wrote ". . . behind all his fun, his bitter satire, his criticism and his pity, was a great dignity, the dignity of humanity. Everything Ring started to write had somewhere behind it a point of view essentially noble. His humor was the humor of protest, a demand, by implication, that mankind be something more than the idiocy he was exposing." (pp. 392-93)

Jonathan Yardley, in his Ring: A Biography of Ring Lardner, *Random House, 1977, 415 p.*

V. S. PRITCHETT (essay date 1977)

[Pritchett is a highly esteemed English novelist, short story writer, and critic. Considered one of the modern masters of the short story, his work in this genre is a subtle blend of realistic detail and psychological revelation. Pritchett is also considered one of the world's most respected and well-read literary critics. He writes in the conversational tone of the familiar essay, a method by which he approaches literature from the viewpoint of a lettered but not overly scholarly reader. A twentieth-century successor to such early nineteenth-century essayist-critics as William Hazlitt and Charles Lamb, Pritchett employs much the same critical method: his own experience, judgment, and sense of literary art are emphasized, rather than a codified critical doctrine derived from a school of psychological or philosophical speculation. His criticism is often described as fair, reliable, and insightful. In the following excerpt from a review of Jonathan Yardley's Ring: A Biography of Ring Lardner *(1977), Pritchett praises Lardner's deftness in delineating the ordinary American, and concurs with James T. Farrell (1945) and with Yardley (1977) that Lardner viewed humankind "with compassion rather than contempt, dismay rather than distaste."]*

About 1920, something veiled and sophisticated came into vernacular writing. It seems to me that in the older humorists both the talk and the characters celebrate their comic life. The fact that the characters are always jawing away extends their extravagance until as human beings they become proverbial fantasies. Lardner's originality—a little later taken over by Hemingway and others—lies in showing his characters dismantling themselves unconsciously in their flat, ignorant or nonsensical language. We are made to see the lines of their dumb but pleasant repetitions. The inadequacy and abuse of language (and spelling) are as revealing, in their way, as fullness is. To deal with dumbness is a game of skill and cunning in itself. The very ordinary American was exposed, but not by being earnestly denounced, as he was by Sinclair Lewis, for mindless greed, social climbing and for being an ugly barrel of pathetic or ugly received ideas.

Early critics thought Lardner hated human beings, but Yardley says: ''He understood that it is the fate of most of us to struggle towards insubstantial goals and to fail even in that and he was amused in a sad and pensive way by what he saw from that Olympian peak he occupied, but he watched with compassion rather than contempt, dismay rather than distaste'' [see excerpt dated 1977].

Lardner's mastery of the offhand, the flat and the non sequitur gives him an irony that was the right medicine for a society notoriously given to the bland. He does not condescend. He understands how a game—whether it is baseball or haircutting—forms the speech and character of a man. The barber in **''Haircut''** is every barber in the world. Lardner also knows that our real lives come to the surface in our off moments. The tired-out characters going glumly to their room in **''The Golden Honeymoon''** are universal casualties in their innocent expectations and their hurt. What Lardner tells us is that it takes a lot of courage to be a helpless human being. That story also shows that only an observer and listener as acute as Lardner knows how to make things true by knowing what to leave out. (p. 7)

V. S. Pritchett, ''The Man with the Perfect Ear,'' in The New York Times Book Review, *August 21, 1977, pp. 7, 29.*

DONALD PHELPS (essay date 1978)

[*In the following excerpt from an excellent essay on Lardner's fiction (originally published in* Shenandoah *XXIX, No. 4 (1978) and revised in 1982), Phelps discusses* The Big Town, *judging it to be one of the author's most accomplished works.*]

What Lardner achieved, from story to story, was a kind of *ad hoc* reconciliation of form and formula: formula in a sense superficially familiar to us all (''formula writing'' being Dummy One on the target range of American criticism) yet understood and practised by him with a precision that one wishes might, for a moment, roost on the sights of those doughty hunters, critics and practitioners both. For Lardner understood and observed formula in the sense that brings it closest to ritual and focusing of myth: an imposed order, well defined, yet always admitting improvisation, which is used to keep the momentary (e.g., one's daily observations) in suspension; divining, thereby creating, the little terrain of a fixed present tense (represented by Lardner with the voice of popular journalism); a miniature, a kind of scale-model order, which, yes, inevitably must exclude many of experience's more turbulent and giantly demanding aspects; but which (as he deployed it) not only never denies these, but, as any good scale model must, provides us with a perspective, in small, of where our powers (i.e., of perception and adjustment, when needed) lie, and affords us some precious breathing space.

The majority of Lardner's output was bent toward reconciling formula with form—which, of course, . . . involves no less than the artist's incessant discovery and identification of his boundaries: the boundaries of his present strengths, as signified by the boundaries of his present performance. It is for form in any authentic sense to comprehend both these visible limits and the terrain of aspiration immediately beyond them; which, I think, is what has, not disappointed perhaps, but sometimes perplexed and frustrated me reading Lardner's work; in which he repeatedly seems *detained* by the story-telling function itself from exploration of his own capacities, decision about his final authority: both to declare *his* artistic order and explore, not merely accept, *his* domain.

And yet, his longest, probably darkest, certainly most ambitious work gives us heartening earnest that Lardner was by way of assuming his writer's full vocation before he died. ***The Big Town***—it is novella-length, but displays much of a novel's copiousness and reflective march—follows the rambling but fateful career of an Indiana family group—the husband and narrator, a World War I veteran, his wife, the wife's adored, lint-brained sister—to Manhattan (thence, with astute quick-march, to that millionaires' grazing-ground of the twenties, Long Island), in search of a well-moneyed husband for the sister. (pp. 325-26)

The Big Town does not so much resolve as bring a kind of armature, a virile consideration, to the melancholy and anxiety that glide and skitter through Lardner's lesser writings. Although in the loping tempo of his more anecdotal tales, episode pattering after episode in recognized comic-strip succession, it conveys that exciting gravity of a writer inventorying and mustering his resources to give good account for a store of experience: a feeling I cannot help recalling as slightly more common in the novel's bad old days of parochial convention.

The novella does not in any wise represent an extension of Lardner's strength, but—what can be as creatively fulfilling and, in this context, almost more invigorating—a declaration of his limitations, and an affirmation of them, even as he has affirmed those of his characters; as *his* natural and honorable and defining boundaries. He has pooled his viewpoint with that of his saturnine, ever-appraising narrator, and with a forcefulness not found in much of his other fiction. The brother-in-law not only takes a hand in the match-making pilgrimage from the start, but he blunders (the arrangement with the jockey), takes chances (beating up the Wall Street two-timer) and exposes his fallibilities. (The drinking, presented elsewhere in Lardner's sketches as a cozy social trope, is slightly but significantly more emphatic, more overtly melancholy and more dramatically and rhythmically relevant to the narrative, than in the shorter pieces.) The guarded detachment, the implicit suspension of Lardner's patented ironic drawl in other stories, here becomes more localized and assailable.

And in truth, the entire collision-course Pilgrims' Progress could fairly be labelled ''an epic of vulnerability''. From the title on out, it amounts to a punchinello-spirited inversion of the Balzacian premise: the rustic's conquest of the big city. The title is a triple-layered reference: at its most obvious, to the Hoosier Hotshots's eager downscaling of Manhattan to fit their own provincial lens (e.g., by nesting in Long Island); second, to their village-instinctive bee-lining, with the sister as queen, to any succulent marital prospect or to anyone adequately disposed, and endowed, to aid them in their course; third, and potentially bleakest of all, to the village dimensions of the opulent people whom they court; the gopher-hole range of those peoples' self-seeking; the lack in those people of any impressive astuteness or even genuine power and authority, apart from that implicit in their wealth; above all—beneath all—the tackily romantic sentimentality that pilots them toward the kid sister, and leaves them open to mortal discomfiture, or actual ruin.

The Big Town offers a white blackbird of antiromantic satire, which resists enfolding the weapons—and luxuries—of its opponent. It is not an attack at all; indeed, it is a wearily smiling, slouching rejection of, not merely the vaultings, the flailing projections of romantic attitude, but the basic presumptions, the initial stances, such as are to be found even in the later, presumedly antiromantic works of initially romantic American writers like Stephen Crane and Frank Norris. Lardner seems to me one of the infrequent American authors to have sliced through the Laocoön entanglement of the romantic and the antiromantic, which bedevilled Melville and his legatees, greater and lesser; and which seems to me to involve no lapse or inadequacy at all on their parts, but rather the salients of the terrain, social, geographical and psychic, in which they discover themselves, and for which they must account; however monolithic, or haphazardly free, their construction. The brute space of the territory, versus the imperative to observe and to assess, empirically, all of its footage, represent in tandem the goad and the peremptory censor of the American writer's imagination.

After our delight in the story's process is through, ***The Big Town*** offers not a soup-bone of comfort to our yearning for some tug of intensity, for some earnest of those absolutes that we can fairly see, like reassuring mesas, beyond the little caravan's last stop. Lardner, to be sure, has left our viewing space open, but he has yielded not a square inch more. The girl, at the story's end, has opted for freedom, against the negotiations, well-intended and generally well-aimed, of her own Mr. and Mrs. Fixit; but she is not a penny's-worth wiser than she has shown herself to be throughout the expedition. And the quality of the happiness impending for her, material and spiritual, is as doubtful, surely, as any of her available prospects along the way. Human freedom owes us none of those reassurances, any more than does the freedom with which any animal is born. Such is the leafless branch that Lardner hands us.

We need expect from Lardner no Great Theme, mounted and paraded for us like a trophy Behemoth on Founders' Day; but ***The Big Town*** will yield up, twirling like a shadowy eel in the aquarium case he has provided, the *motif* of human mortality, which his very wakeful scrutiny, and minimal artistic interference, have coaxed out of hiding. The narrator, with his Ph.D. from the War to End All Wars, sounds the key at the outset. When his war profiteering-father-in-law invites him to join the old man's tanning company, baiting the invitation with, "Who knows?" the son-in-law retorts, "My nose knows," not referring only, we may be sure, to the stench of the tanneries. The concern is resumed *a fortiori* with the off-stage death of the test pilot; again, mutedly, by the semi-invalid dowager who engages the sister as companion; finally, resolved with a brassy flair of burlesque by the actor's courtship offering: a play about a man apparently restored from death, a World War I aviation ace. The resolution itself, the most flagrant fantasy and mask.

Lardner's situation as author keeps him this side of the veil that separates, for each author, everything present and negotiable in experience from everything potential, projected. Here, however, he has declared, not merely settled into, his situation; the outlines of this work, confirmed by his decision about what is accessible—observable, transmittable—to him, and what is not; to him, hence to us. In the case of an American writer like Lardner, no veritable representation of the world, the utter world, even as he can intuit it beyond the boundary-markers of his craft, is possible: such is the message of the actor-suitor's dreadful *chef d'oeuvre*. For Lardner was *detained*, like generations of other American writers and artists, Melville being one of the most renowned, from the pre-emption of Eternity by the weaving nonfixity of the story two inches from his eyes. And Lardner, for his part, lacked, nor would cultivate, the antirational will to override; to have, through metaphor, through epiphany, through wish-fulfillment fantasy, that immemorial birthright and prize of artists: the cake that he had eaten, was eating, would eat, *in perpetuum*. Instead, he gives over his imagination, the farthest possible attainments of his artist's will, and, instead, makes an affirmation of his reserve, his detention in the present, that shaky *status quo*, to which, however, his eyes are now opened forever more. He comes closer, in ***The Big Town***, to Nathanael West of *A Cool Million* and *Miss Lonelyhearts* than he ever came before. May we wonder—is there any point in wondering, now—given another five, six years of life to Lardner—what common waterways those two antic, self-reliant, flint-eyed ferrymen might have found? (pp. 327-30)

Donald Phelps, "Shut Up, He Explained," in Word and Beyond, *edited by Harry Smith, The Smith, 1982, pp. 313-30.*

WRIGHT MORRIS (essay date 1979)

[*Morris is an American novelist whose works, which are generally set in the rural and small-town Midwest, examine American myths, traditions, and the character of the American people. His important critical study* The Territory Ahead *(1958) surveys the history of American literature. In the following excerpt from his* Earthly Delights, Unearthly Adornments: American Writers As Image Makers, *Morris discusses the characteristics of Lardner's fiction and briefly compares it to that of Sherwood Anderson.*]

> A long solemn-faced man. The face was wonderful. It was a mask. All the time you were with him you kept wondering . . . "What is going on back there?"

On meeting Lardner in 1933, Anderson recorded this impression.

Much that was going on back there could be read in the daily Chicago *Tribune*, where Lardner had his own column. He reported on what he saw and heard around him, with emphasis on what he heard. The medley of utterance, not necessarily speech, that constituted the American vernacular was in full flower. Lardner had been a sportswriter, with an entrée into the palmy world of baseball. The inwardly tormented, outwardly disfigured, brooding and groping grotesques of Anderson's imagination were also the kith, kin and kissing cousins of the loud-mouthed, horseplaying, four-flushing bush leaguers just emerging from the dark woodwork of rural and small-town life. The country hick was on his way to becoming the big-city slicker. A gap once too broad for leaping separated Winesburg, Ohio, from the ball park in Detroit or Chicago.

> He ast me one time, he says: "What do you call me Ike for? I ain't no Yid."

Humor this broad and slangwich this bad are now part of the new language heralded by Whitman. (pp. 89-90)

Anderson's characters speak plainly enough, but not often, as if speech cost them much effort. The tone of his writing is oral, and the reader seems to intrude into a discourse that has no end. The monologue or dialogue casually breaks off, to begin again the following morning. This style of narration suited the needs of Lardner's column, as well as the attention span of his readers. A Lardner innovation is the use of quotations to emphasize high points of humor. The images are flat, bold as the cartoons in full bloom in the comic pages. On many occasions the cartoon "balloon" would have served Lardner's purpose better than quotation marks. The refrain "You can't get ahead of Mother" would have served as the title of a serial.

Compared with Lardner's slangy, up-to-the-minute reporting, Anderson seems the writer of an earlier decade. Lardner appears to dispense with the familiar distinctions between literature and life. People seldom sound as good as he reports them, but they would if they could. He is at ease in the tradition of the journalist-satirist, given authority and appeal by Mark Twain, but he departs from the humorists that preceded him in the cutting edge of his mockery. The sword of his wit gives the *coup de grâce* to Mother, the back of his hand to Father, the flat of the blade to the reader. The uproarious, guffawing surface of the world of **"You Know Me, Al"** did conceal from Lardner the crassness and vacuity of the life beneath it. Though he was as romantically ready for life as Fitzgerald, the aftertaste of his humor has the bitterness of alum. Like Hemingway, he looked about him and saw a dream corrupted. Increasingly, his humor was that of a man betrayed by the people he had hoped to believe in. In the place of Anderson's brooding grotesques Lardner inserts the caricature, the animated look-alikes shaped by that staple of American life, the wisecrack. (pp. 90-1)

"I Can't Breathe," the diary of a teen-ager besieged on her vacation by old and new boyfriends, is one of the most "hysterically" successful of Lardner's acid portraits. This nameless diary writer anticipates the mindless subspecies of Nathanael West and the remarkable juveniles of J. D. Salinger. There is no hint that Lardner's *jeune fille* is acquiring experience, or that the passage of time will result in a larger awareness, or "growth," or that her nature is complex enough to be probed for its "hurt," its numb core of feeling. The humor seems good clean all-American fun until it goes a bit sour as the diary closes. Is she a moron? In the passage of time will the boy she marries refer to her as Mother? The reader is free to assume she will learn no more than how to breathe.

> This is one about a brother and sister and the sister's husband and the brother's wife. The sister's name was Rita Mason Johnston; she was married to Stuart Johnston, whose intimates called him Stu, which was appropriate only on special occasions. The brother was Bob Mason, originally and recently from Buchanan, Michigan, and in between whiles a respected resident of Los Angeles. His wife was a woman he had found in San Bernardino and married for some reason.

Whatever effect this had on the readers, it would prove unforgettable on the writers. The concreteness, the economy, the irony are all a seamless part of the language; no cues for laughs are necessary. The closing sentence is a story within a story, at once "humorous" and searingly sarcastic. Nevertheless, the impression persists that it is all there, for free, in the language. (pp. 91-2)

Writers other than Lardner, all readers of Lardner, will create the new conscience of the postwar generation. Lardner's remarkable talent seems to be merely part of the language itself. Not a few readers, reading Lardner, would feel that they should try their hand at writing. How could they miss? All he did was see and hear what was free as the air. Only the writer will perceive that these *images,* so artless-seeming, are matchlessly crafty. He is not always so good. If he had been, a decade of writers would have been silenced. In the easeful achievement of his vernacular style we see ourselves like the reflections in shop windows. How lifelike we are! As a rule, neither so handsome nor so dreadful as we feared. Wheezing with laughter, Lardner's readers are often unaware in what way they are being tickled. Sinclair Lewis will be the first to reap the harvest of "types" that the new public seems prepared for. As a laugh purveyor to a nation of "boobocrats," Lardner was well paid, famous and full of self-loathing. The admiration of critics and writers he admired aggravated his suspicions that he had wasted his talents. The measure of his achievement, however, is not in what the "serious" writers said about him, but in the way they absorbed him, more an act of recognition than plagiarism. He was part of the news that had become part of urban life. Like Twain and Stein, he is invisibly present in the images we have shaped of ourselves, the gargoyles and leering comical "mugs" that small fry paint on the benign, reassuring faces in Norman Rockwell's *Saturday Evening Post* covers. (pp. 92-3)

In Lardner's mocking glance there is more of the cutting edge of Swift than the chuckle of Twain. "The laceration of laughter that ceases to amuse" can be heard offstage.

Between vaudeville, the movies, the novels and the horseplay, it was getting harder and harder to recognize *real* life. Americans were long accustomed to laughing at each other: through Lardner they were compelled to laugh at themselves. (p. 93)

Wright Morris, "Ring Lardner," in his Earthly Delights, Unearthly Adornments: American Writers As Image-Makers, *Harper & Row, Publishers, 1979, pp. 89-94.*

ELIZABETH EVANS (essay date 1979)

[In the following excerpt from her critical study Ring Lardner, *Evans examines Lardner's treatment of women in his fiction.]*

Jonathan Yardley has suggested that Lardner "tended to divide women into two separate and absolutely hostile camps." On the one hand were "harpies, gold diggers, and two-timers typified by the women he had seen hanging around ballplayers; these were women who had somehow betrayed their sex because they were just as coarse as the men in their lives, and frequently more clever." Opposite these were women "who remained faithful to his pre-Jazz Age sense of femininity but who also had wit, humor, ebullience and style" and in this group were diverse women he admired—Zelda Fitzgerald, Kate Rice, Dorothy Parker, Claudette Colbert, his sister Anna, his wife Ellis, his mother Lena.

Examples from the first camp exist in Lardner's fiction, but women characters seldom (and never in a fully developed sense) exhibit wit, humor, ebullience and style. The women he portrays vary in temperament, background, and ambition. Generally, they are either unpleasant or unwise, too aggressive or too subservient, too naive or too worldly-wise. Although most of the women characters are married, Lardner rarely shows a marital relationship that is happy, growing, and content. Instead, women characters struggle to survive, spend energy (and money) pursuing frivolous and senseless goals, and fail to act positively or to rebel successfully. (p. 51)

A clever and amusing view of women was ***Say It with Oil,*** Lardner's 1922 answer to Nina Wilcox Putnam's attack on husbands, *Say It with Bricks.* Here humor overrides satire and wit tempers Victorian views. The persona's grammar alone dispels any pretense or seriousness. (p. 52)

While Lardner's stories have many funny episodes and quick lines as ***Say It with Oil*** does, the humor usually arrives with a painful self-revelation, a display of naiveté, ignorance, or self-consciousness. The easy-going banter found in ***Say It with Oil***, **"Marriage Made Easy,"** and **"Love Letters Made Easy"** is missing. The fiction treats women and men seriously, pointing out their foibles, exposing their weaknesses, and satirizing their pretentiousness.

A frequent female type in Lardner's fiction is the insensitive, aggressive, harsh woman who centers her attention on material things and good times; domestic concerns are of no interest, children of little consequence. Such a character has always been an apt target for the satirist. For Lardner, such women reflected the newer times when maintaining a home for the pleasure and comfort of husband and children was not the ideal life to which all women aspired. In his fiction this character type remains especially unpleasant: she does not strike out for a challenging career, but simply maintains her role, neither feminine nor feminist.

In **"Mr. and Mrs. Fix-It,"** . . . the two husbands play active and almost interchangeable roles with their wives. Furthermore, the victims (Ada and her husband, the narrator) are satirized as soundly as are the aggressors (Belle and Tom Stevens). Of all the meddlesome friends Ada has forced on her husband, the worst is the Stevens couple whom Lardner portrays as the busiest of busybodies. (pp. 52-3)

While it is easy to find the behavior of the Stevens couple maddeningly officious as they insensitively disregard the other couple's tastes, preferences, and plans, Ada and her husband are not faultless. When Lardner has the narrator describe Ada as "one of these kinds of people that just can't say no. Which is maybe why I and her is married," he portrays ineffectual characters ill-equipped to deal with problems. Indeed, issuing insults is the only recourse the narrator has against Stevens "and nothin' we could say was an insult." Furious complaints about Stevens do not stop the narrator from asking him to fix a speeding ticket—"it's silly to not appreciate favors like that." As much as Ada wants to keep the Miami trip a secret, she blurts out the news rather than have Belle and Tom think them too poor to join a California excursion the Stevenses proposed. In short, Lardner exposes all four: Belle and Tom are not malicious, but they are meddlesome and insensitive; Ada and her husband resent being pushed around, but will profit when the occasion suits and will protect their pride at all costs.

While **"Liberty Hall"** . . . also deals with the busybody, Lardner sets the story in the East and Mrs. Thayer easily surpasses Belle Stevens in brashness. Ben Drake, a successful song writer and rival of Gershwin, has his privacy protected by his wife (who declines social invitations because they interfere with his work) and by his secretary (who sends a bogus telegram on his rare visits in case he needs an escape). Previous visits have been marred because Drake's demands were not all met: the bathtub filled too slowly, the breakfast was skimpy, the reporters still reached him, no bedside lamp was provided. **"Liberty Hall"** recounts the visit that ended visits for Drake. (pp. 54-5)

Lardner's satire remains relatively mild here, but his treatment of the four characters is critical nonetheless. Mrs. Thayer displays no feminine charm; instead, she pushes, manages, and arranges. Her husband is given little to do or say, powerless against her domineering ways. Ben takes his wife for granted, leaving her to endure solitary days and nights when his play is in rehearsal. Lonely, she needs the invitations he refuses. The social rank of the respective couples in **"Mr. and Mrs. Fix-It"** and **"Liberty Hall"** shifts from a modest Chicago flat to the Thayers' estate, Landsdowne; instead of the elevated train, characters travel in a limousine; the narrator can only insult Tom Stevens, but Ben Drake goes on a binge after escaping from the Thayers. His wife shows little surprise when she says, "small wonder that Ben was credited at the Lamb's Club with that month's most interesting bender." Higher social position with affluent surroundings does not improve people and while Lardner makes us laugh, we are laughing at undesirable traits.

Not only is the nurse Miss Lyons in **"Zone of Quiet"** . . . an insensitive woman, she also lacks all of the expected qualities of her profession. As the doctor leaves the patient who is not fully awake from anesthesia, he tells Miss Lyons not to let the man talk "and don't talk to him; that is, if you can help it." Once the doctor is out of ear shot, Miss Lyons begins with a ceaseless chatter. (pp. 55-6)

To dismiss the nurse as a mere featherbrain, as some have done, is to judge the story too lightly. Miss Lyons's youth and good looks do not compensate for her inept and somewhat sadistic behavior. She does not give the patient time to say that he slept poorly and she stands far removed from the ideal nurse who is kind, efficient, prompt, alert, and sensitive. Just as Jack Keefe in ***You Know Me Al*** flagrantly disregarded baseball training rules and managerial orders, so Miss Lyons has no sense of duty, no concern for her patient's well-being.

Women play an important role in the life of Jack Keefe, Lardner's baseball player-boob who became a familiar figure when **"A Busher's Letters Home"** appeared in the *Saturday Evening Post* in 1914. Writing to his hometown friend Al Blanchard, Jack relates his ups and downs as a baseball player, as a husband, and later as a none-too-willing soldier. His common theme is steadfast: whatever has gone wrong is no fault of his. The letters quickly reveal his naiveté, his willfulness to break rules, and his irresponsibility. With such undesirable traits, he is at best a dubious judge of others. A disingenuous narrator, Jack reports and the reader evaluates. What Jack says about marriage and his wife Florrie is colored with snide and bitter remarks. Whether or not Florrie deserved the sorry opinion Jack held about her is debatable; however, what he tells and how he tells it strongly suggest that Florrie used him, spent his money, and ignored his difficulties. (p. 57)

Abrasive and unfeminine, Florrie is one of Lardner's most unpleasant women characters, quite the opposite of the ideal woman he saw in his mother and his wife.

In contrast, many of the women characters are (or seem to be) patient, quiet, and faithful. Ironically, the best example of this type never appears, but is merely referred to. Bertha Blanchard, Al's wife, supports her husband's willingness to remain Jack Keefe's friend, loaning him money, arranging house rental, accepting the various responsibilities Jack casts upon him. The reader pictures Bertha as implicitly a good woman, possessing all the domestic interests and virtues Florrie lacks.

Representative of the patient woman is Mabelle Gillespie, that quiet, thrifty, efficient girl in **"Some Like Them Cold,"** . . . who in reality just connives to get a man. Radically different are Julie Gregg (**"Haircut"** . . .) as well as Ellen Kelly and Emma Hersch Kelly (**"Champion"** . . .), who are victimized by wicked men. The Missus in **"Gullible's Travels"** . . . is socially ambitious, but when her Palm Beach fiasco is done, she quietly admits her failure and returns to her dependable domestic scene. Celia Gregg (**"The Love Nest"** . . .) marries false expectations and confronts her misery with heavy drinking and silent protests. Finally, Bess Taylor in **"Anniversary"** . . . pays a bitter price for being the respectable wife in a respectable and model marriage.

"Some Like Them Cold" (adapted in 1929 as ***June Moon,*** Lardner's one successful theatrical venture) presents Mabelle Gillespie, a young woman working in Chicago who by chance meets Chas. F. Lewis in the Lasalle Street railroad station. Mabelle is waiting for her sister; Lewis is waiting for the New York train, bound he thinks for fame and fortune as a Broadway song writer. An epistolary courtship of sorts ensues.

Portraying herself as thrifty, hard-working, and domestic, Mabelle catalogs her virtues and casts herself as a woman dedicated to making a husband happy. The truth, however, is that Mabelle merely wants to get a man and lures Lewis with her amusing conversation, expert housekeeping, and enviable cooking. Lewis's letters are full of poor grammar, misspellings, clichés, and confused words, but Mabelle flatteringly calls him a genius. Although Lewis had said he did not want a wife "that don't know a dishrag from a waffle iron," he does not propose to the hopeful Mabelle, but instead marries his librettist's sister. (pp. 59-61)

Mabelle and Lewis are typical of Lardner's middle-class characters who lack charm and manners and who are destined for mediocrity.

Unlike Mabelle, women in two of Lardner's most celebrated stories, **"Haircut"** and **"Champion,"** are ill-treated by men—physically abused, neglected, humiliated. Jim Kendall and Midge Kelly lack all vestige of humane conduct and distort the roles of the husband and son as provider and protector. The women are rendered powerless and the surrounding characters (the town population in **"Haircut"** and the prize fighter's public in **"Champion"**), while innocent of violent deeds, are still culpable because they do not act against these men. (pp. 61-2)

Probably Lardner's most anthologized story, **"Haircut"** portrays Kendall's wife as helpless in her dilemma: life with Kendall is unspeakable but divorce is impossible because she has no means of support. The humiliation scene for Julie is all the more frightening because it occurs at night, Kendall and the pool room crowd are drunk, and Julie expected Ralph Stair to greet her so convincing had Kendall's voice imitation been. Critical commentary on the story has praised Lardner's excellent use of the disingenuous narrator and his thorough condemnation of a small town that tolerates a Jim Kendall. The women characters should also be carefully considered for in their helplessness against sheer brutality, they confirm that society can tolerate astonishing behavior without serious protest.

A catalog of Midge Kelly's exploits in **"Champion"** sounds like exaggerated melodrama, but like the adventures in *Candide* where the rapid cumulative effect creates the sense of unreality, no one doubts the truth of the individual deed. (pp. 62-3)

Like Jim Kendall, Kelly is an amoral creature, vicious to women or anyone else who gets in his way.

Lardner salvages the story from complete melodrama by keeping Midge's road to success unbroken and by never giving him the slightest regret for his behavior. Instant pleasure fills his mind; no suffering touches him. Singular in his callousness, Midge will not protect, support, or love the women dependent on him. Wife and mother and child are left destitute and helpless. (p. 64)

The vulgarity and menace of wealth are clearly shown in **"The Love Nest"** where motion picture producer Lou Gregg has successfully transformed his talented starlet wife into drunken chattel without ever letting the public suspect the slightest flaw in his happy home. . . . Considered a great home girl, Celia goes through the motions Lou demands: constantly greeting him with "Sweetheart," she strikes the pose of a woman for whom "home and kiddies come first."

On the surface, nothing about the plot is unusual: big money can buy everything, even the appearance of happiness. What distinguishes the story is the extent of Celia's despair, made bearable only through liquor. To Barlett, the magazine interviewer, Celia confesses her state. Since Gregg is often away and does not seriously question Celia's evening headaches, her late risings, or the half-filled bourbon bottles, he thinks that his money has bought him a happy wife and family. The pathos of Celia's life is revealed in the game she plays to keep Lou Gregg content. Further, allusions to famous theatrical greats—Francois Delsarte, Ina Claire, Ethel Barrymore, and Anna Pavlova—suggest Celia's efforts to keep alive remnants of the career she has lost. When Barlett arrived, she "made an entrance so Delsarte as to be almost painful" and greeted the guest "in a voice reminiscent of Miss Claire's imitation of Miss Barrymore." When she danced alone to the radio's music, she impressed Barlett with her skill but she protests, "I'm no Pavlowa." [sic] At twenty-seven, she is imprisoned in elegance, surrounded by wealth, children, and a husband she loathes.

Not entirely blameless ("I married him to get myself a chance"). Celia can only rue her life. Should she live long enough to witness her daughters grow up, she will advise Norma, who resembles her, "to run away from home and live her own life. And *be* somebody! Not a *thing* like I am!" Contemplation of divorce amounts to nothing: Gregg has done nothing indiscreet, and men avoid Celia because they fear him. Not a slick story about the idle rich, **"The Love Nest"** is a vicious picture of success. Gregg has built the image he wants the world to believe and Celia must play her part, relieved only by the senselessness that liquor brings. Denigrated, she is a *thing* and as much a victim of her fate as Midge Kelly's battered wife.

Death by boredom is what Bess Taylor faces in **"Anniversary"** as her husband Louis proves year after year how solid, respectable, and thrifty he is. When she married nine years ago, Bess was one of the town's "most charming and beautiful women"; now at thirty-three, her evening activities consist of forty games of solitaire (with occasional cheating) before bedtime. Louis will not learn to play bridge, the picture show hurts his eyes, and he will not allow Bess to go out alone at night. (pp. 66-7)

The imprisonment of wives in respectable comfort draws Lardner's satire to a fine point. His sympathy goes to the women; the men, whether the Lou Greggs in the mansions or the Louis Taylors in their houses, are villains. The women are irrevocably stuck. They do not like Nora Helmer, leave home or like Hedda Gabler, shoot themselves or like Mrs. Alving, quietly run the business. They are left to drink, solitaire, or death. At the end of *Candide* when the old farmer proclaims that work saves men from vice, poverty, and boredom, boredom may seem the least threatening. For many women in Lardner's fiction, boredom rivals vice and poverty.

Characterized as late Edwardian and suited to an age of extended courtship and proper marriage, Lardner did not portray the fallen woman frequently in his fiction. Sex, for him, was not a subject for polite conversation nor a situation for fictional satire. However, he did include some immoral women whose explicit activities are assumed rather than detailed—Midge Kelly's friend Grace, Conrad Green's mistress Rose, and Hurry Kane's would-be mistress Evelyn.

Grace, in **"Champion,"** is a kept woman, well dressed and well financed. While one hardly believes she attached herself to Midge Kelly with matrimony in mind, she does finally suggest it. Midge refuses by remembering for once his lawful wife, Emma. What becomes of Grace is another story. Midge discards her as he does other people when he finishes with their usefulness.

In **"A Day with Conrad Green,"** . . . the successful, semiliterate producer goes through an eventful day: his and his wife's names do not appear in the society page as expected; he decides not to attend his faithful secretary's funeral; his wife surprises him and to save face, he gives her pearls intended for his mistress, Rose. (pp. 68-9)

Green is a liar, a cheat, a thief; the women around him are greedy and self-serving, quite deserving the shabby treatment they get from him.

"Hurry Kane" . . . gives wide range for Lardner's satirical attack: the talented, but slow-witted and greedy baseball rube, Elmer Kane, nicknamed "Hurry Kane"; ball players who can be bribed; and a glamorous woman who arranges a bribe. Convinced that the theatrical star Evelyn Cory likes him, Kane accepts the first installment of a $20,000 bribe. In truth, Evelyn "belongs to Sam Morris, the bookie," who has six to one odds on the game in question. Brought into the story to effect the exploitation of Kane, Evelyn is a static character, stereotyped by her good looks and her desire for money. Ironically, her questionable virtue looks innocent enough beside Kane who is temperamental and self-centered, keeps a girl at home and one away from home, and neither returns the bribe nor throws the game.

Finally, in **"Old Folks Christmas,"** . . . Lardner lashes out at the bitter price people pay for making money. The parents, Tom and Grace, unwisely buy a ridiculous number of extravagant gifts for their children—a beaver coat, an opal ring, a roadster—only to find these gifts are declassé to Ted and Caroline who ask tactlessly if they can be exchanged. All the pleasure cherished with past Christmas times is gone since the children prefer going about with the younger set until all hours, are too tired to open presents at the accustomed time, and forget when Christmas dinner has always been served. Caroline (née Grace) may not be or may not become a fallen woman, but from Lardner's point of view, she displays the distressing characteristics of the modern generation. (pp. 70-1)

In summing up Ring Lardner's attitude toward women, Donald Elder said, "He idealized women, and when he wrote of those who fell short of his ideal, the portraits were harsh and bitter. There are very few admirable women in all his stories; there are very few admirable men, either, but when women were coarse, egotistical or pretentious, they were much worse because he had expected them to be so much better." (p. 71)

Lardner in his later years. The Granger Collection, New York.

Elizabeth Evans, in her Ring Lardner, *Frederick Ungar Publishing Co., 1979, 150 p.*

JAMES DeMUTH (essay date 1980)

[In the following excerpt, DeMuth compares Lardner's work with that of George Ade and Peter Finley Dunne, two Chicago writers who are considered Lardner's most significant influences.]

Lardner engages his reader's sympathy by consistently writing in the first person singular and by adopting, as his own voice, the idiom of the common man. He restricts his language to the ordinary diction of workingmen, well-laced with their colloquialisms, and he composes his writing to reflect the rather haphazard syntax of common speech. . . . Lardner's idiomatic speech, for all its apparent laxity in syntax and grammar, is nevertheless a terse satiric instrument. By adopting the semiliterate idiom of a "wise boob," Lardner could express, in the language his popular audience best understood, his sense of the generally debased character of their urban lives. In reading Lardner's fiction, one is always aware of a muffled belligerence threatening to erupt into abuse, complaint, or even obscenity. (p. 70)

With his apparently ill-disciplined idiom, Lardner suggests the disintegration of moral and social standards in the city; his characters exhibit little respect for the standards of courtesy, modesty, or good taste. Their humor is sarcasm and rude practical jokes. Dunne and Ade, by contrast, had expressed, through their characters' comic language, a quite different sense of urban culture. For Dunne, Chicago had stimulated the Irish immigrant to sharpen his folk dialect into an accurate, humorous, and perceptive urban idiom. The speech of Mr. Dooley, particularly his concise, ironic aphorisms ("I care not who makes th' laws iv a nation if I can get out an injuction," for example), indicates self-control, intelligence, and abounding confidence. George Ade suggests the same qualities in his richly figurative Chicago slang. And, by his modification of actual Chicago slang into an appropriate "parlor slang," Ade indicated a keen respect for the moral scruples of average Chicagoans.

In Lardner's fiction, though, one misses the sense of affirmation, restraint and propriety which had imbued Dunne and Ade's work. They had affirmed Chicago as a healthy, moral community by representing certain Chicago neighborhoods as the novel re-creations of stable, rural community cultures. Lardner could not sustain their effort in assimilating the two dissimilar cultures, urban and rural, industrial and agrarian. Like the Chicago novelists of the 1890s, Lardner perceived Chicago as a radically unique environment which incited its people to selfish, immoral, and aggressive behavior. He translated the novelists' tragic themes of alienation and moral corruption into the modest lives of "thirty-five dollar a week" Chicagoans. Dunne and Ade had always distinguished the modest citizen from other Chicagoans; he, if not his economic masters, still preserved the moral values of an earlier, simpler village culture. Lardner demonstrated that the common man could not be distinguished from the city in which he lived.

Lardner's first, and still most widely appreciated, urban comic character was Jack Keefe, the "busher" who became a successful pitcher for the Chicago White Sox. Lardner's portrait of professional baseball in ***You Know Me, Al*** . . . , the epistolary novel of Jack Keefe's two-season career, is detailed and knowledgeable. He drew on an eight-year experience as a sports writer, six years of which he had spent traveling with the Chicago Cubs and Chicago White Sox. In his book he expresses his esteem for baseball and the game's accomplished players through his distinction, scrupulously maintained, between the "bushers" (always fictional characters) and the "regulars" (always actual baseball players). Jack Keefe, a "raw recrut" from Terre Haute of the Central League, is a "busher," inexperienced, overconfident, and irresponsible. It is the duty of the White Sox "regulars"—manager "Cal" Callahan, coach "Kid" Gleason, and veteran pitcher Ed Walsh, principally—to season him into a professional pitcher. The task is formidable, but with patience, insults, fines, and occasional praise, they succeed. In one season, they turn "bonehead" Keefe into the most capable pitcher on the mediocre White Sox team.

The story of Jack Keefe's "education" as a player for the Chicago White Sox is instructive for what it tells us of Ring Lardner's values, attitude, and style as a comic artist. He represents the ball team as a close-knit and responsible community; it is the equivalent, in his work, of Mr. Dooley's "Bridgeport" or George Ade's boardinghouses, offices, and social clubs. As is the case with the neighborly communities evoked by the earlier humorists, Lardner's ball team is humanly satisfying; however, unlike Dunne and Ade, Lardner represents the community of the ball team as artificial, its work as professional entertainment, and its season as short-lived. It does not focus the political and social life of Chicago as Bridgeport does or as Artie Blanchard's office does; the ball team simply has a place and a season within the city. (pp. 71-2)

Professional baseball, as Lardner represents it, is unquestionably valuable for Jack Keefe; the game disciplines him to work with an uncharacteristic dedication, and it justly rewards him on the merits of his performance. Lardner consistently represents the seasoned players and managers, those who have mastered baseball's rigorous competitive standards, as intelligent, fair men genuinely dedicated to serving their team. Obviously, such a portrait glosses over the often ruthless competition which baseball encouraged between veterans and rookies, as well as the petty tyranny in which managers and owners frequently indulged. Many of the players of Lardner's time—Fred Snodgrass, "Wahoo Sam" Crawford, Tommy Leach, "Chief" Meyers, Al Bridwell, and Paul Waner, to name a few of the more outspoken—protested their frustration with the sabotage of their play as rookies. Jealous veterans, they protested, often monopolized practice time or deliberately confused rookies with contradictory instructions; piqued managers and coaches often vented their anger by harassing new players. (p. 74)

As an experienced sports writer, Lardner certainly knew the abuses rookies frequently suffered. However, he acknowledges these abuses in only two brief incidents in ***You Know Me, Al:*** manager Callahan's harassment of Jack during his loss to the Tigers and owner Comiskey's shrewd manipulation of Jack into an underpriced, long-term contract. Otherwise, Lardner generously portrays baseball as a productive, moral, and fraternal activity. His portrait, however, does not appear sentimental or false because the baseball "regulars" express themselves in an abrasive "wise boob" language of sarcasm and profanity. Manager Callahan and coach Gleason do not solicit Jack's cooperation; they discipline him with ridicule and, when necessary, with fines and suspensions. Significantly, the measure of Jack's maturity as a ball player, after his apprenticeship with the San Francisco team, is his mastery of the veteran's wit. . . . In ***You Know Me, Al,*** unlike Lardner's later fiction, the wise-boob language signifies control, self-discipline, and quick intelligence because it is the polished idiom of professionals. As a rookie, Jack Keefe's language was crude, literal, and abusive—his response to every joke, criticism, and mishap was the same: "If he ever talks to me like he done to him I will take a punch at him." With experience, though, Jack begins to understand and speak—to manager Callahan's surprised delight—the quick, confident, and sarcastic idiom of a seasoned player; he is even able to talk down Ty Cobb.

In Lardner's descriptions of Jack Keefe as a ball player, we see that baseball's discipline is valuable; however, its effect is short-lived. During the off season, Jack's language degenerates into vulgarity, and his moral character declines into sloth, greed, and temper. In South Side Chicago, Jack freely indulges those appetites which the White Sox had carefully curbed: he sleeps until noon, eats and drinks to excess, wastes all his money, and on several occasions assaults the waiters, bartenders, and strangers who, he fancies, have affronted him. It is this degeneration of character, rather than Jack Keefe's competent performance as a professional ball player, which has earned ***You Know Me, Al*** its reputation as an uncompromising satire on the American athlete.

Jack's moral and physical corruption is quickened by his novel experience of freedom and anonymity in Chicago. As a stranger on the South Side, he is freed of the public opinion which, in his hometown of Bedford, Indiana, would have disciplined his behavior much as the vigilant coaches and manager of the White Sox had during the season. It should be noted in Jack's defense, and Lardner carefully establishes this qualification, that he did not seek the moral freedom of living anonymously in Chicago. Throughout his first season, he never questioned the value of a settled domestic life in quiet Bedford. His wife, though, a woman he marries after a five-day courtship at the end of the season, does not share his enthusiasm for Bedford. Instead, Florrie wants swell clothes, "mohoggeny" furniture, jewelry, entertainment, and a hired girl; she wants, and she gets, Chicago. (pp. 74-6)

You Know Me, Al entertained thousands of readers by confirming familiar and comfortable attitudes about baseball. In Lardner's early comic fiction, as well as in several sports essays, until the stunning revelations of the 1919 "Black Sox" scandal disturbed his opinion, baseball represented an enduring but—regrettably—increasingly anachronistic moral society. It epitomized the values of honest labor, democratic opportunity, self-reliance, and community cooperation ideally associated with the traditional ways of American small towns—particularly, for Lardner, the ways of his hometown of Niles, Michigan. In baseball, a small-town man like Jack Keefe could feel welcome and needed; he worked in a close-knit community of thirty players and coaches, and his talents, proven in fair competition, were essential to the team's success.

In limiting Jack Keefe's competence to baseball, and to the type of traditional community it represented, Lardner established the moral criteria by which he would measure all his urban characters. None of Lardner's Chicago characters, beginning with Jack Keefe, can control the base appetites which the city excited; none, except Jack Keefe, could retreat from the city to compete, without favor or disability, for an honorable place in a secure and fraternal society. Lacking Jack Keefe's exceptional opportunity, Lardner's wise boobs flounder pathetically. They are routinely victimized by the bores, *poseurs,* and phonies whom they attract, and they are scorned by the affluent, fashionable Chicagoans whose recognition they eagerly seek.

The power of Lardner's urban humor, developed first in his satires of ordinary Chicagoans and refined in his many short stories written after moving to New York City in 1919, lies in his deft ability to gradually alter a reader's perception of the wise boob's moral character. When introduced, Lardner's wise boobs are, for the popular audience he entertained, familiar and roughly sympathetic characters. By the usual standards of middle-class achievement, they are comfortably successful people: one is the assistant chief of detectives of the Chicago Police Department; another is a shrewd investor enjoying an early retirement. Lardner's readers, one would imagine, could easily identify with the apparently modest and decent ambitions of his characters. The characters simply desire more comfortable homes; additionally, they desire a wider and more distinguished circle of friends and a social status commensurate with their incomes. One's sympathy is further engaged by the frustration and expense which the characters endure and suffer in pursuing their simple ambitions. Fred Gross, for example, the assistant chief of Chicago detectives, wants to build a house in the suburbs for his growing family. This simple ambition bankrupts him. His architect underestimates the building cost and neglects to design essential features; the contractor defaults on debts; and the workmen do shoddy work. The final cost of the $2,000 house is $5,300. When Fred Gross moves in, he finds that windows won't open and doors won't close; the roof also leaks and the basement floods. In addition to these difficulties, the Gross family lives in their new home from May until August without receiving one visitor.

One's sympathy for Fred Gross and other wise boobs gradually evaporates, though, as one watches envy and greed consume their good sense and modesty. On moving into his new home, Fred Gross immediately understands and covets the snobbish exclusiveness of suburbanites. . . . Though he hungers for their recognition, Fred Gross never gets acquainted with the fine people of his suburb. They shun his overtures and even, at one point, expel him from a local charity ball because, they insolently explain, he could only have received his written invitation by mistake. Hurt and angered by his neighbors' disdain, Fred Gross begins a vendetta against Hamilton, his next-door neighbor and the suburb's leading citizen. He places a quarantine sign on the Hamiltons' porch the night they give a party, he deflates the tires of Hamilton's car, and he arranges with his friend the county sheriff to send deputies to raid Mrs. Hamilton's bridge club as a gambling house. (pp. 77-9)

A more attractive wise boob than Fred Gross, whose boorish and spiteful behavior soon exhausts one's sympathy, is Gullible, the protagonist of ***Gullible's Travels***. . . . Gullible seems mature, quick-witted, and candid; he enjoys, without apology or self-consciousness, his mundane pleasures of spectator sports, gin rummy, and tavern conviviality; and he unerringly sees through the pretensions of others. His sarcastic humor and blunt expression remind one of the confident, ironic banter of Lardner's "regular" ball players. One laughs heartily at Gullible's burlesque summaries of the operas his wife persuades him to attend, and one applauds the success of his clever campaign to rid his home of the unemployed actor courting his sister-in-law. However, when Gullible maneuvers, at his wife's insistence, to ingratiate himself into fashionable society, his rude habits render him a ridiculous, ill-mannered, and vindictive person. He becomes, in effect, the abusive boor Fred Gross became when confronted with the disdain of suburbanites. (p. 80)

For Lardner, bridge succinctly dramatized the frustration and inadequacy his wise boobs experienced in trying to establish themselves in an urban society. It is a game which Lardner wholly identifies with urban culture, particularly the culture of those educated and affluent urban citizens who use it as a weapon of invidious social discrimination. The game, relatively new at the time Lardner wrote his stories, is utterly beyond the experience and capacity of the gin-rummy playing "thirty-five dollar a week men" of his stories. . . . In Lardner's fiction, bridge symbolizes, in the petty jealousies, vulgar recriminations, and harsh quarrels it inevitably provokes, the breakdown of manners, community, and tradition in the city. Whereas baseball, an accessible, common man's entertainment, had figured prominently in Lardner's early, largely genial fiction and journalism, the strange, intimidating game of bridge appears more frequently in his later, increasingly bitter, stories of the urban middle class. As an urban sport, baseball had reflected the traditional small-town culture of its origins; it had remained an open and leisurely summer's entertainment for fans from all social classes. Unlike bridge, with its esoteric "sines," baseball was common property and an enriching influence on the common language. For Jack Keefe, baseball developed his talent, sharpened his wit and disciplined his impulses. For Fred Gross, Gullible, and a host of later Lardner characters, bridge is a degrading experience; it denies them the pleasure of comfortable social intercourse, it draws out their ill-suppressed greed and envy, and it breaks their fragile self-esteem.

Lardner's generally demeaning characterizations of his wise boobs exhausts the effort of the Chicago popular humorists, beginning with Finley Peter Dunne, to extend to an urban audience the appeal of a traditional American comic type, the plain-spoken and coarse-mannered rustic moralist. For Dunne, the effort had presented no great difficulty. In all essential features of personality, social status, and experience, Mr. Dooley is simply a transplanted crackerbarrel philosopher. He lives in a parochial community, respects its traditional culture, and is accorded respect because of his age, community service, and property. (pp. 83-4)

George Ade did not endow his common-folk characters with the full measure of Mr. Dooley's wisdom and confidence, though they embodied, essentially, the same nostalgic values of village domesticity, economic self-reliance, and simple moral rectitude. Unlike Dunne, Ade firmly distinguished himself from his characters; one always recognizes the distinction between Ade, the accomplished storyteller, and the naive characters he describes. (p. 84)

In Lardner's characterization of the wise boob, the irony separating the Chicago humorist from the common Chicagoan expands dramatically. His characters, introduced as self-satisfied and practical-minded people, quickly alienate the reader's sympathy as they succumb to envy and ill temper. For Lardner, the city—Chicago, later New York City—was responsible for the moral degeneration of its common citizens. By exciting the wise boobs' dormant appetites for privilege and conspicuous consumption, the city denied them the stability, intimacy, and modesty which they had known in the small hometowns they had left.

In his many short stories written after his move to New York City in 1919, Lardner repeated, with little variation, the moral characterization of Chicago and its wise boobs. The only significant difference between Lardner's later stories (excepting ***The Big Town,*** written in 1920) and his Chicago stories is, occasionally, the image of the American small town. In Lardner's Chicago fiction, and in ***The Big Town,*** the small hometowns of the urban characters—Bedford, Indiana; South Bend, Indiana; St. Joseph, Michigan—are nostalgically described as stable, comfortable, and moral communities. The people of Bedford, as Jack Keefe's wife Florrie knows and dreads, would influence Jack by their moderate habits and discipline him by their public opinions. In Lardner's later fiction, however, the distinct, nostalgic, moral quality of the American small town occasionally dissolves and disappears. **"Haircut,"** generally considered Lardner's masterpiece, is a bitter indictment of the sleazy morality which small towners could accommodate. In the story, a vicious, jealous practical joker, Jim Kendall, is tolerated and envied by his more cautious confederates in the town's barber shop. The moral standards of decency and responsibility, which small towns had embodied in Lardner's earlier fiction are in **"Haircut"** only enforced when the town half-wit murders Kendall for exposing the gentle and virtuous Julie Gregg to public ridicule.

Lardner's stories of urban boobs and, occasionally, of small town brutes parodied, with devastating effect, the worn conventions of nineteenth-century American popular humor. Reviewing Lardner's work in her influential *American Humor,* published shortly before Lardner's death, Constance Rourke grimly evaluated his fiction as the "final product of a humor that had worn away idiosyncrasies, taking with it all the edged elements of character" [see excerpt dated 1931]. . . . (pp. 85-6)

James DeMuth, "Ring Lardner," in his Small Town Chicago: The Comic Perspective of Finley Peter Dunne, George Ade, Ring Lardner, *Kennikat Press, 1980, pp. 69-86.*

CHRISTIAN K. MESSENGER (essay date 1981)

[*In the following excerpt Messenger, an American educator and essayist, discusses Lardner's sports fiction, placing it in the tradition of the rustic Southwestern humor of the nineteenth century.*]

The most talented sportswriter was Ring Lardner, the innovative chronicler of American games, comic players, and their foibles. He allied himself to popular sport and the realist tradition while irrevocably fixing the stereotype of the professional athlete for modern fiction. Lardner stands at the center of any discussion of popular sport in modern American literature. He knew professional sport and suburban recreation to be the average citizen's obsessions, and he worked out of a rich Chicago tradition of sports writers and humorists. He had none of the energy and rawness of American Naturalism and he knew little about it. Throughout his career he affected a classic antiintellectual pose, a stance traditionally feigned by American humorists to enhance satiric thrusts; in Lardner's case, the pose became permanently identified as a trait of his characters, specifically his baseball players. His defensive posture against the world of ideas and, indeed, the world of art as well, seems in retrospect to have been genuine. He was a fearful man, suspicious of his own best and worst impulses, mistrustful of the franker, more open life of the 1920s, proud of his craft as he saw it yet ultimately less than candid about his motivations, both in life and in literature. (p. 108)

Like the Southwestern Humorists a half-century before, Lardner presented the athlete or gamester and his environment as representative of society. In his own reticent fashion he was as angry a stern moralist as [Augustus Baldwin] Longstreet, as skillful at creating vernacular speech as [George Washington] Harris; his characters could be as sly as [Johnson Jones] Hooper's Simon Suggs or, in another vein, as full of comic bombast as any western roarer. Lardner's links to the Southwestern tradition can be seen most clearly in the role of the narrator as social commentator. The Southwesterners had lashed the rural citizens for their manners; Lardner dissected the urban mass man in his ignorance and insensitivity. Like the Southwestern Realists, Lardner participated in a profound social upheaval, in his case, the twentieth-century urbanization of life and letters.

A philologist of sorts and a writer committed to the vernacular, he found his first congenial subject on the ball field, where his deadpan, laconic narrators related the tallest of baseball tales as in [**"Horseshoes," "Alibi Ike,"** and **"Hurry Kane"**.] . . . He was the first writer to assume a role critical of the sportswriter's position; he introduced women into sports fiction; he scaled the professional sports hero down into a realistic subject, investing him with physical prowess while comically divesting him of judgment, maturity, and self-knowledge.

Did Lardner mean to criticize athletes as a group? The evidence overwhelmingly suggests that he did not. By making White Sox pitcher Jack Keefe a simple young man with a shrewish wife, unpaid bills, and an apartment he could not afford, Lardner suggested that the athletic hero was not much of a heroic figure and not a symbol of anything, certainly not of the crassness and boobery of all baseball players. Many other Lardnerian urban and suburban citizens shared Keefe's blustering vanity and unrealistic self-image. Lardner mistrusted not ballplayers but popular heroes with self-inflated egos. (p. 109)

At the center of diffuse modern American life, Lardner found a cluster of social games that revealed what passed for reality in social relations. The tensions in this most uncommunicative of men are shown most strongly in his scores of characters who talk past each other in their attempts at finding a link with other human beings. The shallow surface life of his bragging characters is relieved only occasionally by a wise narrator or by their own unconscious hilarity. His work is replete with ballplayers, fans, newsmen, bridge players, and golf caddies, all filling what seemed to be endless days, isolated in one sort of competition or another.

Lardner had a vision of suburban America at play throughout the 1920s, and he wrote that new social freedoms would dictate a widened scope of "games." He saw that the new age's social disorder could be depicted through its games and game players, the roarer sitting in the big league dugout, the con man sitting at the bridge table at a suburban country club, the competitor as a potential menace to the spirit. Lardner was no apologist for organized sport and competition but then he was no advocate of free play either. He discerned no higher American values or common good to come out of a national obsession; he mistrusted obsessions of any kind, communal or personal. (p. 110)

Jack Keefe, Lardner's first baseball protagonist, grew out of Lardner's association with ballplayers, their speech, and their lives. The vernacular that Keefe uses in writing letters home to his old friend, Al, is the speech of Niles and semiliterate America. Lardner made a clean break with the dialect tradition. His characters were always representative of the new middle class, suggesting that the new urban and suburban citizen was bound to his neighbor by immersion in the common milieu of the present rather than the linguistic roots and customs of an ethnic past. Baseball, the great unifying force of American popular sport, was a superb choice for creating a bewildered representative of mass man—at once a hero to thousands yet under financial and emotional stress, a character caught in a commercial system against which he blusters with all the instincts of a frontier roarer.

Standing at the center of popular athletic fame in Lardner's work are isolated, ignorant, and frightened men caught in an unreal world of adulation that they could not assimilate into their personal lives. The tension between an individual American athletic hero and his restriction to a commercial team is highlighted in Keefe, the "busher," a young man lacking self-knowledge, control, and tenderness. The role of Keefe suggests not that ballplayers are all braggarts and louts, but that the modern popular hero is an artificial creation fed by the hero's knowledge of his own heroism in the public eye; however, he is mystified by how to transfer this leverage and notoriety into his personal life, which remains a romantic and financial shambles. Nothing in Jack Keefe's life in Bedford has prepared him for the daily stresses of life in Chicago, performance on a major league team, the advances of designing women, and the frustration of his own appetites. He learns nothing; his teammates, manager, and owner alternately write him off as not worth the trouble in spite of his talent.

The epistolary form is here almost that of a diary, a perfect format for a ballplayer's life that moves slowly, day by day and game by game. Jack reports incidents that fix him in the reader's mind while passing over his own head. His run-on quotations and repetitive word choice add to the dreariness of his accounts. He knows nothing of why the joke is so often on him; fully half the remarks made in the novel are beyond him. His own gaffes are seized on by others in derision, causing him to become belligerent and to withdraw further into the shell of his wounded vanity. (pp. 112-13)

His bragging is hollow; he has no free will; his public performance is controlled by the team; his private life is manipulated by his wife and her relatives. Ostensibly a hero figure, Jack is, in actuality, a little man to whom things happen.

Increasingly after the Civil War, the Popular Sports Hero had to perform in the arena for spectators; he was a diminished figure in relation to the backwoods heroes of the almanacs and Southwestern Humor tales. Natty Bumppo's conflict with Judge Temple had been over substantive issues in American conduct. In contrast, Jack Keefe has no sporting code, no ideals. His only issue is money, and he loses his salary battle with Comiskey, owner of his own "settlement." Jack's only function is to win, and by that criterion alone is he judged. Lardner reinforces the *agon* as the only valid category of play in the modern Popular Sports Hero's experience. There is no higher order of sport than competition.

Lardner loaded Jack's letters with references to actual ballplayers and teams. Their appearances enhanced the realism of Jack's letters and allowed Lardner to rework the consistent theme of Jack's overestimation of his own worth. (pp. 113-14)

Jack himself is not a hero-worshipper because, in his view, no ballplayer can measure up to his own skills, except by luck or trickery. In an inversion of a conventional pulp fiction ending, Jack throws a ball at a batter's head in extra innings with the bases loaded and the score tied because he has a grudge against him. Jack gets his man, loses the game, and earns a fifty-dollar fine from his manager. Jack then writes, "And how could a man go to 1st base and the winning run be forced in if he was dead which he should ought to of been the lucky left-handed stiff . . . ." . . . This violent reaction is stronger because it comes from Jack who is usually all bluster with little real animosity. However, Lardner's most intriguing baseball story, **"My Roomy,"** . . . ends with Buster Elliott, the disturbed hero, in an asylum for having attempted to murder his girlfriend and her new lover with a baseball bat. Elliott writes to his former roommate, the story's narrator, "Old Roomy: I was at bat twice and made two hits; but I guess I did not meet 'em square. They tell me they are both alive yet, which I did not mean them to be."

The similarities between these two passages, written at approximately the same period, show how Lardner could take comic material and turn it into a personal tragedy. Jack's bragging turns chilling with Elliott's attempted murder of his girl. The pugnacity always lurking in Jack in response to what he feels is a hostile world is carried through by Elliott, who relates, "That's my business, busting things." Whereas Jack is a sometime-success, showing just enough promise to be suffered for years by the White Sox, Elliott is a thorough outsider, a prodigious slugger who refuses even to attempt to catch fly balls. Indeed, Elliott is a modern athletic reincarnation of a Bartleby, albeit with some manic energy. Elliott's antics are so bizarre as to dictate his release by the team because his mockery of procedure digs at unity; there is a submerged terror evinced by the player who does everything backwards, who sees nothing in conventional threats, who relies on personal quirks to dictate his actions at any given moment. The game is mocked by his aberrations. Tension increases between Elliott and his mates. His loneliness is best described by his sympathetic roommate who comments, "What could you say to a guy who hated himself like that?"

The sports frame throws into bold relief every personal peculiarity. Tales of ballplayers' inability to abide by curfew, meal times, train schedules, and simple field procedures are legion. Elliott's disorientations are overwhelming and all the more so since they literally take place in the public eye. He is rejected even by the narrator who is the only player who would finally consent to room with him. The greatest ballplayer of the time, Ty Cobb, manifested serious personality disorders both on and off the field; however, Cobb's performance was of such brilliance that often his frightened teammates put up with his violence and paranoia. During Cobb's career, Lardner had nothing but praise for his brainy play and competitive drive. It is probable that he was glossing over the facts; as his sports-writer learns in **"Champion,"** "the people don't want to see him knocked. . . ."

As a member of the team, the problem of belonging, of performing day after day, defeats Elliott and highlights his isolation. Lardner complicated both a ballplayer's psyche and the question of his fundamental duties and relations. The individual problems of a team member would become a major theme in later sports fiction. The theme chronicled an American social dilemma which far transcended the playing field, but the field served as an excellent microcosm for investigation of American society. What is the cost of personal freedom? What allegiances are owed to the team, the group, the company, the family, or the society?

Lardner raised questions but he did not answer them. A sober insider in the life of the teams he covered as a newspaperman, Lardner was always with them but not of them; he always preserved a solitary core. This could be ascribed to the traditional role of the artist; but since Lardner himself would have rejected that notion, one must say that the distance he kept in all his relations was one of fear of deeper emotions spilling over, of scenes that could not be controlled. Control is what his narrators possess over their feelings and desires, what his rubes and bushers never achieve. A game with rules and rigid logic was most congenial to his need for an external order. So many of his disordered characters are kept at arm's length from the reader, their bizarre or foolish actions filtered through a cool narrator who stands between the reader and their anarchy. However, the narrator of **"My Roomy"** does stand up for Elliott; Al, we assume, reads, thinks about, and answers his old friend Jack Keefe at some length, trying to help him cope with city life.

Most of Lardner's early baseball fiction is lighter than **"My Roomy,"** but still portrays a variety of characters. In **"Horseshoes,"** an exasperated player-narrator relates the impossible luck of a teammate in staying clear of responsibility for on-the-field blunders; however, the reader perceives that it is the narrator's self-hatred and inferiority complex that keeps him from success. In **"Harmony,"** an older player is credited with scouting a young slugger for his team. In reality, he never saw the youth play but championed him because of his excellent tenor voice; the team was short one member in its barbershop quartet. The "harmony" is extended from a musical term to the well-being of the team in general. **"Alibi Ike"** as a title is almost self-evident; it refers to the insufferable player with an excuse for every miscue whom the team razzes but ultimately nurtures.

As early as 1921, Lardner was revealing his disenchantment with the emphasis on the slugger in baseball. . . . Along with his dislike of what he felt to be a poor caliber of play, Lardner also criticized the audience: "We don't play because (1) we lack imagination, and because (2) we are a nation of hero worshippers. . . . But hero worship is the disease that does the most to keep the grandstands full and the playgrounds empty." The heart of Lardner's quarrel with baseball can be seen in **"Hurry Kane"** when the ignorant but amazing young pitcher, a 36-game winner as a rookie, consents to fix the World Series to enable him to obtain the money he needs to impress a showgirl. When he learns she is only stringing him along, he reverses form to win the deciding game, a cynical transformation of the conclusion of **"Along Came Ruth."** . . . Such tainted reformations had their bitter irony. Jack Keefe was many things but one could hardly imagine him as a fixer. Elmer Kane's "moral" decision to go against the gamblers did not exist in reality. In [**"The Battle of the Century," "The Venomous Viper of the Volga,"** and **"Greek Tragedy"**] . . . Lardner satirized the fans at wrestling and boxing matches even more pointedly than the performers, who at least knew what they were doing.

Lardner did change his views about sport in the 1920s to some extent but he did not regret his years of writing about it. His defects as a writer were, if anything, masked by his early work in an environment in which he was most comfortable. His creation of baseball "boobs" was extended by others, who attributed to ballplayers qualities ranging from limited intellect to utter boorishness. No small amount of the public's conception of the professional athlete today springs directly from Lardner's early success at creating humorous sports characters in his fiction. Lardner's triumph made the professional athlete a subject for comedy for decades. Lardner's prototypes remain both on the field and in the literary imagination where writers have appropriated his comic ballplayers for more sophisticated ends. Lardner's continual mastery of popular sport consisted in part in his doing what any innovative popular artist does, in giving back mass experience through art with a heightened awareness of its meaning. He identified the Popular Sports Hero and shaped the conventions of his presentation. (pp. 114-17)

Lardner's temperament and aims were, in general outline, similar to those of Longstreet, [Thomas Bangs] Thorpe, Hooper, and Harris, while his characters were more akin to the first-generation urban citizens of Dunne and Ade. Lardner's conservatism was evidenced in many ways. He was always slightly out-of-date in the songs he preferred, in the kind of baseball he liked to watch, and in his own writing, in which he eschewed any mention of sex at a time when strictures of presentation were being relaxed. Late in life, he led a quixotic campaign against suggestive lyrics in popular music, a crusade that dismayed both Fitzgerald and Hemingway. (pp. 119-20)

He implicitly mourned a passing life by criticizing the new order just as the Southwesterners had criticized backwoods manners and mores to show their distance from that scene. His ballplayers and fans existed in the same social stratum, that of the middle class. Just as surely as Longstreet, Hooper, and Harris, Lardner knew that the social bonds of a community were reported through its games.

One of the ways in which Lardner worked with the elements of comic realism was to highlight the disparity between the almanac physical-prowess hero such as Crockett and Fink and the outcast Southwestern hero such as Ransy Sniffle or Sut Lovingood. The character of Jack Keefe has both a public and private role as he is both Crockett and Sut. He performs feats in the full glare of modern spectacle on the diamond, but in his private life he feels rejected and duped and looks to battle his enemies, real and imagined. Jack is constantly contesting his tormenters off the field. He should have heroic stature because of his public role but he does not.

In **"Champion,"** . . . Lardner took on an entire society's cherished beliefs about its athletic heroes when he wrote about middleweight champion Midge Kelly. Boxers, managers, fans, sportswriters—no one is spared in this tale in which Lardner created not simply a picture of a brutal fighter but of a character who was nothing more than a thug in love with violence. Midge's personality is well known to all who have the personal misfortune to depend upon or interact with him. Yet the public is force-fed conventional lies by the sportswriters about his upstanding character. The tone is established at the outset: "Midge Kelly scored his first knockout when he was seventeen. The knockee was his brother Connie, three years his junior and a cripple. The purse was a half dollar given to the youngster by a lady whose electric had just missed bumping his soul from his frail little body." This paragraph parodies the line account of a fight by a wire service, giving all essential information as to fighter, opponent, and purse. However, the tone is one of derision and even bemused acceptance of Midge's character. The effect of "frail little body" and "knockee" gives the reader an early gauge to the moral stance of the tale. The narrator already knows the truth about Midge Kelly; the reader learns it brutally at the outset but it takes him longer to realize why the narrator is so cynical. (pp. 120-21)

Lardner directed the brunt of his message in **"Champion"** at the sportswriting profession rather than solely at Kelly, whom he never really attempts to make into a believable villain. The cartoon monster Kelly is intentionally as unsatisfactory a portrait as the saccharine family man presented in the Sunday sports section. Lardner very neatly balanced these two polarized descriptions to give the reader a chance to be influenced by his final point about the responsibility of the sporting press. In his view, it was a continuing dilemma, one that still rages between those writers who gloss over the peccadilloes of popular heroes and those reporters who sensationalize the men behind the heroic postures or humanize them, all in the name of selling the heroes for the widest possible commercial consumption. (p. 121)

Lardner's conception of American fandom was to become increasingly pessimistic in the 1920s. The atmosphere of hero-worship is criticized in a number of Lardner tales of athletes, usually by the wise narrator, a teammate, roommate, umpire, or writer, who knows the hero behind the scenes. These figures—the sympathetic teammate of **"My Roomy"**; Al, by implication in ***A Busher's Letters;*** the narrators of such tales as [**"Sick 'Em," "Alibi Ike," "Harmony," "The Holdout," "The Battle of the Century," "Hurry Kane," "The Venomous Viper of the Volga,"** and **"Take a Walk"**] . . .—give testimony to the fact that Lardner's ballplayers were not all dolts and blusterers. The stories are invariably related by a wise, sane, and often kind member of the athletic fraternity whose balance and good humor enable him to characterize the comic hero. **"Harmony"** includes a touch of pathos in the sportswriter's story of a veteran ballplayer's search for companionship in the team's barbershop quartet. An umpire in **"Take a Walk"** sympathetically recounts another umpire's lonely life in rented rooms and his fruitless love for a young girl who prefers a vain young slugging third baseman. The manager of **"Holdout"** stands up for a raise for his first baseman who is about to become a father. The baby is then named after the manager by the grateful player.

Such reporter-narrators were reminiscent of the Southwestern tradition. Longstreet always wrote from the gentleman's viewpoint, a man above the comic action. . . . Even Harris' Sut was relating all his adventures to "George," the author/confidant, who transcribed Sut's tales just the way he spoke them as one must believe Al has turned over Jack Keefe's letters for publication. The position of reporter is assumed by an insider in Lardner's athletic tales. He functions as an observer of comic heroes, both those of prowess and of wit; he records their boasts, their deeds, and their essential lack of self-control and self-knowledge. However, his status presupposes an alternative world of order and reason within the team itself, a motive force that enables the unit to withstand the stress put on it by the clown or troublemaker. This character has never been given his due by Lardner's critics. This bemused insider, a rejoinder to the stock conception of Lardner's dumb ballplayers, also appears in Lardner's nonsports narratives, most notably as Finch, the put-upon husband in ***The Big Town***. . . . (pp. 121-22)

The role of the reporter, so ingrained in Lardner as a newspaperman, was first utilized in his baseball tales and then transferred to his other fiction. Lardner came to the frame narrator in his own way through his newspaper experience, his temperamental role as an observer, and his critical view of modern life. He needed to appropriate a form that would enhance portraits of comic heroes who could only lose force if made the focal point of the narration, since they did not have the depth, moral sense, or self-irony to criticize themselves. (p. 123)

Far from being the source of amusement to their teammates, the Keefes, Elliotts, and Kanes are exasperating and are suffered by the team in the hope that their performance will cancel out their personal foibles. The player who drew attention because of his personality or off-the-field affairs might have been the best fictional subject but his performance was the opposite of what Lardner admired, namely smart play and consistency as he carefully explained in a 1915 *American Magazine* series. A definite split existed between the comic athletes of his short stories and the winning players he respected most: those who evinced professionalism in their work.

It is erroneous to see Lardner as a descendant of Twain. His narrators finally lacked the breadth of humanity that characterized so many of Twain's narrators. Whole areas of human pathology which Twain vividly exposed were closed to Lardner, the student of surface manners. In this way, too, Lardner can more truthfully be placed in a direct line from the more provincial Southwestern Humorists. His attitude toward undisciplined ballplayers is analogous to the Southwesterners' jaundiced view of the backwoods athlete and confidence man. Both Lardner and the Southwesterners wrote in a mixture of amusement and dismay at their subjects' vitality and energy. They reproduced with fidelity their speech and habits. Lardner's narrators are the equivalents of the Southwestern gentleman travellers and hunters, raconteurs, collectors of tall tales. He, too, wrote of a society in flux and created the Popular Sports Hero as one of its representative men. (pp. 123-24)

The general movement in contemporary sports fiction has been for the reporter, player, or player-as-reporter to be the controlling narrator, most often in first person. Lardner's fiction firmly established this convention. (p. 124)

Christian K. Messenger, "Lardner: The Popular Sports Hero," in his Sport and the Spirit of Play in American Fiction: Hawthorne to Faulkner, *Columbia University Press, 1981, pp. 108-28.*

ADDITIONAL BIBLIOGRAPHY

Anderson, Sherwood. "Meeting Ring Lardner." In his *No Swank*, pp. 1-7. Philadelphia: Centaur Press, 1934.

Recounts two meetings with Lardner. Anderson believed that Lardner was an essentially warm, shy man who hid his true nature behind a mask of wit and gregariousness.

Broun, Heywood. "Nature the Copycat." In his *It Seems to Me: 1925-1935*, pp. 297-99. New York: Harcourt, Brace and Co., 1935.

Salutes Lardner as the "inventor" of such colorful baseball heroes as Dizzy and Daffy Dean, Schoolboy Rowe, and other participants in the 1934 World Series. Broun quotes a friend's comment that "Lardner invented Dizzy Dean. Here is Elmer the Great come to life. Could any author ask for more?"

Geismar, Maxwell. *Ring Lardner and the Portrait of Folly*. New York: Thomas Y. Crowell Co., 1972, 166 p.

An introductory critical biography by one of Lardner's longtime admirers and critics.

Goldstein, Melvin. "A Note on a Perfect Crime." *Literature and Psychology* XI, No. 3 (Summer 1961): 65-7.

A psychological interpretation of "Haircut." The critic holds that the story is "essentially concerned with a man whose self-destructive impulses are so intense and so close to the level of consciousness that all of his acts are performed in a search for final punishment."

Hasley, Louis. "Ring Lardner: The Ashes of Idealism." *The Arizona Quarterly* 26, No. 3 (Autumn 1970): 219-32.

Surveys Lardner's career, which Hasley divided into three phases similar in progression to the career of Mark Twain. The first period, dominated by humor, ended in 1921 with *Symptoms of Being Thirty-Five* and *The Big Town*. The second, which ended in 1929, produced Lardner's most famous stories and was dominated by satire. The final period, which ended with his *New Yorker* articles and his death, was pervaded by pessimism, despair, and nihilism.

Ingram, Forrest L. "Fun at the Incinerating Plant: Lardner's Wry Waste Land." In *The Twenties: Fiction, Poetry, Drama*, edited by Warren French, pp. 111-22. Deland, Fla.: Everett/Edwards, 1975.

Surveys the major works of Lardner's career, finding them reflective of the pessimistic spirit of T. S. Eliot's poem "The Waste Land."

Kasten, Margaret Cotton. "The Satire of Ring Lardner." *The English Journal* XXXVI, No. 4 (April 1947): 192-95.

On the deceptive nature of Lardner's satire. To illustrate, Kasten discusses three stories—"Champion," "The Golden Honeymoon," and "Haircut"—and reprints excerpts from the essays of college students who failed to perceive the satire in "Haircut," one of whom saw the loutish Jim Kendall as "a man with whom one could spend a delightful evening."

Masson, Thomas L. "Ring W. Lardner." In his *Our American Humorists*, pp. 186-208. 1931. Reprint. Freeport, N.Y.: Books for Libraries Press, 1966.

Praise for Lardner's humor, including several sizable and entertaining excerpts from Lardner's own writings.

Mencken, H. L. "Pongo Americanus." *The American Mercury* XXIX, No. 113 (June 1933): 254-55.

Praises Lardner as a perceptive portrayer of American stupidity. In a short final paragraph, Mencken favorably reviews *Lose with a Smile*.

Moseley, Merritt. "Ring Lardner and the American Humor Tradition." *South Atlantic Review* 46, No. 1 (January 1981): 42-60.

Finds Lardner to be "firmly in the tradition" of the late nineteenth- and early twentieth-century "literary comedians."

Overton, Grant. "Ring W. Lardner's Bell Lettres." *The Bookman*, New York LXII, No. 1 (September 1925): 44-9.

An amusing and admiring overview of Lardner's life and work, written in semiliterate slang reminiscent of one of Lardner's own characters.

Pritchett, V. S. "The Talent of Ring Lardner." *New Statesman* LVII, No. 1467 (25 April 1959): 580-81.

Discusses Lardner's skill in "yarning" in the tradition of Mark Twain and contrasts American and English humor, noting differences in attitude towards sports.

Sheed, Wilfrid. Review of *The Lardners: My Family Remembered*, by Ring Lardner, Jr. In his *The Good Word, and Other Words*, pp. 254-58. New York: E. P. Dutton, 1978.

Makes several revealing references to Lardner's life and work. This essay originally appeared in *The New York Times Book Review* in 1976.

Sherman, Stuart. "Ring Lardner: Hard-Boiled Americans." In his *The Main Stream*, pp. 168-75. New York: Charles Scribner's Sons, 1927.

Reprints an admiring review of *The Love Nest, and Other Stories* and surveys Lardner's major works.

Smith, Leverett T., Jr. "'The Diameter of Frank Chance's Diamond': Ring Lardner and Professional Sports." *Journal of Popular Culture* VI, No. 1 (Summer 1972): 133-56.

Posits reasons for the change in Lardner's attitude toward professional sports after 1919, a change reflected in his fiction. Smith holds that "after 1919 Lardner became concerned with two developments that he felt were hurting the quality of professional sports: a new, and, to Lardner, inferior style of play was introduced and this style appealed to the fan's lowest impulses. After 1919, much of his writing that did concern itself with sports was concerned with attacking the new style of play, particularly in baseball, or with attacking the fans for their stupidity in enjoying it."

Spatz, Jonas. "Ring Lardner: Not an Escape, but a Reflection." In *The Twenties: Fiction, Poetry, Drama*, edited by Warren French, pp. 101-10. Deland, Fla.: Everett/Edwards, 1975.

A general survey of Lardner's short stories that places the major stories in the literary tradition of despair that had begun in the early 1920s with T. S. Eliot's "The Waste Land."

Webb, Howard W., Jr. "Mark Twain and Ring Lardner." *The Mark Twain Journal* XI, No. 2 (Summer 1960): 13-15.

Comparison showing that Lardner's "background, the sources of his interest in language, the nature and function of the vernacular in his writings—all these place him in marked contrast with Twain." And although Twain was the greater writer, Lardner's "use of the common speech was a tributary to that stream which Hemingway and others were to swell to a flood."

Yates, Norris W. "The Isolated Man of Ring Lardner." In his *The American Humorist: Conscience of the Twentieth Century*, pp. 165-93. Ames: Iowa State University Press, 1964.

Surveys Lardner's career and holds that "the implied message of his work is one of nihilism and despair. His nice guys finish last, and very few of them are even nice guys. In a wasteland of 'normalcy' where there are no heroes and the common man is commonly too much of a boob—however 'wise'—to be worshipped according to the democratic dogma of the liberals, there isn't much left."

Thomas Mann

1875-1955

German novelist, short story and novella writer, essayist, and critic.

The following entry presents criticism of Mann's novella *Der Tod in Venedig (Death in Venice)*. For a complete discussion of Mann's career, see *TCLC*, Volumes 2 and 8.

Death in Venice is considered among the finest novellas in world literature. The work skillfully combines psychological realism and mythological symbolism to create a multi-dimensional story that explores the moral transformation undergone by the artist in quest of perfect beauty. This classic situation is depicted in the decline and ultimate collapse of Mann's artist-hero Gustave von Aschenbach, a renowned German author who, after years of living a morally and artistically ascetic life, surrenders to the sensual side of his nature during a sojourn in Venice. There, the sultry Venetian setting incites Aschenbach's homoerotic passion for Tadzio, a beautiful, godlike youth. As Aschenbach succumbs to long-repressed spiritual and physical desires, he loses control of his will, and his resulting degradation leads to his death.

Published in 1913, *Death in Venice* marks the end of the earliest phase of Mann's career and the beginning of a transitional phase in which the author wrote only nonfiction works for several years. *Death in Venice* was preceded by his first novel, *Buddenbrooks,* which had won him immediate literary recognition, and by two other successful novellas, *Tonio Kröger* and *Tristan*. While these early compositions foreshadow many of the themes found in Mann's later works, including the seductiveness of death and disease, the isolation of the artist in society, and the degenerative effects of art on the individual psyche, *Death in Venice* is the most representative of the decadent, poetic, and ironic stories Mann wrote throughout his career. It was not until *Der Zauberberg (The Magic Mountain),* published eleven years after *Death in Venice,* that he attempted to reconcile the dualism of the spiritual and the physical that troubled his own artistic life and dominated his early works. Although Mann had achieved literary success by the time he wrote *Death in Venice,* he had also met with a measure of failure, as with his drama *Fiorenza,* the novel *Königliche Hoheit (Royal Highness),* and several essays he was unable to complete. Some critics believe that Aschenbach's artistic stagnation in *Death in Venice* depicts a similar impasse experienced by Mann around 1910. He originally conceived the novella as a short tale that would recount the unrequited love of the aged Johann Wolfgang von Goethe for seventeen-year-old Ulrike von Levetzow, but he found that the widely known facts of the story inhibited his creativity. Then in 1911, inspired by Austrian composer Gustave Mahler's death and by a series of incidents witnessed while vacationing on the Lido near Venice, Mann developed a simple story of ''forbidden love'' informed by Friedrich Nietzsche's concept of the Apollonian-Dionysian conflict, which contends that irresolvable discord exists between reason and emotion, or the carnal and the spiritual. It is this basic duality of human nature—long suppressed by the austere Aschenbach—that emerges, compels him to seek respite from his work, and lures him to the exotic, cholera-ridden Venetian seashore.

The Granger Collection, New York

A complex work inviting a diversity of critical interpretations, *Death in Venice* is so infused with vivid images, rich symbolism, and Mann's ironic vision of life that every detail of the novella is vital to the work as a whole. While some commentators consider the novella to be simply another of Mann's ''artist-fables'' after the pattern of his earlier fiction, many others believe that Aschenbach represents the sophisticated European society of 1911 as it stood on the brink of World War I. For this reason critics, as well as Mann himself, have attributed the novella's early popularity to its timeliness in portraying the decadence of modern Europe. Praised for its symphonic structure and perfect form, *Death in Venice* is often compared to the compositions of Richard Wagner, who died in Venice and whose works similarly depict the tension evoked by the ambiguities of love, death, and beauty. Critics observe that in addition to its Wagnerian overtones and Nietzschean philosophy, *Death in Venice* is informed by the philosopher Arthur Schopenhauer's contention that all is nothingness except the amoral ''cosmic will.''

Critics agree that one of the most striking features of Mann's technique in *Death in Venice* is his use of mythological symbolism in combination with psychological realism. The work alternates between realistic depictions of events as Aschenbach sees and experiences them, and symbolic episodes that allude to Greek mythology: a grotesque stranger in a cemetery who melds into the form of a beautiful Greek statue; Tadzio's momentary resemblance to Narcissus, Hermes, and Eros; and images of Dionysian ritual which permeate mundane events within the story. It is acknowledged that *Death in Venice* borrows its mythological elements from other works, particularly Homer's *Odyssey,* Euripides' Bacchae, and the ancient myth of Cupid and Psyche. Mann also utilized dialogues from Plato's *Symposium* and *Phaedrus,* and Plutarch's *Erotikos* to impose a "classical antiquity" and profundity upon the work. With respect to the masterful weaving of "myth plus psychology" in *Death in Venice,* André von Gronicka has concluded that Mann's "bifocal view of life that encompasses both the transcendent and the real develops steadily to reach . . . a degree of perfection which Mann has rarely if ever excelled." According to some critics, elevating *Death in Venice* to a mythical level allowed Mann to more easily broach the sensitive subject of homosexuality. Ignace Feuerlicht has observed that "the allusions to antiquity and its different moral and religious standards definitely softened the blow that many readers felt at the time of the publication of the novella because of the theme of homosexuality."

In Aschenbach's aesthetic appreciation of and lustful infatuation with Tadzio, whom he worships as the apotheosis of beauty and form, critics perceive Mann's questioning of the morality of the artist who seeks art as an end in itself. Many have noted that the outcome of Aschenbach's desire, his death, does not readily resolve the moral issue of the work, but rather asserts Mann's own ambivalent attitude regarding the question. Concerning Mann's ambivalence, T. J. Reed has suggested that Mann was a "reluctant moralist" who first sought a "hymnic" approach to the novella. Similarly, Erich Heller has proposed that "Thomas Mann from beginning to end . . . is both fascinated and agonized by the spirit and passion in their lonely pursuit of themselves. . . . This is why he burst out with the dictum 'Literature is death' . . . , and why he achieves such mastery in a story which offers the exactly appropriate scope to both his sympathy with, and his moral critique of, that love which is death." Regarding *Death in Venice* as one of his most important works, Mann himself was aware of its ambivalent, enigmatic nature, and in a summation of the novella stated: "*Death in Venice* is indeed a crystallization in the true sense of the word; it is a structure, and an image, shedding light from so many facets, by its nature of such inexhaustible allusiveness, that it might well dazzle the eyes of its creator himself as it took shape."

(See also *Contemporary Authors,* Vol. 104.)

D. H. LAWRENCE (essay date 1913)

[*Lawrence, an English novelist and poet, was one of the first novelists to introduce themes of modern psychology into his fiction. In his lifetime he was a controversial figure, both for the explicit sexuality he portrayed in his novels and for his unconventional personal life. Much of the criticism of Lawrence's work concerns his highly individualistic moral system, which is based on absolute freedom of expression—particularly sexual expression. Human sexuality was for Lawrence a symbol of the Life Force, and is frequently pitted against modern industrial society, which he believed was dehumanizing. His most famous novel,* Lady Chatterley's Lover *(1928), was the subject of a landmark obscenity trial in Great Britain in 1960, which turned largely on the legitimacy of Lawrence's inclusion of hitherto forbidden sexual terms. In the following excerpt, Lawrence assesses* Death in Venice *as "well done" while objecting to its "unwholesome" subject and contrived structure. His review originally appeared in a 1913 issue of* The Blue Review, *a short-lived literary magazine that was edited by J. Middleton Murry and Katherine Mansfield. Lawrence's appraisal of* Death in Venice *is itself discussed in the excerpt by Geoffrey Galt Harpham (1982).*]

[Thomas Mann] is personal, almost painfully so, in his subject-matter. In **"Tonio Kröger,"** the long *Novelle* at the end of the ***Tristan*** volume, he paints a detailed portrait of himself as a youth and younger man, a careful analysis. And he expresses at some length the misery of being an artist. "Literature is not a calling, it is a curse." Then he says to the Russian painter girl: "There is no artist anywhere but longs again, my love, for the common life." But any young artist might say that. It is because the stress of life in a young man, but particularly in an artist, is very strong, and has as yet found no outlet, so that it rages inside him in *Sturm und Drang*. But the condition is the same, only more tragic, in the Thomas Mann of fifty-three. He has never found any outlet for himself, save his art. He has never given himself to anything but his art. This is all well and good, if his art absorbs and satisfies him, as it has done some great men, like Corot. But then there are the other artists, the more human, like Shakespeare and Goethe, who must give themselves to life as well as to art. And if these were afraid, or despised life, then with their surplus they would ferment and become rotten. Which is what ails Thomas Mann. He is physically ailing, no doubt. But his complaint is deeper: it is of the soul. (pp. 308-09)

"For endurance of one's fate, grace in suffering, does not only mean passivity, but is an active work, a positive triumph, and the Sebastian figure is the most beautiful symbol, if not of all art, yet of the art in question. If one looked into this portrayed world and saw the elegant self-control that hides from the eyes of the world to the last moment the inner undermining, the biological decay; saw the yellow ugliness which, sensuously at a disadvantage, could blow its choking heat of desire to a pure flame, and even rise to sovereignty in the kingdom of beauty; saw the pale impotence which draws out of the glowing depths of its intellect sufficient strength to subdue a whole vigorous people, bring them to the foot of the Cross, to the feet of impotence; saw the amiable bearing in the empty and severe service of Form; saw the quickly enervating longing and art of the born swindler: if one saw such a fate as this, and all the rest it implied, then one would be forced to doubt whether there were in reality any other heroism than that of weakness. Which heroism, in any case, is more of our time than this?"

Perhaps it is better to give the story of ***Der Tod in Venedig,*** from which the above is taken, and to whose hero it applies.

Gustav von Aschenbach, a fine, famous author, over fifty years of age, coming to the end of a long walk one afternoon, sees as he is approaching a burying place, near Munich, a man standing between the chimeric figures of the gateway. This man in the gate of the cemetery is almost the *Motiv* of the story. By him, Aschenbach is infected with a desire to travel. He examines himself minutely, in a way almost painful in its frankness, and one sees the whole soul of this author of fifty-three. And it seems, the artist has absorbed the man, and yet the man is there, like an exhausted organism on which a parasite has fed itself strong. Then begins a kind of Holbein *Totentanz* ["dance of death"]. The story is quite natural in appearance, and yet there is the gruesome sense of symbolism throughout. The man near the burying ground has suggested travel—but whither? Aschenbach sets off to a watering place on the Austrian coast of the Adriatic, seeking some adventure, some passionate adventure, to which his sick soul and unhealthy body have been kindled. But finding himself on the Adriatic, he knows it is not thither that his desire draws him, and he takes ship for Venice. It is all real, and yet with a curious sinister unreality, like decay, the "biological decay." On board there is a man who reminds one of the man in the gateway, though there is no connexion. (pp. 310-11)

Aschebach takes a gondola to the Lido, and again the gondolier reminds one of the man in the cemetery gateway. He is, moreover, one who will make no concession, and, in spite of Aschenbach's demand to be taken back to St. Mark's, rows him in his black craft to the Lido, talking to himself softly all the while. Then he goes without payment.

The author stays in a fashionable hotel on the Lido. The adventure is coming, there by the pallid sea. As Aschenbach comes down into the hall of the hotel, he sees a beautiful Polish boy of about fourteen, with honey-coloured curls clustering round his pale face, standing with his sisters and their governess.

Aschenbach loves the boy—but almost as a symbol. In him he loves life and youth and beauty, as Hyacinth in the Greek myth. This, I suppose, is blowing the choking heat to pure flame, and raising it to the kingdom of beauty. He follows the boy, watches him all day long on the beach, fascinated by beauty concrete before him. It is still the *Künstler* ["artist"] and his abstraction: but there is also the "yellow ugliness, sensually at a disadvantage," of the elderly man below it all. But the picture of the writer watching the folk on the beach gleams and lives with a curious, gold-phosphorescent light, touched with the brightness of Greek myth, and yet a modern seashore with folks on the sands, and a half-threatening, diseased sky.

Aschenbach, watching the boy in the hotel lift, finds him delicate, almost ill, and the thought that he may not live long fills the elderly writer with a sense of peace. It eases him to think the boy should die.

Then the writer suffers from the effect of the *sirocco,* and intends to depart immediately from Venice. But at the station he finds with joy that his luggage has gone wrong, and he goes straight back to the hotel. There, when he sees Tadzin again, he knows why he could not leave Venice.

There is a month of hot weather, when Aschenbach follows Tadzin about, and begins to receive a look, loving, from over the lad's shoulder. It is wonderful, the heat, the unwholesomeness, the passion in Venice. One evening comes a street singer, smelling of carbolic acid, and sings beneath the veranda of the hotel. And this time, in gruesome symbolism, it is the man from the burying ground distinctly.

The rumour is, that the black cholera is in Venice. An atmosphere of secret plague hangs over the city of canals and palaces. Aschenbach verifies the report at the English bureau, but cannot bring himself to go away from Tadzin, nor yet to warn the Polish family. The secretly pest-smitten days go by. Aschenbach follows the boy through the stinking streets of the town and loses him. And on the day of the departure of the Polish family, the famous author dies of the plague.

It is absolutely, almost intentionally, unwholesome. The man is sick, body and soul. He portrays himself as he is, with wonderful skill and art, portrays his sickness. And since any genuine portrait is valuable, this book has its place. It portrays one man, one atmosphere, one sick vision. It claims to do no more. And we have to allow it. But we know it is unwholesome—it does not strike me as being morbid for all that, it is too well done—and we give it its place as such.

Thomas Mann seems to me the last sick sufferer from the complaint of Flaubert. The latter stood away from life as from a leprosy. And Thomas Mann, like Flaubert, feels vaguely that he has in him something finer than ever physical life revealed. Physical life is a disordered corruption, against which he can fight with only one weapon, his fine aesthetic sense, his feeling for beauty, for perfection, for a certain fitness which soothes him, and gives him an inner pleasure, however corrupt the stuff of life may be. There he is, after all these years, full of disgusts and loathing of himself as Flaubert was, and Germany is being voiced, or partly so, by him. And so, with real suicidal intention, like Flaubert's, he sits, a last too-sick disciple, reducing himself grain by grain to the statement of his own disgust, patiently, self-destructively, so that his statement at least may be perfect in a world of corruption. But he is so late.

Already I find Thomas Mann, who, as he says, fights so hard against the banal in his work, somewhat banal. His expression may be very fine. But by now what he expresses is stale. I think we have learned our lesson, to be sufficiently aware of the fulsomeness of life. And even while he has a rhythm in style, yet his work has none of the rhythm of a living thing, the rise of a poppy, then the after uplift of the bud, the shedding of the calyx and the spreading wide of the petals, the falling of the flower and the pride of the seed-head. There is an unexpectedness in this such as does not come from their carefully plotted and arranged developments. Even *Madame Bovary* seems to me dead in respect to the living rhythm of the whole work. While it is there in *Macbeth* like life itself.

But Thomas Mann is old—and we are young. Germany does not feel very young to me. (pp. 311-13)

D. H. Lawrence, "Literature and Art: German Books, Thomas Mann," in his Phoenix: The Posthumous Papers of D. H. Lawrence, *edited by Edward D. McDonald, Viking Penguin, 1936, William Heinemann, 1936, pp. 308-13.*

THOMAS MANN (letter date 1920)

[*In the following excerpt from a letter to the German poet and critic Carl Maria Weber, Mann responds to Weber's critique of* Death in Venice *and provides several insights that have been useful to critics in their interpretation of the work. For further discussion of Mann's letter to Weber, see the excerpt by T. J. Reed (1974). For further insight into* Death in Venice *by Mann himself, see the excerpt dated 1936.*]

I have read a great many of your poems and found much I liked and much to admire. It is certainly not by chance that you achieve your best effects where your emotion attains the highest degree of freedom and unselfconsciousness, as in the "Swimmers," which contains much of the humaneness of the younger generation, and in "Voluptuousness of Words," a poem of incontestable beauty. I say this although I have written ***Death in Venice,*** for which you have such kind words of defense in your letter—against objections and rebukes which may well be only too familiar to you yourself. I wish you had taken part in the conversation I had about these matters recently, one evening that stretched on and on, with Willy Seidel and another colleague, Kurt Martens. For I should not want you and others to have the impression that a mode of feeling which I respect because it is almost necessarily infused with *mind* (far more necessarily so, at any rate, than the "normal" mode) should be something that I would want to deny or, insofar as it is accessible to me (and I may say, with few reservations, that it is), wish to disavow.

You cleverly and clearly recognized the *artistic* reason why this might seem to be the case. It is inherent in the difference between the Dionysian spirit of lyricism, whose outpouring is irresponsible and individualistic, and the Apollonian, objectively controlled, morally and socially responsible epic. What I was after was an equilibrium of sensuality and morality such as I found perfected in [Johann von Goethe's] *Elective Affinities*, which I read five times, if I remember rightly, while working on ***Death in Venice.*** But that the novella is at its core of a hymnic type, indeed of hymnic origin, cannot have escaped you. The painful process of objectivation, imposed on me by the inner necessities of my nature, is described in the introduction to the otherwise miscarried ***Gesang vom Kindchen.***

Do you recall? Higher frenzy, extraordinary emotion
Once may have come over you too, casting you down
So that you lay, brow in hands, your soul rising
In hymnic praise. Amid tears the struggling spirit
Pressed forward to speak in song. But alas there was no change.
For a sobering effort began then, a chilling command to control.
Behold, *the intoxicate song turned into a moral fable*.

But the artistic reason for the misunderstanding is just one among others; the purely intellectual reasons are actually more important. For example, there is the naturalistic bent of my generation (so foreign to you young people), which compelled me to see the "case" *also* in a pathological light, and to alternate this motif (the climacterium) with the symbolic motif (Tadzio as Hermes Psychopompos). Something still more a matter of intellect, because more personal, was added: the altogether non-"Greek" but rather Protestant, Puritan ("bourgeois") basic state of mind not only of the story's protagonists but also of myself; in other words, our fundamentally mistrustful, fundamentally pessimistic relationship to passion in general. Hans Blüher, whose writings fascinate me (certainly the idea of his "Role of the Erotic," etc., is greatly and profoundly Germanic), once defined eros as the "affirmation of a human being, irrespective of his worth." This definition comprehends all the irony of eros. But a moralist—whose point of view, to be sure, can be only taken *ironice*—would have to comment: "That's a fine kind of affirmation, 'irrespective of worth.' No thanks!"

But more seriously: Passion as confusion and as a stripping of dignity was really the subject of my tale—what I originally wanted to deal with was not anything homoerotic at all. It was the story—seen grotesquely—of the aged Goethe and that little girl in Marienbad whom he was absolutely determined to marry, with the acquiescence of her social-climbing procuress of a mother and despite the outraged horror of his own family, with the girl not wanting it at all—this story with all its terribly comic, shameful, awesomely ridiculous situations, this embarrassing, touching, and grandiose story which I may someday write after all. What was added to the amalgam at the time was a personal, lyrical travel experience that determined me to carry things to an extreme by introducing the motif of "forbidden" love. . . .

I have had to put this letter aside for a while. I did not want to close without having said something further about my relationship to that emotional tendency. You will not demand of me that I place it absolutely above the more common variety. There could be only one reason to place it absolutely *below:* that of its "unnaturalness," a term which Goethe long ago rejected on good grounds. Obviously the law of polarity does not hold unconditionally; the male need not necessarily be attracted by the female. Experience refutes the idea that an attraction to the same sex is necessarily allied to "effeminacy." Experience also teaches, to be sure, that degeneracy, hermaphroditism, intermediate creatures, in short, repulsively pathological elements may be and frequently are involved. That is the medical side of it, which is important but has nothing to do with the intellectual and cultural side of it. On the other hand, it can scarcely be suggested that, say, Michelangelo, Frederick the Great, Winckelmann, Platen, Stefan George were or are unmanly or feminine men. In such cases we see the polarity simply failing, and we observe a masculinity so pronounced that even in erotic matters only the masculine has importance and interest. It does not surprise me for a moment that a natural law (that of polarity) ceases to operate in a realm that in spite of its sensuality has very little to do with nature, far more to do with mind. I see nothing unnatural and a good deal of instructive significance, a good deal of high humanity, in the tenderness of mature masculinity for lovelier and frailer masculinity. In matters of culture, incidentally, homoerotic love is obviously as neutral as the other kind. In both, the individual case is everything; both can generate vulgarity and trash, and both are capable of highest achievement. King Ludwig II of Bavaria is no doubt a type, but the typicality of his instincts seems to me amply balanced by the noble austerity and dignity of such a phenomenon as Stefan George.

As for myself, my interest is somewhat divided between Blüher's two basic forms of social organization, the family and associations of men. I am a family founder and a father by instinct and conviction. I love my children, deepest of all a little girl who very much resembles my wife—to a point that a Frenchman would call idolatry. There you have the "bourgeois." But if we were to speak of eroticism, of unbourgeois intellectually sensual adventures, things would have to be viewed a little differently. The problem of eroticism, indeed the problem of beauty, seems to me comprehended in the tension of life and mind. I have intimated as much in an unexpected context. "The relationship of life and mind," I say in the ***Betrachtungen,*** "is an extremely delicate, difficult, agitating, painful relation charged *with irony and eroticism.*" And I go on to speak of a "covert" yearning which perhaps constitutes the truly philosophical and poetical relationship of mind to life. "For yearning passes back and forth between mind and life. Life, too, longs for mind. Two worlds whose relation is erotic *without clarification of the sexual polarity,* without the one representing the male and the other the female principle: such are life and mind. *Therefore there is no union between them, but only the brief, inebriating illusion of union and understanding, an eternal tension without resolution. . . . It is the problem of beauty* that the mind feels life and life feels mind as 'beautiful.' . . . The mind that loves is not fanatical; it is ingenious, political; it woos, and its wooing is erotic irony. . . ."

Tell me whether one can "betray" oneself any better than that. My idea of eroticism, my *experience* of it, is completely expressed in those lines. But finally, what else have we here if not the translation of one of the world's most beautiful love poems into the language of criticism and prose, [Friedrich Hölderlin's] poem whose final stanza begins: "Wer das Tiefste *gedacht*, liebt das *Lebendigste*" ["He whose thought has plumbed deepest loves life at its height"]. (pp. 102-05)

This wonderful poem contains the whole justification of the emotional tendency in question, and the whole explanation of it, which is mine also. To be sure, Stefan George has said that in ***Death in Venice*** the highest is drawn down into the realm of decadence—and he is right; I did not pass unscathed through the naturalistic school. But disavowal, denunciation? No. (p. 105)

Thomas Mann, in a letter to Carl Maria Weber on July 4, 1920, in his Letters of Thomas Mann: 1889-1955, *edited and translated by Richard Winston and Clara Winston, Alfred A. Knopf, 1971, pp. 102-06.*

CUTHBERT WRIGHT (essay date 1925)

[*In the following excerpt, Wright favorably reviews the first English translation of* Death in Venice.]

[When ***Death in Venice***] was first translated in *The Dial* I recall someone saying to me: "It is astonishing with what art the author introduces details and episodes which heighten in the reader a cumulative sense of excitement, disquiet, almost of terror, the preparation for some ultimate spiritual disaster which the artist never completely reveals even to the last sentence of the book." This is true. One recalls the meeting with the strange traveller on the steps of the Funeral Hall at Munich in the setting sun; the episode of the aging and painted fop gesticulating on the quay; and the sinister voyage in the gondola, shaped like a coffin, headed unaccountably for the open sea. The symbolism is so delicately implicit that in comparison the symbolism of Ibsen himself seems artificial and obtrusive, dragged in by all its hairs. (p. 422)

[Mann's] motive for writing such a story, like the emotion of his hero, may have been nameless or irreducible to language; nevertheless the artist has intensely felt something, and partly by his intensity, partly by his persuasive art, has so transmitted it that the reader dimly feels it also. Only it was amusing and perhaps essential to transform the primary emotion into the stuff of a purely intellectual problem, an adventure in fiction; to invent, in short, a secondary value, a device repeated any number of times in great literature, and familiar to us, in a highly ingenious and perverse form, in Henry James's *Turn of the Screw*. The factual elements of ***Death in Venice*** are so simple as to be what the French call *simplistes*. An aging artist in need of a vacation comes upon a little boy at a watering-place. In the presence of the child he experiences a sense of happiness and well-being, so intense that he feels his tired energies stirring in a last and perfect manifestation, and composes a book which is classically linear and beautiful like the boy himself. So far a comprehensible and innocent idyll. Then the *deus ex machina* emerges in the form of the cholera; the authorities are silent fearing for their trade; the boy and his family, unwarned, stay on in the plague-stricken city; and the great writer, knowing the danger, oblivious of his reputation and noble past, stays on also, refrains from warning them, and braves death and disgrace for the sake of his obsession, for a daily sight of the beauty, the idol, he has never even spoken to. . . . The catastrophe is all prepared; and the illustrious man of fifty, the national mirror of discipline and dignity, is shaken by an abnormal emotion so intense that he commits what is substantially a crime.

So much for the actual story. It is a little *simpliste*, I have said, but it is very beautifully wrought, and is the sort of thing that might have occurred to a German, especially since the war. As for the latent story, "the inner and spiritual grace," as says the Prayer Book, it is unnecessary, and indeed impossible, to follow it in a notice merely intended to praise a delicate achievement on the part of a distinguished writer. (pp. 424-25)

Cuthbert Wright, "Eros," in The Dial, *Vol. 78, No. 5, May, 1925, pp. 420-25.*

THOMAS MANN (essay date 1936)

[*In the preface to his* Stories of Three Decades, *from which the following excerpt is taken, Mann recalls the occasion and inspiration of* Death in Venice. *For a more revealing discussion of the novella's genesis by Mann, see the excerpt dated 1920.*]

The immediate occasion of the tale [***Death in Venice***] was a chance stay on the Lido; it was conceived as modestly as are all my enterprises, a kind of improvisation, to be written as quickly as might be, and serving as an interlude to work on ***Felix Krull***. But creation has its own laws. ***Buddenbrooks***, planned with Kielland as a model for a novel of merchant life, to run to some two hundred and fifty pages at most, displayed a will of its own. ***The Magic Mountain*** when its turn came was to be quite as headstrong; and the story of Aschenbach, the hero of ***Death in Venice***, proved persistent well beyond the terminus which I had fixed for it. Every piece of work is in fact a realization—piecemeal if you like, but each complete in itself—of our own nature; they are stones on that harsh road which we must walk to learn of ourselves. No wonder, then, that each one in turn is a surprise to us! ***Death in Venice*** is indeed a crystallization in the true sense of the word; it is a structure, and an image, shedding light from so many facets, by its nature of such inexhaustible allusiveness, that it might well dazzle the eyes of its creator himself as it took shape. It had its place in time almost immediately before the war—it appeared in 1912—and if at this distance I may judge it objectively, it possesses in its way the same intense timeliness of mood that ***Tonio Kröger*** had—which may explain the impression it produced when it appeared in the *Neue Rundschau*, and also in other countries, in France and in America. Despite its small compass I incline to reckon this book as well as ***Tonio Kröger*** not with my slighter but with my more important works. (pp. vii-viii)

Thomas Mann, in a preface to his Stories of Three Decades, *translated by H. T. Lowe-Porter, Alfred A. Knopf, 1936, pp. v-ix.*

CYRIL CONNOLLY (essay date 1936)

[*Connolly was an English novelist and critic who reviewed books for the* New Statesman, The Observer, *and* The Sunday Times *from 1927 until his death in 1974. Considered a remarkably hard-to-please critic, he was the founding editor of the respected literary monthly* Horizon *(1939-1950). In the following excerpt from a 1936 review of Mann's* Stories of Three Decades—*a collection which includes* Death in Venice—*Connolly compares the inevitability of Aschenbach's doom in* Death in Venice *to the decline of the great protagonists of classical Greek tragedy.*]

I am inclined to think that though perfect in many details, and in form especially, there is something a little artificial, almost arty, about the homosexual element [in ***Death in Venice***]—which is not deep and honest enough—and something a little vulgar about the thick palette which is used to describe the plague in Venice—but how, if one can't read German, can one lay down the law?

Death in Venice is based on a fundamental but neglected principle of tragedy: the sequence of cause and effect. When von Aschenbach, the austere great writer, is suddenly prompted to go to Venice by the appearance of a wayfarer in a Munich cemetery, we feel that he is doomed as any bull that enters the arena, creature of equal dignity or fire. All von Aschenbach's elaborate spartanism crumbles under the strain of his passion for a Polish boy whom he sees when he arrives on the Lido. During the whole book they never speak, but Aschenbach goes through all the stages of a desperate and irremediable passion, blundering through Venice in pursuit of his idol as the bull blunders after the sword that will kill it, and as the one sinks down to die, its back planted with absurd streamers, so Aschenbach, now painted, powdered, and rejuvenated by dyed hair, is carried off by the plague. The plague in Venice forms the background, as if the author had understood that the city's essential spirit, torrid, sinister, pagan and decayed, could reveal itself only in such a décor. Death appears in many shapes through the book which, in spite of the Wagnerian union of love and death and the heavy quality of German Hellenism, has the frozen completeness of a work of art, a classic example of the tragic breaking-up of a fine character through the fatal abandon of age to its "sola et sera voluptas" ["solitary belated pleasures"]—love for what Proust called "la jeunesse féroce et légère" ["beastly and thoughtless youth"]. (pp. 66-7)

Cyril Connolly, "The Position of Joyce: Thomas Mann," in his The Condemned Playground, Essays: 1927-1944, *The Macmillan Company, 1946, pp. 63-7.*

VERNON VENABLE (essay date 1938)

[*In the following excerpt, Venable discusses the symbolic structure of* Death in Venice *and praises Mann's poetic style, which enables the symbolic associations throughout the story to subtly impress themselves upon the reader. For further discussions of Mann's use of symbolism in* Death in Venice, *see the excerpts by Frank Donald Hirschbach (1955) and J. R. McWilliams (1967).*]

"Death in Venice" is a powerful, strangely haunting, and tragic story about a middle-aged artist who takes a holiday from his work, and finds himself held in Venice by the charms of a twelve-year old boy until he goes to seed in a most shocking way, and at last succumbs to the plague which he might otherwise have fled. There is no more of a plot than that. There are other people, however, who wander in and out of the story apparently at random, but who leave their mark both on the artist, Aschenbach, and on the reader: a red-haired, snub-nosed traveler, whose vitality and air of distant climes first suggest to Aschenbach that he himself go off on a trip; a painted and primped old scapegrace from Pola who gets on Aschenbach's Venice-bound steamer with a coterie of young men; a gondolier, sinister of aspect, who rows Aschenbach from Venice to the Lido and vanishes without collecting his money; a mendicant singer who, shortly before Aschenbach's death, goes through his comic turns on the porch of the hotel, smelling all the while of the carbolic acid which has become associated with the plague.

These people seem to serve only as atmosphere, to be quite unrelated both to one another and to the development of the story, but in truth they constitute the very structure of its elaboration. One is reminded of the musical form known as the passacaglia, where a ground bass, repeating the same theme over and over again for progressive variations in the upper register, occasionally emerges into the treble itself, with the effect of affirming emphatically the singleness of the thematic material in both registers.

In **"Death in Venice,"** the treble is the simple narrative sequence of Aschenbach's voyage, his life on the Lido, his love for the boy Tadzio, and his death. The ground bass is the "life and death" theme repeated as a sort of undertone to the story by those characters who seem to have no very obvious connection with the proper narrative content. (pp. 64-5)

This is a comparatively easy accomplishment for the musician, whose medium does not involve meaning, but it demands rare subtlety from a writer. Mr. Mann's deftness is, of course, prodigious, and he contrives to keep his formalized meanings from the explicit attention of the reader largely by the simple technical expedient of hiding them from Aschenbach himself.

For example, Aschenbach never notices—and hence the reader seldom does—that the vital stranger who aroused in him the desire to stop working and to try merely living for a while, is the same man as the sinister gondolier who later ferries him to the Lido and his eventual death, and that the clowning beggar of the hotel porch is none other than the gondolier still further down at the heel. Nor is he ever aware that this ubiquitous person bears a shocking resemblance to the loathsome old fop from Pola. Least of all does it occur to him that all of these questionable people, as morbid caricatures of the heroes of his own novels, are really merely images of himself and his loved-one Tadzio, though it is this final identification which constitutes the meaning and effect of the entire story.

If, as readers, we are not supposed to be consciously aware of these relationships, we may, as critics, proceed to seek them out. The life and death theme is announced at the very beginning of the story: Aschenbach is waiting by the North Cemetery when he sees a wandering stranger. His reveries proper to the funereal setting, sober, necroscopic, are changed by this man's striking vitality into extravagant fancies of the jungle, lush with phallic imagery. Death and life, entering the scene thus hand-in-hand, induce their characteristic emotions, and Aschenbach's heart knocks "with fear and with puzzling desires."

At this point, a retrospect of Aschenbach's life as man and artist breaks the narrative, and we are introduced to the second important symbol. This time, it is not a person of the story, but a *type* of person found in Aschenbach's own stories—a kind of character that proclaims much the same virtues as does the figure of Saint Sebastian in painting, and that represents to Aschenbach's readers a new ideal for spiritual and moral heroism. This figure is really Aschenbach's artistic projection of his own personality, an apotheosis of his own "distinguishing moral trait," and though it is not yet at this place associated with the first symbol, the stranger of the cemetery, it already begins, obviously, to reflect its symbolism on Aschenbach. Equally important, it reintroduces the life-death theme of the ground bass, for this paradoxical "hero-type" combines "a crude and vicious sensuality capable of fanning its rising passions into pure flame" with "a delicate self-mastery by which any inner deterioration, any biological decay was kept concealed from the eyes of the world."

These are the grounds for a gruesome association which soon follows; the shameless old fraud from Pola—Aschenbach's fellow-traveler to the southland where he has been drawn by his "puzzling desires"—this revolting old man, weazened and rouged, decayed and feeble, but more waggish and gay than any of his young companions, is none other than a loathsome travesty of the Sebastian-like hero-type: in him, the hero's "crude and vicious sensuality" burns no "pure flame" but reeks of perversion; the "delicate self-mastery" which distinguishes Aschenbach's characters and is the controlling principle of his own art, appears here as ugly artifice, and "biological decay" shows doubly horrible through the old man's paint.

But Aschenbach fails to see the image of himself; indeed, even when, towards the end of the story, he himself resorts to cosmetics in his wooing of Tadzio, the kinship does not occur to him. And though he is now "fascinated with loathing" at the old man on the boat, he does not remember his "fear and desire" of the cemetery, or even the vital stranger, whose insolence and habit of grimacing were not unlike the old dandy's. Neither does the reader make this association consciously, but the ground is nonetheless well prepared for the reappearance of the stranger when the ship docks at Venice.

This time the stranger is not framed in the portico of a funeral hall, to be sure, but he *is* riding a gondola: "strange craft . . . with that peculiar blackness which is found elsewhere only in coffins—it suggests silent, criminal adventures in the rippling night, it suggests even more strongly death itself, the bier and the mournful funeral, and the last silent journey." And as Aschenbach transfers from the ship to be rowed by this modern Charon on his own last journey, he observes guilelessly "that the seat of such a barque, this arm-chair of coffin-black veneer and dull black upholstery, is the softest, most luxurious, most lulling seat in the world." This time the "desire" has taken the form of a "poisonous but delectable inertia." But "fear" is there also, deriving from the illicit aspect of the gondolier, whose present dilapidation hides his identity both from us and from Aschenbach and renders his vitality and pugnacious insolence distinctly menacing. The red hair, however, the snub nose, the long, white savage teeth and the frail build are those of the vital stranger; there are even certain frayed remnants of his former costume if we were but to observe them, and his second disappearance is quite as uncanny as his first.

The life-death theme, firmly established by these devices, is now taken up for development by the story proper. . . . Rumors of the plague run an increasingly sinister counterpoint to Aschenbach's growing love for Tadzio, his young fellow-guest at a hotel on the Lido. An ominous odor of death thus conditions but intensifies the seductiveness of this new life-symbol until the climax of the story when the stranger, entering for the third and last time, performs his antics for the hotel audience.

He is a beggar now, and he smells of disinfectant. Even his arrogance has become tainted with obsequiousness. In the repulsively suggestive movements of his mouth, in "his gestures, the movements of his body, his way of blinking significantly and letting his tongue play across his lips," our symbol of organic life reveals himself to be as rotten at the core as the sleazy old cheat of Pola. The latter, we may remember, "showed a deplorable insolence . . . winked and tittered, lifted his wrinkled, ornamented index finger in a stupid attempt at bantering, while he licked the corners of his mouth with his tongue in the most abominably suggestive manner." And the vital stranger's smell is the smell that has become associated with the constant rumors of death. Aschenbach goes, the next day, to the tourist office to inquire about these rumors. He learns that they are true: there is death in Venice, death that was hatched as pestilence in jungle swamps. And the jungle had meant *life* to Aschenbach, had lured him away from the stern and desiccating discipline of his existence to seek "an element of freshness" for his blood, to live!

That night he has a dream in which he joins a fertility dance in the heart of the jungle—an orgiastic nightmare, compounded of fear and desire, which completes the annihilation of his "substance . . . the culture of his lifetime." "His repugnance" at the awful carousal, "his fear, were keen—he was honorably set on defending himself to the very last against the barbarian, the foe to intellectual poise and dignity. But . . . his heart fluttered, his head was spinning, he was caught in a frenzy, in a blinding, deafening lewdness—and he yearned to join the ranks of the god." When the obscene symbol was raised at last, he could resist no longer; he abandoned himself to the hideous debauchery and "his soul tasted the unchastity and fury of decay."

A short coda-like section completes the development of the symbol of imposture; then, in a concluding synthesis, the hero-type symbol is resolved. The symbol of fraud is no longer the old fop, but Aschenbach himself. Harassed by chronic apprehensiveness, ravaged by his illicit passion, undone by the anguish of his dream, Aschenbach begins to show the marks of death. But "like any lover, he wanted to please. . . ."

And when, after a scandalous pursuit of his loved one through the infected alleys of Venice, he sits by the cistern in the deserted square with his mouth hanging open, panting for breath, sticky with sweat, trembling, lugubrious and old, but with blossoming youth painted on his lips and cheeks, dyed into his hair, sketched about his eyes—as he sprawls thus in ghastly caricature of his own spiritual and moral ideal, we not only do not loathe him, but we temper with a new access of sympathy the loathing we originally felt for the old cheat of Pola. For when the magnificent stranger showed his frailty, we felt how it must be with everyone.

The synthesis which brings the story to an end reveals the full meaning of the hero-type symbol, and effects at the same time a final merger of all the other meanings. At the sacrifice of his art, of his ideals, of his very life itself, Aschenbach found Tadzio; now Tadzio, the object of his sacrifice, the goal of his desire, the instrument of his death, reveals that he *is* Aschenbach's art, his own ideal creation, and thus is Aschenbach himself no less than are the stranger and the cheat.

The scene which accomplishes this dénouement was prepared for in Aschenbach's first meeting with Tadzio. After days of worshiping the god-like beauty of the boy at a distance, but of giving no outward sign of his feelings, indeed scarcely admitting them even to himself, Aschenbach chanced to come face-to-face with him so suddenly one evening that "he had no time to entrench himself behind an expression of repose and dignity," but smiled at him in infatuated and undisguised admiration. And the exquisite smile which Tadzio gave back to his smitten admirer was "*the smile of Narcissus* [the italics throughout are mine] bent over the reflecting water, that deep, fascinated, magnetic smile with which he stretches out his arms *to the image of his own beauty* . . . coquettish, inquisitive and slightly tortured . . . infatuated and infatuating.'' Quite broken up by the episode, Aschenbach sought solitude in the darkness of the park, and as he whispered fervently the ''fixed formula of desire . . . 'I love you!''' his voice was for none but his own ears. That the *''night-smell of vegetation''* pointed up the frenzy of his passion in this scene, is typical of the faithfulness and subtlety with which Mr. Mann introduces fragments of his bass theme into the details of the treble.

Unknowing, Aschenbach was confronted with the image of his own beauty. What was this image but the Sebastian-like hero-type, his own apotheosis, his spiritual essence—parodied in the old cheat, revealed in its uncompromising duplicity in the stranger, and displayed in its pathos in the painted Aschenbach?

Now, in the final scene, that ideal is at last glorified again by the frail, the exquisite Tadzio. Tadzio is out on a sandbar in the ocean. His playmates of the beach have brutalized and humiliated him, but he stands haughty and graceful, ''separated from the mainland by the expanse of water, separated from his companions by a proud moodiness . . . a strongly isolated and unrelated figure . . . placed out there in the sea, the wind, against the vague mists.'' Here he is the true Sebastian, the living hero-type—that figure which by a power of ''more than simple endurance,'' by ''an act of aggression, a positive triumph . . . [is] poised against fatality . . . [meets] adverse conditions gracefully . . . stands motionless, haughty, ashamed, with jaw set, while swords and spear-points beset the body.'' He is Aschenbach's ideal incarnated. (pp. 65-71)

Now, at the last, Tadzio is standing [outlined against the sea] . . . beyond the shore this time, out in the vast expanse itself. Slowly he turns from the hips, looks over his shoulder with twilight-grey eyes toward the artist seated on the shore, and seems to beckon to Aschenbach to come. Once more arousing himself to the call of his own spiritual form—out from the incommensurate, the incommunicable, the non-existent—the stricken artist stands up to follow, then collapses in his chair.

This is an outline, by no means exhaustive, of the symbol structure of **"Death in Venice."** The clearest view of Mr. Mann's synthetic technique, and of the nature of the change that occurs in an individual symbol during the process of synthesis, is furnished by the episodes which involve the vital stranger, first in the cemetery, second in the gondola, and third on the hotel porch.

To connote the life-death antithesis in the episode of the cemetery, three pairs of symbols are used: the stranger versus the funeral hall, Aschenbach's jungle fancies versus his necroscopic reveries, his desire versus his fear. These fall roughly into the three realms of physical things, of ideas, and of emotions.

In the gondola episode, the same three realms are preserved, each with two symbols: in the world of things the gondola opposes the stranger; ideally, Aschenbach's attention is divided between the gondola's luxurious comfort and the illicit aspect of the stranger; and feelings of fear still mingle with his desire.

Some interesting things follow from this rather dull arithmetic. In the first episode, the symbols were for the most part unambiguous: the stranger meant life and life only; the cemetery, death and death only. Further, they were mutually exclusive in their functions: the stranger supplanted the cemetery as a focus of attention, the jungle images disposed entirely of thoughts of the grave. Finally, the causal progression between Aschenbach's physical impressions and his emotional reactions seemed also to be without ambiguity: the stranger was solely responsible for his jungle fancies and these fancies alone aroused his desire, just as the funeral hall alone inspired his morbid reveries and these, presumably, his fear. But let it be noted that even in this first episode, fear and desire held the emotional stage together! Ambiguity had already begun.

In the gondola episode the situation is very different. Synthetic activity is well under way, and the ambiguity which marked the emotional realm in the first instance, extends here to the other two realms. The stranger still seems to be the physical symbol of life and the gondola of death, but in the realm of Aschenbach's ideas the whole thing is confused; the vital stranger looks ''illicit'' and ''perverse'' to him, capable, indeed, of those very ''criminal adventures in the rippling night'' which were originally brought to mind by the death-symbol, the gondola. And the gondola, ''coffin-like barque'' though it be, is by this time, in Aschenbach's dreamy fancy, naught but the ''most luxurious seat in the world.'' Thus his desire—that ''poisonous but delectable inertia''—issues from the death-symbol, ''from the seat of the gondola itself,'' while his fear is of the vital stranger!

The merging of the life and death symbols, initiated in the emotional realm during the scene in the cemetery, now absorbs the symbols in the realm of Aschenbach's ideas, and, because one is never sure which of his ideas is caused by the gondola and which by its conductor, even the symbols of the physical realm begin to be drawn in.

It remains for the third episode to complete the synthesis. Here the same three realms are preserved: the stranger goes through his physical antics on the hotel porch; Aschenbach indulges in some new reflections about the jungle, and his dream is an orgy of emotion. But in each realm there is now only one symbol, no longer two: the fuzzy boundaries distinguishing life from death have disappeared entirely and these antitheses have become functions of single symbols: decay is seen in the vital stranger himself; the lush jungle is known as the source of the plague; the fertility-dance is felt as a carousal of death. Even the causal chain which, in the other episodes, connected the three realms, is missing here; indeed, the three realms are quite separate in time. (pp. 72-4)

The most interesting product of the complicated structural relations which this analysis has brought to light is, to me at least, the poetic simplicity of mood which distinguishes one's response to **"Death in Venice."** The type of control which makes it possible has been rejected by most contemporary poets, probably under the influence of the tradition of *symbolisme*. Two points are usually raised against it: first, that the rational or logical element in it tends to falsify poetry's true object—indeterminate, fluctuating, concrete reality as presented to immediate experience; and, secondly, that it leaves no room for that exquisite quality of response which, under the name *sens du mystère,* is often identified with what Poe referred to as the ''vague and therefore spiritual effect'' of ''suggestive indefiniteness.'' How Mr. Mann provides for what Poe was talking about we have already remarked. His control operates entirely below the reader's conscious attention; meanings are never forced, they are intimated and suggested rather than stated, and the reader is allowed the illusion, at least, of a good deal of imaginative freedom.

But the feeling of mystery which characterizes authentic poetic response is not, I believe, merely this feeling of freedom of reference. The problem is less simple; it is probably not a technical one at all. Poor poets fail to conjure up mystery even with methodical mystification, yet it often flourishes in classical poetry in the full light of logical reference from symbol to meaning. I suspect that *mystère* is to be sought rather in the aspect of experience comprehended in a poem than in the form of its elaboration. At this level there is essential, not artificial, mystery, deriving, perhaps, from the nature of experience itself. Both the nuance of private feeling, the "immediate experience" of the *symbolistes,* and Mr. Mann's "infinity" where, "in a matter of eternal contraries," harmony lies—both of these are, in the last analysis, quite un-understandable, and hence, unsusceptible of totally adequate communication. At the level of *mystère,* the mediated experience is no less valid a poetic object than the immediate one.

These, however, are properly questions for aesthetics rather than for literary criticism. Here I have been concerned less with the latent content of poetry, with its mystery, than with that other quality which is often forgotten today but which Mr. Mann has so richly remembered—the quality of lucidness, of intelligibility, by whose virtue the incommunicable *seems,* at least, to be communicated. (pp. 75-6)

Vernon Venable, "Poetic Reason in Thomas Mann," in The Virginia Quarterly Review, *Vol. 14, No. 1 (Winter, 1938), pp. 61-76.*

JOHN BOVEY (essay date 1940)

[*In the following excerpt, Bovey maintains that* Death in Venice *is more than just a story of individual degradation, suggesting that the novella may be interpreted as a representation of the decline of European society before World War I. To support his argument, he offers a detailed examination of the symbolism in* Death in Venice. *For a similar discussion, see the excerpt by R. Hinton Thomas (1956).*]

Thomas Mann is perhaps more completely aware of the meaning of ***Death in Venice*** today than he was when he composed it in 1911. And though he might entirely refuse to accept any such interpretation as I am about to suggest, his own words are certainly an irresistible invitation to read between the lines. ***Death in Venice,*** he says, in the Preface to his collected stories [see excerpt dated 1936] "is indeed a crystallization in the true sense of the word; it is a structure, and an image, shedding light from so many facets, by its nature of such inexhaustible allusiveness, that it might well dazzle the eyes of its creator himself as it took shape."

The narrative content of the story is by now well known. A hard working, lonely, and inhibited artist, whose genius has gained universal recognition, goes to Venice for a vacation. There, in the lush and sensual atmosphere of the South, the desires which he has hitherto sublimated in his writing break forth in a lustful but unconsummated passion for a beautiful young Polish boy, who is staying at his hotel. After a number of adventures, the artist catches the cholera, which has broken out in the city, and dies on the beach during the last morning of the Polish family's stay.

Reduced to the mere shell of its narrative, the story may appear to be simply a study in the breakdown of the human will, or another portrait in Thomas Mann's long gallery of frustrated artists. The phenomenon of the ivory tower has always fascinated him; reared, as ***Tonio Kröger*** and the ***Coming Victory of Democracy*** both show, in the *fin de siècle* tradition, he has never been able to find any completely satisfactory answer to the troublesome problem of the artist's position in society. And on one level ***Death in Venice*** is merely another posing of the problem. Unless I am very much mistaken, however, the history of Gustave Aschenbach's degradation has much wider implications, and I can hardly believe that the disaster which overtakes him is wholly unconnected with the disaster which was about to overtake Europe. For what is Gustave Aschenbach really but the embodiment of the European intelligence? And what are these insane, plague-stricken creatures, trapped in the dark alleys and fashionable hotels of Venice, but European society itself on the brink of the abyss of 1914?

It is significant that the first paragraph of the story arouses the mood of uneasiness to which in our day the world is so accustomed that any other state seems happily anomalous: "It was a spring afternoon in that year of grace 19—, when Europe sat upon the anxious seat beneath a menace that hung over its head for months." The reference is presumably to the Agadir crisis of 1911, but it would perhaps be a mistake to infer that Mann was entirely and consciously aware of the meaning of that crisis, or that the symbol of the artist was deliberately chosen as an illustration for a theme. The deluge of 1914 was, after all, a considerable surprise to most of those who were swept away by it. Intellectuals and statesmen, no less than the man in the street, appear to have been blissfully unaware of what was to occur—unaware, at any rate, of the scope and magnitude of the coming disaster. . . . Mann was probably as much taken in as any one else; indeed no specific foreboding or symptom of perturbation appears in any of the stories which he wrote during the period. And the ominous rumble which sounds through the first sentence of ***Death in Venice*** is not so clearly audible in any other section of the story. From this point forward, the impending disaster must be understood entirely in terms of the protagonist's fate; it has been absorbed and taken up into the symbols among which he moves. One's reading of those symbols may of course be entirely gratuitous, but one cannot, especially at present, resist the conclusion that they bear some relation to their author's surroundings.

It is not altogether accidental that Aschenbach, despite his cold and impassive isolation from the world, is described as "too busy with the tasks imposed upon him by his own ego and the European soul, too laden with the care and duty to create." And like the Europe of the Edwardian era, he feels played out without quite knowing why. His accomplishments are already secure: he has achieved the mastery of his medium, and the world of letters has paid him homage. But he no longer feels any joy in his work, and his proud isolation stifles the energy of his imagination. An overwhelming sense of flagging will-power is Aschenbach's chief attribute, and its symptoms recur innumerable times in the course of the story. (pp. 238-40)

Later in the story, as the degraded artist sits on the beach, musing over his inability to break the spell that binds him, Mann draws a kind of clairvoyant picture of the moral and intellectual Saturnalia of the war:

> Aschenbach was no longer disposed to self-analysis. He had no taste for it; his self-esteem, the attitude of mind proper to his years, his maturity and single-mindedness, disinclined him to look within himself and decide whether it was constraint or puerile sensuality that had prevented him from carrying out his project.

Such a state of mind it was that produced Bergson's picture of the war as a conflict between life and matter, that made

Royce call pro-Germans the enemies of humanity, that made even Mr. Santayana dwell scornfully on egotism in German philosophy. In our own day, and on a somewhat lower level, this failure of the critical faculty produces the *ex cathedra* pronouncements of Alfred Rosenberg or the ingenious equivocations of Virginio Gayda. Nor are the signs of its failure absent from the American scene. Like Gustave Aschenbach, the lords of the intellectual world, then as now, resorted to the most pitiful rationalizations to cover their own inability to cope with the real issues. And like him, they surrendered completely to emotions which had been starved by a discipline of empiricism and weary reasonableness.

Mann seems to have sensed the inevitable future even more clearly in the dreadful irony of the scene in which Aschenbach soothes his pride and justifies his lust with perverted quotations from the *Phaedrus*. The effectiveness of the episode arises from the reader's awareness that the Platonic *rapprochement* between physical and spiritual beauty—the very reconciliation in which Aschenbach attempts to find comfort—has been utterly destroyed. And nothing could sum up more completely the essential sickness of western civilization than that one of its most distinguished representatives should sit, painted and bedraggled, in a sordid little square in Venice, misquoting from the works which constitute the corner-stone of European thought. So far had the Europe of 1911 come from the shadows of the plane-tree on the banks of the Ilissus, and such were the last exertions of the European intellect.

The setting in which Aschenbach's tragedy takes place is equally significant. The strange Venetian amalgam of the classic, the Oriental, and the Western, associating the monuments of a glorious history with the sordid realities of social decay, has particularly attracted writers of the last fifty years—James, for example, and Proust and Eliot. Viewed in certain lights, Venice is a kind of microcosm of European civilization, a meeting place where the bustle of bourgeois "tourism" has not quite succeeded in obliterating the traces of a past which only makes the present seem more appalling. No setting could underscore more aptly the eschatological feelings which Mann attempts to convey; the final agonies of the European mind take place fittingly in the hot, semi-barbaric atmosphere, where "subdued voices speak most of the principal European tongues," and where primitive emotions are apt at any moment to erupt violently on the scene. Thus the theme of ***Death in Venice*** is, in a sense, a foreshadowing of Eliot's *Burbank with a Baedeker,* though Mann treats it with a more leisurely seriousness and gives it more solid intellectual and emotional extensions.

Mann has been at pains also to surround the figures who serve to arouse the fatal unbalance in Aschenbach with an aura of submerged violence, of underlying primitivism. The first of these symbols appears suddenly, in an almost Hawthornesque manner, at the opening of the story, when Aschenbach catches sight of the stranger on the steps of the chapel in Munich. . . . (pp. 240-41)

This curious, Pan-like figure appears no less than six times in the story, and the reader's dim perception that each disguise only conceals the same phantasm is confirmed by the subtle reiteration of these same attributes, especially the Adam's apple, the withered neck, and the long, white animal teeth. (p. 242)

At last even the stern countenance of the artist himself takes on the barbarity of these dreadful beings. Wearied by his pursuit of Tadzio through the streets of Venice, he casts himself down by a fountain in an obscure and filthy little square. "His eyelids were closed, there was only a swift, sidelong glint of the eyeballs now and again, something between a question and a leer; while the rouged and flabby mouth uttered single words of the sentences shaped in his disordered brain by the fantastic logic that governs our dreams."

The forces that propel the story forward are thus objectified in creatures whose essential animality is subtly and painstakingly established. Viewed in the light of their symbolic significance, these figures are manifestations of the persistent barbarity which lies beneath the surface of civilized life, and each step that Aschenbach takes along the path of degradation marks one more stage in the movement of the European mind, "reeling back to the beast" at the close of an era. I think it is equally true that the persons who tend to check Aschenbach's emotional frenzy suggest at once the forces of social order and ethical stability—religion, tradition, and adherence to accepted codes of decent behavior. There are, for example, the Polish boy's sisters, who assume in the artist's eyes the appearance of nuns; there are the governess, the mother ("the arrangement of her lightly powdered hair had the simplicity prescribed in certain circles whose piety and aristocracy are equally marked"), and the English clerk who obeys the dictates of social duty and gives Aschenbach his last chance for expiation by telling him the truth about the plague.

It is remarkable also how many of the symbols employed in the story are exactly those through which the unconscious mind projects its content in dreams. Thus after encountering the sinister stranger in Munich, visions of landscape float before Aschenbach's eyes—"a tropical marshland, beneath a reeking sky, steaming, monstrous, rank." Nearly every apparition of the mysterious animal being arouses in the artist a trance-like state, in which apathy mingles with desire. . . . The Polish boy himself, the central symbol, calls forth a whole train of sensual impressions in the artist's mind, beginning with a lush classical imagery which is appropriate to the voluptuous warmth of the Venetian setting—Eros, Orion, Pan, Hyacinthus, Narcissus—and culminating, near the close of the story, in the terrific orgiastic dream, whose symbols seem almost consciously Freudian—the mountain scene, the serpents, and the strange centaur-like participants. In projecting the unbridled primitivism which has invaded Aschenbach's consciousness, Mann uses these symbols with an apparently deliberate frequency, and one is somewhat surprised to find, from his own testimony, that ***Death in Venice,*** unlike ***Joseph and His Brothers,*** was written without any direct knowledge of Freud's investigations. It is only natural, however, that in the eulogistic lecture on Freud, published two years ago, Mann should have recognized the profound affinity between the imagery of the story and the discoveries of the great Viennese. So close is the world into which we are hurled at night to our primitive state, and such is the relevance of the dark truths that psychoanalysis has revealed to the teachings of the moralist and the necessities of social discipline.

Another symbol which deserves attention is introduced, almost in the manner of a Wagnerian *leit-motiv,* toward the close of the story. This is the plague and the external signs, such as the stench of germicide, which denote its presence in the city. If Aschenbach and the strange spirit who haunts him have any of the wider social significance I have attempted to attach to them, it follows that the plague too must be considered in this light. It perhaps signifies the universal corruption which infects the whole social structure, once the moral barriers of its individual members have given way. It is not entirely accidental that Aschenbach notices the odor of disease in the air only after four weeks on the Lido have succeeded in undermining his own conscience. After that it becomes an obsession with him; he smells the carbolic acid everywhere, inquires about it wherever he goes, and takes delight in sneering at the perfunctory explanations of the officials. He associates it with the possible death of the boy and is horrified to discover that he is indifferent, even favorably disposed, to such an eventuality. And at last he takes frank delight in it, as the broken spirit always takes delight in social corruption. . . . The plague as a symbol of social decay must be associated in some way with the bestiality from which it springs: one notes that cholera is the product of just such a tropical scene as that which swims before Aschenbach's eyes at the beginning of the story, and that the two themes of the mysterious stranger and the cholera merge in the person of the clown who dances in the hotel garden. . . . (pp. 242-44)

In a sense then, Mann's published lectures on Goethe, Wagner, and Freud are only footnotes to ***Death in Venice,*** just as the remarks on fascism in ***The Coming Victory of Democracy*** form a pendant to the allegory of ***Mario and the Magician.*** The elements which are abstractly formulated in those three lectures are already present in the story of Gustave Aschenbach: the problem of his sacrifice to his art brings to mind the lofty devotion of Goethe to his calling; the contrapuntal resources which Mann employs in handling his themes suggest at once the method of Wagner; and the unfolding of Aschenbach's inner consciousness displays a profound grasp of the mysterious workings of the unconscious mind upon which the analysis of Freud has since shed such a flood of light.

Dimly discernible in the unconscious were the forces which continually threaten the foundations of civilization and which were at work beneath the surface of the liberal society of 1911. The fate of Gustave Aschenbach was the fate of his era, and in projecting his catastrophe Mann's sensitivity enabled him to trace the direction of the motions which were carrying a blissfully ignorant world to its destruction. The brilliance of his clairvoyance can be appreciated more fully today, when subsequent events in the external world have proven the reality of that rank corruption, mining all within, which Mann seems to have sensed at the time he wrote ***Death in Venice.*** (p. 245)

Death in Venice is, in fact, one of those rare stories whose symbols possess a peculiar force because they have been conceived in the throes of the sacred rage which enables the artist to discharge into his work, without conscious deliberation, his full sense of the age. It thus became a startling prognosis of disaster for the world of 1911; it remains a terrifying diagnosis of the maladies of the present. (p. 246)

John Bovey, "'Death in Venice': Structure and Image," in Twice a Year *(copyright 1940 by Dorothy S. Norman,* Twice a Year*), No. 5, Fall-Winter, 1940 and No. 6, Spring-Summer, 1941, pp. 238-46.*

CHARLES NEIDER (essay date 1948)

[*Neider is a Russian-born American critic and editor who has written extensively on the works of Mark Twain and Franz Kafka. In the following excerpt, he discusses the symbolism in* Death in Venice *and compares its structure to the development of a musical composition.*]

Mann's ***Death in Venice*** is widely considered to be one of the most perfect novellas ever written, in its immaculate style and form, and in the astonishing union of form, idea, and passion. Its perfect fusion of northern discipline with Mediterranean sensuousness, its masterly effect of growing orchestral power, its beauty of scene and linguistic envelope, make it clear that the author is a poet working in the prose medium. The novella is modern in its appreciation of music, myth, symbol, and the unconscious. On the surface it relates the death of an artist of importance, but beneath this lurks a study of the artist as a type, his devotion to discipline and form, and his yearning for bohemia and the dissolute; it is also a story of the interplay of different kinds of awareness in a complex and sensitive personality: the desperate struggle, transmuting itself at times into gleaming symbols, between the unconscious and the conscious minds.

Few modern tales cast so magical a spell, beguiling the reader by every means into a desperate and sick, even criminal although very beautiful Italian journey. (p. 48)

The novella is among other things a tissue of symbols, the primary one being death—in the form of a cemetery, cholera, the black gondolas, the sea and, foremost, five men with odd features in common. These five are the stranger in the portico near the cemetery, the sailor with the goatee, the ancient dandy, the obstinate gondolier, and the singing buffoon. The second and third are secondary symbols; their symbolic weight is carried by their physical decrepitude. The others are primary symbols; it is they who chiefly share common characteristics, one of which is a life-death dualism suggested by their aggressiveness and strength as well as by their physical appearance. All three are below medium height and of slight build, belong to the blond or red-haired type, and are strikingly snub-nosed (suggesting a death's head). All are outlanders: the first is "obviously not Bavarian," the second is "of non-Italian stock," the third is "scarcely a Venetian type." This alien status is a musical leitmotif hinting at the symbolic, mythical, unconscious meaning of journey, the journey as death. The life-death dualism is heightened by an emphasis on the naked Adam's apple and fangs and gums. A minor motif, indicative of Mann's detailed interest in such matters, is the "two pronounced perpendicular furrows" on the forehead. Mann's repetitions are carefully nuanced to avoid crudeness and to increase variation and suggestiveness. The life-death motif is epitomized by the jungle symbol. At the beginning of the story Aschenbach, yearning to travel, experiences almost a seizure of the imagination, and visualizes a jungle containing crouching tigers. Near the end he learns that Asiatic cholera springs from the jungle of the Ganges delta, "among whose bamboo thickets the tiger crouches." In this novella, as in most of Mann's work, the musical motif and the thematic symbol are indistinguishable.

The musical form is remarkably evocative. The first scene at the cemetery is like a first movement. The second section is like an adagio, the third section is accelerated. The Tadzio motif is brought in almost at once and is subtly developed while time is made to pass unobtrusively. Aschenbach's crisis, his panic, and revolution, is a fine complication to distract attention from Tadzio so that the boy's image will not grow too familiar, and to indicate how strong is the writer's passion for him. The crisis has still another and more subtle function: to indicate the futility of Aschenbach's attempts to escape his fate. He himself is the cause of the misadventure: if he had left the hotel when the porter requested, and had accompanied his trunk to the station, as was usual, the trunk would not have gone astray. The fourth section, the ecstatically lyrical one, is a renewed evidence of Mann's lyrical genius, seen throughout his career. The fifth and final section is an orchestration of all the familiar themes. The invention seems inexhaustible, the grasp of detail always rich and striking. The result in its riotous romantic color reminds one of a Strauss tone poem, as well as of Wagner, master of Mann as well as Strauss. In Mann's invention the sordid is made to seem surpassingly beautiful. Perhaps not since Plato has the homosexual motif been handled in so classical and exquisite a manner. Mann's sonorousness, texture, and weight remind one also of Brahms. It is odd that Mann has almost nothing to say of Brahms in his essays, whereas he has written so lavishly of Wagner. Both in temperament as well as in art he seems to have a greater affinity with the comparatively sober Brahms than with the ecstatic, vainglorious, exceedingly daemonic Wagner. In this musical connection, it is worth noting that Mahler was the physical and in some ways psychological model for Aschenbach.

Aschenbach is a Jamesian figure. Like the Jamesian heroes, he possesses a fine conscience and lives a life of renunciation. But whereas the Jamesian heroes generally continue to renounce, this being their tragedy, Aschenbach's tragedy is his late and sudden acceptance of disorder, the passions, and the depths. He is a symbol of the age, which is exhausted, stunted. His moral and physical decline symbolizes the decline of the European world, which is too formalistic and cerebral, a world soon to be rent by the upsurge of passion, of desperate inner need. Mann's symbol of the depths is characteristically Eastern: Tadzio is a Pole, a fact which recalls Chauchat, the Russian bohemian of ***The Magic Mountain.***

Death in Venice is a study of the flight toward death, of the will to death, on the part of a man who believes that he is in complete control of himself. The flight is sketched with mythical symbols. Aschenbach is the victim of energies which he has been repressing for years. These overthrow him on two counts, moral and physical. They seduce him to the illicit level of homosexuality and, having witnessed his progressive degeneration, slay him with the plague. Fatigued by his sapping work and worn out by a lifetime of repression, Aschenbach unconsciously seeks a new life, a rebirth. That is why he heads instinctively toward the sea, symbol of woman, womb, and parturition. He travels south because the south symbolizes for him the sensuous, the feminine, and disorder, traits he has inherited from his mother, the daughter of a Bohemian musical conductor. (The coupling of music and the illicit, as well as music and the sea, is prominent in Mann's work.) Aschenbach's yearning for rebirth is suggested even by his repugnant attempts to beautify himself at the Venetian barber's. Rebirth entails death, and that is why Aschenbach must die. Aschenbach's "yearning for new and distant scenes," his "craving for freedom, release, forgetfulness" are cravings for death so that he may be reborn. Aschenbach, in brief, is the artist as Oedipus. (pp. 49-51)

Charles Neider, in an introduction to Short Novels of the Masters, *edited by Charles Neider, 1948. Reprint by Holt, Rinehart and Winston, 1967, pp. 3-51.**

FRANK DONALD HIRSCHBACH (essay date 1955)

[*In the following excerpt from his* The Arrow and the Lyre: A Study of the Role of Love in the Works of Thomas Mann, *Hirschbach discusses the conflict between erotic passion and the rational control of individual will in* Death in Venice, *examining this struggle on both a naturalistic and a symbolic level. For further discussion of symbolism and character psychology in Mann's novella, see the excerpts by André von Gronicka (1956) and J. R. McWilliams (1967).*]

Seen from a naturalistic point of view, ***Death in Venice*** is the story of an aging, successful, highly sensitive writer who feels in need of a vacation, travels to Venice, remains there because of his passion for the fourteen-year old Polish boy, Tadzio, contracts cholera and dies of it. There are no incidents in the story which cannot be explained naturally. Everyone has encountered remarkable-looking people, such as the man whom Aschenbach meets at the streetcar stop in Munich. There is nothing astounding about an insolent and unlicensed gondolier who flees when he fears the intervention of the police. A mix-up in baggage was probably a common occurrence in a pre-Fascist Italy in which the trains did not yet run on time.

A good many other elements contribute to the naturalistic tenor of the story. The names of real streets in Munich and Venice are employed. The works of the fictitious Gustav von Aschenbach bear a close resemblance to those already written or planned by Thomas Mann. The descriptions of people are drawn with great attention to detail (such as the false teeth of the old man on the steamer) and the unpleasant is described along with the pleasant. The use of the cholera element is in itself a naturalistic device.

When the story is read on a naturalistic level, Aschenbach's homosexual tendencies fit well into the picture. It would appear that Aschenbach has repressed these tendencies for many years, and we are constantly told about his tremendous self-discipline in sentences like "the pattern of self-discipline he had followed ever since his youth," "a proud, tenacious, well-tried will," "he had bridled and tempered his sensibilities", or later on when it is said:

> Forgotten feelings, precious pangs of his youth, quenched long since by the stern service that had been his life, now returned so strangely metamorphosed . . .

It is the sight of a man, who in some way attracts Aschenbach, that is the innocent cause of his trip to Venice. Beginning with the chance meeting with the mysterious stranger in Munich, Aschenbach's will fights a losing battle with his desires. The use of such terms as "a longing inexplicable," "contagion", "vice, passion," "the embers of smouldering fire," "to strengthen . . . the ethically impossible" leave no doubt about the erotic character of his emotions which Aschenbach at first tries to characterize as merely "longing to travel."

Once in Venice, where he is unknown, his once-repressed desires fix upon a beautiful fourteen-year old boy, and from here on Aschenbach's reactions and actions are much the same as those of any undeclared lover. He pursues his beloved, gradually throwing all caution to the winds; he only feels happy when the object of his love is within his sight; he tries to exchange glances with him; he stands at his door at night; he feels the pangs of jealousy; and he finally even uses cosmetics in order to be pleasing to him. By the time that he reaches the high point of his passion for Tadzio he is almost completely unaware of the "impropriety" or unconventionality of his love, and even launches into a defense of homosexuality on the basis of historical fact.

When the story, on the other hand, is read on a symbolic level, it becomes the case study of the gradual deterioration and abdication of the human will and of the artistic will in the face of beauty. . . . Aschenbach's rise and greatness are due to a colossal effort of the will to subdue his natural inclinations. All his life he was said to be too busy with the tasks which his ego and his European conscience provided for him. His favorite term is "Durchhalten" ("Stick to it!"). . . . The hero of Aschenbach's writings is a masculine, intellectual and virginal youth who clenches his teeth and stands in silent defiance of the swords and spears that pierce his side. The picture is that of the martyr, Saint Sebastian; the ideal is that of Stefan George. Aschenbach's efforts are on one occasion labelled ecstasy of will ("Willensverzückung"), an achievement as well as a means to further achievement.

The irony and tragedy of Gustav Aschenbach lie in the fact that this iron will, which has carried him to such great heights, collapses utterly within a matter of weeks, and it collapses of itself. Tadzio, who might be regarded as the prime agent in Aschenbach's negation of the will, is in reality only the main station on a road which has begun long before. There are perhaps four other stations on this road, each symbolized by one of the strangers whom Aschenbach meets, three of them before his acquaintance with Tadzio is made. The stranger in Munich, set against the background of a cemetery, acts as the catalytic agent who sets off the reactions that lead to Aschenbach's downfall and death. This first stranger indirectly causes Aschenbach to have a daydream of symbolic import. He dreams of an exotic, tropical landscape, the type where cholera breeds. Thus, his death is forecast for a second time. But it is also the type of region where all living organisms, plants and animals alike, are able to grow and act free of inhibitions and restraints. During the dream Aschenbach feels his heart pounding with horror and mysterious desire. In Venice he seeks his dream landscape in a civilized setting.

The second stranger, the ancient adolescent on the steamer, "a painted and primped old scapegrace", represents the point to which a man can fall when he lets his urges overpower his will—a warning to Aschenbach, and yet the second stranger, who sidles up to him at the end of the trip and whispers a significant "Pray keep us in mind" into his ear, already sees an ally in the aging man.

The gondolier asserts his will over Aschenbach's will in a most decisive manner. Although Aschenbach has taken the gondola in order to make a steamship connection at San Marco, the gondolier takes him to the Lido. Twice during the trip Aschenbach tries to protest, but "the wisest thing—and how much the pleasantest!—was to let matters take their own course." Thus, Aschenbach is borne to his destination in a black barque which resembles a coffin.

Much is said in the story about the extraordinary beauty of the boy Tadzio. But his beauty is not perfect, and in fact, if he were not seen through the eyes of his lover, he would probably turn out to be just a very handsome boy of fourteen. He is the symbol of a passion which cannot come to any fruition and which Aschenbach does not really want to be fulfilled. If he and Tadzio were to become friends, if he had spoken to him, if he had a chance to observe Tadzio more intimately, no doubt his love would die and his will return.

After the gondola episode his will makes one last attempt to assert itself: the attempted flight from Venice. It is perfectly obvious that Aschenbach does not really wish to leave Venice, since he could have done so even without his baggage. After this, his will deteriorates step by step. His realization that it was Tadzio who kept him in Venice; his enraptured contemplation of Tadzio's body on the beach; his passivity toward the disease which later grows into complete carelessness; finally his use of cosmetics are all steps on the way to a total abdication of the will.

One is reminded of the devil in *Doctor Faustus,* who constantly changes shapes during his conversation with Leverkühn, when one encounters the fourth stranger, the guitar player. He has the prominent Adam's apple and the two furrows of the Munich stranger; he lets his tongue run from one corner of the mouth to the other like the stranger on the steamer; and he frequently bares his strong teeth like the gondolier. This fourth stranger no longer has any particular function except to signify the demon's complete victory over Aschenbach. His familiarity and his bawdy gestures symbolize that Aschenbach is now considered vanquished. Shortly before it had already been said:

> Mind and heart were drunk with passion, his footsteps guided by the demonic power whose pastime it is to trample on human reason and dignity.

After all the strangers have led their victim a little bit on his way to death, it is finally again Tadzio, "the pale and lovely Summoner" who leads the soul of the dying artist into the lower regions.

Aschenbach's downfall is projected within the frame of an erotic dream which he has shortly before his death. He dreams of a tremendous, communal sex orgy, in which humans and animals alike participate, a voluptuous adoration of the phallic symbol which he approaches with a combination of anxiety and desire and in which he finally takes full part. Here for the first time, Thomas Mann uses the term "the stranger god" for God's Mephistophelian counterpart, who rules the drives and urges within us.

Love and the uncontrolled contemplation of beauty play their part in this story of the gradual disintegration of the will: the will to create, the will to remain dignified, and finally the will to live. For death itself here becomes a symbol of the inevitable last step on the road to the renunciation of the will. (pp. 17-21)

Frank Donald Hirschbach, in his The Arrow and the Lyre: A Study of the Role of Love in the Works of Thomas Mann, *Martinus Nijhoff, 1955, 195 p.*

ANDRÉ VON GRONICKA (essay date 1956)

[*In the following excerpt from an essay originally printed in* The Germanic Review *in 1956, Gronicka discusses the locale, plot, and characters of* Death in Venice, *focusing on Mann's use of psychological realism and mythological symbolism. Gronicka maintains that "myth plus psychology" imbues the novella with both a contemporary realism and a mythological timelessness. For further discussion of symbolism and character in* Death in Venice, *see the excerpts by Frank Donald Hirschbach (1955) and J. R. McWilliams (1967); for further discussion of mythological symbolism, see the excerpts by James B. Hepworth (1963) and A. E. Dyson (1971); also see the excerpt by Isadore Traschen in* TCLC, *Vol. 2.*]

In an exchange of letters with the Hungarian anthropologist Karl Kerényi, Thomas Mann has pointed to a basic quality of his writings by revealing that he had early recognized "mythos plus psychology" as his natural "element" and that he had been for a long time "passionately fond of this combination." Mann's formula calls for a brief amplification. "Myth" as used in it stands for rather more than the term conventionally defines. It encompasses legend, history, and the literary traditions of the more recent past; it calls for a language that is cleansed of the colloquial and the commonplace, is marked by lyric pathos, or evokes the monumental and the statuesque. "Psychology," on the other hand, implies a penetrating analysis and a carefully controlled statement in an all but naturalistic idiom, of the reality of the psychophysical world. The "plus" in the formula does not represent simple addition but a most subtle combination and permutation of disparate elements resulting in a unique *"Steigerung"* [heightening and intensification]. (p. 46)

This bifocal view of life that encompasses both the transcendent and the real develops steadily to reach, in the masterly *novella* ***Death in Venice,*** a degree of perfection which Mann has rarely if ever excelled. (p. 47)

In the *novella* . . . everything springs with a surprisingly unbroken vitality and directness from that bifocal view of life: the locale, the plot, and especially the characters. Here everything is rooted both in this-worldliness and in the realm of myth and legend. Here Thomas Mann lays hold of life in all its concrete outer-inner, psychophysical reality, while reaching deep into the rich storehouse of myth and legend, as well as of modern literature. He does this with an uninhibited creative energy that informs reality with myth's timeless grandeur, while rescuing myth from abstract remoteness and endowing it with a vibrant immediacy far removed from "persiflage."

In the "Sketch of my Life," written in 1930, Mann recollects that he had never before or since the composition of ***Death in Venice*** experienced "such a splendid sensation of uplift." Of the hero of the *novella,* of Gustav von Aschenbach, he says: "His spirit struggled to give birth, his memory flung up primal thoughts inherited in youth, but never before made vivid by his own fire." We are safe in reading this characterization of Aschenbach's creative state of mind as a fragment of self-revelation on the part of the author. It was surely in a similar state of supreme creative élan that Mann achieved the well-nigh miraculous, and could write both as the soberly meticulous analyst and delineator of physis and psyche and as the inspired recreator of the world of myth. Thus, in this *novella* Mann's cultivated mind, oriented Janus-like toward the past as well as the present, becomes a potent synthesis of the meticulously observed and recorded world of contemporary, bourgeois civilization and the timeless and measureless vistas of man's cultural heritage. It creates a unique work of art, suspended in an unceasing tension between the poles of psychological realism and the symbolism of myth. . . . (p. 48)

The central locale of the *novella,* Venice, "the sunken queen" is caught by Mann's bifocal vision as the "flattering and dubious beauty . . . half fairy tale, half tourist trap," in its sordid reality and mythical splendor. We are not spared the oppressive sultriness and fetid stench of its alleyways, nor the garbage floating on its canals with their evil exhalations; yet above these very waters there rises the "graceful splendor" of its palaces, bridges, churches, of its "fairy tale temples," rendered in a rhythmical prose of exquisite limpidity and grace. This *ambiente* is done with the most painstaking precision of detail, yet not in order to produce a naturalistic picture of the city, but to create, by way of an ever alert selectivity, a highly stylized composition characterized by a tense equilibrium of realism and idealization. There is modern Venice drawn in a decidedly up-to-date idiom, liberally sprinkled with technical terms and with foreign loan-words and entire phrases, particularly French. . . . And next to, superimposed upon, and integrated into this modern Venice is the timeless, exotic city par excellence, the "very seat of all dissoluteness," the perfect stage for the "noiseless and criminal adventures in the plashing night" as fashioned by the imagination of Elizabethan poets and dramatists and by the Italian novelists, Venice of Oriental "fabled splendor," Romantic Venice risen from the dreams of Byron, Platen, Wagner, and Nietzsche, that magical city of ruthless passions, of passions-unto-death, of the *Liebestod.* And on this complex *montage,* this subtle composite of reality and literary tradition, Mann superimposes the world of classical antiquity, its scenery, historical figures (Socrates, Phaedros, Critobolus) and the gods of Olympus. . . . (pp. 49-50)

The bifocal vision of Thomas Mann is clearly at work when the stage is set for Aschenbach's fateful meeting with the stranger. Time and place are stated in an exact factual manner which could well serve to open a realistic, even naturalistic tale, yet the apparent realism of the "English Garden" and the "busy garden restaurant next to which some cabs and carriages were standing," of the Ungerer Strasse with its streetcar tracks, is subtly modified by interwoven elements of description: the "more and more quiet paths," the sinking sun, Aschenbach's "way home across the open meadow [!]," his tiredness and the thunderstorm that broods threateningly over Föhring, are elements which charge this realism with a significant *Stimmungsgehalt* [mood content] and lend it a symbolical quality which gradually becomes dominant. Our attention is drawn to the desolate "stonemason's yard, where crosses, commemorative tablets and monuments, displayed for sale, form a second graveyard," to the "cemetery chapel, a building in the Byzantine style . . . in the reflected light of departing day," to a setting which causes Aschenbach's inner vision ("geistiges Auge") to lose itself "in the translucent mystic meaning [of the inscriptions]."

When the stage is set in this manner, the stranger makes his unobserved, uncanny entrance to stand-elevated-at the portals of the funeral hall: "Whether he had come out of the hall through its bronze gate or had climbed up there from outside, unnoticed, was uncertain." Here, surely, is more than a suggestion of the mysterious and eerie which, however, is at once counteracted by the very next sentence: "Aschenbach, without devoting particular thought to the question, inclined to the earlier assumption." Both the content and tone of this sentence, especially the matter-of-fact, off-hand phrase "inclined to the earlier assumption" are calculated to break or at least weaken the spell of spectral other-worldliness that might have been worked by the description of the cemetery, the funeral hall with its "hieratic paintings" and "apocalyptic beasts," and of the "not quite ordinary appearance" of the stranger.

The manner in which the stranger's appearance is characterized reminds one at first of an official identification, abrupt, curt, exact in its phrasing: "moderately tall, spare, beardless, and strikingly snub-nosed." Suddenly, however, we become aware that the figure is raised above commonplace reality, acquires a statuesque quality, a striking monumentality. No longer merely a Bavarian tourist, the stranger has grown to the stature of a mythical figure. He *is* the archtempter Satan, he *is* also the imperious, ruthless liberator from life's toil, Death with his characteristic mask: "his short turned-up nose," with lips "completely drawn back from his teeth, so that they, exposed down to his gums, appeared white and long between them," the skull as it appears in many a Dance of Death. To be sure, in this composite figure the hoof of Satan is decorously hidden.

Yet the stranger's long, scrawny neck with its starkly protruding Adam's apple, red eyelashes over pale eyes, would amply identify the Lord of Hell even if it were not for the two "vertical, energetic furrows" etched on his forehead and drawn down between his eyes, which—ever since Dante's day—have served to symbolize the devil's mythical horns. But while shaping this mythical figure, Mann is ever intent to justify and explain its existence on realistic and psychological grounds. "Perhaps his elevated and elevating position contributed to this impression . . ." he ventures to suggest, and again, in explanation of the mask of death and the marks of the devil, he offers as the realistic cause, the sun's blinding rays which may well have forced the stranger to grimace.

The effect of the stranger upon Aschenbach, though powerful, is rendered in a pointedly realistic manner. The bellicose gaze of the stranger, "so militant . . . so straight into his eye, so obviously intending to drive the matter to the extreme . . ." causes no sudden surrender, no petrifaction nor casting down upon bended knees with head thrown back and arms spread wide. To suggest such a typically expressionistic gesture is to point up the absurdity of all excess and eccentricity and sudden "break-through" within the context of Thomas Mann's worldview and corresponding style. His Aschenbach is merely "painfully moved," turns away, and "had forgotten him [the stranger], the next minute." It is difficult to imagine a more sobering denouement of a highly charged situation.

But then the author switches to the psychological plane and here unfolds a masterful analysis of the effect of the meeting upon Aschenbach's psyche, his "imagination," shows how the indefinable "physical or psychic influence . . . of the stranger" releases a flood of long and ruthlessly repressed emotions which crystallizes into a waking dream of such poignancy as to leave Aschenbach shaken, his heart throbbing "with horror and enigmatic desire."

Yet is this transfer to the realistic plane of psychoanalysis complete? Does the mythical figure of the stranger vanish altogether in the light of this analysis? Are his "not quite ordinary appearance and enigmatical influence really "explained" on rational grounds? Can we agree with Aschenbach when he attempts to rationalize the encounter as the upshot of a sudden onset of "desire to travel, nothing more"? By no means. It is precisely the paradox of Mann's style that, despite its thorough realism, it leaves myth and legend in their very palpable existence. (pp. 51-3)

The figure of Tadzio is also the creature of the two worlds of reality and myth, a creation of Mann's bifocal view. We see him, almost exclusively through Aschenbach's eyes, both "at the most advantageous distance, aesthetically," as a "statue, imaging and mirroring intellectual beauty" as well as from close range. We see him as the little Polish boy of pale complexion, with carious teeth, we hear his high-pitched voice, observe a fit of his high-strung temper. But we also behold him as the paragon of beauty whose flawless profile awakens in Aschenbach memories of "Greek statues of the best period," "mystical concepts . . . of primeval times, of the origin of form and of the birth of the gods." In fact, Tadzio's shortcomings serve to support rather than weaken in Aschenbach's mind the ideal qualities of his figure. (pp. 54-5)

This "intensification" of the realistic figure into a figure of myth is carried out with the greatest circumspection. Nowhere is the reader required to relinquish reality in favor of myth. To be sure, Tadzio is set apart from his sisters, he is "desired, courted, admired." That in itself, however, would not lift him above the plane of reality. Only in Aschenbach's inflamed imagination is the figure likened to or identified with the immortal beings of Greek mythology. Even Tadzio's final appearance as Hermes in that impressive setting of complete isolation on the sea-encircled sand bar as a "figure most isolated and apart . . ." is at once rationalized as a vision of the dying poet: "But to him it seemed as if the pale and lovely psychagogue out there were smiling, beckoning to him, as if, lifting his hand from his hip, he were pointing ahead, flying before him into the realm of promise and tremendousness." . . . Analysis, then, proves psychological realism unbetrayed. Tadzio's identification with figures of myth can in every instance be explained on solidly rational grounds as a figment of Aschenbach's overwrought imagination.

And yet, such is the vividness of Mann's evocation of the mythical figures and their identification with Tadzio that we experience their fusion as palpably real and must exert a conscious effort to disengage in our imagination the "real" boy from the mythical overlay of the divine figures. Here Mann achieved a truly perfect *montage,* a splendid example of what Vernon Venable [see excerpt dated 1938] aptly calls his "new technique for the exploitation of poetic meaning . . . in which no symbol is allowed unequivocal connotation or independent status, but refers to all the others and is bound rigorously to them by means of a highly intricate system of subtly developed associations." Neither Tadzio as the Polish boy nor Tadzio-Hyacinthus, nor Tadzio-Narcissus, nor even Tadzio-Hermes are "allowed independent status" but they "are identified with each other and finally fused into the single, nuclear, paradoxical meaning which Mann wishes to emphasize." . . . Tadzio is, paradoxically, the inspiration and challenge to the artist's creative urge that measures and molds and bodies forth, and is its nemesis, the tempter to lassitude, stupor, and final disintegration of body and mind.

When Aschenbach first catches sight of the youth, he is at once impressed by his beauty as a magical combination of a uniquely personal charm, of the "purest perfecton of form." He is stimulated to musings on the secret of the "mysterious union which the normative must form with the individual element, so that human beauty may be born . . ." It is this "mysterious synthesis" which Thomas Mann has achieved in his figure of Tadzio. He has created in him the human being of flesh and blood with its unique charm, with its flaws and failings that bring him close to us and rouse in us the compassion which goes out only toward our fellow men; and he has raised this "real" being into a complex symbol whose existence is beyond time and space in the realm of eternal myth. In sum, he has achieved in Tadzio a perfect combination of "psychology plus myth."

It is not at all surprising to find in Mann's portrayal of Gustav von Aschenbach his skill of psychological analysis and realistic description at a high pitch of perfection, for Aschenbach is, to a significant degree, a self-portrait and is the representative of a way of life, the artist's life, which Mann has explored with such uncompromising, sharp-eyed penetration. What is more impressive is to find the author able to maintain in his portraiture of the protagonist the same subtle balance and tension between reality and symbol, psychology and myth which we had found in the other chracters of the *novella*. Mann's delineation of Aschenbach oscillates tensely between the poles of apotheosis and deflation, of idealization and searching analysis touched with gentle irony, between grandiloquence and understatement, between rhetorical flourish and sober naturalistic prose, without, however, ever quite touching either extreme.

The dialectical polarity of style is rooted in Mann's attitude toward his hero, which is at once detached and empathetic, marked by an urge to elevate to the prototypical and to deflate to the problematical, characterized by sincere admiration, even adulation and by that smiling irony that has discovered the Achilles' heel. This double-visioned manner of portrayal is also predicated upon Mann's basic concept of the protagonist as an "unheroic" hero, as the "hero of creative work" par excellence. This heroism is a heroism of weakness, a heroism of the "despite" *despite* frailty of body, *despite* a problematical, overfastidious, quickly exhausted mind. Such heroism cannot be conveyed except by way of realistic description and searching psychoanalysis, while at the same time the urge to ennoble must also be operative. Thus, Mann's favorite combination of "psychology plus myth" proves to be the perfect means to body forth such a "heroic" figure. Gustav von Aschenbach is raised upon a pedestal as *the* poet-laureate of exemplary achievement, but he is also examined as a "case" on the psychiatrist's couch. He is associated in the reader's mind with figures of the glorious Grecian past and of Christian legend, with Socrates and Saint Sebastian. Yet these figures are themselves brought down from their lofty plane. To be sure, Socrates is shown as a man of mature wisdom but he is also characterized with quite unGrecian pathos as the human-all-too-human mark of youth's seductive beauty, and the figure of Saint Sebastian is introduced, significantly, by a "clever analyst"—none other, of course, than the "analyst" Thomas Mann himself—who proceeds to modernize the figure by way of an analysis which is both "brilliant" and "precise" into the representative of an "intellectual and youthful manliness, which clenches its teeth in proud bashfulness and stands quietly while the swords and spears transfix its body." It is interesting to note how this passage in its choice of descriptive vocabulary holds the finest balance between the elevated and the realistic style, moving closer to the former in such a traditionally "heroic" phrase as: "while the swords and spears transfix its body," tending toward the realistic in the expression: "clenches its teeth" which serves to render a carefully observed physiological detail from the workaday world. Unquestionably, the sacrosanct figure of the Saint loses some of its patina in the hands of the "analyst." In fact, it may be argued that the very opposite of "myth-building" is taking place, that it is not Aschenbach who is elevated, by the process of association and approximation, to the Saint's immortal plane, but rather that it is the figure of saintly legend that suffers a loss of imposing other-worldliness in changing into an "unheroic" hero of our times. The juster view would seem to be that of a well-nigh perfect ambivalence with the patina lost by the Saint being transferred to the figure of Mann's hero.

Aschenbach's way to his doom is traced with extreme economy on the level of plot, in keeping with the demands of the *novella* genre and, more significantly, with Mann's view of the highest function of narrative art. With Schopenhauer he holds that the epic writer's aim should be to conjure up the richest possible inner life by means of a minimum of external action. . . . Thus every detail of Aschenbach's outward life is so chosen as to illuminate the deepest recesses of his mind and to furnish the richest symbolical meaning. Aschenbach is drawn, on the psychological level, as the aging man whose rational, disciplined self is overwhelmed by a late and sudden eruption of emotional drives which had been all too long and ruthlessly suppressed; he is also the artist "who, sacrificing in the spirit, engenders beauty." This delineation is most searching in its statement of the unique case, yet at the same time it is most effective in raising the unique to the typical. Aschenbach transcends the individual, his fate too is set up as the symbol and mirror of the lot of creative man who follows the danger-beset path, that "erring and sinful way" which leads by the senses toward the goal of ultimate cognition and beauty. In fact, Aschenbach's figure gains its importance precisely by transcending the unique and individual "case" and rising to the typical and the eternal. Thus ***Death in Venice*** is once again seen to be an important step in Mann's reorientation, with growing maturity, from the "middle-class and individual" to timeless myth. . . . (pp. 55-9)

It is but natural that Aschenbach's figure and fate, being central to the *novella,* would have received extensive and intensive treatment. To enter upon a full-scale analysis would be to move along well-beaten paths. Nevertheless, one important theme seems to have received no more than passing mention and deserves elaboration. It is the typically Romantic theme of the fatal fascination held by the sunlit, idyllic South for the denizen of the mist-shrouded North. The *locus classicus* of this theme in the *novella* is that seemingly realistic description of Aschenbach's summer place in the mountains and the subsequent passage quoted all but verbatim from Homer's *Odyssey*.

Just prior to complete surrender to the lure of Venice and his long yearning for "freedom," Aschenbach thinks back to the place of his creative toil in the North: "He remembered his country place in the mountains, the scene of his creative struggles in the summers, where the low clouds passed through the garden, frightful evening storms put out the lights of his house, and the ravens which he fed swung in the tops of the spruce trees." Surely, on the level of realism, it is rather startling to have Aschenbach keep "ravens" for pets. Yet this eccentricity of description with its attention-provoking "cue" is, of course, intentional. It serves to switch the mind of the reader attuned to the "combination" of realism and myth to the mythological plane. With a start one becomes aware of Aschenbach's approximation to Odin-Wodan whose mythological bird was, in fact, the raven. Now the other elements of the montage fall neatly into place and reveal their full significance: the mountainous setting, the low-hanging clouds, the terrifying storms that extinguish the lights of the house, the ravens swinging in the wind-tossed "tops of the spruce trees." With what calculated effect the words are chosen to conjure up the mythological setting without entirely cancelling out reality! We see Aschenbach's "country place" but at the same time we see, as if superimposed upon it, mighty Thor in his ram-drawn chariot laying about him with hammer and lightning, threatening the home, extinguishing the hospitable fire of helpless mortals; we see the typical setting which Romantic imagination has formed into the timeless abode of the Nordic gods, especially stark and forbidding when contrasted with the idyllic shores of the Mediterranean and the sunlit heights of Olympus.

It is precisely this Romantic antithesis that patterns Aschenbach's feelings and thoughts. As he recalls his Northern home, his present surroundings turn into a veritable Elysium: "Then it would seem to him as if he had been transported to the land of Elysium, to the limits of the earth, where the lightest of lives is granted to men, where there is no snow nor winter, no storm nor streaming rain, but Oceanos ever sends up the gently cooling breeze and in blissful idleness the days slip by without effort, without struggle, and entirely devoted to the sun and its festivals." (pp. 59-60)

In the supreme achievement of his master *novella* Thomas Mann draws equally from both fountainheads of truly great art, from the immediate, sensible present and the endless vistas of the past, from the fleeing reality of life and the timeless reality of art. Throughout he maintains, with an unerring touch, a unique equilibrium between the realism of coldly controlled observation, of self-critical analysis and that Dionysiac intoxication, that inspired creative élan, that "splendid sensation of uplift" capable of infusing the specters of a mythical past with a new vibrant vitality and thus creates what must be adjudged a masterpiece of "psychology plus myth." (p. 61)

André Von Gronicka, "Myth Plus Psychology: A Stylistic Analysis of 'Death in Venice'," in Thomas Mann: A Collection of Critical Essays, *edited by Henry Hatfield, Prentice-Hall, Inc., 1964, pp. 46-61.*

R. HINTON THOMAS (essay date 1956)

[*Thomas is the author of the critical study* Thomas Mann: The Mediation of Art, *which focuses on Mann's major works. In the following excerpt from that work, Thomas discusses* Death in Venice *and the decline of the artist Aschenbach as representative of the deterioration of German society. For a similar, though somewhat broader view of the novella, see the excerpt by John Bovey (1940).*]

Mann has described the modest origins of his story [***Death in Venice***], how certain personal observations on the Lido suggested themselves as suitable for a short story appropriate for such a journal as *Simplicissimus* and how in the process of composition they formed themselves together in a manner that he could not have anticipated [see excerpt dated 1936]. Without prior intention the elements of the story, as he put it in an image bearing the stamp of Goethe, 'shot together, in the actual sense in which one might speak of a crystal, to form a pattern which, playing in the light of different facets and hovering amid manifold sets of relationships, could well make its author, actively watching over its growth, dream in astonishment'. He goes on: 'I love this word: association (*Beziehung*). However relative it may be, the idea of what is significant coincides in my mind entirely with it. That which is significant is nothing other than that which is rich in associations.' The meaning of this passage becomes clearer in conjunction with some words from ***The Magic Mountain:*** 'We will put it like this: a spiritual—that is to say, a significant—thing is "significant" precisely through the fact that it points beyond itself, that it is the expression and manifestation of a spiritual generality, of a whole world of feeling and outlook which has found in it its more or less perfect symbol—and it is in accordance therewith that the degree of its significance is measured.'

Now, one important feature of ***Death in Venice,*** as compared with Mann's earlier works, is that the problems of the artistic existence are not seen here in contrast to the bourgeois world but that in a full and integral sense the artist becomes the focus and symbol of society. Aschenbach, the 'born deceiver', was the 'poet of all those who labour on the brink of exhaustion' and, combatting weakness with redoubled efforts of will and organization, 'at any rate for a time secure the effects of greatness. There are many of them, they are the heroes of the age. And they all recognized themselves in his work, they found themselves confirmed and proclaimed in it, they were conscious of their gratitude to him, they honoured his name.' In this work Mann writes, as it were, in advance the epitaph of a Germany still at the height of power, whose outward power and prosperity are felt as 'an elegant façade which up to the last moment conceals an inner undermining and biological decay from the eyes of the world'. Aschenbach 'represents' Prussianized Germany. The symbol for art such as Aschenbach's, we are told, and the words bear equally on Mann's view of Germany, would be the figure of St. Sebastian, the Roman soldier and Christian martyr, killed by arrows under Diocletian—an art infused with a 'manliness' 'which in proud modesty grits its teeth and remains calmly standing while swords and arrows pierce its body'. In his ***Thoughts on the War*** Mann was shortly from rather the same angle to portray Frederick the Great's struggle as a 'heroic' fight against weakness and fearful odds and in the ***Reflections*** the 'heroism' of Germany's war effort against overwhelming difficulties.

Aschenbach shuns the impurities of common life, but the artistic products of his withdrawal embody—contrary to his will and intention—some of the deepest aspects of the world around him. ***Death in Venice,*** Lukacs declared many years later, can be regarded as a great forerunner 'of that tendency which signalizes the danger of a barbarous underworld within modern German civilisation as its necessary complementary product'. Of course, this had no part in Mann's conscious purpose in writing the story, but he commented favourably on Lukacs's statement. For the only correct perspective, he said, is to see the poet as a 'seismograph, a medium of sensitivity', unclear as to his organic function, often guilty of wrong-headed judgements, but capable nevertheless of embodying in his work the deeper realities of his age and society'. The statement, which certainly does not indicate the whole truth about Mann's view of the writer, is nevertheless helpful in approaching the question of Mann's realism, in understanding its nature and its limitations. No other major work of his was in its conception so far removed from social or ideological intention, none more 'artistic', none more concentrated than this in its manipulation of the resources of symbolism, and in none is so much social truth, and of such profundity, caught in so small a compass. (pp. 82-4)

R. Hinton Thomas, in his Thomas Mann: The Mediation of Art, *1956. Reprint by Oxford at the Clarendon Press, Oxford, 1963, 188 p.*

ERICH HELLER (essay date 1958)

[*Heller is a Czechoslovakian-born British essayist, translator, and educator who has written and edited numerous studies of the works of such German and German-language authors as Friedrich Nietzsche, Franz Kafka, and Mann. In the following excerpt from his comprehensive critical study* Thomas Mann: The Ironic German, *originally published in 1958, Heller offers a detailed discussion of Mann's literary techniques and parodistic style in* Death in Venice.]

One of the tests of an artistic creation lies in its hold on the memory, in its manner of staying there. Works of art often provoke the memory to play the tricks of a child's mind: to abstract from the adult wholeness of the impression the random and mysteriously significant detail which with the passing of time assumes a monumental quality. Particularly with a minor work it may easily happen that, coming upon it again, we find to our dismay that the remembered monument is a mere trifle within the composition. This is less likely to occur in the case of a major work, for there every detail is infused with the meaning of the whole. In ***Death in Venice*** there is indeed hardly a detail which is not "telling," which does not tell in its miniature way the entire story. Yet the total effect is not one of overloading, but of complete lucidity. In fact, what stays in the mind and absorbs every detail is a truly monumental vision: a man meeting his fate in beauty, a man on his own, whom we never see in the company of other people, and of whose past life we know next to nothing. But this monumental quality is achieved without the slightest deviation from strict realism. Everything is what it is: the tramp is a tramp, the street-musician is a street-musician, the hotel is a hotel, and Venice is Venice. No attempt is made—say, in the manner of Kafka—to unsteady our trust in the reliability of everyday experience. Nevertheless the ordinary world is under notice of dismissal. We feel that at any moment we may be left with the purest extract from reality: man, sea, sky, an empty beach—playthings in the hand of Fate. ***Death in Venice,*** alone among all the works of extreme psychological realism, achieves in all seriousness the parodistic semblance of mythic innocence. It is a triumph of deliberation and intuition, helped not a little by the limited scope of the chosen form. (pp. 98-9)

This may be the place to show in some detail the working and great efficiency of Thomas Mann's literary technique, for ***Death in Venice*** is the quintessential proof of its power. (p. 100)

An overture which contains *in nuce* the whole drama and is yet the beginning of the story proper—this is what Thomas Mann achieves on the first pages of ***Death in Venice.*** Being made explicit, this condensation may appear overdeliberate and obtrusive. It is not. Such are the literary tact and economy of the author, that only repeated readings will reveal the technique. What then, it may well be asked, is its point and immediate effect? To work the first and decisive spell of seduction. The reader's imagination is made to accept, unknowingly yet, the final consummation, just as the hero of the story is set on a road which looks harmless enough and is yet paved with the intentions of doom. What these first pages describe is a dramatically very modest situation: Aschenbach, his mind overstrained by repeated and repeatedly vain attempts to maneuver his work over an obstinate difficulty, has been out for a lengthy walk. Having returned to the outskirts of the city, he is now waiting for the tram to take him back. The stopping-place is in front of a stonemason's yard and opposite the entrance to a cemetery. At the gates of the cemetery stands a tramplike figure with rucksack and walkingstick. The sight awakens in Aschenbach the strong desire to travel. He decides that he will do so.

Most of the powerful insinuations of the scene are brought out even in a translation which, however, cannot help adding a note of slightly clumsy portentousness. This is the literary drawback, almost unavoidable, of all English renderings of Thomas Mann, and so often his undoing in the eyes of English critics. What the translation invariably misses is the ironical elegance and the overtone of mockery, subtly ridiculing the habitual posturing of the German language. In English, alas, the ironically draped velvet and silk often look like solemnly donned corduroy and tweed. . . .

> The mortuary chapel opposite, a structure in Byzantine style, caught and threw back into the silence the gleam of the ebbing day. Its façade, adorned with Greek crosses and hieratic designs in light colors, displayed symmetrically arranged inscriptions in gilded letters, select scriptural texts concerning the future life, such as "They are entering into the House of the Lord," or "May the Light Everlasting shine upon them." Aschenbach passed a few minutes of his waiting immersed in the transparent mystical meaning of those words, until his attention was diverted by the sight of a man standing in the portico, above the two apocalyptic beasts that guarded the flight of steps. Something not quite usual in this man's appearance gave his thoughts a fresh turn.

This is how both death and Venice make their first appearance at the Munich opening of ***Death in Venice.*** For it is, of course, already Venice which is present in the glistening desertion, the gleam of the departing day, the Byzantine structure, the ornate façade, the hieratic designs, and the apocalyptic beasts, while the untenanted graveyard may somehow belong to the domain of the stranger of whom it is impossible to tell "whether he had come out of the chapel through the bronze doors or mounted unnoticed from outside," as suddenly as he will soon vanish again out of Aschenbach's sight. What is unusual about him? Only if we impress the details of his appearance upon our memories shall we recognize him, as Aschenbach will not, in three future disguises. He is "of medium height, thin, beardless, and strikingly snub-nosed," and "obviously not Bavarian." His "broad, straight-brimmed straw hat makes him look distinctly exotic." (pp. 101-02)

If we add the bare teeth to the description of his physical attitude, as he supports himself with the iron-shod stick resting slantwise on the ground, then a mere extension of stick and iron, and a mere disregard of the meager flesh, bring before our eyes a Durer image of Death, the first in a little procession which will accompany Aschenbach on his journey. And journey he must, for at the sight of the journeyman the urge to do so comes upon him with hallucinatory violence; and his imagination, not quite at rest yet after the hours of work, seizes upon "a model of the marvels and terrors of the manifold earth." (p. 103)

[The] hallucination of the jungle completes, in anticipation, the story of Gustav Aschenbach. He, the classical writer of his age and country, who has "rejected the abyss" and entered into a covenant with Apollo, determined as he is to let his art do service in the humanization of man, unwittingly goes out in search of Dionysus and dies in his embrace. As the messenger of Death will come back, so the vision of the fertile chaos will recur, and each time death will be in an ever-closer alliance with the chaotically brooding sources of life, an alliance irresistibly strong in its attack upon the disciplined forms of the human spirit. But as the disciplined forms of art require for their being the most intimate association with the dark ground of creativity, ***Death in Venice*** is Thomas Mann's first tragic allegory of art. (p. 104)

If Gustav Aschenbach had no choice, neither had Thomas Mann. He could not have chosen another scene for Aschenbach's doom. Venice is its inevitable location. For it seems a city built by the very Will to Power in honor of Death. Teeming with Life, it is yet entirely Art, the residence of Eros Thanatos, the *Liebestod,* the music of which it has inspired, just as it has inspired Nietzsche's one almost perfect lyrical poem. Venice is to Nietzsche "another word" for both music and the South, of that happiness of which he was unable to think without a "shudder of fear." It is the city too of Platen's poetry—and "Tristan" is the prophetic title of the poem which begins with the best line he ever wrote: *"Wer die Schönheit angeschaut mit Augen, ist dem Tode schon anheimgegeben,"* handing over to death him who has set eyes on beauty. And, indeed, it is

Death himself who rows Gustav Aschenbach to this consummation. (p. 105)

That very evening Aschenbach sees Tadzio for the first time—and Charon may be sure of his obol. Thomas Mann now tells the history of a passion with an economy and intensity unsurpassed in all his work. It is as if the art of writing tried to gather into itself some of the resources of architecture and music in order to produce transparent clarity of form by means of ceaseless musical allusiveness—a parody of the classical manner achieved with Wagnerian methods. Tristan in hexameters—the obvious absurdity of the suggestion is the measure of the startling success of ***Death in Venice.*** (p. 106)

[For a time,] the classical mood dominates Aschenbach's mind as well as the style of the narrative. In the beach scene . . . , however, another ingredient is faintly added to it: the soft, melodious sound of Polish. Aschenbach, not without curiosity to learn the boy's name, tries to catch the word by which he is called. First, he can only make out "two musical syllables, something like Adgio—or, more often still, Adjiu, with a long-drawn-out *u* at the end." But even before he has found out the full name—Tadzio, a shortened form of Thaddeus, with its vocative Tadziu—we are back again in classical antiquity: Tadzio has a playmate on the beach, another Polish boy, most affectionately devoted to him; once he even embraces and kisses Tadzio. "But you, Critobulus," Aschenbach socratically quotes to himself with a smile, "you I advise to take a year's leave. That long, at least, you will need for complete recovery." Meanwhile Tadzio is bathing far out in the sea; and at once the Dionysian flute breaks in. Mother and governess anxiously call out to him, and his name "with its soft consonants and long-drawn *u*-sound, seems to possess the beach like a rallying cry; the cadence had a quality at once sweet and wild: Tadziu! Tadziu!"

This would suffice to show the extraordinary and yet unforced consistency of Thomas Mann's composition. There is hardly a moment in the narrative which is not reached by an echo at least of the war which is its subject—the war between form and chaos, serenity of mind and consuming passion, articulate names and enticingly melodious syllables, hexameters and long-drawn *u*-sounds, with Death presiding over it as judge and ultimate conqueror. What happened at a Munich tram-stop, where an upholder of the classical virtues of writing was momentarily lost in a vision of the jungle, is tentatively repeated on the Lido beach where the Apolline contemplation of beauty is ever so slightly disturbed by the first quiver of the Dionysian carnival. Aschenbach is still in high spirits as from his deck-chair he delights in the sight of Tadzio while tasting fresh strawberries he has purchased from a vendor. Yet this piling of deliciousness upon delight already savors of excess, and before too long it will be strawberries again, but then overripe and soft, possible carriers of the deadly infection, bought in an unclean corner of the plague-infested city to quench an intolerable thirst. Aschenbach will greedily swallow them, almost fainting with exhaustion after a mad and vain pursuit of his idol through the sirocco-sultry maze of Venetian alleys.

But before the story of Aschenbach reaches this dissolute climax, Thomas Mann traces with consummate skill all the stages of passion: how the aesthetic enjoyment changes to infatuation, infatuation to love, love to degrading abandon, abandon to death. And Venice joins in: the temperature on the beach rises from day to day, the blue sky turns leaden, a sirocco sets in, the streets begin to smell of carbolic acid, nothing can any longer stop the spreading disease. At one point, before he has acknowledged to himself the nature and power of his passion, Aschenbach, suffering badly from the sirocco, determines to leave. It is the last exercise of his moral will; and it fails. The virtuosity of the narrator is at its highest in the delineation of this incident: how Aschenbach, resentful at being hurried over breakfast, but in fact only desirous of seeing Tadzio once more, allows his luggage to be taken to the station ahead of him on the hotel's private motorboat, while he himself will follow later—for there is plenty of time—on the public vaporetto; how his sadness mounts, sadness at losing Venice forever, as he travels along the palaces of the *Canal Grande;* how he curses his rash decision as the weather seems to improve; how at the station he finds that his luggage has gone on the wrong train; how he is easily persuaded to await its return on the Lido; how his innermost soul rejoices at the accident as if secretly celebrating the successful conclusion of a subtle maneuver; and how, as he settles down again in the hotel, he realizes that he will be in no haste to leave again, for it is Tadzio to whom he has come back. And indeed, the weather changes, the sky is clear, and the prose itself seems now to worship the sun god with Homeric metaphors and rhythms which are yet disquietingly upset by adjectives and inflections announcing the wilder deity.

As he lies by the sea, Aschenbach's mind weaves image after image from the glitter and haze of sun and water; and one is of the ancient plane-tree where Socrates holds forth to young Phaedrus. "For beauty, my Phaedrus, beauty alone is lovely and visible at once. Mark you, it is the sole aspect of the spiritual which we can perceive through our senses, or bear to perceive. . . . So beauty, then, is the lover's way to the spirit—but only the way, only the means, my little Phaedrus." Soon, however, this wanderer will miss his way and arrive at another destination. It happens one evening when the Polish family are absent from dinner. Aschenbach, restless after his meal, walks up and down in front of the hotel. Suddenly, in the light of the arc-lamp, he sees them approach and, caught unawares, his face may perhaps express more than he normally permits it to show in the sight of Tadzio. And Tadzio responds, and smiles at him: "Such must have been the smile of Narcissus as he bent over the mirroring pool, a smile, profound, infatuated, lingering, as he put out his arms to the reflection of his own beauty; the lips just slightly strained, perhaps by the vanity of his desire to touch the lips of his shadow—with a mingling of coquetry and curiosity and a faint unease, enthralling and enthralled." "And he who had received that smile turned away with it as though entrusted with a fatal gift." As Aschenbach flees into the darkness of the garden, words strangely mixed of tenderness and reproach burst from him: "Listen, one must not smile like that at anyone! How dare you smile like that!" And Aschenbach knows that he is lost in love.

"Mirror and image," these are the names which Aschenbach once gave to the beauty embodied in a work of art. Mirror; and now Narcissus. Addressed to Narcissus, Aschenbach's declaration of love is at the same time his declaration of defeat. For Narcissus is in love with himself, and no passion is more disastrous than the love he calls forth from others. (pp. 107-09)

Death himself makes yet another, his last, appearance in the story, this time in the shape of a musical buffoon, a guitarist, leader of a band of street-musicians. . . . It is in this street-musician that the various features distributed among the previous messengers of Death are merged and enriched: the thin, snub-nosed face, and teeth showing, vagrancy—they all appear to come from another place—poverty oddly combined with the signs of a despotic will, an existence unconventional to the point of the illicit, lasciviousness and the power to bring about the relaxation of all rules of discipline, and, added now, the odor of disease and a rather dubious association with the art of music. Also, Tadzio is now part of the scene; and as if to hint at his having a place among the images of death, Thomas Mann makes him stand at the balustrade of the terrace in a position reminiscent of the stranger in Munich: "with his legs crossed" and one of his arms "propped against his waist."

Aschenbach tries in vain to extract from the guitarist the secret behind the smell of disinfectant. He comes to know it on the following day. The English clerk of a travel bureau tells him the truth "in his honest and comfortable language." Asiatic cholera has made its way into Venice, that pestilence which has its source "in the hot, moist swamps of the Ganges delta, breeding in the mephitic air of the primeval jungle where the tiger crouches in the bamboo thickets." Aschenbach's mind goes back to those cemetery gates in Munich, but the very thought of return, sobriety, labor, and mastery appalls him beyond endurance. No, he will not warn Tadzio's mother, he will keep the secret; and indeed, his sharing in it fills him with a sense of wild conspiracy, with giddy and unreasoning hopes. Virtue and art count for nothing compared to the "advantages of chaos," and Aschenbach's feverish brain seizes upon the abominably sweet prospect of a deserted island, emptied by death and panic, and his remaining there alone with Tadzio. (pp. 110-12)

Death in Venice is not only "parody," it is also paradox: a work of art embodying so radical a critique of art that it amounts to its moral rejection. Aschenbach's scruples read like that letter . . . which Keats wrote to Richard Woodhouse (October 27, 1818): "The poetical character . . . has no character," and "what shocks the virtuous philosopher delights the Chameleon Poet"—a deficiency of character which Keats views with equanimity: "It does no harm from its relish of the dark side of things any more than from its taste for the bright one; because they both end in speculation." But Thomas Mann—perhaps because he has in him less of the poet and more of the virtuous philosopher—fears harm. His, or at least Aschenbach's Platonic speculations lead straight into the Platonic Republic from which the poet is banned for the sake of civic order and moral dependability. In this respect, too, Schopenhauer is left behind. For Schopenhauer accepted, transforming it into a metaphysical psychology of art, Kant's definition of beauty as something that pleases without appealing to any self-interest in the beholder, something that gives pure, disinterested pleasure. Nietzsche, however, mocks so saintly a conception. Quoting Stendhal's definition of beauty as *"une promesse de bonheur"* ["a promise of happiness"], he asks: "Who is right, Kant or Stendhal?—When our aesthetic philosophers never tire of protesting, in support of Kant, that under the spell of beauty one may *even* behold statues of female nudes 'without interest,' one may well laugh at their expense. The experience of *artists* is, with regard to this delicate point, more 'interesting,' and, surely, Pygmalion was not a man without 'aesthetic judgment.'" Neither is Gustav Aschenbach, whose fate places ***Death in Venice*** at an extreme point in the endless debate about the moral significance of art.

It may, of course, be asked whether so paradoxically *artistic* a presentation of the case against art deserves to be taken seriously. The answer may be found in the fact that the "speculation" in which ***Death in Venice*** ends has none of the Keatsean "harmlessness." It is the speculation of a radical moralist who ironically asserts his moralism in a subject of seemingly modish morbidity. With ***Death in Venice*** Thomas Mann has closed the circle of doubts besetting his moral existence as a writer. In ***Buddenbrooks*** art emerges as the destroyer of life. The artist Tonio Kröger, on the other side of life, can only justify himself by holding on to his love for the artless world. The artist's love for the artless world is psychologically scrutinized and monstrously suspected in ***Fiorenza.*** And Gustav Aschenbach, having seemingly risen beyond suspicion in the disciplined service of art, is brought down by the revengeful forces of life. The circle seems to be as vicious as can be, and so firmly drawn that it is hard to break. To be sure, no book of Thomas Mann's, apart from the essay on Frederick the Great, was written between 1911—the year of ***Death in Venice***—and 1918; and what did appear in 1918, ***Meditations of a Nonpolitical Man,*** was no work of art. It was a vast volume of speculations, all bearing the mark of deep and passionate concern, about the moral state and possible self-defense of writer and writing in a world which, not unlike Aschenbach, had upheld the virtues of moral discipline and civilized achievement only to sink into chaos and war. (pp. 113-14)

Erich Heller, in his Thomas Mann: The Ironic German, *The World Publishing Company, 1961, 303 p.*

EUGENE McNAMARA (essay date 1962)

[McNamara is a Canadian poet, fiction writer, and critic. In the following excerpt, he discusses imagery employed by Mann in Death in Venice *to reveal both the physical and spiritual natures of the individual as well as the emotional and moral conflict that results when either portion of human nature is suppressed.]*

Through an ambiguous structuring of the imagery in the story, **"Death in Venice,"** Thomas Mann made an observation about a problem common to all men: living in harmony with a diverse nature.

Hence, **"Death in Venice,"** often regarded as an "artist-fable," like Kafka's "Hunger Artist" or James's "The Figure in the Carpet," can be read as a parable of the unexamined life and its dangers. Mann seems to say that no one can live a splintered existence. A human being is not an angel; neither is he completely an animal. Being both spirit and matter, he must somehow reconcile these two diverse natures and live in harmony with them. Failure to do so ends in destruction of the self.

Gustave Aschenbach had lived for too long as an austere stoic. His submerged animal nature, long repressed, struggled for expression. But it was not only the atmosphere of Venice ("Southern," artistic, and corrupt) and the presence of Tadzio that brought the hidden self into full eruption—an eruption that not only gave expression to the buried self but destroyed the unity of the human being. A hint could be seen in Aschenbach's "new type of hero" that appeared in his latest works. This "new type of hero" might be a disguised expression of the artist's hidden nature: It is an image taken from Botticelli's painting of St. Sebastian ("an intellectual and virginal manliness, which clinches its teeth and stands in modest defiance of the swords and spears that pierce its side.") This could either indicate a sublimated masochism or give rise to a new prototype: the suffering homosexual as hero. (p. 233)

A close look at Mann's image patterns in the story gives ample indication of this more generalized theme. It is more a matter of inference, of mood generated by atmosphere, than it is one of direct reference. The time of the story gives added impetus to this universal meaning. It is immediately before World War I, which Mann has elsewhere seen as the great watershed of modern times, separating the old corrupt world from the new, healing a sick civilization through amputation.

Aschenbach's ruminations before the deserted graveyard are interrupted by the apparition of the foreign traveller. The word "apparition" is used quite literally here. "Whether he had come out of the hall through the bronze doors or mounted unnoticed from outside, it was impossible to tell." Immediately before the manifestation of this bizarre figure from the house of death, Aschenbach had been reading the Byzantine texts carved on the tomb: "They are entering the House of the Lord." Then the sight of the stranger sets off a chain of feelings in Aschenbach: "He felt the most surprising consciousness of a widening of inward barriers, a kind of vaulting unrest, a youthfully ardent thirst for distant scenes."

This is certainly in keeping with the connotations of the traveller's garb, but is surprising in the context of death and the future life suggested by the graveyard and tomb. And the malevolent quality of the stranger's gaze is hardly an incentive to feelings of youthful unrest. Surely the stranger, in the context of the scene, suggests more a Summoner for Everyman, an emissary of death, than merely a fortuitous image of travel. The lines, "True, what he felt was no more than a longing to travel; yet coming upon him with such suddenness and passion as to resemble a seizure, almost a hallucination" reinforce the notion of a vision, giving the entire scene outside the graveyard the quality of the supernatural. In light of this, Aschenbach's whole adventure can be seen as a dream-journey, as a parable.

It is in this scene too that the image of the jungle with its rank vegetation and a "crouching tiger" looms up. This landscape vision fades, never to recur in the story. The land Aschenbach visits is no jungle, but a civilized city. Yet the tiger appears again. When Aschenbach first learns of the plague from the English travel clerk, he thinks of the breeding place of cholera, "that primeval island-jungle, among whose bamboo thickets the tiger crouches."

In light of the close and careful structure of the story, the tiger does not appear again by chance. In the initial vision, outside the graveyard, he not only brings up thoughts of the far-off and exotic, but occasions a set of ambiguous feelings in Aschenbach: "He felt his heart throb with terror, yet with a longing inexplicable." Even so does he regard the plague. It is dangerous and horrible; yet it keeps him near Tadzio and seems, moreover, to represent his own hidden corruption. The crouching tiger might represent Aschenbach's destiny, lying off in the future, as the crouching beast waited for John Marcher in James's *The Beast in the Jungle*. It might also represent Aschenbach's long-repressed animal nature, coiling for its spring.

The image of the malevolent foreign traveller who summons Aschenbach to the journey recurs in the same ambiguous manner. As the elderly artist lies on the beach, just before his death, it seems to him that the far-off figure of Tadzio moves and changes. "It seemed to him the pale and lovely Summoner out there smiled at him and beckoned; as though, with the hand lifted from his hip, he pointed outward as he hovered on before into an immensity of richest expectation." If the traveller before the tomb was an ambiguous messenger, calling him either to death and judgment or simply to far places, there is no question here. The "pale and lovely Summoner" beckons him to death.

This ambiguous shift in context occurs in the use of sun imagery throughout the story too. From a light of pagan joy it becomes a source of corruption. Aschenbach's approach to his relationship with Tadzio undergoes the same ambiguous treatment. He begins, naturally enough, in literary allusion. With a host of mythological and literary rationales (Socrates and Phaedrus, Apollo and Hyacinthus, Narcissus, Oceanus, Eros) he tries to "poetize" his feelings for the boy. But the Platonized structure soon breaks down into the physical, the sentimental, and the erotic. This double-leveled imagery lends itself to the central ironies of the story: the divided self, the hidden forces suppressed within, the coming downfall of intellectual pride. As much as Aschenbach invokes Apollo and Hyacinthus or tries to sublimate his interest in "a page and a half of perfect prose" the tiger lies in wait within the bamboo thickets of the secret self.

This same element of ambiguity is seen in the theme of disguise that pervades the imagery. The mysterious traveller may be a disguised Summoner for Death. Aschenbach is alone and incognito in Venice. The terrible old man on the boat who is imperfectly disguised as a youth becomes Aschenbach disguised to himself in the final stages of his disintegration. Tadzio, the beckoning fair one on the beach, is really a Summoner for Death. And Venice itself disguises its hidden sickness under a fog of lies, official silence, sweet-smelling disinfectants. The imagery creates a mood in which the disintegration of Aschenbach the artist can be seen as an example of what Robert Penn Warren called "the tragic division of our age." Man lives a splintered, truncated existence. Either he lives in an impossibly idealistic intellectuality or he lives as the most bestial of beasts. To live as either, and not as both, is to invite destruction. The "opening of inward barriers" left Aschenbach without human balance. His moral rigidity, a weapon of his intellectual creativity, left him vulnerable and open to invasion from the world of the senses. (pp. 233-34)

Eugene McNamara, "'Death in Venice': The Disguised Self," in College English, *Vol. 24, No. 3, December, 1962, pp. 233-34.*

JAMES B. HEPWORTH (essay date 1963)

[In the following excerpt, Hepworth draws parallels between the Dionysian myth as depicted in Erwin Rohde's Psyche *and the symbolic aspects of the myth as evidenced in* Death in Venice. *He posits that the character of Tadzio is Mann's own recreation of the god Dionysus, and that Aschenbach is a votary of the god. For further discussions of the use of myth in* Death in Venice, *see the excerpts by André von Gronicka (1956) and A. E. Dyson (1971); for further discussion of the influence of Rohde's* Psyche *on* Death in Venice, *see the Herbert Lehnert entry in the Additional Bibliography.]*

Approximately fifty years have passed since Thomas Mann wrote his finest and best known short story, **"Death in Venice."** In the course of this half century it has been the subject of a never-ending stream of essays and critical analyses. Thus, it would seem that any further comment would necessarily have to be a rehash or re-evaluation of that which has already appeared in print. However, I should like to submit that, up to now, one of the most significant aspects of the story has gone unnoticed or at least (to my knowledge) has not been published.

Soon after Gustav Aschenbach's arrival in Venice his ears ring with the sound of an unusual name with a "long-drawn-out *u* at the end" as it issues forth from the throats of the women on the beach. The name sounds to him at first like "Adgio" then again like "Adjiu." And, as he pondered over the strange sounds, the name "conjured up mythology" in his mind.

It seems strange indeed that so little attention has been paid to this all-important phrase since it is, so to speak, the key to a better understanding of **"Death in Venice."** In short, it is only when we realize precisely what this particular mythology is that we are able to correctly interpret a great amount of the symbolism which hitherto has escaped the eyes of the critics.

A considerable number of deities and mythological figures are mentioned in the story but, with the possible exception of Zeus, none of the names of these could possibly have any connection with that with the long-drawn-out *u* sound at the end. Hence, we must turn our attention elsewhere. The solution to the problem, I am sure, is to be found in the myth of Dionysos whose name, strangely enough, is not to be found anywhere in the story.

Information concerning Dionysos can be obtained from a variety of ancient sources of which Euripides' *The Bacchae* is the most enlightening. Perhaps the best single short summary of the essential features of the Dionysiac rites, however, is to be found in Erwin Rohde's *Psyche*. Here we are provided with a composite picture of the nocturnal festivals held in honor of this strange god. While space does not permit a reprinting of Rohde's description here, I should like to point out that it conforms in almost every detail to Thomas Mann's description of Aschenbach's dream except, of course, that Rohde lacks the poetic talent of Thomas Mann. Both refer to the wild music and dancing, the shrill cries of the votaries of the god, the peculiar uniform dress of the maddened women participants, the eating of the raw flesh and the drinking of the warm blood of the sacrificial animal.

Rohde, however, mentions one very important item which is only vaguely implied by Thomas Mann and it is precisely this one point around which the substance of my argument revolves. In speaking of the Bacchanals, *i.e.*, the votaries of Dionysos, Rohde says "they carried snakes sacred to Sabazios." Now Sabazios is simply one of the many names by which Dionysos was known and it appears that this was the name which was most frequently used by his intoxicated followers when calling upon the god to make his appearance in order that they could become possessed by him and become one with him. Thus, when in Aschenbach's dream he once again hears "the shrill haloos and a kind of howl with the long drawn out *u* sound at the end," he is most certainly hearing the votaries of the god calling out his name and at the same time he once again hears the identical sounds which conjured up mythology in his mind earlier in the story.

The point I wish to make, of course, is that the name "Tadzio" when called out by the women on the beach reminded Aschenbach of the name "Sabazios" and consequently of the myth of Dionysos. The similarity of the sounds contained in these two names is even closer in German since the *d* in "Tadzio" becomes unvoiced before the *z*, which is pronounced *ts*. At any rate, we can be certain that Thomas Mann's choice of this name for the young Polish boy was not an accidental one.

At least one version of the Dionysian myth informs us that the Theban-born god was brought up by a group of women somewhere in the East—probably Thrace. Although male worshippers were not unknown, the Dionysian world is primarily a feminine one. Women accompany him in all his comings and goings; they wait upon him and are most susceptible to his charms. It is the women in *The Bacchae* who were the first to be overcome by the strange madness attributed to the god. Also in **"Death in Venice"** it is interesting to note that Tadzio (who, like Dionysos, comes from the East) is constantly surrounded by women.

Among the others who form a group which attracts Aschenbach's attention early in the story . . . are two women and three girls who are sisters of the young boy. These are identically dressed and their appearance, according to Aschenbach's observation, suggests that of nuns, *i.e.*, of women who have dedicated themselves to a life of religious devotion. This is significant since it suggests the uniform dress of the Bacchanals who are religious devotees not entirely unlike the brides of Christ. The analogy becomes more convincing when we learn that the Dionysian myth tells of groups of sisters attaching themselves to the god. Furthermore, we are informed that almost always there are *three* sisters who stand in particularly close relationship with him.

One of the essential features of the Dionysian rites is phallicism. The thyrsoswand, which is also mentioned by Rohde, was closely associated with phallic worship, since this iron-tipped staff was, at times, adorned with a pine cone which is commonly considered to be a phallic symbol. On occasions more vivid phalli were used, such as the "obscene symbol of the godhead . . . monstrous and wooden" which Aschenbach sees in his dream. On the ship bound for Venice this phallic symbolism is once more vividly brought out. Among the passengers is a group of reveling youths from Pola. One, however, is young only to the extent that his use of cosmetics is effective. He is drunk and his tongue keeps "seeking the corner of his mouth in a suggestive motion ugly to behold". . . . The iron-shod stick which the beardless snub-nosed stranger at the beginning of the story . . . holds in his hand was, I believe, intended by Mann to symbolize the thyrsos-wand.

Perhaps the most startling result of my research in connection with the Dionysian myth as it appears in **"Death in Venice"** concerns the omophagic aspects of the rites of the god. According to ritual a young beast—usually a goat, *i.e.*, one of the animal incarnations of Dionysos—was selected as an offering and the worshippers ate the raw flesh and drank the warm blood of the victim. Rohde, as has been pointed out, makes some mention of this. So too, Aschenbach describes the drinking of the blood by the maddened women, and he too flung himself upon the animals and "bit and tore and swallowed smoking gobbets of flesh." . . . (pp. 172-74)

Now this Dionysiac dream which Aschenbach has is but the culmination of a series of events and experiences which precede it—some of which have already been noted. I should like now to point out that these last mentioned elements of his dream are also not without their antecedents.

It will be recalled that on two occasions . . . Aschenbach buys and eats "dead-ripe strawberries." It must also be remembered that he eats these berries for the first time while listening to the sounds which conjure up the myth of Dionysos. Hence, it is not difficult for us to assume that it was still on his mind and that he would naturally be impressed with the similarity between this blood-red fruit and raw flesh. If, however, this assumption places too great a strain on the imagination, perhaps

I can be more convincing by citing another instance of symbolic omophagia which should leave little doubt as to the intent of the author.

One evening after dinner Aschenbach finds himself sitting not far from Tadzio as both are listening to a group of street musicians who are entertaining the guests at the hotel. . . . He is aware that his reason is tottering and, though outwardly he manages to exercise some control of himself, his inner being is shaken with excitement. He forces himself to watch the singers, casting only now and then a glance at his beloved. He is in a state of complete intoxication. Yet this intoxication is not the result of having drunk too much—he has not ordered wine but rather pomegranate juice. A strange drink indeed for one who is possessed by the "stranger god." Wine, of course, is one of the gifts of Dionysos and, if we are consciously seeking to establish some relationship with the omophagic drinking of the blood of Dionysos, we should be somewhat disappointed here to find Aschenbach sitting before this seemingly innocent drink instead of before a glass of red Burgundy or claret. The intent of the author becomes clear however when we learn that pomegranates, according to the myth, sprang from the blood of Dionysos.

Thus, Tadzio appears unmistakably as the reincarnation of the "stranger god." Surrounded by his women votaries, he exerts his wondrous powers on the ill-starred Aschenbach and sends him headlong but willing into the abyss. Indeed, it is the spirit of Dionysos which becomes the motivating force behind the entire chain of events which lead to the hero's destruction.

It might be pointed out, furthermore, that although Mann's use of the Dionysian myth reaches its climax in **"Death in Venice,"** it also appears in a number of his other works—notably in the Joseph novels where Dionysos reveals himself in the guise of his Egyptian counterpart, Osiris. (pp. 174-75)

James B. Hepworth, "Tadzio—Sabazios: Notes on 'Death in Venice'," in Western Humanities Review, *Vol. XVII, No. 2, Spring, 1963, pp. 172-75.*

RONALD GRAY (essay date 1965)

[*In the following excerpt, Gray discusses Mann's deceptive technique in* Death in Venice: *he maintains that Mann intentionally deceives the reader into assuming the standard interpretation of the artist's quest for perfect beauty and the consequent failure of this vain pursuit, whereas the work in fact contains numerous details that contradict this reading. These ambiguities, in Gray's view, nullify the moral issues of the artistic quest and ultimately are a reflection of Arthur Schopenhauer's concept of the amoral "cosmic will." For further discussion of the ambiguities in* Death in Venice, *see the excerpts by T. J. Reed (1974) and Martin Swales (1980).*]

Der Tod in Venedig, like ***Tonio Kröger,*** has the appearance of illustrating an argument, in the literary as well as the logical sense of the word. It seems to be about an artist of great distinction who abandons the disciplined life he has led, yielding to the elemental temptation of perfect beauty. Aschenbach, dissatisfied with the ambiguities of his situation as a writer, gives way to the impulse to seek a more untrammelled life, goes to Venice and there succumbs both to love of the boy Tadzio and to the plague which he is too infatuated to avoid. The whole seems to be summed up in Aschenbach's dream of Socrates, one or two pages from the end, in which he hears the philosopher affirm that all true poets and artists must inevitably come to disaster, by virtue of the very fact that it is beauty they pursue. 'Our magisterial style is all folly and pretence', Socrates is made to say, with evident application to Aschenbach, 'our honourable repute a farce, the crowd's belief in us is merely laughable . . .'. If the artist abandons his pretence at dignity and his role as a leader of society, as Aschenbach has done—if he goes in search of beauty, he will come to disaster nevertheless. These thoughts are, it is true, introduced as 'the strange logic of dreams' and an examination of the argument would reveal the mass of illogicalities usually found in Mann's work, of which, here at least, he was evidently aware himself. Yet, standing where it does, the Socrates passage can easily give the impression of summing up the argument of the story as a whole.

Such an impression encounters difficulties as soon as the details are considered. The talk is always of 'the artist', and 'the poet', and evidently we must see Aschenbach as essentially representative if we are to make sense of the whole in this way. Here the difficulties arise. It is all too clear that Aschenbach is representative of no writer, unless of Mann himself. His fundamental desire for fame at the expense of truth is in itself enough to put him outside the conception of artistry as it had existed until his day. (It might be argued that both Aschenbach and Mann speak the truth as they see it, to those who have eyes to see, namely that there is no truth. But this paradox cannot be called a concern for truth; it is an abrupt denial of truth, overweeningly pre-judging the issue, and leads directly to the untruthfulness of this story.) Aschenbach's style, also, bears the mark of this desire for an acclaim not based on appreciation of his work but on conventional misreadings. It is not a genuine way of writing, not one which attempts to convey the author's perceptions, but rather one which is calculated to impress by its 'deliberate imprint of mastery and classicizing style'. These words are carefully chosen; they express precisely the impression one has from reading ***Death in Venice:*** the 'imprint' of masterliness is there, and yet the writing has a curious pose, as though drawing attention to the quality; the whole thing is deliberate. The 'classicizing' is there too: neither 'classical' nor 'classic', but an imitation designed to deceive. (pp. 147-49)

What, then, can be the purpose of the story; was Mann aware of this seeming deception, or was he so identified with Aschenbach for the time being that he could not stand outside him? The answer must be in terms of ambiguity, for the story does not, despite its ending, plainly conclude with Aschenbach's defeat and decay. From the outset, his position was ambiguously described: even in his initial situation he was described both as a born deceiver and as a martyred saint. His situation as a public man was, thanks to this dichotomy, unbearable, although it also seemed at times to be portrayed as an ideal one. Leaving Munich for Venice, Aschenbach looked for some escape, yet this situation too proved ambiguous. His love for Tadzio was felt, even by himself, to be iniquitous, and yet at the same time holy: 'he whispered the hackneyed phrase of longing—impossible in these circumstances, absurd, iniquitous, ridiculous enough, yet sacred too, and not unworthy of honour even here: "I love you!"'. This dual image of a man who is both saint and devil persists into the heart of the story, and continues through to the last page. In his final moment, as Aschenbach sits in his deck-chair on the beach, he sees, or thinks he sees Tadzio walking out into the sea in the likeness of Hermes, the conductor of souls into the world of the dead. It seems to him that the boy is beckoning him on, 'as though, with the hand he lifted from his hip, he pointed outward as he hovered on before into an immensity of richest expectation [ins Verheißungsvoll-Ungeheure]. And as he had done so many times before, he made as if to follow him.' This is in fact the moment of Aschenbach's final collapse, but the word 'Verheißung' ('promise', here rendered 'expectation') used in this passage invites our attention. It is the word used by Mann at those moments when his characters' visions seem on the point of realization: it is used of Thomas Buddenbrook's vision and of Hanno's music, and of course the word does have a more solemn, religious import than the usual word for 'promise', 'Versprechen'. What, then, is this immensity or monstrousness ('Ungeheure' has both senses) which is full of promise? It must surely be the sea, which had been for Aschenbach earlier the object of his 'seductive allurement towards the unorganized, the immoderate, the eternal—in short, towards nothingness'. The sea was the symbol or living reality of that nothingness which is the final goal of Schopenhauer's philosophy; Aschenbach had longed to rest in it as in perfection, and, he or Mann had asked, 'is not nothingness a form of perfection?' If we can answer yes to this question, then the story leads not only to Aschenbach's ignominious collapse, his cheeks cosmetically tinted with the appearance of youth, himself driven to the 'abyss' in his pursuit of perfect beauty, but also to his assimilation at the very end into a greater perfection, perhaps the Will itself which had produced the perfection of his own style and of Tadzio's body. . . . There is, in a way, no change. The beauty and the perfection were themselves both ambiguous, the Will is ambiguous in its promise and its monstrousness. Ultimately there is only the 'endless present' of Thomas's vision, the constant reiteration of the ambiguous Being which can only be either accepted or totally rejected, although even the rejection must lead to assimilation in the same Being.

The apparent pattern of the story is thus of little consequence. We can, if we choose, read many patterns into it: Aschenbach can be seen as a Faust lured away from his study by diabolical promises of delight, as a symbol of Germany or of Europe succumbing to the 'disease' which spreads from the East, the 'yellow peril' perhaps, or neo-Buddhism; or again the disease may be the impending war of 1914. Hints here and there invite us to make such readings, but they are all a part of the world of appearances, a play of illusions. 'In this world of appearances', Schopenhauer wrote, 'there is as little possibility of genuine loss as of genuine gain. The Will alone exists, and it is this, the thing-in-itself, which is the source of all those appearances.' On these terms, the question whether Aschenbach loses by his decline or gains by his entry into the vastness full of promise is irrelevant. Mann draws the story together in such a way that contradictory readings are possible for some of his readers; for himself, he seems rather to stand like the camera seen on the beach shortly before Aschenbach's death: 'A camera on a tripod stood at the edge of the water, apparently with no-one to operate it [scheinbar herrenlos]; its black cloth snapped in the freshening wind.' The lens may be open, but there is, apparently at least, no one in charge. One image after another passes through on to the plate, but when the picture is sought there is, from over-exposure, nothing on the negative. We are left with nothing but the recording apparatus—a seismograph was the term used by Mann at another time—the black cloth, and the cold wind.

That ***Der Tod in Venedig*** records the fatalism which has predominated in Germany for at least two centuries is undeniable. If Mann is right in his assumption that the artist's task is to be a 'medium of sensitivity', he has succeeded here supremely well, so far as certain tendencies in German thinking are concerned. His word does reveal, however, what seems to be an inevitable consequence of such an assumption, in its constant attempt at deluding the reader. The pretence is made, throughout the story, of dealing with issues familiar to the reader from long acquaintance: the nature of art, beauty, truth and so on. In fact, these are never properly dealt with: instead, some substitute is offered at every turn. The supreme qualities of Aschenbach's style are seen to be deceptive, the beauty of Tadzio is already corrupt. If the reader accepts these tokens of beauty at face value he is left with a pernicious sense of the corrupting influence of high ideals. If he does not accept them, he may be left with the impression, nevertheless, that there is something illusory about these ideals: he may be tempted to rank himself with the discerning few who see through to the heart of Mann's writing. But it is not a matter of illusion here, rather of delusion. Mann continually offers a suggested meaning which his incidents do not bear out, arguments whose evasiveness requires constant alertness, a style which is for the greater part of the story a mockery of the reader's ability to discern. It is not a matter of persuading the reader to perceive a genuine illusoriness in the world, but of tricking him into thinking he does. Or, to put it another way, Mann behaves here like a conjurer who, by means of hidden devices, tries to persuade his audience not merely that he is a first-rate conjurer, a first-rate deluder, but that reality is veritably as illusory as he makes it appear (whereas the real enjoyment of watching a conjurer lies in the wondering how he manages to trick us so well). Of course, if the trick fails to work, the grounds for mocking the reader disappear and no harm is done, or at least not so much harm. What is really pernicious, however, is the ease with which Mann implants his suggestions, the contempt which, with cause enough though little justification, he shows towards his audience. It is not because he shows a really corrupting power in truth and perfect beauty that he becomes so insidious a force for evil. Had he been able to show such a corrupting power, his regard for truth must still have counted for good: we should have been forced to a tragic recognition in which some uncorrupting truth would still have remained. But Mann does not do this: rather, he presents us with a highly suggestive story in the reading of which we need to keep all our wits about us, if we are not to be hypnotized into acceptance of its apparent purport. More, he offers an equally delusory (not illusory) refuge to those who look beyond his first level of meaning: the refuge of seismographic neutrality, from which one can observe the supposed imperfections of perfection with equanimity. The whole is deceivingly self-contained, and it is only by continual reminders of Aschenbach's and Tadzio's failure to correspond to the roles for which they are cast that its hermetic influence can be countered. (pp. 152-56)

Ronald Gray, "'Tonio Kröger'; 'Death in Venice'," in his The German Tradition in Literature: 1871-1945, *Cambridge at the University Press, 1965, pp. 137-56.*

J. R. McWILLIAMS (essay date 1967)

[In the following excerpt, McWilliams focuses on the psychological aspects of Death in Venice, *maintaining that the novella's symbolism indicates the "psychological justification for Aschenbach's degradation." To support his assessment, McWilliams draws parallels between* Death in Venice *and* Tonio Kröger, *both of which examine an artist who represses his human passions. McWilliams ultimately concludes that* Death in Venice *is the more penetrating psychological study of the two, because Aschenbach's demise is depicted in a more purely psychological manner. For*

further discussions of Mann's symbolism in Death in Venice, *see the excerpts by Vernon Venable (1938) and Frank Donald Hirschbach (1955); for another examination of character psychology in the novella, see the excerpts by Frank Donald Hirschbach (1955) and André Von Gronicka (1956).*]

The reader of ***Der Tod in Venedig*** is repeatedly struck by the signs of death which occur in this novella. At the very beginning the hero Gustav Aschenbach finds himself before a Munich cemetery which is deserted except for a mysterious stranger whose facial description reminds one of a death's head. From this omen of the grave, the first of a series of Stygian figures encountered by Aschenbach, there is a progression to an apocalyptic culmination in the cholera epidemic in Venice. The total effect is a powerful dirge, a paean of death which hinges on the slightest of plots.

These signs and symbols of death are more than external artistic embroidery. They are intimately correlated with the protagonist's inner mental state and are an indispensable factor in his drift towards the abyss. In Gustav Aschenbach's mind death is the penalty which he must categorically pay for his frantic excesses. Up to now critics have not viewed these images as part of the psychological justification for Aschenbach's degradation. Vernon Venable [see excerpt dated 1938] sees them as literary symbols and only touches on their psychological function. In fact, he calls the first stranger a symbol of life. Frank Hirschbach [see excerpt dated 1955] finds two distinct levels of interpretation in this work: '***Death in Venice*** especially was written and is intended to be read on a naturalistic and symbolic level. Every incident in the story as well as the story as a whole have both a naturalistic and symbolic meaning. . . . When the story . . . is read on a symbolic level, it becomes the case study of the gradual deterioration and abdication of the human will and of the artistic will in the face of beauty'. While this last statement may possibly apply to the beautiful Tadzio, it scarcely fits the spectral strangers who precede him. And to explain Aschenbach's problem as a failure of the will is to obscure a good deal of the psychological penetration with which Mann invests this narrative. It is also questionable whether anything is really gained by such a division into two distinct levels or that it is necessary to distinguish between a human and an artistic will. Instead of being interpreted as mutually exclusive phenomena or as a departure from reality, these and other devices in the story can be regarded as an extension of perfectly natural forces operative within the frame of the narrative. Indeed, it is through these devices that Mann helps to direct his hero's downfall and that he offers us striking evidence of his exceptional understanding of psychology. Thomas Mann's masterpiece will thus be viewed not only as a literary *tour de force* but also as a remarkable psychological document.

In order to comprehend this work more fully, it is essential to go back, as other critics have done, to the hero of Mann's earlier story: ***Tonio Kröger.*** For a knowledge of Tonio Kröger's attitude towards his basic drives is the key to a real understanding of Aschenbach's fatal eruption in sin.

Tonio Kröger is an icy intellectual, a man of impeccable dress and manners who is always careful to keep a proper distance from his fellow men. In his self-imposed isolation Tonio Kröger attempts to live his own dictum of frigid art in which his emotions are reduced to a bare minimum. . . . Tonio knows that his urges, once unleashed, could easily get beyond control and sunder him. He therefore represses his impulses and embarks on a rigid ascetic course which is passive and safe.

Like Tonio, Aschenbach has been living in an emotional vacuum. He has put Tonio Kröger's programme to the fullest test, exhausting himself in dedication to his calling. This fact has not gone unnoticed by critics, who have also pointed out the artistic kinship between Aschenbach and Tonio Kröger as well as the similarities between them and their creator. However, it is vital that we pay even closer attention to the psychological affinity between these two protagonists. Both heroes undergo practically the same experiences in a very similar context, that of a simple journey to a foreign land from their home in Munich. In Tonio's case it is a trip to the colder North, by way of the home of his puritanical father; Aschenbach, on the other hand, travels to a southern clime, where sensuality and animal-like passions hold sway. Otherwise they act, to a great extent, in a similar manner. In his constant sitting and gazing Aschenbach is, if we disregard the erotic overtones, close to the spokesman for frigid art, whose participation in the life at the sea resort where he stays is virtually non-existent. Other parallels to ***Tonio Kröger*** are equally impressive: Tonio's pining sighs for the blonde Inge and Aschenbach's longing for the honey-haired Polish boy; Hans Hansen dressed, like Tadzio, in a sailor's suit; the glass door of the hotel's dining-room overlooking the sea through which Tadzio and his counterparts, Inge and Hans, enter; both heroes suffering silent martyrdom, 'sitting in a corner', so to speak, and whispering their confession of love. Also it can be considered that Aschenbach's venture into sensuality is the pendulum of Tonio's extremes swinging back again. There is as well an indication of the same abhorrence of Italians and their lack of conscience in the allusions to official corruption in the city of Venice. And in the Socratic dialogue near the very end there is the Lisaweta Iwanowna interlude *in nuce:* the artist's self-doubt, his worthlessness and lack of virility, the desirability of detachment in art and the paralysing impact of 'Erkenntnis' ['knowledge']. But most significant is the phenomenon of the sea landscape, the references and descriptions of which are like a leitmotif in the two stories. It is as if both heroes travelled to their vacation spots for no other reason than to contemplate and feast their eyes on the vast expanse of water before them. The sunrise on the sea, viewed from the hotel room in the very early morning, is an awe-inspiring experience which Gustav Aschenbach and Tonio Kröger both have in common.

Tonio's trip north has, to some extent, the same purpose as Aschenbach's journey. It too is an attempt to make contact with life. But it is only a beginning. He is still too much dominated by the force of his repression which extinguishes the spontaneity necessary for involvement. His problem has not reached the critical stage. He can thus enjoy the sea landscape in a symbolic way as a sign of absolution, for the horror of his own death is not consciously a part of his thoughts.

Though Aschenbach's kinship with Tonio Kröger is extremely close, his need for chastisement sets him apart, and in this he represents a kind of culmination of his artistic precursors. Nowhere else has Mann devoted so much space to self-mortification as the necessary prerequisite for the artist hero's existence, to punishment as the means of rehabilitation and salvation and as a means to maintain a check on his turbulent urges. (pp. 233-35)

In the Aschenbach at the beginning of the novella, the high-point of repression is described, but by comparison with his prototype Tonio, Aschenbach has progressed a long way. He needs far more drastic safeguards than those which Tonio consciously and didactically imposed upon himself. So exaggerated is his stoicism that the life he leads is a caricature of the hero he writes about. He has come dangerously close to the breaking-point. In emphasizing the severity of the hero's self-mortification, a kind of penitential exorcism to cleanse the soul of basic urges, the author motivates with fine psychological insight his final abandonment and degradation. Although Aschenbach's excessive and rigid asceticism contrasts violently with his subsequent moral decay, it is nevertheless an indispensable condition for it. The more severe the repressive force, the more violent is the break with propriety. In these terms the impact the mysterious figure in the cemetery makes upon the hero is fully comprehensible. Reality seems to be suspended by the sudden arrival of this ominous figure; like an apparition he appears from nowhere. But rather than see this figure as standing outside natural law or as a symbol of the uncanny as does Hans M. Wolff, we can interpret him as lending greater force to the tension within Aschenbach. He exists logically as the figment of the hero's repressed mind, and the chain reaction of associations unleashed thereby, the vision of the Asiatic landscape, is merely the extension of the same hallucination. What Aschenbach sees is not dependent on an external stimulus, but is rather the result of forces at work within his mind. The luxuriant dream jungle, raw, savage and chaotic, represents the forbidden; it is a place where life runs rampant, and, as such, the source of decay and death to the guilty artist. . . . The sight of this domineering and ruthless stranger who regards him with such hostility triggers the fantasy of the jungle which strikes terror into his heart. He is now fully conscious of the fact that death is the reward for the liberation of his tyrannized senses. But this figure is also the prelude to his coming fall and must precede the jungle vision of life, for the expectation of death is the indispensable condition for the process of dissolution. It provides the penitential factor and prepares the way for the long-desired pleasure. In Aschenbach's mind sensual gratification is associated with his own doom. Only the threat of death could exert the strength needed to maintain the prohibition against his clamouring instincts. But now even this is insufficient. The drive to experience becomes irresistible to him; the immediate aim of gratification takes hold of him and shunts aside the far-reaching consideration of dignity and propriety. Already in the Munich cemetery it is clear that it is only a question of time before his intellect is completely powerless against the imperious claims of his instincts. Aschenbach now acts impulsively; more and more he interprets the world about him in terms of an impatient inner necessity. Unlike Tonio Kröger's, his decision to take a trip resembles a flight into the unknown. (pp. 236-37)

In Aschenbach's vivid artistic fantasy of the steaming jungle we see the derivation from sexual tension. It is thus hardly coincidental that he set out on his walk on a sultry spring day, a time when the blood quickens, and because he is unable to make any progress at all in his writing and is also powerless to check those impulses connected with art. As his urges gain momentum there comes the realization that his artistic fantasy alone is, despite its all-consuming consequences, inadequate to satisfy his inner desires.

Under the influence of Eros, Aschenbach, in sight of Tadzio on the beach at Venice, is once more involved in pursuing his calling. He suddenly wishes to write. The excitement which he feels is directed to the producing of the written word. The sexual ingredient is the *conditio sine qua non* for his artistic creation. Indeed here as with Albrecht van der Qualen, in the short tale ***Der Kleiderschrank*** (1899), it is not fulfilment but free play of fantasy alone which yields the finished work of art. . . .

Here there is still an element of the ***Tonio Kröger*** repression in the artist who numbs and attenuates his passions by the intellectual process of creation. But after Tadzio has once responded by a smile to the voyeuristic sallies of the hero, the latter's striving for beauty assumes the features of the perverse culminating in the orgiastic dream. . . . (p. 238)

In his Bacchanalian vision he achieves instinctual gratification, in essence the revenge of his capped impulses. It is readily seen that love, normally associated with tenderness, is utterly lacking in this scene. The hero's ability to love had long since been severely crippled. What we find in his dream consummation of sex is sensual gratification with unmistakable elements of cruelty, aggression and destruction. This dream offers convincing evidence of Aschenbach's ambivalence; in his mind the sexual is never dissociated from death. As horribly degrading as his dream is, it is still the logical consequence of the harsh stringency he has imposed on his drives. Degradation means for him a measure of punishment and, as such, atonement. It also weakens his carefully constructed prohibitions against unrestrained behaviour. Further, the frenzy of the debauch points to the pleasures in store for him, if he will let himself go. This is why the dream shatters him; it represents an irresistible step towards ruin, helps to pave the way for his death through the plague, and at the same time gives further sanctions to his burning transgressions.

After the dream orgy Aschenbach wears foppish clothes and lets himself be painted with cosmetics, in order to become attractive to Tadzio. He now contrasts strikingly with the impeccably dressed Tonio Kröger who abhors the Bohemian type and all his lax ways. Aschenbach's willingness to experience abasement shows us that he is close to death. For in his self-imposed humiliation he is intentionally seeking out that which he fears in order to steel himself against too sudden exposure. He hopes thereby to prove that he is the arbiter of his own destiny and not totally subject to unknown forces. By arranging the humiliation himself he dispels his fear of the consequences.

The actual cause of Aschenbach's death is treated so casually that the reader is apt to miss the terse statements which describe his eating of the overripe strawberries. Matter of factly and desultorily Aschenbach partakes of them on a stroll through the city. The off-hand and brief manner of this presentation contrasts sharply with the minute history of his adventures in Venice. Yet this description too fits the psychological needs of the hero. Though consciously aware of the dangers of the pestilence, his haphazard and unthinking feast of the moment allays his fear of falling directly a victim to the plague. He does not reflectively dwell on the possible consequences of his act, but rather inadvertently stills his momentary and insignificant need for refreshment. In this way he prevents the knowledge of his own fate from being consciously apprehended by rational thought.

Only after he has exposed himself to the perils of disease can gratification occur. As in the case with Albrecht van der Qualen in ***Der Kleiderschrank,*** a decree of death is a contingency of the penalty for instinctual release. Only then are the ends of retributive justice satisfied. In the final scene Tadzio is overcome in a wrestling bout by his black-haired companion Jaschiu. Through this substitute symbolic contact is made between the lover and the beloved. Moments later Aschenbach dies. Consummation has exacted the final payment.

Nowhere else in his works has Thomas Mann given us such a look at the ghastly and shocking results of unrestricted indulgence. Yet, paradoxically, Gustav Aschenbach's passion for Tadzio is completely passive. Everything is at a distance. From afar he gazes longingly at the object of his love. Once he walks behind Tadzio and is overcome by the desire to touch him, but at the last moment he hesitates and successfully resists the urge. This is the closest he comes to putting his amorous designs into action. It is true that he destroys his *dehors* [''outer appearance''] by letting himself be painted with cosmetics and that he shadows Tadzio through the streets of the city, but his love affair never progresses beyond the point of voyeurism. Consummation is all in his mind.

Though Thomas Mann creates powerful emotions which culminate in a brutish debauch, he manages at the same time to maintain his characteristic reserve and reticence in keeping with his other works. By means of symbolic references to death, Socratic dialogues, the hero's passivity, and the dream which seals off the Bacchic revelry from the objective world, he achieves a certain detachment. And when he described his hero, already debauched and with painted countenance, as the worthy artist who has renounced all sympathy with the abyss and who has rejected Bohemianism and all it stands for, he ironically dissociates himself still further from this artist figure. Finally, the author manages to achieve distance in the narrative by the inclusion . . . of allusions to Greek mythology and of classical figures of speech. . . . (pp. 239-40)

The Socratic dialogues, Aschenbach's procrastination and hesitation in Venice—which contrast rigidly with his sudden flight from Munich—, and the other dilatory devices create a suspension of the mounting tension of the hero. Psychologically they represent the attempt to reassert the Tonio Kröger-like prohibition against the world of the senses, for the life-long fear of consequences cannot be dispelled so easily by the hero. In this work where the emphasis is on the relentless struggle in Aschenbach's mind and in which the reader is never far removed from the hero's thoughts and feeling, the total effect of these stylistic devices is to prolong the tension, not to resolve it. By retarding the action, they give the reader time to participate in the protagonist's agony. In letting his hero enjoy the situation and defer the final payment, Mann perpetuates the state of the unbearable between anxiety and pleasure.

A number of Thomas Mann's works are variations on the same theme of the artist who undergoes an inner struggle to find a hold on life. In ***Der Tod in Venedig,*** more than in any other major work, the author dispenses with the external story-situation and concentrates on the hero's psychic conflict. The tale represents the author's deepest penetration into the psyche of the artist figure and reveals Mann to be strikingly perceptive in the use of the psychology of his time. (p. 241)

J. R. McWilliams, ''The Failure of Repression: Thomas Mann's 'Tod in Venedig','' in German Life & Letters, *Vol. XX, No. 2, January, 1967, pp. 233-41.*

ILSEDORE B. JONAS (essay date 1969)

[*Jonas is the author of* Thomas Mann and Italy, *a comprehensive study of Italian influences in Mann's works, Mann's influence on Italian literature, and the critical reception of Mann's work in Italy. Jonas's study was originally published in Germany in 1969. In the following excerpt from that work, Jonas discusses the importance of the Italian setting to* Death in Venice.]

In the novella ***Death in Venice (Der Tod in Venedig)*** Mann assigned to the city of lagoons . . . a rôle important, actually crucial, to the development of the action. In the drama ***Fiorenza*** of 1905, the Italian landscape is still of very minor importance: in the second act the writer leads us into the garden of the Villa Medici, where ''the open Campagna with cypresses, stone-pines and olive trees'' extended into the distance. The Florence of the Renaissance is only a backdrop in front of which the problematics of the characters are brought into relief. In the novella ***Death in Venice,*** on the other hand, the city of Venice and the landscape surrounding it—that is, in this case, the sea—are of determining significance; indeed, actually a part of the action itself.

Romantic Venice, the Venice of Platen, Wagner, and Nietzsche, reflects an older cultural epoch and is yet at the same time a city of the modern. And Thomas Mann, the stylistic artist, succeeds, through the help of the description of the real world, in fashioning a rich symbolism. (pp. 34-5)

With every fibre Aschenbach drinks in the fabulous beauty of Venice as he glides slowly on the ship through the canal of San Marco, and he is delighted that by the open sea he reaches this city, whose character is so strongly defined by the water surrounding and penetrating it. . . . (p. 35)

Yet the impression of beauty and incredibility becomes supplanted by a feeling of dread as Gustav von Aschenbach enters the gondola which is to bring him out to the Lido. Suddenly he becomes distinctly conscious of how much in form and color it (the gondola) resembles a coffin. . . .

The sweet, exotic fullness of life which seduces the visitor from the north into erotic adventures now becomes intimately fused with the motif of extreme danger, indeed, of inescapable destruction. But simultaneously, in this work Italy, for the first time for Thomas Mann, also signifies the land of antiquity. He described the figure of the boy Tadzio with all the attributes of a noble Greek sculpture, of the kind he had studied closely in the museums on his first visit to Italy. ''The head of Eros, out of the yellowish mellowness of Parian marble, with fine and serious brows, temples and ears duskily and softly hidden by the springing ringlets of his hair.''

The danger to Aschenbach from the ominous atmosphere of the city, hidden beneath the magnificence and ''splendor,'' emerges in the ever more strongly emphasized picture of decay and putrefaction. . . .

Aschenbach recognizes the danger in which he finds himself and decides to flee; but he already begins to regret this decision on the way to the railway station. The air seems to him suddenly fresher and more wholesome, and it becomes clear to him how much he is in the power of Venice, with its atmosphere at bottom so alien to him. (p. 36)

The emotional conflict developed in his soul into a kind of physical defeat before this city. Once before he had to leave it hastily because of a sudden illness. If he now again departed, then it meant a parting forever, since he would ''of course henceforth have to regard it as a place impossible and forbidden to him, which he was not equal to and which it would be foolish to visit again.''

A chance occurrence comes to his aid and within a short time Aschenbach finds himself on the way back to the Lido. Inwardly he feels a deep sense of happiness and satisfaction to be ''turned around and driven back by Fate to see again in the same hour places from which in deepest sadness one has just taken leave forever."

The weather indeed changes and in a true feeling of happiness Aschenbach enjoys the nearness of Tadzio and at the same time the southern surroundings, which form such a strong contrast to the coldness and austerity of his northern homeland. . . .

Aschenbach has inwardly changed: while previously after a short period of relaxation he had always soon longed again for work, hardship, discipline, and order, he now allows himself to become completely caught up in the magic of enjoyment and idleness, "dreaming away across the blue of the southern sea, or in the mild night as well, reclining upon the cushions of the gondola which carried him from the Piazza San Marco, where he tarries long, beneath the vast starry heavens homewards to the Lido."

Aschenbach lives as if in a state of intoxication: Tadzio and the luminous sea, antiquity and present merge into a oneness, into perfect harmony. (p. 37)

A vision of antiquity now rises within him: "Out of the murmur of the sea and the radiance of the sun a charming picture wove itself for him. It was the ancient plane-tree not far from the walls of Athens—that hallowed shady spot filled with the fragrance of the chaste tree blossoms, and adorned with sacred images and devout offerings in honour of the nymphs and of Achelous." More and more Aschenbach becomes caught in his unnatural, forbidden love. And again it is Venice, the beguiling city, which symbolizes the enormous danger in which he finds himself owing to his passion for a fourteen-year-old youth. (pp. 37-8)

In addition to the visual—the seductive exoticness of the city—the acoustic now also entered the scene, the magic of Italian music. In the evening a band of street musicians appears in the hotel garden to entertain the guests with their partly yearning-melancholy, partly rousing melodies. Aschenbach is transported by this music, "his nerves eagerly absorbed the piercing sounds, the vulgar and languishing melodies, for passion paralyses the sense of discrimination, and in all seriousness has dealings with enticements which sobriety would take humorously or indignantly reject."

Death, which for Gustav von Aschenbach is a deliverance—deliverance from himself—does not come to him in the city of Venice, but on the beach, in view of Tadzio and the broad sea which Aschenbach loves, since it is for him "the experience of eternity, of nothingness and of death, a metaphysical dream." In Venice he finds the perfect harmony of city with sea, such as he has longed for. The novella ends with Aschenbach's death just at the moment "when Tadzio beckons to him to follow him into the eternal infinity of the sea." This motif, dealt with again and again in literature, was once expressed by Thomas Mann in another place with the words: "For love of the sea, that is nothing else but love of death."

The Venice which Thomas Mann described in this work is to the smallest detail modern Venice. But at the same time he gave the city a timeless, romantic, exotic character, so that it is not only the background for the tragic event, but also has a share in determining the plot and, so to speak, itself becomes a part of the action.

The sensuous, seductive beauty of Venice is reflected for Aschenbach in the perfection of the boy, and owing to the exotic and fascinating atmosphere of the city the writer is particularly open to the attraction of Tadzio and willingly allows himself to become bewitched by him. One may assume that without the mystical force of the city of lagoons the encounter with the boy would not have become such a devastating experience for Aschenbach. Although in the case of Thomas Mann no such distinct equation of the figure of Tadzio with the concept "Venice" takes place as with Gerhart Hauptmann, in whose glass-factory fairytale Pippa and Venice become fused into a oneness, still the fascination of the boy is increased because of Venice, and perhaps even dependent upon it.

While the outward features of Aschenbach resemble those of the composer Gustav Mahler, of whose death Thomas Mann was apprised during a stay on the island of Brioni in 1911, the true image, however, was the poet August Graf von Platen, the proclaimer of the ancient ideal of beauty and of the close relationship between beauty and death, as he portrayed it in his poem **"Tristan."** . . . Just as in Platen's fate, for Aschenbach, also, beauty and approaching destruction are closely interwoven, and in his love and passion for Tadzio one is reminded of the concept of the arrow of death, which Platen expressed in the second verse of his poem:

> He whom the arrow of beauty has ever hit
> For him the pain of love endures eternally.

Beauty conceals deadly danger: Michel Hellriegel's eyes grow blind, after he has beheld beauty; and Aschenbach, through his passionate love for the boy, is "a prey of death already." The three concepts Venice, beauty, and death become a mystical unity, and Aschenbach must suffer death because he has sought to become at one with beauty.

In ***Death in Venice*** Thomas Mann again dealt with the theme of the longing of the northern individual for the south. Tonio Kröger, as also the heroes of other earlier novellas, had succumbed to the temptations of Italy for some time; but then he had come to his senses, and precisely on account of his erotic adventures in the south and their ultimate conquest, had matured into an artist.

Aschenbach, to the contrary, had already concluded his important literary works when he is swept by an irresistible longing for Italy. The north suddenly seems to him too sober, too disciplined, and therefore cold and sterile. Like Tonio Kröger's nature, that of Aschenbach also exhibits Latin characteristics through inheritance from his southern mother, and because of this mixture the man influenced by "darker, fiery impulse" is predestined to become an artist. For a long time he has suppressed his mother's inheritance through self-control and severe discipline, and the motto "hold fast" had become his favorite maxim and his life's rule of conduct. Now suddenly his literary existence appears questionable to him; he who for some time had become a model and teacher to his public because of the self-discipline reflected in his works, suddenly feels doubts about his profession as a writer, which at bottom is built upon an unnatural and therefore false basis.

So Aschenbach goes to Italy, to Venice, there to discover his true self in order to free himself from all restraint and self-punishment. In the south he desires to do justice to the previously suppressed inheritance of his mother, and through surrender to sensual beauty overcome the numbing of his personality that was brought about by his unnatural asceticism. He finds the fulfillment of his longing in Venice, which offers this beauty in perfect form, for indeed here Italian and fable-like Oriental elements are blended into a oneness. Visual impressions combine with the acoustic of the "languishing" Italian music.

While in the early novella ***Disillusionment*** Thomas Mann had emphasized the marvellous lucidity of Venice, which offers a "sight of incomparable shining and festive beauty," the Venice of Aschenbach is at the same time sinister and full of danger for the visitor intoxicated by this deluding atmosphere. The city has a conflicting character, for behind a façade of the greatest beauty and magnificence are hidden disease, immorality, and crime. Like Hieronymus in the novella ***Gladius Dei*** and Savonarola in ***Fiorenza,*** Aschenbach is conscious of this other side of the southern atmosphere; but while both of the moralists fought the evils with word and deed, Aschenbach lets himself be deluded and overcome by them. He does not possess the moral strength of resistance which made it possible for Tonio Kröger to flee from the dangers of the south by returning to his northern homeland.

Aschenbach, on the other hand, is already in a state of psychical and physical weakness while still in Munich, so that the sight of the stranger at the cemetery puts him in a state of "roving unrest" and evokes in him a "youthful thirsty longing for foreign parts," to which he completely surrenders; indeed, which within his soul heightens to an unrestrained vision. Also in the two encounters during the journey, one on the ship with the perverse old man behaving like a youth, as well as the one with the sinister gondolier, Aschenbach is incapable of resisting. To be sure, he realizes the danger he is in, yet in his exhaustion and susceptibility he lacks the strength to resist the temptation of a total abandonment. In reality, a longing, still unbeknown to him, for chaos, immorality, and death has already won the upper hand in his soul. In this condition Aschenbach is entirely delivered over to the alluring and seductive charms of Venice; indeed, the deceptiveness of the city increases his susceptibility to the utmost. In such surroundings the figure of Tadzio, the youth closely resembling an ancient statue, has to become for Aschenbach a deeply stirring experience. All the previously suppressed emotions are unchained and must lead to the destruction of the hero, to his death in sight of the city of Venice, the beautiful boy, and the infinite sea. (pp. 38-41)

Ilsedore B. Jonas, in her Thomas Mann and Italy, *translated by Betty Crouse, The University of Alabama Press, 1979, 184 p.*

A. E. DYSON (essay date 1971)

[An English educator and critic, Dyson has written and edited numerous studies of European literature. A critic who, like his mentor C. S. Lewis, approaches literature from a scholarly, orthodox Christian viewpoint, Dyson has written: "I suppose I am a traditionalist because I believe in the present. What is worse than provincialism? Almost everything that makes life rich was said or written or created by people who are now no longer living; almost all the colour and joy came from religious men." In the following excerpt from an essay originally published in 1971, Dyson examines the vivid thematic parallels between Euripides' Bacchae *and* Death in Venice, *citing the latter as a work that reflects the spirit of Europe's "post-Christian" era. For further discussions of mythic elements in* Death in Venice, *see the excerpts by André Von Gronicka (1956) and James B. Hepworth (1963).]*

Of all modern novelists, Mann was the most consciously and fruitfully indebted to Wagner. To list the many recurrences, developments, mutations of theme [in ***Death in Venice***] would be tedious; but a few establish themselves as motifs and control the structure. In the opening pages, life and death mingle in alternating visions of swamp and tiger. These in turn colour the still and disquieting mortuary chapel, where Aschenbach sees the uncouth man with a prominent Adam's apple who so powerfully impresses him. . . . This encounter, again, is recalled when the stranger's near simulacrum, more fierce, derisory and depraved, turns up as strolling singer in plague-stricken Venice. . . . The imagery of death is now pervasive; and in the next passage, Aschenbach at last learns what sickness arrived in Venice along with himself. . . . From here, we move to Aschenbach's fearful dream, when the stranger god lurking behind these images and visitations is revealed. It is as if the figures surrounding Aschenbach's adventure might all have been phantoms, emanating from the god into whose hands he falls.

The sense of surrounding presences is further enhanced by the rogue gondolier who rows Aschenbach to the Lido against his explicit orders, yet in accordance with his unspoken desires and eventually—as Aschenbach discovers the impossibility of effectual protest—with his tacit consent. '"I am a good rower, signore"', says the gondolier, '"and will row you well".' When Aschenbach arrives at the Lido it is to fall into a deep sleep, from which he is never to awake again to his normal world. The gondolier is no doubt Charon, ferrying his prey; he is also a type of that other gondolier who will later help Aschenbach to pursue his beloved through Venice, and leer his complicity with the sickened man. To these figures must be added the grotesque and to Aschenbach horrible homosexual on the boat, the 'ghastly young-old man', painted and drunken, whose simulacrum Aschenbach himself is destined to be.

All these people belong to nightmare, as harbingers of the world of unreason; they emerge from and merge back into the shadowy realm of disease and pestilence, which mirrors sweet and terrible joy. They are the landscape of the hidden world where Aschenbach is now to become the 'solitary': the scene where this hitherto successful and lionised public man, the master of words, is to become an outcast, communicating only marginally with anyone, and with his beloved, except in enigmatic glances, not at all. 'He fled from the huddled narrow streets of the commercial city, crossed many bridges, and came into the poor quarter of Venice. Beggars waylaid him, the canals sickened him with their evil exhalations.' . . . (pp. 84-5)

Such symbols are all caught up in Venice, the most beautiful and exotic city in the world. . . . But, serene and apparently untouched by time, she is built on crumbling foundations and polluted waters, the child equally of religious vision and despotic greed. Where else in the plight of fallen man so visibly embodied, the divine promptings, the irrevocable commitment to sin and death? To Aschenbach, Venice is 'the fallen Queen of the seas', but she was always fallen and always Queen. Undoubtedly, this city is the fated stage for his drama, an image encompassing all other images—the pilgrim stranger, the gondoliers, the ghastly young-old man, the labyrinths of pursuit. It is the image of Tadzio—his perfect beauty united with a delicacy and a suggestion of illness; his enchanting face which is capable of 'angry disgust', 'the black and vicious language of hate' directed towards the happy, simple Russian peasants; his enigmatic responses to a lover's pursuit. Above all, it is the image of Aschenbach's own fearful fulfilment, the blazing and exotic beauty of his latter days. The streets where Aschenbach pursues and loses Tadzio are his soul, the sultry and unwholesome airs his consciousness, the depraved and corrupted inmates his destiny, the desperate refreshments his death.

Death and love lock together in single images, as the plague becomes thematically inseparable (its furtive approach, its secrecy, its fatal charm and attractiveness) from the progress of love. In the end, Aschenbach is himself the plague, stalking the boy; he is the menace sensed and shunned by Tadzio's proper guardian, the fascination half-drawing the victim to itself. And it seems only one more Venetian turn—a coming out on the next jewelled church, great palace, unsuspected piazza—that Tadzio should then prove to be the angel of death. In all this, the tale is superbly Venetian, with Aschenbach hardly more than one of the daily sacrifices she might exact.

Do we judge Aschenbach, or envy him? (pp. 85-6)

Before we pursue this matter of appropriate moral judgements, it might be pertinent to speculate on the boy's degree of involvement with Aschenbach's love. We see this largely, of course, through the eyes of his lover, which are not the most perfect instruments for objective report. It is noteworthy that although this tale is not told in the first person, we are often directly admitted to the hero's mind. While we remain sharply enough aware that Aschenbach's situation is not to be equated with his consciousness, much of the experience is mediated directly from himself. For our sense of Tadzio, in particular, we rely very fully on what Aschenbach sees, hopes and fears. Aschenbach becomes aware (we know) of some responsiveness in Tadzio's eyes as they meet his. (p. 87)

The best that Aschenbach can hope for—the violated Aschenbach of this tale is that the boy will be sufficiently mature, and sufficiently brave, reckless or cynical, to have a brief sexual adventure on the threshold of life. The great dream is the old one of *Phaedrus* and *The Symposium,* that the sweetness of love will conquer every barrier placed in its way. Yet for a man like Aschenbach, whose whole philosophy has been a rejection of romantic extravagance and of the rejected, such a sweetly alluring idyll must be the abyss. It could only deprave and destroy his life if heeded—as indeed it does, even before he suffers the disastrous and irrevocable dream. We are forced back on the perception that he is marked out and prepared for destruction: but whether this is through his failure of will at the time of testing, or through the way of life exemplified in such a will, is not resolved.

It is in this area that the Bacchic interpretation is important; and it pervades ***Death in Venice*** intentionally, as we can see from the continual allusions to Euripides' play. In *The Bacchae,* Pentheus conducts a moral crusade against Bacchus' Theban worshippers, and the god destroys him in revenge. To each god his due: this is Greek wisdom; and only a fool would behave towards the god of instinct as Pentheus does. Though his motives are honourable, they do not excuse him. He must suffer a savage personal epiphany of the god. (pp. 87-8)

Pentheus' punishment in Euripides' play . . . is made inevitable by the fact that a man cannot really exile the more dangerous parts of his nature, or successfully cauterise his inner self. To reject Bacchus is as dangerous as accepting him too totally, since the god must and will have his dues. Pentheus eventually agrees (like Aschenbach) to go 'half-way to the tigers', and his hidden instincts leap within their cage. The god first lures him into the fatal breakdown of vigilance, and then addresses insidious suggestions to the traitor within. Deceived by the promise of invisibility (a direct lie, like much else that Bacchus tells him), Pentheus parades through the streets dressed as a woman, and is delivered over to dismemberment and death. His suppressed voyeurism and transvestism are the god's weapons, and no mercy is finally shown. In ***Death in Venice,*** Aschenbach's terrible dream is the parallel incident, and what he dreams *is* the climax of Euripides' play.

Like Pentheus, in fact, Aschenbach must be wrested from his hard-won dignity and propriety, and consigned to the destructive powers he has tried to resist. As the reckless obsession with Tadzio gathers, he must not be spared the delusion of recovered youth and bliss. This must be played off also against those occasional horrifyingly different glimpses of his predicament, thrown up by the suppressed but not extinguished rational powers. There comes the moment when he allows a barber to transform him into the semblance of the 'ghastly young-old man' of the Venice quayside, and throws his concern for respect and survival to the winds. He must suffer this violation of all he has chosen, revered and shaped himself towards, for the joy which seems to transcend a lifetime of work.

Like Pentheus he must wonder whether he recovers sanity in Venice, or whether he is plunged into madness and total shame. Does he belong with Antony and Tristram, Lancelot and Troilus, among the great doomed lovers; or is he any elderly man led to forfeit repute, and the ideals he has lived for, by one forbidden, fierce and seemingly irresistible joy? While any reader who judges too easily will be brutally insensitive, the most brutal condemnations are endorsed in his heart.

In worldly terms, we are challenged to attempt judgements and left to move through the novel's data as we can. The colouring I have pointed to is chiefly Hellenic, but other modes of understanding are also invoked. There is the intellectual analysis which is persistently obtruded, for instance, of Aschenbach as a man irrevocably split into warring halves. These are associated with his 'bourgeois' father and his 'bohemian' mother, who are seen as contributing irreconcilable traits to the mix. In my view, this aspect of the novel is naïve, and its one structural weakness, but it usefully links us back to ***Tonio Kröger*** (1903). It is also of a piece with Aschenbach's role as a typical modern hero, on which my main conclusions will turn.

The young Aschenbach finds himself torn between 'bourgeois' and 'artist', and could echo the words of Tonio Kröger: 'I stand between two worlds. I am at home in neither, and I suffer in consequence.' But even in youth he has shunned indolence, and the vices which Tonio Kröger resorts to, in favour of discipline and will. The desire for fame, which preserves him from despair and dissipation, becomes the guiding passion of his life. Unlike Tonio Kröger, he does not allow 'obscure impulse' to rule him, but learns to reunite impulse with direction and power.

In middle life Aschenbach becomes famous as author of *The Abject,* 'which taught a whole grateful generation that a man can still be capable of moral resolution even after he has plumbed the depths of self-knowledge'. This salvation involves, however, a rejection of all those who fall in life's battle, and a resolute flight from their bitterness and from their claims. 'With rage the author here rejects the rejected, casts out the outcast' . . . 'explicitly he renounces sympathy with the abyss'. Aschenbach pushes the very pains of art into bourgeois service, making art itself a text for disciplined hard work.

In escaping the abyss, then, Aschenbach sacrifices certain freedoms of love and sympathy, including perhaps the inner freedom of his art. This lends an obvious ironic fitness to his nemesis in ***Death in Venice,*** though it could also, of course, be read another way. A stern moralist might decide that Aschenbach dies shamefully because he relapses from chastened insight, and proves unable to evade his private abyss. Was it not St Paul who said, 'I keep under my body and bring it unto subjection: lest that by any means, when I have preached to others, I myself should be a castaway'?

Yet to read ***Death in Venice*** as an artist's warning against himself is surely too literal, if only because it ignores the existence and force of the work itself. Mann is not Aschenbach, nor is ***Death in Venice*** the story of ***Death in Venice;*** there is also the usual miracle of form. If Aschenbach's adventure is in fact surrounded with richness and transmuted to beauty, the form which achieves this cannot be merely a lie. Few readers are likely to judge Aschenbach without fear and pity, or to imagine that they might themselves be exempt from his fate. The moral sensitivity generated is clearly higher than self-righteousness, and more human than any mere armour-plating against suffering and love. As we come to understand the extent to which Aschenbach's 'bourgeois' days were themselves armour-plated, we sense that he dies a finer, though a less reputable, man than he lived.

To point this out is, of course, to risk stating the obvious; but it is also to suggest a coarseness in Mann's intellectual structure when compared with his art. The antithesis between 'bourgeois' and 'bohemian' is bound to seem blunt and unsatisfactory when embedded in so subtle and beautiful a tale. It offers little to our real understanding of Aschenbach's predicament, and is at odds with the novel's manifest power. Whatever we make of Aschenbach's encounter with the god he has made a stranger, we are unlikely to extract simple insights about class, or about art.

That Aschenbach's sufferings turn to beauty in the telling is, as I have insisted, a triumph of form. Whatever doubts about form ***Death in Venice*** expresses, the tale itself is free to whisper and sing. It is one of those works of art which enriches our education, humanises our culture, haunts our imaginations, safeguards our religion itself. In forcing us to take account of the sublime and tragic, it forces us back with its hero, towards the abyss.

Since this triumph is achieved by content and form in indissoluble unity, we can be sure that Apollo as well as Dionysus has his dues. There is a reminder that morality in a work of art is never autonomous, and can never therefore be abstracted on its own. Because the content is inseparable from texture, structure, tone, symbolism and language, there can be no ultimate divide between meaning and form. And since the artist's sensitivity is inevitably incarnate in his creation, refined sensitivity is seen to be one of the conditions of greatness in art.

While such reflections may not answer all the doubts about art which afflict Aschenbach, they direct us away from the cramping framework in which he thinks. Art clearly cannot be simply 'bourgeois' in the sense indicated, but neither can it be simply anarchic in 'bohemian' ways. The tale transcends its intellectual framework by its own achievement; and in doing this, it offers us a useful further clue. Is it possible that other morals can be drawn by a reader of ***Death in Venice,*** perhaps in defiance, almost, of its chosen terms?

With this in mind, I now want to look at Aschenbach's sufferings from a different perspective, and to consider the novel's intellectual framework alongside the novel itself. Aschenbach is specifically linked in Mann's opening pages with the 'soul of Europe', and while his personal fate is unique, and remote from normal experience, we are also invited to see him as 'typical' in certain ways. The 'soul of Europe' is a concept familiar in Arnold, Eliot and many other great writers, and gives a positive nudge in the direction of cultural debate.

My suggestion will be that Aschenbach's whole development as we see it is post-Christian, and that this is even truer of his middle years as author of *The Abject,* than it is of his youthful cynicism, or his last great love. It may indeed be that his experience links so fruitfully with the ethos of Plato and Euripides precisely because he is a distinctively *modern* man. Ancient and modern meet, in certain tragic insights and torments, partly because the great intervening episode of Christian Europe has come and gone. It is almost as though St Paul had never stood before the altar of the Unknown God in Athens, and spoken his marvellous and astonishing words. (pp. 89-93)

As a way of pursuing what I have in mind, I want to return to the nature of Aschenbach's obsession. In one obvious way his love for Tadzio marks him out as a man better than average but less than perfect (an Aristotelian tragic hero, in fact). A perfect person would be as safe from Bacchus as Milton's Lady is from Comus; but such perfection is admittedly rare. A depraved person would also be safe, or at least much safer, since he would hardly obsess himself with erotic impossibilities or be caught by the erotic unawares. Aschenbach's experience is that of a man who is sensitive to beauty, tender and considerate by nature, but also insulated from very much knowledge of his sexual depths.

But, this might suggest, is he not thereby a victim of sexual ignorance, and to this extent a pre-Freudian rather than a post-Christian man? And it may be true that those of us brought up on Freud would be less likely than Aschenbach to overlook a homosexual component, or to imagine that growing love could be totally insulated from sex. But this is not to my mind the important aspect of ***Death in Venice,*** and indeed it seems hardly important at all. What really counts is Aschenbach's reaction to self-knowledge when it comes to him: as soon as he recognises the erotic he submits to it and ceases to experience love apart from his need. It is here that we encounter the particularly and distinctively modern attitude which marks the 'soul of Europe' in our times. One could say that, while post-Freudians are less likely to overlook sexual possibilities in their love than most of their predecessors, they are far more likely to overlook almost everything else. They are more likely to overlook love itself, in its Christian aspect, as Aschenbach clearly and disastrously does. In Christian terms, it would be perfectly possible for him to say of the boy—either in his heart, or aloud—'I love you', and for this to be no matter for concealment or incipient shame. . . . It is surely post-Christian for the words 'I love you' to seem inherently dangerous, as the prelude—where sex is impossible—to suffering and shame.

Now it might be argued that Aschenbach's love is in fact erotic, or becomes so, and that such reflections are therefore beside the point. But I think that his love becomes erotic and obsessive partly, at least, because this is all it can be. When recognised as love, eroticism becomes the sole possibility, with friendship a non-starter in the race. Aschenbach's love becomes his desire to possess Tadzio, and this supersedes his reverence for the boy's beauty and graces—for the boy himself. The betraying fact is not the erotic desire which might happen to anyone, but the egocentric possessiveness also aroused. In the Christian ethos, it would have seemed natural to love widely and passionately across all barriers of age, sex, race and colour, but not natural to regard possessive and erotic demands as a *sine qua non*. On the contrary, such demands would be seen as totally harmful except in marriage, and the surest way of soiling and destroying love. What has disappeared, with this Christian perspective, is the sense that, since love is drawn out in homage to another person, it links only contingently, if at all, with the lover's needs.

It seems probable that Aschenbach's rejection of the rejected directly relates, as a post-Christian phenomenon, to the disastrous turn which his love later takes. The kind of self-discipline which mistrusts love and raises barriers against it may be precisely the kind which responds, as Aschenbach's does, to irresistible love. If the rejection of the rejected is one distinctively post-Christian doctrine, so still more is the related fear of love. Aschenbach lays himself open to nemesis then not only in the terms recognised by the Greeks and by modern psychologists, but in terms central—however neglected they have often been—to the Christian Church.

My suggestion, it will be seen, is that friendship—a love rich and pervasive in Christian life and literature—has been the chief casualty of our modern obsession with sex. That our sexual instincts are better understood today, is of course reassuring, as indeed is our greater tolerance towards deviant sex. But such gains have been won at great cost in confusion and suffering, which Aschenbach's story illustrates especially well. (pp. 95-7)

Turning back to ***Death in Venice,*** I am struck most of all by the absences. Why does Aschenbach never envisage fruitful love between himself and Tadzio, or any healing or beneficial outcome of his love? He could have introduced himself to the family with propriety and sought appropriate expressions of love. Mann makes clear indeed that he precipitates his fate by failing to speak to the family—to warn them of plague, cultivate them, put himself on a friendly footing—and that this isolation is the soil where his sufferings grow.

In this conclusion I am ranging beyond Mann's intellectual context, but in a way which I believe he leaves his readers free to do. To my mind the tragic essence is to be located in the cultural disaster of our times. While Christianity has been continually attacked by enemies for its supposed laws and restrictions against love, the same enemies have created the conditions they deplore. . . . Our most distinctive moral crusades are now for nudity, pornography, obscenity, and, of course, for the inalienable right of children to be depraved. The resulting society is mirrored in Genet, Nabokov, Burroughs, Mailer, Baldwin, *Oh! Calcutta, Hair*—most of our novels, most of our plays and films; where does such a list stop? It is in these places that future generations will find us, and judge what degree of freedom in love we really have.

My suggestion is not that Aschenbach at all shares in so much modern squalor, but that he is a symptom of the forces which shaped it half a century ago. As recently as 1850, Dickens could depict David Copperfield's love for Steerforth, Tennyson could write and publish *In Memoriam;* the traditional Christian channels still flowed. If such relationships are less often expressed and perhaps less often purely experienced in the 1970s, then the absences from ***Death in Venice*** could be one of our clues. And of course it is not only loves like Aschenbach's which are now pertinent: the mass has spread to 'normal' sexuality, including—often—marriage itself. The 'stranger god' Mann refers us to is, we know, Bacchus; but in ***Death in Venice*** there is another, and far greater, stranger God. (pp. 98-9)

A. E. Dyson, "The Stranger God: Mann's 'Death in Venice'," in his Between Two Worlds: Aspects of Literary Form, *Macmillan, 1972, pp. 81-99.*

R. J. HOLLINGDALE (essay date 1971)

[*Hollingdale is the author of* Thomas Mann: A Critical Study, *which examines the "foundation" of Mann's fiction by studying six of its central preoccupations: ideology, decadence, irony, myth, crime, and sickness. In the following excerpt from that work, Hollingdale discusses Mann's literary technique, which skillfully transforms the realism of* Death in Venice *into "phantasmagoria."*]

The total transformation of reality into phantasmagoria—essayed on a small scale in ***The Wardrobe***—is achieved much more successfully and on a much larger scale in ***Death in Venice***. The narrative style of this story is, as is usual with Mann, characterized by a close attention to details—but these details, when closely observed, now serve to deprive the narrative of all realism and to transform it into fantasy, as though the real world were being seen through the sick eyes of Gustav von Aschenbach.

At the beginning of the story Aschenbach, the famous and respected author, feeling unwell takes a walk through the streets of Munich. He halts before a mortuary chapel decorated with such scriptural texts as 'They are entering into the House of the Lord' and 'May the Light Everlasting shine upon them'; here there suddenly appears before him 'a man standing in the portico, above the two apocalyptic beasts that guarded the staircase'. He cannot decide how the man has got there, but he observes him minutely, and the narrator gives us a close description of the man's dress and features. As a consequence of this experience Aschenbach feels 'a longing to travel' so strong as to resemble 'a seizure, almost a hallucination'. The man's dress bears some resemblance to hiking gear, but the connexion between his appearance and Aschenbach's reaction is not naturalistic: the apparition has, for whatever reason, sent him on the route to his death.

Where he is to die is stated immediately: reflecting on the number of places he can travel to, he has a vision of 'a tropical marshland, beneath a reeking sky, steaming, monstrous, rank—a kind of primeval wilderness-world of islands, morasses, and alluvial channels. . . . Among the knotted joints of a bamboo thicket the eyes of a crouching tiger gleamed—and he felt his heart throb with terror, yet with a longing inexplicable.' The fragmentary repetition of this description at later points in the story reveals that what he has visualized is Venice become a 'morass' through the invasion of the 'Asiatic' cholera, and the source of the disease itself, 'the hot, moist swamps of the delta of the Ganges, where it bred in the mephitic air of that primeval island-jungle, among whose bamboo thickets the tiger crouches'. Aschenbach's inexplicable longing is for death.

The figure between the apocalyptic beasts which sends him out to meet death reappears twice: the first time as the unlicensed gondolier who ferries him from his boat across to the death-trap of Venice, the second time as the singer who performs in front of the hotel, smells of carbolic and passes on the cholera.

In all of this there is nothing whatever naturalistic. Aschenbach moves as if in a dream: the dreamlike atmosphere is reinforced by a hundred details. On the boat to Venice he meets a prefiguration, altogether unreal but entirely in place in a scene of phantasmagoria, of his own final condition before death claims him: 'Aschenbach . . . was shocked to see that the apparent youth was no youth at all. He was an old man . . . with wrinkles and crow's-feet round his eyes and mouth; the dull carmine of the cheeks was rouge, the brown hair a wig.' Even as he is experiencing the events of the voyage, Aschenbach feels 'not quite canny, as though the world were suffering a dreamlike distortion of perspective'. The gondola is 'black as nothing else on earth except a coffin' and as he steps into it, it calls up in him 'visions of death itself, the bier and solemn rites and last soundless voyage', he finds it so comfortable he wishes the trip 'might last forever'.

Arrived in his graveyard, Aschenbach begins a long and one-sided romance with the life he is about to depart from. The boy Tadzio is described in dozens of phrases which are all merely variants of one phrase: that he is 'beauty's very essence'. That he is 'real' no one will suppose: that on his first appearance Aschenbach remarks on the contrast his 'perfect beauty' presents to the plainness of his sisters suggests that Aschenbach is bestowing something if not all of this beauty on him himself. His attempted flight from Venice is thwarted by an accident which, as in a dream, is the fulfilment of his own desire; his trip back there is, unlike the first trip, swift and easy: no resistance of any kind is left.

The second stage of Aschenbach's death is written up in language that now frankly abandons the descriptive manner and becomes inordinately florid, baroque and 'mythological': 'Now daily the naked god with cheeks aflame drove his four fire-breathing steeds through heaven's spaces', and so on. Aschenbach as an individual begins to disappear within the mound of words heaped up around him: the concept he embodies is developed more luxuriantly than a 'character' can well survive. The nearer he approaches the end the less restrained is his worship of the beauty he has created and the more unbalanced and 'decadent' does he himself become. At length the baroque manner, overborne by the fantasy it is seeking at once to communicate and suppress, gives way to undisguised phantasmagoria, and Aschenbach, after a terrific erotic dream in which the contents of his decaying soul are vomited up, abandons all restraint and all 'normality'. His love of 'Tadzio' has already forced him to notice how old he is getting: now, as prefigured by the young-old man on the boat, he resorts to cosmetics and becomes a parody of his own ideal of youth and beauty, while the boy, as if to emphasize the grotesqueness of his elderly admirer, grows ever more ethereal. Trailing Tadzio through the narrow streets of Venice, 'where horrid death [cholera] stalked too', it seems to him 'as though the moral law were fallen in ruins and only the monstrous and perverse held out a hope'. He lives as in a dream, and when he talks to himself 'the rouged and flabby mouth uttered single words of the sentences shaped in his disordered brain by the fantastic logic that governs our dreams'. The last thing he sees before his decease is pure dream: Tadzio, standing on the seashore, beckons him out into the ocean of nothingness. And with that he is dead.

On the level of realism, the plot of ***Death in Venice*** is: an elderly and much admired and respected author is tired from overwork; he decides to take a holiday and goes to Venice; there he sees a beautiful boy who arouses in him repressed homosexual feelings of which he is ashamed; he indulges in fantasies about the boy, at first sublimated and artistic (Greek statues and the like), later frankly erotic; but because he has a bad conscience about all this his morale is destroyed and his outward behaviour begins to correspond with his inner constitution. At the same time Venice is invaded by cholera, and the progress of the physical disease parallels that of his psychological and spiritual degradation. This plot—which, although somewhat lurid, is of course in no way impossible in the real world—is made to bear a weight of *leitmotif,* fantasy and 'fine writing' which pushes it down out of the real world into the underworld of dream and phantasmagoria: and this procedure is an extension and consequence of what is in the long run the most striking thing about the story—the total lack of sympathy evidenced for the wretched Aschenbach. As Tonio Kröger is Hanno grown up, so Aschenbach is Tonio grown old. But his author now refuses to enter into him sympathetically: he is viewed with the eye of irony and he is as a consequence transformed into a grotesque and the world in which he moves loses its reality. (pp. 90-4)

R. J. Hollingdale, in his Thomas Mann: A Critical Study, *Bucknell University Press, 1971, 203 p.*

T. J. REED (essay date 1974)

[*In the following excerpt from his critical study* Thomas Mann: The Uses of Tradition, *Reed examines the genesis of* Death in Venice *by discussing Mann's personal correspondence, especially a 1920 letter to Carl Maria Weber. Reed believes that while writing* Death in Venice *Mann altered his affirmative portrayal of homosexual love to accommodate a more conventionally moral treatment of the theme, a change that resulted in the work's ambivalent portrayal of Gustave von Aschenbach. For further discussions of the ambiguities of* Death in Venice, *see the excerpts by Ronald Gray (1965) and Martin Swales (1980); for fuller insight into Mann's revealing letter to Weber, see the excerpt by Mann (1920); for another discussion of homosexuality in Mann's novella, see the excerpt by Jeffrey Meyers (1977).*]

Der Tod in Venedig records the phases of a real experiment; it is not a mere mental construct, manipulating an imagined character through arbitrarily chosen adventures. To begin with, Thomas Mann's own Venetian experiences in 1911 were close to Aschenbach's, at least in embryo. The figure in the Munich cemetery, the sordid ship from Pola to Venice, the aged dandy on board it, the unlicensed gondolier, Tadzio and his family, the attempt to leave Venice foiled by a misdirection of luggage, the cholera epidemic, the honest English clerk at the travel bureau, the street singer—everything was provided by reality, not invented for the later fiction. It all had an 'innate symbolism'. . . . (p. 149)

Equally real was the literary standstill which Mann makes the motive for Aschenbach's journey. Thomas Mann's work in the first decade of the century was in general in a transitional phase, and failure arguably outweighed success: ***Fiorenza*** and ***Königliche Hoheit*** had fallen far short of what was expected of the author of ***Buddenbrooks,*** the projects for 'Maja', 'Ein Elender', the Friedrich novel, and 'Geist und Kunst' had all been abandoned, and now ***Felix Krull*** was hardly moving. In the early months of 1911 Mann wrote very little. Reporting this to [his brother] Heinrich late in March, he speaks of his present low vitality . . . ; the same letter announces a planned holiday in Dalmatia. In mid-May he leaves with his wife for the island of Brioni, but moves to Venice for a short stay . . . : he is at work on a 'recht sonderbare Sache, die ich aus Venedig mitgebracht habe, Novelle, ernst und rein in Ton, einen Fall von Knabenliebe bei einem alternden Künstler behandelnd. Sie sagen "hum, hum!" Aber es ist sehr anständig' (an exceedingly bizarre thing I brought back from Venice, a *Novelle,* serious and pure in tone, treating the case of an elderly artist's passion for a boy. 'Hm, hm!', you say. But it is all very proper).

This jaunty tone is gone altogether the next time Mann reports on progress. He writes to Ernst Bertram on 16 October 1911 that he is 'von einer Arbeit gequält, die sich im Laufe der Ausführung mehr und mehr als eine unmögliche Conception herausstellt und an die ich doch schon zuviel Sorge gewandt habe, um sie aufzugeben' (tormented by a project which in the course of execution has turned out more and more to be an impossible conception and on which I have nevertheless spent too much trouble to give it up now). At the beginning of April he has hopes of finishing the story by the end of the month; although he thinks Heinrich may not approve of it as a whole, he is sure it has 'individual beauties', and is especially pleased with a 'classicizing' chapter. . . . But by the 27th, problems again dominate. Although publication arrangements are already well in hand, Mann writes to Heinrich that he cannot round the story off. . . . And on 3 May he speaks once more of being 'schrecklich angestrengt und besorgt, einer eigenen Arbeit wegen, an die ich—vielleicht instinktloser Weise—beinahe ein Jahr gewandt habe und die nun so oder so fertig werden muss' (terribly strained and worried about a work of my own on which—perhaps I should have known better—I have now spent nearly a year and which must now be finished one way or another).

This is not a picture of issues easily mastered or of an experiment which yielded its conclusions straight away. That is hardly surprising if we remember Mann's difficulties over 'Geist und Kunst'. And if the Venice stay had provided material for working out these teasing problems in fictional form, new factors had added to their complexity. The clearest way to present the matter is to reconstruct the genesis of the story.

The clues Mann provides are suggestive and, although not precise as to time, help us to see essentially what occurred. Our knowledge of his sources and of the dates at which he came upon them also helps. The purpose of our reconstruction, which may seem at times to be suggesting 'earlier versions' of the text (there is some evidence for this) is to point up the possibilities—both literary and moral—of each contribution to the story in such a way that its final form can be grasped in all its richness of reference, and appreciated as a solution which was anything but facile.

The threads we have to follow are drawn together by Mann himself in his letter of 4 July 1920 to Carl Maria Weber [see excerpt dated 1920]. The ethos Mann discerned in Weber's poems led him to declare his own attitude to homosexuality, about which ***Der Tod in Venedig*** had left room for misunderstanding. Mann says that he would not wish to give the impression of rejecting a type of feeling which he honours, which almost of necessity has more spiritual value (*Geist*) than the so-called normal type, and which he is himself no stranger to. He then goes at length into the reasons why his story nevertheless appears to reject it.

First there is the nature of his artistic processes. He distinguishes between the 'Dionysiac spirit of irresponsible-individualistic lyrical effusion' and the 'Apolline spirit of epic with its moral and social responsibilities and objective limitations'. In other words, between the urge to express private and personal feeling, and the requirements of the more public genre of prose narrative. It may not be permissible to endorse in sober prose what one feels a private enthusiasm for. In fact, it may not be possible, for the execution of the literary conception has its own corrective influences, which Mann calls a 'painful process of objectivization'. He says that ***Der Tod in Venedig*** finally strove for a balance between sensuality and morality, analogous to Goethe's achievement in *Die Wahlverwandtschaften*. But in its origin, and still at its core, the story is essentially 'hymnic'.

Mann refers Weber to his account of hymnic origin and objectivization already published in 1919, in the *Vorsatz* [introduction] to ***Gesang vom Kindchen.*** That opens with Mann's old nagging question: 'Bin ich ein Dichter?' ['Am I a poet?']. . . . There follows his defence of the prose moralist as a 'poet', familiar from 'Geist und Kunst'. But what comes next is the confession of a past shame which still rankles, a secret defeat, a never-avowed failure. He means the writing of ***Der Tod in Venedig***. . . . Clearly Mann's Venice experience . . . originally inspired an affirmative rather than critical treatment, perhaps even in verse (***Gesang***) rather than prose. The hexameters in the text of ***Der Tod in Venedig*** could be remnants of this treatment. At all events, the failure to carry the project out in that form still rankled in 1919—even though the final form of the story had turned the shortcoming into a virtue and reaped praise. . . . The heights of *Dichtertum* [poetic method] were not scaled. In his letter Mann names other factors at work in the story's development: first, his Naturalist background, so alien to the younger generation Weber represents, which made him see the 'case' in a pathological as well as a symbolic light. . . . Secondly, there was his personal mistrust of passion as such, a Protestant and puritanical burgher trait which he shares with Aschenbach, and which counteracted any 'Greek' view of homosexual love. The real subject of his fable, he says, was the confusion and degradation caused by passion, a theme he had previously thought of treating in a renarration of the aged Goethe's love for the seventeen-year-old Ulrike von Levetzow.

In the rest of the letter, Mann develops the idea that the erotic attraction of *Leben* [life] for *Geist* [spirit] need not correspond to the attraction between the sexes. He sums it up with a quotation from Hölderlin's poem 'Sokrates und Alkibiades': 'Wer das Tiefste gedacht, liebt das Lebendigste' (whose thought deepest has probed, most loves vitality). And he makes the judgement on homosexual love depend on the nature of the individual instance: it is morally neutral until it shows its value in its works.

This remarkably frank self-interpretation suggests why the 'bizarre thing' Mann brought back from Venice gave him such trouble in the composition, and fills in the background to the letters quoted above. By July 1911 the work was already to be a *Novelle,* though not yet necessarily a 'moral fable': the 'purity of tone' and the 'propriety' may at that stage have meant something other than adverse judgement on Aschenbach. By October of that year the difficulties have set in. Mann finds he is working with an 'impossible conception'. This surely is the point at which an affirmative treatment was abandoned. (pp. 149-54)

So we have a picture of a diametrical change in the conception of ***Der Tod in Venedig.*** (p. 154)

The precariousness of the Artist's claim to dignity and public respect was thus a theme awaiting embodiment. But this does not mean it was from the first the keynote of the new story. Rather, it was an old theme towards which the working out of the story increasingly gravitated. Mann was in this case, it is plain from his accounts, a reluctant moralist.

Picture him as a writer at a cross-roads in his development, with the doubts and possibilities of the 'Geist und Kunst' essay in his mind, with his work seemingly much in need of a revivifying impulse. In Venice he has an intense emotional experience. It inspires him to treat it in a form which is far from his usual literary stock-in-trade and is thereby a kind of creative rebirth: in place of cold analysis and Apolline epic form, an impassioned outpouring, lyrical and Dionysiac. Tadzio is celebrated hymnically, the passion he inspires is affirmed because it is fruitful. In a milder way, ***Tonio Kröger*** asserted that the basis of true *Dichtertum* [poetic method] was emotional. Now the emotion goes deeper: it is nothing less than Nietzsche's Dionysiac spirit, described in the *Geburt der Tragödie* as indispensable for great art. (pp. 154-55)

But it also speaks of a healthier art and of a new classicism —very much the ideals which Aschenbach pursued, and the ideals of the times. For these things equally Tadzio's beauty could serve as an inspiration: a work of celebration was still possible. But if the celebration was not to be drunken and Dionysiac, what was it to be?

The answer is: Platonic. This brings us to the most important source for ***Der Tod in Venedig.*** The text is rich in phrases, images, and ideas from Plato's *Symposium* and *Phaedrus* and from Plutarch's *Erotikos,* a much later dialogue essentially Platonic in style and theme.

The technique of weaving in quotation and allusion to famous texts was one Mann had practised skilfully before, not merely to decorate his fiction but to add a dimension of meaning to what was being narrated. The references to *Don Carlos* in ***Tonio Kröger,*** the retelling of the Tristan story as a burlesque, in different ways place the characters' experience in a broader context than that of the immediate fiction. This is true to a yet greater extent of the Greek sources in ***Der Tod in Venedig.*** Even before being exploited for literary effect, they clearly helped Mann himself to a deeper, more generalized understanding of his theme. If the fate of Aschenbach embodies problems connected with the literary scene of the 1910s and Mann's place in it, the Greek dialogues placed these problems in a wider framework still. For where Mann had been concerned with a fashionable emphasis (*Zeitströmung*) on external beauty in the Germany of his day, and with a defence of intellect in art, the Platonic dialogues stated an all-embracing and timeless theory of the relationship of beauty to men's spiritual and intellectual life, ideally reconciling the two. They also discussed the kinds of love beauty provokes, its potential inspiring quality and potential dangers. . . . They provided an altogether more profound explanation of Aschenbach's artistic development and his passion, and clear criteria for judging it. (p. 156)

Despite the ambiguities which are rooted in the genesis of ***Der Tod in Venedig,*** at least the direction of development is clear: in what it implies about the Artist, the story constitutes a moral victory which is nothing to do with the morality of homosexual love. Through Aschenbach Mann had experimented with a change in his literary ways, a decision to reject the values by which he had so far lived and worked. The forces influencing him in that direction were stated in 'Geist und Kunst'—a work which Aschenbach, significantly, had brought to completion, we can easily infer in what sense. Subjected to the temptation of swimming with the stream, and even for a time actively wishing to do so, Mann nevertheless remained true to himself. The nature of his talent asserted itself against his more superficial motives. In place of the new kind of form he yearned to achieve, it drew him back towards a soberer, more critical, still 'intellectual' work. This is surely what he meant when he spoke in the ***Lebensabriss*** of the surprises the work had in store for its author. . . . The failure to achieve undeniable *Dichtertum* [poetic method] which he still speaks bitterly of in ***Gesang vom Kindchen,*** was thus only a failure in a limited sense.

The ambivalent art which was first brought to maturity in ***Der Tod in Venedig*** was a permanent acquisition. It is the basis for many later ambiguities and for an adroit manipulation of levels of meaning. (p. 177)

The creation of ambivalence was the breakthrough in Mann's long-standing programme to 'elevate' the novel. It rescued the novel of ideas from the mechanical methods of simple allegory. 'Allegory' still fairly describes some aspects of ***Der Zauberberg*** or ***Doktor Faustus;*** but the door has been opened to intellectual complexities of a quite different order from the encoded self-concern of ***Königliche Hoheit.*** From ***Der Tod in Venedig*** on, ambivalence is the central technique of Mann's art, suggesting, but not affirming, layers of meaning which lie beneath the surface of immediate experience. (p. 178)

T. J. Reed, in his Thomas Mann: The Uses of Tradition, *Oxford at the Clarendon Press, Oxford, 1974, 433 p.*

JEFFREY MEYERS (essay date 1977)

[In the following excerpt, Meyers discusses Mann's treatment of homosexuality in Death in Venice. *He believes that the tragic consequences of Aschenbach's homosexual drive symbolize the tragic nature of the artist's search for ideal beauty. For another discussion of homosexuality in Mann's novella, see the excerpt by T. J. Reed (1974).]*

[***Death in Venice,*** like André Gide's] *The Immoralist,* is strongly influenced by Nietzsche. The Apollonian-Dionysian polarity in *The Birth of Tragedy* (1871) is expressed in the opposition of culture, intellect, discipline, serenity and order to instinct, passion, licence, panic and chaos; of society to the individual, life to art, reality to illusion, health to sickness, perfection to decadence. Both Michel and Aschenbach move from the realm of abstract ideas to actual experience; and in the south, outside their own culture, find an instinctual release that leads to a fatal weakening of the will, to homosexuality, decadence, disease and destruction. Both novels question the repressive element in culture, and emphasize the classical wisdom of tempering the emotions with ethical restraint.

But [Albert] Guerard's statement that both books present 'essentially the same story of a latent and unrecognized homosexuality leading to self-destruction' is misleading, for the differences are perhaps more significant than the similarities. Gide's first-person confession is much more subjective and sympathetic to homosexuality than Mann's detached and ironic narrative. Michel condemns the old values, attempts to construct a new morality, maintains a hedonistic and self-consciously immoral attitude toward inversion and achieves his liberation at the expense of Marceline. But in his powerful Dostoyevskian novel, *The Abject,* Aschenbach renounced sympathy with the abyss and 'taught a whole grateful generation that a man can still be capable of moral resolution even after he has plumbed the depths of knowledge'. Though Aschenbach abandons his moral resolution, he retains his asceticism and guilt, and pays for his knowledge with his life. Whereas Michel seeks actual and physical experience with the Arab boys, Aschenbach longs for the ideal and the spiritual; and though he pursues Tadzio, he withdraws from any direct contact which would ruin the purely aesthetic basis of their relationship. As in Huysmans and Wilde, the homosexual theme in Gide's *The Immoralist* is the *covert* but actual subject of the novel. And though this theme is *overt* in ***Death in Venice,*** which carefully describes the development of Aschenbach's homosexual passion, it is not the real subject of the book. Mann employs homosexuality to symbolize the core of passionate feeling that inspires great art, and the theme of his novella is the possibility of self-destruction inherent in creative genius. (pp. 42-3)

Aschenbach justifies the agony of his creative genius—and anticipates the collapse of his discipline and abandonment of moral values—by a belief in 'the idea that almost everything conspicuously great is great in despite: has come into being in defiance of affliction and pain, poverty, destitution, bodily weakness, vice and passion.' . . . By contrast, Tadzio achieves his inspiring 'perfection of form' naturally and effortlessly—like a god. Aschenbach's homosexual passion teaches him that he cannot control his own fate, indeed cannot even save his own life in the face of overwhelming emotion. Tadzio, the love-object, links art with death, and becomes at once the symbol of perfect form that eludes the artist and the rigidly repressed passion that destroys him.

This thematic prelude and the revealing sketch of Aschenbach's character establish the intellectual framework of the novella, suggest the inevitability of his tragic fate, and lead to a series of encounters with menacing and vaguely theatrical figures. The goat-bearded 'circus director' (attended by a hunch-backed sailor) sells Aschenbach the ticket across the northern Adriatic from Pola to Venice and seals their satanic pact with the sand which, like that in his parents' hour-glass, warns of human mortality. The aged and grotesque homosexual with dyed hair, rouged cheeks and false teeth cavorts with the youths on the ship and with his tongue makes 'a suggestive motion ugly to behold'. And Charon, the second messenger of death, complete with straw hat, snub nose and white teeth bared to the gums, conveys Aschenbach, against his will, from the dock to the Lido in a coffin-like gondola, and then suddenly vanishes after the cryptic warning: 'The signore will pay'.

When Aschenbach encounters Tadzio's perfect beauty, delightful charm and expression of pure serenity he does not see him as an actual boy of fourteen, but as an embodiment of Greek art, transmuted and gilded with mythical significance. Aschenbach alludes to Homer, Xenophon and Ovid, and constantly compares the golden-haired youth to Greek sculpture in Parian marble, to Cleitos, Cephalus, Orion, Hyacinthus and, of course, to Narcissus. The classical allusions not only idealize Tadzio but also foreshadow his doom, for all these beautiful Greeks were destroyed by passion. Aschenbach sees Tadzio, as Hallward saw Dorian Gray, as 'the visible incarnation of that unseen ideal' which he hopes to re-create in his own art. His classical idealization of Tadzio, the mirror and image of spiritual beauty whose mellifluous name sounds like the musical syllables of *adagio,* is partly the instinctive habit of the scholar who encounters beauty in a Mediterranean country, partly an expression of his aesthetic taste and partly a defence against his own surging feelings.

The old and ugly Aschenbach imagines his adoration of Tadzio—whose passive response seems to be motivated by adolescent flirtatiousness, vanity and narcissism—as the modern equivalent of Socrates' love for Phaedrus, though Plato does not suggest, in the actual *Phaedrus,* that Socrates is wooing the youth. Aschenbach renounces Socrates' insinuating wit and charming turns of phrase, and seduces Tadzio with meaningful glances that seek and meet the eye of the beloved. Tadzio sees 'himself in his lover as in a glass', and his responsive looks lead Aschenbach to address the boy in his imagination. Though Aschenbach is dominated by passion, he attempts to express—and therefore to control—this passion by means of his intellect, and he represents his feelings as a platonic search for the good. But his paraphrase of Plato merely emphasizes his tragic dilemma and forms an ironic counterpart to his absurd degeneration.

Like Socrates—who was forced to commit suicide for corrupting the youth of Athens—Aschenbach, under the influence of Tadzio, now equates beauty with goodness, and stresses the moral and spiritual qualities of perfect form. (pp. 45-6)

The irony of Aschenbach's futile attempt to idealize his pederastic passion and substitute Elysium for Hades is emphasized by the parallel development of his love and the progress of the cholera that insidiously infects the city. For Aschenbach, the highly respectable widower with one married daughter (he has no son, just as Tadzio seems to have no father), changes from a passive to an active lover, from a purely intellectual and aesthetic admirer of Tadzio's beauty to a man who suddenly realizes that the acute pain he felt during his quite sensible attempt to leave the city (fortuitously prevented by the loss of his trunk) was due entirely to his rapturous though unacknowledged feeling for the youth. His half-hearted attempt to speak to the boy, join body and mind, and effect a sane recovery from his folly fails. Aschenbach's imaginative possession of Tadzio is more intense and more meaningful than physical possession, and he does not want to exchange illusion for reality.

After he whispers the confession of love to himself he throws off the final restraints. The writer whose sternly moral works were adopted as school textbooks is now driven to degeneration by his mania, and openly pursues the boy through the narrow and unclean passages of the town. . . . (p. 47)

Aschenbach's passion is like a crime, and the city's evil secret of the cholera (whose deadly convulsions parody the sexual climax) mingles with the one in the depths of his heart. As Mann writes in **'Goethe and Tolstoy':** 'Disease has two faces and a double relation to man and his human dignity. On the one hand it is hostile: by overstressing the physical, by throwing man back upon his own body, it has a dehumanizing effect. On the other hand, it is possible to think and feel about illness as a highly dignified human phenomenon.' . . .

When Aschenbach learns he is in mortal danger, he realizes that the 'one decent, expiatory course' open to him is to warn Tadzio's mother and urge her to flee at once. Though this advice would save their lives and restore his self-possession, Aschenbach decides to join the conspiracy and hide the guilty knowledge. His irrational and even sinister behaviour is explained not only by his fear of losing Tadzio and desire to be quarantined with him in the abandoned city, but also by his early response to Tadzio's imperfect teeth: '"He is delicate, he is sickly," Aschenbach thought. "He will most likely not live to grow old." He did not try to account for the pleasure the idea gave him. . . . (p. 48)

Tadzio's poor teeth connect him with the aged homosexual on the ship, and this symbol of his anaemic disease and human mortality is pleasurable to Aschenbach because it equalizes youth and age, beauty and ugliness, and diminishes Tadzio's godlike power over him. The writer is possessively jealous of the youth's perfect form, and wants him to die at the height of his beauty, before he is ravaged by decay and old age. He includes Tadzio in his own wish for death, the final release; and the boy's death seems appropriate to Aschenbach, who associates art with disease and suffering.

The actual, as opposed to the idealized meaning of Aschenbach's Socratic 'sacrifice as to an idol or a god' is revealed in the dream that occurs immediately after he discovers the full implications of the cholera and refuses to warn the Polish family about it. This disturbing vision is a powerful contrast to the Apollonian order and reason of the Socratic dialogue and of the 'primeval legend, handed down from the beginning of time, of the birth of form', for it expresses his unconscious fears and desires, and ravages the cultural foundations of his life. As his will disintegrates amidst the stench of wounds, uncleanliness and disease, Aschenbach 'craved with all his soul to join the ring that formed about the obscene symbol [the phallus] of the godhead'. He finally gives himself up to the Dionysian 'orgy of promiscuous embraces—and in his very soul tasted the bestial degradation of his fall.' . . . This terrifying dream denies the relationship of beauty, love and moral goodness, and suggests that Aschenbach's long-sought release is totally negative and destructive: 'it seemed to him as though the moral law were fallen in ruins and only the monstrous and the perverse held out a hope.' . . . (p. 49)

Overwhelmed by passion and disgusted by his ageing body, Aschenbach submits to the cosmetic attentions of the hotel barber, who transforms him into a grotesque replica of the repulsive old invert on the ship. The theatrical make-up is not only a visible manifestation of Aschenbach's corruption, but also an ironic comment on his search for true beauty, for in the *Phaedrus* the effeminate boy also supplies 'his natural deficiency of complexion by use of cosmetics'. Aschenbach, however, is delighted by his sudden rejuvenation, and he pursues Tadzio into Venice wearing a red tie and straw hat which link him to the boy's red-silk breast knot and to the hats of the messengers of death. But he is soon exhausted by his unsuccessful search; and in the little square where he had once conceived the plan of his abortive flight, he eats the over-ripe strawberries that infect him with the fatal cholera, and once again thinks of Socrates' dialogue with Phaedrus. (pp. 49-50)

The doomed Aschenbach then returns to the hotel to discover that Tadzio is leaving. When he rushes to the beach for a final glimpse of the beautiful boy he finds that Tadzio's friend Jaschiu—who once kissed the beloved while Aschenbach compensated himself with 'luscious dead-ripe' strawberries—is avenging himself for his long weeks of subserviency to Tadzio, of stooping (like Aschenbach) beneath his proud sceptre. Jaschiu challenges Tadzio to a fight and presses his 'face into the sand—for so long a time that it seemed the exhausted lad might even suffocate. He made spasmodic efforts to shake the other off, lay still and then began a feeble twitching.' . . . This scene symbolizes the degradation of beauty and form, and at the same time, the spiritual forbearance in the face of fate and constancy of beauty under torture that was represented in the figure of St Sebastian, who 'was specially invoked as a patron against the plague'. After witnessing this scene, the artist is 'summoned' by Tadzio, the final messenger of death.

Though the conclusion of ***Death in Venice*** is ambiguous, it is difficult to agree with [Lionel] Trilling's statement that 'If Mann's Aschenbach dies at the height of his intellectual and artistic powers, overcome by a passion that his ethical reason condemns, we do not take this to be a defeat, rather a kind of terrible rebirth: at his latter end the artist knows a reality that he had until now refused to admit to consciousness'. For Aschenbach does not die at the height of his artistic powers, but expires in a state of profound degeneration as 'the rouged and flabby mouth uttered single words of the sentences shaped in his disordered brain.' . . . Though Aschenbach thought that the figure of Tadzio would be the divine model for his style, that masterpiece of nature never inspires Aschenbach's creative genius nor breaks the artistic impasse that forced him to leave Munich. The only thing he writes in Venice is a page and a half of mannered and decadent prose that barely conceals the dry rot of its intellectual foundations. The thoroughly ironic mode of the novella and Aschenbach's premature death suggest that though he knows a new reality at the end of his life, this self-knowledge cannot be transformed into art: 'It has compassion with the abyss—it *is* the abyss'.

Mann makes Aschenbach a homosexual for several reasons. On one level homosexuality is a manifestation of strain and disorder, a release of psychological repression that results in the vulgar and degrading passion of an elderly gentleman for a rather cruel and unworthy boy. Aschenbach abandons his will, conspires with pseudo-artists like the equivocal musician and the cosmetic barber, sadly deludes himself about his relationship to Tadzio, and condemns himself—and probably his beloved—to death.

More importantly, Aschenbach's homosexual pursuit is symbolic of the artist's noble but tragic quest for perfection. In *Phaedrus* Socrates concludes that the lover who does not seek mere sensual gratification is the one who truly serves the god of love since the contemplation of beauty is more important than the pleasure of the moment, which is lost as soon as it is gratified. Mann adapts this idea to his theme when he makes Aschenbach, who fails to ascend from Tadzio's physical beauty to a higher ideal form, die in a kind of Wagnerian *Liebestod* while contemplating perfect beauty.

Mann's imaginative artist, who paradoxically creates in his work a life that he is unable to live in reality, must maintain a subtle and perilous balance of feeling and thought, and cannot surrender to either without losing his capacity to write. Aschenbach's first dream in Munich reveals the existence of his passionate though repressed feelings, which contribute to the greatness of his art as long as they are controlled by the discipline and restraint of 'the poet-spokesman of all those who labour at the edge of exhaustion; of [those] . . . who yet contrive by skilful husbanding and prodigious spasms of will to produce, at least for a while, the effect of greatness.' . . . Repression is, paradoxically, vital for expression; and without Apollonian form, Aschenbach's Dionysian passion becomes wild and useless, like that of the other artist-types in Mann's stories: Spinell in **'Tristan'**, Siegmund in **'The Blood of the Walsungs'** and Cipolla in **'Mario and the Magician'**. And yet, as Plato writes: 'If a man comes to the door of poetry untouched by the madness of the Muses, believing that technique alone will make him a good poet, he and his compositions will never reach perfection, but are utterly eclipsed by the performances of the inspired madman'. In the doomed love of the suspect and anti-social pederast, Mann found the perfect pattern for the artist's desperate struggle to recapture the ideal form of sensual beauty, and to unite passion with thought, grace with wisdom, the real with the ideal. (pp. 51-3)

Jeffrey Meyers, "Mann and Musil: 'Death in Venice' (1912) and 'Young Torless' (1906)," in his Homosexuality and Literature: 1890-1930, *Athlone Press, 1977, pp. 42-57.**

T. E. APTER (essay date 1978)

[*Apter is the author of the critical study* Thomas Mann: The Devil's Advocate, *which contends that Mann believed "an investigation of evil's force and fascination would result in refreshing disgust with evil." In the following excerpt from that work, Apter provides an overview of* Death in Venice *and discusses the decadence of Gustave von Aschenbach as a man and as an artist.*]

Death in Venice, one of Mann's finest works, reveals his recalcitrant mistrust of those impulses and emotions which are so vividly presented in Wagner's works. This novella does not discuss Wagner directly, as do ***Tristan*** and ***The Blood of the Walsüngs,*** but it presents Mann's attitudes towards death, passion and the debilitating effects of beauty in a way that makes Aschenbach's story similar to one of Wagnerian contagion. The novella reveals the stagnation of Mann's own imagination, yet it treats this impasse so vividly that the negative resolution is transcended by the excellence of the creative presentation.

The story concerns a man who cannot find his way through the maze of sensuality and beauty, who becomes ensnared by a love-fascination that both excites and enervates him. His desires fluctuate among crude sensual longings, tender protectiveness and spiritual cravings. The fluctuation destroys the familiar boundaries of his personality and crushes him with confusion. At the opening of the novella Aschenbach is a respectable, disciplined writer whose forbears were—with the exception of one lively clergyman and a musical grandfather—officers, civil servants and judges. Though he is an artist he retains his forefathers' restraint and regimented lifestyle. This fastidious control is the focal point of his weakness: Aschenbach's impulses have, from childhood, been totally suppressed and, in their neglect, have remained untutored so that when they emerge, they emerge in a thoroughly crude and primitive fashion.

This analysis does not use a specifically Freudian model, for, according to Freud, impulses are always untutored and must always be repressed to some extent, though if they are repressed too severely, they will emerge as a neurotic symptom. The salvation of the civilised personality is achieved by a balance of impulse and control, and, in any person born into any human society, there will be a continuous balance, however precarious or unsatisfactory, between impulse and control. Mann's model of total suppression and then violent release has more in common with Euripide's portrayal of Pentheus's struggle against Dionysus. Here, the man who trusts reason's strength and thus his own self-control is guilty of *hubris*. His punishment is to be torn apart by the Maenads, the representatives of impulse in its crude, orgiastic state. ***Death in Venice*** does not actually contradict a Freudian model, but the pattern of Aschenbach's decay is fashioned upon the Greek myth.

Aschenbach's byword is 'hold-fast'. The type of hero he favours in his writing is one who shows forbearance in the face of fate, or who remains constant under torture. In short, he is interested in heroism born of weakness. He believes that every conspicuously great achievement has resulted from adverse circumstances—from pain, poverty, physical weakness, vice, passion. This view of greatness is similar to that of Nietzsche, who carried the point further by suggesting that since adversity bred greatness, adversity should be propagated. Aschenbach, however, does not so vigorously deny a humanist morality. In highly unNietzschean fashion he bypasses those investigations of human nature which might deprive him of his firm moral line. Since his own impulses and emotions are suppressed, he knows nothing of those creative-destructive energies which blur distinctions between good and evil. Indeed, his safe, sober respectability has little contact with the suffering, vice and passion of which he writes in a fine classical style and which is reproduced in school textbooks. Aschenbach's interest in formal perfection is part of his denial of the vast undergrowth of life; and, at the same time, it makes him particularly susceptible to this amoral, violent undergrowth. Classical form, according to Mann, has two aspects: it reveals a moral strength because it is the result of discipline, but it reveals an immoral tendency in its esteem for beauty—for beauty concerns form and elegance alone; it cares nothing of either good or evil. The artist might turn away from the dark, ugly side of nature and devote himself to beauty and hope thereby to discover a spiritual, sublime image; but beauty, even if it eventually leads to the spiritual, first acts upon the senses. This makes beauty perilous, and for this reason imagination itself is wanton. For imagination is not affected by reason, morality or practicality; it is affected by beauty and good form. Aschenbach's respect for good form (or sensuous manifestation) combined with his detachment (that is, his proud denial of his uncivilised impulses) leads directly to the abyss of irrationality and passion; since beauty appeals to the senses, the detached rationality cannot regulate the impulses thereby aroused, and the impulses follow a rabid, extravagant course.

This is the theoretical outline of the novella. There is, however, little content given to the divine which the artist allegedly tries to approach through beauty or to the special relation beauty might, in the best of circumstances, have with the divine. The quasi-Platonic model (in the *Symposium* love is seen as a link between the sensible world and the world of Forms; it prompts the soul to recapture the vision of the ideal world) is used as an unargued premise. The spiritual is simply posited as the opposite of sensuous fascination, and therefore the assertion that Aschenbach's love for Tadzio is spiritual yearning gone wrong carries no conviction. Indeed, it is impossible to believe, from the very beginning of the tale, that Aschenbach's desires are anything other than sensual. In any great love passion, both sensual and spiritual, will be mingled to the point at which the distinction between them is invidious; but Aschenbach's yearning is always degrading. Moreover, all the seductive arguments in the novella are on the side of decadence and extravagance. The foul-smelling lagoon of Venice whose air Aschenbach inhales with tender, deep, almost painfully sweet draughts, the hateful, insinuating sultriness of the narrow streets in whose stagnant air cigarette smoke remains suspended, the faintly rotten scent of the sea breeze and the sirocco which excites and enervates at once—these command the poetic sympathy of the novella.

A craving for this decay initially motivates Aschenbach, and the longing he suffers is different from anything in Wagner. For decadent though Wagner's sensuousness may at times appear in its enormity and egoism, his characters' desires, even as they emerge from the archaic bed of impulse, are never directed towards the crude and the primitive. The vision which eventually leads Aschenbach to Venice, however, is a regression to the wild and cruel aspects of the primitive. The vision seems to the writer like a 'most surprising widening of the inward barriers' but these barriers are widened only in the sense of being lowered; their profundity is purely regressive. . . . (pp. 50-3)

The compelling realism of this hallucination is ironic and, alongside the constant shift from perception to imagination, enforces the uncanny atmosphere in which decay is more vivid than anything else. The precise detail in which the red-haired, snub-nose man is described is also ironic; as he appears in the portico of the cemetery he allegedly calls Aschenbach back to reality—whereas the red-haired man, in fact, is anything but ordinary reality. He reappears in various guises, at various points in the novella, as a messenger of decay. Similar detail of commonplace occurrences—Aschenbach's smarting eyes the morning he leaves for Venice, the nauseous sensation in his stomach as the boat pushes away from port, the seductively comfortable seat of the gondola, the mincing, hate-filled courtesy of the people in the tourist trade—places them alongside Aschenbach's imaginary visions, so that the balance between imagination and perception is totally destroyed. The often overripe virtuosity of the writing is itself an investigation of the imagination from which the fascination with the overripe springs; there is no stable point from which to judge and resist imagination's seduction.

The sea, in its eternal, unorganised simplicity and vastness, is a symbol of the imagination. When Aschenbach first catches sight of Tadzio, the boy is like a figure rising up from the sea, and it is to the sea that Tadzio points while, dying, Aschenbach observes him for the last time. The immensity of expectation, the rich vastness which the sea, as imagination, represents is, however, merely negative. It is release from the degrading tension of intellect and will. It is salvation for the imagination which is confused and made crude by its receptivity to beauty; but the salvation it offers is only death. There can be no higher resolution, for imagination is an impasse of the soul; its receptivity to beauty leads to degradation.

The smile Tadzio offers the writer in response to his joy at seeing the boy again is over-powerful; its effect is similar to that of Wagner's music in its enervating intoxication. It leads to a thoroughly undisciplined emotional outpouring. Aschenbach whispers 'the hackneyed phrase of loving and longing—impossible in the circumstances, absurd, abject, ridiculous enough yet sacred too, and not unworthy of honour even here: "I love you!" . . .' Only in isolation and in fear of normality can his 'love' survive. Mann does not present a passion which happens to go wrong; he presents a passion which can exist only if it does go wrong.

Aschenbach's debilitating infatuation is closely connected to his meagre store of energy. Mann continually points to the writer's fragile resources—how his strength must be absorbed from outside sources and then put to some special purpose: he sacrifices to his art, in two or three hours of almost religious fervour, the strength he assembles from sleep. His discipline is a necessity, for it is a means of gathering up his meagre capacities and, at the same time, a way of making sure he uses up all his energy, so he has none left to corrupt him. Aschenbach exhibits none of the natural vigour or the joy of activity which characterises someone whose energy is a healthy part of his self. His inability to maintain a relaxed flow of energy is essential to the detachment which eventually leads to his destruction. When he does not release all his energy in his writing, he has no other outlet. The strength that flows into him from the sun and sea and idleness erupts in emotional intoxication; but this is an inward, stagnant intoxication. The energy not released in his art becomes an attack upon his soul.

Passion, as presented in Mann's works, is passive; that is, it is not directed toward the attainment of its object. Its action is to degrade the person who suffers the passion; passion's object remains almost incidental. Mann fails to appreciate the positive aspect of Tristan and Isolde's yearning for night because he fails to see passion as union; he sees passion as an emotion that isolates rather than extends the individual. Moreover, this isolation viciously enforces itself, so that not only does passion make its subject turn aside from society, it also makes its subject seek to destroy society: 'Passion is like a crime: it does not thrive on the established order and the common round; it welcomes every blow dealt the bourgeois structure, every weakening of the social fabric, because it therein feels a sure hope for its own advantage'. Aschenbach would happily see all Venice destroyed by the disease, for a death-ridden city would provide a fine setting for the enactment of his lewd fantasies. When he discovers the severity of the plague he is 'feverishly excited, triumphant in possession of the truth at last, but with a sickening taste in his mouth and a fantastic horror at his heart'. This self-knowledge is abhorrent to him, and he knows that this recklessness presents a danger to his own self as well as to others. The primitive and destructive landscape of his initial vision has been realised in his passion for Tadzio, and this landscape, too, is the cause of the disease; for the cholera has come from the 'hot moist swamps of the Ganges, where it bred in the mephitic air of that primaeval island-jungle, among whose bamboo thickets the tiger crouched . . .'.

Tristan and Isolde's love also destroys the social fabric, in the sense that their love disregards social order; but such destruction is not the point of their passion, as it is the point of Aschenbach's passion. The purpose of the opera characters' passion is a mystical union, a consummation of a love that brings all longing—sensual and spiritual—together. The harm they do is through neglect of everything other than their passion; and even when their society kills them for this neglect, they assert passion's reality above the reality of death. Mann's view of a passion that disregards all else is of a will to destroy all else. Death, then, is the mitigation of violence. Tristan and Isolde pass into death through an assertion of their vision; their death forces home the Romantic metaphor of death as spiritual realisation, infinite promise and mystical union. Aschenbach's imagination is too confused to make this triumphant leap. As he gazes out to the sea, as Tadzio seems to be hovering before an immensity of richest expectation, there is only the vaguest sense that the tension will be resolved; the only real possibility seems to be that the tension will be dissolved in death.

The archaic undergrowth of human impulse cannot enrich imagination or life because any investigation of this undergrowth will destroy life and mind. Mann's Romanticism is that of the moralist whose principles are as rigidly rational as those of Aschenbach (who deals only with the rational aspects of man) but who is intrigued by the amoral energies which, he half realises, are the sources of imagination and emotion. Aschenbach's favourite hero, the man who achieves strength through weakness and adversity, uses his will only in a highly moral fashion. The blackness of the will which appears in the course of the tale reveals the moralist's frenzied self disgust at the true nature of his will.

The closing sentence reads, 'And before nightfall a shocked and respectful world received news of his decease'. Mann assumes that the public wants to believe in the respectability of the artist, that since the public trusts the artist to reveal human truths the artist himself is expected to be a model of morality. Though the opposite is often the case, though the public delight in the artist's eccentricities and vices and sufferings, Mann here reveals his own expectations of the artist, expectations whose disappointment is often his theme. Mann shows the artist's respectable, spiritual purpose being waylaid by his own imagination; he shows how the discipline necessary to art distorts, through detachment, the artist's human impulses. Here Mann gives content to his dictum that the creator cannot live well. 'Life' is the capacity for self-expression and personal interaction; and the artist's need to give form to the chaos of the human psyche, to tease out the various truths that are packed together in ordinary perception, threatens him with the very chaos he, as an artist, so proudly handles. Indeed, Aschenbach's problem is not simply that he is an artist, but that he is not a great artist. He is therefore unable to look upon all life and to mould its horror creatively, and to balance the horror against the good. The artist's creative material is the mass of sensuousness, impulse and longing which threatens the form and morality he craves. The substance of creation is chaos, and this chaos can destroy the creator.

In this novella the tension between art and life is perfectly realised, but the realisation only shows that the tension, as Mann conceived it, is without resolution. Mann's depiction of imagination's defeat before life, and its inability to handle its own creative material, and its tendency to corrupt its own noble impulses, is an artistic triumph; yet this triumph reveals the defeat of Mann's own imagination, which could not participate in deeper emotional impulses without being hopelessly bewildered, without being able to find a salvation other than annihilation. (pp. 53-7)

T. E. Apter, in his Thomas Mann: The Devil's Advocate, *The Macmillan Press Ltd., 1978, 165 p.*

MARTIN SWALES (essay date 1980)

[*In the following excerpt from his* Thomas Mann: A Study, *Swales discusses the ambiguity of meaning in* Death in Venice, *exploring both the novella's realistic and metaphorical levels of interpretation. For similar discussions, see the excerpts by Ronald Gray (1965) and T. J. Reed (1974).*]

[***Der Tod in Venedig (Death in Venice)***] works on two levels. At a metaphorical level it is the tragedy of the creative artist whose destiny it is to be betrayed by the values he has worshipped, to be summoned and destroyed by the vengeful deities of Eros, Dionysus, and Death. At a realistic, psychological level, the story is a sombre moral parable about the physical and moral degradation of an ageing artist who relaxes the iron discipline of his life, who becomes like the pathetic dandy on the boat to Venice, an older man desperately trying to recapture his lost youth. Both these levels of the story—and the kind of reader response which they elicit—co-exist in Thomas Mann's text. One can illustrate this co-existence by examining the function of those passages in the story which draw on a whole tradition of aesthetic philosophy from Plato onwards. I have in mind those paragraphs where we are given discursive reflections about art and beauty, quotations from and allusions to the Platonic dialogues. In one sense, such passages supply a philosophical and metaphysical context for Aschenbach's experience which makes his story illustrative of larger problems. Beauty, so the argument runs, is the one absolute that is perceivable by the senses. When man encounters the Beautiful he is visited almost by a shock recognition that he has come face to face with an intimation of his higher spiritual destiny. Yet Beauty is a subversive value: the very fact that the senses are involved in its perception means that man's excited response may be not spiritual but sensual. The higher love may, on examination, prove to be nothing more than a sexual infatuation. And this is true particularly of homoerotic experience. Because a homosexual attraction cannot lead to physical creation, to procreation, it may promise the higher creativity of the mind, of art. Yet equally the homoerotic can be the source of furtive, degraded and degrading relationships. Such considerations as these figure in the text of ***Der Tod in Venedig*** in two ways. Clearly they function in their own right as philosophical reflections on the ambiguous nature of Beauty. And this philosophical scheme gives Aschenbach's story the dignity of a metaphysical drama. But equally these reflections are inseparable from the particular psychological context of Aschenbach, the ageing artist. He himself uses such considerations to justify—and, ultimately, to deceive himself about—the nature of his feelings for the boy Tadzio. The metaphysical argument is of a piece with the realistic, psychological argument. The Platonic musings on Beauty are vital ingredients of Aschenbach's psychology: they are *his* thoughts—and yet they are also the thoughts enshrined in a major philosophical tradition of the West.

What, then, is the effect of this coexistence of meanings? T. J. Reed [see excerpt dated 1974] has shown how the story has its roots in what was initially a local problem: Mann disliked the enthusiasm in contemporary art circles for work that was sensuous, plastic, 'sculptured', rather than reflective, critical, analytical. From this came the impetus to a moral tale about the degradation that awaits the man, the artist who denies scruple and reflection in the name of a cult of formal beauty and perfection. But the ideas and values that are implicated in Aschenbach's decline are, as we have seen, part of a longer cultural and philosophical tradition with which Mann has to take issue if he is to understand the forces that mould and shape his hero's thinking. And any such cultural tradition is not simply a stable, timeless entity: it is transmitted through the specific sensibility of a particular man, of a particular time, of a particular culture and society. The story makes clear that Aschenbach is very much part of the historical ambience around him. The narrator reflects: . . .

> In order for a significant product of the human mind to make instantly a broad and profound impact there must be a secret affinity, indeed a congruence between the personal fate of its creator and the general fate of its contemporary audience.

In what does this sympathy consist which makes Aschenbach the spokesman of a generation? The narrator answers: . . .

> Once—in an unobtrusive context—Aschenbach had directly suggested that any major achievement that had come about stood as an act of defiance: it had been made in defiance of grief and torment, poverty, destitution, bodily weakness, vice, passion and a thousand other obstacles.

Aschenbach speaks, then, for a generation of 'Moralisten der Leistung' . . . (moralists of effort), a generation which identifies moral good with spiritual struggle and attrition. Virtue is to be found in the 'Trotzdem', in the overcoming of difficulty, scruple, doubt in an exercise of willed self-assertion. This is a Nietzschean legacy, what J. P. Stern has called 'the morality of strenuousness'. The narrator, in a passage of explicit commentary, goes on to imply a critique of the cast of mind that identifies morality with an entity that has, strictly speaking, no room for moral values. . . .

> Does form not have two faces? Is it not moral and immoral at one and the same time? Moral as the result and expression of discipline, but immoral and indeed anti-moral in so far as it is of its very nature indifferent to moral values; in fact is is essentially concerned to make morality bow before its proud and limitless sceptre.

Here the narrator comments upon an aspect of Aschenbach's personality as artist, but such is the 'sympathy' that binds *this* artist to his time that the aesthetic credo implies the cultural and intellectual temper of its age. ***Der Tod in Venedig*** appears some two years before the outbreak of the First World War. It is a text which suggests how the ethos of discipline and order is a questionable value, one which, in its very repudiation of scruple, reflection, analysis, lays itself open to the seductions of untrammelled, orgiastic experience, thereby confusing self-transcendence with self-abasement. Mann's story acquires a particularly sombre colouring when we remember the waves of collective enthusiasm with which a whole European generation acclaimed the outbreak of war in 1914. Significantly, in his essay ***Bruder Hitler (Brother Hitler)*** of 1939 Mann wrote the following: . . .

> ***Death in Venice*** knows a great deal about the repudiation of contemporary psychologism, about a new decisiveness and simplicity in the psyche—all this, admittedly, I brought to a tragic conclusion. I was not devoid of contact with tendencies and ambitions of the time, with what was felt to be—and proved to be—the coming mood: twenty years later it was to be hawked through the streets.

It would, however, be too easy to see ***Der Tod in Venedig*** as simply a cautionary tale. For it is too perceptive in its understanding of the ethos of form, too implicated in the cast of mind which it diagnoses, to be a work of straightforward didacticism. Indeed, it is one of the profoundest ironies of the book that its own formal control, its deliberately 'classicizing' style is of a piece with the artistic and human ethos which it criticizes. And this gives the work an authority richer than unambiguous denunciation could ever achieve. To borrow the term applied to Aschenbach's achievement, Mann's tale is bound to its time by complex ties of sympathy. And sympathy implies 'suffering with', a 'suffering with' which, in this case, embraces analytical understanding and critique. (pp. 41-5)

Martin Swales, in his Thomas Mann: A Study, *Heinemann, 1980, 117 p.*

GEOFFREY GALT HARPHAM (essay date 1982)

[*In the following excerpt, Harpham bases his discussion of* Death in Venice *on the difference between metonymic language, which "designates a relationship between objects characterized by random and possibly meaningless contiguity, such as that between pen and paper," and metaphoric language, which "designates a sharing of essence that cuts across immediate contexts, so that one object is seen as a version of another, such as pen and finger." Harpham then explains that both types of language are fundamental in the creation of parody, which posits a certain type of relationship between language and the objects it refers to in the world. He states that "metonymic language, the language of realism, claims to have its origin in 'the world.' Metaphoric language, on the other hand, breaks the hold of the referential world, locating its origin in language, or the copying process, itself. If, as in grotesque parody, it becomes impossible to segregate origin from copy, then both metonymy and metaphor are subverted or contaminated by each other. For Thomas Mann, suspicious of the pretenses of art to represent reality, and equally suspicious of the pretensions of artists who would claim for art an autonomous existence, grotesque parody was a natural mode."*]

[The] subject of ***Death in Venice*** can be conceived as metaphor seizing metonymy and dragging it toward parody.

To understand metaphor as the maternal ground from which language has arisen and toward which it may degenerate is to begin to understand the extraordinary sense of "inevitability" imparted by the narrative. For although Aschenbach renounces "knowledge," "sympathy with the abyss," and "the flabby humanism of *tout comprendre, c'est tout pardonner*" [*"to understand all, is to forgive all"*] as a means of "obliterating" the maternal metaphor, he is pulled back toward them, toward a sense of the connectedness of things, by the gravitational allure of the natural. Remarkably, the sense of inevitability accelerates as the events become increasingly unusual; it accelerates despite the interweaving of dream into the realistic narrative, the proliferation of mythic figures and references; it accelerates despite the increasingly exotic psychological condition of the protagonist. Inevitability seems inversely proportionate to probability; necessity, to rarity. And this can be only because Aschenbach, in his grotesqueness, rushes toward a "natural" condition.

It was this progression that provoked D. H. Lawrence [see excerpt dated 1913] to accuse Mann of "banality," of falling prey to the "rotten" Flaubertian doctrine of "Nothing outside the definite line of the book." Lawrence's own method, and his morality, were precisely the opposite. The double novel *The Rainbow* and *Women in Love* begins with a vision of the generations of Brangwens living close to the immemorial rhythms of the earth, a celebration of the replicable, the shared, the familial, in which there are no individuals, only Brangwens, and "Brangwen" is a mode of being sanctified by the ages and the place. But the novel moves relentlessly out of the primordial swamp and into the drier air of dis-integrated individuality, ending with Birkin and Ursula, living in a world recognized as contemporary, struggling to achieve a condition for which there is no precedent. Lawrence points toward a new heaven and new earth, one of the most attractive features of which must have been that (as it says in *Revelation*) "there was no more sea." Mann's hero begins at that point of achieved individuality toward which Lawrence's grope, but then half-willingly abandons it. Aschenbach begins in a condition of metonymy: Aschenbach the solitary warrior of the soul, with neither family nor friends, with no interests other than his work—he is his honored self, illuminating but not illuminated by the world, attached to nothing, replicated nowhere. His personal condition is reinforced by the metonymic character of the narrative. We encounter him in the historical, specifiable world, walking down a "realistic" Prince Regent Street in Munich on a spring afternoon in "19—." The uncertainty in the date is the sole de-realizing element, the only opening for the sense of reality to leak out, and the figural or archetypal to enter in. Aschenbach seems, however, no creature of the fancy or imagination, but a dense figure, even one composed from verifiable facts drawn from the lives of Platen, Goethe, Winckelmann, Mahler, and even Mann himself, who attributed his own thinly disguised works to his protagonist, and who had himself vacationed in Venice. Mann went so far as to acknowledge these circumstances by saying that "Nothing is invented in ***Death in Venice.***" In other words, up to a certain point, it seems that nothing at all is "within the line of the book," but all derived or adapted from "life," the category of the external. The tale so offended Lawrence because the hero surrenders rather than acquires his significant features, his differentiating marks. The tale ends in the sea; the hero is diluted, for he replicates and is replicated by all the figures he has encountered—even Venice, even death itself. (pp. 132-34)

We can track Aschenbach's fate by marking the points at which he surrenders his higher degree of organization by accepting kinship. We can begin with the relatively inconspicuous incident following the Dionysian dream, in which Aschenbach visits the barber. He is tempted by the barber's arguments in favor of cosmetic rejuvenation because they mimic his own noble rejection of "the hampering and disintegrating effect of knowledge." . . . The barber's defense is moral and bourgeois, favoring action and artful discipline over nature's betrayals. He equates nature and the human soul not through the creation of extended prose narratives but by dyeing hair, powdering cheeks, and, in general, "restoring" the "natural color" that "belongs" to his client. Aschenbach succumbs to these strategems because, in his weakened state, it seems to him as if the barber is speaking with his own voice; but this is just the beginning, for when he rises from the chair he has become in fact a grotesque parody of himself—which is to say, an image of another parody, the young-old man. When he looks in the mirror he discovers a "young man," and this mirror-image encompasses both "the master" and that hideous creature of rouge and loose dentures. But the image is only the grotesque manifestation of deeper sympathies: like the young-old man, the young Aschenbach had taken away "the breath of the twenty-year-olds with . . . cynic utterances on the nature of art and the artist life." . . . Both teach, both provide models for youth, both are attracted to beauty. Multiplying resemblances, we can see that the barber has created not a smaller, or a false, Aschenbach, but a larger and a true one; a poet who, grotesquely but rightly, contains the young-old man.

Paradoxically, this kind of truth consists of constant dilution of the original self. In the course of the narrative Aschenbach collects attributes in a manner so crude and so mysterious that it seems at once a parody and an apotheosis of literary "devices" such as "foreshadowing" and "symbolism." We know that he goes into the barber shop sporting a straw hat, but we do not know until he leaves the shop that this hat has a "gay striped band," or that he has been wearing a red necktie. These details would be unimportant except for the fact that the young-old man and the gondolier were similarly outfitted, and the necktie and hatband now seem evidence of contamination by them. Such connections are most apparent with the three "messenger" figures who impress the artists so forcefully—the stranger at the cemetery, the gondolier, and the guitarist. It is inadequate merely to point out that these figures share a number of qualities; more accurate to say that they draw on a definable pool of characteristics or traits, to which they each contribute something: an imperious air, a "foreign" quality, an iron-shod stick, a dubious association with music, a prominent Adam's apple, crossed legs, less than middle height, a connection with the sea, an association with disease, a snub nose, pointed teeth, and a pattern of coloration that includes the three primary colors and black, white, and grey. The repetition of these attributes subverts the status of any identity in the text by implying that each individual is merely a partial incarnation, a facet, of some larger concept whose limits are unclear, but always apparently enlarging.

Surprisingly, even Tadzio draws from this well. His colors and nautical aspect are right: he wears a blue and white sailor-suit, with a red breast-knot and white collar; he has yellow hair and blueish teeth. He participates, too, in his taint of illness, his foreignness, and even in his quick contempt for the Russian family whom he spies "leading their lives there in joyous simplicity" . . .—repugnant to the boy in his role as "absolute art-demon" leading Aschenbach to radical foolishness. Tadzio's mother is known as the "lady of pearls"; a pearl is a little perfection formed around a speck of dirt, the lovely product of a pathological irritation, and he is his mother's son. For he is Apollo masking Dionysus—Nietzsche's definition of Greek drama—and is recognizable both as Aschenbach's "own god" and as the "stranger god." Tadzio embraces Jaschiu, his tormentor-lover, who shares his vowel. And he embraces Aschenbach, touching through conspiratorial glances with his grey eyes. As black/white, grey is the color of mediation, of metaphor, of entropy, of the impure union of opposites. The only other grey in the text is masked, or secret: it is the color of Aschenbach's hair. Tadzio is a universal mirror and image, a glass in which everything discovers its double, especially the doubled artist whose task is to mirror both spiritual beauty and the destiny of his contemporaries.

In such ways Tadzio gathers identities unto himself; in this, he complements the last of the messenger-figures, the guitarist, who disperses himself generally. Thus the scene in which Aschenbach and Tadzio regard each other furtively while the guitarist entertains the international clientele of the hotel is especially interesting for its simultaneous and multi-leveled absorptions and dispersals. The guitarist is a truly cosmic figure, constantly breaking the frame that would limit him. First he leaves the area of performance, going up on the terrace to collect money from the assembled guests—who all contribute, even the artless Russians. While collecting, he is also dispersing, for he is drenched in carbolic and each inhales his reek. Then, having collected, he begins his performance, a rowdy song in an "impossible" dialect, with a refrain consisting only of laughter, which comes "whooping, bawling, crashing out of him, with a verisimilitude that never failed to set his audience off in profuse and unpremeditated mirth that seemed to add gusto to his own." At the height of the laughter, he reverses the frame, becoming the spectator by pointing at the audience "as though there could be in all the world nothing so comic as they; until at last they laughed in hotel, terrace, and garden, down to the waiters, lift-boys, and servants—laughed as though possessed." . . . The point of his climactic scene is that they are indeed possessed; that pollution is general and as inevitable as drawing breath; that nothing is separate, nothing is outside the definite line of the poet. The smaller sympathetic contaminations I have been discussing gather here to universal taint. The impure "type" that cannot be kept securely on the outside now engulfs everything: family resemblances have proliferated beyond control or definition. The type is scattered over the map of Europe; the pool threatens to include *all* characteristics. The protagonist has been disbanded as an individual, but has come close to achieving the condition that Northrop Frye attributes to the entire literary universe, "in which everything is potentially identical with everything else."

What is the center of this network, the point of this endless connectedness? Is there a type of types among the replicas, an axle from which all spokes radiate? To these questions many answers seem possible. It could be said that all the characters are "really" images of Tadzio, or that they all group around Aschenbach as manifestations of his psyche. It has been suggested that the three main tempters are images of death like those we encounter in Dürer; or that they are satyrs attendant to Tadzio-Dionysus. One critic has maintained that both Tadzio and Aschenbach are versions of Sebastian, the hero of Aschenbach's works: "'The conception of an intellectual and virginal manliness, which clenches its teeth and stands in modest defiance of the swords and spears that pierce its side'." . . . In finding justice in all these views I am proposing another kind of approach altogether: that we abandon the search for a center within the text, and think instead of the entire narrative as a continuing process of the foreign-becoming-intimate, the metonymic-becoming-the-metaphoric—in other words, of a movement from the center to the margin. The narrative is like a great chain of being, except that it has no definable origin, no source of order.

In making these suggestions I have extended the implications of two images that do seem, if not central, at least pervasive. The first is a metaphor for metaphor itself—the air, which passes through everything, imparting life, infecting, degrading, inspiring. The air of thought is the hateful, sultry air of the sirocco. In and through the air, everything is linked: to see the text from the point of view of the air is to see individual identity as migratory, a provisional configuration.

The second image of images is sweetness. . . . I am not speaking only of literal sweetnesses, such as the strawberries Aschenbach twice consumes, but as it happens these two occasions are instructive of the larger sense of sweetness I have in mind. He first eats strawberries when he sees Tadzio on the beach, early in his stay in Venice. They are delectable, but already savoring of excess (in the same way that "beaded bubbles winking at the brim" in "Ode to a Nightingale" convert instantly to the dangerous "purple-stainèd mouth"), for they constitute his "second breakfast." They are not fresh, but are "luscious, dead-ripe fruit." . . . Within a paragraph, sweetness is linked not with corruption but with the image of Tadzio as a young god, virginally pure and austere: the cry "'Tadzui! Tadzui!'" with its terminal vowel, strikes Aschenbach as "sweet and wild." . . . Tadzio is consistently sweet in both the senses implied in these instances; he can be considered as an epitome of sweetness itself, the kind of ambiguous delight/debauchery, fatality/fertility invoked in an Aschenbach daydream as the "sweet blood" of the slain Hyacinthus, from which the flower springs.

The second time we encounter strawberries, we know both that the food supply in Venice is the source of the plague, and that Aschenbach has emerged from the attentions of the barber with his lips colored carmine, "the color of ripe strawberries." The phrase "sweet and wild" has reappeared, too, in the account of the fearful dream, applied to the "mad rout" in the frenzied pursuit of the goats. The cry of the pursuers is accompanied by flute-notes "of the cruellest sweetness." . . . And we have read, and understood as a sign of the plague, of the "sweetish-medicinal smell" . . . of the carbolic used to disinfect the city. This is a smell not altogether different from "that cloying, sacrificial smell" . . . in St. Mark's, with which it mingles. Horrid death stalks the streets in these evil vapors, much as Aschenbach stalks the delightful, "sweetly idle" Tadzio.

This pursuit is sweet stalking sweet, for Aschenbach and Tadzio are displaying the two sides of sweet: this, indeed, is the idea that unites them. Sweet things delight; and they dissolve: they rot. The strawberries are presented to him not as an assemblage of discrete items, but as a great mass, ambivalently plural and single. Sweet implies ripe, and ripe promises rot. This is precisely the course of Aschenbach's entanglement with Tadzio, which begins with baby cloudlets and images of creation and ends with corruption and death. Tadzio, with his honey-colored ringlets, rots into the stranger god, and then into Hermes, god of duplicity and ambivalence. All figures in this narrative rot. The musicians who accompany the artist's gondola to the Lido rot into the guitarist and his company; the fantasy of Socrates discoursing to Phaedrus, which occurs to Aschenbach when he first sees Tadzio, rots into the drunken dream-Socrates at the end. This version of the philosopher instructs his pupil that beauty represents a path of "perilous sweetness, a way of transgression." . . . Sweet things rot into their own parodies, surrendering their structure and level of organization as they do so.

We can see why "moral fiber" must be based on a renunciation of the sweet. What Aschenbach discovers is that there is no avoiding it. He had favored "lofty purity, symmetry, and simplicity" . . . , opposing these to the "disintegrating effect of knowledge," but suspects from the first that simplicity itself is entropic: the very renunciation which combats rot encourages it, resulting "in its turn in a dangerous simplification, in a tendency to equate the world and the human soul. . . ." . . . His whole aesthetic philosophy is based on entropy, in artfully disguised forms: "Thought that can merge wholly into feeling, feeling that can merge wholly into thought—these are the artist's highest joy." . . . So we cannot be taken by surprise when the scabrous Socrates tells his boy-lover that "simplicity, largeness, and renewed severity of discipline" means "a return to detachment and to form," and that this preoccupation with form leads "to intoxication and desire," and ultimately to "the bottomless pit." . . . As all communication fills in "the gap of evenness," all mergings lead to the pit.

This pit is figured by the sea, the home of largeness and simplicity, and here is the final characteristic of sweet: it dissolves into liquid, into the larger body which absorbs it. Perhaps we call our lovers terms of endearment which summon up images of sweetness to express our desire that their singleness be fused with ours in a third thing, love. Sweet love is like a metaphor, establishing a base of sameness in difference, a sameness that necessarily involves a loss of individuality on both sides. Other sweetnesses also dissolve. Revenge is sweet because, in bringing an enemy low it destroys an odious hierarchy. That parting is a sweet sorrow means that we can blend most blissfully when we are certain of regaining our selves shortly after. Rapture precedes rupture: deep-sea divers speak of "the rapture of the deep," a form of nitrogen narcosis that is reportedly inexpressibly sweet. Aschenbach's dreams are first a delightful, and then a rank, preliminary version of his death, for they break the frame of self, permitting a free flow to the infinite. When Goffman speaks of "breaking frame" he, too, uses the image of "flooding out," and this is Aschenbach's experience—sweet love ending in liquid death. (pp. 139-43)

Like Adam, Aschenbach—and all fictional characters, and all narratives—"stands in the middle." The reader who regards

Death in Venice as a "realistic" narrative will consider this marginality ethically dubious, even disreputable. In "the world," it is. As Sartre says, slime is a symbol of *"Antivalue"* . . . , by which he means that value-judgments follow genre-decisions, and depend upon reliable categories, strict framing. Within an "interim existence" . . . there can be no value. On the other hand, as Sartre says boldly, though the slimy may be repugnant, it is *being*, and embodies "the meaning of the entire world." . . . As a character, and as an emblem of writing, Aschenbach is a "true Amphibium," a creature of divided natures. His impurity, revealed at the point where the alien becomes the intimate, is the impurity of the grotesque. But it is, after all, mistaken to speak of a "point," for the range of impurity in this text reaches from noble sympathy with one's readers to utter debasement. Another student of Venice, John Ruskin, also understood how easy was the descent, how viscous the path, from the "noble grotesque," characterized by terror and pity, to the "ignoble grotesque," marked by obscenity, mockery, and grossness. According to Ruskin, Venice declined from the noble Gothic grotesque to the ignoble form when it became afflicted by a "pestilence . . . that came and breathed upon her beauty. . . ." In ***Death in Venice***, Mann has retold this story with a terrible nobility. (pp. 144-45)

Geoffrey Galt Harpham, "Metaphor, Marginality, and Parody in 'Death in Venice'," in his On the Grotesque: Strategies of Contradiction in Art and Literature, *Princeton University Press, 1982, pp. 122-45.*

ADDITIONAL BIBLIOGRAPHY

Bance, A. F. "*Der Tod in Venedig* and the Triadic Structure." *Forum for Modern Language Studies* VIII, No. 2 (April 1972): 146-61.

Scholarly discussion of the triadic structure of *Death in Venice*.

Baron, Frank. "Sensuality and Morality in Thomas Mann's *Tod in Venedig*." *German Review* XLV, No. 2 (March 1970): 115-25.

Posits that knowledge of Johann von Goethe's *Wahlverwandtschaften* is necessary for an understanding of *Death in Venice*, specifically in relation to the moral perspective of the novella.

Berendsohn, Walter E. *Thomas Mann: Artist and Partisan in Troubled Times*. Translated by George C. Buck. University: University of Alabama Press, 1973, 261 p.

Critical survey of Mann's works.

Braverman, Albert, and Nachman, Larry David. "The Dialectic of Decadence: An Analysis of Thomas Mann's *Death in Venice*." *German Review* XLV, No. 4 (November 1970): 289-98.

Discusses the decline of Gustave von Aschenbach from moral idealist to a degraded sensualist.

Brennan, Joseph Gerard. *Thomas Mann's World*. New York: Russell & Russell, 1962, 206 p.

Examines Mann's artistic personality as revealed in his works.

Bürgen, Hans, and Mayer, Hans-Otto. *Thomas Mann: A Chronicle of His Life*. Translated by Eugene Dobson. University: University of Alabama Press, 1969, 290 p.

Year-by-year chronicle of Mann's life.

Church, Margaret. "*Death in Venice:* A Study of Creativity." *College English* 23, No. 8 (May 1962): 648-51.

Discusses the nature of art and reality in *Death in Venice*.

Consigny, Scott. "Aschenbach's 'Page and a Half of Choicest Prose': Mann's Rhetoric of Irony." *Studies in Short Fiction* 14, No. 4 (Fall 1977): 359-67.

Examines stylistic aspects of the work by Aschenbach inspired by the youth Tadzio.

Egri, Peter. "The Function of Dreams and Visions in *A Portrait* and *Death in Venice*." *James Joyce Quarterly* 5, No. 2 (Winter 1968): 86-102.*

Comparative study examines the importance of dreams and visions in James Joyce's *A Portrait of the Artist as a Young Man* and Mann's *Death in Venice*.

Good, Graham. "The Death of Language in *Death in Venice*." *Mosaic* V, No. 3 (Spring 1972): 43-52.

Proposes that the novella can be read in terms of a crisis of language. Good discusses the conflict between the "pure" classical writing style and language of the character Aschenbach, and the "impure" sensual language characteristic of the inhabitants of Venice.

Kaufmann, Fritz. *Thomas Mann: The World As Will and Representation*. Boston: Beacon Press, 1957, 322 p.

Examines philosophical aspects of Mann's works, especially *Buddenbrooks, The Magic Mountain*, the *Joseph* novels, and *Doctor Faustus*.

Kirschberger, Lida. "*Death in Venice* and the Eighteenth Century." *Monatshefte* LVIII, No. 4 (Winter 1966): 321-34.

Posits that *Death in Venice* is inspired both by eighteenth-century thought and by the life and art of the German poet and dramatist Johann von Schiller.

Kronenberger, Louis. "Finely Wrought Fiction: *Death in Venice, and Other Stories*." *The Saturday Review of Literature* I, No. 48 (27 June 1925): 851.

Review of first English translation of *Death in Venice*.

Lehnert, Herbert. "Thomas Mann's Early Interest in Myth and Erwin Rohde's *Psyche*." *PMLA* LXXIL, No. 3 (June 1964): 297-304.*

Discusses the influence of Erwin Rohde's *Psyche* on Mann's use of myth in *Death in Venice*. For a further discussion of myth in *Death in Venice*, see the excerpts by André von Gronicka (1956) and James B. Hepworth (1963).

Leppmann, Wolfgang. "Time and Place in *Death in Venice*." *The German Quarterly* XLVIII, No. 1 (January 1975): 66-75.

Examines the "timelessness" and "classical" quality of *Death in Venice* through a discussion of Venice as it was in 1911, the year Mann began the novella.

Mann, Erika. *The Last Years of Thomas Mann: A Revealing Memoir by His Daughter, Erika Mann*. Translated by Richard Graves. New York: Farrar, Straus and Cudahy, 1958, 119 p.

Reminiscences.

Marson, E. L. *The Ascetic Artist: Prefigurations in Thomas Mann's "Der Tod in Venedig."* Berne, Switzerland: Peter Lang, 1979, 165 p.

Extensive, detailed study which centers "on the fact that Thomas Mann's *Der Tod in Venedig* uses in a quite crucial, prefigurative sense two models from classic Greek literature and thought—*The Bacchae* of Euripedes, and various Platonic dialogues" (in particular *The Phaedrus*).

McClain, William H. "Wagnerian Overtones in *Der Tod in Venedig*." *Modern Language Notes* 79, No. 5 (December 1964): 481-95.

Proposes that *Death in Venice* portrays the life and work of German composer Richard Wagner. In this interesting discussion, McClain maintains that Wagner's influence on Mann is most evidenced by the "deeper-lying similarities in form and content" between Mann's novella and Wagner's musical dramas.

Nicholls, R. A. *"Death in Venice."* In his *Nietzsche in the Early Work of Thomas Mann*, pp. 77-91. Berkeley and Los Angeles: University of California Press, 1955.

Overview of *Death in Venice* which focuses on the Nietzschean symbolism and psychological conflicts within the novella.

Seyppel, Joachim H. "Two Variations on a Theme: Dying in Venice (Thomas Mann and Ernest Hemingway)." *Literature and Psychology* VII, No. 1 (February 1957): 8-12.*

Comparative study that explores the "vision of beauty and death" in *Death in Venice* and Ernest Hemingway's *Across the River and into the Trees*.

Shuster, George N. "Art at War with the Good (Thomas Mann's *Death in Venice*)." In *Great Moral Dilemmas in Literature, Past and Present*, edited by R. M. MacIver, pp. 25-36. New York: Institute for Religious and Social Studies, 1956.

Discusses the tragedy of Gustave von Aschenbach's unfulfilled search for idealized beauty.

Slochower, Harry. "Thomas Mann's *Death in Venice*." *American Imago* 26, No. 2 (Summer 1969): 99-122.

Psychoanalytical interpretation of *Death in Venice*.

Stavenhagen, Lee. "The Name of Tadzio in *Der Tod in Venedig*." *The German Quarterly* XXXV, No. 1 (January 1962): 20-23.

Focuses on the allegorical and symbolic meanings of the name Tadzio.

Stewart, Walter K. "*Der Tod in Venedig:* The Path to Insight." *The Germanic Review* LIII, No. 2 (Spring 1978): 50-55.

Proposes that an understanding of the Platonic principle of beauty is basic to an understanding of the complexities of *Death in Venice*. Stewart's views are similar to those of T. J. Reed (see excerpt dated 1974) in that both critics' assessment of the novella rely on Mann's own interpretation of his work (see excerpt above, 1920).

Tarbox, Raymond. "*Death in Venice:* The Aesthetic Object as Dream Guide." *American Imago* 26, No. 2 (Summer 1969): 123-44.

Freudian analysis of *Death in Venice*.

Urdang, Constance. "Faust in Venice: The Artist and the Legend in *Death in Venice*." *Accent* XVIII, No. 4 (Autumn 1958): 253-67.

Contends that *Death in Venice* is a parody of the Faustian legend.

Vaget, Hans Rudolf. "Film and Literature: The Case of *Death in Venice:* Luchino Visconti and Thomas Mann. *German Quarterly* LIV, No. 2 (March 1980): 159-75.

Compares Luchino Visconti's 1971 film version of *Death in Venice* with the novella.

Mori Ōgai

1862-1922

(Born Mori Rintarō; also transliterated as Ohgai; although Mori is his family name, Mori Ōgai has traditionally been known by his pseudonymous given name, Ōgai) Japanese novelist, novella and short story writer, dramatist, biographer, autobiographer, translator, critic, essayist, and poet.

From Mori Ōgai and the Modernization of Japanese Culture, *by Richard John Bowring. Cambridge University Press, 1979. Reprinted by permission of Cambridge University Press.*

Ōgai is recognized as one of the most important authors of Japan's modern era, a period inaugurated in 1868 under the rule of the Emperor Meiji. During the Meiji Restoration (1868-1912), the Japanese abandoned the archaic structure of a society based on feudal governors in order to admit the social, political, and technological innovations of Western countries. Over a brief span of years, Japan adopted the modern practices of technologically advanced societies in everything from fashion to scientific discoveries. At the same time there was also an attempt to preserve certain traditions, especially those pertaining to religion and the family, which were integral to Japanese identity and which presumably posed no obstructions to modernization. Nevertheless, conflicts arose between the old and the new social order, instilling a sense of alienation in people who for the first time felt at odds with their own culture. Although Ōgai was in the vanguard of some of the most dramatic changes in Japanese life, both as an author and as a physician who introduced ideas and techniques of Western medicine, his writings reflect many of the ambiguities of this transitional period. In the words of J. Thomas Rimer, a leading critic and translator of Japanese literature: "Ōgai's reaction to these ambiguities have come to epitomize for later generations the spiritual realities of those times."

Ōgai was born in Tsuwano, a small village on the Sea of Japan, far from such major cultural centers as Kyoto or Tokyo. His father was a doctor, as were many of his ancestors, and Ōgai also chose to pursue a medical career. His early education consisted primarily of rote schooling in Chinese and Japanese classics of philosophy and literature. An exceptional student, Ōgai was selected to attend Tokyo University, where he studied German before entering medical school. After receiving his medical degree in 1881, Ōgai enlisted in the army medical service. In 1884 he was sent to Germany to study methods of military hygiene. He lived in German cities for several years, and his experiences there, in particular his romantic affair with a young German woman, became the substance of his first work of fiction, "Maihime" ("The Girl Who Danced"), as well as two subsequent stories, "Utakata no ki" and "Fumizukai" ("The Courier"). Upon his return to Japan in 1888, Ōgai contributed translations from the works of Johann Wolfgang von Goethe and Shakespeare to an influential anthology, *Omokage,* which provided Japan's first significant exposure to Western literature. In addition to his translations, Ōgai's most important work at this time was his literary criticism. In 1891 he entered into a literary debate with Tsubouchi Shōyō, whose *Shosetsu shinzui* (which can be translated as "The Essence of the Novel") was the first example of modern literary criticism in Japan. While Shōyō argued for a naturalistic literature based upon an author's worldly experience, Ōgai advocated a romantic form of writing founded on extra-mundane ideals of truth and beauty.

Ōgai's hostility to Naturalism in literature eventually inspired him to write *Vita Sexualis,* a parody of Naturalist fiction which leaves unfulfilled its promise of an autobiographical rendering of the author's sexual life. But although the novel was parodic in intent and purposely bland in subject matter, it was nevertheless banned by authorities during a period in which Naturalist literature was being suppressed. *Vita Sexualis* was published in 1909, and it was from that time until the end of his life that Ōgai produced his most significant creative works, including such dramas as *Shizuka,* the novel *Gan (The Wild Geese),* and historical writings consisting of both fiction and biography. At the same time that he carried on an influential career as a man of letters, including his editorship of two literary journals, Ōgai was also active in medicine and in the military. He served in the Sino-Japanese and Russo-Japanese wars, and he eventually became the Surgeon General of the army. Although he was strongly opposed by the military-medical establishment, Ōgai effected important medical reforms that promoted modern methods over traditional folk remedies. Ōgai also held various positions in the Japanese government, serving until a few years before his death from a kidney ailment at the age of sixty-one.

"Ōgai's literary sensibility," as critic David A. Dilworth explains, "evolved as a process of integration of his youthful absorption in Japanese classical literature and the popular romance-type literature of the late Tokugawa period (1603-1868), on the one hand, and his pioneer role in introducing the values of German Romanticism through translation, literary criticism, aesthetic theory, and his own creative writing, on the other.'' While Ōgai wrote significant works in a variety of genres, from fiction to dramas to philosophical essays, his work is generally discussed in terms of a few central concerns, primarily the relationship between individual needs and social responsibility, and the continuities as well as the changes in Japanese society during the Meiji Restoration. His earliest fiction—the short stories ''The Girl Who Danced,'' ''Utakata no ki,'' and ''The Courier''—detail the conflicts of the Japanese emigré who returns to his homeland and confronts the dichotomy between his sense of duty to his own country and his attraction to the stimulating new life found in European society. This conflict between tradition and change, either in the form of cultural friction between opposing societies or between radically dissimilar periods in Japanese history, is echoed in various ways throughout Ōgai's works. As Ōgai was anything but a superficial author, the resolution of this central theme in a given work may be highly ambiguous, especially since his strong admiration for Western life and literature coexisted with an appreciation for many of Japan's traditional literary and cultural values. In his discussion of Ōgai's dramas *Tama kushige futari Urashima, Kamen,* and *Ikutagawa,* Frank J. Motofuji contends that in these works Ōgai resolves this conflict through his philosophy of ''resignation.'' Ōgai's essay *Yo ga tachiba* (which can be translated as ''My Point of View'') explains this philosophy as one of emotional detachment from a world in which innovation is often mistakenly equated with improvement. While seemingly a simplistic program for social withdrawal, Ōgai's concept of resignation contains complexities that also suggest new ways of involvement with the world. In a more extensive analysis of Ōgai's literary and intellectual development, David A. Dilworth finds that resignation evolved into a firm idealism in Ōgai's historical writings, ''a kind of transcendent individualism as Ōgai searched for the proper vehicle to express his sense of the true and the beautiful.'' The earliest of these works were written after General Nogi committed ritual suicide following the death of the Emperor Meiji in 1912, thus honoring the samurai code of joining one's master in death. Ōgai wrote two stories based on this tradition of *junshi,* and he set these works in the Tokugawa period. Other works of fiction and biography set in pre-Meiji Japan followed, and critics recognize these last works of Ōgai's literary career as the culmination of his genius.

In his essay on the narrative technique of *Vita Sexualis,* Yoshiyuki Nakai mentions some of the most common criticisms of Ōgai's writing. Among these are Ōgai's tendency toward didacticism and his lack of emphasis on devices which would sustain the interest of readers not concerned with his philosophical premises. Quite often in Ōgai's work the particular ''story'' a reader is led to expect never materializes, displaced by a thoughtful and precise, but seemingly irrelevant, exposition of narrative details. *Vita Sexualis*—a story in which the narrator neglects to recount the ''sex life'' promised in the book's title—is an example of this practice. Critics find that Ōgai's intent often lies in imparting didactic observations on literature, society, and human nature, concerns better suited to nonfiction than to creative writing. Despite these apparent weaknesses, Ōgai's most attentive readers have discovered that his stories excel in a subtle narrative artistry that prompts moral and philosophical reflection rather than emotional and aesthetic diversion. For Ōgai, literature was only a single aspect of his diverse and complex life; and while he is recognized for his profound understanding of literary aesthetics—in his multiple capacities as translator, critic, and creative artist—his works attained their great success as an expression of and a vehicle for personal and social development during a difficult period in Japanese history. In Japanese literature Ōgai assumed much the same role that prominent modern authors of social and psychological crisis, including T. S. Eliot, Jean-Paul Sartre, and Albert Camus, performed in Western literature.

(See also *Contemporary Authors,* Vol. 110.)

PRINCIPAL WORKS

''Maihime'' (short story) 1890
 [''My Lady of the Dance,'' 1906; also published as ''The Girl Who Danced'' (''Maihime'') in *The Language of Love,* 1964; and ''Maihime (The Dancing Girl)'' in journal *Monumenta Nipponica,* 1975]
''Utakata no ki'' (short story) 1890
 [''Utakata no ki'' published in journal *Monumenta Nipponica,* 1971]
''Fumizukai'' (short story) 1891
 [''The Courier'' published in journal *Monumenta Nipponica,* 1971]
Tamakushige futari Urashima (drama) 1903
Nichiren Shōnin tsuji zeppō (drama) 1904
''Hannichi'' (short story) 1909
 [''Half a Day'' (''Hannichi'') published in journal *Monumenta Nipponica,* 1973]
Kamen (drama) 1909
Shizuka (drama) [first publication] 1909
Vita Sexualis (novel) 1909
 [*Vita Sexualis,* 1972]
''Asobi'' (short story) 1910
''Chinmoku no to'' (short story) 1910
''Fushinchū'' (short story) 1910
 [''Under Reconstruction'' published in *Modern Japanese Stories,* 1961]
''Hanako'' (short story) 1910
 [''Hanako'' published in *Paulownia: Seven Stories from Contemporary Japanese Writers,* 1918]
Ikutagawa (drama) 1910
Gan (novel) 1911
 [*The Wild Geese,* 1959]
Hyaku monogatari (novella) 1911
''Mōsō'' (short story) 1911
 [''Delusion'' published in journal *Monumenta Nipponica,* 1970]
''Abe ichizoku'' (short story) 1912
 [''The Abe Family'' published in *The Incident at Sakai, and Other Stories,* 1977]
''Ka no yō ni'' (short story) 1912
 [''As If'' published in *Tokyo People: Three Stories from the Japanese,* 1925]
''Okitsu Yagoemon no isho'' (short story) 1912
 [''The Last Testament of Okitsu Yagoemon'' published in *The Incident at Sakai, and Other Stories,* 1977]
''Gojiingahara no katakiuchi'' (short story) 1913
 [''The Vendetta at Gojiingahara'' published in *The Incident at Sakai, and Other Stories,* 1977]
''Sahashi Jingorō'' (short story) 1913
 [''Sahashi Jingorō'' published in *Saiki Kōi, and Other Stories,* 1977]
''Sakai jiken'' (short story) 1914
 [''The Incident at Sakai'' published in *The Incident at Sakai, and Other Stories,* 1977]

"Sanshō dayū" (short story) 1914
["Sansho Dayu" published in *Sansho Dayu, and Other Stories,* 1952; also published as "Sansho Dayu" in journal *Asian Scene,* 1956; and "Sanshō Dayū" in *The Incident at Sakai, and Other Stories,* 1977]
"Yasui Fujin" (short story) 1914
["The Wife of Yasui" published in *Saiki Kōi, and Other Stories,* 1977]
"Kanzan Jittoku" (short story) 1915
"Kanzan Jittoku" published in *The Incident at Sakai, and Other Stories,* 1977]
"Takasebune" (short story) 1915
["Takase-bune" published in *Paulownia: Seven Stories from Contemporary Japanese Writers,* 1918; also published as "The Takase-Boat" in *Sansho Dayu, and Other Stories,* 1952; and "The Takase Boat" in journal *Monumenta Nipponica,* 1971; and "The Boat on the River Takase" in *The Incident at Sakai, and Other Stories,* 1977]
Izawa Ranken (biography) 1916
Shibue Chūsai (biography) 1916
Hōjō Katei (biography) 1917
Mori Ōgai zenshu. 53 vols. (novels, novellas, short stories, dramas, biography, autobiography, translations, essays, criticism, poetry, and letters) 1951-56
Sansho Dayu, and Other Stories (short stories) 1952
The Incident at Sakai, and Other Stories (short stories) 1977
Saiki Kōi, and Other Stories (short stories) 1977

Translated selections of Ōgai's poetry have appeared in the following publications: *Masterpieces of Japanese Poetry, Ancient and Modern* and *The Current of the World.*

TADAO KUNITOMO (essay date 1938)

[*In the following excerpt from his critical survey* Japanese Literature Since 1868, *Kunitomo provides a general estimate of Ōgai's contribution to modern Japanese literature as a translator, fiction writer, dramatist, literary critic, and biographer.*]

It was Shôyô, Futabatei, and Ohgai who made serious efforts in translating works of pure literary merit. Shôyô went to Shakespeare, Futabatei took up the Russian writers, while Ohgai tried his part in original German literature. This was a striking contrast to most of the translations of political novels which were retranslated from English translations of the original. Ohgai's translation was rendered in a lucid classical style as he was an earnest student of Japanese classics and set the new standard for translated literature. This was a sharp contrast to the free use of the colloquial style by Shôyô and Futabatei who were more at home with the literature of the Tokugawa regime.

Ohgai's first works in creative writing and translating were published as ***Minawa-shû*** including three of his own and sixteen translated short stories. They were mostly done while he was in Germany studying medicine by order of the Army Department. Three short stories, ***Maihime, Utakatano-ki,*** and ***Fumizukai*** dealt with lyrical and romantic love affairs which the writer had seen or experienced in Germany. The style was unique and the plot well organized, which established the standard for new short story writing in Meiji literature. His translation of Anderson's *Improvisator,* entitled *Sokkyô-shijin* was another favorite of the young Japanese and its fresh romantic life and rhythm resulted in the perfect harmonization of classical beauty in Japanese mingled with the newly introduced European syntax.

Ohgai was a scientist and so his scholarly attitude did not allow him to be purely romantic. After he outgrew his sensitive youth, his reason got the better of him and during the naturalist period he came back with his high romantic idealism opposing vigorously the objective treatment of life by these naturalists. (pp. 71-2)

[At] the height of the naturalistic movement, Ohgai came out vigorously against it. ***Vita Sexualis*** was an exhaustive work which attacked the naturalists with their own weapon. Sex-instinct, which the naturalists regarded as the sole basis of human life, Ohgai treated merely as its part. This was a strong blow to naturalists for Ohgai was a medical man and knew the sex problem more precisely from its scientific angle. ***Sakazuki (The Wine-cups)*** and ***Asobi (The Play)*** were two short stories which emphasized the legitimacy of his aesthetic attitude in life and art.

Ohgai's contribution to the literature of Meiji and Taishô was manifold and voluminous. He always stood as a pioneer and leader of some new movements with his profound knowledge in art, literature and drama. We have already mentioned that he had set the example for the western type of short stories with ***Maihime, Utakata-no-ki,*** and ***Fumizukai.*** In translations he covered the fields of western poetry, and novel, and modern drama of Continental Europe; the last mentioned served as the ready repertoire for the *Shingeki* movement. It included immortal Goethe, John Gabriel Borkmann, and Henrik Ibsen. His interest in drama was not limited to the modern type only, but it led him into the field of old Kabuki plays. When his younger brother, Miki Takeji, an authority in the Kabuki edited the monthly "Kabuki," he served as a regular contributor, injecting new spirit into a field otherwise inclined to be stale and conventional.

He was also co-founders of the first systematic literary criticism in the history of Meiji literature, for it was through his challenge to Shôyô that literary criticism commenced to occupy a legitimate position in the early twenties of Meiji. Ohgai based his literary theory on [Karl von] Hartmann's aesthetics, the introduction of which was enlightening as it was sensational. (pp. 132-33)

[Ohgai also wrote] authentic biographies of great men whose names had been somehow neglected. In this attempt, too, he marked a new angle of perspective, and many writers of the neo-realism of the middle Taishô period followed his attitude and technique.

Vita Sexualis . . . Meiji 42, 1909.

Ohgai's motive of writing this type of novel was definitely explained in its introductory part. In the year Meiji 42, 1909, naturalism reached its zenith and every ambitious writer was zealously following the path in search of truth. Ohgai saw the situation with the characteristic calm of a scientist. To prove and teach the people that sex-instinct, strong though it is, is only a part of composite human life, he introduced a philosopher, Kanai by name, and let him record his own sex experience with the accuracy of a true scholar. It was rather an amusing irony that the government could not see Ohgai's true motive and put a ban on the book as it was feared that the book might invoke immoral desires in the readers' minds. (pp. 133-34)

Besides the accurate record of Kanai's sex experience, his psychological reaction and fine shades of emotional feeling were so exquisitely pictured in accordance with the gradual stages of his physical growth that the whole story had a fine artistic finish. Its value as Ohgai's autobiography, and as the record of customs in the early Meiji, added greatly to its literary merit.

Asobi . . . Meiji 43, 1910.

In a journal of only half a day's activity, the entire life philosophy of Kimura, who was a petty government official, was significantly described. Although his official status was so trivial that his presence in office was hardly noticed even by his colleagues, his name as an author was widely known among the literary circles. He had the idea that life was one continuous play. And the play, according to him, had two divisions, and people belonged to either of them as long as they lived. One was that which gave pleasure to the players, and the other gave no pleasure but was none the less important to players. His official duties, according to his interpretation, was the second type of play, so he discharged them without any complaint. His writing, which he undertook by faint lamplight far into the night, was the play of pleasure. To him both were the same play. Thus, he kept on playing both without any sense of contradiction. However, this attitude caused bitter criticism among critics of the day. They blamed him for being inconsistent and insincere. But Kimura disregarded such attacks and kept on playing, which was life.

In this story, Ohgai defended his philosophy of life against the supreme reign of naturalism. What critics and even Kimura's close friends criticized was exactly what critics blamed Ohgai for his dual activities in the army and literature. To the naturalists, whose eyes could not see anything but the fact and truth in life through their limited perspective, Ohgai's point of view was intolerable as it was impossible. Ohgai, however, stood adamant in his theory and attacked blind naturalists ruthlessly. This he declared even more precisely through the eighth girl of ***Sakazuki (The Wine-cups)***. She said, *"Mon verre n'est grand, mais je bois dan mon verre"* ["My cup is not big, but I still drink from my own cup"], when all others insisted that she should change her cup to the same size with the rest of the girls. (pp. 135-36)

Tadao Kunitomo, "Literature of Meiji Era (1868-1912): Literature of Idealism and Romanticism" and "Reaction to Naturalism," in his Japanese Literature Since 1868, *The Hokuseido Press, 1938, pp. 67-75, 112-36.**

FRANK T. MOTOFUJI (essay date 1967)

[*In the following excerpt, Motofuji discusses the effects of modernization during the Meiji Restoration and describes how the tension between Western innovations and Japanese traditions is reflected in three of Ōgai's dramas. The critic explains that Ōgai's solution to the conflict between Japanese and Western culture took the form of his philosophy of "resignation," which for Ōgai "was synonymous with non-involvement; he was a bystander who refused to take action." In Motofuji's view, Ōgai's withdrawal was a reaction to zealous and sometimes needless Westernizing reforms in Japanese society.*]

Every major writer in Japan since 1868 has written with one overwhelming fact impinging upon his consciousness: the shattering impact of the West upon traditional values and the concomitant necessity for making an adjustment to this situation. (Even when the works of certain writers like Higuchi Ichiyō, Tanizaki Jun'ichirō, and Kawabata Yasunari reflect little or nothing of this dislocation, there is implied in their activity within areas free of this confrontation, the choice of rejecting, for whatever reason, the alien part of the new hybrid culture.) For Japan, only the defeat in World War II was more traumatic than the reopening of the country after its withdrawal into isolation in 1639 with only a minimal contact with the rest of the world. When the importunities of the Western powers could no longer be put off and the Tokugawa shogunate entered into unilateral treaties with foreign nations, its opponents, rallying around the emperor, quickly established a battle line that brought down the house that had been the political ruler for 265 years. The rallying cry of the anti-shogunate forces had been "Revere the emperor and expel the barbarians," but it was ironically under the new emperor Meiji (r. 1868-1912) that Japan turned to the West for assistance in modernization when the new leaders realized with a sense of urgency the need for overcoming the backwardness of their nation. Convulsive political, economic, and social reforms delivered Japan painfully into the modern world.

Scores of Japanese fanned out on official missions into the advanced countries of the West to study, observe, absorb, and, later, to transmit information that was useful to Japan. In 1884, Mori Ōgai . . . , who was to become one of the leading literary figures of the new Japan, went to Germany as an army officer assigned the task of studying medicine and sanitation in the German army. Two days after his arrival in Berlin, Ōgai recorded in his diary that he called on the Japanese minister to Germany who, on learning what the young man had been sent abroad to study, said, "It is fine to study sanitation, but I feel that you will probably find it difficult to put into practice in Japan right now what you will learn here. What use will theories on sanitation be to a people who walk around gripping the thongs of their clogs between their toes? Learning does not mean only reading books. What are the ideas of the Europeans? How do they live? What are their rules of conduct in society? If these are the only points that you study carefully, you will have discharged your obligations fully." The juxtaposition of theories and thongs is an earthy and vivid commentary on the Japanese view of Japan's position in relation to the West; but there was also the point, which could not have been lost on Ōgai, that not all Western knowledge was going to be immediately applicable in Japan, and that mere form superimposed for its own sake was of little use.

In his diary Ōgai faithfully recorded the activities that took him from the laboratory to the salon and to the coffee houses. The picture the entries provide is that of a sensitive and impressionable young man revelling in the pursuit of scientific knowledge and new experiences in an exotic milieu, undergoing, in the process, a kind of spiritual liberation. This is not to say, however, that he was blindly adulatory of the West. In an extraordinarily lengthy and heated entry for March 6, 1886, he showed himself to be clearly on the defensive about Japan, especially about Japan's progress in westernization. He had attended a meeting of a scientific society at which the speaker, a German who had been invited by the Japanese government to conduct geological surveys and to teach at Tokyo University, made the statement, which Ōgai found disquieting, that Japan's modernization had not been embarked on of her own accord but was a course that had been imposed by external forces. What had upset Ōgai most of all was the fact that the audience seemed to be in complete agreement with the speaker that the changes in Japan were at best only superficial. Later, at dinner, the speaker once again nettled Ōgai with a remark on Buddhism that the latter took as an aspersion. The speaker said that he could show no interest in a religion which excluded women from paradise on the grounds that they had no intelligence. Ōgai, who had been deeply chagrined at not having been able to make a rebuttal during the formal speech now seized the opportunity to set matters right. He rose and said, "In the sutras there are numerous examples of women having attained buddhahood. . . . Women also have been able to become enlightened beings. How could they be said to lack intelligence? Ladies, my only desire is to clear Buddhism of this unjust charge and to offer proof that my respect for women is no less than that of Christians."

Ōgai's attitude in this exchange, at the end of which he quotes with some satisfaction the statement of a German friend that Ōgai had vindicated the position of Japan, is revealing. He was anxious to make it clear to the assembly that Japan had indeed made remarkable progress—much more so than the speech had indicated. But what convincing argument could Ōgai have offered to refute the assertion that external coercion had been a factor in Japan's attempts to modernize? A traditionalist would have accepted the statement and deplored the effects of the forcible reopening of the country. A traditionalist would also have acknowledged the fact that Buddhism has always held that women *are* inferior, and he certainly would not have played the gallant. Only a Western-oriented Japanese anxious to claim for his country a position of equality with Europeans, but whose education and position precluded an open break with tradition would have taken Ōgai's stand. In his Janus-like attempt to face both ways, Ōgai was a microcosm of Japan in this dilemma. A Japanese critic has written as follows about Ōgai: "In their confrontation with the changes that were brought about, whether from within or without, [in the Meiji era,] men have attempted to resist them or to surrender to them; but the majority attempted to make a compromise between the two. It is my opinion that this wholly Japanese solution was reflected in and focused on, in an almost perfect way even into the Shōwa period, in the person of Ōgai, who was born before the Meiji and died in the Taishō."

Ōgai was the nearest thing to a universal man in Japan. He was trained as a physician and rose to the post of Surgeon General of the Army. At the same time he was active in letters as translator of Western poetry and drama, editor of literary magazines, and writer of poetry, criticism, fiction, and plays. He was made Doctor of Literature in 1909.

Many of Ōgai's works deal with his attempts to resolve the conflict of identity within himself. In the end, he arrived at a solution that was to become characteristic—a state of mind he called "resignation." For Ōgai, "resignation" was synonymous with non-involvement; he was a bystander who refused to take action. This characteristic is clearly seen in three of his most important plays—***The Jeweled Casket and the Two Urashima* [*Tama kushige futari Urashima*]** . . . ; ***The Mask* [*Kamen*]** . . . , which is the only one among Ōgai's seven plays with a modern setting; and ***The Ikuta River* [*Ikutagawa*]**. . . . The Urashima play is based on the legend of the fisherman who sojourns in a palace under the sea and, when he returns to land, discovers that generations have passed in what had seemed to him to be only a brief period of time. On his departure from the sea palace, he was given a jeweled casket with the admonition that he must on no account open it if he wishes to return. But Urashima opens it and in a twinkling he turns into an old man and dies.

The play is written in poetic meter, each line being two units of seven and five syllables (more or less). It is in two acts, the first of which takes place in the palace under the sea. The play opens with Urashima awakening from a troubled dream. The princess asks why he is so agitated. . . . He had dreamt that he was once more fishing in calm waters when suddenly a storm broke over him. As he struggled to control his boat, he awoke. He interprets the dream as a sign that he must return to land. The princess asks him if he doesn't appreciate his idyllic existence. . . . Despite the princess' pleas and the doleful descriptions by her attendants of the cruelties that the creatures on land are capable of inflicting, Urashima sets out for land. . . . What is the significance of this marine Eden? Had there been something like it in Ōgai's life? Evidence points to the four years spent in Germany as having been something pretty close to it. He was twenty-two when he went abroad. The years of freedom and discovery were idyllic ones with the joy edged with a sharp sense of poignancy: he knew that he eventually had to return to Japan. (pp. 412-17)

The second act of ***Urashima*** takes place on the beach of Urashima's village where preparations are being made by a young chieftain to lead a fleet of ships to sea. . . . Urashima, who is a stranger in the village, is brought before the leader. . . . Being a stranger Urashima is not trusted. The leader challenged him and grapples with him. He seizes the casket from Urashima and opens it. A white cloud drifts out from it and a quantity of pearls spills out onto the sand. In an instant Urashima ages into a white-haired ancient. The leader then identifies himself as a descendant of Urashima who had rowed out to sea three centuries ago and was never seen again. The tercentenarian declares that he is that very ancestor and demands to know the purpose behind the warlike preparations. . . . The old Urashima then offers his descendant the pearls with which to fill the coffers of the expedition. . . . Urashima does not himself carry out the undertaking he had dreamed of. Grown old, he sees it being consummated by his descendant. The riches in pearls which came from the princess Ōgai means to symbolize the knowledge he had gained from the West. (pp. 417-20)

Ōgai had come to the realization that he was not going to be able to achieve his goals after all. . . . Ōgai's Western training had taught him to value spirit over form. When city planners concerned themselves with the layout of roads and types of buildings, Ōgai stressed the importance of the problems of water supply and sewage. When the movement to abolish rice from the diet and to substitute meat was started, Ōgai wrote that he saw no merit in the movement as rice and fish were extremely digestible. When orthographic changes were introduced, Ōgai opposed them because they would have obliterated historical developments in the language. . . . [In his short story ***Fantasies***] Ōgai has the narrator express a balanced, detached view which would not accept without question the gifts of the West, or question traditional values simply because they were traditional.

In ***The Mask,*** which was written in 1909, seven years after ***Urashima,*** Ōgai has disengaged the two main characters, a physician and a young patient, from the struggle. In ***Urashima*** there had been optimism as the younger man embarked on his journey. (Since the venture is martial in nature, Ōgai may have been suggesting a struggle with a foreign power which, in 1902, meant Russia. To Japan Russia was a Western power, and between 1904-1905 the two nations were to engage in a war.

Or the young chieftain's undertaking could have the larger symbolic meaning of Japan's sending to the West the fruits of her own discoveries after decades of borrowing and adopting from the West.) In ***The Mask,*** however, there is no optimism. There is no pessimism, either—only a chilling retreat into isolation behind a figurative mask. (pp. 420-22)

The problem of identity is more complex in this play. The protagonist is a Western-trained physician who lives by a Western philosopher's dictum of maintaining a detached and superior attitude from the masses who were rushing pellmell, with blinders on, along the course of westernization that had been decreed as official policy from above. Sugimura holds himself aloof from this trend and influences Shiori to do likewise. But there is a deeper significance in this exchange. By advising the young man not to act in accordance with a truth that has been arrived at by scientific methods, Sugimura symbolically disassociates himself from the West. But does this mean that he has tipped the scales in favor of traditional values? He expresses open admiration for the demeanor of the gardener's wife. (She is dressed and coiffed in the traditional way. In contrast, Mrs. Kanai, the modern, emancipated woman, is dressed in a modish style which combines the traditional and the new: with her kimono and Japanese coat, she wears a fur neckpiece and a muff. She has a taste for Western music. For all her outward modern trappings, however, she is fundamentally traditional in outlook: the fear of displeasing her mother-in-law looms large in her consciousness.) The gardener (what could be more traditional than a Japanese garden?) is made to die stoically. The very language used by the gardener and his assistant is the vulgar colloquial of the lower classes, not the polite speech of the upper classes that Sugimura, Shiori, and Mrs. Kanai use. But there is no complete identification with people like the gardener's wife who are not part of the common herd.

What does the disease symbolize if not the aberration resulting from the effort to reconcile two ways of life? The physician has effected a cure in an attitude (or mask) or non-commitment, but the young man, being in the midst of his studies, is in the throes of this struggle and accepts the solution offered by the older man. Although the solution is couched in Nietzschean philosophy, the disengagement from society has resulted basically from a sense of resignation—the key word in Ōgai's work.

In 1910, Ōgai wrote his most important play, ***The Ikuta River.*** As was the case with ***Urashima,*** the plot was taken from traditional sources. There are, in some of the earliest extant Japanese literary works, the legend of a young girl who is courted by two suitors but who, being unable to choose between them, commits suicide. (pp. 424-25)

In this play, the girl who is pressed to make a choice between two men, one a native of her province and the other an alien, is obviously Ōgai himself caught in the pull between tradition and the West. The girl insists that it is beyond her power to choose and would let matters take their course, just as the snowgoose, with whom she feels that her destiny is linked, sits motionlessly on the flowing stream. The snowgoose symbolizes resolution, hope, salvation, and, in fact, a return to life. But it is destroyed by two arrows. The girl decides to go and take a look, but there is no prospect or basis for making a choice, and Ōgai does not provide an answer. The play ends without a resolution and creates a poetic and somber aftereffect. Once again, Ōgai kept the delicate balance necessary in the attitude of resignation where no choice is necessary.

When Ōgai wrote, certain assumptions in native traditions (such as the matter of legend as history) could not be examined closely. That would have come under "dangerous thought." With his Western training, this problem inevitably assumed great importance to Ōgai, but he was well aware of the result of this scrutiny being carried out to a logical conclusion. In modern Japan many of the barriers to scientific inquiry that existed during Ōgai's time (and indeed existed until August 15, 1945) have been removed. The problem of integrity and compromise that was so prevalent is now happily a thing of the past. But in the matter of westernization, which is taking place at a pace more brisk than in Ōgai's time, would he say that the Japanese now adopt substance and not form? Would he say that Japan was returning as much as she borrowed? Ōgai would answer, "Not yet." (pp. 429-30)

Frank T. Motofuji, "Mori Ōgai: Three Plays and the Problem of Identity," in Modern Drama, *Vol. 9, No. 4, February, 1967, pp. 412-30.*

MASAO MIYOSHI (essay date 1974)

[*Miyoshi is a Japanese-born American critic and the author of* Accomplices of Silence: The Modern Japanese Novel. *In the following excerpt from that work, Miyoshi examines Ōgai's first fiction work* "The Dancing Girl," *written just after his return from Germany, and the later novel* The Wild Geese, *which ends with the protagonist's departure for Germany. Observing that "modern Japan exhibits its contradictions most clearly to its returning émigrés," the critic finds that these two works illustrate the dependence of the Japanese on Western literary models (specifically the modern European novel) as well as Western models of social organization, both of which were imperfectly assimilated during Ōgai's lifetime.*]

Mori Ōgai published his first fiction in 1890. To think of **"The Dancing Girl"** ***(Maihime)*** as anything but juvenilia is hard for most of us now, but Meiji readers found it otherwise: with the exception of a very few critics, it was a perfect modern masterpiece for them.

The language of **"The Dancing Girl"** is in a decorous elegant style (*gabun-tai*), although contemporary readers took it as a "mixed style of Japanese, Chinese, and Western" (*wa-kan-yō-setchū-tai*), feeling that the scattering of German words and names through the story was the most important stylistic feature. The elegant style of **"The Dancing Girl"** reads well even today, being neither too difficult to understand nor too familiar as the colloquial style might be. The nostalgia created by the old-fashioned language matches the exotic setting and experience described by the story, which was at least part of the reason for its instant acclaim. But at this particular juncture what mainly interests us is the hero's experience, which provides one of the earliest examples of an attitude toward the West that has since grown into something like a version of pastoral in modern Japanese fiction.

The story runs like this. A young career government worker, assigned to a few years' study in Germany, meets a struggling young ballerina in Berlin and saves her from a threatened seduction. He falls in love with her, and they live together, but this highly irregular behavior invites his superior's censure, and he is dismissed from his position. Down and out in a strange land, he struggles to survive on a few free-lance writing assignments for Tokyo newspapers. Then an old friend of his who happens to be in Berlin as secretary to a visiting official offers to help him on condition that he give up the girl and return to Japan. He accepts the offer. The girl, now pregnant, discovers his plan and suffers a breakdown. He goes home anyway, but on his return voyage he writes of his feelings of guilt and regret, and this first-person record constitutes the story.

In the earlier part, the young man thinks about the meaning of all the hard work that has put him through the highly competitive university system. . . . What he used to believe was great moral dedication to learning is no more than selfish and bureaucratic careerism.

At this point in his critique of self and society he meets his German dancer, with her "pale golden hair," "pure blue inquisitive eyes bedewed with tears," "long eyelashes," and, of course, "white skin." . . . But there is still something else involved. Although the German girl no doubt differs in appearance, in practically every other aspect she is conceived by Ōgai in the familiar terms of a Japanese girl. (pp. 38-40)

There is nothing extraordinary about a writer's projecting his own ideal upon the people his hero encounters in a foreign setting. . . . But there are some specific features that should be mentioned in the case of the Japanese traveler-writer. And here we might look directly at the significance of foreign travel for the Meiji era Japanese.

Going abroad, or *yōkō,* was, at least until very recently, a glamorous affair in which the excitement of the event itself was combined with the promise of an élite career to follow. (p. 40)

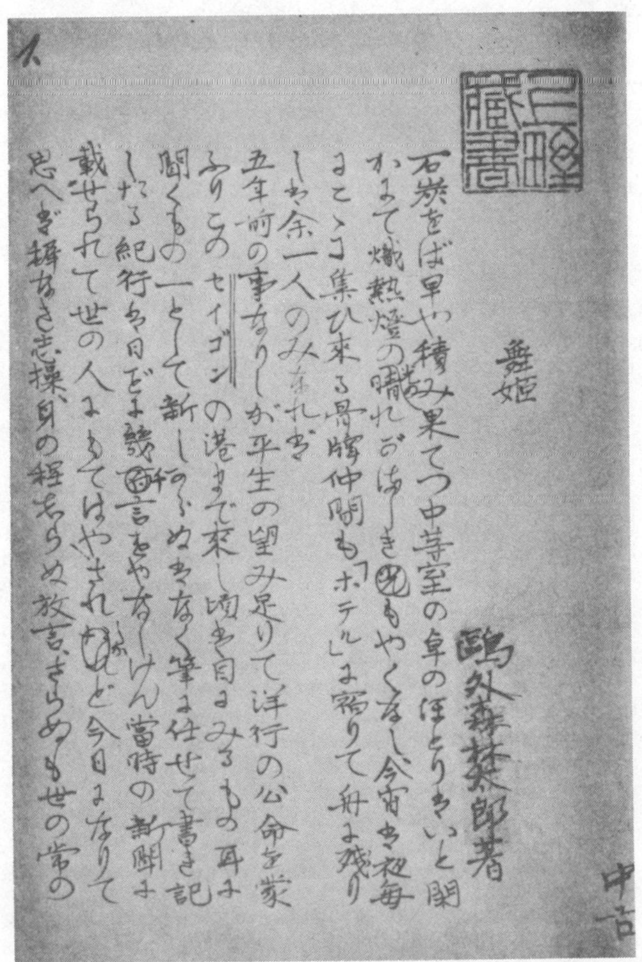
1

舞姫

鷗外森林太郎著

石炭をば早や積み果てつ中等室の卓のほとりはいと閑
かにて熾熱燈の晴れがましきもやくなし今宵は夜毎
にこゝに集ひ来る骨牌仲間も「ホテル」に宿りて舟に残り
しは余一人のみなれば
五年前の事なりしが平生の望み足りて洋行の公命を蒙
りこのセイゴンの港まで来し頃は目に見るもの耳に
聞くもの一として新しからぬもなく筆に任せて書き記
しつる紀行文日ごとに幾千言をかなしけん当時の新聞に
載せられて世の人にもてはやされしかど今日になりて
思へば稚き思想身の程知らぬ放言さらぬも世の常の

中古

Holograph copy of the first page of Ōgai's story "Maihime."

Then, there are of course the differences between [a young man's] former Japanese life and that in which he now finds himself. Undoubtedly, comparison of cultures is a hazardous business, and the supposed vast differences between the East and West may or may not be bridgeable, or may indeed not even exist. But we are more concerned here with the felt contrast, not any absolute or objective difference, and the Japanese traveler is likely to see the West as the diametric opposite of the East, just as the antonyms imply. By him, the unfamiliar paradigms of Western life—respect for the assertion of individuality, the analytic habit of thought, the general tenets of democratic government—are felt to be the opposite of his native ones. (p. 41)

The re-entry shock upon coming home can cause long-term adjustment problems. . . . The West has been inescapably internalized for these men in a way that can deprive their resumed life of the simplest pleasures.

To generalize boldly, modern Japan exhibits its contradictions most clearly to its returning émigrés: the country can no longer sustain the feudal fabric of community, but its corporate institutions insist on the bureaucratic loyalty of their vassals. The vertical relationship of parents and children is weakening rapidly, but more democratic family forms are yet to come. While the Empire expects its "subjects" to give homage to the Emperor, the wider world in various ways undermines nationalism as a source of intellectual and emotional satisfaction. Paternalism persists throughout society, cheek by jowl with rising "democratic" expectations. In short, while the old Japan is fast being secularized, the new myths tend to be stillborn.

"The Dancing Girl" is a convenient early index to this new East-West encounter which involves the fact and metaphor of traveling. . . . Ōgai is inescapably bonded to the vision he shares with the rest of his society. There is nothing "personal" about his Japanizing of the German dancer; it is as though the character—and the author—had not known the independence of the self at all. . . . Thus the hero's blaming his friend at the end of the story is an absurd self-deception. **"The Dancing Girl,"** once hailed as Japan's earliest "romantic" tale, unromantically insists throughout on maintaining safe ties to the work-oriented Japanese society, and thus stops far short of a serious examination of the choice between both work and freedom and social bondage and personal fulfillment.

Ōgai wrote two more elegant-style stories, which, with **"The Dancing Girl,"** form a European trilogy. Both highly successful at the time, they are very much the sort that had great vogue all over Europe in the early nineteenth century. Ōgai, it appears, made use of the exotic "gothic" setting, with its aristocrats and castles and mysterious deaths, to lure the Japanese reader to a land of enchantment far away. (pp. 41-3)

Ōgai is no longer able—either in fiction or outside it—to talk about the problems of modern Japan without directly putting them in a Western frame of reference. Somehow an adequate explanation of one's experience requires a context provided by the West; or, more drastically, Japanese experience is somehow incomplete in itself. In order to become satisfying and significant, it asks for placement in a Western context where it can be viewed from a Western perspective. (p. 45)

The importation of themes from the West is, then, a provisional solution to the identity crisis in Japanese literature. Futabatei's borrowing from Russian and Ōgai's from German are only two cases out of a whole cultural process which for lack of a better term must be called the "Westernization" of both art and life. . . . Along with the methods and the products of Western industry and engineering, many post-Meiji Japanese were eager to import not just the West's literature and literary themes, but a new life-substance itself. And if all this looks like an insignificant ripple on the surface of one's being, we must see that in a man's life no surface change leaves the depths untroubled.

Ōgai's European studies continued, as can be seen in his translations from his characteristically wide range of authors—from Rousseau, Goethe, Lermontov, Hoffmann, Andersen, Turgenev, Daudet, Flaubert, D'Annunzio, Tolstoi, Gorky, Ibsen, Andreyev, Strindberg, and Schnitzler to Shaw, Maeterlinck, and Rilke. During this time, he was also deeply absorbed in rediscovering the roots of his native culture. When, for instance, General Nogi, national hero and Ōgai's personal friend, followed the Emperor Meiji in death by taking his own life in 1912, in accordance with samurai tradition, Ōgai's grief expressed itself in a series of semi-historical fictions treating the samurai code of *junshi* (joining the departed lord by suicide). His return to the past becomes even more dominant in the barely fictional and nonfictional historical studies written after ***The Wild Goose*** up until his death in 1922. And yet, it is as a reaction to the imported West, even as part of the Westernization program itself, that such a resurgence of Japanese themes ought to be considered. . . . (pp. 46-7)

The Wild Goose (Gan . . .) was written precisely at the point in his work where Ōgai turned from Western to Japanese themes. Its subject matter is no longer the East-West encounter, and instead of civil servant and aristocratic repatriates its main characters are a coarse-grained moneylender [Suezō] and his naïve mistress [Otama]. There is a handsome young medical student [Okada], but he is not particularly well versed in the lore of the West, and only at the end does he decide to go to Germany, thus joining the host of Ōgai émigrés. The novel then largely focuses on a style of petty-bourgeois life everywhere observable in Tokyo. . . . For once, Ōgai seems to be writing fiction, as he digs out the life of ordinary Japanese in Japan. But is he really weaned from the West? (p. 47)

The narrative structure of ***The Wild Goose*** is a bit awkward, a frequent problem with Japanese novels. The narrator, Okada's friend, begins by reminiscing on past events, but soon disappears from the tale, almost making it a third-person story. He returns in chapter 18 when it becomes increasingly clumsy to present events which the narrator cannot have been in a position to know. His explanation of his knowledge is offered at the end—"I learned half the story during my close association with Okada [and] I learned the other half from Otama, with whom I accidentally became acquainted after Okada had left the country" . . .—and is unpersuasive. (pp. 48-9)

What might usually flaw a novel, however, is not altogether a weakness in this case. In the opening, the narrator's "I" is very prominent ("That date comes back to me so precisely because at the time I lodged in the Kamijọ . . . and because my room was right next to that of the hero"). This implies that his relationship with Okada is more than just thematic. The "I" meets Okada as a self meets the other and becomes an observer of the other. Interestingly, the hero is himself a passive observer rather than an actor. Thus, as the voice shifts, confusing the hero's with the narrator's, the effect is to distance the events from the reader altogether. (p. 49)

The work explores several possible man-woman relationships in Tokyo life. To begin with Suezō, such an ambitious and energetic man cannot possibly be satisfied with an ugly woman like his wife, Otsune. . . . As his store of wealth increases, his vitality seeks fresher outlets, although not to the extent of breaking up his marriage. With Otama, however, his sexuality does not seem as fully engaged as it ought to be under the circumstances. When he buys linnets for her, feeling "How charming [it is] to see her with them" . . . , he is utterly unironic. He really is in love with his bird-girl in a cage. (p. 50)

The narrator-author is plainly sympathetic toward Otama's growth from a gullible child "bride," to a beautiful young girl willing to sell herself for her father's comfort, and thence to a woman aware of her own need for happiness. This process of maturation is marked by several image notations along the way. . . . She must find the right man.

Her restlessness shows itself, just after she moves into her new house, when she discovers Suezō's true status. A seemingly unrelated incident occurs when a self-announced ex-convict invites himself into the house and forces money from Otama at *knife point*. Thus the intrusion of male sexuality into Otama's consciousness commences, and it is about this time that she begins to notice Okada. When the linnets are attacked, it is Okada who runs to the rescue, cutting the snake's head off—castrating himself, and Suezō, too, at the same time. Thus this St. George, though reputedly a fine athlete and a connoisseur of Chinese erotic literature, is neither a very virile lover, nor any substantial succor to anyone, linnet or girl.

Ōgai's almost too explicit handling of symbols culminates in Okada's killing of the wild goose. Otama's possibility of freedom is annihilated by this one, partly unintentional, act. Okada, the linnet's defender, has become the slayer of a goose, undergoing this change just as his involvement with Otama becomes a possibility. Clearly, she is left here with little but the prospect of frustration.

Accident plays too conspicuous a role toward the end. By accident, Okada is not available for Otama's carefully arranged meeting; by accident, he hits the bird; and by unhappy coincidence, he is to leave for Germany next day. And yet, there is something much more stunning about the story in the way it—not Okada—kills off this "jewel of a girl" (a literal translation of her name). Despite the sympathetic treatment of her growth, the book thoroughly extinguishes any hope she may have for the future when it quenches the possibility of Okada's becoming her lover. It is the same with all the other failed relationships—Suezō and his wife, Otama and her policeman "husband," Suezō and Otama, even Otama and her father—and by the end it is as though her story itself had been stoned to death like the wild goose. Of course, there are the two survivors, Okada and the narrator. But they, too, seem headed toward a dead end. . . . And so, with both appearing all too ready to join the other Ōgai émigrés, we see that the Japanese setting has not after all engaged Ōgai as fully as he might have wished. There is no hope at present for personal happiness in Japan.

But not having a happy life to live is not the same as having no life to write about. In the very culture that Matthew Arnold called "not interesting," Hawthorne and Melville were writing their great novels. And Otama's life, despite its desolate outlook, does provide Ōgai with a subject matter to hang a story on. Yet even here one recalls—as Ōgai's contemporaries must have—that ***The Wild Goose*** was to some extent inspired by *The*

Wild Duck (1884), by Henrik Ibsen, whom Ōgai had been translating off and on since 1903. . . . [Despite] all the real differences between the two, the killing of the wild goose at the end of Ōgai's work cannot be considered without reference to the killing of the wild duck, which in fact turns into the murder of the innocent girl Hedvig. The landscape of Shinobazu Pond may have little in common with the Scandinavian parlor scenes of Ibsen's play, but the climactic emphases given the episodes in both works are remarkably similar in their effect.

A large inference is tempting here. Ōgai requires for his fiction a mode of experience that belongs to a foreign context of life. When he treats ordinary Japanese life, his creativity is not engaged: he either adheres too closely to actual life (as in his émigré cycle or his historical studies), or loses control and turns preposterous (as in the hero's relationship with an older woman in ***The Youth***). In ***The Wild Goose*** the Suezō-wife-Otama relationship is stalemated, and Ōgai clearly had difficulty resolving it. . . . In short, his worry over the ending of ***The Wild Goose*** did not abate until he developed the notion of the bird-killing and the exile of the hero.

The hero's departure for Germany is not just another plot detail. Only by taking him out of Japan and Japanese experience could Ōgai bring the story to its conclusion. . . . Like the church bell in Victorian fiction, "going abroad" says something final and inevitable in the Meiji novel.

Ōgai was not alone with his problem. It may be that Japanese life was not yet amenable to the form of the novel as it is understood in Western literature. Possibly, the novel could not readily be born there at that time, as it could not in, say, seventeenth-century England. The novel needs a particular kind of life—a certain expectation or assumption—which Japanese culture, even today, does not easily make available. This necessary life withheld to greater or less degree, the modern Japanese writer seems to have two choices. He can fall back on his own personal life, which, having been lived, is factual and hence presumably plausible. The consequence of this choice is the tradition of the *shishōsetsu* (beginning around the time of ***The Wild Goose***) which uses details of the writer's daily life, often at the expense of the work's form or even of his life's form. . . . Or he can invent, even fabricate if he will, a life outside the context of ordinary Japanese experience. Characters can be free and events extraordinary in any situation beyond everyday experience. Ōgai sends his characters abroad so that they may behave like the sojourners and outsiders they are for the moment. . . . Either way, abroad or at home, the introduction of Western life offers a solution for the problems that have arisen in the Japanese novel, itself an imported form. And it will continue to do so, until the imported life itself has truly taken root in Japan, making ordinary life a suitable substance for the novel. (pp. 50-4)

Masao Miyoshi, "The Imported Life," in his Accomplices of Silence: The Modern Japanese Novel, *University of California Press, 1974, pp. 38-54.*

J. THOMAS RIMER (essay date 1977)

[*Rimer is a critic and translator of Japanese literature and the author of* Modern Japanese Fiction and Its Traditions: An Introduction, *as well as a study of Ōgai's life and major works. In the following excerpt from his introduction to* The Incident at Sakai, and Other Stories, *Rimer offers a general estimate of the importance of Ōgai's writings, focusing on the later historical works.*]

Despite a lasting reputation in Japan, Mori Ōgai has yet to achieve any satisfactory reception in the West. Natsume Sōseki, the only writer of Ōgai's generation to share his stature, has been widely translated and admired, but Ōgai remains a shadowy figure, austere, even obscure. It often happens, of course, that the work of certain writers cannot be sufficiently understood outside their own cultures. (p. 1)

Nevertheless, there is much in Ōgai that might well appeal to a Western reader. The nature of his mental world, unlike that of a number of his contemporaries, was overwhelmingly cosmopolitan; indeed, he spent a great deal of time throughout his career translating into Japanese such diverse writers as Goethe (Ōgai's version of *Faust* is still the standard), Ibsen, Strindberg, and Hofmannsthal. In a very real sense the stories presented in [***The Incident at Sakai, and Other Stories***] can be considered "translations" by Ōgai of historical Japanese and Chinese materials into contemporary terms. Our difficulties in approaching his art may lie elsewhere.

They may originate, for example, in the relatively narrow boundaries set down around the word "literature" in the Anglo-American tradition. . . . [Ōgai's] early training in the Confucian classics, reinforced by his later studies of German literature and culture, gave him a strong sense of the high importance of literature and of the possibility—indeed the necessity—of its use as a means to convey philosophical ideas. Ōgai's work contains little that is "popular." His seriousness of purpose provides from the first a hurdle to those readers who turn to fiction, oriental or occidental, merely for pleasant entertainment. Nevertheless, these stories, read carefully, reveal a depth and precision of observation that goes far beyond the usual kind of romantic fantasy that so often constitutes "historical fiction" in the West. (pp. 1-2)

The fact that Ōgai chose historical subjects serves as no indication that he necessarily approved of the attitudes of the feudal past (against which he fought during his whole adult life), or that he preferred the old way of doing things to the new. Rather, the writing of these works seemed to serve as a means for him to deal with contemporary moral and philosophical problems from an artistic perspective congenial to him. If the characters and settings represented a vanished age, Ōgai's choice of concerns in dealing with them was thoroughly contemporary. Indeed, during the time he was working on these stories, he was also engaged in publishing a series of highly respected translations of contemporary works by Strindberg, Ibsen, Rilke, and Schnitzler.

Ōgai's contributions to the development of intellectual life in the Japan of his time were enormous. In addition to his work as a writer, his translations introduced to the Japanese a number of important works of philosophy and literature, ranging from Heine and Goethe to Hofmannsthal. He was a noted innovator in the creation of a modern poetic style in Japan, and his early experiments in writing European-style drama helped to create a viable dramaturgy for the modern Japanese theatre. He was an extremely perceptive critic, and his writings on Japanese and foreign literature are still consulted and considered valuable. His role as a public figure, informal adviser to statesmen, and as a physician and student of Western medicine must also be mentioned.

All aspects of Ōgai's intellectual and spiritual life are reflected in varying degrees in his fiction, and nowhere more so than in his late works, composed when he was in full possession of his artistic facilities and in his full maturity as a man.

Even limiting a consideration of Ōgai's work to his historical stories, the amount of material to examine is considerable. There are, first of all, three extensive chronicles that, from their length and complexity, may be classed as historical novels: ***Shibue Chūsai*** . . . , ***Izawa Ranken*** . . . , and ***Hōjō Katei***. . . . The three form something of a unit. In the three books, Ōgai examines the life of Shibue Chūsai, a leading physician and Confucian scholar in the late Tokugawa period, the career of his teacher Izawa Ranken, and, in the third, he reconstructs the biography of Ranken's colleague, Hōjō Katei.

The remaining works . . . are usually divided into two categories by Japanese critics, the fictional pieces (*rekishi shōsetsu*) that deal with historical themes in an artistic and psychological way . . . and the biographical narratives (*shiden*) that remain more closely related to the factual information unearthed on his characters by Ōgai. . . . Ōgai evolved a style appropriate to both genres, but to a Western reader the divisions between them may seem somewhat arbitrary, and many stories show the use of a considerable variety of subject matter and literary technique. Despite all this diversity, however, some generalizations may be useful as an introduction to the general reader in terms of what the stories are meant to represent and what Ōgai's intentions were in writing them.

Ōgai's fidelity to history was certainly an important determinant in their composition. (pp. 5-6)

Ōgai confesses that even his friends debate about whether his use of historical figures permits his works to be called fiction. Ōgai counters by saying that he looks for the "natural" in history, he respects it, and he is loathe to change it. After all, he continues, if people enjoy reading about life "as it is" in modern naturalistic fiction, then they certainly ought to like reading about it as it was. Indeed, he concludes, it is precisely because he respects history that he is all the more bound by it. (p. 6)

Ōgai can be moved by history but not wish to change it, he can be what Nietzsche calls ". . . a new transfiguring light needed to catch and hold in life the stream of individual forms." Coolness and objectivity characterize his attitudes in re-creating the past.

Given these attitudes toward his art, Ōgai's concerns as a thinker and a writer emerge more clearly. As was suggested above, Ōgai experienced in his own lifetime the crisis of civilization in Japan: modern man had shed his feudal sense of community and his superstitions only to find them replaced by spiritual emptiness. The end of the Meiji period seemed to mark an end to that transition period. Even the death of General Nogi seemed a final gesture of the dying past. For Ōgai, the best way to pursue the future was to examine the past; by discovering and articulating the Japanese virtues that existed in the past, the problems of the present and the limitations and possibilities for the future became clearer.

Ōgai drew his metaphysical sketches on the grandest possible scale. None of the stories deal with romantic love (although many of his earlier ones do), but rather with issues he found, at this time in his life, to be of more fundamental importance: loyalty, sincerity, intellectual honesty, independence of spirit, the nature of the spiritual temperament, and the abiding relationships between parents and children. The range of moral choice and action in the stories is perhaps limited by their historical settings, yet Ōgai's selection of events and attitudes to portray reveals his altogether striking modern attitude of mind. In fact, Ōgai's choices often lead him rather far from life "as it was." His concerns are for modern values, and indeed, it is precisely this creative gap between his material and his own mental outlook that gives the stories their remarkable moral power. Without being didactic in any way, the stories are idealistic. Ōgai has located the attitudes in history that have brought spiritual satisfaction to the men and women he portrays, and he holds them up as models for contemporary society, not as models in the conventional sense, but rather as reminders, as shadows cast across the confusions of the present.

Perhaps Ōgai's attitudes can be traced back to his early training in the Confucian classics, with their rational appeal to an ordered, restrained humanitarianism. By this definition, Ōgai can be included among the last generation of Confucian writers in Meiji Japan; yet on the other hand, his attitudes and perceptions were immeasurably broadened and rendered sophisticated through his long and intimate contact with late nineteenth-century European life and literature. As a result, the best of Ōgai's work manifests both the moral power sanctioned in the Confucian tradition and a subtlety and finesse of style derived from the West, both fused into a harmonious whole. These historical stories seem well described in the remark of Stephen Ross [in his *Literature as Philosophy*] that ". . . there is something particularly sublime about novels that not only succeed in purely literary terms but contain and develop ideas of great philosophic worth without destruction of literary values." (pp. 7-8)

One of Ōgai's most important artistic principles is that of selection. The kinds of incidents about which he chose to write show the precision with which he wished to voice his concerns. Most of the stories deal with specific historical events about which at least some documentation exists. (p. 8)

The temptation for most popular writers of historical fiction is to re-create the grand episodes and large figures of the past. Such an attitude is true in Japan as elsewhere: kabuki playwrights and novelists have usually turned to colorful and dramatic incidents for their inspiration. Ōgai, on the other hand, normally chooses as his main character an obscure person who may be close to a great man but who exhibits in his own private person some attitude or quality of mind Ōgai wishes to investigate. (pp. 8-9)

In the same fashion, the stories often take place in the generation before or after some great historical event. The event itself is not depicted, and the times in which the characters live are more often than not outwardly peaceful and normal. These seeming restrictions actually permit Ōgai to concentrate on his characters rather than on the historical events surrounding them. . . . Some Japanese critics have suggested that, because Ōgai's creative powers were limited, he shied away from depicting dramatic historical events. Nevertheless, Ōgai's desire to make his work "all the more contemplative" dictated the means he used.

In particular, Ōgai wrote a number of stories about the great feudal families in Kyushu, especially the Hosokawa family. (p. 9)

If the selection of an incident is one basic artistic technique at work in these stories, then another is Ōgai's method of selection within the context of a single incident. A story like **"Sahashi Jingorō,"** for example, is constructed by the same principles of organization that govern Japanese horizontal scrolls. Major scenes are painted in a very explicit fashion; and these scenes, as they unfold, are interspersed with bits of connecting "narrative" linking them together. In his major scenes, Ōgai provides an extraordinary amount of specific detail, subjecting his narrative to relentless documentation. Yet nothing is chosen at random, for each item Ōgai chooses to mention creates an effect contributing to his total conception. These scenes, in turn, are linked with episodes of historical background, quickly sketched.

Another important technique of Ōgai is his personal assumption of the role of narrator. Ōgai the writer and the man is never far from his reader; he constantly comments, shapes the narrative before the reader's eyes, speculates on the motives for the actions he is in the process of describing. (pp. 9-10)

The direct presentation to the reader of the working out of the author's own mental processes was a style of writing quite new in Japan at that time. . . .

Ōgai's sense of objectivity is chiefly conveyed through the tone of his language, which is terse, brilliant, and precise. Ōgai's style has always received unstinted praise from Japanese critics and writers. He has been admired by such diverse talents as Nagai Kafū and Mishima Yukio. Ōgai may have developed his ability to create his kind of lucid precise Japanese because, like his brilliant predecessor, the novelist Futabatei Shimei, he took an interest in the spoken language. (p. 10)

There are many reasons why these late stories of Ōgai may have a legitimate appeal, even in translation, to a modern reader.

First of all, in terms of literary technique, the stories show considerable distinction. Ōgai's ability to establish an effective relationship between author, reader, and the materials presented in the story provides the necessary means for him to accomplish his complex ends. These ends often concern human virtue. Writers have usually found vice more simple to portray (Chaucer said it was more exciting), but Ōgai's historical stories provide some effective counterexamples. (pp. 10-11)

Secondly, the stories hold considerable interest because of the light they shed on Ōgai as a leading intellectual leader of the Meiji period. Many of the difficulties and enthusiasms of that time are mirrored in these works. . . .

Lastly, many of Ōgai's philosophical ideas, irrespective of his cultural background, are compelling. I should merely like to call attention to the fact that his treatment of the problem of human ego, and his understanding of the close and reciprocal relationship between self and self-sacrifice are as profound as those of any modern writer in the West.

If I may conclude on a personal note, I feel that it is time for us to learn from the Japanese writers. Men of the stature of Natsume Sōseki and Mori Ōgai are worthy of being included in that small circle of serious writers in the modern spirit—James, Dostoevski, Eliot, Sartre, Camus—who consider fearlessly the human condition. None of these men wrote works that can be considered entertainment. Ōgai is as difficult to read as any of them, and his concerns are as profound. (p. 11)

J. Thomas Rimer, "The Historical Literature of Mori Ōgai: An Introduction," in The Incident at Sakai, and Other Stories *by Mori Ōgai, edited by David A. Dilworth and J. Thomas Rimer, The University Press of Hawaii, 1977, pp. 1-12.*

DAVID A. DILWORTH (essay date 1977)

[Dilworth is a critic and translator of Japanese literature. In his introduction to Saiki Kōi, and Other Stories, *he provides a survey of Ōgai's most important works of fiction and criticism, which he divides into three periods: first, the three romantic stories—*"Maihime" ("The Girl Who Danced"), "Utakawa no ki," and "Fumizukai" ("The Courier")*—written after Ōgai's return from Germany; second, the literary criticism, social and philosophical writings, and creative works written before 1912; third, the historical fiction and biographies written after 1912. Dilworth sees a progression from the pre-1912 works, in which themes of romantic love and philosophical resignation are prominent, to the post-1912 historical writings, in which Ōgai transforms "the various polarizations of his public and private, outer and inner, rational and emotional, scholarly and aesthetic, roles into one whole."]*

Mori Ōgai and his contemporary, Natsume Sōseki (1867-1916), towered over their own society as the truly outstanding figures of their time. Their contemporaries looked up to Ōgai and Sōseki as articulators of the important responses to the problems of their day, as well as of deep attitudes toward life in general. For this reason their major writings became classics in their own time.

Confining ourselves to Ōgai, Nakano Shigeharu has written, in another context, that Ōgai remains the most important "historical symbol" in the last century of Japanese history. He contends that the basic concerns and accomplishments of Japanese society are mirrored in Ōgai's career to a greater degree than in that of any other single figure in the first one hundred years since the Meiji Restoration. (p. 2)

Ōgai's was an essentially modern mind. His double career as army medical doctor, teacher, and bureaucrat, on the one hand, and as translator, literary critic, essayist, novelist, poet, short-story writer, and biographer, on the other, helped shape powerful cultural dynamisms at the crucial juncture of late Meiji when international values were being internalized and integrated with their own indigenous culture by the Japanese people. . . .

Ōgai himself . . . was acutely aware of the strains to which his many-sided nature subjected him. A careful study of his career will show that he used the medium of his own literary creations as the chief means to integrate these tensions, and to probe their deeper ground in his own genius.

Japanese critics usually point to the last phase of Ōgai's writing as the time in which he most creatively integrated the dimensions of his career. This was a period of exceptional intellectual vitality during which Ōgai, between 1912 and 1918, reformulated his philosophical and aesthetic ideas in the genre of "historical literature." After the death of the Meiji emperor and the *junshi* ["ritual suicide following the death of an emperor"] of General Nogi and his wife in 1912, Ōgai chose to write almost exclusively in this vehicle of "historical literature"—a term inclusive of fictional (*rekishi shōsetsu*) and biographical (*shiden*) pieces. Here again specialists will find it difficult to sort out the two literary forms, since Ōgai himself did not care to make the distinction. Yet Ōgai's "historical literature" as a whole remains the most praised of his total literary output, and the primary source material for the student of his philosophical ideas. (p. 3)

Ōgai's aesthetic intention in working with historical materials grew out of his long-standing polemic against the self-confessional genre of contemporary "realistic" and "naturalistic" literature. But while the very problematic of this debate grew out of the importation of Western forms of literature and aesthetic theory in his day, Ōgai's use of the genre of "historical literature" to illustrate his own aesthetic ideals resulted in his repossession of concepts of "reality" and "nature" deeply rooted in Oriental civilization. . . .

The stylistic excellence of Ōgai's "historical literature" has been noted by Japanese novelists and critics as well. Both in masterpieces of literary merit such as **"Abe ichizoku"** and **"Sanshō dayū,"** and in outstanding biographical works such as **"Kuriyama Daizen"** and **"Shibue Chūsai,"** Ōgai is said to have achieved a creative fusion of personal, historical, philosophical, and aesthetic dimensions through the medium of an impeccable prose narrative. . . .

In a word, the significance of Ōgai's "historical literature" consists in the fact that it became the final expression of Ōgai's protean genius. At the same time, it functioned as an important vector of Japanese cultural modernization. (p. 5)

Ōgai's works as a whole are a record of [the] continuing struggle with time and circumstance to realize his literary and intellectual gifts. The sometimes rough-hewn, highly condensed, and apparently unfinished character of many of his writings undoubtedly reflect this "relentless everyday fact." On the other hand, his works have the stamp of personal authenticity which this struggle helped produce. We can go further and note that the "unfinished" and "unexpressed" qualities of his stories became an element in his own self-consciousness as an "eternal malcontent" in his middle years, and are a function of his romanticism and idealism in general. His career-long struggle to be creative in the cultural sphere can in fact be found as one symbolic motif in the late historical fiction and biographies. (p. 6)

Ōgai's literary sensibility evolved as a process of integration of his youthful absorption in Japanese classical literature and the popular romance-type literature of the late Tokugawa period, on the one hand, and his pioneer role in introducing the values of German Romanticism through translation, literary criticism, aesthetic theory, and his own creative writing, on the other. (p. 9)

Ōgai also became a powerful influence on the formation of the Meiji literary consciousness through his polemics in the field of literary criticism and in the philosophy of aesthetics. (p. 10)

As for Ōgai's own literary works, totaling over one hundred twenty titles (mostly short stories and novellas), three general areas of development are discernible. The first was comprised of three romantic novellas written after his return from Germany, namely **"Maihime,"** . . . **"Utakata no ki,"** . . . and **"Fumizukai."** . . . It has been said that Ōgai virtually established the Japanese tradition of the "I novel" (*Ich Roman*) in his own way through **"Maihime,"** although he was ultimately to reject the naturalistic assumptions on the basis of which the same genre was later exploited by Japanese writers.

The second period, which runs from the end of the Russo-Japanese War to the death of the Meiji emperor in 1912, more directly reflects Ōgai's antinaturalistic standpoint, his social criticism and philosophical musings. He composed a prodigious number of works at this time. (pp. 10-11)

Finally, after the *junshi* of General Nogi in 1912, Ōgai wrote **"Okitsu Yagoemon no isho"** and **"Abe ichizoku,"** two stories on the subject of *junshi* set in the Tokugawa period. With this momentum he turned to write, and no less prolifically than before, in the genre of historical literature and biography. . . . This body of literature, to which we shall return below, probably represents one of the outstanding feats of painstaking historical research combined with creative writing, in the twentieth century.

I have said above that Ōgai's early and middle works represent a developing literary sensibility in which conceptual and symbolic elements he discovered in German literature resonated with the stratum of Japanese literature he had internalized as a youth. At the same time, these writings produced an imaginative world that concretely embodied his literary theories and aesthetic ideals. Again, they are a testament to his deepening powers of introspection and self-discipline, on the one hand, and his sensitive reactions to the political and social world, on the other. (p. 12)

The "historical" material of his late writings, which so remarkably repossessed the values of the pre-Meiji past, became the medium through which Ōgai continued to react to and comment upon the "modernization" process as he experienced it in his own day.

Thus in addition to understanding the fusion of Tokugawa and German literary forms in his works, it is imperative for the reader to gain some insight into the philosophical sense of personal cultivation and social order which Ōgai reflects as a creative Meiji figure. The critic Katō Shūichi has indeed suggested that the greatness of Ōgai and Sōseki is bound up with the fact that they flourished in the "transitional" time of the late Meiji period when the essential philosophical values of the Tokugawa period were still a living, though transformed, part of the spiritual landscape. This opinion seems to accord with Okazaki Yoshie's assessment of Ōgai as having been always an "enlightenment scholar" who strove to interpret the impact of Westernization on the indigenous Japanese modernization process. The sympathetic reaction of many Japanese intellectuals who have revered Ōgai up to the present time seems partly based on the fact that they see his life and attitudes as an objectification of their own problems and concerns for meaning as modern Japanese.

But if this is so, we should ponder the implications of this phenomenon for our own interpretation of Japanese culture. In point of fact, Ōgai's "historical literature" gives the reader a vivid sense of his appreciation of a quality of spiritual life he knew had existed in the premodern, Tokugawa culture. On the whole, these writings bear eloquent witness to the continuity of Japan's premodern civilization in his own case. Simple stories such as **"Jiisan baasan," "Suginohara Shina,"** and **"Yasui fujin"** bear the imprint of this appreciation. They are able to communicate Ōgai's sense of the beauty of the lives of men and women who personified the values of love, dedication, self-sacrifice, and self-cultivation, which were social ideals in the Tokugawa culture. The significance of his longer historical biography, ***Shibue Chūsai,*** is usually understood in this light. It probes the public and private life of a medical doctor, scholar, and man of letters of the late Edo period with whom Ōgai came to identify as almost his own earlier incarnation. He brought this project of historical self-recollection to consummation in the sequels to this work, the biographies ***Izawa Ranken*** and ***Hōjō Katei.*** (pp. 12-13)

Let us now briefly work out some of the aspects of Ōgai's inner life as he revealed it in his pre-1912 literary works. In this way we shall be in a better position to understand what he was attempting to do in his post-1912 "historical literature," and what the serious contemporary reader of this literature must have realized was taking place in Ōgai's mature psychology. . . .

[***Vita Sexualis*** furnishes] one clue as to the direction of Ōgai's later writings. The work, a thinly veiled account of his own adolescent sexual life, was at the same time a critique of the self-confessional "I novel" and its underlying credo of Naturalism. (p. 14)

Vita Sexualis is important in Ōgai's developing literary career for exemplifying his basic concern to include the self-confessional approach in a wider, and more spiritual, value orientation. This unique approach, combining a selected reminiscence of personal and historical detail with an effort at imaginative expression, and both in the service of oblique spiritual autobiography, became the essential programmatic of the historical genre to which he turned only three years later.

Ironically, however, ***Vita Sexualis*** was grouped with the naturalistic writings of the day and banned by the authorities in the wake of a famous political trial in 1910. The government's sweeping suppression of free expression, combined with other political issues of the times, drew forth a complex response on Ōgai's part. Not abandoning his aesthetic intention in the face of these pressures and obstacles, Ōgai began to articulate a complex philosophy of "resignation" (*teinen, akirame*) that gave a deep coloration to his already pensive works. If we bear in mind that Ōgai was himself at this time a prominent figure in the governmental bureaucracy—and commanded a wide audience of intelligent readers—we shall be better able to surmise the nuances contained in the themes and symbols of his stories and essays written between 1909 and 1912.

If we follow Okazaki Yoshie's interpretation, the concept of "resignation" formed one side of Ōgai's earliest literary expression. His first romance, **"Maihime,"** . . . revolves around the tension between *giri,* that is, loyalty to the performance values of clan and family, and *ninjō,* that is, the dictates of the human heart and aesthetic emotion. In **"Maihime,"** Ōgai wrote a self-confessional account of his student days in Germany that at the same time symbolized the irreconcilable tension between his career as a public figure in the social structure and his desire to be a writer. In this work, *giri* must conquer *ninjō,* but, as Okazaki maintains, the seed had been sown in Ōgai's writings for the eventual transcendence of the former by the latter.

The tension between *giri* and *ninjō,* between *teinen* ("resignation") and romantic love, reoccurs in Ōgai's next works, **"Utakata no ki"** and **"Fumizukai."** And we have clear indications of *teinen* and Ōgai's romantic idealism in ***Vita Sexualis.*** But for schematic purposes we can say that Ōgai's middle-period works, written between 1906 and 1912, rang various changes on the "resignation" theme, while at the end of this period his **"Ka no yō ni"** . . . signaled a transition to a "new idealism" in which the "resignation" theme was transcended.

In these terms, the conceptual key to Ōgai's middle-period works can be found in an essay entitled **"Yo ga tachiba" [My standpoint]**. . . . In this essay, Ōgai stated that he did not care to be classified or compared with such contemporary authors as Tayama Katai, Shimazaki Tōson, Masamune Hakuchō, Nagai Kafū, and Natsume Sōseki. Here "resignation" signified that Ōgai, in his own words, was "giving up all desire" of being appreciated by the Naturalism-oriented critics, and expressed contentment in his intention of "going his own way." He wrote as follows of the "serenity" (*heiki*) which this resolve had produced in him.

> . . . the word that sums up my feeling best would be that of *resignation.* My feeling is not confined to the arts; every aspect of society evokes this in me. Others may think I must surely be suffering to hold such an attitude, but I am surprisingly serene. Probably there is some suggestion of faint-heartedness in an attitude of resignation, but I do not intend to make any special defense against this accusation.

Despite the typical Japanese manner of self-deprecation, however, Ōgai's continuing output and unflagging energy had nothing to do with a faint-hearted attitude. It was rather a positive spiritual resolve to follow the dictates of his own self-consciousness. Spinoza's philosophy, itself mediated through Ōgai's long interest in Goethe, played a role in the formation of this "resignation" concept. Like Spinoza, Ōgai was impelled to "neither laugh nor weep," but earnestly to seek to understand the ambivalences and contradictions, and the deeper harmonies, of his own life and times. But, like Goethe, Ōgai conceived of this kind of "resignation" in terms of active pursuit of duty and destiny.

We can assume that Ōgai's contemporary readers were able to understand this fusion of Japanese and German spiritual attitudes in his works. In 1910 Ōgai drew out one implication of his "resignation" concept in a short story entitled **"Asobi."** "Asobi" literally means "play." The protagonist, Kimura, who is both an official and a man of letters, represents another self-reflection of Ōgai at this stage in his career. Intrinsically related to the "serenity" concept found in **"Yo ga tachiba," "Asobi"** reexpressed Ōgai's transcendent attitude. But symbolically the *asobi* sensibility functioned as the point of harmony between politics and art, as exemplified in Ōgai's own position in late Meiji society. Other variations on the *asobi* theme appeared in **"Fushigi ga kagami"** and **"Dengaku tōfu,"** . . . and can be traced into Ōgai's historical literature and biographies as well. (pp. 14-16)

It is imperative to be aware of the intricate inner dialogue in Ōgai's writings. If *asobi* was one variation on the *teinen* theme articulated in 1910, Ōgai explored another—and equally autobiographical—dimension of it in **"Mōsō."** . . . (In this work, Ōgai imagines himself in his old age; there is an intrinsic connection between **"Mōsō"** and ***Hōjō Katei,*** a late historical biography which deals with the life in retirement of a spiritual forebear of ***Shibue Chūsai.***) A characteristically introspective pronouncement by Ōgai in **"Mōsō"** has often been cited by Japanese critics as expressive of Ōgai's self-consciousness as an "eternal malcontent" (*eiennaru fuheika*) at this time. He writes of feeling a "hunger of the soul." (p. 17)

Ōgai professed he was not satisfied with the actual world, and by implication, with the actual Ōgai. He felt the call to search after and express the richer possibilities of human life, as manifested in his confessed love of learning and art and his sense of the value of culture.

Another intrinsic dimension of this multipolarized sensibility Ōgai elaborated in literary form the following year in **"Hyaku monogatari."** . . . This was related on the one hand to the "eternal malcontent" theme of the previous year, and on the other to Ōgai's "Apollonian" attitude, which already figured prominently in his uniquely "objective" literary style. Now it became an explicit philosophical attitude, tied to his rejection of the natural, instinctive self. The [*Bōkansha* ("onlooker")] concept thus subsumed the original "resignation," "play," and "eternal malcontent" themes into a new configuration, indicative of Ōgai's spiritual individualism and quest for more adequate self-expression in spite of the internal and external obstacles he felt. (p. 18)

In all of these variations on the general "resignation" concept in Ōgai's middle period, we find the keynote to be a kind of transcendent individualism as Ōgai searched for the proper vehicle to express his sense of the true and the beautiful. (p. 19)

[In] **"Ka no yō ni,"** Ōgai began to shift the center of gravity of his general "resignation" sensibility toward a more explicit idealism which recapitulated his earlier concern for the beautiful and aesthetic value and allowed for the fuller flowering of his genius. (p. 20)

Finally let us observe Ōgai at work in another direction around this time. He published his novel ***Gan*** **[*The wild geese*]** in serial form between 1911 and 1913, and thus it was completed only after the *junshi* of General Nogi and the appearance of Ōgai's **"Okitsu Yagoemon no isho."** . . . ***Gan*** has usually been acclaimed as an outstanding work in the rich canon of modern Japanese literature. Its sophisticated romanticism does not well accord with some characterizations of Ōgai as an aloof or cold writer. As is true of ***Vita Sexualis,*** there is something intensely personal in ***Gan,*** although expressed by Ōgai under the powerful discipline of his "Apollonian" standpoint.

The heroine of ***Gan,*** Otama, appears to be a projection of Ōgai's own feminine *anima* (in Jung's sense). (This is true of the female personages who appear in Ōgai's historical literature as well—for example, Yü Hsüan-chi in **"Gyogenki,"** Sayo in **"Yasui fujin,"** Anju in **"Sanshō dayū,"** Run in **"Jiisan baasan,"** Shina in **"Suginohara Shina,"** and Ichi in **"Saigo no ikku."**) Ōgai, noted for his powerful masculine mind and Apollonian vision of life, appears to have been equally possessed of a delicate feminine sensitivity in the depths of his unconscious. His creative imagination strove to integrate the two sides of his psychological makeup through the medium of his literary expression.

Otama is a hauntingly affecting character into whom Ōgai poured his own mind and soul. She becomes in the course of the novel a transparent symbol of the "onlooker" as she waits each day for the student, Okada, to pass by her house. She is made to take on the full weight of Ōgai's attitude of "resignation" as well. She falls in love with Okada but has no way of revealing or consummating her emotion. She "saves" the situation for her aging father, for whose sake she has become the mistress of a moneylender, Suezō. Through her "resignation" she also saves the situation for Suezō himself. (The novel recollects many of the themes and symbols of Ōgai's earlier works, from **"Maihime"** onward, in the course of events.) *Bōkansha* and *teinen* sensibilities come together in this tragic but beautiful tale of the Meiji value system as internalized by Otama, and of the pull of historical forces that finally take Okada from her through his trip to Germany.

Okada, of course, represents another autobiographical dimension in ***Gan.*** He is another variation on Ōta, the protagonist of Ōgai's early romantic *Ich Roman,* **"Maihime."** We are given to feel that just as Okada and Ōta have their lives permanently touched by the tragedy of unfulfilled love, so Ōgai must ever be the "eternal malcontent" because of his pursuit of the beautiful. Read in the light of such works as **"Mōsō"** and **"Ka no yō ni,"** ***Gan*** also suggests the inner longing, the still unexpressed genius, of Ōgai's own psyche.

Gan, at any rate, is a highly nuanced, personal expression. It is full of an intense but subdued emotion. It is clear that these sensibilities were carried over into the "historical literature" which Ōgai began to write in 1912. (pp. 20-1)

In retrospect, Okazaki Yoshie seems to be right in contending that the tension between "resignation" and "romantic love" formed the subcurrent of Ōgai's literature from his earliest work, **"Maihime,"** onward. These were the two conflicting aspects of his "double career." But in this light we cannot fail to see that there is an intrinsic link between **"Maihime"** . . . and ***Gan***. . . . We have now to see that Otama and Okada of ***Gan*** were, in turn, metamorphized by Ōgai into the various personages of his "historical literature." The essential thrust of his post-1912 writings involved Ōgai in transforming the various polarizations of his public and private, outer and inner, rational and emotional, scholarly and aesthetic, roles into one whole. Far from being merely "historical," his literary writings after 1912 represent Ōgai's final phase of self-expression, and the most adequate realization of his aesthetic conception of the beautiful. (p. 22)

The questions of "love" and "self" in Ōgai's earlier writings become the themes of self-transcendence and the worth of high ideals in his later stories. Ōgai's earlier preoccupation with the question of domestic relations and the broader issues of social order and authority similarly return in the coherent spiritual humanism of his "historical literature." From **"Okitsu Yagoemon no isho,"** which was written immediately after the *junshi* of General Nogi and his wife, Ōgai's historical stories and biographies usually depict characters who, by transcending the instinctive, natural self, establish a deeper, "ideal" self in relation to lord, or parent, or husband, or wife, or the honor of their house and ancestors, or of the Japanese nation. (p. 23)

Ōgai did not endeavor to write *realistic* historical fiction. The subject matter of his historical literature, accordingly, was not that of feudal values per se, but rather the universal spiritual qualities Ōgai endeavored to distill from the given historical context he portrayed.

The thematic of his first historical story, **"Okitsu Yagoemon no isho,"** for example, is that of the value of the tea ceremony—itself a symbol of cultural sensibilities in general—in a military age. It was Ōgai's shrewd comment on Japan's modernization process in his day—and on ours, and every modernization process. The "spiritual pragmatism" of this work is directly relatable to the theme of **"Ka no yō ni,"** as we have seen. Even Ōgai's response to General Nogi's *junshi* was expressed in this same universalizing intentionality—he obliquely commemorates General Nogi's deed as an act of *beauty* in the standpoint of universal humanity. (p. 25)

Ōgai's next work, **"Abe ichizoku,"** took a typically more ambivalent attitude toward the subject of *junshi*. But it would again be a mistake to read this masterpiece in realistic terms. The main theme, as Okazaki Yoshie has pointed out, is rather the ideals of loyalty and sincerity, and the tragic consequences of their absence, as universal human values. And **"Gojiingahara no katakiuchi,"** while dealing with the subject of a feudal vendetta sanctioned by the Edo shogunate, has its primary aesthetic intention in the presentation of the sterling qualities of Kurōemon, Bunkichi, and Riyo, in contrast to the "modern" rationalistic doubts and consequent spiritual collapse of the son Uhei. But Kurōemon's manly pride, Bunkichi's unswerving loyalty, and Riyo's single-minded resolve are not so much depicted as customs of the late feudal age as universal forms of man. Ōgai achieved a similar aesthetic effect in the tale of multiple *seppuku* in **"Sakai jiken."**

Ōgai's "spiritual naturalism," then, involved the predominant intentionality of presenting the beauty of the lives of persons who have lived and died according to a basically *ideal* conception of "self." He succeeds sublimely at times in capturing the self-transcending "will" and "pride" that are essential elements in the Japanese national character. But the final impact of his historical literature is not precisely the ethical quality of his characters, but rather the aesthetic beauty they embody as human beings. (pp. 25-6)

Ōgai wrote of his devotion to "history in itself," in contrast to giving free play to his fictional imagination, in his essay **"Rekishi sono mama to rekishibanare."** . . . This essay was in fact written directly after he published **"Sanshō dayū,"** and can be read as an exegesis on that work. At the same time, we must bear in mind that Ōgai used the historical, or in this case legendary, medium as a vehicle of his hermeneutical discovery of ontological dimensions of personal and cultural experience—and as a vehicle of his literary typology of ideal human qualities. **"Sanshō dayū"** was a tour de force in that Ōgai worked within a predetermined story frame to create an idealization of Anju, the central expression of his creative imagination, in his own version of the legend. But even Zushiō is a reincarnation of other male characters—of Ōta of **"Maihime,"** Okada of ***Gan,*** of many of the samurai personages of the late stories and biographies. (p. 28)

Anju's death, as well as her parting from Zushiō, retell the tragically beautiful endings of **"Maihime," "Utakata no ki,"** ***Gan,*** and other works. (p. 29)

From this brief sampling of the themes of some of the historical stories we can conclude that Ōgai created his "historical literature" in an imaginative horizon which transcended the domain of formal historiography. The concepts of "history in itself" and "history as nature" which Ōgai set forth in **"Rekishi sono mama to rekishibanare"** were primarily *aesthetic* concepts, and not a retreat by Ōgai into the domain of scientific fact. Accordingly they do not represent a conversion to literary "realism" either, but rather an innovative effort at synthesis of his classicism and romanticism. (pp. 29-30)

Like every authentic artist, Ōgai succeeded in finding his own inimitable material and style, that of historical literature as oblique spiritual autobiography. (p. 30)

David A. Dilworth, "The Significance of Ōgai's Historical Literature," in Saiki Kōi, and Other Stories *by Mori Ōgai, edited by David A. Dilworth, The University Press of Hawaii, 1977, pp. 1-31.*

Ōgai in 1909, two years after his promotion to Surgeon General. From Mori Ōgai and the Modernization of Japanese Culture, *by Richard John Bowring. Cambridge University Press, 1979. Reprinted by permission of Cambridge University Press.*

RICHARD JOHN BOWRING (essay date 1979)

[*Bowring is the author of* Mori Ōgai and the Modernization of Japanese Culture, *the most extensive English-language study of Ōgai's works. In the following excerpt from that work, Bowring examines Ōgai's contribution to the modernization of Japanese drama.*]

[One] tends to ignore the work [Ōgai] did towards a modernization of Japanese drama.

In September 1889 he was made one of seventeen committee members of the newly formed Nihon Engei Kyōkai (Japan Entertainments Society), and began in characteristic style to inveigh against the idea put forward by Suematsu Kencho and his Engeki Kairyōkai (Society for Theatre Reform) of building a new theatre. Although the Kairyōkai itself had only lasted from 1886 to 1888 and so was already disbanded, the proposals lingered on. The main theme of Ōgai's two articles, **'Engeki kairyō ronja no kenken ni odoroku' (On being shocked at the distorted views of those who are in favour of the Society for Theatre Reform . . .)**, and **'Futatabi geki o ronjite yo no hyōka ni kotau' (A second essay on the theatre in answer to critics of the age . . .)**, was that to erect a brand new European-style theatre while ignoring the content of the plays themselves was putting the cart before the horse. Ōgai's priorities were play (*gikyoku*), performance (*engeki*) and lastly theatre (*gekijō*); modernization had to start with a renovation of the content and style of the plays, and it was perfectly possible to act modern plays in the theatres which already existed. He was totally opposed to the idea that the *kabuki* stage and techniques be abandoned, and astutely pointed out that they were in some ways closer to the theatres of Shakespeare's England than were modern European stages. His was the voice of sanity and gradualism at a time when there was uncritical acceptance of most things Western. (p. 157)

He emphasized the role of the author in modern drama (*shōgeki*) in contrast to his position in traditional Kabuki, a prerequisite to which he was to return later. As the idea of a new type of drama was, of course, only in its infancy at this stage, and it was to be some time before any actual results were seen, Ōgai's articles were primarily concerned with explaining simple, basic truths. . . .

Ōgai never lost contact with the development of *shimpa,* the style of acting that was an attempted modernization of *kabuki,* and the later *shingeki* movement at the turn of the century, which was modern theatre in the Western sense. But he produced very little, except for the occasional review, until his first play. . . . (p. 158)

Tamakushige Futari Urashima is a two act play based on the Japanese legend of Urashima who returns from a dream world to find he is three hundred years old; on opening a casket he has been given, however, he suddenly ages the full span and dies. Ōgai's adaptation is interesting for a number of reasons. In the first act Urashima wakes up in the sea palace having had a troubled dream. He tells the princess that he dreamt he was back in the world above and was once again fishing in a calm sea when he was overtaken by a storm which threatened to sink the boat. While struggling for his life, he awoke to find himself still in the beautiful dream world beneath the sea. Despite the pleas of the princess that he should stay in this land of eternal peace and idyllic charm, he cannot resist the urge to return to the land of men. . . . Eventually, as he is adamant, she weeps for his departure and her tears turn to pearls. These pearls are placed in the jewelled casket which she gives him, telling him not to open it until they meet again.

In contrast to this lyrical scene the second act is more robust and takes place on the shore by his native village. He has returned to find that one of his descendants is making preparations to set sail with a large fleet and subjugate a foreign land for the greater glory of Japan. Urashima is captured on the shore and after a struggle the casket is dropped, the pearls fall out and he becomes a white-haired old man. All is revealed and Urashima is overjoyed that his descendant is to carry out the 'enterprise' that he had been yearning to undertake: 'It is for the forefathers to dream and for their descendants to act out those dreams.' . . . He gives the pearls to his descendant to pay for the expedition and decides to retire in seclusion deep in the mountains, content in the knowledge that his dream is to be carried out, for 'that is one form of immortality.' . . . (pp. 158-59)

Among the elements which Ōgai could be said to have added to the legend are the comparison of the incompatibility between the princess and Urashima to that between Nature and Man, the drive that Urashima feels towards an 'enterprise', and his gift of the pearls to his warlike descendant at the end. (p. 160)

Nichiren Shōnin Tsujizeppō, which Ōgai wrote the following year and which was acted at the Kabukiza in April 1904 just before his departure for the front in the Russo-Japanese War, is a slight work of little importance. The action is set in Kamakura where Nichiren is proselytizing and warning the country of the possibilities of a Mongol invasion. Yoshiharu, a retainer of the Hōjō regents, is in love with Tae, the daughter of a devout believer in Nichiren's teachings. The father refuses them permission to marry because Yoshiharu is critical of Nichiren. All this background is skilfully introduced in a short economical exchange between the two lovers, which is interrupted by the arrival of Nichiren himself. The great preacher begins to harangue the crowd, argues vigorously with a Zen priest, and is protected from assault by Yoshiharu. Then there follows a succession of questions and answers which are used to explain Nichiren's convictions. Yoshiharu is won over by his persuasive arguments of the danger to the nation and the threat from the mainland. Tae's father sees him talking with Nichiren, hears of his conversion and allows the marriage to take place.

The main interest of this one act play is not the plot, which is extremely thin, but the realistic way in which Ōgai portrays Nichiren, his forceful street sermonizing, and the freedom with which he adapted the historical details. (pp. 161-62)

Compared to these two early plays, the four that Ōgai wrote in 1909 and 1910 are far more modern in both diction and conception, reflecting the contacts he had with the *shingeki* movement. . . .

Concomitant with the rise of *shingeki* Ōgai's interest in producing some original plays was reawakened and the first of these was the two act ***Purumūla*** published in January 1909 in *Subaru* but never in fact staged. (p. 162)

The first act is set in Sind which is being invaded by Arab forces. Defeat being imminent, the Queen Lala, her sister Sati, and her two daughters Surug and Purumūla make the decision to commit suicide when the news of defeat reaches them; before they can do so, however, the enemy surprises them and they are arrested. The enemy General Kāsim decides he will stay to rule the country and chooses Sati as his queen. He tells how he has been told in a dream that one of the first women he should meet in Sind would be his eventual murderer and the only way he can avoid this is to marry her. Up to this moment Purumūla has said and done nothing, but she suddenly springs to her feet and demands to be crowned herself. Despite her willingness and her beauty Kāsim decides that she and her sister Surug should be sent back to Arabia to enter the harem of his master in Damascus. The act ends as he calls for preparations to be made for their journey.

The second act is set in Dasmascus three years later. Despite the efforts of her sister to keep her happy in the idyllic surroundings, Purumūla broods on her fate. We learn that the Caliph Valid, who had ordered the expedition against Sind, is dead and that his place has been taken by his younger brother Sūlemān. She had already managed to avoid being made Valid's concubine by lying to him that she was raped by Kāsim in Sind and was therefore no longer a virgin. Because of his trust in Kāsim and the counsel of his chief adviser, Valid had refused to take action. Sūlemān enters her apartments and asks her if her story is true. When she repeats the lie he has the corpse of Kāsim brought in on a bier, telling her that he had already taken appropriate measures. Now that the deed is done she admits that the whole story was a fabrication. Sūlemān is furious when he sees he has been duped and condemns both her and her sister to be drawn and quartered the next morning. The play closes as Purumūla is bending over Kāsim's corpse with the words 'The seeds of a lie which I made up on the spur of the moment when pressed by Valid have somehow ripened to a fruit and become my revenge, but in truth the deed was not accomplished with such pure intent.' . . . (pp. 162-63)

What Ōgai has done in this case is add to the original story as he found it in his researches a further subtler motive for Purumūla's lies. The basic story of the revenge carried out by a single-minded daughter for the death of her father has been amplified with the second theme of her love for the conqueror Kāsim, which she herself only fully comprehends at the end of the play. In typical Ōgai fashion this slight adaptation is treated with such restraint that it is never made explicit. Ōgai is here beginning to reveal the fascination with strong-minded noble women in a historical context that is a feature of his historical novellas, and which is reflected in the heroines of a number of his drama translations of this period. (p. 163)

The style and content are not as modern as one might expect from Ōgai writing in 1909; one can see from the stage directions, which mention the use of *hanamichi* among other traditional elements, that it was written with *kabuki* rather than *shingeki* in mind. Secondly, one sees the extraordinary attention to detail which characterizes Ōgai's meticulous approach to literature and research. (p. 164)

Kamen (Masks) on the other hand is a modern one act play in a contemporary setting using everyday speech. . . . The action takes place in the waiting room of a doctor Sugimura. A young student called Shiori has been to see the doctor because he is afraid he has contracted tuberculosis. . . . We know from his expression that he has seen the report on the doctor's desk and knows that the tests were in fact positive. He works himself up into such a terrible state of fear that the doctor decides to take him into his confidence and reveals that he himself found he was suffering from tuberculosis seventeen years previously. He told no one about it at the time, preferring to keep his own counsel and cure the disease on his own. He himself is not sure whether it was from purely selfish motives. Then, out of the blue, he asks Shiori whether he has ever read Nietzsche.

> *Shiori:* I was stimulated to read him by Professor Kanai's lectures, but only *Beyond Good and Evil*.
>
> *Doctor:* I see. He often mentions the idea of masks in that book too. He says that what we call the Good is merely having the same attitudes as the common herd of humanity and Evil is when one tries to destroy those attitudes. We should not concern ourselves with Good or Evil. He said he wanted to stand aloof from the common herd, strengthen his resolve and place himself high above them in an aristocratic position of lonely eminence. Such eminent men wear masks and those masks are to be respected. Tell me, do you respect mine?
>
> (p. 165)

Shiori understands that the doctor is enjoining forbearance, self-control and self-reliance and he restates his determination to carry on attending lectures while not breathing a word of his illness. The doctor replies:

> . . . as a doctor I must forbid you to attend school and I must order you to move to your brother's house but that would be to prescribe for one of the common herd. I will let you do what you want and strive as best I know to prevent your disease from endangering those around you. We shall cure it. I will do all I can and stand with you beyond Good and Evil.
>
> (pp. 165-66)

The play ends as Shiori and the doctor prepare to go out for lunch and a Chopin concert.

It is with this play that we find ourselves on more familiar ground in the sense that the theme is typical of Ōgai's stories of this period. While the mention of Nietzsche can be explained as an example of his conscious and often obtrusive didacticism, it does bring into question the exact connection between the ideas expressed by the doctor and Ōgai's own attitudes. Given the fact that Ōgai was rather sceptical about Nietzsche's Overman, ***Kamen*** can hardly be taken at face value.

What is significant here is the adoption of a mask which was to appear again as a strong theme in the pessimistic **'Kaijin'.** The elitism is not a natural one built on a foundation of aristocratic birth and therefore including an element of social responsibility but a kind of excuse for a 'disengagement from society'. The doctor's claim that the mask is something to be respected rings somehow hollow and avoids the more basic reason—it is a refuge in which the man who is afraid of death can preserve his outward calm. There is more than a suspicion in this play of ambivalence in the attitude of the author. Although no preference is actually stated in so many words, the doctor's philosophy is not above criticism. He lies blatantly . . . about Shiori's health, he sees his mask as eminently worthy of respect and is willing to endanger the lives of others for the sake of a fellow 'aristocrat'; he sees both Shiori and himself as standing 'beyond Good and Evil'. Are we to identify Ōgai with this attitude? The play is surely more subtle than this. Ōgai has written as a detached author but his very treatment of the theme gives away his underlying distrust of such extremes. Even the doctor worries that the masking might be from purely selfish motives, and the fact that at the end of the play they go off to a Chopin concert seems to ring a little false. (p. 166)

Kamen stands out at this period as a work of some maturity, showing a sense of detachment and irony. Reminiscent of the Austrian playwright Schnitzler, some of whose works Ōgai was concurrently translating, it is a good one act play which has not received the attention it perhaps deserves. . . .

Shizuka was the next play that Ōgai wrote. It was published in *Subaru* in November 1909 but not acted until 1921. It is an historical play dealing with the famous feud between the two Minamoto brothers Yoritomo and Yoshitsune, Shizuka being the name of Yoshitsune's mistress. It is also one of the first examples of modern everyday speech being used in conjunction with such a classical theme. The first scene takes place at Yui Bay where Shizuka's son is about to be drowned on the orders of Yoritomo. In a dream-like sequence Adachi orders his men to put a stone into the boat and then puts out to sea by himself. This very short introductory scene ends with a sudden outburst from a 'strange fisherman' who has been silently staring into the distance. The rest of the people on stage are not supposed to see him and his role is purely symbolic. . . .

The second scene takes place in an inn at Kamakura two months later when Shizuka is preparing to depart for Kyoto. While her maids play *sugoroku* Adachi comes to collect her and there follows a conversation in which their attitude to fate is revealed. Shizuka is described as having an 'attitude of resignation tinged with light irony' and she has decided not to become a nun or to kill herself but to resign herself to her fate and continue living. (p. 167)

Ōgai was clearly interested in the original story because he wished to investigate why Shizuka had not in fact committed suicide on the death of her son. She was fated never to see Yoshitsune again, had lost hope and yet decided to live on. Rather than ascribing it to any motive of selfishness, he preferred to see in this story an example of human fortitude in the face of a cruel fate. . . . The play itself, rather than the theme, is an interesting experiment in symbolic drama and shows the influence of Maeterlinck in construction and treatment. (p. 168)

The next play, ***Ikutagawa (The Ikuta River)***, was commissioned by the Jiyū Gekijō, written in April 1910 and performed at their second programme in the May. . . . The story was based on a tale from the *Yamato Monogatari* as Ōgai noted in a short postscript to the play. The legend is of a beautiful girl who cannot decide between two men who come to court her. In the end she is forced to commit suicide. Ōgai's play opens with a conversation between mother and daughter which explains the situation. The girl complains that she has headaches caused by the spring weather, but they are only a symptom of the indecision with which she is wracked. She is worried that the man she rejects will kill himself and so stand between her and the man she chooses. The problem appears to be intractable. The two men, Unai and Chinu, come to visit the girl and each brings with him a duck that he has shot over the river. While the girl is out of the room, her mother proposes to the two men that they should hunt a swan which they have seen on the river; the man who manages to shoot it and bring it back will be given her daughter to marry. They both agree to the idea and leave the house.

When her mother tells her of the proposal the girl is upset because she had seen the swan that morning and thought how beautiful it looked. She then looks out of the window and describes the shooting of the swan. Both arrows pierce the bird. Feeling that the matter must be decided that day because of the death of the swan, the girl goes out to take a closer look. The play ends as her mother thinks about what she has just said, feels worried and decides to follow her out. The girl's suicide is left untold, but we are left in little doubt as to the outcome. In the short space of time between the discovery that both men had managed to shoot the bird and her decision to leave the house, a Buddhist priest comes outside the window and intones a number of chants from the *Yuishikiron*, the doctrine that all phenomena are in essence Mind. The four chants, which propound in turn the ideas that all human suffering lies in man's wayward desires, that the five senses are illusory, that the concrete world is not true reality and that duality is a false doctrine, mirror the gradual formation of a firm decision in the girl's mind.

There can be little doubt that Ōgai has here used an old legend to express his own acute sense of indecision and impotence, using a treatment which has more than a suggestion of Ibsen. Ōgai is at pains to point out that Unai comes from the same province as the girl—who is also known as the 'Maiden of Unai'—but Chinu comes from a different part of Japan. In this case we can see them symbolizing the pull of traditional Japan versus modern Europe which was Ōgai's main concern in this period. If this is so, what does the swan stand for? The girl had been content to leave the problem unresolved until the death of the swan, which brought the impossibility of reconciliation into sharp relief. She was aware of the ultimate conflict but had achieved a kind of modus vivendi by a resigned acceptance of the contradictions. If she came down on any one side it would cause the death of the other. To avoid this she was prepared to hold the balance indefinitely hoping for an eventual solution both natural and gradual. The problem was not to be forced. It is when both men find their arrows in the swan that the confrontation is brought out into the open. The girl is destroyed when a solution is attempted but fails.

Ōgai is here arguing for the necessity of making no choice at all but rather accepting a precarious balance. This is not a cowardly act but a practical decision. For Ōgai the vague ennui was preferable to a direct battle in which the self would be driven to destruction. On an even deeper level this attitude can perhaps be related to the priest's incantations. Duality means inevitable conflict and the only true concept is the oneness of things; if all reality is Mind then opposition becomes meaningless.

The importance of Ōgai's plays therefore lies not only in the pioneering elements, such as the use of modern colloquial language in historical plays and the conscious use of symbolism, but also in their content and themes. It will be seen that he was exploring exactly the same problems in his plays as in his short stories of 1909 to 1912 and the fact that five out of six were concerned with historical or legendary material is a further pointer to later developments. (pp. 168-70)

Richard John Bowring, in his Mori Ōgai and the Modernization of Japanese Culture, *Cambridge University Press, 1979, 297 p.*

YOSHIYUKI NAKAI (essay date 1980)

[In the following excerpt, Nakai analyzes Ōgai's fictional technique, focusing on the mock-autobiographical novel Vita Sexualis. *Nakai explains that although Ōgai's fiction has been criticized for its lack of conventional narrative interest and its cumbersome use of factual data, that criticism is inadequate because Ōgai was concerned with more complex themes and subtler artistic effects than those commonly associated with the autobiographical novels he was satirizing. The following excerpt also contains a lengthy excerpt of critical commentary on Ōgai's narrative technique by Yukio Mishima, one of the most celebrated authors of post-World War II Japan.]*

Appraisal of Mori Ōgai as a writer . . . ranges from that of Uchida Roan, who recognized little literary value in his works, to that of Mishima [Yukio], for whom Ōgai was an inimitable master novelist. One might think that the general view of Ōgai would be situated somewhere between these two poles. For some reason, however, this is not the case. People tend either to be negative about—even hostile to—Ōgai, or passionate devotees. So long as a person is seriously involved in the issue, it appears impossible to stay on middle ground.

The division over Ōgai's literary merits has its source in his very approach to the writing of fiction. One's initial encounter with an Ōgai story is often perplexing, if not disappointing. The story tells very little, virtually nothing. It may be a dull narrative of some insignificant happening—if anything happens at all—that took place in his personal life, whether long before (as in ***'Daihakken'*** [***'A Great Discovery'***], . . . or ***'Niwatori'*** [***'The Chickens'***] . . .), or more recently (as in ***'Hannichi'*** [***'A Half Day'***] . . . , or ***'Kitsugyaku'*** [***'Hiccups'***] . . . ; a meticulous account of historical facts—just that—such as **'Yasui Fujin' ('The Wife of Yasui Sokken')** . . . , or ***'Gojiingahara no Katakiuchi' ('The Vendetta at Gojiingahara')*** . . . ; or else a children's tale such as ***'Kanzan Jittoku' ('Han-shan and Shih-te')*** . . . , or ***'Sanshō-daiu'***. . . . In fact, if anything novel-like can be found in an Ōgai story, the reader is lucky. His works of fiction appear to be stories that failed to be stories. ***'Maihime'*** and ***Gan ('The Wild Goose')*** . . . are perhaps the only exceptions. These two pieces, with their recognizable plots, have been far more popular than any other novels or stories by Ōgai and have been referred to as his masterpieces. But Ōgai himself did not value the popular elements of love and romance in these works very highly. And if Ōgai had nothing else to offer than the love stories of ***'Maihime'*** and ***Gan,*** then Uchida Roan was surely correct in ranking him as a second-rate novelist.

The lack of 'novelistic' interest is not the only difficulty in Ōgai's fiction. The reader may also be put off by the didactic and pedantic manner in which Ōgai tells his stories, by the unreadable *kanji,* the long names and official titles, the foreign words that crop up constantly, the display of all sorts of bookish knowledge, the endless self-indulgent references to his own personal life, and, worst of all, the tedious moralizing. Even an apologist such as Kinoshita Mokutarō, 1885-1945, had to admit that some of Ōgai's stories contain elements of sermonizing (*odangi*). And then, after all that bragging and preaching, the story usually appears devoid of significant content. The reader would seem justified in concluding that Ōgai either is making a fool of him or is a fool himself.

Despite such negative features, however, many people, including a number of literary figures, have found that Ōgai's stories make a strong impression on them. Discussing ***'Gojungahara no Katakiuchi',*** Saitō Mokichi, 1882-1953, noted that emanating from the pages of what seemed to be a mere narration of historical facts was a 'heart-heat'. Speaking of the character of Chūsai's wife, Oio-san, in ***'Shibue Chūsai',*** 1916, Kinoshita remarked that Ōgai had achieved what was termed in Chinese painting 'transmission of spirit'.

The vast majority of Ōgai's admirers have found it difficult to define just what this ineffable 'heart-heat' or 'transmission of spirit' is or wherein lies its source. The one critic to elucidate with some precision the origin of the mysterious impression left by Ōgai's stories is Mishima. In so doing Mishima also provides sharp insight into the nature of Ōgai's craft as a writer. Mishima writes, 'In a short story, the theme or moral tends to stand out too conspicuously. A well-written short story often has this flaw. Ōgai's short stories, however, are scarcely troubled by this problem. . . . His narrative style is placid and the reader feels as if he is reading a catalogue. A while after finishing the story, however, he begins to recognize its awesome theme, which grows increasingly clear to him.'

To illustrate his point, Mishima uses the example of ***'Hyakumonogatari' ('The Hundred Tales')*** . . . , a story about a party given by a millionaire named Shikamaya, at which a hundred people are supposed to tell a ghost story, each in a setting appropriate to the event.

> In an Ōgai story, there are many useless elements which serve his purpose. For instance, he may interrupt his narration without warning and begin a long, pedantic lecture instead. Such an insertion is clearly out of balance with the rest of the story. Suppose one is going to write a twenty-page story. One typically first lays out a plan: two pages for introduction, three pages for introduction of characters, one page for description of the scene, two pages of psychological analysis, three pages of conversation, seven pages for the climax, etc. . . .
>
> Ōgai never wrote his stories in this manner. The narrative of ***'Hyakumonogatari',*** for example, may be regarded as 'useless' from beginning to end. As early as the seventh line from the beginning, Ōgai interrupts his narration, saying, 'I understand that one should not explain things in a piece of fiction, but self-indulgence is our common fault. . . .' This is truly outrageous. This is followed by the explanation of the background of the man named Shitomi, who invited the narrator to the event; this also has nothing to do with the main line of the story. At length, the narrator reaches the inn where the guests are to rendezvous. But he is still giving a sarcastic comment on the word *shoken* ('reading'); the reader begins to grow impatient, wondering when Ōgai is going to tell the main part of the story.
>
> Finally, the narrator arrives at the house where the party takes place, but by then the story is half-over, and it ends abruptly when he goes home without waiting for the beginning of Thc Hundred Tales. The ghost stories have been postponed. The reader is dumbfounded, but, after finishing the story, he suddenly begins to see its awesome theme, which soon overwhelms him. He realizes that the host, Shikamaya, was the ghost of boredom. Such an acrobatic way of telling a story is not something anyone can imitate; such a long-lasting, dark impression is not something any writer can create. . . .

Ōgai's technique as explained by Mishima may be compared with that used by painters such as Archimboldo or Salvador Dali. At first glance, a picture seems to be a mere sketch of a peaceful countryside—a field with some trees, gentle lines of hills in the background, and some clouds in the sky above. As the viewer ponders it, however, he experiences a strange sensation. The disturbing feeling grows increasingly distinct, and when the viewer is finally able to name it as something resembling the uneasiness felt in the presence of large animals, he suddenly recognizes the humpbacked camel formed by the clouds in the sky; the hills are in the shape of an angry giant whale, while a fleeing weasel is drawn by the lines of the branches of the trees. The picture now begins to tell a fantastic story which the viewer had hardly imagined an instant before.

In the introduction to ***Vita Sexualis,*** . . . Ōgai seems to have explained his artistic method as something comparable to this hidden-picture technique. Describing the style adopted by the protagonist, Kanai Shizuka, a professor of philosophy, in his lectures, Ōgai writes,

> In his lectures he seeks communication through immediate perception, occasionally casting an intense light on something. On such an occasion his listeners receive an indelible impression. They are startled into comprehension, realizing that he has explained something while talking about another matter entirely unrelated to it, something which has nothing to do with it. Schopenhauer, I understand, kept notes of various current events reported in the newspapers and used them as materials for his philosophical discussions. Dr Kanai uses everything and anything for his lectures on the history of philosophy. While giving a serious lecture, he may quote, for instance, from some novels currently popular among young people, much to the surprise of his students.

In writing the novel which follows on this introductory remark, Ōgai experimented with just such a narrative technique. For the framework of ***Vita Sexualis*** he adopted the style of 'novels currently popular among young people', namely, the *shizenshugi shishōsetsu,* or the Naturalist I-novel, which had rapidly gained popularity after the publication of Tayama Katai's *Futon* ('The Quilt') in 1907. Ōgai tells his readers that Dr Kanai has noted the success of this confessional mode in which the author writes about his own personal life with particular attention to sexual matters: 'A great many authors have appeared at the same time and started to write much the same thing; the critics acknowledge it as the truth of life.' Observing this phenomenon, Dr Kanai 'thought that he might take this opportunity to write the history of his own sexual desire. He realized that he had never really considered how his own sexual desire had emerged and developed, and decided that he would think about it and write it down.'

With this introduction by Ōgai, Dr Kanai begins to tell in the first person various incidents which occurred in his childhood and early youth. The reader is expected to identify the narrator, Dr Kanai, as the author Ōgai himself, only transparently fictionalized, and to follow Dr Kanai's account with the pleasure of peeking into the personal life of the famous author/surgeon-general, easily locating each situation in the story in such and such period of Ōgai's life, and identifying each character as such and such person around Ōgai.

'I was six,' Dr Kanai begins. 'I lived in the castle town of a certain minor daimyo in Chūgoku. After the abolition of the domains, the new prefectural capital was established in the adjoining region and our castle town rapidly became deserted. My father stayed in Tokyo with his lord. . . . My father was only a *kachi* [samurai of low rank], but we lived in at least a samurai house with a formal gate surrounded by earthen walls. . . .

The reader presumably knows that Ōgai was born in the small castle town of Tsuwano in Chūgoku and that his father was a domain doctor, a peripheral member of the local samurai society. As the narrative proceeds, the reader is confirmed in his assumption that Ōgai is telling about his own life. Dr Kanai moves to Tokyo at the age of eleven and lives in Mukōjima. At thirteen he enters the Tokyo English School, which corresponds to the Tokyo Medical School attended by Ōgai; he advances to the university at sixteen and graduates from it at nineteen. Ōgai's friends appear in the story with easily decipherable pseudonyms, such as Koga Kokusuke (Kako Tsurudo), Waniguchi Gen (Taniguchi Ken), Kojima Jūnirō (Ogata Shūjirō), and Bitō Eiichi (Itō Magoichi).

However, as he follows the development of Ōgai's 'I-novel', the reader gradually begins to feel disappointed because the experiences to which Dr Kanai confesses seem largely anticlimatic. For each year of his childhood and early youth, Dr Kanai relates one or two episodes. These events may be somehow associated with sexual matters, such as the boy's accidental encounters with pornography or his overhearing some sexual jokes, but by no means are they particularly interesting. Their account can hardly be regarded as a confession of the naked truth of life appreciated by the *shizenshugi* writers. And most of the episodes seem only remotely related, if at all, to anything sexual. Indeed, Dr Kanai declares chapter after chapter that he did *not* feel sexual desire and thus has nothing significant to mention concerning his sexual life. At long last, after the chapter 'I Turned Twenty-one . . .', he stops. The author Ōgai comes into the story again to explain what is happening to Dr Kanai. Ōgai writes:

Ōgai in 1916. From Mori Ōgai and the Modernization of Japanese Culture, *by Richard John Bowring. Cambridge University Press, 1979. Reprinted by permission of Cambridge University Press.*

> When he put down his pen for a moment to think, he began to suspect that to write about that unnecessary bumping, haphazardly repeated, might be meaningless. . . . Dr Kanai did not want to write something which had no artistic value. . . . There cannot be passion in sexual desire without love, and a subject about which one does not feel passion is not appropriate for an autobiographical narration. Even Dr Kanai could not help recognizing this. He resolutely made up his mind to abandon his story. . . .

The reader is, of course, put out to hear Ōgai make such a statement at this point. However, he has only himself to blame. Ōgai made it clear at the beginning that Dr Kanai did not think highly of the *shishōsetsu* that he set out to imitate.

> Dr Kanai reads much fiction. When he reads newspapers and magazines, he does not care for the editorials and articles, but goes straight to the fiction section. If the authors knew why he wanted to read their works, however, they would be upset. He does not read them as works

> of art. He has particularly high demands regarding the quality of works of art, and the kind of *shōsetsu* that one finds everywhere these days does not satisfy his standards. He is simply interested in the psychological states of the authors in writing their stories. When an author believes what he has written is sad or tragic, Dr Kanai may find it extremely funny; when the author thinks that he is writing a comic story, Dr Kanai may feel sad.

Dr Kanai observes that when he read the works of Mr Natsume Kinnosuke (Sōseki), he felt his arms twitch, that is, he was anxious to compete with him; but the novels of the *shizenshugi* school did not make his arms twitch particularly, although he was very curious about these works. He also raises a question about the claims of the *shizenshugi* authors to write the truth of life, wondering whether he might be the only person in Japan who has failed to see this 'truth of life'.

Given Dr Kanai's low opinion of the *shishōsetsu,* there is no reason why his own work should be any better. But while mocking the reader in this way, Ōgai also reminds him of the warning given in the introduction that Dr Kanai might tell 'something' while talking about another matter which has nothing to do with it. On the last page, after making Dr Kanai state that what he has narrated so far is quite useless, Ōgai remarks that Dr Kanai's passion may look dead on the surface, but, 'Although the poles of the earth may be covered with eternal ice, a raging fire, which may thrust up in a volcanic eruption, burns below.'

Is there a fiery lava rumbling deep below the dead surface of the I-novel of ***Vita Sexualis***? Has Ōgai indeed told 'another' story in the course of writing his anticlimatic *shishōsetsu*? In fact, while on one level Ōgai parodies the confessional style of the *shizenshugi* writers with a story about Dr Kanai's evident lack of passion, he simultaneously engages in an exploration of the inner depths of his protagonist's sexual psychology. Ōgai gives notice of the direction of this exploration in the clinical title of his novel. '*Vita sexualis*' was the term used by Richard von Krafft-Ebing to describe the case studies of various sorts of sexual anomalies contained in his *Psychopathic Sexualis,* 1886.

As a medical student in Berlin, more than twenty years before he published ***Vita Sexualis,*** Ōgai had read Krafft-Ebing's *Psychopathia Sexualis*. He continued his studies of sexual psychology after returning to Japan, reading recent European publications on the subject. In a two-part article published in 1902-1903, he quoted more than fifty European scholars of sexual psychology and discussed, among other things, Sigmund Freud's new theory of psychoanalysis, introducing some of the repercussions it had caused among European scholars. . . . Ōgai regarded Freud's thesis as a hypothesis yet to be proven and quoted European opinions both for and against it. He had reservations about Freud's view that the repression of sexual desire necessarily leads to psychological problems. However, there is no doubt that Ōgai understood Freud's idea that sexual desire is reflected in the subconscious, and that visions and dreams which do not make rational sense may reveal matters of great significance on the deeper level of a person's psychological life.

In relating the story that lies below the banal surface of ***Vita Sexualis*** Ōgai makes double use of these Freudian notions. In light of his knowledge about human sexual psychology, Dr Kanai strongly suspects that he might be 'anomalous' and sexually frigid. It is for the purpose of knowing whether this suspicion is valid or not that he wants to write his own *vita sexualis*. (pp. 223-29)

There is no ambiguity that the 'serious lecture' Dr Kanai is going to give concerns his own *vita sexualis,* the history of his sexual desire studied objectively from the medical point of view, and that this *vita sexualis* may not be fully congruent with the surface reality of his life.

Ōgai, however, did not intend his ***Vita Sexualis*** to be simply a clinical record. He has Dr Kanai make derogatory remarks not only about the claim of the *shizenshugi* writers to pursue the truth of life when in fact they did not, but also about the artistic mediocrity of their works. For Ōgai art was something universally valid, something endowed with the power to touch its audience on the deepest level of human existence. To attain these standards, a writer had to have full command of such professional skills as the use of the conventional language of symbols, allegory, and allusion, and be familiar with the achievements of past masters. A person could not create a work of art by recording at random the facts about his own personal life, as advocated by the *shizenshugi* writers. In ***Vita Sexualis,*** Ōgai aimed to write something that would satisfy these high standards as to what constitutes a work of art as well as being a scientifically accurate analysis.

In ***'Chinmoku no Tō' ('The Tower of Silence'),*** . . . a short story that Ōgai wrote in protest of the government's ban on ***Vita Sexualis,*** he explains some of the implications of the artistic method that he sought to use in ***Vita Sexualis.*** He writes,

> The domain of arts has been expanding from the ideas on the surface of one's consciousness to the impulses hidden at the bottom of one's subconscious. Just as in recent painting colors are mixed indistinguishably and in current music indistinct feelings are expressed by chromatic modulations, in literature writers try to express their impressions in sentences, exploring their impulses, and when they do so, their sexual impulses are necessarily revealed.

What Ōgai refers to here is the theory of impressionism underlying Monet's paintings and Debussy's music, and the possibility of applying the same method to the writing of fiction. The central idea of impressionism is to cease delineating a distinct theme or making a statement in a work of art, and instead to express in toto certain psychological states of the artist which represent a more integral truth at the deeper level of his life. In ***Vita Sexualis*** Ōgai seeks to apply Monet's technique of painting, to leave some shapeless but intense impressions on the reader's psyche, just as Monet's painting of the cathedral in the sun has an indefinable but brilliant effect on the viewer. However, acting not only as an impressionist artist but also as a sexual psychologist familiar with the subconscious meaning of the language of symbols, Ōgai also sets out to organize the impressions he presents to his readers in such a way as to produce a calculated effect.

Vita Sexualis thus has a trifold structure. On the most immediate level it is a commentary on the current sad state of literature in Japan in the form of a parody of an I-novel. Simultaneously it is an exploration of human sexual psychology at a depth not ventured by the *shizenshugi* authors for all their efforts at 'raw confession'. And this analysis of the protagonist's psychology is carried out and raised to the level of art by means of an impressionistic presentation of a series of related images. (pp. 229-30)

> *Yoshiyuki Nakai, "Ōgai's Craft: Literary Techniques and Themes in 'Vita Sexualis'," in* Monumenta Nipponica, *Vol. XXXV, No. 2, Summer, 1980, pp. 223-39.*

ADDITIONAL BIBLIOGRAPHY

Izumi, Hasegawa. "Mori Ōgai." *Japan Quarterly* XII, No. 2 (April-June 1965): 237-44.

Biographical essay detailing Ōgai's literary, military, and medical careers, and providing pertinent background material on Japanese culture of the period.

Jansen, Marius B., ed. *Changing Japanese Attitudes toward Modernization*. Princeton: Princeton University Press, 1965, 546 p.

A publication of the first Conference on Modern Japan of the Association for Asian Studies. Ōgai is mentioned throughout. The purpose of this conference was "to become freshly aware of the complexity of interrelationships between elements of 'tradition,' imported and indigenous, as they changed during the period of modernization."

Nakai, Yoshiyuki. "Mori Ōgai's German Trilogy: A Japanese Parody of *Les contes d'Hoffmann*." *Harvard Journal of Asiatic Studies* 38, No. 2 (December 1978): 381-422.

In-depth discussion of Ōgai's German trilogy—"The Girl Who Danced," "Utakata no ki," and "The Courier"—as a parody of the three acts of the French opera *Les contes d'Hoffmann* by Jacques Offenbach.

———. "Mori Ōgai: The State of the Field." *Monumenta Nipponica* XXXV, No. 1 (Spring 1980): 99-106.

Discusses the reasons for Ōgai's popularity and reviews Richard John Bowring's book *Mori Ōgai and the Modernization of Japanese Culture*.

Rimer, J. Thomas. *Mori Ōgai*. Boston: Twayne Publishers, 1975, 135 p.

Biographical and critical study.

———. "Nagai Kafū and Mori Ōgai: The Past versus the Present—*The River Sumida* and *Sanshō the Steward*." In his *Modern Japanese Fiction and Its Traditions: An Introduction*, pp. 138-61. Princeton: Princeton University Press, 1978.

Compares Ōgai and Kafū as members of a generation of Japanese authors whose exposure to European society influenced their individual literary careers as well as the general course of Japanese literature.

Swann, Thomas E. "The Problem of 'Utakata no Ki'." *Monumenta Nipponica* XXIX, No. 3 (Autumn 1974): 263-81.

Examines this early story written soon after Ōgai's return from Germany. The critic summarizes "Utakata no ki" as "a striking work combining a story of romantic love and tragedy with a complex theme that expresses the Romantic view of perfect art."

Émile Nelligan

1879-1941

French Canadian poet.

Nelligan is considered by many critics to be Canada's first major poet. An heir to the poetic legacy of Charles Baudelaire and Arthur Rimbaud, he is credited with introducing the ideology and techniques of French Symbolism to the conservative literary community of Montreal, which still clung to the mid-nineteenth century Romanticism of Victor Hugo and Alfred de Vigny. Although Nelligan has had a profound impact on French-Canadian poetry, problems with translating his poetic forms and imagery have caused him to remain relatively unknown to the English-speaking world.

Nelligan was born in Montreal, Quebec, to an Irish father and a French-Canadian mother. From his mother, who was a moderately accomplished singer and pianist, Nelligan inherited a deep sensitivity for music, and commentators attribute the strong rhythmic and lyrical quality of his verse to this early influence. As a boy, Nelligan was a voracious reader of French poetry and had a particular fondness for the work of Baudelaire and Paul Verlaine. An unenthusiastic student at the Jesuit college he attended, Nelligan dropped out of school in 1896 at the age of seventeen. It was at this time that he committed his life to writing poetry, and the next three years were devoted to intense poetic activity. All of his important poetry was written in this period.

During 1898 and 1899, Nelligan occasionally attended meetings of the École littéraire du Montréal (the Literary School of Montreal), which was composed of an enthusiastic group of young writers dedicated to reforming French-Canadian intellectual life and literature. Quebec society at that time was characterized by a repressive parochialism. To a large extent, the social and political environment of nineteenth-century Quebec was determined by a strong bond between the provincial government and the Catholic Church. Termed a "theocratic establishment," this alliance of power very effectively circumscribed forms of behavior and the intellectual life of the province well into the twentieth century, fostering that sense of desperation and solitude which critics find reflected in much French-Canadian writing. The École littéraire du Montréal was one of several groups that sought to circumvent the repressive nature of Quebec society through assimilating European artistic and intellectual influences. Nelligan was the École's youngest member, and although he was unknown to general readers and most of Montreal's literary community, he was regarded by many members of the École as that group's most talented and promising poet. In fact, the only moment of public recognition that he received during his career occurred at a meeting of the École in May 1899. Nelligan read "La romance du vin" ("The Poet's Wine"), a turbulent and defiant poem that addressed the plight of the French-Canadian artist, for which he was given a standing ovation and escorted home by his audience of fellow poets.

Despite the acclaim of his peers, Nelligan became more alienated from the world around him; and during his three year creative period, his personality, which had always been extremely neurotic, grew increasingly disturbed. Aware of his

Les Editions Fides

own impending mental collapse, Nelligan continued to obsessively devote himself to poetry. He once remarked, "I shall go mad like Baudelaire." Three months after his triumphant reading at the École, Nelligan lapsed into a catatonic state. Diagnosed as schizophrenic, he was committed to a mental institution, where he remained in a hopelessly withdrawn state until his death forty years later.

Although a few of Nelligan's poems appeared in Montreal literary magazines while he was still writing, his work was not collected and published in book form until after his hospitalization, when his friend Louis Dantin edited *Émile Nelligan et son oeuvre,* which appeared in 1903. From this collection Dantin omitted any of Nelligan's poems that he considered too despairing or controversial. It is believed that some of the poems Dantin rejected for publication were lost or destroyed, although a 1952 edition of the *Poésies complètes* included many poems that were not included in Dantin's collection.

Nelligan is considered a master of French prosody whose work artfully combines the aspirations of the French Symbolist poets—who sought to evoke indirectly and symbolically a realm of mood or feeling beyond the material world of the five senses—with the adherence of the French Parnassian poets to fixed poetic and metric forms. Like the Symbolist poet Rimbaud, with whom he is often compared, Nelligan attempted to create a personal myth of his despair, burgeoning madness, and inability to adapt to an imperfect world. Utilizing vivid dream imagery, his poems are often lyrical complaints on the inequities of society, the impermanence of human life, and the ultimate reality of death. The most common symbolic element of Nelligan's work is the dream landscape, which consists of images from nature that form pictorial analogies of the poet's consciousness and thereby enable the reader to experience more effectively the poet's interior world. These dream landscapes are often modeled after the northern Canadian terrain, where the brutal extremes of darkness and cold seemed to correspond with the emotional isolation and spiritual desolation Nelligan experienced as an artist alienated from his society. A prominent device employed by the poet to convey this imagery is that of viewing a landscape through a window, which emphasizes both his inner distance and his separation from the exterior world. This alienation is also reflected in the consistent use of images that demonstrate his fear of and fascination with death. In numerous poems the grandeur of death is exalted by the isolated poet who has no proper place in society, and whose longing for death is often compared to longing for a happier past. Critics note Nelligan's preoccupation with morbid themes as evidence of his strong death wish, and often discuss this in conjunction with his decades of madness, or living death. Nelligan's obsession with death and madness has in turn assumed the level of a national myth in French Canada among later generations of poets fascinated with his work and the example of his troubled life.

On the basis of slightly less than two hundred poems, Nelligan has been credited with modernizing French-Canadian literature. His work had a profound effect on the poetry being written in his day, which, as Gerard Tougas remarked, "had been lagging at least a generation behind French and European taste." Nelligan accomplished this by breaking away from the traditional themes of Canadian poetry—Canadian history and domestic life—to incorporate the cosmopolitan French influences of Symbolism and the modern preoccupation with individual consciousness. For this reason he is widely considered the most influential figure in twentieth-century French-Canadian poetry.

PRINCIPAL WORKS

Émile Nelligan et son oeuvre (poetry) 1903
Poésies complètes: 1896-1899 (poetry) 1952
Selected Poems (poetry) 1960

Translated selections of Nelligan's poetry have appeared in *A Century of Canadian Literature*, *The Oxford Book of Canadian Verse in English and French*, and *The Poetry of French Canada in Translation*.

E. K. BROWN (essay date 1930)

[In the following excerpt, Brown discusses the two dimensions of Nelligan's isolation: his neglect by the Montreal literary milieu and his increasingly severe psychological withdrawal.]

[Nelligan's] life has been almost ideally tragic. Too proud to submit to any kind of manual or clerical work, derided and neglected by the pretentious mutual-admiration societies of literati in Montreal, he got his food from garbage-cans and slept where he could. One must not blame too bitterly the poets who rejected him. For them the acme of poetry was the romanticism of Victor Hugo, muscular and brilliant, or the demi-romanticism of Lamartine, or, which was even more threatening to Emile Nelligan, the stiff glittering pomp of the Abbé Delille. Nelligan was a precursor of a new poetic movement fatal to all the things his Canadian contemporaries held dear, a *confrère* of Rimbaud, and Francis Jammes and Verlaine. Isolated and obdurately refusing to conform, he went from neurosis to neurosis, from megalomania to a destructive mania of persecution: he was quite conscious of his plight, of the path he trod and of the place to which it led: and at eighteen he arrived at the end of his path and passed behind the doors of an asylum and there, after thirty years, he still is. (pp. 724-25)

The poetry of Nelligan is as slight in texture and content as in quantity. It has two principal values,—as a passionate record of the phases in his mental collapse and as a no less passionate record of his very delicate and bizarre perceptions of external objects. The autobiography of Nelligan is simple and tragic. He was aware that to retain or retrieve his sanity he required cordial effective contacts with other people and other things, contacts which should let into his packed, strained mind sun and air and common sights and concepts. He was also aware that he was disqualified for these salutary contacts by that very fullness and tension that they should relieve. He saw himself imprisoned more and more tightly in his own mad self and he acquired little by little a pensive pride in his prison. There could be but one end for such a history; as he himself wrote, his mind a sombré dans l'abime du Reve ["foundered in the abyss of dream"].

His impressions of external things resemble those of his French contemporaries: the thing is perceived sideways, as it were, and at one incalculably rapid glance and is almost at once submerged by curious and often factitious but never vacuous associations. The value of the thing, the value of the instantaneous perception of the thing, are but incidental: the genuine, supreme value is in the complex of associations. (pp. 725-26)

E. K. Brown, "The Claims of French-Canadian Poetry," in Queen's Quarterly, *Vol. XXXVII, Autumn, 1930, pp. 724-31.**

LOUIS DUDEK (essay date 1943)

[Dudek is a Canadian poet and critic who was a central figure in the Canadian poetry revival in Montreal during the 1940s, a period in which the Canadian literary scene saw the emergence of many new, innovative poetic voices and the founding of many literary magazines and small presses. Dudek's verse is marked by keen insight and acerbic, somewhat cynical, commentary on modern society. He has long been regarded as an astute judge of literary talent in Canada and has edited several important anthologies of Canadian poetry. In the following excerpt, Dudek assesses Nelligan's importance in French-Canadian poetry and concludes that his intensely emotional and poetic imagination was inseparable from his mental instability.]

Emile Nelligan had genius: extreme emotional sensitivity, a fine feeling for sounding words, and an absorbing imagination. His images are not separate and striking metaphors, as in much of modern poetry; they are symbolic perceptions in which the whole poem is absorbed. . . . Their explicit lyricism is more than lyricism: it is heavy with poetic perception, because the same visionary perception fills every lyrical image. There is nothing like this among our English Canadian poets.

It is usually argued about a poet like Nelligan that he might have reached "great heights" had he come to maturity as a poet. Keats, for example. But perhaps this speculation is unfounded. An organic disease of this kind which destroys the mind is in itself a cycle, producing extreme sensibility, imagination, suffering: these reached maturity and power, as Nelligan approached his end. They produced the greatness which is in his poetry. Had he been a normal man, he would not have written these poems.

His work, however, is highly subjective, traditional in its technical forms, and growing out of an inner psychology rather than environment and culture. It is also immune to ideas; they are irrelevant to the poetry. But we do not demand more from Nelligan: this only delimits the quality of his poetry. (p. 20)

Louis Dudek, "Three Translations from Emile Nelligan," in First Statement, *Vol. 2, No. 3, October, 1943, pp. 18-20.*

R. CHAUVIN (essay date 1949)

[In the following excerpt, Chauvin discusses Nelligan's association with the Literary School of Montreal. He stresses the influence of the French Symbolists and Parnassians on Nelligan and his generation of French-Canadian poets and contends that Nelligan should be just as important an influence on the next generation of French-Canadian poets.]

The nineties were gay days in Montreal. Poetry made more rapid advances then in ten years than it has since in twenty. Enthusiasm for art was widespread and of the better sort: it aimed at production. Student writers began to meet and discuss. The group grew and, typical of French Canada, organized itself into a society. It was called the Literary School of Montreal. . . .

This school professed no common dogma; rather, its members (Louvigny de Montigny, Charles Gill, Jean Charbonneau, Albert Lozeau) were agreed solely on reaction to the earlier Patriotic School of Quebec. This reaction sprang, of course, from boredom, but also from the discovery of new sources of inspiration. The Quebec poets of 1860 had been disciples of Hugo or Lamartine; in 1895 Montrealers followed Baudelaire, Verlaine, Hérédia. As Canadians seem to be born imitators, at that time as always, change in taste was accompanied by change in style.

Organization frequently hinders intellectual activity—especially literary discussion with a creative end. At any rate, the School of Montreal disbanded after only five years. . . . The school, however, had stirred many ambitions and experienced proud successes—especially so on the night its youngest but most gifted member, Emile Nelligan, had read aloud in Ramezay his **"Romance du vin."**

Opposition to the new school was fierce. Admirers of Hugo, Crémazie and Fréchette criticized the younger poets in print, and bitterly. This **"Romance du vin"** might be considered a species of "credo": it conveys the school's ideal, its passion for art (sometimes carried to art for art's sake), and Nelligan himself, his incurable sadness, despair, hate of the bourgeois. Nelligan's reading of the poem met with an ovation, a rare thing indeed for French Canada.

But the school ceased meeting only six months later, and Nelligan himself was to disappear shortly. Maladjustment had reached a peak. He had already abandoned his B.A. course, was loth to apply for any work, and lived for the day when his poems would be published in Paris and would startle his own country into admiration. He shut himself up in his room and there, like another youthful poet, Rimbaud, fell prey to apocalyptic visions. Moral suffering deliberately cultivated led to madness. Nelligan's career ends at the age of twenty-one.

His poems were collected, prefaced and published by the critic, Louis Dantin. . . . Dantin published only those poems he personally esteemed worthy of Nelligan. Today many of us regret this choice. Dantin excluded from his edition, for instance, Nelligan's last poems, remarkable for their tragic imagery. (p. 277)

[Nelligan's poems] are typical of the Literary School inasmuch as they are lyrical and influenced by French Parnassians and Symbolists. As a matter of fact, Nelligan blended rather uniquely music and symbol with Parnassian rigidity of form. For style, vigor and intensity they are undoubtedly the school's best.

Nelligan was born . . . of an Irish-Canadian father and a French-Canadian mother—a mixture comparable only to a hasty concoction of whiskey and wine. Nelligan's nature was just as fiery. He was inclined to spleen, nostalgia and despair, but he gave the spur to them for literary purposes. With true Irish passion he made of poetry life itself, not its epiphenomenon. This process, of course, proved fatal. Dantin informs us that Nelligan often stated: "I will go mad . . . like Baudelaire."

Precocious reading shaped Nelligan's character. However, this morbidity cannot be reckoned as wholly literary. Nelligan felt truly the grandeur and nakedness of death. Unrequited love, extreme maladjustment to society and ailing introversion accentuated his longing for the beyond—which, characteristically, Nelligan imagines suffused with sweet Cecilia's music.

None of this hints at the child in Nelligan. But Nelligan *is* adolescence typified, in its excesses as in its flashes of depth: his idealistic love, his tender filial devotion, his terrestrial or imaginative notion of the beyond. Nelligan's poetry is never light or even gay, but the reader catches in the midst of despairs, hates and nostalgias, glimpses of an innocence and candor as touching as Rimbaud's. The reader is then deeply moved, for he has Nelligan's own tragedy, that of having been unable to reconcile his own purity with the lesser purity of our world. . . . (pp. 277-78)

Nelligan cared little for ideas. His poems are packed with emotion and imagery. It is this quality which makes him stand out among Canadian poets. However, had Nelligan cultivated ideas as carefully as he did emotions, he might have arrived at a wider scope. He falls short of sustained tension, the depth and unflinching originality of Baudelaire, or of the vastness of Rimbaud. Nevertheless, for impeccability of form and compactness of poetic matter, Nelligan deserves a place in an anthology of the best French-speaking poets. . . .

I do believe that Nelligan made an important contribution to our country's literature. He was the most gifted of French Canada's poets. He is one of our chosen few who can be entrusted in the hands of the young for the development of poetic taste. (p. 278)

R. Chauvin, "Emile Nelligan," in The Canadian Forum, *Vol. XXVIII, No. 338, March, 1949, pp. 277-78.*

A.J.M. SMITH (essay date 1960)

[In the following excerpt, Smith provides a synopsis of Nelligan's brief literary career with emphasis on his innovative contributions to French-Canadian poetry.]

[Nelligan's] poetry, which introduced Baudelairism and Verlainism into the opening circles of the French-Canadian literary consciousness, was hailed with enthusiasm by the poets and critics of the Montreal School. . . . Technical virtuosity, aspirations of more than local scope, and a passionate, if feverish, sensibility combined to produce some of the finest poems ever written in Canada. A new, surprising, and, for French Canada, extremely salutary movement was being inaugurated at the moment it could be most useful, a movement that was at once aesthetic, passionate, cosmopolitan, and exotic, and that gave an immense impetus to the *other,* the non-native tradition in Canadian literature. It was later poets, however, Paul Morin and René Chopin particularly, who were to carry on the movement. Nelligan, like Chatterton or Rimbaud, was a marvellous boy, whose work was done before he reached twenty. In 1899 his mind collapsed, and though he did not die until 1941 he remained hopelessly insane, one of the most tragic figures in the history of North American letters. (pp. xl-xli)

A.J.M. Smith, in an introduction to The Oxford Book of Canadian Verse: In English and French, *edited by A.J.M. Smith, Oxford University Press, London, 1960, pp. xxiii-li.**

P. F. WIDDOWS (essay date 1960)

[In the following excerpt, Widdows discusses Nelligan's influences, themes, and poetic style.]

The happiness of [Nelligan's] childhood was one of the major themes of his poetry. His life contained two great crises: the first, when he lost that happiness and became a poet; the second, when he failed to find a substitute for it in adult life and was driven to despair and madness. (p. v)

It is sometimes said that [Nelligan's] poems are little more than pastiches of his favourite writers, and particularly of Verlaine and Rodenbach. Certainly he is not original in the sense that Rimbaud is original. He did not create a new language of poetry. But our ideas of what constitutes originality have been considerably modified in recent years. Research into the sources of, for example, Coleridge and Keats has shown far more obligation to other writers, on the conscious or unconscious level, than was usually suspected, and it has not lessened the value of these poets. . . . [A poet's] originality consists not in what he uses, but in how he uses it. If he allows himself to be dominated by what he remembers, he is imitative. If he uses what he remembers for his own purposes, absorbing, reshaping and transforming it . . . , the process can be a source of strength and enrichment. There are plenty of examples in Nelligan's poetry of excessive domination by his models. He had, after all, to serve his apprenticeship. (pp. vii-viii)

His range is admittedly a narrow one. His two principal themes are Regret, chiefly for the lost paradise of childhood, and the Ideal, the positive side of Regret. Subordinate to these are Le Rêve, a conception which is not clearly defined but which represents an escape from the disappointment of life, and La Névrose, again a nebulous but nevertheless an eloquent word for the anguish which resulted from the inadequacy of Le Rêve as a philosophy of life. Today he would perhaps have called it Angst or La Nausée. He is an almost entirely introspective poet. His rare outward-looking poems are not as successful as those in which he expresses, and thereby calms, his emotional torments. The only specimens of the objective type in this selection are **"Le Perroquet," "L'Idiote aux Cloches,"** and **"Le Fou."** His central theme of regret for lost childhood is not unique to him, but I do not know of any more immediate and passionate expression of it than his.

Passionate feeling, of course, is not enough to make a poet. The poet works with words. And with words Nelligan was well equipped. He has been compared, like all poets who started young and finished early, with Rimbaud. In general the comparison is absurd, but they did have this in common, that they both came to their tasks fully armed. Nelligan found the images and symbols to express his feelings and embodied them with unerring tact in the appropriate words, rhythms and rhymes. There is no sense of straining after effect. One has the impression of a technique waiting to translate the ideas without distortion into the language of art. This does not mean that he achieved his effects without working for them. The interested reader will find a good example of his sure feeling for words in a comparison between the earlier and later versions of **"Soirs d'Automne,"** where all the changes made are for the better.

It has often been remarked that his verse moves with a natural music. That is true, as can be seen conspicuously in **"Rêve d'Artiste," "Clair de Lune Intellectuel," "Le Jardin d'Antan,"** and **"Sérénade Triste."** He was also, as is not so often recognized, capable of writing poems of great force and power, for example **"Le Vaisseau d'Or," "Châteaux en Espagne,"** and **"La Vierge Noire"**; and capable of combining the two effects in an harmonious whole, as in **"Ruines," "Amour Immaculé"** and **"Devant le Feu."** He is also a poet of resounding and memorable lines; and memorableness is an important test of a poet. (pp. viii-ix)

P. F. Widdows, in an introduction to Selected Poems *by Émile Nelligan, translated by P. F. Widdows, The Ryerson Press, 1960, pp. v-xi.*

EDMUND WILSON (essay date 1965)

[Wilson, considered America's foremost man of letters in the twentieth century, wrote widely on cultural, historical, and literary matters, authoring several seminal critical studies. He is often credited with bringing an international perspective to American letters through his widely read discussions of European literature. Wilson was allied to no critical school: however, several dominant concerns serve as guiding motifs throughout his work. He invariably examined the social and historical implications of a work of literature, particularly literature's significance as "an attempt to give meaning to our experience" and its value for the improvement of humanity. Though not a moralist, his criticism displays a deep concern with moral values. Another constant was his discussion of a work of literature as a revelation of its author's personality. However, although Wilson examined the historical and psychological implications of a work of literature, he rarely did so at the expense of a discussion of its literary qualities. Perhaps Wilson's greatest contributions to American literature were his tireless promotion of writers of the 1920s, 1930s, and 1940s, and his essays introducing the best of modern literature to the general reader. In the following excerpt, Wilson calls Nelligan Canada's finest poet and discusses how several technical and thematic aspects of his work relate to the facts of his life.]

[Nelligan] is at once the Rimbaud and the Gérard de Nerval of French Canada, and he seems to me the only really first-rate Canadian poet, French or English, that I have yet read. . . . At school, the boy did poorly and failed to finish, yet his vocation as a poet was passionate and from his earliest years all-absorbing. His first poems were published when he was sixteen, in 1896, and he was soon the star of an École Littéraire in his native Montreal. He read all the then modern poets, and his work shows a variety of influences: Baudelaire, Verlaine,

Heredia. But he developed his own rich imagery and his own perfection of form, which make him, in the Canada of the end of the century, a quite unfamiliar phenomenon. He has nothing of the dilution and tepidity which were encouraged in the United States by the slack standards of our magazines. All his poems are full of point and close-packed; some are very complex. A virtuosity of meter, rhyme and assonance, a peculiar intensity and strength make something that is Nelligan's own out of even the Verlainean pathos or the metallic Heredian sonnet. In this poetry of stained glass, golden heavens and dawns that bathe the mountains in blood, of celestial visions as dazzling as the luxury of fabrics and gems, one almost loses sight of the milieu in which these brilliant pieces were created, and yet the chill sternness of that milieu lies behind these bright tapestries, in the background; it is suggested by the recurrent rhyme *givre-vivre* [''to cover with frost'' / ''to live''], which reminds one of the recurrent problem of survival in that paralyzing climate, and by the glimpses of family life, in which even the mother's piano, by whose music the boy is enchanted, cannot make him forget the lace curtains, the faded brocade and moire, all the dreary *''mobilier de deuil''* [''articles of mourning''], by which he finds himself surrounded. (pp. 97-8)

He speaks often of his *''névrose''* [''neurosis'']—once it is *''mes troupeaux de névroses''* [''flock of neuroses'']. Nor are his visions of madness mere exercises: the idiot woman who wants to find the church bells in order to hold them in her hands, the ''spectral bull,'' huge and red, *''aux cornes glauques''* [''with glaucous horns''], ''from which we must all flee.'' He had said to one of his friends, *''Je mourrai fou comme Baudelaire''* [''I shall die mad like Baudelaire'']. The *coup de grâce* seems to have been given him when his charming poem ***Le Perroquet*** was criticized by a visiting French journalist at a meeting of l'École Littéraire. At a subsequent meeting of this circle at the end of May, 1899, he recited ***La Romance du Vin,*** which involved a retort to this critic:

> C'est le règne du rire amer et de la rage
> De se savoir poète et l'objet du mépris,
> De se savoir un coeur et de n'être compris
> Que par le clair de lune et les grands soirs d'orage!

> [Kingship of the bitter laughter, and the rage
> Of knowing that one is a poet, pierced by scorn;
> Of being a heart and not understood, forlorn
> To all but the moon's night and thunder's equipage.
> (Translated by George Johnston)]

But he declares that he is full of gaiety and celebrates the ecstasy of his drunkenness.

> Serait-ce que je suis enfin heureux de vivre;
> Enfin mon coeur est-il guéri d'avoir aimé?
> Les cloches ont chanté; le vent du soir odore . . .
> Et pendant que le vin ruisselle à joyeux flots,
> Je suis si gai, si gai, dans mon rire sonore,
> Oh! si gai, que j'ai peur d'éclater en sanglots!

> [Not drunk either—that I'm happy to be alive?
> Has it at last been healed, my old wound of loving?
> The bells cease, and the evening scents follow after
> As the breeze takes them, and the wine rustles and throbs.
> I am more than gay, hear my resonant laughter!
> So gay, so gay, I am breaking into sobs.
> (Translated by George Johnston)]

One of the audience reported that *''les applaudissements prirent la fureur d'une ovation''* [''the applause incited the furor of an ovation''] and his comrades carried him home on their shoulders. Two months later, he was found kneeling and reciting his poems before a statue of the Virgin. He was evidently schizophrenic, and he spent the rest of his life in an institution. Under pressure of a constant struggle with a practical prosaic father who wanted him to be a clerk, he had been desperately concentrating his forces on preparing a volume of verse, which he did not retain his faculties to put into final shape. After his moment of public triumph, he suddenly short-circuited, burnt out and, tragically, became indifferent. For the reader, to come to the end of Nelligan's exciting poetry and to learn of the blankness that followed is like learning of the last years of Nizhinsky. . . . (pp. 99-100)

Edmund Wilson, ''Émile Nelligan,'' in his O Canada: An American's Notes on Canadian Culture, *Farrar, Straus and Giroux, 1965, pp. 97-101.*

GERARD TOUGAS (essay date 1966)

[In the following excerpt, Tougas discusses Nelligan's influence on French-Canadian poetry, emphasizing his assimilation of French verse traditions, his vivid imagery, and his technical accomplishments.]

In the history of French-Canadian literature very few poets can be compared with [Emile Nelligan]. For the spontaneity and quality of his imagery he remains unequalled.

The rapid spread of his reputation as a poet and the quality of the criticism which ensured for his name a place apart among French-Canadian poets, are not isolated phenomena having little relation to Nelligan's poetical work. (p. 73)

Of mixed ancestry . . . Nelligan soon recognized those contradictory attractions to which the adolescent sensibility is exposed. Besides this, aware of the superiority conferred on him by his multiple vision of the world, little by little he withdrew into his dreams, as much through contempt of the Philistines as through necessity. At a time when Fréchette was still writing poems inspired by Victor Hugo and Pamphile Lemay was writing Parnassian verse without being aware of it, here we have this school-boy discovering poets who reveal to him secrets that are *his* secrets: first Baudelaire, then Verlaine, Catulle Mendès, Georges Rodenbach. Melancholy by nature, Nelligan will always remain so, and will not have to go to the Parnassians and the Symbolists for subjects, although at the beginning he borrows from Parnassus. The marmoreal perfection of Parnassian verse echoed some intimate need of this soul tortured by an ideal and remains one of the characteristic features of its brief poetic flight. As early as June of 1897 Nelligan gave this proof of his virtuosity [in his poem **''Moines en Defilade''**]. . . . (pp. 73-4)

What an astounding sonnet for a seventeen-year-old poet! The imagery is not yet the visual creation of the poet that he will become in two years' time; a few lines too commonplace are the price of his inexperience. But the sharpness of the photographic image, the sensuous suggestiveness of the rhythm are undeniable. If the borrowings are obvious, so too is the originality. (p. 74)

Nelligan's poetic work, left in abeyance in mid-evolution, is of necessity only a suspicion of what it might have been. Dead to poetry at the age of nineteen, Nelligan had not yet had time to assimilate perfectly the poets who were his delight as a student. He is all the more remarkable since an original inspiration emerges from the borrowings and reminiscences of which his poetry is woven.

A Romantic in feeling, a Parnassian in form, a Symbolist in vocabulary, Nelligan in his best moments effects a fusion of these elements through his gift of imagery. His thought may be too thin, even empty at times, his prosody borrowed, his epithets often plucked from poets he revered—what difference does it make? He looks around him with keen and seeing eye and the image springs forth. . . .

As if by instinct he finds the right tone, the ideal cadence to make the setting for the delicate impressions of his ***Rêve de Watteau,*** he who has no knowledge of painting except through an intuitive vision. . . . (p. 75)

With the most astonishing facility Nelligan was able at the very beginning to master verse technique, whereas all the French-Canadian poets before him had always had a hard struggle with form. Certain poems of his are fireworks in which he merely exercises his virtuosity. When there is a meeting of the anguish within him and the music of his verse, the effect can be startling. . . . (pp. 75-6)

Nelligan was to exercise a lasting influence on French-Canadian poetry. Before him there had been hardly any variation in the choice of subjects. The history of French Canada, the joys of the home or of life in the fields, vague sadness in the style of René, these were about the only themes that a French-Canadian poet had been able to employ with confidence. Now Nelligan scorned the so-called Canadian subjects and found his inspiration in Symbolism. By the example of his genius he had proved that the authentic poet seeks his subjects according to rules known to himself alone and that these subjects attain value only through the magic of form. He was to be reproached for not having found his inspiration in Canada yet basically Nelligan is the most Canadian of poets. (p. 76)

Gerard Tougas, "The Modern Period (1900-1939)," in his History of French-Canadian Literature, *translated by Alta Lind Cook, second edition, The Ryerson Press, 1966, pp. 73-143.**

KATHY MEZEI (essay date 1979)

[*In the following excerpt, Mezei compares Nelligan's dream landscapes with those of Archibald Lampman, an English-speaking Canadian poet who was Nelligan's contemporary. In the work of both poets, dream landscapes were created as a retreat from the harsh reality of the outer world to a realm where the artist's inner reality could be expressed.*]

In 1899 the poetic careers of Archibald Lampman and Emile Nelligan ended; Lampman had died aged thirty-seven and Nelligan, at nineteen, had been admitted to the Retraite Saint-Benoît, one of the mental hospitals in which he remained until his death in 1941. Although it is doubtful that Lampman and Nelligan had ever heard of one another, their poetry was a response to [what Saint-Denys-Garneau called] 'ce manque d'air' ['the lack of air'] that pervaded their culture and personal lives, and to the haunting vision of a 'spectacle de la dance' ['spectacle of the dance'].

The two poets were writing in the period just after the excitement of Confederation. Both were urban malcontents longing for an ideal place where artists might live and love and work amid beautiful and congenial surroundings. While Nelligan raged against the sordid present, the night streets of the city, and yearned for the sacred gardens of the past—*les jardins d' antan*—Lampman condemned the corruption of modern life, Ottawa as the 'Dominion Cess-pool,' and idealized the 'comfort of the fields.' Nevertheless, in the Ottawa of the eighties and nineties, Lampman was able to participate in the Fabian Society, the Royal Society of Canada, the Ottawa Literary and Scientific Society, and the Audubon Society. . . . During the same period, Montreal, where Nelligan lived, had developed into a lively centre for writers and intellectuals interested in preserving the French heritage; Nelligan was invited to several gatherings of l'Ecole littéraire de Montréal, which was at its most intense and energetic phase in the 1890s. . . .On occassion Nelligan read his poems to l'Ecole and listened to discussions of the parnassian and symbolist movements in France.

Lampman's involvement with the Confederation poets, and Nelligan's with l'Ecole littéraire de Montréal, the two innovative and *engagé* ['engaged' (socially conscious)] Canadian literary movements of the day, and the vision presented in their poetry cast the two poets into the vanguard of modern French- and English-Canadian poetry. . . . Lampman's northern landscapes, socialist sympathies, and tone of longing and alienation, and Nelligan's painful and lyrical revelations of an enclosed and tormented soul have struck sympathetic chords in their successors. The clear, evocative, indigenous images in the natural landscapes painted by Lampman, and the eloquent verbal images of Nelligan's *paysage d'âme* ['landscape of the soul'] contain lessons of form and language for F.R. Scott, A.J.M. Smith, and Al Purdy, and for Saint-Denys-Garneau, Alain Grandbois, and Anne Hébert.

Lying at the periphery of British, American, and French cultures, and just at the threshold of their own, the two poets struggled to possess their place and language, to find a true tone and form, and to present the landscapes of their souls in images that sing of self and place. In the attempt to order their own troubled reality and create an appropriate form, they reverted to dream landscapes, and dream landscapes become the form within which they presented their sense of physical and spiritual place.

Although the landscapes and the relationship between landscape and dream differed in the two poets, their dreams often resembled one another. Their reasons for turning to dream landscapes were also similar. Both Nelligan and Lampman sensed that they were playing important roles as heralds of change in a country struggling to find itself culturally. Both Nelligan and Lampman were exceedingly sensitive to the arrows of reality shot at them by a harsh world, and sought a form in which to shelter and nurture a delicate sensibility. Dream landscapes provided, therefore, an objective framework within which the poet could express his inner state.

Trapped by the lack of a language to express their physical landscape, and hesitating to disclose openly their anxious souls, the two poets turned to this particular form, a form which appears to be far removed from reality but, in fact, carries one deeply into the poet's inner reality. Since the nature of dreams implies the immediacy, inevitability, and inseparability of images and thoughts, dream landscapes become pictoral analogies of the poet's inner world. Images in their poems are arranged so as to present either the topography of dreams as in Lampman's 'The Frost Elves' and 'A Vision of Twilight,' or a surrealistic, dreamlike vision of a natural landscape as in Nelligan's **'Rêve fantasque.'**

Unlike the English language, French makes distinctions between different kinds of dreams: 'rêve'—the night-dream in sleep, 'rêverie'—the act of day-dreaming, and 'songe'—half thought, half day-dream. It is reverie that most closely approximates the poetic process for, in both poems and dreams, truths, visions, and events are revealed through a hidden coherence of images that rise up as 'things.' Dreams and poems are symbolic manifestations of the poet's vision and activity of mind; their logic is the logic of symbols, of the visionary gleam, not of rational, orderly observation. (pp. 151-53)

In the symbolist poets, symbolic landscapes were essentially dream landscapes in which the reader follows a progression that is not logical but associative and, out of the unusual combination of images, reinforced by inverted syntax and bizarre juxtapositions of words, he is drawn into the poet's mental space. Symbolic landscapes were an appropriate mode for Nelligan who, in company with the French symbolists, created [according to Edward Engleberg]

> dreamscapes in which despair, a sense of loss and fear, hunger for beauty and release, and a horrible awareness of sullen leaden reality pervade their work. Such awareness will lead to dream, to nightmare, to seeing the beautiful in the ugly (and vice versa) to boredom, to fatigue—*and* to the magnificient visions that lie beyond the window pane.

Whereas Nelligan begins in dreams, and Lampman in landscapes, when they commence their poetic journeys, Nelligan weaves landscapes out of dreams and Lampman dreams out of landscapes.

Nelligan moves through dream into a landscape of his soul, a conventionalized landscape whose contours are shaped by Baudelaire and Verlaine, and the pastoral tradition. . . . Lampman, on the contrary, moves from the physical landscape to the realm of dreams, pausing at the threshold. . . . (pp. 153-54)

The two poets have different approaches to landscape. Lampman delighted in the details of landscape and sought to find the language of the place. In many poems he described the rolling Gatineau hills around Ottawa, creating pastoral scenes in which nature, like dream, was refuge, solace, and retreat from the bustle and strife of city life. (p. 154)

But observing and describing the natural landscape caused Lampman to fall into reverie and so many of his landscapes melt into dreams. . . . (p. 155)

His landscapes are *Edens d'or,* enclosed gardens, sheltered from nature and located in another realm, beyond reality. The wilderness that is both desolate country and the winter season is a fearful, not a creative solitude, inhabited by fierce wild beasts and gruesome spectres. Clearly, Nelligan's natural landscapes were drawn from literature, not from accurate observation of the country around him. . . . Nelligan on the other hand, viewed the natural landscape as something to be transcended. . . . His landscapes are generalized descriptions, seldom rooted in the blue Laurentians, the rolling countryside of the Eastern townships, or the topography of habitant villages along the St. Lawrence. In fact, his external landscapes are, for the most part, composed of artifacts—the reconstructed world of chapels, formal gardens, manor houses, monasteries, and trinkets. . . . Nelligan's focus being inward, nature, in the form of seasons, turbulent seas, enclosed gardens and bucolic landscapes, is called upon to furnish analogies for the state of the soul, but the objects described by Nelligan are not necessarily related to an external reality; they are intended to evoke an impression, a mood, a feeling of autumnal sadness. . . . This autumnal sadness, while poignant, seems nevertheless vague and literary and removed from any concrete, known landscape. Yet despite the echoes from his continental masters, Nelligan's poem has a sonorous roll of consonants and vowels that do arouse emotions in the reader. Notice, though, how Lampman in, for example, 'In November' focuses on details of the landscape, depressing the reader with his accumulation of bleak physical phenomena: 'black stumps and briers,' 'mulleins long since dead,' 'a silent and forsaken brood,' 'so gray, so haggard, and austere.' While the landscapes of the two poems are in stark contrast to one another, the effect is similar: a mood of sadness and loss is evoked.

Furthermore, although the kind and use of natural landscape differs in the two poets, their attitudes toward dream have much more in common. If one looks closely at the poems of Lampman and Nelligan, one is struck by the recurrence of the word 'dream' or 'rêve.' Lampman's confusing and varied use of 'dream' has already been explicated at great length, and generally condemned by critics. . . . By dream, Lampman variously meant: unreal, real, day-dream, night-dream, poetic imagining, meditation. His constant and changeable use of the word dilutes its impact. However, the most common meaning seems to imply a state or mood in which his imagination was allowed free rein, usually inspired by the solitude and beauty of nature. . . . Nelligan's 'rêve,' like Lampman's 'dream,' recurs with varying shades of meaning but generally Nelligan, too, seems to use it to suggest a state of poetic imagining or an escape from present time and place. . . . Both poets, therefore, make a clear association between the state of poetry and the nature of dreams. . . . Moreover, 'a great lyric poem is a thing which is written, if one may so to speak it, in a dream.' . . . (pp. 155-58)

Lampman (and Nelligan) dreamt in order to escape the harsh realities of work and life for, as Lampman said in the conclusion of 'The Frogs':

> Secure were we, content to dream with you
> That change and pain are shadows faint and fleet,
> And dreams are real, and life is only sweet. . . .

The reality of dreams, with the deliberate juxtaposition of 'dream' and 'real', is expressed in several other poems: 'In November,' 'Winter Hues Recalled' . . . there rose up, / Out of that magic well-stored picture house, / No dream, rather a thing most keenly real'), 'Winter-Thought' ('no longer dreams, but dear realities'). Dreaming appears to be, then, a state of poetic creation, desirable and necessary, firmly removed from the strictures of everyday material reality.

Nelligan, too, views dreams as a refuge from brutal reality. . . . But it is also true that Lampman, unlike Nelligan, was inspired to dream by the physical landscape that he so concretely portrayed; a landscape that has moods and 'communes' with him. (pp. 158-59)

The dream landscape that Lampman prefers is a utopian or visionary one. 'The Land of Pallas' is a socialist dream of a 'happy land where strife and care were dead,' and 'A Vision of Twlight' presents the landscape of a dreamlike city in a twilight time, through surreal images. . . . (p. 159)

Nelligan's dream visions, however, have little to do with social reality and political utopias although when they are optimistic, they bear the imprint of Catholic redemption. Both the poet's vision in **'Rêve d'une nuit d'hôpital'** and Alfus's in **'La Voix**

dans la vision' in Père Alfus' promise salvation and paradise if one's duty on earth is completed. . . . In contrast to Lampman who described the state of dreaming and the entry into dream, but rarely the dream itself, Nelligan habitually dwelt on and in dream landscapes. Out of his memories of childhood, he created nostalagic, idyllic gardens of delight, *jardins de rêve* [''dream gardens'']. . . . Given his background, Nelligan was haunted by Catholicism which pervaded his dreams through images of chapels, stained glass windows, The Virgin Mary, saints, monks, hallucinations of sin and death, and visions of hope and salvation. The enclosed world of dream, like the enclosed chapel fragrant with incense and illuminated by the colours and patterns of stained glass windows, and the enclosed garden of childhood, is a refuge, but a refuge that may disappoint or turn sinister and threatening. . . . In moments of despondency, his castles in Spain and his high desires and dreams crumble before the impurity of his soul. . . . Some of Nelligan's dream landscapes are fantasies, other projections of his despairing soul. (pp. 160-61)

Nelligan, like Lampman, carried the features of a natural landscape into some of his dreams. For example, in **'Rêve de Watteau,'** where Nelligan paints an idyllic scene, the composed and created landscape, like his natural landscapes, echoes the pastoral tradition. . . . Yet the poet merges himself completely into this dream through metaphorical language. . . . Although images of dawn and stars are hardly original, the poet achieves a fusion of natural phenomena with subjective feeling through the technique of symbolic, evocative language. The emphasis is on the resonance of language, not on the statement or idea. Nelligan, in contrast to Lampman, draws us into the landscapes of his dreams. . . . (p. 161)

When Nelligan retreats further and further into the self, these dream landscapes become the landscapes of a soul that he wishes to reveal to the reader: 'Je vous ouvrais mon coeur comme un basilique' ['I exposed my heart to you like a basilicon']. . . . But the soul opens out, not onto the remembered meadows and northlands of Lampman, but onto a desolate, haunted past. . . . Whereas, for Lampman, the separation between reality and dream was too distinct, Nelligan could not distinguish between them, and drowned in his dream and his dream of words. . . . (p. 162)

Certain images recur in these dream landscapes like archetypes that dominate dreams. The dream landscapes of the two poets are often 'composed of pools, caves, hollows, animals.' Pools, for example, attracted Nelligan; he enters a haunted world through a deep pool. . . . This deep, enclosed, and dark body of water that is an invitation to death reflects the poet's narcissistic death-wish. The penetration of the depths of a pool or the seas in which the persona drowns, as in **'Vaisseau d'or,'** is a symbolic penetration of the dark and forboding recesses of the subconscious. The dark pool is the dark antithesis of the green enclosed garden. It is also an inversion of the recurring vertical movement upward toward transcendence that structure many of Nelligan's poems.

Lampman is less attracted to fatal pools than to mysterious groves, which seem to correspond to the imaginative space of poetic creation. (pp. 162-63)

Through dream landscapes of utopian cities, infant days, and haunted houses, we enter the inner world of Lampman and Nelligan. The unusual images, surreal juxtapositions, and a-logical process of dreams that structure the dream landscape poems expose a hidden side of the poet's mind. Since the poet's inner world is so often chaotic and disturbed, dreams often become nightmares, and dream landscapes nightmare or savage landscapes, and both Lampman and Nelligan rise to their most eloquent heights in depicting macabre scenes. When the utopian vision fails, a sterile hell replaces golden Jerusalem as Lampman demonstrates in 'The City of the End of Things'. . . . Nelligan, when possessed by a black vision of the universe, also inverts his pastoral world into a scene of death and destruction, wreaked by a monstrous beast. . . . (p. 163)

But Nelligan reveals a more grotesque nightmare world than Lampman; phantoms of death, madness, and retribution spur him on to describe macabre banquets where the bones of his ancestors come to dance. . . . Like the later generation of Anne Hébert and Saint-Denys-Garneau, Nelligan reverts to images of horror and death to shed off the oppressiveness of ancestors. (p. 164)

Throughout Nelligan's poetry recurring images of funeral processions, coffins, and hearses draped in black create a sense of enclosing space and of the terror invading the poet's soul. His nightmare landscapes are populated with wild animals and skeletal trees. . . . Horror is augmented by associating the anatomy of the landscape with a ravaged human form as in **'Paysage fauve,'** or in Lampman's 'In November' where the mulleins are 'so shrivelled and thin.' The conflicts, fears, and divisions of the poet's soul are transformed into the landscape of a nightmare; the distorted images of skeletal trees and dancing skeletons symbolize his terror as he confronts the wilderness, death, the restrictions of society, or his own troubled being. The dream of the enclosed garden and groves becomes a nightmare of black pools or winter nights. In the nightmare landscape, the dream of refuge has been hideously betrayed.

In the landscapes of dreams and nightmares, Lampman and Nelligan found a framework within which to describe their desires and fears. Lampman's dream landscapes consisted of natural landscapes hazed by dream, or melting into dream, until they reflected the poet's often ambivalent mood or inner being. Except for descriptions of his dream visions of utopia, Lampman seldom explicitly entered his dreams. Nelligan, however, inhabited landscapes that existed only in dreams of the past, of his childhood, of another reality. Consequently his portraits of his inner state were clearer and more insistent while Lampman's landscapes were more tangible and rooted in Canadian soil. It is the poetic attention that Lampman paid to the details of the physical landscape of the Gatineaus and that Nelligan paid to the contours of his soul that resonate in the poems of their successors. Margaret Atwood and Anne Hébert, for example, completely internalized the landscape, creating an inner landscape of the self, while Al Purdy and Paul Chamberland mythologized the landscape, recreating or 'inventing' the land. After the poetic ventures of Lampman and Nelligan, what remained for the moderns to accomplish was a more complete poetic integration of the inner and outer landscapes. (p. 165)

Kathy Mezei, ''Lampman and Nelligan: Dream Landscapes,'' in Canadian Review of Comparative Literature, *Vol. VI, No. 2, Spring, 1979, pp. 151-65.**

KATHY MEZEI (essay date 1980)

[In the following excerpt, Mezei discusses several predominant thematic concerns that Nelligan's work shares with the French Symbolist poets and with later French-Canadian writers. Mezei

devotes most of her attention to Nelligan's preoccupation with alienation, withdrawal, and the exploration of individual consciousness, providing detailed analysis of the symbols he used to convey his meaning.]

Though his flame of genius flickered so briefly, the romantic, tragic and mad Emile Nelligan . . . captured the imagination of Quebec as no writer before or after. . . .

Nelligan spent his youth in Montreal. His father, absent most of the year on behalf of the postal service, was a tyrannical Irishman who refused to learn French, while his mother, a gentle, musical French Canadian, protected her son. As a boy Nelligan seemed indifferent to his studies and as a young man showed no inclination to find regular employment, much to the annoyance of his father. From age sixteen to nineteen he devoted himself exclusively to writing poetry, affecting a bohemian life style. Then he succumbed to the schizophrenia that had been slowly engulfing him and waited out the rest of his days in mental institutions, never writing another word of poetry. One can see, given Nelligan's background and futile rebellion, how his schizophrenia assumed a mythic quality in Quebec, how it came to symbolize the oppressive theocracy and uneasy dual heritage. (p. 81)

Part of this adulation stems from Nelligan's eloquent expression of images and themes that continue to obsess Quebec artists: entrapment, isolation, alienation, exile, ambivalence towards one's Catholic heritage which nevertheless supplies a bottomless fount of aesthetic images. But this tribute also arises from the recognition that Nelligan heralds the arrival of modernism in Quebec. In his poetry, the fetters of a moribund partiotism and artificial romanticism are thrown off, revealing the possibilities of the symbolic use of language and the psychological examination of one's inner being. This is not to deny that Nelligan was—as any youthful poet inevitably is—strongly imitative of his masters—the French and Belgian poets of the parnassian and symbolist schools, as well as Byron and Poe. Despite the conventional, if well-crafted poetic forms (in particular, the sonnet) and the echoes from continental poets, a desperate and moving inner struggle illuminates Nelligan's poems. Unlike earlier Quebec poets, he sought to portray the state of his soul, to reveal the often divided images of the self; thus he created a landscape of the soul that reverberates in the poems of Alain Grandbois, Saint-Denys-Garneau, and Anne Hébert. (pp. 81-2)

By examining the spatial symbols that dominate Nelligan's poems and tracing their development throughout his poetry, we will have a better understanding of Nelligan's main themes, his poetic process, his modernism, and the reason he has had such a strong impact on the Quebec imagination.

Heir to the three great literary movements of the nineteenth century, Nelligan drew out essential characteristics of each that suited his temperament and his art. From romanticism came the concept of the agony of creation and the significance of subjective impressions; from the parnassians came the emphasis on clarity of image; and from the symbolists, the encouragement to pillage nature for symbols to express ideality and intense subjectivity. The symbolists, particularly Baudelaire and Verlaine, provided the rationale for a complex and unnatural use of symbols from nature: they wished to create a literature "in which the visible world is no longer a reality and the unseen world no longer a dream." Nature, then, became a source of symbolic forms and Nelligan's expression of nature is symbolic and far removed from the natural world. Indeed, the concept of ideality is pervasive in Nelligan who constantly strives to flee "La Matière aux yeux ensorcelants / Aux plages de Thulé vers l'île des Mensonges" ["The material world with its bewitching eyes / With its Thulian shores circling an isle of illusions"]. With true Mallarmean horror of "la brute nature" ["coarse, inanimate nature"], Nelligan wishes to escape the ugly realities of winter, stormy seas, and the "earth," symbolically recoiling from "too much reality." . . . However, the contours of Nelligan's ideal remain vaguely defined; occasionally, this ideal resides in the golden age—the personal one of childhood or the historical one of days of chivalry and romance, and occasionally in the future, in the golden Jerusalem. Since the ideal can be visited most freely through "le rêve" ["the night-dream in sleep"], the loose but implicit coherence of dreams structures the ideal.

In his poem **"Rêve d'artiste,"** Nelligan presents the process by which he seeks the space that is his ideal world. Disarmingly, he describes how, were he to possess the elusive muse "une soeur angélique au sourire discret" ["an angelic sister (muse) with a modest smile"], he would fashion an equally angelic and beautiful garden—his poem. . . . Invoking the familiar symbolist vision of "un autre pays" ["a land elsewhere"] or "un pays absolu" ["an unrestricted realm"] through the common image of "azur" ["azure"] which he combines with the religious and romantic images of "lys" ["lily"], "soleil" ["sun"], "gloire" ["glory"], (all symbols of creative energy), Nelligan promises us a distant, ideal space that is both poem and dwelling place. The distance and improbability of the realm are emphasized because Nelligan addresses the reader, not the "soeur bonne et tendre" ["kind and tender sister"], thus setting the possibility of "poem" and personal "glory" in a remote time and place. The **"Rêve d'artiste"** is an exposition of the development of the conditions of artistic creation and of his vision of an "ideal poetic space."

Frequently this ideal space is described as "un rêve enclos" or a "jardin sentimental" or a "jardin d'antan" ["gardens of the past"] nostalgically evoking the sheltered innocence of childhood and a traditional pastoralism (because derived from literature). However, this ideal space is Janus-faced for, on the one hand, Nelligan seeks refuge in "chapelles" ["chapels"] and "jardins" ["gardens"] (religious and childhood sanctuaries). . . . But, on the other hand, the refuge, like Nelligan's soul, has its shadowy, macabre side. . . . In a manner reminiscent of Gaston Bachelard's depiction of houses as souls, Nelligan's "chapelle" in **"Chapelle de la morte"** assumes "les traits / De ton âme qu'elle a humée" ["The traits of your soul which it has drawn in"]. The fear and trembling within the soul are projected outward and the abstract blackness of the soul is often transferred to the concrete ruins of "chapelles." . . . (pp. 84-6)

Similarly the peaceful cloister is occasionally transformed into a ghoulish monastery. **"Le Cloître noir"** is a haunting and ambivalent portrait of monks filing into a chapel that captures, through the rhythmic correspondence of chants and marching feet, the process of attaining grace and salvation. This sonnet rises to a symbolic, surprise open ending so common to Nelligan, which focuses the entire poem and which sends the startled reader back to explore its symbolic evocations. Note, for example, the significance of the difference in the ending between the original 1897 poem **"Moines en défilade"** and the revised version **"Le Cloître noir."** . . . The two versions of **"Le Cloître noir"** are interesting in the light of Nelligan's occasionally demonic vision of the "Church" and because we can see how, here as in other places, Nelligan is torn between the black and the macabre and the pure and the holy. Yet which is more terrifying: the vision of hell and temptation in the earlier poem or the ghostly emptiness of salvation in the latter one?

Here, then, are the two facets that balance the scale pans of Nelligan's precarious soul. First we encounter "l'abîme" ["the abyss"] with its "Suprême Tentateur" ["supreme devil"] and second, l'abîme with "l'espoir triomphant" ["triumphant hope"]. Nelligan's soul is weighed down on one side with exoticism and nostalgia represented by the "bibelots," "négresses," parrots, pieces of Chopin, Liszt, "missels d'ivoire" ["ivory missals"] and portraits of his mother. The other side is weighed down with morbidity and death, represented by images in which the past appears "claquant leurs vieux os" ["clattering their old bones"], or in which the poet gloats over his coffin and approaching death. Either by a retreat into exoticism or nostalgia or by succumbing to morbidity and death, Nelligan seeks to escape reality.

Thus, while Nelligan inhabited and desired to inhabit another reality—a dream world constructed out of his imagination and out of the past recollected in turbulence—that this other reality eventually overwhelmed him is evident in his descent into mental illness. It is clear that Nelligan had little interest in the practical, everyday world and felt trapped and horrified by it. . . . (pp. 86-7)

Wavering between ecstasy and desperation, Nelligan subscribes to the notion dominant among the romantic and symbolist poets that the poet is seer, that he is possessed by superhuman qualities (poetic genius) by which he can reveal to the ordinary man the ideal lurking in the real world. . . . The concept of the poet as more perceptive and tuned to other universes is a recurring motif in Nelligan's poems and further supplements his aura of otherworldliness.

Given the symbolist emphasis on the symbolic possibilities of such natural elements as water, trees, birds, autumn, and on the vivid reconstruction of spiritual worlds through the use of these symbols, it is no wonder that Nelligan found in their poems and in their methods, congenial modes of expressing his dream world. But most of Nelligan's nature symbols are developed from his literary experience rather than his experience of the Canadian landscape. Only with "snow" in **"Soir d'hiver"** and **"Hiver sentimental,"** does Nelligan infuse his image with a local relevance, though cold and even snow are certainly favourite symbolist metaphors. But even with "neige" ["snow"], it is the verbal possibilities of the image that intrigue Nelligan, rather than its "real" properties. (p. 87)

The world of literature is, for the poet, a sacred space. And so is dream. The sacred space is constructed by the poet and, as Verlaine said, "tout le reste est littérature" ["all the rest is literature"], all the rest is profane, worldly, and of little consequence. As archetype, sacred space is inner, and profane space, outer. In his use of images Nelligan continually makes this distinction between the inner, sacred reality, and the outer, profane reality.

Although Nelligan is concerned with illuminating the self, he prefers to view the self from the outside as separate and often abstract. For example, when in **"La Fuite de l'enfance,"** the desire of the poet to escape earthly bounds is rendered as "La Fuite de l'enfance au vaisseau des vingt ans" ["The flight of childhood on the twenty-year-old ship"], the self is distanced, abstracted as "Enfance." But as [Gérard] Bessette points out, Nelligan's greatness lies in his ability to combine the abstract with the self, and more significantly the abstract with the concrete. Therefore, in this poem, the "vaisseau" become the concrete representation of the soul; it is also a recurring symbol for the soul adrift on the seas of change throughout his poetry. . . . Through spatial metaphors of the heavens, abysses, seas, the self is indirectly revealed. These often clichéd metaphors catch our attention first because they do reveal the self, and second, because of their fine verbal quality.

The spatial direction in Nelligan is predominantly vertical: up to the heavens, down into the abyss or the sea; and it is complemented by those metaphors of space (sea, abyss, heavens) that are the recipients of this vertical movement. This preference for the "vertical" further emphasizes Nelligan's desire to evade the real world and to escape into higher realms of being. Although Nelligan does deal with universal themes—**"La Fuite du temps,"** death, nostalgia—it is always within the frame of the self; to intimate the stages of his soul and the tenuousness of his life is the concern of Nelligan's art.

As a consequence, Nelligan's nature pieces are symbolic inner landscapes avoiding any direct involvement with the natural world which is distanced either by window frames or by literary convention. . . . Nelligan does not develop a region-spirit or genius loci; he is a visionary poet who projects the poetic genius which absorbs his whole vision upon place rather than seeking to merge his poetic spirit with the spirit of the place. Moreover, although his "space" is inevitably shaped by clearly delineated Catholic and conservative forces, Nelligan creates a psychological or inner space that requires little in the way of concrete physical ties to the outer space in order to express itself. Thus Nelligan's landscapes are conventional and symbolic. Enclosed gardens, pastoral vistas, and winter scenes predominate, frequently succumbing to macabre visions or formless and vacant landscapes where the Baudelarian nightmare of "le gouffre" ["the abyss"] affirms its dreadful primacy. In Nelligan's poetry, the line of development, therefore, is from "le rêve blanc" ["the white dream"] to "le rêve noir" ["the black dream"], from a fanciful to a gloomier symbolism: the morbid strain is always present in Nelligan's symbolism and, in **"Paysage fauve"** or **"Le Corbeil,"** verbal and thematic elements reveal more of the morbid than of the fanciful or idyllic.

In Nelligan's hands, the pastoral constitutes an artificial world where simplicity, love, the golden age and rural retirement are ideals bolstered by traditional symbols of pastoral flocks (cows), shepherds, and shepherdesses (Gretchen), Pan, song, gardens, flowers. The motifs weaving their way through the pastoral poems are childhood (the past, the golden age); the season of loss and sadness (autumn), the season of death (winter), and of love (summer and spring); song, gardens, and religious faith revealed by the recurring image of bells. These themes and images unite and intermingle to represent a sense of longing, usually for a simpler, happier past. When the tone saddens and the vision darkens, the longing turns towards death. (pp. 88-9)

Three winter pieces, **"Soir d'hiver," "Hiver sentimental,"** and **"Frisson d'hiver"** contrast the cold outside with the warmth inside (a living heart): sacred and profane spaces. However, cold and death (in life and love) slowly invade the heart, and the poems **"Paysage fauve"** ("Pastels et porcelaines") and **"Soirs hypochondriaques"** ("Poèmes posthumes") become hallucinatory and wintery landscapes.

In the section "Virgiliennes" Nelligan repeats his themes of nostalgia, melancholy, innocence, childhood and longing after the ideal. The ringing of the angelus (**"Automne," "Jardin sentimental"**) accompanies the poet's melancholy mood and signals the awakening of memories of the past. For Nelligan, the landscape, as seen repeatedly in these poems, is associated with churchbells and chapels; thus the countryside has a strong religious significance. In **"Jardin sentimental,"** the continual reference to the angelus brings the garden close to another metaphor of enclosed and sacred space, the "chapelle" (which Nelligan portrays in the section "Petites chapelles"). The sacred space of the garden and the chapel are places for the poet to construct his dreams; they are also temporal in that they are places of childhood memory. (p. 90)

In the symbolist poets, symbolic landscapes are essentially dream landscapes in which the reader follows a progression that is not logical but associative, and through the unusual combination of images, reinforced by inverted syntax and bizarre juxtapositions of words, is drawn into the poet's mental space. Symbolic dream landscapes were an appropriate mode for Nelligan, who in company with the French symbolists created [according to Edward Engleberg in his *The Symbolist Poem*]

> dreamscapes in which despair, a sense of loss and fear, hunger for beauty and release, and a horrible awareness of sullen leaden reality pervade their work. Such awareness will lead to dream, to nightmare, to seeing the beautiful in the ugly (and vice versa) to boredom, to fatigue—*and* to the magnificent visions that lie beyond the window pane.

These landscapes . . . are enclosed gardens, sheltered from nature, located in another realm, beyond reality. For Nelligan, the wilderness that is both desolate country and the winter season, is a fearful, not a creative solitude, inhabited by fierce wild beasts and gruesome spectres. In keeping with his temperament Nelligan also has a predilection for the dying season, autumn, while winter becomes the season of despair when the landscape turns to nightmare and is haunted by ghosts. However, because of his ability to draw nuances from common symbols like roses, trees, pools, and to combine them in a rhythmic movement, Nelligan's symbolic landscapes arouse powerful emotions. (pp. 92-3)

In [the poem **"Soir d'hiver"**] the poet appears to be looking out the window, but in actuality he is looking in, at his own soul. Here is the paradox of enclosed space. Except where it provides a vocabulary for the soul, nature in Nelligan's poems, is stylized and conventional ("neige," "roses" ["snow," "roses"]). Bessette has pointed out that Nelligan was attached not to nature, but to artificial objects, particularly objects of cults and of music.

The continual use of exotic and alien images rather than authentic native images to describe the self can be seen as another way of expressing alienation. Being derived from another culture, another land, these images project a distanced and alienated self. Moreover, exotic images of Paris salons, Louisiana, Egypt, Vienna, Spain are twice removed from the poet's reality because they are drawn from literature not experience. This alienation is even more directly and consciously expressed by the images of death, mourning, and enclosure.

To mirror the separation of the subjective from the objective and to project subjective feelings onto a distant and objective space, Nelligan employs formal and imagistic devices in a persistently recurring pattern. His predominant mode of distancing is the window, particularly the frame of the window, which allows the poet to compose the landscape. The window is also a common symbolist metaphor for the poet's realization of the difference between himself, his ideal world and the reality besieging him, and one finds the poet looking out the window, not at the landscape, but at himself: he is [according to Edward Engleberg]

> alienated from an ideal world and also forever acutely conscious not only of this separation, but also of the sordid reality from whose perspective he is obliged to seek the azur of the ideal world. In short, the poet is trapped between his impulse to recover the transcendent world and his awareness of the utter impossibility of ever doing so, except by resorting to the illusion of windowpane.

The window separates the sacred from the profane space, while permitting the poet, seated behind the window, to see both spaces and to follow a controlled exchange between the two different impressions. As already seen, Nelligan prefers to view the landscape through the window; in **"Soir d'hiver,"** the "vitre" ["window"] becomes a metaphor of the soul which is a framed, composed, winter landscape. To use this image is to deliberately separate subjective feelings from the objective phenomena. Even a metaphor as fused as "ma vitre est un jardin de givre" ["my window is a garden of rime (frost)"] which makes a direct association between the self and the landscape (that is, the poet does not use a more detailed and conscious form of simile such as "ma vitre est *comme* un jardin de givre" ["my window is *like* a garden of rime"]) insists upon a separation of the self and on the inevitability of a divided self. The self, because it is symbolized by a "vitre" which looks both inward and outward and is transparent, does not belong wholly to itself but is torn between the inner and outer and hovers at the fringe of the two worlds. (pp. 94-5)

Given his background, Nelligan was naturally haunted by Catholicism; it pervaded his images, his invocations to prayer, his despair over salvation and the other world. This combined with his delight in visual imagery provided another variation on "le vitre"—that of "le vitrail" or stained glass window. This image was particularly rich because "le vitrail" possessed its own integral design and colours as well as permitting the outer world to be reflected upon the inner sanctum. "Le vitrail" presented a clearly defined barrier to outer realities. . . . (pp. 95-6)

In religious iconography and emblematic literature the church is a type of the soul, a constructed sacred place enclosed from the profane, as is the garden. In several poems Nelligan resorts to the image of the church as sanctuary and as symbol of the soul. (p. 96)

The images of the window and "le vitrail," by their very physicality, draw attention to another kind of space—the enclosed space of stuffy rooms or churches or trapped souls. Throughout Nelligan's poems, the enclosed space denotes a sacred place within the profane world of "brutes laideurs" ["coarse ugliness"], a place in which to dream. While gardens, "au jardin clos, scellé, dans le jardin muet" ["to the closed garden, sealed, in the silent garden"], are separated from the real world by paths, "Chapelles" ("le cloître noir"), circled by woods and warmed by prayer, are divided from the profane world by their stained glass windows. Houses, in the shape of villas, châteaux, castles, are protected by windows and represent the spaces of family life, dreams, idyllic childhood days, and sincere religious faith (**"Prière du soir," "Devant le feu"**).

Associated with either the cozy domesticity of familial houses or the glamorous relics of celebrated homes are the even more enclosed spaces of rooms and salons. Within these "circles" lie other small objects that have both temporal and psychological significance: cabinets of dusty memories ("Vieille armoire,") and vases ("Potiche,") containing relics of the soul and of the artistic endeavour. . . . Nelligan is more at home with objects, images, and scenes of the "inside"—of salons, cupboards, hearths with their lingering memories of the past than with the vast and energetic "outside." . . . These enclosed spaces are claustrophobic as well as creative. . . . This image of claustrophobia, a symbol of alienation and withdrawal from the creative forces, is also found later in Anne Hébert's and Saint-Denys-Garneau's images of "chambres de bois," tombs, and decaying ancestral manors, and may be symptomatic of the intellectual trapped by a stifling Quebec milieu. Thus, the metaphors of enclosed space degenerate from symbols of nostalgic memory to symbols of death and entrapment as the poet grows more despairing. (pp. 96-7)

In the celebrated destiny of **"Vaisseau d'or"**—"sombre dans l'abîme du rêve" ["Foundered in the abyss of dream"]—is epitomized the dream that has turned to nightmare and which has capsized the soul into death. The image of the empty and terrifying void of the Baudelairean gouffre permeates Nelligan's verse, a reminder of the perils of the imagination. . . .

From this outline of Nelligan's predominant symbols of space, one can see that his imagination is directed inwards into the self, into enclosed spaces which are unrelieved, for the most part, by the energizing and creative "green" (except for the bitter-sweet **"La Romance du vin"**) and which eventually become the black and eternal enclosures of madness and death. The complex and yet coherent symbolic inner landscape Nelligan created struck and continues to strike a responsive chord in the imagination of the Quebecois. Although his own imagination became a macabre prison, his eloquent expression of it proved to be a liberating force for those who followed. (p. 98)

Kathy Mezei, "Emile Nelligan: A Dreamer Passing By," in Canadian Literature, *No. 87, Winter, 1980, pp. 81-99.*

PAULA GILBERT LEWIS (essay date 1980)

[In the following excerpt, Lewis discusses the predominance of black and white landscapes in Nelligan's poetry and relates them to his extreme moral and artistic values and his psychological collapse.]

Nelligan was essentially a French symbolist poet and, specifically, a *poète maudit* ["accursed poet"]. True to Verlaine's original meaning of *malédiction,* Nelligan saw himself as a poor misunderstood genius scorned by the majority of his fellow "vulgar" Quebecois, isolated in an aesthetic world of his own and dreaming of an absolute purity by means of poetry. His poems express an inner revolt and pathetic cry, more musical than intellectual, against his obsessions with the cruel world, . . . the passing of time, sensations of *le spleen* and *le gouffre* ["the abyss"], and inevitable death. They complain of the impossibility of attaining absolute perfection in art but attest to the poet's wishes to continue the struggle. And, above all, Nelligan's poetry chronicles his macabre voyage toward insanity. (p. 229)

The predominance of poetic themes such as winter, snow, ice, frost, night, a distant past and future, pure unattainable or sterile ideals, *le gouffre, la névrose* ["neurosis"], insanity, and death—all painted either in black or in white in an absence of color and of warmth—can be viewed as exterior or interior psychological décors. They are to be treated, especially when used as interior descriptions of the poet's heart and mind, as *maudit* obsessions. But, in their frequency as exterior décors for his poems, they stress primarily the Canadian landscape, permeating the inner self through a dual window overlooking both wintery scenes and the shuddering soul.

Of 177 known poems by Nelligan, a large percentage are concerned with the presence of an exterior coldness, specifically mentioning winter, the white snow, ice, and frost. The opening verse of **"Soir d'hiver"** offers the reader an idea of the constant décor of Nelligan's poetry: "Ah! comme la neige a neigé!" [O how the snow did snow!" (Translated by Louis Dudek)] . . . In many of Nelligan's poems, this white coldness, associated with purity, possesses positive characteristics; it is good and desired and, perhaps, the only possible warmth available to the poet. . . .

If the poet is referring to Canada in most of these poems, he sees his homeland as related to other northern countries in a fraternal bond. He mentions Belgium, Flanders, and Norway, in particular, all viewed as snowy, white, and cold, as well as melancholy under gray skies. (p. 230)

If Emile Nelligan is the poet of the cold, white winter, he is equally the poet of the cold, black night. At least one quarter of his poems are specifically described as nocturnal. In a few instances that night serves a calm and soothing function for the poet, a form of preferred consolation and inspiration. . . . But generally night is feared. It is a hallucinatory night whose progressive invasion engenders the sensation of a black void, of eternity. . . . It is often seen as evening at the time of vespers just before the death of day when all possible light disappears.

Despite his terror of the encroaching black coldness, this nocturnal poet is obsessed with the absolute blackness of the winter night. Like Mallarmé, haunted by his vision of the frightening sky of his ideals, Nelligan utters the same desperate cry in **"Confession nocturne"**: "je suis hanté" ["I am haunted"]. (pp. 230-31)

Just as twilight serves as a transition between daytime and its death into night, October, or autumn, is often used by Nelligan to symbolize the season immediately preceding the death of nature into winter. If the white snowy coldness of Canadian winters represents at times purity and warmth, more often it can be seen as precipitating the cold blackness of nature's death. (p. 231)

One additional type of exterior coldness surrounding the poet should be mentioned, especially since it appears in Nelligan's best-known poem, **"La Romance du vin."** Here the poet haughtily complains of the coldness of the Canadian public toward him and his art. . . . Such a situation was, of course, typically *maudit,* although also Canadian in that the average Quebecois of the late nineteenth century neither understood nor accepted such French intellectual literary thoughts. Nelligan's reaction to this exterior coldness was also typical: he withdrew into himself, into his own world of artistic dreams and, eventually, into insanity, only to discover, once again, a permeating white and black cold.

Paul Wyczynski states in several of his critical works on Nelligan that the color (or absence of color) white symbolized for the poet his nostalgically remembered childhood, his mother, and, therefore, his former happiness and secure warmth. Despite the truth of this observation, substantiated in several poems, it is also evident that this past life is now dead and, therefore, although still white, cold and silent. . . . Similarly, religion, and especially his beloved Sainte Cécile, are described by Nelligan as being pure and white, but in a form of "cold warmth," distant from the poet and offering him little consolation.

This distant white but cold purity is associated not only with past happiness and memories but also, and predominantly, with the future. Like so many poets before and contemporary to him, Nelligan constantly viewed ideal beauty, both female and artistic, as white, pure, and virginal. For Nelligan in particular, all female beauty, be it real or absolute, was cold and unapproachable. All of his women remained at a distance.

His aesthetic ideals, dreams, and goals of reaching an absolute world were similarly sterile or unattainable. . . . Although Nelligan is often the poet of escape, of the voyage toward the infinite and the absolute, his art soon becomes, as he himself interpreted that of Baudelaire, "un violon polaire" ["a polar violin"], a frigid musical poetry that, according to popular tradition, made dance the Aurora Borealis, the Northern Lights seen in northern latitudes. . . . If nature dies, frozen under the glacial immobility of water, so do the poet's hopes, frozen and fallen like leaves from a tree in winter. (p. 232)

Not only are the poet's artistic ideals described as pure and white (though cold and frozen), but Nelligan sees himself, at times, in an identical manner. . . .

It is noteworthy that Nelligan, himself living in a cold, wintery country, creates his inner artistic ideals as pure, white, and cold. He seldom expresses a desire to escape to a land of warmth and sunshine. His absolutes are not the exotic realms of inner light, but the cold, feared, but desired obsessions of art and the artist, expressed ironically, in moving, personal tones. If there is any light present in his poetry, it is, although examples are rare, that of gold, itself a distant, harsh light, seen almost as white and viewed, in effect, as another "cold warmth." . . .

As Nelligan looks around and sees the cold, white, wintery, nocturnal landscape, while dreaming of pure white aesthetic ideals, he examines his own inner being: his life, his thoughts, and his soul. . . . He experiences the occupational hazard of *l'étouffement* ["suffocation"] and of an inner, cold void. And he is, especially, obsessed with the sensation of depth, with falling into a deep, black, cold *gouffre*. . . .

Emile Nelligan's obsession with falling into a cold, black abyss is dual, with both fates envisioned as inevitable and terrifying. Passing through stages of macabre hallucinations, he fell into *la névrose* ["neurosis"] becoming insane, and, therefore, mentally dying well before his actual death. The poet predicted his own "mental shipwreck" in **"Le Vaisseau d'or,"** where the golden-white vessel, about to reach "l'azur, sur des mers inconnues" ["the azure, on unknown seas"], was coldly struck by the night. . . . (p. 233)

Beyond his immediate mental death, Nelligan was constantly haunted by his actual death. The cold, black night can only precipitate an identical catastrophe for the poet. Images of coffins, tombstones, hearses, mourning crapes, cemeteries, and skeletons abound in his poems. Death and the ensuing funeral procession always arrive on a cold, winter evening when "les noirs des musiques" ["the sorrows of music"] can be heard. And since the cold rigidity of death is inevitable, Nelligan, already experiencing the black coldness of life and of encroaching insanity, may as well hasten the process. . . . [We] may conclude that there exist many interdependences and fluctuations between exterior and interior coldness, both black and white, in the poetry of Nelligan. In anticipation of his cold, black insanity and eventual death, the poet often experiences a shudder (*le frisson*) of his soul, fearful of the future in a cold *néant* ["nothingness"]. This inner shuddering corresponds to the cold, white shudder of wintery nature in the black night. . . . The pure white heart of the poet, melancholy and black with visions of macabre death, becomes immobile, sterile, frozen into the Canadian snow.

In order to effect the passage of this black and white coldness between both exterior and interior décors, the poet views these pervading relationships through a window, the Nelliganian counterpart of the Mallarméan *vitre* ["window"]. . . . Like Mallarmè, Nelligan uses *la vitre* in order to contemplate both the landscape and the distant ideal azure skies. Through the window pass these exterior images into the claustrophobic room and into his closed heart. The movement is, of course, reversible. But the windowpane serves also as a transparent obstacle, for the poet cannot reach his goals, either in the absolute realm of art or in the purity of snow. Everything he sees, touches, and dreams is frozen and imprisoned. (pp. 234-35)

Both [Mallarmé and Nelligan], although fearful of this cold reflection . . . can never turn away from its haunting presence. . . .

It remains accurate to state that Emile Nelligan was esentially a French symbolist *poète maudit* who loved France and her literary traditions. But despite his overt disregard of his Quebecois milieu, his poetry does betray the influence of his Canadian homeland. The poem **"Soir d'hiver"** could only have been written by a northern poet. . . . (p. 235)

Paula Gilbert Lewis, "Emile Nelligan, 'Poète Maudit' of Quebec: The Pervasion of Black and White Coldness," in Pre-Text, Text, Context: Essays on Nineteenth-Century French Literature, *edited by Robert L. Mitchell, Ohio State University Press, 1980, pp. 229-38.*

ADDITIONAL BIBLIOGRAPHY

Collin, W. E. Review of *Poésies complètes: 1896-1899,* by Émile Nelligan. *University of Toronto Quarterly* 22, No. 4 (July 1953): 405-06.

Review which provides information regarding early publication of Nelligan's work by his friend and critic, Louis Dantin.

Andrei (Platonovich) Platonov

1899-1951

(Pseudonym of Andrei Klimentov; also transliterated Andrey) Russian novelist, short story writer, poet, dramatist, folklorist, essayist, and critic.

Platonov was the author of controversial works that examine the failure of the Soviet state to realize the ideals of the Russian Revolution. While his early stories praised the Revolution and its promise of material and cultural rewards, Platonov soon became disillusioned with the Soviet government's neglect of the basic tenets of Marxism, and he used satire to juxtapose an idealized Marxist state with the brutal reality of the USSR. Throughout his works, Platonov sought to return his nation's course to the ideals of the Revolution. Considered ''negative'' and unpatriotic during the author's lifetime, publication of Platonov's fiction was unofficially banned during the 1930s, leaving many of his best works unpublished until after his death.

Platonov was born in the provincial town of Voronezh, three hundred miles north of Moscow. The oldest son of an uneducated metal worker, he ended his formal education at the age of fourteen in order to help support his family. During the civil war a large number of refugee artists, publishers, and writers settled in Voronezh, transforming its cultural life virtually overnight. Inspired by the changing cultural climate, Platonov wrote his first stories and submitted them to a railroad-worker magazine in 1918; by 1920 he was a staff member of the town's Bolshevik newspapers, contributing poetry, short stories, and philosophical essays supportive of the Revolution. He joined the Communist Party in 1920, but left a year later for unknown reasons. During this time Platonov studied electrical engineering and became interested in the development of irrigation systems, just one aspect of a delight in the workings of machinery that is reflected throughout his writings. Although his first book, the poetry collection *Golubaya glidina,* was published in 1922, he abandoned his writing career in 1924 when he was assigned responsibility for the irrigation projects of the entire Voronezh region. Successful in his home province, Platonov was chosen to repeat his success in Tambov. The work went badly, however, for he felt himself an outsider beset with the problems of a burgeoning bureaucracy that thwarted his plans for development. Threatened with imprisonment or death for his lack of progress, Platonov resigned his post in 1927 and moved to Moscow with his wife and son, determined to devote himself to writing.

Platonov's first collection of short stories, *Epifanskie shlyuzy,* was published in 1927. The title story, considered the best in the collection, contrasts the organizational genius of Peter the Great with his brutal implementation of progressive ideas. The theme of incompatibility of noble ends and brutal means was repeated throughout Platonov's career and was a reflection of his disgust with the brutality of Soviet collectivization, which resulted in the systematic murder of millions of people deemed reactionaries or counter-revolutionaries. Another recurring theme of Platonov's work emerged in this story: the necessity of unifying the rigors of Western analytical thought with the more emotional life of Asian Russia. For Platonov, this conflict between ways of life and thought reflected the deeper conflict that exists between humanity and its environment. Platonov consistently sought to eliminate the discord humans felt with both their natural environment and the inanimate objects they created, such as machines.

During this period, Platonov was linked to a group of writers known as the Perevalists. Many of the Perevalists were Communist Party members and all proclaimed devotion to the Revolution and its aims, but they believed that the Soviet state of the 1920s was only a brief passage in the development of a Marxist state, a belief reflected in the name Pereval, which means ''mountain pass'' or ''divide.'' The Perevalists contended that a sincere portrayal of immediate impressions was the basis for art and declared that the writer should be free of programs and parties to explore the human spirit. Their honest portrayal of the problems of the Soviet state and unwillingness to accept the stereotypes of Soviet ideology drew the wrath of party officials. They were severely attacked in the Soviet press and their group was liquidated in 1932 with other autonomous literary groups. Most of the Perevalists disappeared during Josef Stalin's purges. Although Platonov was only associated with the group for a brief period, his writings reflect the aims of the group and his persecution by Soviet authorities has been linked to this involvement.

Platonov's portrayal of the shortcomings of Soviet bureaucracy inspired vituperative attacks in the Soviet press and led to his unofficial blacklisting in the 1930s. Yevgeny Yevtushenko has claimed that the short story "For the Future Good" so infuriated Stalin that the dictator called Platonov and his work "scum." Throughout the next decade Platonov was only able to publish a handful of his stories. In 1941, however, he was drafted as a war correspondent, and during the next few years was able to publish nine books and more than fifty articles and stories. A great proportion of these works were wartime propaganda pieces and antifascist statements, the most popular being "Inspired Men," which depicted the heroic actions of five Soviet soldiers who strapped grenades to their bodies and lay beneath an attacking German tank. Although this work was extremely popular, Platonov was still unable to publish his earlier works of fiction. After the war Platonov again fell from favor and was only able to publish translations of folktales and children's stories for the remainder of his life. He died of tuberculosis in 1951.

Most of Platonov's works, including his novels *Kotlovan (The Foundation Pit)* and *Chevengur,* were not published during his lifetime. During Nikita Khrushchev's cultural thaw of the late 1950s and early 1960s (when the cult of Stalin was repudiated and the Soviets began to confront some of the excesses of his reign) many of Platonov's works were issued to great popular approval. In the late 1960s, however, several of his works that were unavailable in the Soviet Union began to appear in the West and to be read to the Soviet people by Western radio stations. Publication of his work in the USSR was restricted and no new manuscripts were published. Although there has been no attempt to deny his existence and commentaries on his officially approved works continue to appear in Soviet journals, a large number of his writings remain unpublished.

Platonov's best works, including his short stories of the 1920s and 1930s and his novels *The Foundation Pit* and *Chevengur,* portray the corruption of Marxist principles by the Soviet state. Platonov was devoted to the ideals of the Revolution and attacked their perversion by V. I. Lenin and Stalin; he believed that the USSR had a special destiny that was being profaned by the excesses of dictators. In particular, he was a celebrant of the common individual, the workers and peasants, who were the ostensible beneficiaries of a communist state but were the greatest victims of Soviet methods of collectivization. In a bitterly satirical manner, his fiction portrays the destruction by bureaucracies of the very groups and ideals that bureaucracies are formed to serve. Although not a prose stylist, his work masterfully captures the speech and thought processes of both bureaucrats and peasants, depicting through conversation the way that revolutionary ideals are debased by misunderstandings and misinterpretation.

Critical comment on Platonov in English is generally in the form of introductions to his fiction or reviews of those works. In the past decade he has been the subject of several excellent translations and his reputation as a chronicler of the early Soviet state is growing.

PRINCIPAL WORKS

Golubaya glubina (poetry) 1922
Sokrovennyi chelovek (novel) 1928
Epifanskie shlyuzy (short stories) 1929
**Proiskhozhdenie mastera* (novel fragment) 1929
Reka Potudan' (short stories) 1937
Volshebnoe kol'tso (folktales) 1950
Izbrannye rasskazy [censored edition] (short stories) 1958; also published as *Izbrannye* [uncensored edition], 1966
Rasskazy (short stories) 1962
V prekrasnom i yarostnom mire (short stories) 1965
***Kotlovan* (novel) 1968
[*The Foundation Pit,* 1973]
The Fierce and Beautiful World (short stories) 1970
***Chevengur* (novel) 1972
[*Chevengur,* 1978]
Fro and Other Stories (short stories) 1972
Collected Works (short stories, novella, and drama) 1978
Razmyshlenie chitatelya (criticism) 1980

*This work is a fragment of the novel *Chevengur* and was later translated and published in the 1978 English edition of that work.

**These works were written in the late 1920s and early 1930s.

L. ANNINSKY (essay date 1968)

[*Anninsky is a contemporary Soviet critic. In the following excerpt, he discusses Platonov's use of East and West in his works as symbolic and philosophical polarities, with the West signifying a sophisticated, logical frame of mind and the East an unsophisticated natural spontaneity. Anninsky believes that throughout his career Platonov sought to unite the two elements in such a way as to unify the spiritual life of humanity. In particular, Platonov sought a corrective for the failure of Western rationalism, which he felt was denoted by the rise of anti-intellectual fascism in the 1920s and 1930s. This essay was originally published under a different title in* Prostor, *No. 1, 1968. For further discussion of the resolution of polarities in Platonov's works, see the excerpt by Maurice Friedberg (1970).*]

The belated recognition that the reading intelligentsia is now giving the name of Andrei Platonov has a bitter tone. During his life, if his work was treated seriously at all, it was, as a rule, for the purpose of demonstrating its "errors." One critic wrote in 1937: "Platonov seems to pick up and inject into his work that which Soviet literature discarded and swept out—biologism, 'immediate impressions,' a romanticizing of those who have suffered wrongs, naturalism, and tongue-tie. . . ." This was considered a normal tone toward Platonov. Even in the 1920s, when there was a certain tolerance in the attitude toward the still young Platonov, he was most often regarded as merely a talented eccentric, whose particular fantasies in any case were "out of date." In the 1930s he was confidently exposed. In the 1940s he was merely named as long since and irrefutably exposed. Platonov was silent—he died, unknown, in 1951.

Ten years later he was rediscovered. The first positive articles about him had an apologetic tone: naturally this writer had made mistakes, but he knew well the lives of working people in the remote areas of Russia and described their mode of life and emotions with psychological authenticity. The rehabilitation of Platonov's good name began in the realm of literature. No one was looking for a philosopher in him. A few more years passed, two or three more volumes of his stories and tales appeared, and it became possible for everyone to read him. Now he was seen as a master, a stylist, a talent. People began to write about him as a sorcerer of style. In two beautiful articles, V. Turbin provided an acute description of Platonov's style, his "elegant disorganization," his archaic and simulated "helplessness," his "preanalytic" freshness. In the light of this new approach, Andrei Platonov looked not merely like a "worthy" describer of everyday life and a light writer, but a unique master. Now he was not compared with his successful colleagues in prewar literature; rather, people now detected in him a similarity "with the great Leskov."

"The great Leskov," be it noted, is still ranked high for his verbal craftsmanship. We virtually do not look into the depths of the spiritual life that gave birth to this verbal craft. Yet it was a link not only in the history of literary art, but a link in the spiritual development of Russian thought and literature. Behind Platonov stands Leskov. Behind Leskov stands Dostoevsky. Hasn't the time come to assimilate our heritage in terms of its meaning, and not merely its craft? By the will of the fates, Russian imaginative literature has had to bear from time immemorial the heavy burden of philosophy—our literary craftsmen have thought about the destiny of world civilization. We are the heirs not only of authorial craft but of their historical and moral searchings.

These searchings constitute the essence and soul of the work of Andrei Platonov. In the mouths of the wise men from the craftsmen's suburbs in his early stories, philosophical notions seemed to be eccentric babble. Later, when Platonov was compelled to channel his unspent forces into literary criticism, he continued, essentially, to struggle with the same world problems. He wrote about Hemingway, Aldington, Caldwell, Steinbeck, and tried to interpret the course of Western civilization. He wrote about Dzhambul and peered into the regenerating culture of the East. In the contact between these two world principles Platonov continued to seek the overall meaning of man's path through history. (pp. 25-7)

The image of the European as representative of a distinctly Western mind appears in the young Platonov in a historical subject full of symbolism. In the 1920s he resolved this theme by placing a dynamic and honest English engineer in wild and boundless Petrine Russia. In Russian literature and Russian thought, "Tsar Peter" was always the symbolic touchstone against which connections with Western culture were tested with utmost sharpness, as if to the breaking point. Platonov sharply felt and emphasized the contrast in this comparison. He looked at raucous, populous Europe from the silent and empty bowl of Eastern spaces. (pp. 27-8)

[**"The Epifan Locks" (Epifanskie shlyuzy)**] is the story of how an honest English engineer took service with Peter to build a canal between the Don and the Oka in the wild steppes, and how he, the very proper Bertrand Perry, a native of Newcastle, disappeared in this mysterious country.

To Platonov's Englishman, Russia was the same as Asia. He could see neither differences nor borders between the wild and secret spaces. Platonov does see these differences; he knows his beloved Russia amidst the flatness of the Asian continent, and he knows what *secret* spiritual riches are hidden in this revealing country. But at the moment we are interested in another side of the conflict; we are interested in the European engineer Bertrand Perry, emissary of Western culture, and the tests Platonov posed for him in this flat steppe.

The Englishman brings to Peter's Russia his engineer's habits and calculations, his profession, his individual decency, and his "arithmetical reason." The Western mind is logical, speculative, consistent. Platonov is acutely aware of the gap between that kind of thinking and his own, but he seeks the best in the Englishman and draws his engineer with sympathy—his firm confidence in reason and personal nobility cultivated on the narrow British isles.

The tragedy of the Western soul revealed by Andrei Platonov at this stage of his career is the tragedy specifically of the narrowness of the private, individual consciousness—noble, but limited to arithmetical reason.

This boundless and cunning steppe, in which the water from the man-made canal suddenly sinks toward the center of the earth and exposes its helpless bottom—a country where Tsar Peter daily wields his knout to beat logic into muzhik behinds, while the muzhiks continue to escape into the steppe with no purpose at all—is incomprehensible to normal, straightforward reasoning.

"Perry's soul, which feared no horror, now quivered in anxiety, as befits human nature."

The purely "human" mind of the Englishman, nurtured in crowded, sea-intersected Europe, was terrified by the "impenetrable deviousness" of the steppe muzhik, who was "very talkative and in reality shrewd beyond belief. . . ." Bertrand's enterprise ends in failure: the builders run away, and the water from the canal is absorbed by the steppe. For the shame and mockery done the sovereign, the degraded engineer is driven to Moscow "over the mid-Russian continent," and Bertrand Perry, who wants only "to be delivered and killed as fast as possible," honorably surrenders to the executioner.

There are logic and honesty, reason and nobility in this English engineer. But he lacks the chief thing for Platonov—the audacity of a free man. (pp. 28-9)

In **"The Epifan Locks,"** the cultured Western mind is drawn with a complex feeling of sympathy and alarm. The sympathy is understandable because the story was written in 1926, when the brown plague had not yet spread over Europe. . . . Andrei Platonov had joined in the eternal meditation of Russian literature on the strength and weakness of the energetic European soul, but Platonov's alarm was more acute than in what had previously been written. He sensed the limitations of the narrow, precise bourgeois mind of the West; he felt the spiritlessness of its arithmetical energy; he foresaw the catastrophe hidden in that unrestrained and rational energy, which exchanged the freedom of one's soul for the law.

Fascism—that is the tragedy; that is the catastrophe.

For the enlightened 20th century mind, fascism was at one and the same time anticipated and surprising. It was predicted and terrifying. Politicians, economists, sociologists, people of practical intellect and life experience predicted it. (p. 30)

The sociopolitical evaluations that Platonov was able to make of European fascism in the 1930s did not go beyond the bounds of the information then available. To Platonov, fascism was a political plague, a movement that had attracted a mass of declassed petty bourgeois and that trampled on reason and law. In **"The Garbage Wind" [Musornyi veter],** the intellectual, the bearer of thought, is contrasted to the dull, sated fascist crowd. This was the sociopolitical truth of the moment, and Platonov reflected it. But not it alone. As an artist seeking answers to spiritual questions, Platonov meditated bitterly on the human and philosophical sources of fascism. As a witness to and participant in the struggle, he described fascism as a monstrosity. As an artist, he intuitively probed another side of the phenomenon: fascism was strong in that it gave to this crowd of healthy people something they could not get from the tired, refined, rational mind ripped from its native ground.

The tragedy of **"The Garbage Wind"** is determined by the following sensation: essentially, Platonov is once again mourning poor Bertrand Perry, whose straightforward reasoning had finally come into conflict, on the soil of Europe, with an equally straightforward cruelty.

"The Garbage Wind" was written in 1934. Its bitter dedication ("Dedicated to Comrade Zachow, unemployed German, witness at the Leipzig Trial, imprisoned in a Hitler concentration camp . . . and today, probably, already dead . . .") spoke of how much of himself Platonov put into that story.

It described an old European city, crowned with a great Catholic cathedral. In the middle of the city, the cathedral—like a sleeping millennium, like suffering organized in stone—sank its foundations deep into the graves of its builders and soared into the sky as a monument to centuries-long efforts of the dynamic European spirit.

The brown plague swarmed around the cathedral. Several thousand Nazis, a unanimous mob "in the brown workclothes of its world view," were setting up a bronze doll—a monument to Adolf Hitler.

This nightmare was reality, historical reality.

Andrei Platonov wanted to explain it to himself. He tried to compare this triumphant and sated "kingdom of the imaginary" with the historical development of the European critical spirit, hungering "to conquer the universe with reason." Therefore he wanted to confront the sources and the results. In the path of the garbage-brown froth of fascism, Platonov placed a traditional European thinker, a Faust, a bookworm, humanist, and physicist of cosmic space. He gave his hero the name of one of the most witty and ironical German writers of the rational 18th century—he called his hero Lichtenberg.

And so the 20th century Lichtenberg, gray from hunger and despair, comes up to the bronze idol and strikes it with his powerless walking stick. And he is immediately struck down by the well-fed brown mob! And he is cast into a concentration camp, where he dies a meaningless animal death. **"The Garbage Wind"** is a requiem for European thought and humanity, a sad and tired requiem; and at the same time it is Platonov's attempt to understand *from whence* this curse of fascism had fallen upon Europe. (pp. 31-2)

There is something sinister, contrary to nature, internally catastrophic in this scene, not in the fact that the Nazi mob tears an intellectual to pieces, but in the fact that, just a few moments before he had broken his cane on the bronze bust of Hitler, the crowd of fascists *had been agreeing* with his confession of faith, interrupting him with howls of ecstasy. This scene is symbolic. In its tragic absurdity there was embodied, for Platonov, that paradox of Western history by which fascism was born not from savagery but from refined expediency, from mechanical rationality, from "political speculation" gone mad, which sees the human individual as merely a petty obstacle along the triumphal march of a cruel world order. (p. 33)

Poor, honest, noble Bertrand Perry would turn over in his grave at the pictures drawn in **"The Garbage Wind."** Fate was kinder to him in that it sent him to the executioner before he was able to understand that his Euclidean calculations and arithmetical prognoses are incapable of encompassing the infinity of the human soul. The British engineer did not go beyond his linear reasoning—he miscalculated and perished. The German physicist, Albert Lichtenberg, experienced something worse. Before the mob trampled him, he had succeeded in understanding *what* had given birth to these robots. Before death liberated him from consciousness, he sensed where mankind was being taken to by the dynamism of soulless energy and reason, purified of love and sympathy. Lichtenberg could not jump outside his "critical reason"—it was not for nothing that he was a child of the 19th century in Europe. He could only capitulate, die in spirit. The Nazis' boots merely stamped out his remains.

A very acute awareness of the impasse of European bourgeois thought, which tormented Platonov, gave a nuance of hopelessness and absurdity to **"The Garbage Wind."** The German city lacked spaciousness, a steppe into which one might flee. Here there was nowhere for the free insubordinate to save himself. Platonov saw no exit from the Western mind, but no way out was something he could not abide.

Five years later, in 1939, when the war with fascism had already become a reality, Platonov wrote a beautiful fantastic story, **"Under the Midnight Heavens" [Po nebu polunochi],** in which, by the power of his imagination, he created the image of a Nazi military pilot who breaks out of the fascist system, in a virtually linear, improbable, half detective-story plot.

Five Nazi fighter planes are flying to Spain across the night skies of Europe. The people who are guiding these planes have already been spiritually transformed by fascism—they are happy idiots, "children with their eyes gouged out," and in their infantile gaze burns "the energetic light of sincere conviction in the truth of fascism, the light of faith. . . ." But one of them proves to be an exception. (pp. 33-4)

[Erich] Summer shoots down the Nazi planes in the night sky over Europe and takes his own to the Spanish Republicans.

This fantastic attempt on Platonov's part to discover a capacity for resistance in the very depths of the stupefied masses is quite curious. After all, where in the European heavens did this Erich Summer, this avenging angel in the uniform of a Nazi officer, come from (think about the story's title: to Platonov this enlightened pilot was, of course, *an angel*), and how was the element of humanity preserved in his "hidden heart," "his secret soul"?

The story gives no answer. Now the internal philosophical hopelessness of **"The Garbage Wind"** has been replaced by a simple dynamic comparison of the results. The believing idiot from the fascist herd has not become so completely contrasted to any manifestations of rationality and a personal life that the task is simplified. In Platonov's eyes, fascism had been transformed from a rational doctrine into a blind faith, and its adherents from businesslike cynics into happy dumbbells. This simplified his problem. The physicist Lichtenberg, who understood and remembered too much, had by now rotted in his grave. He was no longer necessary. Now it sufficed to give the hero elementary common sense and a hint of that very German *Weltschmerz* that in the splendid 19th century (when the direction in which this "weariness" was leading philosophers was not yet entirely clear) was regarded as "spirituality"; and immediately, in the middle of the herd of happy idiots stupefied by fascism, this symbolic drop of "spirituality" exploded like antimatter. . . . (pp. 34-5)

In Platonov's improbable story, the German avenging angel suddenly shot down his fellow countrymen.

That was the time when the Nazi hordes were tramping uncomplaining down the roads of the real Europe. The world war was coming closer. In the mind of the Western intellectual raised on Spengler and Toynbee, it loomed like the end of civilization, the universal failure of human history. During that period, Platonov saw nothing in the European sky but his hypothetical angel, Summer. But the entire structure of his integral soul rebelled against the moral impasse into which Western bourgeois thought threatened to lead mankind. He did not know how. But he was certain: *not this way*.

At the end of the 1930s, Platonov wrote a number of critical articles on the most outstanding writers of the European "lost generation." In these articles, Platonov's tortured meditations on the fate of human culture as a whole—which was the internal connecting link of his stories in the late 1920s and early 1930s—were gone. (pp. 35-6)

[Human] life itself had a different qualitative value in his eyes. He could not abide the "sportsman's" attitude toward life. He could not endure this break with the integrity of being. He understood too well how the individualist mind gone mad threatened mankind. "The petty proprietor who would remake the world—isn't he a candidate for tyrant?" . . . Give some thought to that aphorism of Platonov's. By the very nature of his talent, Platonov was unable to look on life as an experiment, as an exercise, as a point of application for alien forces. "Who lives life as an experiment? If a life is not successful, it cannot be corrected by living a second time." . . . This is the organic perception introduced by the pen of Platonov the writer.

It was this perception that made his interest in the Western critical mind so acute and so anxious—it was an interest in contrast.

It was this perception that also brought Platonov to the idea that . . . within the Western individualist mind there is no exit from the dead end of dissociation, and that some alternative must be provided for that extreme course.

In Andrei Platonov's writings, Asia appears as a region of unpopulated spaces. It is not a geographic locality, just as Platonov's Europe is not a geographically specific place. The tight and densely populated British isles are as representative to him of the West as—later—the stone verticals of a German Catholic city. To Andrei Platonov, East and West are not geographical but philosophical concepts. They constitute not locale markers but spiritual structures that reveal in their conflict the highest moral truth. The only land on earth in which Platonov sees and loves unique local features is the central Russia of the settlements, counties, and provinces. But this is associated with the genuinely Russian *answer* that the writer Platonov gives to the question of human existence. And he *poses* this question—according to the long Russian tradition—as the question of the total meaning of life. To Platonov, West and East are two principles of existence. He compares them.

The West is densely populated, visible, narrow.

The East is uninhabited. Dead sands extend to the horizon, and a tiny huddle of people, leaving an inhabited place, moves across the scorching mud flats "in the direction of an equally empty space."

The West is tangible, perceptible, fleshy.

The East is intangible. The sands glimmer with disappearing mirages. Rolling clumps of grass skim over the steppe. People wander, losing themselves in invisible spaces, pressing themselves to the ground, circling in endless rings in the steppe in order to take from the ground what has succeeded in growing up since the last time round, and in order not to depart from the ring, not to emerge from the circle.

The West is energetic, rational, filled with an insistent will to live.

The East is guilelessly trustful and direct as a child, as Platonov sees it. (pp. 38-40)

In the early 1930s, when teams of writers moved into Central Asia and Turkestan from the capital cities, Andrei Platonov went there too. Of the two things he wrote as the result of this trip, the lesser, **"Mud Flats,"** was published, while the other waited thirty years for its readers. It was one of Platonov's best works and one of the best works Russian literature has produced about Asia—**"Dzhan."**

We read it now as though it had been written only yesterday. (p. 40)

In **"Dzhan,"** Platonov concentrated and gave definite expression to his general thoughts about mankind living on the earth's expanse, and about the poverty that has eternally tormented people. Penury, the poverty of life, is a leitmotif of all of Platonov's work, just like another leitmotif—unconquered spaces. Platonov was not only a Russian writer who was born and grew up on the great plain; he was a writer born in an epoch of catastrophic earthquakes of history. He witnessed the collapse of the old way of life; he knew devastation. As a provincial land manager, he was the first to organize reclamation and electrification in his native backwoods. As a writer, he remained linked to these two motifs all his life: space and poverty. In Platonov's writing, the East was the theme that concentrated these ideas.

In **"Dzhan,"** Platonov does not paint landscapes of the desert, yet the image of the desert pursues us constantly as we read, and the most important sensation left by **"Dzhan"** is precisely the sensation of the desert—dumb, unresponding, merciless, and surrounding people.

"In the desert there is nothing." This is the core of his descriptions. In the desert you wipe your hands over the earth and they become clean. There is not even dirt in the desert: "the desert is all clean." The image of the intangible, illusory, and spectral horizon becomes symbolic in **"Dzhan."** "The deserted land of the desert." This might have been said of the desert by a poet who reveals in this image not so much an elementary, local content as the structure of his meaning. Platonov too had the structure of meaning in mind. He wrote **"Dzhan"** not as a prose writer but as a poet—but a poet not in the present sense of the word but in its ancient meaning, when a poet composed songs and myths that became an epic of life, philosophy, and faith.

People in the desert. For Platonov, this situation was filled with ancient symbolism. Their existence, their struggle for each instant of life now acquires, as it were, its primeval meaning. Their searches for water constitute an epic, and their quests for food become feats of valor that recall primitive folk tales. The overwhelming scene in which Chagataev, exhausted, dying of hunger, lying flat on his back, shoots at the eagles that are already tearing at his body—a scene of terrible reality described in naturalistic detail (perhaps the critics would have regarded it as "naturalism" had Platonov published it in the period when it was written)—is a scene in which we now detect something quite different—the archaic, legendary heroism of primeval existence. . . . Bertrand Perry, the ill-fated English intellectual in **"The Epifan Locks,"** was compared by [V.] Turbin to Faust. In my view, the climax of the Faustian tragedy was interpreted even better in **"The Garbage Wind."** In **"Dzhan"** we find echoes of different legends. The eagle tearing at a man who dreamed of leading people from the desert of darkness and death and who was ready to sacrifice himself for their sake—this is the legend underlying all humanist morality in its European development; this is the legend of Prometheus, which Platonov transfers to an Asian background.

Platonov's symbolism seems here to expose the primitive essence of things. Food is not merely the dead bird that the people gnaw down to the feathers. It is the meager gift of the earth giving a lump of its own flesh to man—it is Food in the first, universal, and pure sense of the word. The People are a few dozen poverty-stricken nomads of various origins, but it is The People, embodiment of Being, and even when Chagataev leads some fifteen living shadows to life, Platonov remembers that this is "The People," for he writes: "Around the quietly burning campfire of desert brush sat the entire people"; "they cooked a meal for the entire people." (pp. 41-3)

Platonov's prose seems to remove the overlays of millennia—typological, ethnic, particular—from things and concepts. He turns the clock of life back to that Old Testament faith when Adam gave *names to things,* when Evil was not yet called Evil, and the entire structure of human existence was manifested in its undistorted essence.

Naturally, this is a "pre-Turgenev" tradition. Moreover, it is "pre-Renaissance" tradition. It is the tradition of Biblical prose, which enables one to weigh not any particular stage of the humanist tradition of mankind, but that entire tradition as a whole. Prometheus' path is the path of the fall "from God" of heroic individuality, the path of the willful rebellion of the private man who, in European thought, symbolizes pre-Christian humanism, and who has been reborn in the bourgeois era. In trying that road, Platonov seeks a new version for it, confronting this European myth with the Asiatic myth of a people marching across a desert to the promised land. Platonov offers his philosophical version of this Eastern legend.

The Dzhan people are in a state of spiritual community, in that integral oneness of poverty of body and soul in which individuality does not have the strength to manifest itself, and in this sense it is dead (dead *as yet*). It is not for nothing that Platonov has so persistent a leitmotif—it is neither life nor death but something intermediate, out of which life may or may not begin. (pp. 43-4)

In **"Dzhan,"** Andrei Platonov creates a version of human existence opposite to that he presented in **"The Garbage Wind."** In the latter, an energetic life was profaned by a bestial, inhuman will that reduced existence to a rational anthill. But in **"Dzhan"** he presents the blissful primeval state of *pre-life,* not yet separated from the earth, an existence in which there is no principle of will. (pp. 44-5)

[These] "European" and "Asian" themes have a very tenuous relationship to the real picture of life in Platonov's own time. For Platonov, these were philosophical rather than real landscapes. In his work he continued the eternal meditation of Russian literature on mankind's two paths, which go back through Blok, Dostoevsky, and Tolstoy to Belinsky, Gogol, and Herzen, not to speak of the Russian philosophers, who knew well that it is precisely from Russia that the East is seen as the East and the West as the West. Platonov constantly keeps these two extreme principles in his mind. Remember the tragic ending of **"Dzhan"**: the people saved by Chagataev, led out of the desert, settled by him on fertile land, and even hammered together into a cooperative flee in all directions on the very first night. Ten or twelve human beings "depart one by one for all the ends of the earth: to the Caspian, to Turkmenia, to the Amu-Dar'ia. . . ." The people has fallen apart. A life has begun in which each of those he saved would have to recognize individuality in himself, to test his own will, his own powers. The drama of individual, separate existence had begun.

Nonetheless, the close of **"Dzhan"** contains an optimistic note that proves more powerful than the truly Haydn-like minor key of farewell. What is stronger here than disintegration? The smile of Chagataev, who from a high mountain terrace watches these tiny figures disappearing over the horizon. "Chagataev sighed and smiled. . . . People can see for themselves what is best for them. It is enough that he helped them to stay alive; let them find their happiness beyond the horizon. . . ."

It is only in a purely geometrical sense that Chagataev's mission in the desert recalls the mission of poor Bertrand Perry, who wanted to draw the rational line of a canal across the Russian steppe. Chagataev really did introduce into the lives of the Dzhan people the principle of will without which they would perish. . . . Isn't this why, in the most terrible minutes, Chagataev feels in himself a sort of "second man," indifferent, calculating and, as it were, personifying in his living, hungry, desert-exhausted body the principle of will? This willful person in him continually sees the goal, and pulls his entire, barely obedient body toward that goal.

But the rational factor of will personified in Chagataev is made, as it were, of another kind of matter than the evil will that crushed out Lichtenberg's entire intellectual world in **"The Garbage Wind."** Between the two extremes of inhuman existence, Andrei Platonov sought what might be a third component—all his work is a quest for that saving measure that would spare mankind's happiness from both sophisticated mechanical and infantile natural impersonality. Chagataev was a man halfway between, of mixed blood, the son of a Turkmen woman of the Dzhan people and of a Russian soldier. He had gone to school in Moscow and brought to the Asian desert not a will alien to it but, as it were, its own greed for life that for the first time was conscious of itself.

Chagataev's will contains wisdom; his strength contains softness; his reason contains charm—all of which makes this man a typical Platonov creation, one of those truly positive heroes with whom this writer populated the remote places of Russia's counties and provinces.

Platonov's keen interest in West and East, the sharply contrasting way in which these two symbolic principles in human history were seen by him, the continuous implied comparison of these two principles reveal what is most important in Platonov: the constant search for an *answer* to the eternal question of existence, the effort to harness the two principles together, to seek a single meaning in disintegrating history, or, as it is put today, to assert the unifying idea in the spiritual life of mankind. (pp. 45-6)

Today we examine this remarkable writer's heritage in its entirety, in its completeness. Today what emerges into the foreground are its philosophical aspects, its humanistic pathos. In this respect, **"Mud Flats"** is for Platonov a unique variation on the eternal, Shakespearean motif of love destroyed and unconquerable. In Platonov's hands, love was born at the edge of the precipice, and it ended in the chasm that had torn the world apart. But Platonov triumphed as an artist. He did not stop calling love love. He preserved this ideal in its purity, and he composed a sad hymn to this dead love. (p. 49)

Platonov's artistic world seems fantastic. He tried to encompass all extremes of a mankind which had been brought into violent motion. We have pictured only one theme in the beautiful and violent world of Andrei Platonov—West and East. Platonov's attitude toward man and toward the world revealed itself in full in this theme, but it was revealed through contrast, paradox, and negation. All his life Platonov wrote of a world torn by struggle, in which an integral human consciousness suffers and lives. This consciousness was the soul of Platonov's contribution as writer.

The contrast between East and West, to which Platonov's pen gave archaic, almost Biblical forms, revealed in his writings with utmost clarity a longing for the unity of mankind, a hunger to harness together, to combine these extreme points. The range of moral seekings was denoted in Platonov by these extreme points.

He also knew the answer to his question. He knew with what to fill this cycle of quests. He constructed a world of positive emotion, a world of active good, knowing wisdom and measure. (p. 50)

L. Anninsky, "East and West in the Work of Andrei Platonov," translated by William Mandel, in The Soviet Review, *Vol. XI, No. 1, Spring, 1970, pp. 25-51.*

YEVGENY YEVTUSHENKO (essay date 1970)

[Yevtushenko is the most popular contemporary Soviet poet, both in the USSR and throughout the rest of the world. He has toured the United States and Europe several times and is widely known for his dramatic public readings. His travels have been an acknowledged attempt to escape the chauvinistic isolationism of the USSR, and he often addresses in his work the need for world peace and understanding. In this regard, Yevtushenko perceives himself as a poet with a mission to take part in the political process of his age. His verse can be divided into two basic groups—lyrical autobiographical poems, which comprise his most accomplished work, and sociopolitical verses, which explore strengths and weaknesses of both Western and Soviet life. Although considered a propagandist early in his career, in his later work he has struggled for liberalization of Soviet life and a return to the humane ideals of the revolution, which stressed faith in the future of humanity. These works, including Babyi Yar *and* The Heirs of Stalin, *have had a strong political impact in the USSR. His frankness on some issues—particularly anti-Semitism and the tyrannies of Stalinism—have caused him trouble with the Soviet authorities. However, Yevtushenko generally stays within the limits of Soviet censorship and as readily attacks the moral and political problems of Western nations as he does of the Soviet Union. But even though he addresses the most important political issues of the age, critics generally find his civic verse blatantly didactic, prosaic, and often shallow. His personal lyrics are considered more interesting, both verbally and thematically; they portray a man who is unsure of himself and constantly concerned with his development, a portrait that many believe explained his strong appeal to Soviet youth in the 1960s and 1970s. In the following excerpt, Yevtushenko surveys Platonov's career, focusing on his defense of the Soviet people from the excesses of Stalinism. In particular, Yevtushenko discusses Platonov's stories detailing the brutality of collectivization, stories which prompted Platonov's official censorship.]*

Andrei Platonov's face, looking out from one of his last photographs, is the face of a tired Russian worker. It has not a trace of affectation, no hint of what is called "artistic temperament," no monumental profundity, no "oracular brilliance" in the eyes.

People with faces like this do not like eloquence. They prefer the painstaking study of the intricate mechanics of living, and before believing something, they want to feel it all over with their hands.

It's the face of a worker who thinks—the face of a master.

The prose Platonov wrote has just this kind of face.

Not long before the Second World War, a short story called **"The Third Son"** by this Russian writer Platonov, who was almost unknown in the West, fell into the hands of Ernest Hemingway, who was already famous. At a meeting with some Soviet journalists, Hemingway spoke with admiration of the pithiness and the expressiveness of Platonov's style. (Hemingway did not know that Platonov had written a brilliant article about his novels *To Have and Have Not* and *A Farewell to Arms*.) To their shame, by no means all of the journalists taking part in this conversation with Hemingway knew the work of their compatriot. Platonov was not spoiled by fame during his life, either at home or abroad. He belongs among the delayed-action writers, whose talent is like a safety fuse which runs many years in length. This fuse smolders unseen but persistent, staying dry even under the drizzle of time, until finally a blinding explosion destroys bridges that had seemed built for eternity. (p. 7)

[Platonov's] first collection of poetry, ***The Blue Deep***, . . . was published in Krasnodar in 1922 in an edition of 800 copies. It was a remarkably weak collection, and Platonov's poetic talent was shown with much greater strength in the short prose passages quoted in the foreword than in the poems themselves.

It is obvious that he felt this himself, and he stopped writing prose in poetic rhythms and started to write prose as a kind of poetry without rhythm. Some writers don't pay enough attention to the word—for them what is most important is to state their subject, no matter how awkward, how untidy, that statement may be. Others nurse every line, licking it over and over again. For a few writers—and Platonov belongs among them—there is an organic confluence of the poetry of words with the psychological development of the narrative.

He was not a believer in words for their own sake, but at the same time he clearly understood that a message is conveyed not only by the manipulation of its subject but also by the manipulation of the words. Just as we can be attracted by an inherent irregularity in the face of someone we love, in the same way we are charmed in Platonov by the amazingly plastic errors he committed against refined language. There is no question that he worked out his own special, Platonov vocabulary, drawn from folklore and from the living talk of simple people.

"She hadn't been able to stand living for very long" is the way he talks about an old woman dying. (pp. 9-10)

But Platonov achieved his most surprising results when he skillfully showed the crazy invasion of political phrases and neobureaucratic words into the constructions of peasant speech. (p. 10)

Platonov was not an inventor of verbal tricks. He simply had an extraordinary ear, and he brought together in his prose the many-colored, the harsh, and the humorous language of his times. And there was something in those days to listen to. From 1923 until 1927 he worked as a specialist in land reclamation in various provinces in the central regions of Russia, and he saw the terrifying devastation and poverty of the time when things had reached a point where people ate each other.

Platonov met the revolution with an open heart, but he saw that the construction of socialism was turning out in practice to be no simple business. Power in some places fell partly into the hands of people who did not know what to do with it. On one side the Scylla of anarchy frightened Platonov, and on the other the Charybdis of bureaucracy.

The future had to be built, but at what price?

It was no accident that this was when Platonov wrote **"The Locks of Epiphany,"** in which he admired the organizing genius of Peter the Great and was horrified at the same time by his bloody methods. In his novel ***Chevengur,*** of which only one part has been published under the title ***The Origin of a Master,*** Platonov described in symbolic form an attempt to organize communism by almost-illiterate poor peasants. The poor peasants drive out all the propertied people, and then wait for the future to come by itself, since they have already organized their classless society. But the future doesn't show up, and the huts begin to tumble down. (p. 11)

So the question arises—is it perhaps unnecessary to depersonalize people? Does the people's strength perhaps lie precisely in this, in the fact that they are all different? Of course, if they all stay apart from each other, they will never accomplish anything, but maybe a society could be brought into being in which people would be both unlike each other and at the same time together? (pp. 11-12)

Perhaps this . . . expresses Platonov's own hopes for the future more than any other. But he was careful not to write out any prescription for it. Platonov believed in movement. . . .

But Platonov, believing in movement, still did not trust it for its own sake. He was leery of unintelligent reformers for whom the itch to transform humanity is more important than the most valuable thing on earth—an individual human being. Platonov knew that indifference to man in the concrete can hide behind abstract talk about love of humanity. And for Platonov humanity was always concrete. (p. 12)

The development of technology side by side with the backwardness of our ethics seemed to Platonov depressingly immoral. He cherished man for his mastery, but also man just for himself.

The intricacy of the problems developing around him transformed Platonov from a most subtle lyrical poet, which he was by nature, into the sharpest kind of writer about life. He was never a defender of militant private property, but the brutal spreading of collectivization by force, against which Lenin warned in his time, could not fail to move Platonov to stand up for man as both the creator of the earth and its creation.

Platonov had already been criticized for his story called **"Doubting Makar,"** when he wrote another story, **"Profit,"** continuing this line, which was printed in the magazine *Krasnaya Nov* in 1931. Stalin was an attentive reader of all magazines and his sharp observing eye did not allow Platonov's story to pass unpunished. Although Stalin himself spoke often later about "exaggerations" in the work in the villages, nonetheless he wanted jealously to reserve for himself any right to mention these deficiencies. On Platonov's story, in Stalin's red pencil, was written "Scum!" with an exclamation mark.

Platonov's literary life became more difficult. His prose was now seldom published and he lived by writing short critical reviews. He tried to get these published in a collected edition, but he did not succeed. Thanks to regular denunciations of Platonov by the critic Ermilov—the same man about whom Mayakovsky said in the letter written just before his death: "Sorry I didn't quarrel with Ermilov"—the already completed volume was killed and scrapped. (p. 14)

[In 1938 Platonov's] fifteen-year-old son Platon was accused of taking part in some kind of alleged counterrevolutionary conspiracy. This boy wrote poetry, by the way, and, judging by reports of those who saw it, very ably. He was given ten years, and sent to the far north, to Norilsk. Platonov wore himself out, haunting all the thresholds there were to haunt, but nothing helped. Then he wrote a letter to Stalin. At this moment Sholokhov came to Moscow to intercede for his own arrested relatives. Stalin received him, and according to rumor Sholokhov spoke up for Platonov's son, too. The boy returned home in 1940, exhausted, ill with tuberculosis, and he soon died. Platonov must be given credit for the fact that during these most difficult years he did not withdraw into himself,

Caricature of Platonov by David Levine. Copyright © 1969 Nyrev, Inc. Reprinted with permission from The New York Review of Books.

nor become embittered, but continued to write and to turn out some of his clearest writings filled with belief in human goodness, like **"Fro,"** **"The Third Son,"** and other stories. (p. 15)

[He] went to Ufa [during World War II] where in the confusion of evacuation his manuscript ***Travels in Humanity*** was irretrievably lost. But he did not relax behind the lines. Platonov began to work as a war correspondent on the paper *Red Star*, which was the most popular of all at the front, writing sketches and stories, giving all his strength for the victory of his fatherland. For Platonov this was not just a geographical patriotism. He always hated Fascism, and even before the war he had mercilessly held it up to shame in his stories **"An Angel Flew in the Midnight Sky"** and **"The Dusty Wind."**

The war came to an end. It would have seemed that Platonov had showed his love for his country—although he didn't need to prove it. He expected, of course, that a great deal would now change in his life. At that time a collection of Russian tales had already been published, worked up by him and protected by Sholokhov's name as editor. From 1929 until 1941 Platonov had had only one thin little book of his own issued, in 1937!

But after the publication of his short story **"Homecoming"** in 1946, criticism landed on Platonov again, and his name vanished from the pages of magazines and newspapers. When this story is reread now, it is hard to imagine why this most virtuous of stories was so attacked. For its gloominess, it seems, for its savoring of the darker aspects of the rear during the war. . . .

Platonov died in 1951 as a result of wounds he had received in fighting during the liberation of Czechoslovakia. He left behind him two unpublished novels, ***Chevengur*** and ***Kotlovan***, nine unproduced plays, nine unproduced motion picture scenarios, and a great many stories, sketches, and articles which had either never seen the light of day or had not been collected in book form. (pp. 15-16)

Platonov's is a delayed-action talent, and it may be that his safety fuse has burned only halfway to the explosion. Why was he held back, throughout his whole life, to a lower rank?

Because in the whole line of his creativity, which continued the great tradition of Russian literature, the tradition of "defense of the so-called little man," the tradition of "guilt for all," he was fundamentally contradicting the fashionable Stalinist theory of man as "a screw in the machine of government," and the proverb which justifies everything: "If you chop wood, chips fly." He loved locomotives, and he knew how to treat each screw gently so the locomotive would run well. He was concerned with screws and he humanized them; but to treat people as screws would have been intolerable to him. He loved trees, and he understood that every little chip by a merciless axe is a part of the murmuring green greatness. He realized that the theory of the inevitability of sacrificing chips can end up by destroying a whole forest. And although Platonov was disposed, like all men of good character, to forgive the times for blows against himself, he could not forgive them for blows against other people, against the humanity he loved so much, for whose sake he lived and wrote. (pp. 16-17)

Yevgeny Yevtushenko, "Introduction: 'Without Me, the Country's Not Complete'," in The Fierce and Beautiful World: Stories *by Andrei Platonov, translated by Joseph Barnes, E. P. Dutton, Inc., 1970, pp. 7-18.*

MAURICE FRIEDBERG (essay date 1970)

[Friedberg is a Polish-born American critic, editor, and writer on international affairs, as well as a former director of the Russian and East European Institute. In his critical studies, Friedberg focuses on the relationship between political and social conditions in the Soviet Union and literature produced by Soviet writers. These studies include The Party and the Poet in the USSR *(1963),* The Jew in Post-Stalin Soviet Literature *(1970), and* Decade of Euphoria: Western Literature in Post-Stalin Russia, 1954-64 *(1977). In the following excerpt, Friedberg discusses Platonov's attempt to eliminate the discord between humanity and nature or humanity and inanimate objects, another form of the polarity noted by L. Anninsky (1968).]*

In the history of Russian literature the decade and a half since Stalin's death are as significant for the new writers that have come to the fore as they are for their literary excavations. . . .

[Among] the major finds was the novelist and short-story writer Andrei Platonov. Widely acclaimed in preceding decades as one of the most original writers of Russian prose, in the last years of his life Platonov was an unperson to Soviet editors and publishers, and eked out a precarious living as a laborer. He died in obscurity in 1951.

Many of the great Russian writers of the past—Turgenev comes most readily to mind—sought to eliminate the discord between Man and Nature. Platonov continues this tradition, but his Nature reflects the changes that took place in Man's natural environment, which in the 1920s and 1930s no longer consisted solely of birch trees, brooks, and birds. By then, Nature had absorbed, as it were, many man-made objects, sounds and smells, and it is with this totality that Platonov seeks to establish a harmonious relationship. As a very young man, he wrote that "besides the fields, the countryside, my mother, and the sound of bells ringing, I also loved—and the longer I live, the more I love—steam engines, machines, shrill whistles, and sweaty work."

What set Platonov apart from most of his contemporaries who shared these concerns was his insistence that his protagonists blend with their industrialized environment without surrendering their humanity. As a result, the best of Platonov's work constitutes an eloquent refutation of the common misconception that the artistic failure of the bulk of Soviet literature should be traced to its partiality to tractors, cement, and production quotas. Rather, we should blame its regretfully pronounced tendency to obliterate distinctions between man and his inanimate surroundings, instead of viewing them as different even if not necessarily antagonistic universes.

Much of Platonov's appeal lies in his deliberately coarse and highly idiomatic language and in a style that echoes, and frequently also parodies, Communist sloganeering and Soviet newspaper editorials. . . .

[Even] in a superior translation and a better collection [than ***The Fierce and Beautiful World***] . . . Platonov is not likely to gain abroad the recognition he deservedly enjoys among those who can read him in the original Russian. In this respect Platonov's prospects are not unlike those of the great humorist Mikhail Zoshchenko, whose tales are relished by every Russian man, woman and child, but who remains relatively unappreciated outside of Russia. In his introduction Yevgeny Yevtushenko hints darkly that the lack of interest in Platonov abroad is explained by the absence of "noisy scandals connected with his name" and that this makes Platonov unacceptable to unnamed Western "specialists on [sic] Soviet literature" who are presumably interested only in "anti-Soviet" writers. Not only is this tired Soviet claim quite unfounded, but it sounds particularly hollow when voiced by a Soviet poet who owes much of his international fame to precisely such "noisy scandals." Yevtushenko's gratuitous remark recalls a wise Russian saying: "Other cows may moo, but yours should keep quiet."

Maurice Friedberg, in a review of "The Fierce and Beautiful World," in Saturday Review, *Vol. LIII, No. 2, January 10, 1970, p. 44.*

JOYCE CAROL OATES (essay date 1970)

[Oates is an American fiction writer and critic who is perhaps best known for her novel them, *which won a National Book Award in 1970. Her fiction is noted for its exhaustive presentation of realistic detail as well as its striking imagination, especially in the evocation of abnormal psychological states. As a critic, Oates has written on a remarkable diversity of authors from Shakespeare to Herman Melville to Samuel Beckett—and is appreciated for the individuality and erudition that characterize her critical work. In the following excerpt, Oates discusses Platonov's celebration of the Soviet state and collective ideals demonstrated in the story collection* The Fierce and Beautiful World, *wondering why Stalin denounced these almost propagandistic works. She also notes the inartistic nature of Platonov's writings and finds little to recommend in his works when compared to the writings of such contemporaries as Alexander Solzhenitsyn and Mikhail Bulgakov.]*

"The Fierce and Beautiful World" is a striking but somewhat misleading title for this collection of stories, the first publication in English of Andrei Platonov's work. There is not much fierceness in Platonov, and his beauty is likely to be a beauty of abstract strength, moral stability, a celebration of virtues that are perhaps now as old-fashioned in Russia as they are in the West—the equation of a man's soul with the larger, collective and holy soul of his nation. (p. 4)

[But,] unless the stories in this volume do not truly represent him, he seems rather unimpressive when compared with his contemporaries who are better known to Western readers—Solzhenitsyn, Bulgakov, "Yuli Daniel," and Yevtushenko . . . .

Platonov intrigues us with his blunt, primitive innocence. His stories are parables of human strength, the pilgrimages men make in search of "happiness." The first story in the book (written in the mid-1930's) is quite literally about a pilgrimage made by an educated man who is sent back to his homeland in Central Asia, the "middle of the wilderness of Asia," the "hellhole of the ancient world." The story begins realistically and ends in fantasy: the hero's desire is to lead his people out of their hellish lives and into happiness, to introduce the sickly, passive, oppressed nomadic tribe into the modern Russian state. **"Dzhan,"** the title of the story, means a soul seeking happiness, according to popular belief in Turkmenistan (a Soviet republic in Central Asia). "We're not going to allow unhappiness any longer," the hero Chagatayev declares.

At its best, Platonov's writing calls to mind simple religious fables of the kind that seem almost universal and certainly impersonal, gaining their strength from centuries of belief—in Platonov's case the belief is not in a supernatural presence, of course, but in the miraculous power of man's communal spirit as it is expressed through the Soviet Russian peasants or workers and through their machines, which mean salvation to them.

Other Soviet writers impress us as being our contemporaries in every way, writing to us or to Russian readers who resemble us, drawing upon certain literary assumptions which we take for granted. Platonov, however, is just the exceptional case that Yevtushenko judges him: he takes quite seriously the myth of the special destiny of the Communist state and does not hesitate to write glowingly of its soldiers (hence the corpses of enemies are "scoundrels" while the corpses of Russian soldiers are "what was born for good and active living," still "watching in death over our enemies in the earth") and machines are marvelous things, helping to bring fulfillment to men. (In the title story a blind engineer regains his eyesight when he is allowed to work again on his locomotive, helped by his assistant, who states that he derives a happiness from staring at his train "just as wonderful as what I felt when I first read Pushkin.")

Indeed, it is difficult to understand why Stalin denounced Platonov personally and why his writings were suppressed as nonconformist. There is very little evidence of irony or skepticism or European sophistication; Platonov obviously wrote to communicate with all readers, and his later works contain only positive references to the authorities, who are "zealous" and work "with great care" and who demonstrate a most admirable brotherhood with non-Party members. Platonov's narratives are unadorned, except for brief "poetic" passages in which nature is honored (though abstractly); there are paragraphs and paragraphs of unashamed rhetoric in praise of man's spirit, which may be fulfilled now for the first time in history as Soviet Russia attempts to work out its fate. Thus a typical story, **"Aphrodite,"** is only superficially about an ex-soldier's search for his wife, who is missing after World War II; it is really about the conquering of his despair, when a comrade tells him that he has no right to personal unhappiness. "Who has guaranteed us happiness and truth? We've got to make them ourselves, because our party is giving meaning to life for all the world. Our party—it's humanity's honor guard, and you're a guardsman."

Platonov demonstrates no capacity for—or interest in—commonly held esthetic values of dramatic development, emphasis, or pacing. His characters are often no more than names or attitudes; they are interchangeable, and this would no doubt seem a virtue to their creator, who is concerned with man at the point at which individual personality disappears and the mysterious collective personality emerges. We must take our places in the giant machinery of the State and there we will find happiness, but only there. Our way in to this State is through work, either the work of soldiers or of factory workers or farmers (Platonov's favorite characters), like the ambitious peasant volunteers for an electrical power station who became more "profound" in their work and developed an interest in each other and in "their relations to the working class, making turbines for generating the electricity [so] that the wretched loneliness of their hearts . . . disappeared."

Though several stories—**"Fro," "The Homecoming," "The Third Son"**—are ostensibly concerned with family relationships, their deeper concern is with this "profundity," this assimilation of the individual into the mass. Platonov therefore seems to us remarkably foreign. But, perhaps, his foreignness is not a result of his dogmatic theme (which is anticipated by Dostoevsky and Chekhov) but of his extremely earnest, crude, plodding narratives. Even the promising story **"Dzhan"** suffers from an exhausting shapelessness; far too long (111 pages), it seems the preliminary draft for a brutal, powerful story of Kafkaesque adventures.

If the lives of ordinary or oppressed people are empty, then art must faithfully reflect this emptiness; but it must reflect it artistically as well. (pp. 4, 42)

Joyce Carol Oates, in a review of "The Fierce and Beautiful World," in The New York Times Book Review, *February 1, 1970, pp. 4, 42.*

DAVID HAWORTH (essay date 1971)

[*In the following excerpt, Haworth praises the stories of* The Fierce and Beautiful World, *although he acknowledges that appreciation of them may be an acquired taste.*]

Stalin called Platonov 'scum', appropriately forgetting perhaps that scum tends to ride high, keep its level up and remain after the torrents of other words have drained through the memory. In Platonov's case this is precisely what has happened. He wrote his best work in the Thirties (of which there are fine examples [in ***The Fierce and Beautiful World***]) died in 1951, and only recently has Soviet censorship relaxed sufficiently for him to be rehabilitated. He is now enjoying much larger appreciation and currency than he could have hoped for in his tragic life. And no one, I think, would cavil with Paustovsky's comment four years ago that had Platonov's work appeared when it was written, 'our contemporaries would have been immeasurably richer in spirit'.

But the excessively fulsome tribute in Yevtushenko's introduction [see excerpt dated 1970] rather puts one on guard. Can 'a remarkable master' be being introduced to the English-speaking world? To the extent that these seven stories repeatedly drive the reader, in spite of reluctance, back to comparisons with Chekhov the answer must be yes. At the same time there is occasional clumsiness here, evidence of a heated infatuation with words and fine feelings, which can become too much for itself. A question of taste, but Platonov is sometimes just a bit loud with his emotions.

For entirely non-literary reasons it was this quality of his work that pulled down Stalinist rage on his head. He had an exquisite instinct about the deeper drives of human nature and this could not be squared with the rulers' demands for the banalities of political optimism. Such optimism was also supposed to take a controlling interest in affairs of the heart, and would inevitably fail, as Platonov knew. . . .

The finest story is the first, **'Dzhan'**—that is, a soul looking for happiness. It concerns the efforts of a sophisticated native of Turkmenistan to bring his people the fruits of political advance inspired by distant Moscow. It has a dream-like fatalism woven into the minutiae of action and observation which is impressive, and yet it is paradoxically sustained by an almost exotic optimism about the human condition. This strange quality manifests itself again in **'Homecoming'** (for which the author was ostracised) and in **'Aphrodite'**. It's all a rich mixture—often brilliant—but a taste for it may have to be gently acquired.

David Haworth, "Resurrection," in New Statesman, *Vol. 81, No. 2081, February 5, 1971, p. 188.**

VICTOR DOROFEYEV (essay date 1972)

[*Dorofeyev is a contemporary Soviet critic whose views demonstrate the vast change in official estimates of Platonov's talents that have taken place since Stalin's death. In the following excerpt Dorofeyev surveys several of Platonov's stories, describing the author's understanding of the common Soviet citizen and his celebrations of the dignity of work, domestic love, and duty.*]

Platonov was a man of the people. His outlook was essentially the healthy, straightforward "working man's" outlook, based on excellent knowledge of the practical needs of the working man, the "mass" conditions of his existence and everyday life. At the same time it was the outlook of a widely gifted, versatile man who through his own efforts rose to the heights of culture and became an intellectual in the best sense of the word, who took an active part in the people's creative endeavour.

Platonov possessed a powerful, highly original literary talent. He was also a born innovator and explorer of new ground by nature. This quality germinated in him early in life, at the work bench, and it later grew and came to fruition in his work as an engineer. Platonov carried over this same thirst for exploration and discovery to his literary work.

Any blazing of new trails, whether in science, technology or the arts, is always a journey into the unknown, involving danger and risk. Platonov frequently took risks. (p. 6)

The most interesting of Platonov's works of the 'twenties and 'thirties are those in which he describes the changes the revolution had wrought in the lives and minds of people living in the depths of provincial Russia, in its most remote corners. What was happening to the inhabitant of the various "middle-class" townships that abounded in provincial Russia before the revolution? How did the inhabitant of small towns sunk in ignorance and poverty live, what went on in his mind, what were his aspirations? What changes had occurred in the life and mentality of the most ordinary man from the masses, who was in no way outstanding, and perhaps even backward, whose position was akin to that of the poor peasant—the provincial workman, the small town craftsman, the village handy man.

One of Platonov's favourite themes is the moral regeneration of man in the process of revolutionary transformation, the awakening in him of genuinely human features and qualities.

While presenting the situation environment and human behaviour in their full everyday reality, Platonov at the same time always felt it was his duty to depict the intense and varied spiritual life of his hero. Not separate thoughts and feelings ascribed to the character on certain occasions but an uninterrupted flow of thoughts and feelings irradiated by him, illuminating everything around him and the character himself. The reader grasps the two simultaneously as naturally and simply as a man sees at once the object on which a spotlight is directed and the spotlight itself.

There is another aspect involved here. The complexity of a man's mentality consists, among other things, in the way in which all phenomena of the outside world (trees and grass and birds and sky) impinge upon his consciousness and become a part of his inward experience. Indeed, "man is the world of man" (Marx). This is how Platonov always tried to show his heroes, depicting the "power field" of their thoughts and feelings.

There is a school of thought which maintains that over these years Platonov was working mainly in the genre of the so-called "psychological" novella. This is not quite right. Psychology is important, but it is not the only and by no means the first concern, but rather a derivative factor of Platonov's images and works. His heroes always live in the world and not enclosed in themselves, and all of them, even the most primitive, take an interest and wish to take part in what is going on in the world because their feeling for life is social. Isolation is their misfortune and an aspect of poverty they have inherited, and the happiness of spiritual "property" which they have gained is to feel their own lives as a part of the common life of the people.

For instance, in ***The River Potudan,*** . . . Platonov tells the sad story of the love between two wonderful people, or rather of how they found it impossible, for quite a while, to experience a full love such as takes over a person's whole being. The subject is clearly elegiac. Surely, it offers a perfect opportunity to describe the purest essence of emotion and sentiment.

Yet, from the very first lines Platonov interweaves the love story with the most down-to-earth prose, describing the everyday round of life in a difficult period when the highest feeling went hand in hand with active help, with the struggle to ward off cold, hunger and typhus, with care to supply the beloved with his daily bread.

It is this aspect more than all the highest sentiments which convince us of the ideal and profoundly moving nature of the characters' emotions.

In ***The River Potudan*** we seem to see a pure spring of human feelings, pure and subtle in their self-sacrificing humanity. However, that spring is fated to water a barren earth, running through accumulations of dirt, rubbish, even sewage. It is possible that some readers may be shocked by this part of the story and some things in Platonov's tale may seem excessively grim and coarse. The justice of such criticisms cannot be denied. There is only one explanation: the writer was afraid that, if he did otherwise, the theme would immediately take on a conventional, abstract character and the lofty feelings would become "literary", banal and trite. (pp. 6-9)

In ***The River Potudan*** the love story is framed in a mass of other apparently secondary and subsidiary themes; there are also some meditative digressions bound up with the author's reminiscences of his own youth. All this does not only widen the horizon of the story, not only strengthen its philosophical implications, but gives the story a basis in life and features typical of its time.

Fro, which can be described as a song of triumphant love, is also firmly rooted in everyday life in the domestic realities of the 'thirties.

Platonov makes no attempt to idealise his heroine—she is shown as she is, capricious, selfish, and even rather silly. He does not even justify her extravagant behaviour when her husband leaves her and she is left alone with her pining heart. Sensitive artist that he is, Platonov simply realises that "no heart can brook delay", that "it aches and will trust nothing", until it achieves its desire.

A person is the same in his public, social activity as he is in his private, personal life. Platonov demonstrates this convincingly by showing not only Fro's longing for her husband, but also her husband Fyodor's untiring creative endeavour, and her retired engine driver father's fierce passion for his erstwhile work.

It has been suggested that Platonov would have been more in tune with the spirit of the times if, instead of restricting Fro to the circumscribed world of emotions, he had endowed her with some interest in social activities or something like that. To begin with we should then be dealing with a completely different story, and anyway the wisdom and charm of this particular story lie in the fact that far from confining Fro to the sphere of the emotions Platonov actually took her away from it.

In Fro—a bright, romantic, captivating character (despite the fact that she is "moulded" of the most down-to-earth material!)—we are shown the joy and sorrow of a heart captive to a single emotion. But such confinement, such delight in a single feeling conceals a great danger. Selfish love is just as much a spiritual desert as any other kind of selfishness. And, in Platonov's opinion, there is only one way of escape from this desert and that is through changing to a new, more mature feeling.

Fro feels this instinctively, and hence her dreams of having children: "Frossia wanted to have children. She would bring them up, they would grow and finish their father's work—the work of communism and science." And when the dream promises to come true, Frossia takes her second separation from the man she loves far more easily.

Love sickness, dreams of motherhood, of children—and suddenly the idea of communism and science! Is this not perhaps a little forced? With any other writer it might well be, but Platonov had a way of making the sharpest transitions of thought seem a perfectly natural flow of reflections and associations.

During the 'thirties Platonov wrote a number of stories in which children played a prominent part. In ***Adobe House in a Provincial Garden, July Storm, The Old Woman of Iron*** readers were struck by the great psychological wealth of the child characters, by Platonov's ability to give an extremely serious, truly plastic rendering of the emotional currents and changing moods in the child's soul. His attitude to the child and his treatment of the relationships between adults and children were highly original. Platonov regarded the adult's attitude to a child as the primary and most accurate criterion of morality. In ***July Storm*** he writes how it is through adults that the child discovers a kind, mysterious world bending over them for defence and happiness. But for adults, too, it is important not to forget the memory of their childhood and not squander or mutilate their "precise child's heart".

The enchanting child characters—and Platonov's children are just that, enchanting, tender, with a sensitive, precise heart—and the image of the mother as a source of life, light, kindness and boundless love constantly recur in Platonov's writings. He regards them as indestructible human values, making for the individual's strength in the "fierce, fine world", linking him to mankind's whole past and future.

Take ***The Third Son,*** for example, written extraordinarily "economically" (Platonov's expression). Although based on down-to-earth life material it deals with one of the "eternal" themes, and deals with it so profoundly, with such accurate and concise expressiveness that it evoked Hemingway's sincere admiration.

The story features the task-force of Soviet society, a fine, strong working family. It is quite clear to us that the brothers have earned their advancement in life by their services, their intelligence and good work. We feel in everything, in their comportment and behaviour, their strength of character and moral fibre, the noble dignity of the working man. People like this can achieve practically anything, but there are things in life which they, like everybody else, are powerless to control.

They have come together in response to a telegram from their old father to attend their mother's funeral. The sons, like their father, are profoundly distressed. They mourn their mother in silence, concealing from one another "their despair, their memories of childhood and the happiness of love which had welled continuously and undemandingly in their mother's heart and had always found them, even across thousands of miles. They had felt it constantly, instinctively, and this awareness had given them added strength and courage to go about their lives." All this has changed with their mother's death, and they are now left to face life on their own.

The sons are all very different people, and so their grief is also very different in quality and degree. Superb artist that he is, Platonov himself does not need to explain this. It is the characters themselves who tell us, and not by words but simply by their behaviour.

Once late at night the old man heard boisterous talk, laughter, and even singing, from the room where the sons slept. The voice of the eldest son sounded "full and strong". "You could feel his healthy teeth that had been repaired in good time and his deep, red larynx." The sailor brothers were tussling and guffawing, and the actor was trying to sing. Only the third son, a Communist, "had kept quiet, not saying anything or laughing". Then he said something and silence fell instantly. The genuine human grief of the third son had "called to order" hearts either made callous and indifferent by success, or somewhat insensitive by nature.

Platonov once said that "every man's mind is terribly overcrowded with thoughts and memories". The writer's task, as he saw it, was to concentrate a whole past life in a character. ***The Third Son*** shows Platonov's tremendous achievement in this direction.

Platonov regarded the theme of labour as the most important for Soviet writers. Socialism, he wrote, ennobles man in all ways, creating the real conditions for a man to "come to life, cheer up and be inspired", devote himself to creative endeavours "and make poetry even of the miner's pick and the steam engine's movement". Several of his stories, like ***The Engine Driver's Wife, Fresh Well Water*** or ***Fierce, Fine World,*** are fascinating examples of a profoundly meaningful, genuinely artistic treatment of this theme.

Platonov was always delighted by the "work principle" in people. He associated it closely with the awareness of individuality, personal dignity, kindness, wisdom and responsiveness.

He skilfully described the actual process of work, whether driving an engine or digging a well. And it was not so much a question of technology as of psychology, the complex work of human hands, mind and heart engaging with the whole wide world. Thus, in his stories a man driving a steam engine or a man digging a well are in complex relationship with the real world, as though standing at the junction of the main currents of life.

Fierce, Fine World is typical in this respect. The whole story is pervaded with the joy of skilful work, the delight of labour, in which Platonov sees man's true greatness to lie, his invincible "Promethean" spirit. The title is most appropriate, for the story indeed brings the reader the beauty of the world in which man is the master, and the fierce struggle going on in this world between all kinds of opposed forces. The outcome of the struggle, and how it is achieved, again depends on the person himself.

The characters are past masters at their job, people who are joyous and strong in spirit. The best of them combine the two strongest forces of life—industry and intelligence—so that for them work becomes an art and a source of enjoyment.

The engine driver Maltsev is a man of outstanding ability, with a highly developed sense of pride in his work. . . . Yet, Platonov shows us, disaster can overtake even a man like this.

Then Maltsev's workmate comes to the rescue of this innocent victim of circumstances. He engages in single combat with the blind, mechanical power of chance that accidentally and indifferently destroys the finest people, since they are more vulnerable than others. (pp. 10-15)

As a result, not only was the unfortunate man freed from the power of circumstances that threatened to destroy him but a new relationship was born between the two men, a more genuinely human relationship. . . . People are strong and invincible, Platonov asserted, when they stand together, when they come to one another's aid and fight shoulder to shoulder against hostile forces.

Thus, he wrote in one of his articles: Very often in life a man finds himself in a desperate situation. The man of labour seeks, and is bound to find, a way out, not only for himself, for his own personal destiny, but for the destiny of the people, of the state. . . . A man of labour always has hidden, "secret" spiritual reserves and means to save life from destruction.

This eminently correct, life-assertive idea, imbued with genuine popular wisdom, is developed by Platonov in many of his stories and sketches of the war years. Suffice it to recall ***Inspired People*** or ***The Defence of Semidvorie,*** or such stories as ***She Was Rosa, Aphrodite*** and ***The Homecoming.***

Platonov discerns inexhaustible "spiritual reserves and means" in ordinary Soviet people, showing them now on the battle field engaged in life-and-death struggle with the fascists, now in a prison torture-chamber, now on the home front with backbreaking labour and the unquenchable grief of a mother, a wife, or a sister.

It was his profound respect for human life, the desire to defend man from hostile forces that determined the strong anti-fascist current in Platonov's writings. (pp. 15-16)

In [***Garbage-Wind***] Platonov presents life under fascism in all its stark loathsomeness, the misery it brings people, while never for a moment losing sight of the inevitable emergence from darkness and madness into light and sanity. For fascism is but a dirty Garbage-Wind of history at the end of the old world, its delirium and nightmare before its ineluctable collapse.

In ***Through the Midnight Sky*** Platonov represents the typical fascist mentality in the navigator König. He is a specimen of that special kind of brute fascism produces according to its monstrous, inhuman designs. And what should people do in the face of this madness crawling across the world if they retain but a grain of true human essence in their hearts and minds? Retreat into themselves? Conceal their life in "the cave of the head", as Lichtenburg, the hero of ***Garbage-Wind,*** a humanist of the old cast, thinks of doing to begin with? Or simply wait until the brown plague subsides, accommodate themselves to it, even "serve" it, but keep silent about their real sentiments, as Lieutenant Erich Summer, the hero of ***Through the Midnight Sky*** does at first? Or struggle against it, doing everything that is in their power to oppose it, as the same Erich Summer eventually comes round to doing?

All these questions were constantly troubling Platonov in the 'thirties. His stories depict brutal types moulded by fascism, and describe the pain and suffering to which fascism condemns people who have retained the slightest degree of honesty and human decency. But his main aim is to arouse in people a burning hatred for this cruel and wholly hostile force. (pp. 17-18)

The truly mass heroism of the Soviet people, the noble tenor of thoughts and feelings of the Soviet soldier and the hard, wise martial art of the commanders evoked a warm response in Platonov, and was transformed by his talented pen into a virile, impassioned artistic account.

Of great importance in understanding Platonov's life and the evolution of his views is his late and largely autobiographical story ***Aphrodite***. Here Platonov makes various "corrections" and "additions" to his view of the country's path to socialism and the essential spiritual qualities of his contemporaries set forth in the first phase of his life and work. At each new stage the writer was somehow different, while always remaining true to himself.

Several collections of Platonov's short stories were published in the years 1942-45. In these stories, Platonov, one of the first to do so, told of the trials of war, the misery and suffering it caused, of children grown up before their time, of the inevitable hardening of human hearts.

The hero of ***The Homecoming***, Ivanov, a sergeant in the Guards, is no monster. On the contrary, he is a good, kind, though somewhat shallow man. But during the war, he grew unaccustomed to family life, and a certain emotional coarseness and unconscious selfishness that had always been there are brought to the surface at his homecoming. (pp. 18-19)

But when Ivanov saw his children running after the train that was bearing him away from his own family, it was as though the scales had fallen from his eyes. "He suddenly knew everything he had known before much more precisely and really. Before he had felt life through a barrier of pride and selfishness, but now he had touched it with his naked heart."

Here Platonov presents the sudden change of heart that Ivanov experiences with remarkable psychological accuracy and power. There are moments in life that can only be expressed through art, and Platonov could do so admirably.

In this story Platonov was true to himself. Firstly, he is mercilessly frank, sincere and truthful. Secondly, he reveals an extraordinarily sensitive, tender approach to the people he is describing, both children and adults.

Consummate artist, Platonov is always intensely *personal*—his outlook on life, his treatment of a subject and his methods of characterisation, his language and imagery are all unmistakably his own and nobody else's. We are carried along by his fresh, original imagery, his penetrating vision and wisdom, the power and beauty of his feelings, without always realising that this is a special artistic world, the world of Platonov.

We must explore this world, reading into it and living and thinking into it for its full enchantment to be revealed to us. (pp. 19-20)

Victor Dorofeyev, in an introduction to Fro and Other Stories *by Andrei Platonov, Progress Publishers, 1972, pp. 5-20.*

JOSEPH BRODSKY (essay date 1973)

[*Brodsky is a Russian poet and critic who emigrated from the Soviet Union in 1972 and became an American citizen in 1977. His early poems were considered morally and politically subversive by the Soviet government, which exiled him for a time to labor at a remote collective farm. Nevertheless, Brodsky's eventual flight from a repressive communist society was also an estrangement from the Russian culture of which he felt a rightful part, as well as a separation from the language necessary to his vitality as a poet. This latter deprivation is an especially poignant one for Brodsky, who has stated his view of poetry as a relief from the horrors and absurdities of life and the meaningless vacuum of death. In a line from one of his most admired poems,* "Gorbunov and Gorchakov," *he states: "Life is but talk hurled into the void." This temperament, along with the often philosophical cast of his poetry, has led critics to link Brodsky with the modern school of existentialism, an affiliation well supported by the important influence played by such precursors of existentialism as Søren Kierkegaard and Fedor Dostoevski in forming Brodsky's artistic vision. Brodsky's work has been well-received by English and American critics, many of whom have called him the greatest living Russian poet. In the following excerpt Brodsky discusses Platonov's use of language, particularly his incorporation of contemporary political language in his tales of peasant life.*]

The idea of Paradise is the logical end of human thought in the respect that it, thought, goes no further; for beyond Paradise there is nothing else, nothing else happens. And therefore one can say that Paradise is a dead-end. . . . (p. ix)

The same may be said of Hell.

Being in the dead-end is not limited by anything, and if one can conceive that even there being defines consciousness and engenders its own psychology, then it is above all in language that this psychology is expressed. In general it should be noted that the first victim of talk about Utopia—desired or already attained—is grammar; for language, unable to keep up with thought, begins to gasp in the subjunctive mood and starts to gravitate toward timeless categories and constructions; as a consequence of which the ground starts to slip out from under even simple nouns, and an aura of arbitrariness arises around them.

In my view this describes the prose language of Andrei Platonov, of whom it can be said with equal veracity that he drives language into a semantic dead-end and, more precisely, that he reveals in language itself the philosophy of the dead-end. If this statement is even half-justified, that is sufficient to proclaim Platonov one of the eminent writers of our age—for the presence of the absurd in grammar says something not just about a particular tragedy, but about the human race as a whole.

In our age it is not customary to examine a writer outside the social context, and Platonov would be a quite suitable subject for such analysis if that which he performs with language did not go far beyond the framework of the specific utopia (the building of socialism in Russia), witness and chronicler of which he is in ***The Foundation Pit***. ***The Foundation Pit*** is an exceedingly gloomy work, and the reader closes the book in the most depressed state of mind. If at this moment direct transformation of psychic energy into physical energy were possible, the first thing one should do on closing the book would be to rescind the existing world-order and declare a new age.

By no means, however, does this mean that Platonov was an enemy of this utopia, the regime, collectivization, etc. The only thing one can say seriously about Platonov within the social context is that he wrote in the language of this utopia, in the language of his epoch; and no other form of being determines consciousness as language does. But unlike the majority of his contemporaries—Babel, Pilnyak, Olesha, Zamyatin, Bulgakov, Zoshchenko, who concerned themselves more or less with stylistic gourmandizing, i.e., played with language, each at his own game (which in the final analysis is a form of escapism)—Platonov subjected the language of the epoch to himself, having seen in it such abysses that once he had peered into them he could no longer slide along the literary surface, concerning himself with clever manipulations of plot, typographical contrivances and stylistic point-lace.

Of course, if one is to study the genealogy of Platonov's style, one inevitably has to mention hagiographic "plaiting of words," Leskov with his tendency towards individualized first-person narratives, Dostoevsky with his choking bureaucratese. But in Platonov's case the important thing is not lines of succession or traditions of Russian literature, but the writer's dependence on the synthetic (or, more precisely, non-analytical) essence of the Russian language itself, something which, partly as a result of purely phonetic allusions, determines the formation of concepts which are devoid of any real content. Even if Platonov had used even the most elementary means, his "message" would be relevant. . . . But his main weapon was inversion; he wrote in a totally inverted language; more precisely, Platonov put an equals sign between the concepts of *language* and *inversion—"version"* (normal word order) came more and more to play a service role. In this sense I would say that the only real neighbor Platonov had in language was poet Nikolai Zabolotsky during the period of *Scrolls*.

If for Captain Lebyadkin's poetry about the cockroach (in *The Devils*) Dostoevsky can be considered one of the first writers of the absurd, for the scene with the striker-bear in ***The Foundation Pit,*** Platonov should be acknowledged the first serious surrealist. I say "first" in spite of Kafka, for surrealism is not just a literary category, tied in our minds as a rule with an individualistic world-perception, but a form of philosophical madness, a product of the psychology of the dead-end. Platonov was not an individualist, quite the contrary—his consciousness was determined by the mass scale and absolutely impersonal character of what was happening. Therefore his surrealism is non-personal, folkloric, and to a certain degree akin to ancient, or for that matter any mythology—which one might call the classical form of surrealism.

In Platonov those who express the philosophy of the absurd are not egocentric individualists to whom God and literary tradition provide crisis-awareness, but representatives of the traditionally uninspired masses; and due to this fact the philosophy becomes far more convincing and utterly unbearable in its magnitude. Unlike Kafka, Joyce, or, let's say, Beckett, who narrate the quite natural tragedies of their "alter egos," Platonov speaks of a nation which in a sense has become a victim of its own language; or, more precisely, he speaks of this language itself—which turns out to be capable of generating a fictive world and then falling into grammatical dependency on it.

It seems to me that therefore Platonov is untranslatable, and in one sense that is a good thing for the language into which he cannot be translated. But nevertheless one has to congratulate any attempt to recreate this language, a language which compromises time, space, life itself and death, not because of "cultural" considerations, but because in the final analysis it is precisely in this language that we speak. (pp. ix-xii)

Dust jacket of a 1973 translation of Platonov's The Foundation Pit *published by Ardis Publishers. By permission of Ardis Publishers.*

Joseph Brodsky, in a preface to The Foundation Pit *by Andrei Platonov, translated by Thomas P. Whitney, Ardis Publishers, 1973, pp. ix-xii.*

MARION JORDAN (essay date 1973)

[*In the following excerpt from the most comprehensive English-language study of Platonov, Jordan surveys the events of Platonov's career and the primary themes of his works.*]

During [the] years from 1918-1927 Platonov, despite the apparent busyness of his life as soldier, student, irrigation expert, newspaper reporter, also completed his apprenticeship as a writer and adopted the pen-name Platonov. His first truly literary work was the composing of poems which he would read with simplicity and a complete absence of dramatic emphasis to his friends in Voronezh. Even with his early poems, which were often marred by a false sentimentality, he won the respect of his fellow-writers and his poems rapidly changed from ones which were criticised because "their setting was the universe, and the hero was a generalised figure remote from real life" to ones which were "made interesting by the poet's attempt to give a more definite and concrete illustration to the theme of revolution"

It was perhaps the warm reception given to these more mundane poems, which describe "a real revolutionary town, the way of life of the working classes, hard work", which led Platonov to the realisation that the work for which he had a real talent was much nearer to the bread-and-butter articles which he had written for his newspaper than to the romantic transports still expected of a young poet. Certainly ***The Sky-blue Depths*** . . . was the only collection of poems which he issued. (pp. 11-12)

The first stories that Platonov wrote in the early twenties were, though literary in form, very much a continuation of his newspaper reporting. Based on fact, often autobiographical fact, they were usually the expression of social conscience rather than of literary inspiration. (p. 12)

In 1927 Platonov published his first collection of sketches and short stories, ***Epiphany Locks***. (p. 14)

The characters even in the earliest stories are the eccentrics who are to wander elusively through practically the whole of Platonov's later work—the childhood innocent, the homeless wanderer, the deserted old man, the beggar. But the manner of these early stories is unbearably clumsy. This clumsiness arises from a desire to be honest, which is not as yet accompanied by technical competence. Platonov sets out to describe real life. (p. 15)

Platonov was already master of the arresting opening, the striking phrase. What his early stories lack is organisation—they have neither climax, nor conclusion, but only a feeling that they may be continued in the next day's report. (p. 16)

Two stories stand out from the collection ***Epiphany Locks***, one the title story and the other **"The Town of Gradov"**. Platonov's satirical intention is clear from the title of this second story, with its echoes of Shchedrin's "History of a certain town". **"Gradov"** tells how an official, Ivan Shmakov, is sent from Moscow to try to bring some common-sense into local affairs in Gradov. However, Shmakov himself rapidly becomes absorbed into the town under the influence of the chief local official, Bormotov. This story has none of the emotionalism of the earlier Platonov. Its tone is that of a polite and measured scorn. The targets of its satire are bureaucracy and provincial ignorance, targets which seem scarcely to have changed since Shchedrin's time. . . . In so far as the targets are specifically Soviet, they are only coincidentally so. The principal butt is the one so common in a world of officials, the inability of officialdom to encompass the contradictions and singularities of human demands. The officials impose a system of ritual and precedence upon their own social affairs, but life generally defies such categorisation. (pp. 16-17)

Platonov was still experimenting with various forms of story. One of the most successful of these experiments is the title story of the collection, **"Epiphany Locks"**. Its theme, that of the wanderer far from home trying to bring help to an ignorant people, is one that had already been treated by Platonov in early stories and that recurs throughout Platonov's work, notably in the later haunting story **"Dzhan"**. On this occasion, however, the story is given a historical setting, and the technological help is brought to a backward eighteenth century Russia by an English engineer. (p. 18)

[The] feeling engendered by the story is universal, rather than either topical or historical. One is presented with an illustration of the intractability of circumstances, circumstances which arise as a result of man's actions and decisions and yet which are not planned by him to take the form which they do. . . . Any interference with nature is presumptuous. Yet human beings are not discredited by their opposition to nature. Platonov's purpose is to show not merely the harsh inevitability of nature's victory, but also that life's value lies in man's dogged though always doomed resistance to such a victory. (pp. 19-20)

With Gorky's help Platonov was able to publish occasional short stories in 1927 and 1930 in the journals *October* and *New World*, but some of his best stories of this period have never been published in book form even to the present day. **"Doubting Makar"**, for example, still exists only in magazine form . . . despite its beautifully controlled manner. The hero of the title, a simple countryman, goes to seek his fortune in Moscow, where he views industrialized communism with a penetrating naivety which allows Platonov to satirise a simplified version of communist doctrine, interpreted, quite literally, by Makar and his friends as the right to free transport, or to financial support from the state, or to universal employment for manual workers such as themselves in some "thinking capacity", or as the right merely to sit and wait for the state to wither away.

The image which caused most serious offence, however, to Soviet critics of the thirties (and still indeed today) is found in Makar's dream where he sees a learned man on a hill-top. This man is raised so far above the people, his gaze is so far into the future, that he can pay attention only to the general line, not to the particular Makar. Makar strives to climb the hill, to bring himself to the attention of the figure, but when he gets there he finds the man not merely deaf and dumb, as he had supposed, but dead; it is a great statue rather than a person, taking a man's physical shape but not sharing his human sensitivity. The figure symbolises the impossibility, in Platonov's view, of communication between the feeling human being and the unfeeling great new state (modern industrial civilisation, or Communism, or Stalin himself, whichever gloss one cares to put upon it). For neither the figure nor this concept of the state is new in Russian literature. Pushkin's Bronze Horseman had looked equally grand, and had been equally indifferent to the individual in his splendid vision of the future. (pp. 23-5)

"For Future Use" is another story of a man wandering in search of the truth about the new Russia, but it sees a return of all Platonov's old pessimism. It combines a sadness at the foolishness of man in his hopeless schemes for reconstruction with an overwhelming despondency in the face of an unresponsive nature. This account of one man's view of the effects of collectivisation is essentially non-fictional. There is a sense in which it could scarcely be described as "nihilistic" rather than "realistic", even by Soviet critics. (pp. 26-7)

[It] is exactly the kind of situation which suits his style. He is drawn always by the twin compulsions of irony and pessimism. He himself both worships the machine and the mechanic and yet distrusts the hope which they appear to offer since, for Platonov, man is never in charge of his own destiny. The situation, therefore, is essentially both hopeless and ironical. (p. 27)

The pages of *October* were closed to Platonov after Averbakh's attack on **"Doubting Makar"**. The pages of *Red Virgin Soil* were closed after Fadeev's attack on **"For Future Use."** . . .

Gorky was now Platonov's one friend in any position of literary importance. . . . Even he, however, was conscious that he could no longer secure the publication of works such as Platonov wrote. (p. 28)

Platonov could not hope to publish any more satire. (p. 31)

One of Platonov's later heroes looks back over his life and sums up its significance: "We were always hemmed in on all sides, in the womb, the cell or the grave; we were unconscious only." Platonov's stories of the early thirties described three threats to man's survival which coincide with these three states of constraint and lead man finally to unconsciousness. The stories either return to Platonov's early years and describe, retrospectively, man's struggle for survival in the times immediately before and after the Revolution (the time of Platonov's "birth" as a writer); or they concern themselves with man's struggle against the emerging threat of Fascism in Europe in the thirties; or they show man's despairing attempt to survive in the face of a hostile nature.

These struggles never end in victory for humanity. They conclude, at best, with the weary shouldering of an impossible burden; at worst the issue is one of degradation and death. But the adversity with which they concern themselves was a circumstance sufficient to prompt Platonov to produce his best work. (p. 33)

The best of the stories of earlier times is **"The River Potudan"**, which returns to the famine and hardship of the period immediately after the Revolution. Like many of Platonov's best stories it is concerned with man driven to the extremity of life, where survival itself is threatened. (p. 34)

The setting of the story is one of such depression that people have deliberately cultivated a weakening of their vital forces because these involve them only in pain. (p. 35)

Such a setting provides a convincing background to the story's insistent refrain that human relationships are not, as is usually the case in modern literature, to be traced in romantic love as such (whose ultimate goal is usually represented as sexual fulfilment) but in the mutual provision of the even more primary needs of food and warmth—everything here depends upon the supply of gifts in kind. . . .

A story compounded of such extremes clearly involves the danger of falling into sentimentality—a danger which Platonov had not always avoided earlier. Here, however, Platonov escapes the danger, by the avoidance of all emotion in style or vocabulary. The facts themselves, tragic or pathetic, are left to convey their own emotion without emotional elaboration of style. The effect is like that of a ballad or a folk-tale where a laconic brevity or an apparently casual banality of style shows the defencelessness of humanity in the face of repeated tragedy. (p. 36)

Yet Platonov tried hard to conform to the spirit of the thirties in the Soviet Union. He was concerned, as was the whole state, with the growing threat of Fascism in Europe. The threat was seen, as always in Platonov, as extreme, on the one hand as an attempt to wipe man from the face of the earth, and on the other as an attempt to cling to whatever forms of sentient life might persist. "The Imperialist War," Platonov wrote, "and its present-day sequel, Fascism, started an attempt to destroy man in all respects, even physically." It is this attempt of one group of men to destroy another which seizes Platonov's imagination in writing of the growth of Fascism, both in Germany and in Spain.

The most important of these stories is **"The Rubbish-bearing wind"**, which tells of the destruction of a "cosmic scientist", in a South German province who had attacked a statue of Hitler. The scientist's original despondency when taken prisoner is dispelled by the courageous example of a young girl-prisoner. He dies, however, of the wounds he had received when first attacking the statue of Hitler. (pp. 37-8)

[The] story is singularly characteristic of Platonov's sense of pessimism and extremity rather than typical of the literature of the day. Platonov here shows an almost pathological revulsion from mankind. There is throughout the story a ubiquitous suggestion that man's chief function is to despoil the world with his cast-off rubbish. The world, soiled by its own excretions, becomes an enormous rubbish-pit, a rotting compound of human putrefaction. . . . (p. 38)

Nor is it only in this picture of the world as a giant rubbish heap that Platonov shows his revulsion from mankind. For here Platonov does not merely portray particular men as deviating from human norms, he portrays the whole of mankind as an animal species eating, and being eaten by, other animals. Stylistically the story represents it as impossible that the world of decay around the scientist should survive in the world of steel and bronze which the Nazis inhabit. (p. 39)

In the meantime Platonov was occupied in the earlier part of this period with stories which form a third thematic group. A third source of constraint, the hostility of Nature (backed by man's own inhumanity) was perhaps the most powerful source of literary inspiration for him. So potent was Platonov's conviction of the hostility of nature that there were times in the thirties when he confessed himself unable to see how man could develop his spiritual potentialities without it. (p. 40)

[**"Takyr"** and **"Dzhan"**] were a response to a grandiose scheme of Gorky's to bring out a five-volume work devoted to the development of socialism. (p. 41)

The first of these stories, **"Takyr"**, (the title is a regional word for a flat expanse of clay earth in the middle of the desert where nomadic tribes briefly reside) is ostensibly concerned with the transformation from the old tribal ways to the Soviet welfare state. (p. 42)

[The author's] real interest, however, lies in the account of the nomadic life, a life, for Platonov, of perpetual farewells, a life which symbolises the fleeting nature of all existence, and which offers none of the luxury and ease, none of the consolations of companionship or humour or love, which might distract man from the contemplation of his grief. Love here is a matter of sexual commerce or of cruelty. . . . Even the relationship of mother and child offers only the most imperceptible of pleasures—the opportunity for a child to warm itself against its mother's body. So cruel is life that only a deliberate cultivation of indifference will allow man to survive. . . . The account of this life is so vivid that it becomes the raison d'être of the story, whereas the reader's attention is scarcely engaged at all by the perfunctory account of Dzhumal's Soviet regeneration and return to the *takyr*.

This is equally true of the second of the stories which Platonov wrote as a result of his visit to Turkmenistan. This story, **"Dzhan"**, takes its name from a desert tribe who have no ethnic name, since they are compounded of the outcasts and refugees of many tribes, and who therefore take (ironically one feels) the Turkmen name for a spirit which seeks happiness, Dzhan. . . . The main part of the story is concerned with Chagataev's heroic efforts to lead the Dzhan back to their ancestral home. Life for the Dzhan is so hard that the only resolution lies in death, or better, in never having been born—Chagataev's mother comments: "They are luckiest who die within the womb." (pp. 44-5)

Platonov also produced in the thirties two other groups of tales which deal with man in less extreme circumstances. One group of these stories forms a series of domestic comedies (or perhaps tragi-comedies), the second is a series of stories which portray man's devoted relationship to the machine.

The family stories are set generally in a contemporary, civilised Soviet Union, without any feeling of threat from Fascism, or persecution, or natural disaster. Yet, even in the midst of comedy, there is a pervasive air of sadness, for in almost all the stories the characters suffer a particular kind of deprivation—they are deprived of those members of their family who might be expected to care for them. Their vulnerability is that of old age without the care of one's children, of extreme youth without the care of one's parents, of deserted husbands or deserted wives. Nonetheless the feeling is one of sadness rather than of hopeless dejection as it had been in the other stories, where the characters, after all, had to suffer family deprivation along with much more damaging stresses.

Platonov was much occupied by the relationship between mother and child. . . . Platonov suggested that however free from guilt one might appear to be one was always somehow or other guilty with regard to one's parents. . . . **"The Third Son"** . . . was devoted to just this theme. (pp. 49-50)

This cool treatment of the patience and self sacrifice of parents is picked up again in a short story of great charm written about the same time, **"The Old Man and the Old Woman"**. . . . Despite the sadness of the ending there is a pleasure, almost a gaiety, in the picture of the old man and his wife. The comedy lies in the fact that the story is, as it were, a parody of a young love-affair. . . . The tragedy lies in the fact that the couple, who have the feelings of youth, have the bodies of age, and so the old woman dies.

The atmosphere of quiet resignation in the face of a sad but natural blow of fate which characterises the end of this story is repeated in **"Fro"**, which again combines a mild, aching sadness with a certain lighthearted resilience and a humorous mockery of the shifts to which the young wife of the title is driven in her attempts to get her husband, an engineer sent to work in the Far East, to stay at home with her. The story is the most developed of Platonov's attempts at domestic comedy, involving as it does what Platonov calls in the story "that inextricable compound of sadness and happiness which is to be found in real life." (pp. 50-1)

The most promising escape from death and destruction offered by Platonov at this time is for man to abandon his dependence upon other men and to put his trust in the machine, the engine. This theme had been an important one in Platonov's stories in the twenties. In the great stories of the early thirties Platonov had put it aside. Now, around 1936, it was revived. (p. 52)

[The] technology in which Platonov was interested was not the advanced industrialisation of urban settlements, but that technology which might with one grand and magical stroke transform the countryside—irrigation schemes, electrification, railways. And of these it was the last which most readily combined with Platonov's other preoccupations, because it allowed him not only to show his interest in technicalities but also to use as his characters the typical "displaced" people of the earlier sketches, men who had been moved from one station to another in the interests of the railways for which they worked.

But the real promise of the machine, as opposed to man, is in the fact that its faults may, hopefully, be rectified. (p. 53)

In October 1942 Platonov was mobilised, like most Soviet writers, as a war-reporter. For three years he worked chiefly on the Red Army newspaper *The Red Star*. (p. 61)

His duties were, of course, non-combatant, but he went right up to the front-line to make his observations and was repeatedly praised for his endurance and military valour.

Platonov's public life, then, flourished in the adversity of the war years as it never had in the adversity of the years of peace. His literary talents, however, languished. Platonov had never really mastered any straight-forwardly narrative way of writing. In the short story proper he had kept largely to the sketch form with only the slightest of plots. Even in his longer stories interest in the plot, in the sense of movement or action, had always been secondary to Platonov's interest in characters, or the nature of the static situation. He had rarely shown any interest in the interplay of characters or in the development of events—an indifference which had sometimes resulted in a certain structural weakness in his stories. . . . War provides its own plots; it imposes an artificial structure upon events; actions begin at determined moments and their outcomes tend to involve their own conclusive—often fatal—consequences. However, it was clearly not within Platonov's powers to deal happily with clear cut plots of this kind, even when they presented themselves to him. (pp. 63-4)

Moreover, alongside . . . false-sounding heroics, so unfortunately characteristic of most stories written in times of war, there exists the equally prevalent suggestion that all the good, all the bravery, all the ingenuity, all the self-sacrifice, are on one side, and that the enemy is characterised by cowardice and subterfuge only—a fallacy equally destructive of literary conviction. In Platonov it goes peculiarly further than is customary, since he so loved great machines and engines that he could not allow even these most inanimate of aids to work impartially for Germans and Russians alike. (p. 65)

Where [the war stories] succeed they succeed by adapting Platonov's existing themes and methods; where they fail they fail by attempting to introduce the violently heroic. Their unevenness arises from the unhappy combination of realistic and detailed narrative event with the fantasy or the grotesque hyperbole of much earlier Platonov. (pp. 66-7)

A small number of Platonov's war stories are concerned with the more irregular fighting that goes on in occupied territory, where the civilian population tries to outwit its invaders. In general this kind of story does not demand the same concentration of action as do war-stories proper. This kind of irregular scheming behind the lines allows Platonov to follow his natural bent, to concentrate on situation and the display of one leading character, rather than on the development of incident and the interplay of diverse characters, as in the stories about the army. In stories like **"The Good Cow"** or **"Grandfather-soldier"** Platonov is, therefore, much more successful since the incidents of heroic prowess are merely momentary interruptions in a naturalistic setting.

This departure from the artificial heroics of the front-line is even more marked in a group of stories dealing with the effects of war upon the bereaved, which return essentially to the Platonov of the thirties, to the Platonov who saw people so often in situations of family deprivation. For these people war is by no means a time for heroic or decisive action, or indeed for action at all. The stories portray, as had many of those of the thirties, a more or less static situation of suffering. Stories like **"The Peasant Yagafar"** or **"The Little Soldier"** are to this extent better than the general run of the war-stories, though they are so slight as scarcely to bear comparison with the great stories of the thirties.

"Mother" is perhaps the best of them. (pp. 67-8)

Even during the war, however, Platonov was engaged not only in writing war-stories, but also in writing a series of stories about children. He started this series in the late thirties at a time when he was finding it impossible to publish anything, and continued it into the mid-forties. (p. 71)

Many of Platonov's earlier stories had in any case included studies of children considered as an integral part of the adult world, and often acting more responsibly than adults proper. In this series of stories Platonov turned his attention more directly to the world of the child itself, a world in which children were the normal inhabitants and adults merely a necessary intrusion, just as children had been a necessary intrusion in the adult world of the earlier stories. Given this important change in the balance of interests, however, these stories are remarkably similar in tone and style to the earlier ones. For Platonov's stories are not stories *for* children, though a child might well recognise with pleasure the sympathy with which they penetrate his world, but stories *about* children. The overall resemblance to Platonov's general work can be seen in the fact that many of the stories are about the deprived—though in this series of stories deprivation almost always takes the form of being orphaned. . . . [In] these stories, as generally in Platonov, family ties are both weak and mutable; a family is not so much a constant unit bound by marriage and blood-relationship, as a shifting group which finds some ad hoc advantage in temporary co-existence, and which disperses when this advantage is no longer to be found.

Platonov's interest at this time, as always, lies not in the analysis of that relationship between equals which is conventionally regarded as characteristic of mature adults, but in the description of the relationship between the dependent and the protector. The bulk of his stories about children treat characters who are, because of their age, in this position of dependence—the immature dependent upon the mature—but this dependence is not to be relied upon since the seemingly mature turn out to be senile, and, therefore, themselves dependent upon the developing maturity of the children who depend upon them. From this there arises a position of mutual dependence in which neither party is both stable and mature.

One story, **"The World of Life"**, takes this one stage further in that there the same character appears both as a defenceless young boy and, later, as a defenceless old man. . . . Platonov is not interested in the *course* of a life, but only in the *states of vulnerability* which that life involves.

Most of these stories about children, however, are more lighthearted than other stories of the period. The children themselves are resilient in a way quite unknown to the children who occur in earlier stories by Platonov. Stories like **"The Iron Old Woman"**, **"A Flower on the Ground"**, and **"Granny's Hut"** are all concerned with children seeking to find out the truth about life from the old people whom they meet. The conversation which forms the bulk of these stories is superbly managed by Platonov to show the contrasting natures of the young, who are vulnerable because in their optimism they expect too much of life, and the old, who are vulnerable because in their pessimism they have ceased to seek anything from life. (pp. 71-4)

By the end of the war Russia had been regained, but the peasant had still to be restored to his hut. And this forms the twin theme, already so firmly indicated in the war-stories themselves, of Platonov's post-war work—the return of the wanderer and the work necessary to restore him to a viable life. (p. 82)

"The Ivanov Family" [published in 1962 as **"The Homecoming"**], Platonov's last independent publication (though not the last thing he wrote) deals . . . fully and . . . directly with the same theme of the wanderer returning from the wars. The story is a splendidly rounded account of the moral and emotional destruction which war causes alongside the physical destruction; it shows how human relationships must be rebuilt, just as homes and generating stations must. (p. 84)

In this story Platonov comes nearer than ever before to complete psychological realism. Sometimes in earlier stories like **"The Potudan River"** Platonov had attempted to provide a complete psychological motivation, but there the attitudes and behaviour of the characters are so extreme that the account becomes pathological rather than psychological. . . . (p. 85)

Although Platonov lived for another five years he was able to publish no other original work in his own lifetime. (p. 88)

[He] turned to what might seem hack-work, to the writing up of collections of Russian folk-tales, but this hack-work became in Platonov's hands a work of literature in itself. (p. 89)

When one reads . . . collections of Platonov's folk-tales like ***Bashkir Folk Tales*** or ***The Magic Ring*** one finds oneself not unrecognisably far from Platonov's earlier world. These humble peasants are subject to the same deprivation as Platonov's earlier characters, that is to say the bulk of them are either very old or very young, and the old have lost their children and the young have lost their parents. There is scarcely a family which is complete. And this somnolent world of defenceless youth and powerless old age is subject to violent upheaval as Platonov's earlier world had been, though in these folk-tales the violence is even more casual. Events like the deaths from snake-bites in **"The Stepdaughter"** or the sticking of the heads of the unsuccessful suitors upon the gate-posts in **"John the Untalented and Helen the Wise"** are rarely equalled in Platonov's modern stories.

Constantly the characters from these stories are forced to wander from their homes upon interminable quests, as Platonov's earlier characters had wandered, though they never reach the degree of dejection experienced by the characters in the stories of the mid-thirties. When the characters are enabled to assert themselves, to make their mark upon the world despite their humility, it is by just those expedients used in Platonov's earlier work, that is to say, by a combination of patience and industry. It is, indeed, of the essence of almost all these stories that people are called upon to undergo repeated trials. (pp. 94-5)

Where the folk-tales did, in general, demand a change from Platonov's normal manner was in their frequent introduction of happy endings. . . . [But] the body of the stories, with their descriptions of pain and suffering is always more impressive, remains longer in the mind, than the ending. For Platonov never creates, even in the fairy-stories, a wholly enchanted world with its own set of rules. His stories are set rather in an ordinary world into which magic is occasionally admitted. (pp. 97-8)

Marion Jordan, in his Andrei Platonov, *Bradda Books Ltd, 1973, 116 p.*

PAUL THEROUX (essay date 1974)

[*Theroux is an American fiction writer, critic, and travel writer who, since 1963, has lived outside the United States, first traveling to Africa with the Peace Corps and later settling in England. Many of his novels and short stories have foreign settings—Kenya in* Fong and the Indians *(1968), Malawi in* Girls at Play *(1969) and* Jungles Lovers *(1971), Singapore in* Saint Jack *(1973)—and feature characters whose conflicting cultural backgrounds, as well as their personal conflicts, provide the substance of the story. Critics often find Theroux's fictional works to be sardonic expositions of chaos and disillusionment presented with wit, imagination, and considerable narrative skill. Theroux has also produced several nonfiction accounts of his travels, including* The Great Railway Bizarre *(1975) and* The Old Patagonian Express *(1979). As a critic, he has written a study of Trinidadian novelist and essayist V. S. Naipaul and frequently reviews books for several major English and American periodicals. In the following excerpt, Theroux discusses Platonov's masterful use of bureaucratese to record his disgust with Soviet life.*]

The Russian author, Andrei Platonov (1896-1951) is described by Joseph Brodsky in his preface to this bilingual edition [see excerpt dated 1973] as "the first serious surrealist," a philosopher of the dead-end, who argues in the clumsy newspeak of language pushed to its limit. In making this point, Brodsky is less than fair to Zamyatin and Bulgakov who have something of Platonov's fine madness. "Stylistic gourmandizing" does not describe either "We" or "Diaboliad," and what these three writers share is a grim, often comic and always uncompromising skepticism. They are as unpopular with the commissars today as they were in the 1920's. Zamyatin is not read in the Soviet Union (or so a Russian student of literature told me last month in Siberia), Bulgakov is not even in the libraries, the Platonov is circulated in *samizdat* typescripts.

"The Foundation Pit" is obviously a masterpiece, and Thomas P. Whitney's translation is to be praised for its ingeniously dogged faithfulness to a magnificent experiment in debased language. It is, of course, bureaucratese, the impersonal and contemptuous lingo of ministerial hacks. (The Watergate hearings have produced a whole lexicon of it.) Platonov uses the language like a man speaking with a rising gorge, occasionally gasping with disgust. The result, as Brodsky warns, "is an exceedingly gloomy work."

The story itself is lugubriously simple. Voshchev, fired from the machine shop, joins a gang of workmen who are digging a deep pit. It is hard work, and as the men scrabble in the frozen soil they talk to keep their spirits up. ("The proletariat lives for the sake of labor enthusiasm . . ." and "Anyone who has a Party ticket in his britches must incessantly see to it that the enthusiasm of labor be in the body.") Bizarre characters and scenes appear: a naked giant ("swollen with wind and misfortune") demands coffins; an amputee hollers from a little cart; aged wrecked creatures doze in the margins of the prose, and at the very end a hopeful innocent girl, Nastya, dies and is buried near the unfinished foundation pit.

With so much idiocy afoot, both here and abroad, the appearance of this book must be welcomed as an inspired challenge to political barbarism.

Paul Theroux, in a review of "The Foundation Pit," in The New York Times Book Review, *March 17, 1974, p. 40.*

MARC SLONIM (essay date 1977)

[*Slonim was a Russian-born American critic who wrote extensively on Russian literature. In the following excerpt, he discusses the collection* The Fierce and Beautiful World, *noting that Platonov's originality resided in his ability to portray the lives of common people.*]

Most of Platonov's heroes are workmen, artisans, and semiliterate eccentrics. These simple, ordinary individuals are always beset with basic questions: who are we, where do we come from, and where are we going—and what is our relationship to our neighbors, to the state, to nature, to God? Their love of life is deep and strong, and one collection of Platonov's stories has a revealing title: ***This Fierce and Beautiful World.*** Everyone, in his opinion, possesses an inherent need for beauty, justice, equality, and humanity. His characters approach revolutionary events from the inside, and Platonov's originality consists exactly in his capacity to render the common people's attitudes, to describe their torments and painful clashes with ugly reality. Platonov himself was afraid that the popular revolutionary outburst had been subdued and deformed by the stiff dogmatists and their useless projects, by a rationalistic bureaucracy alienated from the natural sources of life, by "giantomania" and by falsification of noble slogans. This anxiety caused the ironic and skeptical mood of his tales—and the Communist critics bombarded him with reproaches and insults. One of them dubbed him "the enemy," and Platonov was forced to hide his identity and sign his articles with various pen names.

Moreover, the conservative reviewers were irritated by his unusual style. Platonov wrote just like his protagonists talked, employing the idiom—and also the slang—of the proletariats and the peasants, and reproducing the crude ungrammatical turns of their speech. In many cases the hazy thoughts of a simpleminded man were reflected in his quest for the right phrase and gave the impression of the painful birth of the right word. The book's terms, borrowed from the Communist press, radio, and television and usually disfigured, are mixed in Platonov's stories with the stuttering efforts of an uneducated person trying to invent a new, hardly adequate locution. What at first appears as the speech of the inarticulate, a kind of mumbling monologue, becomes—on further reading—a highly individualistic style and a rare linguistic achievement. But it was only in the 1970's, twenty years after his death, that Platonov was recognized as one of the most original writers of his time and his comeback in Soviet literature was accepted as an act of justice. Yet many of his manuscripts are still kept in State archives and it is not known when Platonov's complete collected works will be published in the Soviet Union. (pp. 358-59)

Marc Slonim, "Posthumous Revivals: Bulgakov, Platonov, Zabolotsky," in his Soviet Russian Literature: Writers and Problems 1917-1977, *revised edition, Oxford University Press, New York, 1977, pp. 352-62.**

BORIS THOMSON (essay date 1978)

[*In the following excerpt, Thomson contends that* Chevengur *and* The Foundation Pit *demonstrate Platonov's contempt for the past and for art, both of which conflict with Marxist values.*]

Early Soviet literature is, not surprisingly, obsessed by the problem of 'the new and the old'. The Communist victory had not created a new world overnight; old ways and values continued to exist and to pose a challenge to those of the new society. For this reason the apparently simple imagery of birth and death that permeates this literature often proves to be more complex than might seem at first glance. Indeed, even in rejecting the values of the past, writers often tacitly took them as their starting-point. (p. 98)

[Few of Platonov's] heroes ever carry any traces of the past with them into the future. Often enough they have no memories of their parents and no families of their own. Their existence is so minimal, so peripheral, that even their deaths are hardly noticed: all one can do is mark their graves in the hope of sustaining some traces of them a little bit longer before they are finally lost for ever in oblivion. In the face of such a view of human existence to speak of continuity and permanent values seems something of an insult.

Even in Platonov's wartime stories where one might expect some concessions to the natural pressures for a more optimistic attitude to death, one finds the same conviction that nothing but total oblivion awaits man both as an individual and as a species. Seen in this vast perspective the destruction and slaughter brought by the war, for all their horror, are only an acceleration of natural processes. Memory may be a palliative, but it is only a temporary and, in the light of history, insignificant, prolongation of existence. (pp. 117-18)

In . . . [the] story **'At the Hazy Dawn of Youth' ('Na zare tumannoy yunosti'** . . .) Platonov tells of a young girl who loses her parents during the Civil War. However, she soon finds a new family in the Soviet state, and a new father in Lenin; and so there is no need for her to look back or search for any continuity.

At the end of **'A Wattle House in a Provincial Garden' ('Glinyanyy dom v uyezdnom sadu'** . . .) the hero returns to look for the scene of his childhood but cannot find it. . . . The emphasis on the newness and unfamiliarity of everything (even the trees) is not intended to alarm or alienate; it is a guarantee of security against any attempt at subversion by the old world.

In general in Platonov's works the past is ignored or forgotten. Where it does survive into the present it threatens to destroy or corrupt it with an almost Mayakovskian intensity. In the short novel ***The Foundation-Pit (Kotlovan*** . . .), he presents two allegorical figures: the innocent ten-year-old orphan Nastya (the name means 'resurrection'), an image of the fragile and vulnerable new world, shorn of all its attachments to the old; and the legless war-invalid Zhachev, the incarnation of the hideous past of physical and psychological mutilation. In a clearly symbolic scene Voshchev, the central figure, and Zhachev are watching a parade of young girls. Recalling the unpropitious circumstances of their birth and early years, the killings, the famines, the epidemics, Voshchev reflects that these children are now a picture of health, innocence and joy. . . . Zhachev develops a touching but still slightly alarming affection for Nastya. For all that, the story ends with the death and burial of the girl and the continuing survival of Zhachev.

Like Zamyatin Platonov seems to leave no place for the past except as a nightmare in the new age; if anything, then, it is even more surprising that he should make the same exception for art, since his world is generally utterly unaware of its existence. In his long and apparently uncompleted novel ***Chevengur*** (. . . the title is the name of a town) he depicts with bitter irony a group of naive and idealistic Marxists who try to establish a Communist Utopia in the steppes. Old ideas of order and cultivation are rejected as mere class prejudices. The houses of the former bourgeoisie, symbols of the strength and solidity of the old culture, are removed bodily from their sites and dumped higgledy-piggledy in the main square. By analogy with the doctrine of the class struggle the aristocrats of the fields, the crops and the flowers, are now deposed, and favour is shown instead to the down-trodden and despised proletarian flora, the weeds. By these and other such absurd extensions of the logic of Marxism, Platonov shows how his heroes cannot move around their own town or find anything to eat.

The same principles are applied to the creation of a new culture. Literacy becomes suspect as an instrument of class oppression, while the central hero, Dvanov, is confident that if only all traces of the culture of the past could be eradicated, then a new and healthier crop would appear spontaneously. . . . (pp. 119-20)

When Dvanov can apply his policies, needless to say, nothing does grow but weeds. With the expulsion of the last traces of the old world the town suddenly looks uninviting and deserted; something vital seems to have been lost, and an aching void, a sterile desert confronts the revolutionaries. One of the heroes is reminded of the day of his mother's funeral. Having at last cleared the way for the glorious future, he can only look back with a terrible sense of bereavement, which seems to threaten the future too. . . .

But Platonov gives the theme one more twist; for there *is* an image of continuity in the novel, Sonya (her name means 'wisdom'), the first and only true love of the proletarian Dvanov. It is now the rootless Party-official Serbinov who hopes to 'possess' and 'master' her, seeing in her all those qualities that the new world seems to have lost. . . . (p. 121)

But even in [his] impressions Serbinov is succumbing to the Soviet myth of culture. For Sonya is not an aristocrat, but the daughter of a worker. The attraction of culture lies . . . in just these links with a condemned class; the bitter corollary for Platonov is that even when the proletariat does produce its own culture, it is not recognized or appreciated as such. Despite the love for Sonya that both the Communist idealist Dvanov and the Party pragmatist Serbinov feel, neither of them wishes to stay with her for any length of time. (p. 122)

Boris Thomson, "The Difference of Art: Some Soviet Writers of the 1920s and 1930s," in his Lot's Wife and the Venus of Milo: Conflicting Attitudes to the Cultural Heritage in Modern Russia, *Cambridge University Press, 1978, pp. 98-122.**

SIMON KARLINSKY (essay date 1979)

[*In the following excerpt, Karlinsky discusses Platonov's portrayal of the perversion of Marxist values under Lenin and Stalin, calling* Chevengur *and* The Foundation Pit *Russian literature's grimmest portrayals of collectivization.*]

The literary fate of the Soviet writer Andrei Platonov has been compared to that of Herman Melville: a writer of exceptional originality and profundity who was ignored by his contemporaries but rediscovered and given a place of honor in the national literary pantheon by a later generation. . . . Two noted poets, Yevgeny Yevtushenko and Joseph Brodsky [see excerpts dated 1970 and 1973], have provided reverential introductions to American editions of Platonov. For the younger Soviet generation, Platonov has by now become a prominent member of the admired pleiad of post-Revolutionary prose writers that includes Zamyatin, Bulgakov, Babel, Zoshchenko and Olesha.

If the growth of Platonov's reputation continues, he might well end up the brightest star of that pleiad.

But the comparison with Melville is perhaps misleading. Melville, while undervalued, was after all published and available, while Platonov's most significant works—his novels and his best plays—have yet to appear in print in the Soviet Union and are known to his admirers there either through *samizdat* [Russian term for a book or other material published and circulated surreptitiously, often in typescript form] or through foreign editions. Recent Soviet editions of Platonov have as a rule avoided including his more stylistically innovative and philosophically daring stories, which was also the case with the English-language collection, ***Fro and Other Stories,*** brought out by the Progress Publishers in Moscow in 1972. Nevertheless, there is by now enough of Platonov's work in print, in Russian and in English, to permit a tentative evaluation of his significance and achievement. . . .

After the success of his first collection of stories, ***The Locks of Epifan*** . . . Platonov moved to Moscow to become a full-time writer. (p. 25)

[His] biographical background supplied the vantage point and the subject matter of Platonov's writings. His characters are poor peasants or railroad mechanics and engineers, the people who remain on the lowest rung of the economic ladder and for whom food shortage is a constant fact of life from the days before the October Revolution to the eve of World War II. Both the author and his characters love machinery—locomotives, power plants, turbines—with a poetic and lyrical love that is quite different from the artificially instilled cult of tractors and factories typical of other writers of the period. . . . In Platonov's writings about the civil war and the collectivization, his compassion extends not only to the common people whose welfare and comfort are repeatedly sacrificed to political expediency, but also to the tormented and mistreated farm animals and machinery.

By 1931, Platonov was in trouble with the Soviet authorities over his **"For Future Use,"** a burlesqued travelogue through the newly collectivized farms, one of several pieces he wrote satirizing the bureaucratization of village life in the 1920s and 1930s. Stalin himself is reported to have written "scum" in the margin of the journal where **"For Future Use"** appeared. Platonov went on publishing sporadically throughout the 1930s and 1940s, surviving in part through luck and in part through the protection of Maxim Gorky and Mikhail Sholokhov.

With the advent of Socialist Realism as the only permissible mode of expression in Soviet literature, Platonov was forced to tone down or entirely give up the two most distinctive aspects of his personal style: his one-of-a-kind literary language (a blending of workers' slang and the post-Revolutionary Soviet officialese into an unexpectedly poetic amalgam) and the type of imagery that in the West came to be known as surrealistic or absurdist. Platonov's surrealistic inclinations placed him within an important trend that was played down in Soviet criticism and overlooked in the West. It can now be seen that a whole array of Soviet writers perceived the revolutionary transformation of the country as an absurd phantasmagoria, in which guilt and innocence had no logical basis and gratuitous violence erupted in unpredictable and irrational forms. Platonov's prose fiction belongs within this continuum together with the poetry of Nikolai Zabolotsky (perhaps the finest poet to emerge in the post-Revolutionary period, Zabolotsky was given a labor camp sentence for his masterful surrealistic narrative poem about collectivization, "The Triumph of Agriculture"); the nonsense verse of Nikolai Oleinikov, widely circulated in manuscript in the 1930s and 1940s, but not published until the 1970s; and the absurdist plays of Daniil Harms and Alexander Vvedensky, rediscovered and much studied in the West in recent years.

Platonov's two novels now available in English (***Chevengur*** and ***The Foundation Pit***), his satirical stories of the late 1920s and his two important plays, ***The Barrel Organ*** and ***Fourteen Red Huts,*** outline his bleak but remarkably consistent vision of how a Marxist-Leninist revolution impinges upon the poor peasants and the unlettered workers, i.e., the very people in whose name and on whose behalf the revolutions of our century have been made. The revolutionary change itself is dealt with in ***Chevengur,*** Platonov's longest and most ambitious prose fiction, begun in 1926, when the memories of his own experiences during the civil war were still fresh. Only the first few chapters were published during the writer's lifetime as a separate novella called **"Origins of a Master Craftsman."** Maxim Gorky read the complete novel in 1929 and wrote Platonov that he found it extremely interesting, but unpublishable because its portrayal of the Revolution was "lyrical and satiric" and because it painted revolutionaries in an "ironic hue," making them look like "madmen and crackpots." (pp. 25-6)

The greater part of ***Chevengur*** is concerned with the efforts of Sasha Dvanov and several other idealistic young proletarians to achieve universal brotherhood and socialism in their province during the aftermath of the Revolution and civil war. Their main handicap is the absence of a blueprint for converting the hostile and illiterate peasantry into class-conscious Communists. The writings of Karl Marx, they are sure, must contain an infallible recipe for such a conversion, but none of these revolutionaries has read Marx. In the Kremlin there live the infinitely wise and benevolent comrades Lenin and Trotsky, who know how to go about it, but they are inaccessible and Moscow is too far away. . . . Because Lenin had told them that the worst enemy of the working class is the bourgeoisie (those "harmful insects," in Lenin's terminology), anyone in Chevengur who owns a home, no matter how modest, is killed or expelled from the town. The inhabitants submit meekly, convinced that the happiness of mankind will be attained by their demise. (pp. 26-7)

After the proclamation of Lenin's New Economic Policy, which permitted a certain amount of private enterprise and instantly raised the standard of living in the country, the rulers of Chevengur see the cause of communism betrayed and cut the town off from the rest of the Soviet Union. The purity of their own communist faith leads them to expect cosmic changes to follow extermination of the exploiting class, among them the abolition of cold weather in winter, resurrection of the dead and visits from proletarians of other galaxies. Lest we accuse Platonov of fantasy or exaggeration, we should remember that in their poetry written right after the October Revolution, Mayakovsky and Esenin also expected the Revolution to effect changes in the sun and the planets or, closer to our time, that the broadcasts of the recently deposed regime in Phnom Penh urged the Cambodian working people to become "masters of the earth and water, of nature and of the future." The Chevengur experiment is ended when the town leadership is massacred by a military detachment they assume to be "Cossacks and Constitutional Democrats on horseback" (the English translation misses the point of this passage), but which is probably a punitive unit of the Red Army, sent to put an end to an insubordinate leftist splinter of the party. The idealistic Sasha Dvanov drowns himself in a lake, a male Ophelia unable to survive the collapse of his dream of brotherhood.

The next stage of the Revolution is reflected in such Platonov stories of the late 1920s as **"The City of Gradov," "Makar the Doubtful"** (both included in ***Collected Works***), **"Resident of the State"** and **"For Future Use"** (neither one as yet translated into English). It was these stories that Alexander Solzhenitsyn had in mind when he mentioned Platonov in his open letter to the Congress of Soviet Writers in 1967 as one of the first to realize the nature of Stalinism and to warn against it. In these stories Platonov documents the rise of the authoritarian bureaucrats, fanatical inquisitors and opportunistic time servers, that followed on the triumph of Marxist orthodoxy and the ban on all dissent. As Platonov saw it, the total domination of the country by such people was what made possible the next "great leap forward" (to borrow a somewhat later non-Russian term), the collectivization of agriculture by Stalin in 1931. This is the subject of Platonov's novel ***The Foundation Pit,*** surely one of the grimmest literary works of the century. . . . (p. 27)

Once again the country is told that the prosperity and safety of the masses will be assured only if a particular social group is exterminated. This time it is the *kulaks*—defined in the novel as any peasant who owns a horse or a cow or more than two sheep (during the preceding period of the New Economic Policy, peasants were officially encouraged to raise livestock to assure a better food supply for the country).

The hallucinatory sequence of scenes in which a group of activists that includes a tame bear and an angelic six-year-old girl—who speaks entirely in party slogans—marches from home to home determining who is and who is not a *kulak* (with the bear and the child casting the decisive votes), shows that Platonov's surrealistic treatment is far more adequate for conveying the historical nightmare of collectivization than any realistic or objective approach could be. At the end of the novel the *kulaks* and their families are loaded on rafts and allowed to float out into the ocean. . . . The remaining peasants, terrified and demoralized, are herded into collective farms while the head activist who organized the local collectivization is discredited and destroyed after a directive arrives from the central party organization accusing him of slipping "down the right and the left slope from the clear-cut ridge of the proper party line."

In the oddly carnival-like atmosphere of ***Chevengur,*** in the oppressive, nightmarish world of ***The Foundation Pit,*** and in the rarefied desert air of Platonov's wonderful novelette of the mid-1930s **"Dzhan,"** the good men who strive for justice have to work with those whose idea of revolution is violence, coercion or gratification of power lust. Brotherhood remains an unattainable dream so long as the brothers are Cain and Abel, as in Platonov's experience they always are. Proletarian revolution is a shining ideal in all of Platonov's writings, no matter how much misery its implementation may bring to the proletariat. . . . But, as Mikhail Geller has pointed out in his preface to the truncated émigré edition of ***Chevengur,*** Platonov's concept of revolution comes not from Marx or Lenin, but from the enigmatic 19th-century religious philosopher Nikolai Fyodorov (1828-1903).

Extravagantly admired in his day by Dostoevsky and by Tolstoy (who declared that he was proud to live in the same century with Fyodorov), Nikolai Fyodorov is today an obscure figure to both Russians and non-Russians. His philosophy combined a critique of Christianity with utopian socialism. (pp. 27-8)

Portrait of Platonov taken in 1936 or 1937.

When Fyodorov writes that with the establishment of Christianity as the dominant religion "the restoration of those fallen away was turned into coercion and catechizing into a holy war, the baptizers and apostles themselves became swordbearers, repentance took the form of inquisition [and] external incorporation into the Church became internal isolation"—all we need do is substitute "communism" and "party" for "Christianity" and "church" to get the very gist of Platonov's critique of Soviet society in ***Chevengur*** and ***The Foundation Pit.*** It is to Fyodorov that we can trace the persistent parallels in ***Chevengur*** between communism and the age of the Crusades. One of Platonov's very best stories of the 1940s, **"Aphrodite"** (included in ***Fro and Other Stories*** and ***The Fierce and Beautiful World***), contains an excellent outline of the philosophical ideas Platonov shared with Fyodorov, ideas which Platonov ingeniously palmed off in the story as "Leninist."

Much of Platonov's work of the last two decades of his life—his rather tame literary criticism . . . , his wartime reporting, his adaptations of folk tales for children and many of his stories of the 1930s and 1940s with their contrived happy endings—is of the safe and drab variety considered acceptable in the Soviet Union. But during those same years, Platonov also produced a number of unpublished plays in which he continued his social criticism couched in his earlier surrealistic manner.

In ***The Barrel Organ*** (I'd have translated the title as *The Hurdy Gurdy*), a co-op that processes crayfish is demoralized when flocks of migratory birds, said to be fleeing from the "crisis of the bourgeoisie'' in Western Europe, descend unexpectedly upon the village. The arrival of the birds is a welcome alleviation of the chronic food shortage, but the co-op administration is handicapped by lack of directions from the center about what to do with the birds. Later on in the play, the administration tries to solve the food problem by introducing new products made of weeds and bird droppings.

The men who run the co-op in ***The Barrel Organ*** are clearly the Soviet variants of the predatory sharks of capitalism, looking after their own interests as best they can within the stranglehold of the overall production plan. Their opponents are an idealistic poet-inventor Alyosha and his girl-friend Myud. Myud's name is an acronym for ''International Day of Youth'' and she suffers chronic depression because she was born under capitalism and ''groaned under it for the first two years of her life.'' Alyosha invents a near-human robot named Kuzma, programmed to shout slogans about the radiant future of socialism. But because of the inadequacy of Soviet technology, Kuzma periodically lapses into counterrevolutionary and anti-Soviet denunciations. There are also visiting foreigners—a Danish scientist and his daughter who envy the co-op members their poverty and ideological purity and are in turn envied by them for their suitcases full of expensive food and clothing.

In the Soviet literature of Platonov's time, foreign visitors have been portrayed as either men and women of good will who are easily converted from capitalism to communism after a quick tour of the Soviet Union, or else as evil saboteurs, intent on wrecking peaceful socialist progress on orders from international imperialism. Platonov is unique in depicting foreign visitors as victims of their own gullibility, lapping up the rhetoric and the propaganda (''I love it!'' exclaims the visiting Dane upon being shown a circular entitled ''On the Principles of Achieving Enthusiasm Through Self-Stimulation'') and blind to the actual nature of Soviet society.

A visit of a distinguished foreigner is also central to ***Fourteen Red Huts,*** Platonov's play published for the first time in 1972 in the Russian-language literary journal *Grani* in West Germany. Here the visitor is a world-famous English scholar who was once a personal friend of Karl Marx and now, at the age of 101, comes to the USSR in his capacity as head of the ''Commission of the League of Nations on Solving the Universal Economic Riddle, Etc.'' His name is Haws, an anagram of Shaw, as in George Bernard.

Haws stays at a remote collective farm, run with an iron hand by a peasant girl of 19 named Suenita (the Russian word for ''vanity'' as in ''vanity of vanities,'' with the negative particle *ni* stuck in the middle). He witnesses the misery, hunger and casual violence to which the Soviet villagers have been reduced by the collectivization, but, taking a long-range historical view, he still finds their way of life superior to anything that the capitalist West has to offer. On a more superficial level, ***Fourteen Red Huts*** is Platonov's bitter satiric blast at G. B. Shaw's widely publicized propaganda campaign on behalf of Stalin; in his *Rationalization of Russia* and his speeches of the 1930s, Shaw defended Stalin's purges and maintained that the collectivization had brought the Soviet people the highest standard of living in Europe. But in the portions that deal with Suenita's relationship to her lover, her child and to the other villagers, the play is a strikingly poetic, profound and often baffling meditation on the nature of power and cooperation, of loyalty and betrayal. Its key, one suspects, can be found in a detailed study of Fyodorov's *Philosophy of the Common Task*. (pp. 28-9)

Andrei Platonov may well be recognized one day as one of the central figures of 20th-century Russian and Western literature. In his best works, he exploited his social origins, his proximity to momentous historical events and his prodigious imagination to map out some of our century's enduring problems. His roots in the Russian tradition point back to Gogol and Dostoevsky and his closest parallels in the West seem to be Kafka and Joseph Heller's *Catch 22*. (p. 30)

Simon Karlinsky, ''Andrei Platonov, 1899-1951: An Early Soviet Master,'' in The New Republic, *Vol. 180, No. 13, March 31, 1979, pp. 25-30.*

WALENTY CUKIERMAN (essay date 1979)

[In the following excerpt, Cukierman compares Platonov's story "The Cow" *to Alexander Solzhenitzyn's story* "Matrena's Home."]

Aleksandr Solženicyn's ''Matrenin dvor'' (''Matrena's Home,'' 1956) has been accorded wide attention ever since it appeared in print in 1963. Critics invariably pointed out the story's evident ties with nineteenth-century Russian literary traditions. Its colorful, dialectal speech is reminiscent of the styles of such writers as Remizov and Leskov. Prototypes of the heroine, the pure-hearted righteous peasant woman Matrena, have been found in the works of Puškin, Turgenev, Nekrasov, Dostoevskij, and Tolstoj. But while Solženicyn's indebtedness to nineteenth-century styles and types is well known, his Matrena has rarely, if ever, been linked to twentieth-century literary heroines. Just such a ''heroine,'' however, can be found in a short story by Andrej Platonov, **''Korova''** (**''The Cow,''** 1943). The story belongs to a group of works written by Platonov in the late 1930s and early 1940s, in which the author's love for village life is often mixed with his fascination for modern industrialization (**''Fro,'' ''Tretij syn,'' ''Ijul'skaja groza,'' ''Na zare tumannoj junosti,'' ''Žena mašinista''**).

On the surface, **''The Cow''** and ''Matrena's Home'' may seem to have little in common. A children's story, **''The Cow''** deals with a cow whose calf is wrested away from her for sale. The cow is endowed with human attributes and feelings, a clear echo of the familiar Tolstojan technique (''Xolstomer''). The scope of ''Matrena's Home'' on the other hand, is much broader in its portrayal of a righteous woman and the folkways of Russian village life. Because the third-person narration in Platonov's story is conducted as if through the eyes of a village schoolboy, it is quite simple and naive and stands in contrast to the mature vision of Solženicyn's first-person narrator. The differences between the stories extend to their language as well. While Platonov's narrative and dialogue are, for the most part, standard literary Russian, Solženicyn's language implicates the narrator's individualized colloquial speech with the colorful folk idiom of the peasants.

But despite these differences the stories show certain striking similarities in setting, structure, choice of details, theme, and most important, the image and role of the main characters. The setting of both stories is rural Russia. In each work it is stressed that the village where the action takes place is situated far away from the city and the railroad station. Both heroines live alone, the cow in an old barn, Matrena in her dilapidated house. Both the cow and Matrena are perceived through the point of view of narrators—in **''The Cow''** the schoolboy Vasja, and in ''Matrena's Home'' the school teacher Ignatič—who become personally involved with the fates of the heroines.

The first encounters with the heroines reveal their suffering. To Platonov's narrator, the cow appears tired and emaciated. To Solženicyn's narrator, Matrena's yellow, sickly face and clouded eyes give evidence that "illness had drained all the strength out of her." Still, though they may be physically ailing, they display an uncommon spiritual health. Indeed, the essence of their characters is in an unreserved giving of themselves to others, in a proliferation of selfless activity. The reader of **"The Cow"** is informed with childlike simplicity that "the cow did not collect her strength in meat and fat, but gave it away in work and milk." Similarly, Matrena is ready to give her help to anyone in need, be it her neighbors or the nearby collective farm. She works, like the cow, without pay, knowing neither financial incentive nor reward. Their outstanding traits—patience, goodness, and love of work—correspond to the basic features of the Russian peasant as traditionally portrayed.

It is noteworthy that both the cow and Matrena are depicted tilling the soil harnessed to a plow, a most uncustomary task for a woman and a cow alike. But the nature of their work involves direct contact with the land and explains, in the Tolstojan tradition, the source of their spiritual health and goodness. In their treatment of peasants, both Platonov and Solženicyn draw on the rich nineteenth-century tradition, which ranged from the naturalistic descriptions of writers like Grigorovič to Tolstoj's overly idealized *mužiks*. For Tolstoj, peasants were the bearers of a higher truth, though his portrayal of them had little to do with the actualities of village life (with the exception of such works as *Vlast't'my*). But Platonov and Solženicyn succeed in combining a realistic picture with an idealized one. The cow and Matrena are on one hand depicted with such unaesthetic details as dirty clothes, dusty interior, plain food, and daily chores, on the other hand, they emanate an almost mythical aura.

These descendants of the nineteenth-century righteous type stand out against the surrounding milieu, which is strange and baffling to them. The heroines' estrangement is emphasized by their difficulties in communicating with the outside world. Whereas the cow obviously can not articulate her inner torments, Matrena's discourse, if she chooses to speak at all, is laden with folk etymologies, local dialect, proverbs, and peculiar rhythms, which the general reader finds hard to comprehend. Interestingly, the narrator, an outsider who gradually falls under the irresistible spell of Matrena, learns how to understand her and even incorporates her folk expressions into his own speech.

The logical end to the lives of the cow and Matrena, which amount to one great sacrifice, is tragic death. Only in death are their life missions realized. It is a striking coincidence that the cow and Matrena meet their end on the railroad tracks. Both Platonov and Solženicyn painstakingly prepare the reader for the final scene of death. The action in the two stories takes place, for the most part, during the gloomy months of late fall and winter. The aura of impending tragedy is especially intensified in the scene immediately preceding the catastrophe. Platonov captures the mood through the use of eerie sounds and dark, foreboding shades of the ending day. . . . The ominous mood is conveyed by Solženicyn through images of darkness and mysterious silence disturbed only by the unpleasant noises of mice scurrying about. . . . Upon their return from school on the day of the catastrophes, both narrators notice some unusual sights near their houses. . . . There is even a similarity in the narrators' reactions to the news of the deaths. They both feel a sense of profound loss of someone dear to them. In **"The Cow"**, "Vasja sat down on the ground and grew numb from the grief of his first close death." . . . In "Matrena's Home": "Matryona was gone. Someone close to me had been killed." (pp. 163-65)

Though the railroad is the direct cause of death for both heroines, it has a different significance for each author. For Solženicyn, as for Tolstoj, the railroad symbolizes the threat of industrialized civilization on the simplicity and purity of the Russian village. Matrena dies an innocent victim of this evil force. For Platonov, however, whose works display a fascination for technological advances and machines, the railroad is not an agent of destruction. In fact, Vasja is as interested in the technology of the locomotive as he is in the cow. The simultaneous admiration for the cow and the train, symbols of organic and inorganic life, reveals the basic dichotomy of Platonov's vision, which he himself captured in memoirs about his childhood. . . .

In death as in life, the cow and Matrena continue to be misunderstood. The cow's apparently senseless death is interpreted by witnesses as an act of mental aberration: "Is she deaf or crazy, or what?". . . . But while the crowds disparage the cow, her usefulness does not cease even after her death: the onwers hurry to sell her carcass for profit. Matrena meets the same fate. Her death unleashes all the grudges the villagers had held against her. And yet the same people who reproach her for not being attached to material objects greedily claim her belongings after the funeral. Again, Matrena proves useful even after her death.

If there remains any doubt about the cow's and Matrena's "higher mission," both Platonov and Solženicyn dispel it in the final scenes of the stories. The essence of their characters is suddenly revealed to the narrators, who express, each in his own way, the need for such beings in today's world. Thus, Vasja and his parents, who typify the average Russian family, are greatly dependent on the cow's goodness and selflessness. This is expressed with a disarming simplicity in Vasja's school composition. . . . (p. 165)

Solženicyn's narrator voices his revelation with the conviction of an adult who has been granted a sudden and profound insight. . . . If the cow and Matrena hark back to the Tolstojan righteous type, then Vasja and Ignatič, who both possess a searching and understanding consciousness able to learn from these types, call to mind such Tolstojan characters as Pierre, Levin, and Nexljudov.

Yet the cow and Matrena go beyond the traditional righteous type of Russian peasant to symbolize Mother Russia herself. In fact, they can be thought of both as the whole of Russia and as a part of the whole which keeps the whole alive. That the heroines carry such broad, universal implications is suggested even in their names. The cow is referred to only by her generic name, which in Russian connotes bountiful fertility. Matrena's last name is mentioned only once. Her given name, of course, derives from the Latin *matrona* ("matron"). Both heroines are portrayed as lonely, grief-stricken mothers whose children died very young. The cow is forced to sacrifice her only "son" to the outside world of commerce. Matrena's six children all died inexplicably within three months after birth.

When one considers the periods in which these stories were written, the image of suffering Mother Russia acquires special significance. Platonov's story was written at the height of World War II, Solženicyn's in the wake of the exposure of Stalin. Thus both stories invoke those qualities of patience, selflessness, and goodness traditionally ascribed to Russia, and do so at times when the very existence and moral foundation of Russia were being threatened. The pictures of Mother Russia which Platonov and Solženicyn evoke differ considerably, however, from the conventional model of an indestructible, heroic, and monumental woman protectively looming above the helpless masses—the image so pervasive during the Stalinist period. Instead, they portray the antithesis of the Soviet type. Matrena and the cow are meek, humble, and inconspicuous, passively accepting their suffering—the direct descendants of the Tolstoj tradition. And their creators, who hold such disparate views of modern technological society, are unquestionably linked by their shared indebtedness to the Tolstojan image of the righteous soul. (p. 166)

Walenty Cukierman, "Platonov's 'The Cow' and Solženicyn's 'Matrena's Home': The Tolstojan Connection," in Slavic and East European Journal, *Vol. 23, No. 1, Spring, 1979, pp. 163-66.**

HENRYKA YAKUSHEV (essay date 1979)

[*In the following excerpt, Yakushev cites three reasons for Platonov's unpopularity with readers and critics during his lifetime. First was his use of folk speech, which ran counter to the trend toward a common literary language; second was his use of innovation in narrative structure, and third was a general misunderstanding of his political and philosophical views.*]

How can we explain the resurgence of interest in Platonov in the sixties and seventies, as opposed to his relative obscurity during the twenties and thirties?

In the critical literature on Platonov (consisting mainly of introductory articles to various editions, both in the USSR and the West) the question is not discussed, as in the Soviet editions, or, as in the West, a simple explanation such as the following is given: Platonov was hardly published (apart from his stories about the war) between the years 1937 and 1958 because of official disapproval. Hence, many of Platonov's works have simply not been made accessible to a broad reading public. And the question of his previous lack of popularity is automatically dismissed.

Yet this argument is hardly convincing. Platonov's works were published during the twenties and thirties. Consequently, at that time the reader had as much access to Platonov as to, let us say, Pilnyak and Babel. While these writers were well-known to the reading public, however, Platonov remained, for the most part, a writer for critics.

Without a doubt the answer to Platonov's popularity during the sixties and seventies must be linked to a change in the critical standards of the contemporary reader. I would suggest that the fate of Andrei Platonov is a striking example of the extent to which literature depends upon extraliterary changes (education, political, social and esthetic orientation, taste, etc.) which alter the readers' apprehension of a work. Aspects of this problem belong to the realm of sociology rather than literary study, and hence I do not aim to resolve this question in the present work. I only wish to point out the difficulty associated with its solution, and to focus our attention on one purely literary quality of Platonov's work, which I believe has to some extent contributed to his lack of popularity during the thirties—the specific nature of Platonov's language.

Andrei Platonov's writing is characterized by a tendency to use the vocabulary of the people—the speech of the peasant and the worker. This tendency is especially apparent when folk speech has absorbed current political and bureaucratic lexicons. When using these lexicons the people comprehend them in a new way and subject them to a unique kind of folk etymology, forming at times extremely bizarre and logically unexpected word combinations. (pp. 171-74)

In using this kind of speech Platonov was by no means an innovator: almost all of the new Soviet literature of the twenties and thirties introduced a socially-colored jargon into the speech of the characters, as well as the narrator. This was, in part, one of the reasons for the phenomenal success of Zoshchenko. But there is an essential difference between Platonov's and Zoshchenko's use of folk speech. In Zoshchenko (as in all other writers of that time) there is always a contrast between this folk speech and literary language, and in this contrast the latter is considered a language which is both normative and correct, i.e., as language which is held by a certain general consensus to be more *true*, more precisely expressive than the folk language. Platonov, on the other hand, shortly after his first published collection ***The Epifan Locks*** . . . , written in a "traditional" manner, conceived of folk speech in quite a different way—it is folk speech, not normative language, which is more true, more precisely expressive. (pp. 175-76)

In juxtaposing normative to folk language, Platonov saw the folk language as an expression of true feelings about the world, and he considers this language to possess semantics in which the truth resides.

Simple people experience the world directly, like children, discovering it anew for themselves each day. And like children, they express in their own words their first impressions of the world. This primal, "unedited" verbal formulation of observation by simple people is always truthful. They formulate their thought-feelings with difficulty, but in contrast to "intelligent" people who use the formulations and words of others, they find their own definitions which adequately reflect "strivings of the heart not inhibited by the reasonings of the mind," to use Platonov's words. As Platonov writes about one of his characters—Sasha Dvanov from ***Chevengur***—that he ". . . did not give another's name to the nameless life unfolding in front of him. Still, he did not want to leave the world unnamed, he only waited for life to reveal her own name, instead of intentionally thought-up nick-names." Thus, Platonov leaves intact the language of the simple people and operates with this distorted, clumsy often whimsical language not only in the characters' speech, but also in the author's own descriptions.

Folk language is concrete, perceptive and, according to Platonov, it would be difficult, if not impossible, to enlist its semantics in the service of the consciously-oriented life. In his poetics, speech becomes an independent element in the structure of a work, along with characters, motifs, etc. No other Russian prose writer has utilized speech as an independent compositional element.

For example, Platonov used speech as an independent element in the structure of his short novel ***The Innermost Man (Sokrovennyi Chelovek)*** . . . , which was also his first treatment of the theme of communism.

The main character of the work, the railroad machinist Foma Pukhov, dashes about Russia at the end of the civil war, apparently without any visible goal, drawn by simple curiosity and, chiefly, by the absence of any earthly reason for staying in one place: "Pukhov's woman had died and he longed to go to the end of the world." Preparing to leave for the Caucasus, as a volunteer in a technical brigade of the Red Army, Pukhov urges his friends to go with him: "We'll really get around, Peter. . . . At the very least we'll see the South and swim in the sea." When his friend refuses to go, Pukhov buttresses his argument by using words with ideological overtones: "The Revolution will end—and we'll have nothing left. What did you do, they'll say. And what will you say? . . . Where were your true sympathies?"

In following the adventures of Pukhov one could conclude, on the basis of plot alone, that Pukhov is a man whose "true sympathies" lie with the Revolution. But that is not, in fact, the case. Platonov makes it sufficiently clear that Pukhov's attitude to the Revolution is sceptical and suspicious: "He jealously kept track of the Revolution, feeling ashamed of its very stupidity, although he took small part in it." He does not understand the Revolution with his feelings, "with his heart," as Platonov likes to express it, and therefore he does not accept it. For him, as for many of Platonov's folk characters, to understand is "to feel," to find harmony between reason on one hand and the innate feelings of the "natural" man on the other.

The disharmony between Pukhov and the Revolution is expressed by the author in semantic terms, as a reaction of the character to the language of meetings, placards and political stereotypes which were frequent at the time. Platonov constructs Pukhov's image in such a way as to lead the reader to conclude that Pukhov's judgments on the truthfulness or falsehood of an idea expressed in this "revolutionary language" depend on the extent to which he can accept this speech as his own. In turn, Pukhov's acceptance of this language as his own is based on its instrumental indicators, that is, on its style, on who says it, on his trust or distrust of this particular person, on the perceived emotional and emotive sense of the speech. Pukhov relates to speech intuitively and, for him, speech itself contains sufficient indicators of whether it is "his" or "not his." Thus Pukhov's doubts about the revolution are based on the fact that "Revolutionary speech" is alien to many people who think they are participating in the Revolution. He sees that when people act out these alien semantics (i.e., when they turn words into action) this results only in either stupidity or in a new means of bureaucratically controlling others. (pp. 176-78)

"An unburdened man," as Pukhov calls himself, at first glance creates the impression of someone who regards the inconsistencies of the Revolution lightly and sees it simply as a game, as an adventure not to be taken seriously. This first impression of Pukhov is reversed in the dramatic denouement of the final scene where Pukhov appears to commit himself to the Revolution. But the denouement not only serves to deepen our image of Pukhov, it also focuses on the latent problem posed in **"The Innermost Man"** that revolution, unless it is carried out on an emotional level, has no value; and it is only through the language that the degree to which it is carried out, can be expressed. In the concluding scene there is an opposition between two spheres of consciousness—the rational-political and the pragmatic-feeling "folk" consciousness, expressed purely through semantic opposition.

Pukhov, who has turned up at oil-fields near Baku, as if unexpectedly, arrives at a ". . . desperate sympathy toward people, working alone against the matter of the whole world." This leads him to a second feeling, that "revolution is the very best fate for people. . . ." In his soul, a harmony is restored between the expediency of the revolution and his primal feelings about life, about man's relation to nature, to work, and to society. As a result, Pukhov accepts the Revolution, not with his reason alone, but emotionally—"with his heart." Meeting his machinist colleague, Pukhov expresses his acceptance of the Revolution and his sense of a renewed harmony with people and the world in the simplest words: "It's a good morning!" he said to the machinist. He is answered with an indifferent cliche, "Fully revolutionary!". Through this contrast between a strong emotive and spontaneous expression, and an automatic reply, the author focuses our attention on the specifically semantic character of the meta-plot problem: by what means can an individual with a folk mentality understand and accept as true the sense contained in political language?

Platonov strips naked the literary, political and bureaucratic metaphors. He considers the latter two as "socially dangerous" and asserts that the concrete words with a single connotation are the one firm foothold of thought. He seems to imply that scrupulous use of such concrete language is our only salvation from the tyranny of the word, as well as from political and ideological tyranny, which is carried out through language.

Unfortunately the reading public of Russia of that time, to whom Platonov turned, was "moving" on a course directly opposite to the current of his literary thought. The language which he cultivated, which he introduced as authentic because of its inherent "truth," was avoided by the majority of his readers. As their level of education rose they grew ashamed of folk language and thought of it as an illiterate, twisted version of educated, "intelligent," normative speech. They accepted it only within the framework of satire, or as a stylistic quality of a character.

Of course, this is not the only reason for the failure of Platonov's works to attract the contemporary reader. Equally difficult to accept was the unusual, completely uncanonical texture of literature which Platonov presented to the unprepared reader. This was little appreciated even by the critics. The peculiarity of his compositional structure, the device of breaking up the plot development almost to the point of destroying it; the interpenetration of the speech of the characters and the author; the use within a single context, often within a single phrase, of both realistic description and maximal generalization; and a new genre which I call the *hypothetical* novel—these innovations completely escaped the attention of the critic of that time. For many years, Platonov was primarily the object only of *political* criticism.

Platonov was criticized for his world-view, for his distortion and exaggeration of reality. Through what I call the direct "factual" analysis of his work, which was applied to Platonov in the thirties and forties (and frequently applied to him in the West now, but, understandably, resulting in a diametrically opposite appraisal), his critics easily drew conclusions about the nature of Platonov's political, philosophical and artistic position, simply on the basis of the descriptive material he uses. But if one judges Platonov's views on the basis of separate episodes, one can come to opposite, mutually exclusive conclusions. One can, for example, select episodes to prove that he was both a communist and an anti-communist, a champion of Soviet power and its enemy, a collectivist and an individualist, and so on. Platonov suffered more than a little during his lifetime from such "factual," "situational" reading of his works.

Even Gorky, who had a benevolent attitude toward Platonov and valued his talent, read his work in the same vein as everyone else. When Platonov turned to Gorky with the request to evaluate his novel ***Chevengur,*** Gorky replied to him:

> . . . despite the indisputable worth of your work, I do not think it will be published. The obstacle is your anarchistic frame of mind, apparently a quality inherent in your 'spirit.' Whether you wished to or not—you have endowed your interpretation of reality with a lyrical-satirical quality which is, of course, unacceptable to our censor. Despite all the gentleness of your relationship to people, they are painted ironically in your writings and appear before the reader, less as revolutionaries, than as 'eccentrics' and 'half-wits.' I do not claim that this is done consciously—however, it *is done*—such is the reader's opinion—mine, that is. Possibly, I am mistaken.''

Gorky was not mistaken in that he was expressing not only his own opinion, but that of other readers—and, in particular, of the professional critics.

Platonov's reaction to this and similar estimates of ***Chevengur*** is striking in its simplicity and enigmatic meaning:

> They refuse to publish the novel. They say that the Revolution is incorrectly portrayed in the novel, that the entire work would be understood as counter-revolutionary. *But I created it with different feelings*. (My italics, H.Y.)

He goes on to say that the novel is an honest attempt to portray the ''beginnings of a communist society.''

It is the application of unsuitable esthetic criteria to Platonov's prose that has led to the misreading and misunderstanding of his works in the past as well as in the present day. Gorky, the Soviet critics of that time, and, apparently, the readers, found it difficult to imagine that a writer such as Platonov, who posed the pressing political questions of his day, did not express directly his emotional attitudes to these questions—be it acceptance or non-acceptance, sympathy or antipathy, approval or condemnation, etc. They assumed that the images and situations were created by Platonov in accordance with the classical canons of esthetics, and therefore embody the author's own emotional attitudes and are calculated to evoke similar reactions in the reader. And no matter how strange this assertion may seem at first glance, Platonov's attitudes and reactions are not to be found in the particular episodes of his prose. Simply stated, Platonov's literary task and his corresponding method of organizing his material was not to create an emotional effect, but to explore many possible solutions to the pressing political-philosophical problem of his time: the realization of the idea of communism.

However, the question of Platonov's political and philosophical views cannot be regarded as something completely external and irrelevant to his work. Precisely the opposite is true. Platonov is a social and political writer *because* of his very choice of descriptive material (events, situations, characters, motifs, and, above all, language). All this material—either directly (using the terminology and pre-conceptions characteristic of the ''historical'' understanding of that time) or in an abstract, generalized, sometimes highly symbolic form—reflects the major or trivial events of the reality of those years. Furthermore, Platonov also projects wholly imagined events and improbable situations. Neither group of events—realistic or imaginary—has an independent meaning; they are brought into the work only to test certain thoughts and assertions which the author has introduced in order to pose the question of their *solvability*. They are presented within a specific context, built around a given theme, and take on meaning only in connection with this theme. Thus, events in Platonov's novels cannot be evaluated directly, but only through a complex semantic link with this theme. It is only here, on the level of these connections, that one may speak of Platonov's political and philosophical sense of the world and how it found expression in his writings.

The theme-problem, for the resolution of which Platonov created at least three of his fundamental works—the novels ***Chevengur, The Foundation Pit,*** and ***Dzhan***—is the possibility or impossibility of implementing the concept of communism. In essence, this is the single theme-problem of his creative work; with a determination bordering on mania, he pursued it almost all of his life. (pp. 178-82)

Platonov's communism's realization was a problem whose solvability and outcome were unclear. In this he took a decisive step away from the concept of communism as potential (i.e., whose feasibility in the future could not be doubted) toward the appraisal of it as hypothetical (i.e., whose feasibility had yet to be proven). This was a serious step that inevitably led to a rift with official ideology. At the same time, it posited the theme of his works as experimental, a thesis with radical consequences for the composition of these works. Virtually the only way to present the central theme was to organize the descriptive material according to episodes which are connected to the hypothetical concept. In Platonov, episodes assume the role of arguments in a proof. (p. 183)

The conception of the basis of communism as a primal, social feeling, as an expression of man's need for collectivity, is one of the thematic axes around which Platonov's novels revolve. Along this axis he lays out episodes which depict either the presence of the feeling of collectiveness (which in this case is identical with the impulse to communism), or the absence of that feeling. In the latter case, the episodes serve to clarify the reason for that absence. They are like laboratory experiments, in which the ''material'' for analysis is selected in order to be as ''convincing'' as possible for demonstration. For example, the introduction of characters in an episode is never motivated. The author chooses them, as if from a deck of cards, without concerning himself about the connection of a given episode with the other episodes from which the given character was snatched.

The connection of events in the majority of Platonov's works is neither casual, temporal nor spatial. The only link between events is their logical relationship to the main theme that Platonov is demonstrating. Each episode-atom depicts a different internal motif of the need for another person, or shows the absence of this need. Such an episode can be extremely prolonged, then suddenly cut short and followed by an entirely unexpected little scene of a completely different order. Some episodes are saturated with everyday details; others are played out in a symbolic manner. Moreover, in one and the same episode or situation, one character may be described realistically, another as an abstract symbol, as for example, the character of the bear or the socialized horses in ***The Foundation Pit.***

Nowhere do his phrases ''create any framework whatsoever of their own'', only in relation to the overall theme. In his work, Platonov was capable of realizing the high demand which he made of literature. "Every word of the author serves the final meaning and purpose of the theme, carrying the function of work and not of play." (pp. 186-87)

Henryka Yakushev, "Andrei Platonov's Artistic Model of the World," in Russian Literature Triquarterly, *No. 16, 1979, pp. 171-88.*

ADDITIONAL BIBLIOGRAPHY

Ginsburg, Mirra. Introduction to *The Foundation Pit,* by Andrei Platonov, translated by Mirra Ginsburg, pp. v-xiv. New York: E. P. Dutton & Co., Inc., 1975.

Biographical information and criticism. Ginsburg recalls the hostile environment in which Platonov lived and wrote, which added to the pessimism, grotesqueness, and profound pity that informed his works. Ginsburg states: "Mirroring the cruel shambles to which revolution and human will (in all its complexities and motivations) have reduced life Platonov brings the action, the characters, and the language itself down to ultimate absurdity. He carried *The Foundation Pit* beyond irony, beyond satire, to a point where everything becomes a tragic parody of itself."

Lavrin, Janko. "Links with the Poet and the Future." In his *An Introduction to the Russian Novel,* rev. ed., pp. 201-11. London: Methuen & Co., 1945.*

Brief mention of Platonov as a promising writer. Lavrin refers to Platonov's "discreet, fastidious" writing and his use of orphan children to help evoke "the sense of the tragic."

Olcott, Anthony. Foreword to *Chevengur,* by Andrei Platonov, translated by Anthony Olcott, pp. ix-xvii. Ann Arbor: Ardis, 1978.

Biography and critical history. In the first complete publication of Platonov's masterpiece, translator Olcott describes the political pressures under which the artist worked and provides information about the suppression and fragmented publication of the work.

Slonim, Marc. "The Patriotic War and Its Aftermath." In his *Modern Russian Literature: From Chekov to the Present,* pp. 407-36. New York: Oxford University Press, 1953.*

Discussion of Russian literature of World War II. The Platonov short story "Inspired Men" is mentioned as one of the era's heroic treatments of the "common man."

"One More Victim." *The Times Literary Supplement,* No. 3472 (12 September 1968): 979.

Biography and plot description. The critic discusses Platonov's life and the short stories in the collection *V prekrasnom i yarostnom mire.*

Zavalishin, Vyacheslav. "Pereval." In his *Early Soviet Writers,* pp. 240-60. New York: Frederick A. Praeger, 1958.*

Discussion of the moral quality of Platonov's work. Although Platonov began as a member of the Pereval group founded in Russia in the 1920s, he soon rejected the group to pursue his own direction. This essay includes an examination of the critical climate that surrounded Platonov's most productive periods, and the lack of craftsmanship which marked his work and that of the Pereval group members.

José Rubén Romero

1890-1952

Mexican novelist, poet, essayist, short story writer, and biographer.

Romero's fiction explores in great detail the life and customs of his native Mexican state of Michoacán. His novels typically examine the clash of political, economic, and religious forces in the lives of the common people and comment pessimistically on human nature and aspirations. Although his novels are characterized by serious themes, Romero infused his works with various comic elements, and this mixture of the serious and the comic has led to a comparison of his novels with those of Mark Twain. In his greatest work, *La vida inútil de Pito Pérez (The Futile Life of Pito Pérez),* Romero created what many consider the most remarkable character in Mexican fiction—Pito Pérez, a bitter, comic, picaresque hero who comments forcefully on the varied effects of human folly.

The son of a merchant family, Romero was born in Cotija de la Paz, in the province of Michoacán. Although little is known about his formative years, Romero claimed that it was the memories of his youth, more than anything else, that provided the wealth of material for his many novels and stories. Romero launched his writing career, however, not with prose but with poetry, publishing his first book of verse, *Fantasías,* at the age of eighteen. Soon afterward he, like his father, entered the mercantile business, becoming proprietor of a grocery store in Tacambaro. In 1911 Romero joined the revolt against the dictator Porfirio Díaz. Although some sources claim that his involvement in the fighting was negligible, Romero actively participated in drafting the new Mexican constitution after Diaz's downfall later that year. In 1912 he was appointed tax collector for a town in his native province, and in the same year published his second book of verse. There is little information available about the ensuing two decades of Romero's life other than the dates of publication of his numerous collections of poetry. Romero eventually became a lawyer and was appointed Consul General to Barcelona, Spain, in 1930. His first novel, *Apuntes de un lugareño,* a series of autobiographical sketches with a markedly regional flavor, appeared two years later and served as a turning point in his career. For the rest of his life he published only prose. During the period from 1937 to 1938, while serving as ambassador to Brazil, Romero wrote and published *The Futile Life of Pito Pérez*. While his fame had been growing considerably even before this publication, it was this work that led to his widespread popularity and prompted his acceptance into the Mexican Academy of Letters. Romero became closely identified with Pito Pérez in the minds of readers, who began calling him by his character's name. In 1939 Romero was appointed ambassador to Cuba, a position he retained until he retired from diplomatic service five years later. Besides his distinguished diplomatic career, Romero also served as a presidential advisor, rector of the State University of Michoacán, and was a lecturer throughout his life. During his last years he wrote a series of articles addressing the problems in Mexico during the revolutionary period of 1910-1930, works which have come to be regarded as valuable to an understanding of the values, objectives, and cultural mores of Mexican society.

Romero's novels are autobiographical, and for that reason he did not like them to be judged by the same artistic standards applied to more purely fictional works, but rather as chapters in the story of his life. However, Romero's reservations appear to have been unfounded, for critics have praised his fictional technique, particularly his strong characterizations and stylistic accomplishments. Like many other novelists of his generation, Romero abandoned the artificially verbose literary style of nineteenth-century Mexican fiction in favor of a realistic approach that stressed an informal conversational tone. Romero's fiction provides one of the best examples of this modern form: anecdotal and vividly descriptive, his style incorporates interesting similes and metaphors and an ever present humor that features puns, ribald situations, and broad caricature. Critics find that Romero's style masterfully captured the nature of Mexican village life, which was his principal subject. He celebrated the lives of these provincial poor, depicting the wisdom they acquired through hardship and demonstrating his belief that human folly is less destructive among small town dwellers, for hypocrisy is more readily perceived in this more intimate environment. However, while his novels are concerned with the daily affairs of villagers, he also demonstrates the effects of larger social problems on their lives.

Critics contend that Romero's concern with social issues is most fully revealed by his depiction of the Mexican Revolution, which was the most prominent subject of Mexican fiction during the first half of the twentieth century. Most novels concerned with the Revolution were written by adherents to the cause, and although they were often critical of many of the effects of the Revolution, they portrayed the events in sweeping, epic terms. Unlike other novelists of his era, particularly Mariano Azuela and Lopez y Fuentes, Romero did not make the Revolution central to his fiction. Rather, he treated it as a peripheral event that affected the lives of his characters only indirectly. In the rare instances when Romero did focus directly on the Revolution, he usually did so critically or satirically. Although he agreed that the Revolution resulted in a better life for most Mexicans, Romero took no grand view of the revolutionaries, but concluded that many acted in part from personal motives, if not entirely out of base self-interest. Similarly, he disagreed with the popular belief that a new and better society would inevitably proceed from the Revolution. It was true that the Revolution had accomplished much, but Romero believed that there was much more to be done and objected to those who complacently accepted post-Revolutionary conditions. Critics have debated the implications of Romero's position, characterizing him alternately as a perceptive social commentator and as a self-obsessed individual removed from the true struggle of his country. Current critical consensus finds him to be more concerned with the struggles of the Mexican people than previous critics realized, and notes that his criticism of the Revolution was inspired by a general cynicism about the goodness of human nature.

This vision of Mexican life and the Mexican Revolution is captured most effectively in *The Futile Life of Pito Pérez*. *Pito Pérez* is often praised for its revival of the picaresque novel form, which had languished since the seventeenth century. Romero's use of that form is so successful that his work is often favorably compared to Miguel de Cervantes's *Don Quixote*. Traditionally, the picaresque hero is someone from a lower social class who is acutely sensitive to his position in society and whose carefree behavior serves as a way to compensate for feelings of inferiority. Pito Pérez fits this description: he is an incarnation of antisocial habits as well as an anarchical homespun philosopher who sees through others, trusts no one, and considers himself a victim. Pito's social position allows him to remain detached from the life of the town around him, which he views tolerantly and without emotion, an attitude that reflects his cynical philosophy that people are interested only in themselves. Although Pito's life of diversion is ostensibly useless, it nevertheless serves to demonstrate his rejection of what he considers a duplicitous society. Because he cannot change his world, he withdraws and becomes a victim, active only in negation and nonconformism. Romero's skillful portrayal of Pito is enhanced by a style that is both conversational and lyrical, blending pathos, satire, fantasy, and bawdy humor in a manner that has led to comparisons with James Joyce's *Ulysses,* Henry Fielding's *Tom Jones,* Mark Twain's *Huckleberry Finn,* and the films of Charlie Chaplin.

The combination of realism and philosophical speculation is the foremost distinguishing element of Romero's work. Throughout his career as a novelist he defined his own vision of life even as he portrayed in detail the customs of his native province. Unlike the works of other Mexican realistic novelists, the two elements are inextricably linked in the novels of Romero, which led R. Anthony Castagnaro to call him ''the most personally absorbing novelist of contemporary Mexico.''

PRINCIPAL WORKS

Fantasías (poetry) 1908
Rimas bohemias (poetry) 1912
La musa heroica (poetry) 1915
La musa loca (poetry) 1917
Sentimental (poetry) 1919
Tacámbaro (poetry) 1922
Versos viejos (poetry) 1930
Apuntes de un lugareño (novel) 1932
Desbandada (novel) 1934
Mi caballo, mi perro, y mi rifle (novel) 1934
El pueblo inocente (novel) 1934
La vida inútil de Pito Pérez (novel) 1938
[*The Futile Life of Pito Pérez,* 1966]
Anticipación a la muerte (novel) 1939
Algunas cosillas de Pito Pérez que se me quedaron en el tintero (aphorisms) 1945
Rosenda (novel) 1946
Obras completas (poetry, novels, essays, short stories, biography) 1957

BERTA GAMBOA DE CAMINO (essay date 1935)

[In an unexcerpted portion of the following essay, Camino describes in detail the thematic concerns and stylistic elements of the many novels of the Mexican Revolution. In the following excerpt, Camino discusses the regionalistic, or local color, aspects of Romero's fiction and notes his relationship to other writers concerned with social reform.]

Rubén Romero is the regional novelist of the State of Michoacán. His ***Memoirs of a Native*** are memories of a village boy during the Revolution. His realism is not that of a journalist relating the horrors of life in the camps, but that of a humorist describing the life and the bourgeois types in a village. In ***The Innocent Village,*** . . . he narrates the adventures of a young student who returns from Mexico City to his own village. Romero constantly tends towards regionalism. He describes admirably the picturesque customs of the villages, their religious celebrations, their social gatherings, days in the fields. He is essentially anecdotal, and at times it seems that his main object is to tell anecdotes, attributing them here and there to the characters in his novels. He has also, like the writers of social novels, a tendency to criticize the abuses perpetrated by officials in villages and provincial cities. In the title, ***The Innocent Village,*** the word ''innocent'' has the double meaning, ironic and bitter, that the village is ignorant of what is being done to it, and is also an expiatory victim, paying for another's crimes. (pp. 270-71)

Berta Gamboa de Camino, ''The Novel of the Mexican Revolution,'' in Renascent Mexico, *edited by Hubert Herring and Herbert Weinstock, Covici Friede Publishers, 1935, pp. 258-74.**

RUTH STANTON (essay date 1941)

[In the following excerpt, Stanton explores Romero's transformation from poet to novelist and concludes that his poetic temperament shapes the form and themes of several of his novels.]

When José Rubén Romero appeared in the national field of Mexican letters in 1932, he easily obtained one of the first places among the novelists because he brought with him those much-desired traits of humor, graceful picturesqueness, and love for the people of his state of Michoacán, which combined to make him an excellent *"costumbrista"* ["novelist of manners"].

His novels show a wide and humorous understanding of the provincial proprieties, and this has contributed greatly to his position as one of the outstanding painters of Mexican village life. He is also an indefatigable narrator of popular stories, and the maze of Mexican folklore holds no secrets from him. .

His poetry was born in those regions of Michoacán where one contemplates the most beautiful landscapes in Mexico, and which, at the same time, have served as the stage for some of the cruelest episodes in Mexican history. The inquietude and ancestral wounds still stirring in the souls of today's generations are expressed by the provincial poet, who has lived absorbed in the world around him. Thus were born in Rubén Romero, at the same time, the poet and the revolutionist. . . . (p. 423)

Rubén Romero speaks of ***Tacámbaro*** as the book of verse that opened for him the doors of metropolitan literary criticism. He presents in it small pictures of village life and of village people in Tacámbaro. . . . (pp. 423-24)

This type of verse was inspired by the poems of Jules Renard, and by the *"hai-kais"* of José Juan Tablada.

In ***Versos viejos,*** our writer shows himself to be not only a proud idealist, but a realistic lover of life. ***Versos viejos*** has much in common with *Les Méditations* of Alphonse de Lamartine: They evoke with nostalgia the scenes of childhood, demonstrate love for a provincial corner and its special enchantments. Rubén Romero admires with Lamartine the beauty of nature and humanity; he can paint states of feeling, but he fails to make sensitive the nebulous and troubled regions of the human soul as Lamartine does.

Among the circumstances that intervened in the formation of Rubén Romero the novelist, we note first the transformation of the poet into a novelist. There is present in the narrator of today the lyric poet of yesterday: It is the poet who rules the destiny of the novelist. (p. 424)

In reality, Rubén Romero's novelistic procedure is poetical—each chapter of a novel compares favorably to a canto, which in turn obliges him to restrain the ideological breadth of the different parts of the book. Gaston Lafarga in his study of Señor Romero believes that his formation as a novelist was developed from his reading of the European writers of the sixteenth, seventeenth, and eighteenth centuries. By this observation he means that the eighteenth-century French ideology was not important in the formation of Rubén Romero the novelist, because his sensibility drew him away from the learned analysis of that epoch, and attracted him to the individualistic romantic synthesis where he could reaffirm the use of his imagination and utilize his impressions to a greater advantage.

The novel, ***Desbandada,*** shows perfectly the "poetic" procedure of Rubén Romero: As a writer of customs he not only describes vividly the villagers and their problems, but he also succeeds in capturing the soul of an episode, the spirit of an attitude, and in identifying himself with the characters he creates—all without resorting to the use of a cohesive plot.

His third book of prose, ***El pueblo inocente,*** is a story of life in one of the many unnamed villages of Michoacán that the author knows so well. The narrative is full of things typically Mexican: customs, types, and language. It is a hymn in praise of provincial life, of the fields and mountains, and of the placid and taciturn Indians. At the same time it expresses indirectly the philosophy of the writer: his appreciation of the integrity of the Mexican people, and his desire to alleviate the injustice in which so many of his people live. (pp. 425-26)

With the publication of ***La vida inútil de Pito Pérez*** there appears another quality in the writing of José Rubén Romero: the cultivation of the picaresque element, which characterizes him as a distant follower of Don Joaquín Fernández de Lizardi. Pito Pérez is not new among the characters created by Señor Romero. We see him profiled first in ***El pueblo inocente,*** but it is in this later volume that he occupies the central position, with his grotesque figure of a village ne'er-do-well. The writer paints from beginning to end the *"via crucis"* of Pito's varied existence, including all manner of tricks and imbroglios suited to an adventurer of his position who earned his livelihood by his wits. Pito's victims always include the three principal characters of village life: the priest, the judge, and the druggist, and such lesser individuals as may cross his path.

We see in ***La vida inútil de Pito Pérez*** an enlargement of that ideological outlook which we have previously considered. In this story, social ostracism gives Pito Pérez opportunity for meditation and an angle from which to observe certain social problems. . . . (pp. 426-27)

The author has recognized no obligation to be polemic nor has he looked relentlessly for victims of the social order who might be elevated into champions of a higher truth. He has not felt obliged to take many exceptions to the broad, average current of human existence. He has, however, chosen the simpler truths for the reason that these illustrate better the workings of the human heart. He has preferred to make as much of the cheerful aspects of life as possible, even when realizing that a certain amount of unpleasantness has to be tolerated. . . .

In general, Rubén Romero's novels represent a decisive advance in simplicity and reality over the nineteenth-century Mexican novels: His characters are no longer required to speak the stilted language or to feel the quivering sentiments that had once seemed symptoms of nobility of soul. His preoccupation with local color has encouraged love of surfaces, if not a satisfaction with surfaces alone. The lives which his novels present are at times inextricably connected with the clash of political, economic, and religious matters; in other instances, they are purely descriptive. His novels are faithful to Mexican life, at least to those phases which he has chosen to record. (p. 427)

Ruth Stanton, "José Rubén Romero, Costumbrista of Michoacán," in Hispania, *Vol. XXIV, No. 4, December, 1941, pp. 423-28.*

R. ANTHONY CASTAGNARO (essay date 1953)

[In the following excerpt, Castagnaro characterizes Romero as a conversationalist in prose whose novels are informal, direct transcriptions of incidents and characters from his life. For this reason, Castagnaro believes that Romero provides an earthy, humorous view of Mexican life unavailable in the works of other

novelists of that generation. For other discussions of this subject, see the excerpts by William O. Cord (1962), Ewart E. Phillips (1963), and John S. Brushwood (1966). Castagnaro also disagrees with those critics who consider Romero a novelist of the Mexican Revolution of the same stature as Mariano Azuela. Rather, Castagnaro finds that Romero did not examine the Revolution as a historical process, but only as an event that affected his personal life. For differing opinions of Romero's portrayal of the Revolution, see the excerpts by Walter M. Langford (1971) and Daniel E. Gulstad (1973).]

José Rubén Romero is a novelist in name only. His novels, even when compared with those of contemporary European and American writers, appear as unorthodox, informal ramblings of a raconteur. An English translation of the title of his first prose work, **"Jottings of a Villager,"** is particularly appropriate in revealing the informal frame and substance that characterize all his later works. The anecdote—authentic, altered or invented—is the main vehicle of his prose.

With an informal gathering of his fellow villagers as his audience, Romero evokes the interesting incidents of his life and transmits them orally to his listeners. The unschooled nature of his written work clearly points to its oral quality; the egocentric orientation of the typical Hispanic conversationalist is always visible. Whether he is the manifest protagonist (***Apuntes de un lugareño, Desbandada, Anticipación a la muerte, Una vez fuí rico***), the person on whom the protagonist is modelled (***El pueblo inocente, Mi caballo, mi perro y mi rifle***), or whether he shares the spotlight with another character (***La vida inútil de Pito Pérez, Rosenda***), Romero is always writing of himself and, more than most writers, to please himself. This frankly egocentric approach is characteristic of all his novels and explains the most important facets of his literary style.

The characters in Romero's novels—there are more than two hundred in his eight novels—are, for the most part, actual people he has known. His characterizations, therefore, are not character creations in the literary sense. They are, rather, evocations of people he has encountered in his own real life and whom, with a varyingly small amount of retouching and polishing, he introduces in his novels. This being so, it is not surprising to find that a few of Romero's character evocations appear in more than one work.

In keeping with this personal approach to characterization, Romero rarely gives us full-length, detailed portraits, or portraits which follow the precepts of the literary schools of the nineteenth or twentieth century. Most of his characters are sketched in fragmentary fashion, the resulting incompleteness being made up for, in part, by the vividness of the depictions. The presentation of personal peculiarities is frequent, and serves to render the character impression more lasting in the reader's consciousness. The emotional proximity existing between Romero and his character evocations also strengthens this effect. But Romero's most important characters are remembered not for their physical appearance but for what they say.

Romero devotes considerable attention to describing the external appearance of his characters. When he works out a well proportioned and vivid description of Don Vicente's appearance, for example, Romero seems to be so proud of it that he repeats the descriptive paragraph, almost verbatim, later on in the work (***El pueblo inocente***). But neither this device, nor the device of frequently reminding the reader that Rosenda's eyes are green (***Rosenda***), is enough to counteract the vagueness in the physical appearance of the respective characters. And so it is with Romero's other large canvases, Pito Pérez being no exception. It is by means of their speech that his characters reveal their personality.

Most of Romero's portraits are literary transcriptions of real and specific Mexicans. As such, and as a result of their vivid and representative quality, these portraits constitute a valuable contribution to the Mexican novel and to the study of the Mexican scene. Despite their incompleteness, Romero's characterizations fill out one composite and truly representative picture, that of the inhabitant of the small town, the *aldeano*, whom none of the other novelists of the Mexican Revolution has painted more effectively than Romero.

Being the emotional, egocentric raconteur that he is, Romero presents similar peculiarities in his descriptions of physical circumstance. He picks out those portions of observable reality that strike his attention most. Naturally enough, his descriptions of physical objects tend to become more detailed the greater the personal, emotional meaning they have for him. Naturally, too, he makes abundant use of personification. He achieves unusually vivid effects through his flair for simile and metaphor. The use of more than thirteen hundred of these figures in a production of eight relatively short novels is a good indication of this descriptive bent. He has wrought some very effective comparisons, and many of his similes and metaphors can be counted among the most picturesque to be found in the novel of the Revolution. But, as in his oral characterizations, his similes and metaphors are used as vehicles for his conversational wit. Their essence is not an esthetic one; they are not used to suggest a reality that lies behind the clearly visible.

Of great irregularity in orientation, length, and effectiveness, Romero's descriptions of physical reality, his local color, his *costumbrismo* all serve as backdrops for his characters and himself as they act and, primarily, speak.

Essentially a small-town man of limited academic and literary culture, Romero often achieves chaotic literary effects when he seriously undertakes to describe and comment. His vocabulary—the most easily read yardstick of his literary self-consciousness—is marked by several levels of linguistic tone. It is of wide range and includes, in approximate order of frequency, common and colloquial words, regionalisms (including dialectal expressions, archaisms, and Indian terms), academic words (including cultural allusions), scatological terms, and foreign expressions. Like the provincial who feels self-conscious in the presence of cultivated men of letters—we recall his acceptance into the Mexican Academy—Romero tries to compensate for the generally popular level of his vocabulary by inserting an inordinate number of high-sounding terms. In doing so, he produces the spectacle of a "popular," regionalistic writer whose vocabulary contains a proportionately greater amount of learned terms than that of more genuinely educated and well balanced writers like Azuela and López y Fuentes. Occasionally, however, when the self-conscious author casts off his recently acquired and artificial literary trappings, he assumes his more authentic manner and gives literary status to the regionalistic elements of his writings.

The basis for designating Romero as a "novelist of the Revolution" is neither as broad nor as deep as in the case of his fellow novelists. To be sure, his novels contain several chapters on the course of the Revolution in Michoacán. . . . But the reader finds no real analysis, no real criticism of the Revolution's course or significance. The significance of the events that have been taking place around him, and in which he has played at least a small part, either escapes his notice or concerns him little. The coverage by any of the other prominent novelists of the Revolution—even that of Magdaleno, who, for reasons of chronology and literary approach, treats the Revolution less intensively than Azuela, Guzmán, or López y Fuentes—is much more comprehensive than the coverage Romero gives.

When Romero does stop to defend the Revolution, he utters the platitudes to which only non-thinking or unconcerned Mexicans will limit their comment. The reader familiar with the works of Azuela and the rest cannot help suspecting that Romero's praise of the Revolution does not carry deep conviction. The Revolution appears in his works only to the degree that it portrays his own participation in the struggle and in the effects it has had upon his personal life. More than anything else, the Revolution serves as a source of anecdotic material for this primarily anecdotic writer. In one especially noticeable case, Romero uses the same event (the incursion into Tacámbaro of the vandalistic band of Inés García Chávez) as the center of two of his more memorable tales (in ***Desbandada*** and ***Rosenda***).

Yet Romero is as surely a "novelist of the Revolution" as any of the writers usually so designated. Besides scattering his abundant collection of tales throughout his novels, Romero has portrayed, in the person of Pito Pérez, as genuine a product of the Mexican Revolution as any single character of Romero's better known literary colleagues. Despite the undeveloped and inconsistent characterization by which he is presented to the reader, Pito Pérez stands as a highly representative, spiritually sick personification of the disinherited *pelado* of present-day Mexico. In a more significant and paradoxical sense, Romero, absolutely unrevolutionary in style, appears on the literary scene as Mexico's most authentic revolutionary product: an unschooled man of the masses who has risen to literary fame and fortune. Like Diego de Rivera (whom he also resembles physically), Romero is an exponent of the truly "popular" art which the Mexican Revolution has lifted from scorn and obscurity to the high degree of appreciation and universal acclaim which it now enjoys.

The novels of Romero are Romero himself. In every chapter—almost on every page—we feel his presence and personality. To an unusually high degree in the case of Romero, "style is the man," and the works of Azuela, López y Fuentes, Guzmán, and Magdaleno seem like the cold observations of the most impersonal novelist when compared with those of Romero. Subconsciously gathering the personality traits which Romero exhibits in his novels, and adding to these the knowledge gathered from more objective sources, the reader can form a more complete and genuine picture of this author than he can of any other novelist of the Mexican Revolution. Rubén Romero thus emerges as an ideologically undeveloped hedonist for whom the writing of novels is a vital complement to the expression of his deep egocentricity or *egolatría*.

Romero's need is to focus the reader's attention upon himself. In order to achieve this, he resorts to a rambling series of personal stories, often told directly, often interwoven in a plot which is never more than incidental. He is always an orally communicative writer; his personal "humor" always pervades his novels. Interpreted in any of the usual meanings the word has had in its peculiar history, "humor" is the subjective characteristic which most clearly distinguishes Romero's style from that of the other novelists of the Revolution. For Azuela, López y Fuentes, Guzmán, and Magdaleno, the Revolution is too serious, too tragic, and too close for them to achieve the literary objectivity which must some day be achieved, if the Revolution is to be understood in true literary and historical perspective. Moreover, these serious writers apparently have too much cognizance of and respect for the novel's traditional form to allow the more intimately personal intrusions of the novelist the free rein which Romero gives. For Romero, on the other hand, the Revolution represents a basic but bygone period in his life; the violent stages of the struggle were already past when Romero's first novel appeared. . . . Given the incidental role of the Revolution in his literary material, and the sensual, roguish egocentricity that he displays in his own overt life, it is not surprising to find that Romero is the only humorous writer among the most important novelists of the Revolution.

In attempting to define and understand Romero's humor, it is useful to remember that Hispanic humor, in general, has always been distinct from the humor of the Anglo-Saxon world. Hispanic humor, traditionally more restricted in scope, variety, and degree, is usually limited to specific characters and situations, and rarely attains the social, cosmic projections of a Bernard Shaw, for example. Nor does it usually possess the subtleties of an Oscar Wilde. Hispanic humor is more direct and accessible. It is heavier, too, for it is a desperate sublimation of grief. Lacking the Anglo-Saxon's highly developed emotional detachment, the Hispanic is serious and tragic in his general orientation to life. His laughter, therefore, is less refined, his mocking more merciless. (pp. 300-03)

The countless anecdotes that Romero tells in his novels are in the genuine Hispanic tradition. They encompass the humor of circumstance, the humor of character and caricature, the quick, direct, occasionally farfetched wit of verbal play. Scatology is abundantly present, either in isolated or related form. Sex is a fundamental component of Romero's humor—it is the central element of some of his best *chistes*—just as it is a natural, unspectacular component of Romero's orientation to habitual life.

It is in ***La vida inútil de Pito Pérez,*** his best novel in other respects also, that Romero achieves the greatest variety and the highest form of Hispanic humor. From the direct, Quevedesque word-play, from the ingenuity of his similes and metaphors, from the jokes played on the grocery-store clerk and the innkeeper's barrels of wine, from the caricature of the pharmacist, Pito Pérez passes on to the kindly trick played on Padre Pureco, by which he supplies the good priest with Latin quotations from the latter's own book, and, finally, to the sublimely humorous, tragicomic adventure with *la Caneca,* the woman's skeleton which Pito Pérez carries about with him. Here, Death, the greatest of human incongruities, is the butt of all of Pito Pérez's (and Romero's) ingenuity, an ingenuity which also brings together cynicism and kindliness in an extended emotional incongruity within an incongruity.

In Pito Pérez, Romero has channeled all the lyricism that he expresses intermittently in his other novels and not always dexterously in his poems. In this outstanding case of character projection, Romero has used the Mexican rogue to make articulate all his anger at the injustices of the world, all his feelings as a frustrated poet, all his sentimental aspirations to the triumph of ethical beauty. Like Cervantes' greater character projection, Pito Pérez expresses his author's complaint against the world's wrongs; unlike Don Quijote, Pito Pérez is a sentimental anarchist. Especially in the second part of the novel, Pito Pérez could easily have become a repulsive character. He is saved from this literary fate by his pathos. Pito is an intelligent, noble, and sentimental soul who could have realized the worthy qualities of his character if Fate had not conspired against him so frequently and viciously. Moreover, his pathos is a genuine expression of a national or racial quality not easily understood by the average non-Latin reader. Its core lies in the realization that man's fate on earth is frustrated from the very beginning, and in the resulting desire to conquer Fate by a desperately emotional rejection of Nature's impositions. ***La vida inútil de Pito Pérez*** may very well be considered the lyrical compendium of this aspect of Mexican psychology.

In the popular source and the unsophisticated quality of his humor—his *gracia*—Romero is an authentic literary descendant of Juan Ruiz, Miguel de Cervantes, and Francisco de Quevedo.

Rubén Romero's literary style is the lack of formal style. He is temperamentally incapable of constructing a novel. There is no technical consistency or virtuosity in his descriptions. There is no profound analysis, no social projection in his characterizations. Romero lacks the novelistic depth essential to the true novelist. Peculiarly enough, in the dissolved, amorphous cast of his "novels," he unconsciously falls within the technique of the contemporary novel.

Romero's most typical and charming manner is that of the raconteur, the conversationalist in writing. Hence, his stylistic forte is narration and dialogue. His characters, enormous in their variety, are best characterized when they speak; his greatest character is himself—the hedonistically humorous rogue who ambles through all the pages of his novels. Romero's vague literary orientation is the retarded romanticism of the provincial. Essentially and inevitably a provincial, he is the most "popular" writer among the novelists of the Revolution. When he tries to rise above the *lugareño* that he is, he falls out of character and fails as a writer. Undeveloped as an esthetic or social ideologist, he is at his lyrical best when he expresses his own emotion. Not nearly as "literary" as his fellow novelists of the Mexican Revolution, J. Rubén Romero is, nevertheless, the most personally absorbing novelist of contemporary Mexico. (pp. 303-04)

R. Anthony Castagnaro, "Rubén Romero and the Novel of the Mexican Revolution," in Hispania, *Vol. XXXVI, No. 3, August, 1953, pp. 300-04.*

SHERMAN EOFF (essay date 1956)

[*In the following excerpt, Eoff discusses the picaro as a literary type as well as the picaresque traits represented by Pito Pérez. For another discussion of Pito as a picaro, see the excerpt by Arturo Torres-Rioseco (1963).*]

One of the claims that the Spanish picaresque novel has on the attention of the devotee of Spanish literature is the vitality evidenced by its periodic reappearance during the last three centuries. The evidence is to be found not only in reproductions of the old narrative form but in extensions and, sometimes, substantial transformations of themes and ideas. (p. 190)

Attention to the *pícaro*'s psychology has been [an extension] of . . . recent date, and with it the vitality of the old genre has been demonstrated anew. For perhaps the richest potential of the seventeenth-century novel for modern development is its presentment of a situation in which the relationship between character and environment is the real basis of the story. . . . When the *pícaro* is observed from this viewpoint, his most fundamental personality trait is his sensitiveness to an inferior position in society, and his life is seen to be a timorous but continuous striving, sometimes laughable and sometimes pitiable, to compensate for the unfavorable circumstances that envelop him from the time of his childhood.

Underlying this general inferiority complex is the insecurity of home and family typical of the *pícaro*'s early years, and among the pertinent factors the status of being held in slight esteem is one of the most significant. If a writer of the present day were to concentrate upon this psychological factor as the basis of a biographical narrative and were to trace in his central character a growing realization of personal futility at once comical and sad, he would only be expanding on a subject already handled in the Spanish picaresque novel of the sixteenth and seventeenth centuries. An outstanding modern treatment of such a psychological development is found in ***La vida inútil de Pito Pérez***. . . . (p. 191)

In ***La vida inútil de Pito Pérez,*** Rubén Romero allows his protagonist to admit, in fact to emphasize, his own unhappiness, and makes perfectly clear that the basic reason for that unhappiness is a lack of sympathy and recognition from other people. Though Pito Pérez as a child was not ashamed of his family, he felt neglected and ignored. At the time of his birth he was deprived of his full share of milk in favor of a baby that was not even his mother's, and later his brothers were always favored in the use of the family's small resources. His brief experience as an acolyte ends in his being kept at home in almost complete seclusion. Lonely and bored, he runs away, looking for adventure and fame. After a few typically picaresque episodes of trickery and deception with different employers, he returns home, hoping above all to find a welcome, even if it has to be with a switch. He is met, instead, with complete indifference.

Following these early and futile efforts to gain recognition in his own family, Pito begins to associate with idlers and gradually acquires the habit of drink. He seeks with little success the love of young women and becomes more and more a rolling stone, trying to hide with the aid of alcohol his insignificance and unhappiness. There is in his seemingly carefree behavior the same effort to compensate for inferiority by way of humorous bravado and clownishness that one finds in the seventeenth-century *pícaro*. He thus exhibits what is unquestionably a fundamental aspect of picaresque behavior: an effort on the part of an ignored child to attract attention. Unlike the old *pícaro,* however, Pito Pérez withdraws from society in his maturity, becoming more a vagabond (in the role of peddler) than a rogue, seeking companionship with nature and even with the small bells that he carries with him as symbols of belongingness with towns of his native Michoacán. But his indifference to human beings is actually a defensive development that reaches finally an explosive point in his *testamento*. This bitter outburst is the key to his psychology. Standing out clearly as the dominant motive in his caustic social criticism is the castigatory reaction of one who wanted to belong and could not. . . . (pp. 192-93)

Approaching the end of a life of disappointments, Pito Pérez is overwhelmed with self-pity and magnifies his misfortunes, especially his experiences in love. "La caneca," the woman's skeleton that he considers a faithful companion, is a farcical substitute for someone to love, a grotesque display paralleling the bitterness of the *testamento*. The extremism that Pito thus exhibits in his last days is but an intensified manifestation of the loneliness that he had previously expressed in softer tones. . . .

The lyrical style of Rubén Romero, which gives his novel its major charm, creates a dominant tone of melancholic nostalgia for something that was ardently desired and never possessed. The reader may find himself interested primarily in this stylistic aspect but he must not forget that the novel is the lyrical account of an individual drama, and that at the heart of the drama is the intense loneliness of one who tries in vain to counterbalance people's indifference to him. (p. 193)

Sherman Eoff, "Tragedy of the Unwanted Person, in Three Versions: Pablos de Segovia, Pito Pérez, Pascual Duarte," in Hispania, *Vol. XXXIX, No. 2, May, 1956, pp. 190-96.**

WILLIAM O. CORD (essay date 1961)

[*Cord is an American professor of Spanish American literature who has written many works on that subject. He is also the English translator of Romero's* The Futile Life of Pito Pérez. *In recognition of his service to Mexican literature, Cord received a decoration from Romero's home province of Michoacán, Mexico. In the following excerpt, Cord examines Romero's reasons for composing his novels, the relationship of the novels to Romero's life, and Romero's reactions to his own work.*]

Romero did not hesitate to evaluate himself as a writer as well as to effect a judgment of his own work. His most general, and at the same time indicative, remark concerning himself as an author was that he composed without cogitation, in the only style which was natural to him, and about that which was most familiar to him. His style and his themes were reminiscent of the province and his provincial life therein. . . . His devotion to the province furnished the stimulus to write, a theme which he could develop, and literally, a style with which he could compose. . . .

Romero remained steadfast in his literary consecration. His novels, his speeches, his articles and essays continuously reflected the flavor of the province. . . . He also admitted that he, like many of his contemporaries, was imbued with the revolutionary feelings which dominated Mexico and its people. Thus, as he wrote about his own experiences, the events for his story were those of the contemporary history of Mexico. Likewise, the people he included in his story were real people caught in the turmoil of revolution. He admitted that he had never created a single event or character. (p. 431)

Because he had developed themes which were fundamentally based on his own experiences in life, the works of Rubén Romero were essentially autobiographical. Romero freely admitted that he felt no restraint in writing of himself. He could tell his stories much in the same manner as he had lived them. He indicated however, that he had sensed that his works would have a popular appeal. It was not vanity which prompted Romero to think of popularity. Rather, as his life had been so typical of that of thousands in Mexico who had experienced similar, even identical, incidents in their lives, identification of reader with a character, an event, a place, or even a mood would be a common occurrence. Autobiographic composition also afforded him freedom from an exercise of the imagination. He could draw on the facets of his life. He was not burdened with the necessities of plot construction, character development, and artistic imagery. Neither did autobiography, in his mind, demand a meticulous prudence in semantics and syntax. He insisted that he was incapable of creating a work wherein style and form could be evaluated by accepted literary standards.

Romero thus considered his literature to have little literary value in either national or international circles. He wrote for personal pleasure and satisfaction, not in an attempt to display any special creative talent or to create finished artistic masterpieces. The writing of his novels was essentially his method of experiencing vicariously the pleasures of his home while he was away from Mexico. He implied that his books were only those works which would have been achieved by anyone possessed of the power of retention coupled with a desire to exhibit in writing an ardent devotion to one's home and friends. (pp. 431-32)

Despite the enthusiastic acceptance of his works by the public and official recognition by the Academy, Romero was still hesitant to grant that any of his compositions could be accepted as works of art. He insisted that he had merely retold the story of his life. He had written the account in the vernacular rather than in a grand or noble prose. He admitted the presence of many defects in these compositions. But, he explained, these defects were really reflections of similar weaknesses in his own character: indiscretion, pride, inconsistence. If late in life he remained unembarrassed by his actions, he blamed himself for not having composed, during the vast scope of his literary career, at least ". . . un buen libro" ["a good book"]. And in final judgment of himself as a writer, he wrote: ". . . debo sentirme vencido, impotente para expresar mis sentimientos" [". . . I feel past my prime, unable to express my sentiments."]. Thus, despite a pretentious popularity in his country and abroad, Rubén Romero was unwilling to deem popular reaction synonymous with artistic value. Although he was so pleased that so many persons had read his works and expressed the hope that others would come to know them, his ultimate decision was that he had been relatively unsuccessful as an author and that his works ". . . carecen de importancia como obras de arte" ["lack the importance of works of art"].

If Rubén Romero generally belittled his talent as an author and the merit of his works as a whole, he was personally most satisfied with his novel ***La vida inútil de Pito Pérez.*** Although Romero stated that perhaps this work had been too highly praised by the critics, there is no doubt that he reached the height of his literary career with this novel which paradoxically has been termed, as will be explained later, both the most Mexican and the least Mexican of his works. (pp. 432-33)

There is no doubt that Romero's most singular attraction to this novel was occasioned by the protagonist, Pito Pérez. If in his literary haste, Romero had caused Pito to die at the close of the novel, Pito lived on in the mind of the novelist. Substantiation of this statement is evidenced by the publication of a second work which concerned Pito's activities. Romero stated that he found consolation in the character of the rogue. Pito afforded a psychological solace which Romero had not found elsewhere. Although Romero never explained himself in this matter, one can assume that such solace was really identification of self with the novelistic character. (p. 433)

There is evidence to support the statement that Romero's primary purpose [in writing the novel] was not merely to entertain. . . . [In 1949 he wrote] that he had wanted to record the sadness and bitterness which life had inflicted upon an individual for whom everything had always turned out for the worse. He had wanted to portray this person who had known only defeat in business, in society, and in love. It was Romero's desire to picture one of these many persons who was hungry while others ate at leisure, one who lived in misery while others enjoyed the benefits granted by wealth. . . .

Since Romero had once inferred that he had written this novel with a purpose more serious than that of entertainment, and then later detailed a specific objective, it would seem that this latter supersedes the first in importance. In effect, this purpose renders the desire to entertain a technique with which the novel becomes more appealing to a greater number of readers.

Assuming the more serious of the two objectives to be Romero's ultimate goal, the immediate public reaction to the novel was somewhat disconcerting to him. Although readers generously applauded this work which enjoyed two editions during the first year of existence, these same readers seemed to see a comic character in the person of Pito Pérez. To them he was a clown. The element of tragedy apparently made no impression. Romero was disturbed by this reaction of the public. He was further upset when people began to associate him with the protagonist of the novel. They began to address him as "Pito Pérez." Such actions and reactions on the part of the public caused Rubén Romero to assume that he was either a poor judge of human character, or that he was completely incapable of expressing himself clearly and accurately in writing. (p. 434)

Romero's initial impression of the public reaction to this novel soon proved incorrect. If the readers had been amused, they were also acutely aware of the tragedy in a human life. To the Mexican, it was the story of his life and Pito Pérez was every Mexican who had been caught in the turmoil that followed the Revolution. Pito was the personification of rebellion against the inhumanity and injustice of a stagnant country. Pito was an individual whose ideas paralleled those of Romero and he became the mouthpiece for the pessimistic views of his biographer, who in turn was enumerating the attitudes of the people. The people of Mexico easily understood his cries and his pleas. Romero was expressing national attitudes; Pito Pérez was his spokesman. But, if Pito Pérez was essentially Mexican in concept and description, he was like many men in other cultures and other societies. It was in this light that Indalecio Prieto termed this novel both the most Mexican and the least Mexican of Romero's works. The totality of Pito's ideas was at once specific to Mexico and general everywhere. They seemed to reflect the thoughts of many men in many places. As one critic explained, the reader saw himself as Pito Pérez, as a *pícaro,* who like Pito was running from life, attempting to escape a cruel monotony and routine. If Romero had really wanted his work to be the anguished story of a man, he actually had compiled "una visión angustiosa de la Humanidad" ["a magnificent vision of humanity"].

In time Romero became aware of the true public sentiment for his novel and even admitted the truth of these cogent analyses. He acknowledged also that he had succeeded in his overall purpose. But what he had not realized, at least at first, was that this was not the tragedy of a man, but one of men. The protagonist was at once the personification of a people and an epoch, and indirectly, reflected the anguish of men of all ages. Pito's complaints were not restricted by time, they were timeless. Thus, Romero had succeeded in writing a work whose declarations had certain universal applications. (p. 435)

It is obvious that Rubén Romero's remarks concerning himself as a writer and those about his literature are relatively few in number. However, they reveal much information which contributes to the literary knowledge of Romero. By his own admission, his literature was the story of his life as a *provinciano* of Mexico. Because this life was so much like that of others, what he wrote was really the story of life, ideas, and observations of many other Mexicans who had been enmeshed in the confusion of revolution. By means of this picture of Mexico and Mexicans, Romero's popularity, and much of his literary success, was assured.

By his own admission, Romero's literature did not boast those characteristics usually associated with artistic creations. His works lacked literary finesse and refinement. He and his literature consistently reflected the atmosphere of provincial life, whose attention was directed more to the daily affairs, concerns, and activities of struggling human beings than to the subtleties of urban society with its fabricated code of cosmopolitan conduct.

Romero believed that his literature should not be judged with the standards necessary for literary works of art. His works were not creations in that the theme, its development, and the style employed for that development were fashioned solely by talent and creative imagination. He admitted that he wrote more by instinct than because of authentic literary genius. But, if Romero at times was disturbed because he had never written a true literary creation, and if he belittled much of his own writing, he was consoled by the presence in his literature of a value which he considered of an importance equal to that of artistic merit. He had expressed himself honestly and sincerely and he had written, with unwavering dedication, about that life which he believed the real delineator of *lo mexicano*. Although he had written of people and events that were close to the soil and native to a given epoch, he had been able, at least in his favorite work, to portray much of the anxiety endured by men everywhere, at all times. (pp. 435-36)

William O. Cord, "José Rubén Romero: The Writer As Seen by Himself," in Hispania, *Vol. XLIV, No. 3, September, 1961, pp. 431-37.*

WILLIAM O. CORD (essay date 1962)

[In the following excerpt, Cord outlines Romero's thoughts on Mexico's people, problems, and future, paying particular attention to his recommendations for national development. Cord's discussion of Romero's social conscience contrasts with R. Anthony Castagnaro's examination of the egocentricity of Romero's novels (see excerpt dated 1953).]

It may be said with reason that the very essence of José Rubén Romero was Mexico, his fatherland. It was this statesman's stimulus to act, this famed novelist's inspiration to compose, and this private citizen's cause for life. . . . The student of Romeros' literature will avow to the sensitive spirit who wrote, with understanding and compassion, of certain problems which plagued Mexico and its people during the years 1910-1930. However, few persons outside Mexico are aware that Rubén Romero completed a valuable analysis of the stimuli, objectives, and cultural mores which dominate the Mexican societal group. The vehicle for this revealing study was a series of articles published by Romero in the Mexican journal *Hoy* during the last years of his life, 1948-1951. (p. 612)

Romero concerned himself little with specific details. Rather his interest lay in revealing those underlying currents which distinguished Mexico and its people from another nation and its people. His purpose was to uncover the stimuli which prompted the country into action and those which determined the course of action of its people. But, as Romero explained, these currents were difficult to define. It seemed fruitless to attempt to describe them because both the currents and their stimuli were understood by intuition rather than by definition or reason. Because Rubén Romero realized the futility of attempting that definition, he could thus only summarize what was Mexico. In that sonorous but flexible style that had so characterized his novels, Romero wrote that Mexico was the haven of an indefinable attraction which despite the factors of poverty and physical privations, bound the Mexican to his country and, rightly or wrongly, caused him to support the cause of Mexico. (pp. 612-13)

Rubén Romero was not unaware of the fact that any nation in all its numerous endeavors is really only the reflection of the attitudes of its people. Although, as a people, Mexico was aware of its physical weaknesses, it was conscious of a remarkably robust fervor for harmonious internal relationships. Romero admitted that the Mexican people were easily baffled by those distinct attitudes of other peoples which deemed personal growth more important than national growth. He confessed that Mexicans were a naïve people, often unable to comprehend the intellectual reasoning which delineated right from wrong, good from bad, legal from illegal. Romero attributed this confusion, if indeed such it may be termed, to the permeation throughout Mexico of an indescribable sentimentalism which was saturated with both a feeling for gaiety and one of haunting unrest. But, if this nature exhibited certain disconcerting elements, it had produced that distinctive characteristic which Romero considered indispensable for the successful growth and development of a nation: indefatigable allegiance to fatherland. If this people had been deprived of those material things which ease the physical discomforts of life, they had found greater solace in their devotion to country. (p. 613)

Because it was the character of the people which had ultimately determined the temperament and complexion of the nation, Romero turned naturally to the stimulus which had furnished the greatest influence in the formation of that character: the province. In Mexico, the province is more than a mere geographic division, it is a mode of life. . . .

As the province was the mainstay of the nation, so the people of the province were really the substance of national spirit. . . . Because of his intimate knowledge of provincial life and his talent to perceive and to interpret accurately, Romero was able to record the generic qualities of these people.

His first comment concerned their tenacity. These were hard people in that they had lived unpampered by those frills of modern living which rendered a people incapable of becoming truly strong. The existence of this tenacity was confirmed by their display of sincerity and bravery in the face of overwhelming dangers of many types. (p. 614)

Romero considered these people a sage and judicious lot despite their lack of formal education. Their troubled existence of many years duration had forced them to use caution in their actions and to judge wisely in their dealings. If it was true that the people were unlettered and ignorant of even the most elementary of philosophical ideas, Romero was convinced that the elders of the province were capable of a most profound philosophy of life. It was to these people that Rubén Romero would turn for counsel, not to the learned scholar trained in the methods of logic and legal codes. And it was a counsel that he would advise all of Mexico to follow for it had withstood the agonies of hunger, poverty, and ignorance. It was the counsel which provided contentment in life. If other concepts of man and his position in the world had afforded contentment, that joy was only temporary. Unlike that of provincial philosophy, such contentment in life had been the result of a specific effort and thus was beneficial only to a given people during a given epoch.

They were a hungry people but a free people. . . . Their struggle for freedom had rendered them humble and their greatest gift to fellow-man was the respect and equality in justice which they dispensed. And mutual respect was all they asked in return. (pp. 614-15)

It was because of these ingrained qualities that Mexico as a country was to realize a significant transformation by means of the Revolution. It is quite true that this Revolution meant different things to different people. Romero believed that the Mexican Revolution was essentially a mass movement of protest and a struggle for liberation from a dictatorship which prohibited free movement and the rendering of justice in which the people so sincerely believed. In magnitude, Romero would also agree that this conflict was the movement of greatest social and economic significance which the twentieth century had witnessed. There is no doubt that Rubén Romero favored revolution in general and particularly was he a partisan of this modern uprising within his own country. . . .

If revolution was mass revolt whose purpose it was to overthrow an evil regime, Romero wrote that the goal of the Mexican Revolution was the removal of the shackles of injustice, poverty and virtual slavery imposed by a ruthless tyrant. To realize this purpose, all that was considered a part of the Díaz administration must be obliterated. (p. 615)

If the Mexicans of the day had understood that the Revolution had as its primary goal the liberation of an enslaved people, many foreign peoples were apparently unaware of that goal. Even in Mexico, as the movement spread and the violence of the struggle became more intense, its program became less definitive, its leaders less effective and its ideals seemed to be lost in an avalanche of greed. As Romero reviewed the events of that period of time, he realized that the Revolution had really isolated Mexico from the rest of the world. (pp. 615-16)

To those critics, and any others of the modern day, Romero advised patience. He would have them display the same perseverance that characterized Mexican disposition. Romero would have the critic of the Revolution foresee the ultimate results which would surpass in grandeur and importance any specific detail, event, or person. The Revolution was easily the most significant single event in Mexican history. It had proved to a people, and would do so to the rest of the world, that the seeds of liberty had gained roots deep within Mexican society. Its basic ideal of liberation completely overshadowed the horror of personal tragedy which had struck at almost every Mexican family. It was not an impotent movement of action for the sake of action. The Revolution had produced a degree of organization within the people and had made them aware of their rightful place within the society of Mexico. . . . Romero would thus advise the pacifist or other critic to study these results and thus understand the motivations which incited the millions of souls into action and bear with his nation for the realization of its ideals.

It is obvious that Rubén Romero's conclusions regarding the Mexican Revolution are of a comprehensive nature. It is understood that he was in sympathy with all who had suffered losses of a personal nature. But Romero possessed the remarkable facility of being able to stand aside from the specific details of the epoch and view the totality of events as an historic entity. In this position, he viewed the inception of the Revolution and its development and he could analyze the trends it had taken as well as visualize the ultimate results.

Perhaps there are those who would demand a more explicit account of the achievements of the Revolution than that which Romero had offered. If he had heretofore expressed himself somewhat in the manner of the poet, he did outline these achievements in a more matter-of-fact fashion. First of all, the Revolution supplied the people with a new hope and purpose in life. Mexico also realized a solid political, economic, and social foundation on which a moribund nation could be resuscitated and made to thrive. The Revolution had sketched the plan by which a people could retain all that was beneficial in their historic tradition in combination with those benefits that had resulted from the scientific and humanistic progress of the modern age. The struggle had provided an atmosphere in which liberty, equality, and justice could exist. (p. 616)

But, if Romero understood the ultimate potential of his country, as afforded by means of the ideals of the Revolution, he also admitted that this potential had not yet been realized. If, as the interpreter of the Revolution, he was capable of compiling a graphic picture of that struggle, he was not disinterested in specific problems which had beset Mexico. Indeed, he was probably more interested in the most elementary problem of his country than those of greatest magnitude in the world. It is in this concern that Romero avoided any poetic ivory tower and temporarily set aside the ambitions he held for his country to dedicate himself to those immediate problems which plagued Mexico.

Romero expressed his anxiety at what he considered one of the most disquieting problems of his day. Although the Revolution had united idealistically the peoples of Mexico, their complete solidarity had not yet been achieved. Romero had no specific term for this solidarity. . . . He was convinced that even the most powerful of nations could be rendered decadent and weak because of the lack of this indefinable unifying factor. He knew that Mexico had not been undermined to the point where it would surrender itself to foreign offers of assistance with the inevitable restrictions. But he believed certain erroneous self-evaluations had made it susceptible to further internal dissolution.

Rubén Romero advanced the theory that this condition had been arrived at by the people's acquisition of certain false impressions. The first of these was that Mexico was a strong country. As a nation, Mexico at times had considered itself the paladin of law and order, the standard and bulwark for all Hispanic countries. Romero would correct such thinking. He would have all the people aware of the fact that Mexico was withdrawn from the problems of its Latin neighbors. He would have the people aware of the little interest Mexico had shown for the problems of its sister countries. Because of its haughty attitude, Mexico had developed a position of leisurely repose toward those nations and had been consoled by thinking that those nations were poor and weaker. Romero would of course infer that his country had turned away from its own appalling state of inadequacy in comparison, let us say with the United States, and had become cloaked with a false comfort by comparing itself with those countries which possessed a kindred culture.

The second of these false impressions concerned the wealth of Mexico. The nation considered itself rich. . . . Romero would have his country know that what it rejected most often, work, was really the secret of all progress and wealth, economic and spiritual. He would also inform his people that by avoiding toil, both physical and intellectual, they were only supplying a psychological fortification by believing that those whom they vilified [those of the United States] had despoiled the country of its wealth. It was essential, he believed, that Mexico see itself clearly. . . . By assuming that their country had been plundered, the Mexican people had indifferently excused their own indolence. Romero was convinced that so long as such attitudes prevailed, Mexico was condemned to a certain internal insecurity and poverty.

The third false impression alive in the minds of the people was that which concerned Mexico's government. Mexico, he wrote, lauded itself as being a model of democratic principles. Although he was assured that his country had taken great strides to achieve that end, in the present day it still exhibited an incompetency to recognize the value to be gained from minority thinking, legitimate criticism, or even open opposition to any policy. In its present state, Mexican democracy assumed that public power was hereditary. In essence, the people were dominated by the concept that a clan of politicians was above reproach, that brute force determined the powerful, and that authority disseminated blame but was above being disciplined or chastised.

To convince the people of Mexico of the truth of his statements, Rubén Romero would have them ask and then answer a series of questions regarding life in Mexico. These questions were simple ones which, in their totality, probed deeply and sharply into the open wounds of Mexican thinking: Are all people equal? Do foreigners really control the country? Has the granting of special privileges to a select few been eliminated? Has the practice, whereby liberty, even life, are purchased, been erased? Is there no clash between justice and force? Is there respect for the rights to personal property? Do ideas and their originators go unpersecuted? Is education readily available to rich and poor alike?

In substance, the negative answer to each of these questions was the overall problem of Mexico. These disconcerting facts were summed up by Romero as the lack of that special attitude which bound a people together in harmonious unity, both internally and externally. It was that attitude which allowed a people to live unafraid and secure in their positions and their futures. It was also an attitude which allowed the nation to live tranquilly, in peace, without threats from abroad. It was an attitude which would permit the individual to work and to profit personally while all the while he contributed to the national welfare.

To resolve these national problems and to correct the false impressions that seemed to serve as a psychological anesthesia, Rubén Romero suggested that Mexico give special consideration to that effort which it had shirked so efficiently in the past: persistent and disciplined toil. He believed that the people must expend a concerted effort, the kind which Mexico never before had known. Such an effort would convert the lingering memories of those tragic events of the past into dreams and would convince all that the present good is but an iota of the country's potential. (pp. 617-18)

William O. Cord, "José Rubén Romero's Image of Mexico," in Hispania, *Vol. XLV, No. 4, December, 1962, pp. 612-20.*

EWART E. PHILLIPS (essay date 1963)

[In the following excerpt from a paper delivered at a 1963 MLA convention, Phillips discusses the development of the character

Inscription by Romero on a copy of his collection of poetry, Sentimental.

Pito Pérez in the novels of Romero. Phillips's assessment of this development suggests that Romero truly considered Pérez a literary character, an interpretation that contrasts with that of R. Anthony Castagnaro (1953), who believes that Romero's characters are best described as autobiographical, nonliterary creations. For further discussion of Pito Pérez as a picaro, see the excerpts by Sherman Eoff (1956) and Arturo Torres-Ríoseco (1963).]

Pito Pérez is the most outstanding character in the novels of José Rubén Romero and probably the most popular fictional character in Mexican literature, in spite of being relatively a new-comer to the field. Few characters have ever captured the attention of the literary public in so little time. His rapid rise in popularity could easily be explained if he were a military hero or a romantic figure, but he is the antithesis of both. He is not the kind of character with whom the reader associates himself, for he demands sympathy instead of empathy. He is, nevertheless, so commanding a character that he cannot be contained by the covers of a single book, but projects himself into six of Romero's nine novels. . . .

Unlike El Periquillo, Lazarillo, Guzmán de Alfarache, and the other picaros, who were engendered full grown, starring in their own stories, Pito grew as a picaro, appearing first as an incidental character in ***Apuntes de un lugareño,*** then in a supporting role in ***El pueblo inocente,*** before taking the stage as the protagonist of ***La vida inútil de Pito Pérez.*** Reading these novels chronologically gives one the distinct impression that here is a character striving to make his place in literature. One is reminded of the words of Pirandello in the preface to *Sei personaggi in cerca d'autore* [*Six Characters in Search of an Author*]. . . . Pirandello believed that the mystery of artistic creation is similar to that of natural birth, that as no woman can become a mother simply by wanting to be one, so no man can become an author by his desire alone, and that the germ of inspiration at some moment takes on life and grows within the mind of the author until it is more real than reality itself and the author is unable to thwart its headlong rush toward expression. The development of Pito Pérez . . . is very similar to Pirandello's description of his own inspiration. (p. 698)

Although he makes only three brief appearances in ***Apuntes de un lugareño,*** Pito is more clearly defined than any other character in the novel and he stands out more vividly than even the protagonist. Like most of Romero's characters, he was taken directly from real life as a composite of the nameless, faceless victims of the social upheaval that was Mexico. . . .

In describing the town of Santa Clara del Cobre in his first novel, Romero introduces Pito by disagreeing with a quotation reputed to have come from the lips of Pito Pérez. . . . Following this indirect introduction of the person destined to be his most unforgettable character, Romero adds several descriptive paragraphs portraying Pito as an inveterate drunkard whose interminable sprees emulated the orgies of ancient Rome. . . . At one time he was a sleight-of-hand artist in a circus; at another time he took on the duties of a midwife. If there was ever a jack-of-all-trades, Pito was one. He left the village of Santa Clara for long periods of time, but he could always be expected to return and he always signalled the news of his return by ringing the church bells—for the ringing of which he was always thrown into jail. (p. 699)

After his introduction of Pito, Romero drops the subject of the picaro and continues his interrupted description of Santa Clara. The next appearance of Pito Pérez in ***Apuntes de un lugareño*** comes as Romero is talking to Salvador Escalante, the military commander of Santa Clara who later rises to the rank of general. Romero and Escalante are discussing the rather broad general subject of liberty when suddenly the clamor of the church bells announces the return of the flower-bedecked Pito, who must pay for his formal announcement with a night in jail. Rubén intercedes in his behalf with Escalante and that night, for the first time, the prodigal Pito can celebrate his homecoming with a night on the town instead of a night in jail. . . .

Again Romero drops the subject of the picaro, this time for many pages, but near the end of the novel, as Rubén prepares to leave Santa Clara to go to Morelia, Pito interrupts the author's nostalgic meditations, making his final appearance. . . . (p. 700)

After pointedly ignoring Pito in ***Desbandada,*** . . . Romero introduces him very early in his third novel, ***El pueblo inocente.*** . . . It is as though Romero has decided to let Pito develop himself more completely, for here the picaro plays a much more important part in the story. He is a member of a group of young men who take part in a *noche de gallo* (a serenading party) in honor of, and on behalf of, the protagonist Daniel. Pito's leadership ability is such that he is chosen as a matter of course to serve in the capacity of master of ceremonies. . . . In a subsequent appearance, a called meeting of all the civic leaders of Santa Clara finds Pito, uninvited, in its midst. . . . Still later, he appears at a local celebration in honor of the Virgen de Guadalupe, where he entertains himself in a game booth, trying to toss a ring around the neck of a wine bottle and thereby win its contents. . . . He is as unsuccessful at this as he is at everything else in life. . . .

The bonds of friendship between the author and his character are becoming stronger and at this point one may see that the incidental character appearing in ***Apuntes de un lugareño*** has grown into a major character, cast in a supporting role. One might even say, in the language of the theater, that to some extent he "upstages" the protagonist Daniel. It becomes apparent that Pito inevitably must become the central character of the next story in which he appears. Thus, . . . we have the appearance of ***La vida inútil de Pito Pérez.***

With the publication of ***La vida inútil de Pito Pérez,*** the picaro has undergone a subtle change, as though he has reached maturity. He does not appear merely as the village drunkard, loafer, and the butt of all jokes, but as a genial, indigent philosopher who looks at life from a detached point of view and is able to appraise critically his environment without emotion, and, having done so, he is able to enjoy the pleasant things of life and to tolerate the rest. (pp. 700-01)

Further evidence of this change in the picaro may be seen in Romero's use of the name of his character. In ***Apuntes de un lugareño*** he is spoken of as "el *pito* Pérez," with the word *pito* clearly used as a pejorative adjective—it is italicized and begins with a lower-case letter. Thus the name could be translated as "the tick Pérez" or better, as "the whistle Pérez," as explained by Pito himself in ***La vida inútil de Pito Pérez***. . . . A third, but less likely, translation for *pito* is "woodpecker," and therefore he may be called "Pecker Pérez." In ***El pueblo inocente*** . . . the name has become "*El Pito Pérez,*" with the initial letters of all three words capitalized and all three words are italicized. The name is treated as a pseudonym, which it really is, the true name of the person concerned being Jesús Pérez Gaona. . . . With the publication of ***La vida inútil de Pito Pérez,*** the name takes on its final form, deleting the article and being written without italics: Pito Pérez. Thus one may observe that the name of the character went through a series of changes as the character became more and more real to the author.

La vida inútil de Pito Pérez concludes with the death of Pito and the reading of his last will and testament. . . . His strength as a character is such that his influence reaches beyond his grave and forces Romero to publish ***Algunas cosillas de Pito Pérez que se me quedaron en el tintero.*** With this little epilogue, Romero seems to have closed Pito's story a second time, but Pito is still not content to remain unheard and he appears in ***Anticipación a la muerte*** . . . and again in ***Una vez fui rico***. . . . (p. 701)

Ewart E. Phillips, "The Genesis of Pito Pérez," in Hispania, *Vol. XLVII, No. 4, December, 1964, pp. 698-702.*

ARTURO TORRES-RÍOSECO (essay date 1963)

[*Torres-Ríoseco was a Chilean-born American scholar of Spanish-American literature who wrote widely on the subject. In the following excerpt, Torres-Ríoseco discusses the picaresque elements of* The Futile Life of Pito Pérez *and draws a comparison between Pito and the picaresque adventures of the characters portrayed by Charlie Chaplin. For further discussion of the picaresque nature of Pito Pérez, see the excerpts by Sherman Eoff (1956) and Ewart E. Phillips (1963).*]

One of the last efforts to revive [the picaresque novel] is ***The Useless Life of Pito Pérez,*** by the Mexican writer Rubén Romero.

A picaresque novel has three basic elements: humor, real observation of life, and pathos. Originally it also had a moralizing purpose, but this element is no longer considered indispensable. If the picaresque novel has no humor, it is only a moral tract; if it is devoid of exact observation, it is not true to life; if it has no pathos, it becomes cruel buffoonery. (p. 21)

The Useless Life of Pito Pérez belongs very definitely to the picaresque genre. It tells the story of Pito Pérez, a Mexican hobo, who follows rather closely the example of the rascals of the Spanish picaresque. He is a choir boy, drugstore clerk, counselor to a priest, missionary, and finally a traveling salesman. He relates his life to the author, at the pay rate of a bottle of tequila for each episode. Pito describes his unfortunate love affairs, his adventures in various jails in Mexico, and his sad experiences in several hospitals.

Toward the end of the novel, just before Pito Pérez is found dead on a pile of rubbish, he speaks to the author about his most faithful sweetheart, a woman he stole from the Zamora hospital. She is a woman of much virtue and tenderness, a submissive being who watches day and night over Pito's life, an acme of perfection. The author cannot conceive of a human being so perfect and asks: "Who is she, Pito Pérez?" "Who is she?" answers Pito, "The skeleton of a woman that the students of medicine of Zamora used in their anatomical studies."

There is a great deal of humor in this book. Humor is here an act of "devaluation"—it exists in the destruction of the hero's aspirations, in his failure to be; but there is also a good amount of objective humor, observable in the simple fact of the hero's presence. Pito Pérez amuses the reader as a type, a hobo or *peladito,* very much as Cantinflas amuses the Mexican spectator, or Charlie Chaplin the American audience. Besides this "devaluation" of the character, there is another important element: the author's sympathy for his hero, without which there would be no humor.

Pito Pérez is an anarchical philosopher. He does not believe in work; he believes in the Devil rather than in God, in the "poor Devil," hated by everybody; he does not respect anybody because nobody respects him; he loved but was fooled by his sweethearts; only a skeleton of a woman is worthy of being loved. Therefore, he drinks tequila while others work; he steals from the wealthy as an act of justice; he makes love to his master's wife "just to be obliging." He pities the poor and advises them to respect the law and to spit in the faces of lawmakers and politicians. He is true to his beliefs even after death; when he dies in the dump, the useless ashes of a forgotten man are lost forever, mixed with the dust of the earth.

There are many similarities between Pito Pérez and Charlie Chaplin's characters. Pito is a social critic, a satirist, a man with a social outlook and a deep insight into human nature. Romero and Chaplin use their talent in a humorous and pathetic manner to expose social evils and cankers, leaning with great understanding toward the underprivileged. In both authors we frequently find a combination of satire, pathos, and fantasy. In *One Night Out,* "while being dragged along a path by Ben Turpin, Chaplin suddenly plucks a daisy and smells it. In a moment the drunk is transformed into a poet." Pito Pérez, starving and almost naked, goes up to the church's belfry "to fish out memories with the bait of the landscape." In both authors we detect also a richness of invention, tenderness, and gravity, which goes deep into the universal in human nature. (pp. 21-3)

The resemblance between *The Kid* and ***Pito Pérez*** is striking. Chaplin exploits the theme of "the little man who lacks material possessions but is a person of position in his own dream world." He is the gentle tramp-philosopher leading a meager existence but dreaming of a better day. Pito Pérez also has his inner world in which "he achieves what society denies him in real life." In *The Circus* and in *City Lights* we find the same humorous and pathetic resources that are used in ***Pito Pérez:*** the loss of a girl to a happier rival, sentimental scenes fraught with pathos and suffering, and a great penetration into the human soul. (p. 24)

Arturo Torres-Ríoseco, "Humor in Hispanic Literature," in his Aspects of Spanish-American Literature, *University of Washington Press, 1963, pp. 3-30.**

JOHN S. BRUSHWOOD (essay date 1966)

[Brushwood is an American scholar who has written widely on Spanish-American literature; particularly noteworthy are his several studies of the Mexican novel. In the following excerpt, Brushwood discusses the regionalism of Romero's fiction and the pessimism of his most interesting creation, Pito Pérez. Brushwood also praises Romero's expertise as a literary stylist and creator of character, an opinion that contrasts with that of R. Anthony Castagnaro (1953), who finds Romero's writings an amateurish blend of high and low tone, colloquial and scholarly language.]

Romero's ***Apuntes de un lugareño*** is a series of autobiographical sketches. They show an intense regionalism that is probably the outstanding characteristic of his works. Romero is undoubtedly one of the most read of Mexican novelists. He was a highly literate man who enjoyed posing as "just a plain, country boy." His humor is on the salty side. The combination of good writing, pose, and humor brought him a large audience. His ego was colossal, and all his novels are to a large extent autobiographical. One aspect of his egocentricity is the insecurity that tied him to his native state even though he travelled extensively. His pictures of provincial life are usually charming, even if the reader does sometimes tire of the author's presence. I suspect that in addition to Romero's personal need to remain spiritually within his native, provincial environment, his regionalism may be related to Azuela's approval of provincial values. The attitudes of both men seem to me to be a reaction against the movement of society that the Revolution started, a reaction against the uncertainty of society in a state of change. (pp. 211-12)

[***Desbandada*** and ***El pueblo inocente***] extol the virtues of the simple life. It is not a pastoral existence that he describes. Indeed, the simple life sometimes seems to be remarkably full of deceit. But Romero would have us believe that, for reasons which he never makes quite clear, human folly in a small town is less destructive than it is in a large city. Perhaps he believes hypocrisy can be seen more easily in the small town.

Desbandada is remotely related to the Revolution. It is the story of what happens when a group of revolutionaries sweeps through the town where Romero runs a store. Before their arrival, the author introduces a number of the town's personalities who come into the store. I suppose we should have some feeling for the town as a whole, but it never comes satisfactorily clear. We are aware only of the individuals' fear of the revolutionaries' brutality. The people of the town show some disgust with the Revolution, but one of them explains that these men do not represent the real Revolution. They are a perversion of it.

Romero's characterizations are good, though he tends strongly to caricature. Apparently he was so aware of individual differences that he was compelled to emphasize them. His somewhat picaresque view of humanity, including himself, is entertaining but not always convincing. ***El pueblo inocente*** is probably Romero's best gallery of provincial types, and the most successful characterization is Don Vicente, a fountain of practical wisdom who serves as a kind of tutor to a student who is home on vacation. In this book, better than anywhere else, we feel the author's ambivalence toward the province: an undying love for it mixed with a good deal of doubt about the honesty of human beings. One of the minor characters in ***El pueblo inocente*** is the town's philosophical bum, Pito Pérez, who became Romero's obsession and the outlet for his bitterness. (pp. 212-13)

La vida inútil de Pito Pérez (The Useless Life of Pito Pérez) is a modern picaresque novel which is the author's statement of his personal obsession. Pito Pérez was a real person in Romero's home town. He was, in fact, the town bum. Presumably his antisocial habits were combined with some antisocial ideas that impressed Romero deeply. Pito's literary incarnation is probably a combination of the real man and the author himself. The book follows the general picaresque manner: Pito tells his story in his own language, he gets an inside view of the lives of different kinds of people, he trusts no one, and he thinks of himself as a victim of society. No literary form could have suited Romero better. He liked to think of himself—at least part of the time—as a *pícaro*, and Pito's book is a kind of "Walter Mitty" experience for the author.

La vida inútil de Pito Pérez is a very entertaining book. It may be a very serious book. We can never be quite sure about Romero. He was a clever writer, a literary prankster. We feel, on reading ***Pito Pérez,*** that it is the most natural narrative we've ever seen, and it is only on second thought that we realize none but a sure hand could juggle the language as Romero does. He is a natural humorist, though the "corn-fed" quality of his wit is a pretense. ***La vida inútil de Pito Pérez*** contains lots of dirty stories, and I am sure many people read the book for this reason alone. But in addition to the obvious humor, there is a much more subtle current that rides the line between tragedy and comedy in a wonderful fashion. The general tone of the book establishes the paradoxical union, and it is made more specific by various episodes like the re-enactment of the Crucifixion by a bunch of half-drunk jailbirds.

Pito's life is called useless, and indeed it is so from the standpoint of his contribution to society. His opinion of people is that they are just no good. Pito, however, gives people no more reason to trust him than he has to trust them. Still, this useless life may be regarded as the result of Pito's attempt to be himself. It may be that his life was useless because he wasn't permitted to live. His view of society raises questions about the honesty of a large variety of customs and institutions. From the point of view of society, Pito's values are perverted. From his own viewpoint, society makes little or no sense. He cannot change society, so he withdraws from its demands and becomes its victim. His life is active only when it is a negation of society, so the end result of his nonconformism is that his role is essentially passive. He cannot be what he would be, what his inner self would have him be. (pp. 222-23)

John S. Brushwood, "The Mirror Image (1931-1946)," in his Mexico in Its Novel: A Nation's Search for Identity, *University of Texas Press, 1966, pp. 205-34.**

WALTER M. LANGFORD (essay date 1971)

[*Langford is an American scholar who has written extensively on the Spanish language and Latin American literature and culture. Throughout his career he has served in several organizations, including the Peace Corps, that provide various forms of aid to Latin America. In the following excerpt, Langford discusses* The Futile Life of Pito Pérez *as an indirect criticism of the failure of the Mexican Revolution. For a similar interpretation of Romero's portrayal of the Revolution, see the excerpt by Daniel E. Gulstad (1973); for a differing interpretation, see the excerpt by R. Anthony Castagnaro (1953).*]

The most common characteristics of the novel of the Revolution were pretty well established by Azuela and remained rather constant. The theme was the Revolution itself or its effects on the Mexican people in one way or another. The focus was semihistorical, documentary, often personal. As a result, little imagination is found in these works, to the extreme that their sameness of theme becomes almost monotonous and surely constitutes a limitation if not an outright defect.

Experimentation in the approach to the theme was even more rare. Three distinct exceptions are [Carlos] Fuentes's *La muerte de Artemio Cruz,* [Agustín] Yáñez's *Al filo del agua,* and José Rubén Romero's ***La vida inútil de Pito Pérez (The Futile Life of Pito Pérez).*** Those knowledgeable about Mexican literature may be surprised that I cast this latter work as a novel of the Revolution. It is customary to speak of it as a picaresque novel, which it certainly is. A close analysis of the work, however, seems to me to reveal more reasons for calling it a novel of the Revolution than can be adduced for many books commonly put in that category. In any case ***Pito Pérez*** is beyond argument a novel, and its protagonist most surely is launching a call to revolution.

La vida inútil de Pito Pérez . . . is built around an actual flesh-and-blood village character who clearly fascinated Romero. The tempo and the orientation of life in his village of Santa Clara del Cobre can be likened to that created by Yáñez in *Al filo del agua*. Both towns are hermetic, ultraconservative, and religion-dominated. In each work the intent is to demonstrate the rigid, exceedingly pious outlook of the people and to spotlight the crying need for change. Yáñez adopts a lugubrious tone about it all and heightens his effect by repetition and lengthy probing into the inner conscience of many characters; Romero achieves somewhat the same effect by malicious humor, by a happy-go-lucky irreverence, and by contrasting his "rebel," Pito Pérez, with the rest of the townspeople. It should be noted at this point that José Rubén Romero is one of the most humorous of all Mexican novelists. Yáñez placed his novel in the last moments of the prerevolutionary days, while Romero has Pito's biography straddle the period of the Revolution as a military reality. Thus, in the final parts of Romero's novel when we see Pito Pérez embittered by the futility of his continuing one-man campaign against dehumanizing forces, we have to interpret it as Romero's backhanded slap at the Revolution, which has largely failed to change life in the rural villages. (pp. 38-9)

Walter M. Langford, "The Novel of the Mexican Revolution," in his The Mexican Novel Comes of Age, *University of Notre Dame Press, 1971, pp. 36-50.**

DANIEL E. GULSTAD (essay date 1973)

[*In the following excerpt, Gulstad contends, in contrast to several other critics, that* Mi caballo, mi perro, y mi rifle *is important as a documentation of the Mexican Revolution. He examines Romero's use of antithesis throughout the novel and finds it an effective unifying device that emphasizes the Revolution's failure to correct social injustice.*]

José Rubén Romero's novel ***Mi caballo, mi perro y mi rifle*** is structurally divided into four parts. The first and the third present antithetical stages in the life of the protagonist, Julián, while the second acts as a transition between them, and the fourth serves as an epilogue. Critics have generally slighted this novel while discussing Romero's works, or have treated it as one which has some interesting characteristics but lacks unity and other essentials of a successful work. Perhaps there has also been too great a tendency to consider it one of the less important novels of the Mexican Revolution, as opposed to challenging the sincerity of the narrator and searching for deeper ironies than the somewhat hackneyed notion of a revolution that culminates in a restoration of the same old social order. The present study is not intended as a complete vindication of the novel from such criticism; rather, we shall examine one of his major stylistic devices for the possibility of structural and thematic unity in the novel, first identifying the relationship between structure and theme. Too, a systematic analysis of stylistic devices in this earlier (and lesser) work is necessarily of interest if only because it will assist in an overall appraisal of the style which at its height gave us ***La vida inútil de Pito Pérez.***

The title, ***Mi caballo, mi perro y mi rifle,*** appropriately characterizes the second, third, and fourth parts, but not the first, which is Julián's autobiographical account of his childhood and adolescence. From the end of the first part on, the work may be classified as a novel of the Mexican Revolution, somewhat episodic and *costumbrista,* with its theme very obviously spelled out during an imagined dialogue between Julián's horse, dog, and rifle . . . , symbolizing, respectively, the fickle opportunism of the rich, the unrewarded and naïvely placed loyalty of the poor, and the indifference of arms toward causes. This, however, . . . is not the main theme, since Julián is not an unbiased observer but a bitter young man whose narrative reflects a somewhat jaundiced view of events and surroundings. [The critic adds in a footnote that it is plausible that Julián is a parody of Julius Caesar. "Such a parody would fit into the general antithetical atmosphere, in as much as Julián as an antihero is the antithesis of Caesar. . . ."]

In the first part Julián depicts himself as a sickly, passive child, whose only defense against his environment is an exacting candor in his observations. By way of contrast, in the third part he rises to feelings of social responsibility and initiative. This is a turn of events internally motivated by the fact that he has previously shown signs of identification with the underdog and by his manner of reporting military activities, playing down his own participation and portraying the events as more fortuitous than heroic.

At the beginning of the novel, Romero deftly creates a number of characters whose every nuance is based on the play of opposites. Julián's mother is like a daughter to his father rather than a wife, since she is still very young when he is about to die of old age. Owing to his senility she is also his mother and he her decrepit infant. Her son, whom she should be mothering, she leaves in the care of "Doña" Concha la Reyes, who is a coarse antithesis of the more genteel mother. Later the antithesis of his mother's marriage is repeated, discrepancy in ages reversed, with the adolescent Julián incongruously married to Andrea, an old friend of his mother's whom he had known all his life as "aunt." The irony of this is heightened by the complete lack of initiative on the boy's part and the clumsy spontaneity (at least from his viewpoint) of the brief sexual encounter that left Andrea pregnant and him still not knowing how she or any woman would look fully unclothed.

Besides playing antithetical characters against each other, the narrator also employs polarity in his descriptions. (pp. 237-38)

In the pathetic remark attributed to small Julián, "—Mi papá se murió, pero yo seré grande como él" ["My papa is dead, but I will be great like him"] . . . , there is a type of contradiction which, owing to the absurdity of this nevertheless typically childlike remark, is difficult to categorize but plays on the fact that the life and expectations of the dead man are all past, while those of the child are future-oriented, and that a duality separates the child's dream of reaching adult stature (of which his father was the image) from the adult's apprehension that the old man's body represents nothing other than the brevity, triviality, and futility of life—world-weary disillusion opposed to innocent illusion.

Julián's inward aggressiveness, viewed against his outward submission to the constrictive and self-serving deportment of those who were responsible for his welfare, creates a new dimension of contrast as well as a microcosmic private world known only to Julián and the reader. A privileged point of view exists for the reader who can note at first hand how the people of Julián's world respond to his lack of self-assertion and how events are recreated in the boy's imagination, with himself in the center rather than on the periphery. (p. 238)

One senses irreverance in Julián's request to his mother, "—Cómprame recortes de hostia" ["Buy me some wafers"] . . . , even though in the boy's mind it would seem natural, in as much as his mother had denied him the sweets he craves but gives him pennies for the collection plate. Under closer analysis, however, this innocent "weakness of the flesh" in the boy, which his mother, by her behavior, condemns, is eclipsed by the sanctimony of this woman. . . . The exaggerated piety of the mother plays against the boy's innocent sacrilege.

After Julián contracted paralysis he was placed in the care of his old nurse, Concha. When he had begun to recover, his mother "[lo] alentaba con ternura" ["encouraged him with tenderness"], but Doña Concha "parecía *dolerse* de [su] *mejoria* [antithesis in itself] temiendo que . . . se le acabara la pitanza" ["seemed to feel sorrowful to witness his recovery [antithesis in itself], fearing that . . . it meant the end of her days of living on the dole"]. . . . In addition to the antithetical sorrow that Concha shows at an event which ordinarily is received with joy, there are two contrasts visible in the circumstances described: (1) his mother's tenderness for Julián when he is a pitiable invalid, which she lacked when he was well, as if her maternal feelings could be inspired only by infirmity (recall her nursing of her senile, moribund husband); (2) Concha's interest-inspired reluctance to acknowledge his recovery and her loss of sinecure, which is the opposite of the words of encouragement that he received from his mother.

The interest displayed here is typical of that which motivates all the novel's characters, minor or major. Julián's father took a wife in order to have someone to look after him in his old age, but the wife he married was no less pragmatic in her motives, choosing marriage to an aging man of property over the alternative of continuous poverty. Andrea was desperate enough for a man to seduce an adolescent and then to lead him reluctantly to the altar. A bishop haughtily pacing up and down while a gray-haired old priest follows apologetically on his knees, a scene witnessed by Julián during his brief school days . . . , reveals the ignoble interest of the bishop, who feels he has been deprived by the priest of an opportunity to ingratiate himself with the rich, showing as well the servile interest of the priest groveling under the bishop's rebuke not with mere priestly humility but with the obvious subservience of an underling anxious to escape his superior's ire. Julián himself welcomed war as an alternative to his premature domestic responsibilities and was thus acting more out of personal motives than out of social responsibility in joining the revolutionaries.

A play of opposites is present also in Julián's brief school life. One would assume that the pupils of the public school, as the offspring of the lower strata of society, would be most inclined toward brutality and insensitivity, while the pupils of a private school, scions of the privileged classes, would be well-mannered and polite, but we learn that the opposite is true. . . . (pp. 238-39)

In the second section of the novel, which functions as a transition from the first into the third and as the beginning of what really constitutes a revolutionary novel, Julián becomes a soldier, acquires his gear, and allows some of the bravado of his comrades to rub off on him. During these events he is less the central figure of his narrative. Antithetical situations now point up social injustice. . . . (pp. 240-41)

The main contradiction, or paradox, of the novel is developed in the third and fourth parts, which is the irony that winning a revolution does not, in Romero's eyes, advance the cause of the poor, despite their sacrifices. A new caudillo appears from the ranks of the rebels, only to assimilate the ways of the one he helped to depose, and the poor are poorer and more miserable than ever. An episodic account of revolutionary activities climaxes at last in abrupt antithesis as Julián's eyes are suddenly and unexpectedly opened to signs that the revolution was its own antithesis.

A string of ironies foreshadows this denouement, such as the cruel treatment of a dog (which symbolizes the down-trodden poor) by the soldiers (who are the very thing he represents!). Ignacio is the physical antithesis of the Newtonian analogue. Although blind he sees the light of truth before his sighted young comrades. There is also a contradiction in the motives of the various rebels characterized in the novel. . . .

Aurelio is an unreflecting bravo who joins the revolutionary forces for the fight and the glory, with little or no concern for the masses. Rafaelito . . . envies Julián for his revolutionary activities because military life sounded romantic, not because he sees the revolution as a means of bringing sustenance and dignity to his family, or for any higher motive.

The only person with a legitimate cause is Ignacio, yet he perishes midway through the military episodes. Julián, who as narrator is to be the chronicler that immortalizes the exploits of the small contingent he is with, represents a number of contradictions. On the one hand, since his family are capitalists in a small way, they would at first seem to have more in common with the wealthy; however, Julián has always felt more affinity with the poor than the rich, for among the latter he was everyone's social inferior. (p. 241)

But the irony that the poor who rebel are not caught up in the more intellectual idealism of the *petit bourgeois* is further complicated by the ambivalent motives of the latter, personified in Julián. . . .

His sympathy for the poor and his hatred of social injustice are . . . secondary to his personal bitterness. To some degree, at least, his psychological state is a product of the environment he hopes the revolution will change, but in part the social injustices are a mere convenient rationalization for a more personal and deep-seated resentment growing out of his infirmity and failure to compete. . . .

There is an interesting correlation in the death of Julián's respective parents, his father at the beginning of the novel and his mother near its end. In both cases he is in the house during the wake, observing the conduct of the mourners, unnoticed by them. At his father's wake he is too small to be noticed . . . , and at his mother's he must be content to listen from the loft where he is hiding from the Huertistas who occupied the town. . . . The parallelism is broken, though, by the difference in his feelings on the two occasions. As we have seen, his father's funeral caused him no grief—only wonder and entertainment—but his adult grief for his mother was deeply felt. (p. 242)

Part four is appropriately short, a mere epilogue. The story of Julián's anti-heroic life has reached its denouement, but to stop at this point without bringing the Revolution to an end would leave part of the incidental plot dangling, so a rapid (four-page) continuation describes with comic irony the triumphant entry of the Revolutionary troops into Morelia and Julián's realization, after observing his town's former *cacique* in the reviewing stand, that the social order has not changed. At the end, Julián's violently discarded rifle discharges and kills his dog, accidentally but with typical indifference. The rifle, which he had previously referred to as "un camino de luz que conduce a la sombra" ["a highway of light that leads to shadows"] . . . , has lived up to its fame: the revolution has taken its toll of the underdog, and after a brief illusion of light (i.e., escape from the misery at the bottom), he is plunged once more into the darkness of social repression. We learn no more about Julián, but we can surmise from his unremitting bitterness that his return to his wife and child is not likely to result in a happy reconciliation. Nothing has changed, not even Julián!

In the preceding pages we have seen how the numerous antitheses that occur in this novel contribute to its thematic unity. It is permeated by an unrelenting cynicism that displays itself in the narrator's portrayal of frailty even in the more sympathetic characters. His depiction of the poor laborer, the simple farmer, the routine of the sugar mill, reveals Romero's feeling for people and his affection for the rural way of life, but that affection is offset by a deep-seated attitude that all men are at heart selfish. At the bottom the underdog lives in dumb subservience, while his antithesis, the equestrian class at the top, is stupidly arrogant. Julián's naïve hope that from the revolution an egalitarian synthesis will emerge is doomed by the fact that everyone in the revolution is there for personal motives rather than a cause. The hope of seeing a new and better society grow out of the revolution turns out to be based on the same fallacy as the ambition of the little boy in the presence of his father's corpse someday to be "big like papa." There is more to this novel than just a belated criticism of the Mexican revolution: it is a skillful parody of man caught between what he believes he should be and what he knows he is. (pp. 242-43)

Daniel E. Gulstad, "Antithesis in a Novel by Rubén Romero," in Hispania, *Vol. 56, April, 1973, pp. 237-44.*

ADDITIONAL BIBLIOGRAPHY

Berler, Beatrice. "The Mexican Revolution As Reflected in the Novel." *Hispania* XLVII, No. 1 (March 1964): 41-6.*

Discussion of the novelists of the Mexican Revolution that pays particular attention to Romero, Gregorio López y Fuentes, and Mariano Azuela. Crow describes these novelists as "soldier-authors" and chroniclers of Mexico's spiritual development.

Carter, Boyd. "The Mexican Novel at Mid-Century." *Prairie Schooner* XXXVIII (1954): 143-56.

Classifies Romero's works as peripheral accounts of the Mexican Revolution that are more concerned with Romero's life and with local color elements of Mexican life.

Crow, John A. "Man Trapped by Tension." *Saturday Review* L, No. 21 (27 May 1967): 32-3.

Review of the English translation of *The Futile Life of Pito Pérez* that discusses the picaresque elements of the novel.

MacKegney, James C. "Some Non-Fictional Aspects of *La vida inútil de Pito Pérez*." *Romance Notes* 6, No. 1 (Autumn 1964): 26-9.

Briefly examines the life of Jesús Gaona, the model for the character of Pito Pérez.

Romero, Carlos. Preface to *The Futile Life of Pito Pérez,* by José Rubén Romero, pp. v-vi. Englewood Cliffs, N.J.: Prentice-Hall, 1966.

Reminiscence by the son of José Rubén Romero that notes how Pito Pérez mirrors both his father's character and the national character of Mexico.

"Opera for a Penny Whistle." *Time* 89, No. 7 (17 February 1967): 100.

Review of the English translation of *The Futile Life of Pito Pérez* that remarks on Pito's affinity with the characters Ulysses, Tom Jones, and Huckleberry Finn.

Josephine Tey

1897-1952

(Pseudonym of Elizabeth Mackintosh; also wrote under pseudonym of Gordon Daviot) Scottish novelist, dramatist, biographer, short story writer, and poet.

Tey was a noted mystery writer whose works became popular during the golden age of detective fiction, an era spanning the 1920s through the 1950s. Her most famous novel, *The Daughter of Time,* is considered a mystery classic. *The Daughter of Time* and Tey's seven other detective novels are often singled out by critics of mystery fiction for their divergence from the strict formulaic guidelines of the genre. The intricate puzzles, grisly murders, and infallible sleuths that dominated the field are essentially absent from Tey's works, which are noted for their sympathetic, sometimes ambivalent portraits of victims, suspects, and overly sensitive detectives, as well as for Tey's keen observations of personality.

Tey was born in Inverness, where she attended the Royal Academy in preparation for an advanced education in the humanities. However, after graduation Tey embarked upon a rigorous course of study in physical culture at Anstey Physical College, and later taught physical education at several schools in England. Around 1926 she gave up teaching in order to care for her invalid father at her family home. There Tey began writing poetry, short stories, and, eventually, novels and plays. Throughout the rest of her life she pursued few interests except writing. Horse racing and fishing, both of which play a part in her fiction, were Tey's primary diversions. Extremely shy, she refused press interviews, had few friends, and seemingly no confidants. After her death it was discovered that Tey had concealed the secret of a fatal illness for over a year.

The Daughter of Time is Tey's most successful novel and has received more serious critical attention than any of her other works. The popularity of this mystery is due in part to its premise, which sets out to refute a long-accepted explanation of a historical event: Richard III, the long-acknowledged murderer of two princes who were potential rivals for the throne of England, is posthumously exonerated of the crime by Inspector Allan Grant with the help of a scholarly research assistant. There is little action in the story, and the investigators and the principals never meet. Relying on the intrigue of discovery, *The Daughter of Time* is Tey's most controversial work, one which brings into question the reliability of history and historians and suggests that history is a mixture of facts, legends, and blatant fabrications. Most criticism of the work notes the controversial, innovative blend of detection, history, and fiction. Anthony Boucher calls the novel "a real bouleversement of schoolbook and encyclopedia 'history,' treated with compelling logic, precise scholarship and a cumulative intensity." While typical early appraisals of the work were laudatory, later critics question Tey's scholastic competence and describe the novel as neither history nor detective fiction, but instead as a fraudulent treatment of an already well-known theory. Among the harshest critics, Julian Symons has remarked that "this amateur rehashing of a well-known argument is, as one might expect, really rather dull." Historians, whose enterprise, methods, and general character are acridly maligned throughout *The Daughter of Time,* have accused Tey of a personal vendetta. Guy M. Townsend, for example, contends that fictional history must be faithful to the large historical context and cannot take liberties with historical fact. In a direct rebuttal of the Townsend position, M. J. Smith argues that since all novels are creations of the writer, manipulation, omission, and invention can be used at will. As Smith observes, the controversy surrounding the work illuminates Tey's thesis that historians have only second hand evidence at best, and that they tend to manipulate that evidence to substantiate their own conclusions.

Inspector Allan Grant, the protagonist of *The Daughter of Time,* appears in several other mysteries by Tey, though he is neither a trademark nor a unifying presence. While his intelligence, cultural grace, and instincts fit the prototype of the detective popularized by such writers as S. S. Van Dine and Dorothy Sayers, Grant is by no means the infallible, self-confident, and cerebral puzzle-solver who treats victims and suspects with cool detachment. In his initial appearance, Grant ignores his sympathetic feelings toward a suspect and pursues the accused on the strength of evidence that is ultimately proven misleading. Similarly, the spinster detective Miss Pym, who appears in *Miss Pym Disposes,* not only shows her fallibility, but her well-intentioned interference with the workings of justice covers up one crime and sets off a series of events that leads to murder. During the era in which Tey wrote, the victims in mysteries generally possessed negative or criminal qualities and were murdered offstage in gruesome, often unique ways. In contrast, Tey's victims are more complex and realistic. In *A Shilling for Candles,* for example, the murdered actress Christine Clay is described by some as foolish and ambitious, and by others as soft-hearted and self-sacrificing. Tey's characters all suffer in varying degrees, and sometimes the innocent are recipients of irreparable injury. Critics have found that whereas other detective novelists cultivate an emotional distance that allows the reader freedom to concentrate on the puzzle and its solution, Tey's emphasis on characterization is more conducive to reader sympathy.

According to Sandra Roy, many of Tey's characters behave "almost as if Tey were using a stock company with the same actors playing different but similar parts in each novel." Two of the most significant types are the precocious ingenue and the mature, unmarried woman. Unlike most of the other characters in the novels, the ingenue typically appears to be exactly what she is—sure of her own feelings and instincts and correct in her perceptions and judgments. For example, the ingenue Erica in *A Shilling for Candles* not only solves the case for Inspector Grant and saves the life of the inept suspect, but also understands Grant's feelings and the reasons for them before he understands them himself. Unmarried women are not unique characters in mysteries, but in Tey's works they are older and remain unmarried by choice, offering no apology for bachelorhood. Many have careers that they prefer to domestic life, while one, Marion Sharpe in *The Franchise Affair,* simply prefers her independence to marriage and considers her life a satisfying one. This absence of personal attachment is characteristic of both male and female characters in Tey's mysteries, where the protagonists are free of family, romance, and close friends.

In addition to her detective novels Tey wrote seven plays, and all except *The Stars Bow Down* were produced. These dramas are generally based on historical and biblical events. Despite her tenacity and sincerity as a dramatist, Tey's only great theatrical success was *Richard of Bordeaux*, which ran on the London stage for over a year. Unlike earlier works based on the life of Richard II, the play depicts his development from a young man in his teens to a successful king and demonstrates the survival instinct that surfaces during various crises. Sandra Roy and John Mason Brown have praised Tey's selection of critical and dramatic incidents in Richard's life. Brown has also observed that Tey's use of colloquial language enabled her to avoid an imitation of Shakespeare or Bernard Shaw, the "stencils used by most English dramatists" when creating plays based on historical figures. Depicted as variously tender, impulsive, and cruel, Tey's Richard is described by Stark Young as comparable in power to and more intelligent than the Richard of Shakespeare. Young adds that Tey's point of view makes the play more contemporary and applicable "to the world of men and thoughts."

In spite of her goals as a serious dramatist, Tey is remembered for her detective fiction. While she adhered to many of the proprieties of the English detective story, her work is not typical of the genre. Summing up the distinct quality of Tey's detective novels, James Sandoe has observed: "One cannot comprehend any one of these eight tales by recalling its characters or its plot. . . . It is perhaps the infusion into all of them of a singularly delicate and humorous perception that fixes them in remembrance as cheeringly as a friend, a warm hearth, and a bracing glass on a snowy day."

(See also *Contemporary Authors,* Vol. 110.)

PRINCIPAL WORKS

Kif [as Gordon Daviot] (novel) 1929
The Man in the Queue [as Gordon Daviot] (novel) 1929
Expensive Halo [as Gordon Daviot] (novel) 1931
Richard of Bordeaux [as Gordon Daviot] (drama) 1932
The Laughing Woman [as Gordon Daviot] (drama) 1934
Queen of Scots [as Gordon Daviot] (drama) 1934
A Shilling for Candles [as Gordon Daviot] (novel) 1936
Claverhouse [as Gordon Daviot] (biography) 1937
The Stars Bow Down [as Gordon Daviot; first publication] (drama) 1939
Leith Sands, and Other Short Plays [as Gordon Daviot; first publication] (dramas) 1946
The Little Dry Thorn [as Gordon Daviot] (drama) 1946
Miss Pym Disposes (novel) 1947
Brat Farrar (novel) 1949
The Franchise Affair (novel) 1949
To Love and Be Wise (novel) 1950
The Daughter of Time (novel) 1951
The Privateer [as Gordon Daviot] (novel) 1952
The Singing Sands (novel) 1952
Plays. 3 vols. [as Gordon Daviot] (dramas) 1953-54
Three by Tey: Miss Pym Disposes, The Franchise Affair, Brat Farrar (novels) 1954

THE NEW YORK TIMES BOOK REVIEW (essay date 1929)

[The following excerpt is from a generally favorable review of Tey's first detective novel, The Man in the Queue.]

[**"The Man in the Queue"**] has a promising beginning, even though it is a bit preposterous. In a queue of people waiting to secure tickets for a musical comedy a man suddenly drops to the ground and is found to be dead from a stab in the back. The persons who were near him are questioned, but with no success. No one knows the man, no one remembers seeing any one leave the line, and no one knows when he was stabbed, for he was so tightly wedged in the line that he might have been held upright for several minutes after his death. . . . Inspector Grant of Scotland Yard, who is assigned to the case, does some clever sleuthing and has some exciting adventures before he learns the identity of the murdered man and his slayer, and the story might have been rather better than the average detective yarn if the author had only refrained from revealing to us at great length the mental processes of the detective. Judicious pruning would have made the story much more readable.

A review of "The Man in the Queue," in The New York Times Book Review, *July 28, 1929, p. 13.*

THE NEW YORK TIMES BOOK REVIEW (essay date 1931)

[In the following review of Tey's The Expensive Halo, *the critic faults the novelist for her "stilted plot and unavoidably mechanical characters."]*

The venerable theme of rich girl-poor boy always offers a sufficiency of pliable material for a capable craftsman, and Gordon Daviot has been astute enough to take advantage of this truism. Moreover, she has been skillful enough to change the formula slightly, adding a fillip of variety to the familiar situations. **"The Expensive Halo"** departs from the accepted treatment in that there are two sets of contrasting characters; the rich girl-poor boy is neatly if somewhat obviously counterbalanced by a poor girl-rich boy combination. Miss Daviot is at least loyal to the code which demands that the public receive its money's worth. . . .

"The Expensive Halo" is a social drama of errors that occasionally soars above its routine plot and motivations into the realm of entertainment. In Alfred Ellis, father of Sara and Gareth, Gordon Daviot has created a thoroughly interesting and believable character. Alfred Ellis is a man of God, a fanatical sectarian, whose overt piety conceals a vicious avariciousness and a violent, unmanageable temper. His bungling attempts to interfere in the lives of his children make the early chapters of this book far superior to the remainder of the story.

Miss Daviot does not fare so well with her other characters. Her heroes and heroines, rich and poor, are straw-stuffed marionettes whose speeches are a credit to the author's literary ventriloquism rather than to her ability to create authentic conversation. Even the noble Ursula, whose renunciation supplies the expensive halo of the title, is a character fashioned with scant understanding. Handicapped by a stilted plot and unavoidably mechanical characters, Miss Daviot's second novel falls short of her initial effort.

"Rich Girl—Poor Boy," in The New York Times Book Review, *October 25, 1931, p. 24.*

JOHN MASON BROWN (essay date 1933)

[*An influential and popular American critic during the 1930s, 1940s, and 1950s, Brown wrote extensively on contemporary British and American drama. He had a thorough knowledge of dramatic history, and his criticism combines the intellectual depth of scholarly erudition with the accessibility of popular reviewing. In the following excerpt from a review of* Richard of Bordeaux, *Brown praises Daviot's (Tey's) portrait of Richard II, calling it "poignant and arresting." Brown also believes that the author's use of colloquial language and dramatic development save the play from what Brown describes as the "dust and pomposity" so characteristic of English historical dramas.*]

Mr. Daviot's **"Richard of Bordeaux"** is a poignant and arresting portrait of that luckless son of the Black Prince who served Shakespeare as his tragic hero in "Richard II." Though he has turned to history for his materials, Mr. Daviot has succeeded in avoiding the stencils used by most English historical dramatists. Instead of aping Shakespeare or Shaw, or the routine pageant-master episodes of Drinkwater, he has written a straightforward and intensely alive drama in prose that is colloquial without being slangy. He has, moreover, proven himself exceptionally shrewd in sensing and developing what is dramatic in his subject.

His Richard is a man born before his time; a dreamer who, in a warlike age, centers his hopes on peace, particularly with France. He is an unpopular king; too young when the play begins to be more than a pawn in the hands of his contemptuous uncles, and too headstrong, as it advances, to master the tactics of government. His major fight is against himself. But his conquest is his own undoing.

Mr. Daviot follows the varying fortunes of his undisciplined king over a period of twelve years in twelve scenes that are admirable in their simplicity. He begins his drama before Shakespeare does his, and gains by doing so. His incidents are deeply affecting, and fortunately free of the dust and pomposity which are the curse of historical dramas. One misses Shakespeare's language, of course. But for modern audiences Mr. Daviot offers compensations of his own.

John Mason Brown, "Tragic Hero," in The Saturday Review, *London, Vol. X, No. 9, September 16, 1933, p. 112.*

RALPH PARTRIDGE (essay date 1949)

[*In the following excerpt, Partridge notes Tey's "gift for portraying imposters" and finds that the protagonist of* Brat Farrar *is the best among them.*]

Brat Farrar is a well-written crime novel, with an element of mystery for anyone who cares to treat it as detection. The hero is a sort of Tichborne claimant. But when he turns up from America in an English county family and starts impersonating the long-lost heir to the property, why does not the person who recognises him as a fraud expose him immediately? As readers of ***The Franchise Affair*** will remember, Miss Tey has a wonderful gift for portraying impostors; and the character of Brat Farrar, combining charm with deceit, is a triumph of her art. I suppose that her vision of countrylife, where the impoverished gentry keep their end up in the class-war with gymkhanas and jodhpurs, is also a triumph—but one that Mrs. Miniver will appreciate more than I do. (p. 530)

Ralph Partridge, "Detection and Thrills," in The New Statesman & Nation, *Vol. XXXVIII, No. 974, November 5, 1949, pp. 528, 530.**

***NEW YORK HERALD TRIBUNE BOOK REVIEW* (essay date 1951)**

[*In the following excerpt the reviewer concludes that, while it is sometimes a pleasant novel,* To Love and Be Wise *does not have the ironic humor of Tey's earlier works.*]

Josephine Tey is one of the best English mystery writers who has recently appeared on the horizon. In her four first books she was experimenting to find her proper metier. [In **"To Love and Be Wise"**] she has gone back to the sophistication of **"Miss Pym Disposes."** But the plot, which again brings a young American stranger into the midst of an English family, is more reminiscent of **"Brat Farrar."** This reviewer feels that the earlier and more ironic vein of **"Miss Pym"** and the **"Franchise Affair"** was preferable. However, a smattering of that irony does crop up in this newest novel which poses a rather slim story, but does it pleasantly. Leslie Searle was a young American photographer who sought out the British news commentator, Walter Whitmore, and immediately became accepted by his family as a treasured guest. When, however, Searle disappeared one day, the police found that he had exerted a rather disturbing influence not only on Whitmore's family but on the whole surrounding community. The problem was: Had Searle been killed, or merely vanished on his own hook? The answer holds an element of surprise, but it's not as startling as it might be.

A review of "To Love and Be Wise," in New York Herald Tribune Book Review, *April 8, 1951, p. 15.*

JAMES SANDOE (essay date 1952)

[*A critic of mystery and detective fiction, Sandoe has contributed numerous articles on real and fictional crimes to periodicals and has compiled related bibliographies. In the following excerpt, Sandoe reviews* The Daughter of Time *and finds Tey's observations of "people and things" as entertaining as the elements of suspense and details of detection.*]

"Daughter of Time" is equal in graces and interest to **"The Franchise Affair"** and by that measure more satisfying than any of the rest of that still very welcome company which includes **"Miss Pym Disposes," "Brat Farrar"** and **"To Love and Be Wise."**

Truth is the daughter of time and it is Detective Inspector Grant, flat on his back in a hospital bed and very bored indeed, who sets out to discover the truth about the bloody hunchback King of England, Richard III. This may sound like unpromising stuff, but I think you'll discover the search as effective an erasure of boredom as Grant did. Mild curiosity turns to livelier doubts and then to fierce conjecture and deduction. Grant is aided by the charming actress he was squiring in an earlier chronicle, by the stalwart Sergeant Williams and by a rather unconvincing young American scholar.

This is the sort of especially satisfying book we have been led to expect from Miss Tey (whose interest in history has been observable in the books and plays she has written as "Gordon Daviot") and it gains its delight principally in the warmth and discernment of her observation of people and things. It is a rather special gift and if a more enchanting book comes my way this year I shall be surprised.

James Sandoe, in a review of "The Daughter of Time," in New York Herald Tribune Book Review, *February 24, 1952, p. 10.*

ANTHONY BOUCHER (essay date 1952)

[*An American author of mystery, science fiction, and fantasy novels, Boucher also cofounded* The Magazine of Fantasy and Science Fiction *in 1949. In addition to editing works in these and related genres, Boucher concurrently reviewed science fiction novels for the* New York Herald Tribune *and detective novels for the* New York Times. *In the following excerpt from a review of* The Daughter of Time, *Boucher calls the novel "one of the permanent classics in the detective field" and praises both Tey's logical, precise scholarship and her presentation of history as "a body of legend bearing only the faintest relationship to demonstrable fact."*]

[Every] year brings new evidence that true creative talent can freshen any form, however hackneyed may be the run-of-the-mill products; and 1952's entry has an astonishingly different kind of detective story in Josephine Tey's **"The Daughter of Time."** . . .

There have been other attempts by mystery novelists to solve historical puzzles by detectival methods; the classic specimens are John Dickson Carr's "The Murder of Sir Edmund Godfrey" and Lillian de la Torre's "Elizabeth Is Missing" (the latter on the same theme which Miss Tey handled so beautifully in **"The Franchise Affair"**). But Tey goes further: she not only reconstructs the probable historical truth, she re-creates the intense dramatic excitement of the scholarly research necessary to unveil it.

Her unique formula is this: Inspector Alan Grant (of **"To Love and Be Wise"**), convalescent and bored by inactivity, becomes fascinated by a portrait of Richard III, which in no way jibes with the monstrous Wicked Uncle of "history." With the help of the British Museum and a young American scholar, he sets to work to find out what really happened in the late fifteenth century, what kind of man Richard actually was—and who, in fact, murdered the two young Princes in the Tower.

The result is a real bouleversement of schoolbook and encyclopedia "history," treated with compelling logic, precise scholarship and a cumulative intensity which makes the fictional, and even the factual, crimes of 1952 seem drab affairs indeed. It is also an exceedingly healthy demonstration, with many allusions to other instances, of the fact that the history which "everybody knows" is a body of legend bearing only the faintest relationship to demonstrable fact. The relative lack of contemporary action may put a few readers off this book; but most will, I trust, like this reviewer, clasp it to their hearts as one of the permanent classics in the detective field.

Anthony Boucher, in a review of "The Daughter of Time," in The New York Times Book Review, *February 24, 1952, p. 31.*

JAMES KELLEY (essay date 1952)

[*In the following excerpt, Kelley finds that Tey's portrayal of the pirate Henry Morgan in her novel* The Privateer *avoids titillation and gaudiness, while providing an exciting and romantic depiction of historic events.*]

The pre-radio Henry Morgan was a sea-going Robin Hood of the seventeenth century whose raiding expeditions among Spanish Caribbean islands and in Panama added a romantic fillip to the history of the period. Off-stage, Cromwell the Protector, the Spanish Inquisitors, and the tension between England and Spain kept things moving. Joining the growing list of writers attracted to these dramatic materials is Scotland-born Gordon Daviot, whose spanking good yarn of Privateer Morgan [**"The Privateer"**] and his progress from bondsman to knighthood is now posthumously published.

In **"Franchise Affair," "Brat Farrar,"** and some of her earlier plays and mysteries (written under the name of Josephine Tey) Miss Daviot proved that vivid characterization, dispassionate reporting, and crisp writing can lend conviction to improbable melodrama. Although she uses the same tools in her new book [**"The Privateer"**], readers accustomed to the florid "adventure novel" treatment may be dismayed by its Arcadian calm. Here is romance without titillation, action without undue emotional heat. But the author succeeds in her chief purpose: to develop a full-color picture of Morgan's dazzling exploits as a freebooter for England against Spain.

We first meet the hero of **"The Privateer"** as a young bondsman of Barbados. With his eye on the main chance even then, Morgan persuades a group of vagabonds to follow him in an audacious attack upon a Spanish ship lying off-shore. Overnight the polite young man becomes a polite swashbuckler in command of the good ship "Fortune." As self-appointed privateer (not buccaneer!), he becomes the scourge of the Caribbean.

Fearless with the enemy and fair with his men, Captain Morgan becomes a leading citizen of Jamaica, his home port. Here he woos and wins his beloved Elizabeth. Here he returns triumphant after each raid until the disastrous invasion of Maracaibo, South America's inland sea. . . .

For most readers, the special charm of **"The Privateer"** will extend beyond the gaudy allure of its derring-do to the rich background tapestry of contemporary events and personalities which is spun out for us. In her final novel Miss Daviot is at the top of her gifts.

James Kelley, "Gentleman of Fortune," in The New York Times Book Review, *August 24, 1952, p. 17.*

SIR JOHN GIELGUD (essay date 1953)

[*A highly acclaimed English actor, Gielgud has appeared in plays by Shakespeare, Oscar Wilde, and many other classic and contemporary dramatists. In the following excerpt from his introduction to* Plays by Gordon Daviot, *Gielgud notes that* Richard of Bordeaux *is the play in which he became an accomplished actor and director. Gielgud, who has also played Shakespeare's Richard II, finds Tey's depiction of Richard more humorous and charming, and therefore more commercially appealing. In addition to discussing her other plays, Gielgud also comments on Tey's eccentric insistence upon personal and artistic privacy.*]

Gordon Daviot was a strange character, proud without being arrogant, and obstinate, though not conceited. She was distressed by her inability to write original plots, especially when, on two occasions, she was unfairly accused of plagiarism. On the first occasion she was sued by the author of an historical novel about Richard the Second, but the case was settled out of court. These episodes distressed her greatly and made her over-sensitive—though it was difficult to tell what she really felt, since she did not readily give her confidence, even to her few intimate friends. She would rarely show her manuscripts to managers or actors, and she never read her plays to people. She was seldom to be seen in London. She shunned photographers and publicity of all kinds, and gave no interviews to the Press. I know that all the work she published under the name of Gordon Daviot was particularly dear to her, while her novels and other books, some of them published with great success under the name of Josephine Tey, she would refer to as her 'yearly knitting', as if they were of little account to her. She made many friends in the theatre, especially among the lesser members of the companies who acted in her plays, and I would often hear how she had kept in touch with them in after years, but I think she had some slight distrust of the leading players, and feared they might become too autocratic and possessive in their friendships. (pp. ix-x)

I find it difficult to criticise her writing, but I am sure it would please her greatly to know it is now to be given to a generation most of whom have not seen any of her plays acted. Naturally I find ***Richard of Bordeaux*** her most successful piece of work, partly because it gave me such wonderful opportunities, and because it was in that play that I won my spurs, both as actor and director. ***Richard*** brought me confidence as well as success. It was said at the time that Gordon had seen me in Shakespeare's *Richard II* at the Old Vic in 1929, and had me in mind when she wrote her play. I do not know whether this is true or not. At any rate she improved on Shakespeare (from a commercial point of view at any rate) by giving Richard a sense of humour. This attractive quality, allied to a boyish charm in the scenes with his wife, and his gallant behaviour in standing up to the war-mongering nobles, helps to excuse, in Gordon's play, the effeminacy of his character and to condone the essential shallowness of his nature.

In ***Dickon,*** on the other hand (which I have read in this book for the first time), Gordon does not succeed, to my mind, in making the character of Richard III sufficiently convincing as a hero, and her good Richard does not begin to be an adequate substitute for the thrilling monster of Shakespeare's play. She was evidently obsessed by this idea, for she develops it at considerable length in her novel ***A Daughter of Time*** (written under the name of Josephine Tey). But here again she writes, rather sadly, that the idea of Richard's innocence is not an original one, and indeed it has been put forward by several other writers before and since.

Similarly in ***Queen of Scots,*** Gordon tried to refute the accepted popular convention, refusing to depict the *femme fatale* that other writers have suggested in dramatising Mary's story. Nor would she bring herself to make the character wholly sympathetic, the injured heroine and pawn of circumstance, who might have touched an audience by her distresses. She tried to take a middle way, neither praising nor blaming, and, though this treatment might have succeeded in a novel, I do not think she has given sufficiently powerful opportunities in her play for an actress, however brilliant, to carry off with complete success.

The women in the Daviot plays are strongest in their mother-instincts. I do not mean this sentimentally, but in Ann of Bohemia, Sophie Brzewska (in ***The Laughing Woman***) and Sara (in ***The Little Dry Thorn***), the characters are wives, mistresses and mothers more than they are lovers. I do not think Gordon understood either the intriguer or the harlot in Mary Stuart. Her heroes, too, are men who need to be protected, touching, romantic, boyish. These are the heroes she likes and understands. The villains and her older men are effective by contrast, but they are often sketchily drawn, and sometimes a little overdrawn. They are types rather than characters. On the other hand she is thoroughly at home with her simple people, peasants, servants, plain soldiers and the like. Her 'little scenes', in which such characters give background and colour to the main action, are admirably neat and act delightfully on the stage.

Gordon's plays, along with those of Clifford Bax (especially *The Rose Without a Thorn* and *The Venetian*), and Rudolph Besier's *The Barretts of Wimpole Street,* gave fresh life to the romantic theatre of their day. They were produced at a time when audiences were eager for such entertainment (the revival of Shakespeare's popularity in the West End was to come later). Shaw had led the way, of course, with his *Caesar and Cleopatra* and *Saint Joan,* both written in witty modern prose, but these plays of his are discursive, meaty and controversial. Gordon's plays are comparatively light and delicate. They have great charm, humour and delightful acting parts. They have some of the romantic glamour of the old historical melodramas (*The Scarlet Pimpernel, The Only Way, The Wandering Jew*), without the pseudo-period dialogue and fustian sentiment which the authors of those plays had inherited from the Victorian and Edwardian theatres.

It is sad to think Gordon will write no more, but I am very proud to be asked to write the Foreword to these plays of hers. We are not so rich in dramatic authors in this country that, when they are as talented and original as Gordon Daviot, we can afford to lose them. The theatre is poorer for an unique talent, and I for a dearly valued friend. (pp. x-xii)

Sir John Gielgud, in a foreword to Plays: The Little Dry Thorn, Valerins, Dickon, Vol. I *by Gordon Daviot, Peter Davies, 1953, pp. ix-xii.*

JAMES SANDOE (essay date 1954)

[In the following excerpt from his introduction to Three by Tey, *Sandoe notes that while Tey was not an innovator of detective fiction, her realistic, unpretentious characterizations surpassed those of even her most distinguished peers. Sandoe concludes that it is ultimately more than the sum of plot and characterization that makes Tey's mysteries memorable, finding their appeal linked to Tey's "singularly delicate and humorous perception."]*

[It] was as Gordon Daviot and as early as 1929 that Miss MacKintosh made her first appearance as a detective story writer. In that year appeared **"The Man in the Queue,"** . . . anticipating fully in texture and in interest its seven successors. Inspector Alan Grant is apparent here (the ingratiating Williams at his side then as later) and Miss MacKintosh catches up in the net of her plot the same rich, acutely observed diversity of characters—clergymen and bookies, actors and stockbrokers—one remembers from all of the tales.

But plays were Gordon Daviot's larger concern for a number of years. Until, indeed, "Daviot" all but disappeared from lists of forthcoming publications and "Josephine Tey" made her first appearance with **"A Shilling for Candles: The Story of a Crime"** in 1936.

Here Miss Tey, with a characteristic minimum of violence, admits a corpse (drowned?) in the opening pages, turns at once to an investigation of the unfortunate business and to a singularly warming retrospective evocation of the victim. Her manner is leisurely but always telling because she is capable of keeping us quite as much absorbed in Grant's encounter with a grubby Canterbury tobacconist or the coltish Miss Erica's private investigations as with climaxes and revelations.

Any reader unwary enough to mistake this leisure for slowness or the digressions for padding is probably a bird who reads digests of Dickens and Dostoevski or chews up a hamburger because roast beef takes longer to cook. Certainly Miss Tey does not stint her readers. There is a richness of delineation even among the minor players (Dora Siggins in **"To Love and Be Wise,"** for instance) that is particularly contenting. There is savour too in the setting and in the characters' responses to it. This is most integrally apparent in **"Brat Farrar"** but it is present in all of them.

Then of course there is Grant, the least insistently genteel of detectives (a cousin of E.C.R. Lorac's Inspector Macdonald, one would guess) and the most satisfyingly human even in the private adversities which enter the latest novels. One has only to recall some of Grant's older contemporaries (Lord Peter Wimsey, Mr. Campion, Roderick Alleyn) in a *crise de nerfs* to measure the accomplishment.

Grant himself was absent from the third of the mysteries, **"Miss Pym Disposes"** . . . , the earliest of the three novels which make up this volume [**"Three by Tey"**]. For a mystery it is made up of most unpromising stuffs: the students and staff of a girls' physical education college, observed by a visiting "popular psychologist," wound in all but plotless succession of incident which has as its apparent climax the nomination of one of the girls for "the Arlinghurst job." Save for one premonitory brush there is no mystery, much less murder, until the novel has run four-fifths of its course. The fact of murder thereafter is, to be sure, the more shocking on that account.

But meanwhile, and observing through Miss Pym's alert, sardonic-compassionate perceptions, we have been altered (as she is) from perhaps casual observers to fierce advocates. This is due only in part to Miss Pym herself, admirable companion though she is. It is the consequence of meeting a lively and provoking company from the coolly gaudy Nut Tart to the shifty Miss Rouse. In a day when one opens the first page of a detective story to be blasted at once by a tommygun, the skill of sustaining human interest in itself seems as rich as it is certainly rare.

Insisting first that eight mysteries is all too few, one may from affection engage with some spirit in choosing favorites among them, very much as one does among the films of Alec Guinness. (pp. v-vii)

This is not, I think, irrelevant since for me at least Mr. Guinness and Miss Tey have that special capacity for engaging one's affections, catching them up as a friend does and not just as a passing acquaintance.

None of the novels takes any faster or firmer hold on one than **"The Franchise Affair"** . . . where in a few pages at the outset Miss Tey realizes Robert Blair (genteel, comfortable, sheltered and just a little restive) and poises him for adventure.

"The Franchise Affair" owes its idea to the eighteenth century case of Elizabeth Canning (called here "Betty Kane" in acknowledgment). Sir John Gielgud recalls that Miss MacKintosh "was distressed by her inability to write original plots, especially when, on two occasions, she was unfairly accused of plagiarism" [see excerpt above, 1953]. It was a baseless fear as any of you who know the Canning case will see. She has indeed taken its central situation but transformed it so in time and place and realized it with such fresh and telling immediacy, that it is, in fact, entirely her own.

Here too, of course, physical violence all but vanishes (as it does in very rare examples of the *genre:* Dorothy Sayers' "Gaudy Night" for one) and the puzzle is spun from the dilemma in which the accused mother and daughter find themselves and the appalling difficulty (if indeed they *are* innocent, after all) of making their innocence compulsively plain. It is an astonishing accomplishment and remains past rereadings as one of the most richly (and repeatedly) exciting detective stories I know anything about.

Grant, present peripherally in **"The Franchise Affair,"** is absent from **"Brat Farrar"** . . . which is the story of an impostor. Some mystery attaches to the imposition and to its reception but the excitement here is essentially the excitement of watching a tight-rope performer with the assurance that he must fall and the desire that he shan't be hurt.

Miss Tey prepares us for Brat by evoking Latchetts, its family and its rich countryside. The evocation is loving and affecting. Brat himself is an uncommon impostor caught past reluctance into a game which must then be played with fastidiousness and even with honor. He has a very genuine charm and his precarious adventure involves the reader early and firmly and then holds on tightly to the explosive conclusion. But **"Brat Farrar"** is still more a romance than a story of crime, although its romance is no matter of holding hands (much less leaping into beds). It is an expression of devotion to English tradition and the English countryside. Its setting is contemporary but its effect is nostalgic and fetching.

In **"To Love and Be Wise"** . . . Miss Tey employed her boldest deceit and did her most skilful juggling, underscoring her clues and indeed making the very quality of the mystery its principal clue and a gigantic one. To be sure the size of the deceit astonished some readers into protest but a rereading convinces me that, granting one rather large problem not convincingly solved, it is an exceptional and (especially upon a rereading) notably rewarding piece of work.

Orfordshire is its setting and, more particularly, Salcott St. Mary, invaded by a noisy lot of artists seeking a quiet country retreat. Miss Tey's sketches here come closer to caricature than most of her characterizations and lose no pungency by Grant's quiet but penetrating observation as he seeks for evidence about the vanished American photographer, Leslie Searle.

"To Love and Be Wise" was succeeded by the most astonishing detective story of them all, **"The Daughter of Time"** . . . , an account of Grant's search (from a hospital bed) for the truth about Richard III, the venomous, hunchback monster whose firm place among history's villains is countered so oddly by the sensitive face apparent in a contemporary portrait.

Grant's first doubt, succeeded by others, makes a marvellously exciting narrative evolved once again from what, superficially, are unpromising stuffs. Miss Tey was not, of course, the first to champion Richard Plantagenet, but the terms in which she realizes the processes of scholarly detection here are memorably infectious.

Grant appears last in that latest of the novels **"The Singing Sands"** . . . , published posthumously. Again he is sick but here rather in mind than body and the novel is as much an account of his rehabilitation in the Scottish highlands as it is an account of the search for a murderer. On both scores it is absorbing and here, as in the other tales, there are particular delights which return warmingly to mind, among them the scenes of fishing in Highland streams with young Pat and the pungent sequence (complete with *ceilidh*) on Cladda in the Hebrides.

Eight tales there are, all of them (if diversely) contenting for all that Miss Tey was not an innovator. She did not, as Hammett did, give detective fiction a new idiom, nor can she, like Mrs. Christie, be praised for a remarkable sequence of dazzling plots. For that matter, although she succeeded more compellingly than some of her most distinguished peers in evoking character compulsively (and better than some of the most distinguished among them in that her characters never for an instant become pretentious), one cannot comprehend any one of these eight tales by recalling its characters or its plot. And this is because each is more than either and more than the sum of both. It is perhaps the infusion into all of them of a singularly delicate and humorous perception that fixes them in remembrance as cheeringly as a friend, a warm hearth, and a bracing glass on a snowy day. (pp. vii-x)

James Sandoe, in an introduction to Three by Tey: Miss Pym Disposes, The Franchise Affair, Brat Farrar *by Josephine Tey, The Macmillan Company, 1954, pp. v-x.*

DOROTHY SALISBURY DAVIS (essay date 1954)

[Davis is an American author of mystery fiction. Her stories blend tragedy, melodrama, and farce with believable characterization and are among the best in the genre. In the following excerpt from her review of Three by Tey, *Davis finds that Tey's detective novels compensate for their slight plots with a diversity of well-developed characters.]*

It has been said that Hammett took the mystery out of the vicar's garden and put it in the hands of those who knew what murder was about. Allowing the too apparent truth of where the pseudo-Hammetts dragged this body of fiction, I wonder if it cannot be said that Josephine Tay spirited it back to the vicar's garden. And there, I submit, it is neither more nor less seemly, and possibly a bit more newsworthy. . . .

The vicar's garden may seem to imply a small world. It is small only if the vicar is small minded, and of course my allusion is meant only to imply the pleasantness of the company of the late Josephine Tey. She knew her share of vicars: it is quite as impossible to ignore the vicar in England as it is to miss teatime. And as foolish. There was practically no stratum of English society with which she was not conversant, and if any one characteristic most distinguished Miss Tey's work it was her power to evoke character, atmosphere, mores by conversation. Her people talk as though speech comes natural to them. It is good talk as well as story propelling. Indeed it makes one nostalgic for the art of conversation.

''Josephine Tey'' was one of two pseudonyms of Elizabeth Mackintosh. It is not surprising to learn that under the other, ''Gordon Daviot,'' she wrote chiefly plays, the best-remembered of which was ***Richard of Bordeaux.*** Her talent was not changed with a name. The dramatist's evocation runs through all of Tey. And really, as James Sandoe says in his excellent introduction to ***Three by Tey*** [see excerpt above, 1954], choosing a favorite from among the eight mysteries Miss Tey wrote is like trying to select a favorite Alec Guinness film. Something particularly endearing leaps to mind out of one after another of them. I am partial to ***The Daughter of Time*** which is not in this trio, but having said that I am immediately tempted to say: no, rather I think ***The Franchise Affair,*** which is.

Elizabeth Canning provoked a notorious scandal in the eighteenth century. To this scandal Miss Tey acknowledged inspiration, but oh, how lightly she leaned upon history. A mother and daughter, living at The Franchise, an isolated house, are accused of kidnapping and enslaving Betty Kane, a girl of excellent reputation and good upbringing. The *Ack-Emma,* a tabloid, takes up the girl's case and an irate community lends a hand in the administration of ''justice.'' Not much of a plot. All Miss Tey's plots could have been written on the back of a match box. But her characters have the diversity of flame, and the sum of their impact is as irresistible.

Miss Pym Disposes is the gentlest of these welcome reissues, and to me the most flavorsome. There is no violence until near the end, and by then the accumulating tension cries out for it. Along with the modest Lucy Pym, who has written *the* book on psychology but cannot accomodate herself to the fame it brings her, here is as likeable a set of girls as any school could matriculate. (p. 17)

In ***Brat Farrar,*** the third book, violence is again tardy, lamentable and inevitable. Brat is an imposter who falls in love with the family upon whom he imposes. His search for honor in dishonor makes him as touching a figure as any of Miss Tey's reluctant heroes.

Allan Grant, Miss Tey's Scotland Yard man, and himself the most reluctant of heroes, is present here only in ***The Franchise Affair,*** and in that he is the antagonist, bringing the case against the women of the Franchise. This is a truly remarkable putting of a detective in his proper place! It must have given Miss Tey a great deal of pleasure to relegate him now and then. So many of her esteemed colleagues in the field have become slaves to their detectives. Grant is perilously human for a detective of fiction: he sometimes sniffles, as who could escape it in the English clime; in one book he needed to go off to Scotland because of an impending breakdown; and in what I believe is a classic use of the detection technique he pursues that wiliest of demons, history, until it yields an amazingly convincing confession about Richard III, the purported murderer of the princes in the Tower—this while Grant is strung up like a plucked fowl, with a broken leg.

It is amusing to find in ***Miss Pym Disposes*** the prophesy of this adventure met with in misadventure. A teacher, on being invited to see *Richard III,* comments: ''A criminal libel on a fine man, a blatant piece of political propaganda, and an extremely silly play.'' Was this Miss Tey's promise to herself that she should one day set her literate sleuth upon the detractors of an unfortunate king?

I know that upon reading ***The Daughter of Time*** I promised myself that if ever I got to London I should search the National Portrait Gallery for Richard III. I did just that. . . . [The bus driver] put me down at the right stop and told me to be sure to go to another gallery also, and to look up his favorite painting, a Constable. . . . (pp. 17-18)

For this I was indebted to the provocativeness of Josephine Tey, and I thought how she herself would have enjoyed such an encounter. What more can be asked of books than that they provoke laughter, more reading, discussion, a pilgrimage? Much of the praise of Miss Tey has been written since her death, no uncommon occurence surely, but it does make one sad that after all ''truth is the daughter of time.'' (p. 18)

Dorothy Salisbury Davis, "On Josephine Tey," in The New Republic, *Vol. 131, No. 12, September 20, 1954, pp. 17-18.*

JULIAN SYMONS (essay date 1972)

[*Symons is an English man of letters who holds two highly praised literary reputations: that of the serious biographer and critic and that of the detective novelist. His popular biographies of Charles Dickens, Thomas Carlyle, and his brother A.J.A. Symons are considered excellent introductions to those writers. Symons is better known, however, for such crime novels as* The 31st of February *and* The Progress of a Crime. *In the following excerpt, Symons notes that while most of Tey's mysteries exhibit originality,* The Daughter of Time *displays an ignorance of history and is, ultimately, dull.*]

In the late fifties, I produced the dubiously useful list of the Hundred Best Crime Stories. . . . The list was . . . partly cooperative, in the sense that I approached several critics and asked them to select their favorite recent crime stories. Among them was Howard Haycraft, historian and devotee of the classical detective story. It is a striking confirmation of the decay in the classical form that the only postwar writer thought by Haycraft worthy to enter the canon was Elizabeth Mackintosh . . . , who wrote plays under the name of Gordon Daviot and crime stories as Josephine Tey. Her first crime story, ***The Man in the Queue*** . . . , introduced the slight, dapper Inspector Grant, and for its time and of its kind was an unusually interesting performance, although it depends upon the supposition that a man stabbed in a theatre queue will not cry out, or even know what has happened, before he collapses a minute or two later. Other Teys were published intermittently, and all have something original about them, in particular ***The Franchise Affair*** . . . , which translates the eighteenth-century disappearance of Elizabeth Canning into modern terms, and then offers an explanation which really applies to the modern fiction rather than to the eighteenth-century case, and is somehow a little disappointing after the sparkling beginning in which the mystery is set out.

The book selected by Haycraft as her best, with the agreement of several other critics, was a freakish performance called ***The Daughter of Time***. . . . In this, Grant, immobilized after falling through a trap door, provides with the help of an American student a solution to the mystery of the Princes in the Tower on the lines that they were murdered at the instance not of Richard III but of Henry VII. There is nothing new about this theory, as the student discovers at the end of their research, and Grant's almost total ignorance of history is the most remarkable thing about the book. The pleasure taken by critics in the very slow unfolding of a thesis already well known suggests a similar ignorance on their part. But even more to the point is the fact that this amateur rehashing of a well-known argument, interspersed with visits from friends to the detective's bedside, is, as one might expect, really rather dull. (pp. 158-59)

Julian Symons, "'Mr. Queen, Will You Be Good Enough to Explain Your Famous Character's Sex Life, If Any?'' in his Mortal Consequences: A History—From the Detective Story to the Crime Novel, *Harper & Row, Publishers, 1972, pp. 151-66.**

GUY M. TOWNSEND (essay date 1977)

[*A historian who specializes in British and modern European history, Townsend publishes and edits* The Mystery FANcier *and reviews mysteries for the* Memphis Commercial Appeal. *In the following excerpt Townsend argues that* The Daughter of Time *is neither a detective novel nor an accurate presentation of the historical episode it examines. Defending historians against the "paranoid" distrust of the author, Townsend contends that Tey's lack of respect for professional historians and her fabrication and omission of documented historical fact about Richard III lead to a distorted presentation and therefore a false conclusion. For a rebuttal of Townsend's opinion, see the excerpt by M. J. Smith (1977).*]

The Daughter of Time is not a detective novel. The only possible justification for calling it one is the fact that the protagonist is a detective. But, since his being a detective has virtually nothing to do with the story itself, it makes no more sense to call it a detective novel than it would to call it a plumber novel if the protagonist had under normal circumstances been a follower of that profession. The only "detection" in the story is a sophomoric version of what professional historians and other scholars do every day without pretending to be detectives. . . .

Miss Tey makes a mockery of scholarly research by ignoring and distorting evidence so as to present a plausible though patently false picture of a famous episode in English history.

Both as a mystery lover and as a historian I have for years been distressed by the virtually unanimous praise which Miss Tey's novel has received and indeed continues to receive. At last I feel compelled to undertake a task that mystery connoisseurs and historians more knowledgeable and capable than myself have chosen to ignore. . . . I shall attempt to demonstrate that ***The Daughter of Time*** is neither a good detective story nor an accurate portrayal of the historical episode which it purports to illuminate. . . .

[The] protagonist is a Scotland Yard inspector named Allan Grant who has sustained injuries in falling through a trap door while pursuing a criminal. As a result of these injuries he is laid up—immobilized—in a hospital bed for a protracted period of recovery. . . .

One day an actress friend of his named Marta brings him a collection of prints of old portraits to look at to while away the hours, and one of them in particular catches his eye. Judging himself capable of reading a person's character in his face, Grant decides that the subject of the portrait was an essentially noble man who had undergone great suffering. Turning the print over at last he reads with astonishment that this is a portrait of Richard III, that monarch of most wicked and evil reputation who had the two princes in the Tower murdered! Intrigued by the stark contrast between Richard III's historical reputation and the nobility of character which Grant sees in his portrait, he decides to read up on Richard III. (p. 211)

[Reading] books on the subject which his friends bring him, including Sir Thomas More's *History of King Richard III,* Grant concludes that there has been a gigantic conspiracy down through the centuries to defame Richard III, and he determines to get to the truth of the matter by going to the original sources.

Bed-ridden as he is, however, Grant is unable to do the required spade work at the British Museum and elsewhere, so Marta turns up a young American quasi-scholar named Brent Carradine to do the work for him, and together they set out to nail down the truth about Richard III once and for all. The balance of the novel consists of an exposition of how the various pieces of evidence are unearthed and fitted together to form a picture which, Miss Tey contends, not only clears Richard of the crime of murdering the two princes, but pins the guilt for those two murders firmly on Richard's enemy and successor, Henry VII. (pp. 211-12)

One of the most striking things about this work is Miss Tey's very nearly rabid hostility towards legitimate historians. A few examples should make this quite clear: . . .

> Grant: "Historians should be compelled to take a course in psychology before they are allowed to write."
>
> Carradine: "Huh. That wouldn't do anything for them. A man who is interested in what makes people tick doesn't write history. He writes novels, or becomes an alienist, or a magistrate—"
>
> "Or a confidence man." . . .
>
> Grant: "Honestly, I think historians are all mad."
>
> Grant: "I'll never again believe anything I read in a history book, as long as I live, so help me."
>
> "How did you get on with the history books?" Williams had asked.
>
> "Couldn't be better. I've proved them all wrong."
>
> (pp. 212-13)

It is evident, then, that Miss Tey regards the works of professional historians with a degree of suspicion which definitely shades into paranoia. "The real history," she has Carradine say, "is written in forms not meant as history. In Wardrobe accounts, in Privy Purse expenses, in personal letters, in estate books." And, Miss Tey appears to believe, in historical novels. For one entire chapter Miss Tey discusses a historical novel by Evelyn Payne-Ellis titled *The Rose of Raby*. . . . Indeed, while ***The Daughter of Time*** includes a total of five pages of quotations from *The Rose of Raby,* Miss Tey does not on a single occasion quote extensively from any history or, for that matter, from any of the primary sources for which she professes such respect. What makes this even more peculiar is the fact that *The Rose of Raby* is not about Richard at all, but about his mother. Richard appears in it only as a minor and unimportant character. Yet Miss Tey is fulsome in her praise of it. (p. 213)

After having lambasted all historians throughout the novel for their dishonesty, blindness, and stupidity, on page 170 (out of a total of 180 for the entire novel) Miss Tey finally admits that there have been some historical defenses of Richard III already. Carradine, in conversation with Grant, says:

> "A man Buck wrote a vindication in the seventeenth century. And Horace Walpole in the eighteenth. And someone called Markham in the nineteenth."
>
> "And who in the twentieth?"
>
> "No one that I know of."

Aside from the fact that there have been a good many more "vindications" than this written . . . , there are two things wrong with this passage, both of which relate to that "someone called Markham." First, that "someone called Markham" is Sir Clements Markham who, though he published an article and a follow-up letter on Richard III in the *English Historical Review* in 1891, did not publish his great defense of Richard, entitled *Richard III: His Life and Character,* until 1906, which, so far as this historian has been able to determine, is in the twentieth century, not the nineteenth as Miss Tey would have it. The second thing is more serious: although, as shall be demonstrated shortly, Miss Tey cribbed every bit of her information from Sir Clements' work and not from the original sources as she pretended, she never gives him one iota of credit. Indeed, the only mention she makes of Sir Clements in the entire book is reproduced in full in the above quotation. Surely Sir Clements deserves better from someone whose work is little more than a paraphrase of his own. Claiming someone else's work as one's own—otherwise known as plagiarism—is a serious crime among scholars, something that a respectable historian would never do. Miss Tey has done it.

Indeed, in all of Miss Tey's arguments there is not one which she does not lift bodily from Sir Clements. (pp. 213-14)

The prime source for the Tudor version of Richard III is Sir Thomas More's *History of King Richard III*. In it Richard is portrayed as an evil monster, deformed in both body and mind, whose wickedness and hunger for power led him to commit, or have committed, unspeakable crimes, the foremost of which was the murder of his two nephews in the Tower. (Actually, the popular image of Richard as monster is owing more to Shakespeare's play than to More's history; indeed, More frequently qualifies his comments regarding Richard's history and his character.) On the subject of Sir Thomas's *History* Miss Tey makes her opinion quite clear: the *History* is biased, distorted, and totally unreliable, and was, on top of all that, not written by Sir Thomas at all but by Tey's *bête noire,* John Morton. (p. 214)

Now, granting that More's portrayal of Richard as a monster in human form is grossly overdrawn, and his account of Richard's deformity a gross exaggeration of a hardly noticeable irregularity in Richard's shoulders, the central thrust of More's tale is that Richard, overcome by his own ambition to possess the crown, contrived to have his nephews murdered in order to secure his hold on the usurped throne, and, while More's account of precisely how Richard's plan was executed (no pun intended) is not in keeping with the facts as we now know them, one does not discredit the work as a whole by infantile ravings about "hearsay" and "gossip." As for the assertion that the *History* was written not by More but by Morton, it is simply nonsense. Can anyone reasonably picture a man as busy as the 35-year-old More was in 1513, taking the time to sit down and copy out in his own hand a 30,000 word account by John Morton? Assuming for a moment that Morton did write it and that More wanted a copy, would he not have had a copy made by someone else?

Miss Tey is merely following the lead of Sir Clements Markham in denying that More himself wrote the *History*. . . . The Richardists appear to feel more at ease calling Morton, who they go to great lengths to defame, a liar, than calling Sir Thomas More one. Then too, it is much more feasible to contend that a contemptible creature such as they portray Morton to be would produce a malicious lie such as the *History* than it is to assert that Sir Thomas would do so. The fact is, as Alison Hanham has recently observed, the attempt to attribute More's history to Morton is "patently absurd." (pp. 214-15)

Miss Tey pretends to be unable to understand how Richard could have been a faithful brother, with no desire to seize the throne, up until Edward's death, then could all of a sudden have come to desire the throne so much that he was willing to murder his own nephews in order to get it. . . . Miss Tey is being disingenuous. She knows perfectly well that the annals of crime, factual as well as fictional, are overflowing with examples of people who behave in perfectly respectable fashions so long as it is not to their advantage to do otherwise, but who do the most dastardly things, completely out of keeping with their previous behavior, when an alteration of circumstances makes it advantageous for them to do so. At his death, Edward was only forty-one years old, and his son was twelve. Richard had had every reason to believe that Edward still had many years of life ahead of him, and that the king's son would be an adult and capable of ruling for himself by the time his father died. Under these circumstances the question of seizing the throne simply did not arise. It was only Edward's untimely death, while his son was still too young to rule for himself, which presented Richard with an entirely unforeseen opportunity to seize the crown. Since the temptation did not exist before, Richard can hardly be given credit for having resisted it.

There is something else wrong with these assertions of Miss Tey. She pretends to believe that Richard was secure in his position as Regent and was in a position to enjoy all of the powers of kinghood except the title for the six or eight years until Edward V was ready to rule for himself. In fact, however, he was in immediate danger of completely losing control of Edward to the Woodvilles, who were intriguing to terminate his regency and gain control of the young king for themselves. Besides, Miss Tey is incredibly naive if she actually believes that any man with a strong ambition—and Richard certainly had that—could be happy at the prospect of being able to rule as *de facto* king of England for only a few years. Richard was only thirty-one years old; he would still have been under forty when Edward took over control from him. What sort of a prospect was it for a man like Richard to look forward to spending the prime of his life as a hanger-on, after having once enjoyed the exercise of kingly power? Certainly Richard had a motive, and an excellent one at that.

Another point that Miss Tey plays up for all it is worth is that the two princes were not the only ones who stood between Richard and the crown. . . . Miss Tey later has Grant make a list of the heirs to Edward IV—totalling eleven, including one bastard. . . . Once again she is being disingenuous. Richard had had himself proclaimed the legitimate heir to the throne by parliament. It was still possible, given the conditions under which that parliamentary ruling was made, that supporters of Edward V would rise up against Richard. Had they done so successfully there can be little doubt that Edward would then have been widely accepted as the legitimate king of England. So as long as he remained alive the young prince represented a positive threat to Richard's security on the throne. An uprising in support of one of Edward IV's daughters or the duke of Clarence's son was much less likely to have widespread support against Richard, and the threat that they represented to him alive was not great enough to offset the danger of having them killed. Despite Miss Tey's disclaimers, therefore, there is nothing "silly" about the suggestion that Richard had his nephews murdered and yet did not have the other claimants murdered as well. The princes offered an immediate threat to Richard's security; the other claimants did not. It was as simple as that. (pp. 215-16)

Miss Tey repeatedly laments that there are no unbiased contemporary accounts of Richard's reign, declaring that all of the existing accounts were written after Richard's death for the Tudors. She has Carradine say, "there is a monkish chronicle in Latin somewhere that is contemporary, but I haven't been able to get it yet." This was the Croyland Chronicle, and to pretend that it was difficult to find and was available only in Latin is a piece of silly nonsense; an English translation of it by H. T. Riley was published in London in 1854 by Bohn's Antiquarian Library, and a copy of it was certainly readily available to anyone who had access to the British Museum, as Carradine had. This is the source which Miss Tey attempts to discredit by saying that Morton was in the neighborhood at the time that the rumors regarding Richard's having murdered the princes was recorded. Incidentally, the Chronicle's precise words (in translation, of course) regarding the rumors are: "a rumor was spread that the sons of King Edward before-named had died a violent death, but it was uncertain how."

In fact, there is a much better contemporary source now available, which was not available when Sir Clements Markham published his defense of Richard in 1906, but which had been available for a decade and a half by the time Miss Tey published her novel in 1951. Naturally, since Miss Tey slavishly follows Markham's version, she chooses to ignore the existence of this other source. Another probable reason why she ignores it is that it completely demolishes her and Markham's picture of the honorable and guiltless Richard III.

In the summer of 1482 an Italian churchman named Dominic Mancini arrived in England, probably on business for the pope. He remained in England, primarily in London, until the late summer of 1483. By December of that year he had completed his work, *De Occupatione Regni Anglie per Riccardum Tercium,* but for some reason it was not published until this century, after a copy of the manuscript was discovered in the Bibliothèque Municipale at Lille, France. An English translation by C.A.J. Armstrong, entitled *The Usurpation of Richard III,* was published in 1936, fifteen years before Miss Tey wrote ***The Daughter of Time.*** She completely ignores it.

As an Italian, Mancini cannot be accused of having a bias on the question of Richard's character, and particularly not a pro-Tudor bias, since his work was written two years before the first Tudor came to power. (pp. 217-18)

The resemblance between Mancini's version and the traditional one (which had been formulated long before Mancini was rediscovered) is striking. (p. 219)

We come now to the bones. In July 1674 some bones were discovered buried beneath a flight of stairs in the Tower. Widely believed to be the bones of the two princes, they were reinterred in a more respectful fashion in the Henry VII Chapel at Westminster. In June 1933 the urn containing the bones was re-opened and the contents re-examined by Professor William Wright, dean of London Hospital, and Dr. George Northcroft, past president of the British Dental Association. They concluded their examination in five days and the bones were interred once again at Westminster. Their conclusion, which was made public at the end of November 1933, was that the bones were those of two boys of the ages of Edward V and his brother Richard in 1483. (p. 220)

Much has been made of the haste with which the examination of the bones was conducted, and of certain difficulties regarding the medical evidence stemming from that examination, and the implication of these criticisms is that Wright and Northcroft's conclusions regarding the bones are erroneous either because of incompetence or because of deliberate distortion on their part.

Now, given the professional standing of these two gentlemen, it seems more than a little farfetched to suggest that they were not competent to carry out the examination. And the idea that they deliberately distorted the evidence is ridiculous on the face of it; if they had wanted to distort the evidence of the bones—which they knew would be put away again and not available to their critics—why would they not have doctored (if you will excuse the pun) the evidence so that there would have been no question as to the ages of the boys at death? They did not do so. Instead, they presented the world with the actual results of their examination, complete with difficulties and uncertainties, and made public the conclusions which they had drawn from them. Others have since tried to prove that the ages of the boys at the time of death were greater than those ascribed to them by Professor Wright and Dr. Northcroft, but the important fact to remember is that all of their attackers have based their attacks *on Wright and Northcroft's own evidence*. In other words, their critics accept their ability to conduct the examination and record the evidence, but reject the conclusions which they draw from that evidence. . . .

What, then, of the Richardist contention that Henry VII murdered the princes? The earliest that he could have done so was August 1485 after his victory at Bosworth Field, by which time Edward V would have been almost fifteen. The Richardists, however, contend that it was not until June-July 1486 that Henry actually had the boys killed, at which time Edward would have been nearly sixteen and Richard nearly thirteen. That two such men as Wright and Northcroft could have mistaken the bones of two children of nearly sixteen and thirteen for those of two children nearly thirteen and ten is too absurd even to merit comment. Some Richardists, however, manage to get around this by asserting that these are not the bones of the two princes at all, that it is merely a coincidence that the bones of two children the ages of Edward and Richard in 1483 should happen to turn up in the very place where those boys were last seen alive.

It is a revealing fact that professional historians are almost never to be found among the Richardists; advocates of the Richard as saint school come uniformly from the ranks of amateurs. Even Sir Clements Markham, the foremost of Richard's defenders, was not a historian.

Professional historians adhere more or less to the traditional version. Despite Miss Tey's contentions, this near unanimity of opinion springs neither from an occupational stupidity nor from a profession-wide conspiracy, but rather from the nature of the evidence itself. (p. 221)

This is not to say that historians are always or even usually in agreement—far from it. . . . Whenever, therefore, professional historians as a whole are in substantial agreement on a particular question, as they are on the main points of the Richard question, it is an excellent indication that there is little if any evidence to support a contrary opinion.

In an entirely fictional detective story the novelist has absolute control over the evidence. This is not so when a novelist reconstructs an actual crime. In that case the evidence has an existence all of its own, independent of whether the author chooses to put it before the reader or not. I am of the old school which feels that a detective novelist has an obligation to play fair with the reader; that is, to present the reader with all the evidence then convince the reader that the novelist's version of what really happened is the only plausible explanation. Since, as has been adequately demonstrated, Miss Tey's version is, to say the very least, not the only plausible explanation of the events in question, she has chosen to withhold from her reader much evidence which does not support her position. Instead of making a fair presentation of all the evidence in the case and then proving to the reader that her's is indeed the only plausible reconstruction of events, Miss Tey builds up a straw man—the naïve and stupid but at the same time diabolically clever professional historian, who has for centuries managed to keep the world ignorant of the truth about Richard—which she has no trouble knocking down again with her extremely selective presentation of the evidence. (pp. 221-22)

Guy M. Townsend, "Richard III and Josephine: Partners in Crime," in The Armchair Detective, *Vol. 10, No. 3, Summer, 1977, pp. 211-24.*

M. J. SMITH (essay date 1977)

[*Smith is an American author and critic whose works include* Cloak-and-Dagger Bibliography *(1976). In the following excerpt, Smith defends Tey's use of "invented" historical evidence and her omission of non-supportive facts in* The Daughter of Time. *Smith is not concerned with the success of Tey's novel as a detective story, offering instead a general defense of fiction writers who manipulate factual material for artistic purposes. Thus, the value of* The Daughter of Time *as a historical study becomes irrelevant. Smith's essay was written as a rebuttal to an article by Guy M. Townsend (1977).*]

My impression after reading Dr. Townsend's article "Richard III and Josephine Tey: Partners in Crime" [see excerpt above, 1977] is that the chief crime in which Tey and Richard aided and abetted each other is that of writing a bad book. ***The Daughter of Time*** is not primarily a poor detective story, though it might be open to criticism on that count, but a bad history book, which it never pretends to be. The author of a work of fiction is entitled to express his or her opinions and prejudices, even against professors of history. He can omit or invent incidents and minor characters, or merge one into another. He can even invent sources (Sherlock Holmes' "monographs," for example, written by and quoted by Holmes). This is what Tey does when she quotes from "The Rose of Raby," by Evelyn Payne-Ellis, neither book nor author having any existence except in Tey's imagination. (No wonder she has a reverence for it!) However, the supposed novel is not used as authority for facts, but as a device to carry the narrative forward—a story within a story.

While I cannot unreservedly defend either Miss Tey's scholarship or her conclusions, I see no reason why Professor Townsend should be allowed to do many of the things he accuses her of. He says that "Professorial historians adhere more or less to the traditional version," ignoring the work of Paul Murray Kendall, except for a brief footnote in the bibliography. . . . He makes fun of the Richardians' belief that Sir Thomas More copied Morton's account of the *History*—which he considers is based on More's being too "saintly" to have written such a document out of his own head—with the equally laughable and unprovable argument that he was "too busy" to have copied it and therefore must have written it from scratch, an even more time-consuming project, and, by implication, from his own knowledge—of things that took place when he was three years old! . . .

[Attacking] Richard III's detractors, on any grounds, does not prove his innocence, any more than attacking his friends proves his guilt. We must turn to the evidence, and since we can no longer discover fingerprints or the like, it must necessarily be circumstantial evidence.

What about the bones as evidence? Oh yes, the bones. I do not dispute the scientific evidence behind the conclusions of Wright and Northcroft. If only it hadn't been left so far behind! Wright's judgment, for instance, was clearly colored by what he expected to find. "The evidence that the bones in the urn are those of the princes is . . . as conclusive as could be desired" . . . yet he could not prove by any medical tests that they were the skeletons of boys, never mind princes. He first states a "probable age." Now, a glance at any seventh grade classroom would convince one that there is a great variation in rates of growth, with girls generally ahead of boys at this age. But having heard in advance of the disappearance of two boys in 1483, Wright concludes that these are the skeletons of boys (not girls), who were exactly 12½ and 10 years old (not 12 or 10 plus or minus two years, as most reputable anthropologists would say), and who were buried there in the year 1483. No scientific method, not even the radio-carbon clock, can date bones or other objects within even decades, but Wright knows the exact year.

If it is objected that it would be too much of a coincidence for bones to turn up in the Tower which were those of children but not those of the princes, the fact is that another set of bones was found early in the seventeenth century. Believed at first to be those of the princes, they were later deduced, by the scientific means available at the time, to be too small. Their presence does show, however, the strong probability of bones of all types and ages being scattered all over the area. At one time the skeleton of an ape was found and declared to be the bones of the princes! (p. 317)

Townsend argues that Richard had to kill the boys, as they were an immediate threat to his security, and in the next paragraph tells us that if they were officially dead all the other heirs would in turn become immediate threats and have to be disposed of. Not so. Warwick, the heir of Richard's older brother George of Clarence, was under his father's attainder. No pro-Edwardian Yorkist could advocate the attainder be set aside without calling into question the legality of Edward IV's rule *in toto*. The other "threats" were children of Richard's sisters, whose claim was inferior to his own, girls who could not inherit in any case, and until April of 1484, his own son. One of these *could* have plotted an assassination attempt, a la *Kind Hearts and Coronets*, but I doubt if Richard, or even Prof. Townsend, would take that idea seriously. Having the boys dead while officially alive would not have precluded it, anyway. That situation gave Richard the worst of both worlds, not the best. If the boys were alive and in his custody, disaffected Yorkists could be kept from fomenting rebellion or going over to the Lancastrians. The rebels would have to invade London and take the Tower itself in order to get the figurehead without which they could not obtain support to make the invasion in the first place. . . . (pp. 318-19)

Was Henry VII guilty, as Tey claims? I don't think so. First, there is the unlikelihood of the boys surviving into his reign and then disappearing without someone noticing and saying so, if not in England, abroad, where folks were always happy to hear anything to the discredit of the English. Second, Henry had also to produce either the boys, their bodies, or a plausible story, to protect himself from the pretenders with which his reign was plagued, but he did nothing until 1502, *after* the execution of the most prominent candidate. Even then he made no official announcement, merely allowing a well-placed "leak" to spread about. Such inaction on Henry's part is puzzling if he knew the fate of the princes. The conclusion is inescapable; Henry, like Richard, was entirely in the dark. . . .

Unlike most Richardians, I do not think Henry was evil incarnate. Were the boys alive, they would have been no threat to him, legitimate or not, as they were Yorkists. To a good Lancastrian's point of view, no Yorkist had any kind of claim to the throne at all. Henry tolerated John of Lincoln, the legitimate heir to the Yorkist line, for years, and apparently had no fear of him. . . .

There is no definite proof, historical or legal, for either side nearly 500 years after the event. There is only the psychological proof of how people acted and reacted. Both Richard and Henry acted as if they had no idea of what happened to the princes. Elizabeth Woodville acted as if she did know. Is it not possible that she could have conspired with someone—most likely Buckingham—to engineer their escape from the Tower, forgetting that Buckingham, although he was her brother-in-law on the Woodville side, hated her family? Elizabeth was a supreme egoist, who could ride roughshod over people and still expect them to do what she wanted. Did she ever learn what actually happened to her sons, and did knowing—or not knowing—drive her mad? Or did she end up running the convent to which Henry sent her? We'll never know.

I respectfully submit that the verdict must be "Murder by person or persons unknown." Have I come to this conclusion by virtue of being a professional historian? No, but there's the old saw about not having to be a chicken to judge an egg. The chicken would probably be the worst judge. (p. 319)

M. J. Smith, "Controversy: Townsend, Tey, and Richard III, a Rebuttal," in The Armchair Detective, *Vol. 10, No. 4, Fall, 1977, pp. 317-19.*

SANDRA ROY (essay date 1980)

[Roy is an American poet, short story writer, and educator who has designed a course on the history and development of detective and mystery fiction. In the following excerpt from her critical biography Josephine Tey, *Roy provides a discussion of Tey's dramas and her nondetective novels.]*

Miss Mackintosh clearly contemplated a career as a serious dramatist on the London stage as she wrote a series of four full-length plays in the early 1930s. Making consistent use of the Gordon Daviot pseudonym, she completed [***Richard of Bordeaux, The Laughing Woman, Queen of Scots,*** and ***The Stars Bow Down***]. . . . All of the plays but ***Laughing Woman*** were based on historical or biblical sources; all but ***The Stars Bow Down*** received full-scale productions. (p. 21)

Richard of Bordeaux closely follows historical accounts of one of England's less successful kings [Richard II]. Gordon Daviot artfully handles a succession of incidents and personages which leave an impression of tactful regret, "if only it could have been otherwise." Her panoramic scenes are all interiors which subtly emphasize the conflicts of tenderness, impulse, and cruelty beneath Richard's tenacious struggle for survival, even when he is physically absent from the stage. Whatever their ambitions, Daviot's characters are uniformly reasonable, well-spoken, and understated whether in prosperity or defeat. Daviot's themes seem quite consistent: the superiority of an unpopular peace to self-defeating warfare, the perseverance of personal loyalties beneath the appearances of political expediency, the tendency of thrusts toward vengeance greed, and personal triumphs to break through moderation and good sense. The author's sympathies seem quite royalist and paternalistic, with barely concealed hostility toward democratic and fraternal ideals. Behind the plans of ambitious men work unseen the inexorable forces of a shaping historical vitality. (pp. 21-2)

The Laughing Woman is singular among Daviot's early full-length plays for its modern and unhistorical theme. In terms reminiscent of D. H. Lawrence, the author mismatches a high-minded and fairly reserved Northerner with a passionately direct Mediterranean. Their relationship is chaste and male-dominated, unlike *Sons and Lovers,* with a fairly predictable melodramatic ending. Daviot's group portraits of London artistes, their patrons and parasites are drawn with a fresh verve and comic malice. Although the conclusion of her play dips into the pathos [Sir John] Gielgud faulted later in ***The Stars Bow Down,*** Daviot reveals an unsuspected talent for crisp and tersely written romantic comedy.

Queen of Scots . . . follows ***Richard*** closely with another confused and impulsive royal failure from the Elizabethan period. (pp. 22-3)

Even more than ***Richard,*** [***Queen of Scots***] suggests the influence of George Bernard Shaw and Sean O'Casey. [Daviot] manages an artful mingling of commoner and aristocrat with authentic idioms proper to each. And her characters are strongly portrayed, though with a characteristic tendency to talk out rather than act out their passions, pushing violence offstage or leaving it to report. With some notable exceptions, conflict is muffled. We hear about Mary's brother's and courtiers' objections to Darnley, are told about Knox's confrontation with the Queen, and hear the briefest comment on the final disastrous battlefield defeat. Daviot's characters develop powerful personal loyalties, exhibit convincing rationales for their actions, and never slip into bawdy or curses. (p. 23)

In ***The Stars Bow Down*** . . . Daviot closely follows the biblical story of Joseph and his brothers, basing the title on her hero's famous dream in which the sun, moon, and eleven stars (one for each brother) bowed down to him. Yusef's (Joseph's) life is portrayed from adolescence when he is sold into slavery by his jealous brothers, is purchased by Potiphar at an Egyptian market, and rises quickly to become his master's highly efficient steward. (pp. 23-4)

Daviot has continued to mine historical veins with ***The Stars Bow Down,*** while returning to biblical matter of interest to British dramatists since the Mystery plays. Her conventions are drawn from the well-made play in her use of the successive rises and falls of fortune endured by her hero, stock characters such as the Pharaoh as doddering Senex ("old man"), the intriguing priest as biter-bit, the seductive siren, and country-boy-makes-good. Her mastery of dialogue which catches individual nuances of character is impressive, although the action proceeds in an even more leisurely way than that in her earlier two full-length plays. She attributes the play's failure to gain a production to unwillingness to stagger "with imitative gestures in the footsteps of genius," fearing that unfavorable parallels would be drawn between her play and a recent production of Sir James Barrie's *David* play. Daviot's deep interest in historical themes was linked in her mind to what Gielgud terms "her inability to write original plots" [see excerpt above, 1953], adding that she had been sued by the author of an historical novel about Richard the Second. Although the case was settled out of court, suggesting some degree of culpability on Daviot's part, the experience seems to have added to her shyness and spikiness. Daviot's consistent use of prose in her dramas, while T. S. Eliot and W. H. Auden were attempting to reintroduce verse into the theater, reflects an interest in films which far outran her involvement with legitimate theater, which she seldom saw.

After twelve years' absence from the stage, quite possibly prompted by charges of plagiarism and the unlucky coincidence of the production of James Barrie's *David* play just after the completion of ***The Stars Bow Down,*** Daviot published a thin volume of eight one-act plays [***Leith Sands, and Other Short Plays***]. . . . (pp. 24-5)

The short plays in this volume are typical of Daviot's taste for a wide range of comic types, a gift for witty Shavian riposte, and a weakness for neat and stagy curtains. She also is a shrewd and telling observer of hypocritical and impersonal institutions and deception. Her one-acts make economical use of box sets and small casts while she manages a nearly seamless blend of historical verisimilitude with timeless humorous foibles.

One of three posthumous collections of full-length plays was published in 1953, including ***The Little Dry Thorn, Valerius,*** and ***Dickon.*** Since no production records accompany the plays, though Daviot provides her future director with suggestions regarding setting and characterization, the plays were presumably written between 1946 and the author's death in 1952. (p. 27)

While it is impossible to place these plays either by order of composition or even to date them within the six-year period following the 1946 publication of her short plays, they are consistent with the subjects and themes of her earlier dramas. The Bible and English history, though pushed back to the Romans in Valerius, are drawn upon. Her central characters are leaders saddened by the loss of friends, defeated by unthinking opposition, and misunderstood by history. Except for ***The Little Dry Thorn,*** which focuses on the powerful personality of the biblical Sara, the plays relegate women to minor roles or omit them entirely. And Daviot's interest has shifted from youthful to middle-aged characters, perhaps consistent with her own process of aging.

Yet a second volume of plays by Gordon Daviot was published posthumously in 1954. It included three full-length plays, ***The Pomp of Mr. Pomfret, Cornelia,*** and ***Patria,*** along with three one-act plays, ***The Balwhinnie Bomb, The Pen of My Aunt,*** and ***The Princess Who Liked Cherry Pie.*** (p. 29)

While it is difficult to generalize about the development of Daviot's craft as a dramatist in this volume, subjects drawn from the Bible or past English history are absent. Her fondness for aristocrats, politicians, and soldiers is present in all these plays; and all but ***Patria*** provide women with leading roles. All are wryly or good-humoredly comic with detailed stage directions, revealing Daviot's continued interest in stage productions.

The last volume of Daviot's plays published after her death includes three full-length plays: ***Lady Charing is Cross, Sweet Coz,*** and ***Reckoning,*** along with two short plays, ***Barnharrow*** and ***The Staff Room.*** Except for ***Barnharrow,*** they are all set in the present century and combine a love interest with politics, religion, education, or a career. And each of them centers around the stripping away of illusion from a passionate, if confused, central female figure. (p. 32)

Daviot's sustained energy in the creation of drama is as notable as her connection with the Tey novels is unknown. Over a period of two decades, she created over two dozen short and full-length plays. From an artistic point of view her difficulties with plotting are balanced by her interest in biblical and historical actions. Her characters are fairly stock, and conflict rarely if ever bursts through her tightly controlled societies and highly capable prose. Although she probably would have preferred that a few of her plays never see print, she never gave up hope that her drama would receive thoughtful productions from sensitive production companies. (p. 34)

Mackintosh wrote three novels that were not mysteries under the Daviot pseudonym, and one biography. The works were not enthusiastically reviewed and have long been out of print. In the case of ***Kif: An Unvarnished History,*** this is regrettable. ***Kif*** was published in 1929, the same year as ***The Man in the Queue,*** though it was to all intents and purposes ignored in favor of the mystery novel. Perhaps readers were bored with novels about the impact of war on an individual, or perhaps the "unvarnished history" was too familiar and painful a reality. (p. 35)

In ***Kif,*** Daviot first presents the theme of honest rogue. This character appears frequently in her non-detective works and dramas. Surprisingly, he is used only in ***Brat Farrar*** and ***The Daughter of Time*** among the canon of eight mystery novels. This theme obviously aroused some deep and ambivalent feelings in the author.

Essentially, her approach is the same, whether dealing with Richard the Third or the unknown Kif. The central character (in this case *hero* is a most appropriate term) has a catalogue of admirable virtues—honesty, integrity, cleverness, sincerity, etc., in addition to one foible. In the case of Kif, it is his desire for adventure; Richard's is softheartedness regarding the Woodvilles. Obviously, these are scarcely severe drawbacks. Nonetheless, they inevitably bring about the temporary, if not permanent downfall of the individual. Daviot takes pains to point out that, while her hero may seem a criminal to most observers, he is either the victim of circumstance as Kif or Brat, or a misjudged combination of Daniel and Robin Hood, serving justice and good government against the wicked rebels. Their actions should not only be pardoned but praised, the author implies. Ironically, of the historical characters she attempted to vindicate, only Harry Morgan the privateer was officially recognized by his government as performing a useful and valuable function, being knighted as a reward.

Undoubtedly ***Kif*** deserves both reissue and careful study. As a psychological novel it fits neatly into the mainstream of literature between Joseph Conrad and Somerset Maugham. Kif, unable to control outer reality, is equally incapable of dealing with his inner tensions and conflicts. His quests for adventure, excitement, and understanding lead inevitably to an early death. Ironically, like most young men in modern literature, his quest is basically directionless. The reader can see its purpose and aim, but the questor himself is unaware of his goal.

Daviot's second traditional novel, ***Expensive Halo,*** is a disappointment. One expects more than a trite plot, absurd characters, unbelievable motivation, and a mechanical action from the author of ***The Man in the Queue*** and ***Kif.*** Published in 1931, ***Expensive Halo*** is a "woman's novel" in the pejorative sense. Full of improbable love affairs, a self-sacrificing mother, a spurned sweetheart, and a cruel father, the book resembles the bastard offspring of a literary coupling of P. G. Wodehouse and "The Perils of Pauline." (pp. 36-8)

Yet, there is no doubt that the writing of ***Expensive Halo*** was practical and instructive. On the one hand, Daviot discovered that the love story was not her strong suit. However, she also discovered both the virtues and the pitfalls of the doubling motif, while handling the intricacies of balanced and opposing characters. These devices were used successfully later in ***Brat Farrar*** where brothers and sisters interact in an atmosphere of dramatic tension lacking in ***Expensive Halo.***

Daviot's fascination with historical characters first emerged with the 1932 production of ***Richard of Bordeaux,*** foreshadowing the extremely successful ***The Daughter of Time*** which is concerned with the vindication of Richard III. Having used history as a basis for both fiction and drama, the author naturally turned to biography as well. In 1937, Gordon Daviot published her study of John Graham of Claverhouse. It was not a success, and she never again attempted straight biographical work.

Claverhouse covers a period of Scottish history from 1648 to approximately 1689, focusing on the life of John Graham, undoubtedly as unfamiliar to most Americans as to professional historians. A peg for every unpleasant legend according to Daviot, Claverhouse was the eldest son of a conservative family related to the Stewarts. When Charles returned to England, young Claverhouse at age twelve was made a burgess of the town of Dundee. Little is apparently known of his personal life, though the author makes character estimations based on various paintings—a favorite pastime of Inspector Grant in ***The Daughter of Time.*** Ultimately Dundee, as Claverhouse is called, becomes a soldier and officer and is sent by Charles II to deal with the Covenanters in Scotland. Like so many others, his battles against the rebels are inconclusive. According to Daviot, Dundee was not guilty of the cruelty and murderous acts with which he is apparently credited by tradition. Further, she suggests, the fact that he chose a life of responsibility and risk in the service of the king is to his credit. With his handsome manners and appearance, he could easily have been a successful court "climber." (pp. 39-40)

This biography's lack of public appeal is perhaps obvious. While the whole world has heard of Richard III, few individuals are aware of the existence, let alone significance, of John Graham of Claverhouse. Though obviously well researched, the style lacks the polish and balance usually associated with Daviot. Her foreshadowing, for example, is a heavy-handed attempt at sustaining interest where there is none. Finally, American readers will find the historical background obscure. English history before, during, and after Cromwell is difficult to follow at best. And Scottish history, influenced so thoroughly by England and the rebelling Covenanters, is nearly impossible without a detailed chronology. (p. 41)

Of Daviot's non-mystery novels, ***The Privateer*** stands out as the most compelling and readable. Written in the best romantic traditions, this swashbuckling study of "Harry" Morgan, privateer and/or buccaneer, deserves to be reissued. Of all the works written under either the Daviot or Tey names, this one would most easily translate into film. (p. 43)

Daviot captures the intensity and color of a turbulent era, drawing extremely fine distinctions between piracy and patriotism. Once again choosing an historic personage of tarnished reputation, she scrupulously polishes her hero into a gentleman. If not a scholar, Morgan is at least a clever, canny, inspiring leader. As Richard III was a much maligned, talented administrator, and Claverhouse a diplomatic, loyal rebel, so is the name of Henry Morgan cleared. Unlike ***Claverhouse,*** in which the reader and Dundee's personality are lost in the circumlocutions of Scottish history, ***The Privateer*** is more focused. Placed in the same period but centering in the Caribbean, the latter book concentrates more on the character of "Harry" Morgan and less on the history of Jamaica or the islands. Avoiding one of the problems of Claverhouse, Daviot does not attempt to describe Morgan's entire life. She concentrates instead on his progress from bondsman to privateer to knight. Of all her works, ***The Privateer*** is undoubtedly the most dramatic and suspenseful. (pp. 43-4)

In this final work, Daviot adds a surprising twist to her hero's character. Unlike Grant, Kif, Miss Pym, Brat Farrar, and all the others, Morgan is able to relate, communicate, and respond to individuals. He alone of all the Daviot/Tey characters has a believable, honest wife and devoted friends for whom he will put his life on the line. Doubtless the author's final painful and lonely year of life is reflected in this denial of isolation and withdrawal. (p. 44)

Kif, Claverhouse, and ***The Privateer,*** three of the Daviot non-detective works, deal with the theme of the "honest rogue." Daviot insists that appearances may lead the public to believe these men were thieves or murderers. In fact, they were victims of circumstance acting from the best of motives. Richard III in both the play and the Tey novel [***The Daughter of Time***] is also presented in this light. If Tey saw appearances as deceiving in real life, it was also true of history, she postulated.

If the reader were to make judgments regarding the author's philosophy by reading her works, some conclusions could be stated with certainty. Elizabeth Mackintosh was a conservative woman as are most writers of detective fiction. She was strongly in favor of a hard-nosed approach to law and order and felt, like some elected officials, that the press often hindered investigative work in government and was indeed "soft" on criminals. That she herself gave no personal interviews indicates the strength of her feelings. She had a deep distrust of blatantly religious individuals, fearing that they, like so many other aspects of life, would prove deceptive and disillusioning. People, objects, even places were often not what they seemed at all. A private girls school, so serene and Eden-like, could be a surprising setting for cold-blooded crime. History, too, was often misleading and inaccurate, accusing the innocent and pardoning the guilty—sometimes in fact making martyrs of them. Above all, these are the novels of a lonely woman, unable to communicate easily except through her writings. The final irony of her life is that she is remembered not for the dramas she loved, but for "her yearly knitting," the mystery novels she scorned. (p. 182)

Sandra Roy, in her Josephine Tey, *Twayne Publishers, 1980, 199 p.*

NANCY ELLEN TALBURT (essay date 1981)

[*Talburt is an American critic who has contributed articles to* Twentieth Century Crime and Mystery Writers *and is coeditor of an anthology of mystery stories. In the following excerpt from her essay on Tey in the collection* Ten Women of Mystery, *Talburt discusses Tey's examination of human suffering, particularly the innocent sufferers in her novels, and also notes the importance of history, the theater, and the independent woman in her works, which Talburt considers "well above" detective novels of the period.*]

Josephine Tey is justly remembered for ***The Daughter of Time,*** for her subject in it is the most famous murder in English history—that of the princes in the Tower—and her treatment makes use of the most popular fictional form of her day, that of the detective novel.

Although the novel is unrivaled in its pioneering adaptation of detecting to history, and splendidly audacious in its least-likely-suspect as villain, Henry VII of England, evaluations of Tey's success in writing a novel to match her ingenious subject have varied. Dilys Winn picks it as one of the five best detective novels. . . . Julian Symons finds the book "really rather dull" [see excerpt above, 1972]. (p. 42)

Despite her versatility and her reputation as the author of one of the classics of detective fiction, Josephine Tey and her eight diverse and meticulously-written mysteries remain less known than the lives and works of her most famous contemporaries. The reason for this state of things seems clear. There is no great detective in Tey's novels, and there is no series of dazzling and intricate plots. Her use of the traditions of detective fiction is discriminating, informed and effective, but while in many particulars her novels are typical of this tradition, in other ways, such as in her consistent and perceptive exploration of the theme of imperiled innocence, they achieve a unique statement which transcends, and sometimes obscures, their nominal adherence to rule and formula. (pp. 42-3)

Tey began her career with the publication of poems and short pieces, of which two, a ghost story and an account of a violent murder by a woman, suggest an early interest in the mystery. (p. 44)

Her mystery writing was essentially concentrated in the last six years of her life when she published the best, and six out of a total of eight, of her mystery novels. The two earlier novels are competently done, and the first achieves a surprising, though non-detected, climax. ***The Man in the Queue,*** which introduces Detective Inspector Alan Grant of Scotland Yard, explores the favored conventions of contemporary detective novels and ends on a note which brings into question the entire process of "detection." Her second [***A Shilling for Candles***], published at the end of a period of great success as a dramatist, makes a second attempt to illustrate detection but comes instead to focus on the character and relationships of the dead girl. It concludes with a solution confirmed by physical evidence (a button torn from a coat) but arrived at by a chance occurrence and the drawing of a very uncertain inference. Alfred Hitchcock's favorite among his British films, *Young and Innocent* (1937), was based on this novel.

Of the six novels published at the end of her life, the most inspired may be ***The Daughter of Time,*** but the best executed of her novels, and the richest in general interest, is ***The Franchise Affair.*** In it, the eighteenth-century disappearance of Elizabeth Canning is represented in contemporary terms in a novel whose serious theme, the vulnerability of the innocent, is perfectly complemented by the surface lightness of its treatment. This surface is achieved by the skillful combining of an amateur detective (a country solicitor), a cool courtship and the devastating but comic tongue of old Mrs. Sharpe. There is a touch of parody in the treatment of the "artists" among whom the crime in ***To Love and Be Wise*** occurs, and the basic plot stratagem is quite bold. Deduction, reader involvement, fairly-shared clues, and the stunning climax make this novel remarkable. (pp. 44-5)

Standard mystery fiction does exist to produce suspense, to display suspicion of the innocent and the apparent innocence of the guilty until the conclusion, and to depict ill-treated victim and suspects. Tey's practice, on the other hand, is to extend the number of the sufferers, to extend the range of sufferings, and, more important, to reveal the character of her detectives by their participation in the sufferings of others, some of which they cause. Most important, these trials of the innocent raise questions concerning the nature of the world where the innocent suffer so regularly, and so much, and in many novels, no resolution is possible of the sort which regularly dispenses happiness to the innocent and punishment to the guilty at the conclusion of the classic detective novel.

The sufferings of Tey's characters go much beyond the social discomfort of being avoided by one's suspicious acquaintances or having to answer the sharply put questions of the Yard. Innocent sufferers represent every class of character: victim, suspect, criminal and detective. Some victims are wholly innocent (Patrick in [***Brat Farrar***], the princes in ***Time,*** Christine Clay in ***Shilling***). This is often not the case in detective fiction, where the sorrow for the death of the victim must not be allowed to detract from the interest in the investigation of the murder. Thus Roger Ackroyd is stingy, Philip Boyes is self-centered, and the King of Bohemia is a fool, though neither of the two former deserve being murdered. Even when innocent, the victim suffers off-stage, and death is instantaneous in most classic mysteries. (pp. 48-9)

In Tey's third novel the treatment of an innocent sufferer achieves a high point. No one who reads the novel will be likely to forget the sufferings of Mary Innes [(***Miss Pym Disposes***)], whom the detective sentences to an extra-legal lifetime of restitution. Mary is first denied her deserved professional appointment by a prejudiced head mistress. Then she discovers that her best friend has committed murder on her behalf. The resolution of this novel is far from the return to innocence and order of the typical detective novel. The resolution of the fourth novel (***Franchise***), though less harsh, is similar. The innocent women lose their peaceful life and the means, their house and possessions, to an independence which they had only lately received and had much prized. The lightness of treatment and their strength and ability to cope do not detract from the resolution of this novel in which the regaining of their good name cannot begin to compensate them for their wholly undeserved losses. (p. 49)

There are other uses of the suffering of the innocent in Tey, and it becomes one of her most consistent motifs, even when it is not the central theme of a novel. The regular appearance of this situation lessens the distance usually maintained between reader and what are often rather two-dimensional characters in much of detective fiction, and it is their ability to feel and their vulnerability to suffering which distinguish Tey's detectives.

Beyond her emphasis on the trials of the innocent, Tey's uses of the basic elements of detective fiction are less consistently unusual although all of her novels possess some important singularity. (p. 50)

Tey's primary difference from the pattern established by her famous peers is easy to spot. There is no great detective in her works. No one asks for an ''Alan Grant'' novel, or ever did. No ''biography'' of his life appears in any of the standard lists (*The Book of Sleuths, The Great Detectives*).

Detective Inspector Alan Grant does share the basic qualities of the gentlemen detectives of the twenties and thirties: financial and domestic independence, sartorial elegance, educated palate, ease in most surroundings and appearance: ''If Grant had an asset beyond the usual ones of devotion to duty and a good supply of brains and courage, it was that the last thing he looked like was a police officer.'' . . . His distinguishing feature is a Scottish ancestry. Like his peers he also has a special detecting technique (comparable to Poirot's ''little grey cells'') called ''flair.'' Unlike Poirot, Grant is often taxed concerning his ''flair,'' especially by his superiors: ''Now, look here, Grant. Flair's flair. And you're entitled to your whack of it. But when you take to throwing it about in chunks it becomes too much of a good thing. Have a little moderation, for Pete's sake.'' . . . The flair consists of an ability to read faces, an approach to apparent dead ends consisting of leaving them alone and returning later (mentally), and an ability which is never described but which consists of his quick perception of the essence of what is going on, whether or not, at the time, he understands what he sees. . . . In the first novel in which he appears, Grant chases the wrong man across most of Britain to a confrontation in the Highlands in which the innocent man nearly dies. At the end of the novel, Grant thinks: ''It had been so clear a case where evidence was concerned . . . he had been saved by the skin of his teeth and a woman's fair dealing . . . his thought went back over the trail that had led them so far wrong.'' . . . Grant's case is perfect, but wrong. If not for a totally unexpected confession from a completely unsuspected person, Grant's evidence would have hanged an innocent man. Similarly, in the second novel, Grant corners a suspect in his hotel room, and, while Grant watches, the suspect escapes. It is the carefully-sought evidence provided by a girl which demolishes Grant's case against this suspect. In a very minor role, he prepares the Yard's case against the two innocent women in ***The Franchise Affair,*** a case which is demolished in court. Of the last three novels in which he appears, one is spent entirely in a hospital bed (alone), and one is spent on sick leave as Grant struggles with claustrophobia brought on by overwork. As early as the second novel he is reported wishing that ''he was one of these marvelous creatures of super-instinct and infallible judgment who adorned the pages of detective stories, and not just a hard-working, well-meaning, ordinarily intelligent Detective Inspector.'' . . . (pp. 50-1)

Despite this somewhat overstated catalogue of Grant's shortcomings, it appears that divinity was intended to enter in at the nativity of the character, but that a writer of Tey's particular interests and talent ultimately found more appealing the vicissitudes of a more nearly mortal character. He is plainly intended to represent a superior (both logical and imaginative rather than plodding) approach to detection, contrasting with his associates and superiors as Dupin contrasts with Monsieur G., the Prefect of Police. His official ''Watson'' is described: ''Williams was his opposite and his complement. . . . But he had terrier qualities that were invaluable in a hunt. . . . To Williams, Grant was everything that was brilliant and spontaneous.'' . . . Grant has a different ''Watson'' in each of the last two novels; in each case a young American is cast in the role and is duly impressed by the chance to sit at the feet of Scotland Yard. Each has a personal interest in the hunt and both are amateurs (any ''Watson'' might be considered, by definition, to be an ''amateur,'' of course). (pp. 51-2)

Tey is ahead of her time in recognizing while writing her first novel the limitations of the fiction in which the great detective is the center. Later, when her best works were written following the second World War, the frame and shape of things seemed so badly torn that not even a great detective could put them right. The great detective's lack of personal and even sexual relationships was no longer quite plausible, and the grotesquely distinguishing eccentricities of many series figures was an embarrassment. Though he remains an understatement, Grant's capacity for indignation and suffering make him sufficiently human to support his function as Tey's detective.

Tey's amateur detectives are more colorful than Alan Grant, although each appears in only one novel. (p. 53)

Miss Lucy Pym, comfort-loving author of a best seller, shrinks from the role of Providence which her fortuitous possession of otherwise unknown facts assigns to her. She is inquisitive and observant despite a natural indolence and the philosophy that one of the compensations of middle age is not having to do anything uncomfortable. A former schoolmistress and a temporary lecturer in a girls' school, she detects a furtiveness in the behavior of a student during an exam. She prevents the girl's cheating and later discovers the notes that were to have been used. When she discards the evidence of this crime, she sets in motion events which are widely destructive. . . . By using her detecting abilities and deciding upon extra-legal justice of her own devising rather than the punishments of the law, Lucy Pym precipitates tragedy. The apparent wisdom of providing for mitigating circumstances rather than accepting the even-handed and blind justice of the law turns to folly. The results are a stark statement on the very popular tradition in detective fiction of "playing god." . . . Unlike Grant, Pym must live with the knowledge that her wrong case against Mary Innes has resulted in a permanent punishment of the innocent. But what other solution existed? The conclusion of this novel is especially provocative when compared with the resolution of the typical detective novel. And it is not altogether surprising that this is Miss Pym's only venture into detection. (pp. 53-4)

Robert Blair is the only one of Tey's detectives to be given the dual roles of investigator and suitor. In both ***The Franchise Affair*** and Sayers' *Strong Poison,* the detective defends a woman accused of a crime, falls in love with her, and is rejected by her when the reader has been thinking (as Blair does, deep inside) that she would be doing pretty well to accept. Similarly, the ironic mockery that Marion directs toward Blair is very much like that which Harriet uses as a barrier between herself and Lord Peter. Blair is drawn with little subtlety, but his greatest virtue is his enjoyment of, and recognition of the justice of, Marion's mockery of his easeful life. Despite his successes, he too must accept providential help (as Grant does) in achieving a case which will not only free the innocent but also convict the guilty. (pp. 54-5)

The plots of Tey's novels do not confer upon them that sort of indelible stamp which would cause readers to enter a bookstore and ask for "another Tey" as they do for another Christie. One perfect subject, ***The Daughter of Time,*** and one perfect and Ackroydal deceit, ***To Love and Be Wise,*** notwithstanding, Tey's plots are not generally what make her novels memorable. (p. 55)

Historically, chance or accident and suicide have been frowned upon as agents of discovery. The appearance is preserved that the intelligence of the detective is responsible for linking otherwise disparate elements of a case, or for providing the imaginative hypothesis whose testing will elicit the necessary information, or for escaping the confines of a limited view to see things in a new, true perspective and so solve the crime.

In Tey's novels, vital information often comes into the novel through the agency of Providence, the Press or the Public. The Press may be used by the police to circulate information and ask for public assistance, and the detective may then be given credit if such information is forthcoming. On the other hand, if an undesired newspaper story, like that pillorying the Sharpes, turns out to have positive effects, then Providence, or the Public, must be credited with the development, rather than the police. Providence may also be given credit for the solution to a murder which results from confession—Mrs. Wallis' confession, Simon's confession (once Brat has accused him), Beau's claiming of the shoe ornament, Heron Lloyd's confession. In five of her eight novels, Tey makes use of at least one confession. Two of these simply tidy things up: Frankie Chadwick's confession explains Betty Kane's fresh bruises, and Heron Lloyd's confession arrives with details just before Grant learns from his own discoveries that Lloyd's fingerprints were on the books of the murdered man. However, Mrs. Wallis' confession and Beau's are vital to the conclusions of the novels in which they occur. Without them, both novels would end with the reader as well as the detective left in the dark. (pp. 55-6)

Several of the novels make use of an inversion of the normal sequence of events in detective fiction. In ***The Franchise Affair*** we assume the innocence of the accused and must proceed from the related hypothesis that the victim is really a criminal. This is a kind of inversion, though not the usual kind where the criminal is revealed and the reader's interest centers upon reconstruction, alone. A similar kind of inversion actually occurs, and is suggested by a barrage of clues, in ***To Love and Be Wise.*** Here, the ambiguity of the character of Leslie Searle may seem partly to account for his murder but actually provides numerous clues as to what really happened. In ***Brat Farrar*** the reader participates from the beginning in the scheme to defraud the Ashbys. Indeed, so involved does Tey make the reader that the chief interest in this adventure novel is not in what happened to Patrick, but in what will happen to the deserving, though criminal, Brat, when his imposture is, as it must be, discovered.

Clues mislead the reader and the detective. That is what they are put in detective fiction to do. The real clues should not appear to be clues at all—until the conclusion, that is. The best use of clues in Tey occurs in ***To Love and Be Wise,*** where they bombard the reader. Physical clues confirm the guilt of the killer in ***A Shilling for Candles.*** The clue which leads to her identity is a newspaper columnist's comment. Physical clues such as the blood on the dagger from the killer's hand play a large part in an era just before blood typing would have prevented the misuse of such information. A new lipstick and fresh bruises provide good clues to the questionable nature of Betty Kane's story. A wrong initial inference from clues (B Seven's poem) provides Grant a return of his health and the reader with a tour of the Hebrides, before the sands in the poem are equated with the Arabian desert rather than the Hebrides. The novel is much lengthened by this false trail.

In ***The Daughter of Time*** the nature of the subject produces an unusual plot. This novel is an excellent example of the difference between subject (story) and plot. The clues have been gone for hundreds of years. No one can be interrogated. Everyone involved is already dead. . . . Here the focus must be on the investigation. An idea more potentially fascinating than the innocence of Richard III is emphasized. History is not fixed or set. It is not always true. It is, in fact, filled (American,

Scottish and English history) with misinterpretations, half-truths and venerated scoundrels. The theme of the novel is its most important element, and the theme is *The Prevalence of Tonypandy*. Grant's painstaking reconstruction begins with an inversion, his doubt of Richard's guilt, and concludes with a comment on the origins of some kinds of "history."

Whatever the final disposition of clues, turns, surprises, climaxes and denouements, the satisfying conclusion to an engaging work is what counts with most readers. The early days of detective fiction saw the unnatural elevation of plot to the end which justified the novel. Tey's novels, flawed as the plots seem to be from this perspective, satisfy interests other than that for puzzle, although they do contain sufficient suspense and staggered and staggering developments to sustain the interest of any but the complete puzzle addict. And if Tey employs the *deus ex machina* consistently, at least the shape in which he appears varies significantly.

The exotic and flamboyant master criminal, the Moriarty or Fu Manchu, would be as much out of place in Tey's fictions as his counterpart, the Great Detective. . . . Likewise, the most bizarre crime is the stabbing in the back with an Italian dagger of a man in a theatre queue. In treating criminals and in devising crimes, Tey's methods are as restrained and her materials as realistic and lacking in melodrama as is her delineation of her detectives and her developing of plot. . . . There are, on the other hand, a number of surprises in her novels in which the original crime turns out not to be a crime, and another crime is discovered. In two of the best novels, this development reverses the roles of criminal and victim. (pp. 56-8)

Women and children are first in Tey; she uses a woman or an adolescent as the criminal in the first six of her eight novels. She is more consistent with tradition in having her criminals most often find their just desserts outside the punishment of the law, through accident, suicide or through having committed a justifiable crime from which they will somehow be spared the consequences. The use of the motivation of friendship or love—the altruistic motive—and her use of the adolescent as a morally responsible agent of death or malice are her best achievements in treating the criminal. Beau Nash and Betty Kane are particularly chilling beings.

A victim, like a proper Victorian child, should be seen but not heard. Slight acquaintance on the part of the reader prevents messy sympathy from intruding.

A prominent feature of the detective fiction of Josephine Tey is an identification of victim and suspect. Victims turn out to be suspect, as victims, and suspects are threatened, victimized and imperiled, becoming VICTIMS. Official victims have the traditional minor role, except as a reconstructed personality. Nevertheless, the VICTIMS (persecuted innocents who are not the apparent victims of the central or main crime with which the plot is concerned) are found in every category of character, from detective to such minor characters as Mrs. Wynn (Betty Kane's foster mother) and Zoe Kentallen (victim of high taxes, small inheritance, and widowhood—as well as an abruptly curtailed romance with Grant).

There is a natural correspondence of victim and suspect when suicide or careless accident is believed to be the cause of death, as in the deaths of Patrick Ashby and Bill Kenrick. But a cardinal rule of detective fiction is that suicide and accident are not allowed as causes of the chief death. Victims in the Tey novels are not always easily identifiable. The apparent victim in the first novel (***Queue***) is the murdered man. But since he is intent upon killing someone else, and is forestalled by his own death, he cannot be classified unequivocally as victim. On the other hand the woman who actually stabs him to death is herself the VICTIM of a maternally blind view of her actress daughter. In a real sense, Bert Sorrell is a VICTIM of the actress. (pp. 60-1)

In two novels (***Franchise*** and ***Love***) Tey makes the supposed victim the perpetrator of a hoax, and thus the criminal, instead. Both these situations are interesting, although only one involves a surprise. The real victims in each book are the accused criminals, in fact, so that the reversal is complete. The Sharpes are plainly VICTIMS, losing their home and possessions after being subjected to abuse and mob violence. Walter Whitmore is the only VICTIM who might be said to have benefitted (or perhaps it is only his fiance who benefits) from his VICTIMization. (p. 61)

There are second VICTIMS in two novels (***Pym*** and ***Franchise***). Mary Innes is first devastated by not receiving the appointment she deserves for her exceptionally fine record in school, and then by an accusation and punishment for a crime she did not commit. This particular inversion of roles is among Tey's best achievements. The other VICTIM is Mrs. Wynn, whose experience during the trial of her foster daughter is described as a "crucifixion."

In Tey's world, the suspect's lot is not a happy one. And for Inspector Grant, the wrongly-accused person is a recurring nightmare. Whether for readers of detective fiction the criminal serves as a scapegoat for the punishment of a common sin, the suspects in a murder novel are often far from innocent. Still, it is usually true that their guilts do not include involvement in the primary crime. (pp. 61-2)

Grant's flair operates to give him a just assessment of all those he suspects. But he can never disregard the physical evidence that the detective novel of Tey's time seems to be all about. He is a sensitive and reasonable man, caught as detective in a world where figures are supposed to be two-dimensional ciphers, constantly finding his judgment of faces, personalities and other reflections of character refuted by some bit of button, or scar, or left-handedness, or shoe in the river, or suitcase, or legacy. The tension between Grant's judgment and the physical evidence which he collects is one of the graces of Tey's fiction. Her substitution of a detailed and sympathetic presentation of the trials of one suspect for the interrogation and investigation of several red herrings is a major departure from detective tradition and the basis for her favorite theme, the trials of the innocent. Her discerning exploration of the suspect as victim, and her extension of peril to detectives and supposed criminals, provides a new dimension to the arrangement of the basic elements of detective fiction which essentially retain their traditional forms in her novels but which are combined to make new statements and raise new questions. (pp. 62-3)

Tey was not an avowed feminist, but the lives of her main female characters are a feminist statement. They are all happily Not Married. (p. 72)

Four women in Tey's mystery fiction represent a balanced range of reactions to the non-married state, and many minor characters buttress the positions taken by the primary four.

The reasons of each of the four for not being married indicate this range. Marta Hallard has no room in her life for Alan Grant—she plans to become a "Dame," not a "Mrs." Lucy Pym thinks wistfully of being cherished for a change, but is brought up short at the thought that the cherishing would have to be mutual, "she would inevitably have to mend socks, for instance. She didn't like feet." . . . There are several reasons why Marion Sharpe refuses the proposal of Robert Blair: "For one, if a man is not married by the time he is forty, then marriage is not one of the things he wants out of life. Just something that has overtaken him; like flu and rheumatism and income-tax demands. I don't want to be just something that has overtaken you." . . . She goes on to tell Blair . . . that she would not be an asset to his law practice, that he has his aunt and she, her mother, with whom they are accustomed to living. But her last reason is the most revealing: "You see, I am *not* a marrying woman. I don't want to have to put up with someone else's crotchets, someone else's demands. . . . There are a hundred thousand women just panting to look after some man's cold, why pick on me?" . . . Lee Searle makes no comment on the subject, possibly because she has the most original and compelling reason of the four—it would surely be inconvenient to someone habituated to spending half the year as a man (a photographer) and half as a woman (a painter) to be encumbered with a husband. (pp. 72-3)

Unlike the other three, Marion Sharpe has no career. Perhaps she is the only one with the leisure for romance. Marion can hardly be considered modern and is far from being a superwoman. Her "shapes" don't stand up, and she has no career. Nevertheless, she is sensible, perceptive and strong. Unconcerned about housework and cooking, she still has the necessary taste and tact to provide appropriately when necessary for guests. She drives a golfball like a man. To Robert Blair, she looks the sort of woman who would have a stake as her natural prop, if stakes were not out of fashion. When she is told she should have been a nurse, she says: "Not me. I have no patience with people's fads. But I might have been a surgeon." . . . Her gentle mocking of Blair's easy life and formal manner make their "courtship" an entertaining spectacle. When he asks her to marry him (on the ninth green—his plan to ask her in the club house over tea is spoiling his game), and she declines what might be thought a handsome offer, it is perfectly clear that the territory of this novel is not that of ordinary popular fiction. . . .

The Not-Married woman adds a quality to Tey's fiction which takes it beyond the normal boundaries of its kind and time. She is not to be confused with the bright and forthright girl, heir of Beatrice and Rosaline, who appears rather more often in detective fiction (and elsewhere in Tey). She is older (in her thirties and forties) and wiser, and she does not use her wits and energy to attract the right man—she uses them to make and enjoy her own way in the world. (p. 74)

The world of Josephine Tey's mysteries is shaped by a special vision. It also obeys most of the rules which were never written down for members of its exclusive club. Proper language and dress are mandatory. Corrupt police and detectives are not allowed. There is a proper place for everyone, and the social order must not be overturned. Force will not prevail over reason. The *Id* will not triumph over the *Super-ego*. Progress and the superiority of western culture over primitive or eastern cultures are assumed. These rules are seldom questioned in the classic detective novel, and the possibility of alternate views seldom intrudes. But in the works of Tey, some innocent people do suffer, some of the guilty do escape justice, and Robert Blair may not live happily ever after. There is a network of fine cracks in the restored world to which the characters are returned at the end of her novels. (p. 75)

While the readability of Tey's novels derives partly from her improvisations on the standard traditions of mystery fiction, it is primarily her exploration of the sufferings of the innocent and the reflections of her personal experience and views of the theatre, history and women which raise her works well above the level of the average detective novel. She produces a sense of quiet drama in her novels, in splendidly realized scene after scene. The characters come alive, not as deep and complex creations or always as very clever figures in drawing room comedy, but as human figures observantly drawn, caught momentarily up in a small crisis. There are many slight turns in Tey's best novels, and she has an ability to maintain pace and momentum without the more artificial aids such as a body to end each chapter. Moreover, throughout every work is the humorously ironic observation of all that occurs. There is, in fact, more variety and originality in her eight novels than in many longer shelves of her contemporaries' works, and her place in detective fiction is secure. (pp. 75-6)

Nancy Ellen Talburt, "Josephine Tey," in Ten Women of Mystery, *edited by Earl F. Bargainner, Bowling Green State University Popular Press, 1981, pp. 42-76.*

ADDITIONAL BIBLIOGRAPHY

Champion, Larry S. "Myth and Counter-myth: The Many Faces of Richard III." In *A Fair Day in the Affections: Literary Essays in Honor of Robert B. White, Jr.*, edited by Jack D. Durant and M. Thomas Hester, pp. 37-54. Raleigh: Winston Press, 1980.

Comparison of *Daughter of Time* with historical documents. While Champion's investigation covers the same materials mentioned in the excerpt by Guy M. Townsend (1977), the conclusion he draws closely parallels that of M. J. Smith (1977), which supports a novelist's prerogative to manipulate and introduce new material in a work of historical fiction.

Charney, Hanna. *The Detective Novel of Manners: Hedonism, Morality, and the Life of Reason.* Rutherford, N.J.: Fairleigh Dickinson University Press, 1981, 125 p.*

Tey's works mentioned throughout. Charney also discusses *Daughter of Time*, noting the import readers and writers of detective fiction place on the lives and reputations of both historical and fictional characters.

Mann, Jessica. "Josephine Tey." In her *Deadlier than the Male: Why Are English Women So Good at Murder?*, pp. 210-17. New York: Macmillan Publishing Co., 1981.

Discussion of wit, clarity, and other aspects of Tey's style.

Rollyson, Carl E., Jr. "The Detective As Historian: Josephine Tey's *Daughter of Time*." *Iowa State Journal of Research* 53, No. 1 (August 1978): 21-30.

Examines Tey's scholarly methods and conclusions in *Daughter of Time*. Rollyson argues that while the form of the novel closely follows the process of historical investigation, the specific methods and conclusions it depicts are questionable.

Young, Stark. "Three Serious Plays." *The New Republic* LXXVIII, No. 1006 (14 March 1934): 134.*

Generally favorable review of *Richard of Bordeaux*. Young discusses the presentation of characters and dramatic events, drawing parallels to other dramatic treatments of Richard II.

Nathanael West

1903(?)-1940

(Born Nathan Weinstein) American novelist, screenwriter, dramatist, and editor.

Courtesy of Jay Martin

West was a prominent American novelist whose works portray the despair and alienation that many writers and artists have found the prevalent characteristics of twentieth-century existence. Regarded as a stylistic innovator whose works fit no standard literary classification, he combined elements of both traditional literary Naturalism and the new technique of Surrealism in the two novels for which he is best known, *Miss Lonelyhearts* and *The Day of the Locust*. In these, West introduced a distorted, grotesque kind of humor that has led critics to call his novels the forerunners in modern American literature of Surrealism and black humor. West's profoundly negative world view acutely reflects the era in which the author wrote, the Great Depression.

West was born in New York City to fairly well-to-do Lithuanian-Jewish immigrants. He was an undistinguished student, who failed to graduate from high school and was later dismissed from Tufts College because of poor attendance. However, the illegally obtained transcript of an older student with a similar name—and better grades—enabled West to transfer to Brown University, where he earned an English degree. After graduation, he worked briefly in his father's construction business before persuading his family to finance a visit to Europe. West spent two or three months in Paris before dwindling finances compelled him to return to New York, where he worked as manager of Kenmore Hall and later the Sutton Club, two hotels owned by his uncles. West allowed writers who found themselves short of funds to lodge at the Sutton for a nominal rent—or for free—and James T. Farrell, Erskine Caldwell, Lillian Hellman, and Dashiell Hammett were among those who availed themselves of West's generosity. It was while working at the Sutton that West wrote his first novel, *The Dream Life of Balso Snell*. This work was published in a limited edition of five hundred copies and received little critical or popular attention. In 1932 West ventured into publishing, joining William Carlos Williams in coediting the journal *Contact,* of which only three issues appeared. The next year West, with the German artist George Grosz, launched a similarly short-lived publication, *Americana*.

After the humorist S. J. Perelman married West's sister Laura, the three of them bought a farm in Pennsylvania, where West wrote his second novel, *Miss Lonelyhearts*. Although favorably reviewed, *Miss Lonelyhearts* was one of the last books brought out by Liveright before that publisher declared bankruptcy. As a result, few copies were distributed under the Liveright imprint, and a second printing of the novel sold poorly. West found that he required a more regular income than that provided by the sale of his novels, and, encouraged by Perelman—who in the early 1930s was a successful Hollywood screenwriter—he began work in the film industry. He was quickly disillusioned by what he had imagined would be a glamorous job; though well paid, he felt he was rudely treated, and he resented the fact that his work was subjected to revision without his knowledge. However, after the indifferent critical reception and meager sales of his third novel, *A Cool Million; or, The Dismantling of Lemuel Pitkin,* he determined to continue screenwriting. His experiences in Hollywood provided the material for his last novel, *The Day of the Locust*. Shortly after this work was published, West met and married Eileen McKenney, who had served as the subject of Ruth McKenney's popular *New Yorker* sketches that were adapted as the play *My Sister Eileen*. Eight months after their marriage, both were killed in an automobile accident.

West's first and third novels, *The Dream Life of Balso Snell* and *A Cool Million,* are generally regarded by critics as his weakest works and have not received the amount of critical attention given his other novels. Since the publication in 1957 of West's collected novels, however, each of these works has been to some extent reevaluated. *The Dream Life of Balso Snell* was greatly influenced by French Surrealism and evokes the literary and cultural mood of the American expatriate community living in Paris in the 1920s. The novel is a satiric denunciation of literary and artistic poses and poseurs, each represented by a character encountered by Balso Snell as he journeys through the bowels of the Trojan Horse. The episodic nature of the narrative led many early reviewers to criticize the work as disjointed and essentially formless. West's biographer Jay Martin, however, finds that the form of *Balso Snell* indicated West's early realization that "he would need to invent new literary forms and attitudes to express, for the modern sensibility, moral indignation without righteousness, and a tragic sense without a vision of redemption.'' Most criticism of the novel written since the 1960s has been much more favorable than earlier evaluations, which tended, in part because of West's liberal use of scatological humor, to dismiss *Balso Snell* as a piece of juvenilia, an obvious ''first novel.'' In his critical study of West, Carter M. Cramer finds that most commentators have erred in analyzing as a novel a work which should more properly be classified as a satire. From the perspective of the 1970s Cramer has concluded that ''in West's decade, no more strident satirical attack against artistic foolishness exists in American letters.''

A Cool Million has received the more thorough critical reexamination of West's two lesser-known novels. It is most often interpreted as a parody of the classic American success story popularized in the late nineteenth-century novels of Horatio Alger. In the typical Alger story, a young man armed only with complete honesty, a total lack of guile, and an earnest desire to do good, sets out to make his fortune, attaining wealth, love, and happiness through a series of unlikely adventures. In West's reversal of this ''luck and pluck'' formula, his ingenuous hero is unequal to the obstacles he faces and gradually undergoes his ''dismantling''—the loss of an eye, his teeth, a thumb, a leg, his scalp, and eventually his life. *A Cool Million* is written in a pastiche of Alger's style; in fact, one critic has shown that dozens of passages from *A Cool Million* are almost word-for-word recreations of sections from several of Alger's works. Indeed, some critics have found this novel's greatest fault to be the absence of a style of West's own. However, T. R. Steiner has noted that ''it is . . . meaningless to talk of West's style in this book, since his effort must have been to divest himself of style, to become a scarcely literate and dirty-minded adolescent'' in order to thoroughly comprehend and satirize the fiction produced for that segment of the population. Steiner writes that *A Cool Million* is West's least appreciated, because least understood, work. In it, West was presenting not only a skewed version of the ''rags to riches'' myth, but also ''a whole series of American motifs, fictions, and myths, American Dreams certainly, but also American Nightmares.'' The work has also been called an American *Candide* and is often likened to a tradition of grotesque comedy that has as its leading exemplars Edgar Allan Poe, Franz Kafka, and Nikolai Gogol.

Miss Lonelyhearts is generally considered West's most artistically accomplished work. It is the story of a male newspaper advice columnist who becomes obsessed with the suffering of his correspondents and his inability to help them. West has said that the inspiration for this novel came from actual letters shown to him by an advice columnist and from the lives of the transients he observed as a hotel manager. West originally conceived of *Miss Lonelyhearts* as ''a novel in the form of a comic strip,'' with each chapter the equivalent of a cartoon panel, in which one action instigates many reactions. Although he abandoned this idea, he wrote that ''each chapter instead of going forward in time, also goes backward, forward, up and down in space like a picture.'' The novel deals with the loneliness, alienation, despair, and violence that were concomitant with the financial disasters of the 1930s and which, according to Thomas H. Jackson, West saw as ''definitive qualities of modern life.'' Martin has observed that the lonelyhearts columnist was the perfect symbol of the times, and most critics concur that West's decision to identify his protagonist only as Miss Lonelyhearts served to underscore the dehumanizing character of the times by equating the person with his public function.

The Day of the Locust has often been called the finest novel about Hollywood to come out of Hollywood, and subsequent books about the film industry are often compared with it. Critics generally agree that this work demonstrates development in West's skills as a novelist. V. S. Pritchett, for example, called it ''an advance from fable and from fragments of people, to the courageous full statement of the novel.'' West found in Hollywood a representative sampling of everything he believed was wrong with American culture. Within the microcosm of the film capital, West further narrowed his focus to encompass the lives of those whom Edmund Wilson called ''nondescript characters on the edges of the Hollywood studios.'' *The Day of the Locust* differed from other Hollywood novels of the same era, such as F. Scott Fitzgerald's *The Last Tycoon,* in that it is not about the rich and famous—the powerful and influential movie stars and studio executives—but about common people whose dreams are manufactured and manipulated by the movies, and who, West believed, harbored a fierce hatred behind their ostensible adoration of movie stars.

Until the renewal of interest in West in the late 1950s, most critics considered him a minor novelist. Many still insist upon such a classification because of the narrow range of his themes and subjects. However, Randall Reid has demonstrated that, within the limits allowed by his bleak and pessimistic vision, West is a ''complex, wide-ranging, and subtle'' author. His experimental style also caused his works to be overlooked during his lifetime by critics and readers who favored literary Naturalism. West was neither realistic enough to be classified as a Naturalist nor concerned enough with character to have found favor with the proponents of Naturalism's successor, the psychological novel. Because his works are both unclassifiable and stylistically innovative, West has been a difficult author to place within a literary tradition. Similarly, the extent of his influence on later writers is not easily ascertainable. Although not generally found to have been a direct literary influence on subsequent writers, West is noted as one of the progenitors—perhaps the earliest—of black humor and the grotesque in modern American fiction. He has been described by Cramer as second only to Faulkner as ''the most experimental American novelist of any importance to write his major works during the bleak decade of the Great Depression.''

(See also *TCLC,* Vol. 1; *Contemporary Authors,* Vol. 104; *Dictionary of Literary Biography,* Vol. 4: *American Writers in Paris, 1920-1939;* Vol. 9: *American Novelists, 1910-1945;* and Vol. 28: *Twentieth-Century American-Jewish Fiction Writers.*)

PRINCIPAL WORKS

The Dream Life of Balso Snell (novel) 1931
Miss Lonelyhearts (novel) 1933
A Cool Million; or, The Dismantling of Lemuel Pitkin (novel) 1934
The Day of the Locust (novel) 1939
The Complete Works of Nathanael West (novels) 1957

CONTEMPO **(essay date 1931)**

[*The following excerpt is a favorable review of West's first novel,* The Dream Life of Balso Snell.]

[***The Dream Life of Balso Snell***] is a first novel. And, considering the usual unevenness of first novels, Mr. West has effected a splendid and craftsmanlike book. Perhaps it would be rather impertinent to call this facile, buoyant book a novel, but whatever the author ordains to baptize his work it is, not too superlatively, a distinguished performance in sophisticated writing. True, there is nothing tremendously significant in it either of style or technique. Yet there is a suavity of phrase and execution in ***The Dream Life of Balso Snell*** that makes for excellent reading. It is with enthusiasm that we look for Mr. West's next work.

V.N.G., in a review of "The Dream Life of Balso Snell," in Contempo, *Vol. I, No. 8, August 21, 1931, p. 3.*

NATHANAEL WEST (essay date 1933)

[*West provides some random thoughts about the American literary scene and its influence on the structure of* Miss Lonelyhearts.]

I can't do a review of ***Miss Lonelyhearts,*** but here, at random, are some of the things I thought when writing it:

As subtitle: "A novel in the form of a comic strip." The chapters to be squares in which many things happen through one action. The speeches contained in the conventional balloons. I abandoned this idea, but retained some of the comic strip technique: Each chapter instead of going forward in time, also goes backward, forward, up and down in space like a picture. Violent images are used to illustrate commonplace events. Violent acts are left almost bald.

Lyric novels can be written according to Poe's definition of a lyric poem. The short novel is a distinct form especially fitted for use in this country. France, Spain, Italy have a literature as well as the Scandanavian countries. For a hasty people we are too patient with the Bucks, Dreisers and Lewises. . . .

Forget the epic, the master work. In America fortunes do not accumulate, the soil does not grow, families have no history. Leave slow growth to the book reviewers, you only have time to explode. (p. 1)

Psychology has nothing to do with reality nor should it be used as motivation. The novelist is no longer a psychologist. Psychology can become something much more important. The great body of case histories can be used in the way the ancient writers used their myths. Freud is your Bullfinch; you can not learn from him.

With this last idea in mind, Miss Lonelyhearts became the portrait of a priest of our time who has a religious experience. His case is classical and is built on all the cases in James' *Varieties of Religious Experience* and Starbuck's *Psychology of Religion*. The psychology is theirs not mine. The imagery is mine. Chapt. I—maladjustment. Chapt. III—the need for taking symbols literally is described through a dream in which a symbol is actually fleshed. Chapt. IV—deadness and disorder; see Lives of Bunyan and Tolstoy. Chapt. VI—self-torture by conscious sinning: see life of any saint. And so on. (p. 2)

I was serious therefore I could not be obscene.
I was honest therefore I could not be sordid.
A novelist can afford to be everything but dull.

Nathanael West, "Some Notes on Miss L.," in Contempo, *Vol. III, No. 9, May 15, 1933, pp. 1-2.*

WILLIAM CARLOS WILLIAMS (essay date 1933)

[*Williams was one of America's most renowned poets of the twentieth century. Rejecting as overly academic the Modernist poetic style established by T. S. Eliot, he sought a more natural poetic expression and attempted to replicate the idiomatic cadences of American speech. Perhaps Williams's greatest accomplishment is* Paterson, *a cycle of poems depicting urban America. He is best known, however, for such individual poems as* "The Red Wheelbarrow," "To Waken an Old Lady" *and* "Danse Russe." *In the following excerpt (in which he mistakenly identifies* Miss Lonelyhearts *as West's first novel), Williams praises West's skilled presentation of highly unpleasant subject matter and his "fine feeling for language," which Williams terms "plain American."*]

It's not only in the news section but among the feature sections also that newspapers show they have been published to conceal the news. [In ***Miss Lonelyhearts***] West takes for his theme "The Miss Lonelyhearts of The New York *Post-Dispatch* (Are-you-in-trouble? Do-you-need-advice? Write-to-Miss-Lonelyhearts-and-she-will-help-you)". It is of course a man who runs the column.

Now this is a particularly sordid piece of business, this sort of feature, for it must be obvious that no serious advice can be given to despairing people who would patronize and even rely on such a newspaper office. The fact is that the newspaper by this means capitalizes misfortune to make sales, offering a pitiful moment's interest to the casual reader while it can do nothing but laugh at those who give it their trust.

Imagine a sensitive man running such a column, a man of imagination who realizes what he is doing and the plot is wound up. What cure? Why the only cure, so far as Nathanael West is concerned, the only truth possible is "the truth"—along with the effects of the evil upon his protagonist. A particularly interesting short novel.

And for this, because the subject matter is sometimes rather stiff, a critic (after all, one must call them something) writing in one of our daily papers has branded the book itself as "sordid." Good God.

How much longer will it take, I wonder, for America to build up a cultural ice of sufficient thickness to bear a really first rate native author? It will happen sooner or later, it must, for we already have a few excellent craftsmen. But—to paraphrase the late Bert Williams—when? Apparently we still make the old and puerile error of finding a work, because its subject matter is unsmiling, serious or if the matter smiles then naturally the book must be light. And so, taking a sordid truth of city making and carrying the facts of the case through to an engrossing climax in brilliant fashion, the book cannot be anything else but sordid also!

If this is so, why then so is *Macbeth* sordid, so *Crime and Punishment*, so nearly the whole of Greek tragedy. And so's your old man. Blah. And that's what our standard American criticism amounts to: Roxy and the statues. Thin ice. We fall through it into mud up to our knees. And there is scarcely a place we can turn to for relief.

This isn't a perfect book, few first books are. But it is excellently conceived and written and it cannot be thrust aside in such slipshod fashion. There are many reasons why nearly everyone who would pick it up would enjoy it.

One thing which has perhaps aided in a careless dismissal of the book is West's insistence on extreme types in his narrative—really the people that newspapers do get letters from: the girl without a nose, the simpleminded child who was raped on the roof of a tenement, "Sick-of-it-all," "Broken-hearted," "Desperate," "Disillusioned-with-tubercular-husband." But after all the use of such extreme types is preeminently the business of literature or we should never have had either Romeo and Juliet, Klytemnestra or Lazarus, whose function it has been to reveal and emphasize a point under observation from a logical intelligence of the facts. (pp. 5, 8)

The letters-to-the-papers which West uses freely and at length must be authentic. I can't believe anything else. The unsuspected world they reveal is beyond ordinary thought. They are a terrific commentary on our daily lack of depth in thought of others. . . .

The characters in West's book, these people whom the newspapers make a business of deceiving, are the direct incentive to his story, the seriously injured of our civic life—although the cases occur everywhere, even worse, perhaps, in the rural districts. The unbearable letters are cited and then the moral bludgeoning which they entail is rapidly sketched out before our eyes. Nothing more clearly upon the track of classical precedent.

If our thought would evade such matters West doesn't. But it is done with skill and virtuosity. It can skate. What is the figure that Dante uses in the Inferno? It is Virgil. It is poetry (that is, good writing) which permits a man, but no ordinary man, to descend to those regions for a purpose. It is the art of writing, in other words, which permits the downward motion since when writing is well made it enlivens and elevates the whole reader—without sweetening or benumbing the sense—while he plunges toward catastrophy.

I'm not dragging in Dante to say West writes poetic prose. He doesn't. But I am saying the book is written with skill, we are not wiped around by sloppy narrative. The story, dreadful as it is, is presented tolerably to us, do what we may about the things presented. It's no treatise, no cold dissection. It is the intelligence feelingly going beside us to make it possible for us at the very least to look and to understand. . . .

It's plain American. What I should like to show is that West has a fine feeling for language. And this is the point I shall stop on. Anyone using American must have taste in order to be able to select from among the teeming vulgarisms of our speech the personal and telling vocabulary which he needs to put over his effects. West possesses this taste. (p. 8)

William Carlos Williams, "'Miss Lonelyhearts' Is Reviewed: Sordid? Good God!" in Contempo, *Vol. III, No. 11, July 25, 1933, pp. 5, 8.*

FRED T. MARSH (essay date 1934)

[*Marsh praises* A Cool Million *as a successful parody of the success stories of Horatio Alger, in which hard work and scrupulous honesty on the part of an ingenuous protagonist typically result in great financial success and personal fulfillment. For another discussion of* A Cool Million, *see the excerpt by T. R. Steiner (1973).*]

[**"A Cool Million; or, The Dismantling of Lemuel Pitkin"**] is a plain, unadorned tale in the good old Horatio Alger Jr. tradition of an American boy who made good—at least posthumously. For Lemuel Pitkin, although he never gets his cool million and is finally murdered, becomes the hero of the American Leather Shirts, the nation's martyr. His whole life stands for the ideals of the Fascist National Revolutionary party bent on restoring the lore and legendry of the plain American people and ridding our fair land of sophistication, Marxism, international capitalism and other sinister alien forces and elements. With the rise of Shagpoke Whipple to dictatorship, American "Know Nothingism" in modern form comes into its own. And the "Lemuel Pitkin Song" is the new national anthem.

Mr. West's hilarious parody-satire is a good deal of fun. You will read it at a sitting and enjoy it. But like "Candide" it strikes a good many notes that sound a little too close to truth to make you altogether comfortable. And there is a good deal of that typically American humor of the comic strip and the vaudeville act—here part of the satire—which depends upon the spectacle of physical pain for its guffaws.

Lemuel Pitkin, according to American tradition of pre-war days, should have become President or at least a millionaire. But times have changed, and although he follows in the prescribed course he receives nothing but indignity and abuse. Something is wrong with the old formula, just as something seemed to be wrong with the teachings under which Voltaire's hero grew up. Neither Lemuel nor Shagpoke Whipple question the virtue of the tradition or how much truth there had ever been in it. . . .

"A Cool Million" is not so brilliant and original a performance as Mr. West's extraordinary **"Miss Lonelyhearts."** Here he is inhibited by the style he has chosen, a parody of the writing in the old "success" stories that used to be aimed at firing American youth with the ambition to make money. But as parody it is almost perfect. And as satire it is a keen, lively and biting little volume, recommended to all and sundry. It is funny, but there's method in its absurdity.

Fred T. Marsh, "'A Cool Million' and Other Recent Works of Fiction," in The New York Times Book Review, *July 1, 1934, p. 6.**

LOUIS B. SALOMON (essay date 1939)

[*In the following excerpt, Salomon notes that West's intent in* The Day of the Locust *was not only to criticize the film industry, but also to sketch "an acidulous melange of Southern California grotesques." Salomon finds, however, that West provided at best only a two-dimensional outline of what could have been a scathing satire or thorough social study.*]

Hollywood-baiting is a branch of literature that began brilliantly with "Once in a Lifetime" and is still drawing noteworthy contributions, some good-humored and some bitter. But [**"The Day of the Locust"**] is a book that attempts to do a great deal more than just pillory the foibles and flimflammery of the movie industry. While its setting is Hollywood, and the miasma of the studio naturally permeates the lives of all the people concerned, Mr. West has sketched an acidulous melange of Southern California grotesques, including not only the usual figures of the disillusioned artist and the self-centered ham actress and the mother of the would-be child star, but some samples of the queer folk you don't read so much about: the Middle Westerners who have saved up a few thousand dollars and moved to California to end their days basking in its vaunted sun. These people, mostly middle-aged, often semi-invalid, invariably bored with their self-chosen life of idleness, inhabit an appalling spiritual wasteland in which the only plants that take firm root are the "crank" cults you will find advertised flamboyantly in cheap psychology magazines under names like "The Search for Truth," "The Quest for Life," "Power Through Mental Force," and, on a slightly different plane, the "Ham and Eggs" Utopias.

Around the central character of Tod Hackett, a young painter attached to one of the big studios, Mr. West has grouped such a galaxy of spongers, misfits, and eccentrics as will give a sensitive reader the crawling horrors. Even Tod himself, while generous and likable, suffers from lack of will-power; though he recognizes the cheapness and artificiality of blond Faye Greener, he has not the strength either to put her out of his mind or to demand from her the favors she withholds only from those who are considerate of her. The story ends on a particularly nightmarish note, when Tod, trying to help a poor lumbering dolt who has also been blighted by Faye's fascination, is injured by the star-worshipping, irresponsible mob outside a world première.

There is abundant material here for scathing satire or careful social study, and the principal objection to **"The Day of the Locust"** is apt to be that it merely scratches the surface. To make the picture less sketchy, less like the strongly highlighted scenes of a bad dream, it needs more thorough characterization, more documentation—most of all, perhaps, a few ordinary, everyday people (of whom there must be a few even in Hollywood), to lend perspective. Perhaps this very sketchiness was part of the author's plan, but by presenting only a two-dimensional picture it detracts from the impressiveness of what could well be a very striking arraignment of America's most unbelievable menagerie. (pp. 78-9)

Louis B. Salomon, "California Grotesque," in The Nation, *Vol. 149, No. 3, July 15, 1939, pp. 78-9.*

EDMUND WILSON (essay date 1940-41)

[*Wilson, considered America's foremost man of letters in the twentieth century, wrote widely on cultural, historical, and literary matters, authoring several seminal critical studies. Wilson was allied to no critical school: however, several dominant concerns serve as guiding motifs throughout his work. He invariably examined the social and historical implications of a work of literature, particularly literature's significance as "an attempt to give meaning to our experience" and its value for the improvement of humanity. Though not a moralist, his criticism displays a deep concern with moral values. Another constant was his discussion of a work of literature as a revelation of its author's personality. Perhaps Wilson's greatest contributions to American literature were his tireless promotion of writers of the 1920s, 1930s, and 1940s, and his essays introducing the best of modern literature to the general reader. The following addendum to* "The Boys in the Back Room," *a discussion of several California writers, was made when Wilson learned of the deaths of West and of F. Scott Fitzgerald. In this excerpt, Wilson praises West's depiction of life in Hollywood in the novel* The Day of the Locust.]

On December 21, 1940, F. Scott Fitzgerald suddenly died in Hollywood; and, the day after, Nathanael West was killed in a motor accident on the Ventura boulevard. Both men had been living on the West Coast; both had spent several years in the studios; both, at the time of their deaths, had been occupied with novels about Hollywood.

The work of Nathanael West derived from a different tradition than that of [James M. Cain, John O'Hara, William Saroyan, Hans Otto Storm, and John Steinbeck]. He had been influenced by those post-war Frenchmen who had specialized, with a certain preciosity, in the delirious and diabolic fantasy that descended from Rimbaud and Lautréamont. Beginning with ***The Dream Life of Balso Snell,*** a not very successful exercise in this vein of phantasmagoria, he published, after many revisions, a remarkable short novel called ***Miss Lonelyhearts.*** This story of a newspaper hack who conducts an "advice to the lovelorn" department and eventually destroys himself by allowing himself to take too seriously the sorrows and misfortunes of his clients, had a poetic-philosophical point of view and a sense of phrase as well as of chapter that made it seem rather European than American. It was followed by ***A Cool Million,*** a less ambitious book, which both parodied Horatio Alger and more or less reproduced *Candide* by reversing the American success story. In his fourth book, ***The Day of the Locust,*** he applied his fantasy and irony to the embarrassment of rich materials offered by the movie community. I wrote a review of this novel in 1939, and I shall venture to append it here—with apologies for some repetition of ideas expressed above—to make the California story complete:

> Nathanael West, the author of ***Miss Lonelyhearts,*** went to Hollywood a few years ago, and his silence had been causing his readers alarm lest he might have faded out on the Coast as so many of his fellows have done. But Mr. West, as this new book happily proves, is still alive beyond the mountains, and quite able to set down what he feels and sees—has still, in short, remained an artist. His new novel, ***The Day of the Locust,*** deals with the nondescript characters on the edges of the Hollywood studios: an old comic who sells shoe polish and his filmstruck daughter; a quarrelsome dwarf; a cock-fighting Mexican; a Hollywood cowboy and a Hollywood Indian; and an undeveloped hotel clerk from Iowa, who has come to the Coast to enjoy his savings—together with a sophisticated screen-writer, who lives in a big house that is "an exact reproduction of the old Dupuy mansion near Biloxi, Mississippi." And these people have been painted as distinctly and polished up as brightly as the figures in Persian miniatures. Their speech has been distilled with a sense of the flavorsome and the characteristic which makes John O'Hara seem pedestrian. Mr. West has footed a precarious way and has not slipped at any point into relying on the Hollywood values in describing the Hollywood people. The landscapes, the architecture and the interior decoration of Beverly Hills and vicinity have been handled with equal distinction. Everyone who has ever been in Los Angeles knows how the mere aspect of things is likely to paralyze the aesthetic faculty by providing no *point d'appui* ["point of support"] from which to exercise its discrimination, if it does not actually stun the sensory apparatus itself, so that accurate reporting becomes impossible.

But Nathanael West has stalked and caught some fine specimens of these Hollywood lepidoptera and impaled them on fastidious pins. Here are Hollywood restaurants, apartment houses, funeral churches, brothels, evangelical temples and movie sets—in this latter connection, an extremely amusing episode of a man getting nightmarishly lost in the Battle of Waterloo. Mr. West's surrealist beginnings have stood him in good stead on the Coast.

The doings of these people are bizarre, but they are also sordid and senseless. Mr. West has caught the emptiness of Hollywood; and he is, as far as I know, the first writer to make this emptiness horrible. The most impressive thing in the book is his picture of the people from the Middle West who, retiring to sunlit leisure, are trying to leave behind them the meagerness of their working lives; who desire something different from what they have had but do not know what they desire, and have no other resources for amusement than gaping at movie stars and listening to Aimee McPherson's sermons. In the last episode, a crowd of these people, who have come out to see the celebrities at an opening, is set off by an insane act of violence on the part of the cretinous hotel clerk, and gives way to an outburst of mob mania. The America of the murders and rapes which fill the Los Angeles papers is only the obverse side of the America of the inanities of the movies. Such people—Mr. West seems to say—dissatisfied, yet with no ideas, no objectives and no interest in anything vital, may in the mass be capable of anything. The daydreams purveyed by Hollywood, the romances that in movie stories can be counted on to have whisked around all obstacles and adroitly knocked out all ''menaces'' by the time they have run off their reels, romances which their fascinated audiences have never been able to live themselves—only cheat them and embitter their frustration. Of such mobs are the followers of fascism made.

I think that the book itself suffers a little from the lack of a center in the community with which it deals. It has less concentration than ***Miss Lonelyhearts.*** Mr. West has introduced a young Yale man who, as an educated and healthy human being, is supposed to provide a normal point of view from which the deformities of Hollywood may be criticized; but it is also essential to the story that this young man should find himself swirling around in the same aimless eddies as the others. I am not sure that it is really possible to do anything substantial with Hollywood except by making it, as John Dos Passos did in *The Big Money,* a part of a larger picture which has its center in a larger world. But in the meantime Nathanael West has survived to write another distinguished book—in its peculiar combination of amenity of surface and felicity of form and style with ugly subject matter and somber feeling, quite unlike—as ***Miss Lonelyhearts*** was—the books of anyone else. (pp. 52-5)

Both West and Fitzgerald were writers of a conscience and with natural gifts rare enough in America or anywhere; and their failure to get the best out of their best years may certainly be laid partly to Hollywood, with its already appalling record of talent depraved and wasted. (p. 56)

Edmund Wilson, in a postscript to his Classics and Commercials: A Literary Chronicle of the Forties, *Farrar, Straus and Giroux, Inc., 1950, pp. 51-6.**

JULIAN SYMONS (essay date 1957)

[*Symons holds two highly praised literary reputations: that of the serious biographer and that of the detective novelist. His popular biographies of Charles Dickens, Thomas Carlyle, and his brother A.J.A. Symons are considered excellent introductions to those writers. Symons is better known, however, for his literate, witty crime novels. In the following excerpt, Symons provides a generally negative assessment of West's novels, noting that West satirized contemporary life without suggesting any alternative values. (Symons's essay on West originally appeared in* The Times Literary Supplement *in 1957 and was reprinted in his collection* Critical Occasions.)]

West was not ignored during his lifetime because, as some writers do, he deliberately swam against the stream of fashion. On the contrary, it is because he was so obviously part of the stream that his work received little attention. In a sense he was a more 'revolutionary' writer than, say, John dos Passos and James T. Farrell: what alienated him from other writers, and from a wide audience, in the 1930s was the extreme pessimism of his attitude towards society and its institutions. It is this nihilistic pessimism, the sense that all social institutions are shams and that the act of love is merely 'the incandescence that precedes being more lonely than ever', that plays a large part in earning respect for West today. If this is a decade when intellectuals are without obvious illusions, it is also one when they are without ideals.

The motive power of West's work, from beginning to end, was a fascinated disgust with the processes of the body and an accompanying obsession with physical violence. The limitation of range imposed upon a writer by such a disgust and such an obsession may be compensated by the intensity of his feeling. West's effective social satire, his scabrous wit, his adolescent desire to shock and his sometimes embarrassing self-pity, all spring from the same source.

In ***The Dream Life of Balso Snell,*** published in 1931 but written some while earlier, the desire to shock is immediately evident. This short fantasy recounts the experiences of the eponymous hero, whose name must surely have some anagrammatic significance, in the rectum of the Trojan Horse. The narrator's exclamatory comment on Balso's entry: 'O Anus Mirabilis!' sets the story's tone of fantastic obscenity. Typical incidents concern Maloney the Areopagite, who in the intervals of attempting to crucify himself with thumb-tacks is writing a biography of Saint Puce, a flea who passed his life beneath the armpit of Christ, the diary of a schoolboy murderer 'written while smelling the moistened forefinger of my left hand', and a love passage between Balso and a beautiful hunchback, who says that she has been seduced by a man named Beagle Darwin, and carries his child in her hump.

Before making a long nose at ***The Dream Life of Balso Snell*** as a piece of scatological juvenilia . . . one should remember that it was written at a time when literary fantasy of a free-associative surrealistic kind was by no means the commonplace that it is today. ***Balso Snell*** is a work of some originality which contains images, and even scenes, of remarkable power: the schoolboy's murder of an idiot, for instance. . . . (pp. 99-100)

The Dream Life of Balso Snell does not really stand apart from West's other fiction; rather, it prefigures the virtues and defects of his later writing. The blasphemy, the obscenity, the deep sense of personal anguish about his own life and the condition of the world, they are all in this early fantasy, and with them the insistent self-mockery, the determination to turn the blood and excrement, the suffering and cruelty, into a joke, that weakens so much of his work. . . .

The theme of ***Miss Lonelyhearts*** . . . is by now fairly well known. The hero writes a newspaper column of advice to those in trouble. (p. 101)

The story is told in short episodes which concern Miss Lonelyhearts' feeble, flickering attempts to escape from his fate, chiefly through drink and lovemaking. (pp. 101-02)

West's books reflect reality in the mirror of personal pain. They are moving and distasteful, sometimes horrifying, but he never had the control over his material necessary for the production of a formal work of art, and structurally ***Miss Lonelyhearts*** splits off into a number of brilliant fragments which could be put together again in another order without any very noticeable effect on the story's emotional impact. The book's undeniable power as a morality is diminished by the fact that it is often written in a style of bright impersonal smartness ('Goldsmith smiled, bunching his fat cheeks like twin rolls of smooth pink toilet paper'), and by West's characteristic hesitancy to commit himself to any positive viewpoint. Pity and disgust are there, and they are finely communicated, but there is no indication that West himself believed these feelings to be valid or helpful, except perhaps as a solvent for his personal unhappiness.

In a way West's next book, ***A Cool Million*** . . . , is the most interesting work he produced. It is, as Mr. Wilson has said, the American success story in reverse [see excerpt dated 1940-41]. The central character, Lemuel Pitkin, wishes only to make a fortune by employing the honest American virtue of free enterprise, so that he may redeem the mortgage on his old mother's home. 'America', that former President of the United States Shagpoke Whipple assures him, 'is the land of opportunity. She takes care of the honest and industrious and never fails them as long as they are both.' Honest, industrious Lemuel Pitkin is dismantled of his teeth, an eye, a leg and his scalp, during his search for a fortune. At last he is shot by a Communist at a mass meeting and becomes a martyr of the National Revolutionary (Fascist) Party which, headed by Shagpoke Whipple, takes power in the country.

The theme is a magnificent one for a satirist, but in the event this is one of those books which sounds like a masterpiece when summarized but in the reading proves something of a disappointment. This is partly because West lacked the range of mind to handle satire upon such a grand scale; but ***A Cool Million*** fails principally because the tale is told in an uncertain pastiche of the style of the American success story. . . . As a conscious literary device the style was, inevitably, ineffective. Here as elsewhere West seems subconsciously to have sought

West in 1931, the year The Dream Life of Balso Snell *was published. Courtesy of Jay Martin.*

for a way of making farce out of material which, if seriously rendered, must have been intolerably painful to him.

The most successful scenes are those in which he expresses quite nakedly his sense of life's cruelty and injustice. (pp. 102-03)

The passionate intensity of feeling that marks such scenes is somewhat diminished in ***The Day of the Locust***. . . . In the sense that here West attempted to fit his talent into the common form of a novel, and actually achieved a background portrait of Hollywood and its architecture that has a fine, brittle brilliance, the book marks an advance on his previous work: but he paid the price for it—perhaps one should say that it was a price exacted by Hollywood—in a slackening of energy and concentration. The characters are fantastic—a hotel clerk pathologically concerned about his sexual unattractiveness, a furious hydrocephalic dwarf, a Hollywood cowboy, a film-struck girl intently preserving her virginity—but their frustrations are treated with an attempted realism that sits uneasily on West, although it should be added that the scene of crowd violence with which the book ends is of a brilliance equal to anything he ever wrote. A mass of people who have come out to watch the celebrities arriving at a first night, are transformed suddenly into a single monster, good humoured and cheerful, but violent by its very nature. West's hero uses this mob scene in a picture called *The Burning of Los Angeles*, and there is a hint of Fascism in his vision of the people in it. 'The people who come to California to die . . . all those poor devils who can only be stirred by the promise of miracles and then only to violence'; but, as in ***A Cool Million,*** the political and social points are never pushed very far. (p. 104)

West was underestimated in his lifetime, but his work has surely been grossly overpraised in recent years. . . . [It] is true that he had a rare originality in the choice of a theme, and showed a fantastic imaginative power in the treatment of the themes he chose. His books are always interesting, and even exciting, to read. The finest passages in them are those in which violence, and particularly mob violence, is described and analysed, in which a real attempt is made to give universal significance to personal agonies and fears. But this sad moralist was too often facetious; this careful and even finicky writer never developed a personal style, but relied for the most part on the ready-made conventional smartness of the period. West was by intention a satirist, and the limitations of his work are suggested by a comparison with the most important modern English satirists, George Orwell, Wyndham Lewis, Evelyn Waugh. Unlike them he has no positive idea to offer, no belief in the values of Socialism or of art or of tradition: beneath the chromium brightness of its surface his work suggests only a self-corrosive despair. (pp. 104-05)

Julian Symons, "The Case of Nathanael West," in his Critical Occasions, *Hamish Hamilton, 1966, pp. 99-105.*

V. S. PRITCHETT (essay date 1964)

[Pritchett is a highly esteemed English novelist, short story writer, and critic. Considered one of the modern masters of the short story, his work in this genre is a subtle blend of realistic detail and psychological revelation. Pritchett is also considered one of the world's most respected and well-read literary critics. He writes in the conversational tone of the familiar essay, a method by which he approaches literature from the viewpoint of a lettered but not overly scholarly reader. A twentieth-century successor to such early nineteenth-century essayist-critics as William Hazlitt and Charles Lamb, Pritchett employs much the same critical method: his own experience, judgment, and sense of literary art are emphasized, rather than a codified critical doctrine derived from a school of psychological or philosophical speculation. His criticism is often described as fair, reliable, and insightful. In the following excerpt, Pritchett discusses West's two best-known and most critically acclaimed novels, Miss Lonelyhearts *and* The Day of the Locust. *Pritchett praises the characterization in* Miss Lonelyhearts *as a "selection of hard, diamond-fine miniatures" and calls the novel "a true American fable"; he finds* The Day of the Locust *to be West's most completely realized work.]*

Nathanael West is one of the novelists of the breakdown of the American dream in the thirties. . . . Two of his novels, ***Miss Lonelyhearts***—which is very well known—and ***The Day of the Locust*** show that a very original talent was cut short. He was preoccupied with hysteria as the price paid for accepting the sentimentalities of the national dream. He feared hysteria in himself, he was morbidly conscious of it in his people; he was attracted and repelled by its false dreams as one might be by a more poisonous way of mixing gin. West did not feel that life was tragic, for the sense of tragedy was lost in the moral collapse of the period he lived in. Like Chekhov—but only in this respect—he was appalled by the banality of city civilization. Instead of being tragic life was terrible, meaningless and without dignity. . . . Americans like West were thrown helplessly among the brute economic facts. For them the experience was emotional and even theatrically so, because hysterical violence is very near the surface in American life.

West's resources were Art—he learned from the surrealists—and compassion. Except in his satire, ***A Cool Million,*** which is an American *Candide* done in the manner of a parody too obvious and prolonged, he was not a political writer in the literal sense. He explored the illness behind the political situation. Human beings have always fought misery with dreams, Miss Lonelyhearts observes; the dream and its ignoble deceits, the panic, anger and frustration these deceits expose, gave him his material. In ***The Day of the Locust,*** his mature novel, it is the boredom exposed by the failure of the Californian dream of an earthly Paradise that puts an expression of hate and destructiveness on the faces of the weary middle-aged population who have retired to Los Angeles. As they pour in to gape at the stars arriving for some world première, they have the look of lynchers. Lynch, in fact, they do and for no reason.

This does not convey that West was a comic writer. He had freakishness, wit and a taste for the absurd from the surrealists, also their sophistication in parody and styles, but moved quickly away from their gratuitous and perverse humor. He became comic and humane. ***Miss Lonelyhearts*** is a potent and orderly distillation of all the attitudes to human suffering. Miss Lonelyhearts himself is the drunken writer of an Advice Column in a newspaper who begins running it as a joke, a sort of sobbing *Americana,* and ends by becoming overwhelmed by the weight of human misery and by his inability to do anything about it. (pp. 276-77)

This might have been a slushy book, the derelict lot behind James Barrie's hoardings. It is, instead, a selection of hard, diamond-fine miniatures, a true American fable. West writes very much by the eye and his use of poetic images has a precision which consciously sustains his preoccupation with the human being's infatuation with his dream and inner story. (All his people are spiders living in the webs they spin out of their minds.) . . . If we call ***Miss Lonelyhearts*** a minor star it is because we feel that the Art is stronger than the passion; that, indeed Miss Lonelyhearts himself is capable only of pathos. His advice to the nymphomaniac who is torturing her husband, to "let him win once," is just wise old owlishness; her happiness is to accuse and torture, his to drag his loaded foot. West has not considered that human beings overwhelmingly prefer suffering to happiness and that their sobbing letters are part of the sense of the role or drama that keeps them going. Still, as a performance, ***Miss Lonelyhearts*** is very nearly faultless.

The Day of the Locust is an advance from fable and from fragments of people, to the courageous full statement of the novel. I say "courageous" because in this kind of transition the writer has to risk showing the weakness of his hand. The artificial lights of the freak show are off in this book and we see human absurdity as something normal. This is a novel about Hollywood. West worked in the hum of the American dream generators and he chose those people who have done more for American culture than their coevals in Europe have done for theirs: the casualties, the wrecks, the failures, the seedy and the fakes. They are the people to whom the leisureless yea-sayers have said "No." The observer is a painter from the East who is dreaming up what sounds like a very bad picture, a sort of Belshazzar's Feast. (He is a vestige of West, the aesthete.) He has fallen for Faye, a daydreaming creature who secretly earns money as a call girl for a "cultured" brothel, and who hopes, like the rest of the people, to get into pictures. She lives among a ramshackle group which includes old stage hangers-on, a ferocious dwarf, a woman who is grooming her son to be a wonder child of the screen, an absurd, fairly genuine cowboy extra and a pathetic hotel clerk from the Middle West. Faye is carefully observed. She is the complete daydreamer, insulated to such an extent by the faculty that it acts as an effective alternative to innocence; she is sexually provoking, cold, little-minded and cruel, but puts gaiety into the roles she takes on and has the survival power of a cork in a storm. If Los Angeles were destroyed by fire she would easily survive, not because she is hard but because she is flimsy. Already, in ***Miss Lonelyhearts,*** West had been a delicate student of the American bitch.

This Hollywood novel is mature because the compassion has no theatrical pressure; because now West is blocking in a sizeable society, and because his gift for inventing extraordinary scenes has expanded. The novel is dramatized—in Henry James's sense of the word—in every detail, so that each line adds a new glint to the action. His sadistic streak comes out in an astonishing description of an illegal cockfight in a desert lot. His comic powers fill out in the scenes with the angry dwarf and in the pages where the hero gets lost in a film Battle of Waterloo. The psychological entangling is brought to an appalling climax when Faye leaves her exhausted hotel clerk for a Mexican and this leads on to the great final staging of the world première, where riot and lynching are sparked off by the wonder boy of the screen, and the hate behind the Californian myth comes out. . . . (pp. 279-81)

The Day of the Locust has the defect of insufficient ambition. It calls for a larger treatment and we have a slight suspicion that the painter-observer is slumming. But West had not the breath for full-length works. Script writing snaps up the clever. His important contribution to the American novel was his polished comedy, which he displayed with the variety of a master and on many levels. If his talent was not sufficiently appreciated in the moral thirties, it was because comedy as a world in itself and as a firm rejection of the respected was not understood. West had something of Europe in him, where it is no crime to know too much. (pp. 281-82)

V. S. Pritchett, "'Miss Lonelyhearts'," in his The Living Novel & Later Appreciations, *revised edition, Random House, Inc., 1964, pp. 276-82.*

RANDALL REID (essay date 1967)

[*Reid's* The Fiction of Nathanael West: No Redeemer, No Promised Land *is a comprehensive study of West's life, works, and critical reputation, devoting a chapter to each of West's novels. In the following excerpt, Reid discusses many of the elements and themes common to American fiction that are not found in West's novels and concludes that West's works are difficult to classify in any literary genre. Reid describes West as a "pictorial parodist" who verbally "drew" his characters and scenes in styles borrowed from the graphic media.*]

A critical study of Nathanael West is hardly a novelty. After years of being out of fashion, his work now suffers from another danger, that of being taken for granted. West is routinely cited as a precursor of current literary trends, his name is sure to be dropped in any discussion of the grotesque, and book reviewers automatically compare new Hollywood novels with ***The Day of the Locust. Miss Lonelyhearts*** has even undergone that ceremony which, in some literary circles, constitutes ritual initiation—two recent critics have detected in it a case of repressed homosexuality. . . . His work is obviously being read, and it deserves to be. But it does not deserve to be fashionable. That West's name should come into vogue at a time when "black humor" is as marketable as sex—and often as synthetic as the Playmate of the month—is just a depressing, and peculiarly Westian, joke. It is true that West was in many ways the enemy of his own time, but he was no herald of ours.

West's vogue has not, of course, been complete. None of his books has ever become a campus fad, and none is ever likely to. He frustrates too many of the common motives for reading. West does not invite the reader to see himself as a sensitive soul in a cruel world, a world made cruel by the stupidity and heartlessness of others. Nor does he allow a reader the comforts of superior laughter. In the deflationary world of his books, simple mockery collapses as completely as simple self-pity. So do all the customary poses: ironic detachment, passionate involvement, heartfelt compassion. A reader who wants a simple attitude to take toward his world will therefore get no help from West.

There are other limitations on West's vogue. Though he is now officially recognized even by those scholars and critics who do not like him, he is still classified, often with an almost passionate insistence, as a minor writer. The most obvious reason is that he did not write very much. But many writers—Stephen Crane and F. Scott Fitzgerald, for example—are known for a very small body of work, and if they are not ranked with Tolstoi and Shakespeare, neither are they emphatically denied major status. West is called minor, I suspect, because of what he did write, not because of what he left unwritten. His vision is too narrow, his subjects are too extreme, there are no normal people in his books, and life isn't all like that. Of course it isn't, but the same objection could be brought to bear against any work of fiction—or against any view of life whatever. The myth of comprehensive genius is only a myth, even when it is applied to Shakespeare. Yet it is obviously true that some writers are more comprehensive than others, and it is obviously silly to suggest that West's range was Shakespearean. There are good reasons, as well as bad ones, for calling him narrow. But there are also good reasons for calling him complex, wide-ranging, and subtle; and there are even better reasons for saying that, when applied to his work, our usual categories make no sense at all.

Many critics of the thirties ignored West because his books did not conform to the "gravymashpotato" [the critic adds in a footnote: "I have borrowed the phrase from Angel Flores' review of ***Miss Lonelyhearts***" (see Additional Bibliography, "***Miss Lonelyhearts*** Is Reviewed")] school of social realism. That was only a temporary and particular form of a general complaint: those who believe that the novel must portray with detailed fidelity the surface of life—whether natural or social—must necessarily feel that West fails as a novelist. No one, however, has satisfactorily explained why the novel must attempt such a portrayal, except that most nineteenth-century novels did. The partisans of another and somewhat more recent tradition must also find West unsatisfactory—those who believe that the novel must portray with detailed fidelity the interior of life, whether that portrayal be Jamesian, Joycean, or Proustian. In West's work, the stream of consciousness is almost nonexistent. He disappoints a good many other expectations too. He contrived no ethos of courage (like Hemingway), created no myth of passionate renewal (like Lawrence), portrayed no great external dramas (like Tolstoi), refurbished no traditional beliefs (like Eliot), advanced no dogmas, bolstered no hopes, soothed no fears. It is therefore fair to ask what he did do, for he begins to sound narrow indeed.

Perhaps, as is so often remarked, he anticipated literary trends which have flourished since. Perhaps, but West's influence on contemporary writing still seems to me hard to evaluate. A few writers—notably John Hawkes and Flannery O'Connor—have acknowledged him as a literary ancestor, but neither his tone nor the peculiar logic which controlled his use of the grotesque is widely reflected in current fiction. And I see no reason why they should be. Much of West's interest lies in his odd relationship to all literary fashions, even those which have succeeded him. He resists assimilation. And the easy vagueness of our literary definitions betrays us totally when we apply them to West. Except in its worst and most imitative forms, the grotesque is not a single mode. William Burroughs and Thomas Pynchon, for example, have only a limited connection with each other, let alone with West, and we achieve nothing but confusion by classifying them together. We achieve even less by making West the precursor of something so inclusive as "anti-realism." He was often an extremely realistic writer. Though his name is invoked to sanction the distortion of reality, though distortion is obviously present in his novels, he frequently dropped it in favor of a scrupulous attention to the external scene which Flaubert would have admired. The cock fight in ***The Day of the Locust*** is, for example, as fine a bit of realistic description as anyone could want. (pp. 1-5)

It is not, therefore, much easier to find West a niche which will hold him now than it was when he was alive. He is a curious figure. Though his work was obviously "original," he is almost as hard to parody as he is to imitate. Most grotesque characters—Steinbeck's Lennie and O'Neill's Hairy Ape are obvious examples—are so easy to ridicule that they are exploited by popular comedians. West's characters, despite their grotesqueness, somehow evade the parodist's grasp. Even his style is elusive. Unlike the various styles of Hemingway, Faulkner, and the later James, it does not invite easy burlesque. Why? Perhaps for the same reason that West resists easy classification by literary critics. Parody, like caricature, usually hunts for the distinctive feature which can be exaggerated, but it is hard to extract the distinctive feature from West's work. He was always the writer of mixed vision, mixed attitudes, mixed modes. And parody, again like caricature, also hunts for the pretentious feature, but West's style is least pretentious when it is most distinctive. At its best, it is a style so simple that it does not even strive for the effect of simplicity. There is a final reason, of course: West was a parodist himself, as completely a parodist as anyone who ever wrote "serious" novels. (pp. 5-6)

[The parodist] is extraordinarily sensitive to banality, but his vocabulary is restricted to clichés—indeed, to him the resources of the language may seem restricted to clichés. The alternatives are mockery and fatuity. Obviously, these alternatives are inadequate. But to the parodist they may seem inescapable—unless, that is, he can make banality eloquent or turn mockery against itself. Or unless he can find a substitute for language. West attempted each of these methods—even, in a curious sense, the last of them.

I am, of course, aware of an immediate objection. To say that West used a substitute for language is, in every normal sense, obviously absurd—his pages contain nothing but words, nearly all of which can be found in any standard dictionary—but it is an absurdity which I shall retain. We naturally borrow the vocabulary of other arts and other experiences whenever we talk about literature: we speak of the "architecture" of novels, of the "orchestration" of dialogue, of the "painting" of scenes, even of the "fragrance" of a style. Such talk is dangerous—it is always threatened by the risks inherent in metaphors on the one hand and clichés on the other—but it is sometimes useful. In talking about West, it is very nearly inescapable. When he remarked that he originally conceived of ***Miss Lonelyhearts*** as a novel in the form of a cartoon strip, he was not, of course, simply being cute. The conception was serious, and much of it shows in the final version of ***Miss Lonelyhearts.*** His images, like those in cartoons, have a way of detaching themselves from the text. Even though they are conveyed through words, they form in the reader's consciousness a distinct set of pictures—pictures which are somehow different from those which a novelist usually evokes by describing a scene. The reason is simple. West was a pictorial parodist quite as much as he was a literary one. He "drew" his characters and scenes in recognizable styles borrowed from nearly all the graphic media. The odd juxtaposition of these styles with each other and with the speech of West's characters creates much of the peculiar tension of his novels. It also distinguishes him from such "painterly" writers as Hawthorne and James who, in their different ways, worked in fairly constant styles. West's style was never constant. At times his pictorial technique closely resembles collage—but only at times. It also resembles cartoon strips, movies, and several different schools of painting, as well as such non-graphic visual arts as the tableau and the dance.

It should begin to be apparent that West was, in several ways, a "formal" writer. He deliberately employed an intricate set of conventions, and if we do not understand these conventions we are not likely to understand his novels. We have often been told, by Aristotle and others, that art is imitation. We usually assume that it is in some sense an imitation of life. But in what sense? In West's novels, the immediate object of imitation is often neither "reality" nor "fantasy" as we commonly define those terms. Instead, it is some form of "art." The distinction is fundamental but by no means simple. To begin with, it separates West from both "realism" and "anti-realism," though he has some characteristics of both schools. (pp. 8-9)

For a "narrow" writer, West begins to seem rather complicated. There is, of course, no necessary contradiction between "narrow" and "complicated," and there is no point in applying either term until we have examined West's novels more closely. I think West is worth the examination. In a century which has made experimental writing almost an absolute value, he is one of the more interesting innovators. The words we like to use to describe modern literature—"violence," "the grotesque," "decadence," "dream," "irony," "allusion," "distortion," "realism," "tradition," "experiment"—are all applicable to his work. So are a good many other words, both in and out of fashion. Though West anticipated new literary trends, he also incorporated many trends which had already flourished, some of them for centuries. (p. 10)

Though he was a formal writer who made deliberate use of conventions, it is also true that he dealt explicitly and pointedly with themes. No one was ever less the disinterested aesthete. And perhaps no one has understood so well, or revealed so accurately, the nature of our favorite lies. We have not lost our taste for lying and we have not improved on West's analysis. Neither those who denounce television nor those who have made Batman a Camp hero can tell us as much about popular culture as West does. Here, as always, he is the enemy of simple enthusiasms—of both the denouncers and the applauders, the hip and the square, the hot and the cool. He regarded popular culture with ruthless sympathy; he understood it too well to like it and too well to feel superior to it. If there is "nothing to root for" in such an attitude, there is something to learn from.

Ruthless sympathy is seldom comforting. Dreams were West's special subject, but absolute clarity was his special tool, and clarity is not kind to dreams. Perhaps it is the *absence* of distortion which really shocks. West chose to reveal his "peculiar half-world" without the softening effect of half-light. His subjects are acutely focused, his style is lucid and exact, and his plots culminate in a violence whose logic is unpleasantly plain. The ease with which West made familiar premises yield disastrous conclusions is disturbing in itself—far more disturbing than the usual cries of personal anguish or cosmic despair. And it is quite different from them. Apocalypse is, in West, not an assertion but the natural consequence of a process. Irreconcilable truths breed disruptive forces. In his mixed vision it is simultaneously true, for example, that dreams are destructive and false and that dreams are inescapable. He denies our fantasies but leaves us prisoners of them. The implications of this paradox, whether or not they are final, are as serious as they are unpleasant. Our debt to West is that he revealed them so clearly, revealed them in ways no one else has. He is still a curious figure. He repudiated social realism but focused on sociological themes, dismissed psychological novels but was an acute literary psychologist, laughed at art but was a conscious and dedicated artist. He was a dandy with proletarian sympathies, a comic writer who specialized in unfunny jokes. (pp. 11-12)

[We] cannot know how West would have developed if he had not been killed. He might have done things which would overshadow both ***Miss Lonelyhearts*** and ***The Day of the Locust***, and he might never have written another novel. What he did do is small but irreplaceable. It gives him a permanent importance beyond any might-have-been. (p. 158)

American writers, we are told, drift inevitably into artistic disintegration and personal collapse, but such a fate seems quite irrelevant to West. He obviously matured as he got older. The excessive cleverness which sometimes mars his early books yields to an increasing candor. In ***Balso Snell***, the only "confessional" moments—the John Gilson and Beagle Darwin sections—are surrounded by such contortions of comic disguise that "serious" interpretation is impossible. ***Miss Lonelyhearts*** drops the protection of total ridicule and seriously examines some of West's own preoccupations, but it embodies them in a character from whom West remains distinct and toward whom his attitude is still, in part, ironic. In ***The Day of the Locust***, protective irony entirely disappears. Tod's character is defined exactly, without deprecation or indulgence. He is a witness whose authority and limitations are equally clear.

Confessional sincerity is not, of course, an adequate test for a novel, especially that form of sincerity which merely adds another footnote to the history of egoism. But in a writer like West, disguise is a far more natural and therefore dangerous tendency than exhibitionism. Even Miss Lonelyhearts reflects a double fantasy whose terms seem appropriate to West himself—the dream of being a savior, the fear of being a fool. Given such preoccupations, mockery becomes ambiguously a threat to the self and a tempting alternative to its fears. It offers the illusion of immunity. The mocker can deny both his inadequacies and his sufferings, asserting a triumphant cleverness in their place. And for West, the mocker's stance had an obvious fascination. Throughout his first three novels, he alternately identifies with it and rejects it, but is always obsessed by it. Shrike's rhetoric is as persistent as a refrain. Beagle Darwin speaks it in ***Balso Snell*** and Israel Satinpenny drops into a variation of it in ***A Cool Million***. In ***The Day of the Locust***, however, West briefly revives the same rhetoric for Claude Estee and then drops it as if he were bored with it. It now seems tired, as habitual and meaningless as the shop talk, gossip, and self-conscious smut of Estee's guests. (pp. 158-59)

The Day of the Locust suggests, I think, that West had grown beyond the alternatives of mockery and pity. The world he confronts in it is repellent, but sensitive young men cannot save it and sardonic intellectuals cannot jeer it away. Roles which were inadequate are now simply irrelevant. They no longer interest West. What does interest him is the power latent in mass discontent, a power which will find its release quite independent of anyone's attempt to redeem it or laugh at it. The people who occupy West's attention now are, even in their deformities, more various and more subtly examined than the brilliant stereotypes of ***Miss Lonelyhearts***. They cannot be reduced to the single quality of suffering. Nor, despite the truisms about West's distorted grotesques, can they be called Gothic or synthetically perverse. Their counterparts are depressingly common, visible in any bus station, and West quietly recognizes both his own kinship with them and his alienation from them. The problem itself now absorbs his interest, not the question of appropriate stances toward it.

West's style establishes the cool precision of his portraits. Despite his love of masks, his prose is both unmannered and unadorned, so bare that any lapse will show. There is no adverbial padding in his sentences, no swell of rhetoric, no self-conscious terseness or muscular lyricism. The idiom is, in Williams' phrase, "plain American" [see excerpt dated 1933], but it absorbs without strain anything from parody to abstract comment. And, unlike many of our literary fashions, West's style emphasizes lucid interpretation. He always reduces incoherence to summary paraphrase. The chaotic speeches of Doyle [in ***Miss Lonelyhearts***] and Homer [in ***The Day of the***

Locust] are, for example, interpreted, not recorded. The reveries of his characters are equally succinct, expressed in images which are both psychologically and thematically appropriate. Violent action in his novels always carries a clear sense of its motives and its consequences; it is always gesture, not just melodrama. Obviously, as I have already remarked, clarity has its limitations as well as its virtues. West was not the complete literary artist or the definitive stylist of our time. He was, however, a distinctive and intelligent analyst of materials which are everywhere in modern literature and modern life.

West's recurrent themes—actor-audience, order-disorder, deadness-violence, dream-misery—are finally reducible to terms so banal they are probably profound. Inarticulate desire supplies the eruptive force in each of these themes, a force so common in life that it is reflected in clichés as wearily familiar as "I can't express it." And even in literature it is hardly the special property of Anderson and West. Faulkner's Benjy, Steinbeck's Lennie, and O'Neill's Hairy Ape are only a few of the more obvious variants upon a familiar type. And the masses, especially in the thirties, have commanded nearly as much literary attention as individual primitives. The theme of decadent exhaustion is equally familiar. It is everywhere in the symbolists, the *fin de siècle* writers, and the early poetry of T. S. Eliot. It is also reflected in the attempt to revitalize—even rebarbarize—language, an attempt which has obsessed many of the century's best writers. Lawrence's urge to discover a pure sensual communication, to destroy consciousness and all the traditional gods which inhabit it, derived, of course, from his conviction that our gods had died, that our language—the things by which we define and express ourselves—had worn out. Hemingway's famous repudiation of abstract words is perhaps another example. And we need only recall Joyce's experiments in language—or the ubiquity of ironic parallels in which the banality of the present is compared to a myth of the past—to realize how common the theme of decadence and exhaustion has been. In many ways, primitive seeking and mass suffering and decadent collapse are all aspects of a single theme. "I can't express it" could almost be called *the* modern problem. Or, if an assertion so broad seems fatuous, I shall merely point out that modern fiction has long been obsessed with the submerged—with those individuals who are submerged in society and those impulses which are submerged in consciousness, with all that is buried, thwarted, denied expression, all that cannot speak. (pp. 160-62)

West's anatomy of collapse is as relevant to the politics of the self as it is to the politics of any state. Perhaps more clearly than any writer we have had, West understood the connection between neurotic aesthetes and vulgar masses, between the dreams of art and the stereotypes of popular culture, between the violence of a mob and the violence in himself. And he revealed the implications of decadence with equal clarity. Parody was, for him, a diagnostic instrument. He used it to identify the familiar themes of our culture, expose their characteristic weaknesses, and express the fact of their decadence. When "classic" ideas or actions collapse into banalities, parody becomes a disturbingly adequate description of them. They are dead, they have no capacity for further change, and the implications of their fates assume syllogistic certainty. In West's novels, decadence is nearly absolute. The violence and suffering he portrays are the inevitable accompaniments of collapse. Though life is not all like that, some life is always like that and all life is in perpetual danger of becoming like that. His "prophetic" vision need not come true at any particular time. It defines the failure which always awaits us, the possibility against which all affirmative action contends. (pp. 162-63)

Randall Reid, in his The Fiction of Nathanael West: No Redeemer, No Promised Land, *The University of Chicago Press, 1967, 174 p.*

CARTER M. CRAMER (essay date 1971)

[*Cramer's essay* "The World of Nathanael West: A Critical Interpretation" *provides a critical overview of West's four novels. In the following excerpt from that work, Cramer summarizes the various critical responses to* Balso Snell *and* A Cool Million *and contends that critics err when analyzing as novels works which are more properly categorized as satires.*]

Critics who implicitly equate the word "novel" with the word "fiction" are often faced with the problem of where to place the large number of works of literature that refuse to fit their novelistic cupboard. Some must be crammed, beaten, and shoved into place; others, too individual in form, must be stored in the back closet, marked "odds and ends," never to be displayed in the central showcase reserved for the works of writers belonging to the tradition of Fielding, Austen, Meredith, and James. . . . [In his *Anatomy of Criticism*] Northrop Frye, in opposition to the Procrustean measurements too prevalent in this age, suggests that critics approach fictional narration by the use of four classifications he designates "specific continuous forms," which in their rare, pure states are of four distinct fictional forms: novel, romance, confession, and anatomy. (p. 5)

Nathanael West's ***The Dream Life of Balso Snell*** is a satirical attack against literary "games" and against the perversion of art in a mass culture by those who use the arts as a tool for deception and as a mechanism for escape from their own fragmented psyches. By the use of scatological imagery, West attempted to shock the jaded nerve-endings of the pseudo-creators of avant-garde literature and their middle-brow intellectual audience. The work is not a fragmented novelistic parodying of such giants as Joyce and Dostoevski, as has been suggested by some critics; instead the focus centers on the pseudo-sophisticates of the late 1920's for whom the despair of having ". . . seen the mornings and the afternoons" was only a pathetic stance and a call for escape to "Anywhere Out of This World," the title of Balso's first song in chapter one.

Thus the actual focus of West's first work is essentially much narrower than has been generally recognized. By interpreting the work as an eccentric, dadaistic novel rather than as a satire or anatomy, most critics have had to argue that ***Balso Snell*** is essentially formless; thus, the thematic purposes ascribed to it are widely divergent. (p. 10)

As a satire, the characters in ***Balso Snell*** are presented as purveyors of ideas, myths, and attitudes native, in less exaggerated form, to the cultural and artistic escapists of the 1920s. The spirit of escapism prevalent during the era is recorded by Malcolm Cowley in *Exile's Return* [see Additional Bibliography]. . . . West's primary concern in ***Balso Snell*** is to lampoon the choice of art as escapism and to criticize the divorce of the artist from society and the perverting of art by the dream makers of a consumer society.

West's satirical assault is not against art itself but against deceit and delusion in the art world. The characters are "flat" and exaggerated in the same manner as the characters in *Candide,* for both works attack particular ideas and attitudes. The focus of each is "extroverted and intellectual." The attention in ***Balso***

Snell to the dreams of a single man, the inclusion of confessional letters, and the parodying of romantic sentimentalism are all elements that link the work to the novel, confessional, and romance forms, respectively. However, these forms are but minor currents in the main stream of an anatomy. The vast array of literary and artistic allusions utilized belong to the encyclopedic aspect of that form, as do the verses interlaced into the prose:

> The Menippean satirist, dealing with intellectual themes and attitudes, shows his exuberance in intellectual ways, by piling up an enormous mass of erudition about his theme or in overwhelming his pedantic targets with an avalanche of their own jargon.

An analysis of ***Balso Snell*** in light of Frye's above observation reveals that its most consistent method of attack is an attempt to bury its opposition in their own clichés and abuses of logic.

Balso Snell's dream begins at the perimeter of the city of Troy, now symbolically surrounded by grass and in a state of decay. Balso comes upon the famous wooden horse of the Greeks—a traditional symbol of artifice, inventiveness, and deceit. Balso, the artistically impotent, clandestine poet, remembers Homer's ancient song and seeks entrance into the interior of the wooden horse:

> On examining the horse, Balso found that there were but three openings: The mouth, the navel, and posterior opening of the alimentary canal. The mouth was beyond his reach, the navel proved a cul-de-sac, and so, forgetting his dignity, he approached the last. O Anus Mirabilis!

By having Balso make such a choice, West serves notice to the reader of the work's intended effect: to shock and shatter any complacency of sensibility which the reader may feel. West's persistent use of scatological imagery is analogous to the same technique as evidenced in Swift's *Gulliver's Travels*. West's purpose was to establish a tenor and tone of disgust similar to that which Swift evoked when he described the Yahoos, for Balso is a comic-pathetic hero haunted by a vision of modern man's having deteriorated into the obscene and the bestial. . . . (pp. 12-13)

The first chapter is extremely important, for it serves to establish Balso as the spiritually and emotionally effete poet of a commercialized mass society. (p. 14)

Balso Snell has a definitive structure, and all of the work's episodes can be accounted for in terms of their form and content, rather than through pseudo-psychoanalysis. The ordering of time and events is sequential. . . . [The] reader is chronologically transported through a mad-house gallery of characters, beginning with a modernized tour guide for Greek heritage and ending with Balso's adventures in a sexual fantasy of the kind printed by the tons by a modern consumer press. (p. 15)

Unquestionably, ***Balso Snell*** was not a hastily written first novel. . . . West first carefully engages the reader in a literary game of allusion hunting, mixing these allusions with interesting satirical sketches, only to reveal, later, through Gilson, the attack he has thus made on the reader. Once the first two episodes are partially recognized as such an attack, the work's remaining structure is greatly clarified.

The first two episodes also contain incidents which are other than an attack on the reader. The first of these two episodes begins with Balso's meeting the Jewish Guide with "Tours" embroidered on his cap. The guide relates a ribald joke about the philosopher-saint, Appolonius of Tyana, and is immediately hired by Balso. West, himself a Jew, portrays the guide as a confidence-man only too willing to extol the virtue of any culture for profit. . . . (pp. 16-17)

Balso next meets the pseudo-religious mystic, Maloney the Areopagite, who wears no clothes except for a derby hat complete with a crown of thorns. Maloney is feigning to crucify himself with thumb tacks when Balso discovers him. Maloney introduces himself as a Catholic mystic. . . . All of West's characters are grotesque incongruities—fragmented men living a life of literary sham. The sham in Maloney's instance is his dedication to writing a biography of Saint Puce, a martyred member of the vermin family who lived on Christ's body and died with him on the cross. After listening to the story of St. Puce's life, Balso advises Maloney:

> "I think you're morbid," he said. "Don't be morbid. Take your eyes off your navel. Take your head from under your armpit. Stop sniffing mortality. Play Games. Don't read so many books. Take cold showers. Eat more meat.

Balso is the product of a matter-of-fact world in which even pathological fixations are to be cured by the simplest remedies. His advice of games and books as a cure would do credit to any modern advice columnist.

As in the first episode, the literary allusions are numerous, and many may be unfamiliar to most readers. Though an encyclopedic cataloguing of the names and allusions dropped in arty conversation may be a legitimate aspect of the anatomy, by such an attack West slows the momentum of his work, and the creation of dramatic momentum was West's structural forte in his later works. Fortunately, he wisely economized on the length of the Guide and Maloney episodes. With the third episode, however, the clutter of decorative allusions cease in favor of functional allusions.

The episode begins with Balso's discovery of the diary of John Raskolnikov Gilson of Class 8B, Public School 186. The source of the Gilson episode is Dostoevski's *Crime and Punishment;* however, the sincerity of that journal of torment contrasts sharply with the pseudo-superman post of Gilson, the self-confessed phony. (pp. 18-19)

Gilson's middle-aged teacher, Miss McGeeney [is] a writer as gifted as Balso at triteness. . . . Through Miss McGeeney, West attacks the academy. . . . West uses the character of Miss McGeeney to attack the straining of logical systems characterizing the academician much in the same sense that he used the Guide to ridicule the abuses of logic evident in "arty" cocktail-party chatter. . . . The entire episode is highly comparable to Swift's "Flying Island" in which Swift lampoons the abstractness of mathematicians. (pp. 22-3)

Having satirized the avant-garde writer and audience as well as the academy, West then focuses on the stereotyped bohemian writer as visualized by the movies and "pulp" fiction of a mass culture. Balso Snell, the vulgate and lyric poet and cliché expert, has been repulsed by both Gilson, the self-confessor, and McGeeney, the academician. In his dream, Balso has momentarily freed himself from Miss McGeeney by shoving her into the fountain. He seeks refuge in a cafe, orders a beer, and then falls asleep, having a dream within a dream. His interior dream is a parody of the rhetoric of romance in second-rate

rwise unnamed hero, Miss Lonelyhearts,
sion in too simplified a fashion, and he is
ummarizing his transformation as crystal-
fusions. Still, the novel does move from
of Shrike—to an exploration of the arche-
ine suffering" of both Miss Lonelyhearts
ents. Perhaps West's own phrase, "moral
ibes the mixed character of this novel. Like
Lonelyhearts is an anatomy of illusion. But
asks illusions only to find that people cannot
He himself is at last appealing only because
lf to the greatest of illusions—the personal
mass. Yet, though his compulsions and sym-
to the Christ dream, his intellect drives him
He is impaled by his antagonist, the butcher-
the thorns of this dilemma. West originally
e the cartoon strip in the structure of his book,
ins some of the stylized motionless-movement
p frame. In a series of episodes Miss Lone-
lplessly from any compulsion to its opposite.
n in the final episode of the book when, fully
sane illusion that he can win and change the
sses, he is shot by the person he wants most
4-6)

earts West made an art-form out of his bitter
ling upon the secret life of the crowds of people
hrough the streets with dreamlike violence."
s and combines aspects of both his dreams of
d his bitterness over its betrayal. Deeply re-
loneliness of the crowd, West was the discov-
xplorer of the geography of modern mass sol-

el, ***A Cool Million*** . . . , West explored directly
Dream of Success, the myth which lay, as he
at the heart of so many other frustrations and
ainly, success had never before seemed so un-
for personal success so vain as in the early 30s.
me that Adolf Hitler was coming to power West
g that there was little essential difference between
's success stories and *Mein Kampf,* and he par-
n ***A Cool Million.*** In ***Miss Lonelyhearts*** he had
ally of the breakdown of faith in modern America;
e of the perversion of the traditional American
ess.

r aesthetic problem in writing ***A Cool Million*** was
special character of economic and political wish-
inking. . . . Influenced by the technique and point-
S. J. Perelman, to whom the book is dedicated,
ted to reveal the absurdity of the myth of success
ng it directly with the reality of the 30s. The result
nic. Though the novel is ostensibly, as Perelman
e most comic of West's books, as in *Candide* and
ravels, books which it closely resembles, bitterness
ion flow just beneath its comic froth. (pp. 6-7)

last five years of his life West labored in the dream
Republic, R.K.O., Universal, and Columbia. But
Scott Fitzgerald and many other writers, he never
make great films. He preferred to work on B- or
de pictures, since these did not touch the sources
tive energy for his fiction; he regarded movies simply
of support.

ortant, perhaps, than the money that West made in
as the material that Hollywood life provided for his fiction. As early as 1933 he formed a plan to write a novel about the subterranean life of the dream capital. In the spring of 1935 he began to collect materials and to sketch out his new book. By choosing with calculation to live near Hollywood Boulevard, West explored a seamy area where dreams, violence, and deception mixed, affecting "the cultists of all sorts, economic as well as religious . . . who can only be stirred by the promise of miracles and then only to violence . . . a great united front of screwballs and screwboxes." The frustrated cultists and those who excited them; victims and victimizers; the starers and the dancers—these provided the material and form for West's fourth novel, ***The Day of the Locust***. . . . (pp. 7-8)

West gave his novel two opposing curves of development. The first consists of the story of the relations between the "dancers" and the "torchbearers," the "super-promisers" and their dupes. The middle-aged émigrés to California are represented by Homer, the man of the crowd, and the Hollywood underworld by Faye, Earle, Abe, and Miguel. Both groups move downward, from desire to frustration and from discontent to frenzy. The upward curve of development in the novel occurs in the art of Tod Hackett, a graduate of the Yale School of Fine Arts who has been hired by National Films to design costumes and sets. Dissatisfied with the kind of merely illustrative painting that he had been trained to do and with the masters—Homer and Ryder—whom he had been taught to admire, Tod attempts to renew his art by learning the secrets of Hollywood life. He learns to use new painting techniques of the surreal and grotesque, resembling those of James Ensor; and he adopts new masters, the painters of mystery and decay, like Salvator Rosa, Monsu Desiderio, and Alessandro Magnasco.

Certainly, Tod's personality, disintegrating during the novel, intersects the first curve of development: beginning as an illusion-maker, an employee of a film studio, he is tormented into becoming one of the frustrated, violent crowd and ends the book as a prophet of mass violence. But in his meditations on the principles of a modern art he expresses the upward curve—of understanding and artistic accomplishment. William Dean Howells once told Stephen Crane that through its sharpened perceptions the novel taught "perspective" to people who could not use their eyes. West used Howells's painterly conception in his novel. Even as Tod's personality dissolves, his artistic perception sharpens. For a moment he can express sanity through aesthetic order, if only by being willing to give himself up to the ugly, the nightmarish, and the insane. (p. 8)

West's world, however distorted its people may sometimes be, is perfectly clear and complete. If it seems to lack the largeness of Tolstoy's—or of what West himself called "the broad sweep, the big canvas, the shot-gun adjectives, the important people, the significant ideas, the lessons to be taught, the epic Thomas Wolfe, the realistic James Farrell"—still it is precisely drawn to scale, richly complete in its own terms, and boldly direct in its concentrated vision. Malcolm Cowley once remarked that West wrote as if he were sending telegrams to a distant land. His world is a writer's world, as his style is an artist's: his vision and style issue powerfully from his precision and creative intelligence. (p. 9)

West is popularly known as the progenitor of the black humor of the 60s. But his permanent reputation will hardly rest upon this. West never attempted to correct society through satire or abandon it through irony; he held no dark mirror up to life. But he created a permanently true artistic vision, unaffected by alterations in the actual world. His works remain parallel

movies and consumer fiction. In the episode, Balso meets a strange lady in the lobby of Carnegie Hall. In typical romance fashion, he tips his hat to her. . . . The technique West uses for ridicule in this episode is singularly grotesque and undoubtedly repulses some readers, for the girl is a huge hunchback with an enormous hump. . . . Balso attempts to seduce Janey Davenport. She refuses him, then consents, provided Balso proves his love ". . . as did the knight of old." First, he must kill Beagle Darwin, whose child Janey carries in pregnancy.

Yet another pretender and fake, Beagle Darwin is the consumer press's concept of the young bohemian artist, professing love to every woman he meets and promising them life in Paris and an artist's studio. Janey gives to Balso two letters written by Beagle. In the first he jilts Janey and creates a melodramatic play out of her imagined suicide that reads like any of a thousand modern confessionals. . . . (pp. 23-4)

Balso awakens from his interior dream to find Miss McGeeney at his side. . . .

Balso, the ambassador of mass culture and defender of sentimental romance, had realized earlier in the satire that the wooden horse ". . . was inhabited solely by writers in search of an audience." He had avowed not to be tricked into listening to another story: "If one had to be told, he would tell it." Balso's only "story," however, is a long speech delivered at the book's conclusion in which he catalogues the "literary reasons" Miss McGeeney may assume for allowing Balso to seduce her. He delivers a hoarde of clichés in exposition of the artistic, political, and philosophical poses which Miss McGeeney may assume. Then, Balso concludes with the maudlin sentimentality of the "Time-argument." . . . (p. 25)

West creates a superb burlesque out of Balso's seduction speech—an effusive oration for which there was no need, for Miss McGeeney has listened from the very beginning stretched out on her back ". . . with her hands behind her head and her knees wide apart."

The satire ends with the culmination of Balso's dream in a sexual fantasy. In parodying consumer fiction, West has chosen a particularly suitable conclusion for his work, for so much of the "art" and sexual fantasies marketed in a mass culture have as their appeal vicarious sexual experience. Balso is the ambassador of such a culture. (pp. 25-6)

Balso Snell is rich in allusions contrasting sharply with the spiritually and morally effete banalities and fantasies of its central character. There are no Swiftian humane men, no Portugese captains to rescue Balso or to give to the work a suggestion of a standard of ethics men should follow. Yet the echoing of the great literary works of both antiquity and the modern age serve as such a standard when contrasted with the stances of the literary snobs and charlatans in Balso's dream.

Once the nonsensical elements in the two brief introductory episodes are recognized as nonsensical, as a "game" played on the reader by West, much as Gilson plays "games" with his audience, the structure of the work takes on a completeness and unity of scope and attack many critics have denied it. The only significant structural weakness of ***Balso Snell*** is its unevenness of dramatic effect—a weakness in proportioning the episodes. Only the Gilson attack on the avant-garde audience and the Smeller incident have the necessary concentrated dramatic fullness demanded. The episodes prefacing these incidents are anemic in comparison, while those following are mostly overdeveloped, except for the seduction scene itself. However, in West's decade, no more strident satirical attack against artistic foolishness exists in American letters. (p. 26)

In ***A Cool Million,*** West wrote the satirical history of a naive All American boy, whose innocent optimism rivals that of Dr. Pangloss and Candide. The same episodic structure is used in both ***A Cool Million*** and *Candide;* furthermore, both of these anatomies or satires feature protagonists innocently victimized by the bromides and clichés of their respective eras. The simple-minded, honest Candide is sent into the world to test the maxim, "This is the best of all possible worlds," while West's Lemuel Pitkin seeks "a cool million" through the mythical methods of Horatio Alger. Both characters are dismantled in the process. Candide ultimately retreats into tending his garden; on the other hand, Pitkin, the country bumpkin, becomes a martyred dupe for political myth-makers and fanatical American nationalists.

In writing his satirical warning of the dangers of a latent fascism in America, West abandoned his own style to parody the Horatio Alger novels. Stripped of his singular style, West fails ultimately to write a work rivaling the universality of *Candide.* Thus, ***A Cool Million*** is West's only work that appears dated after some thirty years. However, the anatomy remains the best American effort of its kind written during West's decade and is perhaps the most successful political satire in American literature. Despite the stylistic limitations inherent in the parody form chosen by West, much of the work emerges as a significant, ironic commentary of America during the painful years of the 1930's.

As with ***Balso Snell,*** critics have too often evaluated ***A Cool Million*** as a novel rather than as an anatomy to be approached by the dictates and "touchstones" of that genre. . . . [West's] purpose in ***A Cool Million*** is to present characters who embody the ideas and myths offered for popular consumption by America's mass media and politicians. Though comic in his attack, he warns of a latent totalitarianism which he feared existed in American society. He makes significant comments on a complex of themes: economic myths propagated by consumer romance, Aryan supremacy, latent social violence in the heritage of the myths of the frontier West, mob behavior, and the fantasies and psychology of demagogues. (pp. 27-8)

In its attack on political, intellectual, and artistic quackery, ***A Cool Million*** is predominately a universal satire.

West's attack on the Alger myth echoes his preoccupation with literary frauds in ***Balso Snell,*** his portrayal of the Hollywood dream-factory in ***The Day of the Locust,*** and his attack on literary escapism in ***Miss Lonelyhearts.*** (p. 28)

His Grosz-like characters spasmodically jerk and blindly reel through comic-pathetic episode after episode, the victims of fraudulent myths. In a romantic-realistic style, John Steinbeck portrayed an anonymous heroic mass working nobly for a selfless cause in the proletarian novel, *In Dubious Battle,* while West portrayed only the abjectly ridiculous and grotesque which he felt inherent in the sham rhetoric and deluded dreams of mass movements.

As an Alger parody, protagonist Pitkin is the ironic embodiment of the white-Protestant American Dream; he mortgages the family cow and heroically leaves Ratsville, Vermont, to seek his fortune by emulating the hard work and honesty of Lincoln and Henry Ford. More unfortunate than even Candide, Pitkin suffers from the teachings of a man who is not only a successful fool but also a swindler; Pitkin's teacher is Nathan "Shagpoke" Whipple, an ex-president of the United States and present president of Rat River National Bank. Whipple lies so well and so often that the reader ultimately comes to realize that Whipple not only deludes his followers but also himself. (p. 29)

In the back of his garage Whipple keeps all of the necessary adornments: a cracker-barrel, boxes, spittoon, a hot stove, and a picture of Lincoln. Also, he owns a wealth of bromides and homilies: "This is the land of opportunity and the world is an oyster." He preaches, "America . . . takes care of the honest and industrious and never fails them as long as they are both." He champions John D. Rockefeller and Henry Ford, as he urges the gullible Pitkins to emulate their honesty and industry. Whipple is anti-Catholic, anti-Jewish, and anti-Negro. His destiny is to organize the National Revolutionary Party or "Leather Shirts," whose uniform is a coonskin cap, a deer-skin shirt, a pair of moccasins, and squirrel rifle. As a true demagogue, he ultimately promises the panacea of total employment; he rants against the Jewish International Bankers and the Bolshevik labor unions—his favorite scapegoats aside from non-Aryans. Advocating the triumph of the revolutionary middle class, he calls for violence: "We must purge our country of all the alien elements and ideas that now infest her. America for Americans!" In lampooning Shagpoke's folksy rhetoric, West makes this pseudo-patriot a crook, a swindler, and a fantastic fool. Having secured the family cow as collateral, Shagpoke lends Pitkin thirty dollars for ninety days at twelve per cent interest collected in advance.

With money in his pocket and a myth in his head, Pitkin leaves for New York City to make his fortune. He is quickly victimized by confidence men, policemen, lawyers, judges, wardens, and politicians (capitalists, fascists, and communists alike). In quick sequence, Pitkin's naive optimism costs him his money, his teeth, a thumb, an eye, a leg, his scalp, and ultimately his life. Pitkin must endure witnessing his feminine counterpart and girl friend be raped, kidnapped and forced into white slavery, rescued, and raped again. Mangled in riot after riot, Pitkin is constantly the victim, whose dismantling occurs against the backdrop of the Great Depression, with its hungry mobs. Every time Pitkin innocently turns to the police for help, he is falsely arrested, often kicked in the groin and head, beaten senseless, tried, prosecuted, and jailed. (pp. 29-30)

The humor and absurdity, the pursuit of a logic to its exaggerated, insane conclusion is the same technique used later by novelists of the absurd. (p. 30)

The countless coincidences, the slapstick action, the use of stereotyped characters, and the mocking of cliché after cliché, are all additional techniques West used to ridicule the mannerisms of the Alger novels. In addition to Shagpoke Whipple, Lemuel Pitkin, and Betty Prail, West introduces the following Alger types in the first three chapters: Sarah Pitkins, mother of Lemuel, an aging, kind, poor, helpless widow; Mr. Slemp, villainous, rich lawyer; Squire Bird, villainous land owner; and Tom Baxter, the town bully. (p. 31)

Pitkin has been pardoned from prison, but before he is reunited with Betty Prail, he first experiences a series of episodes that cost him his health, the additional money he has earned, and an eye. Finally, he manages to escape New York in the company of General Shagpoke Whipple, Betty, and Jake Raven, an Indian chief. Their destination is the Sierra Mountains of California, where Whipple and Raven intend to dig for gold to finance the National Revolutionary Army. The Sierra Mountain episodes serve West as a means to broaden greatly his attack on the myth-makers of America. Having lampooned the morality and wisdom of the Alger myth, and by implication, the pulp romance, he next attacks the violence propagated through the American myth of the Western badman and the social irresponsibility incited by certain members of the intellectual class. Two characters are introduced to implement the attack; the Missouri Pike County Man and the Indian Chief, Israel Satinpenny. (p. 32)

The badman's one solution to any personal affront is to shoot his offender. West has included him in ***A Cool Million*** to ridicule the violence, brutality, and lawlessness of the primitive myth of frontier justice that is so large a part of the inheritance of America. . . .

West's Pike County Man ultimately rapes and kidnaps Betty, shoots Jake Raven ("The only good Injun is a dead one, is what I alluz say."), and severs Pitkin's leg by placing a bear trap in his path. Indians who come to avenge the wounds of Jake Raven find Pitkin and, believing him to be their enemy, loot his glass eye and false teeth. The leader of this raiding party is Israel Satinpenny, Harvard graduate. An anarchist disgusted with the society which has educated him, he becomes within the economic context of the satire ". . . the necessary product of capitalism and a reflection of the 'inner-contradictions' which will eventually destroy middle-class society." Satinpenny's prototype in West's fiction is John Gilson of ***Balso Snell***, who shares the same animosities toward the middle class.

The choice of "Israel" for a first name is appropriate for the apocalyptic Old Testament predictions of doom the Indian preaches, much as does West himself. Yet unlike West, he is an advocate of violence, who calls for revolution. As an Indian and an intellectual, Satinpenny belongs in part to a tradition of American primitivism that celebrates the beauties of nature over the evils of civilization. (p. 33)

Nostalgic romanticism offered no exits for West, and he viewed with horror America's nurturing of violence. The horror he feared most was the communal spirit of the mob aroused by the Shagpokes and Satinpennys of America. When Satinpenny speaks, however, of America's "dying of a surfeit of shoddy," he does become the voice of West. (p. 34)

West's ability to criticize a society while he is also satirizing many of its critics gives the work a universality of attack, elevating it above mere satirical propaganda and accounting for its significance and appeal some thirty years after its publication. (p. 36)

By his strident ridicule of the crass aspect of the American Dream, by his lampooning of a cross-section of American myths and mythmakers, and by his satiric dissection of the demagogue's fantasies and the psychology of the mob animal, West suggests that much in American culture and thought passes beneath the lowest levels of art, myth, and imagination, reaching the depth ". . . at which an imaginative vision of an eternal world becomes an experience of it." When West spoke of violence being idiomatic to American art, he was attesting in part to mass man's proclivity to a savagery in which the boundaries between myth, fantasy, symbol, and reality dissolve. Victimized by myths, West's mass man seeks flesh-and-blood Messiahs, and attempts literally to live his dramas and his fantasies. He seeks comedy through the witnessing of actual brutality, and primitive catharsis through the communal mob's search for a *pharmakos* or scapegoat.

West wrote his work during an era when hob-nailed boots clicked on the streets of Berlin, as Hitler acted out in Germany's arenas a savage, demonic melodrama that exploded into the monstrous violence of World War II. Hitler's propagandistic weapon was his ability to rejuvenate primitive myths, long half-dormant, and to make of life a savage drama. West saw in America the potential threat of similar myths and warned of a latent social savagery constantly nursed by violence and by a primitively naive, melodramatic search for scapegoats for our social ills. Thus, West, ironically, reverses the consumer fiction versions of the American Dream, and Lemuel Pitkin, the American Boy, becomes the real life *pharmakos* of America's confidence men and the absurd saint of a deceived populace.

As an anatomy of American myth, ***A Cool Million*** deserves the status of a minor classic. Its one major flaw resides in West's curbing in part his own style to parody the Alger books. Nor does ***A Cool Million*** have the richness and complexity that is achieved by the combination of the anatomy, the romance, and the novel forms present in ***The Day of the Locust***, or the intense dramatic effect of ***Miss Lonelyhearts***. Such, however, is more an inherent self-limitation of the parody and the anatomy than a weakness in West's artistry. To criticize ***A Cool Million*** or ***Balso Snell*** as inferior novels in comparison to West's other works is to state a preference for the novel form over the anatomy—little more. (p. 38)

Carter M. Cramer, "The World of Nathanel West: A Critical Interpretation," in The Emporia State Research Studies, *Vol. XIX, No. 4, June, 1971, 72 p.*

JAY MARTIN (essay date 1971)

[Martin wrote the authorized biography of West, Nathanael West: The Art of His Life *(1970; see Additional Bibliography), and is the editor of* Nathanael West: A Collection of Critical Essays. *The following excerpt from Martin's introduction to the latter work provides a critical summary of West's career.]*

His novels, of course, were the major expressions of the labyrinths of West's personality. The chief source of his personal complexity lay in the contrast between his intellectual and emotional life, between his ability passively to understand experience and his initial lack of capacity for deeply active involvement in it. (p. 3)

The Dream Life of Balso Snell . . . , West's first novel, was largely the product of his wit, the sardonic side of his personality. . . . It is the account of a journey that an American Babbit takes through the anus of the Trojan Horse, and of his encounters there with various forms of deception, pretense, and illusion. West at once set his innocent, innocuous mock-hero upon an investigation into the Western tradition itself. Imaginative, witty, and wildly inventive, this book well expresses the sense of literary internationalism that West shared at this period with his peers. In form it resembles, of course, the short, tight French novella that West and his contemporaries most admired. Many of its themes, too, are closely allied with continental preoccupations. Breton, Picasso, Klee, Joyce and others had experimented with the dream life of man, the night-life of the soul. Scorning ordinary social values and emphasizing man's interior life, the whole tendency of experimental literature between 1920 and 1930 had been to turn values inside out—to declare the primacy of dreams over acts, of violence over order, of Sade's sexual gospel over that of the churches; of arbitrary over calculated action; and then to announce the

superiority
bourgeois c

West first p
Kurt Schwit
At the last m
he changed l
in ***Balso Snell***
travail. The T
called his boo
the deceitfuln
dreams symbo
through illusio
atole France's
an anatomy of

In this first nov
occupy all of hi
seem necessary
illusion seems to
how to assign gu
has been rendere
tragic when both
very nature of ma
tatively in this boo
he would need to
express, for the mo
righteousness, and
tion.

West was thus to t
personal involvemen
dinary capacity for c
the masses. His intell
and complex craftsma
deep artistic sympathy

Even while West was
Snell he was pondering
modern world. In 1929
upon a collection of lett
of a Brooklyn newspap
merged cries of pain fro
ple, despairing and yet
Deeply moved by the lett
own capacities, West wo
four years, completing hi

Miss Lonelyhearts . . . is
casually takes on the job
quence, however, he poses
had, like his fellows, been
haps I can make you unde
fiancée. "Let's start from
give advice to the readers
culation stunt and the whole
comes the job, for it might le
he's tired of being a leg man
but after several months at i
He sees that the majority of t
pleas for moral and spiritual
expressions of genuine suffer
correspondents take him seriou
he is forced to examine the
examination shows him that h
not its perpetrator."

Doubtless the othe
understands his mi
here not so much
lizing his own co
comedy—the joke
types of the "gen
and his correspon
satire," best desc
Balso Snell, Miss
here, the hero unn
live without them
he commits hims
redemption of the
pathies drive him
from belief in it.
bird, Shrike, on
intended to imita
and the novel ret
of the comic str
lyhearts moves h
All opposites jo
accepting the in
hearts of the m
to comfort. (pp

In ***Miss Lonely***
and comic broo
who "moved t
His book share
a noble life a
sponsive to the
erer and first
itude.

In his third no
the American
understood it
illusions. Ce
likely or hope
At the same t
was suggestin
Horatio Alge
odied both i
written gene
now he wro
faith in succ

West's maj
to convey th
fulfillment t
of-view of
West attem
by confront
is highly i
has said, t
Gulliver's
and disillu

During the
factories o
unlike F.
aspired to
even C-gr
of the crea
as a sour

More im
movies w

to our lives, brilliant instruments through which we can measure and understand the crucial issues of our age. In them, West offered no comprehensive criticism of the temporal world; rather, he created a more permanent perspective by which that world, at any time, might be understood and judged. Satirists who construct their own complete worlds, such as Persius, Rabelais, Johnson, and Dickens, are the writers to whom West may most accurately be compared. However our world changes (and, admittedly, since West's death it has come to resemble more and more the chaotic world of his fiction), his art seems likely to possess the same interest and power. (p. 10)

Jay Martin, in an introduction to Nathanael West: A Collection of Critical Essays, *edited by Jay Martin, Prentice-Hall, Inc., 1971, pp. 1-10.*

THOMAS H. JACKSON (essay date 1971)

[*Jackson is the editor of* Twentieth-Century Interpretations of "Miss Lonelyhearts": A Collection of Critical Essays. *In the following excerpt from his introduction to that collection, Jackson finds that the actions of West's characters illustrate a "two-fold dilemma" central to his novel: "human energies and potentialities are confined and repressed within an agonizing and horrifying finitude; and yet something in these people drives them to* enforce *this finitude, to disable or eradicate any agency that seems to offer a way out."*]

Miss Lonelyhearts is about despair, alienation, violence, fragmentation, dehumanization, victimization, and sterility—about all of these things as definitive qualities of modern life. And though some of them are more nearly central than others, they are so ineluctably interrelated in the novel that to speak of any one as a "cause" of the others is but an academic exercise. Consequently, the book seems unusually multifaceted and susceptible to differing interpretations, all suggestive, and all at least partly valid, depending on which facet first catches the eye. (p. 1)

Suppose, for example, one begins by considering the motif of order. This branches into all sorts of directions. In the chapter "Miss Lonelyhearts in the Dismal Swamp" Miss Lonelyhearts imagines himself inundated by a sea of civilization's junk; he tries to form the random objects that roll up into a cross, but "every wave added to its stock faster than he could lengthen its arms." Coming as it does after his sexual encounter with Fay Doyle, this phenomenon is not a bad figure for some of the main concerns of the novel. The tendency of the cross to grow toward the shape of a phallus by sheer pressure of mechanical flotsam and jetsam is not just a threatening of the spiritual by the appetitive; it is the threatening of order by disorder, and it is emblematic of a widespread disintegration of human experience. Miss Lonelyhearts' appeals to Christianity are solely on behalf of order; again and again in the novel he refers to it as "the answer" to the misery and moral disorder he sees around him, and hardly at all as a devotional consideration. His invocation of the Christ answer, furthermore, is always conscious, and at one point we are told that its unavailability for Miss Lonelyhearts is due to Shrike's having taught him to handle the Christ myth with a "thick glove of words"—that is, too consciously and too deliberately. It is thus opposed to the "Pan" impulse with which it struggles in the novel. Christ is love, and thus rooted in the irrational, but He is also control and order; Pan is spontaneity, but spontaneity gone bad—riot, violence, chaos. That the invocation of Christ reaches down to activate the lurking Pan-energies in the self reveals how wrong is the sundering of the rational from the irrational that characterizes West's world. (pp. 2-3)

The sundering of rational and irrational is intimately related to other troubles in the world of Miss Lonelyhearts. The characters in the book are only half persons or worse and cannot act as whole persons. The men cannot love, and the women could not accept them if they did—consider the reductive emotional outlook of Mrs. Shrike, who cannot join "love" and sex in her mind, or of Mrs. Doyle, who knows sex but not love. As male and female are cut off from each other, the person is cut off from society: Miss Lonelyhearts' colleagues jest truthfully in their speakeasy conversation that the individual's experience cannot be socially meaningful. Even language is disabled: it is words, as we have seen, that spoil the Christ escape for Miss Lonelyhearts. When Peter Doyle attempts to converse with Miss Lonelyhearts, his speech is an incomprehensible jumble "of retorts he had meant to make when insulted and the private curses against fate that experience had taught him to swallow"—that is, language reduced to merely reproducing, not helping to order, a jumble of feelings. Similarly with Shrike, whose conversation is a bitter revelation of moral chaos in its besliming of all sources of order. The letters, though more innocent, are also but a reproduction of the disorder they bring forward for cure. Language, West's novel implies, can be a cry of anguish or a cry of hatred; it cannot be an expression of reason. At no point in the novel does speech or writing function in the service of anything closer to reason than an imitation or burlesque of it.

A moral order presupposes some coincidence of thought and feeling: morality is in part how we feel about what we perceive, how we value it, how we think it ought to be. The divorce of thought and feeling evident in the breakdown of language in Miss Lonelyhearts' world produces violence: emotion divorced from reason or control means chaos and destruction. (pp. 3-4)

Miss Lonelyhearts, then, is a deflation of the heroic novel whose hero confronts the flux and attempts to order it. The flux, as always, is the world with its cruelties and sufferings. The letters Miss Lonelyhearts is assigned to answer are its expression, and ultimately Fay and Peter Doyle are its embodiment. West's extensive use of the Doyles for this purpose (we shall pursue the implications of his mechanical treatment of them later) takes various forms. Through suggestive and often shared imagery, through echoed speech, and through various conceptual and situational parallels the Doyles and their state become a summary of other characters and situations. . . . Fay's comic-pathetic attempt to seem a victim of seduction makes her a perhaps imperfect approximation to the many women in the novel who are in fact victims of lust and depravity; yet she herself has literally been such a victim, at the hands of the father of her ironically-named child Lucy. She is also in some sense a recapitulation of Mary Shrike and Betty in being simultaneously a victim of human sexual appetites and a narrow-minded wielder of sex for her own purposes.

Peter Doyle is a walking manifestation of the disorder and misrule implicit in a world of flux ("His eyes failed to balance; his mouth was not under his nose; his forehead was square and bony; and his round chin was like a forehead in miniature. He looked like one of those composite photographs used by screen magazines in guessing contests"). He is a Miss Lonelyhearts letter in the flesh, doubly a victim with his lameness and his status as an insulted and then a betrayed husband. And like Fay, he echoes other characters in the novel: in the speakeasy, Shrike "raised his fist as though to strike" Miss Farkis; in the

Doyles' apartment at one point Doyle "made as though to strike his wife." His queerly incommunicative speech at his first meeting with Miss Lonelyhearts (later he barks like a dog) is surely representative of the malfunctioning of language endemic to the whole ***Miss Lonelyhearts*** world. At the same time Doyle is also a version of Miss Lonelyhearts. He, too, according to his letter near the end of "Miss Lonelyhearts and the Cripple," wants to know "what is it all for . . . what in hell is the use day after day . . . what is the whole stinking business for." That he and Miss Lonelyhearts twice end up holding hands is suggestive not of homosexuality, . . . but of identity—or is it the hero succumbing to one aspect of flux as he has already been engulfed by the other?

The nearly loveless disorder of the Doyles' marriage is but a realization of the disorder of the letters and the self-centered cruelties and neglects they reveal. Neither Fay nor Peter seems much aware of the other as a person. . . . Their marriage is a little world made as uncunningly as the big one, marred by violence, obliterative of selfhood and dignity, unlovely and utterly beyond the rational control of either victim.

These facts all suggest, then, that we should read the Doyles as, among other things . . . , the principle of flux come to life. But they perform their function in a more complicated way as well, a way implied by the title of the episode immediately following Fay's seduction of Miss Lonelyhearts, "Miss Lonelyhearts in the Dismal Swamp." Through the letters, the flux has already wrought a grave spiritual effect on Miss Lonelyhearts; bearing in mind the full sense of the term *spirit,* we may say that the letters are the spiritual manifestations of suffering. The Doyles are its physical manifestation. The effect of Fay Doyle's sexual ingestion of Miss Lonelyhearts is to demonstrate for the only time in the novel what its climate as a whole would deny—unity of soul and body, as Miss Lonelyhearts retires to his bed physically—as well as spiritually—ill. The sum of the episodes with Peter Doyle is but a fatal intensification of this theme. Driven by his spiritual miasma to the physical morass of Fay Doyle, Lonelyhearts succumbs irrevocably to the principle of flux in the figure of Peter, who shoots him. The hero is physically destroyed in the midst of a spiritual fantasy of himself as Christ—an additional irony being that he *is* a Christ; but at this point the narrative yields to the facts of real life: Miss Lonelyhearts is Christ only physically, and his death has no valid spiritual content.

West, I said, "uses" the Doyles. It is a measure of the bitterness in his view of modern life that his version of the heroic plot is expressed through a set of almost purely symbolic characters whose essential claims as persons are undercut and denied by their reductive symbolic values. Obviously a character can be symbolic without being dehumanized; but in West's fable the two go together, and the condition symbolizes his world. His technique becomes an embodiment of his theme in the sense that his people have no being, only symbolic value. Miss Lonelyhearts himself is apprehended less as a character than as a state of mind, or worse, a plight (his name, of course, is not his name, but the name of his public function). . . . West sedulously avoids any suggestion that his hero has a realistic inner life, and when he dies we have seen but the completion of a diagram. Late in the novel Betty is reduced to "the party dress," and in fact she is little more than that anywhere in the book: a mere emblem of naive, detached, simplistic (and implicitly self-involved) thoughtlessness. Shrike, the emblem of caustic, cynical disbelief, is a more compelling—and repellent—presence, but he is not really a character in the traditional sense; he is, like T. S. Eliot's Prufrock, a voice, not a person, a category, to be filled in by each reader for himself out of his own experience.

The status of West's characters as non-persons is underscored by their tendency to blur into each other. When Peter Doyle "made as though to strike his wife," he mirrors Shrike, who had made as though to strike Miss Farkis. Miss Lonelyhearts is assimilated to Shrike in his theatrical posing before Betty in "Miss Lonelyhearts and the Fat Thumb," and Betty, perhaps, to Miss Farkis, when she "raised her arm as though to ward off a blow." . . . Furthermore, all the women in the book are alike in sharing a common torment—all are seduced, raped, deceived, or otherwise abused.

But if these two strategies underscore West's deliberate dehumanization of his characters by weakening their individual identities, they can be seen in another light as well. Miss Lonelyhearts acts throughout the book as though the possible solutions to his plight were limited by his actual surroundings. For example, he tries to palm off on the Doyles shoddy pieties that are partly what he got from Betty and partly what he peddles in his column. He lives, in fact, in a terribly finite world, and the Christ dream, his one nonmaterialist escape, is no longer, for him, dreamable, partly because he is afraid to let himself go and dream it. He applies for "escape," therefore, only within the dreary limits of the people around him—Betty, Mary Shrike, the drunkenness of his colleagues, violence of his own (e.g., against the "clean old man") inspired by the violence he sees around him, even Shrike's kind of wordmongering. What is true for Lonelyhearts is true for the world of the book as a whole. The facts of life are hideous, yet the one potential universal palliative—dreaming—has been discredited by deceitful, grasping, cynical, and powerful men, who treat the less powerful as starfish treat oysters. With no way to turn except to turn on each other, these people find themselves trapped in a world of terribly limited possibility. . . . Almost without exception in this novel, female suffering real or imagined stems from the repression of women to purely sexual potentialities. Mrs. Doyle has been reduced to an object of sexual pleasure by her Italian businessman; Betty is left at the end of the novel pregnant, a victim of Miss Lonelyhearts' detached sexuality; the first letter in the book comes from a woman who has been reduced to the status of pleasure-and-child-machine by her husband's sexual appetites combined with his religious "convictions." The next letter but one tells of a thirteen-year-old girl who has been raped. The most telling case of all, perhaps, is the jocularly brutal discussion of lady novelists in the speakeasy, where Miss Lonelyhearts' colleagues decide that all lady writers need "a good rape"—which would presumably cure their presumably unwarranted urges to ascend into the realm of the imaginative, there to exercise a potentiality other than that conventionally allotted to women. And this is surely West's point: the world is designed—and if it is not designed, the men in it will see to it that it gets designed—to limit the function of women to one and only one thing. It is not necessary to adduce the traditional literary use of women as symbolic of potentiality, or salvation through passivity, or fruitful irrationality, or the surrender of dominion and the sublimation of ego, though there are various well-known analogies to what West is doing here—Sonia, for one, in *Crime and Punishment*. As with women, so with Christ and the slaughtered lamb in Miss Lonelyhearts' dream: none of these, apparently, will subsist quietly and dependably—and narrowly—as the men in the book want them to; they are constantly threatening to break out into unwanted (unknown and therefore frightening) potentialities. The dilemma of West's world, then, is two-fold: human energies and potentialities are confined and repressed within an agonizing and horrifying finitude; and yet something in these people drives them to *enforce* this finitude, to disable or eradicate any agency that seems to offer a way out. Why this should be raises some interesting questions about West's writing and its relationship to the times in which he lived.

Those times included two great landmarks in the emotional and psychic history of the United States, the economic boom of the 1920s, and the Great Depression of the 1930s. After ***The Dream Life of Balso Snell,*** West's first and least worthwhile novel, his books focused on the popular mythology of democratic capitalism, its effect on the lives of his fellow citizens, and its major instruments for propagating the faith—***Miss Lonelyhearts*** fixes on the advice column dodge, ***The Day of the Locust*** deals with Hollywood-movie-house culture, and ***A Cool Million*** satirizes Horatio Alger. In all these books West sees the commercial spirit to be in absolute control of American life, and he sees it to be the father of lies. In ***Miss Lonelyhearts*** the "dream" has been betrayed, betrayed by agencies with a stake in its betrayal and in replacing it with prepackaged, over-the-counter fantasies—for the dream is freedom; the dream is inner, private, uncontrollable, and never made anyone a dime. West's three last novels depict a world that has been reduced to the coarsest materialism, but which is constantly being foisted off on people as not materialistic, a world in which the commercial movie magazine is offered in lieu of dreams, the commercially motivated newspaper columnist in lieu of spiritual adviser, phony nightclubs in lieu of pleasure gardens. For such a world to survive, of course, delusion is a crucial necessity. It only adds to the irony that West's characters, like the denizens of any Inferno, help forge the chains that keep them from the truth.

The vulgarization or betrayal of the dream is an old theme in American literature—one need only recall Mark Twain—and as a child of the 'twenties West must have been thoroughly alive to it. . . . (pp. 4-10)

The time of the writing of Miss Lonelyhearts was an excited period, when American literature seemed about to go places, when a great deal of romanticism surrounded the idea of being a professional writer, and when many serious writers were deluded into thinking they could do honest and creative work in the promising medium of films. We know now that American literature did not go anywhere special; the romanticism of the intellectual or creative life has largely vanished, what with government and academic grants and positions, and as for films, one can only say that up to now no first-class literary talent has ever been allowed to function fully in that baldly commercial air. At any rate Nathanael West was very much of that climate. Specifically American writing he saw as a kind apart, and so did the artists around him—witness, for example, the last paragraph of William Carlos Williams' review of ***Miss Lonelyhearts*** [see excerpt dated 1933]. Whatever West may have felt about the quality of modern American life, moreover, he seems to have been willing to see the artist trim his sails to its wind, praising the short "lyric" novel as better suited to American life than more agglutinative styles. I bring this up because of the peculiar kind of appeal that ***Miss Lonelyhearts*** seems to make. It is a book many people discover, with delight, in college, and it seems then the perfect expression of creative writing as part of a truly intellectual life style. Yet it is also a book that tends not to be reread over the years: few who first read it in college will have reread it ten years later, though they will remember it as an "exciting" book.

One reason for the neglect which tends to follow upon one's admiration for the book is its deliberate economy. Compared to more ambitious works it seems narrow and therefore less of an achievement and certainly a less inclusive imitation of human life. But this narrowness is a part of its success. There are, as has already been noted, no interesting people in West's book, no elaborate situations, whether narrative as in Dickens, structural as in Doris Lessing, or psychological as in Dostoevsky or even Hemingway. ***Miss Lonelyhearts*** cultivates a spareness daring in its intensity and the result is an astonishingly successful economy of means. West was a child of the first really great age of American gadgetry, and ***Miss Lonelyhearts*** reflects an odd faith in mechanical decisions. West's own comments on the book [see excerpt dated 1933] . . . , speak much in terms of mechanics, and of writing as the deliberate application of premeditated mechanical principles. Thus he toys with the idea of using comic strip techniques in a novel, then does just that in ***Miss Lonelyhearts*** . . . . He theorizes about the propriety of short novels as such, then produces a very short novel. ("Leave slow growth to the book reviewers," he writes, "you only have time to explode.") He theorizes further that "Psychology has nothing to do with reality," and therefore in ***Lonelyhearts*** eschews it, except for "cases" from William James and E. E. Starbuck. West speaks, in fact, of using the findings of psychology the way one might use mythology, as a compendium of *types* or *emblems,* the way Euripedes "uses" Hippolytus to depict the type of one-sided man, or the way Sophocles "uses" Oedipus to create an emblem of overweening self-confidence.

This manner of West's reminds one of the techniques of other writers more or less of his day—the Imagists, William Carlos Williams, Ezra Pound: a whole generation of writers whose work was directed by what Hugh Kenner has called "an aesthetics of glimpses," which involved stripping expression down to its barest essentials. . . . West did not share Pound's aesthetic, but he knew a version of it in the admired work of his colleague Williams, and he could write, "For a hasty people we are too patient with the Bucks, Dreisers and Lewises. . . . Forget the epic, the master work. In America fortunes do not accumulate, the soil does not grow, families have no histories." Such an attitude exemplifies what I have characterized as the romanticism of West's ambience. So sentimentalized a view of the anxiety-laden bustle of the American life-style would hardly find public utterance in intellectual circles of today. The contrast between this and West's bitter contempt of the commerce-ethic is striking in the extreme, and further exemplifies, perhaps, that readiness to make an intellectual silk purse out of a substantial sow's ear so typical of the period in which he worked. (pp. 11-13)

The novel as an institution has certainly gone on to other things since West's day, and it is doubtful that he would have had much more influence than he has had even if he had not died so young; his technical experiments were simply not that radical or far-reaching. In this he is like rather than unlike his countrymen, for it is arguable that the really seminal experiments in the form of the novel have not been carried out by Americans. Melville, Hemingway, Dos Passos, Faulkner, West: all are writers who consciously forged new forms useful to themselves only. Yet of West's vision of American life, who today can truthfully say that it was wrong? The apocalyptic riot at the end of ***The Day of the Locust,*** which enacts the violent upheaval implicit in ***Miss Lonelyhearts,*** has not taken place in quite that form. But we have the gruesome memory of Chicago in 1968, of southern (and northern!) university campuses since 1960, and of the perpetration of individual hideousness we do not lack examples. (p. 13)

Thomas H. Jackson, in an introduction to Twentieth Century Interpretations of "Miss Lonelyhearts": A Collection of Critical Essays, *edited by Thomas H. Jackson, Prentice-Hall, Inc., 1971, pp. 1-17.*

IRVING MALIN (essay date 1972)

[*Malin teaches at New York's City College and has written extensively on Jewish-American authors. His works include* Jews and Americans *(1965),* Saul Bellow's Fiction *(1969), and* Isaac Bashevis Singer *(1972). In the following comprehensive survey of West's novels, Malin provides a close analysis of each, maintaining that an examination of the text of the work in isolation from social or biographical contexts results in a more valuable criticism.*]

[West's] novels are constructed tightly. ***Miss Lonelyhearts*** and ***The Day of the Locust,*** the best ones, demand that we explore intensively images, metaphors, and symbols because they are the heart of the matter. The symbols are as important, if not more important, than characterization and theme. They incarnate the latter elements. The novels are formal designs which create their powerful effects by the accumulation of significant recurring details. They are perfectly suited to explication.

I am interested in West because he is so ambivalent. Although he creates his art with great care . . . , he does not possess a closed mind. He gives us no final solutions. When we read the last sentence of any of his novels, we are not completely relieved of the tensions and ambivalences preceding it. ***Miss Lonelyhearts,*** for example, concludes with: "They both rolled part of the way down the stairs." I underline "part of the way"—it symbolizes his refusal to write an easy conclusion, fixing guilt and offering rewards. Miss Lonelyhearts, Peter Doyle, and Betty are implicated in the violence—they share responsibility; they are all on the stairs. The novels reverberate with such ambiguities. (p. 2)

[West] goes beyond psychology. He refuses to give us the childhoods of Lemuel Pitkin, Balso Snell, Tod Hackett, and Miss Lonelyhearts. His heroes may remember a few incidents from their pasts, but they never stop to analyze their parents or their traumas. They exist in a kind of vacuum; their present condition is all that matters—and this condition has as much to do with religious transcendence as violent sex. (p. 4)

The heroes are fascinated with their bodies in such a way that they cannot cope with reality. They keep thinking about holes, wounds, deformities, and even beauties. Their bodies become totemic, holding secret and mysterious power. Their narcissism is strikingly ambiguous. They are in love-and-hate with their physical being; they would like to surrender it or, to use West's word, "dismantle it," but they cannot let go. Thus they are caught in a vicious cycle. They hate what they need to live with. This psychological phenomenon is the novelistic axiom.

West stops here. He does not inform us where the narcissism began; he omits parental training, childhood rituals of excretion, Oedipal romance. He destroys the past. At the same time he makes his heroes act strangely toward other people. Women are usually maternal (see Betty and Fay in ***Miss Lonelyhearts;*** Mrs. Pitkin in ***A Cool Million***; or Miss McGeeney in one of her transformations in ***The Dream Life of Balso Snell***) or destructive creatures (see Faye Greener in ***The Day of the Locust***). Men are threatening authorities (Shrike in ***Miss Lonelyhearts,*** the various guides in ***The Dream Life of Balso Snell,*** and the police and judges in ***A Cool Million***). The heroes are out of place in the adult world. Wherever they turn for comfort and instruction, they find danger. It is no wonder that they retreat into their beds (or shells or enclosures), preferring to play mentally with their own bodies. Perhaps this is the secret of the novels' endings. A wet dream (***Balso Snell***); a shooting and falling down the stairs (***Miss Lonelyhearts***); a final dismantling and martyrdom (***A Cool Million***); a hysterical laugh (***The Day of the Locust***)—these various endings rehearse the flight into sleep, dreams, the womb of self.

West's novels are childish. Although they are written with great authority, they lapse into silliness (***A Cool Million***) and exhibitionism (***The Dream Life of Balso Snell***). These lapses are often noted—what critic could neglect them?—but they are usually dismissed without analyzing their sources. I suggest that they are the clue to the shaping spirit behind all the novels.

Dust jackets of the first editions of Nathanael West's works. From The Dream Life of Balso Snell. *Contact Editions, 1931./From* A Cool Million: The Dismantling of Lemuel Pitkins. *Covici, Friede, 1934. Copyright 1934 by Nathanael West. Used by permission of Crown Publishers, Inc./ From* The Day of the Locust. *Random House, 1939. Reprinted by permission of Random House, Inc.*

The novels deal with the fears (and rages) that an innocent child feels in the adult world; heroes vent their feelings in primitive ways—they have fits or tantrums when they discover that their bodies are mere objects to others. The fact that ***The Dream Life of Balso Snell*** is a closed dreamworld should alert us to this narcissistic quality.

Closed dreamworld! The phrase, once we think of it, applies to the underlying structure of all the novels. ***Balso Snell*** is a series of dreams-within-dreams, centering in the hero's unconscious desires for sexual fulfillment. Despite the many episodes, it returns to the adolescent wet dream as the source of the preceding art. ***Miss Lonelyhearts*** has many more realistic characters than the first novel, but they seem to be extreme projections of the hero; they are aspects of his tormented personality. It is impossible at times to separate Miss Lonelyhearts from Shrike or Peter Doyle. There is a dreamlike quality because events and characters are melodramatic, stylized, and self-serving. ***A Cool Million*** describes the American dream (the freedom to gain success), but behind this dream lies the same narcissistic desires and attitudes we have seen. Mr. Whipple, Jake Raven, Wu Fong, and Lemuel Pitkin are drawn in heavy strokes as a child would portray them. ***The Day of the Locust*** is set in the closed dreamworld of Hollywood. Here childish feelings are given professional status because they are the creative forces behind our movies. (pp. 5-6)

West's novels are "on the edge." They begin with quest (or, better yet, wish-fulfillment) and end with nightmarish failure. Balso Snell dreams of completion as an artist (and man); Miss Lonelyhearts wants to save the world; Lemuel Pitkin, on a lower level of aspiration, travels extensively to find money for his mother's house; and Tod Hackett hopes to paint "The Burning of Los Angeles." These heroes are defeated. They are overwhelmed by dark violence (bred of frustration). West is shrewd enough to underline the dreams of his heroes by writing dreams-within-the-basic-dream. His novels are full of dreams—to the point that it becomes difficult to separate or define clearly the waking state. By emphasizing dreams, he compels us to realize that rationalism, sanity, and daylight thinking are less important (and creative) than the irrational dreams we share.

I believe that West writes about compulsive designs. His heroes try to plot their lives to reach the goals they have set for themselves, but they act obsessively. They do not see much of reality—only those aspects which fit or mirror their needs. . . . West's novels are very American in their portrayal of these designs.

They resemble the romances described by Richard Chase. [The critic cites in a footnote Chase's *The American Novel and Its Tradition* "for this representative statement: 'Oddity, distortion of personality, dislocations of normal life, recklessness of behavior, malignancy of motive—these the English novel has included. Yet the profound poetry of disorder we find in the American novel is missing, with rare exceptions, from the English.' West surely gives us the 'poetry of disorder.'"] They shy away from the full-bodied, substantial materials used by George Eliot or Jane Austen. They are flat, stylized, and nocturnal. Their very strength lies in such qualities. They refuse to accept the world as it is; they rage against it as they cry for more—for more wisdom and goodness. They want to believe in the values of everyday life—as the English novel does—but they know that such values cannot exist with certainty in a world of illusion, deception, and violence. The oddity, the narrowness, the intensity—aren't these, finally, the only clear method to capture the American experience? (pp. 6-7)

West employs many opposing symbols—the house and the voyage (or "field-trip"—to use his word); the actor and the spectator; the real and the unreal et al. These couples establish the frame of reference for his narcissistic heroes. Because Miss Lonelyhearts or Tod Hackett cannot solve his religious-psychological problems (who can?), he tends to have double vision. He is unable to see reality clearly; he tends to view it as a set of ambivalent forces. The objects which surround him (aside from his body) become terrifying. Thus Miss Lonelyhearts cannot merely accept his room and forget about it. It gets out of control; it suddenly becomes imbued with all sorts of meaning (enclosure, womb, tomb), and these meanings shake him because he cannot take a stand. He cannot commit himself to one meaning. His ambivalence, of course, is much greater when he has to cope with various metaphysical symbols. Christ disturbs him more than his room, but the two externals share this perplexing quality.

Rooms: the "horse" in ***The Dream Life of Balso Snell;*** the newspaper office in ***Miss Lonelyhearts;*** the interior decoration in ***A Cool Million;*** the frame-devices in ***The Day of the Locust.*** These basic rooms are echoed in so many other symbolic structures that West almost gives us the "other voices, other rooms" of Capote. The important thing is that they are all haunted. Balso feels trapped (as he is in his own body), and he cannot get out. When he journeys forth, he is destroyed by violent, frenetic movement.

Voyage: all the novels are built on a journey as the epigraph to ***The Dream Life of Balso Snell*** would lead us to believe: "After all, my dear fellow, life, Anaxagoras has said, is a journey." But the journey is "to the end of night" because the heroes do not move steadily. Their "pilgrim's progress" is interfered with by repetitions, coincidences, and crowds. Any page of West's novels stresses such unbalanced movement. I need only cite the army "jumbled together in bobbing disorder" at the beginning of ***The Day of the Locust*** to point the way.

I have compulsively stressed unclear vision of the heroes (not of West who sees clearly and independently). This vision also functions symbolically. Balso perceives "strange foreshortenings" (he is describing the girl cripples) throughout his adventures; Miss Lonelyhearts stares at the crucifix and "it becomes a bright fly"; Lemuel Pitkin has a glass eye; and Tod is a painter who uses fantastic, deformed models to get at reality. The novels are visionary, but like those of new American Gothic, they propose that epiphanies are duplicitous, warped, and somehow unbelievable. (pp. 8-10)

The four novels vary in quality—the two most powerful ones are, of course, ***Miss Lonelyhearts*** and ***The Day of the Locust***—but they share remarkable similarities of theme, character, and symbol. We would expect this kind of similarity because West is, like such other American writers as Poe, Hawthorne, Melville, and Faulkner, an obsessive artist. I underline the noun to indicate that he does not merely throw "narcissism," quest, etc. at us and force us to pattern them; he shapes his dreams in complex ways that demand the close readings I have given.

The novels resemble lyrics. They are constructed tightly—except for ***A Cool Million***—because they stress image, not idea. This is not to imply that they do not deal with important themes—West writes about the most important ones we can consider: destiny, wisdom, "reality"!—but to suggest that they are, after all the analyses, symbolist designs. If we neglect the performer, the mirror, or the room, we misread (misunderstand) the meaning. Image is idea; form is content. (p. 119)

But there is one more point. We are given some hope because we recognize that no matter how much we may hate art, calling it false or inhuman as Balso Snell did, we are pleased that it can illuminate the inadequacy of our designs. We are comforted by art—if it cannot rescue us from life's painful details, it can, nevertheless, alert us to them and by doing so, help us to scrutinize ourselves squarely and ironically. For this pleasurable, terrifying insight we are grateful to West's best novels. (pp. 123-24)

Irving Malin, in his Nathanael West's Novels, *Southern Illinois University Press, 1972, 141 p.*

T. R. STEINER (essay date 1973)

[*Steiner's was the winning essay in a contest seeking critical studies of Nathanael West's work. In the following excerpt, he discusses the basic structure of the typical Horatio Alger success story, which West employed in writing* A Cool Million, *and finds that West incorporated numerous other "American motifs, fictions, and myths" into the work. For another discussion of* A Cool Million, *see the excerpt by Fred T. Marsh (1934).*]

Nathanael West's ***A Cool Million*** remains the least appreciated of his works, to a large extent because it has not been read properly. Its mode of operation is only partially understood at best; hence readers' responses are at the same time not serious enough and too serious. Like the Horatio Alger novels, on which it is based (and in a way like *Gulliver's Travels,* from which it draws the name of its hero, Lemuel Pitkin), ***Cool Million*** frequently purports to be a children's book. As such, although its literary mode may be parody or mock-heroic, West's novel is also fantasy, myth, dream-wish identification, imaginative "redemption" and pure play. Because of this important "latent content," the book much more resembles ***The Dream Life of Balso Snell*** and ***Miss Lonelyhearts*** (called a modern myth by Victor Comerchero) [see *TCLC,* Vol. 1] than one might first have suspected. Its great difference from these earlier works is that they are more arty—a quality toward which West manifested much ambivalence.

I do not deny that the book has "serious" social and political content, and clearly shows West's anxiety that a Hitlerian dictatorship may come to Depression-fragmented America. But this content is trite: demagoguery and the blind force of mass-man had been staples of cultural and political analysis since de Tocqueville, Burckhardt and Nietzsche had outlined them as particular dangers of democracy. West seems not so much interested in the fact of these monstrosities as in the popular imagination which makes it easier for them to thrive. That, rather than Nathan "Shagpoke" Whipple, is the arch-villain of his book. As overt pulp-magazine fiction, ***Cool Million*** is a mirror of the popular imagination—an early piece of pop art, like Rauschenberg or Lichtenstein, using American cultural materials to comment on them, chanting American themes in a skewed, that is to say, "true," fashion. Here, the novel insinuates, is the landscape of the American psyche, which needs and creates Horatio Alger, racial stereotypes, pulp pornography. If we required yet another foil to make the mode of ***Cool Million*** clear, it would be the many commentators on mass culture from Freud to Robert Warshow and Susan Sontag, but most notably George Orwell in his examination of boys' weekly papers and lewd postcards to get at the common Englishman. For a comparable reason, West consciously wrote a pornographic penny dreadful.

It is, therefore, meaningless to talk of *West's* style in the book since his effort must have been to divest himself of style, to become a scarcely literate and dirty-minded adolescent. West "supplies" only the invisible frame—the skewing of speeches, the introduction of super-grotesqueries, the revelation of what happens after the jump-cut, in short, the consciousness which the reader perceives above and controlling the naive materials, the consciousness revealed by the mere fact of West's recognizable name on the book. So, the Alger material becomes very sophisticated and the skeleton for, as well as merging with, a whole series of American motifs, fictions and myths, American Dreams certainly, but also American Nightmares. The American Boy wants to succeed and honorably have the boss's daughter (or at least a clean "white" girl like Fiedler's Blonde Maiden) but he also wants to destroy (in fantasy-roles like the gangster) and to brutally deflower. He wouldn't mind being Tom Baxter piggishly taking frail Betty; he lusts after the international, dark sex of Wung's House of All Nations, and like the American Girl desires exotic experience but preferably with fabricated authenticity. Alger's hero becomes the picaro (the myth tends readily toward this metamorphosis because of American cultural and geographic mobility), touching North and South, mine and corral, farm and frontier. Here are Davy Crockett, Abe Lincoln and the martyr Patrick Henry; here, introduced in one of Whipple's speeches, the great military landmarks—"Remember the Alamo! Remember the Maine!" Here Chingachgook and the comity of American bloods like that in Cooper and Melville. In outline, sketchy, fragmented, jocose form, then, ***Cool Million*** is the encyclopedia of mythic "America." And West realizes that the Dreams mask horrors and coexist with nightmares—American xenophobia, anxiety, fear of the cultural exotic. Hence the racial stereotypes: cops are always Irish and revel in brutality; Chinese are inscrutable "celestials"; Indians retain the redness of their savagery; Jews, in their craft and cunning, deceive and steal. American populism hates, fears, but also identifies with the foreign, which enables it to have its darker fantasies. It is like Hitler, who (according to Alan Ross and Norman Cohn) turned the Jew into both the dark father whom he strove to destroy and the dark actor who fulfilled his erotic wishes. Although the Deep South riot which West describes could happen, West is least concerned with describing present reality, or predicting the future; the riot is a "sign of the times," a symbolic probability (very much in the Aristotelian sense) given the real nature of the native American psyche. It is a pleasing fiction to that psyche, the inverse corollary to the "constructive" egoism of the Alger myth. West sees, indeed, that whatever their outward manifestation, however much self-control or sacrifice even our good myths demand, they are power-myths either in essence or application, violent by nature as is every page of ***Cool Million.***

The dreams of power are analyzed to their archetypes; so is the dream of martyrdom. The essential structure of the book is not the successful life of an Alger protagonist but the creation of a martyr-hero for Whipple's National Revolutionary Party—the life not of J. P. Morgan but a mock-Christ. Strangely, those critics who see West as a symbolist—his central fictions as quest and sacrifice, and Lonelyhearts as a modern Christ—have not recognized the underlying fable of ***Cool Million.*** Like Christ but without His consciousness, Pitkin bears a Revealed New Life, suffers and dies for his Dream, leaving his "message" to American youth. Lemuel (the name means literally, "belonging to God") has no earthly father; we are asked to see him (through the name of his widowed mother Sarah) as Isaac, Christ's type as sacrificial victim in the Old Testament. Whipple is his spiritual father, sending him into the world with a blessing (and, ironically, like Judas "selling" him to that world with the loan of thirty dollars). Before the quest—an attempt quite literally to "save his house"—begins, Lem kills the "furious animal" which assails the innocent Betty, conquers the bestial, pig-eyed Tom Baxter, but is tricked by that fraudulent "butcher boy," in an incident prefiguring his future defeats. Still, Lem tries to live the destined life, is kind, charitable, self-sacrificing; experiences degradation and poverty for Whippleism (the avatar of the Dream); and is slowly destroyed by the world his message is trying to "save." (Modern America here is Sodom, the Cities of the Plain, Roman Judaea or their modern manifestation, Eliot's Wasteland which West clearly seems to call on.)

At least once, Pitkin is explicitly likened to Christ. Having been arrested for trying to accuse the powerful brothel-keeper Wu Fong, he protests: "But I'm innocent. . . . I'm innocent," repeated Lem, a little desperately. "So was Christ," said Mr. Barnes with a sigh, "and they nailed Him." . . . And they nail Pitkin, in the mock-crucifixion of the music-hall scene. Standing between the two comics, Riley and Robbins (is it far-fetched to see this name as deliberately evoking the two thieves?), who use his destroyed body as a comic prop, Pitkin begins the revolutionary speech prepared for him by Whipple: "'I am a clown . . . but there are times when even clowns must grow serious. This is such a time. I . . .' Lem got no further. A shot rang out and he fell dead, drilled through the heart by an assassin's bullet." . . . Brilliantly, West prevents Lem from stepping out of his role. He must be interpreted by Whipple on the national holiday, Pitkin's Birthday, which combines in a socio-religious ceremony elements of Washington's or Lincoln's Birthday, Armistice Day and Christmas: "Simple was his pilgrimage and brief, yet a thousand years hence, no story, no tragedy, no epic poem will be filled with greater wonder, or be followed by mankind with deeper feeling, than that which tells of the life and death of Lemuel Pitkin . . . although dead yet he speaks . . . he did not live or die in vain. Through his martyrdom, the National Revolutionary Party triumphed, and by that triumph this country was delivered. . . . America became again American." Pitkin the redeemer; although "dismantled," his mantle has fallen on other shoulders. The book ends with a striking triptych: on the reviewing stand, as thousands of American youth "March for Pitkin," are Pitkin's mother (his Mary), Betty Prail (surely in her prostitution the Magdalene) and Whipple, at once the God, Judas and Pope of Pitkinism.

So, West jocoseriously sees Christ the hero in Horatio Alger, and a large degree of the Alger quality in Christ. The Greatest Story Ever Told has become in this book pulp-magazine uplift, and West realizes that for the popular imagination Christ (or the archetypal questing hero) can function either as victor or victim. The risen "Christ" is an identificatory model; the fallen, a defenseless recipient of our yearning aggression. We worship the powerful, successful "Christ"; we prey on the meek, submissive, idealistic. Indeed, what West seems most responsive to in the Alger myth, and in some of the other American myths he parodies, is that they are exploitative. In the fallen world of modern America, the promises of the American Dream are used to harness the idealism, energy, altruism of the young. The culture myth, in this novel transmitted by Whipple to Pitkin, implicitly says to the child, "The world is your oyster. Go out and succeed." But it does not prepare him for social and political realities; indeed by its lie, disables him in the inevitable competition with knowing adults and boys who have wised up. Yet, the cultural ideal endures, virtually through the destruction of the idealistic child, betrayed promiscuously to sharper, con-man, Indian, Southerner, WASP, Jew. However sympathetic Whipple may be at times, however consciously idealistic, he is the exploiter (already in the first scene bilking the innocent Lem). And however much of a booby Pitkin is, he functions—like Candide or Parson Adams—as the ingenu in satire, establishing—Pitkin obviously without force or validity—an unshakeable blind belief in the right, the good, the committed. (pp. 157-62)

In ***Cool Million*** West's Jewishness begins to be seen in the intertwining of native American and Christian (and New Testament) with Jewish (and Old Testament) strains. The hero, his mother, his spiritual father, indeed almost every character in the book, has at least one Jewish (or Hebrew) name: Yankees like Nathan Whipple, Levi Underdown, Ephraim Pierce; Indians like Jake Raven and Israel Satinpenny; an Irish Moe Riley; and Jewish Patriarchs like Asa Goldstein, Ezra Silverblatt, Seth Abromovitz. There is a lot of incidental fooling with these names—Jake Raven is violent ("raving," "ravin"), Satinpenny's first name reminds us of the commonplace equation of Red Indians with the Lost Tribe, two characters "pierce" and "rile," two Jews are associated with pelf—but I think that their main point is to posit modern America as a kind of conglomerate ironic Chosen People, sharing not only names but characteristics and cultural "artifacts." Thus, Asa Goldstein sells "Colonial Exteriors and Interiors" and Ezra Silverblatt supplies coonskin caps and other accessories to Whipple's Party. (For their trading in Americana, even at their own expense, Jews are indeed satirized heavily.) But the Yankees and Indians also are characterized by their greed and financial rapacity, while the two lawyers who "get" Pitkin are Seth Abromovitz and Elisha Barnes. The characteristic which all share is their violence, whether overt like that of Irish cops, Southern lynch mobs, and Indians, or disguised like that of Warden Purdy who has all of Pitkin's teeth knocked out "to prevent infection." By taking the melting-pot metaphor seriously, making it one constructive principle of his book, West suggests that the Hebrew, Christian, and American myths are interpenetrable, indeed, interchangeable for "explaining" life in these eclectic United States. All of them talk about one life, which is man's. (pp. 162-63)

It may be late in the day to speak of any important American writer, much less Nathanael West, as a Jewish writer, and to involve one's own experience of Jewishness in a discussion of him. To do so invites scorn and misunderstanding. To do so, now that the Jews have made it very nearly to the center of the White Establishment, and other groups are suffering even more intensely their traditional fate of exclusion, runs the risk of seeming dated. Yet Leslie Fiedler in a recent *Partisan* (Summer 1967) called West for ***Balso Snell*** the first of the modern American Jewish writers, and he is right—at least as far as ***Balso*** and ***Cool Million*** are concerned. It is valuable, even necessary, to approach West with some understanding of the Jewish cultural milieu, if only to counteract the effect of his near-convert's fascination with Christ in ***Miss Lonelyhearts*** and to open up the body of Jewish-Hebrew reference in his books. It may be helpful, although certainly not necessary, for the critic to be personally familiar with the particular cultural shocks which West seems to have been an heir to, however much he tried to avoid or deny them. For whatever degree of universality there is in West's fictions about the American scene, I am convinced that he was an intensely personal writer, with a Freudian's heightened awareness that an author, by indirections, talks of his own wishes and fears, and that his symbols plot his own inner landscape. (pp. 169-70)

T. R. Steiner, "'Cool Million': West's Lemuel and the American Dream," in Nathanael West, the Cheaters and the Cheated: A Collection of Critical Essays, *edited by David Madden, Everett/Edwards, Inc., 1973, pp. 157-70.*

KINGSLEY WIDMER (essay date 1973)

[*Widmer is an American literary and social critic and the author of* Nathanael West *(1982; see Additional Bibliography), a comprehensive survey of West's writings. In the following excerpt from his essay* "The Day of the Locust: The Last Masquerade," *Widmer examines West's novel in the context of other Hollywood novels and considers it "probably the best of that curious subgenre."*]

In ***The Day of the Locust*** Nathanael West describes his denizens of the Hollywood tide pools as "masqueraders." As with the anguished dead horse at the bottom of a swimming pool in one scene, they all turn out to be rubber imitation bad jokes. Yet West's sardonic detailing suggests that the masquerade applies not only to his characters and the dream factories but to the houses, the costumes, the relationships, and the sensibilities of all southern California, and beyond. (p. 179)

[West is] a sharply sad-eyed documentor of a particular reality. I enter this as a caveat against those who see the author of ***The Day of the Locust*** as primarily a fantast of the grotesque. West, I agree, is an artful stylist, one of the important American adaptors—along with such as Henry Miller—of the surrealist image and the concretely fantastic disjunction. But they apply to an actual world. West, I would also argue, is to American fiction what Zamiatin is to Russian: the small but brilliant descendent of Dostoyevsky, who very specifically influenced them both in their compulsive victims and ironic crucifixions and mockingly anguished prophecies of suffering and destruction and nihilism. And ***The Day of the Locust,*** from my reading of about four dozen Hollywood novels, is probably the best of that curious subgenre of the reality of fictional corruption. West achieved distinction in his intense mannerist expressiveness. Some of his descriptions—with dusk a "violet piping, like a Neon tube, outlined the tops of the ugly, hump-backed hills"; with night "through a slit in the blue serge sky poked a grained moon that looked like an enormous bone button"—not only most aptly catch the scene (at least back in the times when you could see the mountains and the moon) but also most pertinently suggest the synthetic fabrication which is part of the larger masquerade theme. Similarly, West's precision catches the fusion of corruption and naivete and of apathy and violence which marks his so American characters.

We can also see West as the progenitor of the bitterly wry laugh at the ornately grotesque and sardonically pitiful which became known as "black humor" in his descendents. That victim's smile, as with his narrating Tod Hackett, covers a desperate ambivalence. As with the writer Tod describes in ***The Day of the Locust,*** the author, too, played out "an involved comic rhetoric that permitted him to express his moral indignation and still keep . . . [his] worldliness and wit." But the mature West is no Pynchon or Barth—not nearly so clever and uncommitted. For he is—how shall we say it?—more simply suffering and serious about the actual. In the first chapter of ***The Day of the Locust*** he describes his Hollywood masqueraders and bemusedly reports on the grotesquery but concludes with earnest poignancy that "few things are sadder than the truly monstrous." (pp. 180-81)

The masquerades are monstrous, comic and bitter pathetic gestures and roles by which one lives, and dies. The more one pursues West's Hollywood, the more actual rather than merely artful it becomes. I once thought the cockfight scene in ***The Day of the Locust*** a fancying of the bizarre only digressively related to the rest of the novel by the motif of fraudulent violence. In fact, as news files from the Thirties confirm, that banned sport was widespread—as central to the subculture of California then as the briefer fad of marathon dancing in McCoy's *They Shoot Horses, Don't They?*—and can still be viewed in Latin ghettos such as East Los Angeles or Atascadero. West's cockfight scene may revealingly masquerade the characters' violent fraud but also reports their immediate reality. Just as West sees (in ***Miss Lonelyhearts***) human warping and suffering as real, not as something to be explained or ameliorated away, so, in ***The Day of the Locust,*** he sees the unreality represented by Hollywood as devastatingly real, in an actual time and place. Hollywood simply realizes the destruction of cultural vitality—West's major preoccupation—which Miss Lonelyhearts summarized: "Men have always fought their misery with dreams. Although dreams were once powerful, they have been made puerile. . . . Among many betrayals, this one is the worst."

Thus ***The Day of the Locust*** might appropriately be related to its special subgenre, the literature of cultural betrayal, the "Hollywood novel" or "Southern California rococco," as long as we do not reduce it to mere literature. The grotesqueries of such fictions belong to the continuing historical reality of California which, of course, becomes the all-American future. The main issue is a desperate meaninglessness. (pp. 182-83)

[Absurd] contrast between material and meaning, appearance and reality, characterized the earliest Hollywood novels, such as *Merton of the Movies.* Harry Wilson's genially elaborate playfulness emphasized the discrepancies between his hero's serious intentions and the comic results. A doggedly simple Iowa boy plays his heart out as the great lover and sterling hero. In the mechanical jogging of early film technique, his moral intensity can come out only as Sennett farce. Given the technology, sincere American idealism provides slapstick. The moral still holds for our culture.

More than a generation later, in *Love Among the Cannibals,* Wright Morris puts his Hollywood songwriter in the Lawrencean love of his life. In the absurdity of the late-Hollywood ethos, his passionate intensity can only create a third-rate popular song. Peeling off the masquerade, like peeling away at Peer Gynt's onion, leaves nothing—"You strip down to / The Essentially / Inessential you," as his song has it. The masquerade is all.

The Day of the Locust appeared midway in time between *Merton of the Movies* and *Love Among the Cannibals,* and seems continuous with them. The mock-heroic comedy, then, goes beyond art to the thing itself: Hollywood. In the initial studio scene of West's novel, we have the filming of the Battle of Waterloo; it ends in the disastrous collapse of the prop—Mont St. Jean—a production judgment ironically analogous to Napoleon's. History itself turns into the mock-heroic. For the novelist, as for the tourist who stared in charmed disbelief at

228.

him laugh and he began to imitate the siren as loud as he could.

XXVIII

Claude was home when the police car brought Tod. He helped carry him into the house and then went to phone a doctor. When he came back to undress him, he found him sitting on the edge of the bed, talking very rapidly and very loudly to himself. He kept on while Claude pulled off his shoes and trousers and helped him into a pair of pajamas. Although he was delirious, it wasn't difficult to understand what he was saying.

He was describing a project for an enormous canvas to be called "The Burning of Los Angeles." In it he would show the people who come to California to die, the fruit and grass eaters, the cultists of all sorts, economic as well as religious, the wave, aeroplane and preview watchers, the whole united front of screwboxes and screwballs; all those poor devils, in fact, who can only be stirred by the promise of miracles and then only to violence. But in this picture they wouldn't be bored. They would be shown dancing joyously around the flames of one city and running to fire others.

When he had finished describing the painting, he forced Claude to argue with him. Claude said that he was

229.

exaggerating the importance of Southern California's screwballs. He admitted that they might be desperate enough to burn a few houses in Hollywood, but said that they were the pick of America's madmen and not at all typical of the country as a whole.

This made Tod still more angry. He changed the image Claude had used from "pick" to "cream of America's madmen" and shouted that the milk from which it had been skimmed was just as rich in violence. The Angelenos would be first, but their brothers all over the country would follow. Only the working classes would resist. There would be civil war.

He raved on until the doctor came and put him to sleep.

The last two pages of the manuscript of The Day of the Locust, *with a complete final chapter that West deleted. Courtesy of Jay Martin.*

the one-dimensional grandeur of the sets, everything turns into a prop.

The characters in ***The Day of the Locust,*** as in most of the more perceptive Hollywood fictions, turn out to be the props of artists who fear they have themselves become the properties of an unbelievable and puerile myth. As with West's would-be starlet, Faye Greener, who acquires the money for her father's fancy funeral as a call girl not as an act of guilt or love but simply as mock-heroic role playing of the devoted daughter—the people are as amoral as the fake scenery. It is all a question, as the writer within the novel says of Mrs. Jennings whore-house, of ''skillful packaging . . . a triumph of industrial design.''

Even F. Scott Fitzgerald, who described himself as a ''spoiled priest'' and always desperately tried to give moral weight to his American success stories, cannot avoid turning a moral scene into a pratfall in Hollywood. The sweet young narrator in *The Last Tycoon* lectures her producer-father on charity. Then she opens a closet door and a naked secretary falls out. Or, in a crucial scene, two women ride on the gigantic statue head of the Goddess Siva in a studio lot flood. Not only is the prop absurd, but, when we later learn that one woman is the heroine and the other a prostitute, so is all symbolic portentousness of the scene.

Thus, almost inspite of themselves, the Hollywood novelists force us to see symbols and morals as merely props to other props. In Norman Mailer's *The Deer Park* the ostensibly love-struck narrator and the beautiful movie queen carry on sexually while she carries on a telephone conversation with someone else. The prop takes over, with the lovely lady fornicating later with someone else in a phonebooth. The incongruities, as with West's scene of a lascivious dwarf and an over-sized prostitute, or Mailer's scene of a producer lecturing his stenographer on morals and then dropping her between his knees for *fellatio,* become subject and norm of the Hollywood material.

When you can't tell phonebooths from boudoirs and prostitutes from heroines and grotesqueries from moralities, then the material may properly be called ''Hollywood.'' By similar twisting, the erotic fantasies become desexed. All but the catatonic audience soon recognize the Manly Hero as really a faggot, the Sweet Innocent Girl as a whore, the Passionate Artist (like West's Tod Hackett) as really an impotent voyeur. The figures of virtue, of course, such as Mailer's power-elite or West's fanatic lower-middle class refugees from the Protestant ethos, use moral assertion as warmup for nasty perversion. It adds up to an inverted morality play, in which the only moral is the inversion.

West elaborates at some length the masquerading of Harry Greener, ex-vaudevillean become silver polish huckster. Harry puts on an obviously phony misery act for sympathy and then suddenly finds himself actually ill and dying. The masquerade has become the reality but the very counterfeiting makes him unable to realize, or know how to respond to, his own reality. A generation later, Allison Lurie in *The Nowhere City* (probably the best of the Hollywood novels of the 1960s), has her prim, repressed and disdainful New England heroine act-out in Hollywood as a bleached, free-wheeling sex-pot, and then with smooth mockery suggests that as her authentic character. The masquerade, like the Hollywood prop, has taken over. (pp. 183-86)

In almost all the stories, when we find intelligence at work in Hollywood it insists upon its impotence. Granted, the tone varies from James T. Farrell's exposing flat sarcasm ("$1,000 A Week") about the irrelevance of the artist through the urbane mannering of exactly the same point by Bemelmans (*Dirty Eddy*). Morris' cynical "ex-cornbelt Shelley," Earl Horter, is no more exempt than Fitzgerald's naively literary Bennington girl, Cecelia Bradley. Yet with hardly any exceptions—we can allow a misplaced touch of it to Schulberg's ponderous melodrama-memoir around Fitzgerald (*The Disenchanted*)—such fictions do not even pretend to be tragedies of the defeated artist but only of artists-as-masqueraders. (p. 186)

Tod, West's artist-narrator, finds himself hopelessly loving the vacuous heroine, Faye, whom he must also despise. The degraded muse diabolically attracts, even with her narcissistic egotism, ruthlessness combined with stupidity, and bitch-goddess' call to destruction (Tod reflects that "her invitation wasn't to pleasure, but . . . closer to murder than to love"). The fatuousness, even the very dehumanization, seem the essential appeal. In ***The Day of the Locust*** no man escapes the yearning—sophisticated writer, primitive Mexican, voracious dwarf, drugstore cowboy, middle-aged puritan, perceptive artist. For each, she is the masturbatory muse. (p. 187)

As the American novelists record it, the studios did for onanistic images what Ford did for automobiles. The Big Con of Hollywood becomes a penultimate image of American aggrandizement. . . . Thus West (and Henry Miller in the Hollywood sketches of *The Air-Conditioned Nightmare*) rightly see the surreal congregations of the dissociated and defeated and deranged as the new America. Nothing fully human can sustain itself behind the poses; the aggrandizement now leads nowhere—the final price of the masquerade. (p. 188)

I detect in most of the Hollywood novels, with varying degrees of consciousness, a desperate effort to find a bedrock reality under the masquerading. Struggling to explain the pseudo-greatness of the Hollywood "giants," the force with which they pursued shadow shows, the novelists are curiously driven to "inexplicable megalomania" or simply "the urge towards total exhaustion." West shows this emptying of sensibility unto madness as the mass effect. It ends in the sex-and-violence exhaustion of fantasy and resentment in an otherwise valueless world. Nothing really happens, nothing is thought or felt, not even the experience of nothing. West's artist reflects, amidst rape fantasies, on the nature of would-be starlet Faye near the end of ***The Day of the Locust:***

> Nothing could hurt her. She was like a cork. No matter how rough the sea got, she would go dancing over the same waves that sank iron ships and tore away piers of reinforced concrete. . . . Wave after wave reared its ton on ton of solid water and crashed down only to have her spin gaily away . . . a very pretty cork, gilt with a glittering fragment of mirror set in its top. The sea in which it danced was beautiful, green in the trough of the waves and silver at their tips. But for all their moondriven power, they could do no more than net the bright cork for a moment in a spume of intricate lace. Finally it was set down on a strange shore where a savage with pork-sausage fingers and a pimpled butt picked it up and hugged it to his sagging belly. Tod recognized the fortunate man; he was one of Mrs. Jennings [whorehouse] customers. . . .

Vintage West, this devastating playfulness: the disparate images ("spume of intricate lace" and "pimpled butt"); the parody of the media processing (the thing of beauty turned into a burlesque of a South Sea scenario); the insights into the total masqueraders (machined prettiness, narcissistic mirror, invulnerability to experience); and yet the artist-author's mixed enthrallment and disgust with the "pretty cork."

As West wrote in ***Miss Lonelyhearts,*** only in the snake-mirrors of "hysteria" can such deadness "take on a semblance of life." Socially, that hysteria is the mob scene, the day of apocalypse. West's timorously chiliastic artist-narrator, gathering his expressionistic fragments for his masterpiece, "The Burning of Los Angeles," can find reality only in the image of the end. And so with West. Yet we have curious reversals here. "The Burning of Los Angeles" is a highly plausible image—many Angelenos half-expect it to happen each fall, with the frenzied spread of brush fires in the peculiar conditions of the basin, with its greasewood and Santa Ana desert winds. But notice also that West plays with that sense of unreality so obsessive in almost all Hollywood novels. We apparently should see the earlier party scenes as rehearsals for the final scene—one is described as a "mock riot"—but the "real" riot becomes yet another dress rehearsal for the ultimate fantasy of the artist. In three or four senses, the final image is only "another picture"—yet another mock riot, a movie premiere, the artist-narrator's preparatory scenes for his masterpiece of apocalypse, and Nathanael West's riotous mockery, as well as the image of the promised end. (pp. 189-91)

Alone and despairing in Los Angeles one New Year's Eve a generation ago, I drifted about downtown. So did thousands of other young, and not so young, inadequately narcoticized delinquents. The aimlessly circling crowd grew, clotted here and there around a curse that offered a fight or a scream that suggested a rape. There were random bits of violence, several plate glass windows shattered, many dresses furtively torn, a few arrests, a few injuries, but finally nothing, not even an adequate mob scene, could find its form. We were all avid spectators for some image of a promising end but all cheated of even the hysteria for which we longed.

So it is, in spite of the overstatements of some critics, with West's concluding, and quite unZolaesque, mob scene. One stomping, some pressing, ripping, shoving; the sirens going, a few injuries, a half-comic simulated hysteria at the end. But little truly happens. West, yet again, remained faithful to his materials. The desperately bored and cheated crowds of ***The Day of the Locust*** provide only their own image as the end of life. In historic fact, the mob fascism which West, replaying his own ending to the burlesque ***A Cool Million,*** half-prophesied, has yet to come to full life in America. Our totalitarianisms slyly develop from other directions. The "lower middle class'' mob was tricked into safer and isolating fantasies of the lavish boob tube culture, and so their rages usually end in the mechanized passivity which is the basic, and base, condition of the mass technological society.

The ravaging of the land by the petit bourgeoise locusts, as West saw, rests in the culture of social and individual malnutrition which was Hollywood. In combining his Sherwood Anderson Middle American, Homer, with the cheaters, the technological fantasts, West's insight was that the basic American repressed character was to merge with the Hollywood counterfeit—as it has in our puritanic decadence—providing the largest masquerade of civilization. Essentially, the historic Hollywood is dead; but just as essentially, America has become Hollywood. The ''mock riot,'' the rehearsal of debacle, properly epitomizes it. Rather better than most of the other Hollywood fictionists, West compassionately perceived the insatiable longing for some final masquerade-ending negation. Yet the end to a life of masquerade is only a masquerade become all reality. And that is the saddest as well as truest apocalypse of all. (pp. 191-93)

Kingsley Widmer, '''The Day of the Locust': The Last Masquerade,'' in Nathanael West, the Cheaters and the Cheated: A Collection of Critical Essays, *edited by David Madden, Everett/Edwards, Inc., 1973, pp. 179-93.*

JOANNA E. RAPF (essay date 1981)

[*In the following excerpt, Rapf discusses the difficulties encountered in the 1974 motion picture adaptation of West's novel* The Day of the Locust.]

Of the three best-known ''Hollywood novels,'' F. Scott Fitzgerald's *The Last Tycoon,* Budd Schulberg's *What Makes Sammy Run,* and Nathanael West's ***The Day of the Locust,*** only West's focuses on the dangers and evils of movies themselves. *The Last Tycoon* and *Sammy* both deal with the rotten ''business'' of moviemaking and the destruction of individuals by an industry more concerned with money than human values and art, but West's primary concern is different. Like the others, he looks at the destruction of individuals, but it is not the industry that is chiefly responsible; it is the weakness of the individuals themselves. The book is narrated from the single point of view of Tod Hackett, an insignificant set and costume designer, but he is hardly a thematic center or dominant character such as Fitzgerald's Monroe Stahr or Schulberg's Sammy Glick. Fitzgerald and Schulberg are interested in the big men; West looks instead at the ''little people,'' and the thematic center of his novel is not a single individual, not the effect of the industry on an individual, nor even the fate of the industry itself. Rather, it is the monstrous way in which this ''dream factory,'' like the fascism of the thirties, feeds human weakness by fashioning illusions and creating impossible visions of beauty and romance.

All their lives, West's ''little people'' slave at some kind of dull, heavy labor, ''dreaming of the leisure'' that will one day be theirs. Then, from Iowa and Oklahoma, they come to California, the land of sunshine and oranges. But they soon get tired of oranges and don't know what to do with their time. . . . Movies have made them discontented with themselves. The product of the ''dream factory'' has destroyed their minds, their bodies, their faith in human nature; and it is this product, not the producers, not the stars, not the drive for power and money, that is the villain of West's novel.

And this, perhaps, poses an insurmountable problem in making a film of ***The Day of the Locust:*** it must be a film about the bad influence of film. Ironically, then, the film's very existence will undercut its message. It is problem enough to make a film from a novel with no strong central character or situation, but how much more of a problem where the very premise of that novel implies a film should not be made of it!

A central character is an easy structural device for reshaping a novel into film. A large number of successful examples come to mind—*Tom Jones, Great Expectations, The Graduate.* (pp. 22-3)

The other side of the coin, naturally, is that the majority of *un*successful adaptations come from novels focused around a central idea rather than character. And a case can be made for this, too, since some of the most criticized adaptations have been such ''idea'' films as *Moby Dick, The Trial, Catch-22,* and, of course, ***The Day of the Locust.*** In hindsight, the film's director, John Schlesinger, has recognized this problem, commenting that ''one of the reasons that ***The Day of the Locust*** did not find wider acceptance was that there was no one in it that the audience could root for.'' The standard cliché about the novel as a verbal medium and the film as visual is applicable here. A single character is, after all, visible and an idea is not, so it is almost axiomatic that *Tom Jones,* whose title specifically tells you its subject, is easier to transfer to a visual medium than ***The Day of the Locust,*** whose title is symbolic and more difficult *to see.* . . .

The problem, then, in adapting ***The Day of the Locust*** to film initially seems to be two-fold: one, as a novel it is focused not on a main character but on an idea, and two, central to that idea is that film exploits the weaknesses of people by feeding them with violence and dreams. To make a film of the novel, therefore, is, ironically, to undercut some of its substance. . . .

But there are yet two more problems. (p. 23)

Not only does [***The Day of the Locust***] lack a central character, which at least novels such as *Gatsby* and *The Last Tycoon* have, but its plot is neither action-oriented nor heavily comic: two strikes against successful adaptation without even getting into the fact that the content of the novel condemns its film. But the fourth problem is, perhaps, the most significant of all, at least it is from the point of view of the film's screenwriter, Waldo Salt. For him, the main theme of the book is what West calls ''the need for beauty and romance.'' This theme is what he wanted at the center of the screenplay, this ''human need.'' But he failed, he believes, not so much because of the problems of adaptation *per se,* but because the novel itself does not maintain that fine balance between compassion and irony that is necessary to get this theme across. The irony ends up overshadowing the compassion, and the *need* for beauty and romance is, according to Salt, lost in both the book and the film. This, he adds, was a problem for West himself, whom he knew in Hollywood during the thirties: the balance between compassion and cynicism was not resolved. If he had to do it over, Salt says he would take even more liberties with West's novel than he did, stressing in particular the need for beauty and romance in Tod. (pp. 24-5)

Boredom, loneliness, lack of communication, the search for love, the settling for second best, all emerge in one way or another in the transition from childhood to adulthood. The relationship between the two is crucial to Schlesinger's films and basic to West's novel as well, in the figure of Homer Simpson (the only character who can still ''feel''), and the grotesque mockery of childhood in little Adore Loomis, who represents what happens when children are not allowed their childhood and grow up without love. In the film, Salt and Schlesinger expand on the theme, including a speech which is not in the book, just before the final riot, in which Homer remarks on how children need love. In the light of what follows, the speech becomes ironic, for Homer, tormented beyond endurance by Adore, crushes the boy to death, and the irony becomes a bitter comment on man's words versus his deeds. (p. 26)

The Waterloo set . . . is a metaphor both in the novel and film for the contrast between fantasy and reality and for the collapse of illusion. When the set collapses, West writes:

> This time the same mistake had a different outcome. Waterloo, instead of being the end of the Grand Army, resulted in a draw. Neither side won, and it would have to be fought over again the next day. Big losses, however, were sustained by the insurance company in workmen's compensation.

It is this kind of cynicism that dominates the book. Attacking cultists of various sorts, West has set designer Tod, in a search for models, visit outlandish Hollywood churches where the dead are supposed to find lost objects and a woman in male clothing preaches the "Crusade Against Salt." Although this kind of extreme is left out of the film, a similar element is included in a somewhat confused sequence in which Faye, with Tod and Homer, takes her father to be cured at a revivalist-type service where the main emphasis is clearly on money and show. (p. 28)

The final destruction of deeply religious feeling by the facades with which people live their lives comes in the climactic riot before the movie premier. In the novel the movie is nameless, but Salt and Schlesinger significantly give it to deMille, a director notorious for what [Gerald] Mast has called "size and splash," the superficial spectacle of glitter and gore. In his pre-World War II Hollywood setting, Schlesinger tries to capture the spirit of West writing about a world on the verge of fascism by changing the movie premier's master-of-ceremonies from a "young man with a portable microphone" and a "rapid, hysterical voice . . . like that of a revivalist preacher," to a somewhat older man strikingly resembling Adolph Hitler. The hysteria, the panic, the inhumanity that follow thus become a miniature of a world gone mad, the eruption of violence latent in people who have been lied to, and as they angrily lift Homer up from the bloody body of Adore Loomis, he stretches out his arms in a gesture of crucifixion. There is no mistaking the image of Christ. Homer, the last innocent, the only one who really cares and feels, is destroyed by the uncaring, the unfeeling. The camera pans up to burning telephone poles, tumbling like crosses, more dynamic and specifically religious symbols of the death of feeling than anything West narrates. (pp. 28-9)

The Day of the Locust is a subtle film and it uses subtle imagery, not broad action, to capture the spirit of West's novel. For example, West's idea of sterility and death is given a subtle visual metaphor by the use of sprinklers. Everywhere in the film we see shots of things being watered. Nothing grows naturally in California. In the opening and closing shots of the San Bernardino Arms, sprinklers are going in a futile attempt to make grass green, an idea Salt said he got from his own apartment complex in Los Angeles in the thirties. At the cemetery during Harry Greener's funeral, again those omnipresent sprinklers work away in the background. Everything is artificial, even the dead horse in the Estes' swimming pool. This kind of imagery is effective, but it does not do enough to counterbalance the uneasy tension between compassion and cynicism. The overt events in West's novel—the cockfighting, the studio disaster, Harry Greener's clowning—are, of course, visual and impressive on screen. The problem is the subtlety of the book, the strained relationships between the characters, and the bitter, ironic look, not just at middle-class American life, but at a world about to become the victim of its own illusions. (p. 29)

In summary then, Salt and Schlesinger had to wrestle with four crucial problems in adapting ***The Day of the Locust.*** One is the fact that although it is a satiric novel, it is not a comic one, and the world of external action, of comedy, is inherently more adaptable than the inner world of West's "sadness." The second is that the film, like the novel, allows satire to overshadow compassion, and human feeling, what Salt calls "the human need," is lost. Third, the book is not about a central character. It is held together by Tod's narrative point of view, but this point of view is not maintained in the film. Visually, this is effective, particularly in scenes between Homer and Faye, but without a compensating structural center, the film, unlike the book, lacks focus. And finally, one of the moral premises of the novel is that movies can be life-destroying, so that to make a film of it may be to undercut some of the values essential to the content. As a result of these problems, style and content seem to clash. . . . In particular, we have a case where a weakness in a book was "faithfully" translated onto the screen. The human need for beauty and romance, a need which in a real way is satisfied by movies, is, in this movie, *not* satisfied. Paradoxically, the ultimate irony is that West, in condemning the Hollywood "dream factory," might just have wanted it to be that way! (p. 30)

Joanna E. Rapf, "'Human Need' in 'The Day of the Locust': Problems of Adaptation," in Literature/Film Quarterly, *Vol. IX, No. 1, January, 1981, pp. 22-31.*

ADDITIONAL BIBLIOGRAPHY

Buckley, Tom. *"The Day of the Locust":* Hollywood, by West, by Hollywood." *The New York Times Magazine* (2 June 1974): 11-12, 50, 52, 55-6, 58, 68, 70, 72-3.

Account of the filming of the 1974 motion picture version of *The Day of the Locust,* interspersed with anecdotes about West's life and career.

Burgess, Anthony. "American Themes." In his *The Novel Now: A Guide to Contemporary Fiction,* pp. 193-202. New York: W. W. Norton, 1967.*

Names West as "perhaps a prototype of the contemporary Jewish-American author" seeking to define the relationship of the Jew to the Gentile community.

Caldwell, Erskine. "The Middle Years." In his *Call it Experience: The Years of Learning How to Write,* pp. 81-166. New York: Duell, Sloan and Pearce, 1951.*

Recounts the period in 1931 during which Caldwell lived at the Sutton residential hotel at a reduced rate arranged by West.

Cohen, Arthur. "The Possibility of Belief: Nathanael West's Holy Fool." *Commonweal* 64, No. 11 (15 June 1956): 276-78.

Comparative study of both West's and Fedor Dostoevsky's use of the "holy fool," a character who protests against social conditions that lead to the spiritual impoverishment of humanity. Cohen cites Dostoevsky's characters Raskolnikov, Smerdyakov, Stavrogin, and Kirilov, and West's central character from the novel *Miss Lonelyhearts,* as examples of this type.

"*Miss Lonelyhearts* Is Reviewed." *Contempo* III, No. 11 (25 July 1933): 1, 4-5, 8.

Symposium of reviews of West's second novel, by Bob Brown, Angel Flores, Josephine Herbst, S. J. Perelman, and William Carlos Williams. The review by Williams is excerpted above.

Cowley, Malcolm. "No Escape." In his *Exile's Return: A Literary Odyssey of the 1920s,* pp. 235-45. New York: Viking Press, 1951.*

Characterizes the 1920s as a time when writers sought escape from commercial American society. Cowley finds escape to be a central theme in the literature of the 1920s, and he discusses a scene from *Miss Lonelyhearts* in which the editor Shrike examines and ridicules many of the popular "escapes" of the time: into art, hedonism, religion, and toward a primitive culture.

Fitzgerald, F. Scott. "Introductions and Blurbs: Nathanael West's *The Day of the Locust.*" In *F. Scott Fitzgerald In His Own Time: A Miscellany,* edited by Matthew J. Bruccoli and Jackson R. Bryer, p. 160. Kent: Kent State University Press, 1971.

Reprints a dust-jacket blurb that Fitzgerald wrote for *The Day of the Locust*. Fitzgerald praises the novel's "scenes of extraordinary power" and West's depictions of crowd scenes.

Gehman, Richard B. Introduction to *The Day of the Locust,* by Nathanael West, pp. ix-xxiii. New York: New Directions, New Classics, 1950.

Biographical and critical sketch, concluding with discussion of *The Day of the Locust* as a microcosm of "everything that is wrong with life in the United States."

Hyman, Stanley Edgar. *Nathanael West*. Minneapolis: University of Minnesota Press, 1962, 48 p.

Biographical and critical introduction to West's life and career.

Martin, Jay. *Nathanael West: The Art of His Life*. New York: Farrar, Straus and Giroux, 1970, 435 p.

First full-length biography of West. In planning and researching this book, Martin interviewed many of West's friends, associates, and family members, and was given unprecedented access to letters and other unpublished papers pertaining to West. Martin also provides a broad social and cultural history of the time in which West lived and wrote.

Scharnhorst, Gary. "From Rags to Patches, or *A Cool Million* as Alter Alger." *Ball State University Forum* XII, No. 4 (Autumn 1980): 59-65.

Classifies *A Cool Million; or, The Dismantling of Lemuel Pitkin* as a political satire. Scharnhorst demonstrates, by means of printing side-by-side excerpts from *A Cool Million* and from several of Horatio Alger's books, the number of passages that West lifted verbatim, or altered only slightly, from Alger's works.

Scott, Nathan A., Jr. *Nathanael West: A Critical Essay*. Grand Rapids, Mich.: William E. Eerdmans, 1971, 43 p.

Biographical and critical essay.

Tibbets, A. M. "The Strange Half-World of Nathanael West." *The Prairie Schooner* XXXIV, No. 1 (Spring 1960): 8-14.

Criticizes the "half-world" Tibbets believes West portrayed in *Miss Lonelyhearts* and *The Day of the Locust,* arguing that in depicting only grotesque characters and situations, West gives no idea of those standards of which he approves.

White, William. *Nathanael West: A Comprehensive Bibliography*. Kent: Kent State University Press, 1975, 209 p.

Bibliography of works by and about West. As well as giving detailed descriptions of both English- and foreign-language editions of West's major works, White provides complete information on West's screenplays, dramas, and unpublished writings. An appendix reprints "Uncollected Writings of Nathanael West."

Widmer, Kingsley. *Nathanael West*. Boston: Twayne Publishers, 1982, 146 p.

Comprehensive and insightful study of West's fiction.

Appendix

The following is a listing of all sources used in Volume 14 of *Twentieth-Century Literary Criticism*. Included in this list are all copyright and reprint rights and acknowledgments for those essays for which permission was obtained. Every effort has been made to trace copyright, but if omissions have been made, please let us know.

THE EXCERPTS IN TCLC, VOLUME 14, WERE REPRINTED FROM THE FOLLOWING PERIODICALS:

Accent, v. 6, Autumn, 1945.

American Mercury, v. XXXIV, January, 1935./ v. XVIII, December, 1929 for "One Ring Circus" by George Jean Nathan. Copyright 1929, renewed 1956, by American Mercury Magazine, Inc. Reprinted by permission of Associated University Presses, Inc. for the Literary Estate of George Jean Nathan.

American Quarterly, v. XII, Winter, 1960 for "The Development of a Style: The Lardner Idiom" by Howard W. Webb, Jr. Copyright 1960, Trustees of the University of Pennsylvania. Reprinted by permission of the publisher and the author.

The American Scandinavian Review, v. XXVII, September, 1939. Copyright 1939 by The American-Scandinavian Foundation. Reprinted by permission of *Scandinavian Review*.

The Armchair Detective, v. 10, Summer, 1977; v. 10, Fall, 1977. Copyright © 1977 by *The Armchair Detective*. Reprinted by permission.

Australian Journal of French Studies, v. XVI, January-April, 1979. Reprinted by permission.

Black American Literature Forum, v. 15, Summer, 1981 for "'Let Me Make the Songs for the People': A Study of Frances Watkins Harper's Poetry" by Patricia Liggins Hill. © Indiana State University 1981. Reprinted by permission of Indiana State University and the author.

The Bookman, New York, v. XXXIX, May, 1914; v. XLVII, July, 1918; v. LIX, July, 1924; v. LXX, November, 1929./ v. LVII, June, 1923 for "The Fate of the Funny Men" by Robert C. Benchley. Copyright © 1923 by George H. Doran Company. Reprinted by permission of International Creative Management, Inc.

The Canadian Forum, v. XXVIII, March, 1949. Reprinted by permission.

Canadian Literature, n. 87, Winter, 1980 for "Emile Nelligan: A Dreamer Passing By" by Kathy Mezei. Reprinted by permission of the author.

Canadian Review of Comparative Literature, v. VI, Spring, 1979. *Canadian Review of Comparative Literature*, © Canadian Comparative Literature Association. Reprinted by permission.

The Centennial Review, v. XIV, Summer, 1970 for "'Our Gatsby, Our Nick'" by Barry Gross. © 1970 by *The Centennial Review*. Reprinted by permission of the publisher and the author.

CLA Journal, v. XXI, September, 1977. Copyright, 1977 by The College Language Association. Used by permission of The College Language Association.

College English, v. 14, October, 1952./ v. 24, December, 1962 for "'Death in Venice': The Disguised Self" by Eugene McNamara. Copyright © 1962 by the National Council of Teachers of English. Reprinted by permission of the publisher and the author.

College Literature, v. X, Fall, 1983. Copyright © 1983 by West Chester State College. Reprinted by permission.

Commonweal, v. II, June 3, 1925. Copyright © 1925 Commonweal Publishing Co., Inc. Reprinted by permission of Commonweal Foundation.

Comparative Literature Studies, v. XIV, September, 1977 for "Mallarme and the Poetry of Innokenty Annensky: A Study of Surfaces and Textures" by Richard Byrns and M. Kotzamanidou. © 1977 by The Board of Trustees of the University of Illinois. Reprinted by permission of the publisher and Richard Byrns.

Contempo, v. I, August 21, 1931; v. III, May 15, 1933; v. III, July 25, 1933.

Contemporary Review, v. CXLVII, June, 1935. Reprinted by permission.

The Crisis, v. 1, April, 1911. Copyright 1911 by The Crisis Publishing Company, Inc. Reprinted by permission.

The Dial, v. 78, May, 1925.

The Double Dealer, v. III, February, 1922 for "An Appreciation of Havelock Ellis" by Arthur Symons. Copyright, 1922, by The Double Dealer Publishing Co., Inc. Reprinted by permission of the Literary Estate of Arthur Symons.

Educational Theatre Journal, v. XIX, December, 1967. © 1967 University College Theatre Association of the American Theatre Association. Reprinted by permission.

The Emporia State Research Studies, v. XIX, June, 1971. Reprinted by permission.

English Studies in Canada, v. V, Fall, 1979 for "Another Reading of 'The Great Gatsby'" by Keath Fraser. © Association of Canadian University Teachers of English 1979. Reprinted by permission of the publisher and the author.

Esquire, v. II, September, 1934 for "Defense of Dirty Words: A Cuban Letter" by Ernest Hemingway. Copyright © 1934 Esquire Associates. Copyright renewed 1961 Mary Hemingway. Reprinted by permission of Charles Scribner's Sons.

The Evening Sun, Baltimore, May 2, 1925.

Evergreen Review, v. 4, May-June, 1960 for a letter from J. Torma to René Daumal on October 20, 1929, translated by Neal Oxenhandler. Copyright © 1960, by Evergreen Review, Inc. Reprinted by permission of the translator.

The Explicator, v. XXXI, May, 1973. Copyright 1973 by Helen Dwight Reid Educational Foundation. Reprinted by permission of Heldref Publications.

First Statement, v. 2, October, 1943 for "Three Translations from Emile Nelligan" by Louis Dudek. Reprinted by permission of the author.

The Fortnightly Review, n.s. v. 130, November, 1931. Reprinted by permission of Contemporary Review Company Limited.

Forum and Century, v. CII, December, 1939. Copyright, 1939, by Events Publishing Company, Inc. Reprinted by permission of Current History, Inc.

The Freeman, v. VII, August 8, 1923.

German Life & Letters, v. XX, January, 1967. Reprinted by permission.

The German Quarterly, v. VII, March, 1934 for "Stefan George, 1868-1933" by Arthur Burkhard. Copyright © 1934 by the American Association of Teachers of German. Reprinted by permission of the publisher and the Literary Estate of Arthur Burkhard.

The Germanic Review, v. XXXI, October, 1956. Copyright 1956 by Helen Dwight Reid Educational Foundation. Reprinted by permission of Heldref Publications.

Harper's Magazine, v. 179, October, 1939. Copyright 1939, renewed 1966, by *Harper's Magazine*. All rights reserved. Reprinted from the October, 1939 issue by special permission.

Hispania, v. XXIV, December, 1941./ v. XXXIX, May, 1956 for "Tragedy of the Unwanted Person, in Three Versions: Pablos de Segovia, Pito Pérez, Pascual Duarte" by Sherman Eoff. © 1956 The American Association of Teachers of Spanish and Portuguese, Inc. Reprinted by permission of the publisher and the Literary Estate of Sherman Eoff./ v. XXXVI, August, 1953 for "Rubén Romero and the Novel of

Mexican Revolution'' by R. Anthony Castagnaro; v. XLIV, September, 1961 for ''José Rubén Romero: The Writer As Seen by Himself'' by William O. Cord; v. XLV, December, 1962 for ''Jose Rubén Romero's Image of Mexico'' by William O. Cord; v. XLVII, December, 1964 for ''The Genesis of Pito Pérez'' by Ewart E. Phillips; v. 56, April, 1973 for ''Antithesis in a Novel by Rubén Romero'' by Daniel E. Gulstad. © 1953, 1961, 1962, 1964, 1973 The American Association of Teachers of Spanish and Portuguese, Inc. All reprinted by permission of the publisher and the respective authors.

Horizon, London, v. IV, September, 1941./ v. IV, September, 1941 for a review of ''The Forge'' by George Orwell. Reprinted by permission of the Estate of the late Sonia Brownell Orwell and Martin Secker & Warburg Ltd./ v. IV, September, 1941 for a review of ''The Forge'' by Antonia White. Reprinted by permission of the Literary Executrices of Antonia White.

The International Fiction Review, v. 9, Winter, 1982. © copyright 1982 International Fiction Association. Reprinted by permission.

The Journal of Negro History, v. II, October, 1917.

The Listener, v. 102, November 22, 1979 for ''Raising the Glass'' by Malcolm Bowie. © British Broadcasting Corp. 1979. Reprinted by permission of the author.

Literary Digest, v. 116, October 14, 1933.

The Literary Review, v. 26, Fall, 1982. Copyright © 1982 by Fairleigh Dickinson University. Reprinted by permission.

Literature/Film Quarterly, v. IX, January, 1981. © copyright 1981 Salisbury State College. Reprinted by permission.

Louisiana Studies, v. IX, Fall, 1970. Copyright © 1970 by The Southern Studies Institute. Reprinted by permission of *Southern Studies: An Interdisciplinary Journal of the South.*

Modern Drama, v. 9, February, 1967. Copyright Modern Drama, University of Toronto. Reprinted by permission.

Modern Fiction Studies, v. I, November, 1955; v. XV, Winter, 1969-70; v. 28, Autumn, 1982. © 1955, 1970, 1982 by Purdue Research Foundation, West Lafayette, Indiana 47907. All reprinted with permission.

Modern Language Notes, v. XXXIV, January, 1919. © copyright 1919 by The Johns Hopkins University Press. Reprinted by permission.

The Modern Language Review, v. LII, January, 1957 for ''Nietzsche's Problem of the Artist and George's 'Algabal''' by M. Boulby. © Modern Humanities Research Association 1957. Reprinted by permission of the publisher and the author.

Monumenta Nipponica, v. XXXV, Summer, 1980. Copyright in Japan, 1980, by *Monumenta Nipponica.* Reprinted by permission.

The Nation, v. LVIII, June 28, 1894; v. LXVI, June 9, 1898; v. CXIX, December 10, 1924; v. CXLII, March 25, 1936; v. 149, July 15, 1939./ v. 191, August 20, 1960; v. 220, May 3, 1975. Copyright 1960, 1975 *The Nation* magazine, The Nation Associates, Inc. Both reprinted by permission./ v. 149, July 22, 1939 for ''Havelock Ellis—1859-1939'' by Karl Menninger. Copyright 1939 *The Nation* magazine, The Nation Associates, Inc. And renewed 1966 by Karl Menninger. Reprinted by permission of the author.

The New Republic, v. LV, August 15, 1928; v. 127, December 8, 1952; v. 131, September 20, 1954./ v. 155, December 3, 1966 for ''The Really Lost Generation'' by Stanley Kauffmann; v. 160, February 1, 1969 for ''Stanley Kauffmann on Norway's Forgotten Giant'' by Stanley Kauffmann. Copyright © 1966, 1969 by Stanley Kauffmann. Both reprinted by permission of Brandt & Brandt Literary Agents, Inc./ v. 180, March 31, 1979; v. 183, August 2 & 9, 1980. © 1979, 1980 The New Republic, Inc. Both reprinted by permission of *The New Republic.*

New Statesman, v. XIX, April 29, 1922. © 1922 The Statesman Publishing Co. Ltd. Reprinted by permission./ v. 73, May 12, 1967; v. 81, February 5, 1971. © 1967, 1971 The Statesman & Nation Co. Ltd. Both reprinted by permission.

The New Statesman & Nation, n.s. v. V, March 18, 1933; n.s. v. XI, March 14, 1936; n.s. v. XVIII, July 22, 1939; v. XXXI, May 18, 1946; v. XXXVIII, November 5, 1949. © 1933, 1936, 1939, 1946, 1949 The New Statesman & Nation Publishing Co. Ltd. All reprinted by permission.

New York Herald Tribune Book Review, March 18, 1951; February 24, 1952./ April 8, 1951; February 15, 1953; August 14, 1960. © I.H.T. Corporation. All reprinted by permission.

New York Herald Tribune Books, May 22, 1927; April 7, 1940. © I.H.T. Corporation. Both reprinted by permission.

New York Herald Tribune Weekly Book Review, October 16, 1949.

The New York Review of Books, April 17, 1980. Copyright © 1980 Nyrev, Inc. Reprinted with permission from *The New York Review of Books.*

The New York Times, August 25, 1918; September 25, 1928. Copyright © 1918, 1928 by The New York Times Company. Both reprinted by permission.

The New York Times Book Review, June 24, 1899./ November 17, 1912; July 28, 1929; October 25, 1931; July 1, 1934; June 18, 1944; January 1, 1950; February 24, 1952; August 24, 1952; July 10, 1960; February 1, 1970; August 22, 1971; March 17, 1974; August 21, 1977. Copyright © 1912, 1929, 1931, 1934, 1944, 1950, 1952, 1960, 1970, 1971, 1974, 1977 by The New York Times Company. All reprinted by permission.

The New Yorker, v. XLI, October 2, 1965; v. LIV, October 23, 1978. © 1965, 1978 by The New Yorker Magazine, Inc. Both reprinted by permission.

Nineteenth-Century French Studies, v. VIII, Spring & Summer, 1980. © 1980 by T. H. Goetz. Reprinted by permission.

Partisan Review, v. XIV, Spring, 1947 for "Personal History" by Irving Howe. Copyright © 1947, renewed 1974, by *Partisan Review*. Reprinted by permission of *Partisan Review* and the author.

Public Opinion, v. XXVI, June 22, 1899.

The Quarterly Journal of Speech, v. LVII, February, 1971. Copyright 1971 by the Speech Communication Association. Reprinted by permission.

Queen's Quarterly, v. XXXVII, Autumn, 1930 for "The Claims of French-Canadian Poetry" by E. K. Brown. Reprinted by permission of Margaret Brown.

Renaissance and Modern Studies, v. XVII, 1973. Reprinted by permission.

Revue de Louisiana, v. 1, Winter, 1972. Copyright © 1972 by the University of Southwestern Louisiana. Reprinted by permission.

Russian Literature Triquarterly, n. 16, 1979. © 1979 by Ardis Publishers. Reprinted by permission.

Saturday Review, v. LIII, January 10, 1970. © 1970 Saturday Review Magazine Co. Reprinted by permission.

The Saturday Review, London, v. X, September 16, 1933.

Scandinavian Studies, v. 32, August, 1960 for an extract from "The Three Hamsuns: The Changing Attitude in Recent Criticism" by Knut Hamsun. Reprinted by permission of the publisher and Gyldendal Norsk Forlag, on behalf of Tore Hamsun./ v. 39, November, 1967 for "Knut Hamsun and America" by Harald Naess. Reprinted by permission of the publisher and the author.

Scrutiny, v. XV, December, 1948. Reprinted by permission of Cambridge University Press.

The Sewanee Review, v. XL, Summer, 1932. Published 1932 by The University of the South. Reprinted by permission of the editor.

Slavic and East European Journal, v. 21, Spring, 1977; v. 23, Spring, 1979; v. 23, Winter, 1979. © 1977, 1979 by AATSEEL of the U.S., Inc. All reprinted by permission.

The Slavonic and East European Review, v. XXII, December, 1944. © University of London (School of Slavonic and East European Studies) 1944. Reprinted by permission.

The Smart Set, v. XXXVIII, December, 1912 for "A Visit to a Short Story Factory" by H. L. Mencken. Copyright, 1912, by John Adams Thayer Corporation. Used by permission of The Enoch Pratt Free Library of Baltimore in accordance with the terms of the will of H. L. Mencken.

Smith College Studies in Modern Languages, v. III, October, 1921-January, 1922. Reprinted by permission.

The Southern Literary Journal, v. X, Spring, 1978. Copyright 1978 by the Department of English, University of North Carolina at Chapel Hill. Reprinted by permission.

The Soviet Review, v. XI, Spring, 1970. Translation © 1970 by International Arts and Sciences Press, Inc. Reprinted by permission.

The Spectator, v. 64, March 29, 1890.

Studies in Short Fiction, v. 19, Winter, 1982. Copyright 1982 by Newberry College. Reprinted by permission.

The Times Literary Supplement, n. 2622, May 2, 1952; n. 3475, October 3, 1968. © Times Newspapers Ltd. (London) 1952, 1968. Both reproduced from *The Times Literary Supplement* by permission.

Twentieth Century Literature, v. 26, Summer, 1980. Copyright 1980, Hofstra University Press. Reprinted by permission.

Twice a Year, n. 5 & 6, Fall-Winter & Spring-Summer, 1940 & 1941.

The University of Kansas City Review, v. XX, Autumn, 1953. Copyright University of Kansas City, 1953. Reprinted by permission of the publisher.

The Village Voice, v. XXV, February 11, 1980 for "Pwatt's Progress" by Robert Richman. Copyright © News Group Publications, Inc., 1980. Reprinted by permission of *The Village Voice* and the author.

The Virginia Quarterly Review, v. 14, Winter, 1938. Copyright, 1938, renewed 1965, by *The Virginia Quarterly Review,* The University of Virginia. Reprinted by permission.

Wascana Review, v. 4, n. 1, 1969. Copyright, 1969 by *Wascana Review.* Reprinted by permission.

Western Humanities Review, v. XVII, Spring, 1963. Copyright, 1963, University of Utah. Reprinted by permission.

The Yale Review, v. XIII, July, 1924. © 1924 by Yale University. Reprinted by permission of the editors.

THE EXCERPTS IN TCLC, VOLUME 14, WERE REPRINTED FROM THE FOLLOWING BOOKS:

Allen, Priscilla. From "Old Critics and New: The Treatment of Chopin's 'The Awakening'," in *The Authority of Experience: Essays in Feminist Criticism.* Edited by Arlyn Diamond and Lee R. Edwards. University of Massachusetts Press, 1977. Copyright © 1977 by The University of Massachusetts Press. All rights reserved. Reprinted by permission.

Anderson, Sherwood. From *Sherwood Anderson's Notebook.* Boni & Liveright, 1926. Copyright 1926 by Boni & Liveright, Inc. And renewed 1953 by Eleanor Anderson. Reprinted by permission of Harold Ober Associates Incorporated.

Annensky, Innokenty. From "Innokenty Annensky on Mikhail Lermontov," in *The Complection of Russian Literature: A Cento.* Edited and translated by Andrew Field. Atheneum, 1971. Copyright © 1971 by Andrew Field. All rights reserved. Reprinted with the permission of Atheneum Publishers, New York.

Apter, T. E. From *Thomas Mann: The Devil's Advocate.* New York University Press, 1978. Macmillan, 1978. © T. E. Apter 1978. All rights reserved. Reprinted by permission of New York University Press.

Bennett, E. K. From *Stefan George.* Bowes & Bowes, 1954. All rights reserved. Reprinted by permission of The Bodley Head Ltd. for Bowes & Bowes.

Bennett, Warren. From "Prefigurations of Gatsby, Eckleburg, Owl Eyes, and Klipspringer," in *Fitzgerald/Hemingway Annual: 1979.* Edited by Matthew J. Bruccoli and Richard Layman. Gale Research, 1980. Copyright © 1980 by The Gale Research Company, Detroit, Michigan. United States of America. Reprinted by permission.

Bentley, Eric. From *The Cult of the Superman: A Study of Heroism in Carlyle and Nietzsche, with Notes on Other Hero-Worshippers of Modern Times.* Peter Smith, 1969. Copyright © 1944, 1957, by Eric Bentley. Reprinted by permission of the author.

Björkman, Edwin. From an introduction to *Hunger.* By Knut Hamsun. Knopf, 1920. Copyright 1920 and renewed 1948 by Alfred A. Knopf, Inc. Reprinted by permission of the publisher.

Blok, Aleksandr. From an extract from a review of "Tikhie pesnie," in *Studies in the Life and Work of Innokentij Annenskij.* By Vsevolod Setchkarev. Mouton, 1963. © copyright 1963 Mouton & Co., Publishers. Reprinted by permission of Mouton Publishers, a Division of Walter de Gruyter & Co.

Bly, Robert. From "The Art of 'Hunger'," in *Hunger.* By Knut Hamsun, translated by Robert Bly. Farrar, Straus and Giroux, 1967. Copyright © 1967 by Farrar, Straus and Giroux, Inc. All rights reserved. Reprinted by permission of Farrar, Straus and Giroux, Inc.

Bone, Robert. From *The Negro Novel in America.* Revised edition. Yale University Press, 1965. © 1958 by Yale University Press. Revised edition © 1965 by Yale University Press. Reprinted by permission.

Bowring, Richard John. From *Mori Ōgai and the Modernization of Japanese Culture.* Cambridge University Press, 1979. © Cambridge University Press 1979. Reprinted by permission.

Brecher, Edward M. From *The Sex Researchers.* Little, Brown, 1969. Copyright © 1969 by Edward M. Brecher. Reprinted by permission of the author.

Brodsky, Joseph. From a preface to *The Foundation Pit.* By Andrei Platonov, translated by Thomas P. Whitney. Ardis, 1973. © 1973 by Joseph Brodsky and Ardis Publishers. Reprinted by permission.

Brome, Vincent. From *Havelock Ellis, Philosopher of Sex: A Biography.* Routledge & Kegan Paul, 1979. © Vincent Brome 1979. Reprinted by permission of Routledge & Kegan Paul PLC.

Brooks, Cleanth and Robert Penn Warren. From *Understanding Fiction.* Second Edition. Appleton-Century-Crofts, 1959. © 1959. All rights reserved. Reprinted by permission of Prentice-Hall, Inc., Englewood Cliffs, NJ 07632.

Brooks, Van Wyck. From *The Confident Years: 1885-1915.* Dutton, 1952. Copyright, 1952, by Van Wyck Brooks. Copyright renewed 1980 by Gladys Brooks. All rights reserved. Reprinted by permission of the publisher, E. P. Dutton, Inc.

Brushwood, John S. From *Mexico in Its Novel: A Nation's Search for Identity.* University of Texas Press, 1966. Copyright © 1966 by John S. Brushwood. All rights reserved. Reprinted by permission of the publisher and the author.

Camino, Berta Gamboa de. From "The Novel of the Mexican Revolution," in *Renascent Mexico*. Edited by Hubert Herring and Herbert Weinstock. Covici, Friede, 1935. Copyright, 1935, by the Committee on Cultural Relations with Latin America. All rights reserved. Used by permission of Crown Publishers, Inc.

Cargill, Oscar. *From Intellectual America: Ideas on the March*. Macmillan, 1941. Copyright 1941 by Macmillan Publishing Co., Inc. Renewed 1969 by Oscar Cargill. All rights reserved. Reprinted with permission of Macmillan Publishing Company.

Chase, Richard. From *The American Novel and Its Tradition*. Anchor Books, 1957. Copyright © 1957 by Richard Chase. All rights reserved. Reprinted by permission of Doubleday & Company, Inc.

Christ, Carol P. From *Diving Deep and Surfacing: Women Writers on Spiritual Quest*. Beacon Press, 1980. Copyright © 1980 by Carol P. Christ. All rights reserved. Reprinted by permission of Beacon Press.

Cockshut, A.O.J. From *Man and Woman: A Study of Love and the Novel 1740-1940*. Collins, 1977, Oxford University Press, New York, 1978. Copyright © 1977 by A.O.J. Cockshut. Reprinted by permission of Oxford University Press, Inc. In Canada by William Collins Sons & Co., Ltd.

Collis, John Stewart. From *An Artist of Life: A Study of the Life and Work of Havelock Ellis*. Cassell, 1959. © John Stewart Collis 1959. All rights reserved. Reprinted by permission of the Estate of John Stewart Collis.

Connolly, Cyril. From *The Condemned Playground, Essays: 1927-1944*. The Macmillan Company, 1946. Copyright, 1946, by Cyril Connolly. All rights reserved. Reprinted with permission of Deborah Rogers Ltd.

Cowley, Malcolm. From "Introduction: The Romance of Money," in *Three Novels: The Great Gatsby, Tender Is the Night, The Last Tycoon*. By F. Scott Fitzgerald. Charles Scribner's Sons, 1953. Copyright 1953 by Charles Scribner's Sons. Copyright renewed 1981 by Malcolm Cowley. All rights reserved. Reprinted with the permission of Charles Scribner's Sons.

Cushing, G. F. From *Hungarian Prose and Verse*. The Athlone Press, 1956. Reprinted by permission.

Daumal, Réne. From "To Approach the Hindu Poetic Art," in *Rasa; or, Knowledge of the Self: Essays on Indian Aesthetics and Selected Sanskrit Studies*. By Rene Daumal, translated by Louise Landes Levi. New Directions, 1982. Originally published in part as *Les Pouvoirs de la Parole*. Edited by Claudio Rugafiore. Gallimard, 1972. © Èditions Gallimard, 1972. All rights reserved. Reprinted by permission of Èditions Gallimard.

DeMuth, James. From *Small Town Chicago: The Comic Perspective of Finley Peter Dunne, George Ade, Ring Lardner*. Kennikat Press, 1980. Copyright © 1980 by Kennikat Press Corp. All rights reserved. Reprinted by permission of Associated Faculty Press, Inc.

Devlin, John. From *Spanish Anticlericalism: A Study in Modern Alienation*. Las Americas, 1966. Copyright © 1966 by Las Americas Publishing Company. Reprinted by permission of Las Americas Publishing Company, 911 Faile Street, Bronx, NY 10474.

Dilworth, David. From "The Significance of Ōgai's Historical Literature," in *Saiki Kōi and Other Stories*. By Mori Ōgai, edited by David Dilworth. The University Press of Hawaii, 1977. English translation: © UNESCO 1977. All rights reserved. Reprinted by permission.

Dorofeyev, Victor. From an introduction to *Fro and Other Stories*. By Andrei Platonov. Progress Publishers, 1972. Reprinted by permission.

Dyson, A. E. From *Between Two Worlds: Aspects of Literary Form*. Macmillan, 1972. © A. E. Dyson 1972. All rights reserved. Reprinted by permission of Macmillan, London and Basingstoke.

Eliot, T. S. From a letter to F. Scott Fitzgerald on December 31, 1925, in *The Crack-Up*. By F. Scott Fitzgerald, edited by Edmund Wilson. New Directions, 1945. Copyright T. S. Eliot 1945. Reprinted by permission of T. S. Eliot. Reprinted for this publication by permission of Mrs. Valerie Eliot and Faber Faber Ltd.

Ellis, Havelock. From a preface to *Studies in the Psychology of Sex, Vol. I: Sexual Inversion*. London: University Press, Watford, 1897. Reprinted by permission of Francois Lafitte for the Literary Estate of Havelock Ellis.

Erlich, Victor. From "Introduction: Modern Russian Criticism from Andrej Belyj to Andrej Sinjavskij, Trends, Issues, Personalities," in *Twentieth-Century Russian Literary Criticism*. Edited by Victor Erlich. Yale University Press, 1975. Copyright © 1975 by Yale University. All rights reserved. Reprinted by permission.

Evans, Elizabeth. From *Ring Lardner*. Ungar, 1979. Copyright © 1979 by Frederick Ungar Publishing Co. Reprinted by permission.

Fitzgerald, F. Scott. From a letter to Edmund Wilson in 1925, in *The Crack-Up*. By F. Scott Fitzgerald, edited by Edmund Wilson. New Directions, 1945. Copyright 1945 by New Directions Publishing Corporation. Reprinted by permission of New Directions.

Fitzgerald, F. Scott. From an introduction to *The Great Gatsby*. By F. Scott Fitzgerald. The Modern Library, 1934. Introduction copyright 1934 by The Modern Library Inc. And renewed 1961 by Random House, Inc. Reprinted by permission of the publisher.

Forster, E. M. From *Two Cheers for Democracy*. Harcourt Brace Jovanovich, 1951. Copyright 1951 by E. M. Forster. Copyright 1979 by Donald Parry. Reprinted by permission of Harcourt Brace Jovanovich, Inc. In Canada by Edward Arnold Ltd.

Freud, Sigmund. From a letter to Wilhelm Fliess on January 3, 1899, in *The Origins of Psycho-Analysis: Letters to Wilhelm Fliess, Drafts and Notes, 1887-1902*. Marie Bonaparte, Anna Freud, Ernst Kris, eds., translated by Eric Mosbacher and James Strachey. Basic Books, 1954. Copyright, 1954, by Basic Books, Inc. Reprinted by permission of Basic Books, Inc., Publishers.

Garrison, William Lloyd. From a preface to *Poems on Miscellaneous Subjects*. By Frances Ellen Watkins. Merrihew & Thompson, 1857.

Gielgud, Sir John. From a foreword to *Plays: The Little Dry Thorn, Valerins, Dickon, Vol. I*. By Gordon Daviot. Peter Davies, 1953. Reprinted by permission of Sir John Gielgud.

Gloster, Hugh M. From *Negro Voices in American Fiction*. University of North Carolina Press, 1948. Copyright, 1948, by The University of North Carolina Press. And renewed 1975 by Hugh M. Gloster. Reprinted by permission.

Goldberg, Isaac. From *Havelock Ellis: A Biographical and Critical Survey*. Simon & Schuster, 1926. Copyright © 1926 by Simon & Schuster, Inc. Renewed © 1953 by Bernice Stern and Ruth Solomon. Reprinted by permission of Simon & Schuster, Inc.

Goldsmith, Ulrich K. From *Stefan George: A Study of His Early Work*. University of Colorado Press, 1959. Reprinted by permission of the author.

Gray, Ronald. From *The German Tradition in Literature: 1871-1945*. Cambridge at the University Press, 1965. © Cambridge University Press, 1965. Reprinted by permission.

Greene, Graham. From *Collected Essays*. The Viking Press, 1969, The Bodley Head, 1969. Copyright 1951 © 1966, 1968, 1969 by Graham Greene. Reprinted by permission of Viking Penguin, Inc. In Canada by Laurence Pollinger Ltd. for Graham Greene.

Grosskurth, Phyllis. From *Havelock Ellis: A Biography*. Knopf, 1980. McClelland, 1980. Copyright © 1980 by Phyllis Grosskurth. Reprinted by permission of Alfred A. Knopf, Inc. The Canadian Publishers, McClelland and Stewart, Limited, Toronto.

Grossvogel, David I. From *The Self-Conscious in Modern French Drama*. Columbia University Press, 1958. Copyright © 1958 Columbia University Press, New York. Reprinted by permission of the publisher.

Gumilev, Nikolai. From *Nikolai Gumilev on Russian Poetry*. Edited by and translated by David Lapeza. Ardis, 1977. © 1977 by Ardis Publishers. Reprinted by permission.

Hanaford, Phebe A. From *Daughters of America; or, Women of the Century*. B. B. Russell, 1882.

Hardy, Thomas. From a letter to Havelock Ellis on April 29, 1883, in *From Marlowe to Shaw: The Studies, 1876-1936, in English Literature of Havelock Ellis*. By Havelock Ellis, edited by John Gawsworth. Williams and Norgate Ltd., 1950. Reprinted by permission of Miss E. A. Dugdale.

Harpham, Geoffrey Galt. From *On the Grotesque: Strategies of Contradiction in Art and Literature*. Princeton University Press, 1982. Copyright © 1982 by Princeton University Press. All rights reserved. Excerpts reprinted by permission of Princeton University Press.

Hassan, Ihab. From *The Dismemberment of Orpheus: Toward a Postmodern Literature*. Second edition. The University of Wisconsin Press, 1982. Copyright © 1971, 1982 Ihab Hassan. All rights reserved. Reprinted by permission.

Heller, Erich. From *The Ironic German: A Study of Thomas Mann*. Secker & Warburg, 1958. Copyright © 1958, 1961 by Erich Heller. All rights reserved. Reprinted by permission of Martin Secker & Warburg Limited.

Hirschbach, Frank Donald. From *The Arrow and the Lyre: A Study of the Role of Love in the Works of Thomas Mann*. Nijhoff, 1955. Copyright 1955 by Martinus Nijhoff, The Hague, Netherlands. All rights reserved. Reprinted by permission.

Hoffman, Frederick J. From *The Modern Novel in America: 1900-1950*. Henry Regnery Company, 1951.

Hollingdale, R. J. From *Thomas Mann: A Critical Study*. Bucknell University Press, 1971. Copyright © 1971 by R. J. Hollingdale. All rights reserved. Reprinted by permission.

Inge, William Ralph. From *A Pacifist in Trouble*. Putnam, 1939.

Innes, Christopher. From *Holy Theatre: Ritual and the Avant Garde*. Cambridge University Press, 1981. © Cambridge University Press 1981. Reprinted by permission.

Ivanov, Vyacheslav. From "Vyacheslav Ivanov on Innokenty Annensky," in *The Complection of Russian Literature: A Cento.* Edited and translated by Andrew Field. Atheneum, 1971. Copyright © 1971 by Andrew Field. All rights reserved. Reprinted with the permission of Atheneum Publishers, New York.

Jackson, Thomas H. From an introduction to *Twentieth Century Interpretations of "Miss Lonelyhearts": A Collection of Critical Essays.* Edited by Thomas H. Jackson. Prentice-Hall, 1971. © 1971 by Prentice-Hall, Inc. Reprinted by permission of Prentice-Hall, Inc., Englewood Cliffs, NJ 07632.

Jarry, Alfred. From a letter to Lugné-Pöe on January 8, 1896, translated by Simon Watson Taylor, in *Selected Works of Alfred Jarry.* Edited by Roger Shattuck and Simon Watson Taylor. Grove Press, 1965. Copyright © 1965 by Roger Shattuck and Simon Watson Taylor. All rights reserved. Reprinted by permission of Grove Press, Inc.

Jarry, Alfred. From "Of the Futility of the 'Theatrical' in the Theatre," translated by Barbara Wright, in *Selected Works of Alfred Jarry.* Edited by Roger Shattuck and Simon Watson Taylor. Grove Press, 1965. Copyright © 1965 by Roger Shattuck and Simon Watson Taylor. All rights reserved. Reprinted by permission of Grove Press, Inc.

Jonas, Ilsedore B. From *Thomas Mann and Italy.* Translated by Betty Crouse. University of Alabama Press, 1979. English translation copyright © 1979 by The University of Alabama Press, University, Alabama. All rights reserved. Reprinted by permission.

Jones, Anne Goodwyn. From *Tomorrow Is Another Day: The Woman Writer in the South, 1859-1936.* Louisiana State University Press, 1981. Copyright © 1981 by Louisiana State University Press. All rights reserved. Reprinted by permission of Louisiana State University Press.

Jordan, Marion. From *Andrei Platonov.* Bradda Books Ltd., 1973. Copyright © 1973 Marion Jordan. Reprinted by permission of Basil Blackwell Publisher, Limited.

Karlinsky, Simon. From "Frustrated Artists and Devouring Mothers in Čechov and Annenskij," in *Mnemozina: Studia litteraria russica in honorem Vsevolod Setchkarev.* Edited by Joachim T. Baer and Norman W. Ingham. Fink, 1974. © 1974 Wilhelm Fink Verlag, West Germany. Reprinted by permission.

Kazin, Alfred. From *On Native Grounds: An Interpretation of Modern American Prose Literature.* Reynal & Hitchcock, 1942. Copyright 1942, 1970 by Alfred Kazin. Reprinted by permission of Harcourt Brace Jovanovich, Inc.

Kirkconnell, Watson. From "Introduction" and "Michael Babits," in *Hungarian Poetry, 1400-1932.* Edited and translated by Watson Kirkconnell. Kanadai Magyar Ujság Press, 1933. Copyright, 1933 by Watson Kirkconnell. Reprinted by permission of the Literary Estate of Watson Kirkconnell.

Kunitomo, Tadao. From *Japanese Literature Since 1868.* The Hokuseido Press, 1938. All rights reserved, 1938. Reprinted by permission.

Langford, Walter M. From *The Mexican Novel Comes of Age.* University of Notre Dame Press, 1971. Copyright © 1971 by University of Notre Dame Press; Notre Dame, IN 46556. Reprinted by permission.

Lardner, Ring, Jr. From *The Lardners: My Family Remembered.* Harper & Row, 1976. Copyright © 1976 by Ringgold Corporation. All rights reserved. Reprinted by permission of Harper & Row, Publishers, Inc.

Lardner, Ring. From a letter to Miss Seavey on August 24, 1933, in *Letters from Ring.* Edited by Clifford M. Caruthers. Walden Press, 1979. © 1979 by Walden Press. All rights reserved. Reprinted by permission.

Lawrence, D. H. From *Phoenix: The Posthumous Papers of D. H. Lawrence.* Edited by Edward D. McDonald. Viking Press 1936, William Heinemann, 1936.

Levi, Louise Landes. From an introduction to *Rasa; or, Knowledge of the Self: Essays on Indian Aesthetics and Selected Sanskrit Studies.* By Rene Daumal, translated by Louise Landes Levi. New Directions. 1982. Copyright © 1982 by Louise Landes Levi. All rights reserved. Reprinted by permission of New Directions Publishing Corporation.

Le Vot, André. From *F. Scott Fitzgerald: A Biography.* Translated by William Byron. Doubleday, 1983. Copyright © 1983 by Doubleday & Company, Inc. Reprinted by permission of the publisher.

Lewis, Paula Gilbert. From "Emile Nelligan, 'Poète Maudit' of Quebec: The Pervasion of Black and White Coldness," in *Pre-Text, Text, Context: Essays on Nineteenth-Century French Literature.* Edited by Robert L. Mitchell. Ohio State University Press, 1980. Copyright © 1980 by the Ohio State University Press. All rights reserved. Reprinted by permission.

Long, Robert Emmet. From *The Achieving of "The Great Gatsby:" F. Scott Fitzgerald, 1920-1925.* Bucknell University Press, 1979. © 1979 by Associated University Presses, Inc. Reprinted by permission.

Lowenthal, Leo. From *Literature and the Image of Man: Sociological Studies of the European Drama and Novel, 1600-1900*. The Beacon Press, 1957. © 1957 by Leo Lowenthal. Reprinted by permission of the author.

Malin, Irving. From *Nathanael West's Novels*. Southern Illinois University Press, 1972. Copyright © 1972 by Southern Illinois University Press. Reprinted by permission of Southern Illinois University Press.

Mann, Thomas. From a preface to *Stories of Three Decades*. By Thomas Mann, translated by H. T. Lowe-Porter. Knopf, 1936. Copyright 1930, 1931, 1934, 1935, 1936, and renewed 1963 by Alfred A. Knopf, Inc. All rights reserved. Reprinted by permission of the publisher.

Mann, Thomas. From a letter to Carl Maria Weber on July 4, 1920, in *Letters of Thomas Mann: 1889-1955*. Edited and translated by Richard Winston and Clara Winston. Knopf, 1971. Copyright © 1970 by Alfred A. Knopf, Inc. All rights reserved. Reprinted by permission of the publisher.

Mansfield, Katherine. From "A Norwegian Novel," in *Novels and Novelists*. Edited by J. Middleton Murry. Knopf, 1930. Copyright 1930, renewed © 1958, by Alfred A. Knopf, Inc. All rights reserved. Reprinted by permission of The Society of Authors as the literary representative of the Estate of Katherine Mansfield.

Martin, Jay. From an introduction to *Nathanael West: A Collection of Critical Essays*. Edited by Jay Martin. Prentice-Hall, 1971. © 1971 by Prentice-Hall, Inc. Reprinted by permission of Prentice-Hall, Inc., Englewood Cliffs, NJ 07632.

McIlwaine, Shields. From *The Southern Poor-White: From Lubberland to Tobacco Road*. University of Oklahoma Press, 1939. Copyright 1939 by the University of Oklahoma Press. All rights reserved. Reprinted by permission.

Mencken, H. L. From *Prejudices, third series*. Knopf, 1922. Copyright 1922 and renewed 1950 by H. L. Mencken. Reprinted by permission of Alfred A. Knopf, Inc.

Mencken, H. L. From *Prejudices, fifth series*. Knopf, 1926. Copyright 1926 by Alfred A. Knopf, Inc. And renewed 1954 by H. L. Mencken. Reprinted by permission of the publisher.

Messenger, Christian K. From *Sport and the Spirit of Play in American Fiction: Hawthorne to Faulkner*. Columbia University Press, 1981. Copyright © 1981, Columbia University Press. All rights reserved. Reprinted by permission of the publisher.

Metzger, Michael M. and Erika A. Metzger. From *Stefan George*. Twayne, 1972. Copyright © 1972 by Twayne Publishers. All rights reserved. Reprinted with the permission of Twayne Publishers, a Division of G. K. Hall and Co., Boston.

Meyers, Jeffrey. From *Homosexuality and Literature: 1890-1930*. Athlone Press, 1977. © Jeffrey Meyers 1977. Reprinted by permission.

Miller, Henry. From a letter to Anaïs Nin on March 26, 1934, in *Letters to Anaïs Nin*. Edited by Gunther Stuhlmann. G. P. Putnam's Sons, 1965. © 1965 by Anaïs Nin. All rights reserved. Reprinted by permission of Gunther Stuhlmann, Author's Representative.

Miller, James E. Jr. From "Fitzgerald's 'Gatsby': The World As Ash Heap," in *The Twenties: Fiction, Poetry, Drama*. Edited by Warren French. Everett/Edwards, Inc., 1975. © copyright 1975 by Warren French. All rights reserved. Reprinted by permission.

Mirsky, D. S. From *Contemporary Russian Literature: 1881-1925*. Knopf, 1926, G. Routledge & Sons, 1926. Copyright 1926, by Alfred A. Knopf, Inc. Reprinted by permission of the publisher.

Miyoshi, Masao. From *Accomplices of Silence: The Modern Japanese Novel*. University of California Press, 1974. Copyright © 1974 by The Regents of the University of California. Reprinted by permission of the University of California Press.

Morris, Wright. From *Earthly Delights, Unearthly Adornments: American Writers As Image-Makers*. Harper & Row, 1979. Copyright © 1978 by Wright Morris. All rights reserved. Reprinted by permission of Harper & Row, Publishers, Inc.

Nadeau, Maurice. *The History of Surrealism*. By Maurice Nadeau, translated by Richard Howard. Macmillan, 1965. Originally published as *Historie du Surrealisme*. Editions du Seuil, 1945. Copyright © The Macmillan Publishing Company, 1965. All rights reserved. Reprinted by permission of Georges Borchardt, Inc. and Editions du Seuil.

Nalbantian, Suzanne. From *The Symbol of the Soul from Hölderlin to Yeats: A Study in Metonymy*. Columbia University Press, 1977. Copyright © 1977 Suzanne Nalbantian. All rights reserved. Reprinted by permission of the publisher.

Neider, Charles. From an introduction to *Short Novels of the Masters*. Edited by Charles Neider. Holt, Rinehart and Winston, 1948. Introduction copyright © 1948, renewed 1975, by Charles Neider. Reprinted by permission of the author.

Pattee, Fred Lewis. From *A History of American Literature Since 1870*. Century, 1915. Originally published and copyright 1915 by the Century Company. And renewed 1943 by Fred Lewis Pattee. Reprinted by permission of E. P. Dutton, Inc.

Perkins, Maxwell E. From "Maxwell E. Perkins Letter to Ernest Hemingway on November 28, 1934," in *Editor to Author: The Letters of Maxwell E. Perkins*. Edited by John Hall Wheelock. Charles Scribner's Sons, 1950. Copyright 1950 Charles Scribner's Sons. Copyright renewed 1977 by John Hall Wheelock. All rights reserved. Reprinted with the permission of Charles Scribner's Sons.

Phelps, Donald. From "Shut Up, He Explained," in *Word & Beyond*. Edited by Harry Smith. The Smith, 1982. Copyright © 1982 by The Smith. Reprinted by permission of The Smith Publishers.

Poggioli, Renato. From *The Poets of Russia: 1890-1930*. Cambridge, Mass.: Harvard University Press, 1960. Copyright © 1960 by the President and Fellows of Harvard College. Excerpted by permission.

Pritchett, V. S. From *The Living Novel & Later Appreciations*. Revised edition. Random House, 1964. Copyright © 1975 by V. S. Pritchett. Reprinted by permission of Literistic, Ltd.

Redding, J. Saunders. From *To Make a Poet Black*. University of North Carolina Press, 1939.

Redmond, Eugene B. From *Drumvoices, the Mission of Afro-American Poetry: A Critical History*. Anchor Press, 1976. Copyright © 1976 by Eugene B. Redmond. All rights reserved. Reprinted by permission of Doubleday & Company, Inc.

Reed, T. J. From *Thomas Mann: The Uses of Tradition*. Oxford at the Clarendon Press, Oxford, 1974. © Oxford University Press 1974. All rights reserved. Reprinted by permission of Oxford University Press.

Reid, Randall. From *The Fiction of Nathanael West: No Redeemer, No Promised Land*. University of Chicago Press, 1967. © 1967 by The University of Chicago. Reprinted by permission of The University of Chicago Press.

Richings, G. F. From *Evidences of Progress among Colored People*. G. S. Ferguson Co., 1896.

Rimer, J. Thomas. From "The Historical Literature of Mori Ōgai: An Introduction," in *The Incident at Sakai and Other Stories*. By Mori Ōgai, edited by David Dilworth and J. Thomas Rimer. The University Press of Hawaii, 1977. English translation: © UNESCO 1977. All rights reserved. Reprinted by permission.

Robinson, Paul. From *The Modernization of Sex: Havelock Ellis, Alfred Kinsey, William Masters and Virginia Johnson*. Harper & Row, 1976. Copyright © 1976 by Paul Robinson. All rights reserved. Reprinted by permission of Harper & Row Publishers, Inc.

Rourke, Constance. From *American Humor: A Study of the National Character*. Harcourt Brace Jovanovich, 1931. Copyright 1931 by Harcourt Brace Jovanovich, Inc. Renewed 1959 by Alice D. Fore. Reprinted by permission of the publisher.

Roy, Sandra. From *Josephine Tey*. Twayne, 1980. Copyright © 1980 by Twayne Publishers. Reprinted with the permission of Twayne Publishers, a Division of G. K. Hall & Co., Boston.

Sandoe, James. From an introduction to *Three by Tey: Miss Pym Disposes, The Franchise Affair, Brat Farrar*. By Josephine Tey. Macmillan, 1954. Introduction copyright 1954, and renewed 1982, by Macmillan Publishing Co., Inc. All rights reserved. Reprinted with permission of Macmillan Publishing Company.

Setchkarev, Vsevolod. From *Studies in the Life and Work of Innokentij Annenskij*. Mouton, 1963. © copyright 1963 Mouton & Co., Publishers. Reprinted by permission of Mouton Publishers, a Division of Walter de Gruyter & Co.

Seyersted, Per. From an introduction to *The Complete Works of Kate Chopin, Vol. I*. By Kate Chopin, edited by Per Seyersted. Louisiana State University Press, 1969. Copyright © 1969 by Louisiana State University Press. Reprinted by permission of Louisiana State University Press.

Shattuck, Roger. From an introduction to *Mount Analogue: An Authentic Narrative*. By René Daumal, translated by Roger Shattuck. Vincent Stuart Ltd., 1959. English translation copyright © 1959 by Robinson & Watkins Books Ltd. Reprinted by permission of the publishers and Roger Shattuck.

Shaw, Bernard. From a letter to Henry Seymour in August, 1898, in *Collected Letters: 1898-1910*. Edited by Dan H. Laurence. Dodd, Mead & Company, 1972. © 1972 The Trustees of the British Museum, The Governors and Guardians of the National Gallery of Ireland, and Royal Academy of Dramatic Art. Reprinted by permission of The Society of Authors on behalf of the Bernard Shaw Estate.

Sherman, Joan R. From *Invisible Poets: Afro-Americans of the Nineteenth Century*. University of Illinois Press, 1974. © 1974 by Joan R. Sherman. Reprinted by permission of the publisher and the author.

Singer, Isaac Bashevis. From "Knut Hamsun, Artist of Skepticism," in *Hunger*. By Knut Hamsun, translated by Robert Bly. Farrar, Straus and Giroux, 1967. Copyright © 1967 by Farrar, Straus and Giroux, Inc. All rights reserved. Reprinted by permission of Farrar, Straus and Giroux, Inc.

Slonim, Marc. From *Modern Russian Literature: From Chekhov to the Present*. Oxford University Press, New York, 1953. Copyright 1953 by Oxford University Press, Inc. Renewed 1981 by Tatiana Slonim. Reprinted by permission of Oxford University Press, Inc.

Slonim, Marc. From *Soviet Russian Literature: Writers and Problems, 1917-1977*. Revised edition. Oxford University Press, New York, 1977. Copyright © 1964, 1967, 1977 by Oxford University Press, Inc. Reprinted by permission.

Smith, A.J.M. From an introduction to *The Oxford Book of Canadian Verse: In English and French*. Edited by A.J.M. Smith. Oxford University Press, London, 1960. Reprinted by permission of Oxford University Press.

Stanford, Derek. From *Critics of the 'Nineties*. John Baker, 1970. © 1970 Derek Stanford. Reprinted by permission of A. & C. Black (Publishers) Ltd.

Stein, Gertrude. From a letter to F. Scott Fitzgerald on May 22, 1925, in *The Crack-Up*. By F. Scott Fitzgerald, edited by Edmund Wilson. New Directions, 1945. Copyright 1945 by New Directions. And renewed 1973 by Elena Wilson. Reprinted by permission of David Higham Associates, as literary agents for Gertrude Stein.

Steiner, T. R. From "'A Cool Million': West's Lemuel and the American Dream," in *Nathanael West, the Cheaters and the Cheated: A Collection of Critical Essays*. Edited by David Madden. Everett/Edwards, Inc., 1973. © 1973 by David Madden. All rights reserved. Reprinted by permission.

Still, William. From an introduction to *Iola Leroy; or, Shadows Uplifted*. By Frances E. W. Harper. Second edition. James H. Earle, Publisher, 1893.

Stillman, Linda Klieger. From *Alfred Jarry*. Twayne, 1983. Copyright © 1983 by Twayne Publishers. All rights reserved. Reprinted by permission of Twayne Publishers, a Division of G. K. Hall & Co., Boston.

Swales, Martin. From *Thomas Mann: A Study*. Heinemann, 1980. © Martin Swales 1980. Reprinted by permission of Heinemann Educational Books Ltd., London.

Symons, Julian. From *Critical Occasions*. Hamish Hamilton, 1966. Copyright © 1966 by Julian Symons. Reproduced by permission of Curtis Brown Ltd., London, on behalf of Julian Symons.

Symons, Julian. From *Mortal Consequences: A History—From the Detective Story to the Crime Novel*. Harper & Row, Publishers, Inc., 1972. Copyright © 1972 by Julian Symons. Reproduced by permission of Curtis Brown Ltd., London, on behalf of Julian Symons.

Szabolcsi, Miklós. From "The Twentieth Century: The Rise of Modern Hungarian Literature (1905-1914)," translated by István Farkas, in *History of Hungarian Literature*. By Tibor Klaniczay, József Szauder and Miklós Szabolcsi, edited by Miklós Szabolcsi. Collet's, 1964. © Tibor Klaniczay, József Szauder, and Miklós Szabolcsi, 1964. Reprinted by permission.

Talburt, Nancy Ellen. From "Josephine Tey," in *10 Women of Mystery*. Edited by Earl F. Bargainner. Bowling Green State University Popular Press, 1981. Copyright © 1981 by Bowling Green University Popular Press. Reprinted by permission.

Thomas, R. Hinton. From *Thomas Mann: The Mediation of Art*. Oxford at the Clarendon Press, Oxford, 1956. Reprinted by permission of Oxford University Press.

Thomson, Boris. From *Lot's Wife and the Venus of Milo: Conflicting Attitudes to the Cultural Heritage in Modern Russia*. Cambridge University Press, 1978. © Cambridge University Press 1978. Reprinted by permission.

Torres-Ríoseco, Arturo. From *Aspects of Spanish-American Literature*. University of Washington Press, 1963. Copyright © 1963 by the University of Washington Press. Reprinted by permission.

Tougas, Gérard. From *Histoire de la littérature Canadienne-Française*. Presses Universitaires de France, 1964. Second edition. Reprinted by permission of Presses Universitaires de France.

Tucker, Janet Grace. From *Innokentij Annenskij and the Acmeist Doctrine*. Indiana University, 1973. © copyright Janet Grace Tucker. Reprinted by permission of the author.

Wagner, Jean. From *Black Poets of the United States: From Paul Laurence Dunbar to Langston Hughes*. Translated by Kenneth Douglas. University of Illinois Press, 1973. Translation copyright 1973 by The Board of Trustees of the University of Illinois. Reprinted by permission of the author.

Walton, Alan Hull. From an introduction to *My Life*. By Havelock Ellis. Neville Spearman, 1967. Copyright © Alan Hull Walton, 1967. Reprinted by permission.

Weeks, Jeffrey. From "Havelock Ellis and the Politics of Sex Reform," in *Socialism and the New Life: The Personal and Sexual Politics of Edward Carpenter and Havelock Ellis*. By Sheila Rowbotham and Jeffrey Weeks. Pluto Press, 1977. Copyright © Pluto Press 1977. Reprinted by permission.

West, Rebecca. From *Ending in Earnest: A Literary Log*. Doubleday, Doran, 1931. Copyright © 1929, 1930, 1931 by Doubleday, Doran & Company, Inc. All rights reserved. Reprinted by permission of A. D. Peters & Co. Ltd.

Widdows, P. F. From an introduction to *Selected Poems of Émile Nelligan*. By Émile Nelligan, translated by P. F. Widdows. Ryerson Press, 1960. Copyright, Canada, 1960, by The Ryerson Press, Toronto. All rights reserved. Reprinted by permission of McGraw-Hill Ryerson Limited.

Widmer, Kingsley. From "'The Day of the Locust': The Last Masquerade," in *Nathanael West, the Cheaters and the Cheated: A Collection of Critical Essays*. Edited by David Madden. Everett/Edwards, Inc., 1973. © 1973 by David Madden. All rights reserved. Reprinted by permission.

Williams, Kenny J. From *They Also Spoke: An Essay on Negro Literature in America, 1787-1930*. Townsend Press, 1970. Copyright © 1970 by Kenny J. Williams. Reprinted by permission of the author.

Wilson, Edmund. From *Classics and Commercials: A Literary Chronicle of the Forties*. Farrar, Straus and Giroux, 1950. Copyright © 1950 by Edmund Wilson. Copyright renewed © 1978 by Elena Wilson. Reprinted by permission of Farrar, Straus and Giroux, Inc.

Wilson, Edmund. From *O Canada: An American's Notes on Canadian Culture*. Farrar, Straus and Giroux, 1965. Copyright © 1964, 1965 by Edmund Wilson. All rights reserved. Reprinted by permission of Farrar, Straus and Giroux, Inc.

Wilson, Edmund. From a letter to F. Scott Fitzgerald on April 11, 1925, in *Letters on Literature and Politics: 1912-1972*. Edited by Elena Wilson. Farrar, Straus and Giroux, 1977. Copyright © 1957, 1973, 1974, 1977 by Elena Wilson, Executrix of the Estate of Edmund Wilson. All rights reserved. Reprinted by permission of Farrar, Straus and Giroux, Inc.

Wright, Barbara. From an introduction to *The Supermale (Le surmâle)*. By Alfred Jarry, translated by Ralph Gladstone and Barbara Wright. New Directions, 1977. Copyright © 1977 by New Directions Publishing Corporation. All rights reserved. Reprinted by permission of New Directions Publishing Corporation.

Yardley, Jonathan. From *Ring: A Biography of Ring Lardner*. Random House, 1977. Copyright © 1977 by Jonathan Yardley. All rights reserved. Reprinted by permission of Random House, Inc.

Yarmolinsky, Avrahm. From *The Russian Literary Imagination*. Funk & Wagnalls, 1969. Copyright © 1969 by Avrahm Yarmolinsky. All rights reserved. Reprinted by permission of Harper & Row, Publishers, Inc.

Yeats, W. B. From *Autobiographies*. Macmillan, 1955. Copyright 1916, 1936 by Macmillan Publishing Company. Renewed 1944, 1964 by Bertha Georgie Yeats. Reprinted by permission of Macmillan Publishing Company. In Canada by Michael Yeats and Macmillan London Limited.

Yevtushenko, Yevgeny. From "Introduction: 'Without Me, the Country's Not Complete'," in *The Fierce and Beautiful World: Stories*. By Andrei Platonov, translated by Joseph Barnes. Dutton, 1970. English translation copyright © 1970, 1969 by E. P. Dutton & Co., Inc. All rights reserved. Reprinted by permission of the publisher, E. P. Dutton, Inc.